DISTRICT OF COLUMBIA
Death Records

August 1, 1874 to
July 31, 1879

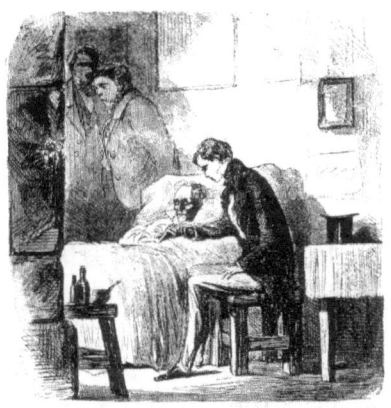

Wesley E. Pippenger

HERITAGE BOOKS
2009

HERITAGE BOOKS
AN IMPRINT OF HERITAGE BOOKS, INC.

Books, CDs, and more—Worldwide

For our listing of thousands of titles see our website
at
www.HeritageBooks.com

Published 2009 by
HERITAGE BOOKS, INC.
Publishing Division
100 Railroad Ave. #104
Westminster, Maryland 21157

Copyright © 1997 Wesley E. Pippenger

All rights reserved. No part of this book may be reproduced or transmitted in any form or by any means, electronic or mechanical, including photocopying, recording or by any information storage and retrieval system without written permission from the author, except for the inclusion of brief quotations in a review.

International Standard Book Numbers
Paperbound: 978-1-58549-446-0
Clothbound: 978-0-7884-8132-1

DISTRICT OF COLUMBIA
Death Records

August 1, 1874 to July 31, 1879

Introduction

Records of death in the District of Columbia (D.C.) are held at two locations. Original certificates of death prior to 1932 are maintained at the D.C. Office of Public Records (commonly called the "D.C. Archives"). Records after 1932 are maintained by the Vital Records Division. The latter is one of several functions of the State Center for Health Statistics (SCHS), part of the Commission of Public Health, Department of Human Services. An earlier series of death records which was kept in a journal inscribed "Interments," covers the period February 1, 1855 to July 30, 1874. Death records and an index for this period can be found on microfilm reels #1994617 and #1994618 that are available through the LDS Church. The journal notes that there were no records kept between August 1, 1862 and January 1, 1866. The original journal is in the custody of the Vital Records Division and cannot be accessed because of its deteriorating condition.

To obtain death records more recent than 1932, one may need to prove a relationship to the deceased and provide the purpose for requesting a copy of the record. Requests to the Vital Records Division for a record made within the last 50 years must be made by a legal guardian or next of kin. Requests for death records may be made in writing by mail to the District of Columbia Department of Human Services, Vital Records Division, 800 9th Street, S.W., First Floor, Washington, D.C. 20004; telephone (202) 727-5314, recording (202) 645-5692. Copies of records previous to 1932 may be obtained without charge, but as staff time permits, from the District of Columbia Office of Public Records, 1300 Naylor Court, N.W., Washington, D.C. 20001. The exact date of death must be provided.

This work is an index to 21,416 certificates of death that were filed with the District of Columbia health officer for the period August 1, 1874 to July 31, 1879. The original certificates from which this work is devised are now maintained at the D.C. Archives. The typical official form contains blanks to enter the date of death, name of the deceased, age, color, sex, occupation, place of birth, length of residence in the District, primary and secondary diseases, duration of diseases, marital status, and where buried. In cases of foreign birth, the original record often notes how long the deceased resided in the United States. Infants are often described without a given name, and certificates frequently give the name of one or both parents. As such, the surname of the father and mother may not be the same, and the race of the parents may differ. One point of confusion in transcribing the place of birth may be with the part of the city called "Island." In some instances, it is suspected this is intended for the country Ireland.

Counts of burials in the 20 most active cemeteries for the period, 1874-1879, are:

1. Mt. Olivet 3,448
2. Congressional 2,169
3. Beckett's 2,104
4. Potters Field 1,786
5. Columbian Harmony 1,671
6. Young Mens 1,305
7. Glenwood 1,204
8. Oak Hill 955
9. Ebenezer 944
10. Mt. Pleasant (Plain) 826
11. Mt. Zion 745
12. Prospect Hill 630
13. Holy Rood 622
14. Graceland 348
15. Presbyterian 266
16. Rock Creek 260
17. St. Mary's 227
18. Payne's 213
19. Moore's 160
20. Washington Asylum 154

Introduction

Frequently the place of burial is listed in a distant location, for example: Alexandria, Va. (138); Annapolis, Md. (10); Arlington, Va. (39); Baltimore, Md. (163); Fairfax County, Va. (25); Leesburg, Va. (15); Montgomery County, Md. (22); Philadelphia, Pa. (46); Prince George's County, Md. (15); and Richmond, Va. (22). Many other burial locations are scattered throughout this work.

Every effort has been made to correctly interpret the sometimes illegible and frequently difficult handwriting that is found in the original records. The compiler was often suspicious that the record creator could not spell, or did not in some way obtain correct and/or complete information about the decedent. Particularly questionable portions are underscored in this work. In many cases the compiler compared death certificate information with that available from extant cemetery records or monuments. Most cemetery office staffs were extremely supportive in assisting the compiler in making such verifications.

Finally, the compiler suggests that this work be used as a finding aid for researchers and not a replacement for original records.

Wesley E. Pippenger
Arlington, Virginia

CONGRESSIONAL CEMETERY.

Cemeteries and Burial Grounds

Death certificates mention numerous different public cemeteries and private burial grounds. The list below contains descriptive details for many of the cemeteries and burial grounds which can be identified. Sources for this information include city directories, personal accounts of the city, and records of the engineer's department. Contrary to what is found today, a surprising number of private burial grounds once existed within the city limits.

On May 15, 1820,[1] a former Act of 1804 was amended to contain provisions affecting the regulation and care of burial grounds within the city limits, and for registering births, deaths, and marriages. On March 30, 1822, the D.C. Board of Health was establsihed.[2] The Board supervised nuisances or sources of disease, and required keeping a register of deaths in the city. Three Commissioners were appointed to oversee activities for the eastern and western burial grounds. They were "appointed for the purpose of dividing the burial grounds into suitable sites for graves, and to dispose of the same, in the manner prescribed by the laws of the Corporation. The Commissioners were also authorized to apply the money arising from the sale of sites for graves, to the improvement and repairs of the fences and burial grounds, and to the purchase of a lot, and the erection of a house thereon, in the neighborhood of each, for the accommodation of the sextons."[3] One sexton was appointed for each burial ground by the Mayor. The sextons or their deputies were the only persons allowed to dig graves in the burial grounds to which they were respectively attached. The sextons were required to keep an exact account of all interments made by them, and make a return thereof to the Register of the city every three months. The 1822 city directory lists the commissioners of the eastern burial ground as John Chalmers, Daniel Rapine, John Crabb, and John L. Brightwell (sexton). The commissioners that year for the western burial ground (Holmead's) were David Easton, Robert King, Benjamin M. Belt, and Phillip Williams (sexton).

By city ordinance passed in June 1852, no new burial grounds could be established within the Boundary Street city limits. In 1853, the city council ordered that the remains buried at the old poorhouse, located between 6th and 7th streets, and on the north side of M Street, N.W., be removed to a new potters field. The latter was located just north of present Congressional Cemetery. It has been said that between the years 1890 and 1940, over 30 burial places were condemned and the remains therein moved out of the city limits. In the 1850's, the Board of Health complained to physicians and undertakers to comply with requirements to return to the Board information regarding cause of death and interment.[4] In 1866,[5] the Board recommended updated legislation on the reporting of births, marriages and deaths. The resulting act can be found transcribed in the Appendix of this work.

In March and April 1909, the Corps of Engineers and others inquired of the District of Columbia Health Officer of a proposed bill to remove bodies from abandoned cemeteries in the District. The legislation would enable a purchaser of ground formerly used as a cemetery, but which was abandoned for that use, to have the bodies removed and reinterred in another cemetery so that the purchaser could extend streets through the ground and sell it for building purposes. At the time there was no intention voiced by city officials to require the general removal of remains from family vaults or private burial places. It was explained that if one should sell the property on which their family vault was located, and the purchaser should desire to remove the remains therein for the purposes of developing the land, the proposed law

---

[1] "Charter of Washington," To incorporate the Inhabitants of the City of Washington, and to repeal all Acts heretofore passed for that purpose. Approved May 15, 1820. Also see The Charter of the City of Washington... (Washington, D.C.: John T. Towers, Printer, 1848), p. 10.
[2] Surviving written proceedings of the Board of Health, beginning April 13, 1822, may be found at the D.C. Archives. At the first meeting, Dr. Frederick May was elected president of the Board, with chairman Charles W. Goldsborough, and Dr. Henry Huntt, secretary.
[3] The Washington Directory... (Washington, D.C.: R.L. Polk & Co., 1822), p. 104.
[4] D.C. Board of Health Minutes, 1848-1871, July 1, 1855.
[5] Ibid., September 17, 1866.

Cemeteries and Burial Grounds

would enable that person to do so, but would not affect the present status of the land.[1] Approvals were advertised 27 MAR 1909 in the Washington Post, that the commissioners approved recommendations that provided for removing remains from abandoned cemeteries in the District.

Many family or private burial grounds vanished from properties once configured as residences-- sometimes of prominent individuals. For instance, the grave of Gen. Robert Brent, U.S. Army paymaster general and first mayor of the City of Washington, was known to be at "Brentwood." The last family interment there was made about July 1874, making 15 known graves. The location was described as being 1-3/4 miles northeast of the capitol building (as the bird flies), just in the rear of the Deaf and Dumb Asylum. An inspector of the property in the 20th century found:

> "The tomb was constructed, so far as can be learned, in the year 1819, and was used from time to time as a receptacle for such members of the family as desired to be interred within it. It is constructed of solid granite blocks, almost square in shape, and surmounted by an arched roof set off by a heavy projecting cornice, resembling somewhat those used by the ancient Egyptians at Luxor and Karnak. An ivy vine, with thick roots and branches, nearly covers the sides and roof of the tomb, while the immediate surroundings are heavily grown with deep underbrush and trees. Just over the doorway is the Latin quotation: *requiescat in pace*. This is the only inscription to be seen."

Such fate of neglect was commonplace among burial grounds in the District of Columbia.

Following is a list of area cemeteries identified on certificates of death, local histories, city directories, and other pertinent source materials. In parenthesis after each entry is the approximate number of burials made (during the years covered in this volume) in the cemetery or burial ground based upon data taken from the certificates of death.

LIST OF CEMETERIES AND BURIAL GROUNDS

Adams (Family) Farm. Death certificate #005985 for Robert Adams describes the place of burial as Mr. Adams' Farm, 3 miles from Bladensburg. Located on property owned by Josiah Adams (d. 1884), said to be a gardener for the Calvert family. Located in Beacon Heights, Prince George's County, Maryland. Later known as Cherry Hill Cemetery. (1)

Adas Israel. First appears under this name in the 1887 city directory (formerly Jews Burial Ground). Burial records, 1870 to 1919, are found on microfiche at the Library of Congress, LC Call Number Microfiche 96/79F. Described in 1891 as being located about 1½ miles from the Insane Asylum. The cemetery office is located at 1400 Alabama Avenue, S.E., Washington, DC 20032. (15)

Addison (Family). In 1879, located on Reason Addison's property near Tennallytown.

Addison's Chapel. Bunker Hill Road (1890). Buried here are Mr. and Mrs. Benjamin Stoddert. (14)

Aurora. In 1899, on Brentwood Road.

Baptist. Baptist Ground in Potomac City (1876), described on death certificate #10395 as being near Chain Bridge (1877). Located near Drovers' Rest (1882, 1890). Edward Palmer, sexton (1883-1887). (c.60)

Barlow (Family). In 1815, the remains of Jacob Barlow were to have been interred on his estate "Kalorama," located off Massachusetts Avenue, N.W. at Rock Creek. Captain Stephen Decatur was buried there in 1820.

[St.] Barnabas Church, Maryland. Located about 5 miles from Upper Marlborough. (8)

Barnes Hospital (see Soldier's Home).

Battle Ground (National). Superintendents were Aug. Armbrecht (1879-1881), Stephen S. Cole (1883),

---

[1] Engineer Department Records, File 77872, L.S. Vol. 218, p. 468.

and Ernest Rittenhouse (1885-1887). The city directory for 1880 shows location at 7th Street Road near Brightwood. Brightwood Avenue near Brightwood (1890). Wall on Georgia Avenue, N.W. repaired in 1916. (1)

Beall (Family). Once located on Gay Street in Georgetown.

Beckett's. Proprietor in 1876 was William Beckett. Described in the 1880 city directory as being on C Street between 16th and 17th streets, S.E. Not listed as Beckett's in city directories after 1882. Found in the 1881 city directory as "Union Beneficial Association Cemetery" at the same location, with William Beckett, sexton. Mr. Beckett resided at 908 E St., S.W. in 1882. Occasionally one finds entries of Beckett's and Ebenezer together. A notice of 27 MAR 1909, in the Washington Post, stated that attorney A.A. Lipscomb, on behalf of Henry G. Freitag, owner of a lot at 16th and C streets, S.E., formerly the cemetery of the Ebenezer African Church, took action regarding the state of the burial ground. Lipsomb's letter stated that the ground is filled with bodies, and that no interments have been made there since 1879. (2,104)

Belt (Family) Farm. Located north of Tennallytown (1882, 1890). Sprigg Belt, sexton (1884-1887). (3)

Berry (Family) Farm. Owned by Richard L. Berry (1883-1888). Earlier the property of Zachariah Berry. Hillsdale (1890). (3)

Blue Plains. In 1901, the D.C. Commissioners bought land at Blue Plains, and in 1907 requested that additional land there be "condemned for a site for a municipal alms house and a burial place for the indigent dead authorized...by Act of Congress, June 27, 1906."[1]

Bridge Street Presbyterian. Georgetown. Location of the church burial ground undetermined. Founded in 1780 by Rev. Stephen Bloomer Balch who was first buried at the front of his beloved church. His remains were removed to the Presbyterian church burial ground, then to Oak Hill Cemetery. Building from 1820, located at the corner of M and 30th streets, N.W., was razed in 1872. The interred remains from the Bridge Street Church graveyard were transferred in 1873 to the Presbyterian burial ground on Market Street.[2]

Brightwood. Brightwood (1882, 1890). Hilleary Green, sexton (1882-1887). (31)

Brown (Family), (see Hillsdale).

Burnes (Family). Graveyard of the Thomas Burnes family (Van Ness' mausoleum), on south side of H Street between 9th and 10th streets.[3] The remains of David Burnes are now found interred in Rock Creek Cemetery.

Carroll Chapel. Located in Forest Glen, Montgomery County, Maryland. (13)

Catholic. The 1822 and 1827 city directories describe the location of the catholic burying ground as near the north end of 3rd Street West, outside the city limits.

Cedars. Once the property of Colonel John Cox. Located where recently stood the Western High School, Georgetown.[4]

Cephas (Family). John Cephas, proprietor (1882-1888). Located on Conduit Road near Drovers' Rest (1882, 1890). (3)

Chapman (Family). Location undetermined (1878). See #16,107 for John Taylor.

Chappel's (Family) Farm. J.E. Chappel, owner (1882-1888). Located on a private farm north of Tennallytown (1890). (11)

Cherry Hill (see Adams Family).

(Georgetown) College Burial Ground. Private, Georgetown (1890). On the present campus of Georgetown University. Graves for those identified on certificates of death may be found in what is now known as the Jesuit community cemetery. (9)

Christian. Located on the Chapel Farm near Tennallytown (1883). R. Dorsey, sexton (1883-1887).

Columbian Harmony Burial Ground. Founded in 1825 by a society primarily composed of freedmen. First situated where bound by 5th, 6th, S and Boundary streets, N.W. Relocated in 1856 to

---

[1] Records of the Columbia Historical Society, 1963-1965, p. 29, "Blue Plains and Bellevue."
[2] James M. Goode, Capital Losses: A Cultural History of Washington's Destroyed Buildings (Washington, D.C.: Smithsonian Institution Press, 1979), p. 208.
[3] Christian Hines, Early Recollections of Washington City (Washington, D.C., 1866), p. 39; Records of the Columbia Historical Society, Vol. 22, pp. 158, 193.
[4] Harold Donaldson Eberlein and Cortlandt Van Dyke Hubbard, Historic Houses of George-town & Washington City (Richmond, Va.: The Dietz Press, Inc., 1958), pp. 64-65; Records of the Columbia Historical Society, Vol. 21, p. 142.

Cemeteries and Burial Grounds

Youngsborough, about 1 mile north of the intersection of H Street North and the Baltimore railroad. Superintendents were John F. Cook (1874), Benjamin McCoy (1880-1884), and Lavina McCoy (1885-1886). The 1890 city directory describes it as the Harmonia Burial Ground at Brentwood Road, 2 miles from the city. This site is now the Rhode Island Metro Station.[1] New location known as the National Harmony Memorial Park in Landover, Maryland.[2] (1,671)

Congressional. Officially named Washington Parish Burial Ground, and established in 1807 on Square 1115. In 1848, expanded to Square 1116 to the south, and in 1853, encompassed Square 1104 to the west.[3] Range locations changed from an alphabetic series to numbers in 1854. Commonly known as Congressional (or Congress) Burial Ground (1874). City directories describe the location as "situated on the eastern branch of the Potomac River, about 1½ miles from the Capitol.," or at 18th Street, S.E. (1890). Superintendents were Charles F. Smith (1874-1882), and J.B. Cross (1883-1887). Comprises about 30 acres. Details on the early particulars of the original cemetery may be obtained from the cemetery office.[4] (2,169)

Convent, Georgetown Visitation. Private, located at 35th and P streets N.W. (1890). On the present Convent of the Georgetown Visitation. Several burial places are in the immediate area. Graves for those identified on certificates of death as being buried at the convent may be found at what is now called "the monastery garden." The convent visitation cemetery is more modern. (12)

Cox's Station (Family). Located in Maryland, 1875-1877. (3)

Danford (Family) Farm. Located on River Road, 1875-1876. See #005047a for Joseph P. Sayles, and #6371 for Mary A. Brackston. (2)

Dangerfield (Family). Henry Dangerfield, superintendent (1884-1886), and John W. Dangerfield, superintendent (1887-1891). No location given in city directories.

Davidson (Family). In his will of 1805, Samuel Davidson requested burial in his intended burying ground at "Evermay."[5]

Dean (Family). Described on death certificate #007919 as "Dr. Deans Family Ground, Bennings Station." On Sheriff Road (1882, 1890, 1891). Julius Dean, superintendent (1882-1886), and Julian W. Dean (1887).

Eastern. Established on February 28, 1798, by the Commissioners of Washington as a public burial ground. The 1827 city directory describes the location as Square 1026, between H and I streets North, and 13th and 14th streets. Located in the square bounded by 14th, 15th, H and I streets, N.E. By 1835, the burial ground was described as being much ornamented and well enclosed. "The numerous handsome monuments and vaults already make this place worthy to be visited by strangers."[6] In 1860, the eastern graveyard, located in the sixth ward of the city, was extended to the west and improved.[7] Marsh conditions led to discontinued use.

Eaton (Family). Location undetermined. (1)

Ebenezer (see Methodist).

Ebenezer African Church (see Beckett's).

Eckton (Family). Location undetermined. (2)

Eldbrooke Methodist (see Methodist). Located adjacent to the Eldbrooke United Methodist Church, 4100 River Road, N.W.

Episcopal. The 1822 and 1827 city directories describe the location as near the Eastern branch, upper bridge.

Episcopal. The 1827 city directory describes the location of the new episcopal burying ground as being in Square 276, between 12th and 13th streets West, and R and S streets.

"Evermay" (see Davidson Family).

---

[1] Washington Post, 23 JUN 1982, "Dispute Surrounds Memorial To Veterans."
[2] Washington Post, 13 FEB 1986, District Weekly, "Learning History From Tombstones of 19th Century."
[3] Records of the Columbia Historical Society, Vol. 11, p. 365.
[4] U.S. Senate, 59th Congress, 2nd Session, Senate Document No. 72, to accompany report H.R. 5972, reprinted as "History of the Congressional Cemetery."
[5] D.C. Wills, Bk. 1, pp. 320-323(178-180); file O.S. 411 in Record Group 21 at the National Archives; original in Box 3 at the D.C. Archives.
[6] Records of the Columbia Historical Society, Vol. 11, p. 308.
[7] Records of the Columbia Historical Society, Vol. 11, p. 383.

Cemeteries and Burial Grounds

"Flint Hill" Burial Ground. Located near Fairfax Courthouse, Va. (1876). (4)
Forrest (Family) Farm. Owned by Catharine Forrest in 1878. See #16,259 for Mauna Bailey.
Francis DeSales. Sometimes referred to as Queens Chapel Roman Catholic, located on Evarts Street, N.E., just off Queens Chapel Road, near Langdon neighborhood.
Franciscan Monastery. Brookland (1900). Located on the grounds of the Franciscan Monastery at 14th and Quincy streets, N.E.

Garden (Family). Colored. Alexander Garden, proprietor (1882-1888). Private, Anacostia Road (1890, 1891). In 1886, the former Uniontown was named Anacostia.
Glenwood. Situated north of the Capitol, about 1½ miles from City Hall (1874). This cemetery was established in 1854 and laid out on the plan of the celebrated Greenwood Cemetery in New York City, of which it is said by travelers to excel in beauty and arrangement anything of the kind in Europe or America. It now comprises about 43 acres. Records begin in June 1878 when a group of lot owners gained control of cemetery management. Glenwood is situated on the high ground overlooking the City of Washington, and on a direct line with North Capitol Street. Andrew J. Deming, superintendent (1879-1881), and Alexander McKerichar (1883-1889). The cemetery was chartered by Congress, and the plots are not liable for debt, taxes or any other invasion (1874). On Lincoln Avenue (1890, 1891). (1,204)
Good Hope. The community of Good Hope is in Anacostia, on the Eastern Branch. Much of the area property was owned by the Naylor family. William Batson, proprietor (1882-1886), and Samuel Patterson (1887). On Hamilton Road (1890, 1891). (9)
Graceland. Established in 1872, and comprised about 25 acres.[1] Discontinued in July 1894, because of its location on marsh land. William H. Gafford, superintendent (1874-1891). Terminus of H Street Northeast (1871, 1883); at 15th and H Street Northeast (1890, 1891). Woodlawn Cemetery essentially replaced Graceland. Debate went on between 1907 and 1912, whether the tract was suitable for a park (Anacostia Water Park) or if it should be divided for development as housing.[2] The location is recently occupied by Hechinger Mall at Benning Road, H Street, and Bladensburg Road, N.E. (348)
Green Vale. Ruth Davis in charge (1883-1887). Near Tennallytown (1883, 1890, 1891).
Green (Family) Farm. Location undetermined. See #20,679 for William Green.

Harmonia, Harmoneon, or Harmony (see Columbian Harmony).
Hebbon (Family). Eliza Hebbon, proprietor (1882-1888). Broad Branch Road (1890, 1891). Located in Chevy Chase in the 1900 city directory.
Hebrew (also see Washington Hebrew). (16)
Hillbrook. In August 1907, permission was requested of the Engineer Department to establish a cemetery for the Jewish society, to be located in Square 5145, Hillbrook, D.C.[3]
Hillsdale. A community earlier known as Barry's Farm[4] (or Potomac City as it was sometimes called), and in 1872 renamed "Hillsboro," and by 1874, called "Hillsdale." Solomon G. Brown (1831-d. June 26, 1906), proprietor (1882-1885), John Cook, sexton (1886-1887). Elvans Avenue, Hillsdale (1891), a portion of Anacostia (1890). Frederick Douglass (d. 1895) in 1879 purchased Lot 4 in Section 1. In January 1967, a blanket disinterment permit (No. 67-1) was issued by the D.C. Department of Public Health for Stanton Courts Joint Venture, Inc. to disinter and remove the bodies from those parts of Old Hillsdale Cemetery belonging in the District of Columbia.[5] Reinterments were to be made at a District cemetery located at Blue Plains. (14)
Hines (Family). As near as can be ascertained, the burial plot of the Hines family was located around the rear of stores at 2440 and 2444 18th Street, N.W., and adjoining the southern wall of Crandall's

---

[1] D.C. Engineer Department Records, D.C. archives, #10819/26.
[2] See 60th Congress, 1st Session, proposed bill to in part authorize the purchase for $150,000 the cemetery site.
[3] D.C. Engineer Department Records, D.C. archives, #67544.
[4] Plat recorded in Liber Levy Court No. 2, Folio 1, of the records of the Office of the Surveyor of the District of Columbia, showing location in parts of original lots 13 and 14 in Section 5, of "Barry Farm."
[5] The order for disinterment, filed December 13, 1966, described the location as being Lots 13 and 14 which lie within Bruce Place, S.E., and Jasper Place, S.E., and part of Lot 13 which formerly lay within 13th Street, S.E.

Cemeteries and Burial Grounds

Knickerbocker Theater.[1]

Holmead's (also known as the Western Burial Ground). Established in 1798 on land patented by James Holmead. Occupied Squares 109 and 1026, bound by 19th, 20th, S, and Boundary (now Florida Avenue) streets. Buried here were Rev. Lorenzo Dow; William Seaton, the journalist; James Hoban, architect; and Andrew Way, printer. Joseph Meigs, father of Gen. Meigs, was first buried at Holmead, but removed to Oak Hill.[2] By 1855, the western graveyard had a new substantial fence.[3] In 1881, the Engineer Commissioner was authorized to advertise for proposals for removal of bodies from Holmead.[4] In disrepair by 1884, when the remains for over 3,000 dead were relocated to other cemeteries. Destroyed. (1)

Holy Rood. Georgetown. Established by Holy Trinity Catholic Church by 1832. On 32nd (High) Street extension (1890). John A. Heenan, sexton (1880-1891). Also called Georgetown Catholic Cemetery. In 1942, Georgetown University inherited management responsibilities for the cemetery and maintained the applicable burial records. By 1984, the university wanted to get out of the cemetery business and close the cemetery.[5] Over 7,000 known burials. (622)

Hospital. Often refers to the Government Hospital. Several hospitals were associated with the Washington Asylum. A burial place at the small pox hospital was frequently described as the small pox grounds. The small pox hospital site was due east of the alms house, and practically at the river. This grouping of facilities was adjacent to Congressional Cemetery.[6] (160)

Howard (Family). Robert Howard, superintendent (1882-1886), and Robert S. Howard (1887-1888). Private, Anacostia Road (1890, 1891). (8)

Insane Asylum (see Washington Asylum). (3)

Jenkins (Family). Thomas Jenkins, proprietor (1882-1886), and Henry J. Hoyle (1887). Private, on Jenkins Family farm (1890). (2)

Jewish (see Adas Israel, Washington Hebrew). (16)

Jews Burial Ground (see Adas Israel after 1887). About 1½ miles from the Government Insane Asylum (1874, 1876). George Groner, sexton (1883-1887).

Jones Chapel. William Henson, superintendent (1882-1886), and Frederick Jackson (1887). Bennings Station (1876), Bennings Road (1890, 1891). (40)

"Kalorama" (see Barlow Family).

Lacy (Family) Farm. Location undetermined. (1)

Loughborough (Family). Nathan Loughborough died in 1852 and was buried at "Grassland."[7]

Lutheran. Square 1272 (1899). Discontinued.

Macedonia, or Macedonian. Henry Waddy, sexton (1882-1886), and William Ellis (1887). Given on death certificate #001,857 for Harriet Lyons as being in Uniontown. On the certificate #010,500 for Rose Dobbs, noted as being located in Potomac City; near Sheridan Avenue in Hillsdale (1882, 1890). (40)

Macpelah (Hebrew). George Graner, superintendent (1886-1887). Hamilton Road (1890).

Marlow (Family) Farm. Located near Good Hope. See #004,220 for Stepny Marlow. (1)

McPherson (Family). William Pinney, sexton (1882-1886), and D. Tinney (1887). Private, Hillsdale (1890, 1891).

Methodist (Tennallytown). Set aside in 1855 by deed from William D.C. Murdock and wife to trustees of the church for $50. Used from 1855 through the 1890's by members of both St. Alban's and its Tennallytown mission, St. Columba's. On Murdock Mill Road, N.W., immediately behind Eldbrooke

---

[1] Records of the Columbia Historical Society, Vol. 22, p. 39.
[2] Helen W. Ridgely, Historic Graves of Maryland and the District of Columbia (Grafton Press, 1908), p. 260, gives a partial list of notables once buried at Holmead's.
[3] Records of the Columbia Historical Society, Vol. 11, p. 365.
[4] Report of the Commissioners of the District of Columbia, Fiscal Year 1881, p. 19.
[5] Washington Post, 11 NOV 1984, Metro Scene, "GU to Close Cemetery."
[6] D.C. Engineer Department Records, D.C. archives, E.D. plat attached to #31362/6.
[7] Records of the Columbia Historical Society, Vol. 24, p. 5. The bodies of Mr. and Mrs. Loughborough (1st wife) were removed to Oak Hill.

Cemeteries and Burial Grounds

Methodist Church at River Road, Tennallytown (1890). W.H. Walker, sexton (1883-1886). Here was interred John "Bull" Frizzell in 1879.[1] Later known as the Tennallytown Methodist Cemetery. The neighborhood is today called Tenleytown. (111)

Methodist Episcopal. The burial ground associated with Foundry Methodist Episcopal Church was once located in Square 235, bounded by V, W, 13th and 14th streets, N.W. The property was sold to real estate developers for $18,000 and the 1,800 graves moved to Glenwood Cemetery.[2] The remains of Dr. James Heighe Blake, who died July 29, 1819, were first interred in the Methodist Episcopal Burial Ground of Georgetown, and were removed November 2, 1870 to the William A. Gordon lot in Oak Hill.[3] (1)

Methodist Episcopal. Sexton Joseph Shelton (1871-1879), and John H. Shelton (1881-1883), John S. Shelton (1884-1886), John H. Shelton (1887). Also known as the Eastern or Old Methodist Cemetery. In 1824, the trustees of the Methodist Society at Ebenezer Station, commonly called the Fourth Street Methodist Church, purchased Square 1102, bounded by 17th, 18th, E and D streets, S.E., directly north of Congressional Cemetery. Discontinued in 1892. (13)

Methodist (Ebenezer). Between 16th and 17th streets East, and C and D streets South, near the Congressional burial ground. This is the same location given for Beckett's Cemetery. Sexton is Wm. Brown (1871, 1874). The city directory for 1876 gives location as E Street between 17th and 18th streets, S.E., with sexton John H. Shelton (1876-1877), and G.C.H. Better (1880-1881). Records begin in 1823. Discontinued in 1892. Burials stop about August 1877. (944)

Moore's (Family). Established c.1850 by Jacob Moore, near "T" Street Hill (now Stanton Road and Suitland Parkway). John Gales, sexton (1886-1887). In Hillsdale at 3134 Stanton Road, S.E. An 1881 map by Griffith M. Hopkins shows Jacob Moore having 6.75 acres just east of the bend in Stanton Road. The city directory for 1899 describes the location as Barry Farm, Potomac City. A death certificate in 1876 (#6,951) for Hester Diggs gives location as Union Town, and another (#10,430) for Thomas Barton gives location as Stanton Hill. Renamed c.1927 to Rosemont Cemetery. "Many years after the abandonment of this burying ground, the remains of residents of the old Barry Farm/Hillsdale community were reinterred in National Harmony Memorial Park, Landover, Maryland, in October 1965."[4] (160)

Mount Olivet (Catholic). Situated at 1300 Bladensburg Road, N.E., about a half mile beyond the tollgate (1874). Superintendent is Patrick Duffy (1874-1880), and Philip J. McHenry (1881-1889).

Mount Pleasant Plain(s). Superintendents Joseph Shorter (1876, 1877), Aaron Talbert (1878-1881), James Talbert (1883), Isaac Talbert (1884), and James F. Herbert (1885-1887). Near Mount Pleasant (1890, 1891). Adams Mill Road (1899) at Calvert Street, N.W. Established by the Colored Union Benevolent Association, first located between 12th, 13th, V and W streets, N.W. Also known as the Free Young Mens Burial Ground. The ground became marshy due to proximity of the headwaters of Reedy Branch. Inactive by 1890, some reinterments made in Columbian Harmony. Discontinued, and about 1940 extant remains were removed to Woodlawn Cemetery. (758)

Mount Zion. The ground was conveyed by Thomas Beall to Ebenezer Eliason and others, by deed of October 13, 1808. Care was turned over to Mt. Zion church.[5] On property purchased by the Montgomery Street Church (known as the Dumbarton Methodist Church after 1850). Henry Bolles, sexton (1883-1887). Located on Mill Road near P Street, N.W. (1890, 1891). It was actually located on the creek side of Q Street.[6] The Old Methodist Burying Ground, Mt. Zion Cemetery and the Female Union Band Society Burying Ground are located collectively in Squares 1288 and 1289, just east of Oak Hill Cemetery in Georgetown. About 1879, a portion of the Old Methodist Burying Ground was set aside for use by the Mt. Zion Church. Located off 27th and Q streets, N.W. near Rock Creek

---

[1] Judith Beck Helm, Tenleytown, D.C.: Country Village Into City Neighborhood (Washington, D.C.: Tenleytown Press, 1981), p. 309.
[2] James M. Goode, Capital Losses: A Cultural History of Washington's Destroyed Buildings (Washington, D.C.: Smithsonian Institution Press, 1979), pp. 206-207..
[3] Records of the Columbia Historical Society, Vol. 24, pp. 160-161.
[4] Hutchinson, p. 132.
[5] Richard P. Jackson, The Chronicles of Georgetown, D.C., From 1751 to 1878 (Washington, D.C.: RO. Polkinhorn, Priner, 1878), p. 270.
[6] D.C. Engineer Department Records, D.C. archives, #14884/5.

Cemeteries and Burial Grounds

Park.[1] (745)

Nonesuch Farm. Located in Good Hope Hill. See #000433 for Maria Lewis.

Oak Hill. Established by charter of March 3, 1849. On property formerly known as "Parrott's Woods." Entrance (1874) to the cemetery on Road Street at the head of Washington Street in Georgetown. President (1874) was W.W. Corcoran. (955)

Old Ebenezer. (see Methodist)

Old Methodist Burying Ground. Located just east of Oak Hill Cemetery in Georgetown. Established on property owned by the Montgomery Street Church, known after 1850 as the Dumbarton Methodist Church. A portion was set aside for Mt. Zion church to bury blacks.

Payne's (Family). Founded c.1851; John Payne's Burial Ground (1879). Mary Payne, sexton (1884), and Henry Speeks (1885-1887). Located at Bennings (1890, 1891), at 4600 Benning Road, S.E., just opposite Woodlawn. Boundaries extended in 1929. The last removals at Payne's were made in the 1960's to the National Harmony Memorial Park. (213)

Pearce (Family). Situated on the north side of Pennsylvania Avenue, opposite the President's House, between the southwest corner and south gate of Lafayette Square. About 30 feet square.[2]

Peltz (Family) Farm. Located in Silver Hill, Prince George's County, Maryland. (1)

Potters Field. At the Washington Asylum (1890). W.H. Stoutenburg, superintendent (1883-1888). Established for use in burying indigents. Located at the site recently occupied by D.C. General Hospital.[3] A former potters field is said to have been located until 1846 in the northeast corner of an almshouse square that was on the north side of M Street, S.W., between 6th and 7th streets. In May 1904, the Engineer Department noted that a plat of the cemetery was on file,[4] and that a plat was to be ordered of the new potters field at the Washington Asylum.[5] (1,786)

Presbyterian. Established by 1856, and located between 4th, 5th, Market and Frederick streets in Georgetown. Once buried here were the remains of Robert Peter (d. 1806), first mayor of Georgetown; John Barnes (d. 1826), collector of the port of Georgetown for 20 years, and founder of the poor house; James Gillespie (d. 1805), member of Congress from North Carolina; Mary Bohrer (d. 1844), wife of John P. Bohrer; Elizabeth Thompson (d. 1847); William Waters (d. 1859), a soldier of the Revolutionary War; Col. George Beall (d. 1807), grandson of Ninian Beall. The 1890 and 1891 city directories give the location as 34th Street and Q Street, N.W., Georgetown; Square 1273 (1899). Discontinued by 1896. Purchased as public park in 1903, although remains had not been removed.[6] In 1897, the city taxed for a sewer line adjacent to the burial ground.[7] In 1907, much discussion was made about removal of remains and grading of the burial ground.[8] By October 31, 1907, it was described that the monuments and stones through the entire cemetery, except that part covered by

---

[1] Washington Post, 16 NOV 1989, "A Plot of History Crumbling: In Georgetown, Nature Overrunning D.C.'s Oldest Black Cemetery."
[2] Hines, pp. 39-40.
[3] City Paper, 30 MAY-5 JUN 1986, pp. 1, 16, "Dead Broke..."; Washington Star, 1 DEC 1912, "In Potter's Field, Where Sleep the City's Unknown and Pauper Dead."
[4] D.C. Engineer Department Records, D.C. archives.
[5] D.C. Engineer Department Records, D.C. archives, #80225.
[6] D.C. Engineer Department Records, D.C. archives, #51648-43, letter dated October 28, 1907 from Wm. H. Manogue to H.L. West, "I beg to invite your attention to the fact that some parties are grading the presbyterian Burial Grounds in Georgetown recently purchased by the Commissioners for Play Grounds, and are doing so in violation of the express terms of the contract of sale which required the removal of the remains entered [sic] therein prior to settlement or sale. ...I respectfully protest against the ruthless manner in which the land is being plowed over, and the location of the dead forever destroyed."
[7] D.C. Engineer Department Records, D.C. archives, #2313, letter of S. Thomas Brown in protest against assessments for sewer laid front of Lot P, Square 1273, on 34th Street. Mr. Brown describes that the lot was donated to the church for a burial ground many years ago and has been held as such up to this time--it was supposed that it was not subject to any taxes.
[8] D.C. Engineer Department Records, D.C. archives, #51648-43, letter dated October 28, 1907, from the Corps of Engineers to Mr. William H. Manogue, "In reply to your letter of this date, relative to the grading being done by the trustees of the West Street Presbyterian Church in the old burial ground in Georgetown, I would state that I have, since talking with you, conferred with Mr. Malery, representing the trustees, and he authorizes me to state that the church stands ready to disinter the remains of any of the deceased members of the families of the heirs which you represent if the graves will be pointed out to him, and that it is their intention to disinter and re-inter any remains that may be found in the grading operations." Another letter, dated the same day, infers involvement of the Beatty family.

Cemeteries and Burial Grounds

lot P, "are entirely gone and none of the remains have been removed as provided by our contract with Mr. Malley." (266)

Prospect Hill Farm. In 1901, Rev. R.W. Lowrie submitted to the D.C. Engineer Department a plat of family burial ground called "Prospect Hill Farm."[1]

Prospect Hill (German Lutheran). 2201 North Capitol Street, N.E. Adjoining Glenwood Cemetery on the west. Superintendents Gustav Hartig (1874, 1876, 1877), George C. Walker (1878-1883), Christian Bucheler (1884-1885), and J.A. Griesbauer (1886). Records begin in 1858. Current staff at this cemetery is unwilling to consider assisting with inquiries of any kind without a payment of fees or "donation." (630)

Quaker. Established in March 1807[2] on land provided by Jonathan Shoemaker, provided that the land be used forever as a Friends burial ground. Located on Adams Mill Road (1899), adjacent to the Free Young Mens Burial Ground. By 1953, city officials decided that the seemingly abandoned property could be taxed. Recently configured as a ball diamond and city park.[3] Destroyed.

Queen (Family) Farm. Thought by Paul E. Sluby to be once located in Maryland. Interments in the Queen farm grounds were removed to Rock Creek. Destroyed.

Queens Chapel. Queens Chapel Road (1899). Known as the Francis DeSales Cemetery. In 1901, a survey of the old Queen's Chapel burying ground was submitted to the D.C. Engineer Department. This survey has not been located.[4] Destroyed and remains removed in 1936 to Mt. Olivet Cemetery. (4)

Reform School. Bladensburg Road (1876).

Rock Creek. Located immediately north of the Soldiers' Home on Rock Creek Church Road. On the premises is St. Paul's Episcopal Church. Charles W. Neale, sexton (1881). (260)

Rosemont (see Moore's).

Russian Hebrew. Located in Congress Heights in the 1900 city directory.

St. Albans. Described in the 1890 and 1891 city directories as being on Rockville Turnpike. More commonly known as being in Cathedral close on the heights above Georgetown.

St. Elizabeth's Hospital. Located on Nichols Avenue, Prince George's County, Maryland.

St. John's Episcopal. Established c.1796 on land given by Col. William Deakins. Once described as being located somewhere near Franklin Row.[5]

St. Mary's German Catholic. Lincoln Avenue (1890, 1891). Described on death certificate #5843 as Father Ailig's German Catholic cemetery near Glenwood [Cemetery]. John W. Cord, superintendent (1881-1883, 1887), and W.P Cord (1884-1886). (227)

St. Matthew's Catholic. Once located in the remote corner of Square 236 on U Street, between 13th and 14th streets, N.W. The property was sold by act of Congress in February 1861, and the graves removed to the newly created Mt. Olivet Cemetery.[6] After the sale of St. Matthew's Cemetery, pastors of St. Matthew's, St. Patrick's, St. Peter's and St. Dominic's parishes purchased about 40 acres of the Fenwick farm for the first section of Mt. Olivet Cemetery, a half mile from the toll-gate on the Bladensburg Road.[7] Destroyed.

St. Patrick's Catholic. Located on Boundary (Florida Avenue), off North Capitol between 1st and and 3rd

---

[1] D.C. Engineer Department Records, D.C. archives, #35691-3.
[2] Records of the Columbia Historical Society, Vol. 40-41, p. 37.
[3] Washington Post, 30 DEC 1986, "Lawsuit Revives Dispute Over Quaker Cemetery."
[4] D.C. Engineer Department Records, D.C. archives, #35691, letter dated June 7, 1901, indicates that a careful study of the description of the original deed has been made as well as of a survey made by Howell & Taylor for the Lutheran people. "Our survey is very similar to that Mr. Howell made them, but I think is somewhat better in view of the fact that it ties up to at least one definite monument still standing, and which appears to be very ancient."
[5] Hines, p. 40. The 1832 will of Dr. Thomas Sim, of Washington, D.C., requested the doctor's desire to be decently interred in the site of the burial ground attached to St. John's Episcopal Church, in the City of Washington, parallel with the remains of his beloved wife Hannah L. Sim.
[6] Helene, Estelle and Imogene Philibert, Saint Matthew's of Washington, 1840-1940 (Baltimore, Md.: A. Hoen & Co., 1940), pp. 50-51. The original lot owners of the catholic burial ground included: Benjamin G. Clements, George Vondelehr, Mr. Holmead, Richard Barry, Mr. Newton, William F. Dove, Lucius M. Clements, Jno. F. Bridget, and Col. P. Taylor.
[7] Philibert, p. 51.

Cemeteries and Burial Grounds

streets, N.W., north of Square 551,[1] begun 1810, was the burial ground for St. Patrick's Church which was organized in 1797. In the late 1850's, the remains at St. Patrick's were exhumed and reintered at Mt. Olivet, as were those from St. Peter's and St. Matthew's. Discontinued.

St. Peter's Catholic. Formerly located in Square 808, between 4th, 5th, H and I streets, N.E., as described on an 1855 map of the city of Washington. Remains were reintered at Mt. Olivet. Destroyed.

Scaggs (Family). Sarah Scaggs, superintendent (1882-1887). Anacostia Road (1890, 1891), Bennings. (5)

Sheriff Farm (Family). Established in 1850, and located north of Benning Road, N.E., east of the Anacostia River. Destroyed.

Shoemaker's Farm (Family). Pierce Shoemaker, owner (1882-1888). Private, near Pierce's Mill (1890, 1891), on Pierce Mill Road in 1899.

Shoemaker (Family). Burial ground on property of Isaac Shoemaker near Tennallytown (1890, 1891). David Shoemaker, owner (1883-1888). (1)

Sibley (Family) Farm. Thought by Paul E. Sluby to be once located in Maryland. Interments from the Sibley farm grounds were removed to Rock Creek. Destroyed.

Small Pox Grounds. Located along the north perimter of Washington Asylum. (6)

Smith (Family). A plat of the family cemetery belonging to the heirs of the late Matilda Smith, dated 1900, notes that the old graves are very irregular.[2] Matilda was the daughter of Tobias Henson, a freed slave. In 1813, Henson acquired a 24-acre tract called "The Ridge," located in the community now known as Congress Heights. Richard Smith, sexton (1882-1888). In Good Hope (1879). Located on Hamilton Road (1890, 1891). An order was made February 3, 1950 for all remains to be disinterred. (21)

Soldiers Home (National). Mathias Glynn, superintendent (1880-1887). Harewood Road (1890, 1891); Barnes Hospital. South of Rock Creek Cemetery. (121)

Swartz (or Swarts) Farm (Family). B.T. Swartz, owner (1883-1888). In Washington County near Brightwood (1890, 1891). (7)

Tennallytown (also Tenleytown and other spellings). (59). Methodist (5), and Presbyterian (1).

Thomas (Family). Proprietor Thomas Thomas. (21)

Union Baptist. Established after 1868, northeast of the intersection of MacArthur Boulevard and Chain Bridge Road, N.W. Discontinued. (7)

Union Beneficial Association (see Beckett's). John F.N. Wilkinson, superintendent (1883).

Unknown. A graveyard was on 24th Street west, between H and I streets north. According to Christian Hines, it was said by some to have been the burial ground of soldiers who were quartered in that neighborhood prior to 1800.[3]

Unknown. Possibly located between E and F streets north, and not far from Easby's ship yard. This is said to have been the place where were interred the drowned who were found floating down the river.[4]

Unknown. A "tolerably large grave yard," on the eastern slope of Observatory Hill.[5]

Unknown. Along and partly in F Street north, possibly between 22nd and 23rd streets. May have contained the grave for Casper Yost.[6]

Unknown. Located where "the old race-course used to be," on a farm occupied by a Mr. Myers, near Boundary Street, and nearly south of Commodore Porter's estate.[7]

Veitch (Family). Founded by John Veitch (d. 1864), the grandson of John Veitch who in 1719 married a daughter of Rev. Hugh Conn. About 10 graves of the Veitch family were located at a distance from

---

[1] Records of the Columbia Historical Society, Vol. 24, p. 123, describe the location of St. Patrick's burying ground at the corner of 10th and F streets.
[2] Louise Daniel Hutchinson, The Anacostia Story: 1806-1930 (Washington, D.C.: Smithsonian Institution Press, 1977), p. 45.
[3] Christian Hines, Early Recollections of Washington City (Washington, D.C., 1866), p. 38.
[4] Hines, p. 38.
[5] Hines, pp. 38-39.
[6] Hines, p. 39.
[7] Hines, p. 39.

Cemeteries and Burial Grounds

graves for at least 30 others. On grounds of the reformed school (1899). The property was acquired in 1913 by the government for use as the National Training School for Boys. The last interment was made in 1919.[1] Located northeast of South Dakota Avenue at 33rd Street, N.E. By the 1970's the area was part of the Fort Lincoln Urban Renewal project. In July 1978, remains from about 40 gravesites once in the Veitch family burial ground were relocated to Ft. Lincoln Cemetery, Bladensburg Road, Prince George's County, Maryland. The contract for the removal required that the monuments be set aside and picked up and disposed of by others.

Washington Asylum (also see Potters Field). The 1822 and 1827 city directories describe the location of an asylum in Square 448, bounded by 6th and 7th streeets West, between M and N streets North. Later, the location was on the tract at B and 19th streets, S.E. There were numerous asylums in the area, e.g. insane asylum, orphan asylums, foundling asylums. However, the Washington Asylum is the only one known by this compiler to have maintained a burial ground. One burial ground here was along the Eastern Branch (Anacostia) River, and near the small pox hospital. The Washington Asylum Hospital, founded in 1832, occupied a portion of the grounds belonging to the asylum. It was renamed Gallinger Hospital, and later became D.C. General Hospital. The original Municipal alms house had its name changed to the Home for Aged and Infirm, and in 1954, to the D.C. Village. A volume inscribed "Record of Interments in the Washington Asylum Burial Ground, District of Columbia," can be found at the D.C. Archives. It is volume three of a series, and covers the period September 18, 1875 to December 18, 1903. (164)

Washington Hebrew (see Adas Israel). (47)

Western Burial Ground (see Holmead's).

Wighht (Family). Located near what is now 12th and Monroe streets, N.E. The Wightt, Queen, Brooks tract was divided to form the Brookland neighborhood.[2]

Woodlawn. Woodlawn Cemetery Association was incorporated on 8 JAN 1895. The cemetery was founded the same year at 4611 Benning Road, S.E. Remains from more than 6,000 burials were reintered here from the now destroyed Graceland Cemetery. Closed between 1972 and 1975.[3] Reopened for burials,[4] but conditions further deteriorated.[5] In 1997, members of the AmeriCorps national service program worked to remove brush at Woodlawn.[6]

Young (Family). Remains of Notley Young were interred in the family lot on Square 390. They were subsequently disinterred and buried by Robert Brent in Carroll Chapel Graveyard, Forest Glen, Maryland.[7]

Young Mens (see also Mt. Pleasant Plain(s), and Free Young Mens Burying Ground). About one half mile northwest of Columbian College. Sexton is Mr. Talbert (1874). Mount Pleasant (1899). Discontinued, reinterments after 1890 to Woodlawn. (1,305)

---

[1] The News Leader (Laurel, Md.), 10 JAN 1968, "Final Notes on the Veitch Family," final part in a series of three articles. See also The News Leader, 27 DEC 1867, "County History Unconfined." As of October 1973, a monument for Isabella Veitch, 1826-1919 could be found.
[2] Records of the Columbia Historical Society, Vol. 22, pp. 193-194; Vol. 50, p. 114.
[3] Washington Star, 4 MAR 1973, "Sad Story of a Cemetery"; Washington Times, 16 APR 1987, "Woman Wages Lonely Battle to Preserve Black Cemeteries."
[4] Washington Star, 27 FEB 1975, "New School Helps Renewal of Old Cemetery."
[5] Washington Post, 13 DEC 1980, "Are Our Dead Truly Gone and Forgotten?"
[6] Washington Post, 6 FEB 1997, "New Life for a Neglected Cemetery."
[7] Records of the Columbia Historical Society, Vol. 21, pp. 148-149.

Abbreviations

Certificate numbers followed with "f" indicate that the place of death given on the certificate was classified by recordkeepers as "foreign," e.g. not in the District of Columbia. Such certificates usually note how the remains entered the District—by train, boat, or other means.

On occasion there will be duplicate certificate numbers, particularly for October 1875. For these, the compiler has inserted an alpha suffix, for example "005020a."

Common Abbreviations Used

C	Colored; black; Negro
d	Day
f	Foreign Death, see further explanation above
h	Hour(s)
I	Indian; I.T. for Indian Territory
m	Month(s)
M	Mulatto, offspring of a European and a Negro
min	Minute(s)
Q	Quadroon, offspring of a white person and a mulatto
w	Week(s)
W	White
y	Year(s)

DISTRICT OF COLUMBIA
Death Records
August 1, 1874 - July 31, 1879

No.	Name	Age	Race	Birth	Death Date	Burial Place
A						
004103	ABBOT, Elizth.	c.87y	W	Pa.	13 JUL 1875	Oak Hill
000898	ABBOT, George D.	65y	W	D.C.	22 OCT 1874	Oak Hill
014925	ABBOT, Harrieg Byron	87y	W	Mass.	03 MAR 1878	Oak Hill
007296	ABBOTT, Thomas F.	32y	W	D.C.	14 MAY 1876	Glenwood
008301	ABEL, Sarah P.	15y	W	Va.	17 JUL 1876	Congressional
004055	ABELL, Annie M.	18y	W	Va.	09 JUL 1875	Congressional
009265	ABENDSCHEIN, William	63y	W	Ger.	01 OCT 1876	Presbyterian
010247	ABENDSHEIN, Elizabeth	72y	W	Ger.	10 JAN 1877	Presbyterian
017148	ABERT, Jane Stone	11m	W	Ky.	23 AUG 1878	Rock Creek
017325	ABNER, Lewis	11m	W	D.C.	05 SEP 1878	Prospect Hill
013657	ABNER, Louise	43y	W	Prus.	28 OCT 1877	Prospect Hill
021017	ABRAHAM, Dennis	7y	C	D.C.	20 JUL 1879	Mt. Pleasant
008494	ABRAHAM, Isaac	11m	C	D.C.	30 JUL 1876	Young Mens
007142	ABRAHAM, Levi	68y	W	Pol.	28 APR 1876	N.Y. City
013157	ABRAHAM, Rebecca	27y	W	Ga.	11 SEP 1877	Graceland
007287	ABRAHAMS, Grace	40y	C	N.C.	13 MAY 1876	Young Mens
011963	ABRAMS, Alonza	3y	M	D.C.	19 JUN 1877	Mt. Zion
002484	ABRAMS, Catharine	30y	C	Va.	09 MAR 1875	Harmony
010359	ABRAMS, Harry R.	7m	W	D.C.	21 JAN 1877	Congressional
007604	ABRAMS, Jessie Blair	9y	W	N.Y.	12 JUN 1876	Congressional
011118	ACKER, Infant of H.B.	1d	W	D.C.	26 MAR 1877	Congressional
013665	ACKER, Nicholas	59y	W	Ger.	29 OCT 1877	Oak Hill
020371	ACTON, Allace Louisa	6y	C	D.C.	10 JUN 1879	Nonesuch[1]
015588	ACTON, Ann M.	56y	W	Va.	03 MAY 1878	Presbyterian
015007	ACTON, Henry J.	4m	W	D.C.	10 MAR 1878	Congressional
009155	ACTON, Henry T.	36y	W	D.C.	21 SEP 1876	Congressional
014719	ACTON, Martha E.	26y	W	D.C.	09 FEB 1878	Congressional
019928	ACTON, Martha Elizabeth	1y	W	D.C.	29 APR 1879	Congressional
016893	ACTON, William	45y	W	Ire.	04 AUG 1878	Presbyterian
011098	ADAMS, Addie DeLeon	40y	W	S.C.	23 MAR 1877	Oak Hill
005235	ADAMS, Alice	21y	W	D.C.	22 OCT 1875	Congressional
005603	ADAMS, Alice O.	62y	W	D.C.	29 NOV 1875	Congressional
002261	ADAMS, Annie Campbell	19y	W	Va.	21 FEB 1875	Fauquier Co., Va.
003931	ADAMS, Ara	8y	C	Va.	30 JUN 1875	Freedmen's Village
014053	ADAMS, Arthur	1y	C	Md.	10 DEC 1877	Young Mens
005318	ADAMS, Cora Omelia	2y	W	D.C.	31 OCT 1875	Oak Hill
020099	ADAMS, Edgar D.	35y	W	Va.	15 MAY 1879	Glenwood
001758	ADAMS, Edward	9m	C	D.C.	16 JAN 1875	Young Mens
016285	ADAMS, Elizabeth J.	35y	W	D.C.	24 JUN 1878	Oak Hill
009621	ADAMS, Frank D.	1y	C	D.C.	05 NOV 1876	Ebenezer
000308	ADAMS, Harriet A.	22y	W	Va.	24 AUG 1874	Leesburg, Va.
009309	ADAMS, Harry	2½d	W	D.C.	05 OCT 1876	Glenwood
017067	ADAMS, Harry	1m	C	D.C.	16 AUG 1878	Brightwood

---

[1] "Nonesuch" was the name of a 150-acre tract in Anacostia, D.C. which George Washington Young inherited from his father in 1826.

District of Columbia Death Records, August 1, 1874 to July 31, 1879

No.	Name	Age	Race	Birth	Death Date	Burial Place
001337	ADAMS, Henrietta	75y	C	Md.	07 DEC 1874	Baltimore, Md.
017334	ADAMS, Ida	7m	C	D.C.	06 SEP 1878	Beckett's
013618	ADAMS, Infant of Gabe	1m	C	D.C.	24 OCT 1877	Beckett's
012752	ADAMS, James	83y	W	Mass.	10 AUG 1877	Congressional
010411	ADAMS, James T.	64y	W	Md.	26 JAN 1877	Congressional
018736	ADAMS, Jane	58y	C	Md.	20 JAN 1879	Harmony
009126	ADAMS, Jane W.	48y	W	N.Y.	18 SEP 1876	Binghamton, N.Y.
012097	ADAMS, Janet	6m	C	D.C.	27 JUN 1877	Arlington, Va.
017850	ADAMS, John	18y	W	D.C.	25 OCT 1878	Congressional
006474	ADAMS, John Carrol	15y	W	Md.	26 FEB 1876	Baltimore, Md.
021167	ADAMS, John G.	62y	W	D.C.	31 JUL 1879	Glenwood
002959	ADAMS, John Q.	34y	W	Ind.	11 APR 1875	Oak Hill
013755	ADAMS, John Quincy	60y	W	Eng.	07 NOV 1877	Potters Field
009403	ADAMS, John Richard	2y	C	D.C.	13 OCT 1876	Beckett's
014877	ADAMS, Joseph Thornton	8y	W	N.H.	26 FEB 1878	Congressional
020672	ADAMS, Josephine	2y	C	D.C.	30 JUN 1879	Mt. Olivet
019981	ADAMS, Laura L.	11m	W	D.C.	04 MAY 1879	Mt. Olivet
006304	ADAMS, Laura V., Mrs.	42y	W	U.S.	11 FEB 1876	Congressional
018432	ADAMS, Lizzie	2y	C	D.C.	23 DEC 1878	Potters Field
018991	ADAMS, Lottie	1y	C	D.C.	08 FEB 1879	Harmony
005567	ADAMS, Margaret	25y	W	D.C.	26 NOV 1875	Congressional
001699	ADAMS, Martha	19y	C	Md.	11 JAN 1875	Young Mens
018483	ADAMS, Martha	28y	C	D.C.	28 DEC 1878	Harmony
019553	ADAMS, Martha	39y	C	Va.	26 MAR 1879	Potters Field
008664	ADAMS, Mary A.	69y	W	Md.	12 AUG 1876	Congressional
020919	ADAMS, Mary Ellen	1m	W	D.C.	14 JUL 1879	Congressional
009585	ADAMS, Mary F.	2y	W	D.C.	31 OCT 1876	Presbyterian
006241	ADAMS, Mary Jane	59y	W	D.C.	05 FEB 1876	Methodist
004165	ADAMS, Mary W.	1m	W	D.C.	17 JUL 1875	Congressional
004945	ADAMS, Maude Gertrude	11m	W	D.C.	07 SEP 1875	Congressional
004026	ADAMS, Nancy	19y	C	D.C.	07 JUL 1875	Mt. Olivet
013537	ADAMS, Nicholas	40y	W	Calif.	17 OCT 1877	Hospital
006328	ADAMS, Robert	22y	C	Va.	13 FEB 1876	Potters Field
005985	ADAMS, Robert	4y	C	Md.	10 JAN 1876	Adams Farm
013443	ADAMS, Robert	7m	C	D.C.	09 OCT 1877	Young Mens
019678	ADAMS, Sarah Jane	25y	C	D.C.	07 APR 1879	Young Mens
009385	ADAMSON, Edward	22y	W	D.C.	12 OCT 1876	Washington Asylum
003653	ADAMSON, Franklin C.	22y	W	D.C.	15 JUN 1875	Congressional
003736	ADAMSON, Joseph L., Jr.	25y	W	Pa.	21 JUN 1875	Congressional
001358	ADDISIN, Mary Ann	47y	C	Md.	10 DEC 1874	Harmony
014765	ADDISON, Alice	73y	C	Md.	15 FEB 1878	Harmony
019136	ADDISON, Charles	42y	C	D.C.	21 FEB 1879	Smith's
014760	ADDISON, Edmund B.	83y	W	Md.	14 FEB 1878	Alexandria, Va.
019496	ADDISON, Ella Beale Thurlow	28y	W	Pa.	22 MAR 1879	Chester, Pa.
014438	ADDISON, George	42y	C	Md.	16 JAN 1878	Harmony
006269	ADDISON, Infant of Rezin	4d	M	D.C.	08 FEB 1876	Tennallytown
005773	ADDISON, James	1y	C	D.C.	17 DEC 1875	Mt. Zion
004038	ADDISON, James	6y	C	D.C.	08 JUL 1875	Addison's
000031	ADDISON, John	5m	C	D.C.	02 AUG 1874	Washington Asylum
020933	ADDISON, John	26y	C	Md.	15 JUL 1879	Mt. Olivet
005088	ADDISON, Joseph	12m	C	D.C.	18 SEP 1875	Mt. Olivet
000232	ADDISON, Judso C.	39y	W	D.C.	18 AUG 1874	Oak Hill
019860	ADDISON, Mary J.	67y	W	Va.	22 APR 1879	Congressional
013421	ADDISON, Mary Watkins	6m	W	D.C.	07 OCT 1877	Oak Hill
002399	ADDISON, Samuel	33y	C	Md.	02 MAR 1875	Mt. Olivet
007027	ADDISON, Sarah Jane	8y	C	D.C.	17 APR 1876	Smith's

District of Columbia Death Records, August 1, 1874 to July 31, 1879   3

No.	Name	Age	Race	Birth	Death Date	Burial Place
010375	ADDISON, William	87y	C	Md.	22 JAN 1877	Mt. Olivet
000680	ADELE, Raphard	20y	W	Ger.	30 SEP 1874	Mt. Olivet
008857	ADISON, Mary Frances	14m	C	D.C.	28 AUG 1876	Harmony
010566	ADKINS, Infant of David	7d	C	D.C.	08 FEB 1877	Mt. Olivet
004473	ADLER, Charles	5m	W	D.C.	06 AUG 1875	Prospect Hill
007062	ADLER, Emil Albert	13y	W	N.J.	21 APR 1876	Prospect Hill
001774	ADLER, Ewald	1y	W	D.C.	18 JAN 1875	Prospect Hill
012608	ADLER, Henry Michael Jacob	7m	W	D.C.	30 JUL 1877	Prospect Hill
005359	ADT, Infant of Francis J.	½d	W	D.C.	05 NOV 1875	Congressional
006278	AFFLICK, Bessie B.	2y	W	Tenn.	09 FEB 1876	Congressional
017952	AGER, Mary Emily	51y	W	D.C.	05 NOV 1878	Oak Hill
013622	AGES, Agnes	1y	C	D.C.	25 OCT 1877	Young Mens
007131	AHEM, Stephen	24y	W	Mass.	27 APR 1876	Hospital
016754	AHEN, Arcseca	9m	C	D.C.	25 JUL 1878	Harmony
016354	AHERN, Helena M.	54w	W	Ire.	29 JUN 1878	Mt. Olivet
018549	AIGLER, Sophia	77y	W	Ger.	03 JAN 1879	Prospect Hill
017194	AIKEN, Eliza M.	24y	W	D.C.	25 AUG 1878	Congressional
018431	AIKEN, Fredrick Argyle	41y	W	Mass.	23 DEC 1878	Oak Hill
020590	AINGER, Brainard Rhodes	1y	W	Mich.	24 JUN 1879	Charlotte, Mich.
019767	AKER, Lucy Maud	20d	W	D.C.	14 APR 1879	Glenwood
012658	ALBERT, James Edward	1y	C	D.C.	04 AUG 1877	Beckett's
017904	ALBERT, John	8h	W	D.C.	30 OCT 1878	Prospect Hill
018616	ALBRECHT, Charles Henry	7y	W	D.C.	09 JAN 1879	Oak Hill
000858	ALBRECHT, Clara Henrietta	1y	W	D.C.	19 OCT 1874	Oak Hill
000416	ALBRIGHT, Harry	2y	W	D.C.	03 SEP 1874	Oak Hill
018851	ALBURGER, Robert V.	20y	W	Pa.	28 JAN 1879	Philadelphia, Pa.
002188	ALCORN, Mary Elizabeth	7w	C	D.C.	16 FEB 1875	Laurel, Md.
005039	ALDEN, Mabel H.	1y	W	D.C.	14 SEP 1875	Glenwood
002066	ALEXANDER, Ada	39y	C	Va.	07 FEB 1875	Baptist Church Potomac
003160	ALEXANDER, Elizabeth	38y	M	Va.	28 APR 1875	Baptist
016808	ALEXANDER, Fredie	18m	C	D.C.	29 JUL 1878	Young Mens
004770	ALEXANDER, George S.	2y	C	D.C.	27 AUG 1875	Potters Field
000250	ALEXANDER, Ida	9m	C	D.C.	20 AUG 1874	Harmony
017360	ALEXANDER, Ida	12y	C	D.C.	10 SEP 1878	Macedonia
005447	ALEXANDER, Infant of Andrew	7d	C	D.C.	13 NOV 1875	Potters Field
007453	ALEXANDER, Infant of Harvy	1d	C	D.C.	01 JUN 1876	Young Mens
014088	ALEXANDER, Infant of Robert	2d	C	D.C.	13 DEC 1877	Swartz's
010574	ALEXANDER, James	c.45y	C	Va.	10 FEB 1877	Potters Field
014823	ALEXANDER, Jane	51y	C	Md.	20 FEB 1878	Montgomery Co., Md.
008594	ALEXANDER, Jane B.	57y	W	N.Y.	07 AUG 1876	Oak Hill
014694	ALEXANDER, John	1y	C	D.C.	07 FEB 1878	Young Mens
004362	ALEXANDER, Lizzie	1y	C	D.C.	29 JUL 1875	Young Mens
005906	ALEXANDER, Marria, of Sarah	4m	C	D.C.	01 JAN 1876	Young Mens
010558	ALEXANDER, Mary F.	12y	C	R.I.	08 FEB 1877	Young Mens
011487	ALEXANDER, Rebeka	4m	W	D.C.	02 MAY 1877	Adas Israel
004327	ALEXANDER, Rosie Lee	1y	C	D.C.	27 JUL 1875	Mt. Pleasant Plain
003514	ALEXANDER, Samuel	84y	C	Md.	02 JUN 1875	Ebenezer
009962	ALEXANDER, Susan C.	64y	W	Ver.	14 DEC 1876	Vergennes, Ver.
012315	ALEXANDER, Thomas	51y	C	Va.	11 JUL 1877	Mt. Zion
002083	ALEXANDER, Walter	5m	M	D.C.	08 FEB 1875	Beckett's
017419	ALEXANDER, William	6y	C	D.C.	16 SEP 1878	Young Mens
015701	ALEXANDER, Willie	4m	C	D.C.	13 MAY 1878	Potters Field
017087	ALEXANDRIA, Sally	60y	C	Va.	18 AUG 1878	Mt. Pleasant
015318	ALEY, Patrick N.	27y	W	D.C.	08 APR 1878	Mt. Olivet
013957	ALFEST, Gustave	50y	W	Den.	29 NOV 1877	Congressional
015106	ALGIE, John	35y	W	Pa.	18 MAR 1878	Congressional

District of Columbia Death Records, August 1, 1874 to July 31, 1879

No.	Name	Age	Race	Birth	Death Date	Burial Place
020235	ALLAN, James	65y	C	Md.	31 MAY 1879	Beckett's
004646	ALLAN, Katie Murph	1y	W	D.C.	18 AUG 1875	Congressional
004761	ALLAN, Rosa	1y	C	D.C.	26 AUG 1875	Young Mens
002791	ALLAN, William	27y	C	Md.	29 MAR 1875	Harmony
010144	ALLEGER, Grace M.	4y	W	N.Y.	01 JAN 1877	Booneville, Wyo.
006193	ALLEMAN, Emma A.	26y	W	Ohio	31 JAN 1876	Oak Hill
006042	ALLEMAN, H.C.	17h	W	D.C.	17 JAN 1876	Congressional
001352	ALLEN, Ada Sophia	4y	W	Ind.	10 DEC 1874	Congressional
001920	ALLEN, Alfred	40y	C	Ky.	27 JAN 1875	Young Mens
011928	ALLEN, Alice Vini	1y	C	D.C.	16 JUN 1877	Harmony
010265	ALLEN, Anna	39y	W	Pa.	12 JAN 1877	Mt. Olivet
002534	ALLEN, Annie	2m	M	D.C.	12 MAR 1875	Mt. Olivet
013071	ALLEN, Betsey	37y	C	Va.	04 SEP 1877	Young Mens
000902	ALLEN, Butler	90y	C	Md.	22 OCT 1874	Smith's
003497	ALLEN, Carrie Stevens	30y	W	D.C.	31 MAY 1875	Congressional
016122	ALLEN, Charles Ashford	2y	M	D.C.	12 JUN 1878	Harmony
014474	ALLEN, Christianna	67y	W	N.J.	19 JAN 1878	Hightstown, N.J.
007651	ALLEN, David	1y	C	Pa.	15 JUN 1876	Mt. Zion
004424	ALLEN, Edgar	1m	C	N.W.	03 AUG 1875	Beckett's
019902	ALLEN, Edward R.	13d	W	D.C.	26 APR 1879	Holy Rood
008215	ALLEN, Ella Zena	11m	C	D.C.	12 JUL 1876	Harmony
017572	ALLEN, Francis	1m	C	D.C.	30 SEP 1878	Mt. Olivet
019543	ALLEN, Frank	30y	C	Va.	25 MAR 1879	Beckett's
000467	ALLEN, Geo.	14y	W	Md.	10 SEP 1874	Potters Field
013385	ALLEN, George C.	10m	W	Va.	03 OCT 1877	Holy Rood
013898	ALLEN, Henry	1y	C	D.C.	24 NOV 1877	Potters Field
020891	ALLEN, Henry	69y	C	Va.	12 JUL 1879	Potters Field
003276	ALLEN, Infant of Carrie	2d	C	D.C.	09 MAY 1875	Mt. Olivet
002704	ALLEN, Infant of Robert	1d	C	D.C.	23 MAR 1875	Harmony
013429	ALLEN, Jacob M.	1y	W	D.C.	08 OCT 1877	Congressional
007410	ALLEN, Jeremiah	3y	C	Pa.	26 MAY 1876	Mt. Zion
017979	ALLEN, John Henry	7m	C	D.C	08 NOV 1878	Washington Asylum
013939	ALLEN, June	1y	W	Md.	27 NOV 1877	Glenwood
017289	ALLEN, Loney	7y	W	Md.	02 SEP 1878	Rock Creek/Oak Hill
002309	ALLEN, Margaret Cath. Forsyth	28y	W	Eng.	24 FEB 1875	Mt. Olivet
008498	ALLEN, Margaret N.	6m	W	Ark.	31 JUL 1876	Mt. Olivet
001900f	ALLEN, Maria A.	c.35y	W	D.C.	26 JAN 1875	Oak Hill
019794	ALLEN, Marie L.	12h	W	D.C.	16 APR 1879	Holy Rood
004605	ALLEN, Mary	1y	W	D.C.	15 AUG 1875	Harmony
013765	ALLEN Mary	35y	C	Md.	08 NOV 1877	Beckett's
016121	ALLEN, Mary	8m	W	D.C.	12 JUN 1878	Mt. Olivet
018906	ALLEN, Mary	c.28y	C	Md.	01 FEB 1879	Beckett's
020192	ALLEN, Mary	16y	C	Md.	25 MAY 1879	Potters Field
001185	ALLEN, Mary A.	19y	W	D.C.	19 NOV 1874	Congressional
009904	ALLEN, Mary A.	77	W	Eng.	08 DEC 1876	Methodist, East
005212a	ALLEN, Mary E.	28y	C	D.C.	20 OCT 1875	Mt. Zion
003579	ALLEN, Mary Gertrude	1y	W	D.C.	09 JUN 1875	Oak Hill
018907	ALLEN, Philip	1y	C	D.C.	01 FEB 1879	Mt. Pleasant
016713	ALLEN, Rachel	2½y	C	D.C.	22 JUL 1878	Mr. Lion's Cem., G.T.
012538	ALLEN, Raymond	21y	M	Md.	26 JUL 1877	Harmony
008762	ALLEN, Rebecca	62y	C	Md.	21 AUG 1876	Mt. Olivet
017455	ALLEN, Robert	25y	M	Md.	19 SEP 1878	Hospital, Government
012199	ALLEN, Sallie Ann	40y	C	Va.	03 JUL 1877	Young Mens
013681	ALLEN, Sedonia	5y	M	D.C.	31 OCT 1877	Harmony
006053	ALLEN, Virginia	24y	C	D.C.	18 JAN 1876	Baptist
019766	ALLEN, Willie	3y	C	D.C.	14 APR 1879	Potters Field

District of Columbia Death Records, August 1, 1874 to July 31, 1879   5

No.	Name	Age	Race	Birth	Death Date	Burial Place
016497	ALLEN, Wm.	47y	W	D.C.	08 JUL 1878	Presbyterian
003022	ALLEN, Wm. Clinton	6y	C	D.C.	17 APR 1875	Harmony
007808	ALLEN, Wm. Henry	6m	C	D.C.	24 JUN 1876	Mt. Olivet
002210	ALLENS, Hattie	4m	C	D.C.	17 FEB 1875	Lanham Sta., Md.
002707	ALLEY, Lee H.	37y	W	N.C.	23 MAR 1875	Filmore, Ind.
016230	ALLISON, Jennie L.	5m	W	D.C.	20 JUN 1878	Rock Creek
015153	ALLISON, John	65y	W	Pa.	23 MAR 1878	Beaver Co., Pa.
003203	ALLISON, Thomas D.	c.59y	W	Va.	03 MAY 1875	Glenwood
020135	ALLMAN, Thomas	4y	W	D.C.	18 MAY 1879	Mt. Olivet
007940	ALLMANN, William	20y	W	Va.	30 JUN 1876	Mt. Olivet
008602	ALLYN, Lucius B.	66y	W	Conn.	07 AUG 1876	Glenwood
007303	ALMAN, Francis	1y	W	D.C.	15 MAY 1876	Mt. Olivet
005078a	ALMAN, Margaret	19y	W	Pa.	07 OCT 1875	Mt. Olivet
003449	ALPINS, Jno. Thos.	20y	C	Va.	26 MAY 1875	Harmony
010093	ALTEMUS, Benjamin C.	61y	W	Pa.	27 DEC 1876	Congressional
020847	ALTON, Jane	80y	C	Md.	09 JUL 1879	Young Mens
009625	ALTROGGEN, Christopher	58y	W	Ger.	05 NOV 1876	Hospital
002800	ALTSCHUH, Arvilla A.T.	21y	W	Ala.	30 MAR 1875	Glenwood
001691	ALTSCHUH, Francis Joseph	9m	W	D.C.	11 JAN 1875	Richmond, Va.
003295	ALVEY, Mary	20y	W	Va.	12 MAY 1875	Mt. Olivet
012247	ALVORD, Henry Jones	66y	W	Mass.	07 JUL 1877	Detroit, Mich.
002319	AMBLER, Claudie	2y	C	D.C.	25 FEB 1875	Mt. Pleasant
015070	AMBLER, Jesse Eugene	16m	M	D.C.	15 MAR 1878	Harmony
019304	AMBLER, William Russell	34y	W	Ky.	07 MAR 1879	Glenwood
000973	AMBUSH, Andrew	1m	C	D.C.	29 OCT 1874	Potters Field
018833	AMBUSH, Charles Augustus	1y	C	D.C.	27 JAN 1879	Young Mens
007544	AMBUSH, Enoch	69y	C	Md.	08 JUN 1876	Harmony
000627	AMBUSH, Florance Hellen	6m	C	D.C.	24 SEP 1874	Mt. Pleasant Plain
005883	AMBUSH, James Delaware	12y	C	D.C.	28 DEC 1875	Harmony
006986	AMBUSH, Joseph	40y	C	D.C.	11 APR 1876	Mt. Pleasant Plain
021166	AMBUSH, Millie	65y	C	Md.	31 JUL 1879	Baptist
002572	AMES, Infant of John	1d	C	D.C.	15 MAR 1875	Harmony
009915	AMES, Maria	30y	C	Va.	10 DEC 1876	Potters Field
002700	AMES, Mary	2m	W	D.C.	23 MAR 1875	Mt. Olivet
003961	AMOS, Ferdinand Pomeroy	5m	M	D.C.	02 JUL 1875	Young Mens
005011	AN, Johanna	7m	W	D.C.	01 OCT 1875	Prospect Hill
020868	ANDEESAR, Appoloni	13y	W	D.C.	10 JUL 1879	St. Mary's
020563	ANDERMOTT, George	39y	W	Ger.	22 JUN 1879	Hospital, Government
000790	ANDERSON, Alberta	1y	W	D.C.	12 OCT 1874	Congressional
006043	ANDERSON, Alice	10m	C	D.C.	17 JAN 1876	Young Mens
007174	ANDERSON, Alice	19y	C	Va.	01 MAY 1876	Ebenezer
009638	ANDERSON, Alice	80y	W	D.C.	08 NOV 1876	Holy Rood
014119	ANDERSON, Andrew J.	33y	W	Den.	17 DEC 1877	Hospital, Government
020848	ANDERSON, Annie	37y	C	Md.	09 JUL 1879	Potters Field
021109	ANDERSON, Arthur P.	17m	W	D.C.	26 JUL 1879	Mt. Olivet
004489	ANDERSON, Beckie	3y	C	D.C.	07 AUG 1875	Harmony
007574	ANDERSON, Camille	2y	C	N.Y.	10 JUN 1876	Ebenezer
013570	ANDERSON, Charles	5m	C	D.C.	20 OCT 1877	Harmony
014452	ANDERSON, Charles A.	5d	C	D.C.	17 JAN 1878	Harmony
005426	ANDERSON, Charlotte	36y	C	Va.	11 NOV 1875	Mt. Zion
005371	ANDERSON, Chas. Melvin	8m	C	D.C.	06 NOV 1875	Harmony
000410	ANDERSON, Corinna Georgia	28y	W	N.Y.	02 SEP 1874	Oak Hill
003679	ANDERSON, Cornelia	24y	C	Md.	17 JUN 1875	Mt. Zion
017055	ANDERSON, Cornelius	24y	C	Va.	15 AUG 1878	Mt. Zion
009339	ANDERSON, Cortney	19y	C	Va.	08 OCT 1876	Young Mens
011222	ANDERSON, E.F., Col.	38y	W	Pa.	05 APR 1877	Congressional

District of Columbia Death Records, August 1, 1874 to July 31, 1879

No.	Name	Age	Race	Birth	Death Date	Burial Place
011793	ANDERSON, E.J.	3m	W	D.C.	03 JUN 1877	Graceland
013911	ANDERSON, Edward	4y	C	D.C.	25 NOV 1877	Potters Field
013044	ANDERSON, Eleanor	81y	W	S.C.	01 SEP 1877	Congressional
016763	ANDERSON, Elizabeth	79y	W	Va.	26 JUL 1878	Congressional
006475	ANDERSON, Eva	14y	C	D.C.	26 FEB 1876	Young Mens
012946	ANDERSON, Frances	30y	C	Va.	25 AUG 1877	Harmony
004270	ANDERSON, Frank	14y	C	Va.	24 JUL 1875	Beckett's
020934	ANDERSON, Frederick Marion	2y	W	Ill.	15 JUL 1879	Rock Creek
007028	ANDERSON, George	52y	W	Md.	17 APR 1876	Soldier's Home
007194	ANDERSON, George	2m	C	D.C.	03 MAY 1876	Ebenezer
019813	ANDERSON, George Samuel	11y	W	D.C.	18 APR 1879	Old Fields, Md.
005566	ANDERSON, George W.	21y	W	D.C.	26 NOV 1875	Oak Hill
011767	ANDERSON, Harriet	7d	C	D.C.	01 JUN 1877	Mt. Pleasant
020890	ANDERSON, Henrietta	10y	C	D.C.	12 JUL 1879	Young Mens
000266	ANDERSON, Henry	3y	C	D.C.	21 AUG 1874	Beckett's
003186	ANDERSON, Howard	5y	C	D.C.	01 MAY 1875	Mt. Pleasant
019293	ANDERSON, Infant of George	4d	C	D.C.	06 MAR 1879	Mt. Pleasant
007259	ANDERSON, Infant of George	4d	C	D.C.	10 MAY 1876	Mt. Pleasant
006027	ANDERSON, Infant of Henry	1d	C	D.C.	15 JAN 1876	Beckett's
001317	ANDERSON, Infant of Lewis	1d	C	D.C.	05 DEC 1874	Potters Field
018877	ANDERSON, Infant of Lizzie	9w	W	D.C.	30 JAN 1879	Potters Field
014860	ANDERSON, Infant of Matthew	6d	C	D.C.	24 FEB 1878	Beckett's
001633	ANDERSON, Infant of William	7d	C	D.C.	04 JAN 1875	Potters Field
014947	ANDERSON, Isabella	27y	W	D.C.	05 MAR 1878	Rock Creek
010175	ANDERSON, James	c.1y	C	D.C.	05 JAN 1877	Young Mens
012216	ANDERSON, James	57y	W	N.Y.	04 JUL 1877	Mt. Olivet
010179	ANDERSON, Jeremiah	63y	W	U.S.	05 JAN 1877	Potters Field
007559	ANDERSON, John	30y	C	Va.	09 JUN 1876	Potters Field
007445	ANDERSON, John	39y	C	Va.	31 MAY 1876	Potters Field
013264	ANDERSON, John	11y	C	D.C.	21 SEP 1877	Moore's
020301	ANDERSON, John	29y	W	Va.	05 JUN 1879	Mt. Olivet
007317	ANDERSON, Josephine	18y	C	Va.	16 MAY 1876	Potters Field
019063	ANDERSON, Judy	70y	C	Va.	14 FEB 1879	Mt. Pleasant
009390	ANDERSON, Leavy	14y	C	Md.	12 OCT 1876	Mt. Olivet
009911	ANDERSON, Leonard J.	56y	W	D.C.	09 DEC 1876	Oak Hill
019156	ANDERSON, Lewis	23y	C	Md.	23 FEB 1879	Harmony
015870	ANDERSON, Louis	17m	W	D.C.	28 MAY 1878	Young Mens
003326	ANDERSON, Lucinda	c.40y	C	Va.	14 MAY 1875	Young Mens
003768	ANDERSON, Margaret	1y	C	D.C.	22 JUN 1875	Ebenezer
008791	ANDERSON, Maria	50y	C	Md.	23 AUG 1876	Harmony
017213	ANDERSON, Martha	1y	C	D.C.	27 AUG 1878	Beckett's
007329	ANDERSON, Martha Ann	47y	C	Va.	18 MAY 1876	Mt. Olivet
015209	ANDERSON, Martha W.	56y	W	Md.	28 MAR 1878	Bladensburg, Md.
019597	ANDERSON, Mary	69y	C	Va.	30 MAR 1879	Moore's
007346	ANDERSON, Mary Elizabeth	20y	C	D.C.	20 MAY 1876	Ebenezer
001053	ANDERSON, Mary Ellen	3m	W	D.C.	05 NOV 1874	Congressional
003710	ANDERSON, May A.	5m	W	D.C.	19 JUN 1875	Mt. Olivet
004135	ANDERSON, Richard	12h	W	D.C.	15 JUL 1875	Oak Hill
014101	ANDERSON, Richard	1y	C	D.C.	15 DEC 1877	Harmony
012848	ANDERSON, Robert Milton	2y	W	D.C.	17 AUG 1877	Congressional
002329	ANDERSON, Salie	c.55y	C	Va.	26 FEB 1875	Richmond, Va.
001242	ANDERSON, Saml.	9y	C	D.C.	27 NOV 1874	Harmony
003299	ANDERSON, Saml.	c.30y	C	U.S.	12 MAY 1875	Potters Field
002109	ANDERSON, Samuel	60y	C	Md.	10 FEB 1875	Mt. Zion
008850	ANDERSON, Samuel	50y	C	Va.	28 AUG 1876	Harmony
001681	ANDERSON, Susan Matilda	44y	W	D.C.	10 JAN 1875	Congressional

District of Columbia Death Records, August 1, 1874 to July 31, 1879   7

No.	Name	Age	Race	Birth	Death Date	Burial Place
010058	ANDERSON, William	9d	C	D.C.	24 DEC 1876	Harmony
012788	ANDERSON, William	70y	C	Md.	13 AUG 1877	Mt. Zion
013428	ANDRE, Bertha E.	4y	W	D.C.	08 OCT 1877	Congressional
008555	ANDRES, Louis	3d	W	D.C.	04 AUG 1876	Holy Rood
020849	ANDREW, Thomas, Rev.	53y	W	Eng.	09 JUL 1879	Rock Creek
000445	ANDREWS, Cecilia	42y	C	D.C.	07 SEP 1874	Potters Field
009026	ANDREWS, Eliza	78y	W	D.C.	11 SEP 1876	Rock Creek
010431	ANDREWS, George W.	17y	W	D.C.	28 JAN 1877	Congressional
015702	ANDREWS, Henrietta Maria	85y	W	Eng.	13 MAY 1878	Congressional
009753	ANDREWS, Lizzie	26y	C	D.C.	20 NOV 1876	Harmony
002796	ANDREWS, Lotta	5m	W	D.C.	30 MAR 1875	Mt. Olivet
003972	ANDREWS, Mary Eliza Ada	4m	C	D.C.	03 JUL 1875	Harmony
008027	ANDREWS, Samuel	6m	C	D.C.	05 JUL 1876	Mt. Olivet
008007	ANDREWS, William	72y	W	Va.	04 JUL 1876	Winchester, Va.
019725	ANDREWS, William	54y	W	Ohio	11 APR 1879	Hospital, Government
008394	ANGEL, Ada M.	10m	W	D.C.	23 JUL 1876	Methodist
020589	ANGEL, Emily	c.73y	C	Va.	24 JUN 1879	Young Mens
007872	ANGEL, Ida	9m	W	D.C.	27 JUN 1876	Methodist
019859	ANGEL, Mary C.	45y	W	Md.	22 APR 1879	Mt. Olivet
013322	ANGELL, Flawrence V.	1y	W	D.C.	27 SEP 1877	Mt. Olivet
014668	ANGELL, Joseph W.	30y	W	D.C.	05 FEB 1878	Oak Hill
007809	ANGELL, Mary E.	64y	W	D.C.	24 JUN 1876	Oak Hill
011996	ANGERMAN, Adolph	25y	W	Ger.	21 JUN 1877	Prospect Hill
005121	ANGERMAN, Infant of Adolph	13d	W	D.C.	21 SEP 1875	Ebenezer
003505	ANGNEY, Isaac	78y	W	Pa.	02 JUN 1875	Congressional
001881	ANNBRICHT, John	21y	W	La.	24 JAN 1875	Battle Ground
005213	ANTHONY, Henry	38y	W	Pa.	29 SEP 1875	Glenwood
014878	APPECH, Louisa	30y	W	Ger.	26 FEB 1878	Prospect Hill
001311	APPERMANN, Ulrich	39y	W	Ger.	05 DEC 1874	Glenwood
008751	APPICH, Emma	1y	W	D.C.	20 AUG 1876	Prospect Hill
007950	APPILUCHI, Margaret	5d	W	D.C.	01 JUL 1876	Congressional
013876	APPLEBY, Edith	85y	C	Va.	21 NOV 1877	Baptist
012797	APPLEBY, Elizabeth	77y	W	Eng.	14 AUG 1877	Oak Hill
008597	APPLEBY, Laura Maud	1y	W	D.C.	07 AUG 1876	Oak Hill
001436	APPLER, Isabella A.	66y	W	Md.	19 DEC 1874	Baltimore, Md.
001868	ARANDES, Henry Joseph	29y	W	Prus.	24 JAN 1875	St. Mary's
016237	ARBUCKLE, Robert C.	45y	W	Ohio	21 JUN 1878	Graceland/Arlington
007619	ARBUCKLE, Robert Edward	4m	W	D.C.	13 JUN 1876	Graceland/Arlington
011381	ARCHER, Agnes	36y	W	D.C.	21 APR 1877	Holy Rood
018713	ARCHER, Albert	c.55y	C	Va.	18 JAN 1879	Potters Field
008692	ARCHER, Emma F.	11y	C	Mass.	15 AUG 1876	Harmony
004874	ARCHER, John	11m	W	D.C.	02 SEP 1875	Holy Rood
012763	ARCHER, John T.	5m	W	D.C.	11 AUG 1877	Holy Rood
004537	ARCHER, Robert A.	62y	W	Md.	11 AUG 1875	Baltimore, Md.
002059	ARCHIBALD, Walter	2m	W	DC.	07 FEB 1875	Glenwood
017744	ARDEESER, Mary A.	78y	W	Ger.	15 OCT 1878	St. Mary's
004326	ARDUSER, Martin	65y	W	Ger.	27 JUL 1875	St. Mary's
018852	ARENDES, Annie Regina	2m	W	D.C.	28 JAN 1879	Mt. Olivet
008905	ARENDT, Samuel	55y	W	U.S.	31 AUG 1876	Hospital, Government
018391	ARENZ, Emma	1y	W	D.C.	20 DEC 1878	Prospect Hill
003110	ARINGTON, Mary A.	67y	W	Va.	25 APR 1875	Presbyterian
010759	ARMES, Mary Elizabeth	8d	W	D.C.	23 FEB 1877	Oak Hill
003039	ARMISTEAD, Anne	58y	M	Va.	18 APR 1875	Mt. Zion
006173	ARMISTEAD, Sarah Elizabeth	30y	W	D.C.	29 JAN 1876	Glenwood
015606	ARMOR, John E.	1y	W	D.C.	04 MAY 1878	Congressional
012472	ARMOUR, Robert, Jr.	3m	W	D.C.	22 JUL 1877	Oak Hill

District of Columbia Death Records, August 1, 1874 to July 31, 1879

No.	Name	Age	Race	Birth	Death Date	Burial Place
010295	ARMSTEAD, Andrew	16y	C	Va.	15 JAN 1877	Potters Field
003451	ARMSTEAD, Infant of Henry	9d	C	D.C.	27 MAY 1875	Young Mens
009029	ARMSTEAD, Infant of Wm.	8h	M	D.C.	11 SEP 1876	Ebenezer
007382	ARMSTRONG, Alice	10m	C	D.C.	23 MAY 1876	Young Mens
005425	ARMSTRONG, Ella	11m	C	D.C.	11 NOV 1875	Ebenezer
019064	ARMSTRONG, Ezekial	10m	C	D.C.	14 FEB 1879	Young Mens
019858	ARMSTRONG, Jeffrey	71y	C	Va.	22 APR 1879	Potters Field
004516	ARMSTRONG, Jessie May	7m	W	D.C.	08 AUG 1875	Perkins' Chapel, Md.[1]
004604	ARMSTRONG, John Wm.	1y	W	D.C.	15 AUG 1875	Congressional
001122	ARMSTRONG, Julia	1m	C	D.C.	11 NOV 1874	Young Mens
018593	ARMSTRONG, Mary E.	2m	W	D.C.	07 JAN 1879	Graceland
009433	ARMSTRONG, Robezet	1y	C	D.C.	16 OCT 1876	Harmony
012704	ARMSTRONG, Willianna	1y	C	D.C.	07 AUG 1877	Potters Field
013553	ARNETH, William H.	3y	W	D.C.	18 OCT 1877	Prospect Hill
012204	ARNOLD, Eva May	2m	W	D.C.	03 JUL 1877	Glenwood
015767	ARNOLD, Frank Joseph	3m	W	D.C.	19 MAY 1878	St. Mary's
006268	ARNOLD, George H.	31y	W	N.Y.	08 FEB 1876	North Cohocton, N.Y.
013360	ARNOLD, Harrison H.B.	49y	W	Va.	01 OCT 1877	Alexandria, Va.
001372	ARNOLD, Henry	2h	W	D.C.	12 DEC 1874	St. Mary's
015315	ARNOLD, Henry A.	36y	W	Va.	08 APR 1878	Alexandria, Va.
008417	ARNOLD, Joseph J.	87y	W	Va.	25 JUL 1876	Hospital
003277	ARNOLD, Julia Ann	4m	W	Md.	10 MAY 1875	Mt. Olivet
000443	ARNOLD, Maria, Mrs.	76y	W	Va.	07 SEP 1874	Oak Hill
004136	ARNOLD, Mary Elizabeth	9m	C	D.C.	15 JUL 1875	Moore's, Hillsdale
014167	ARNOLD, Mary Geneveve	14y	W	Va.	22 DEC 1877	Glenwood
007490	ARNOLD, Mary Kate	6m	W	D.C.	04 JUN 1876	St. Mary's
005305	ARNOLD, Maurice Emerrey	1y	W	D.C.	29 OCT 1875	Congressional
020348	ARNOLD, Rebecca	28y	W	Md.	09 JUN 1879	Prospect Hill
005226	ARNOLD, Sarah Rebecca	30y	W	Va.	30 SEP 1875	Congressional
004179	ARNOLD, Thomas F.	8m	W	D.C.	18 JUL 1875	Prospect Hill
014948	ARNOLD, Toner	4y	W	D.C.	05 MAR 1878	Baltimore, Md.
003528	ARNOLD, William	51y	W	Md.	04 JUN 1875	Mt. Olivet
010211	ARNOLD, William	3w	W	D.C.	07 JAN 1877	St. Mary's
001663	ARTH, Anthony	3m	W	D.C.	09 JAN 1875	Mt. Olivet
011503	ARTH, John Philip	77y	W	Ger.	04 MAY 1877	Congressional
007161	ARTH, Philip L.	23y	W	D.C.	30 APR 1876	Congressional
000633	ARTH, Reuben Winfield	7y	W	D.C.	24 SEP 1874	Congressional
002273	ARTH, William	3y	W	D.C.	22 FEB 1875	Congressional
016187	ARTHUR, Hezekiah	34y	C	Md.	16 JUN 1878	Payne's
011914	ARTHUR, James	76y	W	Scot.	15 JUN 1877	Rock Creek
003439	ARTHUR, Jane	68y	W	N.Y.	25 MAY 1875	Glenwood
007506	ASCHENBACH, Henry	4y	W	D.C.	05 JUN 1876	Prospect Hill
017751	ASCHENBACH, John Valentine	38y	W	Ger.	16 OCT 1878	Prospect Hill
004472	ASCHENBACK, Herman	4y	W	D.C.	05 AUG 1875	Prospect Hill
020673	ASH, Blanche Stella	9d	W	D.C.	30 JUN 1879	Congressional
017288	ASH, Francis L.	45y	W	Md.	02 SEP 1878	Presbyterian
018627	ASH, Henrietta Maria	74y	W	Md.	10 JAN 1879	Rock Creek
019938	ASH, Henry T.	43y	W	Ky.	30 APR 1879	Rock Creek
007790	ASH, Mary	9m	W	D.C.	23 JUN 1876	Mt. Olivet
008461	ASHBY, Eddie	4m	C	D.C.	28 JUL 1876	Potters Field
004910	ASHBY, John Robert	51y	W	Va.	05 SEP 1875	Congressional
003557	ASHDOWN, Emma	30y	W	D.C.	07 JUN 1875	Congressional
006482	ASHDOWN, Francis Edgar	11m	W	D.C.	27 FEB 1876	Congressional

[1] Located in Prince George's County, Md.

District of Columbia Death Records, August 1, 1874 to July 31, 1879   9

No.	Name	Age	Race	Birth	Death Date	Burial Place
015218	ASHDOWN, William W.	34y	W	D.C.	29 MAR 1878	Congressional
013890	ASHE, John G.	69y	W	N.Y.	23 NOV 1877	Congressional
006279	ASHFIELD, Alfred	38y	W	N.Y.	09 FEB 1876	Mt. Olivet
010136	ASHFORD, Craven	70y	W	Va.	31 DEC 1876	Rock Creek
014778	ASHFORD, Emerella	66y	W	Va.	16 FEB 1878	Rock Creek
005764	ASHFORD, George Thomas	2y	W	D.C.	16 DEC 1875	Congressional
002690	ASHLEY, Joseph R	42y	W	Pa.	22 MAR 1875	Glenwood
008918	ASHLEY, Susie	6m	C	D.C.	01 SEP 1876	Beckett's
008957	ASHTON, Alberta	17y	C	Va.	03 SEP 1876	Beckett's
010204	ASHTON, Alice	1y	C	D.C.	07 JAN 1877	Young Mens
018390	ASHTON, Charles	46y	W	Va.	20 DEC 1878	Congressional
016496	ASHTON, Edmonia	8m	C	D.C.	08 JUL 1878	Mt. Pleasant
000864	ASHTON, Georgianna	2y	C	D.C.	19 OCT 1874	Beckett's
014258	ASHTON, Henry	45y	C	Va.	30 DEC 1877	Potters Field
012047	ASHTON, Henry	7y	C	D.C.	25 JUN 1877	Ebenezer
001136	ASHTON, Howard	5m	C	D.C.	13 NOV 1874	Mt. Pleasant Plain
017560	ASHTON, Infant of Isaac	7d	C	D.C.	29 SEP 1878	Payne's
003962	ASHTON, Isabella	74y	C	Va.	02 JUL 1875	Beckett's
018878	ASHTON, Isabella	35y	C	Va.	30 JAN 1879	Beckett's
011157	ASHTON, Jacob	3y	C	D.C.	30 MAR 1877	Ebenezer
019826	ASHTON, John	4m	C	D.C.	19 APR 1879	Payne's
017782	ASHTON, John Lewis	2y	C	D.C.	18 OCT 1878	Beckett's
010842	ASHTON, Laura	3y	C	D.C.	02 MAR 1877	Ebenezer
019812	ASHTON, Maggie	3y	C	D.C.	18 APR 1879	Payne's
007182	ASHTON, Mary	9d	C	D.C.	02 MAY 1876	Beckett's
013506	ASHTON, Mary E.	8d	C	D.C.	14 OCT 1877	Beckett's
017573	ASHTON, Mary Ellen	9m	C	D.C.	30 SEP 1878	Potters Field
019192	ASHTON, Sarah	1y	C	D.C.	25 FEB 1879	Potters Field
000395	ASHTON, Wallace	26y	C	D.C.	01 SEP 1874	Beckett's
007756	ASHWORTH, Dixon	70y	W	Pa.	21 JUN 1876	Soldier's Home
007258	ATCHISON, Charles B.	38y	W	Ill.	10 MAY 1876	Galena, Ill.
002601	ATCHISON, Harris Herbert	5y	W	D.C.	16 MAR 1875	Congressional
018318	ATCHISON, James Evan	66y	W	Md.	13 DEC 1878	Mt. Olivet/Holy Rood
019694	ATHERTON, Hattie May	11y	W	D.C.	08 APR 1879	Glenwood
000954	ATHEY, Alice	23y	W	Va.	27 OCT 1874	Oak Hill
008135	ATKINS, Charles	2m	C	D.C.	10 JUL 1876	Mt. Olivet
017195	ATKINS, Samuel	2m	C	D.C.	26 AUG 1878	Mt. Olivet
015900	ATKINSON, Bertha Josephine	3m	C	D.C.	30 MAY 1878	Harmony
014154	ATKINSON, Fannie Pratt	43y	W	Va.	21 DEC 1877	Glenwood
009273	ATLER, Blanche G.	15m	W	D.C.	02 OCT 1876	Mt. Olivet
002934f	ATOCHA, Alce A.	41y	W	La.	09 APR 1875	Mt. Olivet
008054	ATRICK, Walter	3m	W	Va.	07 JUL 1876	Mt. Olivet
001673	ATTSCHUH, Caspar	61y	W	Bav.	10 JAN 1875	Richmond, Va.
015540	ATWELL, Julia	63y	W	Va.	28 APR 1878	Alexandria, Va.
011439	ATZ, John	9d	W	D.C.	27 APR 1877	Congressional
010374	ATZEL, Annie, Mrs.	35y	W	Ger.	22 JAN 1877	Prospect Hill
018697	AUE, Sophia	2y	W	D.C.	17 JAN 1879	Prospect Hill
019608	AUFFORT, Sarah V.	2y	W	D.C.	31 MAR 1879	Congressional
010753	AUGERER, Augustus W.	45y	W	Ger.	23 FEB 1877	Prospect Hill
001853	AUGUST, Ada	15y	W	D.C.	23 JAN 1875	Congressional
005694	AUL, Wilemena	1y	W	D.C.	08 DEC 1875	Prospect Hill
008954	AULDRIDGE, Benjamin F.	13y	W	D.C.	03 SEP 1876	Congressional
006483	AUSTIN, Addison	1y	C	D.C.	27 FEB 1876	Ebenezer
007383	AUSTIN, Ellen	37y	C	Va.	23 MAY 1876	Ebenezer
003385	AUSTIN, George L.	10y	W	Md.	21 MAY 1875	Congressional
004517	AUSTIN, James B., Jr.	1y	W	D.C.	09 AUG 1875	Congressional

District of Columbia Death Records, August 1, 1874 to July 31, 1879

No.	Name	Age	Race	Birth	Death Date	Burial Place
019407	AUTH, Frank	8m	W	D.C.	15 MAR 1879	St. Mary's
001707	AVERT, Samuel	25y	C	Va.	13 JAN 1875	Washington Asylum
005858	AVERY, Ernest Aloysius	7m	W	D.C.	25 DEC 1875	Congressional
011170	AVERY, James Forrest	5m	W	D.C.	30 MAR 1877	Congressional
011461	AVERY, Robert Franklyn	29y	W	D.C.	29 APR 1877	Mt. Olivet
000069	AWKARD, Daniel Webster	5m	M	D.C.	05 AUG 1874	Mt. Pleasant
015946	AXE, Chas. C.	3d	W	D.C.	01 JUN 1878	Congressional
012513	AXE, John C.	50y	W	Pa.	24 JUL 1877	Congressional
016393	AYER, Infant of Martha	21d	C	D.C.	02 JUL 1878	Mt. Pleasant
009930	AYERS, Lewis	1y	C	D.C.	11 DEC 1876	Mt. Zion
013702	AYES, Infant of Henry	11d	C	D.C.	02 NOV 1877	Potters Field
001524	AYLMER, Mrs. Henry	97y	W	Ire.	28 DEC 1874	Holy Rood
020213	AYLMER, Robert Henry	31y	W	Va.	28 MAY 1879	Holy Rood

B

No.	Name	Age	Race	Birth	Death Date	Burial Place
003107	BABBINGTON, Bridget	2y	W	D.C.	24 APR 1875	Mt. Olivet
008213	BABCOCK, Charles P.	72y	W	N.H.	12 JUL 1876	Grand Rapids, Mich.
013405	BABINGTON, Pierce	55y	W	Ire.	05 OCT 1877	Mt. Olivet
001563	BACCHUS, Baily	25y	C	N.C.	01 JAN 1875	Young Mens
005062	BACCHUS, Willie	1y	C	D.C.	16 SEP 1875	Young Mens
016062	BACH, Ella	7y	C	D.C.	08 JUN 1878	Mt. Pleasant
009144	BACIGALUPPO, Maria Madalena	61y	W	Italy	20 SEP 1876	St. Mary's
015084	BACKERS, Eddie	7m	C	D.C.	16 MAR 1878	Young Mens
020334	BACKUS, Allen	60y	W	Va.	08 JUN 1879	Glenwood
020279	BACON, Adeline	9m	C	D.C.	03 JUN 1879	Payne's
001962	BACON, Agnes Virginia	21d	W	D.C.	31 JAN 1875	Mt. Olivet
008551	BACON, Nettie	8m	C	D.C.	04 AUG 1876	Beckett's
012947	BACON, Rosanna	5d	C	D.C.	25 AUG 1877	Young Mens
016667	BACON, W.H.	6y	W	D.C.	19 JUL 1878	Mt. Olivet
009223	BADDY, William	1y	C	D.C.	28 SEP 1876	Smith's
001194	BADEN, Joseph	30y	W	Md.	20 NOV 1874	Congressional
000463	BADGER, Lizzie E.	12y	C	D.C.	09 SEP 1874	Mt. Pleasant
019704	BAER, Michael	80y	W	Prus.	09 APR 1879	Hebrew
001756	BAEUR, Dorther	64y	W	Ger.	16 JAN 1875	Prospect Hill
001550	BAGA, Scharlott	12d	C	D.C.	31 DEC 1874	Beckett's
001241	BAGBY, Charlotte	40y	C	Va.	27 NOV 1874	Beckett's
015435	BAGBY, Cora	7m	C	D.C.	18 APR 1878	Mt. Pleasant
003096	BAGBY, Infant of Frances	7h	C	D.C.	23 APR 1875	Potters Field
010120	BAGBY, Infant of Walter	6d	C	D.C.	30 DEC 1876	Potters Field
010109	BAGBY, Milard Fillmore	19y	C	Va.	29 DEC 1876	Potters Field
020350	BAGBY, Randolph	29y	C	Va.	09 JUN 1879	Young Mens
001215	BAGBY, Simon	1d	C	D.C.	23 NOV 1874	Beckett's
000022	BAGGETT, Willie	4m	M	D.C.	02 AUG 1874	Mt. Pleasant
017511	BAGGOTT, George Wm.	4y	W	D.C.	24 SEP 1878	Glenwood
017486	BAGGOTT, Mary Frances	5y	W	D.C.	22 SEP 1878	Glenwood
019930	BAGLY, Jenie	13y	W	D.C.	29 APR 1879	Mt. Olivet
005006	BAGNAN, Mary Catherine	10m	W	D.C.	12 SEP 1875	Mt. Olivet
005096	BAHLMAN, Rosa	11m	W	D.C.	19 SEP 1875	German Catholic
019939	BAILEY, Carrie	14m	C	D.C.	30 APR 1879	Mt. Olivet
016157	BAILEY, Elizabeth	66y	W	Va.	14 JUN 1878	Mt. Olivet
013175	BAILEY, Emma G.	16d	W	D.C.	13 SEP 1877	Methodist
020574	BAILEY, Florance A.	5m	W	D.C.	23 JUN 1879	Congressional
016725	BAILEY, Frank	19y	C	D.C.	23 JUL 1878	Potters Field
017546	BAILEY, George	5y	C	D.C.	27 SEP 1878	Beckett's

District of Columbia Death Records, August 1, 1874 to July 31, 1879   11

No.	Name	Age	Race	Birth	Death Date	Burial Place
016498	BAILEY, Infant	6w	C	D.C.	08 JUL 1878	Young Mens
016714	BAILEY, Infant of Charlotte	10d	C	D.C.	22 JUL 1878	Beckett's
014439	BAILEY, Infant of Martha	9d	C	D.C.	16 JAN 1878	Potters Field
018557	BAILEY, Infant of Wm.	7d	C	D.C.	04 JAN 1879	Potters Field
013949	BAILEY, James	73y	C	Va.	28 NOV 1877	Beckett's
021144	BAILEY, James	22-23y	C	Va.	29 JUL 1879	Beckett's
008414	BAILEY, Jane	c.70y	C	Va.	25 JUL 1876	Young Mens
016499	BAILEY, Jane E.	59y	W	Va.	08 JUL 1878	Congressional
017701	BAILEY, John G.	3y	W	Minn.	11 OCT 1878	Glenwood
010046	BAILEY, John R.	35y	W	Va.	21 DEC 1876	Potters Field
020805	BAILEY, John Thomas	3m	W	D.C.	07 JUL 1879	Congressional
018353	BAILEY, Joseph I.	16y	W	Md.	16 DEC 1878	Mt. Olivet
018175	BAILEY, Katie G.	24y	W	Iowa	27 NOV 1878	Glenwood
010702	BAILEY, Louisa	1y	C	D.C.	20 FEB 1877	Potters Field
019157	BAILEY, Louisa	23y	C	D.C.	23 FEB 1879	Beckett's
011408	BAILEY, Lucinda M.	58y	W	Md.	23 APR 1877	Glenwood
008649	BAILEY, Lucy Betty	17y	C	Va.	11 AUG 1876	Young Mens
018014	BAILEY, Mary	1y	W	D.C.	11 NOV 1878	Mt. Olivet
011252	BAILEY, Mary E.	35y	W	Md.	07 APR 1877	Mt. Olivet
011004	BAILEY, Mary Maud	1y	W	D.C.	16 MAR 1877	Graceland
016259	BAILEY, Mauna	100y	C	Md.	22 JUN 1878	Catharine Forest Farm
007959	BAILEY, Robert	1y	C	D.C.	01 JUL 1876	Young Mens
007605	BAILEY, Robert	3m	M	D.C.	12 JUN 1876	Ebenezer
006360	BAILEY, Sarah	6m	C	D.C.	15 FEB 1876	Ebenezer
015341	BAILEY, Silas	4y	C	D.C.	10 APR 1878	Beckett's
003074	BAILEY, Susan	2y	C	D.C.	21 APR 1875	Beckett's
011837	BAILEY, Teresa	2y	W	D.C.	08 JUN 1877	Holy Rood
010578	BAILEY, Theodorus	71y	W	N.Y.	10 FEB 1877	Oak Hill
019515	BAILEY, Virginia Mason	31y	W	D.C.	23 MAR 1879	Hollywood, Richmond
005034a	BAILEY, Willie	7m	C	D.C.	03 OCT 1875	Mt. Pleasant
011735	BAILEY, Willie	1y	C	D.C.	29 MAY 1877	Ebenezer
010351	BAILLEY, Wm. H.	53y	W	Va.	20 JAN 1877	Holy Rood
008382	BAILOR, Annie	1y	W	D.C.	22 JUL 1876	Ebenezer
003752	BAILOR, Horace	57y	C	Va.	21 JAN 1875	Harmony
014180	BAILOR, Infant of James	8d	C	D.C.	23 DEC 1877	Potters Field
004153	BAILY, Ada	1m	W	D.C.	16 JUL 1875	Presbyterian
015618	BAILY, Catharine	50y	C	Va.	05 MAY 1878	Beckett's
006807	BAILY, Henrietta	16y	C	D.C.	25 MAR 1876	Beckett's
009123	BAILY, Henry	28y	C	Va.	18 SEP 1876	Young Mens
006903	BAILY, James	50y	C	Va.	03 APR 1876	Mt. Pleasant Plain
011042	BAILY, Joanna	80y	C	Md.	19 MAR 1877	Ebenezer
006689	BAILY, Rosa E.	5y	W	D.C.	16 MAR 1876	Congressional
017333	BAILY, Ross	1y	W	Md.	06 SEP 1878	Glenwood
008720	BAILY, Thomas	1y	C	D.C.	18 AUG 1876	Beckett's
001221	BAIN, Samuel M.	6d	W	D.C.	24 NOV 1874	Glenwood
002071	BAINES, Josie	5m	W	D.C.	07 FEB 1875	Congressional
006716	BAINES, Mary Frances	c.25y	W	Va.	18 MAR 1876	Congressional
015091	BAIRD, Infant of Elizabeth	3w	W	D.C.	17 MAR 1878	Potters Field
004092	BAIRD, John James	55y	W	Eng.	12 JUL 1875	Congressional
000173f	BAIRD, Wm. S., Rev.	--	--	--	13 AUG 1874	--
012343	BAKER, Charles H.	85y	W	Mass.	13 JUL 1877	Glenwood
013324	BAKER, Edward S.	6y	W	D.C.	27 SEP 1877	Congressional
009514	BAKER, Eliza	74y	W	D.C.	24 OCT 1876	Rock Creek
018541	BAKER, Elizabeth	82y	W	Md.	02 JAN 1879	Congressional
014168	BAKER, Emma V.	21y	W	D.C.	22 DEC 1877	Presbyterian
001951	BAKER, Georgiana	26y	W	D.C.	30 JAN 1875	Glenwood

District of Columbia Death Records, August 1, 1874 to July 31, 1879

No.	Name	Age	Race	Birth	Death Date	Burial Place
018056	BAKER, Henry	c.21y	C	Md.	15 NOV 1878	Mt. Zion
011772	BAKER, Irma E.	1y	W	D.C.	01 JUN 1877	Hagerstown, Md.
008668	BAKER, Isaac	2y	C	D.C.	13 AUG 1876	Harmony
003604	BAKER, John	54y	C	Va.	11 JUN 1875	Harmony
020648	BAKER, John	6m	C	D.C.	28 JUN 1879	Harmony
014090	BAKER, John T.	75y	W	Va.	14 DEC 1877	Oak Hill
009368	BAKER, Josepha A.	30y	W	Pa.	10 OCT 1876	Glenwood
007038	BAKER, Josephine	13m	C	D.C.	18 APR 1876	Mt. Zion
013096	BAKER, Lewis H.	39y	W	Ger.	06 SEP 1877	Glenwood
001244	BAKER, Lilly Kirk	6y	W	D.C.	27 NOV 1874	Congressional
002017f	BAKER, Mary E.	64y	W	Md.	04 FEB 1875	Baltimore, Md.
007347	BAKER, Mary Francis	4m	W	D.C.	20 MAY 1876	Holy Rood
003166	BAKER, Michael	c.30y	C	Va.	29 APR 1875	Young Mens
013444	BAKER, Sallie	6y	C	D.C.	09 OCT 1877	Harmony
019314	BAKER, Sophia	62y	W	Ger.	08 MAR 1879	Glenwood
016412	BAKER, Virginia	c.85y	C	Va.	03 JUL 1878	Harmony
013323	BAKER, Washington	37y	C	Va.	27 SEP 1877	Potters Field
016169	BAKER, Wesley	27y	C	Va.	15 JUN 1878	Potters Field
009603	BAKER, Wilson Lewis	5y	W	Md.	02 NOV 1876	Glenwood
018360	BALDWIN, Annie	30y	W	N.Y.	17 DEC 1878	Graceland
007356	BALDWIN, Elizabeth Taylor	41y	W	D.C.	21 MAY 1876	Congressional
017936	BALDWIN, Honorah	51y	W	Ire.	03 NOV 1878	Mt. Olivet
010159	BALDWIN, John S., Jr.	15y	W	N.Y.	03 JAN 1877	Oak Hill
012859	BALDWIN, Sarah Little	20d	W	D.C.	18 AUG 1877	Congressional
011955	BALER, William	1y	W	D.C.	18 JUN 1877	Beckett's
000049	BALEY, Emma	15y	W	Md.	04 AUG 1874	Mt. Olivet
014578	BALEY, Maud Agnes	1y	W	D.C.	28 JAN 1878	Mt. Olivet
013398	BALILEY, Julia	6y	C	D.C.	04 OCT 1877	Beckett's
020373	BALL, Ada	16y	C	Va.	10 JUN 1879	Potters Field
008015	BALL, Alx.	38y	W	Md.	04 JUL 1876	Glenwood
002426	BALL, Griffin	70y	C	Va.	04 MAR 1875	Young Mens
001891	BALL, J.N.	64y	W	N.J.	26 JAN 1875	Glenwood
011263	BALL, James	80y	C	Va.	07 APR 1877	Potters Field
011744	BALL, John George Thomas	4y	W	D.C.	30 MAY 1877	Prospect Hill
017789	BALL, Lewis	7m	C	D.C.	19 OCT 1878	Potters Field
012522	BALL, Robert J.	6m	C	D.C.	25 JUL 1877	Ebenezer
012508	BALL, Rosetta	11y	W	Md.	24 JUL 1877	Tennallytown
003198	BALL, Rosier Augustus	2y	M	D.C.	02 MAY 1875	Young Mens
020774	BALL, Thos.	6m	C	Va.	05 JUL 1879	Beckett's
001976	BALLARD, Dennis	30y	C	Va.	01 FEB 1875	Alexandria, Va.
020144	BALLARD, George	6m	C	D.C.	19 MAY 1879	Graceland
016533	BALLARD, George J.	1y	C	D.C.	10 JUL 1878	Graceland
010480	BALLAUF, Emilie L.	4y	W	D.C.	02 FEB 1877	Glenwood
000038	BALLAUF, William	8m	W	D.C.	03 AUG 1874	Glenwood
003894	BALLENGER, Ada Grace	5m	W	D.C.	28 JUN 1875	Mt. Olivet
002621	BALLENGER, Rebecca	50y	W	Md.	17 MAR 1875	Congressional
020804	BALLINGER, Abraham A.	33y	W	Pa.	07 JUL 1879	Potters Field
001434	BALMAIN, Andrew	67y	W	D.C.	19 DEC 1874	Congressional
000254	BALSER, Infant of Conrad	6d	W	D.C.	20 AUG 1874	Prospect Hill
016549	BALSTEN, Laura	4m	W	D.C.	11 JUL 1878	Prospect Hill
010966	BALSTER, Theodore N.	14m	W	D.C.	14 MAR 1877	Glenwood
019483	BALTIMORE, William Henry	28y	C	D.C.	21 MAR 1879	Harmony
012913	BALTOMORE, Virginia	40y	W	Pa.	23 AUG 1877	Washington Asylum
003762	BALTZER, Anney	3m	W	D.C.	22 JUN 1875	Congressional
015517	BANCROFT, Mary H.	25y	W	Mass.	26 APR 1878	Canton, Mass.
002411	BANERMAN, Mary Ann, Mrs.	67y	W	Md.	03 MAR 1875	Glenwood

District of Columbia Death Records, August 1, 1874 to July 31, 1879   13

No.	Name	Age	Race	Birth	Death Date	Burial Place
001071	BANES, Lot	65y	W	Pa.	06 NOV 1874	Congressional
002759	BANESTER, William	70y	C	Md.	27 MAR 1875	Mt. Pleasant
013843	BANGS, George S.	54y	W	Ohio	17 NOV 1877	Chicago, Ill.
004788	BANGS, Mary Jane	53y	W	Md.	28 AUG 1875	Oak Hill
003256	BANKET, Agnes	88y	C	Va.	07 MAY 1875	Ebenezer
015674	BANKET, Infant of Daniel	7d	C	D.C.	10 MAY 1878	Young Mens
008516	BANKETT, Mary Ann	2y	C	D.C.	01 AUG 1876	Young Mens
010537	BANKS, Abbey	26y	C	Va.	06 FEB 1877	Mt. Zion
004211	BANKS, Ann M.	2y	C	D.C.	20 JUL 1875	Young Mens
012653	BANKS, Aquilla	1y	C	D.C.	03 AUG 1877	Beckett's
006305	BANKS, Charlotte Gertrude	7m	C	D.C.	11 FEB 1876	Mt. Pleasant Plain
020257	BANKS, Edward	7m	C	D.C.	01 JUN 1879	Young Mens
003453	BANKS, Eliza	4d	C	D.C.	27 MAY 1875	Mt. Pleasant
018352	BANKS, George	18y	W	Va.	16 DEC 1878	Congressional
020750	BANKS, George	3m	C	D.C.	04 JUL 1879	Young Mens
011811	BANKS, George H.	7m	C	D.C.	05 JUN 1877	Young Mens
002133	BANKS, Infant of Ireen	2m	C	D.C.	12 FEB 1875	Potters Field
011448	BANKS, Infant of William	4d	C	D.C.	28 APR 1877	Ebenezer
016183	BANKS, Infant of Battle	1y	C	D.C.	15 JUN 1878	Potters Field
004662	BANKS, Julius	19y	C	Va.	19 AUG 1875	Potters Field
013457	BANKS, Robert	80y	C	Va.	10 OCT 1877	Potters Field
020955	BANKS, Rosco T.	1y	C	D.C.	16 JUL 1879	Mt. Pleasant
000985	BANKS, Sophia	54y	C	Va.	30 OCT 1874	Va.
010474	BANKS, William	1y	C	D.C.	01 FEB 1877	Ebenezer
019679	BANKS, Willie	3m	C	D.C.	07 APR 1879	Potters Field
008166	BANNING, Elizabeth Emma	35y	W	Pa.	11 JUL 1876	Glenwood
017732	BANNISTER, John	41y	W	D.C.	14 OCT 1878	Methodist
016600	BANNISTER, Wm. F.	1y	W	D.C.	15 JUL 1878	Presbyterian
011565	BANNON, William	48y	W	Ire.	11 MAY 1877	Mt. Olivet
002515	BANTUM, Leah	60y	M	Md.	11 MAR 1875	--
019828	BANYON, Wm.	80y	C	Va.	19 APR 1879	Young Mens
013623	BAPTIST, Harriet	60y	C	Va.	25 OCT 1877	Potters Field
020516	BAPTISTE, Edward	1y	C	D.C.	19 JUN 1879	Potters Field
012535	BAPTISTE, Emma	1y	W	D.C.	26 JUL 1877	Congressional
016446	BAR, Sarra E.	1y	W	D.C.	05 JUL 1878	Congressional
013507	BARBAR, Joseph	80y	W	Ger.	14 OCT 1877	St. Mary's
009896	BARBER, --	c.35y	C	D.C.	07 DEC 1876	Potters Field
017150	BARBER, Ada	16m	C	D.C.	23 AUG 1878	Potters Field
008448	BARBER, Carrie	2d	C	D.C.	28 JUL 1876	Potters Field
013252	BARBER, Clinton	3y	M	Va.	20 SEP 1877	Washington Asylum
016140	BARBER, Edward	1m	C	D.C.	13 JUN 1878	Beckett's
014411	BARBER, George	57y	W	Va.	14 JAN 1878	Congressional
015541	BARBER, Infant of Lewis	14h	C	D.C.	28 APR 1878	Beckett's
000914	BARBER, Julia Irine	4m	W	D.C.	24 OCT 1874	Oak Hill
015129	BARBER, Lewis F.	54y	W	Ger.	20 MAR 1878	St. Mary's
012723	BARBER, Netty	6m	C	D.C.	08 AUG 1877	Ebenezer
013595	BARBOUR, Mercer	30	W	Va.	23 OCT 1877	Harmony
000699	BARBOUR, Patsey	53y	M	Va.	03 OCT 1874	Harmony
002403f	BARGHANSEN, George	1y	W	D.C.	26 FEB 1875	Prospect Hill
002565	BARGHAUSEN, Henry	3y	W	D.C.	14 MAR 1875	Prospect Hill
010279	BARGY, Hannah J.	80y	W	D.C.	13 JAN 1877	Rock Creek
006852	BARKER, Andrew L.	2m	C	D.C.	29 MAR 1876	Harmony
001630	BARKER, Ann	30y	C	Va.	06 JAN 1875	Beckett's
014375	BARKER, Benijah M.	38y	W	N.Y.	10 JAN 1878	Rock Creek
020280	BARKER, Charles	9m	C	D.C.	03 JUN 1879	Beckett's
009950	BARKER, Elizabeth	77	W	Eng.	13 DEC 1876	Oak Hill

District of Columbia Death Records, August 1, 1874 to July 31, 1879

No.	Name	Age	Race	Birth	Death Date	Burial Place
009539	BARKER, Elizabeth	77y	W	Va.	26 OCT 1876	Congressional
015962	BARKER, Infant of C.W.	2h	W	D.C.	02 JUN 1878	Presbyterian
004897	BARKER, Infant of Jas. L.	1h	W	D.C.	04 SEP 1875	Congressional
001687	BARKER, Infant of William	4m	C	D.C.	10 JAN 1875	Beckett's
002445	BARKER, James A.	9m	C	D.C.	05 MAR 1875	Harmony
018037	BARKER, John	23y	C	D.C.	13 NOV 1878	Mt. Olivet
001091	BARKER, John Henry	48y	W	Md.	09 NOV 1874	Congressional
010731	BARKER, Joseph L.	37y	W	Va.	22 FEB 1877	Congressional
011349	BARKER, Leon W.	14d	C	D.C.	16 APR 1877	Harmony
004747	BARKER, Margaret	25y	C	D.C.	25 AUG 1875	Mt. Olivet
007277	BARKER, Margaret	60y	W	Ire.	12 MAY 1876	Mt. Olivet
013958	BARKER, Mary E.	1m	C	D.C.	29 NOV 1877	Mt. Zion
016220	BARKER, Mary, Mrs.	45y	C	D.C.	19 JUN 1878	Mt. Olivet
002878	BARKER, Sarah Ann	58y	W	Va.	05 APR 1875	Glenwood
019241	BARLEY, Alice	73y	W	Md.	01 MAR 1879	Ellicott City, Md.
003270	BARLEY, Cornelia M.	40y	C	N.J.	09 MAY 1875	Mt. Pleasant
017561	BARLOW, Arthur	3d	M	D.C.	29 SEP 1878	Harmony
008522	BARNARD, Edward	10m	W	D.C.	02 AUG 1876	Oak Hill
007560	BARNARD, Fanny	3m	C	D.C.	09 JUN 1876	Smith's
000618	BARNARD, Henry S.	61y	W	Eng.	23 SEP 1874	Oak Hill
016971	BARNARD, James S.	85y	W	Eng.	09 AUG 1878	Oak Hill
001587	BARNARD, Joshua	80y	C	Va.	02 JAN 1875	Smith's
014660	BARNARD, Richard	5y	C	D.C.	04 FEB 1878	Potters Field
001070	BARNARD, Roberta	2m	W	D.C.	06 NOV 1874	Congressional
002828	BARNARD, Walter Sinclair	2y	W	Ind.	01 APR 1875	Glenwood
018173	BARNARD, William H.	19y	W	D.C.	27 NOV 1878	Congressional
007530	BARNES, Adams	6m	W	D.C.	07 JUN 1876	Glenwood
012131	BARNES, Albert	1y	W	D.C.	30 JUN 1877	Leesburg, Va.
010744	BARNES, Allen	102y	C	Md.	23 FEB 1877	Mt. Olivet
007719	BARNES, Ann	70y	C	Md.	19 JUN 1876	Ebenezer
001201	BARNES, Annie	1y	C	D.C.	20 NOV 1874	Mt. Pleasant
003932	BARNES, Benjamin Walter	10m	W	D.C.	30 JUN 1875	Congressional
003129	BARNES, Catharine	74y	W	Md.	26 APR 1875	Congressional
019236	BARNES, Charles Edward	9y	W	D.C.	28 FEB 1879	Tennallytown
012923	BARNES, Duke William	4y	C	D.C.	24 AUG 1877	Harmony
014907	BARNES, Gamaliel Randolph	28y	W	Va.	01 MAR 1878	Presbyterian
005987	BARNES, Geo. J.	7m	C	D.C.	10 JAN 1876	Ebenezer
017937	BARNES, George	68y	W	D.C.	03 NOV 1878	Arlington, Va.
017915	BARNES, George	49y	C	Md.	01 NOV 1878	Harmony
000797	BARNES, Infant of G.W.	7y	C	D.C.	13 OCT 1874	Mt. Pleasant
001347	BARNES, Infant of James	10d	C	D.C.	09 DEC 1874	Potters Field
010821	BARNES, Infant of Rachel	6d	C	D.C.	01 MAR 1877	Potters Field
019929	BARNES, James	43y	C	N.C.	29 APR 1879	Harmony
004689	BARNES, James Grant	1y	C	D.C.	21 AUG 1875	Potters Field
005193	BARNES, Jane	28y	C	Md.	27 SEP 1875	Mt. Olivet
001177	BARNES, John M.	6m	M	D.C.	18 NOV 1874	Harmony
019952	BARNES, John T.	70y	C	Md.	01 MAY 1879	Beckett's
000205	BARNES, Joseph	25y	W	D.C.	16 AUG 1874	Mt. Olivet
015637	BARNES, Joseph	66y	C	Md.	07 MAY 1878	Potters Field
006092	BARNES, Josephus John	29y	W	D.C.	22 JAN 1876	Mt. Olivet
016431	BARNES, Judias	1y	C	D.C.	04 JUL 1878	Young Mens
010869	BARNES, Laura	35y	W	D.C.	05 MAR 1877	Congressional
010496	BARNES, Louisa	84y	C	Md.	03 FEB 1877	Young Mens
012432	BARNES, Mary Elizabeth	5y	W	D.C.	19 JUL 1877	Prospect Hill
003423	BARNES, Mary Jane	34y	W	D.C.	24 MAY 1875	Congressional
008661	BARNES, Mesia M.	11m	W	D.C.	12 AUG 1876	Tennallytown

District of Columbia Death Records, August 1, 1874 to July 31, 1879 15

No.	Name	Age	Race	Birth	Death Date	Burial Place
002740	BARNES, Rachel	65y	C	Md.	27 MAR 1875	Washington Asylum
019107	BARNES, Walter W.	3y	W	D.C.	18 FEB 1879	Presbyterian
007892	BARNES, William	8m	C	D.C.	28 JUN 1876	Ebenezer
018753	BARNES, William H.	46y	W	N.Y.	21 JAN 1879	Glenwood
007430	BARNES, William Henry	10m	W	D.C.	29 MAY 1876	Prospect Hill
005589	BARNES, Winnefurt	23y	C	Md.	28 NOV 1875	Hospital
006532	BARNES, Wm. H.	1y	W	D.C.	03 MAR 1876	Mt. Olivet
018433	BARNET, Madison	28y	C	Va.	23 DEC 1878	Potters Field
004346	BARNETT, Levi Woodbury	3m	C	D.C.	28 JUL 1875	Smith's
008201	BARNETT, William	56y	W	Pa.	12 JUL 1876	Philadelphia, Pa.
011302	BARNETT, Wm. Henry	3y	C	D.C.	11 APR 1877	Harmony
007944	BARNETT, Wm. James	12y	W	D.C.	01 JUL 1876	Holy Rood
000803	BARNEY, Mary	7m	M	D.C.	14 OCT 1874	Young Mens
008340	BARNITZ, D. Wagner	47y	W	Pa.	20 JUL 1876	York, Pa.
001410	BARNS, Annie	1m	W	D.C.	16 DEC 1874	Oak Hill
006250	BARNS, Annie	60y	C	Md.	06 FEB 1876	Mt. Zion
000289	BARNS, Aurther	17y	C	Md.	22 AUG 1874	Baptist
006715	BARNS, Charles E.	21d	W	D.C.	18 MAR 1876	Birch Farm, Va.
014054	BARNS, George	9y	C	D.C.	10 DEC 1877	Mt. Zion
011723	BARNS, George V.	21y	C	Md.	27 MAY 1877	Jones Chapel
018013	BARNS, Rachel	75y	C	Md.	11 NOV 1878	Mt. Olivet
002511	BARNS, Thomas	40y	W	Ire.	11 MAR 1875	Mt. Olivet
013285	BARQUE, Charles, Rev., S.J.	68y	W	Switz.	24 SEP 1877	College, Georgetown
000229	BARR, Blanchard Maria	10m	W	D.C.	18 AUG 1874	Congressional
020973	BARR, Elizabeth Stockton	47y	W	Del.	17 JUL 1879	Oak Hill
001233	BARR, Sarah Ann	c.54y	W	D.C.	26 NOV 1874	Congressional
013891	BARRETT, Allen	28y	W	Miss.	23 NOV 1877	Oak Hill
013127	BARRETT, Catharine	57y	W	D.C.	09 SEP 1877	Queen's Chapel, Md.
019054	BARRETT, Catharine	17m	W	D.C.	13 FEB 1879	Mt. Olivet
015316	BARRETT, Catherine Anna	41y	W	N.Y.	08 APR 1878	Oak Hill
016045	BARRETT, Dennis A.	8m	W	D.C.	07 JUN 1878	Mt. Olivet
000009	BARRETT, Edward	69y	W	Ire.	01 AUG 1874	Mt. Olivet
014568	BARRETT, Elizabeth	7y	W	Md.	27 JAN 1878	Mt. Olivet
010148	BARRETT, Francis Joseph	1y	W	D.C.	01 JAN 1877	Mt. Olivet
000650	BARRETT, George Henry	10m	W	D.C.	27 SEP 1874	Mt. Olivet
004057	BARRETT, Ida E.	3y	W	D.C.	09 JUL 1875	Glenwood
007030	BARRETT, John W.	31y	W	D.C.	17 APR 1876	Mt. Olivet
016300	BARRETT, Julia	6m	W	D.C.	25 JUN 1878	Mt. Olivet
000148	BARRETT, Laura Rosecilla	2y	W	D.C.	11 AUG 1874	Glenwood
012651	BARRETT, Roberta	50y	W	D.C.	03 AUG 1877	Oak Hill
012420	BARRON, Benj. F.	1y	W	D.C.	18 JUL 1877	Congressional
017078	BARRON, Ed Oliver	8m	W	D.C.	17 AUG 1878	Congressional
004437	BARRON, Henry	67y	W	Md.	04 AUG 1875	Oak Hill
018045	BARRON, James	5y	C	D.C.	13 NOV 1878	Young Mens
012205	BARRON, Julia Ann	72y	W	Md.	04 JUL 1877	Congressional
005122	BARRON, Willie	3y	W	D.C.	21 SEP 1875	Congressional
009352	BARROW, Emily	46y	W	Va.	09 OCT 1876	Glenwood
010546	BARROWS, Infant of Samuel	1h	C	D.C.	06 FEB 1877	Moore's
019350	BARRY, Bridget	37y	W	Ire.	10 MAR 1879	Mt. Olivet
013158	BARRY, Cora L.	27y	W	Va.	11 SEP 1877	Glenwood
005742	BARRY, Eliza, Mrs.	74y	W	D.C.	14 DEC 1875	College, Georgetown
004607	BARRY, Eugene Creed	1y	W	D.C.	15 AUG 1875	Mt. Olivet
003309f	BARRY, George	68y	W	Ger.	13 MAY 1875	St. Mary's
003553	BARRY, H.W.	35y	W	Ky.	07 JUN 1875	Mt. Olivet
017752	BARRY, Henrietta	78y	W	Md.	16 OCT 1878	Laurel, Md.
000929	BARRY, Infant of P.C.	½h	W	D.C.	25 OCT 1874	Mt. Olivet

No.	Name	Age	Race	Birth	Death Date	Burial Place
009868	BARRY, James	65y	W	Eng.	04 DEC 1876	Mt. Olivet
018270	BARRY, James E.	10m	W	D.C.	08 DEC 1878	Mt. Olivet
017897	BARRY, Johanna	36y	W	Ire.	29 OCT 1878	Mt. Olivet
020607	BARRY, John Paul	9m	W	D.C.	25 JUN 1879	Mt. Olivet
014466	BARRY, Katie S.	3m	W	D.C.	18 JAN 1878	Mt. Olivet
009378	BARRY, Mary	24y	W	D.C.	11 OCT 1876	Mt. Olivet
005752	BARRY, Mary E.	30y	W	N.Y.	15 DEC 1875	Mt. Olivet
007318	BARRY, Patrick	c.42y	W	Ire.	16 MAY 1876	Mt. Vernon, Ohio
002077	BARRY, William	23y	C	S.C.	08 FEB 1875	Washington Asylum
002509	BARTEN, Lucy Elen	8y	W	Va.	10 MAR 1875	Mt. Olivet
012271	BARTEN, William	9m	C	D.C.	08 JUL 1877	Mt. Olivet
020351	BARTHOLOMAE, Christopher	5m	W	D.C.	09 JUN 1879	Prospect Hill
011806	BARTLETT, Edith	30y	W	Pa.	05 JUN 1877	Greenwood, N.Y.C.
002518	BARTLETT, Elizabeth	81y	W	Mass.	11 MAR 1875	Glenwood
014939	BARTLETT, John	4d	W	D.C.	04 MAR 1878	Glenwood
006165	BARTLETT, Julia Mary	18y	W	D.C.	28 JAN 1876	Oak Hill
019768	BARTLETT, Susan Hendrick	53y	W	Va.	14 APR 1879	Richmond, Va.
000916	BARTLEY, Samuel	33y	W	Md.	24 OCT 1874	Congressional
005986	BARTLEY, Susan Sherman	50y	W	Ohio	10 JAN 1876	Glenwood
018698	BARTON, Catherine	2m	C	D.C.	17 JAN 1879	Mt. Olivet
002597	BARTON, Edward	1y	C	D.C.	16 MAR 1875	Harmony
020527	BARTON, James	1y	C	D.C.	20 JUN 1879	Potters Field
012708	BARTON, John	1y	C	D.C.	07 AUG 1877	Potters Field
011315	BARTON, Martha	7m	C	D.C.	13 APR 1877	Harmony
010430	BARTON, Thomas	48y	C	Md.	28 JAN 1877	Moore's
006843	BARWOOD, James	38y	W	Eng.	28 MAR 1876	Utica, N.Y.
013406	BASFIELD, Wm. H.	1y	C	D.C.	05 OCT 1877	Harmony
007348	BASFORD, William E.	58y	W	Md.	20 MAY 1876	Graceland
000703	BASHEARS, Infant of McClain	9d	C	D.C.	03 OCT 1874	Beckett's
017349	BASKER, John	58y	C	Va.	07 SEP 1878	Harmony
017126	BASKER, John H.	8y	C	D.C.	21 AUG 1878	Harmony
014244	BASS, Joseph	3m	C	D.C.	29 DEC 1877	Young Mens
020674	BASSETT, Annie	22y	W	R.I.	30 JUN 1879	Mt. Olivet
009027	BASSETT, Olive	84y	W	Conn.	11 SEP 1876	Congressional
017746	BASSIMAGIAN, O.	54y	W	Tur.	15 OCT 1878	Congressional
008317	BASTEN, L.M.A.	7y	W	N.Y.	18 JUL 1876	Glenwood
011012	BASTERFIELD, Edna, Mrs.	23y	W	D.C.	16 MAR 1877	Harmony
003356	BATCHELDER, George A.	42y	W	Mass.	18 MAY 1875	Arlington, Va.
020528	BATEMAN, Jane E.	68y	W	D.C.	20 JUN 1879	Holy Rood
007894	BATEMAN, Sabra	75y	M	Md.	28 JUN 1876	Mt. Pleasant
000290	BATEMAN, Sarah A.	63y	W	Md.	22 AUG 1874	Congressional
002763	BATES, Ann Wright	63y	W	Eng.	27 MAR 1875	Glenwood
003464	BATES, Catharine A.	58y	W	Md.	28 MAY 1875	Oak Hill
018144	BATES, Edwin W.	8y	W	D.C.	25 NOV 1878	Glenwood
007529	BATES, Eugene	6m	W	D.C.	07 JUN 1876	Congressional
003964	BATES, Henriette	75y	C	Va.	02 JUL 1875	Potters Field
001854	BATES, Horatio	34y	W	N.Y.	23 JAN 1875	Glenwood
002815	BATES, Josephine	1m	C	D.C.	31 MAR 1875	Potters Field
002029	BATES, Mary	45y	C	Va.	04 FEB 1875	Mt. Olivet
001314	BATES, Mary V.	10d	C	D.C.	05 DEC 1874	Young Mens
016989	BATES, Samuel	1y	C	D.C.	10 AUG 1878	Freedmen's Village
005614	BATES, Sarah E.	25y	C	Ohio	01 DEC 1875	Oak Hill
009351	BATES, Sarah Taylor	54y	W	Md.	09 OCT 1876	Glenwood
000657	BATES, Virginia Shirley	29y	W	Va.	28 SEP 1874	Oak Hill
013666	BATES, Willie Patton	5y	W	D.C.	29 OCT 1877	Oak Hill
000687	BATSON, E.A.	19d	C	D.C.	01 OCT 1874	Potters Field

District of Columbia Death Records, August 1, 1874 to July 31, 1879   17

No.	Name	Age	Race	Birth	Death Date	Burial Place
001023	BATSON, Eliza Ann	64y	M	Md.	02 NOV 1874	Thomas'
019998	BATSON, Helean	61y	C	Md.	05 MAY 1879	Good Hope
005502	BATSON, Mary Ellen	9d	C	D.C.	19 NOV 1875	Ebenezer
004343	BATT, John	36y	W	Va.	28 JUL 1875	Alexandria, Va.
015675	BATTENFIELD, Anna Elizabeth	7y	W	D.C.	10 MAY 1878	Prospect Hill
013737	BATTERS, Catherine T.	45y	W	Ire.	05 NOV 1877	Mt. Olivet
012469	BATTIE, Wm. H.	6m	C	D.C.	22 JUL 1877	Moore's
001174	BATTLE, Rachel Ann	1y	C	D.C.	17 NOV 1874	Mt. Olivet
000276	BATTLEFIELD, Katie	5m	W	D.C.	21 AUG 1874	Prospect Hill
009822	BATTLES, Harriet E.	18y	C	D.C.	29 NOV 1876	Harmony
003974	BATTLES, Susan	39y	C	Md.	03 JUL 1875	Ebenezer
003522	BATTS, Sarah Ann	33y	W	Md.	04 JUN 1875	Chappel's
006644	BATTY, Henry	38y	W	Eng.	11 MAR 1876	Presbyterian
006038	BAUER, Joseph F.	26y	W	Md.	16 JAN 1876	Congressional
005993	BAULHAUER, Frederick	31y	W	Ger.	11 JAN 1876	Hospital
011890	BAUM, Elizabeth	60y	W	Va.	14 JUN 1877	Glenwood
019379	BAUM, John Raymond	1y	W	D.C.	13 MAR 1879	Glenwood
012707	BAUM, Katie	9d	C	D.C.	07 AUG 1877	Beckett's
017905	BAUMANN, Chas. F.	2y	W	D.C.	30 OCT 1878	St. Mary's
007773	BAUMANN, Mary	1y	W	D.C.	22 JUN 1876	St. Mary's
004213	BAUMGARTEN, Benjamin	1m	W	D.C.	20 JUL 1875	Hebrew
005183a	BAUSCH, Maria	19y	W	Ger.	18 OCT 1875	Prospect Hill
001664	BAXTER, Harry	1d	W	D.C.	09 JAN 1875	Methodist, S.E.
017138	BAXTER, John Towers	17d	W	D.C.	21 AUG 1878	Graceland
015688	BAXTER, Mary Ella	2w	W	D.C.	12 MAY 1878	Congressional
000507	BAXTER, Sarah Elizabeth	1y	W	D.C.	14 SEP 1874	Oak Hill
000649	BAYLER, Annie E.	12y	C	Va.	27 SEP 1874	Beckett's
002738	BAYLER, Wm. Thomas	4m	C	D.C.	25 MAR 1875	Ebenezer
020022	BAYLEY, Infant of Walker	15min	C	D.C.	07 MAY 1879	Potters Field
004067	BAYLISS, William	33y	W	D.C.	10 JUL 1875	Congressional
016784	BAYLISS, William	70y	W	Va.	27 JUL 1878	Mt. Olivet
015488	BAYLOR, Lillie G.	2y	C	D.C.	23 APR 1878	Beckett's
019970	BAYNE, Robert Ashby	1y	W	Md.	03 MAY 1879	Barnabas Church
008284	BAYNE, Robert S.	31y	W	N.C.	16 JUL 1876	Glenwood
015092	BEACH, David J.	53y	W	N.Y.	17 MAR 1878	Congressional
001838	BEACH, Elizabeth A.	65y	W	Va.	22 JAN 1875	Congressional
017475	BEACH, Eveline	35y	W	Md.	21 SEP 1878	Congressional
017339	BEACH, Geo. S.	2y	W	D.C.	07 SEP 1878	Alexandria, Va.
007545	BEACH, Harrold	6m	W	D.C.	08 JUN 1876	Philadelphia, Pa.
012501	BEACH, Helen Adelaide	5m	W	D.C.	24 JUL 1877	Glenwood
000936	BEACH, James B.	4m	W	D.C.	26 OCT 1874	Glenwood
010167	BEACH, Jas. D.	29y	W	Ohio	03 JAN 1877	Glenwood
019661	BEACH, Mary Ellen	5m	W	Va.	05 APR 1879	Mt. Olivet
006831	BEACH, Nathaniel	71y	W	Va.	27 MAR 1876	Congressional
013992	BEACH, Susan Henneretta	49y	W	Va.	03 DEC 1877	Glenwood
021032	BEACH, William	10m	W	D.C.	21 JUL 1879	Mt. Olivet
019801	BEAKMAN, Albertine	30y	W	D.C.	17 APR 1879	Glenwood
017030	BEAL, Alice A.	9y	W	D.C.	13 AUG 1878	Congressional
020622	BEAL, Annie	38y	C	D.C.	26 JUN 1879	Mt. Pleasant
009181	BEALE, Harry	11m	W	D.C.	23 SEP 1876	Congressional
003525	BEALE, Mary	3d	W	D.C.	04 JUN 1875	Mt. Olivet
001459	BEALL, Henry Edward	7y	W	Md.	22 DEC 1874	Mt. Olivet
013072	BEALL, Johana	35y	C	Md.	04 SEP 1877	Mt. Zion
018792	BEALL, John	7m	W	Va.	24 JAN 1879	Congressional
016894	BEALL, Josephine	1y	W	D.C.	04 AUG 1878	Mt. Olivet
011538	BEALL, Lloyd Simms	30y	W	D.C.	07 MAY 1877	Oak Hill

No.	Name	Age	Race	Birth	Death Date	Burial Place
000573	BEALL, Margaret Ann	67y	M	D.C.	20 SEP 1874	Mt. Zion
007325	BEALL, Mary Ann	3m	W	D.C.	17 MAY 1876	Mt. Olivet
018145	BEALL, Mary Francis	43y	W	D.C.	25 NOV 1878	Glenwood
014475	BEALL, Polly	87y	W	Md.	19 JAN 1878	Washington Asylum
012397	BEALL, Rachel	93y	W	Md.	17 JUL 1877	Oak Hill
013746	BEALL, Rebecca	32y	C	Md.	05 NOV 1877	Mt. Zion
008593	BEALL, Susie May	5m	W	D.C.	07 AUG 1876	Glenwood
017803	BEALL, Valinda	53y	W	Md.	20 OCT 1878	Congressional
002684	BEALL, William Dent	72y	W	R.I.	22 MAR 1875	Oak Hill
001375	BEALL, Willis J.	25y	W	D.C.	13 DEC 1874	Congressional
013959	BEALL, Wm. B.	59y	W	Md.	29 NOV 1877	Rock Creek
001336	BEAM, William	2y	W	D.C.	07 DEC 1874	Methodist
002406	BEAMAN, Bertha	1y	W	D.C.	03 MAR 1875	Loudoun Park, Md.
015528	BEAMAN, Elizabeth Gertrude	2y	W	D.C.	27 APR 1878	Rock Creek
011801	BEAMAN, Lillie E.	19y	W	Md.	05 JUN 1877	Baltimore, Md.
020000	BEAN, Colley	55y	W	D.C.	05 MAY 1879	Methodist
018764	BEAN, Emma	4y	C	D.C.	22 JAN 1879	Beckett's
003912	BEAN, Francis	34y	C	D.C.	29 JUN 1875	Mt. Olivet
010466	BEAN, Maggie	1m	W	D.C.	01 FEB 1877	Congressional
001049	BEAN, Mary A.	23y	W	D.C.	04 NOV 1874	Mt. Olivet
018909	BEAN, Rosa	1y	C	D.C.	01 FEB 1879	Potters Field
009473	BEAN, Samuel	1y	C	D.C.	20 OCT 1876	Ebenezer
005412	BEANS, Henry	19y	C	Md.	10 NOV 1875	Ebenezer
018328	BEANS, John Walker	18y	C	D.C.	14 DEC 1878	Mt. Pleasant
003573	BEANS, Theodore	75y	C	Va.	08 JUN 1875	Ebenezer
007489	BEANY, Patsey	82y	C	Va.	03 JUN 1876	Harmony
004691	BEAR, Frank Hallett	6m	W	Md.	21 AUG 1875	Queen's Chapel, Md.
001940	BEARD, Eliza	10m	C	D.C.	29 JAN 1875	Mt. Pleasant Plain
018649	BEARD, Jno.	1d	C	D.C.	12 JAN 1879	Harmony
002311	BEARD, Mary Ann	57y	W	Mass.	25 FEB 1875	Oak Hill
003072	BEARD, Richard F.	75y	W	Scot.	21 APR 1875	Washington Asylum
019116	BEARD, William	53y	W	N.Y.	19 FEB 1879	Hospital, Government
016753	BEATTIE, Sarah	22y	W	Mass.	25 JUL 1878	Mt. Olivet
018217	BEATTY, Charles F.	65y	W	D.C.	02 DEC 1878	Presbyterian
016646	BEAUMAS, Infant of Peter	5d	W	D.C.	18 JUL 1878	Presbyterian
016700	BEAUMAS, Infant of Peter	9d	W	D.C.	21 JUL 1878	Presbyterian
010730	BEAVERS, Sarah H.	45y	W	D.C.	22 FEB 1877	Glenwood
002301	BECK, Harry	1y	W	D.C.	24 FEB 1875	Glenwood
019331	BECK, John H.	41y	C	Va.	09 MAR 1879	Graceland
016096	BECK, Lenora	6m	M	D.C.	10 JUN 1878	Mt. Pleasant
018038	BECK, Mary	76y	W	Pa.	13 NOV 1878	Glenwood
003703	BECK, Robert	4m	W	D.C.	19 JUN 1875	Prospect Hill
004690	BECK, William	2y	W	D.C.	21 AUG 1875	Prospect Hill
012686	BECK, William	11m	W	D.C.	06 AUG 1877	Prospect Hill
019726	BECK, William	2m	W	D.C.	11 APR 1879	Mt. Olivet
018083	BECKER, Anna Maria	50y	W	Ger.	18 NOV 1878	Mt. Olivet
016258	BECKER, Hugh	15y	W	N.Y.	22 JUN 1878	Oak Hill
016257	BECKER, Michael H.	12d	W	D.C.	22 JUN 1878	Mt. Olivet
001232	BECKER, Nicholas	2y	W	Va.	26 NOV 1874	Fluvanna Co., Va.
005815	BECKER, William Joseph	3y	W	D.C.	21 DEC 1875	Oak Hill
018640	BECKERT, Christian Martin	51y	W	Ger.	11 JAN 1879	Prospect Hill
015436	BECKET, Austin	2m	C	D.C.	18 APR 1878	Young Mens
012482	BECKET, Edward	7m	C	D.C.	23 JUL 1877	Harmony
018955	BECKET, Elizabeth	50y	C	Va.	05 FEB 1879	Young Mens
014384	BECKET, Ellen	6y	C	D.C.	11 JAN 1878	Harmony
001487	BECKET, Eugene Clement	1y	C	D.C.	26 DEC 1874	Mt. Zion

District of Columbia Death Records, August 1, 1874 to July 31, 1879   19

No.	Name	Age	Race	Birth	Death Date	Burial Place
003503	BECKETT, Charles	12y	C	D.C.	01 JUN 1875	Beckett's
020374	BECKETT, Ferdinand	2y	C	D.C.	10 JUN 1879	Young Mens
001551	BECKETT, Francis	89y	C	Md.	31 DEC 1874	Harmony
019583	BECKETT, Henry	71y	C	Md.	29 MAR 1879	Harmony
004117	BECKETT, Infant of David	6d	C	D.C.	13 JUL 1875	Young Mens
016827	BECKETT, James Albert	4m	C	D.C.	30 JUL 1878	Young Mens
016988	BECKETT, Maria	74y	W	Md.	10 AUG 1878	Oak Hill
018674	BECKETT, Mary	33y	C	D.C.	15 JAN 1879	Mt. Olivet
005165	BECKETT, Mary E., Mrs.	24y	C	D.C.	25 SEP 1875	Beckett's
019554	BECKETT, Mary Genevieve	11y	C	D.C.	26 MAR 1879	Mt. Olivet
002713	BECKETT, William H.	22y	C	D.C.	24 MAR 1875	Beckett's
020881	BECKETT, Wm.	65y	C	Md.	11 JUL 1879	Mt. Zion
011032	BECKLEY, Mary C.	30y	W	Ire.	18 MAR 1877	Mt. Olivet
013747	BECKLEY, Sarah	18y	C	D.C.	06 NOV 1877	Harmony
016688	BECKLY, John William	60y	C	Va.	20 JUL 1878	Harmony
018063	BECKLY, Maggie	2y	C	D.C.	16 NOV 1878	Harmony
014808	BECKLY, Rachel	52y	W	Pa.	18 FEB 1878	Glenwood
006484	BECKS, Edwin	10m	M	D.C.	27 FEB 1876	Young Mens
010742	BECKS, Woodie	4m	M	D.C.	22 FEB 1877	Young Mens
003407	BECKWITH, Emma L.	35y	W	Ver.	23 MAY 1875	Norwich, Conn.
010642	BECKWITH, George W.	4m	W	D.C.	15 FEB 1877	Holy Rood
010334	BECKWITH, Harriet S.	18y	W	D.C.	19 JAN 1877	Holy Rood
003339	BECKWITH, Infant of John A.	1d	W	D.C.	16 MAY 1875	Graceland
008128	BECKWITH, Mary E.	1y	W	D.C.	10 JUL 1876	Holy Rood
004663	BECKWITH, Samuel	10m	C	Md.	19 AUG 1875	Potters Field
019378	BECRAFT, Caroline J.	60y	C	D.C.	13 MAR 1879	Holy Rood
005822	BEDLO, Thomas	56y	W	Ire.	22 DEC 1875	Mt. Olivet
017769	BEE, Infant of Isaac	7d	C	D.C.	17 OCT 1878	Potters Field
001506	BEE, Wm.	10y	C	Va.	27 DEC 1874	Mt. Zion
005658	BEECH, Henrietta, Mrs.	67y	W	Md.	05 DEC 1875	Methodist
003394	BEECHUM, Albert	2y	C	D.C.	22 MAY 1875	Mt. Olivet
020128	BEEKMAN, Allie H.	1m	W	D.C.	17 MAY 1879	Glenwood
017291	BEEKMAN, Rose	1y	W	D.C.	02 SEP 1878	Presbyterian
008771	BEETMAN, William Henry	66y	C	Va.	22 AUG 1876	Potters Field
011481	BEHLE, Edward H.	11y	W	Ky.	01 MAY 1877	Prospect Hill
015413	BEHLE, Matilda Maria S.	35y	W	Pa.	15 APR 1878	Prospect Hill
009860	BEHREND, Elijah	30y	W	Ger.	03 DEC 1876	Washington Hebrew
014682	BEHREND, Emma	38y	W	Boh.	06 FEB 1878	Washington Hebrew
019695	BEHREND, Henriette	41y	W	Ger.	08 APR 1879	Washington Hebrew
019829	BEHREND, Moritz	4m	W	D.C.	19 APR 1879	Washington Hebrew
011494	BEHREND, Rachel	11y	W	Ky.	03 MAY 1877	Hebrew
015358	BEHRENS, Lillie	8m	W	D.C.	11 APR 1878	Prospect Hill
010661	BEINEM, Leuvenia	3d	C	D.C.	16 FEB 1877	Mt. Zion
001429	BELFORD, Jane	35y	C	Va.	18 DEC 1874	Mt. Pleasant
007082	BELFORD, Sarah Jane	33y	C	Va.	23 APR 1876	Potters Field
000458	BELFORD, Willie	16m	C	D.C.	08 SEP 1874	Young Mens
000418	BELFOUR, George	28y	C	Va.	03 SEP 1874	Mt. Pleasant
001879	BELL, Alice	3y	C	Va.	24 JAN 1875	Beckett's
001469f	BELL, Alpheus	1y	C	D.C.	23 DEC 1874	Harmony
011782	BELL, Ann Eliza	61y	W	N.C.	03 JUN 1877	Congressional
017315	BELL, Ann Elizabeth	9d	C	D.C.	04 SEP 1878	Mt. Zion
012813	BELL, Annie	6m	C	D.C.	15 AUG 1877	Union Baptist
009348	BELL, Arthur	1y	C	D.C.	09 OCT 1876	Mt. Olivet
000659	BELL, Caroline	18y	M	Va.	28 SEP 1874	Beckett's
000014	BELL, Charles	1y	C	D.C.	01 AUG 1874	Harmony
017656	BELL, Christopher	55y	C	Md.	07 OCT 1878	Beckett's

No.	Name	Age	Race	Birth	Death Date	Burial Place
019220	BELL, Cora	4y	C	D.C.	27 FEB 1879	Mt. Pleasant
002321	BELL, Dolly	58y	C	Md.	25 FEB 1875	Mt. Zion
008035	BELL, E.B.	7m	W	D.C.	05 JUL 1876	Oak Hill
007688	BELL, Eliza	9m	C	D.C.	17 JUN 1876	Jones Chapel
012860	BELL, Eliza	3y	C	D.C.	18 AUG 1877	Young Mens
016972	BELL, Eliza	62y	C	Md.	09 AUG 1878	Harmony/Graceland
004704	BELL, Emily	13y	C	D.C.	22 AUG 1875	Mt. Zion
015359	BELL, Enoch G.	64y	C	D.C.	11 APR 1878	Harmony
020749	BELL, Eulalie	1y	M	D.C.	04 JUL 1879	Young Mens
014071	BELL, Flora	12d	C	D.C.	12 DEC 1877	Potters Field
016111	BELL, Frank	1y	C	D.C.	11 JUN 1878	Mt. Zion
015627	BELL, Freddie	7m	C	D.C.	06 MAY 1878	Payne's
005123a	BELL, Frederick N.	7d	C	D.C.	13 OCT 1875	Ebenezer
013967	BELL, George	65y	W	Ohio	30 NOV 1877	Hospital, Government
015731	BELL, Gilbert	32y	C	Va.	15 MAY 1878	Mt. Pleasant
015328	BELL, Harriet	1y	M	D.C.	09 APR 1878	Potters Field
019193	BELL, Hattie	4y	C	Va.	25 FEB 1879	Potters Field
002721	BELL, Hellen	4y	C	Md.	24 MAR 1875	Mt. Olivet
009036	BELL, Henrietta	45y	C	Va.	12 SEP 1876	Potters Field
012296	BELL, Hiram	42y	C	W.Va.	10 JUL 1877	Shepherdstown, W.Va.
002310	BELL, Infant of Alexander	2d	C	D.C.	25 FEB 1875	Mt. Zion
007588	BELL, Infant of Anthony	28y	C	D.C.	11 JUN 1876	Jones Chapel
014850	BELL, Infant of Edward	14h	W	D.C.	23 FEB 1878	Methodist
018340	BELL, Infant of Joseph	1m	C	D.C.	15 DEC 1878	Beckett's
007252	BELL, Infant of Louis W.	20d	C	D.C.	09 MAY 1876	Moore's
003283	BELL, Infant of Martha	1h	C	D.C.	11 MAY 1875	Potters Field
011114	BELL, Infant of Thomas	7d	C	D.C.	25 MAR 1877	Ebenezer
004308	BELL, Irene	4m	C	D.C.	26 JUL 1875	Mt. Zion
006998	BELL, James Edward	16m	C	D.C.	12 APR 1876	Beckett's
014413	BELL, James Elwood	2m	C	D.C.	14 JAN 1878	Young Mens
015947	BELL, James Thomas	2y	C	D.C.	01 JUN 1878	Payne's
005901	BELL, Jane	27y	C	Va.	31 DEC 1875	Young Mens
006000	BELL, Jas. Henry	60y	C	Md.	12 JAN 1876	Potters Field
003417	BELL, John	86y	C	Ky.	24 MAY 1875	Washington Asylum
006476	BELL, John	13m	M	Va.	26 FEB 1876	Young Mens
008234	BELL, John	50y	W	Eng.	13 JUL 1876	Arlington, Va.
003097	BELL, Joseph	8y	C	D.C.	23 APR 1875	Beckett's
018853	BELL, Joseph Warren, Gen.	64y	W	N.C.	28 JAN 1879	Glenwood
001482	BELL, Julia	58y	C	Va.	25 DEC 1874	Beckett's
000281	BELL, Louisa	29y	M	La.	22 AUG 1874	Harmony
005272	BELL, Louisa	c.22y	C	U.S.	26 OCT 1875	Ebenezer
008313	BELL, Maria Agnes	19y	C	Va.	18 JUL 1876	Mt. Zion
004845	BELL, Mary	48y	C	D.C.	31 AUG 1875	Mt. Zion
013675	BELL, Mary	1y	M	D.C.	30 OCT 1877	Beckett's
004518	BELL, Mary Ellen	19y	C	D.C.	09 AUG 1875	Young Mens
020184	BELL, Mary Ellen	7y	C	D.C.	24 MAY 1879	Harmony
000010	BELL, Mary, Mrs.	75y	C	Md.	01 AUG 1874	Mt. Olivet
004253	BELL, Melinda	1y	M	D.C.	23 JUL 1875	Young Mens
002897	BELL, Moses	4m	C	D.C.	06 APR 1875	Harmony
005999	BELL, Nellie	c.100y	C	Md.	12 JAN 1876	Mt. Zion
013724	BELL, Nicholas	22y	C	D.C.	04 NOV 1877	Mt. Zion
013508	BELL, Rachael	77y	C	Md.	14 OCT 1877	Mt. Zion
004210	BELL, Rachael Ann	7m	C	D.C.	20 JUL 1875	Jones Chapel
002113	BELL, Randolph	8y	C	Va.	10 FEB 1875	Beckett's
012709	BELL, Regina T.	4y	W	D.C.	07 AUG 1877	St. Mary's
009540	BELL, Richard	2m	C	D.C.	26 OCT 1876	Young Mens

District of Columbia Death Records, August 1, 1874 to July 31, 1879					21

No.	Name	Age	Race	Birth	Death Date	Burial Place
001021	BELL, Robert	3y	C	D.C.	02 NOV 1874	Harmony
006583	BELL, Robt. Edward	1y	C	D.C.	07 MAR 1876	Harmony
012414	BELL, Sarah	c.40y	W	Md.	18 JUL 1877	Congressional
018628	BELL, Sarah Broadus	62y	W	Va.	10 JAN 1879	Oak Hill
001229	BELL, Sophia	9y	C	D.C.	25 NOV 1874	Mt. Zion
009374	BELL, William	20y	C	Md.	11 OCT 1876	Mt. Olivet
020691	BELL, William	70y	W	Va.	01 JUL 1879	Congressional
011146	BELLE, Daniel	76y	M	D.C.	29 MAR 1877	Harmony
005646	BELLEW, Robert	56y	W	Ire.	04 DEC 1875	Mt. Olivet
013977	BELLFIELD, Alice	4y	C	D.C.	01 DEC 1877	Potters Field
005124a	BELLMAN, Maria	29y	M	Va.	13 OCT 1875	Potters Field
012530	BELLOWS, Infant of Mary	3d	C	D.C.	25 JUL 1877	Potters Field
004192	BELLOWS, Sarah	50y	W	Ire.	19 JUL 1875	Mt. Olivet
016286	BELSFIELD, Charles A.	2m	W	D.C.	24 JUN 1878	Mt. Olivet
015462	BELSHAW, Francis Young	24y	W	N.Y.	21 APR 1878	Congressional
018199	BELT, Bridget Anna	c.46y	W	Pa.	29 NOV 1878	Mt. Olivet
004272	BELT, Carrie May	10m	W	D.C.	24 JUL 1875	Congressional
018532	BELT, Dinah	75y	C	Md.	01 JAN 1879	Potters Field
005556	BELT, Harvey C.	40y	W	D.C.	25 NOV 1875	Glenwood
002341	BELT, Hester A.	3y	C	Md.	27 FEB 1875	Potters Field
014761	BELT, Ida Elizabeth	1y	C	D.C.	14 FEB 1878	Mt. Olivet
020113	BELT, Infant of Spring	2h	W	D.C.	16 MAY 1879	Belt's Farm
005399	BELT, Mary E.	30y	C	D.C.	09 NOV 1875	Potters Field
007575	BELT, Melvin	4m	W	D.C.	10 JUN 1876	Glenwood
018803	BELT, Winney Ann	51y	C	Md.	25 JAN 1879	Harmony
004457	BELT, Wm. H.	3y	W	D.C.	05 AUG 1875	Congressional
003876	BELTER, Anna Elvina	26y	C	Va.	27 JUN 1875	Ebenezer
014807	BEMBRY, John Richard	1y	C	D.C.	18 FEB 1878	Beckett's
006149	BEMBRY, Lucy	19y	C	Va.	27 JAN 1876	Ebenezer
003973	BENDER, Joseph	3m	W	D.C.	03 JUL 1875	Prospect Hill
013073	BENDER, Nora	5m	W	D.C.	04 SEP 1877	Graceland
011781	BENDER, Thomas Henry	1y	W	D.C.	02 JUN 1877	Harmony
012582	BENDZ, Violet	5m	W	D.C.	28 JUL 1877	Congressional
016355	BENETT, Lilie	10m	C	D.C.	29 JUN 1878	Young Mens
004028	BENIT, James	1y	C	D.C.	07 JUL 1875	Ebenezer
002451	BENJAMIN, Frances	34y	W	Mass.	06 MAR 1875	Dixon, Ill.
018026	BENJAMIN, Infant of Lewis	1½d	W	D.C.	12 NOV 1878	Adas Israel
014588	BENJAMIN, James S.	4m	C	D.C.	29 JAN 1878	Mt. Olivet
007063	BENJAMIN, Lewin	3y	C	D.C.	21 APR 1876	Holy Rood
010912	BENJAMIN, P.F.	60y	W	N.Y.	08 MAR 1877	Shelbina, Mo.
006184	BENKERT, George Felix	44y	W	Pa.	30 JAN 1876	Oak Hill
017547	BENNER, Anna C.	64y	W	Del.	27 SEP 1878	Congressional
015214	BENNER, Louis C.	c.30y	W	D.C.	22 APR 1878	Congressional
005214	BENNER, Spencer	16y	W	D.C.	29 SEP 1875	Congressional
011268	BENNET, Annie	12y	C	D.C.	08 APR 1877	Graceland
013795	BENNET, Charles W.	6y	W	N.Y.	11 NOV 1877	Lewinsville, Va.
004137	BENNET, Daisy	3m	W	D.C.	15 JUL 1875	Glenwood
000260	BENNET, Elen	38y	W	Ire.	20 AUG 1874	Mt. Olivet
009487	BENNET, Richard	60y	W	Ire.	21 OCT 1876	Mt. Olivet
005570	BENNETT, Birdie	6y	C	D.C.	26 NOV 1875	Ebenezer
015500	BENNETT, Clayton Lee	1y	W	D.C.	24 APR 1878	Congressional
015239	BENNETT, Cornelius	7m	W	D.C.	31 MAR 1878	Mt. Olivet
000449	BENNETT, Edward	10d	C	D.C.	07 SEP 1874	Young Mens
002220	BENNETT, George	11m	C	D.C.	18 FEB 1875	Mt. Olivet
018158	BENNETT, Gertrude	4m	C	D.C.	26 NOV 1878	Potters Field
018411	BENNETT, Gustavus	3y	C	D.C.	21 DEC 1878	Young Mens

District of Columbia Death Records, August 1, 1874 to July 31, 1879

No.	Name	Age	Race	Birth	Death Date	Burial Place
010514	BENNETT, Harry T.	24y	W	Pa.	04 FEB 1877	Trenton, N.J.
015142	BENNETT, Ida L.	7y	W	D.C.	22 MAR 1878	Congressional
007493	BENNETT, Infant of Patrick	15min	W	D.C.	04 JUN 1876	Mt. Olivet
016896	BENNETT, John	c.40y	C	Mass.	04 AUG 1878	Harmony
018303	BENNETT, John E.	10y	W	N.Y.	11 DEC 1878	Lewinsville, Va.
000032	BENNETT, John H.	19m	C	D.C.	02 AUG 1874	Beckett's
004286	BENNETT, Joseph	23y	C	D.C.	25 JUL 1875	Mt. Zion
003379	BENNETT, Julia	36y	W	Ire.	20 MAY 1875	Mt. Olivet
012237	BENNETT, Maria	32y	W	Ga.	06 APR 1877	Mt. Olivet
018738	BENNETT, Mary Jane	36y	W	Md.	20 JAN 1879	Congressional
014926	BENNETT, Michael	46y	W	Ire.	03 MAR 1878	Holy Rood
017896	BENNETT, Michael L.	1y	W	D.C.	29 OCT 1878	Mt. Olivet
012298	BENNETT, Sarah H.	39y	W	N.Y.	10 JUL 1877	Iroquois Co., Ill.
010010	BENNETT, William H.	35y	C	N.C.	19 DEC 1876	Young Mens
000372	BENNETT, Wm. H.	25y	W	D.C.	30 AUG 1874	Congressional
007589	BENNETT, Wm. J.	33y	W	Eng.	11 JUN 1876	Philadelphia, Pa.
009738	BENNIT, Jane W.	26y	W	D.C.	19 NOV 1876	Glenwood
009800	BENSINGER, Frederick	2y	W	D.C.	25 NOV 1876	Congressional
008796	BENSON, Bessie	4m	W	D.C.	23 AUG 1876	Rock Creek
006622	BENT, Anthony	57y	W	Ger.	10 MAR 1876	Glenwood
004844	BENTER, F.E.	9m	W	D.C.	31 AUG 1875	Prospect Hill
017420	BENTER, Infant of F.A.	22h	W	D.C.	16 SEP 1878	Prospect Hill
004027	BENTLEY, Lilly Virginia	4m	W	D.C.	07 JUL 1875	Mt. Olivet
004040	BENTLY, William Thomas	10m	C	D.C.	08 JUL 1875	Mt. Olivet
003933	BENTON, John F.	4m	W	D.C.	30 JUN 1875	Presbyterian
011202	BENTON, Sarah Ann	56y	W	Md.	03 APR 1877	Presbyterian
003099	BENTZ, Emilea	21y	W	D.C.	23 APR 1875	Prospect Hill
000087	BENTZLER, Mary Adelaide	11m	W	D.C.	07 AUG 1874	Holy Rood
009690	BENZLER, Johanna Ch. Fredericka	6m	W	Ger.	13 NOV 1876	Prospect Hill
001847	BERBER, Burdette	5w	C	D.C.	23 JAN 1875	Potters Field
016170	BERBERICH, Barbara	70y	W	Ger.	15 JUN 1878	St. Mary's
004556	BERCKMAN, Mary A., Mrs.	61y	W	D.C.	12 AUG 1875	Congressional
015745	BERCKNER, Eleanor	1m	C	D.C.	17 MAY 1878	Harmony
013216	BERENS, Catherine	3y	W	D.C.	16 SEP 1877	St. Mary's
013061	BERGEMAN, Elizabeth L.	4m	W	D.C.	03 SEP 1877	Congressional
013333	BERGER, Infant of J.C.S.	5h	W	D.C.	28 SEP 1877	Congressional
018765	BERGMAN, Charley Adelphy	3y	W	Md.	22 JAN 1879	Glenwood
006690	BERGMAN, William J.	75y	W	Ger.	16 MAR 1876	Prospect Hill
015890	BERGMANN, Friedericke Caroline	45y	W	Ger.	29 MAY 1878	Prospect Hill
001106	BERKELEY, Anna Betsy	75y	W	D.C.	10 NOV 1874	Congressional
008782	BERKLEY, Clara V.	11m	W	D.C.	22 AUG 1876	Congressional
010220	BERKLEY, Daniel P.	29y	W	D.C.	08 JAN 1877	Congressional
005098a	BERKLEY, Jenny	18y	C	Va.	10 OCT 1875	Young Mens
014034	BERKLEY, Joseph	38y	C	Va.	08 DEC 1877	Macedonia
012973	BERKLEY, Martin B.	2m	W	D.C.	27 AUG 1877	Congressional
008496	BERKLEY, Sarah A.	3m	W	D.C.	30 JUL 1876	Congressional
015168	BERKLEY, Sarah E.	7m	W	D.C.	24 MAR 1878	Congressional
012724	BERKLY, Allie	1y	C	D.C.	08 AUG 1877	Young Mens
004041	BERLIN, Isabella	4m	W	S.C.	08 JUL 1875	Oak Hill
001795	BERMAN, Adline	31y	C	Va.	19 JAN 1875	Young Mens
017747	BERMAN, Cathrene	62y	W	Ger.	15 OCT 1878	Prospect Hill
015303	BERMAN, Samuel	2m	W	D.C.	07 APR 1878	Adas Israel
005343	BERNARD, Infant of Chas.	26d	C	D.C.	03 NOV 1875	Potters Field
018098	BERNARD, Mary E.	29y	W	Md.	20 NOV 1878	Mt. Olivet
013538	BERNARDE, Henry	4y	W	D.C.	17 OCT 1877	Graceland
008615	BERNARDINI, Jiorlio	24y	W	Italy	08 AUG 1876	Mt. Olivet

District of Columbia Death Records, August 1, 1874 to July 31, 1879   23

No.	Name	Age	Race	Birth	Death Date	Burial Place
010508	BERNAUGH, Martha	57y	C	Va.	04 FEB 1877	Harmony
009218	BERNETT, Anna	8m	W	D.C.	28 SEP 1876	Prospect Hill
020175	BERNHEIMER, Samuel	1y	W	D.C.	23 MAY 1879	Alexandria, Va.
006444	BERRET, Alice S.	35y	W	D.C.	23 FEB 1876	Holy Rood
014142	BERRETT, Charles Brown	42y	W	D.C.	20 DEC 1877	Congressional
001101	BERRETT, Infant of William	3d	C	D.C.	09 NOV 1874	Potters Field
009789	BERRIMAN, John	21y	C	Va.	24 NOV 1876	Ebenezer
016685	BERRY, Alice	1y	C	D.C.	19 JUL 1878	Mt. Zion
008697	BERRY, Annie	3y	W	D.C.	15 AUG 1876	Oak Hill
011959	BERRY, Arianna	16y	C	Md.	18 JUN 1877	Eastern Shore, Md.
012439	BERRY, Arthur	1y	C	D.C.	20 JUL 1877	Beckett's
007150	BERRY, Charles A.	17y	C	D.C.	29 APR 1876	Mt. Zion
009510	BERRY, Infant of John	2m	C	D.C.	23 OCT 1876	Ebenezer
020802	BERRY, Iva Virginia	5m	W	D.C.	07 JUL 1879	Congressional
006014	BERRY, James W.	34y	W	Ill.	14 JAN 1876	Hospital
008694	BERRY, Jane	23y	C	Md.	15 AUG 1876	Mt. Zion
016645	BERRY, Josephine	27y	C	Md.	18 JUL 1878	Harmony
004746	BERRY, Lee	43y	C	Md.	25 AUG 1875	Potters Field
005992	BERRY, Margaret	c.81y	W	Md.	11 JAN 1876	Oak Hill
016885	BERRY, Maria	5m	C	D.C.	03 AUG 1878	Beckett's
010651	BERRY, Mary Ella	9m	C	D.C.	16 FEB 1877	Ebenezer
020851	BERRY, Mary J.	19y	W	D.C.	09 JUL 1879	Congressional
003263	BERRY, Milton Elsworth Meyers	6m	W	D.C.	08 MAY 1875	Howard's/Uniontown
016188	BERRY, Moses	84y	C	Md.	16 JUN 1878	Eastern Shore, Md.
001187	BERRY, Nimrod	40y	C	Va.	19 NOV 1874	Harmony
018629	BERRY, Philip Tayloe	78y	W	Md.	10 JAN 1879	Oak Hill
002945	BERRY, Rachael	8d	W	D.C.	11 APR 1875	Congressional
013097	BERRY, Richard	6m	W	D.C.	06 SEP 1877	Beckett's
010193	BERRY, Thomas	67y	W	N.Y.	06 JAN 1877	Mt. Olivet
012234	BERRYMAN, Infant of Louisa	14d	M	D.C.	06 JUL 1877	Potters Field
006999	BERRYMAN, Jno.	3y	C	N.J.	12 APR 1876	Mt. Pleasant
012705	BERRYMAN, Louisa	17y	C	Va.	07 AUG 1877	Potters Field
013509	BERRYMAN, Mary Verlinda	27y	W	D.C.	14 OCT 1877	Mt. Olivet
013399	BERRYMAN, Winnie	80y	C	Va.	04 OCT 1877	Young Mens
001138	BERTREIL, Fidele	68y	W	Ger.	13 NOV 1874	Graceland
004591	BESSLER, Minnie	7m	W	D.C.	14 AUG 1875	St. Mary's/Glenwood
011430	BESTOR, Chauncey	89y	W	Conn.	26 APR 1877	Congressional
013578	BESTOR, Sarah S.	83y	W	Va.	21 OCT 1877	Glenwood
005089	BETHAM, John	30y	W	Md.	18 SEP 1875	Potters Field
017819	BETLOW, Margaret	85y	C	D.C.	21 OCT 1878	Payne's
020494	BETTER, Effie Estella	1y	C	D.C.	18 JUN 1879	Payne's
001818	BETTER, Emma	14d	C	D.C.	21 JAN 1875	Ebenezer
006413	BETTER, Thomas H.	1m	C	D.C.	19 FEB 1876	Ebenezer
000028	BETTES, Martha Rebecca	1y	C	D.C.	02 AUG 1874	Beckett's
010947	BETTS, George	34y	W	U.S.	12 MAR 1877	Soldier's Home
018835	BETTS, John E.	4y	W	Va.	27 JAN 1879	Accotink, Va.
005703	BETTS, Mary	9y	W	D.C.	09 DEC 1875	Congressional
005569	BETTUS, Lucy	2y	C	D.C.	26 NOV 1875	Ebenezer
000529	BETZ, Henry Leonard	6y	W	D.C.	16 SEP 1874	Prospect Hill
020647	BETZ, Lilly Blanche	16d	W	D.C.	28 JUN 1879	Prospect Hill
006182	BETZ, Thomas B.	7d	W	D.C.	30 JAN 1876	Prospect Hill
003963	BEUEHL, Anna	14y	W	Ger.	02 JUL 1875	Prospect Hill
014231	BEVAN, John H.	40y	W	Pa.	28 DEC 1877	Philadelphia, Pa.
000786	BEVANS, James P.	29y	W	D.C.	12 OCT 1874	Congressional
007475	BEVANS, Lucy A.M., Mrs.	61y	W	Md.	03 JUN 1876	Holy Spring, Md.
016356	BEVANS, Samuel	95y	C	Md.	29 JUN 1878	Potters Field

District of Columbia Death Records, August 1, 1874 to July 31, 1879

No.	Name	Age	Race	Birth	Death Date	Burial Place
007742	BEVELY, Mary	11m	C	D.C.	20 JUN 1876	Potters Field
003658	BEVERIDGE, Charles	19y	C	D.C.	15 JUN 1875	Harmony
004555	BEVERIDGE, John G.	9m	W	D.C.	12 AUG 1875	Baltimore, Md.
019117	BEVERLEY, Alice	1y	C	D.C.	19 FEB 1879	Beckett's
008390	BEVERLY, Anson	8d	M	D.C.	23 JUL 1876	Potters Field
013310	BEVERLY, Caroline	17y	C	Va.	26 SEP 1877	Beckett's
011475	BEVERLY, Elvira	9m	C	D.C.	01 MAY 1877	Ebenezer
001735	BEVERLY, Emily	35y	C	Va.	14 JAN 1875	Beckett's
017335	BEVERLY, John	6y	C	D.C.	06 SEP 1878	Macedonia
019097	BEVERLY, John	5y	C	D.C.	17 FEB 1879	Young Mens
006290	BEVERLY, John Prescott	1y	C	D.C.	10 FEB 1876	Ebenezer
010409	BEVERLY, Lettie	22y	C	Va.	26 JAN 1877	Ebenezer
013756	BEVERLY, Mary	2m	C	D.C.	07 NOV 1877	Young Mens
001085	BEVERLY, Robert	60y	C	Md.	08 NOV 1874	Potters Field
011258	BEVERLY, Sarah	9y	C	D.C.	07 APR 1877	Macedonia
017103	BEYER, Jenie	2y	W	D.C.	19 AUG 1878	Mt. Olivet
012187	BEYNON, Peter Levi	6m	W	D.C.	02 JUL 1877	Holy Rood
016828	BEYNON, Sarah	5m	W	D.C.	30 JUL 1878	Holy Rood
019416	BEYPRECHT, John Thomas	9m	W	D.C.	15 MAR 1879	Prospect Hill
009538	BIAS, John	11m	C	D.C.	26 OCT 1876	Mt. Olivet
019649	BIAS, John	2y	C	Md.	04 APR 1879	Annapolis, Md.
020800	BIAS, Martha	2m	C	D.C.	07 JUL 1879	Mt. Olivet
015304	BIDDERSON, Mary A.S.	3y	W	Md.	07 APR 1878	Baltimore, Md.
016950	BIDENHARN, Eulalia	44y	W	Ger.	08 AUG 1878	Mt. Olivet
014579	BIEGLER, Catherine	60y	W	Ger.	28 JAN 1878	Congressional
007668	BIELASKI, Eugene	20y	W	D.C.	16 JUN 1876	Congressional
003680	BIGER, Mary Catharine	7m	W	D.C.	17 JUN 1875	Glenwood
005515	BIGGES, Ann	48y	W	D.C.	20 NOV 1875	Congressional
017224	BIGGS, Augustus C.	2d	C	D.C.	28 AUG 1878	Beckett's
019971	BIGGS, James A.	2y	W	D.C.	03 MAY 1879	Rock Creek
003798	BIGGS, John H.	40y	W	D.C.	24 JUN 1875	Presbyterian
014669	BIGGS, Maria	80y	W	D.C.	05 FEB 1878	Holy Rood
016535	BIGGS, Thomas H.	8m	W	D.C.	10 JUL 1878	Graceland
005891	BIGLEY, David R.P.	36y	W	Va.	29 DEC 1875	Glenwood
003177	BIGLEY, Martha	35y	W	Va.	30 APR 1875	Potters Field
000984	BILLS, Sarah Jane	1y	W	D.C.	30 OCT 1874	Mt. Olivet
008739	BILLUPS, Mary J.	14y	W	Md.	19 AUG 1876	Congressional
016065	BINARDY, Willie	4y	W	France	08 JUN 1878	Graceland
018919	BINGER, John	64y	W	Ger.	02 FEB 1879	Md.
001842	BINGHAM, Albert	1y	W	D.C.	22 JAN 1875	Mt. Olivet
005912	BINGHAM, Caroline	55y	C	Va.	02 JAN 1876	Arlington, Va.
007267	BINGHAM, Farrand Godfrey	4y	W	D.C.	11 MAY 1876	Eel River, Ind.
019234	BINGHAM, George	85y	C	Md.	28 FEB 1879	Potters Field
019555	BINGHAM, John Frederick	10m	W	D.C.	26 MAR 1879	Mt. Olivet
017149	BINGHAM, Louisa	77y	C	Va.	23 AUG 1878	Arlington
002905	BINNIX, Julia, Mrs.	46	W	Md.	07 APR 1875	Congressional
011144	BINNS, George	45y	C	Va.	28 MAR 1877	Loudoun Co., Va.
002613	BIRCH, Ann Rebecca	1y	W	D.C.	17 MAR 1875	Congressional
011189	BIRCH, Elizabeth S.	80y	W	Va.	01 APR 1877	Oak Hill
011231	BIRCH, Isaac	80y	W	Va.	05 APR 1877	Oak Hill
012837	BIRCH, John Dillon	35y	W	D.C.	16 AUG 1877	Mt. Olivet
019997	BIRCH, Nancy	80y	C	Va.	05 MAY 1879	Potters Field
007739	BIRCH, Nathaniel King	28y	W	D.C.	20 JUN 1876	Oak Hill
000722	BIRCH, Rebecca	60y	W	D.C.	06 OCT 1874	College
014259	BIRCKHEAD, Amelia A.	54y	W	Md.	30 DEC 1877	Congressional
007876	BIRCKHEAD, Elizabeth	79y	W	Md.	27 JUN 1876	Glenwood

District of Columbia Death Records, August 1, 1874 to July 31, 1879   25

No.	Name	Age	Race	Birth	Death Date	Burial Place
004285	BIRCKHEAD, Franklin M.	47y	W	D.C.	25 JUL 1875	Glenwood
020850	BIRD, Amelia Ann	1y	C	D.C.	09 JUL 1879	Harmony
009295	BIRD, Amos	1y	C	D.C.	04 OCT 1876	Ebenezer
018281	BIRD, Celia	32y	C	Va.	09 DEC 1878	Mt. Zion
020549	BIRD, Ethel W.	2m	W	D.C.	21 JUN 1879	Glenwood
001693	BIRD, Frank	1y	M	D.C.	11 JAN 1875	Mt. Zion
015719	BIRD, Harriet	25y	C	Va.	14 MAY 1878	Beckett's
014832	BIRD, Henry	65y	C	Md.	21 FEB 1878	Potters Field
016028	BIRD, Henry	1m	C	D.C.	06 JUN 1878	Potters Field
005042a	BIRD, Infant of Reuben	2h	C	D.C.	03 OCT 1875	Mt. Zion
010121	BIRD, Infant of Mark	45y	C	D.C.	30 DEC 1876	Ebenezer
015921	BIRD, James C.	2y	W	D.C.	31 MAY 1878	Glenwood
002325	BIRD, John	38y	C	Va.	26 FEB 1875	Washington Asylum
013128	BIRD, John W.	52y	W	Va.	09 SEP 1877	Leesburg, Va.
015814	BIRD, Mary E.	10m	C	D.C.	23 MAY 1878	Holy Rood
007743	BIRD, Mary Edna	3m	W	D.C.	20 JUN 1876	Glenwood
016783	BIRD, Robert	3y	M	D.C.	27 JUL 1878	Fairfax Co., Va.
020957	BIRD, Sarah	26y	C	Va.	16 JUL 1879	Graceland
006120	BIRD, William	2y	C	D.C.	24 JAN 1876	Ebenezer
000465	BIRD, William H.	6m	C	D.C.	09 SEP 1874	Beckett's
004808	BIRTH, Charles William	30y	W	Tenn.	29 AUG 1875	Congressional
001293	BISCHOF, Gertrude	45y	W	Ger.	02 DEC 1874	St. Mary's
019159	BISCHOFF, Alma	1y	W	D.C.	23 FEB 1879	Prospect Hill
014185	BISH, Sarah E.	2w	C	D.C.	24 DEC 1877	Young Mens
017316	BISHOP, Celia	27y	C	Va.	04 SEP 1878	Potters Field
002748	BISHOP, Charles	46y	W	Va.	26 MAR 1875	Congressional
013645	BISHOP, Henry	87y	W	Eng.	27 OCT 1877	Glenwood
001376	BISHOP, Henry H.	32y	W	Md.	13 DEC 1874	Oak Hill
000770	BISHOP, Jemima	67y	W	Md.	10 OCT 1874	Congressional
008761	BISHOP, John	c.65y	C	France	21 AUG 1876	Young Mens
018257	BISHOP, Sarah Anna	19d	W	D.C.	07 DEC 1878	St. Mary's
007336	BISSHAN, Robert	7d	W	D.C.	19 MAY 1876	Montross, Va.
020221	BITNER, William G.	85y	W	Ger.	29 MAY 1879	Congressional
019889	BIVENS, John	70y	C	Md.	25 APR 1879	Potters Field
013373	BLACK, Allen	20y	C	Va.	02 OCT 1877	Young Mens
007652	BLACK, Antony	21d	C	D.C.	15 JUN 1876	Mt. Olivet
011830	BLACK, Augustine	1m	C	D.C.	07 JUN 1877	Mt. Olivet
007000	BLACK, Austin	9m	C	D.C.	12 APR 1876	Mt. Olivet
012725	BLACK, Chas. Fredk.	1y	W	Md.	08 AUG 1877	Prospect Hill
015703	BLACK, Eliza	47y	C	Va.	13 MAY 1878	Potters Field
005539	BLACK, Elizabeth	10d	C	D.C.	23 NOV 1875	Ebenezer
006796	BLACK, Henry	1m	C	D.C.	24 MAR 1876	Mt. Olivet
000980	BLACK, John	44y	W	Ire.	29 OCT 1874	Oak Hill
007288	BLACK, John Henry	2y	W	D.C.	13 MAY 1876	Philadelphia, Pa.
003068	BLACK, Joseph	2m	W	D.C.	21 APR 1875	Mt. Olivet
010954	BLACK, Louise	4m	W	Md.	12 MAR 1877	Baltimore, Md.
004329	BLACK, Margaret	1m	C	D.C.	27 JUL 1875	Mt. Olivet
011995	BLACK, Margaret	2m	W	U.S.	21 JUN 1877	Mt. Olivet
013192	BLACK, Mary Ann	8m	W	D.C.	14 SEP 1877	Presbyterian
006869	BLACK, Wm.	50y	W	Eng.	31 MAR 1876	Potters Field
000304	BLACKBURN, Elizabeth	15d	C	D.C.	24 AUG 1874	Harmony
017485	BLACKBURN, Elizabeth	95y	W	Va.	22 SEP 1878	Presbyterian
009946	BLACKBURN, Emma	3y	C	D.C.	13 DEC 1876	Mt. Zion
004852	BLACKBURN, Infant of Robert	11d	C	D.C.	31 AUG 1875	Potters Field
013860	BLACKBURN, Susan	15y	C	Va.	19 NOV 1877	Potters Field
019098	BLACKESTONE, Samuel Joseph	1y	C	D.C.	17 FEB 1879	Harmony

District of Columbia Death Records, August 1, 1874 to July 31, 1879

No.	Name	Age	Race	Birth	Death Date	Burial Place
012232	BLACKFORD, Homer	3m	W	D.C.	05 JUL 1877	Oak Hill
011518	BLACKFORD, Infant of Kate	c.3 min	W	D.C.	05 MAY 1877	Presbyterian
009965	BLACKFORD, James S.	69y	W	Eng.	14 DEC 1876	Oak Hill
011847	BLACKLEY, William	1y	C	D.C.	09 JUN 1877	Mt. Pleasant
005450	BLACKMORE, Charlott Ann	1y	C	D.C.	14 NOV 1875	Ebenezer
006949	BLACKSON, Florence Geneva	8m	C	D.C.	07 APR 1876	Harmony
001986	BLACKSON, Henrietta	85y	C	Md.	01 FEB 1875	Harmony
020091	BLACKSTON, Charity	29y	C	Va.	14 MAY 1879	Harmony
005908	BLACKSTON, Henriette	60y	C	Md.	01 JAN 1876	Mt. Olivet
003316	BLACKWELL, Anna S.	29y	W	D.C.	14 MAY 1875	Congressional
008059	BLACKWELL, Charles	3y	C	D.C.	07 JUL 1876	Mt. Pleasant
010067	BLACKWELL, Edward	14d	C	D.C.	25 DEC 1876	Potters Field
006996	BLACKWELL, Elijah	1y	C	D.C.	12 APR 1876	Young Mens
019861	BLACKWELL, Florence	2y	C	D.C.	22 APR 1879	Beckett's
015948	BLACKWELL, Harriet	2y	C	D.C.	01 JUN 1878	Mt. Zion
020726	BLACKWELL, Infant of Josephine	13d	C	D.C.	03 JUL 1879	Potters Field
010230	BLACKWELL, Jefferson	c.65y	C	Va.	09 JAN 1877	Ebenezer
012075	BLACKWELL, Mary	1y	C	D.C.	26 JUN 1877	Mt. Olivet
018969	BLACKWELL, Sarah	46y	C	Va.	06 FEB 1879	Lincolnville, Va.
009259	BLAGBORN, Jennie	80y	C	Va.	01 OCT 1876	Young Mens
012074	BLAGDON, Charles Andrew	1y	C	D.C.	26 JUN 1877	Ebenezer
016097	BLAGMAN, Cornelius	11m	C	D.C.	10 JUN 1878	Beckett's
019394	BLAIR, Gertrude	8m	C	D.C.	14 MAR 1879	Harmony
014737	BLAIR, Henry	9d	C	D.C.	11 FEB 1878	Mt. Olivet
018039	BLAIR, Josephine	25y	C	Md.	13 NOV 1878	Mt. Olivet
005069a	BLAIR, Lizzie	42y	C	Md.	06 OCT 1875	Mt. Olivet
019417	BLAIR, Rebeca	2y	W	D.C.	14 MAR 1879	Washington Hebrew
014538	BLAIR, Travis	55y	C	Va.	24 JAN 1878	Macedonia
001322	BLAKE, Bridget	35y	W	Ire.	06 DEC 1874	Mt. Olivet
013107	BLAKE, Charles	50y	W	Ire.	07 SEP 1877	Soldier's Home
001323	BLAKE, Dennis	35y	W	Ire.	06 DEC 1874	Mt. Olivet
010509	BLAKE, George Anna	1y	C	D.C.	04 FEB 1877	Mt. Olivet
005961	BLAKE, James	1y	W	D.C.	07 JAN 1876	Mt. Olivet
019025	BLAKE, Joseph	7y	C	D.C.	11 FEB 1879	Mt. Olivet
020349	BLAKE, Mary A.	55y	C	Md.	09 JUN 1879	Mt. Olivet
014015	BLAKELY, William Nowell	2m	W	D.C.	06 DEC 1877	Methodist, E.
016462	BLAKEY, Elizabeth J.	37y	M	Va.	06 JUL 1878	Mt. Zion
008100	BLAKEY, Sophy	28y	C	Va.	09 JUL 1876	Potters Field
017404	BLANCH, Emma	84y	C	Va.	14 SEP 1878	Harmony
003872	BLANCH, Maria	3m	W	D.C.	27 JUN 1875	Mt. Olivet
012892	BLANCHARD, Samuel B.	c.60y	W	N.H.	21 AUG 1877	Rock Creek
003582	BLAND, Agnes	10m	C	Md.	09 JUN 1875	Young Mens
018028	BLAND, Agnes	c.70y	C	Va.	12 NOV 1878	Baptist
001110	BLAND, Dolly	83y	C	Va.	10 NOV 1874	Bluff Point, Va.[1]
015188	BLAND, Edmund	75y	C	Va.	26 MAR 1878	Potters Field
020573	BLAND, Elijah	4m	C	D.C.	23 JUN 1879	Beckett's
014001	BLAND, Hattie	3m	C	D.C.	03 DEC 1877	Beckett's
010248	BLAND, James	7y	C	D.C.	10 JAN 1877	Ebenezer
012243	BLAND, James Henry	28d	C	D.C.	06 JUL 1877	Beckett's
011654	BLAND, John	3y	C	D.C.	20 MAY 1877	Mt. Pleasant
015963	BLAND, Joseph	2m	C	D.C.	02 JUN 1878	Potters Field
004538	BLAND, Laura	7y	C	D.C.	11 AUG 1875	Ebenezer
002099	BLAND, Laura Marie	33y	W	Pa.	09 FEB 1875	Congressional

[1] Located in Westmoreland Co., Va.

District of Columbia Death Records, August 1, 1874 to July 31, 1879

No.	Name	Age	Race	Birth	Death Date	Burial Place
004039	BLAND, Loula	12d	C	D.C.	08 JUL 1875	Beckett's
014747	BLAND, Simie	2y	C	D.C.	12 FEB 1878	Beckett's
005216	BLAND, Spencer	7y	C	D.C.	29 SEP 1875	Beckett's
002870	BLAND, Willie	3y	C	D.C.	04 APR 1875	Ebenezer
008740	BLANDFORD, Annie C.	13y	W	Md.	19 AUG 1876	Congressional
016001	BLANDFORD, Frederick	4m	C	D.C.	04 JUN 1878	Young Mens
009414	BLANFORD, Jesse W.	3y	C	D.C.	15 OCT 1876	Mt. Pleasant Plain
018668	BLASLAND, Willie	4y	W	D.C.	14 JAN 1879	Glenwood
000039	BLECKHEIM, Jacob	9d	W	D.C.	03 AUG 1874	Washington Asylum
018216	BLEISER, Elizabeth	71y	W	Ger.	02 DEC 1878	St. Mary's
015143	BLENCK, Eliza	49y	W	Ire.	22 MAR 1878	Congressional
019851	BLENCK, William	50y	W	Ger.	21 APR 1879	Congressional
007039	BLENHAM, Matilda	61y	M	Va.	18 APR 1876	Potters Field
011209	BLINCOE, Marie A.	26y	W	Va.	04 APR 1877	Tennallytown
006539	BLISS, Jeremy W.	64y	W	Conn.	04 MAR 1876	Hartford, Conn.
013045	BLOCK, Cornelius	1y	C	D.C.	01 SEP 1877	Young Mens
006505	BLODGETT, Monah H.	40y	W	N.Y.	29 FEB 1876	Albany, N.Y.
003841	BLONDHEIM, Albert	6m	W	D.C.	26 JUN 1875	Jewish
003819	BLONDHEIM, Olivia	35y	W	Md.	25 JUN 1875	Jewish
020550	BLOOMER, Sarah Augusta	6m	W	D.C.	21 JUN 1879	Glenwood
013637	BLOOMQUIST, Oscar	31y	W	Ger.	25 OCT 1877	Prospect Hill
001598	BLOSS, Mary	2y	W	D.C.	03 JAN 1875	Glenwood
007260	BLOUNT, David E.	2y	W	Ga.	10 MAY 1876	Congressional
012000	BLUE, Charles Henry	5m	W	D.C.	21 JUN 1877	Oak Hill
016298	BLUE, Lucy	19y	C	Va.	25 JUN 1878	Harmony
007134	BLUE, Lucy Ann	29y	C	Md.	27 APR 1876	Ebenezer
001530	BLUE, Robt.	8y	C	Va.	28 DEC 1874	Holy Rood
010936	BLUM, Caroline	38y	W	Ger.	10 MAR 1877	Prospect Hill
016923	BLUM, Johanna	78y	W	Ger.	06 AUG 1878	Baltimore, Md.
003529	BLUME, Conrad	39y	W	Ger.	04 JUN 1875	Hospital
018854	BLUNDON, Joseph C.	1y	W	D.C.	28 JAN 1879	Oak Hill
010707	BLUNDON, Marja E.	6	W	D.C.	20 FEB 1877	Oak Hill
010663	BLUNT, Edward	3m	C	D.C.	17 FEB 1877	Potters Field
003071	BOADLEY, Nellie	2m	C	D.C.	21 APR 1875	Mt. Zion
010428	BOAN, Edward	3y	C	D.C.	28 JAN 1877	Young Mens
006541	BOARMAN, Henry	34y	C	Va.	04 MAR 1876	Potters Field
017927	BOARMAN, Lizzie	6d	C	D.C.	02 NOV 1878	Mt. Zion
018229	BOARMAN, Maria Josephine	6y	W	D.C.	03 DEC 1878	Mt. Olivet
003265	BOARMAN, Mary	3m	W	D.C.	09 MAY 1875	Mt. Olivet
015423	BOCK, George	61y	W	Ger.	16 APR 1878	Tennallytown[1]
018510	BODAY, Eva Jane	9y	C	D.C.	30 DEC 1878	Mt. Pleasant
003842	BODELER, Wm.	3m	W	D.C.	26 JUN 1875	Congressional
002909	BODIN, Winfield S.	22y	W	Va.	07 APR 1875	Congressional
016969	BODREY, George	1m	C	D.C.	09 AUG 1878	Payne's
011757	BODY, Caroline	47y	C	Va.	31 MAY 1877	Mt. Pleasant
013968	BODY, Lucy	1y	C	D.C.	30 NOV 1877	Mt. Pleasant
013218	BODY, Margarett E.	43y	W	Va.	16 SEP 1877	Glenwood
011552	BODY, Mary Magdaline	6y	C	D.C.	09 MAY 1877	Young Mens
003763	BODY, Wm. []	2y	C	D.C.	22 JUN 1875	Mt. Pleasant Plain
019084	BOEGLER, Frederick	76y	W	Ger.	15 FEB 1879	Prospect Hill
010848	BOGAN, Gilbert	64y	W	Ire.	03 MAR 1877	Soldier's Home
016357	BOGART, James N.	30y	W	N.Y.	29 JUN 1878	Rock Creek

---

[1] Grave for George M. Bock is found at Eldbrooke Methodist Cemetery adjacent to the Eldbrooke United Methodist Church, 4100 River Road, N.W., Washington, D.C.

No.	Name	Age	Race	Birth	Death Date	Burial Place
000758	BOGGESS, Joanna C.	54y	W	Pa.	08 OCT 1874	Congressional
011498	BOGGESS, Thomas L.	63y	W	Va.	03 MAY 1877	Congressional
020417	BOGGS, Genevieve	1y	W	D.C.	13 JUN 1879	Congressional
002512	BOGGS, William Bunton	64y	W	N.J.	11 MAR 1875	Oak Hill
013801	BOGIA, Infant of Mattena	4h	W	D.C.	12 NOV 1877	St. Mary's
010548	BOGUE, Charles	c.50y	W	Ire.	07 FEB 1877	Potters Field
018594	BOHANAH, Amanda	26y	C	Md.	07 JAN 1879	Potters Field
006183	BOHANAH, Deliah	8m	C	D.C.	30 JAN 1876	Mt. Pleasant
012009	BOHANNAH, Cornelia	5m	C	D.C.	22 JUN 1877	Mt. Pleasant
010336	BOHANNAN, Carrie R.	4y	W	D.C.	19 JAN 1877	Congressional
006645	BOHLMAN, John	27y	W	Ger.	12 MAR 1876	Hospital
012327	BOHRER, Chlorine	3y	W	D.C.	12 JUL 1877	Presbyterian
000331	BOHRER, Infant of John S.	9d	W	D.C.	27 AUG 1874	Montgomery Co., Md.
009991	BOIL, Martin	32y	W	Ire.	17 DEC 1876	Hospital
012088	BOISEAU, Rose Marie	1y	W	D.C.	27 JUN 1877	Mt. Olivet
000378	BOLAND, John	40y	W	Ire.	30 AUG 1874	Mt. Olivet
014073	BOLAND, Winnifred	8y	W	D.C.	12 DEC 1877	Mt. Olivet
008098	BOLDEN, Diana R.	10m	C	D.C.	09 JUL 1876	Young Mens
000380	BOLDEN, Lula I.	6m	C	D.C.	31 AUG 1874	Mt. Zion
010557	BOLDEN, Thomas	52y	C	Va.	08 FEB 1877	Harmony
002121	BOLDEN, William	2y	C	D.C.	11 FEB 1875	Harmony
004789	BOLDIN, Benjamin	32y	C	Va.	28 AUG 1875	Potters Field
003021	BOLES, Bridget	50y	C	Ire.	17 APR 1875	Mt. Olivet
013725	BOLING, Alice	28y	W	Va.	04 NOV 1877	Balls Farm, Va.
017076	BOLING, Mary Martina	40y	W	D.C.	17 AUG 1878	Mt. Olivet
011123	BOLL, Catharine	10m	W	D.C.	26 MAR 1877	St. Mary's
016484	BOLL, Infant of Agnes	1d	W	D.C.	07 JUL 1878	Mt. Olivet
018073	BOLLES, Anna May	1m	W	D.C.	17 NOV 1878	Mt. Olivet
015831	BOLLES, John Augustus	69y	W	Conn.	25 MAY 1878	Boston, Mass.
002827	BOLLING, Anna Maria	61y	W	N.H.	01 APR 1875	Boston, Mass.
019235	BOLLING, Gracie	2y	C	Me.	28 FEB 1879	Young Mens
006485	BOLSTON, James N.	3y	M	D.C.	27 FEB 1876	Potters Field
007116	BOLTON, Diana	40y	C	Md.	26 APR 1876	Mt. Pleasant
014194	BOLTON, William	2m	C	D.C.	25 DEC 1877	Hillsdale
017658	BOLZ, Caroline	1y	C	S.C.	07 OCT 1878	Mt. Olivet
007133	BOMBARY, Theresa	27y	C	Md.	27 APR 1876	Mt. Olivet
005035a	BOMBREY, Lizza	9m	C	D.C.	03 OCT 1875	Potters Field
008682	BOND, Birdie	c.8m	C	D.C.	14 AUG 1876	Mt. Pleasant Plain
006705	BOND, Frederick Wales	7m	C	D.C.	17 MAR 1876	Harmony
019409	BOND, George H.	1y	C	D.C.	15 MAR 1879	Holy Rood
016855	BOND, Ida	7m	C	D.C.	01 AUG 1878	Young Mens
006892	BOND, Ignatius	71y	C	Md.	02 APR 1876	Mt. Pleasant
001739	BOND, Infant of J.D.	9d	W	D.C.	15 JAN 1875	Mt. Olivet
020728	BOND, James	39y	W	U.S.	03 JUL 1879	Soldier's Home
005942	BOND, John	8y	C	Md.	05 JAN 1876	Young Mens
015437	BOND, John Wesly	35y	C	Md.	18 APR 1878	Potters Field
004896	BOND, Sarah F.	35y	W	Va.	04 SEP 1875	Oak Hill
010379	BOND, Wesly	23y	C	Md.	23 JAN 1877	Harmony
002732	BOND, William	28y	W	Md.	25 MAR 1875	Mt. Olivet
006868	BOND, William	c.73y	W	Pa.	31 MAR 1876	Glenwood
001723	BONFANTIE, Frances Marian	21y	W	D.C.	14 JAN 1875	Mt. Olivet
019598	BONIVERES, Marietto	5m	W	D.C.	30 MAR 1879	Mt. Olivet
011637	BONNER, Ann Milissa	11m	C	D.C.	18 MAY 1877	Young Mens
011640	BONNER, Ellen	35y	C	Va.	18 MAY 1877	Young Mens
006419	BONNER, Frederick Richard	37y	C	Va.	20 FEB 1876	Young Mens
012556	BONNER, George	7m	C	D.C.	27 JUL 1877	Mt. Pleasant

District of Columbia Death Records, August 1, 1874 to July 31, 1879   29

No.	Name	Age	Race	Birth	Death Date	Burial Place
014169	BONNER, Susan	12y	C	D.C.	22 DEC 1877	Young Mens
018983	BONSALL, Esther	1m	W	D.C.	07 FEB 1879	Congressional
013940	BONTZ, Daisy Estelle	6m	W	D.C.	27 NOV 1877	Congressional
007667	BONTZ, Ernest Irving	1m	W	D.C.	16 JUN 1876	Congressional
006966	BONTZ, Geo. E.	26y	W	D.C.	08 APR 1876	Methodist Navy Yard
018239	BONTZ, Taylor	25d	W	D.C.	05 DEC 1878	Carlin Springs, Va.
007791	BONTZE, Grace	5d	W	D.C.	23 JUN 1876	Congressional
021130	BOOKER, Chas. H.	9m	C	D.C.	28 JUL 1879	Mt. Pleasant
011203	BOOKER, Lucy	70y	C	Va.	03 APR 1877	Harmony
005197a	BOOKMAN, Sarah A.	11m	C	D.C.	19 OCT 1875	Young Mens
012476	BOOMS, Jane	13y	C	Md.	22 JUL 1877	Ebenezer
008247	BOON, Edward	9m	C	D.C.	13 JUL 1876	Ebenezer
002107	BOON, Harriet	74y	C	Md.	10 FEB 1875	Ebenezer
017112	BOON, Samuel	4m	C	D.C.	20 AUG 1878	Mt. Pleasant
015189	BOONE, Henrietta H.	65y	W	Va.	26 MAR 1878	Mt. Olivet
020958	BOONE, John A.	42y	W	Pa.	16 JUL 1879	Hospital, Government
000886f	BOONE, Rebecca	34y	C	Md.	21 OCT 1874	Harmony
010293	BOONE, Sarah	85y	C	Md.	15 JAN 1877	Potters Field
019368	BOONE, Teresa	93y	C	Md.	12 MAR 1879	Potters Field
002217	BOOSE, James L.	35y	W	D.C.	18 FEB 1875	Rock Creek
011106	BOOTEN, Lewis	40y	C	Va.	24 MAR 1877	Potters Field
001937	BOOTES, Samuel A.	71y	W	D.C.	29 JAN 1875	Oak Hill
005627	BOOTH, Benjamin	70y	C	Va.	02 DEC 1875	Mt. Zion
013075	BOPP, Jane	78y	W	Md.	04 SEP 1877	Congressional
013098	BORBECK, Marie	10y	W	D.C.	06 SEP 1877	Mt. Olivet
002450	BORELAND, Winnia E.	4y	W	D.C.	06 MAR 1875	Glenwood
011983	BORLAND, Mary	4d	W	D.C.	20 JUN 1877	Oak Hill
007772	BORMAN, Bertha R.	3m	C	Md.	22 JUN 1876	Holy Rood
009845	BOSHAN, Thomas	1m	C	D.C.	02 DEC 1876	Potters Field
012861	BOSLEY, Cornelia	15y	C	Pa.	18 AUG 1877	Young Mens
000785	BOSMAN, Wm. T.	2m	W	D.C.	12 OCT 1874	Congressional
011677	BOSS, John	54y	C	Va.	22 MAY 1877	Mt. Zion
008780	BOSS, Mary Ellen	23y	W	D.C.	22 AUG 1876	Congressional
012764	BOSS, William F.	42y	W	Va.	11 AUG 1877	Richmond, Va.
013253	BOSSE, Walter J.	3y	W	D.C.	20 SEP 1877	Glenwood
013063	BOSSY, Susie	7m	C	D.C.	03 SEP 1877	Potters Field
012628	BOSTIC, Mary Elizabeth	14y	C	D.C.	01 AUG 1877	Potters Field
018234	BOSTIN, Frederick William	42y	W	D.C.	03 DEC 1878	Baltimore
019291	BOSTON, Infant of Wm.	1m	W	D.C.	05 MAR 1879	Potters Field
017804	BOSTON, Lettie	24y	C	Md.	20 OCT 1878	Potters Field
011367	BOSTON, Martha Letta	3m	C	D.C.	18 APR 1877	Ebenezer
005005	BOSTON, Rosetta	72y	C	Md.	12 SEP 1875	Graceland
007162	BOSTON, Rosetta	21y	M	D.C.	30 APR 1876	Harmony
018282	BOSWELL, E.V.B.	39y	W	Md.	09 DEC 1878	Oak Hill
013493	BOSWELL, Edward	3y	W	D.C.	13 OCT 1877	Congressional
012278	BOSWELL, Elnora	27y	W	D.C.	09 JUL 1877	Washington Asylum
010032	BOSWELL, Infant of Henry	15min	W	D.C.	20 DEC 1876	Congressional
019680	BOSWELL, John	40y	W	D.C.	07 APR 1879	Congressional
008345	BOSWELL, Laura	23y	C	Va.	20 JUL 1876	Young Mens
017596	BOSWELL, Lucas	5d	C	D.C.	02 OCT 1878	Beckett's
007918	BOSWELL, Mary	7d	C	D.C.	29 JUN 1876	Congressional
016781	BOSWELL, Mary Julia	11m	C	D.C.	27 JUL 1878	Mt. Olivet
008426	BOSWELL, Rebecca Ann	62y	W	D.C.	26 JUL 1876	Congressional
009528	BOSWELL, Richard Henry	2y	W	D.C.	25 OCT 1876	Congressional
020237	BOSWELL, Sarah	76y	W	Md.	31 MAY 1879	Tennallytown
009122	BOSWELL, Wm. Phil.	1m	W	Md.	18 SEP 1876	Montgomery Co., Md.

District of Columbia Death Records, August 1, 1874 to July 31, 1879

No.	Name	Age	Race	Birth	Death Date	Burial Place
017075	BOSWORTH, Cora A.	10m	W	D.C.	17 AUG 1878	Mt. Olivet
004406	BOSWORTH, Edward F.	2y	W	D.C.	02 AUG 1875	Mt. Olivet
020023	BOTELER, Austin	2m	C	U.S.	07 MAY 1879	Mt. Olivet
014072	BOTELER, Eva May	16d	W	D.C.	12 DEC 1877	Glenwood
002287	BOTELER, Fannie Willson	6y	W	D.C.	23 FEB 1875	Glenwood
018434	BOTELER, Harry D.	3y	W	D.C.	23 DEC 1878	Glenwood
020445	BOTELER, John	1m	C	D.C.	15 JUN 1879	Mt. Olivet
009033	BOTELER, John A.	4m	W	D.C.	11 SEP 1876	Glenwood
008515	BOTELER, Overton Carr	1m	W	D.C.	01 AUG 1876	Glenwood
020551	BOTELER, Susan	15d	C	D.C.	21 JUN 1879	Mt. Olivet
016464	BOTELER, Susan E.	32y	W	Md.	06 JUL 1878	Congressional
008398	BOTHELMER, Charles	9m	W	D.C.	24 JUL 1876	Prospect Hill
001559	BOTLER, Edward M.	45y	W	D.C.	01 JAN 1875	Congressional
000377	BOTTCHER, Wilhelm	4y	W	D.C.	30 AUG 1874	Prospect Hill
008845	BOTTOMLY, Eliza	14y	W	D.C.	27 AUG 1876	Glenwood
017056	BOTTS, John M.	47y	C	Va.	15 AUG 1878	Mt. Pleasant
011087	BOTTS, Julia	8m	W	D.C.	23 MAR 1877	Congressional
014621	BOTTS, Nancy	2y	C	D.C.	01 FEB 1878	Potters Field
007221	BOUCHER, Edward	10m	W	D.C.	06 MAY 1876	Mt. Olivet
015919	BOUCHER, Victor Emile	18y	W	Md.	31 MAY 1878	Baltimore
008485	BOUDAN, Infant of W.	3m	C	D.C.	30 JUL 1876	Young Mens
012445	BOUHER, Amanda	23y	C	Md.	20 JUL 1877	Mt. Pleasant
007968	BOUIE, Lizzie	21d	W	D.C.	02 JUL 1876	Potters Field
019528	BOUIE, Stephen, Sr.	68y	W	Md.	24 MAR 1879	Baltimore, Md.
015305	BOULDEN, Mary Ann	58y	C	Md.	07 APR 1878	Harmony
020464	BOULDER, Mercer	1y	C	D.C.	16 JUN 1879	Young Mens
002973	BOULDIN, Catharine	84y	C	Va.	12 APR 1875	Harmony
011462	BOULDIN, Silva A.	47y	C	Ala.	30 APR 1877	Harmony
019999	BOULDIN, William	5y	C	D.C.	05 MAY 1879	Beckett's
012380	BOULDING, Rebecca	82y	C	Va.	16 JUL 1877	Beckett's
020001	BOULTER, Harry E.	4y	W	D.C.	05 MAY 1879	Congressional
007984	BOUMBRA, Mary	1y	C	D.C.	03 JUL 1876	Young Mens
016548	BOUNDS, Anna L.	5m	W	D.C.	11 JUL 1878	Holy Rood
014262	BOURN, Adolph	5y	W	D.C.	30 DEC 1877	Jewish, Alexandria, Va.
000002	BOURNS, Jane Alicia	3y	W	D.C.	01 AUG 1874	Washington Parish
005613	BOUTCH, John C.	75y	W	Ger.	01 DEC 1875	Soldier's Home
019662	BOUTWELL, Edward E.	73y	W	Va.	05 APR 1879	Mt. Olivet
003168	BOUVET, Mathias	69y	W	France	29 APR 1875	Oak Hill
004734	BOWDEN, Samuel Jackson	2y	W	Va.	24 AUG 1875	Glenwood
016550	BOWDIN, Annie M.	2y	W	D.C.	11 JUL 1878	Glenwood
002666	BOWDLER, Margaret	20y	C	D.C.	21 MAR 1875	Congressional
008681	BOWDOIN, Infant of Haus	5d	C	D.C.	14 AUG 1876	Ebenezer
015803	BOWDWIN, Emma	4m	C	D.C.	22 MAY 1878	Graceland
006624	BOWEN, Benjamin L.	48y	W	Md.	10 MAR 1876	Glenwood
015109	BOWEN, Charles M.	32y	W	Ind.	18 MAR 1878	Graceland
008978	BOWEN, Cora J.	1y	C	D.C.	05 SEP 1876	Harmony
000991	BOWEN, Edith A.	1y	W	D.C.	31 OCT 1874	Presbyterian
008326	BOWEN, George Y.	70y	W	Md.	19 JUL 1876	Glenwood
010249	BOWEN, James L.W.	37y	C	D.C.	10 JAN 1877	Harmony
013985	BOWEN, James Milton	4y	C	D.C.	02 DEC 1877	Harmony
003589	BOWEN, Laura	20y	W	Md.	10 JUN 1875	Glenwood
009977	BOWEN, Mary Matilda	1m	W	D.C.	16 DEC 1876	Mt. Olivet
012480	BOWEN, Rosalee Elizabeth	6m	W	D.C.	23 JUL 1877	Glenwood
004854	BOWEN, Saml. Walker	26y	W	D.C.	01 SEP 1875	Glenwood
002784	BOWEN, Samuel	1y	W	D.C.	29 MAR 1875	Mt. Olivet
015648	BOWEN, Susan D.	68y	W	D.C.	08 MAY 1878	Glenwood

District of Columbia Death Records, August 1, 1874 to July 31, 1879

No.	Name	Age	Race	Birth	Death Date	Burial Place
008274	BOWENS, Mary	27y	C	Md.	15 JUL 1876	Mt. Zion
013926	BOWER, Cornelia H., Mrs.	56y	W	Md.	26 NOV 1877	Baltimore, Md.
018113	BOWER, Infant of E.T.	2d	W	D.C.	22 NOV 1878	Congressional
018581	BOWERS, H.P.	2y	W	D.C.	06 JAN 1879	Congressional
015747	BOWES, Joseph	½d	W	D.C.	17 MAY 1878	Graceland
010845	BOWEY, Annie E.	1m	C	D.C.	02 MAR 1877	Mt. Zion
008688	BOWIE, Charles	2w	C	D.C.	15 AUG 1876	Potters Field
008232	BOWIE, Charles Williams	4m	W	D.C.	13 JUL 1876	Glenwood
000059	BOWIE, Edward	1m	C	--	04 AUG 1874	--
003577	BOWIE, George W.	21y	W	D.C.	09 JUN 1875	Glenwood
011509	BOWIE, Harry Williams	8y	W	D.C.	04 MAY 1877	Glenwood
009034	BOWIE, Infant of Allen L.	½h	W	D.C.	11 SEP 1876	Glenwood
012275	BOWIE, Infant of Augustus	15min	C	D.C.	09 JUL 1877	Ebenezer
003106	BOWIE, Infant of Frank	5d	C	D.C.	24 APR 1875	Potters Field
006194	BOWIE, John O.	44y	W	Va.	31 JAN 1876	Glenwood
006531	BOWIE, Maria	9d	C	D.C.	03 MAR 1876	Harmony
004042	BOWIE, Mary E.	2m	C	D.C.	08 JUL 1875	Mt. Olivet
018055	BOWIE, Mary E.	57y	C	Md.	15 NOV 1878	Mt. Pleasant
018146	BOWIE, Maud	1y	W	D.C.	25 NOV 1878	Philadelphia, Pa.
018667	BOWIE, Matilda	97y	C	Md.	14 JAN 1879	Harmony
003949	BOWIE, Teressa	3y	C	D.C.	01 JUL 1875	Ebenezer
014721	BOWIE, Thomas H.	45y	C	Md.	09 FEB 1878	Mt. Olivet
011192	BOWIE, Thyrza	35y	W	Md.	02 APR 1877	Rock Creek
009072	BOWIE, William J.	54y	C	Md.	14 SEP 1876	Mt. Pleasant
011159	BOWLER, Marissa	69y	W	Va.	30 MAR 1877	Graceland
011571	BOWLES, Ellen	35y	C	Va.	12 MAY 1877	Young Mens
012443	BOWLES, Frances A.	1y	C	D.C.	20 JUL 1877	Mt. Zion
005714	BOWLES, Harriet Ann	2y	C	D.C.	10 DEC 1875	Mt. Zion
019330	BOWLING, Benjamin	50y	W	Va.	09 MAR 1879	Potters Field
005886	BOWLING, Edward M.	16y	W	D.C.	28 DEC 1875	Mt. Olivet
006288	BOWLING, Eliza	65y	W	Md.	10 FEB 1876	Mt. Olivet
015861	BOWLING, Henry	38y	W	Md.	27 MAY 1878	Congressional
010493	BOWLING, Mary M.	72y	W	Md.	03 FEB 1877	Mt. Olivet
005184a	BOWLS, Luke	42y	C	Va.	18 OCT 1875	Young Mens
012533	BOWMAN, Ana Cath.	3y	W	D.C.	26 JUL 1877	Prospect Hill
016752	BOWMAN, Chas. A.	1y	C	D.C.	25 JUL 1878	Young Mens
012411	BOWMAN, Eda R.E.	27y	W	Va.	18 JUL 1877	Congressional
012685	BOWMAN, George	53y	W	Mass.	06 AUG 1877	Clinton, Mass.
006289	BOWMAN, George Francis	2y	C	D.C.	10 FEB 1876	Holy Rood
018393	BOWMAN, Infant of Annie	1m	W	D.C.	20 DEC 1878	Potters Field
003215	BOWMAN, John	28y	W	N.Y.	04 MAY 1875	Soldier's Home
007965	BOWMAN, Louis Abguen	7m	C	D.C.	02 JUL 1876	Harmony
012442	BOWMAN, Mary E.	1y	C	D.C.	20 JUL 1877	Mt. Zion
006891	BOWMAN, Nellie	5m	C	D.C.	02 APR 1876	Potters Field
002160	BOWMAN, Rachel A	48y	C	Va.	14 FEB 1875	Harmony
015130	BOWMAN, Sarah	55y	C	Md.	20 MAR 1878	Young Mens
008965	BOWMAN, Spencer	19y	C	D.C.	04 SEP 1876	Potters Field
017370	BOWMAN, William	6d	C	D.C.	11 SEP 1878	Beckett's
015194	BOWSER, Mamie	7y	C	D.C.	27 MAR 1878	Harmony
008770	BOXALL, Joseph	2y	W	D.C.	21 AUG 1876	Mt. Olivet
018580	BOYAN, Josepn V.	6m	C	D.C.	06 JAN 1879	Potters Field
009424	BOYAR, Charles H.	16y	W	N.Y.	16 OCT 1876	Buffalo, N.Y.
000279	BOYCE, Andrew W.	1y	W	D.C.	22 AUG 1874	Congressional
020976	BOYCE, Mary McIrven, Mrs.	75y	W	Pa.	17 JUL 1879	Oak Hill
006329	BOYD, Abraham	20y	C	Md.	13 FEB 1876	Harmony
018821	BOYD, Abraham	24y	C	Md.	26 JAN 1879	Mt. Pleasant

District of Columbia Death Records, August 1, 1874 to July 31, 1879

No.	Name	Age	Race	Birth	Death Date	Burial Place
014356	BOYD, Ann	10h	W	D.C.	08 JAN 1878	Graceland
001431	BOYD, Charles	21y	C	Md.	18 DEC 1874	Harmony
020775	BOYD, Edna	6m	W	D.C.	05 JUL 1879	Oak Hill
015659	BOYD, Infant of L.R.	3m	W	D.C.	09 MAY 1878	Glenwood
015649	BOYD, Infant of L.R.	4m	W	D.C.	08 MAY 1878	Glenwood
013738	BOYD, James W.	30y	W	D.C.	05 NOV 1877	Soldier's Home
000762	BOYD, Jane	51	W	Va.	09 OCT 1874	Congressional
015785	BOYD, John C.	21y	W	N.Y.	21 MAY 1878	Prospect Hill
016689	BOYD, William	73y	W	Ire.	20 JUL 1878	Congressional
020676	BOYD, William Fred	5m	W	Tex.	30 JUN 1879	Mt. Olivet
016843	BOYED, Margeret	42y	W	Ire.	31 JUL 1878	Glenwood
014260	BOYER, Carollin	c.40y	W	Ger.	30 DEC 1877	Adas Israel/Portland, Ore.
010012	BOYER, Infant of John	4d	W	D.C.	19 DEC 1876	Adas Israel
018354	BOYER, Louisa	5y	W	D.C.	16 DEC 1878	Prospect Hill
014488	BOYKEN, Katie	9m	C	D.C.	20 JAN 1878	Young Mens
011760	BOYKEN, Lewis	1m	M	D.C.	01 JUN 1877	Mt. Pleasant
017353	BOYLAN, Henry Edward	1y	W	D.C.	09 SEP 1878	Mt. Olivet
003613	BOYLE, Ann	1m	W	Md.	12 JUN 1875	Mt. Olivet
013714	BOYLE, Ann Eliza McLeod	c.68y	W	Md.	03 NOV 1877	Oak Hill
015020	BOYLE, Cornelius, Dr.	60y	W	D.C.	11 MAR 1878	Glenwood
011688	BOYLE, Daisy C.	4y	W	D.C.	24 MAY 1877	Mt. Olivet
000444	BOYLE, David	9y	W	D.C.	07 SEP 1874	Mt. Olivet
001852	BOYLE, George B. McClellan	6d	W	D.C.	23 JAN 1875	Mt. Olivet
005971	BOYLE, James	43y	W	Ire.	08 JAN 1876	Mt. Olivet
001988	BOYLE, John	4m	W	D.C.	02 FEB 1875	Mt. Olivet
007019	BOYLE, John Franklin	65y	W	Md.	15 APR 1876	Mt. Olivet
008126	BOYLE, Mary	7m	W	D.C.	10 JUL 1876	Congressional
002653	BOYLE, Sarah Cecelia	23y	W	Va.	20 MAR 1875	Congressional
006150	BOYLE, Wm.	40y	W	Ire.	27 JAN 1876	Mt. Olivet
013219	BOYNTON, Susan N.	32y	W	D.C.	16 SEP 1877	Oak Hill
020777	BOYNTON, William McLean	40y	W	Mass.	05 JUL 1879	Oak Hill
018304	BOZEMAN, Benjamin Antonio	67y	C	Fla.	11 DEC 1878	Troy, N.Y.
006371	BRACKSTON, Mary Ann	3m	C	D.C.	16 FEB 1876	Danfords River Road
012317	BRADBURN, Sarah	1y	W	D.C.	11 JUL 1877	Congressional
012016	BRADBURY, Bessie	10m	W	D.C.	22 JUN 1877	Arlington
011842	BRADBURY, Samuel Benjamin	8y	W	D.C.	08 JUN 1877	Congressional
002434	BRADFORD, George W.	48y	W	Ind.	05 MAR 1875	Glenwood
010710	BRADFORD, Helen	5y	W	Me.	20 FEB 1877	Congressional
013850	BRADFORD, John West	24y	W	N.Y.	18 NOV 1877	Graceland
020852	BRADFORD, Mary Eudora	26y	W	Tenn.	09 JUL 1879	Graceland
013445	BRADFORD, Norah Frances	30y	W	Md.	09 OCT 1877	Mt. Olivet
014968	BRADFORD, Stricker	8m	W	D.C.	07 MAR 1878	Graceland
002982f	BRADFORD, Winslow J.	44y	W	N.Y.	28 JUN 1870	Congressional
005380	BRADLEY, Alice Emeline	10y	W	Wisc.	07 NOV 1875	Congressional
010146	BRADLEY, Arthur Lee	4m	W	D.C.	01 JAN 1877	Congressional
019026	BRADLEY, Cora	14d	C	D.C.	11 FEB 1879	Potters Field
009806	BRADLEY, Henry	68y	W	D.C.	26 NOV 1876	Oak Hill
018822	BRADLEY, Henry	62y	W	D.C.	26 JAN 1879	Congressional
002327	BRADLEY, Jno. Thomas	62y	W	D.C.	26 FEB 1875	Congressional
009098	BRADLEY, John Thomas	3m	C	D.C.	16 SEP 1876	Payne's
018174	BRADLEY, Joseph	2d	W	D.C.	27 NOV 1878	Mt. Olivet
000346	BRADLEY, Joseph Henry, Jr.	42y	W	D.C.	28 AUG 1874	Oak Hill
019752	BRADLEY, Mary M.	6m	C	D.C.	13 APR 1879	Young Mens
011689	BRADLEY, Mattie E.	6y	W	D.C.	24 MAY 1877	Congressional
014261	BRADLEY, Oliver C.	1m	W	D.C.	30 DEC 1877	Congressional
011924	BRADLEY, Sue Young	1y	W	D.C.	16 JUN 1877	Oak Hill

District of Columbia Death Records, August 1, 1874 to July 31, 1879   33

No.	Name	Age	Race	Birth	Death Date	Burial Place
008554	BRADLEY, William A.H.	44y	W	D.C.	04 AUG 1876	Congressional
020220	BRADLEY, Willie	3y	C	D.C.	29 MAY 1879	Payne's
013030	BRADLY, Catharine	102y	W	Ire.	31 AUG 1877	Mt. Olivet
004748	BRADLY, Georg	1y	C	D.C.	25 AUG 1875	Ebenezer
003800	BRADLY, Jennie	32y	C	D.C.	24 JUN 1875	Potters Field
005050a	BRADSHAW, Ann M.	35y	W	Va.	04 OCT 1875	Glenwood
013607	BRADSHAW, Catharine E.	45y	W	Md.	24 OCT 1877	Presbyterian
009858	BRADSHAW, Charles	31y	W	N.J.	03 DEC 1876	Woodbury, N.J.
006729	BRADSHAW, David	4m	W	D.C.	19 MAR 1876	Congressional
003460	BRADSHAW, Infant of Alexander	36h	W	D.C.	28 MAY 1875	Mt. Olivet
001638	BRADSHAW, William	12d	W	D.C.	07 JAN 1875	Congressional
015757	BRADY, Ann	62y	W	Ire.	18 MAY 1878	Mt. Olivet
009797	BRADY, Elizabeth	35y	W	Ire.	25 NOV 1876	Congressional
010935	BRADY, Mary	84y	W	Md.	10 MAR 1877	Congressional
017689	BRADY, Sister Agnes	21y	W	La.	10 OCT 1878	Mt. Olivet
020576	BRAHLER, John T.	1y	W	D.C.	23 JUN 1879	Prospect Hill
015980	BRAHNAM, Allen	7d	C	D.C.	03 JUN 1878	Moore's
005765	BRAINARD, Lucy	43y	W	N.Y.	16 DEC 1875	Congressional
014476	BRANAN, Maria, Mrs.	33y	W	Ger.	19 JAN 1878	Congressional
001248	BRANBIEHL, David R.	31y	W	Ger.	28 NOV 1874	Congressional
012159	BRANCH, Elizabeth	6y	W	D.C.	01 JUL 1877	St. Mary's
004056f	BRAND, Edgar E.	6m	W	Md.	09 JUL 1875	Oak Hill
005580	BRAND, Louis A.	60y	W	Md.	27 NOV 1875	Baltimore, Md.
002728	BRANDEBURRY, Lemuel G.	65y	W	Pa.	10 MAR 1875	Glenwood
019395	BRANDON, Elvira B.	c.37y	W	Ind.	14 MAR 1879	Glenwood
005023a	BRANDON, Henry	2y	C	D.C.	02 OCT 1875	Mt. Olivet
014175	BRANDON, Richard	6y	C	Va.	23 DEC 1877	Potters Field
011060	BRANDON, Robert H.	3m	C	D.C.	21 MAR 1877	Bladensburg, Md.
014060	BRANDON, Thomas	56y	W	Md.	11 DEC 1877	Mt. Olivet
004427	BRANDSTETTER, Anna	66y	W	Aus.	03 AUG 1875	Potters Field
005715	BRANDT, John D.	50y	W	S.C.	10 DEC 1875	Congressional
018074	BRANNAN, Maria	3y	M	D.C.	17 NOV 1878	Mt. Zion
014303	BRANNAN, Minnie	8m	W	D.C.	03 JAN 1878	Congressional
017680	BRANNINGER, Lena	11m	W	D.C.	09 OCT 1878	St. Mary's
001131	BRANNON, Martin	35y	W	Ire.	01 NOV 1874	Holy Rood
014412	BRANNON, Samuel Joseph	1y	W	D.C.	14 JAN 1878	Holy Rood
006606	BRANSON, Annie	26y	C	Md.	09 MAR 1876	Mt. Olivet
002200	BRANSON, Catharine	4y	W	D.C.	17 FEB 1875	Congressional
017649	BRANSON, Catharine	83y	W	Md.	06 OCT 1878	Mt. Olivet
009417	BRANSON, Henrietta	7m	C	D.C.	15 OCT 1876	Potters Field
013693	BRANSON, Henry	65y	C	Md.	01 NOV 1877	Mt. Olivet
011386	BRANSON, Infant of Catherine	3h	C	D.C.	21 APR 1877	Young Mens
014527	BRANSON, Jos. R.	8m	W	D.C.	23 JAN 1878	Congressional
020920	BRANSON, Susie	2m	W	D.C.	14 JUL 1879	Congressional
014274	BRANSON, William	42y	C	Va.	31 DEC 1877	Young Mens
016394	BRANSON, Wm. Joseph	3m	C	D.C.	02 JUL 1878	Potters Field
011227	BRANTZELL, Ellen	6y	W	D.C.	05 APR 1877	Holy Rood
011356	BRANTZELL, Emma E.	4y	W	D.C.	16 APR 1877	Holy Rood
012872	BRANTZELL, Thomas W.	1y	M	D.C.	19 AUG 1877	Holy Rood
016326	BRANUM, Daisy	1y	C	D.C.	27 JUN 1878	Mt. Pleasant
016447	BRANZELL, Charles B.	6m	W	D.C.	05 JUL 1878	Holy Rood
005311	BRASELL, Lucy	1y	M	D.C.	30 OCT 1875	Beckett's
014342	BRASHEARS, Joseph J.	1y	W	D.C.	07 JAN 1878	Glenwood
013167	BRASS, James E.	13y	W	D.C.	12 SEP 1877	Holy Rood
010301	BRASS, Mary, Mrs.	43y	W	Ire.	15 JAN 1877	Holy Rood
012351	BRAUCH, William	21m	W	D.C.	13 JUL 1877	St. Mary's

District of Columbia Death Records, August 1, 1874 to July 31, 1879

No.	Name	Age	Race	Birth	Death Date	Burial Place
001722	BRAUMAN, Johanna	39y	W	Ger.	14 JAN 1875	Mt. Olivet
001522	BRAUMANN, Mary	4d	W	D.C.	28 DEC 1874	St. Mary's
003007	BRAUNER, Eleanor Harrison	75y	W	Md.	16 APR 1875	Congressional
011180	BRAUNER, Frank	19y	W	Tenn.	31 MAR 1877	Knoxville, Tenn.
007211	BRAWNER, Memie	6m	W	D.C.	05 MAY 1876	Rock Creek
011382	BRAXTON, Betsy	30y	C	Va.	21 APR 1877	Baptist Church
012110	BRAXTON, Bettie	3m	C	D.C.	28 JUN 1877	Scagg's
005558	BRAXTON, Burtha	1y	C	D.C.	25 NOV 1875	Mt. Pleasant
017445	BRAXTON, Infant of Annie	7d	C	D.C.	18 SEP 1878	Potters Field
001034	BRAXTON, Infant of Joseph	2d	C	D.C.	03 NOV 1874	Beckett's
009215	BRAXTON, James	63y	C	Va.	27 SEP 1876	Young Mens
005148a	BRAXTON, John	33y	C	Va.	15 OCT 1875	Young Mens
017770	BRAXTON, Martha Jane	2m	C	D.C.	17 OCT 1878	Young Mens
017403	BRAXTON, Martha Jane	19y	C	Va.	14 SEP 1878	Young Mens
010769	BRAXTON, Mary Etta	1y	C	D.C.	24 FEB 1877	Young Mens
017371	BRAXTON, Mary Louisa	15y	C	Va.	11 SEP 1878	Young Mens
000502	BRAXTON, Thomas	5m	C	D.C.	13 SEP 1874	Harmony
000426	BRAXTON, William	3m	C	D.C.	04 SEP 1874	Eaton's B.G.
012350	BRAZIL, Matilda	1y	C	D.C.	13 JUL 1877	Beckett's
015746	BRECHT, Theodore C., Jr.	2y	W	D.C.	17 MAY 1878	Oak Hill
007415	BRECKENRIDGE, Dorah	3y	C	D.C.	27 MAY 1876	Mt. Pleasant
020304	BRECKHAUER, George Henry	54y	W	Ger.	05 JUN 1879	Soldier's Home
012518	BREEN, Emma	1y	W	D.C.	25 JUL 1877	Oak Hill
003845	BREEN, James Henry	1y	W	D.C.	26 JUN 1875	Mt. Olivet
017125	BREEN, Jane	30y	W	Ire.	21 AUG 1878	Mt. Olivet
011449	BRELSFORD, Mary Elizabeth	1y	W	D.C.	28 APR 1877	Congressional
007811	BREMER, John	65y	W	Eng.	24 JUN 1876	Soldier's Home
013827	BREMMERMAN, Katy M.	1y	W	D.C.	15 NOV 1877	Barndsville, Md.
018049	BRENNAN, Ann	86y	W	Ire.	14 NOV 1878	Mt. Olivet
011285	BRENNAN, Bernard A.	48y	W	Ire.	09 APR 1877	Rock Creek
013521	BRENNAN, James H.	15y	W	D.C.	15 OCT 1877	Mt. Olivet
017924	BRENNAN, John A.	18y	W	Ind.	01 NOV 1878	Mt. Olivet
001791	BRENNAN, Laura Ann	24y	W	D.C.	19 JAN 1875	Congressional
013386	BRENNAN, Mary E.	1y	W	D.C.	03 OCT 1877	Mt. Olivet
003652	BRENNAN, Robert Patrick	3m	W	D.C.	15 JUN 1875	Mt. Olivet
005479	BRENNON, Margaret	5m	W	Tex.	17 NOV 1875	Mt. Olivet
004664	BRENNON, Mary Catherine	14y	W	Fla.	19 AUG 1875	Mt. Olivet
012739	BRENT, Arthur	30y	C	Va.	09 AUG 1877	Young Mens
016782	BRENT, Arthur B.	3m	C	D.C.	27 JUL 1878	Potters Field
017164	BRENT, Burnet	8m	C	D.C.	24 AUG 1878	Payne's
020185	BRENT, Charles	1y	C	D.C.	24 MAY 1879	Jones Chapel
016698	BRENT, Delia	32y	C	Va.	21 JUL 1878	Hospital
011604	BRENT, Hannah	23y	W	Md.	15 MAY 1877	Potters Field
005328	BRENT, Infant of Robert	1y	C	D.C.	01 NOV 1875	Payne's
014505	BRENT, Jane R.	73y	C	Va.	21 JAN 1878	Harmony
006291	BRENT, John Carroll	62y	W	D.C.	10 FEB 1876	Mt. Olivet
018687	BRENT, Lulie	2y	C	D.C.	16 JAN 1879	Young Mens
012960	BRENT, Maria A.	17y	C	Va.	26 AUG 1877	Harmony
001433	BRENT, Samuel	8m	M	D.C.	19 DEC 1874	Young Mens
002961	BRENT, Thomas	12y	C	Md.	11 APR 1875	Thomas'
002618	BRENT, Thos. C.	5y	W	Md.	17 MAR 1875	Mt. Olivet
017151	BRENT, Virginia	2y	C	D.C.	23 AUG 1878	Potters Field
000821	BRENT, Wallace	43y	C	Va.	16 OCT 1874	Washington Asylum
011684	BRENT, Warrenton	40y	C	Va.	23 MAY 1877	Young Mens
001218	BRERETON, John H.	23y	W	D.C.	23 NOV 1874	Glenwood
007438	BRERETON, Samuel	47y	W	D.C.	30 MAY 1876	Rock Creek

District of Columbia Death Records, August 1, 1874 to July 31, 1879   35

No.	Name	Age	Race	Birth	Death Date	Burial Place
003319	BRESHNAN, Mary	9d	W	D.C.	14 MAY 1875	Mt. Olivet
002913	BRESNAHAN, Catharine	80y	W	Ire.	07 APR 1875	Mt. Olivet
011889	BRESNAHAN, Edward	14y	C	D.C.	14 JUN 1877	Mt. Olivet
018235	BRESNAHAN, Infant of Cornelius	2h	W	D.C.	04 DEC 1878	Mt. Olivet
004043	BRESNAHAN, Joseph	2y	W	D.C.	08 JUL 1875	Mt. Olivet
013074	BRESNAHAN, Margaret	48y	W	Ire.	04 SEP 1877	Mt. Olivet
019418	BRESNAHAN, Thos.	7y	W	D.C.	16 MAR 1879	Mt. Olivet
011267	BRESNEHAN, Mary	16y	W	D.C.	08 APR 1877	Mt. Olivet
009577	BREWER, Eunice V.	7m	W	D.C.	30 OCT 1876	Congressional
014908	BREWER, Infant of M.S.	20h	W	D.C.	01 MAR 1878	Congressional
002007	BREWER, Mary	5m	C	D.C.	03 FEB 1875	Young Mens
004458	BREWER, Mary Rebecca	7m	W	D.C.	05 AUG 1875	Congressional
007307	BREWER, Rebecca	86y	W	Md.	15 MAY 1876	Falls Church, Va.
012659	BREWER, Sarah F.	8m	W	D.C.	04 AUG 1877	Presbyterian
009553	BREWER, Wm. H.	2y	W	D.C.	27 OCT 1876	Presbyterian
001596	BREWTON, Charles S.	21d	W	D.C.	03 JAN 1875	Congressional
001438	BREWTON, Emma E.	38y	W	Md.	20 DEC 1874	Congressional
015008	BRIANERD, Jehu	70y	W	Ohio	10 MAR 1878	Cleveland, Ohio
020429	BRICE, Anie	1y	C	D.C.	13 JUN 1879	Brightwood
007434	BRICE, Oliver O.	33y	C	Md.	29 MAY 1876	Potters Field
003993	BRICE, Rachel	3m	C	D.C.	04 JUL 1875	Holy Rood
012510	BRICE, Theodore	2y	C	D.C.	24 JUL 1877	Potters Field
012601	BRIDGE, Margaret Rebecca	65y	W	D.C.	29 JUL 1877	Carroll Chapel, Md.
011239	BRIDGE, Raymond R.	16y	M	Pa.	06 APR 1877	Mt. Olivet
016141	BRIDGES, Elizabeth D.	51y	W	Md.	13 JUN 1878	Rock Creek
006931	BRIDGES, Julia Ann	57y	W	D.C.	05 APR 1876	Mt. Olivet
012789	BRIDGES, Susan	5m	W	D.C.	13 AUG 1877	Rock Creek
005600	BRIDGES, Virginia	46y	M	Md.	29 NOV 1875	Mt. Olivet
003677	BRIDGETS, Mary	1m	W	D.C.	17 JUN 1875	Mt. Olivet
021121	BRIELL, Lewuen Virginia	29y	W	Va.	26 JUL 1879	Mt. Olivet
003799	BRIEN, Mary J. Virginia	5m	W	D.C.	24 JUN 1875	Mt. Olivet
019014	BRIEN, William George	7y	W	D.C.	10 FEB 1879	Mt. Olivet
005581	BRIGETT, John H.	24y	W	D.C.	27 NOV 1875	Mt. Olivet
007528	BRIGGER, Richard	9d	C	D.C.	07 JUN 1876	Ebenezer
014426	BRIGGS, Maria	8m	C	D.C.	15 JAN 1878	Beckett's
010745	BRIGGS, Richard	56y	C	Va.	23 FEB 1877	Potters Field
000095	BRIGHAM, Laura J.	25y	W	Ohio	07 AUG 1874	Presbyterian
000079	BRIGHT, Charles	18d	W	D.C.	06 AUG 1874	Beckett's
003480	BRIGHT, George S.	37y	W	D.C.	29 MAY 1875	Mt. Olivet
012948	BRIGHT, John	77y	W	Md.	25 AUG 1877	Congressional
018686	BRIGHTWELL, John	42y	W	Md.	16 JAN 1879	Congressional
013715	BRINEY, George	16y	W	D.C.	03 NOV 1877	Prospect Hill
020621	BRINKLEY, Jennie E.	1m	W	D.C.	26 JUN 1879	Methodist
002652	BRINKLEY, John	8y	C	D.C.	20 MAR 1875	Mt. Olivet
002094	BRINKLEY, Mary Ann	71y	W	Md.	09 FEB 1875	Methodist
008198	BRINKLY, William	21y	C	Va.	12 JUL 1876	Potters Field
011662	BRISBY, Mamie	5y	W	N.Y.	21 MAY 1877	St. Mary's
009193	BRISCO, Annie	1m	W	D.C.	24 SEP 1876	Prospect Hill
000238	BRISCO, Annie Marie	1y	C	D.C.	18 AUG 1874	Mt. Olivet
002314	BRISCO, Benjamin	86y	C	Va.	25 FEB 1875	Holy Rood
009196	BRISCO, Betty	1y	W	D.C.	25 SEP 1876	Prospect Hill
014044	BRISCO, Emma Teresa	4y	C	D.C.	09 DEC 1877	Mt. Olivet
014304	BRISCO, John	8m	C	D.C.	03 JAN 1878	Young Mens
006805	BRISCO, Wm. Oliver	5y	W	N.Y.	25 MAR 1876	Congressional
003517	BRISCOE, Alice Virginia	5m	C	D.C.	03 JUN 1875	Mt. Olivet
007370	BRISCOE, Ann	29y	C	Md.	22 MAY 1876	Young Mens

District of Columbia Death Records, August 1, 1874 to July 31, 1879

No.	Name	Age	Race	Birth	Death Date	Burial Place
004590	BRISCOE, Catherine	70y	C	Md.	14 AUG 1875	Mt. Zion
020248	BRISCOE, Edward W.	14d	C	D.C.	01 JUN 1879	Beckett's
014851	BRISCOE, Francis Ann	13y	C	D.C.	23 FEB 1878	Beckett's
007740	BRISCOE, Frederick	5w	C	D.C.	20 JUN 1876	Potters Field
010291	BRISCOE, George	2m	C	D.C.	14 JAN 1877	Mt. Olivet
001497	BRISCOE, Henrietta F.	2y	C	D.C.	26 DEC 1874	Mt. Pleasant
014155	BRISCOE, Infant of Richard	13d	C	D.C.	21 DEC 1877	Mt. Olivet
011297	BRISCOE, Isaac	50y	C	Md.	10 APR 1877	Harmony
006939	BRISCOE, James	6y	C	D.C.	06 APR 1876	Harmony
013206	BRISCOE, James	1y	C	D.C.	15 SEP 1877	Mt. Olivet
010779	BRISCOE, Josephine	34y	C	Va.	25 FEB 1877	Ebenezer
014852	BRISCOE, Julia	8m	C	D.C.	23 FEB 1878	Beckett's
014949	BRISCOE, Lula	1y	C	D.C.	05 MAR 1878	Beckett's
010688	BRISCOE, Maria	70y	W	Md.	18 FEB 1877	Glenwood
005713	BRISCOE, Martha	31y	C	Va.	10 DEC 1875	Harmony
000311	BRISCOE, Mary	20y	C	Va.	25 AUG 1874	Washington Asylum
000091	BRISCOE, Mary Agnes	6m	C	D.C.	07 AUG 1874	Mt. Olivet
003911	BRISCOE, Melville	2h	W	D.C.	29 JUN 1875	Glenwood
019841	BRISCOE, Rachel	75y	C	Va.	20 APR 1879	Potters Field
019565	BRISCOE, Willie	7m	C	D.C.	27 MAR 1879	Beckett's
009975	BRISCOLL, Melvina	30y	C	Md.	16 DEC 1876	Mt. Olivet
001564	BRISLAUN, Abraham	51y	W	Ger.	01 JAN 1875	Baltimore, Md.
008868	BRISTOE, Infant of Henry	9d	C	D.C.	29 AUG 1876	Mt. Olivet
020530	BRISTOW, Rebecca	72y	W	Eng.	20 JUN 1879	Congressional
013757	BRISTOW, Rebecca Jane	43y	W	N.Y.	07 NOV 1877	Congressional
011643	BRITHAUPT, Virginia L.	15y	W	Va.	18 MAY 1877	Prospect Hill
002591	BRITON, Heartley	1d	W	D.C.	16 MAR 1875	Graceland
011330	BRIXLEY, Margaret	3d	W	D.C.	14 APR 1877	Congressional
013062	BRIZZOLARI, Bartolomeo	26y	W	Italy	03 SEP 1877	St. Mary's
014636	BROADICE, Richd.	45y	C	Va.	02 FEB 1878	Young Mens
005244	BROADISE, Carrie	12d	C	D.C.	23 OCT 1875	Young Mens
011423	BROCK, Charles	43y	W	Ger.	25 APR 1877	Washington Asylum
003875	BROCK, Infant of Toles	27d	C	D.C.	27 JUN 1875	Young Mens
002233	BROCK, Martha	43y	W	Me.	19 FEB 1875	Congressional/Arl.
008042	BROCKENBERRY, Jacob	55y	C	Va.	05 JUL 1876	Potters Field
020316	BROCKENBURG, Joseph	17m	C	D.C.	06 JUN 1879	Harmony
011204	BROCKENBURY, Fanny	85y	C	Va.	03 APR 1877	Potters Field
000012	BROCKETT, Mattie	1y	C	D.C.	01 AUG 1874	Young Mens
014279	BROCKETT, William	11m	C	D.C.	01 JAN 1878	Young Mens
017456	BROCKSON, Sarah	26y	W	Va.	19 SEP 1878	Young Mens
005909	BRODEGAN, Ida	14y	W	D.C.	01 JAN 1876	Mt. Olivet
001597	BRODEN, Frank	27y	W	Ire.	03 JAN 1875	Mt. Olivet
009741	BRODERICK, Mary A.	c.25y	W	D.C.	19 NOV 1876	Mt. Olivet
016699	BRODHAG, Harry	8m	W	D.C.	21 JUL 1878	Prospect Hill
006400	BRODHEAD, Mary Octave	1y	W	D.C.	18 FEB 1876	Oak Hill
014506	BRODINE, Mary Agnes	1y	W	D.C.	21 JAN 1878	Mt. Olivet
013057	BRODRICK, Cath. May	15m	W	D.C.	02 SEP 1877	Mt. Olivet
018805	BRODRICK, John M.	3m	W	D.C.	25 JAN 1879	Mt. Olivet
016715	BRODUS, Infant of Lewis	2d	C	D.C.	22 JUL 1878	Young Mens
008532	BROKENBERRY, Lillie	1y	C	D.C.	02 AUG 1876	Beckett's
006893	BROKENBERY, Florence	3y	C	D.C.	02 APR 1876	Harmony
021168	BROKENBURG, Matilda	1y	C	D.C.	31 JUL 1879	Beckett's
000212	BROKS, Viola C.	7m	C	D.C.	16 AUG 1874	Young Mens
015066	BROM, Chas.	27y	W	Fla.	14 MAR 1878	Young Mens
009074	BROMZELL, Gertrude L.	10m	W	D.C.	14 SEP 1876	Holy Rood
003992	BRONAUGH, George D.	1y	W	Va.	04 JUL 1875	Hay Market, Va.

District of Columbia Death Records, August 1, 1874 to July 31, 1879					37

No.	Name	Age	Race	Birth	Death Date	Burial Place
005514	BRONAUGH, Sarah M.	60y	W	D.C.	20 NOV 1875	Congressional
000436	BRONAUGH, Wilie M.	11m	C	D.C.	06 SEP 1874	Mt. Zion
015360	BRONSON, Annie	7m	W	D.C.	11 APR 1878	Mt. Olivet
014557	BRONSON, John	29y	W	D.C.	26 JAN 1878	Mt. Olivet
010192	BRONSON, Mary	17y	W	D.C.	06 JAN 1877	Mt. Olivet
001539	BRONSON, William A.	4m	C	D.C.	30 DEC 1874	Beckett's
005533	BROOK, Hester	50y	C	Md.	22 NOV 1875	Mt. Olivet
013950	BROOK, Infant of Thomas	1m	C	D.C.	28 NOV 1877	Potters Field
006860	BROOK, Jane Eliza	68y	C	Md.	30 MAR 1876	Mt. Pleasant
014453	BROOK, John	79y	C	Md.	17 JAN 1878	Potters Field
017280	BROOKE, Arthur	19m	M	D.C.	01 SEP 1878	Beckett's
005050	BROOKE, Emma E.	29y	W	Md.	15 SEP 1875	Mt. Olivet
011635	BROOKE, Francis Pence	2y	W	D.C.	18 MAY 1877	Mt. Olivet
005307	BROOKE, George	6d	C	D.C.	30 OCT 1875	Ebenezer
019205	BROOKE, Henrietta	60y	W	Md.	26 FEB 1879	Holy Rood
016564	BROOKE, Jack B.	41y	W	Md.	12 JUL 1878	Glenwood
020529	BROOKE, Judith	20y	W	France	20 JUN 1879	Mt. Olivet
000356	BROOKE, Lewis	10m	C	D.C.	29 AUG 1874	Young Mens
011097	BROOKE, Louis	7m	W	D.C.	23 MAR 1877	Oak Hill
011218	BROOKE, Maggie	2m	W	D.C.	05 APR 1877	Congressional
016239	BROOKE, Walter T.	76y	W	Va.	21 JUN 1878	Mt. Olivet
003045	BROOKE, William Walter	1y	M	D.C.	19 APR 1875	Ebenezer
014580	BROOKES, John	25y	C	Md.	28 JAN 1878	Potters Field
018330	BROOKES, Mary Louise	4y	W	D.C.	14 DEC 1878	Glenwood
018296	BROOKES, Stanley	6y	W	D.C.	10 DEC 1878	Glenwood
006468	BROOKS, Aaron	37y	C	Va.	25 FEB 1876	Ebenezer
018866	BROOKS, Albert Augustus	8m	C	D.C.	29 JAN 1879	Payne's
018476	BROOKS, Andrew	19y	C	Va.	27 DEC 1878	Beckett's
009972	BROOKS, Andrew Jackson	14d	C	D.C.	15 DEC 1876	Mt. Zion
005951	BROOKS, Ann M.	68y	W	D.C.	06 JAN 1876	Rock Creek
000225	BROOKS, Anna	11m	C	D.C.	17 AUG 1874	Beckett's
012566	BROOKS, Anna D., Mrs.	68y	W	Pa.	27 JUL 1877	Glenwood
006997	BROOKS, Antonett	19y	W	D.C.	12 APR 1876	Glenwood
019940	BROOKS, Augustus	9m	C	D.C.	30 APR 1879	Payne's
018834	BROOKS, Caroline	9y	C	D.C.	27 JAN 1879	Harmony
020620	BROOKS, Carrie	4m	C	D.C.	26 JUN 1879	Harmony
002372	BROOKS, Catherine S., Mrs.	64y	W	N.Y.	01 MAR 1875	Holy Rood
020044	BROOKS, Charles Edward	9m	C	D.C.	09 MAY 1879	Beckett's
016079	BROOKS, Charles Henry	9y	C	D.C.	09 JUN 1878	Payne's
004661	BROOKS, Charlott	92y	C	Md.	19 AUG 1875	Mt. Olivet
000953	BROOKS, Clara	32y	M	Va.	27 OCT 1874	Mt. Pleasant
020591	BROOKS, Clara	9m	C	D.C.	24 JUN 1879	Potters Field
020258	BROOKS, Clement	55y	C	Md.	01 JUN 1879	Harmony
010317	BROOKS, Cora A.	4m	W	D.C.	17 JAN 1877	Graceland
015660	BROOKS, Dennis	2y	C	D.C.	09 MAY 1878	Payne's
019814	BROOKS, Dennis	17y	C	D.C.	18 APR 1879	Mt. Pleasant
015272	BROOKS, Edward	8y	C	D.C.	03 APR 1878	Harmony
000189	BROOKS, Edward Augustus	9m	C	D.C.	14 AUG 1874	Mt. Pleasant
009225	BROOKS, Elias	18y	C	D.C.	28 SEP 1876	Mt. Zion
012626	BROOKS, Elijah	8m	C	D.C.	31 JUL 1877	Beckett's
008151	BROOKS, Elizabeth	74y	C	Va.	10 JUL 1876	Graceland
016014	BROOKS, Elizabeth	11y	C	D.C.	05 JUN 1878	Mt. Pleasant
019351	BROOKS, Elizabeth	11m	C	D.C.	10 MAR 1879	Mt. Zion
004426	BROOKS, Ellen	35y	C	Md.	03 AUG 1875	Mt. Zion
012447	BROOKS, Ellerweder	1y	C	D.C.	20 JUL 1877	Ebenezer
018114	BROOKS, Emaline	42y	C	Md.	22 NOV 1878	Harmony

District of Columbia Death Records, August 1, 1874 to July 31, 1879

No.	Name	Age	Race	Birth	Death Date	Burial Place
003843	BROOKS, Emma	1m	W	D.C.	26 JUN 1875	Young Mens
010526	BROOKS, Estelle	4m	C	D.C.	05 FEB 1877	Harmony
002176	BROOKS, Eugene	10m	C	D.C.	15 FEB 1875	Potters Field
002162	BROOKS, Evelina	6m	C	D.C.	14 FEB 1875	Mt. Zion
021073	BROOKS, Francis J.	67y	W	Ire.	24 JUL 1879	Mt. Olivet
020787	BROOKS, Frederic	50y	W	Ger.	06 JUL 1879	Washington Asylum
016884	BROOKS, Genevieve	3m	C	D.C.	03 AUG 1878	Mt. Zion
005411	BROOKS, George	c.40y	M	Md.	10 NOV 1875	Harmony
020801	BROOKS, George	15y	C	D.C.	07 JUL 1879	Potters Field
019484	BROOKS, George	39y	C	Md.	21 MAR 1879	Payne's
013411	BROOKS, George Annery	21y	C	D.C.	06 OCT 1877	Mt. Pleasant
019842	BROOKS, Georgia	4m	C	D.C.	20 APR 1879	Payne's
000967	BROOKS, Gracie	54y	C	Va.	28 OCT 1874	Beckett's[1]
009721	BROOKS, Hanson	3y	C	D.C.	18 NOV 1876	Harmony
001332	BROOKS, Henrietta	66y	C	U.S.	07 DEC 1874	Washington Asylum
005750	BROOKS, Henry	52y	C	N.C.	15 DEC 1875	Harmony
003322	BROOKS, Henry	8y	C	D.C.	14 MAY 1875	Beckett's
010184	BROOKS, Henry	50y	C	Va.	06 JAN 1877	Ebenezer
014074	BROOKS, Henson	85y	C	Va.	12 DEC 1877	Young Mens
016046	BROOKS, Infant of Maria	1m	C	D.C.	07 JUN 1878	Mt. Zion
003244	BROOKS, Infant of Susanah	7h	C	D.C.	06 MAY 1875	Preserved for Science
007306	BROOKS, Infant of Walker	36h	C	D.C.	15 MAY 1876	Harmony
014156	BROOKS, James	1y	C	D.C.	21 DEC 1877	Beckett's
004557	BROOKS, James Edward	15y	C	D.C.	12 AUG 1875	Mt. Zion
005813	BROOKS, Jesse	120y	C	Va.	21 DEC 1875	Ebenezer
002719	BROOKS, John A.	4m	C	D.C.	24 MAR 1875	Moore's
004647	BROOKS, John L.	32y	W	D.C.	18 AUG 1875	Holy Rood
008348	BROOKS, Julia A.	55y	C	Md.	20 JUL 1876	Mt. Zion
008921	BROOKS, Maggie	1y	C	D.C.	01 SEP 1876	Mt. Olivet
005063	BROOKS, Malindia	2y	C	D.C.	16 SEP 1875	Ebenezer
018982	BROOKS, Margaret	25y	C	Md.	07 FEB 1879	Harmony
006829	BROOKS, Margaret F.	23y	C	D.C.	27 MAR 1876	Harmony
013608	BROOKS, Margarette E.	4y	C	D.C.	24 OCT 1877	Harmony
003609	BROOKS, Margret	7m	C	D.C.	11 JUN 1875	Potters Field
008605	BROOKS, Martha B.	74y	C	Md.	08 AUG 1876	Mt. Zion
003846	BROOKS, Mary	2h	C	D.C.	26 JUN 1875	Young Mens
002260	BROOKS, Mary Elizabeth	1y	C	D.C.	20 FEB 1875	Young Mens
013802	BROOKS, Mary J.	6m	C	D.C.	12 NOV 1877	Potters Field
010156	BROOKS, Mary Jane	49y	C	D.C.	02 JAN 1877	Harmony
012912	BROOKS, Mary L.	4y	C	D.C.	23 AUG 1877	Beckett's
006455	BROOKS, Nathan	60y	C	Md.	24 FEB 1876	Posey's B.G.
005628	BROOKS, Peter	84y	C	Va.	02 DEC 1875	Mt. Pleasant
007531	BROOKS, Philip	26y	C	Va.	07 JUN 1876	Potters Field
003321	BROOKS, Rachael	65y	C	D.C.	14 MAY 1875	Harmony
006930	BROOKS, Rachael	2m	C	D.C.	05 APR 1876	Young Mens
004029	BROOKS, Rebecca	6y	C	D.C.	07 JUL 1875	Ebenezer
003222	BROOKS, Robert	3y	C	N.J.	05 MAY 1875	Young Mens
015979	BROOKS, Rosa	3y	C	D.C.	03 JUN 1878	Beckett's
002490	BROOKS, Rosetta	c.60y	C	Md.	09 MAR 1875	Young Mens
003286	BROOKS, Ross	6m	C	D.C.	11 MAY 1875	Mt. Pleasant
013346	BROOKS, Samuel Eugene	4d	C	D.C.	29 SEP 1877	Harmony
003465	BROOKS, Sarah A.	46y	C	U.S.	28 MAY 1875	Mt. Zion
005907	BROOKS, Silvia	68y	C	Md.	01 JAN 1876	Potters Field

[1] Place of burial given on certificate of death reads Ebenezer Beckett's.

District of Columbia Death Records, August 1, 1874 to July 31, 1879

No.	Name	Age	Race	Birth	Death Date	Burial Place
019024	BROOKS, Stepney	21y	C	D.C.	11 FEB 1879	Beckett's
000745	BROOKS, Susan	30y	C	Md.	08 OCT 1874	Mt. Olivet
014792	BROOKS, Thomas	2m	W	D.C.	17 FEB 1878	Mt. Olivet
015901	BROOKS, Thos.	7y	C	D.C.	30 MAY 1878	Beckett's
007893	BROOKS, William	2y	C	D.C.	28 JUN 1876	Ebenezer
001905	BROOKS, William Henry	1y	C	D.C.	26 JAN 1875	Young Mens
010397	BROOME, Mary V.	5m	W	D.C.	24 JAN 1877	Congressional
011072	BROOMS, Jane	70y	C	Md.	22 MAR 1877	Potters Field
004875	BROSNAHAN, Edward	1m	W	D.C.	02 SEP 1875	Mt. Olivet
006706	BROSNAN, Mary	49y	W	Ire.	17 MAR 1876	Mt. Olivet
013522	BROSNAN, Patrick Joseph	7m	W	D.C.	15 OCT 1877	Mt. Olivet
006605	BROTT, Rawlins Shepperd	7m	W	La.	09 MAR 1876	Glenwood
009766	BROUGHTON, Sally	80y	W	D.C.	21 NOV 1876	Congressional
001286	BROUMAN, Katie	3y	W	D.C.	02 DEC 1874	St. Mary's
013579	BROWER, Arthur Winfield	2y	W	D.C.	21 OCT 1877	Prospect Hill
000460	BROWN, Acotta	10m	M	D.C.	09 SEP 1874	Mt. Zion
001877	BROWN, Ada	2m	C	D.C.	24 JAN 1875	Ebenezer
010424	BROWN, Adam	20y	C	Md.	28 JAN 1877	Potters Field
006774	BROWN, Addison	3y	W	Kan.	22 MAR 1876	Hutchinson, Kan.
007212	BROWN, Agnes	3w	C	D.C.	05 MAY 1876	Mt. Pleasant
012180	BROWN, Albert	1y	C	D.C.	02 JUL 1877	Ebenezer
017521	BROWN, Alexander	9y	C	D.C.	25 SEP 1878	Young Mens
001589	BROWN, Alfred	56y	C	Va.	02 JAN 1875	Harmony
001217	BROWN, Alice	45y	C	Md.	23 NOV 1874	Mt. Zion
003190	BROWN, Alice	17y	C	Va.	01 MAY 1875	Mt. Zion
020315	BROWN, Alice	5m	C	D.C.	06 JUN 1879	Beckett's
016156	BROWN, Amelia	4y	C	Md.	14 JUN 1878	Mt. Olivet
011516	BROWN, Americus	4y	W	D.C.	05 MAY 1877	Glenwood
012836	BROWN, Andrew	6m	C	D.C.	16 AUG 1877	Payne's
002002	BROWN, Anie	8m	C	D.C.	03 FEB 1875	Mt. Zion
007029	BROWN, Ann A.	43y	C	Md.	17 APR 1876	Harmony
020636	BROWN, Anna E.	15y	C	D.C.	27 JUN 1879	Baptist
017678	BROWN, Annie	60y	C	Md.	09 OCT 1878	Potters Field
007368	BROWN, Annie Elizabeth	55y	W	D.C.	22 MAY 1876	Congressional
004912	BROWN, Archibald	4m	C	D.C.	05 SEP 1875	Harmony
009931	BROWN, Archibald	85y	C	Md.	11 DEC 1876	Mt. Olivet
013265	BROWN, Augustus	4m	C	D.C.	21 SEP 1877	Mt. Olivet
020465	BROWN, Augustus	6m	C	D.C.	16 JUN 1879	Potters Field
005786	BROWN, Basil	c.76y	C	D.C.	19 DEC 1875	Harmony
005591	BROWN, Bazil	68y	C	Md.	28 NOV 1875	Thomas'
001946	BROWN, Betsey	5y	C	D.C.	29 JAN 1875	Beckett's
005557	BROWN, Betsey (Stone)	60y	M	Md.	25 NOV 1875	Mt. Olivet
007774	BROWN, Betsy	10y	C	Md.	22 JUN 1876	Charles Co., Md.
007812	BROWN, Betsy	57y	C	Va.	24 JUN 1876	Potters Field
011982	BROWN, Blanch R.	4m	C	D.C.	20 JUN 1877	Beckett's
006582	BROWN, Burnet	75y	M	Va.	07 MAR 1876	Potters Field
018639	BROWN, Burrell	38y	C	Va.	11 JAN 1879	Beckett's
007384	BROWN, Calphus	33y	C	Md.	23 MAY 1876	Ebenezer
006809	BROWN, Campbell F.L.	10y	C	D.C.	25 MAR 1876	Beckett's
008880	BROWN, Caroline Christifor	1y	C	D.C.	30 AUG 1876	Young Mens
011930	BROWN, Carrie Celia	2m	C	D.C.	16 JUN 1877	Ebenezer
012373	BROWN, Carrie E.	1y	C	D.C.	15 JUL 1877	Harmony
007720	BROWN, Catharine E.	60y	W	Ire.	19 JUN 1876	Mt. Olivet
003225	BROWN, Catharine F.	1y	C	D.C.	05 MAY 1875	Glenwood
013340	BROWN, Celestia	9m	W	N.Y.	04 OCT 1877	Graceland
000147	BROWN, Celia Delany	20y	C	Md.	11 AUG 1874	Mt. Olivet

No.	Name	Age	Race	Birth	Death Date	Burial Place
020432	BROWN, Cemia Ann	2y	C	D.C.	14 JUN 1879	Payne's
005568	BROWN, Charles	2y	C	D.C.	26 NOV 1875	Graceland
012547	BROWN, Charles	3m	C	D.C.	27 JUL 1877	Harmony
013726	BROWN, Charles	62y	C	Md.	04 NOV 1877	Mt. Olivet
019442	BROWN, Charles	21m	C	D.C.	18 MAR 1879	Mt. Zion
001958	BROWN, Charles E.	1y	C	D.C.	30 JAN 1875	Ebenezer
013077	BROWN, Charles F.	2y	C	D.C.	04 SEP 1877	Mt. Olivet
014186	BROWN, Charles Wm.	8y	W	D.C.	24 DEC 1877	Holy Rood
005074	BROWN, Charlott	5m	C	D.C.	17 SEP 1875	Harmony
011295	BROWN, Charlotte	55y	C	Va.	10 APR 1877	Mt. Pleasant Plain
012505	BROWN, Charlotte	9m	C	D.C.	24 JUL 1877	Potters Field
004375	BROWN Charly	3m	C	D.C.	30 JUL 1875	Young Mens
006794	BROWN, Chas.	3m	C	D.C.	24 MAR 1876	Mt. Zion
010506	BROWN, Clara	25y	C	Va.	04 FEB 1877	Potters Field
013076	BROWN, Columbus	42y	W	Md.	04 SEP 1877	Glenwood
015009	BROWN, Daisy	2y	C	D.C.	10 MAR 1878	Payne's
000924	BROWN, Daniel	1y	C	D.C.	24 OCT 1874	Harmony
012035	BROWN, Daniel	34y	C	Va.	24 JUN 1877	Alexandria, Va.
012574	BROWN, David	82y	W	Scot.	28 JUL 1877	Congressional
018918	BROWN, Delia Francis	1y	C	D.C.	02 FEB 1879	Payne's
020174	BROWN, Dominick	22y	C	Md.	23 MAY 1879	Mt. Olivet
015844	BROWN, Dora E.	3y	C	D.C.	26 MAY 1878	Mt. Zion
020302	BROWN, Eddward	9m	C	D.C.	05 JUN 1879	Potters Field
006013	BROWN, Edmonia	42y	C	Va.	14 JAN 1876	Mt. Zion
007093	BROWN, Edward	49y	C	Md.	24 APR 1876	Mt. Olivet
020236	BROWN, Edward	64y	C	Va.	31 MAY 1879	Mt. Zion
011860	BROWN, Ela	11y	C	D.C.	11 JUN 1877	Mt. Olivet
001944	BROWN, Elanor	49y	C	Md.	29 JAN 1875	Potters Field
014327	BROWN, Elijah	54y	C	Va.	05 JAN 1878	Mt. Zion
006232	BROWN, Eliza	6y	C	D.C.	04 FEB 1876	Mt. Olivet
012326	BROWN, Eliza	50y	C	Va.	12 JUL 1877	Potters Field
015704	BROWN, Eliza	36y	C	D.C.	13 MAY 1878	Mt. Pleasant
015489	BROWN, Eliza S.	70y	W	Md.	23 APR 1878	Oak Hill
005036a	BROWN, Elizabeth	44y	W	Ire.	03 OCT 1875	Mt. Olivet
008262	BROWN, Elizabeth	c.66y	C	Md.	14 JUL 1876	Mt. Pleasant
021029	BROWN, Elizabeth	35y	C	Va.	21 JUL 1879	Mt. Zion
020372	BROWN, Elizabeth	60y	C	Md.	10 JUN 1879	Harmony
007175	BROWN, Ella	20y	C	Va.	01 MAY 1876	Young Mens
014720	BROWN, Ella	1y	C	D.C.	09 FEB 1878	Young Mens
019174	BROWN, Ella	1y	C	D.C.	24 FEB 1879	Beckett's
006270	BROWN, Ellen	37y	C	D.C.	08 FEB 1876	Ebenezer
016142	BROWN, Ellen Small	67y	W	W.Va.	13 JUN 1878	Oak Hill
006420	BROWN, Emily	38y	C	Md.	20 FEB 1876	Harmony
008214	BROWN, Emma	8m	C	D.C.	12 JUL 1876	Ebenezer
009491	BROWN, Emma	71y	C	D.C.	22 OCT 1876	Baptist
012908	BROWN, Emma	8y	C	D.C.	22 AUG 1877	Mt. Olivet
002845	BROWN, Emma V.	1y	W	D.C.	02 APR 1875	Presbyterian
019085	BROWN, Emmeline	53y	C	D.C.	16 FEB 1879	Harmony
003874	BROWN, Eva	9m	C	D.C.	27 JUN 1875	Mt. Zion
005236	BROWN, Eva Roberta	2y	C	D.C.	22 OCT 1875	Ebenezer
015577	BROWN, Fannie	34y	C	N.C.	02 MAY 1878	Potters Field
017020	BROWN, Frances E.	26y	M	D.C.	12 AUG 1878	Mt. Olivet
012753	BROWN, Francis	50y	C	Md.	10 AUG 1877	Harmony
010149	BROWN, Francis	2m	C	D.C.	01 JAN 1877	Ebenezer
015547	BROWN, Francis Winston	3m	M	D.C.	29 APR 1878	Harmony
011308	BROWN, Frank	5y	W	D.C.	12 APR 1877	Congressional

District of Columbia Death Records, August 1, 1874 to July 31, 1879

No.	Name	Age	Race	Birth	Death Date	Burial Place
002859	BROWN, Frankie	3m	C	D.C.	03 APR 1875	Young Mens
020776	BROWN, Fred L.	1y	C	D.C.	05 JUL 1879	Mt. Zion
000362	BROWN, Frederick	18m	C	D.C.	29 AUG 1874	Potters Field
005960	BROWN, Frederick	8y	C	Va.	07 JAN 1876	Mt. Zion
019497	BROWN, Genevieve	1y	W	D.C.	22 MAR 1879	Mt. Olivet
015107	BROWN, Geo.	50y	C	Md.	18 MAR 1878	Young Mens
019909	BROWN, Geo.	7m	C	D.C.	27 APR 1879	Payne's
004271	BROWN, George	4m	C	D.C.	24 JUL 1875	Mt. Zion
007083	BROWN, George	69y	C	Md.	23 APR 1876	Mt. Zion
014222	BROWN, George	19y	C	Md.	27 DEC 1877	Mt. Zion
013900	BROWN, George H.	17y	C	Va.	24 NOV 1877	Baptist [Union]
005258	BROWN, George M.	1y	W	D.C.	24 OCT 1875	Glenwood
004525	BROWN, Gertrud	8m	C	D.C.	10 AUG 1875	Potters Field
012441	BROWN, H.M.	2m	W	D.C.	20 JUL 1877	Presbyterian
009956	BROWN, Hannah	22y	C	Va.	14 DEC 1876	Young Mens
011559	BROWN, Harriette	12y	C	D.C.	10 MAY 1877	Ebenezer
016883	BROWN, Harry	8m	M	D.C.	03 AUG 1878	Mt. Pleasant
003232	BROWN, Henrietta	17y	C	Md.	05 MAY 1875	Ebenezer
004436	BROWN, Henry	8m	C	D.C.	04 AUG 1875	Harmony
009226	BROWN, Henry C.	34y	C	D.C.	28 SEP 1876	Ebenezer
007081	BROWN, Herbert	1y	C	D.C.	23 APR 1876	Ebenezer
016599	BROWN, Hester Ann	6m	C	D.C.	15 JUL 1878	Mt. Pleasant Plain
007741	BROWN, Horace E.	11m	C	Md.	20 JUN 1876	Young Mens
006830	BROWN, Howard	4m	C	D.C.	27 MAR 1876	Ebenezer
008842	BROWN, Ida	15m	C	D.C.	27 AUG 1876	Harmony
012949	BROWN, Ida	8m	C	DC.	25 AUG 1877	Mt. Olivet
012389	BROWN, Ida	5m	C	D.C.	16 JUL 1877	Ebenezer
011388	BROWN, Ignasious	79y	C	Md.	21 APR 1877	Mt. Olivet
018566	BROWN, Infant of Allen	20d	C	D.C.	05 JAN 1879	Mt. Olivet
009281	BROWN, Infant of B.	1m	M	D.C.	03 OCT 1876	Ebenezer
020326	BROWN, Infant of Edward	½h	C	D.C.	07 JUN 1879	Payne's
017894	BROWN, Infant of Elizabeth	7d	C	D.C.	29 OCT 1878	Swartz's
002492	BROWN, Infant of Francis M.	6d	W	D.C.	09 MAR 1875	Holy Rood
000714	BROWN, Infant of Frederick	20d	C	D.C.	04 OCT 1874	Potters Field
000710	BROWN, Infant of George P.	4d	W	D.C.	04 OCT 1874	Congressional
001601	BROWN, Infant of James	1m	C	D.C.	03 JAN 1875	Mt. Pleasant
009684	BROWN, Infant of John	11h	C	D.C.	13 NOV 1876	Ebenezer
012089	BROWN, Infant of Julia	1m	C	D.C.	27 JUN 1877	Ebenezer
015846	BROWN, Infant of Laura	9d	C	D.C.	26 MAY 1878	Payne's
016463	BROWN, Infant of Lizzie	6h	C	D.C.	06 JUL 1878	Harmony
004589	BROWN, Infant of Louis	1d	C	D.C.	14 AUG 1875	Mt. Olivet
007958	[Brown?], Infant of Mary	2m	C	D.C.	01 JUL 1876	Mt. Olivet
012417	BROWN, Infant of Philip	8m	C	D.C.	18 JUL 1877	Potters Field
001284	BROWN, Infant of Samuel	13d	C	D.C.	01 DEC 1874	Beckett's
001149	BROWN, Infant of Thos.	8d	C	D.C.	14 NOV 1874	Mt. Olivet
007084	BROWN, Infant of Victoria	4d	C	D.C.	23 APR 1876	Potters Field
016325	BROWN, Irena	90y	C	Va.	27 JUN 1878	Harmony
005896	BROWN, Isabella	16y	C	D.C.	30 DEC 1875	Harmony
014124	BROWN, Isabella	3y	C	D.C.	18 DEC 1877	Mt. Olivet
008268	BROWN, J.W.	1y	C	Va.	15 JUL 1876	Mt. Olivet
001509	BROWN, James	42y	C	Pa.	27 DEC 1874	Mt. Pleasant
004606	BROWN, James	58y	W	Va.	15 AUG 1875	Congressional
015871	BROWN, James	4m	C	D.C.	28 MAY 1878	Beckett's
018392	BROWN, James Henry	9m	C	Md.	20 DEC 1878	Mt. Olivet
015736	BROWN, James M.	2m	W	D.C.	16 MAY 1878	Graceland
012378	BROWN, James M.A.	26y	W	D.C.	16 JUL 1877	Tennallytown

District of Columbia Death Records, August 1, 1874 to July 31, 1879

No.	Name	Age	Race	Birth	Death Date	Burial Place
013003	BROWN, Jane	65y	W	D.C.	29 AUG 1877	Congressional
013986	BROWN, Jane	39y	C	Va.	02 DEC 1877	Harmony
013495	BROWN, Jane R.	3w	C	D.C.	13 OCT 1877	Potters Field
013176	BROWN, Jas. E.	3m	C	D.C.	13 SEP 1877	Harmony
013334	BROWN, Jemima	9m	C	D.C.	28 SEP 1877	Harmony
010311	BROWN, Jesse Morris	3y	C	D.C.	16 JAN 1877	Baptist
007875	BROWN, Jessie A.	7m	C	D.C.	27 JUN 1876	Cooney, Va.[1]
014969	BROWN, Jno.	35y	C	Va.	07 MAR 1878	Payne's
001231	BROWN, John	1y	C	D.C.	25 NOV 1874	Mt. Zion
005451	BROWN, John	41y	C	Md.	14 NOV 1875	Harmony
005934	BROWN, John	50y	C	Va.	04 JAN 1876	Washington Asylum
021122	BROWN, John	13d	C	D.C.	27 JUL 1879	Payne's
019648	BROWN, John Albert	8y	C	D.C.	04 APR 1879	Beckett's
009169	BROWN, John H.	14y	C	Va.	22 SEP 1876	Mt. Zion
019485	BROWN, John Henry	1y	W	N.S.	21 MAR 1879	Potters Field/Congressional
006443	BROWN, John M.	6m	C	D.C.	23 FEB 1876	Mt. Olivet
012544	BROWN, John T.	3m	W	D.C.	27 JUL 1877	Presbyterian
005466	BROWN, John Wesley	4m	C	D.C.	16 NOV 1875	Ebenezer
006181	BROWN, Jos.	55y	C	Md.	30 JAN 1876	Mt. Olivet
004745	BROWN, Joseph	4m	W	D.C.	25 AUG 1875	Mt. Olivet
006987	BROWN, Joseph	1y	C	D.C.	11 APR 1876	Young Mens
006950	BROWN, Joseph	1y	C	Md.	07 APR 1876	Ebenezer
007507	BROWN, Joseph	4m	W	D.C.	05 JUN 1876	Mt. Olivet
000844	BROWN, Joseph D.	2y	C	D.C.	17 OCT 1874	Young Mens
010481	BROWN, Joseph Wm.	2m	W	D.C.	02 FEB 1877	Prospect Hill
015144	BROWN, Josephine	4m	C	D.C.	22 MAR 1878	Potters Field
019467	BROWN, Josiah	18y	C	Md.	20 MAR 1879	Young Mens
004330	BROWN, Julia	1y	M	D.C.	27 JUL 1875	Young Mens
015735	BROWN, Julia	65y	C	Md.	15 MAY 1878	Beckett's
009440	BROWN, Katie S.	1y	C	D.C.	17 OCT 1876	Potters Field
010876	BROWN, Laura	4y	C	D.C.	05 MAR 1877	Harmony
015845	BROWN, Laura	24y	C	D.C.	26 MAY 1878	Payne's
010539	BROWN, Laura E.	21y	M	D.C.	06 FEB 1877	Harmony
008586	BROWN, Lavina	10m	C	D.C.	07 AUG 1876	Ebenezer
004396	BROWN, Lavinia	70y	M	Va.	01 AUG 1875	Potters Field
006623	BROWN, Lelia Vernon	19y	W	Va.	10 MAR 1876	Glenwood
009568	BROWN, Lewis	1y	C	D.C.	29 OCT 1876	Young Mens
004809	BROWN, Lewis Crouse	2y	W	D.C.	29 AUG 1875	Glenwood
013580	BROWN, Lilly E.	2m	C	D.C.	21 OCT 1877	Mt. Zion
016211	BROWN, Linney	c.80y	C	Va.	18 JUN 1878	Mt. Pleasant
020024	BROWN, Lize	6y	C	D.C.	07 MAY 1879	Harmony
002369	BROWN, Lizzie	7y	C	Va.	01 MAR 1875	Young Mens
015689	BROWN, Lizzie	5m	C	D.C.	12 MAY 1878	Moore's
009438	BROWN, Lorenzo Carter	3y	C	D.C.	16 OCT 1876	Ebenezer
001296	BROWN, Louisa	17m	C	D.C.	03 DEC 1874	Beckett's
019466	BROWN, Louisa	45y	C	Md.	20 MAR 1879	Mt. Olivet
016143	BROWN, Luceba N.	62y	W	Mass.	13 JUN 1878	Glenwood
011090	BROWN, Lucie	78y	C	Md.	23 MAR 1877	Harmony
017960	BROWN, Lucinda C.	60y	C	D.C.	06 NOV 1878	Mt. Olivet
015705	BROWN, Lucy	7m	C	D.C.	13 MAY 1878	Potters Field
017627	BROWN, Lucy	60y	C	Md.	04 OCT 1878	Potters Field
017720	BROWN, Lucy	6y	C	W.Va.	13 OCT 1878	Beckett's
001386	BROWN, Luley	1y	C	D.C.	14 DEC 1874	Mt. Pleasant

[1] Located near Chain Bridge.

District of Columbia Death Records, August 1, 1874 to July 31, 1879   43

No.	Name	Age	Race	Birth	Death Date	Burial Place
017181	BROWN, Lulu	9m	C	D.C.	25 AUG 1878	Beckett's
011843	BROWN, Madison	24y	C	Va.	08 JUN 1877	Ebenezer
015108	BROWN, Maggie	7m	C	D.C.	18 MAR 1878	Mt. Olivet
016686	BROWN, Maggie E.	5m	C	D.C.	20 JUL 1878	Mt. Olivet
001612	BROWN, Margaret	75y	C	--	04 JAN 1875	Potters Field
005150	BROWN, Margaret	60y	W	Va.	24 SEP 1875	Gaines' Farm[1]
010657	BROWN, Margarite	37y	C	D.C.	16 FEB 1877	Greensvale
005097	BROWN, Maria	74y	C	Va.	19 SEP 1875	Moore's
011716	BROWN, Maria E.	57y	W	Md.	26 MAY 1877	Graceland
008518	BROWN, Marshal	c.54y	C	D.C.	01 AUG 1876	Harmony
004540	BROWN, Martha	1y	C	D.C.	11 AUG 1875	Ebenezer
020194	BROWN, Martha	31y	C	Md.	25 MAY 1879	Mt. Olivet
001328	BROWN, Mary	15y	C	Md.	07 DEC 1874	Young Mens
001162	BROWN, Mary	49y	C	D.C.	16 NOV 1874	Harmony
004397	BROWN, Mary	1y	M	D.C.	01 AUG 1875	Holy Rood
002326	BROWN, Mary	2y	C	Md.	26 FEB 1875	Mt. Olivet
001714	BROWN, Mary	1m	C	D.C.	13 JAN 1875	Beckett's
004373	BROWN, Mary	2m	C	D.C.	30 JUL 1875	Potters Field
015463	BROWN, Mary	20y	C	Md.	21 APR 1878	Mt. Olivet
014738	BROWN, Mary	77y	W	D.C.	11 FEB 1878	Rock Creek
015920	BROWN, Mary	4d	C	D.C.	31 MAY 1878	Beckett's
021033	BROWN, Mary	24y	C	Va.	21 JUL 1879	Potters Field
004425	BROWN, Mary Ann	72y	C	Va.	03 AUG 1875	Ebenezer
010901	BROWN, Mary Ann	20y	W	Pa.	07 MAR 1877	Mt. Olivet
005398	BROWN, Mary Bently	67y	W	Md.	09 NOV 1875	Oak Hill
012237	BROWN, Mary E.	6m	C	D.C.	06 JUL 1877	Young Mens
016430	BROWN, Mary E.	20y	C	Md.	04 JUL 1878	Beckett's
009114	BROWN, Mary Elisabeth	1y	C	D.C.	17 SEP 1876	Beckett's
003870	BROWN, Mary Eliza	1y	C	D.C.	27 JUN 1875	Mt. Olivet
006130	BROWN, Mary Elizabeth	1y	C	D.C.	25 JAN 1876	Mt. Zion
015210	BROWN, Mary Elizabeth	16y	C	Md.	28 MAR 1878	Mt. Olivet
003314	BROWN, Mary Ellen	26y	W	Va.	13 MAY 1875	Glenwood
016429	BROWN, Mary F.	24y	M	D.C.	04 JUL 1878	Harmony
012710	BROWN, Mary H.	27y	C	D.C.	07 AUG 1877	Holy Rood
002547	BROWN, Mary L.	2y	C	D.C.	13 MAR 1875	Mt. Zion
014170	BROWN, Mary M.	1y	W	D.C.	22 DEC 1877	Rock Creek
011587	BROWN, Matilda	70y	C	Md.	13 MAY 1877	Potters Field
006054	BROWN, Matilda Ann	6y	C	D.C.	18 JAN 1876	Mt. Zion
011126	BROWN, Matthew	3m	C	D.C.	27 MAR 1877	Young Mens
005751	BROWN, Melinda	27y	C	Md.	15 DEC 1875	Ebenezer
013276	BROWN, Minie Alice	1y	C	D.C.	22 SEP 1877	Harmony
015455	BROWN, Minnie	5m	C	D.C.	20 APR 1878	Beckett's
005900	BROWN, Minty	70y	C	Md.	31 DEC 1875	Mt. Zion
010364	BROWN, Murry	10y	C	D.C.	21 JAN 1877	Harmony
005629	BROWN, Myra	60y	C	Va.	02 DEC 1875	Ebenezer
008177	BROWN, Nancy	c.25y	C	Md.	11 JUL 1876	Mt. Olivet
012181	BROWN, Nancy	72y	C	Va.	02 JUL 1877	Harmony
018495	BROWN, Nancy	50y	C	Md.	29 DEC 1878	Mt. Olivet
020057	BROWN, Nathan Henson	25y	C	Md.	10 MAY 1879	Mt. Pleasant Plain
013624	BROWN, Nathaniel B.	3m	M	D.C.	25 OCT 1877	Harmony
005237	BROWN, Nellie	90y	C	D.C.	22 OCT 1875	Ebenezer
005865	BROWN, Noah	30y	C	D.C.	26 DEC 1875	Ebenezer
021060	BROWN, Percilla	25y	C	D.C.	23 JUL 1879	Beckett's

[1] Located near Tennallytown.

No.	Name	Age	Race	Birth	Death Date	Burial Place
002277	BROWN, Philip	28d	C	D.C.	22 FEB 1875	Mt. Olivet
005381	BROWN, Philip	1y	C	D.C.	07 NOV 1875	Ebenezer
014210	BROWN, Philip	77y	C	Md.	26 DEC 1877	Young Mens
019751	BROWN, Philip	7m	C	D.C.	13 APR 1879	Young Mens
008815	BROWN, Priscilla	3y	C	Md.	25 AUG 1876	Potters Field
003844	BROWN, Rachael Ann	108y	C	Md.	26 JUN 1875	Mt. Olivet
004824	BROWN, Rachel	8m	C	D.C.	30 AUG 1875	Young Mens
003414	BROWN, Rachel	128y	C	Md.	23 MAY 1875	Young Mens
003948	BROWN, Rebecca	1y	C	D.C.	01 JUL 1875	Ebenezer
007942	BROWN, Rebecca	11d	C	D.C.	30 JUN 1876	Ebenezer
013374	BROWN, Rebecca	30y	C	Md.	02 OCT 1877	Potters Field
013667	BROWN, Rebertha Island	3y	W	D.C.	29 OCT 1877	Alexandria, Va.
003404	BROWN, Richard	40y	C	Va.	23 MAY 1875	Potters Field
017380	BROWN, Richard	37y	W	Md.	12 SEP 1878	Prospect Hill
017499	BROWN, Richard Benjamin	2y	C	D.C.	23 SEP 1878	Young Mens
001692	BROWN, Robert	21y	W	Pa.	11 JAN 1875	Congressional
002423	BROWN, Robert	36y	C	Md.	04 MAR 1875	Thomas'
014176	BROWN, Robert E.	3y	W	D.C.	23 DEC 1877	Holy Rood
013596	BROWN, Robt. A.	34y	C	Md.	23 OCT 1877	Good Hope
004307	BROWN, Rosa	8m	C	D.C.	26 JUL 1875	Beckett's
018802	BROWN, Rosella	49y	C	Md.	25 JAN 1879	Young Mens
002956	BROWN, Ruben	21y	C	Va.	11 APR 1875	Washington Asylum
014157	BROWN, Ruben R.	51y	W	Md.	21 DEC 1877	Glenwood
013899	BROWN, Sallie	45y	C	Va.	24 NOV 1877	Beckett's
005814	BROWN, Salmon Rich	58y	W	N.Y.	21 DEC 1875	Graceland
005787	BROWN, Samuel	3y	C	Va.	19 DEC 1875	Alexandria, Va.
005606	BROWN, Samuel	57y	W	Pa.	29 NOV 1875	Prospect Hill
018891	BROWN, Samuel G.	4y	C	D.C.	31 JAN 1879	Mt. Olivet
011850	BROWN, Sandy	2m	C	D.C.	09 JUN 1877	Potters Field
019328	BROWN, Sara Clarke	64y	M	Md.	09 MAR 1879	Mt. Olivet
019086	BROWN, Sarah	30y	C	Va.	16 FEB 1879	Young Mens
016064	BROWN, Sarah A.	2y	W	Pa.	08 JUN 1878	Graceland
017637	BROWN, Sarah A.	74y	C	Va.	05 OCT 1878	Mt. Zion
019445	BROWN, Sarah A.	50y	C	Va.	19 MAR 1879	Harmony/Graceland
005950	BROWN, Sarah Ann	2y	C	D.C.	06 JAN 1876	Ebenezer
010090	BROWN, Sarah E.	2m	W	D.C.	27 DEC 1876	Congressional
011166	BROWN, Susan	53y	W	Md.	30 MAR 1877	Methodist
000839	BROWN, Susan Anne E.	1y	C	D.C.	17 OCT 1874	Mt. Olivet
001302	BROWN, Teco Jane	30y	C	D.C.	04 DEC 1874	Mt. Pleasant
005582	BROWN, Thomas	52y	C	Va.	27 NOV 1875	Young Mens
007001	BROWN, Thomas	34y	C	Md.	12 APR 1876	Washington Asylum
008603	BROWN, Thomas	9d	C	D.C.	08 AUG 1876	Potters Field
014055	BROWN, Thomas	8d	C	D.C.	10 DEC 1877	Young Mens
012620	BROWN, Thomas	1y	C	D.C.	31 JUL 1877	Potters Field
015607	BROWN, Thomas	65y	C	D.C.	04 MAY 1878	Harmony
019910	BROWN, Thomas	45y	C	Md.	27 MAR 1879	Potters Field
011055	BROWN, Thos. P.	5d	W	D.C.	20 MAR 1877	Mt. Olivet
020956	BROWN, Ursula	26y	C	Va.	16 JUL 1879	Potters Field
014187	BROWN, Virginia	48y	W	D.C.	24 DEC 1877	Oak Hill
007810	BROWN, Wagmond	1y	C	D.C.	24 JUN 1876	Mt. Pleasant
006730	BROWN, Waldo	47y	W	Ohio	19 MAR 1876	Oak Hill
001164	BROWN, Walter	19y	C	Md.	16 NOV 1874	Beckett's
016616	BROWN, Walter	1m	C	D.C.	16 JUL 1878	Young Mens
003197	BROWN, Watson	80y	C	Va.	02 MAY 1875	Harmony
007492	BROWN, William	4m	C	D.C.	04 JUN 1876	Potters Field
011633	BROWN, William	80y	C	Md.	18 MAY 1877	Potters Field

District of Columbia Death Records, August 1, 1874 to July 31, 1879   45

No.	Name	Age	Race	Birth	Death Date	Burial Place
013851	BROWN, William	54y	W	N.J.	18 NOV 1877	Potters Field
016299	BROWN, William	9m	C	D.C.	25 JUN 1878	Beckett's
015815	BROWN, William	18m	W	Pa.	23 MAY 1878	Graceland
019329	BROWN, William	4y	C	D.C.	09 MAR 1879	Potters Field
003192	BROWN, William Francis	10y	C	Md.	02 MAY 1875	Mt. Olivet
001736	BROWN, William H.	2y	C	D.C.	14 JAN 1875	Beckett's
020256	BROWN, William H.	1m	C	D.C.	02 JUN 1879	Mt. Zion
002427	BROWN, William Henry	2y	C	DC.	05 MAR 1875	Mt. Olivet
006870	BROWN, William Henry	2y	C	D.C.	31 MAR 1876	Ebenezer
013254	BROWN, William Henry	67y	C	Md.	20 SEP 1877	Mt. Pleasant
008476	BROWN, Willie	8m	C	D.C.	29 JUL 1876	Potters Field
009142	BROWN, Willie	1y	C	D.C.	20 SEP 1876	Harmony
015154	BROWN, Willie	3y	M	D.C.	23 MAR 1878	Young Mens
009755	BROWN, Wilson	1y	C	D.C.	20 NOV 1876	Ebenezer
010164	BROWN, Wilson E.	51y	W	Md.	03 JAN 1877	Oak Hill
009209	BROWN, Wm.	1m	C	D.C.	26 SEP 1876	Alexandria, Va.
002873	BROWN, Wm. Henry	1d	C	D.C.	04 APR 1875	Ebenezer
007546	BROWN, Wm. Henry	4m	C	D.C.	08 JUN 1876	Harmony
005885	BROWN, Wm. Joseph	2y	C	D.C.	28 DEC 1875	Young Mens
009586	BROWN, Wm. S.	6m	C	D.C.	31 OCT 1876	Harmony
000258	BROWNAN, Joseph	5d	C	D.C.	20 AUG 1874	Young Mens
004104	BROWNE, Elizabeth Montgomery	81y	W	Ire.	13 JUL 1875	Brooklyn, N.Y.
008483	BROWNE, Ella	11m	C	D.C.	30 JUL 1876	Potters Field
004374	BROWNE, Harriet M.	27y	C	D.C.	30 JUL 1875	Harmony
000893	BROWNE, Louisa	63y	M	Va.	21 OCT 1874	Young Mens
020853	BROWNE, Marion W.	38y	W	N.Y.	09 JUL 1879	Congressional
017707	BROWNING, George T.	21y	W	D.C.	12 OCT 1878	Oak Hill
009892	BROWNING, Minnie Anna	6m	W	Md.	06 DEC 1876	Congressional
006372	BROWNING, Saml. Gilbert	6y	W	D.C.	16 FEB 1876	Gettysburg, Pa.
013571	BROWNING, Sarah Francis	30y	W	Md.	20 OCT 1877	Congressional
008766	BROWNING, William Theodore	9m	W	D.C.	21 AUG 1876	Congressional
002055	BRUBECKER, Amanda	26y	W	Md.	06 FEB 1875	Potters Field
009360	BRUCE, Addie	39y	C	D.C.	09 OCT 1876	Harmony
006064	BRUCE, Alfred	31y	W	Pa.	19 JAN 1876	Hospital
009626	BRUCE, Annie	40y	C	D.C.	06 NOV 1876	Mt. Olivet
008094	BRUCE, Charles	82y	C	Md.	09 JUL 1876	Harmony
018754	BRUCE, Charles	68y	W	Md.	24 JAN 1879	Washington Asylum
008507	BRUCE, Ella	1y	C	D.C.	31 JUL 1876	Mt. Zion
015240	BRUCE, Fanny	103y	C	Va.	31 MAR 1878	Young Mens
016534	BRUCE, Francis	11m	C	D.C.	10 JUL 1878	Harmony
012738	BRUCE, Henry W.	6d	C	D.C.	09 AUG 1877	Mt. Zion
007305	BRUCE, Hermoine C.	10m	C	D.C.	15 MAY 1876	Harmony
010819	BRUCE, James	2y	C	D.C.	01 MAR 1877	Beckett's
000149	BRUCE, Jane	60y	C	Md.	11 AUG 1874	Harmony
012241	BRUCE, Louisa	30y	W	D.C.	06 JUL 1877	Congressional
015273	BRUCE, Margaret	16y	C	D.C.	03 APR 1878	Moore's
014970	BRUCE, Maria	80y	C	Md.	07 MAR 1878	Mt. Pleasant
005333	BRUCE, Mariha	6y	C	D.C.	02 NOV 1875	Ebenezer
013277	BRUCE, Peter	40y	W	France	22 SEP 1877	Annapolis, Md.
013528	BRUCE, Richd. G.	3y	C	D.C.	16 OCT 1877	Harmony
013005	BRUCE, Robert J.	35y	W	Md.	29 AUG 1877	King George Co., Va.
012263	BRUCE, Willie Clifford	11y	C	D.C.	08 JUL 1877	Harmony
002084	BRUCHHEISER, Jacob	56y	W	Ger.	08 FEB 1875	Prospect Hill
001094	BRUEHL, Emanuel	80y	W	Ger.	09 NOV 1874	Prospect Hill
003871	BRUESCKE, Frederick A.	2y	W	Ger.	27 JUN 1875	Prospect Hill
009059	BRUFF, Joseph Goldsborough	11m	W	D.C.	13 SEP 1876	Congressional

District of Columbia Death Records, August 1, 1874 to July 31, 1879

No.	Name	Age	Race	Birth	Death Date	Burial Place
010871	BRUFF, Mary	c.95y	W	Md.	05 MAR 1877	Congressional
011607	BRUGGBECKER, Francis	35y	W	Ger.	15 MAY 1877	Soldier's Home
018956	BRUMAGIM, John W.	48y	W	N.J.	05 FEB 1879	Glenwood
019315	BRUMMEL, Elizabeth	68y	W	Md.	08 MAR 1879	Carroll Co., Md.
020045	BRUNENGER, Barbara	41y	W	Ger.	09 MAY 1879	Prospect Hill
018329	BRUNGER, Fannie	6y	W	Va.	14 DEC 1878	Glenwood
001236	BRUNK, Jane	2m	C	D.C.	26 NOV 1874	Potters Field
011067	BRUNNA, David	2m	W	D.C.	21 MAR 1877	Mt. Olivet
006221	BRUNSTEAD, Mary E.	45y	W	Md.	03 FEB 1876	Congressional
004924	BRUST, Ada	3y	W	N.Y.	06 SEP 1875	Congressional
011437	BRUTUS, George	22y	C	Va.	27 APR 1877	Mt. Zion
000020	BRYAN, Alice	6m	W	D.C.	02 AUG 1874	Congressional
007251	BRYAN, Eddie	3y	W	D.C.	08 MAY 1876	Congressional
009258	BRYAN, Infant	1m	C	D.C.	01 OCT 1876	Ebenezer
009792	BRYAN, John V.	44y	W	D.C.	25 NOV 1876	Congressional
004212	BRYAN, William	3m	C	D.C.	20 JUL 1875	Ebenezer
011007	BRYAN, William M.	5y	W	D.C.	16 MAR 1877	Mt. Olivet
003310	BRYAN, Wm. S.	30y	W	D.C.	13 MAY 1875	Congressional
007518	BRYANT, Alice M.	9m	W	D.C.	06 JUN 1876	Congressional
012484	BRYANT, Ann H.	69y	W	Del.	23 JUL 1877	Congressional
007835	BRYANT, Clara	11m	W	D.C.	25 JUN 1876	Mt. Olivet
013494	BRYANT, Cora E.	1y	W	D.C.	13 OCT 1877	Congressional
001454f	BRYANT, Emma	55y	W	Md.	21 DEC 1874	Oak Hill
000837	BRYANT, Fannie	39y	C	Va.	17 OCT 1874	Beckett's
018138	BRYANT, Garrett Daniel	27y	W	S.C.	24 NOV 1878	Congressional
001945	BRYANT, Geo. Edmund	7m	C	D.C.	29 JAN 1875	Young Mens
018027	BRYANT, Helen A.	3y	W	D.C.	12 NOV 1878	Graceland
001146	BRYANT, Henrietta	24y	C	Va.	14 NOV 1874	Potters Field
007874	BRYANT, Infant of George	6d	C	D.C.	27 JUN 1876	Potters Field
002524	BRYANT, Infant of Walker	7d	C	D.C.	11 MAR 1875	Potters Field
020822	BRYANT, Joseph	58y	C	Va.	08 JUL 1879	Potters Field
019305	BRYANT, Mary	58y	W	Va.	07 MAR 1879	Alexandria, Va.
000838	BRYANT, William	17y	W	Va.	17 OCT 1874	Lynchburg, Va.
004344	BRYANT, William C.	9m	C	Va.	28 JUL 1875	Wilson's Farm[1]
014195	BRYANT, William C.	47y	W	Pa.	25 DEC 1877	Potters Field
009105	BRYNE, Margaret	43y	W	Ire.	17 SEP 1876	Mt. Olivet
016500	BRYON, Ada	3y	W	D.C.	08 JUL 1878	Congressional
010011	BRYSON, Araminta	53y	W	Md.	19 DEC 1876	Methodist
002169	BSHOP, Henry Percy	2y	W	D.C.	15 FEB 1875	Oak Hill
003611	BUCH, Samuel H.	30y	W	S.C.	12 JUN 1875	Glenwood
009284	BUCHANAN, Adeline	42y	C	Va.	03 OCT 1876	Grace Church, Md.
000755	BUCHANAN, Celia	60y	C	Va.	08 OCT 1874	Beckett's
014477	BUCHANAN, Chas. Wm.	1y	C	D.C.	19 JAN 1878	Harmony
006675	BUCHANAN, Martha	49y	C	D.C.	15 MAR 1876	Mt. Olivet
018198	BUCHANAN, Robert C., U.S.A.	67y	W	Md.	29 NOV 1878	Rock Creek
020416	BUCHANNAN, Lewis	2m	C	D.C.	13 JUN 1879	Potters Field
009953	BUCHLER, John	56y	W	Ger.	13 DEC 1876	Prospect Hill
002076f	BUCHLY, Rudolph	46y	W	D.C.	08 FEB 1875	Congressional
001554	BUCK, Caroline Belmont	c.55y	W	Ver.	01 JAN 1875	Congressional
004648	BUCK, Ebenezer	65y	W	Mass.	18 AUG 1875	Hospital
005227	BUCK, Margaret	22y	W	Pa.	30 SEP 1875	Rock Creek
003481	BUCKANNON, Christopher Lewis	8m	C	D.C.	29 MAY 1875	Harmony
010307	BUCKEY, Jane	56y	W	D.C.	16 JAN 1877	Oak Hill

[1] Located in Good Hope, D.C.

District of Columbia Death Records, August 1, 1874 to July 31, 1879　　　　　　　　　　　　　47

No.	Name	Age	Race	Birth	Death Date	Burial Place
002756	BUCKHANON, Walter	2y	W	D.C.	27 MAR 1875	Ebenezer
011730	BUCKHIND, Columbus	1y	C	D.C.	28 MAY 1877	Mt. Pleasant Plain
011463	BUCKINGHAM, Leana	46y	W	Va.	30 APR 1877	Congressional
008502	BUCKLER, Mary Alice	2y	W	D.C.	31 JUL 1876	Greenmount, Balt., Md.
007411	BUCKLEY, Ellen	19y	W	D.C.	26 MAY 1876	Mt. Olivet
007980	BUCKLEY, Geo. M.	1y	W	D.C.	03 JUL 1876	Mt. Olivet
000799	BUCKLEY, James S.	64y	W	Md.	13 OCT 1874	Congressional
011694	BUCKLEY, Jeremiah	30y	W	Ire.	24 MAY 1877	Soldier's Home
000110	BUCKLEY, Jobe	3y	C	Va.	08 AUG 1874	Harmony
008666	BUCKLEY, John J.	4m	W	D.C.	12 AUG 1876	Mt. Olivet
005149	BUCKLEY, Mary	67y	W	Ire.	24 SEP 1875	Mt. Olivet
010195	BUCKLEY, Mattie	2y	W	D.C.	06 JAN 1877	Mt. Olivet
008755	BUCKLEY, Michael	37y	W	Ire.	20 AUG 1876	Mt. Olivet
010172	BUCKLEY, William	3y	W	D.C.	04 JAN 1877	Mt. Olivet
002664	BUCKLY, Patrick	3y	W	D.C.	21 MAR 1875	Mt. Olivet
019584	BUCKMAN, Enoch	22y	C	Md.	29 MAR 1879	Potters Field
012464	BUCKMAN, Jacob H.	10m	M	D.C.	22 JUL 1877	Young Mens
013658	BUCKMAN, Martha	3m	W	D.C.	28 OCT 1877	Tennallytown
003273	BUCKMASTER, Jasper N.	30y	W	Ohio	09 MAY 1875	Hospital
015628	BUCKNER, Ages Irene	3m	C	D.C.	06 MAY 1878	Harmony
003462	BUCKNER, Emeley	75y	C	D.C.	28 MAY 1875	Harmony
013031	BUCKNER, Infant of Amanda	11m	C	D.C.	31 AUG 1877	Beckett's
007706	BUCKNER, John Arthur	3m	C	D.C.	18 JUN 1876	Beckett's
016166	BUCKNER, Joseph	1y	C	D.C.	16 JUN 1878	Beckett's
007873	BUCKNER, Lenard	9m	C	D.C.	27 JUN 1876	Harmony
000456	BUCKNER, Margaret	18m	M	D.C.	08 SEP 1874	Beckett's
004490	BUCKNER, Mary E.	8m	C	D.C.	07 AUG 1875	Beckett's
009246	BUCKNER, Sarah V.	1y	W	D.C.	30 SEP 1876	Mt. Zion
008175	BUCKNER, Victoria	1y	C	D.C.	11 JUL 1876	Potters Field
019982	BUDD, Birdie	8m	C	D.C.	04 MAY 1879	Harmony
015819	BUDD, Fannie	5m	C	D.C.	24 MAY 1878	Harmony
004539	BUDD, Ida	11m	C	D.C.	11 AUG 1875	Mt. Pleasant
011948	BUDD, Jessie	1y	C	D.C.	17 JUN 1877	Mt. Pleasant
008819	BUECHLER, Elisabeth	2y	W	D.C.	25 AUG 1876	Prospect Hill
018737	BUELL, Catharine	5y	W	D.C.	20 JAN 1879	Oak Hill
006976	BUERGER, Ferdinot	5m	W	D.C.	10 APR 1876	Prospect Hill
013129	BUFFET, Jacob	6y	C	Md.	09 SEP 1877	Mt. Pleasant
004456	BUHLER, Harry	6y	W	N.J.	05 AUG 1875	Morristown, N.J.
006584	BUIE, David J.	11d	W	D.C.	07 MAR 1876	Congressional
012018	BUIE, Francis	14d	W	D.C.	22 JUN 1877	Congressional
000535	BUIE, Mary E.	28d	W	D.C.	17 SEP 1874	Congressional
017970	BUIE, Maud	1m	W	D.C.	07 NOV 1878	Congressional
020675	BULKLEY, John Wells	5m	W	D.C.	30 JUN 1879	Congressional
007547	BULKLEY, Kate	3y	W	D.C.	08 JUN 1876	Mt. Olivet
000919	BULKLEY, Michael	12d	W	D.C.	25 OCT 1874	Mt. Olivet
016413	BULLEN, William	1y	C	D.C.	03 JUL 1878	Potters Field
010053	BULLOCH, Amanda W.	68y	W	Ver.	22 DEC 1876	Cornish, N.H.
020975	BULLOCH, Lottie	18m	W	D.C.	17 JUL 1879	Glenwood
006330	BULLOND, Lee Thompson	22y	C	W.Va.	13 FEB 1876	Young Mens
017679	BUMBERY, George	80y	C	Va.	09 OCT 1878	Beckett's
020974	BUMBREY, Kate	70y	C	Va.	17 JUL 1879	Prince William Co., Va.
013255	BUMBREY, Richard	19y	C	Va.	20 SEP 1877	Young Mens
003334	BUMBREY, Rosannah	4y	C	D.C.	15 MAY 1875	Moore's
005215	BUMBREY, William	72y	C	Va.	29 SEP 1875	Mt. Pleasant Plain
012925	BUMBRY, Infant of Sarah	8d	C	D.C.	24 AUG 1877	Young Mens
008209	BUNCE, Veaney	7m	W	D.C.	12 JUL 1876	Methodist

No.	Name	Age	Race	Birth	Death Date	Burial Place
003583	BUNDAY, William	2y	C	D.C.	09 JUN 1875	Potters Field
017928	BUNDY, Harry	5y	C	D.C.	02 NOV 1878	Beckett's
014478	BUNDY, Infant of Daniel	7d	C	D.C.	19 JAN 1878	Moore's
010285	BUNDY, Infant of Harrison	1d	C	D.C.	14 JAN 1877	Ebenezer
002777	BUNDY, Infant of Matilda	2d	C	D.C.	28 MAR 1875	Potters Field
003037	BUNDY, Matildia	20y	C	Va.	18 APR 1875	Ebenezer
010171	BUNDY, Moses	80y	C	Va.	04 JAN 1877	Butler's
008714	BUNDY, Susan	8y	C	D.C.	17 AUG 1876	Beckett's
012907	BUNDY, Walter	1y	C	D.C.	22 AUG 1877	Ebenezer
006828	BUNELL, Wm.	4d	C	D.C.	27 MAR 1876	Young Mens
012906	BUNYEA, Emmet Washington	4y	W	D.C.	22 AUG 1877	Congressional
017196	BURCH, Addie Alberta	2y	W	D.C.	26 AUG 1878	Congressional
017895	BURCH, Charles Jesse	58y	W	D.C.	29 OCT 1878	Glenwood
000439	BURCH, Elizer, Mrs.	62y	C	Md.	06 SEP 1874	Beckett's
002596	BURCH, George W.	45y	W	Va.	16 MAR 1875	Presbyterian
018595	BURCH, Henry	26y	C	Md.	07 JAN 1879	Potters Field
007304	BURCH, Ida Virginia	18y	W	D.C.	15 MAY 1876	Congressional
005202	BURCH, Lucinda	30y	C	Md.	28 SEP 1875	Ebenezer
009369	BURCH, Margaret E., Mrs.	54y	W	D.C.	10 OCT 1876	Glenwood
016627	BURCH, Martha	3y	W	D.C.	17 JUL 1878	Moore's
013266	BURCH, Mary V.	1y	W	D.C.	21 SEP 1877	Mt. Olivet
012924	BURCH, Nathaniel R.	8m	W	D.C.	24 AUG 1877	Oak Hill
005213a	BURCH, Richard	88y	W	Md.	20 OCT 1875	Congressional
002552	BURCH, Sallie Rebecca	1y	W	D.C.	13 MAR 1875	Oak Hill
019890	BURCH, Sarah Frances	36y	W	D.C.	25 APR 1879	Mt. Olivet
016371	BURCH, Thomas Edward	3y	W	D.C.	30 JUN 1878	Mt. Olivet
020706	BURCHARD, Abbie Cornelia	26y	W	Conn.	02 JUL 1879	Lebanon, Conn.
002980	BURCHE, Kate Hewitt	22y	W	D.C.	13 APR 1875	Rock Creek
001366	BURCHE, L.M., Mrs.	89y	W	Md.	11 DEC 1874	Rock Creek
008178	BURDEN, Lily Gertrude	1y	W	D.C.	11 JUL 1876	Glenwood
016274	BURDETT, Cora	1y	W	D.C.	22 JUN 1878	Glenwood
016327	BURDETT, Debora	2y	W	D.C.	27 JUN 1878	Glenwood
009601	BURDINE, George	2d	W	D.C.	02 NOV 1876	Congressional
018295	BURELL, Harriet Alice	4y	W	Va.	10 DEC 1878	Rock Creek
010575	BUREN, Julius	c.30y	W	France	10 FEB 1877	Hospital
004345	BURGDORF, Anna	47y	W	Ger.	28 JUL 1875	Hospital
004214	BURGEE, Gertrude	8m	W	D.C.	20 JUL 1875	Glenwood
020433	BURGEE, Infant of John R.	24h	W	D.C.	14 JUN 1879	Glenwood
007454	BURGER, Eleanor, d/o J.G.S.	7m	W	D.C.	01 JUN 1876	Congressional
007491	BURGER, Harry Candy	7m	W	D.C.	04 JUN 1876	Congressional
020293	BURGER, Jacob F.	63y	W	Va.	04 JUN 1879	Congressional
017223	BURGESS, Blanche W.	6y	W	D.C.	28 AUG 1878	Congressional
004121	BURGESS, Edith M.	2m	W	D.C.	14 JUL 1875	Congressional
007369	BURGESS, Elizebeth Matilda	27y	W	Md.	22 MAY 1876	Congressional
008439	BURGESS, Enoch	8y	C	Md.	27 JUL 1876	Jones Chapel
016666	BURGESS, Geo. Washington	88y	C	Md.	19 JUL 1878	Potters Field
008675	BURGESS, Grace C.	3m	W	D.C.	13 AUG 1876	Congressional
016465	BURGESS, Harvey C.	5m	W	D.C.	06 JUL 1878	Congressional
002844	BURGESS, James	2y	C	D.C.	02 APR 1875	Beckett's
000054	BURGESS, John	9m	C	D.C.	04 AUG 1874	Mt. Pleasant
015589	BURGESS, John	59y	W	Md.	03 MAY 1878	Rock Creek
008724	BURGESS, Mary E.	10m	W	D.C.	18 AUG 1876	Congressional
016897	BURGESS, Preston Tucker	8y	W	D.C.	04 AUG 1878	Congressional
010804	BURGESS, Samuel J.T.	2m	W	D.C.	27 FEB 1877	Congressional
001118	BURGESS, Silas	37y	C	Va.	12 NOV 1874	Beckett's
020773	BURGESS, Susan Maria	9m	M	D.C.	05 JUL 1879	Washington Asylum

District of Columbia Death Records, August 1, 1874 to July 31, 1879   49

No.	Name	Age	Race	Birth	Death Date	Burial Place
012068	BURGESS, Willard	8m	W	D.C.	26 JUN 1877	Chester, Pa.
007220	BURGUSSON, Chas.	39y	C	Va.	06 MAY 1876	Potters Field
002964	BURGWINE, Georgianna	13m	C	Md.	11 APR 1875	Berry's Farm
004843	BURHORST, Frank	19y	W	Ind.	30 AUG 1875	Congressional
020214	BURK, artha	65y	W	Ire.	28 MAY 1879	Mt. Olivet
007975	BURK, Benjamin	22y	C	U.S.	02 JUL 1876	Potters Field
007576	BURK, George H.	12m	C	D.C.	10 JUN 1876	Young Mens
001435	BURK, Mary	20y	C	D.C.	19 DEC 1874	Mt. Zion
009005	BURK, Rodoup	6y	C	D.C.	08 SEP 1876	Mt. Pleasant
015195	BURK, Thomas	41y	W	Ire.	27 MAR 1878	Hospital, Government
019498	BURKE, Bridget	39y	W	Ire.	22 MAR 1879	Mt. Olivet
016895	BURKE, Briget	56y	W	Ire.	04 AUG 1878	Mt. Olivet
013220	BURKE, Eliza	66y	W	Ire.	16 SEP 1877	Mt. Olivet
020333	BURKE, Elvira W.	31y	W	Md.	08 JUN 1879	Glenwood
006359	BURKE, George McD.	6y	W	D.C.	15 FEB 1876	Glenwood
004193	BURKE, James	43y	C	Va.	19 JUL 1875	Harmony
006565	BURKE, James	2h	W	D.C.	06 MAR 1876	Holy Rood
003082	BURKE, James Thomas	33y	C	W.I.	22 APR 1875	Ebenezer
003067f	BURKE, John	6y	W	Pa.	08 SEP 1853	Oak Hill
006566	BURKE, John	12h	W	D.C.	06 MAR 1876	Holy Rood
014748	BURKE, John E.	35y	W	Va.	12 FEB 1878	Langley, Va.
002861	BURKE, Josiah	60y	C	Ga.	03 APR 1875	Potters Field
000706	BURKE, Julia	45y	W	Ire.	03 OCT 1874	Mt. Olivet
000738	BURKE, Lizzie	39y	W	Ire.	07 OCT 1874	Washington Asylum
007967	BURKE, Mary Catherine	4m	C	D.C.	02 JUL 1876	Mt. Olivet
015368	BURKE, Nellie	19y	C	Va.	12 APR 1878	Mt. Pleasant
012421	BURKE, Patrick	34y	W	Ire.	19 JUL 1877	Washington Asylum
017887	BURKE, Sallie C.	39y	W	Va.	28 OCT 1878	Rock Creek
009913	BURKE, Thomas	79y	W	Ire.	09 DEC 1876	Mt. Olivet
009121	BURKHARDT, A.F.	4m	W	D.C.	18 SEP 1876	Prospect Hill
008412	BURKHARDT, John M.	40y	W	Switz.	25 JUL 1876	Prospect Hill
008940	BURKHARDT, Minnie	2y	W	N.J.	02 SEP 1876	Prospect Hill
014357	BURKHART, Louis	6y	W	Pa.	08 JAN 1878	Hebrew
011160	BURKLEY, Lottie	37y	C	Va.	30 MAR 1877	Young Mens
010933	BURKLEY, Martha Ellen	11y	C	D.C.	09 MAR 1877	Young Mens
017413	BURL, Samuel	1y	C	D.C.	15 SEP 1878	Beckett's
004725	BURLEIGH, Hagar A.	36y	C	Va.	23 AUG 1875	Young Mens
011095	BURLEY, Isaiah Thomas	28y	C	D.C.	23 MAR 1877	Mt. Pleasant
019727	BURLEY, John Henry Wesley	46y	C	Md.	11 APR 1879	Graceland
002098	BURLEY, Millie	2d	C	D.C.	09 FEB 1875	Young Mens
000364	BURLEY, Sarah	78y	C	Md.	29 AUG 1874	Young Mens
020665	BURLL, Elizabeth	77y	C	Md.	29 JUN 1879	Mt. Olivet
003567f	BURNELL, Cobb	21d	W	Va.	09 APR 1873	Congressional
003566f	BURNELL, Elizabeth	24y	W	D.C.	17 FEB 1873	Congressional
006902	BURNELL, Frank	33y	W	N.Y.	03 APR 1876	Mt. Olivet
003565f	BURNELL, James Alexander	3y	W	Va.	29 AUG 1872	Congressional
020748	BURNETT, Alice	3y	W	D.C.	04 JUL 1879	Mt. Pleasant Plain
018137	BURNETT, Enoch	81y	W	Md.	24 NOV 1878	Glenwood
007854	BURNETT, Francis	3m	W	D.C.	26 JUN 1876	Holy Rood
018981	BURNETT, Henrietta	3m	C	D.C.	07 FEB 1879	Beckett's
016970	BURNETT, John	1m	C	D.C.	09 AUG 1878	Beckett's
009730	BURNETT, Laura C.	25y	W	D.C.	18 NOV 1876	Mt. Olivet
017249	BURNETT, Levinia	71y	C	Va.	29 AUG 1878	Beckett's
013375	BURNETT, Margarett	77y	W	N.Y	02 OCT 1877	Glenwood
013217	BURNETT, Maria	10d	C	D.C.	16 SEP 1877	Beckett's
007394	BURNETT, Martha	3d	C	D.C.	24 MAY 1876	Potters Field

District of Columbia Death Records, August 1, 1874 to July 31, 1879

No.	Name	Age	Race	Birth	Death Date	Burial Place
008695	BURNETT, Mary	7m	C	D.C.	15 AUG 1876	Ebenezer
007395	BURNETT, Mary	3d	C	D.C.	24 MAY 1876	Potters Field
005049	BURNETT, Mary Gertrude	22y	W	Pa.	15 SEP 1875	Philadelphia, Pa.
014833	BURNETT, Virginia	28y	C	Va.	21 FEB 1878	Harmony
009256	BURNETT, Walter	9m	C	D.C.	01 OCT 1876	Harmony
005108	BURNETT, William F.	11m	C	D.C.	20 SEP 1875	Harmony
015843	BURNHAM, Joseph	c.50y	W	N.H.	26 MAY 1878	Norwich, Ver.
017980	BURNS, Bridget	50y	W	Ire.	08 NOV 1878	Mt. Olivet
014982	BURNS, Charles W.	26y	C	Va.	08 MAR 1878	Young Mens
009375	BURNS, David	53y	W	Ire.	11 OCT 1876	Mt. Olivet
010041	BURNS, Elias	60y	C	N.H.	21 DEC 1876	Potters Field
002385	BURNS, Elizabeth	37y	W	Md.	02 MAR 1875	Mt. Olivet
001246	BURNS, Ellen	18d	C	D.C.	27 NOV 1874	Young Mens
011958	BURNS, Florence E.	11m	W	D.C.	18 JUN 1877	Oak Hill
007474	BURNS, James	11y	W	D.C.	02 JUN 1876	Mt. Olivet
016002	BURNS, John	65y	W	Ire.	04 JUN 1878	Alexandria, Va.
019158	BURNS, Mary	c.60y	W	D.C.	23 FEB 1879	Mt. Olivet
001534	BURNS, Mary Jane	2y	C	D.C.	29 DEC 1874	Young Mens
009574	BURNS, Mary Jane	22y	W	N.Y.	30 OCT 1876	Mt. Olivet
019566	BURNS, Millard F.	32y	W	D.C.	27 MAR 1879	Presbyterian
018368	BURNS, Thomas	54y	W	Ire.	18 DEC 1878	Mt. Olivet
001330	BURNS, William	33y	W	U.S.	07 DEC 1874	Glenwood/Arlington
016922	BURNS, Wm.	1y	W	D.C.	05 AUG 1878	Mt. Olivet
015978	BURNSIDE, Kate	11m	C	D.C.	03 JUN 1878	Mt. Olivet
015288	BURNSIDES, Lizzie	9m	W	D.C.	05 APR 1878	Mt. Olivet
006174	BURR, Charles C.	55y	W	Conn.	29 JAN 1876	Hartford, Conn.
008837	BURR, George L.	1y	W	D.C.	26 AUG 1876	Congressional
003337	BURR, Henry C.	31y	W	D.C.	16 MAY 1875	Oak Hill
000636	BURR, Mary E.	11m	W	D.C.	25 SEP 1874	Oak Hill
018375	BURR, Richard W.	49y	W	D.C.	19 DEC 1878	Rock Creek
011486	BURRELL, Fanny	29y	C	Va.	01 MAY 1877	Young Mens
000910	BURRELL, John	72y	C	Va.	23 OCT 1874	Beckett's
017290	BURRELL, Thomas	8y	C	Va.	02 SEP 1878	Hillsdale
013979	BURRILL, Augustine	11m	C	D.C.	01 DEC 1877	Young Mens
001115	BURRILL, Silvey	30y	C	Va.	10 NOV 1874	Young Mens
017745	BURRISS, Hester	63y	C	Md.	15 OCT 1878	Mt. Olivet
007989	BURROUGHS, Cordelia	31y	W	N.Y.	03 JUL 1876	Congressional
013004	BURROUGHS, H. Wailes	47y	W	Md.	29 AUG 1877	Congressional
006389	BURROUGHS, Wm. T.	67y	W	D.C.	17 FEB 1876	Holy Rood
007587	BURROW, Mary P.	77y	W	Md.	11 JUN 1876	Presbyterian
004328	BURROWS, Francis Thomas	10m	W	D.C.	27 JUL 1875	Presbyterian
004154	BURROWS, Hezekiah	65y	W	Md.	16 JUL 1875	Presbyterian
016842	BURROWS, Mary	1m	C	D.C.	31 JUL 1878	Moore's
020575	BURROWS, Percival	7m	W	D.C.	23 JUN 1879	Tennallytown
021031	BURT, Alice Penrose	5y	W	D.C.	21 JUL 1879	Mt. Olivet
011869	BURT, Minerva W.	69y	W	N.Y.	12 JUN 1877	East Saganaw, Mich.
003515	BURTON, Carrie	6m	C	D.C.	03 JUN 1875	Alexandria, Va.
001407	BURTON, Cary	25y	M	Va.	16 DEC 1874	Alexandria, Va.
011352	BURTON, Henry H.	36y	W	Pa.	16 APR 1877	Boston, Mass.
006390	BURY, John Calvert	5m	W	D.C.	17 FEB 1876	Glenwood
005151	BURY, John F.	6y	W	D.C.	24 SEP 1875	Congressional
013638	BURY, Julia Rebecca	11y	C	D.C.	26 OCT 1877	Smith's
008884	BUSCHER, Elizabeth	27y	W	D.C.	30 AUG 1876	St. Mary's
017657	BUSCHER, Francis	12y	W	Md.	07 OCT 1878	St. Mary's
005040	BUSCHER, Mary Elizabeth	1d	W	D.C.	14 SEP 1875	St. Mary's
002304	BUSCZARD, L.S.	28y	W	Ohio	24 FEB 1875	Cincinnati, Ohio

District of Columbia Death Records, August 1, 1874 to July 31, 1879   51

No.	Name	Age	Race	Birth	Death Date	Burial Place
007210	BUSEY, Clarance	9m	W	D.C.	05 MAY 1876	Congressional
007532	BUSEY, Milo Baily	10m	W	D.C.	07 JUN 1876	Congressional
007132	BUSEY, Sarah	3y	W	D.C.	27 APR 1876	Congressional
010532	BUSH, Mary A.	36y	W	Mass.	05 FEB 1877	Mt. Olivet
005360	BUSH, Rebecca	31y	W	D.C.	05 NOV 1875	Congressional
002225	BUSH, Richard	80y	C	Md.	18 FEB 1875	Potters Field
001917	BUSH, Wm. A.	11m	C	D.C.	27 JAN 1875	Ebenezer
008332	BUSHBY, Catharine Ann	58y	W	D.C.	19 JUL 1876	Glenwood
001125	BUSHER, Henry	53y	W	Ger.	11 NOV 1874	St. Mary's
008662	BUSHING, Hermina	17y	W	D.C.	12 AUG 1876	Prospect Hill
016726	BUSHMAN, Joseph	3d	W	D.C.	23 JUL 1878	Glenwood
015715	BUSSEL, Annie	3m	C	D.C.	13 MAY 1878	Beckett's
020127	BUSSEY, Mary	17m	C	D.C.	17 MAY 1879	Mt. Pleasant
014909	BUSSINS, Wm. F.	21y	W	D.C.	01 MAR 1878	Glenwood
003051	BUSSY, Simon	20y	C	Va.	19 APR 1875	Mt. Olivet
017412	BUSTER, Jeannette Josephine	4y	W	D.C.	15 SEP 1878	Stafford, Ver.
016445	BUSTOW, Richard	14y	C	D.C.	05 JUL 1878	Mt. Olivet
016123	BUSY, Martha	25y	M	D.C.	12 JUN 1878	Mt. Zion
011698	BUTCHER, Caroline	45y	C	Md.	25 MAY 1877	Harmony
011884	BUTCHER, Ida	9m	C	D.C.	13 JUN 1877	Beckett's
001147	BUTCHER, Isabela	3m	C	D.C.	14 NOV 1874	Beckett's
014608	BUTCHER, Lafayette Burk	7m	C	D.C.	31 JAN 1878	Harmony
000160	BUTCHER, Mary M.	1m	C	D.C.	12 AUG 1874	Young Mens
004439	BUTLAR, Richard	60y	C	Md.	04 AUG 1875	Moore's
013458	BUTLER, Alcinda M.	49y	W	Va.	10 OCT 1877	Frederick, Md.
000041	BUTLER, Alice Ardella	4m	C	D.C.	03 AUG 1874	Harmony
014766	BUTLER, Ann	60y	W	Ire.	15 FEB 1878	Mt. Olivet
003817	BUTLER, Ann Virginia	29y	C	D.C.	25 JUN 1875	Mt. Olivet
020803	BUTLER, Annie	14y	C	D.C.	07 JUL 1879	Potters Field
010486	BUTLER, Annie E.	6m	C	D.C.	02 FEB 1877	Freedmen's Village
018804	BUTLER, Arthur	11m	C	D.C.	25 JAN 1879	Mt. Pleasant
002182	BUTLER, Belle	5m	M	D.C.	15 FEB 1875	Harmony
008195	BUTLER, Benjamin	4m	C	Md.	12 JUL 1876	Ebenezer
013659	BUTLER, Berlinda	80y	C	Md.	28 OCT 1877	Holy Rood
011337	BUTLER, Bridget	40y	W	Ire.	15 APR 1877	Holy Rood
016764	BUTLER, Cassy	2y	C	D.C.	26 JUL 1878	Mt. Olivet
004975	BUTLER, Ch. S.	1y	M	D.C.	10 SEP 1875	Harmony
004459	BUTLER, Charity	10m	C	D.C.	05 AUG 1875	Mt. Olivet
000058	BUTLER, Charles	5m	C	D.C.	04 AUG 1874	Mt. Pleasant
003994	BUTLER, Charles	35y	C	W.Va.	04 JUL 1875	Young Mens
011293	BUTLER, Charles	2y	C	D.C.	10 APR 1877	Mt. Pleasant
021072	BUTLER, Charles E.	7m	C	D.C.	24 JUL 1879	Harmony
011805	BUTLER, Charles Robert	70y	C	Md.	05 JUN 1877	Potters Field
016578	BUTLER, Charlotte	1m	C	D.C.	13 JUL 1878	Moore's
008955	BUTLER, Charlotte E.	2m	C	D.C.	03 SEP 1876	Mt. Olivet
010717	BUTLER, Chas.	10y	C	D.C.	21 FEB 1877	Ebenezer
011223	BUTLER, Chas. H.	1y	C	D.C.	05 APR 1877	Beckett's
006063	BUTLER, Chloe Ann	55y	C	D.C.	19 JAN 1876	Harmony
008138	BUTLER, Cornelia	40y	C	Va.	10 JUL 1876	Potters Field
010132	BUTLER, Daniel	37y	C	D.C.	31 DEC 1876	Mt. Olivet
010215	BUTLER, Eleanor	14d	C	D.C.	07 JAN 1877	Mt. Olivet
006151	BUTLER, Eliza	37y	C	Md.	27 JAN 1876	Potters Field
003172	BUTLER, Emily	17y	C	Md.	29 APR 1875	Charles Co., Md.
014853	BUTLER, Emily	53y	C	Va.	23 FEB 1878	Mt. Pleasant
004438	BUTLER, Eugene Francis	4m	W	D.C.	04 AUG 1875	Congressional
006806	BUTLER, Ferdinand	52y	W	D.C.	25 MAR 1876	Oak Hill

District of Columbia Death Records, August 1, 1874 to July 31, 1879

No.	Name	Age	Race	Birth	Death Date	Burial Place
015832	BUTLER, Frank	3y	C	D.C.	25 MAY 1878	Potters Field
020592	BUTLER, Geo. Thomas	1m	C	D.C.	24 JUN 1879	Beckett's
010320	BUTLER, Georgana	1y	C	D.C.	17 JAN 1877	Young Mens
005788	BUTLER, George	6m	C	D.C.	19 DEC 1875	Mt. Zion
005260	BUTLER, George	3m	C	D.C.	25 OCT 1875	Ebenezer
017265	BUTLER, George	21d	C	D.C.	31 AUG 1878	Mt. Zion
016221	BUTLER, George W.	3y	W	D.C.	19 JUN 1878	Congressional
001521	BUTLER, George Washington	27y	M	D.C.	28 DEC 1874	Harmony
015619	BUTLER, Gracie	4y	C	D.C.	05 MAY 1878	Mt. Zion
001797	BUTLER, H.	65y	C	Md.	19 JAN 1875	Mt. Zion
012893	BUTLER, Henry D.	1y	C	D.C.	21 AUG 1877	Harmony
009976	BUTLER, Ida	14d	C	D.C.	16 DEC 1876	Holy Rood
015329	BUTLER, Ida	5y	C	D.C.	09 APR 1878	Beckett's
009678	BUTLER, Infant of Buck	1m	C	D.C.	12 NOV 1876	Potters Field
018777	BUTLER, Infant of Chas.	2d	C	D.C.	23 JAN 1879	Potters Field
014385	BUTLER, Infant of Cornelius	12h	C	D.C.	11 JAN 1878	Potters Field
011840	BUTLER, Infant of Ignatius	8d	C	D.C.	08 JUN 1877	Mt. Olivet
012987	BUTLER, Infant of L.J.	3h	W	D.C.	28 AUG 1877	Congressional
012988	BUTLER, Infant of L.J.	3½h	W	D.C.	28 AUG 1877	Congressional
014910	BUTLER, Infant of Levi	13d	C	D.C.	01 MAR 1878	Potters Field
015802	BUTLER, Infant of Robert	30min	C	D.C.	22 MAY 1878	Beckett's
020303	BUTLER, Isadora	5y	C	D.C.	05 JUN 1879	Beckett's
000101	BUTLER, James	27y	C	Md.	08 AUG 1874	--
002974	BUTLER, James	5y	C	D.C.	12 APR 1875	Potters Field
002297	BUTLER, James	75y	C	Md.	23 FEB 1875	Mt. Olivet
016687	BUTLER, James B.	c.60y	M	Md.	20 JUL 1878	Mt. Olivet
005834	BUTLER, James E.	9y	C	D.C.	23 DEC 1875	Mt. Zion
013539	BUTLER, James H.	5y	C	D.C.	17 OCT 1877	Mt. Zion
016939	BUTLER, Jane	87y	C	D.C.	07 AUG 1878	Mt. Olivet
016938	BUTLER, John	1h	C	D.C.	07 AUG 1878	Holy Rood
004665	BUTLER, John F.	11m	W	D.C.	19 AUG 1875	Mt. Olivet
005083a	BUTLER, John Francis	1y	C	D.C.	08 OCT 1875	Moore's
001295	BUTLER, John R.	7m	C	D.C.	02 DEC 1874	Potters Field
002018	BUTLER, Joseph	55y	C	Md.	04 FEB 1875	Potters Field
009763	BUTLER, Joseph	5y	C	D.C.	21 NOV 1876	Harmony
021030	BUTLER, Laura Lu	70y	W	D.C.	21 JUL 1879	Congressional
002525	BUTLER, Luvina	6m	C	D.C.	11 MAR 1875	Young Mens
017986	BUTLER, Mamie	2y	C	D.C.	09 NOV 1878	Payne's
010893	BUTLER, Margaret	5m	C	D.C.	07 MAR 1877	Moore's
005949	BUTLER, Margret	75y	C	Md.	06 JAN 1876	Baltimore, Md.
016826	BUTLER, Maria	28y	C	Md.	30 JUL 1878	Potters Field
008807	BUTLER, Mariah C.	35y	C	Va.	24 AUG 1876	Harmony
019827	BUTLER, Martha	2y	C	D.C.	19 APR 1879	Harmony
014467	BUTLER, Martha Ellen	36y	C	Va.	18 JAN 1878	Potters Field
003818	BUTLER, Mary	9m	C	D.C.	25 JUN 1875	Ebenezer
005022	BUTLER, Mary	73y	M	Va.	13 SEP 1875	Mt. Olivet
016238	BUTLER, Mary E.	c.40y	C	Md.	21 JUN 1878	Moore's
004574	BUTLER, Mary Ellen	1y	C	D.C.	13 AUG 1875	Mt. Olivet
009136	BUTLER, Mary Jane	48y	C	D.C.	19 SEP 1876	Potters Field
001018	BUTLER, Matthew	55y	C	Md.	02 NOV 1874	Potters Field
001069	BUTLER, Melvina	20y	C	Md.	06 NOV 1874	Beckett's
000306	BUTLER, Nathan	4y	M	D.C.	24 AUG 1874	Potters Field
011358	BUTLER, Nathaniel	12d	C	D.C.	17 APR 1877	Young Mens
013960	BUTLER, Nellie	113y	C	Md.	29 NOV 1877	Carroll Chapel, Md.
000956	BUTLER, Nora	7y	C	D.C.	27 OCT 1874	Mt. Zion
001072	BUTLER, Pernell	12h	C	D.C.	06 NOV 1874	Beckett's

District of Columbia Death Records, August 1, 1874 to July 31, 1879   53

No.	Name	Age	Race	Birth	Death Date	Burial Place
012849	BUTLER, Rachel	33y	C	Va.	17 AUG 1877	Washington Asylum
019879	BUTLER, Robert	5y	C	D.C.	24 APR 1879	Beckett's
000007	BUTLER, Sarah	23y	C	Md.	01 AUG 1874	Harmony
011617	BUTLER, Sarah	68y	W	Ire.	16 MAY 1877	Oak Hill
011739	BUTLER, Sarah	48y	C	Va.	29 MAY 1877	Ebenezer
014879	BUTLER, Sarah	60y	C	Md.	26 FEB 1878	Mt. Olivet
004306	BUTLER, Sophia	26y	C	D.C.	26 JUL 1875	Brightwood
020114	BUTLER, Stewart	53y	C	Md.	16 MAY 1879	Potters Field
017583	BUTLER, Strother	80y	C	Va.	01 OCT 1878	Baptist
012972	BUTLER, Thomas O.	5h	C	D.C.	27 AUG 1877	Beckett's
012722	BUTLER, Thomas S.	68y	W	Va.	08 AUG 1877	Marshall Hall, Md.
006540	BUTLER, Walter	c.63y	C	Md.	04 MAR 1876	Harmony
000106	BUTLER, William	18y	C	D.C.	08 AUG 1874	Harmony
006081	BUTLER, William	85y	C	Va.	21 JAN 1876	Baptist
015361	BUTLER, William	8m	C	D.C.	11 APR 1878	Mt. Olivet
018533	BUTLER, William Edward	3y	W	D.C.	01 JAN 1879	Graceland
010394	BUTLER, William George F.C.	1m	C	D.C.	24 JAN 1877	Holy Rood
019737	BUTLER, William Henry	41y	C	Va.	12 APR 1879	Graceland
021143	BUTLER, William Howard	1m	C	D.C.	29 JUL 1879	Mt. Olivet
005615	BUTLER, Willie	1m	C	D.C.	01 DEC 1875	Harmony
020136	BUTLER, Willie	2y	C	D.C.	18 MAY 1879	Mt. Pleasant
017077	BUTLER, Wm.	1y	C	D.C.	17 AUG 1878	Mt. Zion
012706	BUTLER, Wm. J.	3y	C	D.C.	07 AUG 1877	Mt. Olivet
004911	BUTS, Anna Eliza	2y	W	D.C.	05 SEP 1875	Prospect Hill
012117	BUTT, William B.	48y	W	Md.	29 JUN 1877	Rock Creek
015737	BUTTERFIELD, Elizabeth Catherine	3y	W	D.C.	16 MAY 1878	Prospect Hill
013716	BUTTLER, Edwin	11m	C	D.C.	03 NOV 1877	Beckett's
014102	BUTTLER, Elisha	24y	C	Md.	15 DEC 1877	Beckett's
010599	BUTTLER, Lula	4y	C	D.C.	12 FEB 1877	Young Mens
001468	BUTTLER, Matilda	100c	C	Md.	23 DEC 1874	Smith's
012619	BUTTONER, Emma	7m	C	D.C.	31 JUL 1877	Mt. Zion
003873	BUTTS, James Wesley	43y	W	W.Va.	27 JUN 1875	Knoxville, Md.
017893	BUTTS, Susan	48y	C	Va.	29 OCT 1878	Mt. Pleasant
006808	BUTTS, Wm. Henry	1y	W	D.C.	25 MAR 1876	Alexandria, Methodist
020375	BUXTON, Otis S.	60y	W	N.Y.	10 JUN 1879	Congressional
005122a	BYAS, Joseph Hunter	1y	M	D.C.	13 OCT 1875	Potters Field
018351	BYBE, Eliza	22y	C	Md.	15 DEC 1878	Potters Field
018367	BYERS, Richard	11d	C	D.C.	18 DEC 1878	Beckett's
004976	BYNAN, Ella	18y	W	D.C.	10 SEP 1875	Congressional
006688	BYNG, Frederick	3m	C	D.C.	16 MAR 1876	Harmony
020292	BYNG, John	69y	W	Md.	04 JUN 1879	Oak Hill
007115	BYNG, Robert	53y	C	S.C.	26 APR 1876	Harmony
001981	BYRD, Harry J.	27y	W	Md.	01 FEB 1875	Congressional
006012	BYRNE, Charles	c.60y	W	Ire.	14 JAN 1876	Mt. Olivet
003576	BYRNE, Eva	6m	W	D.C.	09 JUN 1875	Congressional
006445	BYRNE, Henry W.	9m	W	D.C.	23 FEB 1876	Auburn, N.Y.
016313	BYRNE, Mary	12y	W	D.C.	26 JUN 1878	Mt. Olivet
002535	BYRNES, Annie E.	1y	W	N.J.	12 MAR 1875	Mt. Olivet
015392	BYRNES, James William	11y	W	D.C.	14 APR 1878	Glenwood
014365	BYRNS, Annie F.	26y	W	D.C.	09 JAN 1878	Congressional
013951	BYRNS, Thomas	17y	W	D.C.	28 NOV 1877	Mt. Olivet
020193	BYRON, Elizabeth E.	52y	W	Ber.	25 MAY 1879	Glenwood
012083	BYRON, John, Sr.	77y	W	Va.	27 JUN 1877	Congressional
020727	BYSON, John	2y	W	D.C.	03 JUL 1879	Congressional

District of Columbia Death Records, August 1, 1874 to July 31, 1879

No.	Name	Age	Race	Birth	Death Date	Burial Place
C						
006988	CABEL, Frank Edward	1y	W	D.C.	11 APR 1876	Alexandria, Va.
006695	CADY, Annie	35y	W	Ire.	16 MAR 1876	Holy Rood
019739	CADY, Infant of B.J.	11h	W	D.C.	12 APR 1879	Congressional
014971	CADY, John	85y	W	Ire.	07 MAR 1878	Holy Rood
008381	CADY, Margaret	6m	W	D.C.	22 JUL 1876	Holy Rood
009174	CADY, Margaret	70y	W	Ire.	23 SEP 1876	Holy Rood
012115	CADY, Martin	42y	W	Ire.	29 JUN 1877	Holy Rood
012287	CADY, Michael	40y	W	Ire.	09 JUL 1877	Holy Rood
000997	CADY, Patrick	70y	W	Ire.	31 OCT 1874	Holy Rood
018503	CADY, Sarah	31y	W	Ire.	29 DEC 1878	Holy Rood
005635	CADY, Thomas	4m	W	D.C.	03 DEC 1875	Holy Rood
014081	CAFFREY, Nicholas, Jr.	4d	W	D.C.	13 DEC 1877	Mt. Olivet
011876	CAGAY, John Thomas	5y	C	D.C.	12 JUN 1877	Mt. Olivet
020807	CAHIL, John James	7m	W	D.C.	07 JUL 1879	Mt. Olivet
012283	CAHILL, Catherine	22y	W	Tex.	09 JUL 1877	Mt. Olivet
015110	CAHILL, Edith B.	1y	W	D.C.	18 MAR 1878	Oak Hill
007372	CAHILL, Martin	32y	W	Ire.	22 MAY 1876	Soldier's Home
016015	CAIN, Ella Leo Caddie	11y	C	D.C.	05 JUN 1878	Graceland
015067	CALAHAN, Mary E.	21y	W	D.C.	14 MAR 1878	Holy Rood
010068	CALBERT, Francis	c.70y	C	Md.	25 DEC 1876	Young Mens
006635	CALDWELL, Alice Ames	14y	W	Mass.	11 MAR 1876	West Bridgewater, Mass.
007856	CALDWELL, Alonzo	6m	C	D.C.	26 JUN 1876	Mt. Pleasant
017300	CALDWELL, John	8y	W	D.C.	02 SEP 1878	Oak Hill
011773	CALDWELL, Margaret	3y	W	D.C.	01 JUN 1877	Oak Hill
014972	CALDWELL, Mariah H.	81y	W	Va.	07 MAR 1878	Congressional
018230	CALDWELL, Mary Letitia	8m	W	D.C.	03 DEC 1878	Shade Gap, Pa.
010160	CALDWELL, Sarah V.	77y	W	Va.	03 JAN 1877	Oak Hill
011817	CALDWELL, Tacy	c.75y	W	Va.	06 JUN 1877	Glenwood
011998	CALDWELL, William	1y	W	D.C.	21 JUN 1877	Oak Hill
011614	CALHOUN, Charles B.	2y	W	D.C.	16 MAY 1877	Presbyterian
014328	CALHOUN, Gracie J.	4y	W	D.C.	05 JAN 1878	Presbyterian
000598	CALHOUN, Stephen L.	49y	W	N.Y.	22 SEP 1874	Presbyterian
019361	CALLAGHAN, Wm. Mattingly	16m	W	D.C.	11 MAR 1879	Mt. Olivet
000541f	CALLAHAN, Alice	4m	W	Md.	17 SEP 1874	Mt. Olivet
005571	CALLAHAN, John	35y	W	Ire.	26 NOV 1875	Mt. Olivet
011981	CALLAHAN, Maggie	2m	W	D.C.	20 JUN 1877	Mt. Olivet
018147	CALLAHAN, Maggie	7y	W	Mo.	25 NOV 1878	Holy Rood
019556	CALLAHAN, Matthew Jarboe	6y	W	Md.	26 MAR 1879	Mt. Olivet
008473	CALLAHAN, Mercano A.	2m	W	D.C.	29 JUL 1876	Pottstown, Pa.
013941	CALLAHAN, Michael	46y	W	Ire.	27 NOV 1877	Soldier's Home
002435	CALLAHAN, P.T.	9y	W	D.C.	05 MAR 1875	Holy Rood
005217	CALLAHAN, Patrick	103y	W	Ire.	29 SEP 1875	Mt. Olivet
006456	CALLAHAN, Redmond	52y	W	Ire.	24 FEB 1876	Alexandria, Catholic
013459	CALLAHAN, Thomas	2y	W	D.C.	10 OCT 1877	Westmoreland Co., Va.
012372	CALLAN, Annie G.	1y	W	D.C.	15 JUL 1877	Mt. Olivet
004692	CALLAN, Edward N.	30y	W	D.C.	21 AUG 1875	Mt. Olivet
000371	CALLAN, Lawrence Earnest	11m	W	D.C.	30 AUG 1874	Mt. Olivet
000452	CALLAN, Margaret Eliz.	30y	W	Ire.	08 SEP 1874	Mt. Olivet
012741	CALLAN, Sarah	6m	W	D.C.	09 AUG 1877	Mt. Olivet
018569	CALLISHER, Samuel Asher	2y	W	D.C.	05 JAN 1879	Washington Hebrew
010260	CALLISS, James H.	2	C	D.C.	12 JAN 1877	Potters Field
014779	CALVER, Louis T.	7m	W	D.C.	16 FEB 1878	Congressional
009321	CALVERT, Charles	19y	C	Md.	06 OCT 1876	Jones Chapel
017930	CALVERT, Eleanora	27y	W	Md.	02 NOV 1878	Rosenville, Md.

District of Columbia Death Records, August 1, 1874 to July 31, 1879

No.	Name	Age	Race	Birth	Death Date	Burial Place
012539	CALVERT, Henrietta	18y	C	Md.	26 JUL 1877	Jones Chapel
005007	CALVERT, Infant of Mary	7d	C	D.C.	12 SEP 1875	Potters Field
008378	CALVERT, Mary Alice	11m	C	D.C.	22 JUL 1876	Ebenezer
002364	CAMBELL, Charity	18y	C	Va.	28 FEB 1875	Ebenezer
004107	CAMBELL, David	6m	C	D.C.	13 JUL 1875	Ebenezer
014844	CAMBELL, Mayr Jane	13y	C	Va.	22 FEB 1878	Young Mens
016871	CAMBELL, Nellie	1y	C	D.C.	02 AUG 1878	Beckett's
008787	CAMEL, Eugene	1y	C	D.C.	23 AUG 1876	Potters Field
012026	CAMEL, Lucy	1y	C	D.C.	23 JUN 1877	Beckett's
003965f	CAMERON, Charles C.	76y	W	W.Va.	04 OCT 1865	Oak Hill
021075	CAMERON, J.W.	66y	W	Pa.	24 JUL 1879	Sinking Valley, Pa.
009841	CAMERON, James	c.50y	W	Scot.	01 DEC 1876	Congressional
002196	CAMERON, Mary Frazier	41y	W	Md.	16 FEB 1875	Holy Rood
000488f	CAMERON, Mary G.	26y	W	Md.	12 SEP 1874	Congressional
011711	CAMERON, Nelly	89y	C	Va.	26 MAY 1877	Harmony
009363	CAMMACK, Christopher	44y	W	D.C.	10 OCT 1876	Oak Hill
011478	CAMMACK, Edmond	41y	W	D.C.	01 MAY 1877	Oak Hill
014427	CAMMACK, Edmund	82y	W	Eng.	15 JAN 1878	Oak Hill
018550	CAMMACK, Forence	1d	W	D.C.	03 JAN 1879	Congressional
008973	CAMMEL, John	40y	C	Md.	05 SEP 1876	Good Hope
008396	CAMP, Rhoda	78y	W	N.Y.	24 JUL 1876	Sandusky, Ohio
017182	CAMPBELL, Ann May	6m	C	D.C.	25 AUG 1878	Beckett's
008550	CAMPBELL, Annie	8m	C	D.C.	04 AUG 1876	Ebenezer
016261	CAMPBELL, Benjamin Dixen	4m	W	D.C.	22 JUN 1878	Glenwood
018124	CAMPBELL, Cassie	12h	C	D.C.	23 NOV 1878	Potters Field
018534	CAMPBELL, Catharine Elizabeth	1m	W	D.C.	01 JAN 1879	Mt. Olivet
020064	CAMPBELL, Charles	8d	C	D.C.	11 MAY 1879	Beckett's
008161	CAMPBELL, Elizabeth	89y	W	Md.	11 JUL 1876	Glenwood
012279	CAMPBELL, Eugenaria	c.16y	C	D.C.	09 JUL 1877	Young Mens
000366	CAMPBELL, Frances	5d	C	D.C.	29 AUG 1874	Beckett's
017971	CAMPBELL, Frederick	3y	C	Md.	07 NOV 1878	Brightwood
019352	CAMPBELL, Frederick	49y	W	Scot.	10 MAR 1879	Soldier's Home
006106	CAMPBELL, George	58y	M	Md.	23 JAN 1876	Mt. Olivet
016433	CAMPBELL, George Robert	15m	W	D.C.	04 JUL 1878	Congressional
018015	CAMPBELL, Henrietta	40y	W	Md.	11 NOV 1878	Mt. Olivet
013078	CAMPBELL, Infant of Thomas	1h	C	D.C.	04 SEP 1877	Potters Field
001675	CAMPBELL, James W.	47y	W	Scot.	10 JAN 1875	Potters Field
020882	CAMPBELL, Jane S.	73y	W	Eng.	11 JUL 1879	Oak Hill
006212	CAMPBELL, Jinnie	1y	W	D.C.	02 FEB 1876	Young Mens
000626	CAMPBELL, John	1m	C	D.C.	24 SEP 1874	Beckett's
002259	CAMPBELL, John	7m	C	D.C.	20 FEB 1875	Beckett's
005140a	CAMPBELL, John	46y	C	Va.	14 OCT 1875	Young Mens
017152	CAMPBELL, John	80y	C	Md.	23 AUG 1878	Mt. Olivet
019681	CAMPBELL, John A.	62y	W	Pa.	07 APR 1879	Congressional
017534	CAMPBELL, John G.	2y	W	D.C.	25 SEP 1878	Mt. Olivet
010340	CAMPBELL, Lilly May	1y	W	D.C.	19 JAN 1877	Glenwood
013540	CAMPBELL, Mariah R.	86y	W	D.C.	17 OCT 1877	Mt. Olivet
017105	CAMPBELL, Minnie	85y	C	Va.	19 AUG 1878	Alexandria, Va.
011743	CAMPBELL, Nancy Ann	8m	C	D.C.	30 MAY 1877	Potters Field
019499	CAMPBELL, Peter	65y	C	Ga.	22 MAR 1879	Potters Field
006334	CAMPBELL, Sarah	4y	C	D.C.	13 FEB 1876	Beckett's
004559	CAMPBELL, Thomas B.	53y	W	N.Y.	12 AUG 1875	Congressional
016448	CAMPBELL, Virginia	8y	W	D.C.	05 JUL 1878	Congressional
001566	CAMPBELL, William	24y	C	Md.	01 JAN 1875	Washington Asylum
008306	CAMPBELL, William G.	6y	W	D.C.	17 JUL 1876	Glenwood
008222	CANAAN, Infant of Mary	½h	W	D.C.	13 JUL 1876	Potters Field

No.	Name	Age	Race	Birth	Death Date	Burial Place
000945	CANDY, Anthony Parkinson	1y	W	D.C.	26 OCT 1874	Congressional
020824	CANFIELD, Margaret J.	55y	W	D.C.	08 JUL 1879	Congressional
016551	CANN, Mary E.	7m	W	D.C.	11 JUL 1878	Congressional
000181	CANN?, Infant	2h	W	D.C.	14 AUG 1874	Mt. Olivet
000748	CANNON, Margret D.	38y	W	Ire.	08 OCT 1874	Mt. Olivet
001272	CANTIN, Jeremiah	30y	C	Md.	30 NOV 1874	Washington Asylum
005276	CANTWELL, Infant of James	3d	W	D.C.	26 OCT 1875	Mt. Olivet
008427	CAPERTON, Allen T.	65y	W	W.Va.	26 JUL 1876	Union, W.Va.
013193	CAPERTON, Hugh	55y	W	W.Va.	14 SEP 1877	Holy Rood
002042f	CAPLE, Edward	60y	W	Eng.	-- --- 1863	Congressional
002043f	CAPLE, Ruth	58y	W	Eng.	-- --- 1873	Congressional
019500	CAPRON, Ann M.	71y	W	Md.	22 MAR 1879	Congressional
007031	CARAWAY, Catherine A.	45y	C	Md.	17 APR 1876	Mt. Pleasant
012418	CARBERY, Annie E.	41y	W	Va.	18 JUL 1877	Mt. Olivet
019530	CARBERY, Frank	1y	W	D.C.	24 MAR 1879	Mt. Olivet
016668	CARDOZA, Rebecca Cole	2y	C	D.C.	19 JUL 1878	Graceland
019804	CAREW, Charlotte Marion	1y	W	D.C.	17 APR 1879	Mt. Olivet
019177	CAREY, Abraham	23y	C	Va.	24 FEB 1879	Young Mens
011161	CAREY, John	29y	C	Va.	30 MAR 1877	Mt. Zion
015241	CAREY, Michael	38y	W	Ire.	31 MAR 1878	Soldier's Home
013007	CAREY, Tampa	66y	C	N.C.	29 AUG 1877	Arlington
015804	CAREY, William	6m	C	Va.	22 MAY 1878	Beckett's
011082	CAREY, Wm.	67y	W	Ire.	22 MAR 1877	Holy Rood
003440	CARKIN, John	70y	W	Ire.	25 MAY 1875	Soldier's Home
003260	CARLIN, George Thomas	40y	W	Md.	08 MAY 1875	Oak Hill
011651	CARLISLE, James Mandeville	63y	W	Va.	19 MAY 1877	Rock Creek
005065	CARLISLE, Josehine F	23y	W	Va.	16 SEP 1875	Congressional
019651	CARLISLE, Minnie	19y	W	Me.	04 APR 1879	Bangor, Me.
012740	CARLTON, Joseph M.	40y	W	Me.	09 AUG 1877	Graceland
016501	CARMADY, Simon	5y	W	D.C.	08 JUL 1878	Mt. Olivet
001787	CARMICHAEL, Jamie	6y	W	N.Y.	19 JAN 1875	Cortland, N.Y.
019262	CARMICK, Infant of Thos. G.	3h	W	D.C.	03 MAR 1879	Graceland
001955	CARMINE, Geo.	1y	C	D.C.	30 JAN 1875	Young Mens
010603	CARMINE, Phebe E.	20m	C	D.C.	12 FEB 1877	Young Mens
010683	CARMON, Martin	35y	W	Ire.	18 FEB 1877	Mt. Olivet
007187	CARNEY, Andrew	6y	W	D.C.	02 MAY 1876	Mt. Olivet
012454	CARNEY, John	c.60y	W	Ire.	21 JUL 1877	Piedmount, W.Va.
005344	CARNEY, Winnifred	10d	W	D.C.	03 NOV 1875	Mt. Olivet
008759	CAROLAN, Daniel	3m	W	D.C.	20 AUG 1876	Mt. Olivet
008295	CAROLL, Mable V.	7m	W	Va.	17 JUL 1876	Oak Hill
018807	CAROLTON, Mary	53y	W	Ire.	25 JAN 1879	Mt. Olivet
002691	CARPENTER, Benjamin T.	78y	W	N.Y.	22 MAR 1875	Rock Creek
007857	CARPENTER, C.H.	6m	W	D.C.	26 JUN 1876	Congressional
015196	CARPENTER, Catherine B.	63y	W	N.Y.	27 MAR 1878	Congressional
004558	CARPENTER, Diana	60y	W	Ohio	12 AUG 1875	Congressional
000537f	CARPENTER, Edna	--	--	--	17 SEP 1874	--
000922	CARPENTER, Elen	60y	M	D.C.	24 OCT 1874	Mt. Zion
014061	CARPENTER, Hattie E.	22y	W	Wisc.	11 DEC 1877	Congressional
010268	CARPENTER, Infant of J.E.C.	17d	W	D.C.	12 JAN 1877	Congressional
012139	CARPENTER, James Henry	9y	W	Tenn.	30 JUN 1877	Congressional
008772	CARPENTER, John	3y	C	D.C.	22 AUG 1876	Young Mens
016125	CARPENTER, John Henry	20y	W	D.C.	12 JUN 1878	Mt. Olivet
016647	CARPENTER, Leland	50y	C	Va.	18 JUL 1878	Harmony
011476	CARPENTER, Michael	48y	W	Ire.	01 MAY 1877	Mt. Olivet
013803	CARPENTER, Roman	3y	C	D.C.	12 NOV 1877	Graceland
003544	CARR, Charles L.	40y	W	Miss.	06 JUN 1875	Glenwood

District of Columbia Death Records, August 1, 1874 to July 31, 1879   57

No.	Name	Age	Race	Birth	Death Date	Burial Place
001422	CARR, Frances	38y	W	D.C.	18 DEC 1874	Mt. Olivet
013694	CARR, Infant of John	3d	W	D.C.	01 NOV 1877	Glenwood
018149	CARR, Infant of Joseph	1h	C	D.C.	25 NOV 1878	Beckett's
009053	CARR, James	40y	C	Va.	13 SEP 1876	Harmony
012614	CARR, John A.	1y	W	N.C.	30 JUL 1877	Mt. Olivet
018856	CARR, Sophia	8m	W	N.Y.	28 JAN 1879	Holy Rood
021020	CARR, Thomas	3m	W	D.C.	20 JUL 1879	Mt. Olivet
018394	CARR, William Edward	2m	W	D.C.	20 DEC 1878	Glenwood
007337	CARR, Winnie	c.45y	W	Ire.	19 MAY 1876	Holy Rood
019028	CARRICK, Henry	39y	C	D.C.	11 FEB 1879	Harmony
002231	CARRICO, Mary L.	11d	W	D.C.	19 FEB 1875	Congressional
014177	CARRICO, William H.	20y	W	D.C.	23 DEC 1877	Congressional
004890	CARRIER, Charles Edward	21y	W	D.C.	03 SEP 1875	Oak Hill
010888	CARRInGTON, Oscar H.	23y	M	Va.	06 MAR 1877	Mt. Pleasant
001265	CARRINGTON, Julia	48y	C	Va.	29 NOV 1874	Mt. Pleasant
018084	CARROL, Bertha	2y	W	D.C.	18 NOV 1878	Potters Field
019652	CARROL, James	45y	W	Mass.	04 APR 1879	Mt. Olivet
001186	CARROL, Lillie	1m	C	D.C.	19 NOV 1874	Harmony
018676	CARROL, William	64y	C	Md.	15 JAN 1879	Beckett's
014767	CARROLL, A.J.	16d	W	D.C.	15 FEB 1878	Congressional
015922	CARROLL, Benjamin	4½m	W	D.C.	31 MAY 1878	Beckett's
010631	CARROLL, Bryan	31y	W	Ire.	14 FEB 1877	Mt. Olivet
019911	CARROLL, Catharine Ellen	50y	W	Md.	27 APR 1879	Carroll Chapel
002523	CARROLL, Charles	15y	C	D.C.	11 MAR 1875	Washington Asylum
018879	CARROLL, Charles	77y	C	Md.	30 JAN 1879	Potters Field
019380	CARROLL, Charlotte	66y	C	Md.	13 MAR 1879	Harmony
020481	CARROLL, Clara Belle	1½m	C	D.C.	17 JUN 1879	Young Mens
006429	CARROLL, Emma B.	27y	W	Miss.	21 FEB 1876	Oak Hill
000928	CARROLL, Frank G	4m	C	D.C.	25 OCT 1874	Young Mens
013877	CARROLL, George	1y	C	D.C.	21 NOV 1877	Potters Field
014062	CARROLL, Grace	2y	C	D.C.	11 DEC 1877	Potters Field
014632	CARROLL, Hattie	10m	M	D.C.	04 JUL 1878	Harmony
014940	CARROLL, Henrietta	71y	C	Md.	04 MAR 1878	Harmony
010465	CARROLL, Hilary	24y	C	Md.	31 JAN 1877	Rockville, Md.
013485	CARROLL, Infant of George	6d	C	D.C.	11 OCT 1877	Potters Field
017942	CARROLL, Infant of Martha	½h	C	D.C.	04 NOV 1878	Potters Field
018596	CARROLL, Infant of Samuel	2½h	W	D.C.	07 JAN 1879	Holy Rood
001089	CARROLL, Infant of Wm.	1d	C	D.C.	08 NOV 1874	Potters Field
016301	CARROLL, James	1m	W	D.C.	25 JUN 1878	Mt. Olivet
004309	CARROLL, Jane	73y	W	Md.	26 JUL 1875	Congressional
020808	CARROLL, John	94y	W	Ire.	07 JUL 1879	Soldier's Home
019585	CARROLL, John	73y	W	Ire.	29 MAR 1879	Holy Rood
008699	CARROLL, John Henry	55y	C	D.C.	16 AUG 1876	Harmony
020479	CARROLL, Joseph	1m	C	D.C.	17 JUN 1879	Holy Rood
013510	CARROLL, Lizzie	c.32y	C	S.C.	14 OCT 1877	Harmony
007877	CARROLL, M.C.	4m	W	D.C.	27 JUN 1876	Mt. Olivet
017805	CARROLL, Maria C.	44y	W	D.C.	20 OCT 1878	Congressional
011790	CARROLL, Martha	55y	C	Md.	03 JUN 1877	Mt. Olivet
003206	CARROLL, Mary A.	65y	W	Ire.	03 MAY 1875	Holy Rood
001360	CARROLL, Mary A.E.	c.50y	C	D.C.	11 DEC 1874	Harmony
013660	CARROLL, Mary Ann	50y	C	Md.	28 OCT 1877	Harmony
020328	CARROLL, Mary Elizabeth	2d	C	D.C.	07 JUN 1879	Potters Field
020531	CARROLL, Mary Ellen	1y	W	D.C.	20 JUN 1879	Congressional
013446	CARROLL, Mildred A.	18m	W	D.C.	09 OCT 1877	Congressional
010547	CARROLL, Rose	6m	C	D.C.	06 FEB 1877	Potters Field
017414	CARROLL, Sarah Ann	6d	C	D.C.	15 SEP 1878	Beckett's

No.	Name	Age	Race	Birth	Death Date	Burial Place
018793	CARROLL, Sarah V.	26y	W	D.C.	24 JAN 1879	Congressional
011271	CARROLL, Susan E., Mrs.	69y	W	Md.	08 APR 1877	Congressional
011748	CARROLL, Sylvester C.C.	17y	W	Md.	30 MAY 1877	St. John's Chapel, Md.
004150	CARROLL, Thomas	9m	W	D.C.	16 JUL 1875	Mt. Olivet
013361	CARROLL, Tobias	60y		Md.	01 OCT 1877	Harmony
000899	CARROLL, Virginia	7y	C	D.C.	22 OCT 1874	Holy Rood
014196	CARROLL, William	36y	W	Ire.	25 DEC 1877	Baltimore, Md.
020960	CARROLL, William	2m	C	D.C.	16 JUL 1879	Harmony
003520	CARROLL, Wm.	50y	C	Md.	03 JUN 1875	Harmony
017562	CARROLL, Wm. J.	58y	W	Ire.	29 SEP 1878	Holy Rood
004347	CARROLL, Wm. W.	48y	W	Md.	28 JUL 1875	Congressional
013130	CARRUTHERS, Henry	34y	W	Scot.	09 SEP 1877	Mt. Olivet
007416	CARSON, Edward Bangs	1y	W	D.C.	27 MAY 1876	Glenwood
015369	CARSON, Henry	30y	W	Ire.	12 APR 1878	Hospital, Government
016275	CARSON, Mary R.	42y	W	Ohio	23 JUN 1878	Congressional
009367	CARSON, Rose DeLina	1y	W	D.C.	10 OCT 1876	Oak Hill
013717	CARSTENS, William	5y	W	D.C.	03 NOV 1877	Glenwood
002016	CARSTINE, Geo.	8y	W	D.C.	04 FEB 1875	Glenwood
020047	CARTE, Thomas	3d	C	D.C.	09 MAY 1879	Potters Field
000335	CARTER, Ada	2m	C	D.C.	27 AUG 1874	Harmony
003230	CARTER, Ada Spilman	1y	W	D.C.	05 MAY 1875	Glenwood
004575	CARTER, Addison	1y	C	D.C.	13 AUG 1875	Potters Field
020854	CARTER, Aggie	112y	C	Va.	09 JUL 1879	Fredericksburg, Va.
009388	CARTER, Albert	52y	C	Va.	12 OCT 1876	Potters Field
010676	CARTER, Albert	50y	C	Va.	18 FEB 1877	Potters Field
005503	CARTER, Alice	1y	C	D.C.	19 NOV 1875	Mt. Zion
007002	CARTER, Alice	9m	M	D.C.	12 APR 1876	Harmony
011933	CARTER, Andrew	21y	C	D.C.	16 JUN 1877	Potters Field
017681	CARTER, Anna	30y	C	Md.	09 OCT 1878	Mt. Olivet
014622	CARTER, Annie	10y	C	D.C.	01 FEB 1878	Beckett's
007385	CARTER, Arthur	40y	C	D.C.	23 MAY 1876	Harmony
011969	CARTER, Benjamin	9y	C	D.C.	19 JUN 1877	Moore's
008591	CARTER, Bernard T.	c.63y	W	Va.	07 AUG 1876	Baltimore, Md.
004164f	CARTER, Caroline R.	47y	C	D.C.	24 MAY 1875	Oak Hill
001390	CARTER, Catharine	33y	C	Va.	14 DEC 1874	Beckett's
020196	CARTER, Cecelia	6d	C	D.C.	25 MAY 1879	Holy Rood
010986	CARTER, Charles	4m	M	D.C.	15 MAR 1877	Mt. Zion
015608	CARTER, Charles E.	3y	C	D.C.	04 MAY 1878	Mt. Zion
014623	CARTER, Dasey Marine	6m	C	D.C.	01 FEB 1878	Young Mens
000891	CARTER, Eddie	5m	C	D.C.	21 OCT 1874	Harmony
004592	CARTER, Edward	41y	C	Va.	14 AUG 1875	Ebenezer
006306	CARTER, Eliza	50y	C	Va.	11 FEB 1876	Ebenezer
009791	CARTER, Eliza	70y	C	Va.	24 NOV 1876	Potters Field
016485	CARTER, Elizabeth	4m	C	D.C.	07 JUL 1878	Potters Field
016765	CARTER, Ellen	26y	C	Va.	26 JUL 1878	Beckett's
013099	CARTER, Emma	16y	C	Va.	06 SEP 1877	Potters Field
002495	CARTER, Emma Virginia	2y	C	D.C.	09 MAR 1875	Mt. Pleasant
013787	CARTER, Fannie	9m	C	D.C.	10 NOV 1877	Mt. Zion
018823	CARTER, Fannie	40y	C	Va.	26 JAN 1879	Young Mens
003916	CARTER, Florene	4m	C	D.C.	29 JUN 1875	Mt. Zion
014280	CARTER, Frances	20y	C	Va.	01 JAN 1878	Beckett's
006747	CARTER, Francis	6m	C	D.C.	20 MAR 1876	Potters Field
016287	CARTER, Frank	6w	W	D.C.	24 JUN 1878	Methodist
000619	CARTER, Fred. Thos.	4m	C	D.C.	23 SEP 1874	Mt. Zion
000025	CARTER, George	21y	C	Va.	02 AUG 1874	Mt. Pleasant
001541	CARTER, George	21y	C	Va.	30 DEC 1874	Harmony

District of Columbia Death Records, August 1, 1874 to July 31, 1879   59

No.	Name	Age	Race	Birth	Death Date	Burial Place
011652	CARTER, George	87y	C	Va.	19 MAY 1877	Young Mens
005060a	CARTER, Hager	70y	C	Md.	05 OCT 1875	Ebenezer
011680	CARTER, Harriet	28y	C	Va.	23 MAY 1877	Potters Field
003435	CARTER, Henry	35y	C	Va.	25 MAY 1875	Beckett's
015891	CARTER, Henry	45y	C	Md.	29 MAY 1878	Beckett's
003238	CARTER, Herbert Petty	2m	W	D.C.	06 MAY 1875	Glenwood
012422	CARTER, Hezekiah	85y	C	Va.	19 JUL 1877	Potters Field
013520	CARTER, Infant of Addison	3m	C	D.C.	14 OCT 1877	Young Mens
016785	CARTER, Infant of Jluia	1m	C	D.C.	27 JUL 1878	Payne's
019138	CARTER, Infant of Martha	7d	C	D.C.	21 FEB 1879	Potters Field
004519	CARTER, Infant of Sarah Ann	1d	C	D.C.	09 AUG 1875	Potters Field
005165a	CARTER, Infant of Thomas	1d	C	D.C.	16 OCT 1875	Mt. Olivet
000921	CARTER, J.B.	84y	C	Md.	24 OCT 1874	Baltimore, Md.
000272	CARTER, Jacob	14d	C	D.C.	21 AUG 1874	Mt. Zion
001075	CARTER, James	18y	C	Va.	07 NOV 1874	Potters Field
003368	CARTER, James	54y	C	Va.	19 MAY 1875	Harmony
011446	CARTER, James B.	5m	C	Pa.	28 APR 1877	Harmony
020327	CARTER, James William	70y	C	Md.	07 JUN 1879	Potters Field
005178	CARTER, Jarrett	c.73y	C	Va.	26 SEP 1875	Young Mens
012208	CARTER, Jeremiah	c.45y	C	Va.	04 JUL 1877	Young Mens
008458	CARTER, John	8m	C	D.C.	28 JUL 1876	Baptist
020294	CARTER, John	1y	C	D.C.	04 JUN 1879	Beckett's
015342	CARTER, John A.	49y	M	N.C.	10 APR 1878	Beckett's
014376	CARTER, John T.	26y	C	Va.	10 JAN 1878	Young Mens
005914	CARTER, John Thomas	2y	C	D.C.	02 JAN 1876	Mt. Pleasant
021018	CARTER, John W.	14d	C	D.C.	20 JUL 1879	Payne's
007638	CARTER, Joseph	10m	C	Va.	14 JUN 1876	Potters Field
011729	CARTER, Joseph	6d	M	D.C.	28 MAY 1877	Ebenezer
009081	CARTER, Joseph F.	3y	C	D.C.	15 SEP 1876	Mt. Zion
013079	CARTER, Joseph M.	22y	C	D.C.	04 SEP 1877	Harmony
007590	CARTER, Josephine Ferguson	1m	C	D.C.	11 JUN 1876	Ebenezer
004166	CARTER, Julia	4m	C	D.C.	17 JUL 1875	Harmony
015362	CARTER, Lee Etta	1y	C	D.C.	11 APR 1878	Harmony
009444	CARTER, Lena	11m	C	D.C.	17 OCT 1876	Moore's
016513	CARTER, Lewis	80y	C	Va.	09 JUL 1878	Potters Field
020228	CARTER, Lewis	50y	C	Va.	30 MAY 1879	Potters Field
018053	CARTER, Lewis C.	4m	C	D.C.	15 NOV 1878	Mt. Pleasant
020446	CARTER, Louisa	21y	C	Md.	15 JUN 1879	Mt. Zion
018617	CARTER, Lucy	23y	C	Va.	09 JAN 1879	Beckett's
003570	CARTER, Maggie	8d	C	D.C.	08 JUN 1875	Mt. Pleasant
001712	CARTER, Maria	2y	C	D.C.	13 JAN 1875	Harmony
015276	CARTER, Marth E.	24y	C	Va.	03 APR 1878	Mt. Zion
009346	CARTER, Martha	6m	C	D.C.	09 OCT 1876	Mt. Zion
011490	CARTER, Martha	22y	C	Va.	02 MAY 1877	King George Co., Va.
020552	CARTER, Martha L.	9d	C	D.C.	21 JUN 1879	Mt. Zion
005866	CARTER, Mary	59y	C	Md.	26 DEC 1875	Harmony
005245	CARTER, Mary	16y	C	Ga.	23 OCT 1875	Mt. Olivet
015738	CARTER, Mary	10m	C	D.C.	16 MAY 1878	Mt. Zion
005774	CARTER, Mary Ann	4d	C	D.C.	17 DEC 1875	Harmony
019931	CARTER, Mary E.	26y	C	Va.	29 APR 1879	Harmony
002417	CARTER, Mary Elizabeth	39y	W	Va.	04 MAR 1875	Glenwood
003689	CARTER, Mary Magdalana	1y	C	D.C.	18 JUN 1875	Mt. Zion
017535	CARTER, Matilda	72y	C	Va.	26 SEP 1878	Payne's
006028	CARTER, Milly	45y	C	Va.	15 JAN 1876	Young Mens
011419	CARTER, Nancy	65y	C	Va.	24 APR 1877	Potters Field
014768	CARTER, Nancy Ann	28y	W	Va.	15 FEB 1878	Glenwood

District of Columbia Death Records, August 1, 1874 to July 31, 1879

No.	Name	Age	Race	Birth	Death Date	Burial Place
000601	CARTER, Peter	22y	C	Va.	22 SEP 1874	Washington Asylum
018766	CARTER, Rachel	2y	C	D.C.	22 JAN 1879	Payne's
006292	CARTER, Rebecca	9m	C	D.C.	10 FEB 1876	Harmony
007152	CARTER, Robert	1y	C	D.C.	29 APR 1876	Holy Rood
020115	CARTER, Robert	3y	C	D.C.	16 MAY 1879	Mt. Zion
000602	CARTER, Rosena	6y	C	D.C.	22 SEP 1874	Mt. Olivet
007020	CARTER, Sallie	52y	C	Va.	15 APR 1876	Ebenezer
014366	CARTER, Sallie	20y	C	Va.	09 JAN 1878	Harmony
000620	CARTER, Sophia	2y	M	D.C.	23 SEP 1874	Potters Field
001465	CARTER, Susan	35y	C	Va.	23 DEC 1874	Washington Asylum
013108	CARTER, Thomas	5y	C	D.C.	07 SEP 1877	Holy Rood
017898	CARTER, Thomas	35y	C	Va.	29 OCT 1878	Potters Field
015924	CARTER, Thomas F.	7m	C	D.C.	31 MAY 1878	Mt. Zion
013236	CARTER, Vincent	60y	C	Va.	18 SEP 1877	Potters Field
016414	CARTER, Walter	10m	C	D.C.	03 JUL 1878	Young Mens
010099	CARTER, Willi	35y	C	S.C.	28 DEC 1876	Potters Field
013912	CARTER, William	80y	C	Va.	25 NOV 1877	Potters Field
002730	CARTER, William E.	3m	C	D.C.	25 MAR 1875	Mt. Zion
014056	CARTER, Willis Edward	6y	M	D.C.	10 DEC 1877	Harmony
015036	CARTER, Yondora	6y	C	D.C.	12 MAR 1878	Young Mens
010832	CARTHEY, Denis	57y	W	Ire.	02 MAR 1877	Soldier's Home
012214	CARTLET, Philip	47y	C	Md.	04 JUL 1877	Beckett's
008741	CARTMAN, Emma J.	7m	W	D.C.	19 AUG 1876	Glenwood
001768	CARTRIGHT, John	23y	C	Md.	17 JAN 1875	Holy Rood
002461	CARTWRIGHT, Elizebeth	50y	M	Md.	07 MAR 1875	Mt. Olivet
020806	CARTWRIGHT, Infant of Hamilton L.	2m	C	D.C.	07 JUL 1879	Mt. Zion
002424	CARTWRIGHT, Lewis	57y	C	Va.	04 MAR 1875	Mt. Zion
018211	CARTWRIGHT, Mary Elizabeth	25y	W	D.C.	01 DEC 1878	Oak Hill
005052	CARTWRIGHT, William	33y	C	Va.	15 SEP 1875	Ebenezer
008078	CARTWRIGHT, Zacharia	58y	C	Va.	08 JUL 1876	Harmony
019959	CARTWRIGHT, [blank]	c.35y	C	--	02 MAY 1879	Potters Field
007814	CARUSI, John	45y	C	D.C.	24 JUN 1876	Potters Field
012885	CARUSI, Nathaniel	84y	W	Italy	20 AUG 1877	Oak Hill
000157	CARVALHO, Ellen	5y	M	D.C.	11 AUG 1874	Macedonia?
013529	CARVER, George William	3y	W	D.C.	16 OCT 1877	Glenwood
002768	CARY, Frank	35y	C	Va.	28 MAR 1875	Ebenezer
019780	CARY, Joshua	1y	C	Va.	15 APR 1879	Harmony
020893	CARY, Robert	5m	C	D.C.	12 JUL 1879	Mt. Zion
003087	CASALEGGI, Angela R.	8d	W	D.C.	22 APR 1875	St. Mary's
014343	CASANAUGH, Michael	65y	W	Ire.	07 JAN 1878	Congressional
002857	CASASA, Teresa	50y	W	Italy	03 APR 1875	St. Mary's
014171	CASE, Charles Dorsey	3y	W	D.C.	22 DEC 1877	Congressional
009003	CASE, Ephraim	45y	W	Pa.	08 SEP 1876	Troy, Pa.
009048	CASE, Harriet R.	39y	W	Pa.	12 SEP 1876	Troy, Bradford Co., Pa.
016083	CASE, Thomas	1m	W	D.C.	09 JUN 1878	Mt. Olivet
011366	CASELL, Katie Julian	8m	W	D.C.	18 APR 1877	Congressional
014386	CASEY, Eliza Anna	20y	C	Va.	11 JAN 1878	Harmony
003245	CASEY, Hanorah	5m	W	D.C.	06 MAY 1875	Mt. Olivet
020170	CASEY, James	55y	W	Ire.	22 MAY 1879	Mt. Olivet
019118	CASEY, Johanna	80y	W	Ire.	19 FEB 1879	Mt. Olivet
000076	CASEY, John	88y	W	Ire.	06 AUG 1874	Mt. Olivet
011585	CASEY, John	42y	W	Ire.	13 MAY 1877	Mt. Olivet
019015	CASEY, Joseph	c.64y	W	Md.	10 FEB 1879	Oak Hill
013625	CASEY, Lucy A.	23y	C	Va.	25 OCT 1877	Harmony
001403	CASEY, Morries	49y	W	Ire.	15 DEC 1874	Mt. Olivet
005064	CASEY, Nelson	29y	C	Va.	16 SEP 1875	Ebenezer

District of Columbia Death Records, August 1, 1874 to July 31, 1879   61

No.	Name	Age	Race	Birth	Death Date	Burial Place
004726	CASH, Abram	49y	C	Va.	23 AUG 1875	Mt. Zion
011378	CASH, Caroline	28y	C	Va.	20 APR 1877	Ebenezer
010914	CASH, John C.	60y	W	Pa.	08 MAR 1877	Philadelphia, Pa.
016112	CASIE, Susan	70y	C	D.C.	11 JUN 1878	Mt. Olivet
010390	CASON, James Robert	24y	W	Ind.	24 JAN 1877	Congressional
004913	CASPER, Cris	1y	W	D.C.	05 SEP 1875	St. Mary's
008293	CASPER, Gertrude	5m	W	D.C.	16 JUL 1876	St. Mary's
013046	CASPER, Joseph	24y	W	D.C.	01 SEP 1877	Mt. Olivet
008428	CASSADY, Julia	6d	W	D.C.	26 JUL 1876	Mt. Olivet
000907	CASSASA, Agusta	16y	W	Italy	23 OCT 1874	St. Mary's
005024a	CASSELL, Laura A.V.	23y	W	D.C.	02 OCT 1875	Glenwood
008459	CASSELL, Laura Virginia	10m	W	D.C.	28 JUL 1876	Glenwood
004542	CASSELL, Maud	7m	W	D.C.	11 AUG 1875	Oak Hill
010967	CASSIDAY, Burnett	20y	W	N.Y.	14 MAR 1877	Mt. Olivet
017748	CASSIDAY, Mary C.	34y	W	D.C.	15 OCT 1878	Oak Hill
014440	CASSIDAY, Peter	40y	W	Ire.	16 JAN 1878	Mt. Olivet
006810	CASSIDY, Elizabeth	26y	W	Md.	25 MAR 1876	Glenwood
013117	CASSIDY, James T.	36y	W	Va.	08 SEP 1877	Glenwood
017821	CASSIDY, Mattie G.	7y	W	D.C.	21 OCT 1878	Oak Hill
016701	CASSIDY, Melissa	35y	W	Va.	21 JUL 1878	Glenwood
010173	CASSIDY, Roger	6m	W	D.C.	04 JAN 1877	Mt. Olivet
018106	CASSIDY, Samuel	65y	W	Pa.	21 NOV 1878	Glenwood
018370	CASSIN, Richard Walter	1y	W	D.C.	18 DEC 1878	Glenwood
007358	CASTAGNATTA, John	7d	W	D.C.	21 MAY 1876	St. Mary's
005308	CASTEL, Margaret	45y	W	Md.	30 OCT 1875	Williams Port, Md.
001019	CASTEL, Martha	62y	W	D.C.	02 NOV 1874	Congressional
006001	CASTELL, Charles J.	19y	W	D.C.	12 JAN 1876	Congressional
003221	CASTELL, Edward O.	63y	W	D.C.	05 MAY 1875	Mt. Olivet
012543	CASTELL, John B.	71y	W	Md.	26 JUL 1877	Congressional
001726	CASTELLO, Timothy	1y	W	D.C.	14 JAN 1875	Mt. Olivet
012509	CASTLE, Lula A.	4y	W	D.C.	24 JUL 1877	Oak Hill
020466	CASWELL, Calvin B.	61y	W	Pa.	16 JUN 1879	Congressional
017574	CATE, Aaron B.	46y	W	N.H.	30 SEP 1878	Congressional
008904	CATE, Leavitt Eugene	10m	W	D.C.	31 AUG 1876	Glenwood
019973	CATE, Mary E.	52y	W	N.Y.	03 MAR 1879	Graceland
011395	CATER, Clarence	15y	C	D.C.	22 APR 1877	Mt. Olivet
014809	CATHCART, Lucy Ann Durkee	54y	W	Pa.	18 FEB 1878	York, Pa.
006533	CATHELL, Sarah T.	79y	W	Del.	03 MAR 1876	Oak Hill
006428	CATHOLIC, Joseph	2y	C	D.C.	21 FEB 1876	Young Mens
007396	CATLETT, John H.	25y	C	Va.	24 MAY 1876	Young Mens
016809	CATLETT, Nelson	50y	C	Va.	29 JUL 1878	Potters Field
008124	CATLETT, William W.	4m	C	D.C.	10 JUL 1876	Potters Field
005089a	CATON, Annie	35y	W	Va.	09 OCT 1875	Presbyterian
019529	CATON, John A.	4y	W	Md.	24 MAR 1879	Presbyterian
008818	CATON, Mary Margaret	1y	W	D.C.	25 AUG 1876	Mt. Olivet
020229	CATON, Sarah Agnes	8m	W	D.C.	30 MAY 1879	Mt. Olivet
016066	CATON, Sarah E.	34y	W	D.C.	08 JUN 1878	Mt. Olivet
008146	CATON, William	7y	W	D.C.	10 JUL 1876	Holy Rood
021019	CATOR, Effie Maud	4m	W	D.C.	20 JUL 1879	Poolesville, Md.
001176	CAUGHLAN, James P.	1m	W	Ill.	18 NOV 1874	Chicago, Ill.
002289	CAUGHLIN, Wm.	22y	W	Va.	23 FEB 1875	Mt. Olivet
009151	CAULDWELL, Infant of Mary	2d	C	D.C.	21 SEP 1876	Potters Field
001659	CAULFIELD, Anie A.	28y	W	Mass.	08 JAN 1875	Marion, Mass.
000727	CAULFIELD, Annie Louisa	10m	W	N.Y.	06 OCT 1874	Glenwood
018767	CAUSINS, Fredrick	2y	C	D.C.	22 JAN 1879	Mt. Pleasant
000965	CAUSTEN, James Hyman	86y	W	Md.	28 OCT 1874	Congressional

No.	Name	Age	Race	Birth	Death Date	Burial Place
015242	CAUSTEN, Manuel Carvalla	36y	W	D.C.	31 MAR 1878	Congressional
008660	CAUTHORN, Robert	66y	W	Va.	12 AUG 1876	Congressional
019912	CAVANAGH, Andrew Mahony	1y	W	D.C.	27 APR 1879	Mt. Olivet
014468	CAVANAUGH, Arthur R.	47y	W	Ire.	18 JAN 1878	Mt. Olivet
000005	CAVANAUGH, Laurence	1d	W	D.C.	01 AUG 1874	Mt. Olivet
014178	CAVANAUGH, Mary	60y	W	Ire.	23 DEC 1877	Potters Field
019532	CAVANAUGH, Mary Philemena, Sister	50y	W	Ire.	24 MAR 1879	Convent
005873	CAVENNAUGH, Rosa	6y	W	D.C.	27 DEC 1875	Mt. Olivet
014695	CAYNOR, William	2y	W	D.C.	07 FEB 1878	Glenwood
010802	CEPHAS, Infant of Bayliss	3d	C	D.C.	27 FEB 1877	Young Mens
008948	CEPHAS, John	3m	C	D.C.	03 SEP 1876	Cephas Farm
012927	CHADVILLE, Francis	63y	W	France	24 AUG 1877	Washington Asylum
002194	CHAMBERS, Agnes	7y	C	Md.	16 FEB 1875	Young Mens
012550	CHAMBERS, Allen	2y	C	D.C.	27 JUL 1877	Ebenezer
020154	CHAMBERS, Harriet	70y	C	Md.	20 MAY 1879	Harmony
019903	CHAMBERS, Martha A.	47y	C	Va.	26 APR 1879	Graceland
017690	CHAMBERS, Mary Jane	18y	W	D.C.	10 OCT 1878	Mt. Olivet
011736	CHAMBERS, Patrick	51y	W	Ire.	29 MAY 1877	Mt. Olivet
015145	CHAMP, Alfred	50y	C	Va.	22 MAR 1878	Harmony
013177	CHAMP, Georgianna	15y	C	Va.	13 SEP 1877	Harmony
018542	CHAMPION, Martha	6y	W	D.C.	02 JAN 1879	Congressional
014063	CHAMPLIN, Job C.	67y	W	N.Y.	11 DEC 1877	Congressional
010672	CHANCEY, Bridget	75y	W	Md.	17 FEB 1877	Congressional
018855	CHANDLEE, Mattie	6y	W	D.C.	28 JAN 1879	Glenwood
017066	CHANDLER, Elizabeth	2y	M	D.C.	16 AUG 1878	Mt. Pleasant
018260	CHANDLER, Hilleray	67y	C	D.C.	07 DEC 1878	Holy Rood
004705	CHANDLER, James	1y	C	D.C.	22 AUG 1875	Mt. Pleasant
007279	CHANDLER, Mary	26y	C	Va.	12 MAY 1876	Mt. Pleasant
008136	CHANDLER, Mildred	4m	C	D.C.	10 JUL 1876	Young Mens
007371	CHANEY, Dennis	30h	W	D.C.	22 MAY 1876	Mt. Olivet
009334	CHAPLITT, Nathaniel	1y	C	D.C.	07 OCT 1876	Beckett's
002265	CHAPMAN, Annie	12y	C	Md.	21 FEB 1875	Ebenezer
016124	CHAPMAN, Annie	6m	C	D.C.	12 JUN 1878	Moore's
006362	CHAPMAN, Catharine L.	2y	W	Va.	15 FEB 1876	Fairfax Co., Va.
014414	CHAPMAN, Charles	1y	C	D.C.	14 JAN 1878	Graceland
004180	CHAPMAN, Daniel	8m	C	D.C.	18 JUL 1875	Moore's
016222	CHAPMAN, Edward Morten	4y	W	D.C.	19 JUN 1878	Congressional
015093	CHAPMAN, Emeline	26y	C	Md.	17 MAR 1878	Young Mens
019705	CHAPMAN, Emma	24y	C	Md.	09 APR 1879	Payne's
018700	CHAPMAN, Emma R.	16y	W	N.Y.	17 JAN 1879	Mt. Olivet
015981	CHAPMAN, Guy R.	2y	W	D.C.	03 JUN 1878	Congressional
016198	CHAPMAN, Harry F.	7y	W	D.C.	17 JUN 1878	Congressional
015230	CHAPMAN, Infant of Thomas Franklin	68h	C	D.C.	30 MAR 1878	Potters Field
018669	CHAPMAN, Infant of Emma	2d	C	D.C.	14 JAN 1879	Potters Field
006677	CHAPMAN, James	54y	C	Va.	15 MAR 1876	Hospital
014305	CHAPMAN, Mary E.	4y	C	D.C.	03 JAN 1878	Graceland
015572	CHAPMAN, Mary Elizabeth, Mrs.	32y	W	Del.	01 MAY 1878	Oak Hill
017140	CHAPMAN, Peter	1y	C	D.C.	22 AUG 1878	Beckett's
011672	CHAPMAN, R.H.	6d	C	D.C.	22 MAY 1877	Mt. Pleasant
016047	CHAPMAN, Rachel	78y	C	Md.	07 JUN 1878	Mt. Olivet
005008	CHAPMAN, Samuel Forrer, Jr.	7m	W	Va.	12 SEP 1875	Fairfax Co., Va.
015071	CHAPMAN, Stephen	3m	C	--	15 MAR 1878	Mt. Olivet
010074	CHAPMAN, Winne	41y	C	Va.	26 DEC 1876	Scagg's Church
005952	CHAPPEL, Celinda	45y	W	N.Y.	06 JAN 1876	Plattsburgh, N.Y.
010646	CHAPPLE, Bernard	25y	W	N.Y.	15 FEB 1877	Washington Asylum
001319	CHAPPLE, James	58y	W	Ire.	06 DEC 1874	Mt. Olivet

District of Columbia Death Records, August 1, 1874 to July 31, 1879

No.	Name	Age	Race	Birth	Death Date	Burial Place
001728	CHARLES, Mary Francis	3y	W	D.C.	14 JAN 1875	Rock Creek
004588f	CHARLTON, Sarah H.	49y	W	D.C.	13 AUG 1875	Congressional
000853	CHARLTON, William Harold	8½d	W	D.C.	19 OCT 1874	Oak Hill
004992	CHASE, Agustus	1y	C	D.C.	11 SEP 1875	Mt. Olivet
013739	CHASE, Alfred	7y	C	D.C.	05 NOV 1877	Mt. Pleasant
003031	CHASE, Ann	70y	C	Md.	18 APR 1875	Washington Asylum
014960	CHASE, Augustus	40y	C	Md.	06 MAR 1878	Mt. Olivet
016974	CHASE, Elizabeth	43y	C	Md.	09 AUG 1878	Mt. Olivet
015253	CHASE, Emanuel	c.70y	C	Md.	01 APR 1878	Harmony
010501	CHASE, Frances Ann	1y	C	D.C.	03 FEB 1877	Mt. Zion
009785	CHASE, Frank	4y	C	D.C.	24 NOV 1876	Mt. Pleasant
007478	CHASE, Grace Ellen	9m	W	D.C.	03 JUN 1876	Methodist White
008223	CHASE, Harriet	75y	C	Va.	13 JUL 1876	Potters Field
005972	CHASE, Henry Cutter	13y	W	N.H.	08 JAN 1876	Portsmouth, N.H.
003112	CHASE, Infant of Wm.	1d	C	D.C.	25 APR 1875	Harmony
018251	CHASE, James William Henry	6m	C	D.C.	06 DEC 1878	Mt. Olivet
004058	CHASE, John	11m	C	D.C.	09 JUL 1875	Ebenezer
008952	CHASE, John	50y	C	Md.	03 SEP 1876	Mt. Zion
010589	CHASE, John	106y	C	Md.	11 FEB 1877	Mt. Zion
005805	CHASE, Joseph	4y	C	Va.	20 DEC 1875	Mt. Olivet
006093	CHASE, Lillie	2y	C	D.C.	22 JAN 1876	Mt. Olivet
002537	CHASE, Louisa	16y	C	Md.	12 MAR 1875	Mt. Olivet
011429	CHASE, Mary	61y	C	Md.	25 APR 1877	Washington Asylum
019516	CHASE, Mary	35y	C	Md.	23 MAR 1879	Mt. Olivet
000813	CHASE, Michael	15d	W	D.C.	15 OCT 1874	Mt. Olivet
003209	CHASE, Susan	35y	C	Md.	03 MAY 1875	Mt. Olivet
020352	CHASE, Thomas Fletcher	8m	C	D.C.	09 JUN 1879	Young Mens
015456	CHASE, William	6m	C	D.C.	20 APR 1878	Mt. Pleasant
018271	CHASE, William	45y	C	D.C.	08 DEC 1878	Mt. Pleasant Plain
002849	CHASE, Wm. H.	5m	C	D.C.	02 APR 1875	Harmony
004876	CHASE, Wm. Henry	3m	C	D.C.	02 SEP 1875	Beckett's
017733	CHASLY, Mary Francis	5m	C	D.C.	14 OCT 1878	Holy Rood
017487	CHATHAM, Julia	22y	C	Va.	22 SEP 1878	Moore's
013541	CHEEKS, Lucy Anderson	29y	W	Ky.	17 OCT 1877	Glenwood
006940	CHEESE, Mary	87y	C	Md.	06 APR 1876	Holy Rood
013407	CHENEY, George Warren	27y	W	D.C.	05 OCT 1877	Oak Hill
009132	CHERRY, Alfred	2y	C	D.C.	19 SEP 1876	Mt. Zion
012457	CHERRY, Charles A.	11m	C	D.C.	21 JUL 1877	Mt. Zion
007612	CHESLEY, Thomas Lee	15y	C	Md.	12 JUN 1876	Young Mens
015949	CHESLEY, W.S.	88y	W	N.S.	01 JUN 1878	Presbyterian
021131	CHESLY, Lewis	8m	C	D.C.	28 JUL 1879	Mt. Zion
019798	CHEVREMONT, Eugene	35y	W	France	16 APR 1879	Mt. Olivet
019126	CHEW, Amelia A.	9y	C	D.C.	20 FEB 1879	Mt. Olivet
001291	CHEW, Anna	24y	C	D.C.	02 DEC 1874	Harmony
005988	CHEW, Arthur	58y	C	Md.	10 JAN 1876	Ebenezer
002191	CHEW, Ella	6m	C	D.C.	16 FEB 1875	Harmony
016973	CHEW, Eva	13m	C	D.C.	09 AUG 1878	Harmony
017563	CHEW, George	10y	C	D.C.	29 SEP 1878	Beckett's
013901	CHEW, Henry Littleton	10d	C	D.C.	24 NOV 1877	Beckett's
008760	CHEW, Infant of Joseph	2min	C	D.C.	21 AUG 1876	Beckett's
015370	CHEW, Infant of William	8d	C	D.C.	12 APR 1878	Beckett's
002019	CHEW, Joseph	1y	M	D.C.	04 FEB 1875	Mt. Olivet
019055	CHEW, Joseph	6y	C	D.C.	13 FEB 1879	Beckett's
012100	CHEW, Liza	81y	C	Md.	28 JUN 1877	Harmony
004030	CHEW, Lubenia	8m	C	D.C.	07 JUL 1875	Harmony
010678	CHEW, Marria Jane	13m	C	D.C.	18 FEB 1877	Beckett's

District of Columbia Death Records, August 1, 1874 to July 31, 1879

No.	Name	Age	Race	Birth	Death Date	Burial Place
002788	CHEW, Mary Ellen	1y	C	Md.	28 MAR 1875	Potters Field
007922	CHEW, Nancy	60y	C	Va.	29 JUN 1876	Young Mens
011627	CHEW, Rebecca	47y	M	Md.	17 MAY 1877	Mt. Olivet
002943	CHEW, Richard S.	31y	W	D.C.	10 APR 1875	Oak Hill
005766	CHEW, Robert	24y	C	Md.	16 DEC 1875	Mt. Olivet
000152	CHEW, Somervill B.	17d	M	D.C.	11 AUG 1874	Harmony
012581	CHEW, Walter S.	3m	W	D.C.	28 JUL 1877	Oak Hill
010852	CHICK, Edger	13y	W	D.C.	03 MAR 1877	Oak Hill
018806	CHICK, Lilie M.	2y	W	D.C.	25 JAN 1879	Oak Hill
020869	CHIDISTIC, Thos. E., Jr.	1h	W	D.C.	10 JUL 1879	Rock Creek
007477	CHILDS, Alice	1m	W	D.C.	03 JUN 1876	Graceland
020387	CHILDS, Effie Mary	2y	W	D.C.	11 JUN 1879	Congressional
015650	CHILDS, Infant of Charles	3m	W	D.C.	08 MAY 1878	Mt. Olivet
020160	CHILDS, Lucy	2y	C	D.C.	21 MAY 1879	Payne's
013351a	CHILDS, Rose Gaye	5y	W	D.C.	29 SEP 1877	North Fairfield, Ohio
011584	CHILTON, William	15y	C	Va.	13 MAY 1877	Washington Asylum
006933	CHINN, Jessie	42y	C	Va.	05 APR 1876	Bristoe Station, Va.
005823	CHIPMAN, Anna C.	51y	W	Conn.	22 DEC 1875	Rock Creek
003820	CHIPMAN, Charles B.	40y	W	Mich.	25 JUN 1875	Congressional
019815	CHIPMAN, Maggie E.	9y	W	D.C.	18 APR 1879	Congressional
008424	CHISHOLM, Emily Jane Willson	76y	W	Md.	26 JUL 1876	Congressional
019714	CHISLEY, Alice	2y	C	D.C.	10 APR 1879	Mt. Olivet
004541	CHISLEY, John Francis	11m	C	Va.	11 AUG 1875	Potters Field
009550	CHISLEY, Lucy	12d	C	D.C.	27 OCT 1876	Mt. Zion
008072	CHISLEY, Mary Agnes	1y	C	D.C.	08 JUL 1876	Mt. Olivet
019065	CHISLEY, Mary E.	10m	C	D.C.	14 FEB 1879	Mt. Olivet
010640	CHISLEY, Mary Ellen	11m	C	D.C.	15 FEB 1877	Mt. Olivet
004195	CHISLY, Henry	13y	C	Md.	19 JUL 1875	Young Mens
014646	CHISLY, Lulu	2y	C	D.C.	03 FEB 1878	Harmony
006332	CHITAINS, Frederick	43y	C	Md.	13 FEB 1876	Ebenezer
018420	CHITHAM, Eliza	35y	C	Md.	22 DEC 1878	Payne's
019444	CHITTANE, Josephene	1y	C	D.C.	18 MAR 1879	Mt. Olivet
019650	CHLITON, James Henry	4m	C	D.C.	04 APR 1879	Potters Field
000403	CHOATE, Warren Christopher	75y	W	Me.	02 SEP 1874	Congressional
012990	CHOPARD, Maria	5m	W	D.C.	28 AUG 1877	Potters Field
015548	CHREAHAN, Thomas	7m	W	D.C.	29 APR 1878	Mt. Olivet
003421	CHRISMAN, John	56y	W	Ger.	24 MAY 1875	Prospect Hill
014539	CHRISTIAN, George	7y	C	D.C.	24 JAN 1878	Young Mens
006333	CHRISTIAN, James	2m	C	D.C.	13 FEB 1876	Ebenezer
003572	CHRISTIAN, Jane	17y	C	Va.	08 JUN 1875	Ebenezer
012886	CHRISTIAN, Lutitia	14m	M	D.C.	20 AUG 1877	Mt. Zion
012285	CHRISTIAN, Tuson	9m	C	D.C.	09 JUL 1877	Beckett's
008046	CHRISTIAN, William H.	17y	W	Ohio	06 JUL 1876	Cleveland, Ohio
004407	CHRISTMAN, Emilie A.C.	32y	W	D.C.	02 AUG 1875	Oak Hill
006560	CHRISTMAN, Margaret J.	32y	W	D.C.	04 MAR 1876	Presbyterian
011818	CHRISTMAN, Philip	73y	W	Pa.	06 JUN 1877	Pa.
018957	CHURCH, Annie	21y	C	Va.	05 FEB 1879	Potters Field
010134	CHURCH, Catharine Hull	21y	W	D.C.	31 DEC 1876	Congressional
005887	CHURCH, George C.	59y	W	Mass.	28 DEC 1875	Congressional
014507	CHURCH, Mary	82y	C	Va.	21 JAN 1878	Mt. Zion
005152	CHURCHILL, Adelia	11y	C	Va.	24 SEP 1875	Potters Field
020892	CHURCHILL, Lewis	35y	C	Va.	12 JUL 1879	Potters Field
018064	CHURCHILL, Maria	88y	C	Va.	16 NOV 1878	Potters Field
004168	CHURCHMAN, Dicey	75y	C	Va.	17 JUL 1875	Mt. Pleasant
011318	CHURM, Charles Henry	1y	C	D.C.	13 APR 1877	Mt. Olivet
017734	CHURN, John H.	34y	W	D.C.	14 OCT 1878	Methodist

District of Columbia Death Records, August 1, 1874 to July 31, 1879

No.	Name	Age	Race	Birth	Death Date	Burial Place
016466	CHURN, Mariah	45y	C	Md.	06 JUL 1878	Mt. Zion
001104	CHURNS, Precilla	46y	W	Md.	10 NOV 1874	Potters Field
012765	CISEL, George	83y	W	Md.	11 AUG 1877	Mt. Olivet
018258	CISSEL, Christena	61y	W	Md.	07 DEC 1878	Glenwood
006319	CISSEL, Edward McCauley	3y	W	D.C.	12 FEB 1876	Glenwood
014596	CISSEL, Infant of Mary	2d	W	D.C.	30 JAN 1878	Jenkins Farm
017753	CISSELL, Clarance H.	2y	W	D.C.	16 OCT 1878	Congressional
005443	CLABORNE, Charles	2y	C	D.C.	13 NOV 1875	Young Mens
011595	CLAGETT, Cornelius Harrison	34y	W	Md.	14 MAY 1877	Congressional
019027	CLAGETT, Harriet H.	59y	W	Md.	11 FEB 1879	Davidsonville, Md.
017845	CLAGETT, Margarett	46y	W	D.C.	24 OCT 1878	Rock Creek
016617	CLAGETT, Parris	2y	C	Va.	16 JUL 1878	Beckett's
019127	CLAGGET, Grandison	22y	W	Va.	20 FEB 1879	Mt. Pleasant
018511	CLAIBORNE, Charlotte	99y	C	Va.	30 DEC 1878	Harmony
016829	CLAIBORNE, Mary E.	2m	C	D.C.	30 JUL 1878	Mt. Pleasant
017639	CLANCY, Catherine Cecelia	5y	W	D.C.	05 OCT 1878	Mt. Olivet
004194	CLANCY, Hanora	5m	W	D.C.	19 JUL 1875	Mt. Olivet
002432	CLANCY, Michael	20y	W	Va.	05 MAR 1875	Mt. Olivet
011085	CLANCY, William	30y	W	Conn.	23 MAR 1877	Soldier's Home
012224	CLANNIGAN, Eliza	69y	C	Va.	05 JUL 1877	Arlington
008878	CLARANCE, William	6m	C	D.C.	30 AUG 1876	Harmony
014824	CLARENCE, Edward	6m	W	U.S.	20 FEB 1878	Mt. Olivet
017127	CLARICE, Cecelia	3m	C	D.C.	21 AUG 1878	Mt. Olivet
009942	CLARK, Albert	67y	W	Conn.	12 DEC 1876	Cleveland, Ohio
015037	CLARK, Alexander	77y	W	Md.	12 MAR 1878	Alexandria, Va.
011529	CLARK, Alice	1y	C	D.C.	06 MAY 1877	Jones Chapel
017421	CLARK, Anna	27y	W	D.C.	16 SEP 1878	Mt. Olivet
017820	CLARK, Barbara	70y	C	Va.	21 OCT 1878	Arlington
011925	CLARK, Catharine	43y	C	Md.	16 JUN 1877	Harmony
003470	CLARK, Catharine E.	68y	W	Va.	29 MAY 1875	Oak Hill
014999	CLARK, Catharine H.	8y	W	D.C.	09 MAR 1878	Congressional
013523	CLARK, Catherine	10m	C	D.C.	15 OCT 1877	Beckett's
008786	CLARK, Cecil Seaton	17d	W	D.C.	22 AUG 1876	Congressional
001278	CLARK, Charles	46y	W	Ver.	30 NOV 1874	Lisbon, N.H.
012699	CLARK, Charlotte	1y	C	D.C.	06 AUG 1877	Potters Field
003122	CLARK, Danl. D.	45y	W	N.Y.	26 APR 1875	Congressional
018148	CLARK, Ed M.S.	3m	C	D.C.	25 NOV 1878	Mt. Olivet
011370	CLARK, Edith Sherman	6m	W	D.C.	19 APR 1877	Congressional
013118	CLARK, Edna Elizabeth	7m	C	D.C.	08 SEP 1877	Mt. Pleasant Plain
013927	CLARK, Edward	1y	C	D.C.	26 NOV 1877	Young Mens
014126	CLARK, Eliza	27y	C	Va.	18 DEC 1877	Beckett's
013928	CLARK, Ella	27y	C	Va.	26 NOV 1877	Potters Field
010592	CLARK, Ellen	87y	W	Va.	11 FEB 1877	Oak Hill
014581	CLARK, Ellen S.	42y	W	Ver.	28 JAN 1878	Congressional
010577	CLARK, Ellenora	60y	W	Md.	10 FEB 1877	Congressional
013942	CLARK, Emeline G.	5m	C	D.C.	27 NOV 1877	Mt. Olivet
006732	CLARK, Enis	2y	M	D.C.	19 MAR 1876	Graceland
018240	CLARK, Eugene	9m	C	D.C.	05 DEC 1878	Payne's
000615	CLARK, Florence	12d	C	D.C.	23 SEP 1874	Mt. Pleasant
000176	CLARK, Frances	23y	W	U.S.	13 AUG 1874	Glenwood
017536	CLARK, Frances	25y	C	D.C.	26 SEP 1878	Harmony
009883	CLARK, Frank	1y	C	D.C.	06 DEC 1876	Graceland
009685	CLARK, Frank	1y	C	D.C.	13 NOV 1876	Young Mens
012270	CLARK, Frank	10m	C	D.C.	08 JUL 1877	Potters Field
013581	CLARK, Freeman	10d	C	D.C.	21 OCT 1877	Young Mens
010944	CLARK, George	2y	C	D.C.	11 MAR 1877	Beckett's

District of Columbia Death Records, August 1, 1874 to July 31, 1879

No.	Name	Age	Race	Birth	Death Date	Burial Place
016514	CLARK, George Duvall	25y	W	N.Y.	09 JUL 1878	Auburn, N.Y.
014722	CLARK, Harriet Ann	20y	C	D.C.	09 FEB 1878	Young Mens
013913	CLARK, Henry	50y	C	Va.	25 NOV 1877	Beckett's
016766	CLARK, Infant of Edward	5min	C	D.C.	26 JUL 1878	Potters Field
004167	CLARK, Infant of Gabe	2m	C	D.C.	17 JUL 1875	Payne's
008323	CLARK, Infant of Margaret	1d	C	D.C.	19 JUL 1876	Mt. Olivet
008164	CLARK, Infant of Philip	1h	C	D.C.	11 JUL 1876	Young Mens
004891	CLARK, Infant of Robt. T.	7d	W	D.C.	03 SEP 1875	Fairfax Co., Va.
018911	CLARK, Infant of Wm.	5d	C	D.C.	01 FEB 1879	Young Mens
018740	CLARK, Isaac Spencer	60y	W	N.Y.	20 JAN 1879	Congressional
009999	CLARK, James Edward	8d	C	D.C.	18 DEC 1876	Ebenezer
014415	CLARK, Jas. P., Dr.	50y	W	Ire.	14 JAN 1878	Washington Asylum
011409	CLARK, John	55y	W	Ire.	23 APR 1877	Mt. Olivet
013530	CLARK, John	80y	W	Md.	16 OCT 1877	Presbyterian
018496	CLARK, John	31y	W	Ire.	29 DEC 1878	Hospital, Government
013880	CLARK, John A.	c.53y	W	N.Y.	22 NOV 1877	N.Y. City
020421	CLARK, John D., Jun.	30y	W	D.C.	13 JUN 1879	Congressional
007085	CLARK, John James H.	1y	C	D.C.	23 APR 1876	Young Mens
014428	CLARK, John W.	43y	C	Va.	15 JAN 1878	Harmony
019175	CLARK, Joseph	19y	C	Va.	24 FEB 1879	Potters Field
021169	CLARK, Josephine	36y	C	D.C.	31 JUL 1879	Holy Rood
019567	CLARK, Josephine	38y	C	D.C.	27 MAR 1879	Harmony
004044	CLARK, Julia	4m	W	D.C.	08 JUL 1875	Prospect Hill
015457	CLARK, Julia	11m	C	D.C.	20 APR 1878	Mt. Zion
001401	CLARK, Lilly May	4y	W	D.C.	15 DEC 1874	Congressional
005659	CLARK, Lucinda J.	31y	W	Md.	05 DEC 1875	Glenwood
017851	CLARK, Malinda	c.80y	C	Md.	25 OCT 1878	Harmony
016003	CLARK, Margaret	45y	W	Ire.	04 JUN 1878	Mt. Olivet
021170	CLARK, Margaret, Mrs.	70y	W	Pa.	31 JUL 1879	Glenwood
002520	CLARK, Martha	50y	C	Va.	11 MAR 1875	Harmony
007758	CLARK, Martha	39y	C	Va.	21 JUN 1876	Harmony
001424	CLARK, Mary	30y	C	D.C.	18 DEC 1874	Payne's
008263	CLARK, Mary C.	49y	W	D.C.	14 JUL 1876	Mt. Olivet
017079	CLARK, Mary G.	6m	C	D.C.	17 AUG 1878	Beckett's
002706	CLARK, Mary Jane	20y	M	D.C	23 MAR 1875	Harmony
019137	CLARK, Mary R.	9m	W	D.C.	21 FEB 1879	Congressional
018017	CLARK, Nelson	26y	C	D.C.	11 NOV 1878	Young Mens
002355	CLARK, Raymond	6m	W	D.C.	28 FEB 1875	Presbyterian
010111	CLARK, Robert C.	71y	C	D.C.	29 DEC 1876	Harmony
006676	CLARK, Robert F.	7m	C	D.C.	15 MAR 1876	Holy Rood
007465	CLARK, Rosa	8y	C	D.C.	02 JUN 1876	Harmony
012780	CLARK, Rose G.	1y	C	D.C.	12 AUG 1877	Mt. Olivet
019921	CLARK, Rush	45y	W	Pa.	28 APR 1879	Iowa City, Iowa
002720	CLARK, Samuel	1y	C	D.C.	24 MAR 1875	Mt. Olivet
011253	CLARK, Sarah A.	34y	W	Va.	07 APR 1877	Bailey's X Roads, Va.
017523	CLARK, Susan	27y	C	Md.	25 SEP 1878	Mt. Pleasant
007403	CLARK, Teresa A.	86y	W	D.C.	25 MAY 1876	Mt. Olivet
000720	CLARK, Thomas	75y	W	Ire.	05 OCT 1874	Mt. Olivet
003950	CLARK, Thomas	40y	C	Va.	01 JUL 1875	Ebenezer
003369	CLARK, Thomas	8y	C	D.C.	20 MAY 1875	Mt. Olivet
020201	CLARK, Virginia	54y	C	Va.	26 MAY 1879	Harmony
018631	CLARK, Walter	1d	W	D.C.	10 JAN 1879	Congressional
001474	CLARK, William	14y	M	Md.	24 DEC 1874	Baltimore, Md.
020707	CLARK, William	37y	W	N.Y.	02 JUL 1879	Congressional
021123	CLARK, William H.	18m	C	D.C.	27 JUL 1879	Beckett's
020778	CLARK, Willie	8m	C	D.C.	05 JUL 1879	Beckett's

District of Columbia Death Records, August 1, 1874 to July 31, 1879   67

No.	Name	Age	Race	Birth	Death Date	Burial Place
014609	CLARKE, Adeline R.	70y	W	N.Y.	31 JAN 1878	Oak Hill
010520	CLARKE, Alossius	2y	C	D.C.	04 FEB 1877	Holy Rood
016240	CLARKE, Arethusa M.	4m	W	D.C.	21 JUN 1878	Oak Hill
004239	CLARKE, Arvina	10m	M	D.C.	22 JUL 1875	Mt. Zion
005516	CLARKE, Cathran	25y	C	D.C.	20 NOV 1875	Mt. Olivet
017041	CLARKE, E.O.	8m	C	D.C.	14 AUG 1878	Mt. Pleasant
000658	CLARKE, Elizabeth	51y	W	Eng.	28 SEP 1874	Rock Creek
017611	CLARKE, Frank Baxter	1y	W	D.C.	02 OCT 1878	Glenwood
012412	CLARKE, Franklin P.	24y	W	D.C.	18 JUL 1877	Congressional
015094	CLARKE, James H.	50y	C	Md.	17 MAR 1878	Harmony
013486	CLARKE, Leonard	48y	C	Md.	12 OCT 1877	Holy Rood
016470	CLARKE, Lillie	1y	W	D.C.	06 JUL 1878	Congressional
001661	CLARKE, Lucy Miller	28y	W	Mo.	08 JAN 1875	Oak Hill
013131	CLARKE, Margaret	81y	W	Md.	09 SEP 1877	Congressional
001130	CLARKE, Mary Anna	33y	W	D.C.	13 NOV 1874	Oak Hill
008171	CLARKE, Reba Sarah	36y	W	Conn.	11 JUL 1876	Glenwood
002279	CLARKE, Sarah	2y	C	D.C.	22 FEB 1875	Mt. Pleasant
020977	CLARKE, Walter	2y	C	D.C.	17 JUL 1879	Mt. Pleasant
008227	CLARKE, William H.	22y	W	D.C.	13 JUL 1876	Mt. Olivet
006972	CLARKE, Wm. H.	45y	W	Ire.	09 APR 1876	Rock Creek
007533	CLARKSON, John F.	72y	W	N.S.	07 JUN 1876	Glenwood
019638	CLARKSON, Mary C.	29y	W	Fla.	03 APR 1879	Mt. Olivet
018543	CLARKSON, Mary E.	1y	W	D.C.	02 JAN 1879	Glenwood/Mt. Olivet
018945	CLARVOE, John A.W.	47y	W	D.C.	04 FEB 1879	Congressional
000540	CLARVUE, George W.L.	42y	W	D.C.	18 SEP 1874	Graceland
008872	CLARY, Johannah	10m	W	D.C.	29 AUG 1876	Mt. Olivet
010043	CLARY, Michael	2y	W	D.C.	21 DEC 1876	Mt. Olivet
016924	CLASH, Mary	9m	C	Md.	06 AUG 1878	Young Mens
010776	CLAXTON, James William	8d	W	D.C.	25 FEB 1877	Potters Field
000013	CLAXTON, John	45y	C	Md.	01 AUG 1874	Mt. Zion
015169	CLAY, Elizabeth	1y	C	D.C.	24 MAR 1878	Payne's
021006	CLAY, Gertrude	8y	C	D.C.	19 JUL 1879	Harmony/Graceland
011110	CLAY, Infant of Henry	2m	W	D.C.	25 MAR 1877	Ebenezer
009263	CLAY, Nora	7d	C	D.C.	01 OCT 1876	Harmony
012838	CLAYBORN, Ella Olivia	9m	C	D.C.	16 AUG 1877	Young Mens
015732	CLAYBORN, Mary Barron	1y	W	D.C.	15 MAY 1878	Congressional
013487	CLAYBORN, Willie	2m	C	D.C.	12 OCT 1877	Beckett's
020083	CLAYBOURN, Mary	6d	C	D.C.	13 MAY 1879	Mt. Pleasant
012499	CLAYBURN, Polly	72y	C	Va.	23 JUL 1877	Young Mens
007534	CLAYBURN, Wm.	4m	C	D.C.	07 JUN 1876	Ebenezer
007920	CLAYTON, Bettie	60y	C	Va.	29 JUN 1876	Mt. Pleasant Plain
002172	CLAYTON, Champin	1y	C	D.C.	15 FEB 1875	Harmony
016603	CLAYTON, Charles Benson	6y	W	Pa.	15 JUL 1878	Rock Creek
007744	CLAYTON, Henry	35y	C	Va.	20 JUN 1876	Harmony
017626	CLAYTON, Susan	51y	W	N.Y.	04 OCT 1878	Graceland/Glenwood
001529	CLAYTON, Thomas G.	69y	W	Pa.	28 DEC 1874	Glenwood
020046	CLAYTON, Ursula Hope	9m	W	D.C.	09 MAY 1879	Graceland
000043	CLAYTON, Walter	11y	M	Va.	03 AUG 1874	Beckett's
013089	CLEAN, Lillie Helen	2y	W	D.C.	05 SEP 1877	Congressional
018630	CLEAR, Robt. Bradley	8y	W	D.C.	10 JAN 1879	Oak Hill/Congressional
010667	CLEAR, Thomas	59y	W	Pa.	17 FEB 1877	Oak Hill
017691	CLEARY, Agnes	5y	W	Pa.	10 OCT 1878	Holy Rood
020420	CLEARY, Charles Tyler	8m	W	D.C.	13 JUN 1879	Mt. Olivet
008404	CLEARY, Cornelius	14d	W	D.C.	24 JUL 1876	Holy Rood
017638	CLEARY, Katie	6y	W	Md.	05 OCT 1878	Holy Rood
007934	CLEARY, Patrick	48y	W	Ire.	30 JUN 1876	Holy Rood

District of Columbia Death Records, August 1, 1874 to July 31, 1879

No.	Name	Age	Race	Birth	Death Date	Burial Place
016449	CLEARY, Paul	3m	W	D.C.	05 JUL 1878	Mt. Olivet
019221	CLEARY, William	72y	W	Va.	27 FEB 1879	Mt. Olivet
006634	CLEGGITT, Lemuel	50y	C	Md.	11 MAR 1876	Potters Field
001124	CLEMENTS, A. Sidney	25y	W	D.C.	11 NOV 1874	Congressional
015414	CLEMENTS, Alfius	2y	M	D.C.	16 APR 1878	Young Mens
014489	CLEMENTS, Edward	40y	W	Md.	20 JAN 1878	Mt. Olivet
016909	CLEMENTS, Eliza	3y	C	D.C.	05 AUG 1878	Harmony
013332a	CLEMENTS, Forence R.	9y	W	D.C.	27 SEP 1877	Mt. Olivet
008885	CLEMENTS, James Theopolus	5m	W	D.C.	30 AUG 1876	Holy Rood
020991	CLEMENTS, Jane N., Mrs.	53y	W	D.C.	18 JUL 1879	Oak Hill
010092	CLEMENTS, Joseph S.	1y	W	D.C.	27 DEC 1876	Fairfax Co., Va.
011974	CLEMENTS, M.J., Mrs.	31y	W	Pa.	19 JUN 1877	Glenwood
003661	CLEMENTS, Martha E.	7y	C	D.C.	16 JUN 1875	Mt. Zion
017721	CLEMENTS, Mary Louisa	23y	W	Md.	13 OCT 1878	Glenwood
013639	CLEMENTS, Samuel H.	71y	W	Md.	26 OCT 1877	Mt. Olivet
017488	CLEMENTS, Sophia Jane	51y	W	D.C.	22 SEP 1878	Holy Rood
001631	CLEMENTS, W.D.	35y	W	D.C.	06 JAN 1875	Trinity Church
002896	CLEMENTS, Walter S.	2y	W	D.C.	06 APR 1875	Congressional
003069	CLEMENTS, William	4y	C	D.C.	21 APR 1875	Mt. Zion
005306	CLEMENTS, Wm.	32y	W	D.C.	29 OCT 1875	Congressional
007620	CLEMENTSON, George W.	32y	W	D.C.	13 JUN 1876	Holy Rood
014211	CLEMENTSON, Mary Cornelia	4y	W	D.C.	26 DEC 1877	Presbyterian
005103a	CLEMESSON, John W.C.	1y	W	D.C.	11 OCT 1875	Presbyterian
000887	CLEMINS, James G.	1y	C	D.C.	21 OCT 1874	Mt. Pleasant
019753	CLEMONS, Ida	7d	C	D.C.	13 APR 1879	Mt. Pleasant
002392f	CLENDENIN, Lottie Campbell	11y	W	D.C.	02 MAR 1875	Glenwood
020650	CLEVELAND, Catherine L.	26y	C	Va.	28 JUN 1879	Graceland
002418	CLEVELAND, Nellie	23y	W	Wisc.	04 MAR 1875	Graceland
006665	CLEVER, Huldah	39y	W	N.Y.	14 MAR 1876	Fairfax C.H., Va.
020402	CLIFFORD, John Gray	7y	W	N.Y.	12 JUN 1879	Mt. Olivet
006107	CLIFT, Eliza R., Mrs.	39y	W	Va.	23 JAN 1876	Congressional
013609	CLIFTON, Sarah	30y	C	Va.	24 OCT 1877	Young Mens
006607	CLIFTON, Vara Genevieve	2y	W	D.C.	09 MAR 1876	St. Mary's
020753	CLINCKETT, Fanny	55y	C	Va.	04 JUL 1879	Harmony
005872	CLINCKINS, Virginia	7m	C	D.C.	27 DEC 1875	Ebenezer
019242	CLINE, Charles Henry	1y	W	D.C.	01 MAR 1879	Presbyterian
010201	CLINKET, Barney	30y	C	Va.	07 JAN 1877	Harmony
019517	CLINKINS, Luvenia	5y	C	D.C.	23 MAR 1879	Payne's
004693	CLINTON, Judie	104y	C	Md.	21 AUG 1875	Mt. Zion
013280	CLINTON, Maga	15y	C	D.C.	23 SEP 1877	Mt. Zion
004045f	CLINTON, William	70y	W	Ire.	22 JUN 1871	Mt. Olivet
020025	CLOSE, Jerome B.	c.55y	W	N.Y.	07 MAY 1879	Glenwood
020008	CLOSE, Louis C.	3y	W	D.C.	06 MAY 1879	Congressional
014740	CLOSS, Charley Taylor	32y	W	Ohio	11 FEB 1878	Glenwood
002337	CLUBB, John Louis	69y	W	D.C.	27 FEB 1875	Congressional
008809	CLUSS, Robert	2y	W	D.C.	24 AUG 1876	Oak Hill
013447	CLUTE, Elizabeth R.	41y	W	N.Y	09 OCT 1877	Congressional
006861	CLYMER, Alexander	80y	C	Va.	30 MAR 1876	Potters Field
005389	COAKLEY, Francis D.	76y	C	D.C.	08 NOV 1875	Holy Rood
000963	COAKLEY, Frank	2y	C	D.C.	28 OCT 1874	Mt. Pleasant Plain
001086	COAKLEY, Infant of George F.	1d	C	D.C.	08 NOV 1874	Mt. Zion
016016	COAKLEY, John R.	4m	C	D.C.	05 JUN 1878	Mt. Zion
001127	COAKLEY, Lucy E.	21m	M	Va.	11 NOV 1874	Holy Rood
009633	COAKLEY, May E.	40y	C	D.C.	06 NOV 1876	Holy Rood
013237	COAKLEY, Wm. L.	27y	C	D.C.	18 SEP 1877	Holy Rood
003006	COAL, Matilda	88y	C	Md.	16 APR 1875	Baltimore, Md.

District of Columbia Death Records, August 1, 1874 to July 31, 1879   69

No.	Name	Age	Race	Birth	Death Date	Burial Place
000628	COATES, Benjamin	4m	C	D.C.	24 SEP 1874	Ebenezer
018522	COATES, Cardwell	2y	C	D.C.	31 DEC 1878	Beckett's
013221	COATES, Charles	9d	C	D.C.	16 SEP 1877	Potters Field
013335	COATES, John	1y	C	Md.	28 SEP 1877	Holy Rood
013401	COATES, Kandus	6y	C	Md.	04 OCT 1877	Mt. Zion
019557	COATES, Mathew	42y	C	Md.	26 MAR 1879	Potters Field
001102	COATES, Susanna	35y	C	Md.	09 NOV 1874	Beckett's
020377	COATS, Charles	10m	C	D.C.	10 JUN 1879	Tennallytown
015021	COATS, Edward	70y	C	Md.	11 MAR 1878	Mt. Zion
007919	COATS, Henry	4m	C	D.C.	29 JUN 1876	Dean's Family
012576	COATS, Ida F.	1y	C	D.C.	28 JUL 1877	Potters Field
012353	COATS, Infant of Columbus	14h	C	D.C.	14 JUL 1877	Ebenezer
014091	COATS, Jane	70y	C	Va.	14 DEC 1877	Mt. Zion
000536	COATS, Lillie	2y	M	D.C.	17 SEP 1874	Washington Asylum
015501	COATS, Lillie	1y	C	M.	24 APR 1878	Mt. Zion
016951	COATS, Mary Elizabeth	4m	C	D.C.	08 AUG 1878	Mt. Zion
000913	COBAUGH, Frederick W.	2w	W	D.C.	24 OCT 1874	Congressional
014367	COBAUGH, Helen J., Mrs.	36y	W	Va.	09 JAN 1878	Congressional
000771	COBAUGH, James	4h	W	D.C.	10 OCT 1874	Congressional
019803	COBB, Jane Melissa Parker	55y	W	Ver.	17 APR 1879	Glenwood
013311	COBETH, Mary	27y	W	Md.	26 SEP 1877	Graceland
009485	COEVY, John	23y	C	S.C.	21 OCT 1876	Potters Field
005540	COFFEE, Robert	46y	W	Eng.	23 NOV 1875	Hospital
011923	COFFEY, Joseph Nathaniel	61	C	D.C.	15 JUN 1877	Holy Rood
013554	COFFEY, Martina Ardella	19y	C	D.C.	18 OCT 1877	Holy Rood
006493	COFFREN, Jeremiah	33y	W	Md.	28 FEB 1876	Prince George's Co., Md.
000986	COGAN, Thomas	48y	W	Ire.	30 OCT 1874	Mt. Olivet
014158	COGGINS, Anna May	1y	W	D.C.	21 DEC 1877	Mt. Olivet, Balt., Md.
006717	COGGINS, John	42y	W	Eng.	18 MAR 1876	Mt. Olivet
002448	COGGINS, Thomas	71y	W	Eng.	06 MAR 1875	Mt. Olivet, Balto.
017080	COGSWELL, Sarah	4y	W	D.C.	17 AUG 1878	Mt. Pleasant
015424	COGWELL, Nelson	28y	C	Va.	17 APR 1878	Young Mens
016538	COHEN, Lilly	4m	W	D.C.	10 JUL 1878	Hebrew
015022	COHEN, Rosa	2y	W	D.C.	11 MAR 1878	Washington Hebrew
015847	COHILL, Sadie A.	7y	W	D.C.	26 MAY 1878	Congressional
002352	COHN, Fany	2y	W	D.C.	28 FEB 1875	Jewish
005497	COHN, Margaret	55y	W	Ire.	18 NOV 1875	Mt. Olivet
007757	COHN, Moses	5m	W	D.C.	21 JUN 1876	Adas Israel
000782	COKE, William, Jr.	34y	W	D.C.	11 OCT 1874	Harmony
016158	COLAMER, Amanda C.	24y	W	D.C.	14 JUN 1878	Congressional
009595	COLBACH, John	67y	W	Ger.	01 NOV 1876	Mt. Olivet
001827	COLBATH, Francis Adams	26y	W	Mass.	21 JAN 1875	Glenwood
003504	COLBATH, George Harris	30y	W	N.H.	01 JUN 1875	Glenwood
013542	COLBERT, Charles	2y	C	D.C.	17 OCT 1877	Mt. Zion
015170	COLBERT, Cynthia	50y	C	Md.	24 MAR 1878	Holy Rood
007548	COLBERT, Eliza A.	9d	C	D.C.	08 JUN 1876	Ebenezer
003620	COLBERT, Ellen	1y	C	D.C.	12 JUN 1875	Mt. Zion
020532	COLBERT, Ellen	51y	W	Ire.	20 JUN 1879	Mt. Olivet
001770f	COLBERT, Francis	16y	C	D.C.	17 JAN 1875	Young Mens
006832	COLBERT, Hattie	1y	C	D.C.	27 MAR 1876	Ebenezer
015690	COLBERT, James	2m	C	D.C.	12 MAY 1878	Beckett's
005361	COLBERT, James Robert	1y	C	D.C.	05 NOV 1875	Harmony
014111	COLBERT, Joanna	64y	W	Ire.	16 DEC 1877	Mt. Olivet
008450	COLBERT, Joseph Samuel	15d	C	D.C.	28 JUL 1876	Prince George's Co., Md.
008816	COLBERT, Lula	2y	C	D.C.	25 AUG 1876	Mt. Olivet
013943	COLBERT, Mary A.	2y	C	D.C.	27 NOV 1877	Harmony

District of Columbia Death Records, August 1, 1874 to July 31, 1879

No.	Name	Age	Race	Birth	Death Date	Burial Place
020752	COLBERT, Robert F.	4d	C	D.C.	04 JUL 1879	Harmony
008440	COLBERT, Rosie Martina	14d	C	D.C	27 JUL 1876	Prince George's Co., Md.
003539	COLBERT, Willie Thomas	1y	C	D.C.	06 JUN 1875	Oxen Hill Church
007549	COLBURN, Harry Eugene	5d	W	D.C.	08 JUN 1876	Oak Hill
010792	COLBUT, May Blanch	1y	C	D.C.	26 FEB 1877	Young Mens
012989	COLE, Alphonso	8m	C	D.C.	28 AUG 1877	Holy Rood
011800	COLE, Anna	26y	C	Va.	05 JUN 1877	Baptist
001825	COLE, Annie (of Sandy Shaw)	16y	C	D.C.	21 JAN 1875	Harmony
016241	COLE, Bernhard	6m	W	D.C.	21 JUN 1878	Mt. Olivet
020823	COLE, Charles	75y	C	D.C.	08 JUL 1879	Holy Rood
017326	COLE, Clinton	9y	C	Md.	05 SEP 1878	Beckett's
016468	COLE, Daniel N.	1m	C	D.C.	06 JUL 1878	Potters Field
002708	COLE, Eliza	4y	C	D.C.	23 MAR 1875	Mt. Olivet
007670	COLE, Francis A.	7m	W	D.C.	16 JUN 1876	Graceland
011655	COLE, Francis A.	5m	C	D.C.	20 MAY 1877	Baptist
014143	COLE, Frederick	22y	C	Md.	20 DEC 1877	Payne's
009318	COLE, Fredrick A.	9m	W	D.C.	06 OCT 1876	Congressional
003788	COLE, George Reginald	7m	C	D.C.	23 JUN 1875	Mt. Olivet
020911	COLE, Harry Johnson	1y	C	D.C.	13 JUL 1879	Harmony
009527	COLE, Infant of Henry	7d	C	D.C.	25 OCT 1876	Ebenezer
011906	COLE, Isabella	32y	C	D.C.	15 JUN 1877	Mt. Olivet
000207	COLE, Jas. Henry	4y	C	D.C.	16 AUG 1874	Mt. Olivet
003450	COLE, John	26y	W	Va.	27 MAY 1875	Glenwood
015786	COLE, John	5m	C	D.C.	21 MAY 1878	Potters Field
012546	COLE, Julia T.	8m	C	D.C.	27 JUL 1877	Mt. Olivet
003076	COLE, Lizzie	22y	C	Va.	21 APR 1875	Ebenezer
007464	COLE, Mary	22y	W	Va.	01 JUN 1876	Fredericksburg, Va.
009606	COLE, Mary	38y	C	Va.	03 NOV 1876	Ebenezer
011016	COLE, Millie	32y	C	Va.	17 MAR 1877	Ebenezer
003033	COLE, Nellie	10m	W	D.C.	18 APR 1875	Mt. Olivet
005452	COLE, Rachel A.	54y	C	D.C.	14 NOV 1875	Harmony
008319	COLE, Robert	2m	C	D.C.	18 JUL 1876	Mt. Zion
016601	COLE, Robert	39y	C	Va.	15 JUL 1878	Beckett's
001660	COLE, Samuel	11y	M	Va.	08 JAN 1875	Mt. Olivet
017513	COLE, Samuel	24y	C	Va.	24 SEP 1878	Potters Field
007745	COLE, Sarah Frances	2y	W	D.C.	20 JUN 1876	Congressional
017104	COLE, Theodore	9y	C	D.C.	19 AUG 1878	Mt. Olivet
018567	COLE, Virginia	39y	C	Va.	05 JAN 1879	Harmony
019076	COLE, William H.	42y	C	Va.	15 FEB 1879	Graceland
010918	COLE, Wm. Henry	9d	W	D.C.	08 MAR 1877	Graceland
020593	COLE, Wm. Henry	4m	C	D.C.	24 JUN 1879	Potters Field
004068	COLEMAN, Anthony	1y	C	D.C.	10 JUL 1875	Young Mens
004762	COLEMAN, Benj.	5d	C	D.C.	26 AUG 1875	Mt. Zion
016098	COLEMAN, Burril	44y	C	Va.	10 JUN 1878	Potters Field
020101	COLEMAN, Catherine	42y	W	Ire.	15 MAY 1879	Mt. Olivet
012781	COLEMAN, Charlotte	65y	C	Md.	12 AUG 1877	Holy Rood
010608	COLEMAN, Cornelius	5m	C	D.C.	13 FEB 1877	Potters Field
016733	COLEMAN, Delphi	40y	C	Va.	24 JUL 1878	Arlington
004846	COLEMAN, Eddie	1y	C	D.C.	31 AUG 1875	Young Mens
001473	COLEMAN, Edward	11m	C	D.C.	24 DEC 1874	Mt. Pleasant
019802	COLEMAN, Eleonora	3y	C	D.C.	17 APR 1879	Beckett's
003282	COLEMAN, Elizabeth	29y	C	Md.	10 MAY 1875	Harmony
010470	COLEMAN, Elmira	17y	C	Va.	01 FEB 1877	Ebenezer
008843	COLEMAN, Emma J.	4y	C	Va.	27 AUG 1876	Ebenezer
011746	COLEMAN, Frank	c.24y	C	Md.	30 MAY 1877	Ebenezer
014875	COLEMAN, Gracie	5y	W	Mich.	28 FEB 1878	Congressional

District of Columbia Death Records, August 1, 1874 to July 31, 1879   71

No.	Name	Age	Race	Birth	Death Date	Burial Place
016145	COLEMAN, Henry G.	3y	W	N.Y.	13 JUN 1878	Mt. Olivet
001933	COLEMAN, Hester	3y	C	D.C.	28 JAN 1875	Ebenezer
013871	COLEMAN, Infant of Eli	10min	C	D.C.	20 NOV 1877	Potters Field
017940	COLEMAN, Infant of Florence	7d	C	D.C.	04 NOV 1878	Macedonia
017040	COLEMAN, Infant of John	12h	C	D.C.	14 AUG 1878	Potters Field
015211	COLEMAN, Infant of John	c.3min	C	D.C.	28 MAR 1878	Potters Field
008937	COLEMAN, Infant of Patric	15min	W	D.C.	02 SEP 1876	Mt. Olivet
006691	COLEMAN, Infant of Sarah	1m	C	D.C.	16 MAR 1876	Potters Field
015264	COLEMAN, Isabella	7w	C	D.C.	02 APR 1878	Harmony
005803	COLEMAN, James	7y	M	Md.	20 DEC 1875	Mt. Olivet
017836	COLEMAN, John	14d	C	D.C.	23 OCT 1878	Mt. Zion
000692	COLEMAN, Jos. Hopkins	1y	C	D.C.	01 OCT 1874	Young Mens
000565	COLEMAN, Laura (illeg.)	3y	C	D.C.	19 SEP 1874	Potters Field
010151	COLEMAN, Leana	65y	C	Va.	02 JAN 1877	Young Mens
006446	COLEMAN, Lony	32y	C	Ky.	23 FEB 1876	Potters Field
013281	COLEMAN, Malinda	50y	C	Md.	22 SEP 1877	Washington Asylum
016467	COLEMAN, Margaret	24y	C	Va.	04 JUL 1878	Hospital
003915	COLEMAN, Mary	5m	C	D.C.	29 JUN 1875	Ebenezer
011852	COLEMAN, Mary C.	2y	C	D.C.	09 JUN 1877	Young Mens
020480	COLEMAN, Nellie	2y	C	D.C.	17 JUN 1879	Moore's
014647	COLEMAN, Nettie	45y	C	Va.	03 FEB 1878	Beckett's
000075	COLEMAN, Randle	35y	C	Va.	06 AUG 1874	Beckett's
001645	COLEMAN, Robert	69y	C	Va.	07 JAN 1875	Beckett's
006585	COLEMAN, Robert	29y	C	Va.	07 MAR 1876	Potters Field
010513	COLEMAN, Robert	32y	C	Md.	04 FEB 1877	Harmony
012138	COLEMAN, Rosa	3y	C	D.C.	30 JUN 1877	Beckett's
007669	COLEMAN, Rosetta	3m	W	D.C.	16 JUN 1876	Potters Field
007446	COLEMAN, Roy Thomas	10m	C	D.C.	31 MAY 1876	Young Mens
008449	COLEMAN, Sarah	45y	C	Va.	28 JUL 1876	Mt. Pleasant
016502	COLEMAN, Secelia	7y	C	D.C.	08 JUL 1878	Young Mens
015155	COLEMAN, Thos.	25y	C	Va.	23 MAR 1878	Potters Field
018016	COLEMAN, Tulip	7m	C	D.C.	11 NOV 1878	Potters Field
011079	COLEMAN, Viola	9m	C	D.C.	22 MAR 1877	Ebenezer
009312	COLEMAN, William	76y	W	Ire.	05 OCT 1876	Mt. Olivet
011348	COLEMAN, William	47y	C	Va.	15 APR 1877	Ebenezer
018341	COLEMAN, William Grinnell	2m	W	N.Y.	15 DEC 1878	Glenwood
016469	COLEMAN, Willis	1y	C	D.C.	06 JUL 1878	Beckett's
017197	COLES, Infant of Lucy	4d	C	D.C.	26 AUG 1878	Potters Field
015502	COLES, Rosa	40y	C	Va.	24 APR 1878	Beckett's
006055	COLFLISH, Catherine	85y	W	Pa.	18 JAN 1876	Baltimore, Md.
016081	COLIN, Beverly	2y	C	D.C.	09 JUN 1878	Mt. Pleasant
016844	COLIN, Julia	3y	C	Va.	31 JUL 1878	Mt. Pleasant
008673	COLLAMER, Frank W.	6m	W	D.C.	13 AUG 1876	Congressional
015578	COLLEDGE, Charles Moorehead	9y	W	D.C.	02 MAY 1878	Glenwood
012599	COLLEDGE, Wm. H.	52y	W	Eng.	29 JUL 1877	Glenwood
000466	COLLENS, Elizabeth, Mrs.	46y	C	Va.	09 SEP 1874	Harmony
020751	COLLETTE, Coudrette	7y	C	D.C.	04 JUL 1879	Graceland
000808	COLLIER, William H.	4y	W	D.C.	15 OCT 1874	Glenwood
003252	COLLINS, Agnes	9m	W	D.C.	07 MAY 1875	Mt. Olivet
008578	COLLINS, Andrew Jackson	62y	W	D.C.	06 AUG 1876	Tennallytown
004877	COLLINS, Arthur Leonard	1y	W	D.C.	02 SEP 1875	Presbyterian
009503	COLLINS, Bernard Patrick	2y	W	D.C.	23 OCT 1876	Mt. Olivet
014075	COLLINS, Catherine E.	4m	W	D.C.	12 DEC 1877	Holy Rood
018369	COLLINS, Clifton S.	7m	W	D.C.	18 DEC 1878	Holy Rood
005962	COLLINS, Daniel	54y	W	Ire.	07 JAN 1876	Mt. Olivet
018116	COLLINS, Edward M.	4y	C	D.C.	22 NOV 1878	Mt. Olivet

No.	Name	Age	Race	Birth	Death Date	Burial Place
017564	COLLINS, Edwin M.	9y	C	D.C.	29 SEP 1878	Harmony
012687	COLLINS, Elias	30y	C	S.C.	06 AUG 1877	Potters Field
016171	COLLINS, Eliza	31y	C	Va.	15 JUN 1878	Potters Field
014950	COLLINS, Elizabeth A.	1y	C	D.C.	05 MAR 1878	Mt. Olivet
004856	COLLINS, Elizabeth L.	1y	C	D.C.	01 SEP 1875	Harmony
001399	COLLINS, Francis	60y	C	N.C.	15 DEC 1874	Mt. Pleasant
018313	COLLINS, Genevieve	38y	W	D.C.	12 DEC 1878	Holy Rood
012688	COLLINS, George	11y	C	Md.	06 AUG 1877	Reform School
005790	COLLINS, George C.	26y	W	Md.	19 DEC 1875	Glenwood
019891	COLLINS, George Washington	62y	W	Md.	25 APR 1879	Rock Creek
019381	COLLINS, Infant of Virginia	8d	C	D.C.	13 MAR 1879	Potters Field
012377	COLLINS, Isabell M.	1y	W	D.C.	15 JUL 1877	Presbyterian
004649	COLLINS, James Albert	4m	W	D.C.	18 AUG 1875	Holy Rood
000097	COLLINS, James William	1y	W	Ill.	07 AUG 1874	Mt. Olivet
008013	COLLINS, Jeremiah	38y	W	Ire.	04 JUL 1876	Hospital
001063	COLLINS, Joanna	54y	W	D.C.	06 NOV 1874	Glenwood
009739	COLLINS, Johanna	70y	W	Ire.	19 NOV 1876	Mt. Olivet
013460	COLLINS, John	65y	W	Ire.	10 OCT 1877	Mt. Olivet
014076	COLLINS, John O.	20y	W	D.C.	12 DEC 1877	Mt. Olivet
017227	COLLINS, John Patric	4y	W	D.C.	28 AUG 1878	Rock Creek
009611	COLLINS, Joseph	65y	C	Va.	04 NOV 1876	Young Mens
019640	COLLINS, Joseph	8m	W	D.C.	03 APR 1879	Glenwood
005059a	COLLINS, Joseph Wilmer	2y	W	D.C.	05 OCT 1875	Presbyterian
007105	COLLINS, Julia A.	73y	W	D.C.	25 APR 1876	Holy Rood
004254	COLLINS, Katie	14y	W	D.C.	23 JUL 1875	Mt. Olivet
016372	COLLINS, Lavina	2m	C	Md.	30 JUN 1878	Payne's
012711	COLLINS, Lilly	4m	C	D.C.	07 AUG 1877	Beckett's
005647	COLLINS, Lucy Ann	2y	M	D.C.	04 DEC 1875	Ebenezer
006318	COLLINS, Luvenia	10y	W	D.C.	12 FEB 1876	Tennallytown
019194	COLLINS, Maggie	19y	W	D.C.	25 FEB 1879	Holy Rood
021145	COLLINS, Maggie Bridget	3m	W	D.C.	29 JUL 1879	Mt. Olivet
010187	COLLINS, Maria, Mrs.	88y	W	Md.	06 JAN 1877	Presbyterian
007606	COLLINS, Mary	28y	W	Ire.	12 JUN 1876	Mt. Olivet
007222	COLLINS, Mary	60y	W	D.C.	06 MAY 1876	Chappel's Farm
009049	COLLINS, Mary	37y	W	Ire.	13 SEP 1876	Fairfax, Va.
015095	COLLINS, Mary	5m	W	Md.	17 MAR 1878	Tennallytown
016536	COLLINS, Mary Clara	25y	C	Md.	10 JUL 1878	Mt. Olivet
005480	COLLINS, Mary Eliza:	1y	W	D.C.	17 NOV 1875	Mt. Olivet
012440	COLLINS, Mary Ellen	3y	W	D.C.	20 JUL 1877	Mt. Olivet
020467	COLLINS, Mary Kate	7m	W	D.C.	16 JUN 1879	Mt. Olivet
008006	COLLINS, Mary, Mrs.	68y	W	Ire.	04 JUL 1876	Congressional
003895	COLLINS, Matilda	44y	C	Va.	28 JUN 1875	Mt. Pleasant
019715	COLLINS, Michael	29y	W	Can.	10 APR 1879	Hospital, Government
003156	COLLINS, Morice	4y	W	D.C.	28 APR 1875	Mt. Olivet
002901	COLLINS, Nancy	1y	C	D.C.	06 APR 1875	Beckett's
002548	COLLINS, Patrick	29y	W	Ire.	13 MAR 1875	Mt. Olivet
011137	COLLINS, Patrick	64y	W	Ire.	28 MAR 1877	Soldier's Home
006430	COLLINS, Peter	24h	C	D.C.	21 FEB 1876	Beckett's
009787	COLLINS, Sarah L.	5y	W	D.C.	24 NOV 1876	Presbyterian
008266	COLLINS, Sidney Chas.	15m	W	D.C.	15 JUL 1876	Mt. Olivet
006065	COLLINS, Susan	7y	C	D.C.	19 JAN 1876	Young Mens
011550	COLLINS, Teresa	18y	W	D.C.	09 MAY 1877	Mt. Olivet
017522	COLLINS, Thomas J.	38y	W	Ire.	25 SEP 1878	Alexandria, Va.
000192	COLLINS, Timothy	50y	W	Ire.	15 AUG 1874	Mt. Olivet
017463	COLLINS, Virginia R.	10m	W	D.C.	20 SEP 1878	Presbyterian
020482	COLLINS, William	3y	W	D.C.	17 JUN 1879	Mt. Olivet

District of Columbia Death Records, August 1, 1874 to July 31, 1879

No.	Name	Age	Race	Birth	Death Date	Burial Place
016537	COLLINS, Williams Elias	7m	C	D.C.	10 JUL 1878	Beckett's
010942	COLLISON, Ann Elizabeth	64y	W	Va.	11 MAR 1877	Presbyterian
016082	COLLISON, Cathrine L.	5y	W	D.C.	09 JUN 1878	Glenwood
001238	COLMAN, Francis	m	C	D.C.	26 NOV 1874	Beckett's
016940	COLMAN, Joseph Olway	6m	C	D.C.	07 AUG 1878	Beckett's
020419	COLMAN, Virginia Etta	2m	C	D.C.	13 JUN 1879	Payne's
012782	COLMAN, Zachariah	8m	C	D.C.	12 AUG 1877	Payne's
002803	COLSON, Arthur	10m	C	D.C.	30 MAR 1875	Young Mens
003757	COLSON, Lewis	11m	M	D.C.	21 JUN 1875	Young Mens
004946	COLTER, George	50y	W	Ire.	07 SEP 1875	Holy Rood
007476	COLUMBUS, Francis S.	2m	W	D.C.	03 JUN 1876	Glenwood
003724	COLUMBUS, Jos.	2d	W	D.C.	20 JUN 1875	Glenwood
011039	COLVERT, John H.T.	4m	C	D.C.	19 MAR 1877	Mt. Olivet
018099	COLVERT, Loyd	46y	C	D.C.	20 NOV 1878	Young Mens
008907	COLVIN, Imogene Williams	1y	W	Va.	01 SEP 1876	Alexandria, Va.
021074	COLVIN, Jeremiah	70y	C	Va.	24 JUL 1879	On the Farm
003220	COLVIN, John	31y	W	Eng.	05 MAY 1875	Mt. Olivet
014973	COMBS, Annie C.	1y	W	D.C.	07 MAR 1878	Mt. Olivet
004182	COMBS, Annie E.	28y	W	D.C.	18 JUL 1875	Mt. Olivet
020058	COMBS, Joseph	78y	W	N.J.	10 MAY 1879	Rock Creek
005608	COMMODORE, Anny	70y	C	Md.	30 NOV 1875	Moore's
017057	COMMODORE, Mary A.	27y	C	D.C.	15 AUG 1878	Young Mens
006039	COMMODORE, Sarah	21y	C	Md.	16 JAN 1876	Moore's
001526	COMPTIN, Martha	3m	C	D.C.	28 DEC 1874	Harmony
009834	COMPTON, Caroline	23y	C	Md.	30 NOV 1876	Harmony
013833	COMPTON, Henry	53y	C	Md.	16 NOV 1877	Harmony
011009	COMPTON, John H.	c.40y	W	U.S.	16 MAR 1877	Washington Asylum
017941	COMPTON, John W.	57y	W	D.C.	04 NOV 1878	Congressional
004287	COMPTON, Joseph Blair	2m	M	D.C.	25 JUL 1875	Mt. Pleasant
005139a	CONARD, Brewis	5y	W	D.C.	14 OCT 1875	Congressional
005262	CONAWAY, Margaret L.	19y	C	Va.	25 OCT 1875	Ebenezer
005727	CONE, Ellen B.	49y	W	D.C.	12 DEC 1875	Congressional
008102	CONKLIN, Jerinna	c.34y	W	Ire.	09 JUL 1876	N.Y. City
011583	CONKLIN, Roberta	1y	W	Va.	13 MAY 1877	Winchester, Va.
001048	CONKLY, Samuel	9d	C	D.C.	04 NOV 1874	Mt. Pleasant
005140	CONLAN, Peter	67y	W	Ire.	23 SEP 1875	Glenwood
009900	CONLIN, Thomas	54y	W	Ire.	07 DEC 1876	Mt. Olivet
014291	CONN, Margaret A.	49y	W	Va.	02 JAN 1878	Congressional
002429	CONNEL, Maggie	4y	W	D.C.	05 MAR 1875	Mt. Olivet
013100	CONNELL, Anna	26y	W	Ire.	06 SEP 1877	Mt. Olivet
013448	CONNELL, Anthony	47y	W	Ire.	09 OCT 1877	Soldier's Home
004106	CONNELL, Cath.	27y	W	Ire.	13 JUL 1875	Mt. Olivet
018670	CONNELL, Johanna	61y	W	Ire.	14 JAN 1879	Mt. Olivet
008060	CONNELL, Joseph E.	6d	W	D.C.	07 JUL 1876	Mt. Olivet
004156	CONNELL, Mary	3m	W	D.C.	16 JUL 1875	Mt. Olivet
017225	CONNELL, Mary	1y	W	D.C.	28 AUG 1878	Mt. Olivet
014558	CONNELL, Mary J.	6y	W	D.C.	26 JAN 1878	Mt. Olivet
000778	CONNELL, Rebecka A.	34y	W	D.C.	11 OCT 1874	Glenwood
000937	CONNELL, William Chas. Sam.	4m	W	D.C.	26 OCT 1874	Rock Creek
006251	CONNER, Alberta	1y	W	D.C.	06 FEB 1876	Methodist
018465	CONNER, Bridget	38y	W	Ire.	26 DEC 1878	Mt. Olivet
003742	CONNER, Briget	45y	W	Ire.	21 JUN 1875	Mt. Olivet
019892	CONNER, Charles Edward	2m	W	D.C.	25 APR 1879	Congressional
000361	CONNER, Joseph	1y	C	D.C.	29 AUG 1874	Mt. Pleasant
002130	CONNER, Patrick	55y	W	Ire.	12 FEB 1875	Mt. Olivet
019754	CONNER, Robert	35y	C	Va.	13 APR 1879	Potters Field

District of Columbia Death Records, August 1, 1874 to July 31, 1879

No.	Name	Age	Race	Birth	Death Date	Burial Place
016358	CONNER, S. Virginia	52y	W	Va.	29 JUN 1878	Congressional
006608	CONNER, Sarah A.	3y	W	D.C.	09 MAR 1876	Methodist
012436	CONNER, William	1y	W	D.C.	20 JUL 1877	Methodist
012712	CONNOLLY, Catharine	14d	W	D.C.	07 AUG 1877	Mt. Olivet
011922	CONNOLLY, Francis	7y	W	U.S.	15 JUN 1877	Mt. Olivet
005789	CONNOLLY, John	48y	W	Ire.	19 DEC 1875	Hospital
001213f	CONNOLLY, John E.	31y	W	Md.	22 NOV 1874	Mt. Olivet
018605	CONNOLLY, Martin	67y	W	Ire.	08 JAN 1879	Mt. Olivet
016067	CONNOLLY, Patrick	46y	W	Ire.	08 JUN 1878	Soldier's Home
015096	CONNOLLY, Thomas C.	65y	W	Md.	17 MAR 1878	Rock Creek
012641	CONNOR, Annie	4d	C	D.C.	02 AUG 1877	Mt. Olivet
013461	CONNOR, Benjamin	8m	C	D.C.	10 OCT 1877	Payne's
014082	CONNOR, Charles O.	7m	W	D.C.	13 DEC 1877	Mt. Olivet
011334	CONNOR, Edmond	77y	W	Ire.	14 APR 1877	Mt. Olivet
012248	CONNOR, Edward	11y	C	D.C.	07 JUL 1877	Ebenezer
010549	CONNOR, Estelle	17m	C	D.C.	07 FEB 1877	Young Mens
014696	CONNOR, George	20	C	Md.	07 FEB 1878	Potters Field
019281	CONNOR, George Frederick	11y	C	D.C.	05 MAR 1879	Harmony
003740	CONNOR, Helen	7m	W	D.C.	21 JUN 1875	Mt. Olivet
018463	CONNOR, James	35y	C	Va.	26 DEC 1878	Holy Rood
003478	CONNOR, Jessy Amos	11m	W	D.C.	29 MAY 1875	Glenwood
001243	CONNOR, Joanna	80y	W	Ire.	27 NOV 1874	Lancaster, Pa.
013476	CONNOR, Johana	15y	W	D.C.	11 OCT 1877	Mt. Olivet
020281	CONNOR, John	32y	W	Ire.	03 JUN 1879	Potters Field
013325	CONNOR, John O.	25y	W	Ire.	27 SEP 1877	Hospital
019769	CONNOR, Katie	7h	W	D.C.	14 APR 1879	Holy Rood
008628	CONNOR, Mary Agnes	19y	W	Md.	09 AUG 1876	Mt. Olivet
004441	CONNOR, Mary Elizabeth	1y	C	D.C.	04 AUG 1875	Harmony
009298	CONNOR, Mary L.	26y	W	Va.	04 OCT 1876	Congressional
009511	CONNOR, Michael R.	70y	W	Md.	23 OCT 1876	Congressional
006331	CONNOR, Patrick	2y	W	D.C.	13 FEB 1876	Holy Rood
013376	CONNOR, Patrick	60y	W	Ire.	02 OCT 1877	Mt. Olivet
013032	CONNOR, Sarah	35y	W	Ire.	31 AUG 1877	Holy Rood
002036	CONNOR, Thomas	33y	W	Ire.	05 FEB 1875	Mt. Olivet
003581	CONNOR, Thomas	3m	W	D.C.	09 JUN 1875	Mt. Olivet
017548	CONNOR, Thomas	56y	C	Va.	27 SEP 1878	Alexandria, Va.
006846	CONNOR, William	13y	W	D.C.	28 MAR 1876	Mt. Olivet
003513	CONNORS, Catherine	65y	W	Ire.	02 JUN 1875	Mt. Olivet
014670	CONNORS, Ellen	22y	W	D.C.	05 FEB 1878	Mt. Olivet
001855	CONNORS, James	10m	W	D.C.	23 JAN 1875	Holy Rood
003308	CONNORS, John	75y	C	Md.	13 MAY 1875	Mt. Olivet
019972	CONNORS, Katie	8m	W	D.C.	03 MAY 1879	Mt. Olivet
001850	CONNORS, Mary, Mrs.	50y	W	Ire.	23 JAN 1875	Mt. Olivet
015383	CONNORS, Samuel	37y	W	Md.	13 APR 1878	Mt. Olivet
009336	CONNTEE, Fortie	2y	C	D.C.	07 OCT 1876	Ebenezer
018241	CONOLLY, Jeremiah	82y	W	Ire.	05 DEC 1878	Mt. Olivet
007261	CONOLLY, Mary	4d	W	D.C.	10 MAY 1876	Mt. Olivet
020202	CONOWAY, Willie	4m	C	D.C.	26 MAY 1879	Beckett's
012338	CONQUEST, Margaret	14d	C	D.C.	12 JUL 1877	Potters Field
010007	CONRAD, Chas. E.	42y	W	Va.	18 DEC 1876	Congressional
008488	CONROY, Jane	60y	W	Ire.	30 JUL 1876	Mt. Olivet
019869	CONROY, Wm. F.	29y	W	La.	23 APR 1879	Mt. Olivet
018808	CONSIDINE, Willie	7y	W	D.C.	25 JAN 1879	Mt. Olivet
002886	CONTEE, Alice	8m	C	D.C.	05 APR 1875	Beckett's
018699	CONTEE, Caroline	4d	C	D.C.	17 JAN 1879	Payne's
007262	CONTEE, Charlotte Priscilla	c.21y	C	Md.	10 MAY 1876	Mt. Pleasant

District of Columbia Death Records, August 1, 1874 to July 31, 1879 75

No.	Name	Age	Race	Birth	Death Date	Burial Place
010352	CONTEE, Eliza	58y	C	Va.	21 JAN 1877	Harmony
005695	CONTEE, Frances	11m	C	D.C.	08 DEC 1875	Mt. Zion
014002	CONTEE, Georgeanna	1y	C	D.C.	04 DEC 1877	Beckett's
009970	CONTEE, Infant of Solomon	7d	C	D.C.	15 DEC 1876	Potters Field
011712	CONTEE, Jane	33y	C	Md.	26 MAY 1877	Mt. Olivet
004687f	CONTEE, John	75y	C	Md.	20 AUG 1875	Holy Rood
000268	CONTEE, John Richard	4y	C	D.C.	21 AUG 1874	Harmony
007921	CONTEE, Joseph	13y	C	Md.	29 JUN 1876	Harmony
016588	CONTEE, Leonard	9d	C	D.C.	14 JUL 1878	Harmony
018606	CONTEE, Mary	71y	C	Va.	08 JAN 1879	Potters Field
006543	CONTON, Mary	92y	W	Ire.	04 MAR 1876	Mt. Olivet
007963	CONVAY, Mary Jane	6m	W	D.C.	02 JUL 1876	Mt. Olivet
002346	CONWAY, Alice	2h	C	D.C.	27 FEB 1875	Harmony
009849	CONWAY, Clara	35y	C	Va.	03 DEC 1876	Ebenezer
005897	CONWAY, Elizabeth	40y	C	Va.	30 DEC 1875	Ebenezer
008388	CONWAY, Fanny	110y	C	Va.	23 JUL 1876	Potters Field
001500	CONWAY, James	33y	W	Ire.	16 DEC 1874	Hospital
004634	CONWAY, John Allen	10y	C	D.C.	17 AUG 1875	Macedonia
001706	CONWAY, Josephine	9m	C	D.C.	12 JAN 1875	Beckett's
004093	CONWAY, Marie	50y	C	Va.	12 JUL 1875	Macedonia
005572	CONWAY, Martin A.	33y	W	N.J.	26 NOV 1875	Atlantic Co., N.J.
007689	CONWAY, Mary	1y	W	D.C.	17 JUN 1876	Mt. Olivet
004440	CONWAY, Mary Ann	3y	C	D.C.	04 AUG 1875	Macedonia
003783	CONWAY, Mary Isadora	13d	W	D.C.	23 JUN 1875	Holy Rood
020729	CONWAY, Mathew	9m	C	D.C.	03 JUL 1879	Macedonia
006506	CONWAY, Robert	6d	C	D.C.	29 FEB 1876	Holy Rood
004608	CONWAY, William	22y	M	Va.	15 AUG 1875	Potters Field
006561	COODE, Bettie St. Clair	c.38y	W	Pa.	05 MAR 1876	Lock Port, Pa.
010402	COOGAN, Edward	57y	W	Ire.	25 JAN 1877	Mt. Olivet
001003	COOK, Alberti	9m	C	D.C.	01 NOV 1874	Young Mens
017238	COOK, Ann	c.70y	C	U.S.	29 AUG 1878	Potters Field/Harmony
015549	COOK, Arly	2y	C	D.C.	29 APR 1878	Young Mens
015863	COOK, Arthur	6m	C	D.C.	27 MAY 1878	Payne's
006015	COOK, Augustus	21y	C	Md.	14 JAN 1876	Harmony
009366	COOK, Carrie E.	17m	W	D.C.	10 OCT 1876	Congressional
002880	COOK, Charles	62y	W	Prus.	05 APR 1875	Danville, Pa.
012839	COOK, Charles Ellsworth	14m	W	D.C.	16 AUG 1877	Methodist
017301	COOK, Charles R.	4m	W	D.C.	03 SEP 1878	Prospect Hill
009475	COOK, Christiana	1d	C	D.C.	20 OCT 1876	Ebenezer
014416	COOK, Clara M.	16y	W	Md.	14 JAN 1878	Baltimore, Md.
006152	COOK, Edward	4m	C	D.C.	27 JAN 1876	Mt. Zion
014951	COOK, Edward	76y	C	Va.	05 MAR 1878	Mt. Olivet
019600	COOK, Ella B.	11m	W	D.C.	30 MAR 1879	Congressional
015000	COOK, Emma	1y	C	D.C.	09 MAR 1878	Young Mens
016471	COOK, Eva Ann	3y	W	D.C.	06 JUL 1878	Mt. Olivet
006166	COOK, Evelina	4y	C	D.C.	28 JAN 1876	Mt. Zion
011687	COOK, Fanny	c.30y	W	U.S.	24 MAY 1877	Potters Field
009068	COOK, Francis	1y	W	D.C.	14 SEP 1876	Graceland
019179	COOK, Francis	49y	W	Md.	24 FEB 1879	Mt. Olivet
015111	COOK, George	57y	W	Ire.	18 MAR 1878	Mt. Olivet
004735	COOK, George Clinton	4m	W	D.C.	24 AUG 1875	Congressional
018107	COOK, Grandison	52y	C	Va.	21 NOV 1878	Harmony
010830	COOK, Hannah	5m	C	D.C.	02 MAR 1877	Baptist, Hillsdale
014868	COOK, Hattie	6y	W	D.C.	25 FEB 1878	Rock Creek
018836	COOK, Henrietta	11m	C	D.C.	27 JAN 1879	Mt. Pleasant
017612	COOK, Henry	3m	W	D.C.	03 OCT 1878	Presbyterian

District of Columbia Death Records, August 1, 1874 to July 31, 1879

No.	Name	Age	Race	Birth	Death Date	Burial Place
004409	COOK, Ida	2m	W	D.C.	02 AUG 1875	Presbyterian
005074a	COOK, Infant of Ambrose	18d	C	D.C.	06 OCT 1875	Young Mens
001957	COOK, Jane, Mrs.	66y	C	Va.	30 JAN 1875	Alexandria, Va.
014815	COOK, Jane, Mrs.	62y	C	Pa.	19 FEB 1878	Harmony
005910	COOK, Janie	20m	W	D.C.	01 JAN 1876	Mt. Olivet
008753	COOK, Jennie Atchison	5m	W	D.C.	20 AUG 1876	Congressional
006658	COOK, Jerome	6m	C	N.W.	13 MAR 1876	Mt. Pleasant
002715	COOK, Johanna R., Mrs.	26y	W	Md.	24 MAR 1875	Holy Rood
018115	COOK, John Cartwright	63y	W	Md.	22 NOV 1878	Congressional
011832	COOK, John F.	56y	W	Va.	07 JUN 1877	Congressional
007022	COOK, John H.	11m	C	D.C.	16 APR 1876	Mt. Pleasant
005927	COOK, Joseph	78y	C	Md.	03 JAN 1876	Mt. Olivet
017302	COOK, Kate	3h	W	D.C.	03 SEP 1878	Congressional
004899	COOK, Laura Virginia	24y	W	D.C.	04 SEP 1875	Congressional
012261	COOK, Letitia	75y	W	Del.	04 AUG 1877	Philadelphia, Pa.
019599	COOK, Lewis	37y	C	Va.	30 MAR 1879	Mt. Pleasant
008556	COOK, Lewis G.	45y	W	Conn.	04 AUG 1876	Congressional
014894	COOK, Lizzie	50y	C	Md.	28 FEB 1878	Mt. Olivet
014263	COOK, Marion H.	21y	W	D.C.	30 DEC 1877	Glenwood
001228	COOK, Mary	2y	M	N.Y.	25 NOV 1874	Mt. Zion
020579	COOK, Mary	25d	W	D.C.	23 JUN 1879	Methodist
019456	COOK, Mary	35y	C	Va.	19 MAR 1879	Graceland
011397	COOK, Minnie Viola	9y	W	D.C.	22 APR 1877	Congressional
003913	COOK, Norman A.	2m	W	D.C.	29 JUN 1875	Glenwood
005541	COOK, Patsey	28y	C	Va.	23 NOV 1875	Mt. Pleasant
001753	COOK, Priscilla	64y	M	Va.	16 JAN 1875	Detroit, Mich.
005362	COOK, Rosanna	12y	C	D.C.	05 NOV 1875	Potters Field
005363	COOK, Sarah Ellen, d/o Lewis	9y	C	D.C.	05 NOV 1875	Potters Field
008970	COOK, Sophia	1y	W	D.C.	05 SEP 1876	St. Rosa Chapel, Md.
019862	COOK, Sophia	2m	C	D.C.	22 APR 1879	Hillsdale
007690	COOK, Walter	5m	C	D.C.	17 JUN 1876	Potters Field
007186	COOK, Watson	90y	C	Va.	02 MAY 1876	Potters Field
012926	COOK, William	8y	W	D.C.	24 AUG 1877	Mt. Olivet
015490	COOK, William E.	9y	C	D.C.	23 APR 1878	Young Mens
006361	COOK, William H.	c.58y	C	Md.	15 FEB 1876	Mt. Zion
013944	COOKE, Alfred Barlow	5m	W	D.C.	27 NOV 1877	Congressional
012038	COOKE, Alfred J.W.	37y	M	D.C.	24 JUN 1877	Harmony
015317	COOKE, Bessie E.	1y	W	D.C.	08 APR 1878	Congressional
001536	COOKE, Wm. Washington	46y	W	D.C.	30 DEC 1874	Congressional
017613	COOLEY, William	1m	C	D.C.	03 OCT 1878	Mt. Olivet
020935	COOLIDGE, Mary E.	65y	W	Mass.	15 JUL 1879	Oak Hill
003371	COOLIDGE, Mary J.	75y	W	Md.	20 MAY 1875	Presbyterian
004857	COOMBES, Ann Maria	58y	C	D.C.	01 SEP 1875	Mt. Olivet
014290	COOMBS, Eliza	42y	C	D.C.	02 JAN 1878	Mt. Olivet
012394	COOMBS, Emma Rebecca	9m	C	D.C.	16 JUL 1877	Ebenezer
002675	COOMBS, George Lennan	2y	C	D.C.	21 MAR 1875	Mt. Olivet
018453	COOMBS, James S.	24y	W	N.J.	25 DEC 1878	Trenton, N.J.
001511	COOMBS, John N.	47y	W	Md.	27 DEC 1874	Oak Hill
012660	COOME, George H.	43y	W	D.C.	04 AUG 1877	Congressional
019755	COOMES, Laura V.	15y	W	D.C.	13 APR 1879	Congressional
011036	COOMES, Madison	22y	W	D.C.	19 MAR 1877	Mt. Olivet
003459	COOMES, Sarah Ella	10m	W	D.C.	28 MAY 1875	Congressional
015243	COONEY, Annie Maria	7y	W	D.C.	31 MAR 1878	Glenwood
016602	COONEY, Isabel V.M.	4d	W	D.C.	15 JUL 1878	Glenwood
001781	COONEY, Michael	54y	W	Ire.	18 JAN 1875	Mt. Olivet
009533	COONY, Maggie	6y	W	D.C.	26 OCT 1876	Mt. Olivet

District of Columbia Death Records, August 1, 1874 to July 31, 1879   77

No.	Name	Age	Race	Birth	Death Date	Burial Place
001625	COOPER, Albert	22y	C	Tenn.	06 JAN 1875	Washington Asylum
017476	COOPER, Amelia	35y	C	Va.	21 SEP 1878	Potters Field
003145	COOPER, Anna Bella West	1m	C	D.C.	27 APR 1875	Potters Field
020335	COOPER, Aramanta	1y	C	D.C.	08 JUN 1879	Beckett's
012174	COOPER, Benjamin King	7d	W	D.C.	02 JUL 1877	Congressional
020418	COOPER, Blanche	5m	C	D.C.	13 JUN 1879	Graceland
017806	COOPER, Caroline	40y	C	Va.	20 OCT 1878	Harmony
006666	COOPER, Charles	3y	C	D.C.	14 MAR 1876	Harmony
004636	COOPER, Edgar P.	38y	W	Ga.	17 AUG 1875	Congressional
015085	COOPER, George B.	2m	W	D.C.	16 MAR 1878	Congressional
009695	COOPER, George William	7y	W	D.C.	14 NOV 1876	Laurel, Md.
005037a	COOPER, Harry Ernest	2m	W	D.C.	03 OCT 1875	Congressional
005401	COOPER, Infant of Daniel	10min	C	D.C.	09 NOV 1875	Harmony
016886	COOPER, Infant of Daisy	5d	C	D.C.	03 AUG 1878	Potters Field
020376	COOPER, John	6m	C	D.C.	10 JUN 1879	Mt. Pleasant
005203	COOPER, L.	6d	C	D.C.	28 SEP 1875	Potters Field
012799	COOPER, Lewis	80y	C	D.C.	14 AUG 1877	Potters Field
002786	COOPER, Lizzie	24y	C	Md.	29 MAR 1875	Potters Field
000634	COOPER, Mary	35y	C	Va.	24 SEP 1874	Beckett's
005534	COOPER, Mary Augusta	24y	C	Md.	22 NOV 1875	Harmony
018910	COOPER, Mary E.	7y	C	D.C.	01 FEB 1879	Beckett's
003194	COOPER, Sarah A.	35y	W	Md.	02 MAY 1875	Baltimore, Md.
000420	COOPER, Sarah E.	41y	C	Va.	03 SEP 1874	Beckett's
014704	COOPER, Wm.	1y	C	D.C.	08 FEB 1878	Beckett's
008401	COOPLEY, Annie	71y	W	Va.	24 JUL 1876	Presbyterian
013786	COQUNTINE, Theopl.	90y	C	Md.	10 NOV 1877	Beckett's
007519	COPELAND, Carrie Ellen	3m	C	D.C.	06 JUN 1876	Young Mens
005023	COPELAND, Charles	7m	C	D.C.	13 SEP 1875	Young Mens
017917	COPELAND, Harry	4m	C	D.C.	01 NOV 1878	Mt. Pleasant
014559	COPELAND, Henry	31y	C	D.C.	26 JAN 1878	Suffolk, Va.
006594	COPELAND, Sarah	19y	C	Va.	07 MAR 1876	Young Mens
004387	COPENHAVER, George	54y	W	Va.	31 JUL 1875	Glenwood
015833	COPLAND, Robert	9m	C	D.C.	25 MAY 1878	Graceland
018497	COPOLUCCI, Mary Elizabeth	5y	W	D.C.	29 DEC 1878	Congressional
001191	CORBAN, Samuel	65y	C	Va.	19 NOV 1874	Beckett's
003585	CORBAUGH, Infant of William D.	4h	W	D.C.	10 JUN 1875	Congressional
014974	CORBETT, Infant of John	7d	W	D.C.	07 MAR 1878	Holy Rood
001384	CORBETT, Wm. F.	41y	W	D.C.	14 DEC 1874	Congressional
003428	CORBIN, Elias H.	13m	C	D.C.	25 MAY 1875	Beckett's
012662	CORBIN, Francis	1m	C	D.C.	04 AUG 1877	Washington Asylum
010806	CORBIN, Geo.	4y	C	D.C.	28 FEB 1877	Potters Field
012381	CORBIN, Infant of Wm.	8d	C	D.C.	16 JUL 1877	Potters Field
016343	CORBIN, Nancy	50y	C	Va.	28 JUN 1878	Mt. Pleasant
012228	CORBIN, Philip Henry	1y	C	D.C.	05 JUL 1877	Beckett's
016798	CORBIN, Philip Loving	3y	W	Tex.	28 JUL 1878	Wilmington, Ohio
008604	CORBIN, Wm. H.	1y	C	Va.	08 AUG 1876	Beckett's
001145	CORBITT, James	7y	W	D.C.	14 NOV 1874	Holy Rood
008030	CORBON, Juliann	1y	C	D.C.	05 JUL 1876	Beckett's
004408	CORCORAN, Marion V.	2y	W	D.C.	02 AUG 1875	Glenwood
000402	CORCORAN, Mary J.	5m	W	D.C.	02 SEP 1874	Mt. Olivet
016314	CORCORAN, Nora	16y	W	D.C.	26 JUN 1878	Mt. Olivet
015620	CORCORAN, William Patrick	8m	W	D.C.	05 MAY 1878	Mt. Olivet
014441	CORE, Clarence Griffin	2y	W	D.C.	16 JAN 1878	Graceland
009325	CORE, John F., twin	20h	W	D.C.	07 OCT 1876	Graceland
009326	CORE, W.W., Jr., twin	2h	W	D.C.	07 OCT 1876	Graceland
010349	COREE, Emma	33y	W	D.C.	20 JAN 1877	Mt. Olivet

No.	Name	Age	Race	Birth	Death Date	Burial Place
001798	CORNEDY, Catharine	35y	W	Ire.	19 JAN 1875	Mt. Olivet
018959	CORNELIUS, Blanch	4y	W	D.C.	05 FEB 1879	Congressional
008353	CORNELL, John P.	8m	C	Md.	20 JUL 1876	Mt. Zion
012783	CORNELL, Maria V.	6m	C	D.C.	12 AUG 1877	Mt. Olivet
000159	CORNELL, Patrick	1y	W	Ire.	12 AUG 1874	Mt. Olivet
010778	CORNISH, Gertrude E.	3y	C	D.C.	25 FEB 1877	Harmony
014927	CORNWALL, Jenett Meador	8y	W	D.C.	03 MAR 1878	Congressional
012490	CORNWALL, Mary	72y	W	Eng.	23 JUL 1877	Congressional
014793	CORNWELL, George	2m	W	Md.	17 FEB 1878	Oak Hill
011070	CORNWELL, Iva May	3y	W	D.C.	22 MAR 1877	Congressional
005637	CORRIDON, Ellen	30y	W	Ire.	03 DEC 1875	Mt. Olivet
018929	CORRIGAN, Estella	1m	W	D.C.	03 FEB 1879	Mt. Olivet
003472	CORRIGAN, Rose, Mrs.	50y	W	Ire.	29 MAY 1875	Mt. Olivet
016395	CORRINGTON, Elizabeth Virginia	12d	C	D.C.	02 JUL 1878	Harmony
020959	CORRY, John H.	2m	C	D.C.	16 JUL 1879	Harmony
001786	CORSEY, Junius	16y	C	Md.	18 JAN 1875	Harmony
015219	CORSON, Walter Frederick	7y	W	D.C.	29 MAR 1878	Glenwood
002141	CORSTIN, Mary Margaret	28y	C	D.C.	13 FEB 1875	Mt. Olivet
007151	CORWINE, Richard Mortimer	64y	W	Ky.	29 APR 1876	Cincinnati, Ohio
012961	CORYELL, Harry Elmo	1y	W	D.C.	26 AUG 1877	Glenwood
012215	COSBY, Braxton	19y	C	Va.	04 JUL 1877	Ebenezer
015476	COSGROVE, James Martin	24y	W	Ill.	22 APR 1878	Northfield, Minn.
021061	COSGROVE, Peter	45y	W	Ire.	23 JUL 1879	Mt. Olivet
007520	COSSY, Annie	70y	C	Md.	06 JUN 1876	Holy Rood
020065	COSTELLO, Joseph Francis	7y	W	D.C.	11 MAY 1879	Mt. Olivet
016328	COSTELLO, Laura	2y	W	D.C.	27 JUN 1878	Mt. Olivet
013661	COSTELLO, Mary	c.74y	W	Ire.	28 OCT 1877	Mt. Olivet
007231	COSTELLO, Thomas	46y	W	Ire.	07 MAY 1876	Mt. Olivet
004560	COSTIGAN, Sylvester Q.	65y	W	Ire.	12 AUG 1875	St. Mary's Co., Md.
020195	COSTILLO, Timothy	42y	W	Eng.	25 MAY 1879	Mt. Olivet
008145	COSTIN, Wm. G.	63y	C	D.C.	10 JUL 1876	Harmony
000086	COTTER, Ann	11m	W	N.Y.	07 AUG 1874	Mt. Olivet
010987	COTTON, Charles T.	52y	W	Miss.	15 MAR 1877	Oak Hill
002698	COTTON, Infant of Wm. H.	16h	W	D.C.	22 MAR 1875	Congressional
002656f	COTTON, Sophrona	73y	W	N.H.	20 MAR 1875	Glenwood
014540	COUGHLIN, William	59y	W	Ire.	24 JAN 1878	Mt. Olivet
002663	COUNTE, Margaret	45y	C	D.C.	21 MAR 1875	Montgomery Co., Md.
008826	COUNTEE, Arthur	14y	C	Md.	26 AUG 1876	Mt. Olivet
002283	COUNTEE, Infant of Arther	12d	C	D.C.	22 FEB 1875	Ebenezer
017361	COUNTEE, Issabella	6m	C	D.C.	10 SEP 1878	Young Mens
018568	COUNTEE, Livinia	8y	C	D.C.	05 JAN 1879	Young Mens
012909	COUNTEE, Louisa V.	13y	C	Va.	22 AUG 1877	Harmony
010829	COUNTEE, Walter	80y	C	Md.	02 MAR 1877	Harmony
005179	COURTNEY, Elizabeth	34y	W	Ire.	26 SEP 1875	Mt. Olivet
004576	COURTNEY, Joseph	7m	C	D.C.	13 AUG 1875	Ebenezer
002422	COURTNEY, Judy	100y	C	Va.	04 MAR 1875	Young Mens
012615	COURTNEY, Richard	1y	C	D.C.	30 JUL 1877	Potters Field
008870	COUSENBURY, Caroline	28y	C	Va.	29 AUG 1876	Ebenezer
020100	COUSIE, Wm.	72y	C	D.C.	15 MAY 1879	Mt. Zion
019697	COVER, Charles Page	4y	W	D.C.	08 APR 1879	Mt. Olivet
019457	COVER, James	2y	C	D.C.	19 MAR 1879	Mt. Pleasant
019443	COVER, Mary L.	6y	C	D.C.	18 MAR 1879	Mt. Pleasant
009632	COVINGTON, Anie	15y	C	Md.	06 NOV 1876	Harmony
008987	COWAN, Ellis	5y	M	D.C.	06 SEP 1876	Harmony
005609	COWES, Haven Ladd	1y	W	D.C.	30 NOV 1875	Oak Hill
002384	COWING, Henry	55y	W	Eng.	02 MAR 1875	Washington Asylum

District of Columbia Death Records, August 1, 1874 to July 31, 1879

No.	Name	Age	Race	Birth	Death Date	Burial Place
013422	COWLES, N.M.H.	54y	W	Pa.	07 OCT 1877	Congressional
002962	COWLING, Francis Rebecca	43y	W	Md.	11 APR 1875	Glenwood
018464	COWNE, Eliza	70y	W	Va.	26 DEC 1878	Congressional
000553	COX, Clement	7m	W	D.C.	18 SEP 1874	Mt. Olivet
013119	COX, Cora	8m	C	D.C.	08 SEP 1877	Beckett's
007198	COX, Emeline	30y	C	Ky.	04 MAY 1876	Potters Field
005754	COX, Enass	9m	C	D.C.	15 DEC 1875	Ebenezer
008338	COX, Frank	1y	W	D.C.	19 JUL 1876	Congressional
003914	COX, George Herndon	8m	W	D.C.	29 JUN 1875	Louisa C.H., Va.
001923	COX, Hanna	1m	W	D.C.	28 JAN 1875	Mt. Olivet
017165	COX, Honoria	35y	W	Ire.	24 AUG 1878	Mt. Olivet
007577	COX, Infant of Emeline	9m	C	D.C.	10 JUN 1876	Potters Field
009297	COX, Isah	1y	C	D.C.	04 OCT 1876	Ebenezer
002362	COX, James	54y	W	Mo.	28 FEB 1875	Soldiers' Home
016382	COX, James	78y	C	Va.	01 JUL 1878	Mt. Pleasant
003646	COX, James Dawson	39y	W	D.C.	14 JUN 1875	Congressional
004105	COX, Josephus	9m	C	D.C.	13 JUL 1875	Methodist Ebenezer
003083	COX, Julia A.	3y	W	D.C.	22 APR 1875	Congressional
014886	COX, Julia Ann	76y	W	Va.	27 FEB 1878	Oak Hill
003778	COX, Laura	3m	C	D.C.	22 JUN 1875	Ebenezer
017327	COX, Mary	15y	C	D.C.	05 SEP 1878	Young Mens
021034	COX, Mary	4m	C	D.C.	21 JUL 1879	Beckett's
002442	COX, Mary E.	31y	W	Md.	05 MAR 1875	Barnabas Church
010666	COX, Robert	5y	C	D.C.	17 FEB 1877	Harmony
020921	COX, Thomas	72y	C	Va.	14 JUL 1879	Beckett's
004181	COX, Washington F.	56y	W	Md.	18 JUL 1875	Congressional
015445	COYLE, Elizabeth	7m	W	D.C.	19 APR 1878	Mt. Olivet
013352	COYLE, Fitzhugh	59y	W	D.C.	30 SEP 1877	Oak Hill
011653	COYLE, Francis	45y	W	Can.	19 MAY 1877	Washington Asylum
014281	COYLE, John	65y	W	Ire.	01 JAN 1878	Mt. Olivet
019531	COYLE, John D.	32y	W	Ire.	24 MAR 1879	Mt. Olivet
011719	COYLE, Mary E.	3y	W	D.C.	27 MAY 1877	Mt. Olivet
005636	COYLE, Mary Elenor	51y	W	D.C.	03 DEC 1875	Congressional
005994	COYLE, Mary Ellen	5y	W	D.C.	11 JAN 1876	Mt. Olivet
005753	COYLE, Robert Emet Urell	2y	W	D.C.	15 DEC 1875	Mt. Olivet
002605	COYLE, William Edward	10d	W	D.C.	16 MAR 1875	Mt. Olivet
020026	COYLE, William H.	68y	W	D.C.	07 MAY 1879	Congressional
006731	COZZINS, Cary Ann	9d	M	D.C.	19 MAR 1876	Harmony
019206	CRACRIN, James	38y	W	Ire.	26 FEB 1879	Glenwood
014867	CRAHAN, Thomas	56y	W	Ire.	25 FEB 1878	Mt. Olivet
001464	CRAIG, Adam	90y	C	Md.	23 DEC 1874	Beckett's
011387	CRAIG, Alexander	55y	C	Md.	21 APR 1877	Potters Field
011625	CRAIG, Amanda	2m	C	D.C.	17 MAY 1877	Potters Field
011169	CRAIG, Andrew	c.60y	W	Pa.	30 MAR 1877	Congressional
011298	CRAIG, Benjamin F., M.D.	49y	W	Mass.	10 APR 1877	Oak Hill
017381	CRAIG, Daniel	50y	C	Va.	12 SEP 1878	Mt. Zion
008570	CRAIG, Eliza	73y	W	Md.	05 AUG 1876	Oak Hill
018583	CRAIG, Elizebeth	87y	W	Ire.	06 JAN 1879	Mt. Olivet
012184	CRAIG, Frank	3m	C	D.C.	02 JUL 1877	Potters Field
006694	CRAIG, Infant of John	11h	C	D.C.	16 MAR 1876	Potters Field
006693	CRAIG, Infant of John	15h	C	D.C.	16 MAR 1876	Potters Field
017405	CRAIG, John	37y	C	Md.	14 SEP 1878	Beckett's
013980	CRAIG, Louisa	2y	C	D.C.	01 DEC 1877	Young Mens
018930	CRAIG, May	2y	W	D.C.	03 FEB 1879	Congressional
008096	CRAIG, Morris Alfred	1y	W	D.C.	09 JUL 1876	Congressional
013626	CRAIG, Winnie	32y	C	Md.	25 OCT 1877	Beckett's

No.	Name	Age	Race	Birth	Death Date	Burial Place
019332	CRAIGE, John	36y	W	Mass	09 MAR 1879	Mt. Olivet
006542	CRAIGE, Mary D.	36y	W	D.C.	04 MAR 1876	Mt. Olivet
003527	CRAIGH, Arthur	3m	C	D.C.	04 JUN 1875	Potters Field
018205	CRAIGH, Nellie	55y	C	Md.	30 NOV 1878	Beckett's
016144	CRAIGH, Walter	9m	C	D.C.	13 JUN 1878	Potters Field
015923	CRAIGWELL, Letia Virginia	18m	C	D.C.	31 MAY 1878	Young Mens
013267	CRAMER, Joseph B.	48y	W	Ohio	21 SEP 1877	Glenwood
006349	CRAMER, Lillie	20m	C	D.C.	14 FEB 1876	Mt. Zion
007263	CRAMPTON, Ernest	1y	C	D.C.	10 MAY 1876	Young Mens
011661	CRAMSIE, James	48y	W	D.C.	21 MAY 1877	Mt. Olivet
020677	CRANCH, Frank	4m	C	D.C.	30 JUN 1879	Mt. Pleasant
008546	CRANDELL, William	82y	W	Md.	03 AUG 1876	Graceland
018641	CRANE, Florence L.	4y	W	D.C.	11 JAN 1879	Oak Hill
000903	CRANE, James A.	47y	W	Md.	22 OCT 1874	Mt. Olivet
009078	CRANE, Margueritte Wilson	2m	W	D.C.	14 SEP 1876	Oak Hill
019445	CRANE, Norman	50-55y	W	N.Y.	18 MAR 1879	Ver.
014661	CRAVEN, Michael	49y	W	Ire.	04 FEB 1878	Mt. Olivet
007855	CRAWFORD, Abbertha	2y	C	D.C.	26 JUN 1876	Ebenezer
007836	CRAWFORD, Adam	73y	W	Md.	25 JUN 1876	Congressional
019781	CRAWFORD, Annie M.	24y	W	D.C.	15 APR 1879	Methodist
006121	CRAWFORD, George	36y	C	D.C.	24 JAN 1876	Mt. Zion
008988	CRAWFORD, George	70y	C	Va.	06 SEP 1876	Potters Field
011542	CRAWFORD, Harvey H.	78y	W	N.H.	07 MAY 1877	Potters Field
006348	CRAWFORD, Infant of Harrison	8m	W	D.C.	14 FEB 1876	Montgomery Co., Md.
008159	CRAWFORD, Joseph	67y	W	N.Y.	11 JUL 1876	Glenwood
020692	CRAWFORD, Julia	4m	C	D.C.	01 JUL 1879	Moore's
005141	CRAWFORD, Lily Washington	21y	W	N.J.	14 OCT 1875	Oak Hill
013902	CRAWFORD, Mary F.	19y	W	D.C.	24 NOV 1877	Congressional
015382	CRAWFORD, Nettie	13y	C	D.C.	13 APR 1878	Mt. Olivet
019160	CRAWFORD, Sarah Estelle	5y	W	N.Y.	23 FEB 1879	Congressional
017999	CRAWFORD, William B.	40y	W	N.Y.	10 NOV 1878	Congressional
010014	CRAWFORD, Willie	2y	W	D.C.	19 DEC 1876	Methodist
015393	CRAWLEY, Alice	65y	W	Scot.	14 APR 1878	Mt. Olivet
013006	CRAWLEY, Susan L.	2y	C	Va.	29 AUG 1877	Potters Field
015739	CREAMER, William	2m	W	D.C.	16 MAY 1878	Mt. Olivet
013033	CREECY, James Robert	8m	W	Md.	31 AUG 1877	Mt. Olivet
002004	CREEK, Ellen	100y	C	Md.	03 FEB 1875	Harmony
000784	CREEK, Florence E.	1y	C	D.C.	12 OCT 1874	Young Mens
015297	CREEK, Henry	1y	C	D.C.	06 APR 1878	Jones Chapel
005843	CRESS, John	64y	W	Ger.	24 DEC 1875	St. Mary's
004635	CRESWELL, Thomas	11m	W	Ohio	17 AUG 1875	Prospect Hill
017828	CREVEY, William	41y	W	Ire.	22 OCT 1878	Soldier's Home
017226	CREW, Edward	1y	M	D.C.	28 AUG 1878	Harmony
004428	CREW, Laura	1y	C	D.C.	03 AUG 1875	Harmony
006664	CRIDER, Michael C.	69y	W	Pa.	14 MAR 1876	Graceland
012521	CRIDLAND, John B.	40y	W	Pa.	25 JUL 1877	Congressional
010791	CRIDLER, Augustus M.	64y	W	Va.	26 FEB 1877	Congressional
002105	CRIDLER, Lorana, Mrs.	24y	W	N.J.	10 FEB 1875	Congressional
002142	CRIDLER, Thos. Wilbur, Jr.	7d	W	D.C.	13 FEB 1875	Congressional
000292	CRIENTON?, Charley	9m	C	D.C.	23 AUG 1874	Harmony
017628	CRIER, Benjamin C.	78y	C	Va.	04 OCT 1878	Harmony
018305	CRIER, Thompson M.	31y	C	D.C.	11 DEC 1878	Young Mens
004363	CRIGLER, Roberta	36y	W	Va.	29 JUL 1875	Culpeper C.H., Va.
015343	CRIMMEN, Honora	6y	W	D.C.	10 APR 1878	Mt. Olivet
004736	CRIMMIN, Ellen	1y	W	D.C.	24 AUG 1875	Mt. Olivet
003593	CRIMMIN, Mary	30min	W	D.C.	10 JUN 1875	Mt. Olivet

District of Columbia Death Records, August 1, 1874 to July 31, 1879   81

No.	Name	Age	Race	Birth	Death Date	Burial Place
018231	CRIMMIN, Patrick	34y	W	Ire.	03 DEC 1878	Mt. Olivet
006316	CRIPPS, William McLean	76y	W	N.Y.	12 FEB 1876	Mt. Olivet
006822	CRITCHER, Warrenton R.	27y	W	Va.	26 MAR 1876	Oak Hill
016716	CROCKETT, Susan	78y	W	N.B.	22 JUL 1878	Congressional
009746	CROCKWELL, Frederick Augustine	2m	W	D.C.	20 NOV 1876	Mt. Olivet
018675	CROGGON, Henry Brown	66y	W	Eng.	15 JAN 1879	Rock Creek
002025	CROGGON, Jane	47y	W	D.C.	04 FEB 1875	Glenwood
009857	CROGGON, Roberta V.	37y	W	Md.	03 DEC 1876	Glenwood
001475	CROLLY, George Henry	19y	W	Md.	24 DEC 1874	Mt. Olivet
005928	CROMPTON, William Henry	2½d	C	D.C.	03 JAN 1876	Beckett's
002101	CROMWELL, George W.	7d	C	D.C.	09 FEB 1875	Mt. Pleasant
015579	CROMWELL, Sarah	64y	W	N.Y.	02 MAY 1878	Congressional
015787	CRONIN, Ellen	2m	W	D.C.	21 MAY 1878	Mt. Olivet
004138	CRONIN, James	1m	W	D.C.	15 JUL 1875	Mt. Olivet
000630	CRONIN, Lawrence	2y	W	D.C.	24 SEP 1874	Mt. Olivet
015902	CRONIN, Mary	9m	W	D.C.	30 MAY 1878	Mt. Olivet
016669	CROPLEY, Richard Lester	1y	W	D.C.	19 JUL 1878	Oak Hill
004013	CROPLEY, Thomas Laurence, Jr.	4m	W	D.C.	06 JUL 1875	Oak Hill
015363	CROSBY, Emma	4m	W	D.C.	11 APR 1878	Congressional
013993	CROSMAN, Benjamin	39y	W	D.C.	03 DEC 1877	Mt. Olivet
006845	CROSS, Annie	2m	W	D.C.	28 MAR 1876	Methodist
005775	CROSS, Chas.	45y	C	Va	17 DEC 1875	Swartz's
000689	CROSS, David	c.50	C	Va.	02 OCT 1874	Mt. Olivet
016396	CROSS, Edward F.	31y	W	D.C.	02 JUL 1878	Congressional
003597	CROSS, George Richard	6w	C	D.C.	10 JUN 1875	Harmony
013914	CROSS, Harriet	50y	W	Pa.	25 NOV 1877	Lancaster, Pa.
001997	CROSS, Infant of Robert	3d	W	D.C.	02 FEB 1875	Methodist
000462	CROSS, James C.	39y	W	U.S.	09 SEP 1874	Congressional
019176	CROSS, James Henry	7m	C	D.C.	24 FEB 1879	Potters Field
001195	CROSS, Julia Rose	54y	W	Va.	20 NOV 1874	Congressional
012029	CROSS, Peter Taltavall	6m	W	D.C.	23 JUN 1877	Congressional
014723	CROSS, Redic	2y	C	D.C.	09 FEB 1878	Mt. Zion
012553	CROSS, Samuel	38y	C	Md.	27 JUL 1877	Potters Field
010079	CROSS, Sarah V.	20y	W	D.C.	26 DEC 1876	Congressional
006932	CROSS, Walter	85y	C	Md.	05 APR 1876	Potters Field
008716	CROSSFIELD, James T.	c.63y	W	D.C.	17 AUG 1876	Glenwood
004898	CROTON, John	2y	W	D.C.	04 SEP 1875	Young Mens
005070a	CROUCH, Orah Aleen	1y	W	D.C.	06 OCT 1875	Congressional
014442	CROUCH, Thomas M., Sr.	70y	W	Md.	16 JAN 1878	Baltimore, Md.
006844	CROUNCE, William Conrad	5m	W	D.C.	28 MAR 1876	Harmony
011523	CROUSE, Edward	2y	W	D.C.	15 APR 1877	Presbyterian
016311	CROUSE, Infant of Walter	14d	C	D.C.	25 JUN 1878	Beckett's
009624	CROUSE, Lulu	30y	W	Md.	05 NOV 1876	Congressional
019756	CROUSE, Mary E.	1y	W	D.C.	13 APR 1879	Holy Rood
016618	CROW, Ambrose	3y	W	D.C.	16 JUL 1878	Mt. Olivet
002498	CROW, Charles	1y	W	D.C.	10 MAR 1875	Mt. Olivet
010748	CROW, Elizabeth	67y	W	Va.	23 FEB 1877	Congressional
005720	CROWDY, Moses	24y	C	Md.	11 DEC 1875	Ebenezer
010619	CROWLEY, Agnes	18d	W	D.C.	13 FEB 1877	Mt. Olivet
019757	CROWLEY, Jeremiah D.	65y	W	Ire.	13 APR 1879	Mt. Olivet
010725	CROWLEY, Mary Ann	2y	C	D.C.	21 FEB 1877	Potters Field
008757	CROWLEY, Michael	21y	W	Mass.	20 AUG 1876	Mt. Olivet
012894	CROWLEY, Nicholas	1y	W	D.C.	21 AUG 1877	Holy Rood
004398	CROWN, Christopher	28y	C	D.C.	01 AUG 1875	Ebenezer
015862	CROWN, Jacob	1m	C	D.C.	27 MAY 1878	Beckett's
019178	CROWN, Laura V.	2y	W	D.C.	24 FEB 1879	Oak Hill

No.	Name	Age	Race	Birth	Death Date	Burial Place
016260	CROWN, Madora Alverta	20y	W	D.C.	22 JUN 1878	Congressional
019429	CROWN, Mary E.	38y	W	D.C.	17 MAR 1879	Mt. Olivet
018837	CROWN, Samuel	74y	W	D.C.	27 JAN 1879	Oak Hill
012171	CROWN, Sarah C.	49y	W	D.C.	02 JUL 1877	Glenwood
015758	CROWN, Wm. H.	42y	W	D.C.	18 MAY 1878	Congressional
014610	CROWNER, Wm. H.	50y	C	D.C.	31 JAN 1878	Harmony
019087	CRUGER, Lewis	76y	W	S.C.	16 FEB 1879	Congressional
007813	CRUIKSHANK, A.J., Mrs.	69y	W	D.C.	24 JUN 1876	Oak Hill
007671	CRUIT, Ann	81y	W	Eng.	16 JUN 1876	Oak Hill
007278	CRUIT, Catharine	79y	W	Eng.	12 MAY 1876	Oak Hill
005913	CRUIT, Mary Louise	36y	W	D.C.	02 JAN 1876	Oak Hill
014816	CRUIT, Richard	40y	W	Pa.	19 FEB 1878	Oak Hill
014232	CRUMBAUGH, Anna Virginia	3y	W	Md.	28 DEC 1877	Holy Rood
014292	CRUMMY, Mary Elizabeth	5m	C	D.C.	02 JAN 1878	Harmony
009933	CRUMP, Catharine	49y	W	Va.	11 DEC 1876	Graceland
016845	CRUMP, Edward	7y	W	D.C.	31 JUL 1878	Mt. Pleasant
018259	CRUMP, Elizabeth A.	20y	W	D.C.	07 DEC 1878	Congressional
020577	CRUMP, James	8m	C	D.C.	23 JUN 1879	Mt. Pleasant
010618	CRUMP, Maria Elizabeth	39y	W	D.C.	13 FEB 1877	Congressional
000894	CRUMP, Martha	2y	C	D.C.	21 OCT 1874	Mt. Zion
008674	CRUMP, Mary	5m	W	D.C.	13 AUG 1876	Prince George's Co., Md.
019639	CRUMP, Mary A.	29y	C	Va.	03 APR 1879	Young Mens
007837	CRUMP, Richard N.	20y	C	Va.	25 JUN 1876	Young Mens
013207	CRUMP, Townsend C.	45y	C	Va.	15 SEP 1877	Alexandria, Va.
019738	CRUMP, William Morris Nelson	10y	W	Ohio	12 APR 1879	Cleveland, Ohio
016212	CRUMP, Wm.	1y	C	D.C.	18 JUN 1878	Mt. Pleasant
009139	CRUMWELL, Martha (twin)	5d	C	D.C.	20 SEP 1876	Potters Field
014035	CRUSE, Mary E.	7d	C	D.C.	08 DEC 1877	Potters Field
011861	CRUSOE, Martha	30y	C	D.C.	11 JUN 1877	Mt. Zion
006761	CRUTCHET, Henry P.	1m	W	D.C.	21 MAR 1876	Mt. Olivet
001172	CRUTCHFIELD, Fannie	3y	C	D.C.	17 NOV 1874	Beckett's
004348	CRUTCHFIELD, Lelia	7m	C	D.C.	28 JUL 1875	Ebenezer
015706	CRYER, Benj. F.	6m	C	D.C.	13 MAY 1878	Young Mens
011050	CUDLIPP, Benjamin	73y	W	Eng.	20 MAR 1877	Glenwood
009890	CUDLIPP, George	8y	W	Ala.	06 DEC 1876	Congressional
013377	CUDMORE, Thomas	1y	W	D.C.	02 OCT 1877	Mt. Olivet
004364	CUDMORE, William	10m	W	D.C.	29 JUL 1875	Mt. Olivet
006082	CULHAM, Johana	27y	W	Ire.	21 JAN 1876	Mt. Olivet
009179	CULHANE, Thomas	8m	W	D.C.	23 SEP 1876	Mt. Olivet
014671	CULL, Eliza	26y	W	Ire.	05 FEB 1878	Mt. Olivet
021092	CULLEN, Clemant	7m	W	D.C.	25 JUL 1879	Mt. Olivet
013168	CULLIGAN, John Dolmick	5y	W	D.C.	12 SEP 1877	Mt. Olivet
008416	CULLINAN, Anne	8m	W	D.C.	25 JUL 1876	Mt. Olivet
017153	CULLINAN, Joseph	1y	W	D.C.	23 AUG 1878	Mt. Olivet
012561	CULLINANE, Ellen	45y	W	Ire.	27 JUL 1877	Mt. Olivet
011314	CULLINANE, John	85y	W	Ire.	12 APR 1877	Mt. Olivet
020447	CULVER, Fred. B., M.D.	70y	W	Ohio	15 JUN 1879	Oak Hill
006646	CULVER, Wm. E.	75y	W	Pa.	12 MAR 1876	Congressional
017754	CUMBERLAND, Elizebeth	17y	W	D.C.	16 OCT 1878	Mt. Olivet
016799	CUMBERLAND, Ella G.	1y	W	D.C.	28 JUL 1878	Oak Hill
016786	CUMBERLAND, Eva	4y	W	D.C.	27 JUL 1878	Oak Hill
017139	CUMBERLAND, Fannie	7m	W	D.C.	22 AUG 1878	Mt. Olivet
013178	CUMBERLAND, Helen	6y	W	D.C.	13 SEP 1877	Mt. Olivet
006692	CUMBERLAND, John, Sr.	72y	W	D.C.	16 MAR 1876	Oak Hill
019696	CUMBERLAND, Margaret	40y	W	Eng.	08 APR 1879	Mt. Olivet
012175	CUMMINGS, John	5d	W	D.C.	02 JUL 1877	Presbyterian

District of Columbia Death Records, August 1, 1874 to July 31, 1879   83

No.	Name	Age	Race	Birth	Death Date	Burial Place
009508	CUMMINGS, Margret A.	26y	W	N.Y.	23 OCT 1876	Holy Rood
013952	CUNINGHAM, John M.	3y	W	Va.	28 NOV 1877	Mt. Olivet
012142	CUNNINGHAM, Alice May	1y	W	D.C.	30 JUN 1877	Mt. Olivet
002158	CUNNINGHAM, Archibald	79y	W	Scot.	14 FEB 1875	Oak Hill
016004	CUNNINGHAM, Francis Vincent	7w	W	D.C.	04 JUN 1878	Mt. Olivet
007792	CUNNINGHAM, Franklin	15d	W	Md.	23 JUN 1876	Glenwood
021110	CUNNINGHAM, Infant of Simon	1h	W	D.C.	26 JUL 1879	Mt. Olivet
003659	CUNNINGHAM, James	2m	W	D.C.	15 JUN 1875	Mt. Olivet
006853	CUNNINGHAM, James G.	38y	W	D.C.	29 MAR 1876	Presbyterian
012991	CUNNINGHAM, Rosa A.	73y	W	Pa.	28 AUG 1877	Presbyterian
002580	CUNNINGHAM, Thomas	44y	W	N.Y.	15 MAR 1875	Mt. Olivet
005400	CUNNINGTON, George R.S.	37y	W	Eng.	09 NOV 1875	Glenwood
004621	CUPP, Willy	21d	W	D.C.	15 AUG 1875	Prospect Hill
020564	CURL, Barbara	30y	W	Pa.	22 JUN 1879	Mt. Olivet
010767	CURRAN, Catharine	68y	W	Ire.	24 FEB 1877	Holy Rood
004855	CURRAN, Edward F.	31y	W	Va.	01 SEP 1875	Mt. Olivet
019974	CURRAN, Stephen	15y	W	D.C.	03 MAY 1879	Holy Rood
009556	CURREN, Edgar G.	8y	W	S.C.	27 OCT 1876	Delaware, Ohio
004825	CURRY, Ann Josephine	1y	W	D.C.	30 AUG 1875	Holy Rood
002606	CURRY, Blanch	2y	C	D.C.	16 MAR 1875	Ebenezer
002568	CURRY, Martha Howard	21y	C	Va.	14 MAR 1875	Beckett's
012642	CURRY, Mary	1y	C	D.C.	02 AUG 1877	Beckett's
007954	CURRY, Oscar	21y	C	Va.	01 JUL 1876	Potters Field
004376	CURRY, Randolph	5m	C	D.C.	30 JUL 1875	Beckett's
018958	CURSON, Annie	85y	W	La.	05 FEB 1879	Mt. Olivet
004094	CURSTON, Emeline	1y	C	D.C.	12 JUL 1875	Mt. Olivet
005583	CURTAIN, Honora Mary	1y	W	D.C.	27 NOV 1875	Mt. Olivet
018701	CURTAIN, Infant of Marion	4h	W	D.C.	17 JAN 1879	Congressional
003721	CURTAIN, James	2y	W	Va.	20 JUN 1875	Mt. Olivet
007244	CURTAIN, Michael	79y	W	Ire.	08 MAY 1876	Mt. Olivet
017392	CURTAIN, Richard	48y	W	Md.	13 SEP 1878	Congressional
010004	CURTIN, John	1m	W	D.C.	18 DEC 1876	Mt. Olivet
014293	CURTIN, John J.	3y	W	D.C.	02 JAN 1878	Mt. Olivet
008687	CURTIN, Joseph Francis	5d	W	D.C.	14 AUG 1876	Mt. Olivet
002589	CURTIN, Joseph Patrick	2y	W	D.C.	16 MAR 1875	Mt. Olivet
010536	CURTIN, Margaret E.	4m	W	D.C.	06 FEB 1877	Mt. Olivet
005490	CURTIN, Mary	½d	W	D.C.	18 NOV 1875	Mt. Olivet
018920	CURTIS, Albert	20y	C	D.C.	02 FEB 1879	Mt. Zion
002983	CURTIS, Alexander	1y	C	D.C.	14 APR 1875	Young Mens
013347	CURTIS, Clark E.	34y	W	Ver.	29 SEP 1877	Congressional
008419	CURTIS, Elsie	29y	C	D.C.	25 JUL 1876	Mt. Zion
011062	CURTIS, Francis J.	9m	M	D.C.	21 MAR 1877	Beckett's
002366	CURTIS, Hariett	2m	C	D.C.	01 MAR 1875	Mt. Zion
014172	CURTIS, Henry	28y	C	Va.	22 DEC 1877	Potters Field
006131	CURTIS, Henry B.	54y	W	Va.	25 JAN 1876	Glenwood
005025a	CURTIS, James Henry	½d	C	D.C.	02 OCT 1875	Moore's
010281	CURTIS, Jane	49y	C	Md.	13 JAN 1877	Harmony
001082	CURTIS, John P.	1y	C	D.C.	08 NOV 1874	Catholic
001471	CURTIS, Kate	18y	M	Miss.	24 DEC 1874	Harmony
001830	CURTIS, Lottis	4m	C	D.C.	21 JAN 1875	Potters Field
008089	CURTIS, Martha	8m	C	D.C.	09 JUL 1876	Holy Rood
020317	CURTIS, Roesetta	40y	C	D.C.	06 JUN 1879	Darnestown, Md.
006373	CURTIS, Samuel Prentis	37y	W	Ohio	16 FEB 1876	Rock Creek
020649	CURTIS, Sophia E.	23y	C	D.C.	28 JUN 1879	Mt. Olivet
007072	CURTIS, Thomas	26y	C	D.C.	22 APR 1876	Mt. Zion
014780	CURTIS, Wallace Lincoln	5y	W	D.C.	16 FEB 1878	Oak Hill

No.	Name	Age	Race	Birth	Death Date	Burial Place
017416	CURTIS, William	27y	C	Va.	15 SEP 1878	Beckett's
006317	CURTISS, Albert Washington	5y	C	D.C.	12 FEB 1876	Harmony
016870	CURTISS, Arthur	14d	C	D.C.	02 AUG 1878	Mt. Pleasant
009893	CURTISS, Georgiana	22y	C	Md.	07 DEC 1876	Small Pox Grounds
018089	CURTISS, Jesse	16y	C	Md.	19 NOV 1878	Harmony
018739	CURTISS, Rebecca	8y	C	D.C.	20 JAN 1879	Harmony
013881	CUSENBERRY, Mary Elizabeth	2y	C	D.C.	22 NOV 1877	Beckett's
001420	CUSHING, William B.	32y	W	Wis.	17 DEC 1874	Congressional
002986	CUSHLEY, Robert	37y	W	D.C.	14 APR 1875	Mt. Olivet
007289	CUSICK, Bridget	22y	W	D.C.	13 MAY 1876	Mt. Olivet
011980	CUSILAGIA, John	15m	W	D.C.	20 JUN 1877	St. Mary's
017415	CUSTARD, Francis	3m	W	D.C.	15 SEP 1878	Holy Rood
007591	CUSTARD, Joseph C.	9m	W	D.C.	11 JUN 1876	Holy Rood
017436	CUSTARD, Mary Ellen	21y	W	D.C.	17 SEP 1878	Holy Rood
009449	CUSTER, Alice	46y	W	Ire.	18 OCT 1876	Mt. Olivet
012058	CUSTER, Mima	81y	C	Va.	26 JUN 1877	Beckett's
002692	CUTLER, Bentz	3y	W	Va.	22 MAR 1875	Congressional
008806	CUTLER, Blanch Sarah	15m	C	D.C.	24 AUG 1876	Harmony
018658	CUTLER, George	7w	C	D.C.	13 JAN 1879	Young Mens
018297	CUTLER, Virgie	2y	C	D.C.	10 DEC 1878	Young Mens
002199	CUTRICK, Julia A., Mrs.	29y	W	Md.	17 FEB 1875	Sharpsburg, Md.

D

No.	Name	Age	Race	Birth	Death Date	Burial Place
013090	D'INVILLE, Alexandre D'Aigneaux	75y	W	W.I.	05 SEP 1877	Mt. Olivet
019263	DABNEY, Charles	50y	C	Va.	03 MAR 1879	Mt. Pleasant
007640	DABNEY, Eddie	15m	C	D.C.	14 JUN 1876	Harmony
015590	DABNEY, Elizabeth	75y	W	Va.	03 MAY 1878	Norfolk, Va.
012355	DABNEY, Infant of Dabney	3h	C	D.C.	14 JUL 1877	Harmony
020268	DABNEY, Isaac	1y	C	D.C.	02 JUN 1879	Young Mens
010306	DABNEY, Lilie May	3y	C	D.C.	16 JAN 1877	Mt. Pleasant
012423	DABNEY, Marie	22y	C	Va.	19 JUL 1877	Harmony
005963	DABNEY, Martha Ann	11m	C	D.C.	07 JAN 1876	Ebenezer
016085	DABNEY, William Henry	3y	C	D.C.	09 JUN 1878	Young Mens
010161	DACUS, Charly	29y	C	N.C.	03 JAN 1877	Young Mens
007721	DACY, Bridget	49d	W	D.C.	19 JUN 1876	Mt. Olivet
020267	DADE, Alfred Erskine	9m	C	D.C.	02 JUN 1879	Harmony
007073	DADE, Daisy C.	1y	C	D.C.	22 APR 1876	Harmony
015580	DADE, Jane	70y	C	Va.	02 MAY 1878	Mt. Pleasant
003036	DADE, Matilda	78y	C	Va.	18 APR 1875	Graceland
014854	DADE, Richard Harrington	13m	C	D.C.	23 FEB 1878	Harmony
002407	DADE, Wilie	3m	C	D.C.	03 MAR 1875	Mt. Pleasant
004773	DAGGS, Sarah	1d	M	D.C.	27 AUG 1875	Holy Rood
005215a	DAGGS, Sarah	46y	C	D.C.	20 OCT 1875	Holy Rood
003441f	DAHERTY, William J.	2y	--	Va.	23 MAR 1862	Graceland
012663	DAHLE, Henry	16m	W	D.C.	04 AUG 1877	Prospect Hill
015425	DAHY, Alexander Elijah Wash.	57y	C	Md.	17 APR 1878	Beckett's
008238	DAID, Lizzie Kinley	4y	C	D.C.	13 JUL 1876	Harmony
011844	DAID, Mary L.	4y	C	D.C.	09 JUN 1877	Harmony
004442	DAILEY, Charles	4m	W	D.C.	04 AUG 1875	Congressional
000016	DAILEY, Ellen	2y	C	D.C.	02 AUG 1874	Holy Rood
002249	DAILEY, Margaret	6m	W	D.C.	20 FEB 1875	Holy Rood
013298	DAILY, Elizabeth	70y	W	Eng.	25 SEP 1877	Potters Field
018377	DAILY, Guinnetta	48y	C	Va.	19 DEC 1878	Mt. Pleasant
007878	DAILY, Michael	1y	W	D.C.	27 JUN 1876	Mt. Olivet

District of Columbia Death Records, August 1, 1874 to July 31, 1879											85

No.	Name	Age	Race	Birth	Death Date	Burial Place
016670	DAILY, Winifed	62y	W	Ire.	19 JUL 1878	Mt. Olivet
016173	DAKE, Frederick E.	54y	W	Ver.	15 JUN 1878	Congressional
003692	DALEY, Lawrence	45y	W	Ire.	18 JUN 1875	Mt. Olivet
011799	DALLIS, Permelia	23y	C	Va.	04 JUN 1877	Ebenezer
020238	DALMAS, Marie	30y	W	France	31 MAY 1879	Mt. Olivet
013969	DALTON, James	2y	W	D.C.	30 NOV 1877	Mt. Olivet
007995	DALTON, James Samuel	11y	W	N.Y.	03 JUL 1876	Oak Hill
018376	DALTON, John W.	20y	W	D.C.	19 DEC 1878	Alexandria, Va.
009770	DALTON, Margaret	16y	W	D.C.	22 NOV 1876	Mt. Olivet
006175	DALTON, Thomas	42y	W	Ire.	29 JAN 1876	Mt. Olivet
018412	DALTON, William H.	50y	W	Pa.	21 DEC 1878	Alexandria, Va.
003849	DALY, Infant of Augustus	½h	W	D.C.	26 JUN 1875	Beckett's
005649	DALY, Mary	c.34y	W	Ire.	04 DEC 1875	Mt. Olivet
002241	DALY, Mary Alice	2y	W	D.C.	19 FEB 1875	Holy Rood
021007	DALY, Mary C.	14m	W	D.C.	19 JUL 1879	Mt. Olivet
008088	DALY, Wm. Henry	9m	W	D.C.	09 JUL 1876	Mt. Olivet
005493	DAMSTEAD, Elizabeth Matilda	9y	W	Md.	18 NOV 1875	Baltimore, Md.
004650	DANA, Julia F., Mrs.	27y	W	Md.	18 AUG 1875	Glenwood
017711	DANAHAR, Bridget	82y	W	Ire.	12 OCT 1878	Mt. Olivet
013462	DANAHER, Infant of Henry	6y	W	D.C.	10 OCT 1877	Mt. Olivet
008290	DANDRIDGE, Charles	38y	C	D.C.	16 JUL 1876	Harmony
020605	DANDRIDGE, Grace Ellen	3m	C	D.C.	24 JUN 1879	Payne's
012776	DANDRIDGE, Infant of George	½h	C	D.C.	11 AUG 1877	Potters Field
001992	DANDRIDGE, Mary Eliz.	7m	C	D.C.	02 FEB 1875	Harmony
001165	DANENHOUR, Wm. W.	9y	--	Pa.	-- --- 1854	Rock Creek
017988	DANENHOWER, Cora Belle	5y	W	Ill.	09 NOV 1878	Rock Creek
005263	DANGERFIELD, Infant of Mary	15h	C	D.C.	25 OCT 1875	Potters Field
007013	DANGERFIELD, James	12y	M	D.C.	14 APR 1876	Mt. Olivet
000093	DANGERFIELD, Lucy Ann	2y	C	D.C.	07 AUG 1874	Beckett's
005413	DANGERFIELD, Margaret	29y	C	Md.	10 NOV 1875	Ebenezer
000425	DANGERFIELD, Mary Magd.	8d	C	D.C.	04 SEP 1874	Mt. Olivet
005166a	DANGERFIELD, Pansy	85	C	Va.	16 OCT 1875	Ebenezer
011579	DANGERFIELD, Richard	6y	C	D.C.	13 MAY 1877	Ebenezer
003250	DANGERFIELD, William	30y	W	Ohio	07 MAY 1875	Congressional
008569	DANGLER, Emma Virginia	2d	W	D.C.	05 AUG 1876	Presbyterian
003389	DANIEL, Charley Lee	2m	W	D.C.	21 MAY 1875	Glenwood
003673	DANIELS, Frank G.	29y	W	N.Y.	17 JUN 1875	Glenwood
015190	DANIELS, Frederick	35y	W	Ger.	26 MAR 1878	Congressional
008406	DANIELS, Lydia Ann	1y	C	D.C.	24 JUL 1876	Potters Field
007176	DANIELS, Mary Gilliam	30y	C	Va.	01 MAY 1876	Ebenezer
004826	DANNAHER, Mary Ann	9y	W	D.C.	30 AUG 1875	Mt. Olivet
002586	DANT, Eva Melvina	3y	W	D.C.	15 MAR 1875	Mt. Olivet
008964	DANT, Joseph C.	3y	W	D.C.	04 SEP 1876	Mt. Olivet
011704	DANT, Mary Bernadette	5m	W	D.C.	26 MAY 1877	Mt. Olivet
019294	DANT, Willia	2y	C	D.C.	06 MAR 1879	Mt. Olivet
016671	DANTE, Fenwick Sylvester	2y	W	D.C.	19 JUL 1878	Mt. Olivet
007455	DARBY, Ann, Mrs.	55y	W	Ire.	01 JUN 1876	Mt. Olivet
010922	DARBY, Infant of Geo. W.	c.3m	W	D.C.	09 MAR 1877	Oak Hill
010923	DARBY, Infant of Geo. W.	c.3m	W	D.C.	09 MAR 1877	Oak Hill
005588	DARBY, Martha	11y	C	D.C.	28 NOV 1875	Small Pox Grounds
002491	DARBY, Ralph H., M.D.	46y	W	Ire.	09 MAR 1875	Congressional
005593	DARBY, Steptoe	30y	C	Va.	28 NOV 1875	Small Pox Grounds
001599	DARNE, Joseph A.	7d	W	D.C.	03 JAN 1875	Holy Rood
016887	DARNE, Sarah V.	7y	W	D.C.	03 AUG 1878	Holy Rood
001844	DARNELL, Isabella	14d	W	D.C.	22 JAN 1875	Congressional
020992	DARNES, Robert	8m	C	D.C.	18 JUL 1879	Harmony

No.	Name	Age	Race	Birth	Death Date	Burial Place
021156	DARNIELLE, Edmond P.	6m	W	D.C.	30 JUL 1879	Oak Hill
018355	DARNIELLE, John H.	9y	W	D.C.	16 DEC 1878	Oak Hill
001206	DARR, Martha Jane	22y	W	Md.	21 NOV 1874	Mt. Olivet
018932	DASHIELDS, Columbus W.	48y	W	Md.	03 FEB 1879	Oak Hill
004069	DASY, Samuel	11m	C	D.C.	10 JUL 1875	Beckett's
013412	DATCHER, Eleanor	80y	C	D.C.	06 OCT 1877	Harmony
012962	DATCHER, George Hicks	42y	C	D.C.	26 AUG 1877	Harmony
012963	DAUGHERTY, G. Benet	15d	W	D.C.	26 AUG 1877	Congressional
017032	DAVENPORT, Edwin	1m	W	D.C.	13 AUG 1878	Oak Hill
016262	DAVENPORT, Eliza	71y	C	Va.	22 JUN 1878	Mt. Zion
021093	DAVENPORT, Emily	48y	C	Va.	25 JUL 1879	Washington Asylum
001832	DAVENPORT, Melinda	35y	C	Va.	21 JAN 1875	Mt. Pleasant
013727	DAVID, Sophia	8y	W	D.C.	04 NOV 1877	Washington Hebrew
009286	DAVIDGE, Mary	70y	C	Md.	03 OCT 1876	Potters Field
011208	DAVIDSON, James George	35y	W	D.C.	04 APR 1877	Holy Rood
011361	DAVIDSON, Spencer	34y	W	Md.	17 APR 1877	Baltimore, Md.
002303	DAVIES, Alice	9y	C	Va.	24 FEB 1875	Alexandria, Va.
008304	DAVIES, Charles	2m	C	D.C.	17 JUL 1876	Alexandria, Va.
000925	DAVINE, Infant of Stepney	9d	C	D.C.	24 OCT 1874	Beckett's
001700	DAVIS, Alexander	2d	C	D.C.	11 JAN 1875	Golden's Farm
000989f	DAVIS, Alexander A.	5y	W	U.S.	25 OCT 1874	Mt. Olivet
007040	DAVIS, Alice Amelia	22y	W	D.C.	18 APR 1876	Glenwood
004240	DAVIS, Alice C.	1y	W	D.C.	22 JUL 1875	Glenwood
015156	DAVIS, Amelia	27y	W	Eng.	23 MAR 1878	Mt. Olivet
001871	DAVIS, Ann	92y	W	Mass.	24 JAN 1875	Mt. Olivet
009023	DAVIS, Anna	18y	W	D.C.	10 SEP 1876	Mt. Olivet
013268	DAVIS, Annie	2m	C	D.C.	21 SEP 1877	Beckett's
015982	DAVIS, Barbara	4h	W	D.C.	03 JUN 1878	Congressional
004706	DAVIS, Benjamin	1y	C	D.C.	22 AUG 1875	Mt. Zion
003816	DAVIS, Bernard McGuire	9m	W	D.C.	24 JUN 1875	Mt. Olivet
008325	DAVIS, Bertie	28d	W	D.C.	19 JUL 1876	Potters Field
014294	DAVIS, Caroline V.	22y	W	D.C.	02 JAN 1878	Mt. Olivet
001711	DAVIS, Catharine	78y	W	N.Y.	13 JAN 1875	Methodist, S.E.
009863	DAVIS, Catharine	9m	C	D.C.	04 DEC 1876	Macedonia
009781	DAVIS, Catherine	8m	C	D.C.	23 NOV 1876	Ebenezer
015733	DAVIS, Catherine	9m	C	D.C.	15 MAY 1878	Alexandria, Va.
019468	DAVIS, Charles	1y	C	D.C.	20 MAR 1879	Mt. Zion
008768	DAVIS, Charles H.	5m	W	D.C.	21 AUG 1876	Baltimore, Md.
010684	DAVIS, Charles Henry	70y	W	Mass.	18 FEB 1877	Cambridge, Mass.
000394	DAVIS, Charles W.	37y	W	D.C.	01 SEP 1874	Mt. Olivet
010141	DAVIS, Charlette	60y	C	Va.	01 JAN 1877	Ebenezer
013640	DAVIS, Clara	10y	W	D.C.	26 OCT 1877	Mt. Olivet
001734	DAVIS, Cora	8m	C	D.C.	14 JAN 1875	Beckett's
006486	DAVIS, Cyrus	75y	W	Md.	27 FEB 1876	Baltimore, Md.
009343	DAVIS, Daniel	59y	W	Wales	08 OCT 1876	Potters Field
004707	DAVIS, David C.	75y	W	Md.	22 AUG 1875	Zanesville, Ohio
014336	DAVIS, Edith Lindsey	9m	W	D.C.	06 JAN 1878	Oak Hill
000637	DAVIS, Edward	4m	C	D.C.	25 SEP 1874	Beckett's
010264	DAVIS, Edward	52y	M	Va.	12 JAN 1877	Mt. Zion
013109	DAVIS, Elisabeth, Mrs.	36y	C	Md.	07 SEP 1877	Mt. Olivet
009025	DAVIS, Eliza	55y	W	Md.	11 SEP 1876	Congressional
000835	DAVIS, Eliza V.	39y	W	Md.	17 OCT 1874	Congressional
005282	DAVIS, Elizabeth C.	34y	W	Va.	27 OCT 1875	Congressional
009247	DAVIS, Ellen	28y	W	Va.	30 SEP 1876	Congressional
018233	DAVIS, Ellen Hood	69y	W	Va.	03 DEC 1878	Oak Hill
009935	DAVIS, Ellenora	19y	C	Md.	12 DEC 1876	Ebenezer

District of Columbia Death Records, August 1, 1874 to July 31, 1879 87

No.	Name	Age	Race	Birth	Death Date	Burial Place
005504	DAVIS, Elliott Wiley	1y	W	D.C.	19 NOV 1875	Glenwood
000145	DAVIS, Fannie Estell	1y	W	D.C.	11 AUG 1874	Congressional
019250	DAVIS, Francis Allen	3m	W	D.C.	02 MAR 1879	Mt. Olivet
010732	DAVIS, Francis Leonora	30y	C	Mass.	22 FEB 1877	Harmony
006094	DAVIS, Gandison	65y	C	N.C.	22 JAN 1876	Harmony
019353	DAVIS, George	85y	W	Va.	10 MAR 1879	Alexandria, Va.
001743	DAVIS, George Madison	64y	W	N.Y.	15 JAN 1875	Oak Hill
015384	DAVIS, George Thomas	60y	W	Md.	13 APR 1878	Congressional
020161	DAVIS, Georgeana	2y	C	D.C.	21 MAY 1879	Mt. Olivet
008625	DAVIS, Gertie	11m	W	D.C.	09 AUG 1876	Oak Hill
018512	DAVIS, H., Mrs.	80y	C	Md.	30 DEC 1878	Mt. Olivet
002376	DAVIS, Henry Beamer	27y	W	D.C.	02 MAR 1875	Oak Hill
018435	DAVIS, Henry C.	10y	W	D.C.	23 DEC 1878	Oak Hill
018065	DAVIS, Henson	55y	C	D.C.	16 NOV 1878	Harmony
020318	DAVIS, Howard G.	1y	W	D.C.	06 JUN 1879	Graceland/Glenwood
011434	DAVIS, Hugh	77y	W	Va.	26 APR 1877	Glenwood
017584	DAVIS, Infant of Annie	2m	C	D.C.	01 OCT 1878	Potters Field
000781	DAVIS, Infant of Geo.	1m	C	D.C.	11 OCT 1874	Young Mens
011709	DAVIS, Infant of James	7d	C	D.C.	12 OCT 1878	Young Mens
013008	DAVIS, Infant of Lt. Danl.	8m	W	D.C.	29 AUG 1877	Glenwood
017362	DAVIS, Infant of Wm.	1d	C	D.C.	10 SEP 1878	Payne's
007834	DAVIS, Infant of Wm.	2d	C	D.C.	24 JUN 1876	Ebenezer
013774	DAVIS, Isabella	40y	C	Va.	09 NOV 1877	Potters Field
008179	DAVIS, Jacob	70y	C	Md.	11 JUL 1876	Potters Field
016069	DAVIS, James H.	6m	C	D.C.	08 JUN 1878	Mt. Pleasant
020187	DAVIS, James H.	3m	C	D.C.	15 JUN 1879	Potters Field
010438	DAVIS, James Newcome	59y	W	Va.	29 JAN 1877	Oak Hill
019544	DAVIS, James W.	52y	W	S.C.	25 MAR 1879	Hospital
000338	DAVIS, Jennie E.	18d	W	D.C.	27 AUG 1874	Congressional
006977	DAVIS, Jerome Edward	6m	W	D.C.	10 APR 1876	Mt. Olivet
004708	DAVIS, John	23y	C	Md.	22 AUG 1875	Potters Field
011910	DAVIS, John	1m	C	D.C	15 JUN 1877	Harmony
008877	DAVIS, John C.	2y	C	D.C.	30 AUG 1876	Mt. Olivet
005199a	DAVIS, John F.	58y	W	Pa.	19 OCT 1875	Potters Field
003975	DAVIS, John Montgomery	14d	M	D.C.	03 JUL 1875	Manassas Station, Va.
003294	DAVIS, John Thomas	11m	C	D.C.	12 MAY 1875	Young Mens
014734	DAVIS, John W.	1y	W	D.C.	10 FEB 1878	Congressional
019518	DAVIS, John W.	1y	C	D.C.	23 MAR 1879	Moore's
013804	DAVIS, Joseph	3y	C	D.C.	12 NOV 1877	Harmony
014036	DAVIS, Joseph E.	39y	W	D.C.	08 DEC 1877	Oak Hill
011554	DAVIS, K., Mrs.	50y	C	Va.	09 MAY 1877	Ebenezer
002110	DAVIS, Levi	58y	W	Md.	10 FEB 1875	Oak Hill
019805	DAVIS, Lewis	68y	C	Md.	17 APR 1879	Potters Field
004925	DAVIS, Lillie	1m	C	D.C.	06 SEP 1875	Ebenezer
000772	DAVIS, Lillie C.	2y	C	D.C.	10 OCT 1874	Moore's
003801	DAVIS, Louisa	20y	C	Va.	24 JUN 1875	Potters Field
016976	DAVIS, Louisa	45y	C	Va.	09 AUG 1878	Harmony
019941	DAVIS, Maggie E.	23y	W	D.C.	30 APR 1879	Congressional
003749	DAVIS, Martha	6w	C	D.C.	21 JUN 1875	Mt. Olivet
005402	DAVIS, Martha Ellen	5y	C	D.C.	09 NOV 1875	Ebenezer
003062	DAVIS, Martha J.	15y	W	D.C.	20 APR 1875	Glenwood
000156	DAVIS, Mary	21y	W	Pa.	11 AUG 1874	Holy Rood
005011a	DAVIS, Mary	45y	C	Va.	12 SEP 1875	Harmony
014624	DAVIS, Mary	21y	C	Va.	01 FEB 1878	Mt. Olivet
013299	DAVIS, Mary A.	16y	W	D.C.	25 SEP 1877	Mt. Olivet
008568	DAVIS, Mary Ann	62y	W	Pa.	05 AUG 1876	Oak Hill

No.	Name	Age	Race	Birth	Death Date	Burial Place
006782	DAVIS, Mary Ann	60y	W	Md.	23 MAR 1876	Congressional
017501	DAVIS, Mary C.	33y	W	D.C.	23 SEP 1878	Congressional
001727	DAVIS, Mary Jane	4m	C	D.C	14 JAN 1875	Harmony
018454	DAVIS, Mary Jane	55y	W	Md.	25 DEC 1878	Forestville, Md.
015197	DAVIS, Mary, Mrs.	59y	W	Va.	27 MAR 1878	Mt. Olivet
003141	DAVIS, Media	19y	W	D.C.	26 APR 1875	Mt. Olivet
002657	DAVIS, Melody	72y	C	Md.	20 MAR 1875	Ebenezer
020403	DAVIS, Pearl J.	3m	W	D.C.	12 JUN 1879	Baltimore, Md.
016628	DAVIS, Philip	1d	W	D.C.	17 JUL 1878	Holy Rood
021111	DAVIS, Philip	2m	C	D.C.	26 JUL 1879	Young Mens
016223	DAVIS, Pigeon E.	6m	C	D.C.	19 JUN 1878	Young Mens
005669	DAVIS, Rachel A.	60y	C	Md.	06 DEC 1875	Mt. Olivet
007213	DAVIS, Richmond	35y	C	N.C.	05 MAY 1876	Harmony
014637	DAVIS, Robert Ryland	19y	W	Md.	02 FEB 1878	Congressional
010699	DAVIS, Saml. R.	35y	W	Conn.	19 FEB 1877	Danielsville, Conn.
003896	DAVIS, Samuel	43y	W	Ire.	28 JUN 1875	Glenwood
005382	DAVIS, Samuel	74y	W	Md.	07 NOV 1875	Glenwood
005198a	DAVIS, Sarah	55y	C	Va.	19 OCT 1875	Harmony
021077	DAVIS, Sophia	65y	W	Md.	24 JUL 1879	Congressional
009740	DAVIS, Susan M. Harrison	36y	W	Conn.	19 NOV 1876	Rock Creek
005076	DAVIS, Walter F.	3m	W	D.C.	17 SEP 1875	Methodist
002500	DAVIS, William	57y	W	D.C.	10 MAR 1875	Congressional
015510	DAVIS, William	17y	C	Va.	25 APR 1875	Mt. Pleasant
001918	DAVIS, William A.	31y	W	D.C.	27 JAN 1875	Oak Hill
009443	DAVIS, William S.	35y	W	Me.	17 OCT 1876	Hospital
008876	DAVIS, Wm. Henry	5d	C	D.C.	30 AUG 1876	Harmony
011400	DAVIS, Wm. M.	64y	W	N.H.	22 APR 1877	Methodist
006625	DAVIS, Wm. Milton	1y	W	D.C.	10 MAR 1876	Congressional
007672	DAVIS, Zachariah	13y	C	D.C.	16 JUN 1876	Young Mens
012266	DAW, Charles T.	8m	W	D.C.	08 JUL 1877	Oak Hill
019282	DAW, Infant of Fred	½d	C	D.C.	05 MAR 1879	Potters Field
002850	DAWSEY, Albert	22y	M	Md.	02 APR 1875	Ebenezer
004622	DAWSON, Charles H.	1y	C	D.C.	16 AUG 1875	Harmony
014064	DAWSON, David Paul	3m	C	D.C.	11 DEC 1877	Young Mens
007621	DAWSON, George	1y	C	D.C.	13 JUN 1876	Ebenezer
005492	DAWSON, John A.	46y	W	Ire.	18 NOV 1875	Mt. Olivet
010623	DAWSY, Ellen	70y	M	Md.	14 FEB 1877	Ebenezer
011670	DAY, Anie Elizabeth	12y	W	D.C.	22 MAY 1877	Congressional/Rock Creek
008506	DAY, Annie	21y	C	Va.	31 JUL 1876	Mt. Pleasant
008617	DAY, Blanche Violer	5m	W	D.C.	08 AUG 1876	Methodist
007280	DAY, Charles Julian	7m	W	D.C.	12 MAY 1876	Young Mens
003556	DAY, E. Clifford	6m	W	D.C.	07 JUN 1875	Methodist
006213	DAY, Ella E.	23y	W	D.C.	02 FEB 1876	Congressional
014003	DAY, Gertrude	10m	C	D.C.	03 DEC 1877	Mt. Zion
018261	DAY, Jacob	27y	C	Va.	07 DEC 1878	Payne's
014275	DAY, James	54y	W	Va.	31 DEC 1877	Alexandria, Va.
003705	DAY, John O.	1m	C	D.C.	19 JUN 1875	Mt. Olivet
006374	DAY, John O.	1m	W	D.C.	16 FEB 1876	Mt. Olivet
020305	DAY, Jonia	1y	C	D.C.	05 JUN 1879	Mt. Zion
018688	DAY, Joseph	10m	C	D.C.	16 JAN 1879	Payne's
008019	DAY, Lemuel	22y	W	Md.	04 JUL 1876	Bell's Meeting House
001558	DAY, Margaret A.	20y	W	D.C.	01 JAN 1875	Mt. Olivet
008080	DAY, Martha	63y	C	Md.	08 JUL 1876	Mt. Olivet
000302	DAY, Mary	74y	W	Mass.	24 AUG 1874	Needham Plains, Mass.
014911	DAY, Mary	58y	C	Va.	01 MAR 1878	Mt. Zion
003218	DAY, Mary Catharine	34y	M	Va.	04 MAY 1875	Ebenezer

District of Columbia Death Records, August 1, 1874 to July 31, 1879   89

No.	Name	Age	Race	Birth	Death Date	Burial Place
009716	DAY, Mary Jane	7m	C	D.C.	17 NOV 1876	Young Mens
013970	DAY, Solomon	3m	C	D.C.	30 NOV 1877	Mt. Olivet
016070	DAY, Thomas	26y	C	Va.	08 JUN 1878	Mt. Zion
015212	DAY, William	63y	C	Va.	28 MAR 1878	Young Mens
018582	DAY, William	70y	C	Va.	06 JAN 1879	Potters Field
005517	DAYES, George	8y	C	D.C.	20 NOV 1875	Harmony
001731	DAYTON, Joseph Purcell	7y	W	S.C.	14 JAN 1875	Congressional
013953	DEACON, Augustus	68y	W	Prus.	28 NOV 1877	Soldier's Home
014638	DEACONS, Lee	6y	W	D.C.	02 FEB 1878	Glenwood
000327	DEAKIN, Florence	4m	W	D.C.	26 AUG 1874	Congressional
006811	DEAKINS, Dennis E.	40y	W	Md.	25 MAR 1876	Glenwood
003824	DEAN, Charles	88y	W	Md.	25 JUN 1875	Oak Hill
006222	DEAN, George H.	79y	W	Md.	03 FEB 1876	Montgomery Co., Md.
004610	DEAN, Henry	9m	C	D.C.	15 AUG 1875	Ebenezer
007895	DEANE, J. Francis	15m	W	D.C.	28 JUN 1876	Harper's Ferry, Va.
016811	DEANE, James A.	66y	W	Va.	29 JUL 1878	Presbyterian
007952	DEANE, Mary	63y	W	N.Y.	01 JUL 1876	Oak Hill
010180	DEANE, Serena	c.70y	W	N.Y.	05 JAN 1877	Graceland
003551	DEARBORN, Annie	35y	W	Va.	07 JUN 1875	Glenwood
004460	DEARING, Eleanor Beck	4m	W	D.C.	05 AUG 1875	Glenwood
008003	DEARING, John	24y	W	Md.	04 JUL 1876	Prospect Hill
007550	DEARSON, George	4m	W	D.C.	08 JUN 1876	Presbyterian
018356	DeATLEY, Rosa	4y	W	D.C.	16 DEC 1878	Congressional
018558	DeATLEY, Willie Barns	3m	W	D.C.	04 JAN 1879	Congressional
007815	DeBEER, Flora	3m	W	D.C.	24 JUN 1876	Hebrew
017708	DeBIRCHE, Gustav	1m	W	D.C.	12 OCT 1878	Mt. Olivet
013430	DEBOY, John Michael	1m	W	D.C.	08 OCT 1877	Oak Hill
008413	DEBTOR, Elias	68y	C	Md.	25 JUL 1876	Mt. Zion
006609	DeBUTT, Mary Ann	c.70y	W	--	09 MAR 1876	Mt. Olivet
010178	DECKMAN, William Henry	6y	W	D.C.	05 JAN 1877	Prospect Hill
003700	DeCOSTER, Louisa R.	60y	M	S.C.	19 JUN 1875	Harmony
004760	DeCRAFT, Mary Payne, Mrs.	c.50y	W	Va.	25 AUG 1875	Congressional
018117	DEE, Catharine Mary	26y	W	D.C.	22 NOV 1878	Mt. Olivet
001368	DEE, David	44y	W	Ire.	12 DEC 1874	Mt. Olivet
017422	DEE, Patrick	75y	W	Ire.	16 SEP 1878	Mt. Olivet
014880	DEEBLE, Ellen, Mrs.	38y	W	Md.	26 FEB 1878	Presbyterian
018176	DEEBLE, William	49y	W	D.C.	27 NOV 1878	Presbyterian
013852	DEEL, Katie A.	1y	C	D.C.	18 NOV 1877	Young Mens
015157	DEENER, Josiah W.	54y	W	Md.	23 MAR 1878	Oak Hill
021133	DEETH, Arthur B.	2y	W	D.C.	28 JUL 1879	Holy Rood
017317	DEETH, Edward W.	39y	W	N.J.	04 SEP 1878	Presbyterian
001789	DEETH, Julia Anna Compton	4m	W	D.C.	19 JAN 1875	Holy Rood
001505	DEETON, Robert	7y	W	Va.	27 DEC 1874	Alexandria, Va.
007691	DEFFER, Catharine E.	7m	W	D.C.	17 JUN 1876	Dumfries, Va.
005616	DEGGES, William Addison	36y	W	D.C.	01 DEC 1875	Glenwood
010133	DEGGS, Emanuel	36y	C	Va.	31 DEC 1876	Harmony
019770	DEGGS, Mary E.	3y	C	D.C.	14 APR 1879	Mt. Pleasant
014961	DEGRAW, William B.	39y	W	Md.	06 MAR 1878	Glenwood
000530	DEIGLE, Samuel	31y	--	Pa.	16 SEP 1874	Congressional
003537	DEITZ, Emma	4m	W	D.C.	05 JUN 1875	Prospect Hill
004349	DEITZ, Infant of Louise	½h	C	D.C.	28 JUL 1875	Potters Field
004561	DeLACY, Richard	35y	W	Ire.	12 AUG 1875	Mt. Olivet
000170	DeLANEY, D.	60y	M	D.C.	13 AUG 1874	Beckett's
002236	DELANEY, John	33y	W	Ire.	19 FEB 1875	Mt. Olivet
006762	DELANEY, John	1y	W	D.C.	21 MAR 1876	Mt. Olivet
007086	DELANEY, Levi	58y	C	D.C.	23 APR 1876	Harmony

District of Columbia Death Records, August 1, 1874 to July 31, 1879

No.	Name	Age	Race	Birth	Death Date	Burial Place
007797	DELANEY, Margaret	39y	C	D.C.	23 JUN 1876	Mt. Olivet
015621	DELANEY, Margaret	45y	W	Ire.	05 MAY 1878	Mt. Olivet
012514	DELANEY, Marrie	10m	C	D.C.	24 JUL 1877	Harmony
001163	DELANEY, Nancy	80y	C	D.C.	16 NOV 1874	Young Mens
016629	DELANEY, Rosana	9d	C	D.C.	17 JUL 1878	Beckett's
006494	DELANEY, Thomas	54y	W	Ire.	28 FEB 1876	Soldier's Home
004400	DELANIA, Hattie	1y	C	D.C.	01 AUG 1875	Moore's
018931	DELANO, Samuel	3d	W	D.C.	03 FEB 1879	Congressional
011335	DELANY, Daniel Webster	4m	C	D.C.	15 APR 1877	Moore's
000033	DELANY, Harriet	17d	C	D.C.	02 AUG 1874	Young Mens
015768	DELANY, Martha	11y	C	D.C.	19 MAY 1878	Moore's
005444	DELANY, Michael	24y	W	N.Y.	13 NOV 1875	N.Y. City
001033	DELASTACIUS, Rachel	36y	W	Can.	03 NOV 1874	Rock Creek
020651	DELAVERGNE, Henry Barker	1y	W	D.C.	28 JUN 1879	Mt. Olivet
000877	DELAY, Mary	26y	W	N.Y.	20 OCT 1874	Mt. Olivet
005010	DELLWIG, Elizabeth H.	30y	W	Eng.	12 SEP 1875	Congressional
010630	DELOE, Chester H.	4m	W	D.C.	14 FEB 1877	Glenwood
003396	DeLOFFRE, Nora Middleton, Mrs.	27y	W	D.C.	22 MAY 1875	Oak Hill
020388	DELORME, Cleophas T.	1y	W	Mich.	11 JUN 1879	Glenwood
007417	DELZ, David	60y	W	Ger.	27 MAY 1876	Hospital
006029	DeMARTIN, John B.	59y	W	Italy	15 JAN 1876	St. Mary's
007426	DEMARZO, Mary	10y	W	D.C.	28 MAY 1876	Mt. Olivet
010006	DEMENT, Effie Jane	3d	W	D.C.	18 DEC 1876	Congressional
006176	DEMENT, Hezekiah	77y	W	Md.	29 JAN 1876	Congressional
014697	DEMENT, John E.	74y	W	Md.	07 FEB 1878	Congressional
002532	DEMPSEY, John V.	c.38y	W	Pa.	12 MAR 1875	Philadelphia, Pa.
004388	DEMPSEY, Margaret	3y	W	Ire.	31 JUL 1875	Mt. Olivet
000934	DEMPSEY, Marie Louise	1y	W	D.C.	26 OCT 1874	Mt. Olivet
011328	DEMPSY, Mary	14y	W	D.C.	14 APR 1877	Mt. Olivet
013718	DENBY, Andrew	37y	C	Pa.	03 NOV 1877	Young Mens
014896	DENEEL, Edward N.	3m	W	D.C.	28 FEB 1878	Rock Creek
006544	DENEGRI, Chas. A.	15d	W	D.C.	04 MAR 1876	Mt. Olivet
020176	DENEIL, Charity Ann	7y	C	D.C.	23 MAY 1879	Hillsdale
018118	DENHAM, Margaret Elizabeth	53y	W	D.C.	22 NOV 1878	Oak Hill
013047	DENHAM, Olive D.	1m	W	D.C.	01 SEP 1877	Oak Hill
003494	DENHAN, Annie	10m	W	D.C.	31 MAY 1875	Congressional
002328	DENISON, Dudle	3y	W	D.C.	26 FEB 1875	Glenwood
016017	DENISON, Eunice	78y	W	N.Y.	05 JUN 1878	Stillwater, N.Y.
006363	DENISON, George	50y	W	Mass.	15 FEB 1876	N.Y.
019913	DENISON, Harry A.	7m	W	D.C.	27 APR 1879	Glenwood
016755	DENMORE, Lucy	19m	C	D.C.	25 JUL 1878	Beckett's
014490	DENNEY, Henry	3y	C	Ill.	20 JAN 1878	Graceland
016199	DENNIS, Jonathan, Jr.	65y	W	R.I.	17 JUN 1878	Oak Hill
012567	DENNIS, Joseph	2y	C	D.C.	27 JUL 1877	Potters Field
012519	DENNISON, Harry	12y	C	D.C.	25 JUL 1877	Congressional
003259	DENNISON, Hetta	6m	C	D.C.	07 MAY 1875	Harmony
010959	DENNY, Sylvanus	48y	W	N.J.	13 MAR 1877	Soldier's Home
002938	DENO, Maud	1y	W	D.C.	10 APR 1875	Congressional
007654	DENO, Rosalia Gallaher	4y	W	D.C.	15 JUN 1876	Congressional
021047	DENRINGER, Josephine	4m	W	D.C.	22 JUL 1879	St. Mary's
008700	DENT, Abraham	80y	C	Md.	16 AUG 1876	Young Mens
019632	DENT, Charles	53y	C	Md.	02 APR 1879	Moore's
013703	DENT, Edwin A.	16y	W	D.C.	02 NOV 1877	Mt. Olivet
002336	DENT, Elizabeth	59y	C	Md.	27 FEB 1875	Mt. Pleasant
020145	DENT, Feeman	4y	C	D.C.	19 MAY 1879	Beckett's
012742	DENT, Neley Ann	c.51y	C	Md.	09 AUG 1877	Rock Creek

District of Columbia Death Records, August 1, 1874 to July 31, 1879

No.	Name	Age	Race	Birth	Death Date	Burial Place
017021	DENT, Rose Mary Edelin	8m	W	D.C.	12 AUG 1878	Mt. Olivet
016888	DENT, Rosina	38y	W	D.C.	03 AUG 1878	Mt. Olivet
018447	DENT, Sarah	74y	C	Md.	24 DEC 1878	Mt. Zion
011964	DENT, Sarah Francis	2y	C	D.C.	19 JUN 1877	Potters Field
008199	DENT, Simon	35y	W	Ger.	12 JUL 1876	Baltimore, Md.
008804	DENT, Walter	1y	C	D.C.	24 AUG 1876	Young Mens
019354	DENT, Willie	1y	C	D.C.	10 MAR 1879	Mt. Pleasant
014516	DENTON, Josephine	7y	C	D.C.	22 JAN 1878	Harmony
005098	DENTON, Mary	5y	C	Md.	19 SEP 1875	Young Mens
004763	DENZEL, Newnan	45y	W	Ger.	26 AUG 1875	Soldier's Home
007458	DePIESRY, Faffael	2m	W	D.C.	01 JUN 1876	St. Mary's
014103	DEPOILLY, Adolph	2y	W	D.C.	15 DEC 1877	Mt. Olivet
013882	DEPOILLY, Eugenie	5y	W	France	22 NOV 1877	Mt. Olivet
013868	DEPOILLY, Louise	6y	W	France	20 NOV 1877	Mt. Olivet
004139f	DEPONAI, Mary	1y	W	D.C.	15 JUL 1875	Mt. Olivet
014611	DERBIN, Joseph	27y	W	Mich.	31 JAN 1878	Hospital, Government
016619	DERBY, Harry Custor	9m	W	N.J.	16 JUL 1878	Glenwood
007094	DeRESS, Thomas	31y	W	Ire.	24 APR 1876	Hospital
020009	DERHAM, Margret	11y	W	D.C.	06 MAY 1879	Mt. Pleasant
016566	DERKS, Samuel	29d	C	D.C.	12 JUL 1878	Beckett's
017710	DEROY, Sallie	1y	W	Pa.	12 OCT 1878	Adas Israel
017292	DERWAN, Margaret	4y	W	D.C.	02 SEP 1878	Mt. Olivet
010949	DERWIN, George	45y	W	Ire.	12 MAR 1877	Mt. Olivet
001811	DeSAULES, Emily	74y	W	Switz.	20 JAN 1875	Congressional
015740	DESFORD, Infant of Daniel	10min	C	D.C.	16 MAY 1878	Potters Field
007858	DESMOND, Cornelius	1y	W	Va.	26 JUN 1876	Alexandria, Va.
012726	DESMOND, Katie	1y	W	D.C.	08 AUG 1877	Mt. Olivet
016952	DETON, Clarence Oliver	20m	W	D.C.	08 AUG 1878	Alexandria, Va.
008981	DETWEILER, Harry	4d	W	D.C.	06 SEP 1876	Glenwood
020116	DEVAUGHAN, Catharine	81y	W	Va.	16 MAY 1879	Alexandria, Va.
011927	DEVAUGHN, Alberta	1y	W	D.C.	16 JUN 1877	Congressional
019334	DEVAUGHN, Alvides Francis	1y	W	Md.	09 MAR 1879	Barnabas Church
005491	DEVAUGHN, Benjamin T.	55y	W	Md.	18 NOV 1875	Congressional
016990	DEVAUGHN, Blanch Vernon	2m	W	D.C.	10 AUG 1878	Barnabas Church
000129	DEVAUGHN, Charles William	2m	W	D.C.	10 AUG 1874	Glenwood
005075	DEVAUGHN, Julia	1y	W	D.C.	17 SEP 1875	Mt. Olivet
018768	DEVAUGHN, Mary	79y	W	Del.	22 JAN 1879	Congressional
008357	DEVAUGHN, Mary Ellis	1y	W	Md.	20 JUL 1876	Barnabas Church
019412	DEVEILLE, Infant of A.J.	3d	C	D.C.	15 MAR 1879	Young Mens
003199	DEVERIES, Frederick	24y	W	Md.	02 MAY 1875	Mt. Olivet
020553	DEVERS, Fanny	3y	W	Md.	21 JUN 1879	Congressional
009720	DEVERS, Louis	69y	W	Va.	17 NOV 1876	Congressional
013929	DEVERS, Louisa	32y	W	Va.	26 NOV 1877	Congressional
020623	DEVERS, Matilte	5y	W	Md.	26 JUN 1879	Congressional
008641	DEVERS, Wm. H.	80y	W	Va.	10 AUG 1876	Glenwood
019333	DEVINE, Catharine	23y	C	Va.	09 MAR 1879	Potters Field
018075	DEVINE, Emily V.	49y	W	D.C.	17 NOV 1878	Holy Rood
007494	DEVINE, Marian	19d	W	D.C.	04 JUN 1876	Holy Rood
001628	DEVINE, Mary E.	27y	W	N.Y.	06 JAN 1875	Mt. Olivet
017567	DEVLIN, Emily R.	60y	W	La.	29 SEP 1878	N.Y.
001685	DEVLIN, James P.	39y	W	D.C.	10 JAN 1875	Mt. Olivet
008143	DEVLIN, Louis	11m	W	D.C.	10 JUL 1876	Congressional
012060	DEVLIN, Mary Ann	8d	W	D.C.	26 JUN 1877	Congressional
006952	DEVLIN, Peter	45y	W	Ire.	07 APR 1876	Soldier's Home
012195	DEVOTE, Edwd.	6m	W	D.C.	03 JUL 1877	Mt. Olivet
004310	DEWEY, Charles N.	9m	W	D.C.	26 JUL 1875	Congressional

No.	Name	Age	Race	Birth	Death Date	Burial Place
017755	DEWITT, Rosalee S.	16y	W	Va.	16 OCT 1878	Glenwood
017961	DEXTER, Benj. B.	84y	W	Mass.	06 NOV 1878	Groton, N.Y.
004637	DICE, Infant of Christo.	2d	W	D.C.	17 AUG 1875	Prospect Hill
003469	DICEY, Henry Hurley	10m	W	D.C.	29 MAY 1875	Mt. Olivet
006203	DICK, Harriet	45	C	Md.	01 FEB 1876	Harmony
008180	DICK, Moses	79y	C	Md.	11 JUL 1876	Harmony
014197	DICK, Robert	68y	C	Md.	25 DEC 1877	Harmony
011327	DICKERSON, Elizabeth	21y	W	Va.	14 APR 1877	Aquia Creek, Va.
002285	DICKERSON, Henry	21y	C	Va.	22 FEB 1875	Young Mens
003848	DICKERSON, Infant of Edward	4m	M	D.C.	26 JUN 1875	Graceland
006294	DICKERSON, James Fredrick	6m	C	D.C.	10 FEB 1876	Harmony
000656	DICKERSON, Nelson	1y	C	N.Y.	28 SEP 1874	Mt. Pleasant
008352	DICKERSON, Priscilla	1y	C	D.C.	20 JUL 1876	Young Mens
011628	DICKEY, John J.	50y	W	Me.	17 MAY 1877	Graceland
010323	DICKINSON, Ella B.	4h	W	D.C.	17 JAN 1877	Graceland
018159	DICKINSON, Ernest Willie Linwood	1y	C	D.C.	26 NOV 1878	Harmony
003155	DICKINSON, George R.	5m	C	D.C.	28 APR 1875	Harmony
019128	DICKINSON, Ida	38y	W	N.Y.	20 FEB 1879	Oak Hill
003246	DICKISON, Sarah	20y	C	Va.	06 MAY 1875	Potters Field
007607	DICKMAN, Ernest Ulrich	8m	W	N.Y.	12 JUN 1876	Glenwood
007010	DICKSON, Anna Jane	43y	W	D.C.	13 APR 1876	Congressional
005009	DICKSON, Harrit Ellen	1y	W	D.C.	12 SEP 1875	Holy Rood
006431	DICKSON, Infant of Alice	2h	C	D.C.	21 FEB 1876	Potters Field
001688	DICKSON, Infant of Rosa	3d	C	D.C.	10 JAN 1875	Potters Field
000061	DICKSON, James	--	--	--	04 AUG 1874	--
014065	DICKSON, Mary	9m	C	D.C.	11 DEC 1877	Payne's
019056	DICKSON, Minnie	12y	C	Va.	13 FEB 1879	Mt. Pleasant
015371	DICKSON, Theodore	50y	C	Va.	12 APR 1878	Harmony
013336	DICKSON, Virginia	c.24y	C	Va.	28 SEP 1877	Potters Field
000828	DICKSON, Washington	67y	C	Md.	16 OCT 1874	Payne's
003258f	DICKUS, Gustave	85y	W	Ger.	07 MAY 1875	St. Mary's
017477	DIEHL, John	8d	W	D.C.	21 SEP 1878	Prospect Hill
016434	DIEMER, Dennis Francis	2y	W	D.C.	04 JUL 1878	Mt. Olivet
006595	DIESON, Annie	7m	C	D.C.	08 MAR 1876	Ebenezer
007232	DIETZ, Anna Sophie	8d	W	D.C.	07 MAY 1876	Prospect Hill
017553	DIETZ, Christena	44y	W	Ger.	28 SEP 1878	Prospect Hill
008108	DIETZ, Henriette Sophie Carol	8m	W	D.C.	09 JUL 1876	Prospect Hill
004224	DIETZ, Louisa H.M.	15y	W	D.C.	21 JUL 1875	Glenwood
011603	DIETZ, Louise Wilhelmine	59y	W	Ger.	15 MAY 1877	Congressional
000895	DIETZE, Clifford W.	1m	W	D.C.	22 OCT 1874	Prospect Hill
003351	DIGGES, Philip	6y	C	D.C.	17 MAY 1875	Jones Chapel
018702	DIGGLE, Emma E.	30y	W	D.C.	17 JAN 1879	Congressional
014404	DIGGLE, Mary Elizabeth	1m	W	D.C.	13 JAN 1878	Mt. Olivet
016276	DIGGLE, William	25y	W	D.C.	23 JUN 1878	Congressional
010456	DIGGONS, Ellen	2m	W	D.C.	30 JAN 1877	Mt. Olivet
003179	DIGGS, Alebertia	6m	C	D.C.	30 APR 1875	Mt. Pleasant
016099	DIGGS, Chas. H.	62y	C	Md.	10 JUN 1878	Mt. Olivet
001264	DIGGS, Edward	9m	C	D.C.	29 NOV 1874	Young Mens
016734	DIGGS, George	7m	C	D.C.	24 JUL 1878	Potters Field
018778	DIGGS, Harriet	34y	C	Va.	23 JAN 1879	Baptist
010761	DIGGS, Henry	70y	C	Md.	24 FEB 1877	Mt. Pleasant
003457	DIGGS, Hester	110y	C	Md.	28 MAY 1875	Mt. Olivet
006951	DIGGS, Hester	4y	C	D.C.	07 APR 1876	Moore's
004152	DIGGS, Horace	3m	C	D.C.	16 JUL 1875	Harmony
005077	DIGGS, James	15y	C	D.C.	17 SEP 1875	Mt. Zion
011078	DIGGS, Jas.	9m	C	D.C.	22 MAR 1877	Mt. Zion

District of Columbia Death Records, August 1, 1874 to July 31, 1879   93

No.	Name	Age	Race	Birth	Death Date	Burial Place
002264	DIGGS, John	21y	C	Va.	21 FEB 1875	Washington Asylum
000073	DIGGS, John Henry	3y	C	D.C.	06 AUG 1874	Potters Field
003764	DIGGS, Joseph	1y	C	D.C.	22 JUN 1875	Mt. Pleasant
010059	DIGGS, Lewis	95y	C	Md.	24 DEC 1876	Beckett's
010567	DIGGS, Maria	9y	C	D.C.	09 FEB 1877	Potters Field
000708	DIGGS, Rosetta	90y	C	Md.	04 OCT 1874	Beckett's
004900	DIGGS, Samuel Jerome	62y	W	Md.	04 SEP 1875	Glenwood
002091	DIGGS, Thomas	30y	C	Md.	09 FEB 1875	Washington Asylum
020215	DIGGS, William F.	27y	C	Va.	28 MAY 1879	Alexandria, Va.
013971	DIGGS, Wm. Thomas	7y	C	Va.	30 NOV 1877	Arlington Heights, Va.
005467	DIGNEY, Annie	9m	W	D.C.	16 NOV 1875	Mt. Olivet
002416	DIGNEY, Catharine	61y	W	Ire.	04 MAR 1875	Mt. Olivet
007246	DILLENBERG, Levi	39y	W	Ger.	08 MAY 1876	Washington Hebrew
013222	DILLENBERGER, Henry	67y	W	Ger.	16 SEP 1877	Congressional
002781	DILLON, Henry W.	16y	W	N.H.	29 MAR 1875	Wilton, N.H.
001119	DILLON, Mary S.	21y	W	D.C.	12 NOV 1874	Glenwood
001261	DILLON, Roy	2m	W	D.C.	29 NOV 1874	Congressional
020554	DILTZ, Solomon	35y	W	N.Y.	21 JUN 1879	Hospital, Government
017088	DINES, Charles	27y	C	D.C.	18 AUG 1878	Mt. Zion
013269	DINES, Henry	13½d	C	D.C.	21 SEP 1877	Potters Field
015560	DINES, Infant of Joseph	13d	C	D.C.	30 APR 1878	Mt. Olivet
008855	DINES, Infant of Philip	6d	C	D.C.	28 AUG 1876	Mt. Olivet
009628	DINES, Maria	65y	C	D.C.	06 NOV 1876	Holy Rood
001084	DINES, Mary	75y	C	Va.	08 NOV 1874	Potters Field
017659	DINES, Mary	78y	C	Md.	07 OCT 1878	Mt. Olivet
016727	DINES, Mary Ann	7m	C	D.C.	23 JUL 1878	Mt. Olivet
001926	DINGES, Charles	3m	W	D.C.	28 JAN 1875	Prospect Hill
004892	DINNEEN, James	11m	W	D.C.	03 SEP 1875	Mt. Olivet
017792	DINSMORE, Marian	24y	W	Md.	19 OCT 1878	Mt. Olivet
010142	DISBROW, David R.	51y	W	N.Y.	01 JAN 1877	Westchester Co., N.Y.
006795	DISCOE, James D.	8y	W	Md.	24 MAR 1876	Methodist
011415	DISHMAN, Joseph	9d	W	D.C.	24 APR 1877	Methodist
008176	DISHMAN, Martha L.	25y	C	Va.	11 JUL 1876	Baptist
017565	DISNEY, Jonathan	36y	W	Ire.	29 SEP 1878	Soldier's Home
005292	DITTOE, Mary Cecilia	45y	W	Ohio	28 OCT 1875	Mt. Olivet
002876	DIVER, Emily G.	2y	W	D.C.	05 APR 1875	Congressional
012062	DIX, Blanch E.	9y	W	Va.	26 JUN 1877	Presbyterian
011130	DIX, D. Dyer	27y	W	W.Va.	27 MAR 1877	Nicholas C.H., W.Va.
014962	DIXON, Chas.	3m	C	D.C.	06 MAR 1878	Beckett's
006567	DIXON, Chs. A.	15m	C	D.C.	06 MAR 1876	Harmony
017166	DIXON, David	29y	W	Ire.	24 AUG 1878	Hospital
012755	DIXON, Fredie	10m	C	D.C.	10 AUG 1877	Ebenezer
011473	DIXON, John	6y	C	D.C.	01 MAY 1877	Mt. Zion
012318	DIXON, Mary	5m	C	D.C.	11 JUL 1877	Mt. Olivet
003431	DIXON, Mary Genevia	22m	C	D.C.	25 MAY 1875	Harmony
020993	DIXON, Robert	75y	C	Va.	18 JUL 1879	Potters Field
010353	DIXON, Sabrinnia	101y	C	Va.	21 JAN 1877	Harmony
000775	DIXON, Sarah alias Davis	45y	C	Md.	10 OCT 1874	Washington Asylum
001114	DIXON, Sythe	26y	C	Va.	12 NOV 1874	Washington Asylum
003207	DIXON, Willie	4y	C	D.C.	03 MAY 1875	Harmony
000414	DIXSON, George	10d	W	DC.	03 SEP 1874	Glenwood
004288	DIXSON, Mary	47y	C	D.C.	25 JUL 1875	Potters Field
016604	DOAS, Susan	75y	C	Va.	15 JUL 1878	Beckett's
003595	DOBBINS, William Bressup	1y	W	D.C.	10 JUN 1875	Congressional
010500	DOBBS, Rose	93y	C	Va.	03 FEB 1877	Macedonia, Potomac
020146	DOBBYN, James R.	6m	W	D.C.	19 MAY 1879	Mt. Olivet

No.	Name	Age	Race	Birth	Death Date	Burial Place
008024	DOBBYN, Martha Agness	5m	W	D.C.	05 JUL 1876	Mt. Olivet
006667	DOBSON, Fred Joses	3y	W	D.C.	14 MAR 1876	Rochester, N.Y.
011316	DOBSON, Lewis	20y	C	Md.	13 APR 1877	Mt. Olivet
010951	DOCKET, John	18m	M	D.C.	12 MAR 1877	Harmony
002899	DOCKSTADER, Percival V.	5y	W	D.C.	06 APR 1875	Congressional
003098	DODD, Reubin	76y	W	Va.	23 APR 1875	Congressional
014662	DODGE, A.H.	62y	W	D.C.	04 FEB 1878	Oak Hill
016100	DODGE, Amasa	1y	W	D.C.	10 JUN 1878	Congressional
006132	DODGE, Frances Isabella	56y	W	Md.	25 JAN 1876	Oak Hill
005460	DODGE, Walter Edwin	1y	W	D.C.	15 NOV 1875	Congressional
015720	DODSON, Addie R.	11m	C	D.C.	14 MAY 1878	Harmony
004169	DODSON, Allan	64y	C	Va.	17 JUL 1875	Mt. Zion
020922	DODSON, Annie Maria	10y	C	D.C.	14 JUL 1879	Harmony
020495	DODSON, Charity	63y	C	Md.	18 JUN 1879	Graceland
014295	DODSON, Edward	6y	C	D.C.	02 JAN 1878	Beckett's
013682	DODSON, Emanuel	28y	C	D.C.	31 OCT 1877	Beckett's
006797	DODSON, Emily	25y	M	Md.	24 MAR 1876	Mt. Olivet
014845	DODSON, George	4y	C	D.C.	22 FEB 1878	Beckett's
002455	DODSON, Ida R.	5m	C	D.C.	06 MAR 1875	Ebenezer
016172	DODSON, Infant of Christopher	1m	C	D.C.	15 JUN 1878	Mt. Pleasant
007641	DODSON, Jacob	80y	C	U.S.	14 JUN 1876	Ebenezer Methodist
015691	DODSON, James E.	3y	M	D.C.	12 MAY 1878	Beckett's
003437	DODSON, Joseph	5m	C	D.C.	25 MAY 1875	Ebenezer
009435	DODSON, Katie	83y	C	Md.	16 OCT 1876	Mt. Olivet
013646	DODSON, Louis	2m	C	D.C.	27 OCT 1877	Beckett's
014144	DODSON, Lucy	78y	C	Va.	20 DEC 1877	Arlington
019430	DODSON, Mary	6m	C	D.C.	17 MAR 1879	Young Mens
008415	DODSON, Mary E.	7d	C	D.C.	25 JUL 1876	Holy Rood
013065	DODSON, Mary E.	1m	C	D.C.	03 SEP 1877	Beckett's
007937	DODSON, Mary L.	1m	C	D.C.	30 JUN 1876	Rock Creek
007412	DODSON, Rose	35y	C	Md.	26 MAY 1876	Rock Creek
002928	DODSON, Sarah	19y	C	Md.	09 APR 1875	Mt. Olivet
002981	DODSON, Simeo	4m	C	D.C.	14 APR 1875	Harmony
014541	DODSON, Susan Blanche	1y	C	D.C.	24 JAN 1878	Beckett's
011091	DODSON, Willis	79y	C	D.C.	23 MAR 1877	Young Mens
011441	DOERING, Lucy	5y	W	D.C.	27 APR 1877	Oak Hill
005935	DOGANS, Sarah	77y	C	Md.	04 JAN 1876	Harmony
016503	DOGIN, Lucinda	50y	C	Md.	08 JUL 1878	Beckett's
007653	DOHERTY, John	3m	W	D.C.	15 JUN 1876	Mt. Olivet
016450	DOHERTY, Mary Emeline	6y	W	D.C.	05 JUL 1878	Congressional
006636	DOLAN, Annie Daisy	2y	W	D.C.	11 MAR 1876	Mt. Olivet
015629	DOLAN, Elizebeth B.	24y	W	Eng.	06 MAY 1878	Mt. Olivet
017682	DOLAN, John M.	22y	W	N.Y.	09 OCT 1878	Mt. Olivet
015950	DOLAN, Margaret Elizth.	9m	W	D.C.	01 JUN 1878	Mt. Olivet
018570	DOLAN, Margret	73y	W	Ire.	05 JAN 1879	Mt. Olivet
012570	DOLEMAN, Joseph Arthur	1y	W	D.C.	28 JUL 1877	Presbyterian
016159	DOLEMAN, Patsy	25y	C	Va.	14 JUN 1878	Beckett's
005390	DOLLY, Lucretia	c.43y	C	Ga.	08 NOV 1875	Harmony
012182	DOLLY, Olivia	1y	C	D.C.	02 JUL 1877	Young Mens
012928	DOMINICK, Mary	15d	M	D.C.	24 AUG 1877	Mt. Olivet
019558	DOMINIST, Mary	c.30y	C	Md.	26 MAR 1879	Mt. Olivet
015503	DOMINIUS, James Harry	6m	C	D.C.	24 APR 1878	Harmony
015220	DOMINIUS, Mary E.	19y	C	D.C.	29 MAR 1878	Harmony
017829	DONAHUE, Delia	10y	W	D.C.	22 OCT 1878	Holy Rood/Oakland, Md.
004216	DONAHUE, Hugh	60y	W	Ire.	20 JUL 1875	Mt. Olivet
011482	DONAHUE, Robert A.	20y	W	Va.	01 MAY 1877	Westmoreland Co., Va.

District of Columbia Death Records, August 1, 1874 to July 31, 1879   95

No.	Name	Age	Race	Birth	Death Date	Burial Place
004609	DONALDSON, Agnes R.	3m	W	D.C.	15 AUG 1875	Tennallytown M.E.
016767	DONALDSON, James Wesley	6d	W	D.C.	26 JUL 1878	Glenwood
005218	DONALDSON, Julia D.	16y	W	D.C.	29 SEP 1875	Congressional
002034	DONALDSON, Laura E.	5y	W	D.C.	05 FEB 1875	Tennallytown
001304	DONALDSON, Lewis	61y	W	Va.	04 DEC 1874	Holy Rood
015038	DONALDSON, Maggie	1y	W	D.C.	12 MAR 1878	Glenwood
005200a	DONALDSON, Mary A.	1y	W	D.C.	19 OCT 1875	Alexandria, Va.
007793	DONALDSON, Matilda	c.90y	W	Md.	23 JUN 1876	Glenwood
021078	DONALDSON, Samuel H.	47y	W	Va.	24 JUL 1879	Glenwood
014245	DONAVAN, Cath.	80y	W	Ire.	29 DEC 1877	Mt. Olivet
002038	DONDARE, Rosa, Mrs.	29y	W	Italy	05 FEB 1875	St. Mary's
005180	DONDON, Elmer Ellsworth	23d	W	D.C.	26 SEP 1875	Glenwood
010280	DONELAN, Patrick H.	55y	W	D.C.	13 JAN 1877	Mt. Olivet
008141	DONELLY, Cornelius	3y	W	D.C.	10 JUL 1876	Mt. Olivet
001989	DONN, Etta Viola	4m	W	D.C.	02 FEB 1875	Glenwood
014329	DONN, John Young	47y	W	Md.	05 JAN 1878	Glenwood
003546	DONN, Marion A.	38y	W	Md.	07 JUN 1875	Glenwood
000759	DONN, Mary	2y	W	Ire.	08 OCT 1874	Mt. Olivet
004122	DONN, Michael	7m	W	D.C.	14 JUL 1875	Mt. Olivet
017266	DONNELLY, Elizabeth	1y	W	D.C.	31 AUG 1878	Mt. Olivet
010468	DONNELLY, Francis, Private	31y	W	N.Y.	01 FEB 1877	N.Y.
004771	DONNELLY, Lizzie H.	14y	W	Pa.	27 AUG 1875	Mt. Olivet
007245	DONNELLY, Matthew M.	54y	W	Pa.	08 MAY 1876	Chester Co., Pa.
003667	DONNELLY, Mary	1y	W	D.C.	16 JUN 1875	Mt. Olivet
017929	DONNELLY, Peter	42y	W	Eng.	02 NOV 1878	Mt. Olivet
019782	DONNING, Fannie May	7y	W	D.C.	15 APR 1879	Congressional
014517	DONNING, William Hysore	1y	W	D.C.	22 JAN 1878	Congressional
005026a	DONOHO, Margret	6y	W	D.C.	02 OCT 1875	Mt. Olivet
002947	DONOHOE, Henry J.	9m	W	D.C.	11 APR 1875	Mt. Olivet
015707	DONOHOE, Margaret	25y	W	Ire.	13 MAY 1878	Holy Rood
018825	DONOHOE, Maria	50+y	W	Ire.	26 JAN 1879	Congressional
014022	DONOHOE, Martin	72y	W	Ire.	07 DEC 1877	Holy Rood
014810	DONOHOE, Mary E.	20y	W	D.C.	18 FEB 1878	Holy Rood
000409	DONOHOO, Catharine D.	12y	W	D.C.	02 SEP 1874	Glenwood
006057	DONOHOO, Harriet	71y	W	D.C.	18 JAN 1876	Mt. Olivet
006271	DONOHOO, Lewis Minchin	28y	W	D.C.	08 FEB 1876	Mt. Olivet
019586	DONOHUE, Alice Genia	2y	W	D.C.	29 MAR 1879	Oak Hill
011467	DONOHUE, Anne	1y	W	D.C.	30 APR 1877	Mt. Olivet
019161	DONOHUE, Daniel	15d	W	D.C.	23 FEB 1879	Mt. Olivet
002293	DONOHUE, Margaret	1y	W	D.C.	23 FEB 1875	Mt. Olivet
017154	DONOHUE, Margaret	27y	W	Ala.	23 AUG 1878	Mt. Olivet
000190	DONOHUE, Michal	11m	W	D.C.	15 AUG 1874	Mt. Olivet
000121	DONOHUE, Owen Baldwin	6m	W	D.C.	10 AUG 1874	Oak Hill
017629	DONOHUE, Rosanna	61y	W	Ire.	04 OCT 1878	Mt. Olivet
001481	DONOHUE, Timothy	40y	W	Ire.	25 DEC 1874	Mt. Olivet
015438	DONOVAN, Cornelius	56y	W	Ire.	18 APR 1878	Mt. Olivet
000227	DONOVAN, John	14d	W	D.C.	18 AUG 1874	Mt. Olivet
002343	DONOVAN, Julia	21y	W	Ire.	27 FEB 1875	Mt. Olivet
017660	DONOVAN, Julia	42y	W	Ire.	07 OCT 1878	Mt. Olivet
013597	DONOVAN, Mary	43y	W	Ire.	23 OCT 1877	Holy Rood
014897	DONOVAN, William	63y	W	Ire.	28 FEB 1878	Hospital, Government
009147	DOODY, Bridget	1m	W	D.C.	20 SEP 1876	Mt. Olivet
010781	DOODY, John	6m	W	D.C.	25 FEB 1877	Mt. Olivet
015254	DOOLITTLE, Eloise	10m	W	D.C.	01 APR 1878	Oak Hill
008491	DORAN, Clara	5m	W	D.C.	30 JUL 1876	Mt. Olivet
002640	DORAN, John	48y	W	N.Y.	19 MAR 1875	Mt. Olivet

District of Columbia Death Records, August 1, 1874 to July 31, 1879

No.	Name	Age	Race	Birth	Death Date	Burial Place
013194	DOREMUS, Irena, Mrs.	77y	W	N.J.	14 SEP 1877	Varick, Seneca Co., N.Y.
015086	DORMAN, Adelaide	80y	W	France	16 MAR 1878	Mt. Olivet
009427	DORMAN, Anthony D.	14½m	W	D.C.	16 OCT 1876	Alexandria, Va.
019041	DORMAN, James	51y	W	Del.	12 FEB 1879	Harrington, Del.
010491	DORN, Michael	37y	W	N.Y.	03 FEB 1877	Soldier's Home
011695	DORR, Carlotta	6y	W	D.C.	25 MAY 1877	Presbyterian
002569	DORRINGTON, Clarissa	60y	C	Md.	14 MAR 1875	Harmony
015591	DORSCH, Catherine	2y	W	D.C.	03 MAY 1878	St. Mary's
019249	DORSEY, Albert A.	9m	C	D.C.	02 MAR 1879	Beckett's
011288	DORSEY, Alice W.	29y	C	D.C.	10 APR 1877	Young Mens
000044	DORSEY, Anna Frances	10m	C	D.C.	03 AUG 1874	Harmony
016768	DORSEY, Birdie	1y	C	D.C.	26 JUL 1878	Mt. Pleasant
011717	DORSEY, Bradley	5m	C	Md.	26 MAY 1877	Mt. Zion
013120	DORSEY, Celia	18y	C	Md.	08 SEP 1877	Potters Field
011826	DORSEY, Charles	23y	C	Md.	07 JUN 1877	Mt. Olivet
017267	DORSEY, Charles	1y	C	D.C.	31 AUG 1878	Beckett's
016113	DORSEY, Charles H.	66y	C	Md.	11 JUN 1878	Mt. Pleasant
016810	DORSEY, Clara T.	11m	C	D.C.	29 JUL 1878	Holy Rood
010634	DORSEY, Dinah	72y	C	Md.	15 FEB 1877	Mt. Pleasant
004772	DORSEY, George	2m	C	D.C.	27 AUG 1875	Beckett's
015788	DORSEY, Gertie	5m	C	D.C.	21 MAY 1878	Mt. Pleasant
019568	DORSEY, Hamilton	52y	C	Md.	27 MAR 1879	Potters Field
014397	DORSEY, Infant of Taylor	4h	C	D.C.	12 JAN 1878	Potters Field
004146	DORSEY, Infant of William	1m	C	D.C.	15 JUL 1875	Potters Field
000141	DORSEY, James	1m	W	D.C.	11 AUG 1874	Holy Rood
014861	DORSEY, James	2m	C	Va.	24 FEB 1878	Young Mens
019004	DORSEY, James Westley	2y	C	D.C.	09 FEB 1879	Beckett's
020203	DORSEY, Jas. E.	16y	C	D.C.	26 MAY 1879	Harmony
012613	DORSEY, Jenney	75y	C	Va.	30 JUL 1877	Beckett's
005792	DORSEY, John S.	6m	C	D.C.	19 DEC 1875	Young Mens
001417	DORSEY, Julia	20y	C	Md.	17 DEC 1874	Potters Field
013477	DORSEY, Lissey	10d	W	D.C.	11 OCT 1877	Holy Rood
020936	DORSEY, Lizzie	14d	C	D.C.	15 JUL 1879	Potters Field
017198	DORSEY, Louisa	47y	C	Md.	26 AUG 1878	Harmony
018642	DORSEY, Madora	1y	C	D.C.	11 JAN 1879	Beckett's
016539	DORSEY, Mamie	7m	C	D.C.	10 JUL 1878	Payne's
014739	DORSEY, Margaret	22y	C	Md.	11 FEB 1878	Potters Field
014698	DORSEY, Martha	1y	W	D.C.	07 FEB 1878	Mt. Olivet
000516	DORSEY, Mary	40y	C	Md.	15 SEP 1874	Mt. Olivet
015289	DORSEY, Mary	50y	W	Ire.	05 APR 1878	Prospect Hill
000317	DORSEY, Mary E.	2m	C	D.C.	25 AUG 1874	Beckett's
014368	DORSEY, Mary Elizabeth	16d	C	D.C.	09 JAN 1878	Beckett's
009176	DORSEY, Phillip	20y	C	Md.	23 SEP 1876	Mt. Olivet
002966	DORSEY, Rosa	2m	M	D.C.	12 APR 1875	Mt. Zion
001268	DORSEY, Samuel	80y	C	Md.	29 NOV 1874	Potters Field
016830	DORSEY, William	6d	W	D.C.	30 JUL 1878	Holy Rood
020754	DORSEY, William	31y	C	Md.	04 JUL 1879	Graceland
008634	DORSEY, Wm.	10m	C	D.C.	10 AUG 1876	Beckett's
020434	DORSON, John	10m	C	D.C.	14 JUN 1879	Payne's
000879	DORSY, Charles	1y	C	D.C.	20 OCT 1874	Beckett's
001987	DORSY, Eliza	2d	W	D.C.	01 FEB 1875	Potters Field
016898	DOTSON, Henrietta	3m	C	D.C.	04 AUG 1878	Beckett's
012690	DOTSON, Joseph	2y	C	D.C.	06 AUG 1877	Potters Field
005214a	DOTSON, Manuel	35y	C	D.C.	20 OCT 1875	Potters Field
011031	DOTSON, Prince Albert Eugene	10y	C	D.C.	18 MAR 1877	Harmony
000629	DOTSON, Sarah	19y	C	D.C.	24 SEP 1874	Beckett's

District of Columbia Death Records, August 1, 1874 to July 31, 1879

No.	Name	Age	Race	Birth	Death Date	Burial Place
008093	DOTSON, Walter	7y	C	D.C.	09 JUL 1876	Ebenezer
000539	DOUD, James P.	1m	W	D.C.	17 SEP 1874	Mt. Olivet
018779	DOUDAN, Rose	4y	W	D.C.	23 JAN 1879	St. Mary's
008557	DOUDHUGH, Michael	55y	W	Ire.	04 AUG 1876	Mt. Olivet
020608	DOUGERTY, Joseph T.	7m	W	D.C.	25 JUN 1879	Mt. Olivet
001683	DOUGHERTY, Edward F.	2y	W	D.C.	10 JAN 1875	Glenwood
008107	DOUGHERTY, Fanny L.	6m	W	D.C.	09 JUL 1876	Congressional
016397	DOUGHERTY, Gracy	2y	W	D.C.	02 JUL 1878	Glenwood
004082	DOUGHERTY, James	8m	W	D.C.	11 JUL 1875	Glenwood
019264	DOUGHERTY, Jas. E.	5m	W	D.C.	03 MAR 1879	Congressional
010913	DOUGHERTY, Mary Jane	21y	W	D.C.	08 MAR 1877	Mt. Olivet
011435	DOUGHERTY, Nathan	38y	W	Ohio	27 APR 1877	Washington Asylum
019088	DOUGHLASS, John	5d	C	D.C.	16 FEB 1879	Mt. Pleasant
019273	DOUGHTON, Catherine E.	2y	W	D.C.	04 MAR 1879	Congressional
020894	DOUGHTY, John S.	53y	W	Ind.	12 JUL 1879	Indianapolis, Ind.
006626	DOUGLAS, Allan A.	8m	W	D.C.	10 MAR 1876	Oak Hill
018421	DOUGLAS, B.B.	56y	W	Va.	22 DEC 1878	Va.
014223	DOUGLAS, Blanche	4y	W	D.C.	27 DEC 1877	Oak Hill
005617	DOUGLAS, Eleanora	1y	C	D.C.	01 DEC 1875	Mt. Pleasant
005973	DOUGLAS, Francis A.	4m	C	D.C.	08 JAN 1876	Ebenezer
004858	DOUGLAS, Henry H.	1y	C	D.C.	01 SEP 1875	Harmony
011410	DOUGLAS, John	75y	C	Va.	23 APR 1877	Young Mens
002615	DOUGLAS, John W.	7d	C	D.C.	17 MAR 1875	Harmony
017962	DOUGLAS, Kate	22y	C	D.C.	06 NOV 1878	Harmony
007879	DOUGLAS, Maria Jane	25y	C	D.C.	27 JUN 1876	Young Mens
007117	DOUGLAS, Mary	21y	C	Va.	26 APR 1876	Ebenezer
003293	DOUGLAS, Mary E.	2y	C	D.C.	12 MAY 1875	Harmony
016068	DOUGLAS, William	8m	C	D.C.	08 JUN 1878	Mt. Olivet
017650	DOUGLAS, William Henry	67y	C	Md.	06 OCT 1878	Harmony
011631	DOUGLASS, Albert	22y	C	Md.	17 MAY 1877	Mt. Zion
019382	DOUGLASS, Eddie	1y	C	N.Y.	13 MAR 1879	Hillsdale
001289	DOUGLASS, Emma A.	8m	C	D.C.	02 DEC 1874	Young Mens
012002	DOUGLASS, Infant of Charles	26h	C	D.C.	22 JUN 1877	Young Mens
005012	DOUGLASS, John	78y	W	Va.	01 OCT 1875	Alexandria, Va.
019410	DOUGLASS, Laura	2y	C	D.C.	15 MAR 1879	Potters Field
011592	DOUGLASS, Leuisa	5m	C	D.C.	14 MAY 1877	Mt. Pleasant
003590	DOUGLASS, Lewis E.	5m	C	D.C.	10 JUN 1875	Harmony
020259	DOUGLASS, Margaret	40y	C	Va.	01 JUN 1879	Potters Field
011986	DOUGLASS, Maud Ardell	3m	C	D.C.	21 JUN 1877	Harmony
005526	DOUGLASS, Rachel	14y	C	D.C.	21 NOV 1875	Harmony
011547	DOUGLASS, Rachel	28y	C	Va.	08 MAY 1877	Potters Field
015344	DOUGLASS, Sylvester	1y	C	D.C.	10 APR 1878	Mt. Olivet
019222	DOUHERTY, Patrick	42y	W	Ire.	27 FEB 1879	Hospital, Government
017437	DOUHERTY, Wm. H.	44y	W	Pa.	17 SEP 1878	Hospital, Government
013945	DOUX, Maria	60y	M	La.	27 NOV 1877	Graceland
005334	DOVE, Edwin	8m	W	D.C.	02 NOV 1875	Rock Creek
016565	DOVE, Isabella	9m	C	D.C.	12 JUL 1878	Mt. Zion
001413	DOVE, Maggie	90y	C	Ga.	16 DEC 1874	Beckett's
003204	DOVE, Susan	7y	W	D.C.	03 MAY 1875	Glenwood
009133	DOVER, Benjamin	11m	C	D.C.	19 SEP 1876	Mt. Zion
007608	DOVER, James	38y	C	D.C.	12 JUN 1876	Mt. Zion
008959	DOVER, Mary Francis	28y	C	D.C.	04 SEP 1876	Mt. Zion
003014	DOVERSMITH, Mary	4m	W	D.C.	17 APR 1875	Mt. Olivet
019852	DOW, Clarinda Annabella	23y	W	Va.	21 APR 1879	Oak Hill
000846	DOWD, Catherine	3m	W	D.C.	18 OCT 1874	Mt. Olivet
007106	DOWD, Johanna	18y	W	D.C.	25 APR 1876	Mt. Olivet

No.	Name	Age	Race	Birth	Death Date	Burial Place
000932	DOWD, Margaret W.	54y	W	Ire.	25 OCT 1874	Mt. Olivet
011913	DOWD, Patrick	33y	W	Ire.	15 JUN 1877	Mt. Olivet
014387	DOWD, Timothy	22y	W	D.C.	11 JAN 1878	Mt. Olivet
006122	DOWDE, Isabella	95y	C	Va.	24 JAN 1876	Harmony
006707	DOWDY, Harriet	25y	C	D.C.	17 MAR 1876	Ebenezer
003823	DOWDY, Robert	1m	C	D.C.	25 JUN 1875	Ebenezer
009219	DOWEL, Mary C.	7d	W	D.C.	28 SEP 1876	Mt. Olivet
017651	DOWLING, Elizabeth	44y	W	Ire.	06 OCT 1878	Mt. Olivet
000611	DOWLING, Ellen	2y	C	D.C.	23 SEP 1874	Harmony
010957	DOWLING, Griffin	77y	C	Va.	13 MAR 1877	Mt. Pleasant
004474	DOWLING, Jeanob	3m	C	D.C.	06 AUG 1875	Harmony
016232	DOWLING, John	70y	W	Ire.	20 JUN 1878	Mt. Olivet
016359	DOWLING, Michael	17m	W	D.C.	29 JUN 1878	Mt. Olivet
005166	DOWLING, Susie	25y	C	D.C.	25 SEP 1875	Harmony
004108	DOWLING, Thomas	4y	C	D.C.	13 JUL 1875	Harmony
020306	DOWNES, John	64y	W	Md.	05 JUN 1879	Congressional
002521	DOWNES, Margaret	5y	W	D.C.	11 MAR 1875	Mt. Olivet
020708	DOWNEY, Chas. O.	16d	W	D.C.	02 JUL 1879	Congressional
011992	DOWNEY, D.L.	2m	W	D.C.	21 JUN 1877	Congressional
004046	DOWNEY, Frankie C.	19d	W	D.C.	08 JUL 1875	Congressional
014198	DOWNEY, Richard A.	21y	W	D.C.	25 DEC 1877	Mt. Olivet
008867	DOWNEY, William	15y	C	D.C.	29 AUG 1876	Potters Field
009337	DOWNEY, William	44y	W	Ire.	08 OCT 1876	Mt. Olivet
015213	DOWNEY, William T.	6m	W	D.C.	28 MAR 1878	Mt. Olivet
018643	DOWNING, Albert Ford	1y	W	D.C.	11 JAN 1879	Glenwood
003821	DOWNING, Christiana	1y	C	D.C.	25 JUN 1875	Potters Field
004332	DOWNING, Elexena B.	4½m	C	D.C.	27 JUL 1875	Potters Field
016702	DOWNING, Frances T.	32y	W	Ire.	21 JUL 1878	Mt. Olivet
005943	DOWNING, George	54y	C	Va.	05 JAN 1876	Harmony
013145	DOWNING, Lucy	1y	W	D.C.	10 SEP 1877	Glenwood
021132	DOWNING, Wm. H.	32y	W	Va.	28 JUL 1879	Salem, Va.
002741	DOWNS, Francis E.	11m	C	D.C.	27 MAR 1875	Moore's
008547	DOWNS, John	94y	W	Md.	03 AUG 1876	Glenwood
008639	DOWNS, John Thomas	c.59y	W	Eng.	10 AUG 1876	Congressional
019396	DOWNS, Mary Emanuel	2m	W	D.C.	14 MAR 1879	Mt. Olivet
016084	DOWNS, Mary Francis	2y	C	D.C.	09 JUN 1878	Mt. Pleasant
011675	DOWNS, Wm.	8m	W	D.C.	22 MAY 1877	Mt. Olivet
013048	DOWNY, Maggie	11m	W	D.C.	01 SEP 1877	Mt. Olivet
020666	DOYLE, Aloysius	8m	W	D.C.	29 JUN 1879	St. Mary's
021036	DOYLE, Anna	10m	W	D.C.	21 JUL 1879	Mt. Olivet
002181	DOYLE, Edward	4y	W	D.C.	15 FEB 1875	Mt. Olivet
020870	DOYLE, Ellen	10y	W	D.C.	10 JUL 1879	Mt. Olivet
013641	DOYLE, George B.	4y	W	D.C.	26 OCT 1877	St. Mary's
001794	DOYLE, John	11d	W	D.C.	19 JAN 1875	Mt. Olivet
017922	DOYLE, John	63y	W	Ire.	01 NOV 1878	Mt. Olivet
010644	DOYLE, Julia	76y	W	Ire.	15 FEB 1877	Mt. Olivet
017861	DOYLE, Kate	3m	W	D.C.	26 OCT 1878	Mt. Olivet
004095	DOYLE, Mamie	2y	W	D.C.	12 JUL 1875	Mt. Olivet
003365f	DOZIER, Ann Sebella	25y	W	Va.	19 MAY 1875	Oak Hill
013555	DRAIGER, Charles	23y	W	D.C.	18 OCT 1877	Prospect Hill
009192	DRAINE, Sarah A.	35y	W	D.C.	24 SEP 1876	Mt. Olivet
002458	DRAKE, Austin	31y	W	Mo.	06 MAR 1875	St. Louis, Mo.
005648	DRANE, James Washington	12m	W	D.C.	04 DEC 1875	Mt. Olivet
017478	DRANE, William	59y	W	Md.	21 SEP 1878	Glenwood
009398	DRAPER, Alexander H.	43y	W	Pa.	13 OCT 1876	Oak Hill
006260	DRAREY, Frank Madison	1y	W	D.C.	07 FEB 1876	Glenwood

District of Columbia Death Records, August 1, 1874 to July 31, 1879

No.	Name	Age	Race	Birth	Death Date	Burial Place
000423	DRAYDON, Molly, Mrs.	32y	C	Va.	03 SEP 1874	Young Mens
018618	DREIFUS, August	41y	W	France	09 JAN 1879	Washington Hebrew
014104	DREW, Albert	19y	W	D.C.	15 DEC 1877	Oak Hill
002830	DREW, Euphemia	3m	W	D.C.	01 APR 1875	Presbyterian
011935	DREW, Francis T.	12d	W	D.C.	16 JUN 1877	Prospect Hill
008783	DREW, George W.	54y	W	N.H.	22 AUG 1876	Oak Hill
020923	DREW, Mary	5d	W	D.C.	14 JUL 1879	Potters Field
006056	DREW, Roger Preston	5m	C	D.C.	18 JAN 1876	Young Mens
005027a	DREW, Sarah N.	21y	C	Va.	02 OCT 1875	Mt. Pleasant Plain
001090	DRIES, John	51y	W	D.C.	08 NOV 1874	Glenwood
010615	DRINKARD, William Beverly	34y	W	Va.	13 FEB 1877	Oak Hill
011920	DRISCOLL, Dennis O.	30y	W	Ire.	15 JUN 1877	Mt. Olivet
014769	DRISCOLL, Ellen	70y	W	Ire.	15 FEB 1878	Holy Rood
008446	DRISCOLL, James	52y	W	Ire.	27 JUL 1876	Mt. Olivet
017464	DRISCOLL, Mary Ann	23y	W	D.C.	20 SEP 1878	Holy Rood
014125	DRISCOLL, Owen	63y	W	Md.	18 DEC 1877	Holy Rood
018741	DRIVER, George	45y	C	Md.	20 JAN 1879	Mt. Olivet
018824	DRIVER, William James	4m	C	D.C.	26 JAN 1879	Potters Field
017446	DROGE, Jermina	11m	W	D.C.	18 SEP 1878	Prospect Hill
015394	DRONEY, Jas.	20y	W	D.C.	14 APR 1878	Mt. Olivet
014735	DRONEY, Mary	52y	W	Ire.	10 FEB 1878	Mt. Olivet
000683	DROOP, Sophie	29y	W	Md.	01 OCT 1874	Oak Hill
015158	DROWNS, George	75y	W	Ire.	23 MAR 1878	Soldier's Home
004593	DRUMMOND, Gertrude	10m	W	D.C.	14 AUG 1875	Presbyterian
017228	DRUMMOND, Isabelle	20y	W	D.C.	28 AUG 1878	Methodist
016071	DRUMMOND, Kay G.	7m	W	D.C.	08 JUN 1878	Congressional
002688	DRURY, Eben N.	54y	W	Ver.	22 MAR 1875	Congressional
016735	DRURY, Genevieve	1y	W	D.C.	24 JUL 1878	Mt. Olivet
011570	DRURY, John F.	5y	W	D.C.	12 MAY 1877	Holy Rood
016648	DRURY, Marie Cecilia	3y	W	D.C.	18 JUL 1878	Mt. Olivet
018395	DRURY, Michael	72y	W	Ire.	20 DEC 1878	Hospital
010820	DUBANT, Elizabeth	73y	W	Va.	01 MAR 1877	Mt. Olivet
009185	DUBANT, George A.	22y	W	D.C.	24 SEP 1876	Mt. Olivet
003847	DuBOIS, Bennete	2m	M	D.C.	26 JUN 1875	Graceland
008524	DuBOIS, Richard L.	1y	W	D.C.	02 AUG 1876	Rock Creek
012112	DUCKET, Daniel	21d	C	D.C.	29 JUN 1877	Mt. Olivet
013572	DUCKET, Edmonia	18y	C	Md.	20 OCT 1877	Harmony
002979	DUCKET, Francis	1y	C	D.C.	13 APR 1875	Potters Field
000120	DUCKET, Infant	2d	C	D.C.	09 AUG 1874	Potters Field
018867	DUCKET, Infant of Hezekiah	1d	C	D.C.	29 JAN 1879	Mt. Olivet
004410	DUCKET, Infant of Nellie	11d	C	D.C.	02 AUG 1875	Potters Field
011946	DUCKET, Martha	25y	C	Md.	17 JUN 1877	Mt. Olivet
020580	DUCKETT, Charles	5m	C	D.C.	23 JUN 1879	Mt. Olivet
019806	DUCKETT, Daniel	2y	C	D.C.	17 APR 1879	Mt. Olivet
006823	DUCKETT, Fannie	1y	C	D.C.	26 MAR 1876	Mt. Olivet
012077	DUCKETT, Frances	22y	M	Va.	26 JUN 1877	Mt. Pleasant
000124	DUCKETT, Freddie W.	20m	W	D.C.	10 AUG 1874	Oak Hill
015290	DUCKETT, Georgeanna	13y	C	Md.	05 APR 1878	Mt. Pleasant
020448	DUCKETT, Henry	91y	C	Md.	15 JUN 1879	Potters Field
013064	DUCKETT, Rachel	9d	C	D.C.	03 SEP 1877	Potters Field
012155	DUCKETT, Reuben	1y	C	D.C.	01 JUL 1877	Harmony
012497	DUCKETT, William T.	9d	C	D.C.	23 JUL 1877	Mt. Olivet
013562	DUCKETT, Willie	1y	C	D.C.	19 OCT 1877	Harmony
016975	DUDLEY, Albert Eugene	1y	M	D.C.	09 AUG 1878	Mt. Pleasant
011021	DUDLEY, Annie E.	40y	W	Va.	17 MAR 1877	Richmond, Va.
004810	DUDLEY, Gertrude	11m	C	D.C.	29 AUG 1875	Potters Field

District of Columbia Death Records, August 1, 1874 to July 31, 1879

No.	Name	Age	Race	Birth	Death Date	Burial Place
019960	DUDLEY, Henry Hayne	44y	W	Va.	02 MAY 1879	Congressional
013818	DUDLEY, John Pinckney	1y	W	D.C.	14 NOV 1877	Congressional
011109	DUDLEY, Mary Ellen	17y	C	Va.	25 MAR 1877	Harmony
017500	DUDLEY, William Zachariah	11m	W	D.C.	23 SEP 1878	Congressional
006293	DUDLEY, Wm.	50y	W	Ire.	10 FEB 1876	Mt. Olivet
001977	DUFF, Cupid	22y	C	Va.	01 FEB 1875	Ebenezer
019089	DUFFEY, Mary M.	63y	W	D.C.	16 FEB 1879	Oak Hill
017692	DUFFY, Alice	23y	W	D.C.	10 OCT 1878	Mt. Olivet/Holy Rood
008463	DUFFY, Alice Blanch	1m	W	D.C.	28 JUL 1876	Mt. Olivet
014330	DUFFY, Ella May	5y	W	D.C.	05 JAN 1878	Mt. Olivet
004215	DUFFY, Infant of Thomas	6h	W	D.C.	20 JUL 1875	Congressional
016552	DUFFY, Kate	43y	W	D.C.	11 JUL 1878	Holy Rood
010996	DUFFY, Lousa R.	3m	C	D.C.	15 MAR 1877	Mt. Zion
005099	DUFFY, Moriah E.	24y	C	Md.	19 SEP 1875	Young Mens
014405	DUFFY, Owen Edgar John	2y	W	Md.	13 JAN 1878	Mt. Olivet
014546	DUGAN, Bridget	54y	W	Ire.	25 JAN 1878	Mt. Olivet
020260	DUGAN, Cumberland Francis	4y	W	D.C.	01 JUN 1879	Mt. Olivet
015464	DUGAN, Mary	96y	W	Ire.	21 APR 1878	Mt. Olivet
008349	DUGAN, Rebecca	58y	W	W.Va.	20 JUL 1876	Presbyterian
004331	DUGAN, Shean Maria	8m	W	Md.	27 JUL 1875	Mt. Olivet
018188	DUGAY, Frederick	27y	W	N.B.	28 NOV 1878	Potters Field
000385	DUGGAN, Daniel	34y	W	Ire.	31 AUG 1874	Mt. Olivet
020825	DUGLAS, Mary	26y	C	D.C.	08 JUL 1879	Mt. Pleasant
015872	DUKE, George V.	9m	W	D.C.	28 MAY 1878	Mt. Olivet
005618	DUKE, Maggie	2y	C	D.C.	01 DEC 1875	Harmony
003023	DUKEHART, Anna E.S.	22y	C	Pa.	17 APR 1875	Harmony
019772	DUKOWITZ, Infant of Eli	5h	W	D.C.	14 APR 1879	Graceland
014443	DULABON, Wm.	21y	W	Pa.	16 JAN 1878	Washington Asylum
018455	DULANEY, Charles Colbert	7m	C	D.C.	25 DEC 1878	Beckett's
017860	DULANEY, John Francis	35y	C	D.C.	26 OCT 1878	Harmony
003101	DULANEY, Mary Agnes	1y	M	D.C.	23 APR 1875	Ebenezer
006414	DULANEY, Mary Agnes	9d	C	D.C.	19 FEB 1876	Ebenezer
008231	DULANEY, Robert	9m	C	D.C.	13 JUL 1876	Ebenezer
002428	DULANEY, Roderic	58y	C	Md.	05 MAR 1875	Mt. Olivet
021076	DULANEY, Thos.	7d	M	D.C.	24 JUL 1879	Beckett's
000137	DULANEY, William	2y	C	D.C.	10 AUG 1874	Beckett's
013121	DULEY, Irene Temple	2y	W	D.C.	08 SEP 1877	Oak Hill
012929	DULEY, Leah J.	4y	W	D.C.	24 AUG 1877	Oak Hill
014037	DULIN, Alice Marie	28y	W	D.C.	08 DEC 1877	Mt. Olivet
007431	DULIN, Benjamin	7m	W	D.C.	29 MAY 1876	Congressional
010289	DULIN, George Whitfield	17y	W	D.C.	14 JAN 1877	Congressional
018040	DULIN, Infant of J.C.	4d	W	D.C.	13 NOV 1878	Congressional
014344	DULIN, Sarah Kirk	2y	W	D.C.	07 JAN 1878	Congressional
018551	DULIN, Sarah Kirk	64y	W	Va.	03 JAN 1879	Congressional
015072	DUNBAR, John	3y	C	D.C.	15 MAR 1878	Mt. Pleasant
014811	DUNCAN, Alfred	35y	C	Md.	18 FEB 1878	Mt. Zion
005755	DUNCAN, Anna O.	1y	M	D.C.	15 DEC 1875	Mt. Zion
006140	DUNCAN, Elizebeth	87y	M	Va.	26 JAN 1876	Harmony
012914	DUNCAN, Infant of Roselia	½h	C	D.C.	23 AUG 1877	Potters Field
020883	DUNCAN, Judson	2m	C	D.C.	11 JUL 1879	Beckett's
018218	DUNCAN, Louisa P.	71y	W	Md.	02 DEC 1878	Oak Hill
014092	DUNCAN, Maria	62y	C	Va.	14 DEC 1877	Young Mens
011539	DUNCAN, Mary	76y	C	Va.	07 MAY 1877	Harmony
018100	DUNGAN, Celene	10w	W	D.C.	20 NOV 1878	Prospect Hill
010398	DUNGAN, Celine	2d	W	D.C.	24 JAN 1877	Prospect Hill
017911	DUNGAN, Mary Ellen	76y	W	Md.	31 OCT 1878	Oak Hill

District of Columbia Death Records, August 1, 1874 to July 31, 1879

No.	Name	Age	Race	Birth	Death Date	Burial Place
012393	DUNKINS, Gertrude	3m	M	D.C.	16 JUL 1877	Mt. Zion
020092	DUNLAP, Armistead	4y	C	D.C.	14 MAY 1879	Graceland
019716	DUNLAP, James	49y	C	Va.	10 APR 1879	Graceland
015964	DUNLAP, Samuel	17d	C	D.C.	02 JUN 1878	Beckett's
001346	DUNMORE, Lulu	1y	C	D.C.	09 DEC 1874	Beckett's
006914	DUNMORE, Wm. Edward	9m	C	D.C.	04 APR 1876	Ebenezer
006678	DUNN, Agnes Loretta	1m	W	D.C.	15 MAR 1876	Mt. Olivet
018000	DUNN, Annie	74y	C	Va.	10 NOV 1878	Harmony
009832	DUNN, Catherine	2y	W	D.C.	30 NOV 1876	Mt. Olivet
008991	DUNN, Joanna	19y	W	Ire.	06 SEP 1876	Mt. Olivet
015073	DUNN, John	38y	W	Ire.	15 MAR 1878	Potters Field
001954	DUNN, Julia	43y	W	Ire.	30 JAN 1875	Mt. Olivet
001123	DUNN, Mary A.H.	1y	W	D.C.	11 NOV 1874	Congressional
015244	DUNN, Mary W.	6y	W	D.C.	31 MAR 1878	Mt. Olivet
014648	DUNN, Michael	47y	W	Ire.	03 FEB 1878	Soldier's Home
015426	DUNN, Thos. Francis	2y	C	D.C.	17 APR 1878	Mt. Olivet
009250	DUNN, Wm. H., Jr.	4m	W	D.C.	30 SEP 1876	Congressional
005791	DUNNIN, Peter	29y	W	Ire.	19 DEC 1875	Mt. Olivet
003822	DUNNING, George A.	51y	W	D.C.	25 JUN 1875	Congressional
010675	DUNNINGTON, Betty	17y	C	Md.	18 FEB 1877	Potters Field
019706	DUNNINGTON, Laura Estella	7y	W	D.C.	09 APR 1879	Howard
011433	DUNWOOD, Alfred	76y	C	Va.	26 APR 1877	Mt. Zion
012170	DUPRE, Julia C.	11y	C	D.C.	02 JUL 1877	Harmony
001676	DURBIN, J.N.	c.45y	W	--	10 JAN 1875	Prospect Hill
007639	DUREN, John Augustus	44y	W	N.H.	14 JUN 1876	Keene, N.H.
019458	DURFEE, Ida	3m	W	D.C.	19 MAR 1879	Glenwood
012754	DURHAM, Harvey	5y	W	D.C.	10 AUG 1877	Mt. Olivet
017250	DURHAM, Rachel	20y	C	D.C.	30 AUG 1878	Mt. Pleasant
019975	DURKIN, George J.	10y	W	D.C.	03 MAY 1879	Mt. Olivet
000666	DURKIN, Mary	21y	W	Pa.	29 SEP 1874	Mt. Olivet
005743	DURWIN, John	7m	W	D.C.	14 DEC 1875	Mt. Olivet
015542	DUTCH, Henry	65y	C	Md.	28 APR 1878	Mt. Pleasant Plain
003210	DUTCH, Lucy	4y	C	D.C.	03 MAY 1875	Potters Field
003688	DUTCH, Mary F.	6d	C	D.C.	18 JUN 1875	Young Mens
015039	DUTTON, Alexander	9m	C	D.C.	12 MAR 1878	Mt. Zion
010757	DUTTON, Barney	2y	C	Md.	23 FEB 1877	Mt. Zion
005329	DUTTON, Sarah	35y	C	D.C.	01 NOV 1875	Mt. Pleasant
009831	DUTTON, Thomas	56y	W	Conn.	30 NOV 1876	Oak Hill
013543	DUVAL, James Aurena	2y	C	D.C.	17 OCT 1877	Beckett's
016200	DUVAL, Samuel	38y	W	Md.	17 JUN 1878	Congressional
018809	DUVALL, Andrew Jackson	51y	W	Md.	25 JAN 1879	Oak Hill
004196	DUVALL, Ann Elizabeth	73y	W	Va.	19 JUL 1875	Glenwood
013668	DUVALL, Claude	4m	W	D.C.	29 OCT 1877	Tennallytown
019195	DUVALL, Effie May	2y	W	D.C.	25 FEB 1879	Congressional
010772	DUVALL, Ella	15y	W	D.C.	24 FEB 1877	Oak Hill
014246	DUVALL, Emma	1y	C	D.C.	29 DEC 1877	Mt. Zion
010969	DUVALL, Emma	35y	W	D.C.	14 MAR 1877	Rock Creek
000503	DUVALL, Emma L.	16m	W	D.C.	13 SEP 1874	Congressional
013669	DUVALL, Fannie G.	8y	M	D.C.	29 OCT 1877	Beckett's
003716	DUVALL, George	50y	C	Va.	19 JUN 1875	Potters Field
012689	DUVALL, John H.	2y	W	D.C.	06 AUG 1877	Glenwood
001031	DUVALL, Lettie	67y	C	Va.	03 NOV 1874	Mt. Olivet
010227	DUVALL, Lloyd	17m	C	D.C.	08 JAN 1877	Young Mens
019983	DUVALL, Margaret S.	34y	W	Md.	04 MAY 1879	Congressional
000595	DUVALL, Mary Agnes	8m	M	D.C.	22 SEP 1874	Mt. Olivet
004059	DUVALL, Minty	55y	C	Va.	09 JUL 1875	Mt. Zion

District of Columbia Death Records, August 1, 1874 to July 31, 1879

No.	Name	Age	Race	Birth	Death Date	Burial Place
010190	DUVALL, Nellie Virginia	5y	W	D.C.	06 JAN 1877	Glenwood
015465	DUVALL, Percy	8m	C	D.C.	21 APR 1878	Harmony
004504	DUVALL, Robert	1y	C	D.C.	07 AUG 1875	Harmony
000568	DUVALL, Thomas E.F.	7m	W	D.C.	19 SEP 1874	Congressional
001512	DUVALL, Turner	21y	M	Va.	27 DEC 1874	Potters Field
018466	DUZENBURY, Infant of Anna	4m	W	D.C.	26 DEC 1878	Mt. Olivet
001790	DWIGHT, Timothy C.	c.72y	W	Mass.	19 JAN 1875	N.Y. City
000230	DWYER, Margaret	18y	W	D.C.	18 AUG 1874	Mt. Olivet
019932	DYE, Infant of John	5d	W	D.C.	29 APR 1879	Lacy Farm
018232	DYER, Agnes	20y	W	D.C.	03 DEC 1878	Holy Rood
001339	DYER, Andrew Cadwallader	54y	W	Me.	08 DEC 1874	Congressional
009024	DYER, Clara M.	6y	W	D.C.	10 SEP 1876	Holy Rood
017872	DYER, Lewis H.	5y	W	D.C.	27 OCT 1878	Holy Rood
005535	DYER, Mary E.	9d	C	D.C.	22 NOV 1875	Mt. Olivet
016451	DYER, Theodore	9m	W	D.C.	05 JUL 1878	Holy Rood
007521	DYER, William T.	34y	W	D.C.	06 JUN 1876	Holy Rood
005014a	DYMS, Joseph Walter	4d	C	D.C.	01 OCT 1875	Mt. Olivet
011345	DYNES, Julia	70y	C	Md.	15 APR 1877	Holy Rood
012691	DYRE, Nancy Spooner	83y	W	Mass.	06 AUG 1877	Philadelphia, Pa.
007095	DYSON, A.C.	33y	C	D.C.	24 APR 1876	Harmony
009370	DYSON, Adelaide S.	23y	C	D.C.	10 OCT 1876	Holy Rood
007009	DYSON, Adeline	4m	C	D.C.	13 APR 1876	Ebenezer
009842	DYSON, Alice Berlina	1m	C	D.C.	02 DEC 1876	Beckett's
015834	DYSON, Annie L.	13d	C	D.C.	25 MAY 1878	Potters Field
006783	DYSON, Belle Curtis	8m	M	D.C.	23 MAR 1876	Ebenezer
015511	DYSON, Benjamin H.	23y	C	Md.	25 APR 1878	Mt. Pleasant
015561	DYSON, Cassie	5m	C	D.C.	30 APR 1878	Moore's
004109	DYSON, Charles A.	8y	C	D.C.	13 JUL 1875	Ebenezer
015074	DYSON, Francis E.	1y	C	D.C.	15 MAR 1878	Mt. Zion
020855	DYSON, Gabelin, H.	1y	C	D.C.	09 JUL 1879	Mt. Pleasant
004399	DYSON, George	6y	C	D.C.	01 AUG 1875	Mt. Olivet
011262	DYSON, George	80y	C	Md.	07 APR 1877	Ebenezer
007974	DYSON, Harriet Anne	1w	C	D.C.	02 JUL 1876	Young Mens
019411	DYSON, James Garrison	18y	C	Md.	15 MAR 1879	Mt. Pleasant
003381	DYSON, Jennie	1y	C	D.C.	20 MAY 1875	Ebenezer
009696	DYSON, Kate	c.30y	C	D.C.	14 NOV 1876	Beckett's
016728	DYSON, Martha	7m	C	D.C.	23 JUL 1878	Potters Field
016690	DYSON, Mary	7m	C	D.C.	20 JUL 1878	Potters Field
009518	DYSON, Sally	c.80y	C	Md.	24 OCT 1876	Mt. Pleasant
002082	DYSON, Stephen	70y	C	Md.	08 FEB 1875	Holy Rood
005013a	DYSON, Teresa	66y	C	Md.	01 OCT 1875	Holy Rood
010594	DYSON, Ugenevia	8y	C	D.C.	12 FEB 1877	Harmony
007956	DYSON, Wm. A.	11m	C	D.C.	01 JUL 1876	Holy Rood

E

No.	Name	Age	Race	Birth	Death Date	Burial Place
015529	EACRITT, Aaron A.	1y	W	D.C.	27 APR 1878	Prospect Hill
016703	EADES, Bessie	2y	W	D.C.	21 JUL 1878	Glenwood
003474	EAGLETON, Charlotte	4y	C	D.C.	29 MAY 1875	Mt. Zion
003447	EAGLETON, Joshua	36y	C	D.C.	26 MAY 1875	Mt. Zion
017837	EARHART, Garnett	17y	W	La.	23 OCT 1878	Oak Hill
010734	EARL, Bessie Guy	5y	W	Mass.	22 FEB 1877	Oak Hill
008127	EARLE, Bertha Dixon	8m	W	D.C.	10 JUL 1876	Philadelphia, Pa.
019042	EARLEY, Lucy	10m	C	D.C.	12 FEB 1879	Mt. Pleasant
007349	EARLY, Clarissa Coles	20y	C	Md.	20 MAY 1876	Young Mens

District of Columbia Death Records, August 1, 1874 to July 31, 1879

No.	Name	Age	Race	Birth	Death Date	Burial Place
005053	EARLY, Rebecca	15y	C	Va.	15 SEP 1875	Young Mens
004351	EARNER, James	80y	W	Ire.	28 JUL 1875	Holy Rood
005028a	EARNEST, Ida, Mrs.	30y	W	Ire.	02 OCT 1875	Mt. Olivet
000399	EARNEST, Joseph	66y	W	Pa.	01 SEP 1874	Orange Co., Va.
014264	EARNEST, Josephine	24y	W	Va.	30 DEC 1877	Orange C.H., Va.
001584	EARP, Ann	c.90y	W	Md.	02 JAN 1875	Congressional
021112	EARP, Matilda	49y	W	D.C.	26 JUL 1879	Congressional
002247	EASLY, Edward	18y	C	Va.	20 FEB 1875	Washington Asylum
015892	EASTER, Albert	3m	C	D.C.	29 MAY 1878	Mt. Olivet
018262	EASTER, Ellen	9m	W	U.S.	07 DEC 1878	Mt. Olivet
016029	EASTER, Lucy	3m	C	D.C.	06 JUN 1878	Mt. Olivet
020389	EASTLAKE, Abram P.	36y	W	N.J.	11 JUN 1879	Congressional
019162	EASTLY, George W.	1d	W	D.C.	23 FEB 1879	Mt. Olivet
002497	EASTMAN, Harry	23y	W	D.C.	09 MAR 1875	Oak Hill
018319	EASTMAN, John McLean	c.28y	W	Minn.	13 DEC 1878	Oak Hill
000567	EASTMAN, Mrs. A.H. (nee Redruf)	34y	W	Ohio	19 SEP 1874	Congressional
004847	EASTMAN, Seth	65y	W	Me.	31 AUG 1875	Oak Hill
013556	EASTON, Ann	75y	C	Va.	18 OCT 1877	Harmony
006718	EASTON, Catharine L.	4m	W	D.C.	18 MAR 1876	Presbyterian
013009	EASTON, Lilly	1m	C	D.C.	29 AUG 1877	Mt. Zion
003349	EASTON, Living	c.70y	W	Md.	22 MAY 1875	Presbyterian
006280	EATMAN, Mahaley	20y	C	Va.	09 FEB 1876	Ebenezer
003555	EATON, Catharine C.	61y	W	Va.	07 JUN 1875	Congressional
007794	EATON, Emma, Mrs.	35y	W	Md.	23 JUN 1876	Addison's Chapel
016174	EATON, Frederick Charles	10m	W	D.C.	15 JUN 1878	Warner, N.H.
006195	EATON, Jane	50y	W	D.C.	31 JAN 1876	Congressional
013463	EATON, Katie Edwins	5y	W	D.C.	10 OCT 1877	Oak Hill
004225	EATON, Mary A.	61y	W	Eng.	21 JUL 1875	Frederick, Md.
019316	EBAUGH, Anna Isabel	7d	W	D.C.	08 MAR 1879	Brooklyn, N.Y.
000479	EBAUGH, Violet	8d	W	D.C.	11 SEP 1874	Oak Hill
002353	EBER, Anna	2y	W	D.C.	28 FEB 1875	Prospect Hill
008260	EBERLIER, Peter	56y	W	Ger.	14 JUL 1876	Prospect Hill
006016	EBERLY, Christoph Daniel Gilges	56y	W	Ger.	14 JAN 1876	Glenwood
010984	EBERLY, Gertrude	25y	W	Md.	15 MAR 1877	Glenwood
018101	EBERLY, Margaret Mabel	1y	W	D.C.	20 NOV 1878	Glenwood
001380	EBERLY, Mary A.	2y	W	D.C.	13 DEC 1874	Holy Rood
003877	EBERT, Laura M.	5m	W	D.C.	27 JUN 1875	St. Mary's
004047	EBY, Mary L.	2m	W	D.C.	08 JUL 1875	Carlisle, Pa.
003019	ECKERT, William W.	42y	W	Md.	17 APR 1875	Baltimore, Md.
020937	ECKFELDT, Fredrick	2d	W	D.C.	15 JUL 1879	Graceland
010441	ECKFELDT, Infant of Fred	2½h	W	D.C.	29 JAN 1877	Graceland
009927	ECKLOFF, Charles Godfrey	50y	W	D.C.	10 DEC 1876	Glenwood
015581	ECKLOFF, James Edward	1y	W	D.C.	02 MAY 1878	Mt. Olivet
011069	ECKLOFF, Joseph Emanuel	3y	W	D.C.	21 MAR 1877	Mt. Olivet
020337	ECKLOFF, Margaret	54y	W	Md.	08 JUN 1879	Mt. Olivet
005506	EDDS, Augusta	2m	W	D.C.	19 NOV 1875	Congressional
017393	EDDS, Margaret R.	26y	W	D.C.	13 SEP 1878	Congressional
009188	EDELEIN, William Joseph	43y	C	Md.	24 SEP 1876	Charles Co., Md.
009082	EDELEN, Barry	2y	M	Md.	15 SEP 1876	Mt. Olivet
002379	EDELIN, Ann Basilissa	75y	W	Md.	02 MAR 1875	Congressional
009201	EDELIN, Edward H.	74y	W	Md.	25 SEP 1876	Potters Field
004411	EDELIN, Frances	10m	C	D.C.	02 AUG 1875	Mt. Olivet
018283	EDELIN, Kate, Mrs.	32y	W	Va.	09 DEC 1878	Alexandria, Va.
007374	EDELIN, Laura	85y	W	Md.	22 MAY 1876	Mt. Olivet
011520	EDELIN, Nellie	17d	M	D.C.	05 MAY 1877	Mt. Olivet
012176	EDELIN, Wm. H.	38y	W	D.C.	02 JUL 1877	Congressional

District of Columbia Death Records, August 1, 1874 to July 31, 1879

No.	Name	Age	Race	Birth	Death Date	Burial Place
021062	EDENBURGH, William H.	50y	C	D.C.	23 JUL 1879	Harmony
019431	EDES, David	34y	W	D.C.	17 MAR 1879	Oak Hill
000000	EDES, Mary Ann	88y	W	Ire.	28 APR 1874	Baltimore, Md.
015965	EDES, Thos. W.	7y	W	Md.	02 JUN 1878	Glenwood
000972	EDIE, John R.	34y	W	Pa.	29 OCT 1874	Oak Hill
016800	EDIE, Joseph	84y	C	Va.	28 JUL 1878	Potters Field
016189	EDINBURG, Charles Augustus	10m	C	D.C.	16 JUN 1878	Harmony
016486	EDLOW, Joseph	79y	C	Va.	07 JUL 1878	Potters Field
006214	EDMONDS, Girrod	37y	C	M	02 FEB 1876	Young Mens
019099	EDMONDS, Harry	2y	C	D.C.	17 FEB 1879	Mt. Pleasant
017981	EDMONDS, James	11m	C	D.C.	08 NOV 1878	Young Mens
002542	EDMONDS, Olivia Crandall	59y	W	N.Y.	13 MAR 1875	Congressional
001040	EDMONDSON, Amelia	92y	C	Md.	04 NOV 1874	Mt. Pleasant Plain
019335	EDMONS, James E.	2y	C	D.C.	09 MAR 1879	Mt. Olivet
009808	EDMONSON, Amelia	12y	C	Aus.	27 NOV 1876	Young Mens
010720	EDMONSON, Annie Elizabeth	26y	M	Va.	21 FEB 1877	Tennallytown
003897	EDMONSON, Charlotte	81y	W	Md.	28 JUN 1875	Oak Hill
008465	EDMONSON, David	18y	C	Aust.	29 JUL 1876	Young Mens
005216a	EDMONSON, Ettie	2y	C	D.C.	20 OCT 1875	Young Mens
006458	EDMONSON, Mary	3m	C	D.C.	24 FEB 1876	Potters Field
014597	EDMONSTON, Infant of Richard	2d	M	D.C.	30 JAN 1878	Payne's
013627	EDMONSTON, James W.	5d	W	D.C.	25 OCT 1877	Glenwood
014898	EDMONSTON, James W.	40y	W	Pa.	28 FEB 1878	Congressional
014794	EDMONSTON, Mary Ann	73y	W	Md.	17 FEB 1878	Oak Hill
002772	EDMONSTON, Mary M.	18y	W	D.C.	28 MAR 1875	Glenwood
006469	EDMUNDS, Emma	8m	C	D.C.	25 FEB 1876	Graceland
002356	EDMUNDS, William	2m	W	D.C.	28 FEB 1875	Rock Creek
010962	EDSERLLY, Infant of A.K.	1m	W	D.C.	14 MAR 1877	Graceland
004389f	EDWARD, William B.	1y	W	D.C.	31 JUL 1875	Oak Hill
003443	EDWARDS, Alfred	46y	C	Md.	26 MAY 1875	Mt. Zion
008844	EDWARDS, Alice	1y	C	D.C.	27 AUG 1876	Young Mens
006133	EDWARDS, Ann	86y	W	N.J.	25 JAN 1876	Congressional
001015	EDWARDS, Augustine F.	56y	W	Pa.	02 NOV 1874	Philadelphia, Pa.
001124	EDWARDS, Caroline Seymour	c.35y	W	Md.	24 NOV 1874	Congressional
014817	EDWARDS, Catharine	65y	W	D.C.	19 FEB 1878	Glenwood
019459	EDWARDS, Catharine	40y	W	Can.	19 MAR 1879	Barnabas Church
003641	EDWARDS, Catherine Ann	6m	C	D.C.	14 JUN 1875	Mt. Olivet
001963	EDWARDS, Edward	11m	M	D.C.	31 JAN 1875	Young Mens
008592	EDWARDS, Elizabeth	60y	W	D.C.	07 AUG 1876	Congressional
005383	EDWARDS, George Amrose	15m	C	D.C.	07 NOV 1875	Mt. Zion
003213	EDWARDS, George R.	45y	W	Ky.	04 MAY 1875	Shawnee Town, Ill.
000407	EDWARDS, Henry	40y	C	Md.	02 SEP 1874	Beckett's
004289f	EDWARDS, Henry Wilson	1y	W	D.C.	25 JUL 1875	Oak Hill
001168	EDWARDS, Infant of John L.	1h	W	D.C.	17 NOV 1874	Congressional
003719	EDWARDS, Infant of L. & C.	1d	W	D.C.	20 JUN 1875	Prince George's Co., Md.
008244	EDWARDS, John	3m	C	D.C.	13 JUL 1876	Ebenezer
013387	EDWARDS, John Thomas	1y	W	D.C.	03 OCT 1877	Graceland
020533	EDWARDS, Joseph	2m	W	Va.	20 JUN 1879	Mt. Olivet
013766	EDWARDS, Lewis Allison	54y	W	D.C.	08 NOV 1877	Congressional/Oak Hill
007107	EDWARDS, Margt.	74y	W	N.Y.	25 APR 1876	Congressional
018946	EDWARDS, Mary E.	39y	W	D.C.	04 FEB 1879	Congressional
020336	EDWARDS, Rosa May	19y	W	D.C.	08 JUN 1879	Mt. Olivet
019049	EED, Mary	18y	C	D.C.	12 FEB 1879	Young Mens
000644	EGAN, Infant of John	1/2h	W	D.C.	26 SEP 1874	Mt. Olivet
004977	EGLIN, Martina	10m	C	D.C.	10 SEP 1875	Mt. Olivet
000871	EICHELBERGER, Alice C.C.	29y	W	Md.	20 OCT 1874	Mt. Olivet

District of Columbia Death Records, August 1, 1874 to July 31, 1879   105

No.	Name	Age	Race	Birth	Death Date	Burial Place
014315	EICHELBERGER, Edith Wirt	3y	W	Md.	04 JAN 1878	Baltimore, Md.
000596f	EICHELBERGER, Sam'l.	22y	--	Md.	21 SEP 1874	Alexandria, Va.
020809	EICHHORN, Cecelia Bessie	7m	W	D.C.	07 JUL 1879	St. Mary's
010442	EIDLIN, Augustus	8d	C	D.C.	29 JAN 1877	Mt. Olivet
004774	EIMER, Morris Evans	7m	W	D.C.	27 AUG 1875	Loudoun Park, Md.
014247	EISENBEISS, Fred	1y	W	D.C.	29 DEC 1877	Prospect Hill
009726	ELBERT, Jacob Ignatius	4m	W	D.C.	18 NOV 1876	Mt. Olivet
006647	ELBERT, Margaret	2y	W	D.C.	12 MAR 1876	Mt. Olivet
002744	ELDREDGE, Lillie	26y	W	Pa.	26 MAR 1875	Danville, Pa.
005302	ELGINS, Daniel	45y	C	Va.	29 OCT 1875	Leesburg, Va.
011124	ELI, John W.	56y	W	Ger.	27 MAR 1877	Oak Hill
008106	ELI, Latimer B.	27y	W	Pa.	09 JUL 1876	Oak Hill
000211	ELI, Mary A.	19y	W	Pa.	16 AUG 1874	Oak Hill
019984	ELIASON, James M.	50y	W	Md.	04 MAY 1879	Congressional
021146	ELIASON, Katie	19y	W	D.C.	29 JUL 1879	Oak Hill
009941	ELIASON, Mary C.	42y	W	Va.	12 DEC 1876	Oak Hill
016579	ELIOT, Harry Randolph	1y	W	D.C.	13 JUL 1878	Congressional
007456	ELIOTT, George	1y	C	D.C.	01 JUN 1876	Beckett's
011599	ELIOTT, Juliana M.	50y	W	D.C.	15 MAY 1877	Oak Hill
007495	ELISON, Wm. L.	30y	W	D.C.	04 JUN 1876	Oak Hill
007195	ELKIN, Lucy Victoria	33y	W	D.C.	03 MAY 1876	Glenwood
001863	ELKINS, Camilla	25d	C	D.C.	23 JAN 1875	Ebenezer
017466	ELKINS, Edith M.	1y	W	D.C.	20 SEP 1878	Harmony
017953	ELLEN, Annie M.	7y	W	D.C.	05 NOV 1878	Rock Creek
018029	ELLEN, Bertha	1y	W	D.C.	12 NOV 1878	Rock Creek
020826	ELLERBROOK, Annie E.	5m	W	D.C.	08 JUL 1879	Congressional
010863	ELLERBROOK, May	4y	W	D.C.	04 MAR 1877	Congressional
014963	ELLET, Daniel	78y	C	Va.	06 MAR 1878	Beckett's
012743	ELLETT, Annie	1y	W	D.C.	09 AUG 1877	Glenwood
015112	ELLINGER, John A., Jr.	1y	W	D.C.	18 MAR 1878	Congressional
012534	ELLIOT, Henry	10m	W	D.C.	26 JUL 1877	Glenwood
020555	ELLIOT, Jennie F.	2y	W	D.C.	21 JUN 1879	Congressional
014127	ELLIOTT, Ann	82y	W	Va.	18 DEC 1877	Graceland
020066	ELLIOTT, Elenora	7y	W	D.C.	11 MAY 1879	Mt. Olivet
010325	ELLIOTT, Elizabeth	36y	C	D.C.	18 JAN 1877	Mt. Zion
020565	ELLIOTT, Florida	c.60y	W	D.C.	22 JUN 1879	Presbyterian
007622	ELLIOTT, Frances Annie	22y	W	Md.	13 JUN 1876	Mt. Olivet
014004	ELLIOTT, George	8m	C	D.C.	04 DEC 1877	Beckett's
001744	ELLIOTT, Infant of Andrew	4h	C	D.C.	15 JAN 1875	Potters Field
011048	ELLIOTT, Mary Ann	93y	C	Va.	20 MAR 1877	Harmony
008380	ELLIOTT, Moses	9d	C	D.C.	22 JUL 1876	Moore's
006586	ELLIS, Anias	1y	C	D.C.	07 MAR 1876	Young Mens
009350	ELLIS, Ann M.	74y	W	Va.	09 OCT 1876	Oak Hill
005776	ELLIS, Anna Josaphine	11y	W	D.C.	17 DEC 1875	Mt. Olivet
012446	ELLIS, Annie E.	2y	W	D.C.	20 JUL 1877	Oak Hill
001985	ELLIS, Becy	3y	C	D.C.	01 FEB 1875	Mt. Pleasant
005782	ELLIS, Caroline	28y	W	Can.	18 DEC 1875	Toronto, Can.
015748	ELLIS, Clara J.	3m	W	D.C.	17 MAY 1878	Presbyterian
020468	ELLIS, Daphna	5m	C	D.C.	16 JUN 1879	Young Mens
014429	ELLIS, Hannah	67y	W	D.C.	15 JAN 1878	Congressional
004973f	ELLIS, Harvey F.	29y	W	N.Y.	09 SEP 1875	Glenwood
000413	ELLIS, Infant of Benjamin	8d	C	D.C.	02 SEP 1874	Harmony
000468	ELLIS, Infant of George	2d	C	D.C.	10 SEP 1874	Harmony
018273	ELLIS, James F.	2m	W	D.C.	08 DEC 1878	Presbyterian
016992	ELLIS, James L.	2y	W	D.C.	10 AUG 1878	Presbyterian
014224	ELLIS, John	1d	W	D.C.	27 DEC 1877	Congressional

No.	Name	Age	Race	Birth	Death Date	Burial Place
001210	ELLIS, John Dripps	30y	W	D.C.	22 NOV 1874	Congressional
012200	ELLIS, Leonard K.	65y	W	Md.	03 JUL 1877	Congressional
012964	ELLIS, Lillian S.	5d	W	D.C.	26 AUG 1877	Holy Rood
005505	ELLIS, Lucy	3y	C	D.C.	19 NOV 1875	Mt. Zion
009455	ELLIS, Mary A.	23y	W	D.C.	18 OCT 1876	Oak Hill
018219	ELLIS, Mary C.	22y	W	D.C.	02 DEC 1878	Presbyterian
017549	ELLIS, Norma J.	2m	W	D.C.	27 SEP 1878	Congressional
013431	ELLIS, Rebecca	8d	C	D.C.	08 OCT 1877	Potters Field
014928	ELLIS, Richard	70y	W	Md.	03 MAR 1878	Oak Hill
016190	ELLIS, Rita Marie	6m	W	D.C.	16 JUN 1878	Oak Hill
012238	ELLIS, Victoria Rosetta	1y	C	D.C.	06 JUL 1877	Harmony
011638	ELLIS, William H.	6d	W	D.C.	18 MAY 1877	Presbyterian
017972	ELLIS, Wm.	6m	C	D.C.	07 NOV 1878	Mt. Pleasant
011276	ELLISON, Silva A.	26y	C	Ala.	09 APR 1877	Harmony
003612	ELLSWORTH, Allonzo	6m	M	D.C.	12 JUN 1875	Harmony
004491	ELLSWORTH, Arthur Melvill	7m	W	D.C.	07 AUG 1875	Glenwood
014377	ELLSWORTH, Dennis	28y	C	Md.	10 JAN 1878	Mt. Pleasant
012862	ELLWOOD, Mary E.	14m	M	D.C.	18 AUG 1877	Mt. Olivet
016452	ELMORE, Blanche	5m	W	D.C.	05 JUL 1878	Glenwood
000584	ELMORE, Francis Ann	57y	W	Va.	21 SEP 1874	Richmond, Va.
002334	ELSIE, Emma	2d	C	D.C.	27 FEB 1875	Moore's
009465	ELSIE, John T.	3m	C	D.C.	19 OCT 1876	Moore's
013642	ELWOOD, Agnes V.	4y	W	D.C.	26 OCT 1877	Glenwood
003720	ELWOOD, Frances	1m	W	Ill.	20 JUN 1875	Mt. Olivet
003467f	ELWOOD, Francis M.	29y	W	D.C.	28 MAY 1875	Glenwood
015330	ELWOOD, Ida Blanch	19y	W	D.C.	09 APR 1878	Oak Hill
003296	ELWOOD, Joseph	7d	C	D.C.	12 MAY 1875	Mt. Olivet
001483	ELWOOD, Martha A.	34y	W	D.C.	25 DEC 1874	Oak Hill
006659	ELWOOD, Thomas	2y	M	Md.	13 MAR 1876	Ebenezer
009572	ELWOOD, Wm. D.	39y	W	D.C.	29 OCT 1876	Oak Hill
004526	ELY, William	10y	W	N.Y.	10 AUG 1875	Prospect Hill
015051	ELZEY, Letitia	c.75y	W	Md.	13 MAR 1878	Baltimore, Md.
002538f	EMERICK, Henry P.	24y	--	D.C.	12 MAR 1875	Oak Hill
013402	EMERSON, James	4y	W	D.C.	04 OCT 1877	Glenwood
018030	EMMART, Laura V.	18y	W	Md.	12 NOV 1878	Rock Creek
001129	EMMERT, Caroline H.	77y	W	Ger.	13 NOV 1874	Oak Hill
008652	EMMERT, Eleanore	6m	W	D.C.	11 AUG 1876	Glenwood
015214	EMMERT, Ernst	1d	W	D.C.	28 MAR 1878	Glenwood
008508	EMMERT, Isabella	6m	W	D.C.	31 JUL 1876	Glenwood
020038	EMMI, Alin	23m	C	D.C.	08 MAY 1879	Mt. Olivet
004350	EMMONS, William, Sr.	83y	W	Mass.	28 JUL 1875	Congressional
002723	EMORY, John W.	54y	W	Md.	24 MAR 1875	Baltimore, Md.
018689	EMORY, William Hemsley	1y	W	Md.	16 JAN 1879	Congressional
002794	EMRICH, Clara Magdalina	19y	W	D.C.	30 MAR 1875	Oak Hill
013903	ENDERS, Emma	5y	W	D.C.	24 NOV 1877	Prospect Hill
008181	ENGEL, Benjamin Franklin	3y	W	D.C.	11 JUL 1876	Mt. Olivet
008101	ENGEL, Emanuel	47y	W	Ger.	09 JUL 1876	Prospect Hill
009990	ENGEL, Henry	23y	W	D.C.	17 DEC 1876	Prospect Hill
015592	ENGEL, Margaretha	36y	W	Ger.	03 MAY 1878	Prospect Hill
007338	ENGLAND, Henrietta	25y	W	Ind.	19 MAY 1876	Salem, Md.
017783	ENGLAND, John	36y	W	N.Y.	18 OCT 1878	Soldier's Home
016453	ENGLEBRECHT, Jennie L., Mrs.	40y	W	Cuba	05 JUL 1878	Mt. Olivet
011734	ENGLEHART, Louise V.	5m	W	D.C.	29 MAY 1877	Holy Rood
011815	ENGLEHART, Sophronia	2y	W	D.C.	06 JUN 1877	Holy Rood
001555	ENGLER, Edward	20y	W	Prus.	01 JAN 1875	Congressional
006153	ENGLISH, Helen Matilda	1m	W	D.C.	27 JAN 1876	Congressional

District of Columbia Death Records, August 1, 1874 to July 31, 1879   107

No.	Name	Age	Race	Birth	Death Date	Burial Place
014919	ENGLISH, James	57y	W	D.C.	02 MAR 1878	Mt. Olivet
018272	ENGLISH, Rebeca F.	4y	W	D.C.	08 DEC 1878	Congressional
018066	ENNIS, Catherine	4m	C	D.C.	16 NOV 1878	Mt. Olivet
020295	ENNIS, Eliza Ann Elizabeth	60y	C	Md.	04 JUN 1879	Mt. Olivet
014479	ENNIS, Elizabeth Jane	1y	C	D.C.	19 JAN 1878	Young Mens
013238	ENNIS, George Franklin	1y	W	D.C.	18 SEP 1877	Graceland
011823	ENNIS, Ida	8y	C	D.C.	07 JUN 1877	Mt. Olivet
014560	ENNIS, Infant of Harry	6d	C	D.C.	26 JAN 1878	Young Mens
018571	ENNIS, Infant of Jno.	10h	W	D.C.	05 JAN 1879	Mt. Zion
006364	ENNIS, James A.	44y	W	D.C.	15 FEB 1876	Mt. Olivet
017457	ENNIS, Josephine	48y	C	D.C.	19 SEP 1878	Harmony
000501	ENNIS, Louisa	35y	C	Md.	13 SEP 1874	Mt. Olivet
000122	ENNIS, Morgan Sherwood	10d	W	D.C.	10 AUG 1874	Graceland
009891	ENNIS, Philip J.	39y	W	D.C.	06 DEC 1876	Mt. Olivet
019029	ENNISS, Elnora	1m	C	D.C.	11 FEB 1879	Mt. Pleasant
018544	ENTS, Anna Margaret	55y	W	Pa.	02 JAN 1879	Rock Creek
012470	ENTWISLE, Jane N.	7y	W	D.C.	22 JUL 1877	Mt. Olivet
016953	ENTWISLE, Minnie Wilson	1y	W	D.C.	08 AUG 1878	Mt. Olivet
000050	ENTWISTLE, Elizabeth Lucas	65y	W	Eng.	04 AUG 1874	Congressional
017674	EPART, Theresa	49y	W	Ger.	08 OCT 1878	St. Mary's
003825	EPERT, Frances Cathrine	5m	W	D.C.	25 JUN 1875	St. Mary's
009554	EPNER, Chagen	3y	W	Pol.	27 OCT 1876	Adas Israel
015573	EPS, Julia	24y	M	Va.	01 MAY 1878	Payne's
017790	ERBERT, William	1y	C	D.C.	19 OCT 1878	Payne's
009022	ERHMANNTRAUT, Joseph	51y	W	Ger.	10 SEP 1876	Holy Rood
017008	ERIKSON, Ida	13m	W	D.C.	11 AUG 1878	Graceland
017791	ERNER, Charles	13y	W	Ire.	19 OCT 1878	Holy Rood
006242	ERNEST, Elizabeth	39y	W	Md.	05 FEB 1876	Tennallytown
016243	ERNST, Hugh Allen, Jr.	2y	W	Mich.	21 JAN 1878	Glenwood
007982	ERSKINE, Edith May	4m	W	D.C.	03 JUL 1876	Glenwood
008501	ERTMAN, William	5y	W	D.C.	31 JUL 1876	Prospect Hill
002776	ERTMANN, Louis	39y	W	Hun.	28 MAR 1875	Congressional
019057	ERVER, Charles C.	40y	W	Mass.	13 FEB 1879	Glenwood
007722	ERWIN, Rachel H.	1y	W	D.C.	19 JUN 1876	Carlisle, Pa.
002996	ESBEY, Martha	50y	C	D.C.	15 APR 1875	Mt. Zion
013309a	ESCHER, C.H.	2y	W	D.C.	25 SEP 1877	Glenwood
003571	ESCHER, Emma	9m	W	D.C.	08 JUN 1875	Prospect Hill
009817	ESCHER, Mathilde	5y	W	D.C.	28 NOV 1876	Prospect Hill
017661	ESCOE, Elucius	3m	C	D.C.	07 OCT 1878	Mt. Zion
006350	ESHER, Albert O.	22y	W	Pa.	14 FEB 1876	Prospect Hill
001466	ESHLAGHER, Mary	5m	W	D.C.	23 DEC 1874	Prospect Hill
001890	ESHLEMAN, Abraham	67y	W	Pa.	26 JAN 1875	Congressional
013388	ESKRIDGE, Margaret Pope	74y	W	Va.	03 OCT 1877	Oak Hill
006141	ESLIN, Rachel B.	41y	W	Md.	26 JAN 1876	Mt. Olivet
012840	ESLY, Annie	1m	W	D.C.	16 AUG 1877	Mt. Olivet
014649	ESPEY, Dasy V.	1y	W	D.C.	03 FEB 1878	Oak Hill
011821	ESPEY, Henry C.	9d	W	D.C.	06 JUN 1877	Oak Hill
007427	ESPEY, Lydia Ann	49y	W	D.C.	28 MAY 1876	Glenwood
009075	ESPINTA, Susan	72y	W	Spain	14 SEP 1876	Mt. Olivet
000849	ESSEX, Annette Pauline	32y	W	N.Y.	18 OCT 1874	Oak Hill
001806	ESSEX, J.T.W.	45y	W	D.C.	20 JAN 1875	Oak Hill
008261	ESSEX, Josiah, Jr.	39y	W	D.C.	14 JUL 1876	Glenwood
007896	ESSLER, William	8m	W	D.C.	28 JUN 1876	Glenwood
020422	ESTELLE, Ellen	2m	W	D.C.	13 JUN 1879	Mt. Olivet
015776	ESTELLE, Virginia Lorain	63y	W	N.C.	20 MAY 1878	Glenwood
004749	ESTLER, Jennie	8m	W	D.C.	25 AUG 1875	Oak Hill

District of Columbia Death Records, August 1, 1874 to July 31, 1879

No.	Name	Age	Race	Birth	Death Date	Burial Place
020483	ESTLER, Laura	1m	W	D.C.	17 JUN 1879	Oak Hill
017089	ESTRIDGE, Fred H.	14d	C	D.C.	18 AUG 1878	Beckett's
015466	EUELL, Basil	45y	C	Va.	21 APR 1878	Beckett's
002806	EVANIS, Henry	69y	C	Va.	30 MAR 1875	Harmony
001845	EVANS, Agnes Mary	2y	W	DC.	23 JAN 1875	Holy Rood
008971	EVANS, Agnes Sanders	55y	W	Va.	05 SEP 1876	Congressional
003092	EVANS, Annie	c.26y	W	Md.	23 APR 1875	Baltimore, Md.
011788	EVANS, Belle	9d	M	D.C.	03 JUN 1877	Young Mens
005319	EVANS, Bertha M.	1y	W	D.C.	31 OCT 1875	Congressional
018090	EVANS, Berther Marrion	3y	W	D.C.	19 NOV 1878	Rock Creek
012850	EVANS, Catharine Virginia	31y	W	D.C.	17 AUG 1877	Oak Hill
002570	EVANS?, Charlotte Virg.	6w	C	D.C.	14 MAR 1875	Ebenezer
008436	EVANS, Elizabeth Ellen	3m	W	D.C.	26 JUL 1876	Evergreen, P.G., Md.
016991	EVANS, Ernest	8y	C	D.C.	10 AUG 1878	Mt. Pleasant
002927	EVANS, Eva Frances	20y	W	Pa.	09 APR 1875	Downingtown, Pa.
008841	EVANS, Fred	1y	M	D.C.	27 AUG 1876	Ebenezer
009402	EVANS, Geo. Ch.	2y	W	D.C.	13 OCT 1876	Mt. Olivet
016872	EVANS, George Tilden	2y	W	D.C.	02 AUG 1878	Congressional
011184	EVANS, H.R.	10d	W	D.C.	01 APR 1877	Congressional
018960	EVANS, Hattie Virginia	4y	W	D.C.	05 FEB 1879	Congressional
007253	EVANS, Hugh F.	10y	W	Md.	09 MAY 1876	Congressional
013256	EVANS, Isaac	25y	C	Tenn.	20 SEP 1877	Mt. Zion
015135	EVANS, James B.	2y	W	D.C.	21 MAR 1878	Holy Rood
005767	EVANS, James Frederick	10m	W	D.C.	16 DEC 1875	Mt. Olivet
012151	EVANS, Lemuel D., Hon.	68y	W	Tenn.	01 JUL 1877	Congressional
012800	EVANS, Marcus	11m	C	D.C.	14 AUG 1877	Young Mens
016769	EVANS, Martha	35y	C	Va.	26 JUL 1878	Potters Field
006457	EVANS, Robert	6m	C	D.C.	24 FEB 1876	Beckett's
006904	EVANS, Robert Dawson	4y	W	Mass.	03 APR 1876	Boston, Mass.
013573	EVANS, T.L.	61y	W	Wales	20 OCT 1877	Potters Field
000802	EVANS, Wm. H.	7d	C	D.C.	14 OCT 1874	Mt. Olivet
000508	EVANS, Wm. H.	6d	W	D.C.	14 SEP 1874	Prospect Hill
015518	EVARTS, William	27y	W	N.Y.	26 APR 1878	Windsor, Ver.
016242	EVERETT, Ernest	1m	W	D.C.	21 JUN 1878	Presbyterian
002063	EVERETT, Minnie May	9m	W	D.C.	07 FEB 1875	Congressional
009357	EVERHOUT, Jacob F.	1y	W	D.C.	09 OCT 1876	Presbyterian
015661	EVERSON, Jane W.	59y	W	Md.	09 MAY 1878	Congressional
007233	EVERSON, Mark	73y	W	N.Y.	07 MAY 1876	Methodist
020517	EWELL, Clara Philomena	6d	C	D.C.	19 JUN 1879	Mt. Olivet
015721	EWELL, Jane	20y	C	Va.	14 MAY 1878	Mt. Pleasant
018001	EWELL, Lillie	6y	C	D.C.	10 NOV 1878	Mt. Pleasant
019129	EWER, Isaac	65y	C	N.C.	20 FEB 1879	Brightwood
018780	EWIN, Margaret	65y	W	Ire.	23 JAN 1879	Baltimore, Md.
000859	EWING, Annie Lauck	3m	W	D.C.	19 OCT 1874	Oak Hill
000675	EWING, Mary J.	27y	W	D.C.	30 SEP 1874	Oak Hill
012814	EWING, William	53y	W	Ire.	15 AUG 1877	Potters Field
010422	EWING, William B.	4y	W	D.C.	27 JAN 1877	Congressional

F

014023	FAGAN, Mary	78y	W	Ire.	07 DEC 1877	Mt. Olivet
008709	FAGAN, William E.	9m	W	D.C.	16 AUG 1876	Mt. Olivet
019317	FAGANS, Harry	6y	C	N.Y.	08 MAR 1879	Harmony
000681	FAHERTY, John P.	57y	W	Ire.	30 SEP 1874	Mt. Olivet
000617	FAHEY, Margaret	19y	W	Ire.	23 SEP 1874	Mt. Olivet

District of Columbia Death Records, August 1, 1874 to July 31, 1879   109

No.	Name	Age	Race	Birth	Death Date	Burial Place
007655	FAHNESTOCK, Simon Snyder	55y	W	Pa.	15 JUN 1876	Harrisburg, Pa.
008765	FAHRMEIER, Mary J.	2y	W	D.C.	21 AUG 1876	St. Mary's
017757	FAIRBROTHER, Francis A.	41y	W	N.Y.	16 OCT 1878	Oak Hill
019663	FAIRFAX, Douglass	7m	C	D.C.	05 APR 1879	Harmony
015277	FAIRFAX, Eliza	59y	C	Va.	03 APR 1878	Potters Field
017303	FAIRFAX, John H.	8m	C	D.C.	03 SEP 1878	Beckett's
012111	FAIRFAX, Mary Elizabeth	21y	C	D.C.	28 JUN 1877	Harmony
003966	FAIRFAX, Thomas B.	2y	M	D.C.	02 JUL 1875	Potters Field
011747	FAIRFAX, Usher	43y	C	Md.	30 MAY 1877	Mt. Zion
000603	FAIRFAX, Willie	1y	C	D.C.	22 SEP 1874	Beckett's
019986	FAIRFIELD, Fred S.	1y	W	D.C.	04 MAY 1879	Rock Creek
007118	FALCONER, Alexander	57y	W	Scot.	26 APR 1876	Congressional
007561	FALCONER, Gertrude	3m	W	D.C.	09 JUN 1876	Glenwood
017938	FALCONER, James A.	23y	W	D.C.	03 NOV 1878	Glenwood
013961	FALES, Joseph T.	72y	W	Pa.	29 NOV 1877	Glenwood
002571	FALLENN, Michael	40y	W	Ire.	15 MAR 1875	Mt. Olivet
015298	FALLON, Catherine	45y	W	Ire.	06 APR 1878	Mt. Olivet
004255	FANNING, Anna	1y	W	D.C.	23 JUL 1875	Mt. Olivet
008228	FANNING, Bridget	37y	W	Ire.	13 JUL 1876	Mt. Olivet
005177	FANNING, John	51y	W	Ire.	23 SEP 1875	Hospital
011414	FANTROY, John	19y	C	Va.	24 APR 1877	Harmony
017846	FAREY, Burdett Hart	7y	W	Kan.	24 OCT 1878	Graceland
015926	FARIS, Craven	6m	W	D.C.	31 MAY 1878	Rock Creek
020499	FARIS, Grace A.	4m	W	D.C.	18 JUN 1879	Rock Creek
017293	FARLEIGH, F.W.	72y	W	Pa.	02 SEP 1878	Potters Field
006802	FARLEY, James	35y	W	Ire.	24 MAR 1876	Holy Rood
014179	FARLEY, Lilly	3m	M	D.C.	23 DEC 1877	Mt. Olivet
004241	FARMER, John	2y	C	D.C.	22 JUL 1875	Potters Field
017200	FARMER, Winnie	c.65y	C	Md.	26 AUG 1878	Young Mens
016304	FARNUM, Norris Corcoran	3y	W	D.C.	25 JUN 1878	Glenwood
010003	FARRAR, Chester Nicholas	5d	W	D.C.	18 DEC 1876	Graceland
020779	FARRAR, Frank	42d	C	D.C.	05 JUL 1879	Potters Field
013994	FARRAR, Kate Olds	5y	W	D.C.	03 DEC 1877	Graceland
013892	FARRAR, Lewis Parker	6y	W	D.C.	23 NOV 1877	Graceland
006775	FARRAR, Mela Jane	35y	W	Pa.	22 MAR 1876	Philadelphia, Pa.
010031	FARRAR, Susan V. Nichols	40y	W	Mass.	20 DEC 1876	Graceland
003802	FARREL, Sarah	6m	C	D.C.	24 JUN 1875	Mt. Olivet
016620	FARRELL, Bridget	20y	W	Ire.	14 JUL 1878	Mt. Olivet
020093	FARRELL, Ellen	51y	W	Ire.	14 MAY 1879	Mt. Olivet
012916	FARRELL, John	51y	W	Ire.	23 AUG 1877	Mt. Olivet
013146	FARRELL, Patrick	28y	W	Ire.	10 SEP 1877	Mt. Olivet
006234	FARSON, George Tudor	1m	W	D.C.	04 FEB 1876	Glenwood
010282	FARWELL, Sarah S.	81y	W	Ver.	13 JAN 1877	Albion, N.Y.
014382	FAUBERSCHMIDT, Leonhard	20y	W	Ger.	10 JAN 1878	Prospect Hill
018908	FAUBERSMITH, Katherina	9d	W	D.C.	01 FEB 1879	Prospect Hill
005238	FAUNCE, Andrew	2m	W	D.C.	22 OCT 1875	Congressional
011535	FAUNCE, Laura	2h	W	D.C.	07 MAY 1877	Congressional
020730	FAUNCE, William	9m	W	D.C.	03 JUL 1879	Glenwood
008288	FAUNER, Jacob D.	1y	W	D.C.	16 JUL 1876	Congressional
009715	FAUNTLEROY, Hester	45y	C	Va.	17 NOV 1876	Ebenezer
003242	FAUNTLEROY, Infant of Louis	3m	C	D.C.	06 MAY 1875	Ebenezer
014770	FAUNTLEROY, William	26y	C	Va.	15 FEB 1878	Young Mens
020067	FAUNTROY, Edward James	1y	C	D.C.	11 MAY 1879	Mt. Pleasant
001819	FAUTH, Rosenia	43y	W	Ger.	21 JAN 1875	Prospect Hill
020319	FAY, Frank	1y	W	D.C.	06 JUN 1879	Mt. Olivet
010116	FAYE, James	64y	W	Va.	30 DEC 1876	Mt. Olivet

No.	Name	Age	Race	Birth	Death Date	Burial Place
001646	FAYMAN, Thomas H.	20y	W	D.C.	07 JAN 1875	Glenwood
020610	FEARSON, Mary Estelle	1y	W	D.C.	25 JUN 1879	Presbyterian
010365	FEARSON, Samuel	45y	W	Va.	21 JAN 1877	Presbyterian
019486	FEEHAN, Margaret	3y	W	D.C.	21 MAR 1879	Mt. Olivet
001682	FEEHAN, Mary Elizabeth	3y	W	D.C.	10 JAN 1875	Mt. Olivet
001344	FEELY, Bridget	76y	W	Ire.	09 DEC 1874	Holy Rood
017113	FEENEY, Peter	7y	W	D.C.	20 AUG 1878	Holy Rood
010000	FEENEY, Sarah	8y	W	D.C.	18 DEC 1876	Holy Rood
003419	FEENY, Bartlett	27y	W	Ire.	24 MAY 1875	Holy Rood
018650	FEENY, Mary	81y	W	Ire.	12 JAN 1879	Holy Rood
015299	FEETE, Infant of Thos.	12d	W	D.C.	06 APR 1878	Middletown, Md.
020496	FEGAN, Horice	1d	W	D.C.	18 JUN 1879	Mt. Olivet
020205	FELDROP, Oscar Adolph	6d	W	D.C.	26 MAY 1879	Prospect Hill
016018	FELLER, Anna Mary	69y	W	Ger.	05 JUN 1878	St. Mary's
014398	FELLHEIMER, Moses	68y	W	Ger.	12 JAN 1878	Hebrew
008149	FELT, William	8m	C	D.C.	10 JUL 1876	Young Mens
009867	FELTE, William W.	8y	W	D.C.	04 DEC 1876	Presbyterian
010262	FELTUS, Thomas	32y	W	Ire.	12 JAN 1877	Soldier's Home
009591	FENBROY, Lucy	9y	C	D.C.	01 NOV 1876	Ebenezer
008924	FENDAL, Mary Ann	1y	C	D.C.	02 SEP 1876	Moore's
014561	FENDALL, Arthur	34y	W	D.C.	26 JAN 1878	Rock Creek
003281	FENDALL, George	48y	C	Md.	10 MAY 1875	Moore's
008163	FENDALL, Nannie Robinson	30y	W	Md.	11 JUL 1876	Baltimore, Md.
012589	FENDALL, Stratford	28y	W	D.C.	28 JUL 1877	Glenwood
011838	FENDALL, William Henry	5m	C	D.C.	08 JUN 1877	Moore's
018019	FENDLE, Mary	52y	C	Md.	11 NOV 1878	Moore's
000319	FENDNER, Herman	11y	W	D.C.	26 AUG 1874	Prospect Hill
014887	FENDRICK, William	33y	W	Ger.	27 FEB 1878	Hospital
015893	FENLEY, Sarah	47y	W	D.C.	29 MAY 1878	Oak Hill
007898	FENNELL, Joseph Bernard	24y	W	D.C.	28 JUN 1876	Mt. Olivet
006040	FENNER, Benjamin	62y	W	Eng.	16 JAN 1876	Newark, N.J.
008299	FENNING, Lizzie M.	2w	W	D.C.	17 JUL 1876	Congressional
008113	FENNING, Mary S.	42y	W	N.J.	09 JUL 1876	Congressional
011615	FENTON, Barbara	28y	W	Ger.	16 MAY 1877	Congressional
016012	FENTON, Howard Gibbs	17m	W	D.C.	04 JUN 1878	Framingham, Mass.
009754	FENTON, Matthias	2d	W	D.C.	20 NOV 1876	Congressional
009807	FENTON, William Augustus	10m	W	D.C.	27 NOV 1876	Congressional
002143	FENTROY, James	3m	C	D.C.	13 FEB 1875	Ebenezer
001208f	FENWICK, James E.	43y	W	D.C.	21 NOV 1874	Mt. Olivet
000392	FENWICK, John	1m	W	D.C.	01 SEP 1874	Mt. Olivet
020652	FENWICK, Mary Selena	9m	C	D.C.	28 JUN 1879	Mt. Olivet
017318	FENWICK, Susan H.	57y	W	D.C.	04 SEP 1878	Holy Rood
007859	FERBER, Charlie	5y	W	D.C.	26 JUN 1876	Prospect Hill
018396	FERBER, George	8d	W	D.C.	20 DEC 1878	Prospect Hill
010060	FERBER, Katie	8m	W	D.C.	24 DEC 1876	Prospect Hill
014724	FERGERSON, Louis	11m	C	D.C.	09 FEB 1878	Mt. Pleasant
000330	FERGESON, William	7m	C	D.C.	27 AUG 1874	Beckett's
020693	FERGURSON, Annie B.	10m	W	D.C.	01 JUL 1879	Congressional
019985	FERGURSON, Sophia	7y	C	D.C.	04 MAY 1879	Beckett's
005433	FERGUSON, Amelia	3m	C	D.C.	12 NOV 1875	Ebenezer
015749	FERGUSON, Catherine	29y	W	D.C.	17 MAY 1878	Mt. Olivet
007074	FERGUSON, Emilia	24y	C	Md.	22 APR 1876	Ebenezer
020498	FERGUSON, Emma	2y	C	D.C.	18 JUN 1879	Mt. Zion
016540	FERGUSON, Ernest Ambrose	10m	W	D.C.	10 JUL 1878	Mt. Olivet
014672	FERGUSON, Harriet B.	1y	W	D.C.	05 FEB 1878	Mt. Zion
005844	FERGUSON, Infant of Lewis	20h	C	D.C.	24 DEC 1875	Young Mens

District of Columbia Death Records, August 1, 1874 to July 31, 1879   111

No.	Name	Age	Race	Birth	Death Date	Burial Place
001679	FERGUSON, Infant of Lewis	5d	C	D.C.	10 JAN 1875	Mt. Pleasant
005974	FERGUSON, Infant of Lewis	16d	C	D.C.	08 JAN 1876	Young Mens
006058	FERGUSON, Louisa M.	3y	C	D.C.	18 JAN 1876	Young Mens
010399	FERGUSON, Stephen	26y	C	Md.	25 JAN 1877	Ebenezer
004412	FERGUSON, Walter	1y	W	D.C.	02 AUG 1875	Glenwood
012665	FERGUSON, William H.	6m	W	D.C.	04 AUG 1877	Congressional
011908	FERRARI, John Edward	8m	W	Md.	15 JUN 1877	Mt. Olivet
011968	FERRARI, Peter M.	8m	W	Md.	19 JUN 1877	Mt. Olivet
012993	FERRIS, Abraham	44y	W	Conn.	28 AUG 1877	Glenwood
014983	FERRIS, Adin Black	2y	W	D.C.	08 MAR 1878	Graceland
001499	FERRIS, Joseph	52y	W	Ire.	07 DEC 1874	Hospital
019419	FERROL, Anna	67y	W	Va.	16 MAR 1879	Mt. Olivet
000411	FERRY, Bertie	3m	C	D.C.	02 SEP 1874	Young Mens
010305	FERRY, Geo. Ed.	2y	W	D.C.	16 JAN 1877	Glenwood
008255	FETTER, Edward H.	2y	W	D.C.	14 JUL 1876	Prospect Hill
015683	FEY, George	4m	W	D.C.	11 MAY 1878	Prospect Hill
011346	FICKETT, Jane A.	74y	W	N.Y.	15 APR 1877	Rock Creek
006002	FIEDLER, Bertha Clara	20y	W	D.C.	12 JAN 1876	Prospect Hill
018243	FIELD, Lloyd Christopher	2m	C	D.C.	05 DEC 1878	Mt. Olivet
018961	FIELD, Mary Virginia	23y	W	D.C.	05 FEB 1879	Congressional
019148	FIELD, Nelson	5y	C	Va.	22 FEB 1879	Mt. Zion
019670	FIELD, Richard	20y	C	Va.	06 APR 1879	Mt. Zion
016812	FIELDS, Charles R.	8y	W	D.C.	29 JUL 1878	Oak Hill
006017	FIELDS, Elizabeth	45y	C	D.C.	14 JAN 1876	Young Mens
000547	FIELDS, Isabella	1y	C	D.C.	17 SEP 1874	Beckett's
017862	FIELDS, Maria	44y	C	Va.	26 OCT 1878	Mt. Pleasant
010625	FIELDS, Sally	6m	C	D.C.	14 FEB 1877	Ebenezer
004978	FIELDS, Sarah	1y	C	D.C.	10 SEP 1875	Mt. Olivet
008723	FIERSON, Rebecca	3m	C	D.C.	18 AUG 1876	Young Mens
006513	FIFIELD, George Langdon	2y	W	D.C.	01 MAR 1876	Mt. Olivet
001439	FILGATE, Cecilia Jane	2y	W	Va.	20 DEC 1874	Mt. Olivet
000029	FILL, Walter H.	1y	W	D.C.	02 AUG 1874	Mt. Olivet
007041	FILL, Wm. F.A.	41y	W	D.C.	18 APR 1876	Washington Asylum
004290	FILLEY, Rollo	1y	W	D.C.	25 JUL 1875	Rock Creek
015415	FILLINS, Augustus	46y	W	U.S.	16 APR 1878	Rock Creek
002619	FILLINS, Berry	11m	C	D.C.	17 MAR 1875	Young Mens
001377	FILLINS, Elizabeth A.	32y	W	Md.	13 DEC 1874	Rock Creek
002855	FILLINS, Lela	4y	W	D.C.	03 APR 1875	Congressional
020653	FINCH, Absolom Paul	9m	W	D.C.	28 JUN 1879	Mt. Olivet
012965	FINCH, Charles David	16m	W	D.C.	26 AUG 1877	Mt. Olivet
017923	FINDLEY, John F.	7m	W	D.C.	01 NOV 1878	Holy Rood
000550	FINK, Corie May	2m	W	D.C.	18 SEP 1874	Oak Hill
013883	FINKMAN, Conrad	63y	W	Ger.	22 NOV 1877	Oak Hill
019740	FINKS, Jonas	35y	C	Va.	12 APR 1879	Potters Field
020633	FINLY, J.M.	45y	W	Ohio	26 JUN 1879	Coshocton, Ohio
016605	FINN, Mathew F.	17y	W	Ire.	15 JUL 1878	Mt. Olivet
017199	FINNEY, Alice	9m	W	D.C.	26 AUG 1878	Holy Rood
014112	FINNEY, Alice C.	19y	W	D.C.	16 DEC 1877	Holy Rood
005181	FINNEY, Samuel	3m	C	D.C.	26 SEP 1875	Ebenezer
002612	FINNEY, Willie Rea	1y	W	D.C.	17 MAR 1875	Glenwood
009173	FISCHER, Augusta	12y	W	D.C.	23 SEP 1876	St. Mary's
016857	FISCHER, Carrie V.	27y	M	Va.	01 AUG 1878	Harmony
007551	FISCHER, Fannie	65y	C	Va.	08 JUN 1876	Harmony
019587	FISCHER, Frederick Godlieb	49y	W	Ger.	29 MAR 1879	Prospect Hill
018057	FISCHER, Mike	4y	W	D.C.	15 NOV 1878	St. Mary's
016831	FISCHER, Simon	35y	W	Ger.	30 JUL 1878	St. Mary's

No.	Name	Age	Race	Birth	Death Date	Burial Place
020497	FISH, Charly	9y	W	D.C.	18 JUN 1879	Trenton, N.J.
005167a	FISH, Randall	c.70y	W	Me.	16 OCT 1875	Potters Field[1]
017340	FISHBACK, Paul Kauffman	2m	W	D.C.	07 SEP 1878	Rock Creek
020320	FISHER, Amanda	28y	C	Va.	06 JUN 1879	Mt. Pleasant
017889	FISHER, Chas.	15y	C	D.C.	28 OCT 1878	Brightwood
017749	FISHER, David A.	30y	W	D.C.	15 OCT 1878	Harmony
006627	FISHER, Dorothea	6m	W	D.C.	10 MAR 1876	Prospect Hill
004365	FISHER, Edward	1y	C	D.C.	29 JUL 1875	Ebenezer
004066	FISHER, Elizabeth S.	1y	W	D.C.	09 JUL 1875	Oak Hill
003323	FISHER, Geo.	42y	C	Va.	14 MAY 1875	Ebenezer
011177	FISHER, Grey Athohl	8m	W	D.C.	31 MAR 1877	Graceland
005964	FISHER, Henry	42y	W	Pa.	07 JAN 1876	Soldier's Home
009080	FISHER, Ida	10m	W	D.C.	15 SEP 1876	Congressional
005204	FISHER, Isabella	c.30y	C	Va.	28 SEP 1875	Young Mens
012664	FISHER, John Edward	1y	C	D.C.	04 AUG 1877	Harmony
012536	FISHER, John Henry	2y	C	D.C.	26 JUL 1877	Harmony
012507	FISHER, Mary	7m	C	D.C.	24 JUL 1877	Beckett's
007508	FISHER, Mary M.	36y	C	D.C.	05 JUN 1876	Harmony
002879	FISHER, Saml. B.	1y	W	D.C.	05 APR 1875	Graceland
014639	FISHUR, Mary	4y	C	D.C.	02 FEB 1878	Harmony
010049	FISK, Lydia A.	41y	W	Mich.	22 DEC 1876	St. Paul, Minn.
005610	FITCH, George Arthur, M.D.	28y	W	W.Va.	30 NOV 1875	Morgantown, W.Va.
001546	FITCH, Mary	74y	W	Ver.	31 DEC 1874	Glenwood
016277	FITCHEW, Sarah	60y	C	Va.	23 JUN 1878	Beckett's
011372	FITNAM, Edward Bernard	4y	W	D.C.	19 APR 1877	Mt. Olivet
020378	FITNAM, Jerome	39y	W	Pa.	10 JUN 1879	Mt. Olivet
002494	FITSGERALD, James Edward	24y	C	D.C.	09 MAR 1875	Potters Field
006637	FITSPATRICK, Joseph	25y	W	N.Y.	11 MAR 1876	Bridgeport, Conn.
009340	FITTS, John	9d	W	D.C.	08 OCT 1876	Holy Rood
007268	FITTZPATRICK, Margaret	1m	W	D.C.	11 MAY 1876	Mt. Olivet
007313	FITTZPATRICK, Susannah	85y	W	D.C.	15 MAY 1876	Mt. Olivet
015345	FITZCHEW, Ella	6m	C	D.C.	10 APR 1878	Mt. Olivet
010885	FITZGERALD, Agnes	6d	W	D.C.	06 MAR 1877	Mt. Olivet
006447	FITZGERALD, Catherine	12y	W	Ire.	23 FEB 1876	Mt. Olivet
003669	FITZGERALD, Edward	14y	W	Ire.	16 JUN 1875	Mt. Olivet
010766	FITZGERALD, Edward	60y	W	Ire.	24 FEB 1877	Mt. Olivet
001152	FITZGERALD, Ellen	43y	W	Ire.	15 NOV 1874	Mt. Olivet
008975	FITZGERALD, Francis P.	6y	W	D.C.	05 SEP 1876	Mt. Olivet
012622	FITZGERALD, James	21y	W	Ire.	31 JUL 1877	Mt. Olivet
011608	FITZGERALD, James	14y	W	D.C.	15 MAY 1877	Holy Rood
014225	FITZGERALD, Johanna	46y	W	Ire.	27 DEC 1877	Mt. Olivet
019574	FITZGERALD, Johanna	6y	W	D.C.	28 MAR 1879	Mt. Olivet
005079	FITZGERALD, John	8m	W	D.C.	17 SEP 1876	Mt. Olivet
015023	FITZGERALD, John F.	8m	W	D.C.	11 MAR 1878	Mt. Olivet
019976	FITZGERALD, Joseph	1y	W	D.C.	03 MAY 1879	Mt. Olivet
006154	FITZGERALD, Julia	1m	W	D.C.	27 JAN 1876	Mt. Olivet
009393	FITZGERALD, Margaret	c.58y	W	Ire.	12 OCT 1876	Mt. Olivet
010429	FITZGERALD, Margaret	65y	W	Ire.	28 JAN 1877	Mt. Olivet
007153	FITZGERALD, Margret	55y	W	Ire.	29 APR 1876	Mt. Olivet
012801	FITZGERALD, Martin	35y	W	Ire.	14 AUG 1877	Mt. Olivet
002854	FITZGERALD, Mary	48y	W	Ire.	03 APR 1875	Mt. Olivet
004401	FITZGERALD, Mary A.	36y	W	Md.	01 AUG 1875	Mt. Olivet
013647	FITZGERALD, May	2y	W	D.C.	27 OCT 1877	Mt. Olivet

[1] Place of burial on certificate of death gives Potters Field (Dead House), and is noted "Congressional" in the margin.

District of Columbia Death Records, August 1, 1874 to July 31, 1879

No.	Name	Age	Race	Birth	Death Date	Burial Place
007163	FITZGERALD, Michael C.	43y	W	Ire.	30 APR 1876	Mt. Olivet
008825	FITZGERALD, Michael Joseph	4y	W	D.C.	25 AUG 1876	Mt. Olivet
015198	FITZGERALD, Patrick	53y	W	Ire.	27 MAR 1878	Mt. Olivet
000643	FITZGERALD, Sarah	6d	W	D.C.	26 SEP 1874	Mt. Olivet
005736	FITZGERALD, Thomas	55y	W	Ire.	13 DEC 1875	Mt. Olivet
009057	FITZGERALD, Thomas	49y	W	Ire.	13 SEP 1876	Mt. Olivet
019108	FITZGERALD, Thomas	4y	W	D.C.	18 FEB 1879	Holy Rood
015113	FITZGERALD, Thos. P.	2h	W	D.C.	18 MAR 1878	Mt. Olivet
003610	FITZGERALD, Wm. Stephen	4m	W	D.C.	12 JUN 1875	Mt. Olivet
007432	FITZGIBBINS, John	4m	W	D.C.	29 MAY 1876	Holy Rood
006460	FITZGIBBONS, Mary	26y	W	Va.	24 FEB 1876	Holy Rood
009587	FITZGIBBONS, Mary	16y	W	N.Y.	01 NOV 1876	Dunkirk, N.Y.
005384	FITZHUE, John C.	58y	W	Md.	07 NOV 1875	Congressional
020137	FITZHUE, Landon	21d	C	D.C.	18 MAY 1879	Beckett's
010756	FITZHUGH, Burnett	2½m	C	D.C.	23 FEB 1877	Young Mens
009380	FITZHUGH, Eliza J.	25y	W	D.C.	11 OCT 1876	Congressional
017354	FITZHUGH, Ellen, Mrs.	c.56y	W	Md.	09 SEP 1878	Congressional
005142a	FITZHUGH, George	67y	C	Va.	14 OCT 1875	Young Mens
006307	FITZHUGH, Henry	18y	C	Va.	11 FEB 1876	Moore's
005494	FITZHUGH, J.B.	88y	C	Va.	18 NOV 1875	Harmony
021035	FITZHUGH, John W.	16y	W	D.C.	21 JUL 1876	Glenwood
012104	FITZHUGH, Sarah	48y	W	Md.	28 JUN 1877	Congressional
019318	FITZHUGH, Thornton	78y	C	Va.	08 MAR 1879	Harmony
013257	FITZHUGH, Willington	1y	C	D.C.	20 SEP 1877	Harmony
011586	FITZMORRIS, Mary	45y	W	Ire.	13 MAY 1877	Mt. Olivet
017281	FITZMORRIS, Mary Catherine	3m	W	D.C.	01 SEP 1878	Mt. Olivet
004475	FITZPATRICK, Christopher	35y	W	Ire.	06 AUG 1875	Mt. Olivet
007535	FITZPATRICK, Ellen	2m	W	D.C.	07 JUN 1876	Mt. Olivet
007223	FITZPATRICK, James	76y	W	Ire.	06 MAY 1876	Mt. Olivet
019283	FITZPATRICK, James	2y	W	D.C.	05 MAR 1879	Mt. Olivet
006967	FITZPATRICK, Jane	38y	W	Eng.	08 APR 1876	Mt. Olivet
011841	FITZPATRICK, John	56y	W	Ire.	08 JUN 1877	Washington Asylum
002119	FITZPATRICK, Mary Elizabeth	2m	W	D.C.	11 FEB 1875	Mt. Olivet
004492	FITZPATRICK, Mary Ida	10m	W	D.C.	07 AUG 1875	Mt. Olivet
019168	FITZRANDOLPH, Walter	9m	W	D.C.	23 FEB 1879	Glenwood
005150a	FITSSIMMONS, Mary Jane	5y	W	Md.	15 OCT 1875	Mt. Olivet
002906	FITZSIMMONS, Michael	27y	W	R.I.	07 APR 1875	Mt. Olivet
017756	FLAHARTY, Jeremiah	5m	W	D.C.	16 OCT 1878	Mt. Olivet
010570	FLAHERTY, Ann O.	36y	W	Ire.	09 FEB 1877	Mt. Olivet
015593	FLAHERTY, Ellen, Mrs.	44y	W	Ire.	03 MAY 1878	Mt. Olivet
019783	FLAHERTY, Margt.	10d	W	D.C.	15 APR 1879	Mt. Olivet
013132	FLAHERTY, Teresa Agnes	6y	W	D.C.	09 SEP 1877	Mt. Olivet
014480	FLANAGAN, James	27y	W	D.C.	19 JAN 1878	Mt. Olivet
001979	FLANNAGAN, Francis E.	8m	W	D.C.	01 FEB 1875	Mt. Olivet
019066	FLATHER, John	77y	W	Eng.	14 FEB 1879	Glenwood
020556	FLATHER, Joseph Arthur	5m	W	D.C.	21 JUN 1879	Glenwood
020451	FLATHER, Rebecca S.	33y	W	Md.	15 JUN 1879	Glenwood
016039	FLEET, Elizabeth	7m	C	D.C.	06 JUN 1878	Potters Field
007487	FLEET, Infant of Nelson	3d	C	D.C.	03 JUN 1876	Ebenezer
005793	FLEET, John	50y	M	Va.	19 DEC 1875	Potters Field
015662	FLEET, Mendleshon B.	21y	C	D.C.	09 MAY 1878	Harmony
000263	FLEET, Robert	32y	C	D.C.	20 AUG 1874	Harmony
014024	FLEMING, Mary	9y	C	Va.	07 DEC 1877	Harmony
011699	FLEMING, Nellie	24y	C	Va.	25 MAY 1877	Young Mens
018331	FLEMMING, James	41y	C	N.C.	14 DEC 1878	Potters Field
014444	FLEMMING, Mary	79y	W	D.C.	16 JAN 1878	Mt. Olivet

No.	Name	Age	Race	Birth	Death Date	Burial Place
003647	FLEMMING, Susan	68y	W	Va.	14 JUN 1875	Congressional
010755	FLETCHER, Augustus A.	5m	C	D.C.	23 FEB 1877	Mt. Olivet
020828	FLETCHER, C.W.	11m	C	D.C.	08 JUL 1879	Beckett's
003152	FLETCHER, Carrie Ward	8m	W	D.C.	28 APR 1875	Congressional
007860	FLETCHER, Charles Augustine	1y	C	D.C.	26 JUN 1876	Mt. Olivet
021157	FLETCHER, Chas.	6m	C	D.C.	30 JUL 1879	Mt. Pleasant
020788	FLETCHER, Elen	6m	C	D.C.	06 JUL 1879	Harmony
011879	FLETCHER, Ella	1y	W	D.C.	13 JUN 1877	Mt. Olivet
006155	FLETCHER, Francis E.	2y	W	D.C.	27 JAN 1876	Presbyterian
007816	FLETCHER, George	39y	W	D.C.	24 JUN 1876	Congressional
021079	FLETCHER, George	6m	C	D.C.	24 JUL 1879	Mt. Pleasant
005078	FLETCHER, Harriet	12y	C	D.C.	17 SEP 1875	Harmony
021113	FLETCHER, Henry	5y	C	D.C.	26 JUL 1879	Beckett's
016302	FLETCHER, James Thomas	11m	C	D.C.	25 JUN 1878	Young Mens
010025	FLETCHER, Lemuel	5m	C	D.C.	20 DEC 1876	Ebenezer
001686	FLETCHER, Lilly A.	7m	C	D.C.	10 JAN 1875	Young Mens
001718	FLETCHER, Lotta	80y	C	Md.	13 JAN 1875	Beckett's
007297	FLETCHER, Louise R.	28y	W	Pa.	14 MAY 1876	Chester, Pa.
008111	FLETCHER, Marion Smith	2m	W	D.C.	09 JUL 1876	Glenwood
010238	FLETCHER, Matilda Arnold	73y	W	Ire.	09 JAN 1877	Erie, Pa.
015638	FLETCHER, Rosetta	108y	C	Md.	07 MAY 1878	Young Mens
010899	FLETCHER, Susan	60y	C	D.C.	07 MAR 1877	Mt. Olivet
011193	FLETCHER, Virginia	23y	C	Md.	02 APR 1877	Mt. Olivet
013286	FLETCHER, William Henry	1m	C	D.C.	24 SEP 1877	Marshall's, Md.
008745	FLETE, Harrisson	5m	W	D.C.	19 AUG 1876	Middletown, Md.
016672	FLEURY, Chr. Benj.	14m	W	Md.	19 JUL 1878	Congressional
014508	FLEURY, W.R.	7m	W	D.C.	21 JAN 1878	Congressional
010083	FLINK, Albert	27y	W	Ger.	26 DEC 1876	Soldier's Home
005125a	FLINN, Margaret	25y	W	Ire.	13 OCT 1875	Mt. Olivet
012766	FLOOD, Cecelia	1m	W	D.C.	11 AUG 1877	Mt. Olivet
012308	FLOOD, Edith Cragin	1y	W	D.C.	10 JUL 1877	Presbyterian
018690	FLOOD, John	65y	W	Ire.	16 JAN 1879	Mt. Olivet/Alexandria, Va.
011979	FLOOD, John Henry	5m	W	D.C.	20 JUN 1877	Rock Creek
001189	FLOOD, Lillie	14d	M	D.C.	19 NOV 1874	Harmony
007188	FLOOD, Lucinda	45y	C	Va.	02 MAY 1876	Beckett's
010075	FLOOD, Priscilla C.	67y	W	Ky.	26 DEC 1876	Congressional
007838	FLOOD, Thomas	37y	C	Va.	25 JUN 1876	Baptist
003995	FLORENCE, Thomas Birch	63y	W	Pa.	04 JUL 1875	Philadelphia, Pa.
006763	FLOSEKER, Agnes R.	10d	W	D.C.	21 MAR 1876	Mt. Olivet
014134	FLOWERS, Alexander	41y	W	D.C.	19 DEC 1877	Mt. Olivet
019433	FLOYD, Ambrose	3m	W	D.C.	17 MAR 1879	Mt. Olivet
000525	FLYNN, Daniel J.	33y	W	Ire.	15 SEP 1874	Congressional
018770	FLYNN, Daniel W.	45y	W	N.Y.	22 JAN 1879	Glenwood
006044	FLYNN, E. Alexander	53y	W	Va.	17 JAN 1876	Salem, Va.
011147	FLYNN, Johanna	37y	W	Ire.	29 MAR 1877	Mt. Olivet
007601	FLYNN, Mary Elizabeth	15y	W	D.C.	11 JUN 1876	Mt. Olivet
013449	FOALE, Henry J.	39y	W	Eng.	09 OCT 1877	Soldier's Home
009704	FOARD, Harriet	32y	C	D.C.	15 NOV 1876	Good Hope
020129	FOBES, Edson	68y	W	Ver.	17 MAY 1879	Glen Falls, N.Y.
014612	FODOR, Velma Rosina	6y	W	Md.	31 JAN 1878	Congressional
001948	FOGG, Waldo Pierce	2y	W	Pa.	30 JAN 1875	Alexandria, Va.
018677	FOLEY, Alice	27y	W	D.C.	15 JAN 1879	Glenwood
006351	FOLEY, Cornelius	35y	W	Ire.	14 FEB 1876	Mt. Olivet
009661	FOLEY, Ellen	c.54y	W	Ire.	10 NOV 1876	Mt. Olivet
010275	FOLEY, Helen	3y	W	N.J.	13 JAN 1877	Mt. Olivet
006204	FOLEY, Jeremiah	3m	W	D.C.	01 FEB 1876	Mt. Olivet

District of Columbia Death Records, August 1, 1874 to July 31, 1879   115

No.	Name	Age	Race	Birth	Death Date	Burial Place
011907	FOLEY, John	32y	W	Ire.	15 JUN 1877	Mt. Olivet
015372	FOLEY, Margaret	78y	W	Ire.	12 APR 1878	Mt. Olivet
011722	FOLEY, Margt.	45y	W	Ire.	27 MAY 1877	Mt. Olivet
000874	FOLEY, Maria	19y	W	D.C.	20 OCT 1874	Mt. Olivet
005364	FOLEY, Mary	50y	W	Ire.	05 NOV 1875	Mt. Olivet
010816	FOLEY, Mary Florence	5y	W	D.C.	01 MAR 1877	Mt. Olivet
019669	FOLEY, Morris	7y	W	D.C.	06 APR 1879	Mt. Olivet
017304	FOLEY, Patrick	43y	W	Ire.	03 SEP 1878	Mt. Olivet
014407	FOLEY, Sarah Catharine	5y	C	D.C.	13 JAN 1878	Potters Field
002268	FOLEY, Theresa	8m	W	D.C.	21 FEB 1875	Mt. Olivet
009353	FOLK, Blanch	7d	W	D.C.	09 OCT 1876	Glenwood
014518	FOLK, Edith Estelle	7y	W	D.C.	22 JAN 1878	Glenwood
015385	FOLLANSBEE, Emily J.	42y	W	Ohio	13 APR 1878	Oak Hill
008793	FOLLEY, Annie	9m	W	D.C.	23 AUG 1876	Holy Rood
016383	FOLLIN, Eliza	11m	W	D.C.	01 JUL 1878	Glenwood
003743	FOLLIN, Elizabeth H.	24y	W	D.C.	21 JUN 1875	Oak Hill
003878	FOLLIN, Sarah J.	3m	W	D.C.	27 JUN 1875	Oak Hill
013209	FOLLINS, Mary G.	1y	W	D.C.	15 SEP 1877	Glenwood
004312	FOLLY, Katie	1y	C	D.C.	26 JUL 1875	Ebenezer
004710	FONTAIN, Willie	1y	C	D.C.	22 AUG 1875	Ebenezer
008455	FONTLEROY, William	7m	C	D.C.	28 JUL 1876	Young Mens
004926	FONTROY, Dora Ann	2y	C	D.C.	06 SEP 1875	Ebenezer
002255	FONTROY, Infant of Monroe	2d	C	D.C.	20 FEB 1875	Mt. Zion
004014	FONTROY, Milly	19y	C	Va.	06 JUL 1875	Potters Field
008294	FOOS, John A.	10m	W	D.C.	16 JUL 1876	Congressional
003487	FOOSBERG, Harold	1m	W	D.C.	30 MAY 1875	Glenwood
017615	FOOT, Frank W.	36y	W	N.Y.	03 OCT 1878	Congressional
006095	FOOT, Mary Morris	69y	W	N.Y.	22 JAN 1876	Cooperstown, N.Y.
017566	FOOT, William Henry	45y	C	D.C.	29 SEP 1878	Harmony
010378	FORD, Alexander	2m	C	D.C.	23 JAN 1877	Ebenezer
013312	FORD, Bertha V.	1y	C	D.C.	26 SEP 1877	Mt. Olivet
020710	FORD, Blanche H.	5m	C	D.C.	02 JUL 1879	Young Mens
009573	FORD, Catherine	52y	C	Va.	30 OCT 1876	Harmony
006074	FORD, Chloe A.	19y	C	Md.	20 JAN 1876	Prince George's Co., Md.
001041	FORD, Daniel	18d	W	D.C.	04 NOV 1874	Mt. Olivet
009631	FORD, Eliza, Mrs.	87y	C	Md.	06 NOV 1876	Harmony
013464	FORD, Elizabeth	45y	C	Va.	10 OCT 1877	Harmony
020084	FORD, Fredric	84y	C	Md.	13 MAY 1879	Harmony
012784	FORD, Henry	40y	C	Md.	12 AUG 1877	Potters Field
014929	FORD, Infant of Hamilton E.	14h	W	D.C.	03 MAR 1878	Oak Hill
014248	FORD, Infant of Sallie	1m	W	D.C.	29 DEC 1877	Potters Field
021171	FORD, Isaac	19y	C	Md.	31 JUL 1879	Graceland
000437	FORD, James	55y	C	U.S.	06 SEP 1874	Potters Field
009199	FORD, James	3y	C	D.C.	25 SEP 1876	Harmony
015245	FORD, James Elias	18d	C	D.C.	31 MAR 1878	Baltimore, Md.
011814	FORD, James Henry	2y	C	D.C.	06 JUN 1877	Ebenezer
001079	FORD, James P.	21y	W	D.C.	07 NOV 1874	Glenwood
016856	FORD, John Henry	7m	C	D.C.	01 AUG 1878	Potters Field
005100	FORD, John William	19d	C	D.C.	19 SEP 1875	Ebenezer
001252	FORD, Julia	2y	C	D.C.	28 NOV 1874	Beckett's
018067	FORD, Julia	1y	C	D.C.	16 NOV 1878	Mt. Pleasant Plain
014337	FORD, Kitty	24y	C	Va.	06 JAN 1878	Potters Field
008397	FORD, Laura	5d	C	D.C.	24 JUL 1876	Ebenezer
013582	FORD, Lettie	c.49y	C	D.C.	21 OCT 1877	Young Mens
009338	FORD, Lizzie	30y	M	Va.	08 OCT 1876	Graceland
001288	FORD, Louisa	37y	C	Md.	02 DEC 1874	Young Mens

District of Columbia Death Records, August 1, 1874 to July 31, 1879

No.	Name	Age	Race	Birth	Death Date	Burial Place
015873	FORD, Louisa B.	19d	C	D.C.	28 MAY 1878	Mt. Pleasant
009982	FORD, Lucinda	60y	M	Va.	17 DEC 1876	Harmony
002631	FORD, Marcey	4y	C	D.C.	18 MAR 1875	Harmony
005039a	FORD, Mary	74y	W	Va.	03 OCT 1875	Glenwood
005038a	FORD, Mary E.	1y	W	D.C.	03 OCT 1875	Congressional
008482	FORD, Mary Ella	5m	M	D.C.	30 JUL 1876	Harmony
013208	FORD, Mary R.	6m	M	D.C.	15 SEP 1877	Harmony
016303	FORD, Rebecca A.	76y	W	Ky.	25 JUN 1878	Glenwood
002166	FORD, Richard	6m	C	D.C.	15 FEB 1875	Potters Field
014454	FORD, Rosa	c.26y	C	Md.	17 JAN 1878	Beckett's
012767	FORD, Samuel J.T.	13m	W	D.C.	11 AUG 1877	Congressional
017939	FORD, Stephen Calvert	14y	W	D.C.	03 NOV 1878	Mt. Olivet
009230	FORD, Thomas F.	27y	W	Ire.	28 SEP 1876	Mt. Olivet
014589	FORD, Walter Ellis	2y	C	D.C.	29 JAN 1878	Mt. Pleasant
015331	FORD, William	28y	C	D.C.	09 APR 1878	Mt. Zion
015530	FORD, William	1y	C	D.C.	27 APR 1878	Mt. Zion
007817	FORD, Willie Francis	7m	W	D.C.	24 JUN 1876	Mt. Olivet
018485	FORE, Augustus	59y	W	Ky.	28 DEC 1878	Hospital, Government
014057	FOREMAN, Eliza	65y	C	Va.	10 DEC 1877	Harmony
014625	FORESMAN, Charles Edgar	2y	W	Wisc.	01 FEB 1878	Madison, Wisc.
021063	FORREST, Angeline	6m	W	D.C.	23 JUL 1879	Mt. Olivet
011323	FORREST, Elizabeth	50y	C	D.C.	13 APR 1877	Harmony
019030	FORREST, Elizabeth F.	29y	W	D.C.	11 FEB 1879	Rock Creek
003354	FORREST, Gertrude M.	2m	W	D.C.	17 MAY 1875	Glenwood
010689	FORREST, Sarah	94y	C	Md.	19 FEB 1877	Harmony
003786	FORRESTER, J. Ridgway	3m	M	D.C.	23 JUN 1875	Ebenezer
000222	FORSINGER, Lena	1y	W	D.C.	17 AUG 1874	St. Mary's
014345	FORSTER, James H.S.	36y	W	Pa.	07 JAN 1878	Harrisburg, Pa.
020102	FORSTER, John Elder	80y	W	Pa.	15 MAY 1879	Harrisburg, Pa.
018018	FORSYTH, George	51y	W	U.S.	11 NOV 1878	Soldier's Home
012235	FORSYTH, Mary	16y	W	N.Y.	06 JUL 1877	Graceland
017852	FORSYTH, William Thomas	30y	W	Eng.	25 OCT 1878	Mt. Olivet
005678	FORTH, Infant of Bettie	4d	C	D.C.	07 DEC 1875	Harmony
005507	FORTUNE, Infant of Albert	5min	C	D.C.	19 NOV 1875	Mt. Pleasant
015904	FORTUNE, Joseph	1m	W	--	30 MAY 1878	Mt. Olivet
009627	FOSKEY, Olive Levy	2y	C	D.C.	06 NOV 1876	Mt. Pleasant
011667	FOSTER, A. Lawrence	74y	W	Mass.	21 MAY 1877	Glenwood
018215	FOSTER, Ann Eliza	23y	C	D.C.	02 DEC 1878	Holy Rood
011474	FOSTER, Bessie R.	2m	C	D.C.	01 MAY 1877	Mt. Zion
006415	FOSTER, Catherine	19y	C	D.C.	19 FEB 1876	Holy Rood
015651	FOSTER, Catherine	65y	C	Md.	08 MAY 1878	Potters Field
004859	FOSTER, Charles Bradford	61y	W	Pa.	01 SEP 1875	Glenwood
019807	FOSTER, Elizabeth	2y	C	D.C.	17 APR 1879	Mt. Pleasant
018320	FOSTER, Ella Ethel	11m	W	D.C.	13 DEC 1878	Glenwood
003693	FOSTER, Emma	17y	C	D.C.	18 JUN 1875	Ebenezer
006108	FOSTER, Emma	5y	W	D.C.	23 JAN 1876	Congressional
014455	FOSTER, Emma (a waif)	3m	C	--	17 JAN 1878	Potters Field
008708	FOSTER, George	15m	W	D.C.	16 AUG 1876	Mt. Olivet
007096	FOSTER, Harriet	8d	C	D.C.	24 APR 1876	Ebenezer
015750	FOSTER, James	4m	C	D.C.	17 MAY 1878	Potters Field
020856	FOSTER, Jas. D.	11m	C	D.C.	09 JUL 1879	Holy Rood
012220	FOSTER, Jeremiah	4m	C	D.C.	04 JUL 1877	Ebenezer
008934	FOSTER, Lawrence	32y	W	N.Y.	02 SEP 1876	Glenwood
021048	FOSTER, Mary	1m	W	D.C.	22 JUL 1879	Prospect Hill
012992	FOSTER, Mary Ellen	44y	C	Va.	28 AUG 1877	Beckett's
019870	FOSTER, Nancy, Mrs.	80y	W	Va.	23 APR 1879	Winchester, Va.

District of Columbia Death Records, August 1, 1874 to July 31, 1879   117

No.	Name	Age	Race	Birth	Death Date	Burial Place
007405	FOSTER, Samuel Tufts	37y	W	N.H.	25 MAY 1876	Manchester, N.H.
015146	FOSTER, Sarah Catherine	23y	C	Md.	22 MAR 1878	Brightwood
004311	FOSTER, William	27y	W	Eng.	26 JUL 1875	Potters Field
014846	FOSTER, Willie	4y	C	D.C.	22 FEB 1878	Brightwood
010150	FOSTER, Wm. Franklin	7y	W	D.C.	01 JAN 1877	Oak Hill
015983	FOUNTAIN, Eugene Taylor	11d	W	D.C.	03 JUN 1878	Congressional
020810	FOUNTAIN, Mary Agnes	46y	C	Va.	07 JUL 1879	Mt. Pleasant
003183	FOWKE, Mary H.	44y	W	Va.	01 MAY 1875	Congressional
009292	FOWKE, Philip Bond	57y	W	Ill.	03 OCT 1876	Congressional
018091	FOWLER, Alice Maud	3y	W	D.C.	19 NOV 1878	Rock Creek
020404	FOWLER, Ann M.	32y	W	Md.	12 JUN 1879	Horse Head, Md.
011791	FOWLER, Annie	11m	W	D.C.	03 JUN 1877	Oak Hill
002288	FOWLER, Daniel Wall	1m	W	D.C.	23 FEB 1875	Glenwood
009924	FOWLER, Elnora	69y	W	Md.	10 DEC 1876	Methodist Tennallytown
007839	FOWLER, Ernest	2y	W	D.C.	25 JUN 1876	Congressional
002782	FOWLER, Genevieve	6m	W	D.C.	29 MAR 1875	Baltimore, Md.
007707	FOWLER, George	26y	W	D.C.	18 JUN 1876	Oak Hill
007746	FOWLER, Georgeanna	28y	W	Md.	20 JUN 1876	Congressional
009517	FOWLER, Harry	6m	W	D.C.	24 OCT 1876	Congressional
000472	FOWLER, Infant of James	10m	C	D.C.	10 SEP 1874	Mt. Olivet
000933	FOWLER, John	54y	W	D.C.	25 OCT 1874	Oak Hill
011649	FOWLER, Lawrence C.	8m	W	D.C.	19 MAY 1877	Mt. Olivet
009966	FOWLER, Mary Thornton	74y	W	Pa.	14 DEC 1876	Congressional
018552	FOWLER, Owen	9y	W	D.C.	03 JAN 1879	Congressional
003358	FOWLER, Rose Ann, Mrs.	30y	W	Md.	18 MAY 1875	Mt. Olivet
010573	FOWLER, Sarah E.	23y	W	Mass.	09 FEB 1877	Rock Creek
015090	FOWLES, Ella May	8y	W	Md.	16 MAR 1878	Rock Creek
012479	FOX, Alice	1y	W	D.C.	23 JUL 1877	Mt. Olivet
019043	FOX, Alice M.	7y	W	D.C.	12 FEB 1879	Alexandria, Va.
018921	FOX, Edward W.	5y	W	D.C.	02 FEB 1879	Alexandria, Va.
018892	FOX, George A.	2y	W	D.C.	31 JAN 1879	Alexandria, Va.
002219	FOX, Hannah	10d	C	D.C.	18 FEB 1875	Potters Field
018422	FOX, Infant of Martha Ann	7d	C	D.C.	22 DEC 1878	Potters Field
003366	FOX, Jabez, Jr.	15y	W	Mich.	19 MAY 1875	Glenwood
017641	FOX, James	42y	W	Ire.	05 OCT 1878	Hospital
000429	FOX, John	3y	C	Va.	04 SEP 1874	Beckett's
016621	FOX, Joseph Walker	12y	W	D.C.	16 JUL 1878	Prospect Hill
008752	FOX, Mary L.	5y	W	D.C.	20 AUG 1876	Mt. Olivet
009874	FOX, Mary M.	31y	W	Md.	05 DEC 1876	Mt. Olivet
006905	FOX, Matilda	23y	C	Va.	03 APR 1876	Harmony
012312	FOX, Rosea	9d	C	D.C.	11 JUL 1877	Beckett's
010163	FOX, Susan	75y	W	Va.	03 JAN 1877	Congressional
000162	FOX, William	29y	C	Md.	12 AUG 1874	Young Mens
005915	FOX, William	14d	C	D.C.	02 JAN 1876	Young Mens
017515	FRAIN, Mary Ann	40y	W	Ire.	24 SEP 1878	Mt. Olivet
015306	FRALEY, Margareth	65y	W	Ger.	07 APR 1878	St. Mary's
006215	FRANCE, Annabella	52y	W	Va.	02 FEB 1876	Congressional
001562	FRANCE, Sebastian	38y	W	Bav.	01 JAN 1875	Potters Field
007042	FRANCES, Laura A.	22y	C	Va.	18 APR 1876	Young Mens
001953	FRANCES, Mary	40y	C	Md.	30 JAN 1875	Mt. Pleasant
020709	FRANCIS, Eliza	38y	C	Va.	02 JUL 1879	Beckett's
004914	FRANCIS, Infant of Lottie	3d	C	D.C.	05 SEP 1875	Harmony
012430	FRANCIS, Maria	36y	M	Va.	19 JUL 1877	Harmony
009821	FRANCIS, Mary A.	45y	M	Va.	29 NOV 1876	Richmond, Va.
011598	FRANCIS, Philip	32y	W	Ire.	14 MAY 1877	Washington Asylum
012154	FRANCIS, Ruth	1d	C	D.C.	01 JUL 1877	Potters Field

District of Columbia Death Records, August 1, 1874 to July 31, 1879

No.	Name	Age	Race	Birth	Death Date	Burial Place
000820	FRANCIS, William	1y	C	D.C.	16 OCT 1874	Beckett's
004623	FRANCISCOE, Cornelia	7m	C	D.C.	16 AUG 1875	Young Mens
013524	FRANK, Elisabeth	11y	W	N.Y.	15 OCT 1877	St. Mary's
002057	FRANK, Fred	62y	W	Ger.	07 FEB 1875	Mt. Olivet
008421	FRANK, Joseph	42y	W	Bav.	25 JUL 1876	St. Mary's
008049	FRANK, Louisa	5m	W	D.C.	06 JUL 1876	St. Mary's
002070	FRANK, Paul, Gen.	45y	W	Ger.	07 FEB 1875	Brooklyn, N.Y.
009066	FRANK, Wm. Sayres	6d	W	D.C.	14 SEP 1876	Prospect Hill
004827	FRANKE, Lisette	59y	W	Ger.	30 AUG 1875	Lancaster, Pa.
007897	FRANKLIN, Ben	36y	C	S.C.	28 JUN 1876	Harmony
018306	FRANKLIN, Charles	37y	C	Ga.	11 DEC 1878	Potters Field
005149a	FRANKLIN, Christy	3y	C	Md.	15 OCT 1875	Baptist
006223	FRANKLIN, John	2y	C	Md.	03 FEB 1876	Mt. Pleasant Plain
009262	FRANKLIN, John	40y	C	Md.	01 OCT 1876	Harmony
011326	FRANKLIN, Julia	10m	W	D.C.	14 APR 1877	Mt. Olivet
002100	FRANKLIN, Mabel	8m	W	D.C.	09 FEB 1875	Congressional
003479	FRANKLIN, Madison	45y	C	Md.	29 MAY 1875	Young Mens
001441	FRANKLIN, Mary O.	55y	W	Md.	20 DEC 1874	Glymont, Md.
018150	FRANKLIN, Stephen	60y	C	Va.	25 NOV 1878	Potters Field
008005	FRANKS, Annie L.	28y	W	Md.	04 JUL 1876	Holy Rood
007330	FRANKS, Samuel J.	c.40y	W	Pa.	18 MAY 1876	Lewistown, Pa.
008933	FRANZ, Herman	8m	W	D.C.	02 SEP 1876	Glenwood
017873	FRASER, Amelia	15y	C	Va.	27 OCT 1878	Beckett's
005936	FRASER, James A.	21y	W	D.C.	04 JAN 1876	Glenwood
018242	FRASER, John	35y	C	Va.	05 DEC 1878	Mt. Zion
000950	FRASER, Salina	50y	W	Md.	27 OCT 1874	Glenwood
007043	FRASIER, Harriet A.	5m	C	D.C.	18 APR 1876	Mt. Zion
012230	FRASURE, Alberta	2m	C	D.C.	05 JUL 1877	Young Mens
021147	FRAULEY, Michael	8m	W	D.C.	29 JUL 1879	Mt. Olivet
003347	FRAWLEY, Mary Ann	3m	W	D.C.	17 MAY 1875	Mt. Olivet
012674	FRAZER, Georgia	1y	C	D.C.	05 AUG 1877	Mt. Zion
001326	FRAZER, James	c.40y	C	Va.	06 DEC 1874	Mt. Pleasant
008076	FRAZER, Jas.	49y	C	Va.	08 JUL 1876	Ebenezer
005980	FRAZIER, Arthur	5m	W	D.C.	09 JAN 1876	Congressional
014491	FRAZIER, Bertha	1y	W	D.C.	20 JAN 1878	Congressional
001451	FRAZIER, Charles	2m	C	D.C.	20 DEC 1874	Young Mens
010896	FRAZIER, Dewit	18y	C	Va.	07 MAR 1877	Young Mens
018371	FRAZIER, Frank	c.50y	C	U.S.	18 DEC 1878	Potters Field
020609	FRAZIER, Georgeanna	19y	C	Va.	25 JUN 1879	Mt. Pleasant
008493	FRAZIER, Hamilton	45y	C	S.C.	30 JUL 1876	Young Mens
004123	FRAZIER, Hattie	8m	W	D.C.	14 JUL 1875	Glenwood
007190	FRAZIER, Infant of Thomas	3m	C	D.C.	02 MAY 1876	Young Mens
003498	FRAZIER, Infant twin of Harrison	56h	C	D.C.	31 MAY 1875	Young Mens
017874	FRAZIER, Julia Anna Pitt	76y	W	Md.	27 OCT 1878	Baltimore, Md.
006096	FRAZIER, Levi	28y	C	Md.	22 JAN 1876	Young Mens
015663	FRAZIER, Madison	56y	C	Va.	09 MAY 1878	Beckett's
014005	FRAZIER, Margaret	52y	W	Ire.	04 DEC 1877	Glenwood
011155	FRAZIER, Richard	20y	W	Md.	29 MAR 1877	Middletown, Del.
015181	FRAZIER, Sophy	25y	C	Md.	25 MAR 1878	Young Mens
015439	FRAZIER, William	1y	C	D.C.	18 APR 1878	Mt. Pleasant
015925	FRAZIER, Wilson	26y	C	Pa.	31 MAY 1878	Young Mens
001503	FREDE, Louis	31y	W	Ger.	23 DEC 1874	Hospital
005153	FREDERICK, Florence	53y	W	Ger.	24 SEP 1875	Congressional
006878	FREELAND, Alice	5y	C	D.C.	01 APR 1876	Ebenezer
006764	FREEMAN, Anna Elizabeth	31y	W	Va.	21 MAR 1876	Leesburg, Va.
008190	FREEMAN, Arena	1y	C	D.C.	11 JUL 1876	Mt. Olivet

District of Columbia Death Records, August 1, 1874 to July 31, 1879   119

No.	Name	Age	Race	Birth	Death Date	Burial Place
013133	FREEMAN, Benjamin C.	26y	C	D.C.	09 SEP 1877	Harmony
019533	FREEMAN, Blanche	1m	C	D.C	24 MAR 1879	Mt. Pleasant
011407	FREEMAN, Caroline	3y	C	Md.	23 APR 1877	Young Mens
011581	FREEMAN, Catherine, Mrs.	76y	W	Ger.	13 MAY 1877	St. Mary's
004709	FREEMAN, Eliza	74y	W	Va.	22 AUG 1875	Glenwood
019609	FREEMAN, Eliza	74y	C	N.C.	31 MAR 1879	Harmony
018177	FREEMAN, Elizabeth	5y	C	D.C.	27 NOV 1878	Harmony
017042	FREEMAN, Emelia	45y	W	Ger.	14 AUG 1878	Mt. Olivet
008801	FREEMAN, George B.	18y	C	D.C.	24 AUG 1876	Harmony
006261	FREEMAN, Infant of John L.	3h	C	D.C.	07 FEB 1876	Harmony
011500	FREEMAN, John Lewis	57y	C	N.C.	03 MAY 1877	Harmony
020269	FREEMAN, Malinda	9d	C	D.C.	02 JUN 1879	Young Mens
015458	FREEMAN, Mary Jane	1y	C	D.C.	20 APR 1878	Young Mens
014562	FREEMAN, Matline Elizabeth	2y	C	D.C.	26 JAN 1878	Mt. Pleasant Plain
006459	FREEMAN, Noah	29y	C	N.C.	24 FEB 1876	Potters Field
006123	FREEMAN, Rhubertta	2y	C	D.C.	24 JAN 1876	Harmony
005154	FREEMAN, Richard	55y	C	Va.	24 SEP 1875	Ebenezer
006233	FREEMAN, Virginia B.	1d	W	D.C.	04 FEB 1876	Prospect Hill
020469	FREEMAN, Wilhemina	45y	W	Ger.	16 JUN 1879	Prospect Hill
005929	FREER, George	29y	W	Md.	03 JAN 1876	Congressional
004577	FREER, Grant	8y	W	D.C.	13 AUG 1875	Congressional
000694	FREESTONE, Thos. H.	1y	W	R.I.	02 OCT 1874	Mt. Olivet
018284	FREH, Phillip Hamilton	11m	W	D.C.	09 DEC 1878	Prospect Hill
017597	FREITAG, Clara	6d	W	D.C.	02 OCT 1878	Congressional
000686	FREITAG, Paulina	1m	W	D.C.	02 OCT 1874	Congressional
020450	FREMAN, Rebekah	3y	C	D.C.	15 JUN 1879	Harmony
002472	FRENCH, Ann Martha	85y	W	Md.	08 MAR 1875	Convent
019432	FRENCH, Jane	33y	W	Eng.	17 MAR 1879	Philadelphia, Pa.
016954	FRENCH, Martha Ellen	6m	W	D.C.	08 AUG 1878	Congressional
005867	FRENCH, Mary A.	53y	W	Ire.	26 DEC 1875	Baltimore, Md.
019904	FRENCH, Richard H.	59y	C	Md.	26 APR 1879	Harmony
008254	FRENCH, Sallie S.J.	66y	W	Conn.	14 JUL 1876	Glenwood
007775	FRENZEL, Harry A.	22y	W	N.Y.	22 JUN 1876	Presbyterian
008715	FRERE, George D.	21d	W	D.C.	17 AUG 1876	Mt. Olivet
007496	FREW, Walker	19m	W	Va.	04 JUN 1876	Mattox Creek, Va.
001103	FREY, Infant of Andrew	1d	W	D.C.	10 NOV 1874	Oak Hill
010737	FREYE, Joseph	55y	W	Ger.	22 FEB 1877	Soldier's Home
006748	FREYHOLD, Barbara Agnes (Gluemer)	48y	W	Ger.	20 MAR 1876	Glenwood
016086	FREYRE, Manuel, Col.	63y	W	Peru	09 JUN 1878	Mt. Olivet
013300	FRIEBUS, Infant of G.	17h	W	D.C.	25 SEP 1877	Cox's B.G.
016384	FRIEDMAN, Mrs.	c.80y	W	Pol.	01 JUL 1878	Washington Hebrew
017022	FRIEDRICH, Margaret Honor	38y	W	Ind.	12 AUG 1878	Prospect Hill
006848	FRIEDRICHS, John	46y	W	Ger.	28 MAR 1876	Prospect Hill
006596	FRIEDRICKS, Charles William	6d	W	D.C.	08 MAR 1876	Prospect Hill
017090	FRIETSOH, Joseph	4d	W	D.C.	18 AUG 1878	Prospect Hill
010993	FRISBEY, Arther Wm.	3y	W	D.C.	15 MAR 1877	Oak Hill
013034	FRISBY, Mary	1y	C	D.C.	31 AUG 1877	Mt. Olivet
016373	FRISBY, Mattie	10m	C	D.C.	30 JUN 1878	Mt. Olivet
018722	FRISBY, Thomas	50y	W	Eng.	19 JAN 1879	Congressional
014038	FRISBY, William	17y	C	Md.	08 DEC 1877	Potters Field
018160	FRISTOE, Julia	c.40y	W	D.C.	26 NOV 1878	Oak Hill
004750	FRISY, Maria L.	17d	C	D.C.	25 AUG 1875	Mt. Pleasant
010401	FRITCH, Caroline Louisa	39y	W	Ger.	25 JAN 1877	Presbyterian/Oak Hill
018810	FRIZELL, John	62y	W	Va.	25 JAN 1879	Tennallytown
011363	FRIZZELL, Wm. Ignatius	6y	W	D.C.	17 APR 1877	Mt. Olivet
019005	FROHBARTH, Henry	57y	W	Ger.	09 FEB 1879	Hospital

District of Columbia Death Records, August 1, 1874 to July 31, 1879

No.	Name	Age	Race	Birth	Death Date	Burial Place
018484	FROHLICK, Infant of Geo.	5d	W	D.C.	28 DEC 1878	St. Mary's
000188	FROST, Clarence	4y	W	D.C.	14 AUG 1874	Congressional
015075	FROST, Henrietta	3y	C	D.C.	15 MAR 1878	Mt. Pleasant
001335	FROST, Maria C.	32y	C	Va.	07 DEC 1874	Arlington, Va.
009381	FRY, Alice Sophronia	34y	W	D.C.	11 OCT 1876	Congressional
003017f	FRY, Bernetta	c.22y	W	D.C.	17 APR 1875	Oak Hill
015562	FRY, George Dallas	33y	W	D.C.	30 APR 1878	Congressional
020624	FRY, Oscar Edgar	9m	W	D.C.	26 JUN 1879	Congressional
003976	FRY, Smith	23y	C	Va.	03 JUL 1875	Little Falls, Md.
005414	FRY, Washington	66y	C	Va.	10 NOV 1875	Ebenezer
018769	FRY, William	3y	C	D.C.	22 JAN 1879	Harmony
001440	FRYE, James H.	68y	W	D.C.	20 DEC 1874	Presbyterian[1]
010047	FRYE, Lizzie	70y	C	Va.	22 DEC 1876	Young Mens
009578	FRYE, Louis Wesley	1m	C	D.C.	30 OCT 1876	Young Mens
009521	FUCHS, Babet	67y	W	Ger.	25 OCT 1876	Adas Israel
000481	FUCHS, Michael George	21d	W	D.C.	11 SEP 1874	Prospect Hill
012727	FUERSINGER, Bertha	5m	W	D.C.	08 AUG 1877	St. Mary's
010874	FUGAZE, Mary	74y	W	Italy	05 MAR 1877	St. Mary's
020611	FUGH, Caroline	27y	W	Md.	25 JUN 1879	Baltimore, Md.
003134	FUGITT, Alfred	28y	W	Va.	26 APR 1875	Congressional
007466	FUGITT, Eugene	7m	W	D.C.	02 JUN 1876	Congressional
010605	FUGITT, Jarrard Henry	61y	W	Md.	13 FEB 1877	Congressional
001573	FUGITTE, James A.	54y	W	Va.	01 JAN 1875	Congressional
015692	FULLALOVE, Ann A.	50y	W	D.C.	12 MAY 1878	Holy Rood/Oak Hill
000551	FULLER, [blank]	71y	W	N.Y.	18 SEP 1874	Methodist, E.
002689	FULLER, Blanche Williams	12y	W	Ind.	22 MAR 1875	Glenwood
010453	FULLER, David	55y	W	Ire.	30 JAN 1877	Mt. Olivet
016048	FULLER, Josephine Louise	33y	W	D.C.	07 JUN 1878	Oak Hill
010115	FULLER, Jotham B.	52y	W	N.Y.	29 DEC 1876	Congressional
003605	FULLER, Sandy	76y	C	Va.	11 JUN 1875	Brightwood
001081	FULLER, Susannah M.	36y	W	Md.	08 NOV 1874	Oak Hill
006633	FULSE, Infant of Thomas	9d	C	D.C.	10 MAR 1876	Potters Field
020755	FULTON, George Frost	3y	W	N.H.	04 JUL 1879	Glenwood
017514	FULTON, William	34y	W	Scot.	24 SEP 1878	Glenwood
014626	FURCRON, Charles H.	6m	W	D.C.	01 FEB 1878	Congressional
002312	FURGERSON, Benjamin	48y	C	Va.	25 FEB 1875	Beckett's
005185a	FURGERSON, Edwd.	1y	C	D.C.	18 OCT 1875	Ebenezer
001385	FURGERSON, Julia	40y	C	D.C.	14 DEC 1874	Harmony
002318	FURGERSON, Rebecca	40y	C	D.C.	25 FEB 1875	Beckett's
004429	FURGERSON, Roberta	6d	C	N.W.	03 AUG 1875	Harmony
007673	FURGESON, Reuben J.	30y	C	Va.	16 JUN 1876	Ebenezer
017640	FURGISON, Harriet	60y	C	D.C.	05 OCT 1878	Potters Field
020155	FURGUSON, Alex. Marshall	8m	C	D.C.	20 MAY 1879	Beckett's
004769f	FURGUSON, Allen Virginia	1y	W	Pa.	26 AUG 1875	Methodist[2]
010736	FURGUSON, Infant of John	6m	C	D.C.	22 FEB 1877	Young Mens
003054f	FURGUSON, Milton	28y	W	D.C.	20 APR 1875	Methodist
011776	FURLONG, Annie	6m	W	D.C.	02 JUN 1877	Congressional
019610	FURLONG, James Martin Henry	15y	W	D.C.	31 MAR 1879	Mt. Olivet
020678	FURLONG, Margaret, Mrs.	63y	W	Ire.	30 JUN 1879	Mt. Olivet
007674	FUSS, James C.	2m	W	D.C.	16 JUN 1876	Glenwood
015927	FUSS, Lula Blanche	5m	W	D.C.	31 MAY 1878	Congressional
007319	FUSS, Mary	19y	W	Md.	16 MAY 1876	St. Mary's

[1] Removed November 14, 1907 to Congressional Cemetery.
[2] Place of burial given is Methodist burying ground, Ebenezer Station.

No.	Name	Age	Race	Birth	Death Date	Burial Place
G						
010586	GADDIS, Harry Powell	5y	W	D.C.	11 FEB 1877	Congressional
013695	GADDIS, Julia A.	77y	W	Md.	01 NOV 1877	Congressional
017652	GADDIS, Margaret	42y	W	Ire.	06 OCT 1878	Congressional
009238	GADFORD, John W.C.	1m	W	D.C.	29 SEP 1876	Mt. Olivet
011058	GAHAM, Mary Magdalene	11m	C	D.C.	21 MAR 1877	Mt. Olivet
006668	GAINES, Caroline	18y	C	U.S.	14 MAR 1876	Potters Field
002234	GAINES, Collins	30y	C	Va.	19 FEB 1875	Baltimore, Md.
018933	GAINES, Elizabeth	85y	C	France	03 FEB 1879	Mt. Olivet
014358	GAINES, Mary Jane	5y	C	Va.	08 JAN 1878	Beckett's
003402	GAINES, Spencer P.	30y	C	Va.	22 MAY 1875	Young Mens
013740	GAINS, Francis	71y	C	Va.	05 NOV 1877	Harmony
017712	GAINS, William	7d	C	D.C.	12 OCT 1878	Potters Field
001607	GAIT, Willie	1y	W	D.C.	04 JAN 1875	Mt. Olivet
007214	GAITHER, Alice Virginia	5m	M	D.C.	05 MAY 1876	Ebenezer
013904	GAITHER, Catharine	50y	W	D.C.	24 NOV 1877	Potters Field
007135	GAITHER, Eliza Ann	59y	W	D.C.	27 APR 1876	Glenwood
009041	GAITHER, Francis Singleton	40y	W	D.C.	12 SEP 1876	Glenwood
003977	GAITHER, John	4y	C	Md.	03 JUL 1875	Ebenezer
014369	GALER, Walter	6m	W	D.C.	09 JAN 1878	Bladensburg, Md.
010436	GALES, Clarence	1y	C	D.C.	29 JAN 1877	Mt. Zion
000926	GALES, Infant of Louisa	18h	M	D.C.	24 OCT 1874	Beckett's
000861	GALES, John	20y	M	Va.	19 OCT 1874	Potters Field
017807	GALES, Lemuel	4d	C	D.C.	20 OCT 1874	Harmony
018200	GALES, Seaton	51y	W	N.C.	29 NOV 1878	Raleigh, N.C.
001028	GALEY, Infant of Adam	2h	W	D.C.	03 NOV 1874	Congressional
020391	GALLAGHER, Catharine	82y	W	Ire.	11 JUN 1879	Mt. Olivet
008642	GALLAGHER, Francis	2y	W	D.C.	10 AUG 1876	Mt. Olivet
009237	GALLAGHER, James	15m	W	D.C.	29 SEP 1876	Mt. Olivet
007032	GALLAGHER, Louisa	1y	C	D.C.	17 APR 1876	Mt. Pleasant
004493	GALLAGHER, Patrick	67y	W	Ire.	07 AUG 1875	Holy Rood
020790	GALLAGHER, Wm. T.	10m	W	D.C.	06 JUL 1879	Mt. Olivet
010516	GALLAHER, John S.	80y	W	W.Va.	04 FEB 1877	Charlestown, W.Va.
000867	GALLANT, Rebecca	83y	W	D.C.	19 OCT 1874	Mt. Olivet
011574	GALLAUDET, Sophia	79y	W	Conn.	12 MAY 1877	Hartford, Conn.
000560	GALLAWAY, John	59y	W	D.C.	19 SEP 1874	Mt. Olivet
005824	GALLAWAY, Priscilla	70y	C	Va.	22 DEC 1875	Young Mens
012399	GALLAWAY, Van Ness C.	2m	C	D.C.	17 JUL 1877	Mt. Zion
004594	GALLERY, Annie	2y	C	D.C.	14 AUG 1875	Mt. Pleasant
015491	GALLERY, Josephine	36y	C	Md.	23 APR 1878	Young Mens
016652	GALLOWAY, Edgar Sydney	3y	W	D.C.	18 JUL 1878	Baltimore, Md.
011618	GALLOWAY, Isabella	38y	C	Md.	16 MAY 1877	Bladensburg, Md.
012386	GALLOWAY, Joseph	30y	C	Md.	16 JUL 1877	Potters Field
010658	GALLOWAY, Luke	25y	C	Md.	16 FEB 1877	Young Mens
005280	GALLOWAY, Mary	40y	C	Md.	27 OCT 1875	Mt. Olivet
003080	GALOWAY, Amos	32y	C	Md.	21 APR 1875	Mt. Olivet
002749	GALT, Bessie	3y	W	D.C.	26 MAR 1875	Oak Hill
003324	GALT, Edgar Roy	9m	W	D.C.	14 MAY 1875	Oak Hill
003161	GALT, Eliza	76y	W	Md.	29 APR 1875	Congressional
013884	GALT, James V.	40y	W	D.C.	22 NOV 1877	Oak Hill
014781	GALVIN, Luly	2y	W	D.C.	16 FEB 1878	Holy Rood
000664	GALWAY, Tinny	96y	C	Md.	29 SEP 1874	Harmony
017155	GAMER, Infant of S.G.	6h	W	D.C.	23 AUG 1878	Congressional
010803	GANA, Ygnacio Zentens	53y	W	Chili	27 FEB 1877	Mt. Olivet
006733	GANDER, Ewd.	27y	W	Eng.	19 MAR 1876	Graceland

No.	Name	Age	Race	Birth	Death Date	Burial Place
018714	GANGEWER, Edwin E.	52y	W	Pa.	18 JAN 1879	Glenwood
011317	GANN, Infant of Louisa	4h	C	D.C.	13 APR 1877	Potters Field
002415	GANNON, Ada E.	2m	W	D.C.	04 MAR 1875	Congressional
000066	GANNON, Catherine	1y	W	D.C.	05 AUG 1874	Mt. Olivet
020534	GANNON, Patrick	32y	W	Ire.	20 JUN 1879	Mt. Olivet
006587	GANNON, Thomas Joseh	3w	W	D.C.	07 MAR 1876	Mt. Olivet
007985	GANT, Alexander	32y	C	Md.	03 JUL 1876	Ebenezer
010965	GANT, Ann Elizabeth	9d	C	D.C.	14 MAR 1877	Mt. Olivet
005403	GANT, Augusta	5y	C	D.C.	09 NOV 1875	Ebenezer
003436	GANT, Bassil	78y	C	Va.	25 MAY 1875	Potters Field
003135	GANT, Charles	13y	C	D.C.	26 APR 1875	Mt. Pleasant
019641	GANT, Dennis	85y	C	Md.	03 APR 1879	Mt. Olivet
004414	GANT, Elizabeth	110y	C	Va.	02 AUG 1875	Ebenezer
003370	GANT, Elizabeth	4y	C	D.C.	20 MAY 1875	Ebenezer
014265	GANT, Elizabeth	41y	C	Md.	30 DEC 1877	Young Mens
019067	GANT, Ely	10y	C	D.C.	14 FEB 1879	Young Mens
016873	GANT, Infant of Warren	3d	W	D.C.	02 AUG 1878	Stafford C.H., Va.
001055	GANT, Isreal	35y	C	Md.	05 NOV 1874	Mt. Zion
019683	GANT, Jane	10d	C	D.C.	07 APR 1879	Payne's
001287	GANT, Jeremiah	96y	C	Va.	02 DEC 1874	Young Mens
009687	GANT, John William	34y	C	Md.	13 NOV 1876	Harmony
018108	GANT, Joseph	1m	C	D.C.	21 NOV 1878	Mt. Olivet
004712	GANT, Louisa	1y	C	D.C.	22 AUG 1875	Mt. Olivet
015307	GANT, Margaret	c.30y	C	Md.	07 APR 1878	Payne's
019961	GANT, Margaret	33y	C	D.C.	02 MAY 1879	Beckett's
020789	GANT, Margrett	20y	C	D.C.	06 JUL 1879	Beckett's
021080	GANT, Mary J.	30y	C	Va.	24 JUL 1879	Mt. Zion
002809	GANT, Mathilda	71y	C	D.C.	31 MAR 1875	Holy Rood
007309	GANT, Moses	49y	C	Md.	15 MAY 1876	Harmony
000523	GANT, Nancy	60y	C	Md.	15 SEP 1874	Mt. Zion
018880	GANT, Patsey	6m	C	D.C.	30 JAN 1879	Mt. Olivet
006109	GANT, Samuel	58y	C	Md.	23 JAN 1876	Beckett's
007953	GANT, Samuel	4m	C	D.C.	01 JUL 1876	Ebenezer
014346	GANT, Sarah	7m	M	D.C.	07 JAN 1878	Beckett's
011086	GANT, Thomas	2m	C	D.C.	23 MAR 1877	Beckett's
013805	GANT, Tracey	6m	W	D.C.	12 NOV 1877	Alexandria, Va.
002439	GANT, Willie	4d	C	D.C.	05 MAR 1875	Ebenezer
015722	GANT, Willie	1y	C	D.C.	14 MAY 1878	Beckett's
018881	GANTS, James	5m	C	D.C.	30 JAN 1879	Beckett's
000334	GANTT, Louisa	1y	C	Md.	27 AUG 1874	Mt. Olivet
004505	GANTT, Otho T.	55y	C	Md.	08 AUG 1875	Harmony
004928	GANTT, Richard	9d	M	D.C.	06 SEP 1875	Mt. Pleasant
013403	GANTT, Roberta E.	34y	W	Md.	04 OCT 1877	Barnabas Church
004775	GANTZ, Marion	1m	W	D.C.	27 AUG 1875	Baltimore, Md.
010835	GANZHORN, Eva E.	2m	W	D.C.	02 MAR 1877	Prospect Hill
017954	GANZHORN, George H.	6m	W	D.C.	05 NOV 1878	Prospect Hill
007326	GARDNER, Amelia	45y	C	Md.	17 MAY 1876	Mt. Olivet
010081	GARDNER, Ann Eliza McLean, Mrs.	77y	W	N.Y.	26 DEC 1876	Congressional
001359	GARDNER, Ellen	75y	C	Md.	10 DEC 1874	Mt. Olivet
010341	GARDNER, Genevieve	1y	W	D.C.	19 JAN 1877	Mt. Olivet
019420	GARDNER, Hannah Jane	1y	W	D.C.	16 MAR 1879	Glenwood
000546	GARDNER, Henry	33y	C	Va.	17 SEP 1874	Beckett's
008947	GARDNER, Henry	1y	C	D.C.	03 SEP 1876	Beckett's
005174	GARDNER, Infant of George	16h	W	D.C.	17 OCT 1875	Congressional
005660	GARDNER, Mary Anna	67y	W	D.C.	05 DEC 1875	Potters Field
003442	GARDNER, Mary George	37y	C	Md.	26 MAY 1875	Mt. Zion

District of Columbia Death Records, August 1, 1874 to July 31, 1879

No.	Name	Age	Race	Birth	Death Date	Burial Place
009531	GARFIELD, Edward	1y	W	D.C.	25 OCT 1876	Nivus, Ohio?
010174	GARGARI, Dominica	50y	W	Italy	05 JAN 1877	Hospital
006610	GARGAS, C.A.	9m	W	D.C.	09 MAR 1876	Mt. Olivet
004711	GARGENS, Martha Elizabeth	1y	W	D.C.	22 AUG 1875	Rock Creek
002660	GARLAND, Mary	3y	C	D.C.	20 MAR 1875	Young Mens
004494	GARNER, Annie	3m	C	D.C.	07 AUG 1875	Young Mens
006031	GARNER, Charles	2y	C	D.C.	15 JAN 1876	Ebenezer
017771	GARNER, George, Jr.	32y	W	D.C.	17 OCT 1878	Glenwood
015894	GARNER, George W., Sr.	65y	W	Md.	29 MAY 1878	Glenwood
001137	GARNER, Henr	31y	C	Md.	13 NOV 1874	Beckett's
010044	GARNER, James W.	71y	W	Va.	21 DEC 1876	Glenwood
011215	GARNER, John R.	52y	W	Md.	04 APR 1877	Congressional
015427	GARNER, Joseph	1m	C	D.C.	17 APR 1878	Young Mens
016020	GARNER, Lillie	23y	W	Va.	05 JUN 1878	Congressional
011444	GARNER, Mary	75y	C	Md.	27 APR 1877	Ebenezer
016128	GARNER, Vincent	56y	C	D.C.	12 JUN 1878	Potters Field
005061a	GARNET, William H.	10d	C	D.C.	05 OCT 1875	Ebenezer
012654	GARNETT, Charles	10m	C	D.C.	03 AUG 1877	Ebenezer
009882	GARNETT, Eliza	1y	C	D.C.	06 DEC 1876	Potters Field
005584	GARNETT, George	52y	C	Md.	27 NOV 1875	Potters Field
019682	GARNETT, Sally	35y	C	Va.	07 APR 1879	Mt. Pleasant
014113	GARNETT, Sarah Anne	34y	C	Va.	16 DEC 1877	Beckett's
019759	GARNETT, Susan	c.35y	C	Md.	13 APR 1879	Harmony
011610	GARNETTA, Ezra	5m	C	D.C.	16 MAY 1877	Beckett's
016874	GARRETT, Ann Jane	60y	W	D.C.	02 AUG 1878	Congressional
015024	GARRETT, George	4m	W	Pa.	11 MAR 1878	Herndon, Va.
015759	GARRETT, Lucy Arena	1y	C	D.C.	18 MAY 1878	Mt. Olivet
018619	GARRETT, Mary L.	54y	W	Va.	09 JAN 1879	Congressional
001990	GARRETT, Minerva	2y	C	D.C.	02 FEB 1875	Harmony
004197	GARRETT, Oscar	5y	W	D.C.	19 JUL 1875	Congressional
005025	GARRETT, Saml. Jackson	24y	W	D.C.	13 SEP 1875	Congressional
001199	GARRETT, Samuel	32y	W	Ire.	20 NOV 1874	Glenwood
017229	GARRETT, William H.	38y	M	Va.	28 AUG 1878	Harmony
008744	GARRISON, Francis	62y	W	N.Y.	19 AUG 1876	Hospital, Government
001298	GARRISON, Mary Ann	56y	W	Va.	03 DEC 1874	Glenwood
003545f	GARRISON, Thomas	23y	C	D.C.	06 JUN 1875	Harmony
018456	GARROW, Mary Ellen	5y	C	D.C.	25 DEC 1878	Payne's
020711	GARTHWAIT, John A.	34y	W	Md.	02 JUL 1879	Congressional
003851	GARTLAND, Mary C.	2m	W	D.C.	26 JUN 1875	Mt. Olivet
014569	GARTON, Mary C.	38y	W	N.Y.	27 JAN 1878	Congressional
010697	GARTRILL, John M.	40y	W	Md.	19 FEB 1877	Glenwood
016126	GARVER, Bridget Margareth	6w	W	D.C.	12 JUN 1878	Holy Rood
001309	GARVEY, John	35y	W	Ire.	05 DEC 1874	Holy Rood
010489	GARVEY, Matt	6y	W	Va.	03 FEB 1877	Holy Rood
002750	GARVEY, Walter	1y	W	D.C.	26 MAR 1875	Mt. Olivet
010094	GARVEY, Wm.	50y	W	Ire.	27 DEC 1876	Holy Rood
000294	GARY, Sarah Ann	32y	W	Va.	23 AUG 1874	Congressional
004413	GASAWAY, Harriet	75y	C	D.C.	02 AUG 1875	Jones Chapel
020231	GASAWAY, Madelia Delores	19y	C	D.C.	30 MAY 1879	Harmony
008643	GASAWAY, Perry	19y	C	Md.	11 AUG 1876	Ebenezer
016650	GASKIN, James	1y	C	D.C.	18 JUL 1878	Mt. Olivet
000588	GASKINS, Amelia, Mrs.	68y	W	Va.	21 SEP 1874	Oak Hill
005607	GASKINS, Ann	23y	C	Va.	30 NOV 1875	Harmony
013080	GASKINS, Ann Elizabeth	2y	C	D.C.	04 SEP 1877	Payne's
014888	GASKINS, Carrie	7d	W	D.C.	27 FEB 1878	Oak Hill
007234	GASKINS, Catharine Virginia	33y	W	Va.	07 MAY 1876	Oak Hill

District of Columbia Death Records, August 1, 1874 to July 31, 1879

No.	Name	Age	Race	Birth	Death Date	Burial Place
004140	GASKINS, Chlora Ann	17y	C	D.C.	15 JUL 1875	Potters Field
006320	GASKINS, George	1y	W	D.C.	12 FEB 1876	Oak Hill
003336	GASKINS, Robt.	6m	C	D.C.	15 MAY 1875	Potters Field
007841	GASKINS, Virginia C.	1m	W	D.C.	25 JUN 1876	Oak Hill
002611	GASKINS, William	78y	C	Va.	17 MAR 1875	Ebenezer
012458	GASS, Bessie Virginia	c.2y	W	D.C.	21 JUL 1877	Congressional
014347	GASS, Dianthe	38y	W	N.Y.	07 JAN 1878	Congressional
016346	GASS, Frederick William	5m	W	D.C.	28 JUN 1878	Congressional
017081	GASS, Laura V.	27y	W	D.C.	17 AUG 1878	Congressional
007796	GASSAWAY, Emma	1y	C	D.C.	23 JUN 1876	Moore's
018399	GASSAWAY, Margaret	52y	C	Md.	20 DEC 1878	Sligo, Md.
013598	GASSAWAY, Mary Jane	50y	C	Md.	23 OCT 1877	Harmony
010324	GASSAWAY, William Henry	4m	C	D.C.	17 JAN 1877	Ebenezer
009019	GASSNER, Nicholas	35y	W	Ger.	10 SEP 1876	Hospital
004737	GASSWAY, Chas. Joshua	19y	C	Md.	24 AUG 1875	Mt. Olivet
015231	GASTON, Genevieve	3m	W	Pa.	30 MAR 1878	Mt. Olivet
014934	GASWAY, John	10m	C	Md.	03 MAR 1878	Brightwood
009441	GASWAY, Nathan	1m	C	D.C.	17 OCT 1876	Moore's
009190	GASZYNSKI, Malvina	66y	W	Eng.	24 SEP 1876	Glenwood
003048	GATCHEL, Edna R.	4m	W	D.C.	19 APR 1875	Glenwood
007723	GATCHELL, Theodore F.	4m	W	D.C.	19 JUN 1876	Glenwood
005066	GATELY, Malachi	39y	W	Ire.	16 SEP 1875	Mt. Olivet
003200	GATES, Daniel Philip	8m	C	D.C.	02 MAY 1875	Mt. Zion
001666	GATES, Earnest V.	6m	W	D.C.	09 JAN 1875	Congressional
013628	GATES, George H.	31y	W	D.C.	25 OCT 1877	Congressional
001388	GATES, Infant	6d	W	D.C.	14 DEC 1874	Mt. Olivet
004694	GATES, Infant of Louis A.	1d	W	D.C.	21 AUG 1875	Congressional
017268	GATES, Julia May	1y	W	D.C.	31 AUG 1878	Congressional
016329	GATES, Lilly Mabel	2y	W	D.C.	27 JUN 1878	Mt. Olivet
017341	GATES, Mary M.	39y	C	D.C.	07 SEP 1878	Holy Rood
015550	GATES, Samuel Winfield	70y	W	D.C.	29 APR 1878	Congressional
010693	GATEWOOD, John Henry	10m	C	D.C.	19 FEB 1877	Potters Field
006097	GATEWOOD, Robert H.	11m	W	D.C.	22 JAN 1876	Mt. Pleasant
006296	GATEWOOD, William	30y	C	Va.	10 FEB 1876	Young Mens
000796	GATH, John	50y	W	Italy	13 OCT 1874	St. Mary's
003850	GATRELL, Mary	4m	W	D.C.	26 JUN 1875	Glenwood
020338	GATTI, Maria Angela	8m	W	D.C.	08 JUN 1879	St. Mary's
012675	GATTON, John	29y	W	D.C.	05 AUG 1877	Congressional
013478	GAUDEMAR, Mary Frances	50y	W	D.C.	11 OCT 1877	Mt. Olivet
009113	GAUNT, Elizabeth	63y	C	Md.	17 SEP 1876	Montgomery Co., Md.
016398	GAUNT, Raymond	8m	C	D.C.	02 JUL 1878	Harmony
016201	GAUPHEN, Jane	35y	C	Va.	17 JUN 1878	Potters Field
005217a	GAUTIER, Marie Siarnia	29y	W	D.C.	20 OCT 1875	Mt. Olivet
012121	GAWLER, Harry F.	17y	W	D.C.	29 JUN 1877	Oak Hill
011404	GAYER, Bridget	30y	W	Ire.	23 APR 1877	Mt. Olivet
007136	GAYER, Mary C.	37y	W	Ire.	27 APR 1876	Mt. Olivet
015052	GAYLE, Ellis H.	11m	W	D.C.	13 MAR 1878	Oak Hill
005024	GAYNOR, Johanna	2y	C	D.C.	13 SEP 1875	Moore's
000599	GAYNOR, Notley Henry	11m	C	D.C.	22 SEP 1874	Moore's
004048	GEANY, James	2m	W	D.C.	08 JUL 1875	Holy Rood
020147	GEANY, Mary	41y	W	Del.	19 MAY 1879	Holy Rood
016203	GEARY, Geraldine	1y	W	D.C.	17 JUN 1878	Mt. Olivet
009604	GEARY, William	88y	W	Ire.	02 NOV 1876	Mt. Olivet
020830	GEBHARDT, Allai Paulin	11m	W	D.C.	08 JUL 1879	Prospect Hill
015221	GEDDES, Robert	75y	W	Md.	29 MAR 1878	Congressional
009713	GEE, Henry	65y	W	D.C.	17 NOV 1876	Congressional

District of Columbia Death Records, August 1, 1874 to July 31, 1879   125

No.	Name	Age	Race	Birth	Death Date	Burial Place
011108	GEE, Martha	42y	C	Va.	25 MAR 1877	Mt. Zion
014683	GEE, Mary Charlotte	44y	W	D.C.	06 FEB 1878	Congressional
012976	GEIER, Bernard Elarius	2y	W	D.C.	27 AUG 1877	St. Mary's
017675	GEIGER, Alexander	46y	W	Ger.	08 OCT 1878	Prospect Hill
015147	GEIGER, Isabella, Mrs.	42y	W	Md.	22 MAR 1878	Mt. Olivet
005385	GEIGER, Jane Harriet	40y	W	Eng.	07 NOV 1875	Glenwood
011692	GEIGER, John	14d	W	D.C.	24 MAY 1877	Holy Rood
002028	GEIGER, Mary	5d	W	D.C.	04 FEB 1875	Prospect Hill
011479	GEISEKING, Caroline D.	57y	W	Ger.	01 MAY 1877	Oak Hill
000648	GELETZER, Maria Magdalena	1y	W	D.C.	27 SEP 1874	Prospect Hill
004751	GELIYER, Lizzie	8d	W	D.C.	25 AUG 1875	St. Mary's
015319	GELOS, Marie	27y	W	Luce	08 APR 1878	Mt. Olivet
004366	GELTRESS, Wm. T.	3m	W	D.C.	29 JUL 1875	Mt. Olivet
010939	GENT, Schurte	1y	C	D.C.	11 MAR 1877	Ebenezer
020354	GENTES, Ella Maria	1y	W	D.C.	09 JUN 1879	Prospect Hill
006546	GENTHER, Joseph F.R.	2m	W	D.C.	04 MAR 1876	Mt. Olivet
019653	GENTRY, Jacob	34y	W	Tenn.	04 APR 1879	Hospital
013081	GENZEROTH, Otto	12y	W	D.C.	04 SEP 1877	Prospect Hill
013870	GEOFFREY, Thos.	4m	W	D.C.	20 NOV 1877	Mt. Olivet
016019	GEORGE, Ann	3m	C	D.C.	05 JUN 1878	Mt. Olivet
005630	GEORGE, Geo. W.	43y	W	N.H.	02 DEC 1875	Arlington, Va.
005247	GEORGE, Jane	40y	C	Va.	23 OCT 1875	Mt. Pleasant
018322	GEORGE, Maria	2m	W	D.C.	13 DEC 1878	Mt. Olivet
003547	GEORGE, Mary Lee	52y	W	N.Y.	07 JUN 1875	Glenwood
006205	GEORGE, Spencer	11y	C	Va.	01 FEB 1876	Young Mens
003444	GEORGE, Whitson	16y	C	D.C.	26 MAY 1875	Harmony
007990	GEORGE, William	3d	W	D.C.	03 JUL 1876	Mt. Olivet
019319	GEORGIE, Carrie	10y	C	D.C.	08 MAR 1879	Beckett's
013159	GERARD, Nathaniel R.	22y	W	N.Y.	11 SEP 1877	Graceland
018660	GERECKE, Lisette	74y	W	Ger.	13 JAN 1879	Congressional
010538	GERSBACH, Anna D.	7m	W	D.C.	06 FEB 1877	Prospect Hill
017306	GERSBACK, Mary Ann R.	6m	W	D.C.	03 SEP 1878	Prospect Hill
002984	GERTH, Albert	2y	W	Tenn.	14 APR 1875	Prospect Hill
001698	GETT, Henry	36y	C	Va.	11 JAN 1875	Beckett's
015246	GETTINGER, Mary O.	48y	W	D.C.	31 MAR 1878	Glenwood
017305	GETZ, Lizzie	4y	W	D.C.	03 SEP 1878	Prospect Hill
011245	GEYER, Francis	7d	W	D.C.	06 APR 1877	St. Mary's
014684	GHALLAGHE, Elizabeth	70y	W	Pa.	06 FEB 1878	Chester Co., Pa.
015001	GHEEN, Enos W.	28y	W	Pa.	09 MAR 1878	Alexandria, Va.
014627	GHEEN, Malinda	61y	W	Pa.	01 FEB 1878	Philadelphia, Pa.
003734	GIBBINS, Mary, Mrs.	c.45y	W	Ire.	21 JUN 1875	Mt. Olivet
019275	GIBBONS, Irving E.	3y	W	D.C.	04 MAR 1879	Glenwood
005182	GIBBONS, Wm. M.	3y	W	D.C.	26 SEP 1875	Glenwood
017114	GIBBS, Armory B.	21y	W	Mass.	20 AUG 1878	Glenwood
020117	GIBBS, Emma, Mrs.	62y	W	Eng.	16 MAY 1879	Glenwood
006335	GIBBS, Frank	7y	C	D.C.	13 FEB 1876	Harmony
005281	GIBBS, Hattie	1y	C	D.C.	27 OCT 1875	Harmony
014984	GIBBS, James	41y	C	D.C.	08 MAR 1878	Harmony
015136	GIBBS, James	5m	C	D.C.	21 MAR 1878	Harmony
016787	GIBBS, Julia	2y	W	D.C.	27 JUL 1878	Congressional
011416	GIBBS, Laura	2y	C	D.C.	24 APR 1877	Young Mens
002444	GIBBS, Leon	2y	C	D.C.	05 MAR 1875	Harmony
016993	GIBBS, Maria Howard	1y	W	D.C.	10 AUG 1878	Oak Hill
016472	GIBSON, Anakor	52y	C	Va.	06 JUL 1878	Young Mens
003456	GIBSON, Ann, Mrs.	70y	W	Md.	27 MAY 1875	Mt. Olivet
021008	GIBSON, Bessie S.	9m	W	D.C.	19 JUL 1879	Glenwood

District of Columbia Death Records, August 1, 1874 to July 31, 1879

No.	Name	Age	Race	Birth	Death Date	Burial Place
011248	GIBSON, Caroline	64y	C	Va.	06 APR 1877	Moore's
016606	GIBSON, Caroline Elnora	10m	C	D.C.	15 JUL 1878	Family Ground
009289	GIBSON, Catherine	39y	C	Va.	03 OCT 1876	Harmony
010207	GIBSON, Catherine	7y	C	D.C.	07 JAN 1877	Mt. Zion
008969	GIBSON, Catherine T.	17y	W	D.C.	05 SEP 1876	Congressional
013511	GIBSON, Charles E.	7y	W	D.C.	14 OCT 1877	Glenwood
001008	GIBSON, Cora	3m	W	D.C.	01 NOV 1874	Congressional
007359	GIBSON, Daniel	65y	C	Va.	21 MAY 1876	Potters Field
000376	GIBSON, David Emile	8m	W	D.C.	30 AUG 1874	Glenwood
011493	GIBSON, Diana	30y	C	Va.	02 MAY 1877	Potters Field
016554	GIBSON, Edward Smiley	9m	W	D.C.	11 JUL 1878	Rock Creek
006336	GIBSON, Elizabeth	35y	C	Va.	13 FEB 1876	Beckett's
010801	GIBSON, Elizabeth	7y	W	Md.	27 FEB 1877	Mt. Olivet
001046	GIBSON, Elmore	3m	W	D.C.	04 NOV 1874	Congressional
018252	GIBSON, G.W.	35y	M	D.C.	06 DEC 1878	Harmony
001488	GIBSON, George W.	43y	W	D.C.	26 DEC 1874	Congressional
000514	GIBSON, Henry	23y	C	Md.	14 SEP 1874	Mt. Zion
008063	GIBSON, Henry Ellsworth	8m	W	D.C.	08 JUL 1876	Rock Creek
018448	GIBSON, Infant of Walter	8h	C	D.C.	24 DEC 1878	Mt. Pleasant
014952	GIBSON, Infant of William	10min	W	D.C.	05 MAR 1878	Potters Field
008457	GIBSON, Isabella Jane	31y	W	Ire.	28 JUL 1876	Baltimore, Md.
015446	GIBSON, James Jones, M.D.	67y	W	Ind.	19 APR 1878	Congressional
002531	GIBSON, Jas. J., Jr.	32y	W	Tenn.	12 MAR 1875	Alexandria, Va.
020010	GIBSON, Jmaes	24y	C	Va.	06 MAY 1879	Payne's
004096	GIBSON, John	6d	C	D.C.	12 JUL 1875	Harmony
018397	GIBSON, Joseph	79y	W	Ire.	20 DEC 1878	Baltimore, Md.
012091	GIBSON, Joseph H.	5m	W	D.C.	27 JUN 1877	Mt. Olivet
010635	GIBSON, Lula	15y	C	Va.	15 FEB 1877	Beckett's
002245	GIBSON, Lulie May	12y	C	D.C.	19 FEB 1875	Harmony
008900	GIBSON, Margaret G.	1m	W	D.C.	31 AUG 1876	Rock Creek
016263	GIBSON, Maria	80y	W	Va.	22 JUN 1878	Congressional
017793	GIBSON, Martha Emma	16y	W	D.C.	19 OCT 1878	Congressional
006391	GIBSON, Mary Frances	18y	C	Va.	17 FEB 1876	Harmony
001869	GIBSON, Mary J.	58y	W	S.C.	24 JAN 1875	Congressional
006880	GIBSON, Moses	53y	C	Va.	01 APR 1876	Howard Co., Md.
017539	GIBSON, Neley M.	5m	W	D.C.	26 SEP 1878	Mt. Olivet
018321	GIBSON, Philip A.	5m	M	D.C.	13 DEC 1878	Harmony
014795	GIBSON, Prince E.	6m	C	N.Y.	17 FEB 1878	Young Mens
009663	GIBSON, Richard T.	34y	C	D.C.	10 NOV 1876	Harmony
013834	GIBSON, Robert	53y	C	Va.	16 NOV 1877	Potters Field
010632	GIBSON, Sarah Elizabeth	6m	W	D.C.	14 FEB 1877	Oak Hill
017630	GIBSON, Susan	62y	C	Md.	04 OCT 1878	Mt. Pleasant
005026	GIBSON, Victoria	2y	W	D.C.	13 SEP 1875	Congressional
010242	GIBSON, William	6m	C	D.C.	10 JAN 1877	Harmony
002246	GIBSON, William Francis	4y	M	D.C.	19 FEB 1875	Harmony
013648	GIBSON, William H.	8y	C	D.C.	27 OCT 1877	Potters Field
019336	GIBSON, William H.	1m	C	D.C.	09 MAR 1879	Beckett's
018068	GIBSON, Wm. Henry	1y	C	D.C.	16 NOV 1878	Payne's
017411	GIBSON, Woolman	74y	W	Md.	14 SEP 1878	Congressional
015664	GIDDINGS, Alice	7y	W	D.C.	09 MAY 1878	Graceland
012966	GIDDINGS, John Henry	14y	W	D.C.	26 AUG 1877	Mt. Olivet
006461	GIDEON, George S.	60y	W	D.C.	24 FEB 1876	Oak Hill
002638	GIDEON, Hubert	11m	C	D.C.	18 MAR 1875	Young Mens
018076	GIGSBEE, Agnes	4y	W	D.C.	17 NOV 1878	Oak Hill
004811	GILBERT, Cornelia	10m	M	D.C.	29 AUG 1875	Potters Field
019446	GILBERT, Edward E.	42y	W	N.Y.	18 MAR 1879	Oak Hill

District of Columbia Death Records, August 1, 1874 to July 31, 1879

No.	Name	Age	Race	Birth	Death Date	Burial Place
015551	GILBERT, Ella	26y	W	Me.	29 APR 1878	Portland, Me.
020353	GILBERT, Fanny	75y	C	Va.	09 JUN 1879	Beckett's
008788	GILBERT, George Thomas	1y	C	D.C.	23 AUG 1876	Potters Field
015790	GILBET, Harry	10m	C	D.C.	21 MAY 1878	Young Mens
018620	GILES, Harriet	12y	C	N.J.	09 JAN 1879	Young Mens
017336	GILES, Ida	1y	C	Md.	06 SEP 1878	Beckett's
005346	GILES, Maria Catherine	8y	C	Va.	03 NOV 1875	Harmony
014226	GILES, Marinda	22y	C	Md.	27 DEC 1877	Beckett's
018659	GILES, Martha	64y	C	Va.	13 JAN 1879	Potters Field
012321	GILES, Mary	8m	C	D.C.	11 JUL 1877	Beckett's
015789	GILES, Nettia	20y	C	Va.	21 MAY 1878	Beckett's
007199	GILES, Sarah	c.52y	C	N.C.	04 MAY 1876	Beckett's
008832	GILL, Ann J.	11m	W	D.C.	26 AUG 1876	Congressional
016345	GILL, Florence	9y	W	D.C.	28 JUN 1878	Glenwood
017043	GILL, James	23y	C	Va.	14 AUG 1878	Mt. Pleasant
001504	GILL, John	1m	W	D.C.	27 DEC 1874	Congressional
009135	GILL, Mary E.	7d	C	D.C.	19 SEP 1876	Mt. Pleasant
020207	GILL, Mary J.	1y	W	D.C.	27 MAY 1879	Congressional
004791	GILL, Vinnie Viola	8m	W	D.C.	28 AUG 1875	Glenwood
012022	GILLCHRIST, Edward Otis	27y	W	D.C.	23 JUN 1877	Congressional
005186a	GILLEN, Charles F.	3m	W	D.C.	18 OCT 1875	Mt. Olivet
009513	GILLET, Ransom H.	76y	W	N.Y.	24 OCT 1876	Glenwood
012974	GILLIAM, Eliza Jane	56y	W	Va.	27 AUG 1877	Oak Hill
005040a	GILLIAM, William	63y	W	Va.	03 OCT 1875	Presbyterian
003114	GILLMORE, Andrew	64y	W	Ger.	25 APR 1875	Mt. Olivet
020756	GILLS, Cora Christiana	1y	C	D.C.	04 JUL 1879	Harmony
011605	GILLUM, Betsy	40y	C	Va.	15 MAY 1877	Mt. Olivet
006030	GILLUM, Joseph	6m	M	D.C.	15 JAN 1876	Mt. Olivet
005080	GILLUM, Maria	c.55y	C	Va.	17 SEP 1875	Ebenezer
020695	GILMAN, Mary A.	71y	W	Va.	01 JUL 1879	Fredericksburg, Va.
006679	GILMAN, Zedock Douglass	59y	W	Va.	15 MAR 1876	Congressional
019434	GILMON, Arther	2m	C	D.C.	17 MAR 1879	Mt. Pleasant
011714	GILMON, Thomas A.	53y	W	N.H.	26 MAY 1877	Rock Creek
006066	GILMORE, George	1y	C	D.C.	19 JAN 1876	Potters Field
009764	GILMORE, Infant of Robert	6d	C	D.C.	21 NOV 1876	Young Mens
003524	GILMORE, Zachariah	9y	C	D.C.	04 JUN 1875	Young Mens
010652	GINETA, Harry V.R.	1y	W	D.C.	16 FEB 1877	Mt. Olivet
019784	GINFORD, Susan	2m	C	U.S.	15 APR 1879	Mt. Olivet
010232	GINGS, Mary A.	24y	W	D.C.	09 JAN 1877	Congressional
004901	GINNATY, Mary Ann	35y	W	D.C.	04 SEP 1875	Mt. Olivet
019470	GINNS, James Henry	1m	C	D.C.	20 MAR 1879	Potters Field
016876	GIOVANNONI, Amelia	2y	W	D.C.	02 AUG 1878	Mt. Olivet
003445	GIPSON, Albert	17y	C	Va.	26 MAY 1875	Young Mens
012785	GIRARD, Maggie	21y	W	N.Y	12 AUG 1877	Graceland
013954	GIRAUDAN, Antoine Charles	45y	W	Switz.	28 NOV 1877	Glenwood
011141	GISBURNE, Charles Philos	8y	W	D.C.	28 MAR 1877	Glenwood
006879	GIVEAN, Eliza	67y	C	Md.	01 APR 1876	Potters Field
014045	GIVEN, Clara B.	4y	W	D.C.	09 DEC 1877	Congressional
020667	GIVENS, David	12y	C	Va.	29 JUN 1879	Payne's
010958	GIVENS, Gertrude	1m	C	D.C.	13 MAR 1877	Potters Field
006915	GIVIN, Al	65y	C	Va.	04 APR 1876	Harmony
013353	GLADMON, Bertie	3y	W	D.C.	30 SEP 1877	Mt. Olivet
003826	GLADMON, Darius T.	35y	W	D.C.	25 JUN 1875	Oak Hill
012816	GLADMON, Franklin R.	2y	W	D.C.	15 AUG 1877	Oak Hill
010240	GLADMON, Susan	67y	W	D.C.	09 JAN 1877	Rock Creek
013496	GLASCOW, Mary C.	20y	W	Md.	13 OCT 1877	Congressional

No.	Name	Age	Race	Birth	Death Date	Burial Place
016344	GLASGO, Mary	21y	C	N.J.	28 JUN 1878	Mt. Pleasant
000614	GLASGOW, Baby	1m	C	D.C.	23 SEP 1874	Young Mens
010310	GLASGOW, Charles L.	4y	W	Va.	16 JAN 1877	Graceland
013583	GLASGOW, Mable E.	17d	W	D.C.	21 OCT 1877	Congressional
002650	GLASSCO, Lizzie New.	7d	C	D.C.	19 MAR 1875	Young Mens
008105	GLASSGOW, Augustus R.	45y	W	Md.	09 JUL 1876	Glenwood
002853	GLAUM, Peter	72y	W	Ger.	03 APR 1875	Prospect Hill
006834	GLAUM, Peter	35y	W	Md.	27 MAR 1876	Prospect Hill
010448	GLEASON, Any Mary	14m	W	D.C.	30 JAN 1877	Mt. Olivet
014417	GLEASON, Katy	6y	W	D.C.	14 JAN 1878	Mt. Olivet
017458	GLEASON, Matthew W.	21y	W	D.C.	19 SEP 1878	Mt. Olivet
004015	GLEASON, Patrick	70y	W	Ire.	06 JUL 1875	Mt. Olivet
012511	GLEASON, Patrick	1y	W	D.C.	24 JUL 1877	Mt. Olivet
001419	GLEASON, Wm. Patrick	4y	W	D.C.	17 DEC 1874	Mt. Olivet
017489	GLEAVES, Mary Ann	40y	C	Md.	22 SEP 1878	Chestertown, Md.
005716	GLEID, Ella	7m	C	D.C.	10 DEC 1875	Potters Field
014663	GLENROY, Franklin	49y	W	Pa.	04 FEB 1878	Congressional
016580	GLICK, Caroline J.	46y	W	Ger.	13 JUL 1878	Glenwood
019369	GLOVER, Edward	14y	W	D.C.	12 MAR 1879	Alexandria, Va.
009077	GLOVER, Jane, Mrs.	87y	W	Eng.	14 SEP 1876	Oak Hill
017469	GLOVER, Julia	c.46y	C	D.C.	20 SEP 1878	Beckett's
006421	GMELIN, Mary E.	13h	W	D.C.	20 FEB 1876	Holy Rood
010492	GOBRIGHT, Mary Ann	c.65y	W	D.C.	03 FEB 1877	Glenwood
018263	GOCKELER, George Conrad	7w	W	D.C.	07 DEC 1878	Prospect Hill
004060	GODARD, Sarah	89y	W	Md.	09 JUL 1875	Holy Rood
006534	GODDALE, Mary D.	11m	W	D.C.	03 MAR 1876	Oak Hill
011679	GODDARD, Benjamin F.	59y	W	Md.	23 MAY 1877	Mt. Olivet
015693	GODDARD, John Wm.	2m	W	D.C.	12 MAY 1878	Mt. Olivet
001183	GODDARD, Maggie Isabella	10m	W	D.C.	19 NOV 1874	Mt. Olivet
010843	GODDARD, Vinton	27y	W	D.C.	02 MAR 1877	Mt. Olivet
014509	GODEY, Laura Virginia	26y	W	D.C.	21 JAN 1878	Oak Hill
005079a	GODEY, Samuel T.	28y	W	D.C.	07 OCT 1875	Oak Hill
018398	GODFREY, Infant of Wm.	24h	W	Md.	20 DEC 1878	Rock Creek
019922	GODFREY, Martha	50y	C	Va.	28 APR 1879	Chappel's
020261	GODWIN, Josephine Virginia	29y	W	Va.	01 JUN 1879	Oak Hill
015222	GODWIN, Virginia	28y	W	Va.	29 MAR 1878	Graceland
016631	GODWIN, Wright	40y	W	Va.	17 JUL 1878	Richmond, Va.
017907	GOEBZINGER, Ernest J.	3y	W	D.C.	30 OCT 1878	St. Mary's
010384	GOEINGS, Lilly May	5m	W	D.C.	23 JAN 1877	Congressional
013082	GOELITZER, Frank	5m	W	D.C.	04 SEP 1877	Prospect Hill
012557	GOERNER, Elizabeth	42y	W	Ger.	27 JUL 1877	Prospect Hill
013413	GOERNER, Emel	42y	W	Ger.	06 OCT 1877	Prospect Hill
001219	GOETZINER, Ernst Michael	4m	W	D.C.	23 NOV 1874	St. Mary's
018559	GOETZINGER, John V.	6y	W	D.C.	04 JAN 1879	St. Mary's
011198	GOINES, Patrick	72y	M	Va.	02 APR 1877	Harmony
008002	GOLD, Adeline Alma	47y	W	Ver.	04 JUL 1876	Baltimore, Md.
003355	GOLDAN, Catheran	35y	C	Va.	17 MAY 1875	Ebenezer
020470	GOLDEN, Agnes	4m	W	D.C.	16 JUN 1879	Prospect Hill
014818	GOLDEN, Andrew	68y	C	Va.	19 FEB 1878	Young Mens
002888	GOLDEN, Harry R.	16y	W	D.C.	06 APR 1875	Glenwood
015741	GOLDEN, Lewis	15y	W	D.C.	16 MAY 1878	Congressional
019741	GOLDEN, Sally	23y	C	Va.	12 APR 1879	Beckett's
001874	GOLDEN, Silas	21d	C	D.C.	24 JAN 1875	Ebenezer
014282	GOLDER, Mary Eliza, Mrs.	63y	W	N.Y.	01 JAN 1878	Poughkeepsie, N.Y.
012579	GOLDIN, Jacob	2y	C	Va.	28 JUL 1877	Beckett's
010016	GOLDIN, Prabby Steims	21y	C	D.C.	19 DEC 1876	Glenwood

District of Columbia Death Records, August 1, 1874 to July 31, 1879

No.	Name	Age	Race	Birth	Death Date	Burial Place
010711	GOLDSBOROUGH, Louis M.	72y	W	D.C.	20 FEB 1877	Congressional
013704	GOLDSBOROUGH, Mary L.	2y	W	D.C.	02 NOV 1877	Potters Field
005794	GOLDSMITH, John J.	5m	W	D.C.	19 DEC 1875	Mt. Olivet
013885	GOLDSMITH, Joseph A.	44y	W	Md.	22 NOV 1877	Congressional
007563	GOLEY, Mary	21y	W	D.C.	09 JUN 1876	Prospect Hill
006953	GOLLOWAY, Harriet	52y	W	Mass.	07 APR 1876	Hospital
014519	GOLLY, Mary F.	28y	W	Pa.	22 JAN 1878	Prospect Hill
005415	GONZENBACH, Frederick A.	49y	W	Switz.	10 NOV 1875	Congressional
019140	GONZENBACH, Louise Emma	7m	W	D.C.	21 FEB 1879	Congressional
016553	GOOCH, Sarah	82y	W	Eng.	11 JUL 1878	Rock Creek
011174	GOOD, James	1m	W	Va.	31 MAR 1877	Mt. Olivet
013649	GOOD, Thomas	1y	W	D.C.	27 OCT 1877	Holy Rood
017713	GOOD, Thomas G.	36y	W	D.C.	12 OCT 1878	Presbyterian
010927	GOODFELLOW, James Leslie	1y	W	Pa.	09 MAR 1877	Philadelphia, Pa.
015929	GOODING, Bertie Rebecca	2m	W	D.C.	31 MAY 1878	Holy Rood
013835	GOODING, Joseph A.	19y	C	Barb.	16 NOV 1877	Congressional
002205	GOODLAR, James	2d	C	D.C.	17 FEB 1875	Potters Field
005631	GOODMAN, Bernard	100y	W	Ire.	02 DEC 1875	Holy Rood
011360	GOODMAN, Richard	40y	C	Va.	17 APR 1877	Ebenezer
007497	GOODRICH, James S.	1y	C	D.C.	04 JUN 1876	Mt. Olivet
012323	GOODRIDGE, Levi	85y	C	Md.	12 JUL 1877	Ebenezer
003180	GOODRIDGE, Thomas	9m	C	D.C.	30 APR 1875	Beckett's
014725	GOODWIN, Cathrine T.	3m	W	Md.	09 FEB 1878	Cumberland, Md.
015255	GOODWIN, Thomas	58y	W	D.C.	01 APR 1878	Mt. Olivet
012135	GORBUTT, Wm. H.	46y	W	Pa.	30 JUN 1877	Glenwood
004624	GORDAN, Maria	9y	C	Va.	16 AUG 1875	Ebenezer
005345	GORDEN, Elizabeth	1y	C	D.C.	03 NOV 1875	Ebenezer
001837	GORDON, John H.	67y	W	Md.	22 JAN 1875	Baltimore
005054	GORDON, Albert	1y	C	D.C.	15 SEP 1875	Ebenezer
008408	GORDON, Alexandria	4m	M	D.C.	24 JUL 1876	Harmony
014706	GORDON, Ann Mariah	6d	C	D.C.	08 FEB 1878	Mt. Olivet
008484	GORDON, Annie	5m	C	D.C.	30 JUL 1876	Potters Field
011229	GORDON, Annie	65y	C	Va.	05 APR 1877	Mt. Zion
006111	GORDON, Belle	20y	C	Va.	23 JAN 1876	Potters Field
006628	GORDON, Charles A.	4y	C	D.C.	10 MAR 1876	Young Mens
015928	GORDON, Clara	2y	C	D.C.	31 MAY 1878	Mt. Olivet
015531	GORDON, David	28y	M	D.C.	27 APR 1878	Beckett's
007899	GORDON, Ella	10m	C	D.C.	28 JUN 1876	Mt. Pleasant
010797	GORDON, Ella Eliza	24y	W	D.C.	27 FEB 1877	Glenwood
007759	GORDON, Elnora	2m	C	D.C.	21 JUN 1876	Young Mens
020379	GORDON, Franklin	23y	W	D.C.	10 JUN 1879	Congressional
014234	GORDON, George	3m	C	D.C.	28 DEC 1877	Young Mens
017863	GORDON, George A.	c.44y	W	Va.	26 OCT 1878	Oak Hill
014181	GORDON, Gilbert	34y	C	Md.	23 DEC 1877	Mt. Olivet
001480	GORDON, Harriet	65y	C	Md.	25 DEC 1874	Congressional
000816	GORDON, Infant of Isaac	7d	C	D.C.	15 OCT 1874	Potters Field
008276	GORDON, Infant of James	7d	C	D.C.	15 JUL 1876	Ebenezer
010155	GORDON, Infant of Matilda	7d	C	D.C.	02 JAN 1877	Potters Field
015160	GORDON, Jessie	35y	C	Va.	23 MAR 1878	Graceland
015386	GORDON, John	64y	W	Md.	13 APR 1878	Mt. Olivet
018922	GORDON, John	60y	W	Ire.	02 FEB 1879	Soldier's Home
015874	GORDON, Kate	21y	C	Md.	28 MAY 1878	Mt. Olivet
006375	GORDON, Lillie	1m	C	D.C.	16 FEB 1876	Potters Field
010527	GORDON, Louisa	3m	W	D.C.	05 FEB 1877	Mt. Olivet
011804	GORDON, Lucy A.	50y	C	D.C.	05 JUN 1877	Washington Asylum
016649	GORDON, Maria F.	1y	C	D.C.	18 JUL 1878	Mt. Pleasant

District of Columbia Death Records, August 1, 1874 to July 31, 1879

No.	Name	Age	Race	Birth	Death Date	Burial Place
005638	GORDON, Mary	16y	C	Va.	03 DEC 1875	Harmony
008071	GORDON, Mary Ann	42y	C	D.C.	08 JUL 1876	Mt. Olivet
010751	GORDON, Mollie	1y	C	D.C.	23 FEB 1877	Ebenezer
012975	GORDON, Sarah A.	65y	W	Md.	27 AUG 1877	Congressional
000569	GORDON, Thomas	1y	C	D.C.	19 SEP 1874	Beckett's
019758	GORDON, Walter	1y	C	D.C.	13 APR 1879	Young Mens
016622	GORDON, William Sibly	26y	W	D.C.	16 JUL 1878	Glenwood
019601	GORGESS, Edward Brook	1y	W	D.C.	30 MAR 1879	Mt. Olivet
003415	GORMAN, Agnes	25y	W	Ire.	23 MAY 1875	Mt. Olivet
017342	GORMAN, Annie J.	1m	W	D.C.	07 SEP 1878	Mt. Olivet
015652	GORMAN, Edward M.	32y	W	N.Y.	08 MAY 1878	Mt. Olivet
003159f	GORMAN, Frank	2y	W	Md.	28 APR 1875	Mt. Olivet
019787	GORMAN, John	1y	W	D.C.	15 APR 1879	Mt. Olivet
008577	GORMAN, Patrick	67y	W	Ire.	06 AUG 1876	College
020171	GORMAN, Thomas A.	32y	W	N.H.	22 MAY 1879	Hospital, Government
009722	GORMLIE, Mary	14d	W	D.C.	18 NOV 1876	Glenwood
018992	GOSLING, Susan	45y	W	Va.	08 FEB 1879	Woodbridge, Va.
000946	GOSNELL, Martha J.	46y	W	Md.	27 OCT 1874	Congressional
008903	GOSS, Estelle Agnes	9m	W	D.C.	31 AUG 1876	Congressional
012314	GOSS, Hanora	7m	W	D.C.	11 JUL 1877	Mt. Olivet
019698	GOSS, John James	11m	W	D.C.	08 APR 1879	Mt. Olivet
013313	GOSS, Mabel E.	11m	W	D.C.	26 SEP 1877	Congressional
010898	GOSS, Thomas J.	2m	W	D.C.	07 MAR 1877	Congressional
004083	GOSSAGE, Chas. A.	5d	W	D.C.	11 JUL 1875	Glenwood
001898	GOSSAGE, Edgar Lee	6y	W	Va.	26 JAN 1875	Richmond, Va.
016568	GOTTHELP, Julia	58y	W	Ger.	12 JUL 1878	Washington Hebrew
009974	GOUGH, Thomas W.	76y	W	Md.	15 DEC 1876	Mt. Olivet
010747	GOULD, Fredrich Alberta	5y	W	D.C.	23 FEB 1877	Glenwood
006401	GOULD, John A.	83y	W	Eng.	18 FEB 1876	Mt. Olivet
012231	GOULD, Mary Wilkins	7m	W	D.C.	05 JUL 1877	Baltimore, Md.
010975	GOULD, Willie W.	3y	W	D.C.	14 MAR 1877	Glenwood
016926	GOVERSON, Mary	80y	C	Va.	06 AUG 1878	Graceland
009987	GRACE, James B.	1d	W	D.C.	17 DEC 1876	Congressional
009109	GRACE, John	32y	W	Ire.	17 SEP 1876	Mt. Olivet
008393	GRACERN, William Henry	18y	C	D.C.	23 JUL 1876	Harmony
020566	GRACI, Maria	11m	W	D.C.	22 JUN 1879	Mt. Olivet
011895	GRADY, Adison	4m	C	D.C.	14 JUN 1877	Potters Field
015403	GRADY, Francis	2y	W	D.C.	15 APR 1878	Mt. Olivet
012185	GRADY, Franklin	2y	W	D.C.	02 JUL 1877	Potters Field
019588	GRADY, George	7m	C	D.C.	29 MAR 1879	Potters Field
004170	GRADY, Hellen A.	1m	W	D.C.	17 JUL 1875	Mt. Olivet
020108	GRADY, Infant of Jacob	3d	C	D.C.	15 MAY 1879	Potters Field
014212	GRADY, Infant of Jacob	12h	C	D.C.	26 DEC 1877	Potters Field
014590	GRADY, Infant of Washington	5d	C	D.C.	29 JAN 1878	Mt. Zion
019618	GRADY, Rosetta	3m	C	D.C.	01 APR 1879	Harmony
013987	GRADY, Susan Ann	7d	C	D.C.	02 DEC 1877	Potters Field
012010	GRADY, William	7d	W	D.C.	22 JUN 1877	Mt. Olivet
010770	GRAEFF, Ann	81y	W	Va.	24 FEB 1877	Oak Hill
009206	GRAFF, Barbara	5d	W	D.C.	26 SEP 1876	Prospect Hill
012226	GRAFF, Mary Catherine	20y	W	Md.	05 JUL 1877	Congressional
004377	GRAHAM, Ada	6m	C	D.C.	30 JUL 1875	Beckett's
009137	GRAHAM, Alice Christina	14y	C	D.C.	20 SEP 1876	Mt. Olivet
013179	GRAHAM, Caroline	3y	C	D.C.	13 SEP 1877	Potters Field
000716	GRAHAM, Edward	9m	C	D.C.	05 OCT 1874	Mt. Zion
018298	GRAHAM, Elizabeth Web	64y	W	Ver.	10 DEC 1878	Oak Hill
011507	GRAHAM, Ellen	70y	C	Md.	04 MAY 1877	Young Mens

District of Columbia Death Records, August 1, 1874 to July 31, 1879 131

No.	Name	Age	Race	Birth	Death Date	Burial Place
001708	GRAHAM, Emma	9d	C	D.C.	13 JAN 1875	Mt. Pleasant
012084	GRAHAM, Emma	13y	W	N.Y.	27 JUN 1877	Glenwood
009274	GRAHAM, French	75y	W	D.C.	02 OCT 1876	Congressional
000807	GRAHAM, Infant	20d	W	D.C.	14 OCT 1874	Graceland
018467	GRAHAM, Infant of Caroline	8d	C	D.C.	26 DEC 1878	Potters Field
007200	GRAHAM, Jennie	18y	C	Md.	04 MAY 1876	Young Mens
015137	GRAHAM, John	65y	W	Ire.	21 MAR 1878	Oak Hill
020296	GRAHAM, John Robert	13y	W	Md.	04 JUN 1879	Bladensburg, Md.
018947	GRAHAM, Margaret	8m	C	D.C.	04 FEB 1879	Young Mens
015875	GRAHAM, Mary M.	1y	C	D.C.	28 MAY 1878	Mt. Zion
007290	GRAHAM, Polly	80y	C	Va.	13 MAY 1876	Young Mens
000440	GRAHAM, Willie	7m	C	D.C.	06 SEP 1874	Potters Field
010817	GRAHAME, Johanna	25y	C	Md.	01 MAR 1877	Nonesuch, Md.
013160	GRAMM, Fannie	58y	W	Pa.	11 SEP 1877	Harrisburg, Pa.
000493	GRANDISON, Benjamin	45y	M	D.C.	12 SEP 1874	Holy Rood
007900	GRANDISON, John	1m	C	D.C.	28 JUN 1876	Potters Field
003397	GRANDSON, John	67y	C	Va.	22 MAY 1875	Mt. Pleasant
002501	GRANGER, Margaret	62y	W	D.C.	10 MAR 1875	Congressional
001585	GRANGER, Mary	36y	C	Md.	02 JAN 1875	Mt. Pleasant
007386	GRANISON, Ida	8y	C	D.C.	23 MAY 1876	Ebenezer
001846	GRANNINGER, Rudolph	29y	W	D.C.	23 JAN 1875	Congressional
016941	GRANNISON, Sarah Jane	10y	C	D.C.	07 AUG 1878	Beckett's
000438	GRANT, Charles A.	5y	C	D.C.	06 SEP 1874	Harmony
018486	GRANT, Edward	1y	C	D.C.	28 DEC 1878	Potters Field
008403	GRANT, Frances Abigail	29y	W	D.C.	24 JUL 1876	Congressional
002374	GRANT, Harriet S.	50y	W	N.H.	01 MAR 1875	Congressional
019163	GRANT, Helen	7m	C	D.C.	23 FEB 1879	Young Mens
013362	GRANT, Henry	2y	C	D.C.	01 OCT 1877	Harmony
005902	GRANT, Henry Washington	89y	C	Md.	31 DEC 1875	Mt. Zion
011742	GRANT, James	52y	C	Va.	29 MAY 1877	Baptist
006973	GRANT, John	10m	C	D.C.	09 APR 1876	Young Mens
019785	GRANT, John	2m	C	D.C.	15 APR 1879	Young Mens
018857	GRANT, Juliaetta	15d	C	D.C.	28 JAN 1879	Montgomery Co., Md.
013091	GRANT, Nellie	6m	C	D.C.	05 SEP 1877	Young Mens
019180	GRANT, Nettie	3m	C	D.C.	24 FEB 1879	Potters Field
020625	GRANT, William Madison	6y	W	Va.	26 JUN 1879	Portsmouth, Va.
016515	GRANTLIN, James S.	3y	C	D.C.	09 JUL 1878	Beckett's
005335	GRANTLIN, Wm. T.	5y	C	D.C.	02 NOV 1875	Beckett's
014705	GRASON, George A.	5m	C	D.C.	08 FEB 1878	Beckett's
015087	GRASON, Lizzie	7y	C	Md.	16 MAR 1878	Beckett's
006308	GRASS, Charles	7m	W	D.C.	11 FEB 1876	Prospect Hill
007623	GRASS, Rosena M.	7m	W	D.C.	13 JUN 1876	Prospect Hill
006495	GRASSIE, John Milledge	43y	W	Can.	28 FEB 1876	Congressional
000305	GRAVES, Alice	1y	C	D.C.	24 AUG 1874	Mt. Pleasant
014762	GRAVES, Anna P.	2y	W	Va.	14 FEB 1878	Presbyterian
004666	GRAVES, Benjamin	1y	C	D.C.	19 AUG 1875	Mt. Zion
014528	GRAVES, Clarah	12y	W	D.C.	23 JAN 1878	Presbyterian
008865	GRAVES, Edward	4m	W	D.C.	28 AUG 1876	Holy Rood
019164	GRAVES, Frederick	1y	C	D.C.	23 FEB 1879	Potters Field
010551	GRAVES, George	10m	C	D.C.	07 FEB 1877	Young Mens
015404	GRAVES, Infant of Edward	12h	W	D.C.	15 APR 1878	Congressional
000705	GRAVES, Infant of J.	5h	C	D.C.	03 OCT 1874	Young Mens
015076	GRAVES, Isaac	21y	C	Va.	15 MAR 1878	Potters Field
018773	GRAVES, Kate	26y	C	Va.	22 JAN 1879	Beckett's
005527	GRAVES, Louisa	16d	C	D.C.	21 NOV 1875	Harmony
008747	GRAVES, Silas	2y	C	D.C.	20 AUG 1876	Beckett's

District of Columbia Death Records, August 1, 1874 to July 31, 1879

No.	Name	Age	Race	Birth	Death Date	Burial Place
006253	GRAVIN, W. Franklin	1y	W	D.C.	06 FEB 1876	Holy Rood
008951	GRAW, James A.	3y	C	D.C.	03 SEP 1876	Ebenezer
015010	GRAY, Anna	4y	C	D.C.	10 MAR 1878	Harmony
019501	GRAY, Arthur	3y	C	D.C.	22 MAR 1879	Mt. Zion
004256	GRAY, Carie	7y	C	Va.	23 JUL 1875	Harmony
014266	GRAY, Cathran	84y	C	Va.	30 DEC 1877	Young Mens
013326	GRAY, Charlotte	70y	C	Va.	27 SEP 1877	Mt. Pleasant
001634	GRAY, Elen	70y	C	Md.	07 JAN 1875	Washington Asylum
005704	GRAY, Elizabeth	2w	W	D.C.	09 DEC 1875	Oak Hill
010263	GRAY, Elizabeth	22y	C	Md.	12 JAN 1877	Ebenezer
006588	GRAY, Esther T.	86y	W	Md.	07 MAR 1876	Oak Hill
004753	GRAY, George	1y	C	D.C.	25 AUG 1875	Young Mens
011149	GRAY, George	4y	W	D.C.	29 MAR 1877	Mt. Olivet
007404	GRAY, Harriett Delphenah	22y	W	Ill.	25 MAY 1876	Chicago, Ill.
006244	GRAY, Henry	38y	M	Md.	05 FEB 1876	Young Mens
014240	GRAY, Henry	18y	C	Va.	28 DEC 1877	Potters Field
019880	GRAY, Infant of Georganna	5h	C	D.C.	24 APR 1879	Potters Field
012311	GRAY, Infant of George T.	1h	C	D.C.	11 JUL 1877	Young Mens
007272	GRAY, Infant of John	1d	C	D.C.	11 MAY 1876	Ebenezer
012560	GRAY, Infant of John	7d	C	D.C.	27 JUL 1877	Potters Field
009856	GRAY, Infant of Walter	6d	C	D.C.	03 DEC 1876	Harmony
016224	GRAY, Infant of William	8d	C	D.C.	19 JUN 1878	Mt. Pleasant
006555	GRAY, Infant of William	2m	C	D.C.	04 MAR 1876	Young Mens
021159	GRAY, James M.	10d	W	D.C.	30 JUL 1879	Potters Field
015191	GRAY, Jenetta	7y	C	D.C.	26 MAR 1878	Young Mens
018691	GRAY, John	44y	C	Va.	16 JAN 1879	Potters Field
009639	GRAY, John H.	38y	C	Va.	08 NOV 1876	Mt. Zion
019165	GRAY, John Henry	2m	C	D.C.	23 FEB 1879	Beckett's
012590	GRAY, Joseph	1y	W	D.C.	29 JUL 1877	Mt. Olivet
019274	GRAY, Leanna	40y	C	Va.	04 MAR 1879	Mt. Zion
009474	GRAY, Marcellus	4y	C	D.C.	20 OCT 1876	Mt. Zion
015011	GRAY, Martha Ann	2m	C	D.C.	10 MAR 1878	Holy Rood
012915	GRAY, Martha Ella	6m	C	D.C.	23 AUG 1877	Young Mens
011752	GRAY, Marthey E.	52y	W	D.C.	31 MAY 1877	Mt. Olivet
007562	GRAY, Mary	1m	C	D.C.	09 JUN 1876	Ebenezer
013019	GRAY, Mary E.	29y	C	Va.	30 AUG 1877	Harmony
010970	GRAY, Mary E.	7y	C	D.C.	14 MAR 1877	Harmony
001044	GRAY, Mary Jane	11m	C	D.C.	04 NOV 1874	Mt. Pleasant
005481	GRAY, Mary Jane	63y	W	Me.	17 NOV 1875	Oak Hill
009742	GRAY, Mary Virginia	1y	C	D.C.	19 NOV 1876	Mt. Zion
007509	GRAY, Mattie L.	1y	W	D.C.	05 JUN 1876	Glenwood
006849	GRAY, Maud	4m	W	D.C.	28 MAR 1876	Congressional
012863	GRAY, Nichols A.	68y	W	N.Y.	18 AUG 1877	Cleveland, Ohio
009210	GRAY, Phoebe	65y	C	Va.	26 SEP 1876	Potters Field
012294	GRAY, Saward	2y	C	D.C.	10 JUL 1877	Harmony
006018	GRAY, Thomas	84y	C	Md.	14 JAN 1876	Ebenezer
019435	GRAY, Walter	23y	C	Md.	17 MAR 1879	Skagg's
012873	GRAY, William Patrick	8m	W	D.C.	19 AUG 1877	Glenwood
013915	GRAYNOR, George	10y	W	D.C.	25 NOV 1877	Prospect Hill
013122	GRAYSON, George	8m	C	D.C.	08 SEP 1877	Mt. Zion
010476	GREASON, Radgnal	9m	C	D.C.	01 FEB 1877	Beckett's
011883	GREAVES, Johnathan	35y	W	Eng.	13 JUN 1877	Philadelphia, Pa.
016651	GREBORY, Sister	36y	W	Va.	18 JUL 1878	Mt. Olivet
017372	GREDRICH, Elisbeth	46y	W	Ger.	11 SEP 1878	Prospect Hill
019664	GREELEY, John	45y	C	Va.	05 APR 1879	Harmony
016127	GREELY, Jerry	1½m	C	D.C.	12 JUN 1878	Harmony

District of Columbia Death Records, August 1, 1874 to July 31, 1879

No.	Name	Age	Race	Birth	Death Date	Burial Place
017537	GREELY, William Henry	1y	C	D.C.	26 SEP 1878	Harmony
015459	GREEN, Addison Lincoln	8m	C	D.C.	20 APR 1878	Mt. Pleasant
017251	GREEN, Adelia	35y	C	Va.	30 AUG 1878	Potters Field
016204	GREEN, Algenon	26d	W	D.C.	17 JUN 1878	Big Rapids, Mich.
000476	GREEN, Alice	1m	W	--	11 SEP 1874	Mt. Olivet
003996	GREEN, Alice	2m	C	D.C.	04 JUL 1875	Potters Field
014685	GREEN, Alice	1y	C	D.C.	06 FEB 1878	Beckett's
006156	GREEN, Allen	65y	C	Md.	27 JAN 1876	Potters Field
008939	GREEN, Alonzo	11m	C	D.C.	02 SEP 1876	Ebenezer
019707	GREEN, Amanda	2y	C	D.C.	09 APR 1879	Mt. Pleasant
007120	GREEN, Amelia	4y	C	D.C.	26 APR 1876	Mt. Zion
005246	GREEN, Ann	c.28y	C	Md.	23 OCT 1875	Mt. Pleasant
013228	GREEN, Ann Maria	62y	C	D.C.	17 SEP 1877	Harmony
011888	GREEN, Anna	41y	C	D.C.	14 JUN 1877	Mt. Pleasant
013364	GREEN, Anna	21y	C	Va.	01 OCT 1877	Graceland
005090a	GREEN, Anna M.	7d	W	D.C.	09 OCT 1875	Congressional
004476	GREEN, Anna Rebecca	1y	C	D.C.	06 AUG 1875	Mt. Zion
002475	GREEN, Anna Rebekah	2y	C	D.C.	08 MAR 1875	Harmony
004651	GREEN, Annie	17d	C	D.C.	18 AUG 1875	Mt. Olivet
002394	GREEN, Annie	8m	C	D.C.	02 MAR 1875	Young Mens
013363	GREEN, Annie	24y	C	Va.	01 OCT 1877	Potters Field
013020	GREEN, Archibald R.	c.53y	W	Md.	30 AUG 1877	Glenwood
016630	GREEN, Archie	9m	M	D.C.	17 JUL 1878	Mt. Pleasant
014985	GREEN, Ardella	3m	C	D.C.	08 MAR 1878	Young Mens
000223	GREEN, Benjamin	1y	C	D.C.	17 AUG 1874	Moore's
004638	GREEN, Benjamin	1y	C	D.C.	17 AUG 1875	Ebenezer
010799	GREEN, Benjamin	6m	M	D.C.	27 FEB 1877	Ebenezer
009130	GREEN, Bridget	45y	W	Ire.	19 SEP 1876	Mt. Olivet
018781	GREEN, Burton Alexander	4y	C	D.C.	23 JAN 1879	Potters Field
009069	GREEN, Charles	24y	C	Md.	14 SEP 1876	Mt. Olivet
016889	GREEN, Charles	14d	C	D.C.	03 AUG 1878	Payne's
021135	GREEN, Charles	22y	C	Va.	28 JUL 1879	Young Mens
012573	GREEN, Charles Henry	1y	C	D.C.	28 JUL 1877	Moore's
009065	GREEN, Clara H.	1y	C	D.C.	14 SEP 1876	Ebenezer
009877	GREEN, David N.	40y	W	Md.	05 DEC 1876	Holy Rood
017467	GREEN, David S.	53y	W	N.Y.	20 SEP 1878	Oak Hill
004367	GREEN, Delina T.	1y	C	D.C.	29 JUL 1875	Brooks Farm, Md.[1]
013423	GREEN, Eddie	5y	C	D.C.	07 OCT 1877	Potters Field
000974	GREEN, Edmonia	23y	C	Md.	29 OCT 1874	Harmony
006142	GREEN, Edward	6d	C	Md.	26 JAN 1876	Ebenezer
009775	GREEN, Edward	27y	W	N.Y.	22 NOV 1876	Soldier's Home
016487	GREEN, Edward	4m	C	D.C.	07 JUL 1878	Beckett's
018743	GREEN, Edward	4m	W	D.C.	20 JAN 1879	Quantico, Va.
008009	GREEN, Elasebeth R.	33y	C	D.C.	04 JUL 1876	Harmony
012363	GREEN, Elesebeth	80y	C	Md.	15 JUL 1877	Moore's
006611	GREEN, Elijah	2y	C	D.C.	09 MAR 1876	Ebenezer
004461	GREEN, Eliza	5m	C	D.C.	05 AUG 1875	Young Mens
013733	GREEN, Eliza	70y	W	Md.	04 NOV 1877	Congressional
001971	GREEN, Elizabeth Agnes	7m	C	D.C.	31 JAN 1875	Mt. Pleasant
001409	GREEN, Ella	17y	M	Va.	16 DEC 1874	Potters Field
008028	GREEN, Ella	1y	C	D.C.	05 JUL 1876	Ebenezer
004443	GREEN, Emma Isabel	1y	C	Md.	04 AUG 1875	Mt. Pleasant
011122	GREEN, Florence	1y	C	D.C.	26 MAR 1877	Ebenezer

[1] Located in Montgomery Co., Md.

District of Columbia Death Records, August 1, 1874 to July 31, 1879

No.	Name	Age	Race	Birth	Death Date	Burial Place
002186a	GREEN, George H.	50y	C	Md.	03 FEB 1875	Mt. Zion
016691	GREEN, Gertrude	8m	C	D.C.	20 JUL 1878	Mt. Zion
020829	GREEN, Harriet	65y	C	Va.	08 JUL 1879	Mt. Zion
016955	GREEN, Harry	6m	C	D.C.	08 AUG 1878	Beckett's
010200	GREEN, Henrietta	73y	C	Md.	07 JAN 1877	Holy Rood
008165	GREEN, Hester	50y	C	Md.	11 JUL 1876	Young Mens
018314	GREEN, Hettie	9y	W	D.C.	12 DEC 1878	Congressional
008608	GREEN, Ida E.	1y	C	D.C.	08 AUG 1876	Potters Field
004031	GREEN, Ida Jane	4m	C	D.C.	07 JUL 1875	Young Mens
017423	GREEN, Infant of Adelia	14d	C	D.C.	16 SEP 1878	Potters Field
003751	GREEN, Infant of Arthur	8m	C	D.C.	21 JUN 1875	Mt. Zion
018774	GREEN, Infant of Pinkin	24h	C	D.C.	22 JAN 1879	Beckett's
009486	GREEN, Isaac	15y	C	Md.	21 OCT 1876	Potters Field
020329	GREEN, Isaiah	1m	C	D.C.	07 JUN 1879	Young Mens
000333	GREEN, James	1y	C	D.C.	27 AUG 1874	Beckett's
003255	GREEN, James	58y	W	Ire.	07 MAY 1875	Mt. Olivet
005888	GREEN, James Henry	2y	C	D.C.	28 DEC 1875	Ebenezer
011059	GREEN, James Henry	5m	C	D.C.	21 MAR 1877	Beckett's
002401f	GREEN, James L.	40y	W	Ire.	02 MAR 1875	Mt. Olivet
018274	GREEN, Jane	57y	C	D.C.	08 DEC 1878	Harmony
017468	GREEN, Jas.	9y	W	D.C.	20 SEP 1878	Mt. Olivet
005112a	GREEN, John	35y	C	D.C.	12 OCT 1875	Harmony
006776	GREEN, John	2m	C	D.C.	22 MAR 1876	On the Farm
006833	GREEN, John	11y	C	Va.	27 MAR 1876	Mt. Pleasant
016288	GREEN, John	1m	C	D.C.	24 JUN 1878	Young Mens
019633	GREEN, John	12d	C	D.C.	02 APR 1879	Mt. Pleasant
004390	GREEN, John C.	38y	W	Mass.	31 JUL 1875	Glenwood
006185	GREEN, John Francis	2y	C	D.C.	30 JAN 1876	Ebenezer
014233	GREEN, John M., Rev.	65y	W	Pa.	28 DEC 1877	Glenwood
004595	GREEN, Joseph	5m	C	D.C.	14 AUG 1875	Young Mens
007708	GREEN, Joseph	2m	W	D.C.	18 JUN 1876	Mt. Olivet
019575	GREEN, Joshua	7m	C	D.C.	28 MAR 1879	Ebenezer
006110	GREEN, Julia	81y	C	Va.	23 JAN 1876	Potters Field
019871	GREEN, Julian	2y	C	D.C.	23 APR 1879	Potters Field
019139	GREEN, Kate	33y	C	Va.	21 FEB 1879	Harmony
006784	GREEN, Laura Ella	1y	M	D.C.	23 MAR 1876	Harmony
010746	GREEN, Lavina	45y	C	Md.	23 FEB 1877	Potters Field
010838	GREEN, Lawrence E.	2y	C	D.C.	02 MAR 1877	Mt. Olivet
017614	GREEN, Lewis	9m	C	D.C.	03 OCT 1878	Young Mens
002607	GREEN, Lillie	1m	C	D.C.	16 MAR 1875	Young Mens
009119	GREEN, Lilly Julietta	2y	C	D.C.	18 SEP 1876	Beckett's
006462	GREEN, Lizzie	9y	C	Va.	24 FEB 1876	Ebenezer
014016	GREEN, Lottie S.	3y	W	D.C.	06 DEC 1877	Oak Hill
016278	GREEN, Louis	45y	C	Va.	23 JUN 1878	Beckett's
001740f	GREEN, Louisa C.	--	--	-	17 JAN 1875	--
019728	GREEN, Lucy Ann	33y	C	Va.	11 APR 1879	Young Mens
004159	GREEN, Mamie	7m	C	D.C.	16 JUL 1875	Mt. Olivet
006496	GREEN, Margaret	26y	C	Md.	28 FEB 1876	Potters Field
016994	GREEN, Margaret	1y	C	D.C.	10 AUG 1878	Mt. Olivet
005201a	GREEN, Margaret Ann	2y	C	D.C.	19 OCT 1875	Mt. Olivet
017115	GREEN, Maria	38y	C	Md.	20 AUG 1878	Potters Field
006545	GREEN, Martha	1y	C	D.C.	04 MAR 1876	Ebenezer
001024	GREEN, Martha Ellen	1y	C	D.C.	02 NOV 1874	Potters Field
002003	GREEN, Mary	1m	C	D.C.	03 FEB 1875	Mt. Pleasant
002167	GREEN, Mary	68y	W	Md.	15 FEB 1875	Potters Field
014025	GREEN, Mary	14y	C	D.C.	07 DEC 1877	Young Mens

District of Columbia Death Records, August 1, 1874 to July 31, 1879

No.	Name	Age	Race	Birth	Death Date	Burial Place
010590	GREEN, Mary	52y	W	Ire.	11 FEB 1877	Holy Rood
010758	GREEN, Mary	10m	C	D.C.	23 FEB 1877	Potters Field
011950	GREEN, Mary	60y	W	Ire.	17 JUN 1877	Mt. Olivet
000179	GREEN, Mary C., Mrs.	19y	C	Md.	13 AUG 1874	Harmony
000470	GREEN, Mary E.	2m	C	D.C.	10 SEP 1874	Beckett's
004861	GREEN, Mary Elizabeth	1y	C	D.C.	01 SEP 1875	Julia Mack's Farm
003413	GREEN, Mary Jane	26y	M	Ky.	23 MAY 1875	Harmony
005434	GREEN, Mary Jane	44y	W	Md.	12 NOV 1875	Baltimore, Md.
017282	GREEN, Mary V.	24y	W	Va.	01 SEP 1878	Quantico, Va.
000725	GREEN, Mary Virginia	22y	M	D.C.	05 OCT 1874	Young Mens
009266	GREEN, Michael	49y	W	Ire.	01 OCT 1876	Mt. Olivet
005995	GREEN, Montroy	62y	C	Va.	11 JAN 1876	Harmony
012147	GREEN, Nancy	80y	C	D.C.	30 JUN 1877	Potters Field
009331	GREEN, Nannie	22y	C	Va.	07 OCT 1876	Young Mens
001801	GREEN, Nina	14y	C	Va.	19 JAN 1875	Potters Field
007552	GREEN, Paul M.	5m	C	D.C.	08 JUN 1876	Beckett's
009064	GREEN, Pauline	12y	M	D.C.	14 SEP 1876	Young Mens
007592	GREEN, Pauline M.	5m	C	D.C.	11 JUN 1876	Beckett's
011836	GREEN, Philip J.	9m	W	D.C.	08 JUN 1877	Holy Rood
017585	GREEN, Rachael	65y	C	Md.	01 OCT 1878	Beckett's
006954	GREEN, Rebecca Hickey	84y	W	Md.	07 APR 1876	Mt. Olivet
010056	GREEN, Robert	70y	C	Va.	24 DEC 1876	Beckett's
009168	GREEN, Robert	3y	C	D.C.	22 SEP 1876	Mt. Zion
020390	GREEN, Robert	7d	C	D.C.	11 JUN 1879	Beckett's
008269	GREEN, Roberta	1y	C	D.C.	15 JUL 1876	Harmony
018437	GREEN, Roberta	7m	C	D.C.	23 DEC 1878	Potters Field
003997	GREEN, Romulus	77y	C	Md.	04 JUL 1875	Potters Field
015609	GREEN, Rose	9y	C	D.C.	04 MAY 1878	Mt. Pleasant
016087	GREEN, Ruth A.	1m	C	D.C.	09 JUN 1878	Beckett's
015864	GREEN, Samuel Bruce	5y	C	D.C.	27 MAY 1878	Hillsdale
008931	GREEN, Sarah Jane	1y	C	D.C.	02 SEP 1876	Ebenezer
010909	GREEN, Selina	53y	C	Md.	08 MAR 1877	Harmony
018436	GREEN, Shelton	14m	C	D.C.	23 DEC 1878	Graceland
012692	GREEN, Susanah	10m	C	D.C.	06 AUG 1877	Harmony
008859	GREEN, Thomas	35y	W	Ire.	28 AUG 1876	Holy Rood
019130	GREEN, Thomas	35y	C	Va.	20 FEB 1879	Beckett's
019612	GREEN, Thomas	40y	C	Va.	31 MAR 1879	Harmony
018285	GREEN, Thomas H.	43y	W	Ga.	09 DEC 1878	Congressional
009620	GREEN, Vernon	1y	C	D.C.	05 NOV 1876	Young Mens
019962	GREEN, Victoria	7y	C	D.C.	02 MAY 1879	Mt. Pleasant
007642	GREEN, William	1w	C	D.C.	14 JUN 1876	Potters Field
012768	GREEN, William	52y	W	Ire.	11 AUG 1877	Graceland
020679	GREEN, William	8m	C	D.C.	30 JUN 1879	Green's Farm
003675	GREEN, Willie	9m	C	D.C.	17 JUN 1875	Potters Field
004217	GREEN, Wm. H.	1y	C	D.C.	20 JUL 1875	Ebenezer
000674	GREENE, Annie [illegible]	1d	C	D.C.	29 SEP 1874	Beckett's
009985	GREENE, Edward	3m	C	D.C.	17 DEC 1876	Mt. Zion
005989	GREENE, Elizabeth	1y	C	D.C.	10 JAN 1876	Potters Field
010104	GREENE, Frank	6y	W	N.Y.	28 DEC 1876	Albion, N.Y.
015966	GREENE, George M.	41y	W	N.H.	02 JUN 1878	Albion, N.Y.
012465	GREENE, Mary E.	8m	C	D.C.	22 JUL 1877	Harmony
004752	GREENE, Mary Eliza	1y	C	D.C.	25 AUG 1875	Mt. Olivet
008958	GREENE, Nancy	70y	C	Va.	04 SEP 1876	Young Mens
004790	GREENE, Samuel C., Capt.	59y	W	N.Y.	28 AUG 1875	Congressional
011886	GREENFIELD, Sallie	22y	C	Va.	14 JUN 1877	Potters Field
014975	GREENFIELD, Sophia	c.50y	C	Md.	07 MAR 1878	Harmony

No.	Name	Age	Race	Birth	Death Date	Burial Place
011939	GREENFIELD, Willie	3m	C	D.C.	17 JUN 1877	Mt. Olivet
014547	GREENHORN, Elvie	35y	C	Va.	25 JAN 1878	Harmony
019223	GREENHOW, Effie	3m	C	D.C.	27 FEB 1879	Potters Field
007840	GREENHOW, Ernest	16m	C	D.C.	25 JUN 1876	Ebenezer
001294	GREENLEAF, Alice	2y	C	D.C.	02 DEC 1874	Harmony
020282	GREENLEAF, Jimmie	1y	M	D.C.	03 JUN 1879	Potters Field
004828	GREENLEY, Martha	26y	M	Ky.	30 AUG 1875	Harmony
008821	GREENWELL, Benjamin	2y	W	D.C.	25 AUG 1876	Mt. Olivet
011874	GREENWELL, James B.	66y	W	Md.	12 JUN 1877	Congressional
008653	GREENWELL, Marian	14y	W	D.C.	11 AUG 1876	Congressional
010266	GREENWELL, Mary E.	51y	W	D.C.	12 JAN 1877	Mt. Olivet
007119	GREER, Henry	81y	W	Md.	26 APR 1876	Glenwood
012031	GREER, John J.	2y	W	D.C.	23 JUN 1877	Glenwood
021134	GREER, Milton	34y	W	D.C.	28 JUL 1879	Glenwood
021158	GREGG, Barbara	59y	W	Ire.	30 JUL 1879	Congressional
016589	GREGOREY, Lillie	1m	W	D.C.	14 JUL 1878	Graceland
011515	GREGORY, Infant of Jennie	1d	C	D.C.	04 MAY 1877	Potters Field
007818	GREGORY, John C.	9m	W	D.C.	24 JUN 1876	Mt. Olivet
004226	GREGORY, Wm. M.	13y	W	N.Y.	21 JUL 1875	Alexandria, Va.
007479	GREGSLEY, Tapsiley	70y	C	Va.	03 JUN 1876	Potters Field
011243	GRESHAM, Infant of James	5d	C	D.C.	06 APR 1877	Young Mens
002955	GRESSON, William	22y	C	Va.	11 APR 1875	Harmony
011828	GREY, Ann C.	66y	W	Ire.	07 JUN 1877	Mt. Olivet
020230	GREY, Grace Lucinda	8m	C	D.C.	30 MAY 1879	Mt. Olivet
015630	GREY, Ida May	1m	W	D.C.	06 MAY 1878	Graceland
019016	GREY, John Henry	2y	C	D.C.	10 FEB 1879	Young Mens
017141	GREY, Jon H.	1m	W	D.C.	22 AUG 1878	Potters Field
019611	GREY, Joseph	4m	C	D.C.	31 MAR 1879	Beckett's
012815	GREY, May	9m	C	D.C.	15 AUG 1877	Young Mens
016925	GREY, Nettie Virginia	15y	C	D.C.	06 AUG 1878	Beckett's
009140	GREY, Peter	79y	W	Ire.	20 SEP 1876	Mt. Olivet
013465	GREY, Robert	2y	C	D.C.	10 OCT 1877	Young Mens
002051	GREY, Thomas	4m	C	D.C.	06 FEB 1875	Harmony
020694	GRICE, Carrie May	1m	C	D.C.	01 JUL 1879	Graceland
009073	GRICE, Isaiah	9y	C	D.C.	14 SEP 1876	Harmony
018984	GRIER, Elizabeth	10m	W	U.S.	07 FEB 1879	Mt. Olivet
006871	GRIER, Margarette	35y	W	Pa.	31 MAR 1876	Oak Hill
020857	GRIES, Geo.	1y	W	D.C.	09 JUL 1879	Mt. Olivet
019808	GRIESBAUER, Emma L.	4y	W	D.C.	17 APR 1879	Prospect Hill
018584	GRIFFEN, Zackel	59y	C	Va.	06 JAN 1879	Mt. Pleasant
001108	GRIFFETH, Lucindia	9y	C	Va.	10 NOV 1874	Beckett's
008513	GRIFFIN, Ada May	1y	C	D.C.	01 AUG 1876	Glenwood
020557	GRIFFIN, Alphonso	2y	C	D.C.	21 JUN 1879	Mt. Zion
004947	GRIFFIN, Ann Mariah	7m	W	D.C.	07 SEP 1875	Mt. Olivet
009061	GRIFFIN, Anna Cornelius	c.8y	C	D.C.	14 SEP 1876	Young Mens
007254	GRIFFIN, Burke	23y	C	D.C.	09 MAY 1876	Mt. Pleasant
005796	GRIFFIN, Catharine	70y	W	Ire.	19 DEC 1875	Holy Rood
017269	GRIFFIN, Catherine E.	38y	W	Md.	31 AUG 1878	Alexandria, Va.
012655	GRIFFIN, Charlott	1y	C	D.C.	03 AUG 1877	Potters Field
005868	GRIFFIN, Elizabeth A.	38y	W	Md.	26 DEC 1875	Alexandria, Va.
020518	GRIFFIN, Ellen	53y	W	Ire.	19 JUN 1879	Holy Rood
015199	GRIFFIN, Emma	19y	C	Md.	27 MAR 1878	Beckett's
006629	GRIFFIN, Frank	7y	C	Va.	10 MAR 1876	Harmony
003261	GRIFFIN, Infant of Wilson	6d	C	D.C.	08 MAY 1875	Ebenezer
005445	GRIFFIN, Infant of Wm.	20h	C	D.C.	13 NOV 1875	Young Mens
010515	GRIFFIN, Infant of John	7d	C	D.C.	04 FEB 1877	Ebenezer

District of Columbia Death Records, August 1, 1874 to July 31, 1879   137

No.	Name	Age	Race	Birth	Death Date	Burial Place
015429	GRIFFIN, James	33y	C	Md.	17 APR 1878	Payne's
011504	GRIFFIN, Jas. L.	67y	W	D.C.	04 MAY 1877	Congressional
003803	GRIFFIN, Joseph	18d	C	D.C.	24 JUN 1875	Potters Field
005795	GRIFFIN, Josephine	24y	C	Md.	19 DEC 1875	Ebenezer
014542	GRIFFIN, Katie	2d	W	D.C.	24 JAN 1878	Glenwood
007957	GRIFFIN, Lucinda	6m	C	D.C.	01 JUL 1876	Ebenezer
007014	GRIFFIN, Mabel Gertrude	3m	W	D.C.	14 APR 1876	Baltimore, Md.
010082	GRIFFIN, Mary C.	78y	W	Va.	26 DEC 1876	Congressional
014591	GRIFFIN, Michael J.	44y	W	Ire.	29 JAN 1878	Mt. Olivet
004878	GRIFFIN, Richard	1y	C	D.C.	02 SEP 1875	Ebenezer
009364	GRIFFIN, Rinaldo Benson	50y	C	Md.	10 OCT 1876	Ebenezer
002395	GRIFFIN, Rosa	9m	C	D.C.	02 MAR 1875	Mt. Olivet
010528	GRIFFIN, Susie Bell	1y	C	D.C.	05 FEB 1877	Mt. Zion
005176a	GRIFFIN, Thomas	4y	C	D.C.	17 OCT 1875	Mt. Olivet
004927	GRIFFIN, Walter	3y	C	D.C.	06 SEP 1875	Mt. Zion
009439	GRIFFIN, Walter	3y	C	Md.	17 OCT 1876	Baltimore, Md.
016858	GRIFFIN, Winnie Ann	1y	C	D.C.	01 AUG 1878	Beckett's
013599	GRIFFITH, Anastasia	27y	W	Ire.	23 OCT 1877	Mt. Olivet
015665	GRIFFITH, Edward D.	45y	W	Va.	09 MAY 1878	Oak Hill
005547	GRIFFITH, George W.	2y	W	D.C.	24 NOV 1875	Congressional
002802	GRIFFITH, James Francis	2y	C	D.C.	30 MAR 1875	Harmony
018644	GRIFFITH, Job E.	75y	W	Pa.	11 JAN 1879	Glenwood, Phila., Pa.
010545	GRIFFITH, LaFayette	6y	W	Tenn.	06 FEB 1877	Mechanicsville, Md.
006252	GRIFFITH, Richard	37y	C	N.C.	06 FEB 1876	Young Mens
003722	GRIFFITH, Richard C.	9m	W	D.C.	20 JUN 1875	Oak Hill
009869	GRIGGS, Lucy Taylor	24y	C	Va.	05 DEC 1876	Chappel's
006648	GRIGSBY, Florence Tamar	2y	W	D.C.	12 MAR 1876	Congressional
012841	GRIGSBY, Rose Ella	2y	W	D.C.	16 AUG 1877	Congressional
008541	GRIMES, A.K.	8m	W	D.C.	03 AUG 1876	Oak Hill
019619	GRIMES, Amelia Jane	22y	W	Md.	01 APR 1879	Mt. Olivet
004860	GRIMES, Ann E.	67y	W	Va.	01 SEP 1875	Alexandria, Va.
015594	GRIMES, Annie Cecilia	7d	W	D.C.	03 MAY 1878	Congressional
020961	GRIMES, Cesar	2y	C	N.Y.	16 JUL 1879	Harmony
001457	GRIMES, Chloe A.	55y	C	D.C.	21 DEC 1874	Harmony
009664	GRIMES, Eleanor	79y	W	Md.	10 NOV 1876	Mt. Olivet
012887	GRIMES, Francis X.	4m	W	D.C.	20 AUG 1877	Oak Hill
008894	GRIMES, George Robert	7m	W	D.C.	31 AUG 1876	Harmony
016108	GRIMES, Infant of John	6d	C	D.C.	10 JUN 1878	Potters Field
006243	GRIMES, John R.	38y	W	Md.	05 FEB 1876	Poolesville, Md.
002274	GRIMES, Joseph	1m	C	D.C.	22 FEB 1875	Ebenezer
014378	GRIMES, Lucy Anna	1y	C	D.C.	10 JAN 1878	Mt. Pleasant
007413	GRIMES, Mamie	3m	C	D.C.	26 MAY 1876	Ebenezer
017107	GRIMES, Winnie	76y	W	Va.	19 AUG 1878	Harmony
016770	GRIMES, Wm. Thomas	1y	W	D.C.	26 JUL 1878	Congressional
019987	GRIMSHAW, Albert Henry	2y	W	D.C.	04 MAY 1879	Harmony
002941	GRINDALL, Edward	60y	W	Md.	10 APR 1875	Congressional
011424	GRINDALL, James Franklin	29y	W	D.C.	25 APR 1877	Congressional
000513	GRINDER, Ann Eliza	48y	W	D.C.	14 SEP 1874	Methodist
009610	GRINDER, Anthony W.	63y	W	Pa.	03 NOV 1876	Congressional
020884	GRINDER, Effie	4m	W	D.C.	11 JUL 1879	Congressional
008794	GRINDER, Emma A.	1y	W	D.C.	23 AUG 1876	Congressional
009154	GRINDER, John N.	7y	W	D.C.	21 SEP 1876	Congressional
000055	GRINNEL, Mary E.	1y	C	D.C.	04 AUG 1874	Mt. Pleasant
006177	GRINNELL, Ann E.	19y	C	Md.	29 JAN 1876	Mt. Olivet
005175	GRINNELL, Joseph	30y	C	Md.	17 OCT 1875	Mt. Olivet
016567	GRINNELL, Martha L.	18y	C	Md.	12 JUL 1878	Holy Rood

No.	Name	Age	Race	Birth	Death Date	Burial Place
018220	GRINNELL, William H.	17y	C	D.C.	02 DEC 1878	Harmony
003073	GRISCOLL, John	50y	W	Ire.	21 APR 1875	Mt. Olivet
015447	GRISSOM, Richard	47y	W	Ire.	19 APR 1878	Rock Creek
005573	GRISSON, Frederick James	1y	W	D.C.	26 NOV 1875	Congressional
000848	GRISTOCK, Charles F.	41y	W	Pa.	18 OCT 1874	Philadelphia, Pa.
016279	GROANAR, Margaret L.	4m	W	D.C.	23 JUN 1878	Prospect Hill
003879	GROANNER, Henry	1y	W	D.C.	27 JUN 1875	Prospect Hill
013758	GRONINGER, Jacob	20y	W	Ger.	07 NOV 1877	St. Mary's
012136	GROSH, Charles C.P.	65y	W	Pa.	30 JUN 1877	Marietta, Pa.
017784	GROSS, Ann E., Mrs.	51y	C	D.C.	18 OCT 1878	Mt. Zion
009373	GROSS, Benj.	c.50y	C	Md.	11 OCT 1876	Young Mens
007795	GROSS, Catherine Elizabeth	5m	C	D.C.	23 JUN 1876	Ebenezer
011210	GROSS, Charles	c.12y	C	D.C.	04 APR 1877	Ebenezer
016399	GROSS, Charles	35y	C	Md.	02 JUL 1878	Beckett's
016416	GROSS, Charles	9m	C	Md.	03 JUL 1878	Potters Field
016846	GROSS, Chs. Wilford	2m	C	D.C.	31 JUL 1878	Payne's
012300	GROSS, Edward J.	16d	W	D.C.	10 JUL 1877	Prospect Hill
016673	GROSS, Eliza	c.23y	C	Md.	19 JUL 1878	Payne's
011379	GROSS, Fannie	3y	W	D.C.	20 APR 1877	Washington Hebrew
001939	GROSS, Ferdina	7y	C	D.C.	29 JAN 1875	Harmony
000834f	GROSS, Flora	9m	W	D.C.	17 OCT 1874	Hebrew
015182	GROSS, Frances A.	18m	C	D.C.	25 MAR 1878	Mt. Olivet
000021	GROSS, George	1y	W	D.C.	02 AUG 1874	Prospect Hill
019942	GROSS, Georgiana	27y	W	D.C.	30 APR 1879	Holy Rood
008680	GROSS, James W.	22y	W	D.C.	14 AUG 1876	Mt. Zion
001327f	GROSS, Joseph	65y	C	Md.	06 DEC 1874	Mt. Zion
005453	GROSS, Joseph	52y	C	Va.	14 NOV 1875	Harmony
016995	GROSS, Laura	34y	C	Md.	10 AUG 1878	Harmony
013610	GROSS, Lucy	98y	C	Md.	24 OCT 1877	Harmony
011117	GROSS, Mary	90y	C	Md.	26 MAR 1877	Potters Field
006470	GROSS, Rosa E.	1y	W	D.C.	25 FEB 1876	Mt. Olivet
008611	GROSS, Rose Emma	12y	W	D.C.	08 AUG 1876	Harmony
011282	GROSS, Rosie	2y	C	D.C.	09 APR 1877	Mt. Zion
001498	GROSSBECK, Peter	45y	W	Ger.	06 DEC 1874	Hospital
001808	GROVERMAN, Charlie	21m	W	D.C.	20 JAN 1875	Mt. Olivet
006295	GROVES, Anne	60y	W	Va.	10 FEB 1876	Congressional
009597	GROVES, Mildred	8d	C	D.C.	02 NOV 1876	Beckett's
019469	GROVES, Ruth	1y	C	Mass.	20 MAR 1879	Beckett's
002272	GROVES, Virginia	35y	C	Va.	21 FEB 1875	Harmony
014456	GROVIER, Wm. R.	57y	W	N.Y.	17 JAN 1878	Glenwood
014026	GRUBER, John Louis	50y	M	Md.	07 DEC 1877	Graceland
009489	GRUNWELL, Mary Adelle	10d	W	D.C.	22 OCT 1876	Congressional
011047	GRUPE, William	65y	W	Ger.	20 MAR 1877	Prospect Hill
016202	GRUSER, Helene	17y	W	Md.	17 JUN 1878	St. Mary's
003047	GUENTHER, Angelica	71y	W	Ger.	19 APR 1875	Prospect Hill
009079	GUILDFORD, J.C., Mrs.	26y	W	Md.	15 SEP 1876	Mt. Olivet
009796	GUISLA, Maria Lucy	2y	W	Ill.	25 NOV 1876	Mt. Olivet
002787	GULICK, Emma	22m	W	D.C.	29 MAR 1875	Oak Hill
003787f	GULICK, Infant of Geo. F.	8m	W	D.C.	23 JUN 1875	Oak Hill
009532	GUNDERSON, Adolphus	26y	W	Den.	25 OCT 1876	Hospital
014753	GUNNELL, Edith H.	2y	W	D.C.	13 FEB 1878	Congressional
002266	GUNNELL, Henry D.	74y	W	Va.	21 FEB 1875	Congressional
011029	GUNTON, Ann	80y	W	Eng.	18 MAR 1877	Congressional
007994	GUNTON, Mary	88y	W	Eng.	03 JUL 1876	Congressional
005248	GURLEY, Willy Menor	19y	C	D.C.	23 OCT 1875	Mt. Pleasant
014592	GURNEE, Elvira	73y	W	Ver.	29 JAN 1878	Glenwood

District of Columbia Death Records, August 1, 1874 to July 31, 1879   139

No.	Name	Age	Race	Birth	Death Date	Burial Place
013134	GURTLEY, Martha	40y	C	Miss.	09 SEP 1877	Potters Field
018742	GUSSIER, Margaret	44y	C	Va.	20 JAN 1879	Mt. Pleasant
020239	GUSTAMARTI, Harriet	6y	C	D.C.	31 MAY 1879	Potters Field
005027	GUSTIN, Annie Violet	3y	W	Ga.	13 SEP 1875	Mt. Olivet
014235	GUTHRIE, Columbus B.	63y	W	Ohio	28 DEC 1877	Zanesville, Ohio
005605	GUTMAN, Emanuel	53y	W	Ger.	29 NOV 1875	Hebrew
009056	GUTTENSON, Michael	72y	W	Ger.	13 SEP 1876	Prospect Hill
002409	GUTTRIDGE, Infant of Wm. H.	7d	C	D.C.	03 MAR 1875	Ebenezer
005468	GUVENATOR, Christopher	26y	W	Ger.	16 NOV 1875	Prospect Hill
009101	GUY, Ann	59y	W	Va.	16 SEP 1876	Congressional
021114	GUY, Annie	2m	C	D.C.	26 JUL 1879	Beckett's
008764	GUY, Laura A.	2m	W	D.C.	21 AUG 1876	Congressional
020204	GUY, Walter D.W.	1y	W	D.C.	26 MAY 1879	Congressional
003304	GWELIN, Carl Ald	2m	W	D.C.	13 MAY 1875	Holy Rood
005123	GWIN, Wilber	1y	C	D.C.	21 SEP 1875	Macedonia
019384	GWINN, Lilly Rosina	3y	C	D.C.	13 MAR 1879	Hillsdale

H

No.	Name	Age	Race	Birth	Death Date	Burial Place
018632	HAAS, Charlotte	4d	C	D.C.	10 JAN 1879	Young Mens
002125	HAAS, Martha Isabell	20y	W	D.C.	11 FEB 1875	Congressional
016401	HAASE, Benjamin Willis	1y	C	D.C.	02 JUL 1878	Mt. Pleasant
019181	HABERMAN, Charles H.	32y	W	Pa.	24 FEB 1879	Prospect Hill
003665	HABIT, David	4m	C	D.C.	16 JUN 1875	Young Mens
002211	HACKETT, Ann	63y	M	Md.	17 FEB 1875	Montgomery Co., Md.
017308	HACKETT, Lucy	27y	C	Va.	03 SEP 1878	Potters Field
000719	HACKLEY, Lucy	4m	C	D.C.	05 OCT 1874	Beckett's
002163	HACKLEY, Lucy	38y	C	Va.	14 FEB 1875	Ebenezer
005090	HACKLEY, Moses	22y	C	Va.	18 SEP 1875	Ebenezer
002883	HACKLEY, Nelson	41y	C	Va.	05 APR 1875	Ebenezer
009224	HACKLEY, Robert	2m	C	D.C.	28 SEP 1876	Mt. Zion
016977	HACKLING, Betsy	3m	C	D.C.	09 AUG 1878	Beckett's
003852	HACKLY, Rosa	19y	M	Va.	26 JUN 1875	Ebenezer
014529	HACKNEY, Robt. B.	63y	W	Va.	23 JAN 1878	Rock Creek
020405	HAFER, Magnus	4m	W	D.C.	12 JUN 1879	St. Mary's
013497	HAGAN, Catherine	9m	W	D.C.	13 OCT 1877	Mt. Olivet
001141	HAGAN, John	19y	W	Md.	14 NOV 1874	Mt. Olivet
018704	HAGAN, John O.	49y	W	Ire.	17 JAN 1879	Mt. Olivet
017023	HAGAN, Rosean	7m	W	D.C.	12 AUG 1878	Mt. Olivet
008529	HAGAN, Twin Infants of Jas. F.	1d	W	D.C.	02 AUG 1876	Mt. Olivet
018021	HAGAN, William James	27y	W	N.Y.	11 NOV 1878	Mt. Olivet
011205	HAGEMAN, Jarret	88y	C	Va.	03 APR 1877	Potters Field
019337	HAGER, Frederick A.	46y	W	D.C.	09 MAR 1879	Prospect Hill
008679	HAGERMAN, Charles	56y	W	Prus.	13 AUG 1876	Potters Field
000766	HAGERTY, Daniel	67y	W	Ire.	09 OCT 1874	Mt. Olivet
006083	HAGERTY, Katie L.	5y	W	D.C.	21 JAN 1876	Glenwood
018745	HAGERTY, Patrick	40y	W	Ire.	20 JAN 1879	Hospital
000747	HAGERTY, Vincent	6m	W	D.C.	08 OCT 1874	Mt. Olivet
005126a	HAGERTY, William	11y	W	D.C.	13 OCT 1875	Holy Rood
017795	HAGERTY, William	73y	W	Ire.	19 OCT 1878	Mt. Olivet
012053	HAGGENMACKEN, James Daniel	7m	W	D.C.	25 JUN 1877	Howard Family
011596	HAGGENMAKER, Annie	28y	W	Md.	14 MAY 1877	Howard
004477	HAGMAN, Pauline	9m	W	D.C.	06 AUG 1875	Prospect Hill
015761	HAGNER, Evylyn Smith	2m	W	D.C.	18 MAY 1878	Oak Hill
017830	HAGNER, James	2m	W	D.C.	22 OCT 1878	Mt. Olivet

No.	Name	Age	Race	Birth	Death Date	Burial Place
018161	HAHN, Chauncy F.	5y	W	D.C.	26 NOV 1878	Baltimore, Md.
000576	HAHN, Philip H., Jr.	32y	W	Pa.	20 SEP 1874	Morristown, Pa.
010070	HAIGHT, Gracie	2y	W	D.C.	25 DEC 1876	Oak Hill
020118	HAIGHT, Lucy A.	35y	W	Va.	16 MAY 1879	Graceland
000580	HAILSTOCK, Joseph	2m	C	D.C.	20 SEP 1874	Beckett's
001968	HAILSTOCK, Robert Wilson	6m	C	D.C.	01 FEB 1875	Beckett's
015933	HAINES, James	6y	W	D.C.	31 MAY 1878	Prospect Hill
016848	HAINES, James Henry	2y	M	D.C.	31 JUL 1878	Beckett's
010530	HAINES, Rachel	79y	W	Md.	05 FEB 1877	Oak Hill
004964	HAIRESON, Benjamin A.	5y	C	D.C.	09 SEP 1875	Mt. Olivet
016115	HAISLIP, Cora	1y	W	D.C.	11 JUN 1878	Presbyterian
008833	HAISLIP, Mary C.	c.59y	W	Va.	26 AUG 1876	Glenwood
021173	HAITHMAN, Infant of Aaron	7d	C	D.C.	31 JUL 1879	Mt. Olivet
004355	HAITHMAN, Katie	10m	C	D.C.	28 JUL 1875	Mt. Olivet
011561	HALEY, Margarett I.	6y	W	D.C.	11 MAY 1877	Congressional
008883	HALIDAY, Forence Estelle	10m	W	D.C.	30 AUG 1876	Glenwood
000323	HALL, Alice Gertrude	2w	W	D.C.	26 AUG 1874	Congressional
003346	HALL, Alice Mary, Mrs.	27y	W	D.C.	16 MAY 1875	Oak Hill
013651	HALL, Anne M.	62y	C	Md.	27 OCT 1877	Harmony
013123	HALL, Arthur	4m	W	D.C.	08 SEP 1877	Congressional
012950	HALL, Bell	1y	C	D.C.	25 AUG 1877	Young Mens
007842	HALL, Caroline	15d	C	D.C.	25 JUN 1876	Ebenezer
009762	HALL, Caroline	1y	C	D.C.	20 NOV 1876	Mt. Zion
008647	HALL, Carrie	5y	C	D.C.	11 AUG 1876	Beckett's
020626	HALL, Case Rena	5m	C	D.C.	26 JUN 1879	Harmony
010793	HALL, Celia	5y	C	D.C.	26 FEB 1877	Ebenezer
009222	HALL, Charles Nelson	1y	C	D.C.	28 SEP 1876	Ebenezer
005469	HALL, Cornelia L.	60y	W	Va.	16 NOV 1875	Oak Hill
012932	HALL, Edna E.	8m	C	D.C.	24 AUG 1877	Harmony
009552	HALL, Edward	42y	C	D.C.	27 OCT 1876	Ebenezer
007843	HALL, Ella	3m	W	D.C.	25 JUN 1876	Mt. Olivet
002616	HALL, Evelina	26y	C	Md.	17 MAR 1875	Ebenezer
001371	HALL, Frank	8m	C	D.C.	12 DEC 1874	Young Mens
018179	HALL, Franklin W.	4d	W	D.C.	27 NOV 1878	Congressional
019265	HALL, Geo. W.	1y	C	D.C.	03 MAR 1879	Mt. Olivet
003540	HALL, George	c.90y	C	Md.	06 JUN 1875	Mt. Olivet
001690	HALL, Georgiana A.	35y	C	D.C.	11 JAN 1875	Potters Field
016555	HALL, Gracie	79y	C	Md.	11 JUL 1878	Potters Field
019761	HALL, H.V.	3m	W	D.C.	13 APR 1879	Prospect Hill
000011	HALL, Hanson	10m	C	D.C.	01 AUG 1874	Young Mens
013287	HALL, Harriet	75y	C	Va.	24 SEP 1877	Beckett's
018572	HALL, Harry	14y	W	D.C.	05 JAN 1879	Congressional
017424	HALL, Henry	6m	C	D.C.	16 SEP 1878	Beckett's
005845	HALL, Hester	6m	W	D.C.	24 DEC 1875	Congressional
015967	HALL, Ida	18y	C	D.C.	02 JUN 1878	Mt. Olivet
019816	HALL, Ida	2y	W	D.C.	18 APR 1879	Glenwood
013650	HALL, Infant of Cyrus	9d	C	D.C.	27 OCT 1877	Beckett's
019760	HALL, Infant of Ellen	9d	C	D.C.	13 APR 1879	Beckett's
016653	HALL, Infant of Francis	1m	C	D.C.	18 JUL 1878	Potters Field
015019	HALL, Infant of Thomas	36h	C	D.C.	10 MAR 1878	Payne's
004777	HALL, Isaac	1y	C	D.C.	27 AUG 1875	Harmony
011703	HALL, James	61y	C	Md.	26 MAY 1877	Potters Field
015040	HALL, James	5y	C	D.C.	12 MAR 1878	Young Mens
014348	HALL, James Henry	8m	C	D.C.	07 JAN 1878	Potters Field
013314	HALL, James Nathaniel	17d	C	D.C.	26 SEP 1877	Mt. Olivet
000712	HALL, John	60y	C	Va.	04 OCT 1874	Washington Asylum

District of Columbia Death Records, August 1, 1874 to July 31, 1879   141

No.	Name	Age	Race	Birth	Death Date	Burial Place
012905	HALL, John	35y	C	Md.	20 AUG 1877	Potters Field
020654	HALL, John Alfred	3m	C	D.C.	28 JUN 1879	Scagg's
020907	HALL, Joseph F.	8m	W	D.C.	13 JUL 1879	Mt. Olivet
010636	HALL, Joseph H.	3y	C	D.C.	15 FEB 1877	Mt. Zion
015848	HALL, Joseph Theodore	7m	C	D.C.	26 MAY 1878	Mt. Pleasant
004032	HALL, Katie	4m	C	D.C.	07 JUL 1875	Mt. Olivet
013035	HALL, Leina	1y	W	N.C.	31 AUG 1877	Charlotte, N.C.
018993	HALL, Lillie	2½m	C	D.C.	08 FEB 1879	Potters Field
008808	HALL, Lucy	8m	W	D.C.	24 AUG 1876	Mt. Olivet
018180	HALL, Maggie	30y	C	Md.	27 NOV 1878	Harmony
014114	HALL, Martha	30y	C	Md.	16 DEC 1877	Potters Field
013930	HALL, Martha	43y	C	Md.	26 NOV 1877	Mt. Olivet
001153	HALL, Mary Elizabeth	1y	M	D.C.	15 NOV 1874	Harmony
017214	HALL, Mary H.	85y	W	D.C.	27 AUG 1878	Glenwood
014236	HALL, Mary Jane	45y	C	Md.	28 DEC 1877	Potters Field
020567	HALL, Matilda	40y	C	Md.	22 JUN 1879	Beckett's
020355	HALL, Matilda	6y	C	D.C.	09 JUN 1879	Scagg's
002677	HALL, Matilda Anne	41y	C	Md.	21 MAR 1875	Harmony
000898	HALL, Millie	75y	C	Md.	22 OCT 1874	Washington Asylum
017822	HALL, Millie	60y	C	Va.	21 OCT 1878	Potters Field
010879	HALL, Olive W.	49y	W	Me.	06 MAR 1877	Wilton, Me.
005205	HALL, Rachel	70y	C	Md.	28 SEP 1875	Harmony
003952	HALL, Robert	9m	W	D.C.	01 JUL 1875	Glenwood
013135	HALL, Robert	2y	C	D.C.	09 SEP 1877	Beckett's
004071	HALL, Saml.	18y	C	Md.	10 JUL 1875	Rosemont
008992	HALL, Sarah	50y	W	Conn.	07 SEP 1876	Potters Field
001426	HALL, Sarah, Mrs.	88y	W	W.Va.	18 DEC 1874	Prospect Hill
011971	HALL, William	11m	C	D.C.	19 JUN 1877	Ebenezer
001196	HALLAN, Lizzie	4h	W	D.C.	20 NOV 1874	Mt. Olivet
006630	HALLAN, Sarah	22y	C	Va.	10 MAR 1876	Mt. Pleasant
008889	HALLARAN, William Edward	59y	W	N.Y.	30 AUG 1876	Glenwood
020107	HALLECK, Nellie Blanchard	11m	W	D.C.	15 MAY 1879	Oak Hill
011917	HALLER, Rebecca	80y	W	Md.	15 JUN 1877	Glenwood
000561	HALLIDAY, Charlotte Lee	2m	W	D.C.	19 SEP 1874	Glenwood
000842	HALLINAN, John	42y	W	Ire.	17 OCT 1874	Mt. Olivet
017479	HALLING, James	c.38y	C	Md.	21 SEP 1878	Potters Field
009619	HALLOCK, Zernbabel	70y	W	N.Y.	05 NOV 1876	Greenmount, Balt., Md.
005816	HALLORN, Ellen	35y	W	Ire.	21 DEC 1875	Mt. Olivet
013246	HALPHINE, Mary	15y	W	D.C.	19 SEP 1877	Mt. Olivet
010964	HALPIN, Alfred	6d	W	D.C.	14 MAR 1877	Mt. Olivet
000343	HALPIN, Isabella	2m	W	--	28 AUG 1875	Mt. Olivet
003978	HALSON, Harriet J.	9m	W	D.C.	03 JUL 1875	Tennallytown
016590	HALSTON, David K.	28y	W	Ohio	14 JUL 1878	Zanesville, Ohio
016102	HAM, Bryce Alan	6m	W	D.C.	10 JUN 1878	Oak Hill
013258	HAM, Elizabeth	1m	C	D.C.	20 SEP 1877	Potters Field
007777	HAM, Gertrude Luce	8m	W	D.C.	22 JUN 1876	Congressional
004597	HAMANN, Alice Gertrude	11m	W	D.C.	14 AUG 1875	Glenwood
013611	HAMANN, Edith	9m	W	D.C.	24 OCT 1877	Glenwood
008993	HAMANN, Ida	10m	W	D.C.	07 SEP 1876	Glenwood
000337	HAMBLETON, Elizabeth	1y	C	D.C.	27 AUG 1874	Mt. Olivet
003214	HAMBLETON, Martha Ann E.	5m	C	D.C.	04 MAY 1875	Mt. Olivet
020249	HAMERSLEY, Margaret Ann	8m	W	Va.	02 JUN 1879	Alexandria, Va.
008014	HAMESLEY, Arther	1m	C	D.C.	04 JUL 1876	Ebenezer
016089	HAMEY, Edward	11m	C	D.C.	09 JUN 1878	Harmony
013819	HAMILL, Mary	37y	W	Va.	14 NOV 1877	Graceland
010147	HAMILTON, Agnes Josephine	4y	W	D.C.	01 JAN 1877	Congressional

No.	Name	Age	Race	Birth	Death Date	Burial Place
015002	HAMILTON, Charles	24y	C	Md.	09 MAR 1878	Payne's
019266	HAMILTON, Clifford	2y	C	D.C.	03 MAR 1879	Harmony
000112	HAMILTON, Eddie	1y	C	D.C.	08 AUG 1874	Young Mens
004944f	HAMILTON, Ellen Maria Kelso	40y	W	Md.	06 SEP 1875	Oak Hill
002517	HAMILTON, Eugine	2y	C	D.C.	11 MAR 1875	Harmony
000296	HAMILTON, Florence	2m	C	D.C	23 AUG 1874	Beckett's
015934	HAMILTON, Geo. Alex.	8y	W	D.C.	31 MAY 1878	Holy Rood
000676	HAMILTON, Hanson	60y	C	Ky.	30 SEP 1874	Mt. Olivet
011233	HAMILTON, Helena	7m	M	D.C.	06 APR 1877	Mt. Olivet
001887	HAMILTON, Henry	24y	C	Va.	25 JAN 1875	Harmony
017156	HAMILTON, Henry W.	47y	W	Mass.	23 AUG 1878	Oak Hill
001615	HAMILTON, Ida	2m	C	D.C.	04 JAN 1875	Young Mens
017943	HAMILTON, James	37y	W	Md.	04 NOV 1878	Congressional
000526	HAMILTON, Jeannette	29d	W	D.C.	16 SEP 1874	Congressional
003603f	HAMILTON, John F.	18y	W	D.C.	11 JUN 1875	Oak Hill
003078	HAMILTON, John Harris	1y	W	D.C.	21 APR 1875	Mt. Olivet
011623	HAMILTON, Landona	40y	C	Va.	17 MAY 1877	Potters Field
014457	HAMILTON, Laura	1y	C	D.C.	17 JAN 1878	Beckett's
010698	HAMILTON, Laura Virginia	8m	M	D.C.	19 FEB 1877	Mt. Olivet
016623	HAMILTON, Lily	6y	C	D.C.	16 JUL 1878	Beckett's
013466	HAMILTON, Martha, Mrs.	35y	C	Md.	10 OCT 1877	Potters Field
001672	HAMILTON, Mary	40y	W	Ire.	10 JAN 1875	Mt. Olivet
014160	HAMILTON, Mary	7m	C	D.C.	21 DEC 1877	Tennallytown
011641	HAMILTON, Mary	75y	C	Md.	18 MAY 1877	Ebenezer
004830	HAMILTON, Mary Ann	1y	W	D.C.	30 AUG 1875	Congressional
002743	HAMILTON, Mary Ellen	6m	C	D.C.	26 MAR 1875	Mt. Olivet
004356	HAMILTON, Mary F.	40y	W	Can.	28 JUL 1875	Oak Hill
015053	HAMILTON, Samuel Jackson	c.54y	C	Md.	13 MAR 1878	Beckett's
003372	HAMILTON, Sarah	6w	C	D.C.	20 MAY 1875	Harmony
015183	HAMILTON, Thomas	48y	W	N.Y.	25 MAR 1878	Mt. Olivet
015932	HAMILTON, William	11y	W	D.C.	31 MAY 1878	Holy Rood
010005	HAMILTON, William F.	3y	W	D.C.	18 DEC 1876	Congressional
018092	HAMMACK, Letilla Exilma	8y	W	Md.	19 NOV 1878	Chickamuxin, Md.
021174	HAMMER, George H.	6d	W	D.C.	31 JUL 1879	Prospect Hill
005721	HAMMER, Henry	13y	W	D.C.	11 DEC 1875	St. Mary's
008512	HAMMER, John	30y	W	Ger.	01 AUG 1876	Mt. Olivet
017987	HAMMER, John Christian	59y	W	Ger.	09 NOV 1878	Harper's Ferry, W.Va.
003643	HAMMER, Katie Eliza	11m	W	D.C.	14 JUN 1874	Mt. Olivet
003656	HAMMER, Mary Ann	25y	W	Md.	15 JUN 1875	Mt. Olivet
010002	HAMMERS, Edward	62y	W	Prus.	18 DEC 1876	Soldier's Home
008677	HAMMERSLEY, John DeVaughn	8m	W	D.C.	13 AUG 1876	Congressional
019559	HAMMON, Abraham	73y	W	S.C.	26 MAR 1879	Brightwood
001766	HAMMOND, Anna Anthony	9d	C	D.C.	17 JAN 1875	Mt. Pleasant
011936	HAMMOND, Helen	c.85y	M	Md.	16 JUN 1877	Mt. Zion
013084	HAMMOND, Mary	72y	C	Md.	04 SEP 1877	Beckett's
018621	HAMMOND, Otho	45y	C	Md.	09 JAN 1879	Payne's
009543	HAMOND, Debby	71y	C	Md.	26 OCT 1876	Harmony
013931	HANCE, Milton J.	1y	W	D.C.	26 NOV 1877	Congressional
000194	HANCOCK, Barbara E.	2m	W	D.C.	15 AUG 1874	Fredericksburg, Va.
008437	HANDCOCK, Armigel W.E.	1y	W	D.C.	26 JUL 1876	Congressional
019894	HANDY, Infant of Theodore	6h	W	D.C.	25 APR 1879	Holy Rood
012804	HANDY, Josephine	10m	C	D.C.	14 AUG 1877	Mt. Olivet
020039	HANDY, Margaret Wilson	79y	W	Md.	08 MAY 1879	Congressional
017373	HANDY, William	35y	C	D.C.	11 SEP 1878	Mt. Zion
018597	HANE, Catharine	90y	W	Md.	07 JAN 1879	Oak Hill
009096	HANEKE, George A.	1y	W	D.C.	16 SEP 1876	Oak Hill

District of Columbia Death Records, August 1, 1874 to July 31, 1879   143

No.	Name	Age	Race	Birth	Death Date	Burial Place
009007	HANEKE, Louisa	8m	W	D.C.	08 SEP 1876	Holy Rood
019817	HANES, Edward	10m	C	D.C.	18 APR 1879	Payne's
012728	HANEY, Hugh	84y	W	Ire.	08 AUG 1877	Mt. Olivet
003619	HANEY, Jane	c.75y	W	Va.	12 JUN 1875	Mt. Olivet
005470	HANEY, Sarah F.	34y	W	D.C.	16 NOV 1875	Mt. Olivet
016692	HANIE, Lulu	3y	C	D.C.	20 JUL 1878	Potters Field
009379	HANKEY, William F.	2y	C	D.C.	11 OCT 1876	Mt. Pleasant
019320	HANKINS, Mary Paulina	8m	M	D.C.	08 MAR 1879	Mt. Olivet
016790	HANN, Mary E.	1y	W	D.C.	27 JUL 1878	Holy Rood
018883	HANNA, Eliza Frances	60y	W	Pa.	30 JAN 1879	Mt. Olivet
010568	HANNA, Francis	71y	W	Ire.	09 FEB 1877	Mt. Olivet
017394	HANNAN, Lorello	2y	W	D.C.	13 SEP 1878	Holy Rood
020357	HANNEMAN, Helene Olga	5m	W	D.C.	09 JUN 1879	Prospect Hill
019119	HANNIGAN, James	35y	W	N.Y.	19 FEB 1879	Soldier's Home
015930	HANRAHAN, Margaret	c.39y	W	Ire.	31 MAY 1878	Mt. Olivet
009838	HANSBOROUGH, May Etta	3y	W	Va.	01 DEC 1876	Methodist
017215	HANSBURY, Infant of Maria	1m	C	D.C.	27 AUG 1878	Beckett's
009782	HANSCUM, S.P.	53y	W	Me.	23 NOV 1876	Congressional
005259	HANSON, David	40y	W	D.C.	25 OCT 1875	Harmony
011235	HANSON, Fannie	35y	C	Md.	06 APR 1877	Harmony
018772	HANSON, Fred. Lowell	12d	W	D.C.	22 JAN 1879	Congressional
004943f	HANSON, Infant of George	8d	C	Md.	06 SEP 1875	Smith's
007357	HANSON, Infant of Willard	15d	C	D.C.	21 MAY 1876	Young Mens
009602	HANSON, Jonathan P.	c.40y	W	Mass.	02 NOV 1876	Danver, Mass.
012676	HANSON, Laura Virginia	5d	C	D.C.	05 AUG 1877	Ebenezer
013612	HANSON, Margaret	60y	C	D.C.	24 OCT 1877	Smith's
000968	HANSON, Mary E	6y	C	Md.	28 OCT 1874	Mt. Olivet
005372	HANSON, Mary L.	34y	W	Md.	06 NOV 1875	Baltimore, Md.
007467	HANSON, William Thomas	29y	C	D.C.	02 JUN 1876	Harmony
002804	HANSON, Willie A.	1y	C	D.C.	30 MAR 1875	Harmony
013282	HANY, John W.	1y	W	Md.	23 SEP 1877	Rockville, Md.
011551	HAPER, Sarah	11y	C	D.C.	09 MAY 1877	Penny Hill, Alex., Va.
012656	HAPPER, Robert	12d	C	D.C.	03 AUG 1877	Beckett's
010233	HARB, Edward K.	32y	W	Ind.	09 JAN 1877	Keokuk, Ia.
009404	HARBAUGH, Daniel	36y	W	D.C.	14 OCT 1876	Glenwood
002180	HARBAUGH, Joseph Francis	6m	W	D.C.	15 FEB 1875	Glenwood
020500	HARBIN, James R.	5m	W	D.C.	18 JUN 1879	Alexandria, Va.
016910	HARBIN, Jane Eliza	54y	W	Va.	05 AUG 1878	Congressional
010121	HARBIN, Julia A.	58y	W	Md.	30 MAY 1879	Mt. Olivet
004334	HARDEN, Julia	16y	W	Md.	27 JUL 1875	St. Mary's Co., Md.
010415	HARDEN, Mary	80y	W	Va.	27 JAN 1877	Congressional
008942	HARDESTEN, Alice J.	8m	W	D.C.	02 SEP 1876	Congressional
018860	HARDESTER, David	69y	W	Md.	28 JAN 1879	Congressional
013916	HARDESTER, Elmira P.	1m	W	D.C.	25 NOV 1877	Congressional
001653	HARDESTER, Emma Jane	1y	W	D.C.	08 JAN 1875	Congressional
013512	HARDESTON, Elmira	35y	W	Md.	14 OCT 1877	Congressional
021148	HARDESTY, Agnes	7y	C	D.C.	29 JUL 1879	Mt. Zion
004652	HARDESTY, Thomas H.	10m	W	D.C.	18 AUG 1875	Rock Creek
020027	HARDIE, Wm. Henry	4y	C	D.C.	07 MAY 1879	Tennallytown
009964	HARDIN, James Allen	53y	W	N.Y.	14 DEC 1876	Mt. Olivet
017270	HARDING, Kate G.	28y	W	Ire.	31 AUG 1878	Mt. Olivet
014899	HARDING, Mamie Elizabeth	5y	Q	Md.	28 FEB 1878	Harmony
008481	HARDING, Mary Francis	4m	W	D.C.	30 JUL 1876	Mt. Olivet
013337	HARDISTY, John Theodore	4y	W	D.C.	28 SEP 1877	Addison's Chapel
013886	HARDISTY, Kate	2y	W	D.C.	22 NOV 1877	Addison's Chapel
008219	HARDISTY, Rachel	7m	W	D.C.	12 JUL 1876	Rock Creek

No.	Name	Age	Race	Birth	Death Date	Burial Place
010123	HARDY, Ann	98y	W	Md.	30 DEC 1876	Congressional
016454	HARDY, Daniel, Jr.	2y	C	D.C.	05 JUL 1878	Graceland
003171	HARDY, David	3y	C	D.C.	29 APR 1875	Beckett's
005737	HARDY, Elizabeth	63y	W	Md.	13 DEC 1875	Potters Field
014825	HARDY, George	10m	C	D.C.	20 FEB 1878	Beckett's
011279	HARDY, Henry	2y	M	D.C.	09 APR 1877	Graceland
017009	HARDY, Mary C.	18y	W	D.C.	11 AUG 1878	Congressional
017319	HARDY, William H.	4y	C	D.C.	04 SEP 1878	Mt. Olivet
016739	HARFORD, Lucy	34y	W	D.C.	24 JUL 1878	Glenwood
000375	HARFORD, Robert A.	8m	W	D.C.	30 AUG 1874	Glenwood
014964	HARGERSON, Priscilla, Mrs.	78y	C	Pa.	06 MAR 1878	Mt. Pleasant
012250	HARKNESS, Florence Gray	18y	W	D.C.	07 JUL 1877	Oak Hill
007154	HARKNESS, Thomas F.	67y	W	D.C.	29 APR 1876	Oak Hill
002324	HARLAN, Lewis	25y	W	Ohio	26 FEB 1875	Glenwood
006660	HARLESTON, Georgiana	40y	W	N.Y.	13 MAR 1876	Oak Hill
006749	HARLESTON, Kate	35y	W	Mich.	20 MAR 1876	Oak Hill
015346	HARLEY, Aimee E.	1y	W	D.C.	10 APR 1878	Chester Co., Pa.
019503	HARLEY, Jessie Blanche	5y	W	D.C.	22 MAR 1879	Pottstown, Pa.
015077	HARLEY, Maurice Joseph	41y	W	Ire.	15 MAR 1878	Mt. Olivet
008703	HARLOW, Ida	4y	W	D.C.	16 AUG 1876	Congressional
019436	HARMAN, Catherine	38y	W	D.C.	17 MAR 1879	Holy Rood
019990	HARMAN, Charles B.	1m	W	D.C.	04 MAY 1879	Congressional
016705	HARMAN, Charles W.	50y	W	Md.	21 JUL 1878	Dorsey's
015265	HARMER, Hellen A.	6y	W	D.C.	02 APR 1878	Glenwood
005846	HARMON, Aaron	33y	W	Va.	24 DEC 1875	Alexandria, Va.
005619	HARMON, Charles Pascoe	36y	W	Va.	01 DEC 1875	Alexandria, Va.
020148	HARMON, Elizabeth	87y	W	Md.	19 MAY 1879	Presbyterian
018545	HARMON, Freeman Clark	31y	W	Me.	02 JAN 1879	Alexandria, Va.
012786	HARMON, Mary Elizabeth	7m	W	Va.	12 AUG 1877	Alexandria, Va.
005729	HARMON, Rebecca	50y	W	Va.	12 DEC 1875	Alexandria, Va.
011639	HARMON, William D.	3m	W	D.C.	18 MAY 1877	Tennallytown
000068	HARN, Magret	11m	W	D.C.	05 AUG 1874	Mt. Olivet
009166	HARNER, Henry Day	2y	C	D.C.	22 SEP 1876	Beckett's
007011	HARP, Margareth	52y	W	Va.	13 APR 1876	Presbyterian
002212	HARPER, Annie	24y	C	D.C.	18 FEB 1875	Potters Field
016205	HARPER, Austin	1m	C	D.C.	17 JUN 1878	Mt. Olivet
004142	HARPER, Charles Edward	10m	C	D.C.	15 JUL 1875	Ebenezer
013365	HARPER, Christopher	48y	W	Eng.	01 OCT 1877	Albany, N.Y.
019905	HARPER, Elizabeth	46y	W	N.Y.	26 APR 1879	Binghamton, N.Y.
017143	HARPER, Hannah	96y	C	Va.	22 AUG 1878	Beckett's
020732	HARPER, Harry	60y	C	Md.	03 JUL 1879	Smith's
012644	HARPER, James	5m	C	D.C.	02 AUG 1877	Young Mens
020358	HARPER, John Arthur	7y	W	D.C.	09 JUN 1879	Oak Hill
002747	HARPER, John Thomas	2y	C	D.C.	26 MAR 1875	Mt. Pleasant
001623	HARPER, Joseph	104y	C	D.C.	05 JAN 1875	Holy Rood
017933	HARPER, Joseph	7m	C	D.C.	03 NOV 1878	Beckett's
008298	HARPER, Mary Catharine	9m	C	D.C.	17 JUL 1876	Smith's
015519	HARPER, Mary F.	17y	C	Md.	26 APR 1878	Harmony
003034	HARPER, Mary W.	18y	C	D.C.	18 APR 1875	Mt. Pleasant
013544	HARPER, Zachariah Worth, Rev.	29y	W	Va.	17 OCT 1877	Congressional
017253	HARREN, Thomas	40y	W	Va.	30 AUG 1878	Mt. Olivet
001140	HARRIES, Alice	6m	C	D.C.	14 NOV 1874	Harmony
019989	HARRIES, Joseph	7y	C	D.C.	04 MAY 1879	Harmony
003502	HARRIGAN, John	2y	W	D.C.	01 JUN 1875	Mt. Olivet
009466	HARRINGTON, Daniel	6d	W	D.C.	19 OCT 1876	Holy Rood
019386	HARRINGTON, George Dana	55y	W	Ver.	13 MAR 1879	Bennington, Ver.

District of Columbia Death Records, August 1, 1874 to July 31, 1879   145

No.	Name	Age	Race	Birth	Death Date	Burial Place
016090	HARRINGTON, Henry F.	49y	W	Mass.	09 JUN 1878	Soldier's Home
019031	HARRINGTON, J.S.	45y	W	Ire.	11 FEB 1879	Hospital
013917	HARRINGTON, Margaret	7d	W	D.C.	25 NOV 1877	Holy Rood
012852	HARRINGTON, Mary	54y	W	Ire.	17 AUG 1877	Holy Rood
020637	HARRINGTON, Mary	15y	W	D.C.	27 JUN 1879	Mt. Olivet
012324	HARRIOD, Infant of Edward	1h	C	D.C.	12 JUL 1877	Ebenezer
005807	HARRIS, Albert	8d	C	D.C.	20 DEC 1875	Mt. Zion
008256	HARRIS, Alexander	21y	C	Va.	14 JUL 1876	Ebenezer
005051a	HARRIS, Anie	1y	C	D.C.	04 OCT 1875	Young Mens
020068	HARRIS, Ann W.	21y	C	Va.	11 MAY 1879	Baptist
013613	HARRIS, Annie	7y	C	D.C.	24 OCT 1877	Beckett's
018095	HARRIS, Arthur	3m	C	D.C.	19 NOV 1878	Mt. Pleasant
020696	HARRIS, Augustus Cary	7m	C	D.C.	01 JUL 1879	Harmony
020994	HARRIS, Bertie	6m	W	D.C.	18 JUL 1879	Congressional
006507	HARRIS, Catherine	4m	C	D.C.	29 FEB 1876	Young Mens
008583	HARRIS, Charles	2y	C	D.C.	07 AUG 1876	Harmony
015816	HARRIS, Charles Carroll	44y	W	R.I.	23 MAY 1878	Congressional/Arl.
020104	HARRIS, Charlie	1y	C	D.C.	15 MAY 1879	Mt. Pleasant
005041a	HARRIS, Chas.	14d	C	D.C.	03 OCT 1875	Beckett's
012236	HARRIS, Chauncey	39y	C	Va.	06 APR 1877	Potters Field
010884	HARRIS, Dinah	c.58y	C	Va.	06 MAR 1877	Young Mens
013853	HARRIS, Dora	5y	C	D.C.	18 NOV 1877	Harmony
018438	HARRIS, Eberle F.	4h	W	D.C.	23 DEC 1878	Frederick Co.
005916	HARRIS, Eliza	80y	C	U.S.	02 JAN 1876	Potters Field
002333	HARRIS, Elizabeth	35y	W	D.C.	26 FEB 1875	Methodist
009769	HARRIS, Fannie	1m	C	D.C.	22 NOV 1876	Young Mens
000544	HARRIS, Frances	17y	C	Va.	17 SEP 1874	Young Mens
020262	HARRIS, Francis	1y	C	D.C.	01 JUN 1879	Young Mens
000669	HARRIS, Henrietta	70y	C	Va.	29 SEP 1874	Young Mens
015012	HARRIS, Henrietta	c.130y	C	Md.	10 MAR 1878	Mt. Olivet
010743	HARRIS, Infant of Albert	1m	C	D.C.	22 FEB 1877	Mt. Zion
010556	HARRIS, Infant of Auusta	3d	C	D.C.	07 FEB 1877	Potters Field
000486	HARRIS, Infant of Chas.	6m	C	D.C.	12 SEP 1874	Potters Field
000581	HARRIS, Infant of Francis	4m	C	D.C.	20 SEP 1874	Potters Field
003267	HARRIS, Infant of Frank	1h	C	D.C.	09 MAY 1875	Beckett's
008229	HARRIS, Infant of Henry	7d	C	D.C.	13 JUL 1876	Young Mens
001025	HARRIS, Infant of J.	16d	W	D.C.	03 NOV 1874	Congressional
014598	HARRIS, Infant of Levi	15min	C	D.C.	30 JAN 1878	Potters Field
017990	HARRIS, Infant of Sarah	3d	C	D.C.	09 NOV 1878	Potters Field
018178	HARRIS, Infant of Walter	7d	C	D.C.	27 NOV 1878	Beckett's
010621	HARRIS, Irene M.	13y	C	D.C.	14 FEB 1877	Harmony
014941	HARRIS, Isabella	2y	C	D.C.	04 MAR 1878	Young Mens
002839	HARRIS, Ivanetta	12d	W	D.C.	02 APR 1875	Congressional
009372	HARRIS, James	64y	C	Va.	11 OCT 1876	Young Mens
010681	HARRIS, James	1y	W	D.C.	18 FEB 1877	Mt. Olivet
003727	HARRIS, James Edward	1y	C	D.C.	20 JUN 1875	Mt. Olivet
004965	HARRIS, James Henry	6y	C	Va.	09 SEP 1875	Ebenezer
017875	HARRIS, John	3m	C	D.C.	27 OCT 1878	Mt. Zion
019843	HARRIS, John	26y	C	Md.	20 APR 1879	Young Mens
017239	HARRIS, John H.	1y	C	D.C.	29 AUG 1878	Moore's
015935	HARRIS, John William	4y	C	D.C.	31 MAY 1878	Young Mens
000094	HARRIS, Lillian	16d	C	D.C.	07 AUG 1874	Young Mens
004543	HARRIS, Lizza	2y	C	D.C.	11 AUG 1875	Young Mens
019006	HARRIS, Lizzie	19y	W	D.C.	09 FEB 1879	Washington Asylum
019385	HARRIS, Louis	1y	C	D.C.	13 MAR 1879	Mt. Pleasant
014628	HARRIS, Maggie	2m	C	D.C.	01 FEB 1878	Brightwood

District of Columbia Death Records, August 1, 1874 to July 31, 1879

No.	Name	Age	Race	Birth	Death Date	Burial Place
003274	HARRIS, Maria	31y	M	Va.	09 MAY 1875	Potters Field
006254	HARRIS, Maria L.	29y	C	D.C.	06 FEB 1876	Mt. Zion
002073	HARRIS, Marry	45y	C	D.C.	07 FEB 1875	Ebenezer
018607	HARRIS, Martha	24y	C	Md.	08 JAN 1879	Moore's
008489	HARRIS, Mary	17y	M	Va.	30 JUL 1876	Harmony
012304	HARRIS, Mary	65y	C	Va.	10 JUL 1877	Harmony
013136	HARRIS, Mary C.	1m	C	D.C.	09 SEP 1877	Mt. Pleasant
018661	HARRIS, Mary E.	7y	C	D.C.	13 JAN 1879	Harmony
018058	HARRIS, Mary Elizabeth	19y	C	Va.	15 NOV 1878	Harmony
011456	HARRIS, Matilda	21d	C	D.C.	29 APR 1877	Young Mens
008342	HARRIS, Maud M.	3m	C	D.C.	20 JUL 1876	Potters Field
008999	HARRIS, May	9y	C	D.C.	08 SEP 1876	Young Mens
007097	HARRIS, Millie	1y	M	Va.	24 APR 1876	Union Baptist
013338	HARRIS, Minnie	30y	C	Md.	28 SEP 1877	Harmony
008519	HARRIS, Nancy	55y	C	Va.	01 AUG 1876	Ebenezer
016146	HARRIS, Noble	50y	C	Md.	13 JUN 1878	Mt. Zion
004050	HARRIS, Ora Allen	4m	W	Md.	08 JUL 1875	Tennallytown
014613	HARRIS, Owen	3y	C	D.C.	31 JAN 1878	Mt. Pleasant
007709	HARRIS, Robert Lane	19d	C	D.C.	18 JUN 1876	Jones [Chapel]
006281	HARRIS, Samuel	39y	C	Va.	09 FEB 1876	Ebenezer
007643	HARRIS, Samuel	1y	C	D.C.	14 JUN 1876	Baptist
002248	HARRIS, Sarah	10y	M	Tex.	20 FEB 1875	Ebenezer
017343	HARRIS, Sarah	30y	C	Va.	07 SEP 1878	Mt. Pleasant
016488	HARRIS, Sarah E.	2w	C	D.C.	07 JUL 1878	Potters Field
016847	HARRIS, Sarah T.	18m	C	D.C.	31 JUL 1878	Beckett's
007215	HARRIS, Susie	5m	C	D.C.	05 MAY 1876	Potters Field
006019	HARRIS, Walter	32y	W	Ohio	14 JAN 1876	Washington Asylum
016088	HARRIS, Walter	1y	C	D.C.	09 JUN 1878	Arlington, Va.
003140	HARRIS, William	9m	C	D.C.	26 APR 1875	Brightwood
010477	HARRIS, William	32y	C	Md.	01 FEB 1877	Hospital
013378	HARRIS, William	25y	C	Va.	02 OCT 1877	Beckett's
003998	HARRIS, William J.	63y	W	Md.	04 JUL 1875	Glenwood
017448	HARRIS, Willie	1y	C	D.C.	18 SEP 1878	Mt. Pleasant
000421	HARRIS, Wilson	35y	C	Va.	03 SEP 1874	Beckett's
001704	HARRIS, Wm. H.	30y	C	Va.	12 JAN 1875	Harmony
006282	HARRISON, Amelia	8y	C	D.C.	09 FEB 1876	Mt. Olivet
018439	HARRISON, Amelia	65y	C	Md.	23 DEC 1878	Beckett's
015387	HARRISON, Angela	70y	W	U.S.	13 APR 1878	Convent
010267	HARRISON, Anna	70y	W	Md.	12 JAN 1877	Oak Hill
011881	HARRISON, Benjamin	1m	C	D.C.	13 JUN 1877	Potters Field
015760	HARRISON, Bessie	6m	W	D.C.	18 MAY 1878	Prospect Hill
003917	HARRISON, Catherine Elizabeth	8m	C	D.C.	29 JUN 1875	Mt. Olivet
010086	HARRISON, Celia	6y	W	D.C.	26 DEC 1876	Graceland
018094	HARRISON, Edward	9m	C	D.C.	19 NOV 1878	Payne's
018771	HARRISON, Eleanor	58y	W	D.C.	22 JAN 1879	Oak Hill
013861	HARRISON, Ella	7y	M	D.C.	19 NOV 1877	Young Mens
021095	HARRISON, Ellen	79y	C	Md.	25 JUL 1879	Payne's
005482	HARRISON, Fanny	1m	C	D.C.	17 NOV 1875	Mt. Pleasant
019306	HARRISON, Frances A.	31y	W	Md.	07 MAR 1879	Congressional
020452	HARRISON, Fred	1y	C	D.C.	15 JUN 1879	Mt. Pleasant
015622	HARRISON, Fredrick	3y	C	D.C.	05 MAY 1878	Beckett's
006297	HARRISON, George	62y	W	Eng.	10 FEB 1876	Glenwood
005454	HARRISON, Henrietta	c.50y	C	Md.	14 NOV 1875	Mt. Olivet
011619	HARRISON, Henrietta	c.38y	C	Md.	16 MAY 1877	Ebenezer
009846	HARRISON, Henry	39y	C	Md.	02 DEC 1876	Mt. Pleasant
020962	HARRISON, Hiram J.	5m	C	D.C.	16 JUL 1879	Young Mens

District of Columbia Death Records, August 1, 1874 to July 31, 1879   147

No.	Name	Age	Race	Birth	Death Date	Burial Place
021064	HARRISON, Ida Ivey	1y	W	D.C.	23 JUL 1879	Congressional
004979	HARRISON, Infant of Wm.	½h	C	D.C.	10 SEP 1875	Potters Field
006735	HARRISON, Infant of John	30h	C	D.C.	19 MAR 1876	Potters Field
004084	HARRISON, John Edward	4m	W	D.C.	11 JUL 1875	Oak Hill
010432	HARRISON, Juliet G.	5y	W	D.C.	28 JAN 1877	Oak Hill
004611	HARRISON, Lemuel	1y	C	D.C.	15 AUG 1875	Young Mens
016330	HARRISON, Lillie	1y	C	D.C.	27 JUN 1878	Young Mens
004829	HARRISON, Margret	5m	C	D.C.	30 AUG 1875	Ebenezer
012233	HARRISON, Maria	80y	C	Md.	06 JUL 1877	Ebenezer
008817	HARRISON, Mariah	1m	C	D.C.	25 AUG 1876	Potters Field
008829	HARRISON, Martha	1m	C	D.C.	26 AUG 1876	Potters Field
004653	HARRISON, Mary Ann	69y	W	D.C.	18 AUG 1875	Congressional
012274	HARRISON, Priscilla	c.35y	C	Md.	09 JUL 1877	Harmony
011737	HARRISON, Robert	48y	W	D.C.	29 MAY 1877	Congressional
017587	HARRISON, Susan	4y	W	Va.	01 OCT 1878	Va.
016400	HARRISON, Susan Ann	½d	C	D.C.	02 JUL 1878	Beckett's
011891	HARRISON, Walter	1y	W	D.C.	14 JUN 1877	Mt. Olivet
019421	HARRISON, Walter	2y	C	D.C.	16 MAR 1879	Beckett's
007820	HARRISON, William	2d	C	D.C.	24 JUN 1876	Ebenezer
019545	HARRISS, Angelo	58y	C	Va.	25 MAR 1879	Arlington, Va.
010891	HARRISSON, Thomas	46y	W	Md.	07 MAR 1877	Congressional
004313	HARROD, Infant of Nelson	15m	C	D.C.	26 JUL 1875	Harmony
019830	HARROD, Nilem W.	39y	C	D.C.	19 APR 1879	Harmony
018206	HARROD, Robt.	65y	C	Va.	30 NOV 1878	Graceland
007196	HARROD, Samuel	33y	C	D.C.	03 MAY 1876	Mt. Zion
016569	HARROD, Thomas W.	9m	C	D.C.	12 JUL 1878	Harmony
011702	HARROVER, Lucy Ellen	32y	W	Va.	25 MAY 1877	Congressional
004110	HARROVER, Martha Ann	1m	W	D.C.	13 JUL 1875	Glenwood
004049	HARROVER, Martha Ann	39y	W	Ind.	08 JUL 1875	Glenwood
008058	HARROVER, Roberta May	7d	W	D.C.	07 JUL 1876	Congressional
002737	HARRYDAY, William Perry	2y	C	D.C.	25 MAR 1875	Mt. Pleasant
018662	HARSLEY, Emma	1y	C	D.C.	13 JAN 1879	Mt. Olivet
010788	HART, Andrew	40y	W	Prus.	26 FEB 1877	Mt. Olivet
000241	HART, Barnet	60y	W	Pa.	19 AUG 1874	Greenmount, Balt., Md.
004879	HART, Eugene	10m	C	D.C.	02 SEP 1875	Ebenezer
010368	HART, Forence	16y	C	Va.	22 JAN 1877	Arlington
020423	HART, Jno. F.	4m	W	D.C.	13 JUN 1879	Mt. Olivet
012194	HART, Josephine A.	50y	W	Md.	03 JUL 1877	Greenmount, Balt., Md.
005508	HART, Julia	6m	C	D.C.	19 NOV 1875	Ebenezer
012677	HART, Julia	1y	C	D.C.	05 AUG 1877	Ebenezer
014889	HART, Mary	73y	W	Ver.	27 FEB 1878	Guilford, Ver.
005825	HART, Michael	52y	W	Ire.	22 DEC 1875	Mt. Olivet
020162	HART, Thomas	8d	W	D.C.	21 MAY 1879	Mt. Olivet
000165	HARTBRECHT, Anna Eliz.	69y	W	Ger.	13 AUG 1874	St. Mary's
013432	HARTBRECHT, George	7y	W	D.C.	08 OCT 1877	St. Mary's
013719	HARTBRECHT, Wilhelm	5y	W	D.C.	03 NOV 1877	St. Mary's
016101	HARTEGAN, Catharine	1y	C	D.C.	10 JUN 1878	Mt. Olivet
015467	HARTENSTEIN, Anna O.	32y	W	Md.	21 APR 1878	Baltimore, Md.
010076	HARTGROVE, Olion	8m	C	D.C.	26 DEC 1876	Mt. Pleasant
020896	HARTING, John	10m	W	D.C.	12 JUL 1879	Prospect Hill
009998	HARTIWAY, Junius	3m	C	D.C.	18 DEC 1876	Young Mens
018893	HARTLEY, Hattie E.	3y	W	D.C.	31 JAN 1879	Congressional
018498	HARTLEY, James Barnard	3y	W	D.C.	29 DEC 1878	Congressional
010277	HARTMANN, Charles Edgar	17m	W	D.C.	13 JAN 1877	Prospect Hill
018608	HARTRIDGE, Julian	49y	W	Ga.	08 JAN 1879	Savannah, Ga.
015468	HARTSHORN, Sarah	84y	C	Va.	21 APR 1878	Mt. Olivet

No.	Name	Age	Race	Birth	Death Date	Burial Place
011383	HARTZ, Tilie	25y	W	Md.	21 APR 1877	Congressional
007350	HARTZFELD, Lanchen	28y	W	Ger.	20 MAY 1876	St. Mary's
012255	HARVEY, Agnes Veronica	1y	W	D.C.	07 JUL 1877	Mt. Olivet
018032	HARVEY, Augustus F.	5d	C	D.C.	12 NOV 1878	Harmony
020594	HARVEY, Catherine	45y	W	D.C.	24 JUN 1879	Mt. Olivet
019078	HARVEY, Elizabeth Ann	3y	W	D.C.	15 FEB 1879	Glenwood
020581	HARVEY, Francis W.	4m	W	D.C.	23 JUN 1879	Mt. Olivet
007373	HARVEY, Gertrude E.	11m	W	D.C.	22 MAY 1876	Mt. Olivet
010499	HARVEY, Infant of Eliza	27d	C	D.C.	03 FEB 1877	Payne's
001533	HARVEY, Infant of Wm.	2m	C	D.C.	29 DEC 1874	Mt. Zion
006059	HARVEY, James	48y	W	Ire.	18 JAN 1876	Mt. Olivet
002281	HARVEY, James H.	c.30y	C	Va.	22 FEB 1875	Young Mens
015805	HARVEY, Jesse Milton	3y	W	D.C.	22 MAY 1878	Glenwood
006045	HARVEY, Marie Lanorra	4y	W	D.C.	17 JAN 1876	Mt. Olivet
008156	HARVEY, Mary Ann, Mrs.	74y	W	Italy	10 JUL 1876	Mt. Olivet
019923	HARVEY, Nellie M.	6y	W	D.C.	28 APR 1879	Congressional
002863	HARVEY, Sarah Catherine Duffy	32y	W	D.C.	03 APR 1875	Mt. Olivet
004776	HARVEY, Thomas	43y	W	Ire.	27 AUG 1875	Mt. Olivet
002347	HARVEY, Thomas	56y	W	Md.	27 FEB 1875	Congressional
003361	HARVEY, Willie	10y	M	D.C.	18 MAY 1875	Mt. Pleasant
006894	HARVIN, Sarah A.	81y	W	Md.	02 APR 1876	Glenwood
011037	HARVY, Harriett E.	81y	W	D.C.	19 MAR 1877	Oak Hill
001054	HARVY, Infant of G.	10d	C	D.C.	05 NOV 1874	Harmony
015256	HARWOOD, Fannie Belle	27y	W	Va.	01 APR 1878	Richmond, Va.
015232	HASKE, Antony A.	4y	W	D.C.	30 MAR 1878	Mt. Olivet
016160	HASKE, Charles Leo	1m	W	D.C.	14 JUN 1878	Mt. Olivet
013036	HASKE, John Aloysius	1y	W	D.C.	31 AUG 1877	Mt. Olivet
005548	HASKER, Charles	32y	W	Ger.	24 NOV 1875	Hospital
018276	HASKIN, Andrew J.	32y	W	Va.	08 DEC 1878	Alexandria, Va.
003530	HASKIN, Jane E.	55y	W	Md.	05 JUN 1875	Alexandria, Va.
017662	HASKINS, Louisa	26y	I	I.T.	07 OCT 1878	Insane Asylum
010897	HASKINS, Williams	6½m	C	D.C.	07 MAR 1877	Mt. Pleasant
017167	HASLOCK, Thornton	23y	C	Va.	24 AUG 1878	Fairfax Co., Va.
005071a	HASON, Elizer M.	35y	C	D.C.	06 OCT 1875	Harmony
007076	HASSALL, Emma	40y	W	N.J.	22 APR 1876	Hoboken, N.J.
001283	HASSET, Bridget	57y	W	Ire.	01 DEC 1874	Mt. Olivet
000587	HASSETT, Henry E.	2m	W	D.C.	21 SEP 1874	Mt. Olivet
014563	HASSETT, James	21y	W	Va.	26 JAN 1878	Mt. Olivet
008915	HASSETT, James E.	15d	W	D.C.	01 SEP 1876	Mt. Olivet
013584	HASSETT, Michal	41y	W	Ire.	21 OCT 1877	Mt. Olivet
000446	HASTINGS, Fleming H.	1y	C	D.C.	07 SEP 1874	Young Mens
000496	HASTINGS, James	50y	W	Ire.	13 SEP 1874	Presbyterian
006669	HASWELL, Dawson	99y	C	Va.	14 MAR 1876	Potters Field
011304	HASWELL, Margaret Elizabeth	11m	W	D.C.	12 APR 1877	Mt. Olivet
001237	HATCHER, John F.	40y	W	Md.	26 NOV 1874	Glenwood
005650	HATHAWAY, John	45y	C	Va.	04 DEC 1875	Harmony
011455	HATMAKER, Thomas	9m	C	D.C.	29 APR 1877	Ebenezer
017989	HATTEN, Infant of Charles	5m	C	D.C.	09 NOV 1878	Beckett's
020085	HATTEN, Louisa	26y	C	Md.	13 MAY 1879	Thomas'
005483	HATTEN, Millie S.	5y	C	Va.	17 NOV 1875	Beckett's
007320	HATTEN, Mollie	76y	C	Va.	16 MAY 1876	Young Mens
017417	HATTON, George W.	46y	W	Md.	15 SEP 1878	Potters Field
003918	HATTON, James Henry	5m	C	D.C.	29 JUN 1875	Young Mens
002836	HATTON, Martha Maria	2y	C	D.C.	01 APR 1875	Beckett's
007798	HATTON, Richard W.	c.33y	C	Md.	23 JUN 1876	Harmony
019844	HAUPT, Charles A.	3w	W	D.C.	20 APR 1879	Glenwood

District of Columbia Death Records, August 1, 1874 to July 31, 1879

No.	Name	Age	Race	Birth	Death Date	Burial Place
001154	HAUPTMAN, George W.	7m	W	D.C.	16 NOV 1874	Congressional
002641	HAUPTMAN, John D.	19y	W	D.C.	19 MAR 1875	Oak Hill
017524	HAUSBUR, Infant of Albert	2w	C	D.C.	25 SEP 1878	Potters Field
012328	HAUSER, Louisa	42y	W	Ger.	12 JUL 1877	Hospital
011813	HAUSMAN, Robt. Lee	11m	W	D.C.	06 JUN 1877	Congressional
007003	HAUSMANN, Sophie Wilhelmine	49y	W	Ger.	12 APR 1876	Prospect Hill
016348	HAVENER, Ann	50y	W	D.C.	28 JUN 1878	Congressional
005484	HAVENER, Mary F.	13y	W	D.C.	17 NOV 1875	Congressional
016927	HAVENER, Olmsted	62y	W	Va.	06 AUG 1878	Smithfield, Va.
003338	HAVENNER, Charles Clifford	5y	W	D.C.	16 MAY 1875	Congressional
017823	HAWINS, Richard W.	1y	W	D.C.	21 OCT 1878	Mt. Olivet
020103	HAWKESWORTH, Mary, Mrs.	64y	C	W.I.	15 MAY 1879	Harmony
010839	HAWKINS, Alfred	45y	C	Md.	02 MAR 1877	Mt. Zion
011101	HAWKINS, Alfred	8y	C	D.C.	24 MAR 1877	Mt. Zion
001001	HAWKINS, Anna	1½d	M	D.C.	01 NOV 1874	Potters Field
009694	HAWKINS, Arthur	2y	C	D.C.	14 NOV 1876	Mt. Pleasant
003730	HAWKINS, Burndena	2y	C	D.C.	20 JUN 1875	Mt. Zion
004667	HAWKINS, Callie	24y	C	Va.	19 AUG 1875	Beckett's
010562	HAWKINS, Catherine	1y	C	D.C.	08 FEB 1877	Ebenezer
010339	HAWKINS, Charity J.E.	26y	C	Md.	19 JAN 1877	Annapolis, Md.
007844	HAWKINS, Charles	30y	C	Md.	25 JUN 1876	Potters Field
014640	HAWKINS, Clias	1y	C	D.C.	02 FEB 1878	Beckett's
012564	HAWKINS, Elizabeth	11y	C	D.C.	27 JUL 1877	Mt. Zion
007143	HAWKINS, Elizebeth	63y	W	Ire.	28 APR 1876	Mt. Olivet
017157	HAWKINS, Ella	3m	C	D.C.	23 AUG 1878	Beckett's
001725	HAWKINS, Florence	14d	C	D.C.	14 JAN 1875	Potters Field
010244	HAWKINS, Floyd	38y	C	Va.	10 JAN 1877	Potters Field
005041	HAWKINS, Frank	6m	C	D.C.	14 SEP 1875	Ebenezer
007923	HAWKINS, Frank	1y	C	D.C.	29 JUN 1876	Ebenezer
017252	HAWKINS, Frederick	22y	C	Md.	30 AUG 1878	Beckett's
009637	HAWKINS, George	5m	C	D.C.	08 NOV 1876	Ebenezer
016729	HAWKINS, Grace E.	1y	C	D.C.	23 JUL 1878	Harmony
012144	HAWKINS, Gurtie	10m	C	D.C.	30 JUN 1877	Ebenezer
005320	HAWKINS, Hannah	40y	C	D.C.	31 OCT 1875	Smith's
012295	HAWKINS, Helen L.	26y	C	D.C.	10 JUL 1877	Mt. Zion
001907	HAWKINS, Henrietta	80y	C	Md.	27 JAN 1875	Harmony
003169	HAWKINS, Henry	9y	C	D.C.	29 APR 1875	Harmony
014250	HAWKINS, Henry	16y	C	Md.	29 DEC 1877	Mt. Zion
014599	HAWKINS, Henry	1y	C	D.C.	30 JAN 1878	Potters Field
018189	HAWKINS, Henry	85y	C	Md.	28 NOV 1878	Potters Field
017158	HAWKINS, Ida	6m	C	D.C.	23 AUG 1878	Potters Field
010139	HAWKINS, Infant of Charles	1h	C	D.C.	01 JAN 1877	Holy Rood
008310	HAWKINS, Infant of George	5d	C	D.C.	18 JUL 1876	Potters Field
007747	HAWKINS, Infant of Minnie F.	6m	C	D.C.	20 JUN 1876	Ebenezer
008851	HAWKINS, Infant of Thomas	7m	C	D.C.	28 AUG 1876	Ebenezer
001389	HAWKINS, J. Patric	65y	C	Md.	14 DEC 1874	Potters Field
003855	HAWKINS, James	4y	C	D.C.	26 JUN 1875	Ebenezer
017931	HAWKINS, James A.	7d	C	D.C.	03 NOV 1878	Potters Field
013918	HAWKINS, Jane	72y	C	D.C.	25 NOV 1877	Holy Rood
014237	HAWKINS, John Francis	9y	C	D.C.	28 DEC 1877	Beckett's
011107	HAWKINS, Joseph	c.35y	W	Ohio	25 MAR 1877	Washington Asylum
016704	HAWKINS, Josiah	1y	C	D.C.	21 JUL 1878	Mt. Olivet
010124	HAWKINS, Julia	77y	W	Md.	30 DEC 1876	Oak Hill
002775	HAWKINS, Katie	1y	C	D.C.	28 MAR 1875	Beckett's
013049	HAWKINS, Margaret Louise	8m	C	D.C.	01 SEP 1877	Beckett's
002862	HAWKINS, Maria	75y	C	D.C.	03 APR 1875	Potters Field

No.	Name	Age	Race	Birth	Death Date	Burial Place
018755	HAWKINS, Martha	1y	C	D.C.	21 JAN 1879	Mt. Pleasant
018378	HAWKINS, Mary	80y	C	Md.	19 DEC 1878	Holy Rood
002053	HAWKINS, Mary E.	35y	M	Md.	06 FEB 1875	Mt. Olivet
014458	HAWKINS, Mary Elizabeth	9d	C	D.C.	17 JAN 1878	Beckett's
012874	HAWKINS, Patience	c.100y	C	Md.	19 AUG 1877	Mt. Pleasant
017109	HAWKINS, Patience	36y	C	Md.	19 AUG 1878	Beckett's
010952	HAWKINS, Prissilla	48y	C	Md.	12 MAR 1877	Ebenezer
014686	HAWKINS, Richard	38y	C	Md.	06 FEB 1878	Harmony
011018	HAWKINS, Robert	50y	C	Md.	17 MAR 1877	Thomas'
016789	HAWKINS, Robt.	10m	C	D.C.	27 JUL 1878	Harmony
003461	HAWKINS, Robt., Jr.	2y	C	D.C.	28 MAY 1875	Mt. Olivet
020186	HAWKINS, Rosa	8m	C	D.C.	24 MAY 1879	Harmony
002252	HAWKINS, Ruth	115y	C	Md.	20 FEB 1875	Beckett's
010498	HAWKINS, Samuel George	7y	C	D.C.	03 FEB 1877	Ebenezer
004070	HAWKINS, Susannah	57y	W	Md.	10 JUL 1875	Glenwood
017735	HAWKINS, Thomas Edward	7y	C	D.C.	14 OCT 1878	Beckett's
006033	HAWKINS, Virginia	7d	C	D.C.	15 JAN 1876	Ebenezer
008690	HAWKINS, William Alfred	2y	C	D.C.	15 AUG 1876	Ebenezer
000829	HAWKINS, William H.	1y	C	D.C.	16 OCT 1874	Young Mens
015576	HAWKINS, Wm. Henry	33y	C	D.C.	01 MAY 1878	Beckett's
002779f	HAWKS, Hannah Gaston	38y	W	N.C.	22 APR 1874	Mt. Olivet
004353	HAY, Harry	11m	W	D.C.	28 JUL 1875	Rock Creek
011075	HAY, Henry	80y	W	Mass.	22 MAR 1877	Oak Hill
014953	HAYDEN, Edith W.	10m	W	D.C.	05 MAR 1878	Congressional
016436	HAYDEN, Grace	7y	W	D.C.	04 JUL 1878	Oak Hill/Rome, N.Y.
009305	HAYDEN, James	50y	W	Ire.	04 OCT 1876	Mt. Olivet
010660	HAYDEN, Margaret	31y	W	Ire.	16 FEB 1877	Mt. Olivet
019307	HAYDEN, Margaret Teresa	2m	W	D.C.	07 MAR 1879	Mt. Olivet
020011	HAYDEN, Washington	65y	C	Va.	06 MAY 1879	Union Baptist
013101	HAYDEN, Woodley Vincent	3m	W	D.C.	06 SEP 1877	Mt. Olivet
003564	HAYDORN, Ivy	4m	W	D.C.	05 JUN 1875	Prospect Hill
012769	HAYES, Charles Lindsay	19d	C	D.C.	11 AUG 1877	Ebenezer
005874	HAYES, Daniel	60y	W	Ire.	27 DEC 1875	Soldier's Home
010598	HAYES, Elizabeth	65y	C	Va.	12 FEB 1877	Young Mens
003828	HAYES, Henrietta	10m	W	D.C.	25 JUN 1875	Congressional
014349	HAYES, John Wm.	6m	C	D.C.	07 JAN 1878	Mt. Zion
012931	HAYES, Katie	4y	W	D.C.	24 AUG 1877	Mt. Olivet
010360	HAYES, Mary	65y	W	Ire.	21 JAN 1877	Mt. Olivet
021096	HAYES, Nathaniel	49y	W	Del.	25 JUL 1879	Congressional
010614	HAYES, Thomas	3y	W	D.C.	13 FEB 1877	Holy Rood
011575	HAYES, Timothy	38y	W	Ire.	12 MAY 1877	Mt. Olivet
008728	HAYES, Uriah L.	34y	W	Pa.	18 AUG 1876	Hospital
018315	HAYMAN, Barrett	73y	C	Md.	12 DEC 1878	Payne's
009714	HAYMAN, Margaret	56y	W	Va.	17 NOV 1876	Mt. Olivet
016387	HAYNES, David C.	17y	W	Va.	01 JUL 1878	St. Mary's
009560	HAYNES, Grace Heaton	9y	W	D.C.	28 OCT 1876	Oak Hill
006957	HAYNES, James	52y	C	Va.	07 APR 1876	Young Mens
017142	HAYNIE, Willard H.	24y	W	Md.	22 AUG 1878	Montgomery Co., Md.
017058	HAYS, Albert Lindner	9d	W	D.C.	15 AUG 1878	Congressional
004738	HAYS, Elizebeth	26y	C	D.C.	24 AUG 1875	Mt. Pleasant
014582	HAYS, Ella	2m	C	D.C.	28 JAN 1878	Mt. Olivet
002263	HAYS, George	19y	W	D.C.	21 FEB 1875	Congressional
010905	HAYS, George	37y	W	D.C.	08 MAR 1877	Addison's Chapel
002436	HAYS, George W.	11m	C	D.C.	05 MAR 1875	Moore's
008308	HAYS, Infant of Richard	30min	C	D.C.	17 JUL 1876	Young Mens
018812	HAYS, Julia	40y	W	Ire.	25 JAN 1879	Mt. Olivet

District of Columbia Death Records, August 1, 1874 to July 31, 1879

No.	Name	Age	Race	Birth	Death Date	Burial Place
014046	HAYS, Maria	45y	C	Va.	09 DEC 1877	Macedonia
010063	HAYS, Michl.	40y	W	Ire.	24 DEC 1876	Mt. Olivet
012032	HAYS, R.B.	8d	W	D.C.	24 JUN 1877	Potters Field
006750	HAYS, Sarah J.	34y	C	Va.	20 MAR 1876	Moore's
015223	HAYS, Spalding	76y	W	Md.	29 MAR 1878	Brandywine, Md.
003167	HAYS, William Glascoe	3y	C	D.C.	29 APR 1875	Moore's
005127a	HAYS, Willie	5d	C	D.C.	13 OCT 1875	Ebenezer
013180	HAYSE, William H.	3y	C	N.J.	13 SEP 1877	Beckett's
002680	HAYSON, John Hesyl	27y	C	D.C.	21 MAR 1875	Beckett's
018553	HAZARD, Harriet A.F.	60y	W	Va.	03 JAN 1879	Congressional
016956	HAZARD, Lotta E.	3m	W	D.C.	08 AUG 1878	Congressional
021161	HAZBERG, Rosa	2m	W	D.C.	30 JUL 1879	Washington Hebrew
002812	HAZEL, Agnes Cecelia	3y	W	D.C.	31 MAR 1875	Mt. Olivet
013195	HAZEL, Henry Clifford	1y	W	D.C.	14 SEP 1877	Mt. Olivet
004625	HAZEL, Robt.	11m	W	D.C.	16 AUG 1875	Mt. Olivet
012851	HAZZARD, Eddie Warder	9d	W	D.C.	17 AUG 1877	Glenwood
014954	HEAD, George M.	72y	W	Ky.	05 MAR 1878	Oak Hill
016756	HEAD, Joshua	10m	C	D.C.	25 JUL 1878	Potters Field
000386	HEAD, William	58y	W	Va.	31 AUG 1874	Congressional
011926	HEALD, Crosby	4y	W	Mass.	16 JUN 1877	Graceland
002227	HEALD, Jane Standish, Mrs.	77y	W	D.C.	18 FEB 1875	Glenwood
009507	HEALEY, Catharine	42y	W	Ire.	23 OCT 1876	Mt. Olivet
006777	HEALEY, James	33y	W	Ire.	22 MAR 1876	Hospital
013878	HEALY, Catherine, Mrs.	70y	W	Ire.	21 NOV 1877	Mt. Olivet
005029	HEALY, Cecelia Plowden	9y	W	N.J.	13 SEP 1875	Mt. Olivet
018813	HEANEY, Hancock H.	52y	W	Va.	25 JAN 1879	Congressional
001831	HEARD, Mary C.	35y	W	Md.	21 JAN 1875	Holy Rood
006365	HEARD, Salina	12y	C	D.C.	15 FEB 1876	Holy Rood
003951	HEARN, Mary A.	2m	W	D.C.	01 JUL 1875	Mt. Olivet
006084	HEARNS, Ellin	8y	C	Va.	21 JAN 1876	Harmony
016347	HEARNS, Martha	6m	C	D.C.	28 JUN 1878	Young Mens
001880	HEARNTON, Marlend	22y	C	D.C.	24 JAN 1875	Mt. Pleasant
013450	HEASELY, Harry Clay	2m	W	D.C.	09 OCT 1877	Graceland
015820	HEATH, Ann W.	78y	W	Va.	24 MAY 1878	Glenwood
006612	HEATH, Frances M.	55y	W	N.Y.	09 MAR 1876	Waukesha, Wisc.
012994	HEATH, Isabella C.	36y	W	Ire.	28 AUG 1877	Mt. Olivet
004812	HEATON, David	24y	W	Ohio	29 AUG 1875	Glenwood
011275	HEATON, Mae B.	31y	W	N.H.	09 APR 1877	Oak Hill
001392	HEAVNER, Mary E.	38y	W	W.Va.	15 DEC 1874	Buckhannan, W.Va.
016154	HEBB, Carie	1d	C	D.C.	13 JUN 1878	Beckett's
018401	HEBER, Faitz	29y	W	Ger.	20 DEC 1878	Soldier's Home
013995	HEBRON, Sarah	17y	C	Md.	03 DEC 1877	Holy Rood
013946	HECHINGER, Solomon	56y	W	Ger.	27 NOV 1877	Washington Hebrew
014188	HECK, Katie Elizabeth	11y	W	D.C.	24 DEC 1877	Mt. Olivet
009499	HECK, Lucretia Isebia	9m	W	D.C.	22 OCT 1876	Winona, Minn.
020330	HECKMAN, Christianna	4m	C	D.C.	07 JUN 1879	Mt. Pleasant
005869	HEDINGER, Albert P.	2y	W	D.C.	26 DEC 1875	Congressional
019924	HEDRICK, Lillian May	18y	W	D.C.	28 APR 1879	Glenwood
010029	HEDRICK, Susan J.	49y	W	D.C.	20 DEC 1876	Glenwood
003640	HEFFNER, Emma Sarah	2y	W	D.C.	14 JUN 1875	Glenwood
003512	HEFFNER, James Edward	7y	W	D.C.	02 JUN 1875	Glenwood
013587	HEIDE, Henry Vander	42y	W	Ger.	21 OCT 1877	Prospect Hill
002818	HEIDENHEIMER, Eva	78y	W	Ger.	31 MAR 1875	Hebrew
007675	HEIGHT, Sarah Jane	56y	C	Va.	16 JUN 1876	Family Ground
005745	HEIL, Michael	45y	W	Ger.	14 DEC 1875	St. Mary's
020697	HEILPEIN, Hendel	76y	W	Pol.	01 JUL 1879	Washington Hebrew

151

District of Columbia Death Records, August 1, 1874 to July 31, 1879

No.	Name	Age	Race	Birth	Death Date	Burial Place
006497	HEIMER, Carrie	1y	W	D.C.	28 FEB 1876	Congressional
004430	HEINLINE, George W.	34y	W	D.C.	03 AUG 1875	Congressional
005091a	HEINLINE, Lillie C.	7y	W	D.C.	09 OCT 1875	Congressional
008061	HEINMAN, Geo. Wm.	7d	W	D.C.	07 JUL 1876	Methodist
002487	HEINMAN, James	2y	C	D.C.	09 MAR 1875	Ebenezer
016225	HEINTZEL, Catrina Eliz. Clarissa	35y	W	Md.	19 JUN 1878	Methodist
007224	HEINTZEL, Robt. T.	15d	W	D.C.	06 MAY 1876	Methodist
008004	HEINZERLING, George	52y	W	Ger.	04 JUL 1876	Prospect Hill
016757	HEINZTEL, Oscar Emil Jos. Fr.	1y	W	D.C.	25 JUL 1878	Mt. Olivet
002058	HEIRD, Carrie May	8m	W	D.C.	07 FEB 1875	Baltimore, Md.
017759	HEIRD, Clarence Carter	2½m	W	D.C.	16 OCT 1878	Baltimore, Md.
000336	HEISS, George	1y	W	D.C.	27 AUG 1874	Prospect Hill
011269	HEITMAN, Mary Virginia	11y	W	D.C.	08 APR 1877	Holy Rood
010300	HEITMULLER, Augusta	73y	W	Ger.	15 JAN 1877	Glenwood
020028	HEITMULLER, Augusta Laura	39y	W	Ger.	07 MAY 1879	Glenwood
003400	HEITMULLER, Lewis Fredrick	17m	W	D.C.	22 MAY 1875	Glenwood
003359	HELIN, Margaret A.	26y	W	Ind.	18 MAY 1875	Muncie, Ind.
012770	HELLEN, Adelaide	88y	W	Md.	11 AUG 1877	Rock Creek
008119	HELLEN, Charles Washington	29y	W	D.C.	10 JUL 1876	Mt. Olivet
006032	HELLEN, Jane Elizabeth	68y	W	Md.	15 JAN 1876	Mt. Olivet
001297	HELLEN, Thomas Clifton	39y	W	D.C.	03 DEC 1874	Mt. Olivet
017736	HELLER, Joseph Berrows	16y	W	D.C.	14 OCT 1878	Washington Hebrew
018723	HELLMUTH, Geo.	2m	W	D.C.	19 JAN 1879	Prospect Hill
021149	HELLMUTH, Martin W.	2m	W	D.C.	29 JUL 1879	Prospect Hill
016049	HELLMUTH, Willie	1y	W	D.C.	07 JUN 1878	Prospect Hill
020012	HELM, Julius	33y	W	Ger.	06 MAY 1879	Prospect Hill
008110	HELMBUCH, Johnny	17y	W	D.C.	09 JUL 1876	Congressional
005284	HELMICK, George	66y	W	Ohio	27 OCT 1875	Glenwood
006245	HELMODE, Mary Odele	8m	W	D.C.	05 FEB 1876	St. Mary's?
005953	HELMSEN, Isabella	46y	W	Eng.	06 JAN 1876	Congressional
010219	HELMSLEY, Perry	39y	C	Md.	08 JAN 1877	Potters Field
003780	HELPHENSTINE, Lillie	1d	W	D.C.	23 JUN 1875	Glenwood
009459	HEMM, Bartholomew	46y	W	Ger.	18 OCT 1876	St. Mary's
006402	HEMSLEY, Robt.	23y	C	Md.	18 FEB 1876	Beckett's
001458	HEMSLY, Henry	89y	C	Md.	21 DEC 1874	Beckett's
012453	HENAULT, Jules S.	69y	W	France	21 JUL 1877	Congressional
015954	HENDERSON, Adell Alexander	4m	C	D.C.	03 JUN 1878	Harmony
020453	HENDERSON, Albert N.	1y	C	D.C.	15 JUN 1879	Congressional
014047	HENDERSON, Benjamin	17y	C	D.C.	09 DEC 1877	Potters Field
011214	HENDERSON, Charles	66y	C	Va.	04 APR 1877	Beckett's
004183	HENDERSON, Charles E.	37y	W	Va.	18 JUL 1875	Oak Hill
019489	HENDERSON, Edward	1m	C	D.C.	21 MAR 1879	Beckett's
009567	HENDERSON, Eliza	4m	C	D.C.	29 OCT 1876	Young Mens
020897	HENDERSON, Florence	1y	C	D.C.	12 JUL 1879	Mt. Pleasant
010723	HENDERSON, Hattie Ann	1y	C	D.C.	21 FEB 1877	Ebenezer
018400	HENDERSON, Henry	35y	C	Va.	20 DEC 1878	Young Mens
014986	HENDERSON, Henry	47y	C	Md.	08 MAR 1878	Potters Field
019399	HENDERSON, Henry	84y	C	Va.	14 MAR 1879	Union Baptist
013905	HENDERSON, Infant of George	14h	C	D.C.	24 NOV 1877	Beckett's
010616	HENDERSON, Infant of George	15min	C	D.C.	13 FEB 1877	Potters Field
001834	HENDERSON, Infant of Mr.	14m	C	D.C.	21 JAN 1875	Potters Field
017459	HENDERSON, Infant of Susan	4d	C	D.C.	19 SEP 1878	Potters Field
005104a	HENDERSON, Infant of Vennie	2m	C	D.C.	11 OCT 1875	Ebenezer
003827	HENDERSON, James M.	1m	C	D.C.	25 JUN 1875	Mt. Pleasant
014430	HENDERSON, Jane	48y	C	Va.	15 JAN 1878	Potters Field
000983	HENDERSON, John N.	61y	W	Pa.	30 OCT 1874	Congressional

District of Columbia Death Records, August 1, 1874 to July 31, 1879   153

No.	Name	Age	Race	Birth	Death Date	Burial Place
019488	HENDERSON, Joseph	21d	C	D.C.	21 MAR 1879	Beckett's
018469	HENDERSON, Lathema	25y	C	Va.	26 DEC 1878	Payne's
003008	HENDERSON, Luella	20y	C	D.C.	16 APR 1875	Mt. Pleasant
009819	HENDERSON, Lula Lee	13y	W	D.C.	28 NOV 1876	Congressional
020187	HENDERSON, Madison	1y	C	D.C.	24 MAY 1879	Payne's
004463	HENDERSON, Martha Ann	7y	C	D.C.	05 AUG 1875	Mt. Pleasant
003853	HENDERSON, Martha G.	80y	W	Va.	26 JUN 1875	Holy Rood
010700	HENDERSON, Mary	30y	C	Va.	19 FEB 1877	Ebenezer
011320	HENDERSON, Millie	70y	C	Va.	13 APR 1877	Mt. Olivet
009039	HENDERSON, Rachel	25y	C	Md.	12 SEP 1876	Arlington
019207	HENDERSON, Richard	4y	C	D.C.	26 FEB 1879	Graceland
013083	HENDERSON, Robert	5y	C	D.C.	04 SEP 1877	Mt. Zion
005904	HENDERSON, Thomas	1y	C	D.C.	31 DEC 1875	Mt. Pleasant
013147	HENDERSON, Thomas	6y	C	Va.	10 SEP 1877	Mt. Zion
020425	HENDERSON, Thomas	5y	C	D.C.	13 JUN 1879	Harmony
009495	HENDERSON, Walter	3y	C	D.C.	22 OCT 1876	Mt. Pleasant
000621	HENDERSON, William	3m	C	D.C.	23 SEP 1874	Young Mens
012817	HENDERSON, William	2m	C	D.C.	15 AUG 1877	Payne's
014316	HENDERSON, William	12y	C	Va.	04 JAN 1878	Potters Field
009802	HENDLEN, Mary Elizabeth	61y	W	N.Y.	26 NOV 1876	Long Island, N.Y.
000740	HENDLEY, John Richard	54y	W	D.C.	07 OCT 1874	Congressional
000491	HENDLEY, Lela	30y	W	Md.	12 SEP 1874	Glenwood
015532	HENDLEY, Ocenia Allade	20y	W	D.C.	27 APR 1878	Congressional
005757	HENDREE, Sarah A.	85y	W	Va.	15 DEC 1875	Richmond, Va.
005996	HENDRICKS, Jacob	33y	W	Ohio	11 JAN 1876	St. Paris, Ohio
000564	HENDRICKS, Thomas L.	1y	W	D.C.	19 SEP 1874	Glenwood
002600	HENE, Doretha	84y	W	Ger.	16 MAR 1875	Glenwood
001983	HENEGAN, Bertha	1y	C	D.C.	01 FEB 1875	Mt. Pleasant
013389	HENING, Alice Ann	60y	W	Md.	03 OCT 1877	Glenwood
006824	HENISON, Willy	1y	C	D.C.	26 MAR 1876	Young Mens
012203	HENLON, Lulie	5m	W	D.C.	03 JUL 1877	Young Mens
014797	HENLY, Charlie	1y	C	D.C.	17 FEB 1878	Harmony
010798	HENNESSEY, Timothy	62y	W	Ire.	27 FEB 1877	Mt. Olivet
004368	HENNESSY, John H.	26y	W	Md.	29 JUL 1875	Mt. Olivet
008038	HENNING, John Robert	19y	W	Md.	05 JUL 1876	Glenwood
020963	HENNINGS, Thos.	3m	W	D.C.	16 JUL 1879	Mt. Olivet
011900	HENNINGSEN, Charles F.	c.65y	W	Eng.	14 JUN 1877	Congressional
000474	HENRY, Ackrey	1y	C	D.C.	11 SEP 1874	Young Mens
020995	HENRY, Ann Maria	5m	C	D.C.	18 JUL 1879	Mt. Pleasant
007624	HENRY, Bertram	10m	C	D.C.	13 JUN 1876	Beckett's
016693	HENRY, Charles	6d	C	D.C.	20 JUL 1878	Beckett's
006098	HENRY, Daniel	43y	W	Ire.	22 JAN 1876	Mt. Olivet
011033	HENRY, Edith	1m	W	D.C.	18 MAR 1877	Oak Hill
000730	HENRY, Emily	40y	C	D.C.	06 OCT 1874	Washington Asylum
001590	HENRY, George	43y	W	N.Y.	02 JAN 1875	Glenwood
009253	HENRY, Ida	1y	C	D.C.	30 SEP 1876	Potters Field
007184	HENRY, Infant of Chas.	6h	C	D.C.	02 MAY 1876	Potters Field
007183	HENRY, Infant of Chas.	6h	C	D.C.	02 MAY 1876	Potters Field
007185	HENRY, Infant of Chas.	6h	C	D.C.	02 MAY 1876	Potters Field
014741	HENRY, Infant of Cecil	5d	C	D.C.	11 FEB 1878	Potters Field
013683	HENRY, James W.	30y	C	Va.	31 OCT 1877	Beckett's
011185	HENRY, John Chs.	1y	C	D.C.	01 APR 1877	Ebenezer
015708	HENRY, Joseph	80y	W	N.Y.	13 MAY 1878	Oak Hill
007819	HENRY, Leanne	5m	C	D.C.	24 JUN 1876	Ebenezer
009016	HENRY, Louise	1m	C	D.C.	09 SEP 1876	Ebenezer
019267	HENRY, Ludwell Braxton	10y	W	Va.	03 MAR 1879	Graceland

No.	Name	Age	Race	Birth	Death Date	Burial Place
021066	HENRY, Maria Estell	15m	W	D.C.	23 JUL 1879	Mt. Olivet
004354	HENRY, Mary	50y	C	Va.	28 JUL 1875	Ebenezer
018692	HENRY, Patrick	43y	C	Va.	16 JAN 1879	Potters Field/Mt. Pleasant
019341	HENRY, Philip	45y	W	Ire.	09 MAR 1879	Mt. Olivet
000817	HENRY, Robert V.	47y	W	D.C.	16 OCT 1874	Congressional
000843	HENRY, Thomas	3y	C	D.C.	17 OCT 1874	Young Mens
011365	HENRY, Thos. Wm.	86y	C	D.C.	18 APR 1877	Hagerstown, Md.
018724	HENRY, William	30y	W	Ger.	19 JAN 1879	Potters Field
014826	HENSEL, Liza	47y	W	Ger.	20 FEB 1878	Prospect Hill
020964	HENSELL, Charles	9y	W	D.C.	16 JUL 1879	Prospect Hill
002918	HENSER, Wm.	10y	W	D.C.	08 APR 1875	Prospect Hill
014331	HENSLEY, Harry Clay	32y	W	D.C.	05 JAN 1878	Graceland
003403	HENSON, Andrew	77y	C	D.C.	22 MAY 1875	Mt. Olivet
016114	HENSON, Ellen	c.50y	C	Md.	11 JUN 1878	Mt. Pleasant
001193	HENSON, Ellen (Robinson)	c.50y	C	D.C.	17 NOV 1874	Hospital
008736	HENSON, Elsie Ann	10m	C	D.C.	19 AUG 1876	Mt. Olivet
000220	HENSON, George	14y	W	D.C.	17 AUG 1874	Congressional
010327	HENSON, Harriett	18y	C	Md.	18 JAN 1877	Ebenezer
009038	HENSON, Hattie	1y	C	D.C.	12 SEP 1876	Harmony
013741	HENSON, Ida	1y	C	D.C.	05 NOV 1877	Beckett's
013229	HENSON, Infant of John H.	2d	C	D.C.	17 SEP 1877	Beckett's
018093	HENSON, Infant of George	½d	C	D.C.	19 NOV 1878	Beckett's
005113a	HENSON, John B.	6y	C	D.C.	12 OCT 1875	Harmony
007298	HENSON, John Henry	35y	C	Va.	14 MAY 1876	Smith Chapel, Richmond
014664	HENSON, Mary Francis	1y	C	D.C.	04 FEB 1878	Mt. Olivet
020938	HENSON, Mattie Evans	2y	C	D.C.	15 JUL 1879	Smith's
017447	HENSON, Randall	37y	W	Va.	18 SEP 1878	Potters Field
009718	HENSON, Sarah	7d	C	D.C.	17 NOV 1876	Ebenezer
008374	HENSON, Virginia	1m	C	D.C.	22 JUL 1876	Young Mens
018059	HEPBURN, Caroline	17y	W	D.C.	15 NOV 1878	Congressional
018913	HEPBURN, David	79y	W	D.C.	01 FEB 1879	Rock Creek
018020	HEPBURN, Ettie	18y	W	D.C.	11 NOV 1878	Congressional
018077	HEPBURN, Isabella	53y	W	D.C.	17 NOV 1878	Congressional
018693	HEPBURN, Jeny	21y	W	D.C.	16 JAN 1879	Congressional
014251	HEPBURN, Mary B.	21y	W	D.C.	29 DEC 1877	Congressional
003473	HEPBURN, William W.	22y	W	D.C.	29 MAY 1875	Congressional
008944	HEPNAR, Eva	9m	W	D.C.	03 SEP 1876	Adas Israel
009143	HEPRON, Annie	27y	W	Ire.	20 SEP 1876	Alexandria, Va.
000830	HERBEL, Louise	17y	W	D.C.	17 OCT 1874	Prospect Hill
004005	HERBERT, Adaline	57y	M	Md.	05 JUL 1875	Harmony
008704	HERBERT, Agnes	8m	W	D.C.	16 AUG 1876	Mt. Olivet
012493	HERBERT, Albert E.	1y	W	D.C.	23 JUL 1877	Prospect Hill
013354	HERBERT, Ann	24y	C	Md.	30 SEP 1877	Mt. Zion
011347	HERBERT, Antony	c.45y	C	Md.	15 APR 1877	Mt. Olivet
009928	HERBERT, Eliza	63y	C	Md.	11 DEC 1876	Mt. Olivet
005495	HERBERT, Elizabeth	63y	C	D.C.	18 NOV 1875	Holy Rood
017201	HERBERT, Elizabeth	c.100y	C	Md.	26 AUG 1878	Harmony
009497	HERBERT, Henry	1m	W	D.C.	22 OCT 1876	Mt. Olivet
020780	HERBERT, Henry	65y	C	Md.	05 JUL 1879	Mt. Olivet
015131	HERBERT, Infant of Clement	12h	C	D.C.	20 MAR 1878	Harmony
008139	HERBERT, James	56y	C	Md.	10 JUL 1876	Mt. Olivet
017926	HERBERT, James	1y	C	D.C.	02 NOV 1878	Mt. Olivet
005042	HERBERT, James L.	1y	W	Va.	14 SEP 1875	Congressional
001746	HERBERT, Jane Louisa	24y	C	D.C.	15 JAN 1875	Young Mens
007644	HERBERT, Jane Rebeca	5m	C	D.C.	14 JUN 1876	Mt. Zion
011990	HERBERT, John T.W.	8m	W	D.C.	21 JUN 1877	Congressional

District of Columbia Death Records, August 1, 1874 to July 31, 1879   155

No.	Name	Age	Race	Birth	Death Date	Burial Place
003690	HERBERT, Julia	11m	W	D.C.	18 JUN 1875	Mt. Olivet
014650	HERBERT, Julia	46y	M	Va.	03 FEB 1878	Young Mens
020048	HERBERT, Leonard J.	7m	C	D.C.	09 MAY 1879	Mt. Olivet
006272	HERBERT, Maria	22y	C	D.C.	08 FEB 1876	Mt. Zion
015623	HERBERT, Mariah	75y	C	Md.	05 MAY 1878	Harmony
011076	HERBERT, Robert	23y	C	Md.	22 MAR 1877	Jones Chapel
014296	HERBERT, Rosa Ellen	15y	C	D.C.	02 JAN 1878	Harmony
016331	HERBERT, Samuel M.	31y	W	D.C.	27 JUN 1878	Glenwood
016175	HERBERT, Smith	20y	C	Md.	15 JUN 1878	Mt. Olivet
000053	HERBERT, William J.	10m	C	D.C.	04 AUG 1874	Harmony
005639	HERBERT, Willie	1y	C	D.C.	03 DEC 1875	Young Mens
005797	HERBERT, Wm.	59y	M	Md.	19 DEC 1875	Mt. Olivet
007108	HERBERT, Wm. G.	55y	W	D.C.	25 APR 1876	Oak Hill
002173	HERBURT, William H.	11m	C	D.C.	15 FEB 1875	Young Mens
003164	HERFURTH, August	8y	W	D.C.	29 APR 1875	Prospect Hill
016177	HERFURTH, August	49y	W	Ger.	16 JUN 1878	Prospect Hill
019602	HERING, Eleonore	37y	W	Ger.	30 MAR 1879	Prospect Hill
004832	HERLIHY, Catharine	41y	W	Ire.	30 AUG 1875	Mt. Olivet
001617	HERLIHY, Dennis	65y	W	Ire.	05 JAN 1875	Mt. Olivet
002438	HERLIHY, Johanna	71y	W	Ire.	05 MAR 1875	Mt. Olivet
004563	HERLIHY, John T.	16y	W	D.C.	12 AUG 1875	Mt. Olivet
002482	HERMOND, Debbie C.	30y	W	D.C.	09 MAR 1875	Oak Hill
001338	HERMOND, George Everest	3y	W	D.C.	08 DEC 1874	Oak Hill
016706	HERNDON, Harry	1d	W	D.C.	21 JUL 1878	Glenwood
001045	HERNDON, Robert	6w	C	D.C.	04 NOV 1874	Mt. Pleasant
012630	HERNE, Plantry	4y	M	D.C.	01 AUG 1877	Harmony
004352	HERNE, Seborna	9m	W	D.C.	28 JUL 1875	Holy Rood
014481	HEROD, Martha	4y	C	D.C.	19 JAN 1878	Mt. Zion
001382	HEROLD, Frederick William	27y	W	Va.	14 DEC 1874	St. Mary's
019729	HEROLT, Frederick	17d	W	D.C.	11 APR 1879	Congressional
010580	HERON, Fannie E.	41y	W	N.Y.	10 FEB 1877	Newark, N.J.
006785	HERR, Henry	16y	W	Va.	23 MAR 1876	Oak Hill
008373	HERR, Willis	15y	W	W.Va.	22 JUL 1876	Oak Hill
019882	HERRELL, Infant of Jno. R.	2h	W	D.C.	24 APR 1879	Congressional
008362	HERRITEE, Martin	76y	W	Ire.	21 JUL 1876	Mt. Olivet
000191	HERRITY, James	65y	W	D.C.	15 AUG 1874	Mt. Olivet
013288	HERRLE, Annie	1y	W	D.C.	24 SEP 1877	Prospect Hill
001467	HERRMEIN, Edward	3y	W	D.C.	23 DEC 1874	Prospect Hill
000226	HERRON, Maggie A.	7y	W	D.C.	18 AUG 1874	Mt. Olivet
002529	HERRON, Mary	74y	W	Pa.	12 MAR 1875	New Cumberland, Ohio
001155	HERZBURG, Infant of Charles	6d	W	D.C.	16 NOV 1874	Hebrew
005435	HESLIN, Valentine	26y	W	N.Y.	12 NOV 1875	N.Y. City
010383	HESS, Carroline	47y	W	Ger.	23 JAN 1877	Glenwood
010335	HESS, Frances	59y	W	Swed.	19 JAN 1877	Washington Asylum
003053	HESS, Jno. M.	64y	W	Ger.	20 APR 1875	Prospect Hill
012572	HESS, Margaret V.	6m	W	D.C.	28 JUL 1877	Glenwood
009428	HESS, William O.	48y	W	Md.	16 OCT 1876	Mt. Olivet
019642	HESSE, Elizabeth	5y	W	D.C.	03 APR 1879	St. Mary's
014128	HESTER, Alexander	3y	W	D.C.	18 DEC 1877	Prospect Hill
019933	HESTER, Roberta Lee	3y	W	D.C.	29 APR 1879	Oak Hill
008144	HEURICH, Anna	1y	W	D.C.	10 JUL 1876	St. Mary's
008271	HEURICH, Domean	35y	W	Ger.	15 JUL 1876	St. Mary's
004141	HEURICH, Joseph	4y	W	D.C.	15 JUL 1875	St. Mary's
000186	HEWETT, Rena	3y	C	D.C.	14 AUG 1874	Young Mens
002161	HEWIT, C.	35y	C	Va.	14 FEB 1875	Harmony
017231	HEWITT, Annie Maria C.	21y	C	Va.	28 AUG 1878	Harmony

No.	Name	Age	Race	Birth	Death Date	Burial Place
006085	HEWITT, Caroline E.	2m	M	D.C.	21 JAN 1876	Mt. Zion
001581	HEWITT, Mary Elizabeth	46y	W	Md.	02 JAN 1875	Congressional
010908	HEWITT, Mary V.	30y	C	Va.	08 MAR 1877	Mt. Zion
018703	HEWITT, William H.	27y	C	Va.	17 JAN 1879	Harmony
005153a	HEWLETT, Catherine	83y	C	Va.	15 OCT 1875	Baptist
014283	HEWLETT, Hatte Olivia	1y	C	D.C.	01 JAN 1878	Beckett's
013050	HEWLETT, Robert	3y	C	D.C.	01 SEP 1877	Beckett's
016788	HEWLETT, Virginia Josephine	60y	C	N.Y.	27 JUL 1878	Boston, Mass.
005574	HEWSTON, John T.	5y	W	N.C.	26 NOV 1875	Mt. Olivet
005744	HEXTER, Sarah	64y	W	Ger.	14 DEC 1875	Washington Hebrew
011802	HEYLMUN, Clara	17y	W	Pa.	05 JUN 1877	Glenwood
003241	HIBBENS, Lidia	49y	W	Ohio	06 MAY 1875	Gallipolis, Ohio
000949	HIBBS, Marion Francis	28y	W	D.C.	27 OCT 1874	Oak Hill
021172	HICKEY, Catharine Anne	18y	W	D.C.	31 JUL 1879	Mt. Olivet
018499	HICKEY, Dan'l	86y	W	Ire.	29 DEC 1878	Mt. Olivet
014159	HICKEY, Esther C., Mrs.	60y	W	Pa.	21 DEC 1877	Congressional
008184	HICKEY, James	45y	W	Ire.	11 JUL 1876	Mt. Olivet
012416	HICKEY, James	3y	W	D.C.	18 JUL 1877	Mt. Olivet
012415	HICKEY, Margaret	5y	W	D.C.	18 JUL 1877	Mt. Olivet
014083	HICKEY, Patrick	67y	W	Ire.	13 DEC 1877	Soldier's Home
014135	HICKEY, Patrick F.	20y	W	D.C.	19 DEC 1877	Mt. Olivet
015806	HICKMAN, Ann	9y	C	D.C.	22 MAY 1878	Potters Field
015025	HICKMAN, Cassie	1m	C	D.C.	11 MAR 1878	Potters Field
020424	HICKMAN, Daniel	50y	C	Va.	13 JUN 1879	Potters Field
018468	HICKMAN, Gertrude	7d	C	D.C.	26 DEC 1878	Beckett's
014406	HICKMAN, Isalina	8m	C	D.C.	13 JAN 1878	Harmony
012046	HICKMAN, Jane Elizabeth	57y	C	D.C.	25 JUN 1877	Harmony
019339	HICKMAN, John Lewis, Sr.	74y	C	D.C.	09 MAR 1879	Harmony
014418	HICKMAN, Louisa	86y	C	Md.	14 JAN 1878	Potters Field
015931	HICKMAN, Martha	21y	C	Va.	31 MAY 1878	Young Mens
006872	HICKMAN, Thomas C.S.	12d	M	D.C.	31 MAR 1876	Harmony
001737f	HICKMAN, William	51y	C	Va.	14 JAN 1875	Young Mens
006498	HICKOK, James	26y	C	N.C.	28 FEB 1876	Washington Asylum
000667	HICKS, Any	6y	C	D.C.	29 SEP 1874	Harmony
003411	HICKS, Arabella	5y	C	D.C.	23 MAY 1875	Harmony
003360	HICKS, Harriet	25m	M	D.C.	18 MAY 1875	Harmony
015582	HICKS, Helen J.	2y	C	D.C.	02 MAY 1878	Beckett's
001245	HICKS, Ida	4m	C	D.C.	27 NOV 1874	Harmony
020820	HICKS, Infant of Mary	14d	W	D.C.	07 JUL 1879	Prospect Hill
019398	HICKS, Infant of Nancy	1d	C	D.C.	14 MAR 1879	Moore's
014006	HICKS, Isabella	3m	C	D.C.	04 DEC 1877	Harmony
006178	HICKS, James A.	1m	C	D.C.	29 JAN 1876	Harmony
009341	HICKS, James W.	6d	C	D.C.	08 OCT 1876	Harmony
010168	HICKS, Joseph	7m	C	D.C.	03 JAN 1877	Harmony
001896	HICKS, Mary	61y	C	D.C.	26 JAN 1875	Holy Rood
019397	HICKS, Nancy	c.39y	C	Va.	14 MAR 1879	Moore's
017108	HICKS, Robert L.	5y	C	D.C.	19 AUG 1878	Harmony
006376	HICKS, Walter	2y	M	D.C.	16 FEB 1876	Graceland
010780	HICKS, Walter	15m	C	D.C.	25 FEB 1877	Young Mens
011833	HICKS, William Pepper	35y	W	D.C.	07 JUN 1877	Mt. Olivet
019988	HICKY, Thomas	20y	W	D.C.	04 MAY 1879	Mt. Olivet
004218	HIESKELL, William B.	24y	W	Pa.	20 JUL 1875	Oak Hill
013697	HIETZLER, Chas. Theodore	11d	W	D.C.	01 NOV 1877	Methodist
004171	HIGBY, Luella	1m	W	D.C.	17 JUL 1875	Congressional
020712	HIGDEN, Clara	85y	C	Va.	02 JUL 1879	Mt. Pleasant
001340	HIGDON, John	80y	C	Va.	08 DEC 1874	Mt. Pleasant

District of Columbia Death Records, August 1, 1874 to July 31, 1879   157

No.	Name	Age	Race	Birth	Death Date	Burial Place
004831	HIGGINS, Annie Rebecca	30y	W	D.C.	30 AUG 1875	Glenwood
010773	HIGGINS, Henrietta	8m	C	D.C.	25 FEB 1877	Ebenezer
015266	HIGGINS, Mary Ellen	30y	W	Md.	02 APR 1878	Glenwood
004578	HIGGS, Samuel	30y	W	Ind.	13 AUG 1875	Hospital
015520	HIGH, Fredrick A.	3y	W	D.C.	26 APR 1878	Congressional
011812	HIKINGS, William	c.24y	C	D.C.	06 JUN 1877	Mt. Olivet
011878	HILBUS, Ida E.	21y	W	D.C.	13 JUN 1877	Mt. Olivet
010673	HILGARD, Aloysios	6h	W	D.C.	17 FEB 1877	Mt. Olivet
012629	HILGARD, Joseph E.	34y	W	Md.	01 AUG 1877	Congressional
014213	HILINGER, John	28y	W	Ger.	26 DEC 1877	Hospital, Government
012864	HILL, Adolphus H.	1y	M	D.C.	18 AUG 1877	Tappahannock, Va.
020909	HILL, Albert	2m	C	D.C.	13 JUL 1879	Beckett's
005013	HILL, Alfred	1y	C	D.C.	12 SEP 1875	Ebenezer
000597	HILL, Ann	1y	C	D.C.	22 SEP 1874	Harmony
001870	HILL, Anna	6y	W	Md.	24 JAN 1875	Presbyterian
011795	HILL, Anthony	45y	C	D.C.	04 JUN 1877	Harmony
009153	HILL, Benjamin T.	7y	C	D.C.	21 SEP 1876	Beckett's
015876	HILL, Bertha	5m	C	D.C.	28 MAY 1878	Payne's
009902	HILL, Betsy	c.30y	C	Va.	08 DEC 1876	Ebenezer
010851	HILL, Carrie Etta	15m	C	D.C.	03 MAR 1877	Harmony
015676	HILL, Charles Franklin	3y	W	W.Va.	10 MAY 1878	Barnesville, Md.
002727	HILL, Chas. H.	30y	C	Md.	25 MAR 1875	Moore's
009032	HILL, Chas. H.	6m	C	D.C.	11 SEP 1876	Beckett's
008189	HILL, Chas. Wesley	9m	C	D.C.	11 JUL 1876	Moore's
016385	HILL, Clancy	82y	C	D.C.	01 JUL 1878	Moore's
015640	HILL, Claude Kingary	10y	W	Md.	07 MAY 1878	Barnesville, Md.
009686	HILL, Clinton	5y	C	D.C.	13 NOV 1876	Harmony
007861	HILL, Coleman	70y	C	Va.	26 JUN 1876	Potters Field
017758	HILL, Copious	4y	C	D.C.	16 OCT 1878	Moore's
017516	HILL, Dumpsy	8m	W	D.C.	24 SEP 1878	Congressional
016632	HILL, Eddie	4y	C	D.C.	17 JUL 1878	Payne's
020130	HILL, Edward	60y	C	Va.	17 MAY 1879	Potters Field
009469	HILL, Elizabeth	19y	M	Va.	20 OCT 1876	Essex Co., Va.
019355	HILL, Emma	14m	C	D.C.	10 MAR 1879	Beckett's
012477	HILL, Eva Bell	11m	W	D.C.	22 JUL 1877	Mt. Olivet
011225	HILL, Fenwick A.	1y	W	D.C.	05 APR 1877	Mt. Olivet
011798	HILL, Frederick	51y	C	Va.	04 JUN 1877	Potters Field
000988	HILL, George	1m	W	D.C.	30 OCT 1874	Presbyterian
008134	HILL, George	20y	C	Md.	10 JUL 1876	Thomas'
011629	HILL, George	c.64y	W	N.Y.	17 MAY 1877	Glenwood
015723	HILL, George	2m	W	D.C.	14 MAY 1878	Mt. Olivet
019340	HILL, George Oliver	6m	W	Mass.	09 MAR 1879	Glenwood
005859	HILL, Hannah	75y	C	Va.	25 DEC 1875	Young Mens
010727	HILL, Harry	4m	C	D.C.	22 FEB 1877	Young Mens
012125	HILL, Hattie Anna	7d	W	D.C.	29 JUN 1877	Glenwood
017642	HILL, Henry	87y	C	Md.	05 OCT 1878	Mt. Zion
020105	HILL, Henry	60y	C	Va.	15 MAY 1879	Beckett's
006337	HILL, Infant of Daniel	15min	C	D.C.	13 FEB 1876	Payne's
014651	HILL, Infant of David	5h	W	D.C.	03 FEB 1878	Barnesville, Md.
020283	HILL, Infant of Louis H.	27d	C	D.C.	03 JUN 1879	Potters Field
007776	HILL, Jacob	8m	C	D.C.	22 JUN 1876	Young Mens
015132	HILL, Jane F.	44y	C	D.C.	20 MAR 1878	Beckett's
007901	HILL, John	2y	C	D.C.	28 JUN 1876	Ebenezer
008784	HILL, John Edward	25y	W	Ga.	22 AUG 1876	Madison, Ga.
021009	HILL, John H.	11m	C	D.C.	19 JUL 1879	Payne's
015666	HILL, John Robert	7y	W	Va.	09 MAY 1878	Barnesville, Md.

No.	Name	Age	Race	Birth	Death Date	Burial Place
008758	HILL, Joseph	3m	W	D.C.	20 AUG 1876	Mt. Olivet
018307	HILL, Joshua A.	32y	C	D.C.	11 DEC 1878	Graceland
020858	HILL, Lilly May	17m	W	D.C.	09 JUL 1879	St. Ignatius, Md.
001126	HILL, Louisa	30y	C	Md.	11 NOV 1874	Mt. Olivet
007075	HILL, Lucinda	62y	C	Va.	22 APR 1876	Ebenezer
018826	HILL, Lucy	19y	C	Va.	26 JAN 1879	Potters Field
004198	HILL, Lucy A.	3y	C	D.C.	19 JUL 1875	Ebenezer
009148	HILL, Mamie	9d	W	D.C.	21 SEP 1876	Congressional
020069	HILL, Martha Ellen Corcoran	72y	C	D.C.	11 MAY 1879	Oak Hill
019620	HILL, Mary	9y	C	D.C.	01 APR 1879	Young Mens
019708	HILL, Mary	26y	C	Va.	09 APR 1879	Graceland
017383	HILL, Mary A.	26y	W	Me.	12 SEP 1878	Mt. Olivet
009241	HILL, Mary Rebecca	59y	W	N.Y.	29 SEP 1876	Glenwood
017824	HILL, Mary Wilson	5m	W	D.C.	21 OCT 1878	Glenwood/Rock Creek
006958	HILL, Minnie	7y	C	Ill.	07 APR 1876	Mt. Zion
012818	HILL, Minnie B.	3y	W	D.C.	15 AUG 1877	Mt. Olivet
002298	HILL, Nancy	2y	C	D.C.	23 FEB 1875	Potters Field
009261	HILL, Nathan	75y	C	Va.	01 OCT 1876	Mt. Pleasant
019643	HILL, Nehemiah	42y	W	N.J.	03 APR 1879	Glenwood
019487	HILL, Percilla	8m	C	D.C.	21 MAR 1879	Va.
008431	HILL, Richard	30y	C	Va.	26 JUL 1876	Beckett's
013696	HILL, Sarah Catherine	8m	C	D.C.	01 NOV 1877	Mt. Olivet
008334	HILL, Theodore	1y	C	D.C.	19 JUL 1876	Harmony
012093	HILL, Thomas	11m	C	D.C.	27 JUN 1877	Ebenezer
012219	HILL, William	1y	C	D.C.	04 JUL 1877	Harmony
016737	HILL, Williard D.	11m	W	D.C.	24 JUL 1878	Oak Hill
005101	HILL, Willie	8m	W	D.C.	19 SEP 1875	Congressional
007760	HILLDEBRAND, A.G.	43y	W	Ohio	21 JUN 1876	Congressional
011537	HILLEARY, Andrew C.	4y	W	D.C.	07 MAY 1877	Holy Rood
011468	HILLEARY, Jas. E.	3y	W	D.C.	30 APR 1877	Holy Rood
002213	HILLEARY, Mary I.	28y	W	Va.	18 FEB 1875	Congressional
012643	HILLEARY, Stacey	74y	C	Md.	02 AUG 1877	Mt. Zion
009565	HILLEARY, William	c.82y	W	Md.	28 OCT 1876	Three Sisters, Md.
011531	HILLIARY, Arthur U.	2y	W	D.C.	06 MAY 1877	Holy Rood
003285	HILLMAN, Catherine	17y	C	Md.	11 MAY 1875	Mt. Olivet
007693	HILLS, Laura E.	39y	W	N.Y.	17 JUN 1876	Oak Hill
015224	HILTON, Eliza Ann	43y	W	D.C.	29 MAR 1878	Oak Hill
020713	HILTON, George R.	61y	W	D.C.	02 JUL 1879	Glenwood
005143	HILTON, Mary	79y	W	Md.	14 OCT 1875	Mt. Olivet
002599	HINCH, Henrietta	28y	W	Switz.	16 MAR 1875	Prospect Hill
021049	HINCKS, William	56y	W	Eng.	22 JUL 1879	Cohasset, Mass.
006432	HINDMAN, William	29y	C	Md.	21 FEB 1876	Ebenezer
011336	HINDS, Cornelia	31y	W	D.C.	15 APR 1877	Oak Hill
002363	HINDS, Edward M.	31y	W	N.Y.	28 FEB 1875	Oak Hill
006812	HINE, Annie Rebecca Albright	22y	W	Pa.	25 MAR 1876	Mauch Chunk, Pa.
000711	HINE, Harriet Amelia	46y	W	Mass.	04 OCT 1874	Congressional
017183	HINEMAN, Celia Alberta	1y	W	D.C.	25 AUG 1878	Congressional
001266	HINES, Christian	94y	W	Md.	29 NOV 1874	Rock Creek
016738	HINES, Harry B.	2y	W	Va.	24 JUL 1878	Mt. Olivet
001234	HINES, Jacob	96y	W	Md.	26 NOV 1874	Glenwood
011246	HINES, Jane E.	3y	C	D.C.	06 APR 1877	Mt. Zion
001626	HINES, Nathan	56y	C	Md.	06 JAN 1875	Potters Field
001973	HINES, Rebecca	17y	W	Va.	01 FEB 1875	Graceland
002875	HINES, Thomas H.	c.35y	C	D.C.	05 APR 1875	Harmony
018380	HINKLEBEIN, Sarah C	7y	W	D.C.	19 DEC 1878	Mt. Olivet
014912	HIRSCH, Bine	37y	W	Ger.	01 MAR 1878	Washington Hebrew

District of Columbia Death Records, August 1, 1874 to July 31, 1879   159

No.	Name	Age	Race	Birth	Death Date	Burial Place
002714	HIRSCH, Ella	4m	W	D.C.	24 MAR 1875	Washington Hebrew
012196	HIRSCH, Florence	7m	W	D.C.	03 JUL 1877	Washington Hebrew
009761	HISLIP, James	61y	W	Va.	20 NOV 1876	Potters Field
009749	HITZ, Jeann Pauline	6y	W	Switz.	20 NOV 1876	Congressional
013414	HOBAN, Jane	30y	C	Va.	06 OCT 1877	Beckett's
008961	HOBAN, Margaret	31y	C	Va.	04 SEP 1876	Westmoreland, Va.
010344	HOBAN, Mary	80y	C	Va.	20 JAN 1877	Ebenezer
010595	HOBBS, Josphiene	21y	W	Va.	12 FEB 1877	Congressional
002462	HOBSON, Richard	3y	C	Va.	07 MAR 1875	Mt. Pleasant
004962	HOCH, Catherine	77y	W	Ger.	09 SEP 1875	Prospect Hill
004948	HOCKLING, Rosa	17d	C	D.C.	07 SEP 1875	Ebenezer
014120	HODDY, John	2m	C	D.C.	17 DEC 1877	Beckett's
013433	HODGDON, Jacob	75y	W	Me.	08 OCT 1877	Boston, Mass.
012995	HODGE, Sofa	8y	C	D.C.	28 AUG 1877	Mt. Olivet
012585	HODGES, Josephine	60y	W	D.C.	28 JUL 1877	Glenwood
019709	HODGES, Sarah Annette	32y	W	D.C.	09 APR 1879	Congressional
003057	HODGES, Silas H.	71y	W	Ver.	20 APR 1875	Rutland, Ver.
015332	HODGKIN, Robert Edwin	44y	W	Va.	09 APR 1878	Glenwood
006941	HODGKINS, Mary A.	1y	W	D.C.	06 APR 1876	Glenwood
019665	HODGKINS, Mary C.	21y	W	D.C.	05 APR 1879	Oak Hill
010585	HODGKINS, Oscar	5y	W	D.C.	11 FEB 1877	Congressional
005014	HODGKINS, Samuel P.	43y	W	D.C.	12 SEP 1875	Holy Rood
019237	HODSON, Joseph F.	2y	W	D.C.	28 FEB 1879	Congressional
004929	HOE, Gustavus	24y	C	D.C.	06 SEP 1875	Harmony
008486	HOE, Infant of Thomas	14d	C	D.C.	30 JUL 1876	Potters Field
014161	HOESTER, Adara	6y	W	D.C.	21 DEC 1877	Prospect Hill
011738	HOEY, Eliza	c.48y	W	Ire.	29 MAY 1877	Congressional
009178	HOFER, Robert	46y	W	Gre.	23 SEP 1876	Prospect Hill
018459	HOFF, Henry Kuhn	69y	W	Pa.	25 DEC 1878	Philadelphia, Pa.
003979	HOFFMAN, Jacob	54y	W	Ger.	03 JUL 1875	Mt. Olivet
000777	HOFFMAN, John A.	45y	W	Ger.	11 OCT 1874	St. Mary's
008267	HOFFMAN, Rosina	7m	W	D.C.	15 JUL 1876	Congressional
008132	HOFFMANN, John	48y	W	Ger.	10 JUL 1876	St. Mary's
014548	HOFHEINZ, Carolina Wilhelmina	62y	W	Ger.	25 JAN 1878	Prospect Hill
011854	HOGAN, Ann	22y	W	Eng.	09 JUN 1877	Holy Rood
017240	HOGAN, Clara	112y	C	Va.	29 AUG 1878	Potters Field
007144	HOGAN, John	55y	W	Ire.	28 APR 1876	Soldier's Home
012771	HOGAN, John	3m	W	D.C.	11 AUG 1877	Holy Rood
017925	HOGAN, John Millen	2y	W	D.C.	01 NOV 1878	Congressional
001785	HOGAN, Reuben M.	74y	M	Va.	18 JAN 1875	Potters Field
011111	HOGAN, Thomas	73y	W	Ire.	25 MAR 1877	Soldier's Home
017271	HOGAN, Thomas	8y	W	D.C.	31 AUG 1878	Mt. Olivet
001227	HOGAN, William	82y	W	Eng.	25 NOV 1874	N.Y.
010719	HOGANS, Francis	19y	M	Mich.	21 FEB 1877	Mt. Olivet
002926	HOGARTY, John	4m	W	D.C.	08 APR 1875	Mt. Olivet
004415	HOGUE, Frederick A.	1y	W	Ill.	02 AUG 1875	Congressional
013789	HOHMANN, Margaret, Mrs.	61y	W	Ger.	10 NOV 1877	St. Mary's
001677	HOLAND, I. Gaines	24y	W	D.C.	10 JAN 1875	Glenwood
012820	HOLBROOK, Lydia Ann	43y	W	Md.	15 AUG 1877	Congressional
002170	HOLCIER, Henr	3y	W	D.C.	15 FEB 1875	St. Mary's
014707	HOLCOMBE, Florence	35y	W	N.Y.	08 FEB 1878	Congressional
015200	HOLDEN, Charles	32y	W	Ger.	27 MAR 1878	Hospital
016305	HOLDEN, Paul T.	5m	W	U.S.	25 JUN 1878	Graceland
009112	HOLEMAN, John	1m	W	D.C.	17 SEP 1876	Presbyterian
002642	HOLEN, William B.	20d	W	D.C.	19 MAR 1875	St. Mary's
018523	HOLLAND, Annia	2d	W	D.C.	31 DEC 1878	Mt. Olivet

No.	Name	Age	Race	Birth	Death Date	Burial Place
004676	HOLLAND, Charles Edward	1y	C	D.C.	20 AUG 1875	Moore's
005903	HOLLAND, Clement	60y	C	Md.	31 DEC 1875	Potters Field
015114	HOLLAND, Ella S.	29y	W	Va.	18 MAR 1878	Congressional
013110	HOLLAND, Fanie	76y	C	Md.	07 SEP 1877	Harmony
008769	HOLLAND, Felix C.	9m	W	D.C.	21 AUG 1876	Mt. Olivet
018069	HOLLAND, Henry	72y	C	Va.	16 NOV 1878	Harmony
009355	HOLLAND, Isabella	1y	C	D.C.	09 OCT 1876	Harmony
011527	HOLLAND, Lewis	7m	C	D.C.	06 MAY 1877	Good Hope
010543	HOLLAND, Lily A.	1y	C	D.C.	06 FEB 1877	Ebenezer
013996	HOLLAND, Maggie J.	14y	W	Md.	03 DEC 1877	Rockville, Md.
007692	HOLLAND, Margaret	83y	W	Ire.	17 JUN 1876	Mt. Olivet
000970	HOLLAND, Margaret E.	32y	W	D.C.	29 OCT 1874	Glenwood
007044	HOLLAND, Mary	10h	W	D.C.	18 APR 1876	Rock Creek
010299	HOLLAND, Mary	83y	C	Va.	15 JAN 1877	Potters Field
015953	HOLLAND, Mary J.	40y	C	D.C.	01 JUN 1878	Washington Asylum
008363	HOLLAND, Nancy	c.40y	C	Md.	21 JUL 1876	Ebenezer
017438	HOLLAND, Robert	73y	C	Md.	17 SEP 1878	Payne's
019044	HOLLAND, Sarah	87y	C	Va.	12 FEB 1879	Payne's
003104	HOLLAND, Sarah A.	50y	W	Va.	24 APR 1875	Congressional
018379	HOLLAND, Wayman	3m	C	Md.	19 DEC 1878	Bladensburg, Md.
013887	HOLLAND, William Henry	3y	C	D.C.	22 NOV 1877	Beckett's
004257	HOLLAND, Wm. Isaiah	14m	C	D.C.	23 JUL 1875	Ebenezer
001865	HOLLANDER, Carey Hellen	21d	W	D.C.	24 JAN 1875	Prospect Hill
002903	HOLLERAN, John	1y	W	D.C.	07 APR 1875	Mt. Olivet
010054	HOLLIDAY, Daisy	18y	C	Va.	23 DEC 1876	Potters Field
004564	HOLLIDAY, Infant of Robert	8d	C	D.C.	12 AUG 1875	Mt. Pleasant
010609	HOLLIDAY, Joshua	42y	C	Md.	13 FEB 1877	Baltimore, Md.
014708	HOLLIDAY, Spence C.	36y	C	Va.	08 FEB 1878	Harmony
000940	HOLLIDGE, Annie R.	23y	W	Md.	26 OCT 1874	Glenwood
010995	HOLLIDGE, George Sinter	7m	W	D.C.	15 MAR 1877	Glenwood
014452	HOLLIDGE, James Bentley	2y	W	D.C.	28 APR 1877	Glenwood
018970	HOLLIN, Clara	5m	C	D.C.	06 FEB 1879	Mt. Pleasant
020519	HOLLINGSHEAD, Mary Winsor	26y	W	D.C.	19 JUN 1879	Glenwood
013614	HOLLINS, James	3y	C	D.C.	24 OCT 1877	Payne's
011764	HOLLIS, Joseph	6y	C	D.C.	01 JUN 1877	Ebenezer
001629	HOLLISTER, John J.	50y	W	N.J.	06 JAN 1875	Mt. Olivet
005336	HOLLOHAN, Michael	17y	W	D.C.	02 NOV 1875	Mt. Olivet
014492	HOLLY, Fannie	4y	C	D.C.	20 JAN 1878	Payne's
020270	HOLLY, George Robert	5m	C	D.C.	02 JUN 1879	Moore's
009291	HOLLY, John	30y	C	Md.	03 OCT 1876	Potters Field
009460	HOLMEAD, James E.F.	41y	W	Md.	19 OCT 1876	Rock Creek
008585	HOLMES, Ada	7m	C	D.C.	07 AUG 1876	Ebenezer
006765	HOLMES, Albert	45y	C	Va.	21 MAR 1876	Beckett's
004596	HOLMES, Alexander	8m	W	D.C.	14 AUG 1875	Holy Rood
019208	HOLMES, Alice	1h	W	D.C.	26 FEB 1879	Congressional
019338	HOLMES, Annetta	1y	C	D.C.	09 MAR 1879	Chappel's
020895	HOLMES, Barney	48y	C	Va.	12 JUL 1879	Mt. Pleasant
008899	HOLMES, Cath.	26y	C	Va.	31 AUG 1876	Beckett's
013230	HOLMES, Charles	8m	C	D.C.	17 SEP 1877	Harmony
000119	HOLMES, Claiborne	83y	C	Va.	09 AUG 1874	Mt. Pleasant
014199	HOLMES, Clara	18y	C	Va.	25 DEC 1877	Young Mens
013698	HOLMES, Edward	6m	C	D.C.	01 NOV 1877	Beckett's
013289	HOLMES, Ella	5y	C	D.C.	24 SEP 1877	Beckett's
014881	HOLMES, Ellen	30y	C	Md.	26 FEB 1878	Potters Field
019589	HOLMES, Emily V.	9m	C	D.C.	29 MAR 1879	Mt. Zion
018163	HOLMES, Emmie	6m	C	D.C.	26 NOV 1878	Beckett's

District of Columbia Death Records, August 1, 1874 to July 31, 1879   161

No.	Name	Age	Race	Birth	Death Date	Burial Place
007021	HOLMES, Fred	11m	C	D.C.	15 APR 1876	Beckett's
019883	HOLMES, George	52y	C	Va.	25 APR 1879	Hospital, Government
019149	HOLMES, George	1y	C	D.C.	22 FEB 1879	Potters Field
019569	HOLMES, George	3h	W	D.C.	27 MAR 1879	Graceland
011071	HOLMES, Harry	3y	W	D.C.	22 MAR 1877	Rock Creek
008225	HOLMES, Infant	7d	C	D.C.	13 JUL 1876	Ebenezer
006934	HOLMES, Infant of Carter	15min	C	D.C.	05 APR 1876	Potters Field
003753	HOLMES, Infant of Peter	2m	C	D.C.	21 JUN 1875	Beckett's
019590	HOLMES, James Thomas	1y	W	D.C.	29 MAR 1879	Mt. Olivet
011756	HOLMES, Joseph	19y	C	Va.	31 MAY 1877	Harmony
007397	HOLMES, Katharine	33w	C	D.C.	24 MAY 1876	Ebenezer
010881	HOLMES, Lavina D.	2y	C	D.C.	06 MAR 1877	Mt. Pleasant
013037	HOLMES, Lewis	50y	W	Pa.	31 AUG 1877	Soldier's Home
005218a	HOLMES, Lizzie	1y	C	D.C.	20 OCT 1875	Potters Field
011190	HOLMES, Lottie	4m	M	D.C.	02 APR 1877	Young Mens
013161	HOLMES, Louisa	6y	C	D.C.	11 SEP 1877	Young Mens
003898	HOLMES, Lucy A.	7m	C	D.C.	28 JUN 1875	Mt. Zion
006321	HOLMES, Major	4m	M	D.C.	12 FEB 1876	Young Mens
005898	HOLMES, Maria	76y	C	Va.	30 DEC 1875	Young Mens
014796	HOLMES, Marjay	8d	C	D.C.	17 FEB 1878	Mt. Pleasant
006813	HOLMES, Martha	1y	C	D.C.	25 MAR 1876	Ebenezer
010704	HOLMES, Mary E.	3y	C	D.C.	20 FEB 1877	Ebenezer
013728	HOLMES, McKenzie	40y	C	Va.	04 NOV 1877	Mt. Pleasant
003151	HOLMES, Michael	51y	W	Ire.	26 APR 1875	Hospital
009394	HOLMES, Moses	6d	C	D.C.	12 OCT 1876	Ebenezer
005365	HOLMES, Nancy	40y	C	Tenn.	05 NOV 1875	Harmony
000673	HOLMES, Nathaniel	75y	C	Va.	29 SEP 1874	Beckett's
003075	HOLMES, Robert	2y	C	Md.	21 APR 1875	Ebenezer
008701	HOLMES, Robert	11m	C	D.C.	16 AUG 1876	Young Mens
018221	HOLMES, Robert	15y	C	D.C.	02 DEC 1878	Skagg's
012366	HOLMES, Sarah	20y	C	Md.	15 JUL 1877	Ebenezer
013531	HOLMES, Sarah Frances	20y	C	Va.	16 OCT 1877	Harmony
006613	HOLMES, Vernon	30y	W	N.Y.	09 MAR 1876	Glenwood
001282	HOLMES, Wm.	44y	C	Md.	01 DEC 1874	Potters Field
012201	HOLOHAN, John T.	47y	W	D.C.	03 JUL 1877	Mt. Olivet
005670	HOLOHAN, William	2y	W	D.C.	06 DEC 1875	Mt. Olivet
007510	HOLOHAN, Wm.	17d	W	D.C.	05 JUN 1876	Holy Rood
001398	HOLSON, Thomas R.	46y	W	Pa.	15 DEC 1874	Methodist Tennallytown
018458	HOLSORN, Laura	1y	W	D.C.	25 DEC 1878	Tennallytown
016516	HOLST, Amelie	21d	W	D.C.	09 JUL 1878	Prospect Hill
005661	HOLSTEAD, George Washington	2y	C	D.C.	05 DEC 1875	Mt. Pleasant
015161	HOLSTEAD, Malchora	21m	C	D.C.	23 MAR 1878	Mt. Pleasant
014543	HOLT, John E.	3m	W	D.C.	24 JAN 1878	Holy Rood
019224	HOLT, Nancy	22y	C	N.C.	27 FEB 1879	Beckett's
002930	HOLTMAN, George	38y	W	Ger.	09 APR 1875	St. Mary's/Mt. Olivet
002948	HOLTZCLAW, Fannie Jane	24y	W	D.C.	11 APR 1875	Congressional
015821	HOLTZCLAW, Mary E.	25y	W	D.C.	24 MAY 1878	Congressional
015905	HOLTZCLAW, Walter	23d	W	D.C.	30 MAY 1878	Congressional
002562	HOLTZER, Laura M.	23y	W	D.C.	14 MAR 1875	St. Mary's
001603f	HOLTZMAN, Charles Reed	8m	W	Md.	03 JAN 1875	Glenwood
005728	HOLTZMAN, Marcellus	42y	W	D.C.	12 DEC 1875	Oak Hill
003772	HOMAN, Thomas F.	11m	W	D.C.	22 JUN 1875	Holy Rood
000062	HOMER, Clara E.	--	--	--	04 AUG 1874	--
018222	HOMER, Infant of Chs. H.	3h	W	D.C.	02 DEC 1878	Congressional
002023	HOMER, Nellie	4y	W	D.C.	04 FEB 1875	Congressional
006680	HOMES, Mary Antoinette	2m	W	D.C.	15 MAR 1876	Congressional

No.	Name	Age	Race	Birth	Death Date	Burial Place
021010	HOMILLER, Daisy	6m	W	D.C.	19 JUL 1879	Mt. Olivet
016455	HOMILLER, John H.V.	8y	W	D.C.	05 JUL 1878	Mt. Olivet
009934	HONERY, Letty	75y	C	Md.	12 DEC 1876	Mt. Zion
000841	HONESTY, Charles	70y	C	Va.	17 OCT 1874	Balls Cross Roads, Va.
005317	HONESTY, Charles	2y	C	D.C.	30 OCT 1875	Mt. Zion
021022	HONESTY, Henry	1y	C	D.C.	20 JUL 1879	Mt. Pleasant
019017	HONESTY, Infant of Daniel	12h	C	D.C.	10 FEB 1879	Cephas
019502	HONESTY, James L.	1y	C	D.C.	22 MAR 1879	Mt. Zion
003767	HONESTY, Thomas	58y	C	Va.	22 JUN 1875	Fairfax, Va.
009544	HONESTY, Thomas Henry	8d	C	D.C.	26 OCT 1876	Mt. Zion
020908	HOOD, Cora	9y	C	D.C.	13 JUL 1879	Beckett's
003042	HOOD, Sarah	72y	W	Pa.	19 APR 1875	Glenwood
017382	HOOK, Henry Edward	2y	W	Calif.	12 SEP 1878	Mt. Olivet
020859	HOOK, Oscar B.	1y	C	D.C.	09 JUL 1879	Glenwood
008526	HOOK, Willia	2y	C	D.C.	02 AUG 1876	Beckett's
020910	HOOKS, Charles E., Jr.	13m	W	Mich.	13 JUL 1879	Congressional
002159	HOOPER, Samuel	67y	W	Mass.	14 FEB 1875	Oak Hill
009481	HOOPER, Samuel	18d	C	D.C.	21 OCT 1876	Beckett's
010531	HOOVER, Edward	2d	W	D.C.	05 FEB 1877	Graceland
017128	HOOVER, Eliza	22y	W	Va.	21 AUG 1878	Graceland
001305	HOOVER, George M.	8y	W	D.C.	04 DEC 1874	Glenwood
009992	HOOVER, Henry	71y	W	Pa.	17 DEC 1876	Philadelphia, Pa.
006956	HOOVER, James W.	32y	W	Ill.	07 APR 1876	Oak Hill
017663	HOOVER, John	87y	W	Pa.	07 OCT 1878	Oak Hill
015835	HOOVER, John T.	43y	W	D.C.	25 MAY 1878	Rock Creek
006224	HOOVER, John Wm., Rev.	55y	W	Pa.	03 FEB 1876	Oak Hill
014027	HOOVER, Mary	68y	W	D.C.	07 DEC 1877	Glenwood
008995	HOOVER, Mary A.	1y	W	D.C.	07 SEP 1876	Glenwood
008023	HOOVER, Mary E.	1y	W	D.C.	05 JUL 1876	Glenwood
005671	HOPE, John S.	54y	W	Ky.	06 DEC 1875	Paris, Ky.
000505	HOPEWELL, Alexis	3y	C	D.C.	14 SEP 1874	Beckett's
000750	HOPEWELL, Eta	3m	C	D.C.	08 OCT 1874	Potters Field
015563	HOPHEINZ, Mattilda	1y	W	Ill.	30 APR 1878	Prospect Hill
009947	HOPKINS, Edward	7m	C	D.C.	13 DEC 1876	Harmony
008718	HOPKINS, George Leland	5m	W	D.C.	17 AUG 1876	Congressional
005827	HOPKINS, George W.	65y	W	Md.	22 DEC 1875	Oak Hill
007177	HOPKINS, Georgia	3y	C	D.C.	01 MAY 1876	Harmony
010612	HOPKINS, Gorham Edward	2y	W	D.C.	13 FEB 1877	Graceland
010784	HOPKINS, Grace	2y	W	D.C.	26 FEB 1877	Congressional
013906	HOPKINS, Greenbury	83y	W	Md.	24 NOV 1877	Barnes Hospital
007235	HOPKINS, Hattie	1y	C	D.C.	07 MAY 1876	Harmony
017598	HOPKINS, Isaac	90y	C	D.C.	02 OCT 1878	Potters Field
000251	HOPKINS, Jessie	1y	W	Va.	20 AUG 1874	Nonesuch
000275	HOPKINS, Lewis	48y	C	D.C.	21 AUG 1874	Mt. Pleasant
010611	HOPKINS, Luther S.	10y	W	Ill.	13 FEB 1877	Congressional
009906	HOPKINS, Mary	24y	W	Md.	08 DEC 1876	Mt. Olivet
016654	HOPKINS, Mary Ella	1y	W	D.C.	18 JUL 1878	Congressional
005768	HOPKINS, Norman Thompson	5y	W	Va.	16 DEC 1875	Congressional
009407	HOPKINS, Richard	24y	C	Md.	14 OCT 1876	Harmony
009317	HOPKINS, Sarah A.	40y	C	D.C.	05 OCT 1876	Mt. Zion
014652	HOPKINS, William Arthur	33y	W	Ohio	03 FEB 1878	Cleveland, Ohio
010170	HOPP, Rachael	65y	C	Md.	04 JAN 1877	Potters Field
013302	HOPP, William	25y	C	U.S.	25 SEP 1877	Potters Field
012819	HOPPER, Frances	20y	C	D.C.	15 AUG 1877	Beckett's
004184	HOPPERTON, Mary Patience	23y	W	Md.	18 JUL 1875	Oak Hill
017586	HOPSON, Louis C.	19y	W	Wisc.	27 SEP 1878	Congressional

No.	Name	Age	Race	Birth	Death Date	Burial Place
018560	HORAD, Susan	27y	C	Va.	04 JAN 1879	Beckett's
002922	HORAN, Nellie	11y	C	D.C.	08 APR 1875	Mt. Olivet
004963	HORED, Emmet	9m	C	D.C.	09 SEP 1875	Ebenezer
005206	HORIGAN, Daniel	26y	W	Ire.	28 SEP 1875	Mt. Olivet
001262	HORNBACH, Valentine	49y	W	Ger.	29 NOV 1874	St. Mary's
012064	HORNER, Francis T.	24y	M	D.C.	26 JUN 1877	Beckett's
014827	HORNER, William	58y	W	Md.	20 FEB 1878	Mt. Olivet
015295	HORNESTY, Infant of Frank	7d	C	D.C.	05 APR 1878	Mt. Zion
006547	HORNEY, Elizabeth J.	36y	W	Md.	04 MAR 1876	Mt. Olivet
003967	HORNICK, John Dixon	8m	W	Md.	02 JUL 1875	Mt. Olivet
016245	HORNIG, Edward H.	55y	W	Ger.	21 JUN 1878	Prospect Hill
016360	HORNING, Adam	5m	W	D.C.	29 JUN 1878	Glenwood
005202a	HORNING, Amelia	1y	W	D.C.	19 OCT 1875	Glenwood
001184	HORNING, Barbra	78y	W	Ger.	19 NOV 1874	St. Mary's
010290	HORNING, Catharine	26y	W	Ire.	14 JAN 1877	Mt. Olivet
016386	HORNING, George David	33y	W	Md.	01 JUL 1878	Glenwood
011645	HORNING, Philomina	5y	W	D.C.	19 MAY 1877	Mt. Olivet
016315	HORRELL, Thomas John	55y	W	Md.	26 JUN 1878	Grace Church, Md.
011600	HORRID, Thomas	1y	C	D.C.	15 MAY 1877	Ebenezer
015320	HORRIGAN, Margaret	41y	W	Ire.	08 APR 1878	Mt. Olivet
002315	HORSCH, Oscar	11y	W	D.C.	25 FEB 1875	Prospect Hill
018912	HORSEMAN, Infant of Andrew	7d	W	D.C.	01 FEB 1879	Congressional
000532	HORSEMAN, James Ed.	1y	W	D.C.	16 SEP 1874	Congressional
013247	HORSEMAN, Mary F.	38y	W	Md.	19 SEP 1877	Congressional
013196	HORSMAN, Jane E.	69y	W	Va.	14 SEP 1877	Falls Church, Va.
003859	HORTEN, Infant of Robert	2d	C	D.C.	26 JUN 1875	Potters Field
012211	HORTON, Edward	50y	W	Eng.	04 JUL 1877	Mt. Olivet
010143	HORTON, Etha [Linda]	33y	W	Md.	01 JAN 1877	Havre deGrace, Md.
007481	HORWICK, Mary Josephine	1y	W	D.C.	03 JUN 1876	Mt. Olivet
006873	HOSCH, August	47y	W	Ger.	31 MAR 1876	Prospect Hill
009236	HOSK, Otto	11y	W	D.C.	29 SEP 1876	Prospect Hill
014726	HOSMER, Harry M.	19y	W	Pa.	09 FEB 1878	Oak Hill
009909	HOSPITAL, Ann L.	11y	W	Md.	09 DEC 1876	Oak Hill
008823	HOSPITAL, Charles H.	41y	W	Va.	25 AUG 1876	Oak Hill
003046	HOTELY, Reuben	72y	C	Va.	19 APR 1875	Potters Field
009773	HOTTLE, Horace P.	2y	W	D.C.	22 NOV 1876	Congressional
014828	HOUCK, Ida Taylor	1y	W	D.C.	20 FEB 1878	Congressional
020656	HOUGH, Edward H.	15y	W	D.C.	28 JUN 1879	Glenwood
019387	HOUGH, Emory Baxter	2y	W	D.C.	13 MAR 1879	Clark's Gap, Va.
013796	HOUGH, John William	3m	W	D.C.	11 NOV 1877	St. Mary's
009823	HOUGH, Lydia Gibson	40y	W	Va.	29 NOV 1876	Leesburg, Va.
009589	HOUGHLAN, Mary	3y	W	D.C.	01 NOV 1876	Mt. Olivet
019621	HOUGHTON, Isabel	2½d	W	D.C.	01 APR 1879	Oak Hill
009989	HOUNDCHILD, George	27y	W	D.C.	17 DEC 1876	Oak Hill
011755	HOUSE, Susan	57y	C	D.C.	31 MAY 1877	Harmony
012405	HOUSEWRIGHT, John F.	55y	W	Va.	17 JUL 1877	Congressional
018332	HOUSTON, William	4y	M	D.C.	14 DEC 1878	Mt. Olivet
014421	HOVELAND, Hattie Augusta	1y	C	D.C.	14 JAN 1878	Potters Field
016736	HOVEY, Charles E.	45y	W	Swed.	24 JUL 1878	Hospital
014630	HOWARD, Annie	1m	C	D.C.	01 FEB 1878	Harmony
004004	HOWARD, Chas. F.	46y	W	N.Y.	05 JUL 1875	Mt. Olivet
007498	HOWARD, Clarance	4m	W	D.C.	04 JUN 1876	Alexandria, Va.
004097	HOWARD, Douglass	56y	C	Va.	12 JUL 1875	Young Mens
008384	HOWARD, Edward	9m	C	D.C.	22 JUL 1876	Potters Field
013962	HOWARD, Edward	47y	W	Ire.	29 NOV 1877	Mt. Olivet
015078	HOWARD, Ellen	53y	C	Va.	15 MAR 1878	Young Mens

District of Columbia Death Records, August 1, 1874 to July 31, 1879

No.	Name	Age	Race	Birth	Death Date	Burial Place
002726	HOWARD, Emma E.	38y	W	Scot.	24 MAR 1875	Oak Hill
000123	HOWARD, F.M.A.	1y	W	D.C.	10 AUG 1874	Howard Family
000756	HOWARD, Francis	35y	C	Md.	08 OCT 1874	Mt. Pleasant
014930	HOWARD, George Henry	7m	W	D.C.	03 MAR 1878	Mt. Olivet
012358	HOWARD, George Montgomerie	39	W	Scot.	14 JUL 1877	Congressional
001674	HOWARD, Gustavus	4y	C	Md.	10 JAN 1875	Mt. Olivet
001715	HOWARD, Harry C.	6d	W	D.C.	13 JAN 1875	Oak Hill
012011	HOWARD, Henry	1m	W	D.C.	22 JUN 1877	Alexandria, Va.
008912	HOWARD, Henry H.	58y	M	Va.	01 SEP 1876	Harmony
014520	HOWARD, James	4y	C	D.C.	22 JAN 1878	Potters Field
018971	HOWARD, James	75y	C	Md.	06 FEB 1879	Potters Field
001569	HOWARD, James S.	7y	C	Md.	01 JAN 1875	Mt. Olivet
017044	HOWARD, James W.	50y	W	Va.	14 AUG 1878	Presbyterian
019603	HOWARD, Jane (Curtiss)	65y	W	Ire.	30 MAR 1879	Graceland
015333	HOWARD, Joseph	58y	W	D.C.	09 APR 1878	Congressional
018162	HOWARD, Joseph	4m	W	D.C.	26 NOV 1878	Mt. Olivet
007593	HOWARD, Joseph Thornton	2m	W	Md.	11 JUN 1876	Congressional
010273	HOWARD, Levi	76y	C	Md.	13 JAN 1877	Mt. Zion
006734	HOWARD, Lillie	21m	W	D.C.	19 MAR 1876	Congressional
020872	HOWARD, Louis	1y	C	D.C.	10 JUL 1879	Mt. Pleasant
017853	HOWARD, Margaret	5m	W	D.C.	25 OCT 1878	Mt. Olivet
014976	HOWARD, Margaret Eliza	58y	W	Md.	07 MAR 1878	Howard Family
017912	HOWARD, Martha	15y	C	Va.	31 OCT 1878	Potters Field
008131	HOWARD, Marthall R.P.	21y	W	Va.	10 JUL 1876	Fredericksburg, Va.
001788	HOWARD, Mary	36y	C	Md.	19 JAN 1875	Mt. Olivet
003616	HOWARD, Mary	2m	C	D.C.	12 JUN 1875	Mt. Olivet
001703	HOWARD, Mary Frances	5y	C	Md.	12 JAN 1875	Mt. Olivet
005132	HOWARD, Mary L.	1m	C	D.C.	22 SEP 1875	Mt. Olivet
011546	HOWARD, Melisie A.	49y	C	Md.	08 MAY 1877	Ebenezer
006650	HOWARD, Oscar	8m	C	D.C.	12 MAR 1876	Young Mens
009609	HOWARD, Oscar	24y	C	Va.	03 NOV 1876	Arlington
000284	HOWARD, Philip	5m	C	D.C.	22 AUG 1874	Mt. Olivet
005405	HOWARD, Rebecca	6y	C	D.C.	09 NOV 1875	Mt. Pleasant
017033	HOWARD, Regina	1m	C	D.C.	13 AUG 1878	Mt. Olivet
013348	HOWARD, Rosa	30y	W	Md.	29 SEP 1877	Mt. Olivet
017772	HOWARD, Rosie	1y	W	D.C.	17 OCT 1878	Mt. Olivet
019560	HOWARD, Samuel	3y	C	D.C.	26 MAR 1879	Young Mens
008919	HOWARD, Sarah M.	13m	M	D.C.	01 SEP 1876	Harmony
000763	HOWARD, Sarah Rosanna	31y	W	Md.	09 OCT 1874	Congressional
000259	HOWARD, Sidney	2m	W	D.C.	20 AUG 1874	Graceland
006916	HOWARD, Susan	22y	C	Md.	04 APR 1876	Harmony
017888	HOWARD, Theresa	69y	W	D.C.	28 OCT 1878	Alexandria, Va.
018109	HOWARD, Thomas	54y	W	Va.	21 NOV 1878	Presbyterian
002992	HOWARD, Thomas Vincent	4m	C	D.C.	14 APR 1875	Macedonia
016674	HOWARD, Uriah	1y	C	D.C.	19 JUL 1878	Potters Field
009115	HOWARD, Virginia	4y	C	D.C.	17 SEP 1876	Ebenezer
003153	HOWARD, William	29y	W	Pa.	28 APR 1875	Philadelphia, Pa.
003829	HOWARD, Wm.	3m	C	D.C.	25 JUN 1875	Ebenezer
008172	HOWE, Albert	45y	W	Mass.	11 JUL 1876	Potters Field
008614	HOWE, Infant of Thomas	5h	W	D.C.	08 AUG 1876	Congressional
006196	HOWE, William	73y	W	Mass.	31 JAN 1876	Hospital
006906	HOWELL, Elizabeth	40y	W	N.Y.	03 APR 1876	Mt. Olivet
007676	HOWELL, Elizabeth J.	3m	W	D.C.	16 JUN 1876	Congressional
018882	HOWELL, Emmeline Juliet	55y	W	Mass.	30 JAN 1879	Glenwood
015906	HOWELL, Harriet	38y	C	Va.	30 MAY 1878	Young Mens
016911	HOWELL, James Albert	1y	C	D.C.	05 AUG 1878	Young Mens

District of Columbia Death Records, August 1, 1874 to July 31, 1879

No.	Name	Age	Race	Birth	Death Date	Burial Place
013600	HOWELL, Mary A.	24y	W	Md.	23 OCT 1877	Congressional
015026	HOWELL, Mary A.	4m	W	D.C.	11 MAR 1878	Congressional
015003	HOWELL, Mary E.	49y	W	D.C.	09 MAR 1878	Glenwood
013828	HOWELL, Samuel Harrison	55y	W	N.J.	15 NOV 1877	Oak Hill
015742	HOWELL, Sarah C.	68y	W	N.J.	16 MAY 1878	Oak Hill
006514	HOWELL, William Herbert	1m	W	D.C.	01 MAR 1876	Congressional
002545	HOWISON, Alice T.	20y	W	Va.	13 MAR 1875	Alexandria, Va.
009006	HOWISSON, Sandie A.	37y	W	Va.	08 SEP 1876	Leesburg, Va.
001143	HOWLETT, Horace R.	48y	W	W.Va.	14 NOV 1874	Congressional
017091	HOWSER, Philip Gilmore	68y	W	Md.	18 AUG 1878	Glenwood
009186	HOY, Edward	27y	W	Mass.	24 SEP 1876	Mt. Olivet
018705	HOYBERGER, Marg. Louisa	3y	W	D.C.	17 JAN 1879	Rock Creek
004403	HOYES, Paul Raymond	5m	W	D.C.	01 AUG 1875	Mt. Olivet
008050	HOYLE, Rebecca C.	52y	W	D.C.	06 JUL 1876	Oak Hill
013498	HOYNE, John B.	8y	W	D.C.	13 OCT 1877	Mt. Olivet
000832	HOYNE, Patrick	66y	W	Ire.	17 OCT 1874	Mt. Olivet
006719	HOYNES, Julia	75y	W	Ire.	18 MAR 1876	Mt. Olivet
013788	HOYNES, Margaret	32y	W	Ire.	10 NOV 1877	Mt. Olivet
002136	HOYT, Harry Blanchard	1y	W	D.C.	12 FEB 1875	Congressional
004754	HOYTE, Henry	37y	W	Mass.	25 AUG 1875	Washington Asylum
010606	HUBBARD, Ellen	73y	W	D.C.	13 FEB 1877	Congressional
013148	HUBBARD, Loretta M.	39y	W	Cuba	10 SEP 1877	Mt. Olivet
018457	HUBBARD, Luther	3m	C	D.C.	25 DEC 1878	Graceland
007480	HUBBARD, Philip Henry	12y	C	D.C.	03 JUN 1876	Reform School
007121	HUBBARD, Solomon	80y	W	Md.	26 APR 1876	Congressional
000847	HUCHINSON, Gant	26y	C	D.C.	18 OCT 1874	Mt. Pleasant
008731	HUCKLEFORT, James	3m	C	D.C.	19 AUG 1876	Young Mens
012450	HUDDLESTON, Maria	42y	W	D.C.	21 JUL 1877	Mt. Olivet
006569	HUDNELL, Blanche Rousaur	1y	C	D.C.	06 MAR 1876	Harmony
009395	HUDNELL, Dodridge	26y	M	Va.	12 OCT 1876	Harmony
003508	HUDSBERY, Henry	6m	C	D.C.	02 JUN 1875	Ebenezer
005559	HUDSON, Carlos	65y	W	Va.	25 NOV 1875	Kinsale Landing
000520	HUDSON, Charles Herschel	9y	W	D.C.	15 SEP 1874	Presbyterian
009276	HUDSON, Infant of William	1d	C	D.C.	02 OCT 1876	Potters Field
009876	HUDSON, John H.	46y	W	Va.	05 DEC 1876	Congressional
005404	HUDSON, Mary E.	1y	W	D.C.	09 NOV 1875	Congressional
015533	HUELL, Joshua	1y	C	D.C.	27 APR 1878	Beckett's
019356	HUFF, Otis P.	1y	C	D.C.	10 MAR 1879	Mt. Zion
020222	HUFMAN, Henry	1y	W	D.C.	29 MAY 1879	St. Mary's
004333	HUGANIN, Margaret V.	29y	W	D.C.	27 JUL 1875	Holy Rood
008705	HUGH, Edward	55y	W	Me.	16 AUG 1876	Potters Field
005151a	HUGHES, Andrew W.	3y	C	D.C.	15 OCT 1875	Harmony
018811	HUGHES, Anna Augustus	3y	C	D.C.	25 JAN 1879	Beckett's
005240	HUGHES, Benjamin	1y	C	D.C.	22 OCT 1875	Ebenezer
009734	HUGHES, Carrie M.	6y	C	D.C.	19 NOV 1876	Harmony
020454	HUGHES, Catherine	21y	W	Va.	15 JUN 1879	Mt. Olivet
005806	HUGHES, Celia	2m	C	D.C.	20 DEC 1875	Washington Asylum
017538	HUGHES, Charles R.L.	22y	C	Va.	26 SEP 1878	Harmony
012259	HUGHES, Cornelius	40y	C	Va.	08 JUL 1877	Ebenezer
002762	HUGHES, Dangerfield	65y	C	Va.	27 MAR 1875	Mt. Olivet
007625	HUGHES, Daniel	1y	C	D.C.	13 JUN 1876	Ebenezer
021160	HUGHES, Edith	2m	W	D.C.	30 JUL 1879	Methodist
000482	HUGHES, Ellen	60y	C	Md.	11 SEP 1874	Harmony
012384	HUGHES, Emma	28y	C	D.C.	16 JUL 1877	Mt. Pleasant
014614	HUGHES, Ernie William	2m	C	D.C.	31 JAN 1878	Beckett's
007903	HUGHES, Frank Taylor	7d	C	D.C.	28 JUN 1876	Harmony

District of Columbia Death Records, August 1, 1874 to July 31, 1879

No.	Name	Age	Race	Birth	Death Date	Burial Place
005081	HUGHES, Gilbert Thornton	1y	M	D.C.	17 SEP 1875	Mt. Olivet
008211	HUGHES, Harriet Ruth	19d	W	D.C.	12 JUL 1876	Prospect Hill
007056	HUGHES, Henry	3y	M	D.C.	20 APR 1876	Young Mens
003105	HUGHES, Hugh	73y	W	Wales	24 APR 1875	Glenwood
011094	HUGHES, Isaac	22y	C	Va.	23 MAR 1877	Mt. Olivet
001627	HUGHES, John	62y	W	Ire.	06 JAN 1875	Holy Rood
009287	HUGHES, Joseph	28y	C	Md.	03 OCT 1876	Harmony
015364	HUGHES, Joseph Vincent	4y	W	D.C.	11 APR 1878	Mt. Olivet
010414	HUGHES, Julie A.	77y	W	Md.	26 JAN 1877	Mt. Olivet
018181	HUGHES, Kitty	79y	C	Va.	27 NOV 1878	Beckett's
005257	HUGHES, Laura	2y	W	D.C.	24 OCT 1875	Holy Rood
001397	HUGHES, Margaret	47y	W	Ire.	15 DEC 1874	Mt. Olivet
014012	HUGHES, Martha Elizabeth	4y	C	D.C.	05 DEC 1877	Payne's
002764	HUGHES, Mary Ann	37y	W	Ire.	27 MAR 1875	Mt. Olivet
016607	HUGHES, Mary, Mrs.	65y	W	N.Y.	15 JUL 1878	Congressional
021097	HUGHES, Matthew	4m	W	D.C.	25 JUL 1879	Mt. Olivet
005012a	HUGHES, Pythagon	1y	C	D.C.	12 SEP 1875	Harmony
019471	HUGHES, Thomas	40y	W	Eng.	20 MAR 1879	Potters Field
020501	HUGHES, William	49y	W	Ire.	18 JUN 1879	Oak Hill
013111	HUGHES, William B.	3y	W	D.C.	07 SEP 1877	Congressional
009561	HUGHES, Wm. A., Rev.	69y	M	Va.	28 OCT 1876	Harmony
002635	HUGHES, Wm. Henry	6m	C	D.C.	18 MAR 1875	Mt. Zion
002869	HUGHS, Charles Beaty	3y	W	D.C.	04 APR 1875	Glenwood
007122	HUGHS, George	1y	C	D.C.	26 APR 1876	Mt. Pleasant
014093	HUGHS, Maria	32y	C	Va.	14 DEC 1877	Beckett's
017480	HUGHS, Mary Ellen	32y	W	Md.	21 SEP 1878	Congressional
007656	HUGHS, Wm.	4m	C	D.C.	15 JUN 1876	Young Mens
004862	HUHN, Philip	43y	W	Ger.	01 SEP 1875	St. Mary's
011721	HUITT, Emma J.	3m	C	D.C.	27 MAY 1877	Mt. Zion
005944	HULBERT, Mary H.	57y	W	Ver.	05 JAN 1876	Detroit, Mich.
012286	HULSE, Margaret May	19m	W	D.C.	09 JUL 1877	Oak Hill
017307	HUME, Charles	9m	W	D.C.	03 SEP 1878	Mt. Olivet
006255	HUME, George Wilson	1y	W	D.C.	06 FEB 1876	Mt. Olivet
017794	HUME, Robert F.	41y	W	Va.	19 OCT 1878	Culpeper Co., Va.
016758	HUME, Virginia Rawlins	3m	W	D.C.	25 JUL 1878	Glenwood
008212	HUMMER, Wm. M.	1y	W	D.C.	12 JUL 1876	Congressional
012802	HUMPHREY, Infant of Mary	21d	C	D.C.	14 AUG 1877	Potters Field
002331	HUMPHREY, John	70y	W	Eng.	26 FEB 1875	Glenwood
011915	HUMPHREY, Millie	21y	C	Md.	15 JUN 1877	Potters Field
003061	HUMPHREY, Wm.	2m	W	D.C.	20 APR 1875	Potters Field
011530	HUMPHREYS, Clarissa Ann	c.42y	C	D.C.	06 MAY 1877	Harmony
015762	HUMPHREYS, George W.	72y	W	Md.	18 MAY 1878	Congressional
012842	HUMPHREYS, James	10y	C	D.C.	16 AUG 1877	Young Mens
013315	HUMPHREYS, Jas. H.	3m	C	D.C.	26 SEP 1877	Mt. Olivet
006167	HUMPHREYS, John	21y	W	Ia.	28 JAN 1876	Glenwood
010507	HUMPHREYS, Louisa	37y	C	Va.	04 FEB 1877	Public [Va.?][1]
016801	HUMPHREYS, Louisa	5y	C	D.C.	28 JUL 1878	Brightwood
010883	HUMPHREYS, Peter	19y	C	Va.	06 MAR 1877	Potters Field
019881	HUMPHREYS, Rebecca Hollingsworth	25y	W	D.C.	24 APR 1879	Congressional
018110	HUMPHRIES, Daniel Clarence	9m	C	D.C.	21 NOV 1878	Beckett's
015395	HUMPHRIES, Jemima	94y	C	Va.	14 APR 1878	Harmony
005152a	HUMPHRIES, John F.	3y	W	D.C.	15 OCT 1875	Congressional
008730	HUMPHRY, John E.	7m	C	D.C.	19 AUG 1876	Young Mens

[1] Place of burial given is "Publick Bueriel Ground," and undertaker is B. Wheatley of Alexandria, Va.

No.	Name	Age	Race	Birth	Death Date	Burial Place
019863	HUMPHRYS, Margaret	91y	W	Ire.	22 APR 1879	Glenwood
011120	HUMPHRYS, Walter, Jr.	2m	C	D.C.	26 MAR 1877	Ebenezer
016473	HUNGEFORD, Edith Spence	5m	W	D.C.	06 JUL 1878	Oak Hill
020734	HUNGERFORD, Henry	1m	W	D.C.	03 JUL 1879	Oak Hill
013303	HUNGERFORD, Ida	2y	C	D.C.	25 SEP 1877	Young Mens
013181	HUNGERFORD, Lucy	10m	C	D.C.	13 SEP 1877	Young Mens
012291	HUNGERFORD, Mary E.	6m	W	D.C.	10 JUL 1877	Oak Hill
013278	HUNGERFORD, Milton	5y	C	D.C.	22 SEP 1877	Young Mens
016435	HUNGERFORD, Thomas	35y	C	Va.	04 JUL 1878	Hospital
002148	HUNT, Anna	79y	W	Va.	14 FEB 1875	Washington Asylum
003899	HUNT, Benjamin F.	46y	W	Va.	28 JUN 1875	Oak Hill
012871	HUNT, Catharine	58y	W	Va.	18 AUG 1877	Oak Hill
017116	HUNT, Catharine	47y	W	Eng.	20 AUG 1878	Mt. Olivet
004462	HUNT, Charles	81y	W	Mass.	05 AUG 1875	Congressional
003779	HUNT, Charles Edward	28y	W	N.Y.	23 JUN 1875	Oak Hill
002068	HUNT, Daisee	2m	W	D.C.	07 FEB 1875	Prospect Hill
014641	HUNT, Eveline	67y	W	N.Y.	02 FEB 1878	Glenwood
012729	HUNT, Hester	10y	W	D.C.	08 AUG 1877	Glenwood
019634	HUNT, Jeanette	3d	W	D.C.	02 APR 1879	Oak Hill
003854	HUNT, Josephine	33y	M	D.C.	26 JUN 1875	Harmony
005386	HUNT, Louisa D.	30y	W	D.C.	07 NOV 1875	Prospect Hill
016415	HUNT, Margareth	2y	W	D.C.	03 JUL 1878	Congressional
005028	HUNT, Samuel A.	2y	W	D.C.	13 SEP 1875	Congressional
013197	HUNT, Sidney Tweedy	35y	W	D.C.	14 SEP 1877	Oak Hill
020307	HUNT, Taylor	63y	W	Va.	05 JUN 1879	Glenwood
020733	HUNT, Willie	11m	C	D.C.	03 JUL 1879	Beckett's
012744	HUNTER, Albert Lester	1y	W	D.C.	09 AUG 1877	Oak Hill
015984	HUNTER, Annie	1y	C	D.C.	03 JUN 1878	Beckett's
003040	HUNTER, Benjamin	60y	C	Va.	18 APR 1875	Potters Field
004273	HUNTER, Blanch Virginia	18d	W	D.C.	24 JUL 1875	Oak Hill
012821	HUNTER, Cathrine	34y	W	Eng.	15 AUG 1877	Rock Creek
009306	HUNTER, Edwin Custis	10y	C	N.Y.	05 OCT 1876	Moore's
002958	HUNTER, Effa	7m	C	D.C.	11 APR 1875	Mt. Zion
020188	HUNTER, Elinor E.	36y	W	Ky.	24 MAY 1879	Holy Rood
004527	HUNTER, Elizabeth	25d	W	D.C.	10 AUG 1875	Mt. Olivet
003648	HUNTER, Elizabeth	9y	C	D.C.	14 JUN 1875	Mt. Pleasant
002527f	HUNTER, Frank	2y	--	Va.	-- --- 1863	Mt. Zion
014834	HUNTER, George W.	41y	W	Md.	21 FEB 1878	Congressional
005239	HUNTER, Hannah Ralston	91y	W	Scot.	22 OCT 1875	Oak Hill
005870	HUNTER, Henry	8y	C	D.C.	26 DEC 1875	Mt. Pleasant
012463	HUNTER, Ida E.	5m	W	D.C.	22 JUL 1877	Oak Hill
008372	HUNTER, Ignatius Ewing	1y	W	D.C.	22 JUL 1876	Congressional
002361	HUNTER, James	3y	C	D.C.	28 FEB 1875	Young Mens
002155	HUNTER, Jane I.	72y	W	Md.	14 FEB 1875	Glenwood
002821	HUNTER, John	1y	C	D.C.	31 MAR 1875	Young Mens
020757	HUNTER, Kate	6y	C	Va.	04 JUL 1879	Washington Asylum
020627	HUNTER, Lillie	6m	W	D.C.	26 JUN 1879	Graceland
013085	HUNTER, Lucy	1y	C	D.C.	04 SEP 1877	Potters Field
002526f	HUNTER, Martha	7y	--	Va.	-- --- 1863	Mt. Zion
002528f	HUNTER, Matilda	10y	--	Va.	-- --- 1863	Mt. Zion
008273	HUNTER, Nelson	18y	C	Va.	15 JUL 1876	Harmony
018858	HUNTER, Robert	75y	C	Va.	28 JAN 1879	Potters Field
021065	HUNTER, Thomas	3m	C	D.C.	23 JUL 1879	Holy Rood
015115	HUNTER, William A.	1y	C	D.C.	18 MAR 1878	Mt. Zion
015013	HUNTER, William, Jr.	25y	W	D.C.	10 MAR 1878	Oak Hill
018323	HUNTINGTON, Mary E.	5m	W	D.C.	13 DEC 1878	Presbyterian

District of Columbia Death Records, August 1, 1874 to July 31, 1879

No.	Name	Age	Race	Birth	Death Date	Burial Place
002584	HUNTON, Nellie	1m	C	D.C.	15 MAR 1875	Beckett's
019914	HUNTT, Mary A.	11m	W	D.C.	27 APR 1879	Congressional
010597	HUPFER, John F.	1m	W	D.C.	12 FEB 1877	Prospect Hill
004792	HURAH, Mary Ann	67y	W	Md.	28 AUG 1875	Oak Hill
005756	HURBERT, Mary	50y	C	Md.	15 DEC 1875	Rockville, Md.
002838	HURBERT, Wm. H.	2m	C	D.C.	01 APR 1875	Mt. Zion
011401	HURD, Austin	75y	C	Md.	22 APR 1877	Mt. Olivet
007578	HURD, Joseph A.	7m	M	D.C.	10 JUN 1876	Ebenezer
018744	HURD, Matthew	52y	W	D.C.	20 JAN 1879	Congressional
005268	HURDLE, Catherine	34y	W	Ire.	25 OCT 1875	Holy Rood
005133	HURDLE, Clara	5y	W	D.C.	22 SEP 1875	Presbyterian
013304	HURDLE, Isaac H.	42y	W	Va.	25 SEP 1877	Glenwood
018275	HURDLE, John S.	36y	W	Pa.	08 DEC 1878	Mt. Olivet
000253	HURDLE, Minnie Lavinia	11m	W	D.C.	20 AUG 1874	Glenwood
001225f	HURDLE, Washington	40y	W	D.C.	25 NOV 1874	Oak Hill
004227	HURDNELL, Willie	4m	M	D.C.	21 JUL 1875	Beckett's
018859	HURLEBAUS, Frederica	47y	W	Ger.	28 JAN 1879	Prospect Hill
020831	HURLEHEY, Timothy	68y	W	Ire.	08 JUL 1879	Mt. Olivet
017982	HURLEY, Genevieve	2m	C	--	08 NOV 1878	Mt. Olivet
001975	HURLEY, James W.	39y	W	Pa.	01 FEB 1875	Mt. Olivet
018031	HURLEY, Joseph	1m	W	D.C.	12 NOV 1878	Mt. Olivet
010287	HURLEY, Laura Henrietta	30y	W	Pa.	14 JAN 1877	Congressional
008847	HURLEY, Martha Aleathea	79y	W	Md.	27 AUG 1876	Congressional
007201	HURLEY, Mary Ann	42y	W	D.C.	04 MAY 1876	Tennallytown
008220	HURLEY, Minnie Belle	7m	W	D.C.	12 JUL 1876	Presbyterian
008117	HURLEY, Rosie Agnes	12y	W	D.C.	10 JUL 1876	Mt. Olivet
009200	HURLEY, Samuel	4d	W	D.C.	25 SEP 1876	Mt. Olivet
007902	HURLIHY, Infant of Ptk.	8h	W	D.C.	28 JUN 1876	Mt. Olivet
017808	HURNSTEAD, Catharine	56y	C	Va.	20 OCT 1878	Harmony
020106	HURST, Florence	6m	C	D.C.	15 MAY 1879	Harmony
005187a	HURST, Lee	50y	C	Va.	18 OCT 1875	Ebenezer
018119	HURST, Netie S.	20y	W	D.C.	22 NOV 1878	Glenwood
000562	HURST, William B.	25y	W	D.C.	19 SEP 1874	Glenwood
013775	HURT, Harry C.	3m	W	D.C.	09 NOV 1877	Congressional
001047	HURT?, Tasker	33y	C	Va.	04 NOV 1874	Beckett's
001510	HURTS, Infant of Alexander	4m	C	D.C.	27 DEC 1874	Moore's
020873	HUSTON, Susan	8m	C	D.C.	10 JUL 1879	Potters Field
011626	HUSTON, William J.	9m	W	D.C.	17 MAY 1877	Mt. Olivet
014094	HUTCHENS, Ella F.	24y	W	Md.	14 DEC 1877	Glenwood
008909	HUTCHENSON, William	1y	C	D.C.	01 SEP 1876	Mt. Pleasant
015751	HUTCHINS, Bertha Lee	5m	W	D.C.	17 MAY 1878	Glenwood
014338	HUTCHINSON, Blanche	1y	W	D.C.	06 JAN 1878	Mt. Zion
020871	HUTCHINSON, Catharine C.	39y	C	Va.	10 JUL 1879	Harmony
015171	HUTCHINSON, Cornelius	18y	C	D.C.	24 MAR 1878	Harmony
016244	HUTCHINSON, Frederick	10m	C	D.C.	21 JUN 1878	Harmony
014276	HUTCHINSON, Jacob	26y	C	D.C.	31 DEC 1877	Mt. Zion
009723	HUTCHINSON, James Walter	19y	W	D.C.	18 NOV 1876	Congressional
009594	HUTCHINSON, John	79y	W	Ire.	01 NOV 1876	Glenwood
012239	HUTCHINSON, Katie J.	1y	W	D.C.	06 JUL 1877	Congressional
005228a	HUTCHINSON, Mary Elizabeth	5m	C	D.C.	21 OCT 1875	Mt. Zion
007553	HUTCHINSON, Octavia	37y	C	D.C.	08 JUN 1876	Harmony
002842	HUTCHINSON, Rosa	9d	M	D.C.	02 APR 1875	Harmony
008743	HUTCHINSON, Wm.	33y	W	Ire.	19 AUG 1876	Rock Creek
021094	HUTCHISON, Percy	3m	C	D.C.	25 JUL 1879	Harmony
011321	HUTCHISON, Susan W.	66y	W	Va.	13 APR 1877	Congressional
008849	HUTH, Hettie	1y	W	D.C.	27 AUG 1876	Presbyterian

District of Columbia Death Records, August 1, 1874 to July 31, 1879

No.	Name	Age	Race	Birth	Death Date	Burial Place
020655	HUTH, JOhn	2y	W	D.C.	28 JUN 1879	Prospect Hill
014238	HUTMULLER, Henrietta Lelia	1y	W	D.C.	28 DEC 1877	Glenwood
003468	HUTTON, Infant of A.L.	1d	W	D.C.	29 MAY 1875	Congressional
009509	HUTTON, Letitia	17y	W	D.C.	23 OCT 1876	Congressional
005298	HUTTON, Margaret Ann	5m	C	D.C.	29 OCT 1875	Mt. Pleasant Plain
011259	HUTTON, Mary E.	2y	W	D.C.	07 APR 1877	Mt. Olivet
001313	HUTTON, Salome R.	77y	W	Mass.	05 DEC 1874	Congressional
009410	HUTTON, Willam	34y	C	Md.	14 OCT 1876	Harmony
020939	HUXFORD, Samuel Fessenden	2y	W	D.C.	15 JUL 1879	Stamford, Conn.
010823	HUYSMAN, Elizabeth	24y	W	D.C.	01 MAR 1877	Prospect Hill
008318	HYDE, Charles	6y	C	Va.	18 JUL 1876	Potters Field
000019	HYDE, Jerome Roseur	1y	W	Md.	02 AUG 1874	Montgomery Co., Md.
020356	HYDE, Mary	1m	W	D.C.	09 JUN 1879	Mt. Olivet
006955	HYDE, Rebecca	16y	C	Md.	07 APR 1876	Ebenezer
012803	HYDER, Mary	60y	C	Va.	14 AUG 1877	Potters Field
017230	HYSON, Infant of Matilda	17d	W	D.C.	28 AUG 1878	Methodist
001083	HYSORE, Milton Elbridge	37y	W	Md.	08 NOV 1874	Congressional

I

No.	Name	Age	Race	Birth	Death Date	Burial Place
005167	IBEL, Henry	4y	W	D.C.	25 SEP 1875	Prospect Hill
012013	IDDINS, Frederich Harvey Penn	62y	W	Eng.	22 JUN 1877	Congressional
000586	IDDINS, Thomas George	2y	W	D.C.	21 SEP 1874	Congressional
003934	IMHOF, Emma	3y	W	D.C.	30 JUN 1875	Prospect Hill
008848	INGALLS, Helen Eva	5m	W	D.C.	27 AUG 1876	Congressional
020240	INGERSOLL, Ebon C.	47y	W	N.Y.	31 MAY 1879	Oak Hill
018070	INGERSOLL, Rosaline C.	39y	W	Ohio	16 NOV 1878	Berea, Ohio
000506	INGERSOLL, Thomas R.	76y	W	Md.	14 SEP 1874	Glenwood
007308	INGHAN, Lucy	62y	W	Va.	15 MAY 1876	Rock Creek
012319	INGLE, John H.	54y	W	D.C.	11 JUL 1877	Congressional
015807	INGRAHAM, Charles A.	1y	C	D.C.	22 MAY 1878	Mt. Olivet
008280	INGRAHAM, Frank	70y	C	Va.	15 JUL 1876	Ebenezer
015968	INGRAHAM, Geo. W.	4m	C	D.C.	02 JUN 1878	Mt. Zion
006003	INGRAHAM, Thomas Washington	10m	C	D.C.	12 JAN 1876	Mt. Olivet
014084	INGRAM, Violet	83y	C	Md.	13 DEC 1877	Mt. Olivet
017973	INGROME, Thomas	61y	C	Va.	07 NOV 1878	Potters Field
004626	INLOES, Joseph	30y	C	Md.	16 AUG 1875	Mt. Zion
006982	IOMBEY, James	52y	C	Md.	10 APR 1876	Potters Field
018746	IRICK, Frank H.	8y	W	D.C.	20 JAN 1879	Congressional
010026	IRVIN, George Henry	1y	C	D.C.	20 DEC 1876	Young Mens
007171	IRVIN, Mary Coffey	53y	W	Ire.	30 APR 1876	Mt. Olivet
002072	IRVINE, Charles H.	38y	C	D.C.	07 FEB 1875	Harmony
000027	IRVINE, Mary Eliza	19d	M	D.C.	02 AUG 1874	Mt. Pleasant
020271	IRVINE, W.H.	6m	W	D.C.	02 JUN 1879	Harrisburg, Pa.
010235	IRVING, Infant of Edward	2m	C	D.C.	09 JAN 1877	Potters Field
011824	IRVING, Mary Ann	25y	C	Va.	07 JUN 1877	Mt. Zion
011525	IRWIN, Fanny	7m	W	D.C.	06 MAY 1877	Mt. Olivet
009971	ISAACS, Richard	6m	C	D.C.	15 DEC 1876	Ebenezer
009645	ISBEL, Joseph L.	1y	C	Va.	08 NOV 1876	Potters Field
001306	ISDELL, Nelson	63y	W	N.Y.	04 DEC 1874	Congressional
012276	IVERSON, Emily	47y	C	Va.	09 JUL 1877	Young Mens
015985	IVERSON, Robert T.	2y	C	D.C.	03 JUN 1878	Mt. Pleasant
010521	IVES, Harry B.	23y	W	N.Y.	04 FEB 1877	Congressional
003919	IVESON, Willie	9m	C	D.C.	29 JUN 1875	Mt. Pleasant
004006	IZELL, Frederica Amelia	15y	W	Md.	05 JUL 1875	Congressional

No.	Name	Age	Race	Birth	Death Date	Burial Place
J						
007627	JACK, James	52y	W	D.C.	13 JUN 1876	Glenwood
019460	JACKSON, Ada	28y	W	D.C.	19 MAR 1879	Oak Hill
018513	JACKSON, Ada N.	6y	C	D.C.	30 DEC 1878	Mt. Zion
005031	JACKSON, Addison	23y	C	Va.	13 SEP 1875	Harmony
009052	JACKSON, Albert A.	45y	C	Va.	13 SEP 1876	Young Mens
000804	JACKSON, Albert F.M.	4y	C	D.C.	14 OCT 1874	Harmony
018079	JACKSON, Alfonso	1y	M	D.C.	17 NOV 1878	Va.
003311	JACKSON, Alice	28y	C	Md.	13 MAY 1875	Jones Chapel
013557	JACKSON, Alice	8m	C	D.C.	18 OCT 1877	Beckett's
013112	JACKSON, Alice	5y	C	D.C.	07 SEP 1877	Potters Field
016247	JACKSON, Alice	26y	C	N.J.	21 JUN 1878	Beckett's
013391	JACKSON, Anderson	1y	C	D.C.	03 OCT 1877	Beckett's
000177	JACKSON, Andrew	1y	C	D.C.	13 AUG 1874	Mt. Pleasant
005134	JACKSON, Andrew	45y	W	D.C.	22 SEP 1875	Glenwood
016291	JACKSON, Andrew	2m	C	D.C.	24 JUN 1878	Beckett's
016050	JACKSON, Angelo	66y	W	N.Y.	07 JUN 1878	Congressional
002359	JACKSON, Ann	60y	C	Va.	28 FEB 1875	Potters Field
001793	JACKSON, Ann	7d	C	D.C.	19 JAN 1875	Mt. Zion
014200	JACKSON, Ann E.	3y	C	D.C.	25 DEC 1877	Potters Field
011650	JACKSON, Annie	78y	C	Md.	19 MAY 1877	Harmony
004445	JACKSON, Annie Elizebeth	1y	C	D.C.	04 AUG 1875	Harmony
015334	JACKSON, Beckie	107y	C	Va.	09 APR 1878	Mt. Pleasant
010421	JACKSON, Bettie	25y	C	Va.	27 JAN 1877	Potters Field
015278	JACKSON, Carrie	13y	C	Va.	03 APR 1878	Young Mens
011822	JACKSON, Cathran	1y	C	D.C.	06 JUN 1877	Mt. Olivet
008960	JACKSON, Cerena	63y	C	Md.	04 SEP 1876	Potters Field
008239	JACKSON, Chaney	54y	C	Va.	13 JUL 1876	Potters Field
001580	JACKSON, Charles	24y	C	Va.	02 JAN 1875	Alexandria, Va.
004713	JACKSON, Charlotte	2y	C	D.C.	22 AUG 1875	Ebenezer
018440	JACKSON, Chester	3y	M	D.C.	23 DEC 1878	Potters Field
006570	JACKSON, Clara	7d	C	D.C.	06 MAR 1876	Beckett's
016132	JACKSON, Clarence	10m	M	D.C.	12 JUN 1878	Young Mens
011030	JACKSON, Clem J.	42y	C	Va.	18 MAR 1877	Mt. Zion
002477	JACKSON, Cora	1y	C	D.C.	08 MAR 1875	Ebenezer
004314	JACKSON, Corinne	5m	C	D.C.	26 JUL 1875	Young Mens
007629	JACKSON, Cy.	3m	C	D.C.	13 JUN 1876	Potters Field
019225	JACKSON, Daniel	2m	C	D.C.	27 FEB 1879	Beckett's
011911	JACKSON, David	7d	C	D.C.	15 JUN 1877	Young Mens
005696	JACKSON, Edward	36y	C	Md.	08 DEC 1875	Mt. Olivet
009399	JACKSON, Edward	58y	C	Va.	13 OCT 1876	Mt. Pleasant
004654	JACKSON, Elias	2y	C	D.C.	18 AUG 1875	Young Mens
008831	JACKSON, Eliza	40y	C	Va.	26 AUG 1876	Beckett's
017093	JACKSON, Eliza	7d	C	D.C.	18 AUG 1878	Potters Field
016474	JACKSON, Eliza Ann	5y	C	D.C.	06 JUL 1878	Mt. Pleasant
013684	JACKSON, Elizabeth V.	11m	C	D.C.	31 OCT 1877	Beckett's
012364	JACKSON, Ellen	1y	C	D.C.	15 JUL 1877	Potters Field
004125	JACKSON, Ellia	1y	C	D.C.	14 JUL 1875	Beckett's
017963	JACKSON, Elmira	28y	C	Va.	06 NOV 1878	Midland, Va.
016519	JACKSON, Emily	54y	C	Va.	09 JUL 1878	Potters Field
005437	JACKSON, Emma	1y	C	D.C.	12 NOV 1875	Young Mens
014039	JACKSON, Emma	30y	C	Md.	08 DEC 1877	Young Mens
012467	JACKSON, Emma	1y	C	D.C.	22 JUL 1877	Young Mens
015416	JACKSON, Emma	6y	C	D.C.	16 APR 1878	Mt. Olivet
005965	JACKSON, Eugene	1y	C	D.C.	07 JAN 1876	Mt. Zion

District of Columbia Death Records, August 1, 1874 to July 31, 1879

No.	Name	Age	Race	Birth	Death Date	Burial Place
007087	JACKSON, Fannie	15y	C	D.C.	23 APR 1876	Beckett's
021115	JACKSON, Fannie	7d	C	D.C.	26 JUL 1879	Potters Field
020568	JACKSON, Flora	40y	C	Va.	22 JUN 1879	Mt. Zion
020177	JACKSON, Florence	6y	C	Va.	23 MAY 1879	Holy Rood
007711	JACKSON, Frances	4m	C	D.C.	18 JUN 1876	Moore's
020407	JACKSON, Frances	3m	C	D.C.	12 JUN 1879	Potters Field
001961	JACKSON, Francis	70y	C	Md.	31 JAN 1875	Potters Field
015405	JACKSON, Frank	5y	C	Va.	15 APR 1878	Potters Field
010009	JACKSON, Frederick	23y	C	D.C.	19 DEC 1876	Harmony
010824	JACKSON, Frederick M.	27y	W	D.C.	01 MAR 1877	Rock Creek
000979	JACKSON, George	9y	C	D.C.	29 OCT 1874	Harmony
002911	JACKSON, George	1y	C	D.C.	07 APR 1875	Potters Field
003606	JACKSON, George	70y	C	Va.	11 JUN 1875	Louisa C.H., Va.
006403	JACKSON, George	18y	M	Va.	18 FEB 1876	Potters Field
010321	JACKSON, George	1m	C	D.C.	17 JAN 1877	Harmony
017092	JACKSON, George	35y	M	D.C.	18 AUG 1878	Harmony
009235	JACKSON, Georgeanna	19y	M	D.C.	29 SEP 1876	Mt. Olivet
017082	JACKSON, Georgeanna	1y	C	D.C.	17 AUG 1878	Moore's
007024	JACKSON, Georgia	9m	C	D.C.	16 APR 1876	Beckett's
020485	JACKSON, Harriet	3m	C	D.C.	17 JUN 1879	Potters Field
003735	JACKSON, Harriet Ann	2m	C	D.C.	21 JUN 1875	Moore's
001866	JACKSON, Harriet Virginia	1m	W	D.C.	24 JAN 1875	Presbyterian
015697	JACKSON, Harry	1m	C	D.C.	12 MAY 1878	Mt. Olivet
019534	JACKSON, Harry	2m	C	D.C.	24 MAR 1879	Payne's
009670	JACKSON, Harry Wilson	4y	W	D.C.	11 NOV 1876	Presbyterian
010701	JACKSON, Henry	5m	C	D.C.	20 FEB 1877	Ebenezer
012588	JACKSON, Henry	40y	C	Md.	28 JUL 1877	Holy Rood
018308	JACKSON, Hester	5m	C	D.C.	11 DEC 1878	Mt. Pleasant
013290	JACKSON, Hezekiah	31y	C	D.C.	24 SEP 1877	Potters Field
004848	JACKSON, Hillery	1y	C	D.C.	31 AUG 1875	Ebenezer
002284	JACKSON, Ida E.	1y	C	DC.	22 FEB 1875	Young Mens
005697	JACKSON, Ida Gertrude	25y	W	D.C.	08 DEC 1875	Oak Hill
008510	JACKSON, Infant of Andrew	17h	C	D.C.	31 JUL 1876	Potters Field
001749	JACKSON, Infant of Bella	14d	C	D.C.	15 JAN 1875	Potters Field
005229	JACKSON, Infant of Bettie	15min	C	D.C.	30 SEP 1875	Potters Field
017363	JACKSON, Infant of Geo.	6h	C	D.C.	10 SEP 1878	Mt. Pleasant
012478	JACKSON, Infant of Henry	2m	C	D.C.	22 JUL 1877	Ebenezer
003418	JACKSON, Infant of Hiram	4d	C	D.C.	24 MAY 1875	Young Mens
011051	JACKSON, Infant of Humphrey	3h	C	D.C.	20 MAR 1877	Beckett's
013730	JACKSON, Infant of James	8d	C	D.C.	04 NOV 1877	Potters Field
017010	JACKSON, Infant of Jeremiah	1m	C	D.C.	11 AUG 1878	Baptist
015552	JACKSON, Infant of John	7d	C	D.C.	29 APR 1878	Young Mens
007727	JACKSON, Infant of John	8d	C	D.C.	19 JUN 1876	Potters Field
020996	JACKSON, Infant of Louis	1m	C	D.C.	18 JUL 1879	Harmony
011329	JACKSON, Infant of Martha	36h	C	D.C.	14 APR 1877	Potters Field
000707	JACKSON, Infant of Moses	7h	C	D.C.	04 OCT 1874	Young Mens
014214	JACKSON, Infant of Nancy	28d	C	D.C.	26 DEC 1877	Beckett's
014095	JACKSON, Infant of Paul	5d	C	D.C.	14 DEC 1877	Young Mens
017309	JACKSON, Infant of Roseanna	1/4h	C	D.C.	03 SEP 1878	Potters Field
018994	JACKSON, Infant of Sandy	2d	C	D.C.	08 FEB 1879	Mt. Zion
019079	JACKSON, Infant of William	2d	C	D.C.	15 FEB 1879	Mt. Pleasant
019504	JACKSON, Isaac	40y	C	Md.	22 MAR 1879	Mt. Olivet
017575	JACKSON, Isabella	22y	C	Md.	30 SEP 1878	Washington Asylum
001276	JACKSON, James	28y	C	Md.	30 NOV 1874	Beckett's
005177a	JACKSON, James	1y	C	D.C.	17 OCT 1875	Harmony
004051	JACKSON, James Francis	1m	C	D.C.	08 JUL 1875	Potters Field

No.	Name	Age	Race	Birth	Death Date	Burial Place
009030	JACKSON, James Henry	8d	C	D.C.	11 SEP 1876	Mt. Zion
016655	JACKSON, Jane	9d	C	D.C.	18 JUL 1878	Beckett's
018894	JACKSON, Jane A.	1y	C	D.C.	31 JAN 1879	Payne's
002228	JACKSON, Jas. Henry	1m	C	D.C.	18 FEB 1875	Beckett's
014593	JACKSON, Jemima	44y	C	Va.	29 JAN 1878	Potters Field
008792	JACKSON, Jenetta	2y	C	D.C.	23 AUG 1876	Holmes Place
010552	JACKSON, Jennie	75y	C	Va.	07 FEB 1877	Beckett's
016226	JACKSON, John	64y	C	Md.	19 JUN 1878	Harmony
015225	JACKSON, John	50y	C	Md.	29 MAR 1878	Harmony
008386	JACKSON, John W.	1y	C	D.C.	22 JUL 1876	Mt. Zion
000492	JACKSON, Joseph	2y	C	D.C.	12 SEP 1874	Beckett's
008852	JACKSON, Joseph	3y	C	D.C.	28 AUG 1876	Ebenezer
010763	JACKSON, Joseph	14d	C	D.C.	24 FEB 1877	Mt. Olivet
001027	JACKSON, Joseph D.	8m	C	D.C.	03 NOV 1874	Mt. Olivet
006766	JACKSON, Joseph L.	5m	M	D.C.	21 MAR 1876	Mt. Olivet
006084	JACKSON, Josiah	65y	C	Md.	21 JAN 1876	Ebenezer
013390	JACKSON, Judith	35y	C	Va.	03 OCT 1877	Potters Field
004478	JACKSON, Julia	18y	C	Va.	06 AUG 1875	Alexandria, Va.
014146	JACKSON, Julia	14y	C	Md.	20 DEC 1877	Harmony
015907	JACKSON, Julia	9m	C	D.C.	30 MAY 1878	Mt. Pleasant
008399	JACKSON, L.	9m	C	D.C.	24 JUL 1876	Mt. Zion
000737	JACKSON, Lavenia H.	71y	W	Ky.	07 OCT 1874	Congressional
011134	JACKSON, Lavina	90y	C	Va.	28 MAR 1877	Ebenezer
015877	JACKSON, Lawrence	8m	C	D.C.	28 MAY 1878	Mt. Zion
020596	JACKSON, Leon W.	25y	C	Conn.	24 JUN 1879	Mt. Olivet
003041	JACKSON, Levi	106y	C	Md.	19 APR 1875	Washington Asylum
016814	JACKSON, Lewis	60y	C	Va.	29 JUL 1878	Potters Field
016504	JACKSON, Livinia	26y	C	Va.	08 JUL 1878	Harmony
003476	JACKSON, Lizzie	33y	C	D.C.	29 MAY 1875	Beckett's
017517	JACKSON, Lizzie	10m	C	D.C.	24 SEP 1878	Potters Field
007678	JACKSON, Loda	c.20y	C	Md.	16 JUN 1876	Potters Field
005585	JACKSON, Louise	33y	C	Va.	27 NOV 1875	Young Mens
006225	JACKSON, Lucy	4y	C	D.C.	03 FEB 1876	Young Mens
010705	JACKSON, Lula	1y	C	D.C.	20 FEB 1877	Mt. Olivet
008659	JACKSON, Malinda	19y	C	Va.	12 AUG 1876	Potters Field
009103	JACKSON, Margaret	87y	W	Md.	16 SEP 1876	Oak Hill
011880	JACKSON, Maria Lucinda	6m	M	Md.	13 JUN 1877	Harmony
005528	JACKSON, Martha	8y	C	Va.	21 NOV 1875	Young Mens
011182	JACKSON, Martha	c.23y	C	D.C.	01 APR 1877	Mt. Zion
012146	JACKSON, Martha	3m	C	D.C.	30 JUN 1877	Holy Rood
008503	JACKSON, Martha C.	3m	C	D.C.	31 JUL 1876	Md.
004061	JACKSON, Mary	3m	C	D.C.	09 JUL 1875	Ebenezer
005099a	JACKSON, Mary	1y	C	Va.	10 OCT 1875	Young Mens
010664	JACKSON, Mary	5d	C	D.C.	17 FEB 1877	Potters Field
014317	JACKSON, Mary	5y	C	D.C.	04 JAN 1878	Potters Field
014510	JACKSON, Mary	35y	C	Va.	21 JAN 1878	Mt. Olivet
014306	JACKSON, Mary	5d	C	D.C.	03 JAN 1878	Young Mens
016130	JACKSON, Mary	9m	C	D.C.	12 JUN 1878	Mt. Pleasant
015791	JACKSON, Mary	1½m	C	D.C.	21 MAY 1878	Beckett's
019730	JACKSON, Mary	9m	C	D.C.	11 APR 1879	Young Mens
005194	JACKSON, Mary Ann	25y	C	Md.	27 SEP 1875	Harmony
019561	JACKSON, Mary Ann	19y	C	D.C.	26 MAR 1879	Harmony
006440	JACKSON, Mary E.	6m	C	D.C.	22 FEB 1876	Mt. Olivet
009937	JACKSON, Mary Eliza	2m	C	Va.	12 DEC 1876	Potters Field
019685	JACKSON, Mary Elizabeth	9m	C	Md.	07 APR 1879	Harmony
007749	JACKSON, Mary M.	2m	C	D.C.	20 JUN 1876	Mt. Zion

No.	Name	Age	Race	Birth	Death Date	Burial Place
011273	JACKSON, Matilda	2m	C	D.C.	09 APR 1877	Graceland
005115a	JACKSON, Matilda A.	22y	C	Md.	12 OCT 1875	Mt. Zion
019070	JACKSON, Meyer	7y	W	Md.	14 FEB 1879	Washington Hebrew
017774	JACKSON, Mina	3y	C	Va.	17 OCT 1878	Brightwood
003488	JACKSON, Nancy	7y	C	D.C.	30 MAY 1875	Young Mens
019362	JACKSON, Nancy	3y	C	R.I.	11 MAR 1879	Beckett's
003935	JACKSON, Nathaniel	70y	C	Md.	30 JUN 1875	Young Mens
007712	JACKSON, Osbourne	70y	C	Md.	18 JUN 1876	Jones Chapel
002035	JACKSON, Persilla	80y	C	Va.	05 FEB 1875	Beckett's
005052a	JACKSON, Peter	65y	C	Va.	04 OCT 1875	Young Mens
018868	JACKSON, Richard	2y	C	D.C.	29 JAN 1879	Young Mens
012700	JACKSON, Richard F.	65y	W	Va.	06 AUG 1877	Fairfax Co., Va.
006338	JACKSON, Robert	6m	M	D.C.	13 FEB 1876	Young Mens
007904	JACKSON, Robert	14d	C	D.C.	28 JUN 1876	Potters Field
007269	JACKSON, Robert	3y	C	D.C.	11 MAY 1876	Baptist
011343	JACKSON, Robert	1y	M	D.C.	15 APR 1877	Ebenezer
016815	JACKSON, Robert	2y	C	D.C.	29 JUL 1878	Mt. Olivet
019058	JACKSON, Robert	8d	C	D.C.	13 FEB 1879	Potters Field
013729	JACKSON, Rose	25y	C	Md.	04 NOV 1877	Potters Field
006862	JACKSON, Samuel	63y	C	Md.	30 MAR 1876	Potters Field
009189	JACKSON, Samuel	2y	C	D.C.	24 SEP 1876	Young Mens
017916	JACKSON, Samuel	1y	C	D.C.	01 NOV 1878	Beckett's
003830	JACKSON, Sarah	8m	C	D.C.	25 JUN 1875	Harmony
002508	JACKSON, Sarah	1y	C	D.C.	10 MAR 1875	Mt. Olivet
009815	JACKSON, Sarah	3m	W	D.C.	28 NOV 1876	Presbyterian
011864	JACKSON, Sarah	3y	C	Md.	11 JUN 1877	Mt. Zion
014297	JACKSON, Sarah	5m	C	D.C.	02 JAN 1878	Payne's
013270	JACKSON, Sarah Ann	4y	C	D.C.	21 SEP 1877	Mt. Olivet
009523	JACKSON, Sarah Elizabeth	42d	C	D.C.	25 OCT 1876	Mt. Zion
008395	JACKSON, Sarah Frances	27y	C	Va.	24 JUL 1876	Young Mens
013790	JACKSON, Sarah Francis	1y	C	D.C.	10 NOV 1877	Beckett's
002627	JACKSON, Sephronia	4y	C	Va.	18 MAR 1875	Ebenezer
018524	JACKSON, Susan	81y	C	Md.	31 DEC 1878	Hillsdale
007821	JACKSON, Susan Ann	c.40y	C	Md.	24 JUN 1876	Mt. Pleasant
005835	JACKSON, Theodore	5d	C	D.C.	23 DEC 1875	Young Mens
007880	JACKSON, Theresia	4m	C	D.C.	27 JUN 1876	Ebenezer
014549	JACKSON, Thomas	88y	W	Va.	25 JAN 1878	Oak Hill
000831	JACKSON, Thomas E.	68y	W	Eng.	17 OCT 1874	Congressional
006907	JACKSON, Victor	5m	M	D.C.	03 APR 1876	Mt. Pleasant
006298	JACKSON, Whitfield	2m	C	D.C.	10 FEB 1876	Harmony
007124	JACKSON, William	4y	C	D.C.	26 APR 1876	Mt. Olivet
007065	JACKSON, William	21y	C	Va.	21 APR 1876	Moore's
010387	JACKSON, William	1y	C	D.C.	23 JAN 1877	Young Mens
019864	JACKSON, William	4y	C	D.C.	22 APR 1879	Beckett's
003717	JACKSON, Willie	15m	C	D.C.	19 JUN 1875	Young Mens
001100	JACKSON, Winne	80y	C	Va.	09 NOV 1874	Potters Field
015595	JACKSON, Wm. H.	2y	C	D.C.	03 MAY 1878	Mt. Pleasant
007609	JACKSON, Wm. J.	4m	C	D.C.	12 JUN 1876	Mt. Zion
005154a	JACKY, Paulina	35y	W	Ger.	15 OCT 1875	St. Mary's
019068	JACOB, Eugene	50y	W	France	14 FEB 1879	Mt. Olivet
013907	JACOBI, Frederica Elizabeth	35y	W	D.C.	24 NOV 1877	Oak Hill
014388	JACOBS, A. Murray	4y	W	Md.	11 JAN 1878	Annapolis Junction
007052	JACOBS, Asbury Roszell	36y	W	Va.	19 APR 1876	Congressional
005918	JACOBS, Catharine	40y	W	Ger.	02 JAN 1876	Mt. Olivet
001932	JACOBS, Eldridge T.	9m	W	D.C.	28 JAN 1875	Congressional
001984	JACOBS, Frank	39y	C	Va.	01 FEB 1875	Harmony

District of Columbia Death Records, August 1, 1874 to July 31, 1879

No.	Name	Age	Race	Birth	Death Date	Burial Place
013759	JACOBS, Harry Franklin	3y	W	D.C.	07 NOV 1877	Congressional
007159	JACOBS, Infant of James	7d	C	D.C.	29 APR 1876	Mt. Pleasant
019671	JACOBS, William H.	6m	W	D.C.	06 APR 1879	Alexandria, Va.
017991	JACOBS, Willie	21d	W	D.C.	09 NOV 1878	Annapolis Junction
000909f	JACOBS, Wm. A.	52y	--	--	23 OCT 1874	Glenwood
004391	JACQUES, Eadith Maria	1y	W	D.C.	31 JUL 1875	Philadelphia, Pa.
002187	JACRITZ, Mary	3y	W	D.C.	16 FEB 1875	Prospect Hill
014913	JAMES, Annie	36y	W	Eng.	01 MAR 1878	Oak Hill
001883	JAMES, Catherine Ann	62y	W	Va.	25 JAN 1875	Oak Hill
010826	JAMES, Chas.	1y	C	D.C.	01 MAR 1877	Mt. Olivet
008657	JAMES, Fannie	19y	C	Va.	12 AUG 1876	Stafford Co., Va.
008750	JAMES, Florence	8m	C	D.C.	20 AUG 1876	Harmony
013806	JAMES, Francis	52y	M	Va.	12 NOV 1877	Harmony
016978	JAMES, Infant of Andrew	7d	C	D.C.	09 AUG 1878	Young Mens
011242	JAMES, Infant of Henry	2d	C	D.C.	06 APR 1877	Potters Field
001767	JAMES, Infant of John	2d	C	D.C.	17 JAN 1875	Harmony
004833	JAMES, Isaac	40y	C	Va.	30 AUG 1875	Mt. Pleasant
016505	JAMES, John Thomas	9m	C	D.C.	08 JUL 1878	Mt. Olivet
002908	JAMES, John Walter	7m	W	D.C.	07 APR 1875	Graceland
000904f	JAMES, L.E.	38y	W	U.S.	-- OCT 1874	Rock Creek
007748	JAMES, Lillie	2y	C	D.C.	20 JUN 1876	Mt. Pleasant
015694	JAMES, Lula	10m	C	D.C.	12 MAY 1878	Beckett's
001949	JAMES, Lulie	11y	C	D.C.	30 JAN 1875	Young Mens
000090	JAMES, Margaret	3m	C	D.C.	07 AUG 1874	Mt. Olivet
012977	JAMES, Mary	26y	C	Md.	27 AUG 1877	Mt. Olivet
012424	JAMES, Mary	24d	C	D.C.	19 JUL 1877	Mt. Zion
015172	JAMES, Mary	c.50y	C	Md.	24 MAR 1878	Harmony
013021	JAMES, Mary E.	1y	C	D.C.	30 AUG 1877	Beckett's
017328	JAMES, Paulina	1y	C	D.C.	05 SEP 1878	Young Mens
003391	JAMES, Thomas	48y	C	Md.	21 MAY 1875	Mt. Pleasant
005091	JAMES, Thomas	9m	C	D.C.	18 SEP 1875	Young Mens
020898	JAMES, William	9m	C	D.C.	12 JUL 1879	Mt. Zion
018402	JAMES, William H.	45y	W	Eng.	20 DEC 1878	Oak Hill
011763	JAMES, William I.	2m	C	D.C.	01 JUN 1877	Mt. Olivet
017320	JAMES, Wm. Henry	5y	C	D.C.	04 SEP 1878	Beckett's
001885	JAMESSON, Mary W.	51y	W	D.C.	25 JAN 1875	Congressional
002132	JAMIESON, Maria	100y	C	Md.	12 FEB 1875	Mt. Olivet
002864	JAMISON, Catherine	56y	C	D.C.	03 APR 1875	Mt. Zion
019795	JAMISON, Millie	65y	C	Va.	16 APR 1879	Potters Field
002208	JAMISON, Samuel	60y	C	Md.	17 FEB 1875	Mt. Olivet
002837	JANEY, Ellen Rebecca	4y	C	D.C.	01 APR 1875	Ebenezer
004291	JANEZACK, Mary Cath.	6m	W	D.C.	25 JUL 1875	Mt. Olivet
014955	JANIE, Lara Ann	1y	C	D.C.	05 MAR 1878	Payne's
001678	JANNEY, Infant of Fannie	6m	C	D.C.	10 JAN 1875	Harmony
006751	JAQUES, Sarah	75y	W	N.J.	20 MAR 1876	Warren Co., N.J.
017540	JARBOE, Mary	77y	W	Md.	26 SEP 1878	Mt. Olivet
019742	JARBOE, Mary	33y	C	Va.	12 APR 1879	Mt. Zion
004923f	JARVIS, Blanche Gibson	1y	W	D.C.	05 SEP 1875	Glenwood
000721	JARVIS, Elizabeth	48y	W	Ire.	05 OCT 1874	Mt. Olivet
017944	JARVIS, Joseph	50y	C	Md.	04 NOV 1878	Potters Field
011918	JARVIS, Rosa	25y	C	Va.	15 JUN 1877	Ebenezer
019342	JASON, James Edward	5m	C	D.C.	09 MAR 1879	Potters Field
001540	JASPER, Harriet	77y	C	Va.	30 DEC 1874	Alexandria, Va.
013259	JAVANS, John	2m	W	D.C.	20 SEP 1877	Mt. Olivet
015734	JAVIN, Mary Blair	14h	W	D.C.	15 MAY 1878	Rock Creek
007511	JEBKINS, Mary	27y	C	Va.	05 JUN 1876	Young Mens

District of Columbia Death Records, August 1, 1874 to July 31, 1879

No.	Name	Age	Race	Birth	Death Date	Burial Place
002147	JEFFERIS, Mabel	20d	W	D.C.	14 FEB 1875	Congressional
001813	JEFFERS, Georganna	2m	W	D.C.	20 JAN 1875	Congressional
000679	JEFFERS, Mary E.	79y	W	Md.	30 SEP 1874	Congressional
004072	JEFFERS, Nannie	2y	W	D.C.	10 JUL 1875	Congressional
005509	JEFFERSON, Agnes	1y	C	D.C.	19 NOV 1875	Mt. Olivet
016730	JEFFERSON, Catherine	73y	W	Va.	23 JUL 1878	Mt. Olivet
018514	JEFFERSON, Catherine Cecelia	20y	C	D.C.	30 DEC 1878	Mt. Olivet
017168	JEFFERSON, Ferdinand	69y	W	Md.	24 AUG 1878	Mt. Olivet
019896	JEFFERSON, Jeremiah	9m	C	D.C.	25 APR 1879	Beckett's
015406	JEFFERSON, Julia	5y	C	D.C.	15 APR 1878	Mt. Pleasant
009303	JEFFERSON, Maggie	7d	C	D.C.	04 OCT 1876	Young Mens
004627	JEFFERSON, Mary	8d	C	D.C.	16 AUG 1875	Mt. Olivet
010475	JEFFERSON, Willie	6m	C	D.C.	01 FEB 1877	Ebenezer
001586	JEFFERSON, Winnie	70y	C	Va.	02 JAN 1875	Mt. Pleasant
005030	JEFFRIES, Infant of Annie	5d	C	D.C.	13 SEP 1875	Harmony
002251	JEMMERSON, Charles H.	1m	C	D.C.	20 FEB 1875	Mt. Olivet
008702	JENIFER, Willie	6m	C	Conn.	16 AUG 1876	Beckett's
000789	JENKIN, John W.	36y	C	Va.	12 OCT 1874	Mt. Zion
010512	JENKINS, Albertie	1y	M	D.C.	04 FEB 1877	Young Mens
018924	JENKINS, Ann M.	58y	W	Va.	02 FEB 1879	Glenwood
009635	JENKINS, Eliza Fields	75y	C	Va.	07 NOV 1876	Harmony
005472	JENKINS, Ellen Lavinia	52y	W	Va.	16 NOV 1875	Mt. Pleasant
005461	JENKINS, George	21y	C	W.Va.	15 NOV 1875	Harmony
016543	JENKINS, George	65y	C	D.C.	10 JUL 1878	Harmony
007361	JENKINS, Hannah	7d	C	D.C.	21 MAY 1876	Harmony
015097	JENKINS, Harriet	70y	C	Va.	17 MAR 1878	Harmony
000274	JENKINS, Infant of Wm.	9d	C	D.C.	21 AUG 1874	Beckett's
012406	JENKINS, Infant of Rebecca	1m	C	D.C.	17 JUL 1877	Potters Field
017945	JENKINS, John H.	80y	C	N.C.	04 NOV 1878	Potters Field
012979	JENKINS, John Henry	14y	W	Va.	27 AUG 1877	Lewinsville, Va.
009412	JENKINS, John W.	22y	W	Va.	15 OCT 1876	Mt. Olivet
006974	JENKINS, Lucretia	80y	C	Md.	09 APR 1876	Mt. Olivet
001423	JENKINS, Mary	35y	C	D.C.	18 DEC 1874	Potters Field
008471	JENKINS, Mary	26y	C	Md.	29 JUL 1876	Mt. Zion
012506	JENKINS, Mary	15y	C	Md.	24 JUL 1877	Potters Field
007594	JENKINS, Mary Elizabeth	4m	C	D.C.	11 JUN 1876	Mt. Zion
001943	JENKINS, Mary Ellen	8m	C	D.C.	29 JAN 1875	Mt. Zion
001178	JENKINS, Miles	28y	C	Ga.	18 NOV 1874	Harmony
019535	JENKINS, Mollie Kullen	26y	W	Ky.	24 MAR 1879	Glenwood
008300	JENKINS, Nellie	2y	C	D.C.	17 JUL 1876	Potters Field
008183	JENKINS, Richard	74y	C	Md.	11 JUL 1876	Mt. Olivet
009483	JENKINS, Richard	23y	C	Md.	21 OCT 1876	Jones Chapel
005436	JENKINS, Robert	30y	C	Md.	12 NOV 1875	Harmony
011454	JENKINS, Rose	80y	C	Md.	28 APR 1877	Potters Field
011668	JENKINS, Samuel	92y	C	Va.	21 MAY 1877	Mt. Zion
013022	JENKINS, Solomon	9m	C	D.C.	30 AUG 1877	Beckett's
020380	JENKINS, Virgi	4d	C	D.C.	10 JUN 1879	Mt. Olivet
010790	JENKINS, W.W.	22y	W	Va.	26 FEB 1877	Glenwood
011306	JENKINS, William L.	5m	C	D.C.	12 APR 1877	Mt. Zion
008103	JENKS, James	22y	W	Ire.	09 JUL 1876	N.Y.
014931	JENNIFER, Thomas	78y	C	Md.	03 MAR 1878	Mt. Olivet
017294	JENNINGS, Cleopatra	7m	M	D.C.	02 SEP 1878	Harmony
011693	JENNINGS, Eliza Henson	31y	C	Md.	24 MAY 1877	Harmony
007948	JENNINGS, Selena	4m	C	D.C.	01 JUL 1876	Young Mens
013974	JEROME, Peter	42y	W	Ger.	30 NOV 1877	Mt. Olivet
008204	JESSOPS, Hannah	70y	C	Va.	12 JUL 1876	Potters Field

No.	Name	Age	Race	Birth	Death Date	Burial Place
008672	JESSUP, Susan	8m	C	Md.	13 AUG 1876	Ebenezer
003981	JESSUP, Worthington	11m	C	D.C.	03 JUL 1875	Mt. Zion
007064	JETT, Fannie	4y	W	D.C.	21 APR 1876	Alexandria, Va.
003125	JETT, Jetty	15m	C	D.C.	26 APR 1875	Mt. Pleasant
007800	JETT, Mary E.	28y	W	D.C.	23 JUN 1876	Presbyterian
007724	JETT, Wm. E.	10d	W	D.C.	19 JUN 1876	Presbyterian
012072	JEWETT, Lewis P.	8m	W	D.C.	26 JUN 1877	Mt. Olivet
017838	JEWITT, Arthur	4y	W	D.C.	23 OCT 1878	Mt. Olivet
009557	JILLARD, George E.	55y	W	Md.	28 OCT 1876	Glenwood
003193	JILLARD, Kate	22y	W	D.C.	02 MAY 1875	Glenwood
011277	JILLARD, William H.	24y	W	D.C.	09 APR 1877	Glenwood
016306	JIRDINSTON, John Ellinger	7m	W	D.C.	25 JUN 1876	Oak Hill
018519	JIROKEY, Hugh Stanislaus	28y	W	D.C.	30 DEC 1878	Mt. Olivet
006917	JOACHIM, John J.F.	78y	W	Ger.	04 APR 1876	Glenwood
002648	JOACHIM, Louise	32y	W	Ger.	19 MAR 1875	Prospect Hill
001280	JOEDAN, Mary L.	3d	C	D.C.	01 DEC 1874	Harmony
002127	JOHNES, Betsy	80y	C	Va.	11 FEB 1875	Ebenezer
005219	JOHNES, Elizabeth	24y	C	Va.	29 SEP 1875	Mt. Zion
011634	JOHNS, Florence	3m	W	D.C.	18 MAY 1877	Mt. Olivet
010072	JOHNS, Mary Josephine	1y	W	D.C.	25 DEC 1876	Mt. Olivet
017502	JOHNS, Mira Sinclair, Mrs.	35y	W	Ohio	23 SEP 1878	Bainsboro, Ohio
006752	JOHNSON, Aaron	1y	C	D.C.	20 MAR 1876	Ebenezer
015291	JOHNSON, Aaron	48y	C	Va.	05 APR 1878	Payne's
015792	JOHNSON, Abe	8d	C	D.C.	21 MAY 1878	Potters Field
003376	JOHNSON, Abraham	c.45y	C	--	20 MAY 1875	Potters Field
012413	JOHNSON, Abraham	9y	C	D.C.	18 JUL 1877	Potters Field
011727	JOHNSON, Adison	5y	C	Va.	27 MAY 1877	Ebenezer
020535	JOHNSON, Agnes Claire	4m	W	D.C.	20 JUN 1879	Mt. Olivet
005758	JOHNSON, Albert	6y	C	D.C.	15 DEC 1875	Beckett's
012028	JOHNSON, Albert	7m	C	D.C.	23 JUN 1877	Potters Field
011954	JOHNSON, Alberta	5m	C	D.C.	18 JUN 1877	Harmony
007098	JOHNSON, Aleck	7m	C	D.C.	24 APR 1876	Mt. Pleasant
005314	JOHNSON, Alexander	26y	C	Va.	30 OCT 1875	Ebenezer
012096	JOHNSON, Alice	10d	C	D.C.	27 JUN 1877	Mt. Olivet
004881	JOHNSON, Allen W.	36h	C	D.C.	02 SEP 1875	Mt. Zion
016437	JOHNSON, Ally	11m	C	D.C.	04 JUL 1878	Young Mens
016608	JOHNSON, Alonza	13m	C	D.C.	15 JUL 1878	Beckett's
005599	JOHNSON, Amanda	56y	C	D.C.	29 NOV 1875	Hospital
006786	JOHNSON, Anderson	51y	C	Va.	23 MAR 1876	Graceland
003536	JOHNSON, Andrew	2y	C	D.C.	05 JUN 1875	Ebenezer
002823	JOHNSON, Andrew	40y	W	Mich.	31 MAR 1875	Hospital
006597	JOHNSON, Andrew	6m	C	D.C.	08 MAY 1876	Young Mens
016541	JOHNSON, Andrew	3y	C	D.C.	10 JUL 1878	Mt. Pleasant
019472	JOHNSON, Anie	22y	C	Md.	20 MAR 1879	Mt. Zion
000214	JOHNSON, Ann	17y	C	Md.	16 AUG 1874	Mt. [illegible]
020297	JOHNSON, Ann	2m	W	D.C.	04 JUN 1879	Mt. Olivet
003831	JOHNSON, Ann Hughes	72y	W	Va.	25 JUN 1875	Oak Hill
004930	JOHNSON, Ann Rebecca	11d	C	D.C.	06 SEP 1875	Mt. Pleasant
014987	JOHNSON, Anna V.	6m	W	D.C.	08 MAR 1878	Oak Hill
003920	JOHNSON, Annie	1m	C	D.C.	29 JUN 1875	Potters Field
007433	JOHNSON, Annie	5m	W	D.C.	29 MAY 1876	Young Mens
010796	JOHNSON, Annie	55y	C	Va.	27 FEB 1877	Ebenezer
016051	JOHNSON, Annie	1d	C	D.C.	07 JUN 1878	Beckett's
014399	JOHNSON, Annie Elizabeth	8y	W	Md.	12 JAN 1878	Mt. Olivet
006256	JOHNSON, Annie Maria	44y	C	Va.	06 FEB 1876	Mt. Zion
011128	JOHNSON, Arena	2y	C	D.C.	27 MAR 1877	Ebenezer

District of Columbia Death Records, August 1, 1874 to July 31, 1879 177

No.	Name	Age	Race	Birth	Death Date	Burial Place
020223	JOHNSON, Ariana	4y	C	D.C.	29 MAY 1879	Potters Field
004902	JOHNSON, Arrabella	3m	C	D.C.	04 SEP 1875	Mt. Pleasant
016248	JOHNSON, Arthur	6m	C	D.C.	21 JUN 1878	Harmony
002847	JOHNSON, Avinna	1y	M	Va.	02 APR 1875	Mt. Pleasant
005836	JOHNSON, Benjamin	c.40y	C	Va.	23 DEC 1875	Harmony
008314	JOHNSON, Benjamin	66y	C	Md.	18 JUL 1876	Mt. Pleasant
012980	JOHNSON, Benjamin Alexander	72y	W	Md.	27 AUG 1877	Mt. Olivet
013813	JOHNSON, Benjamin, s/o Samuel	9m	C	D.C.	13 NOV 1877	Jones Chapel
015321	JOHNSON, Bessie	1y	C	D.C.	08 APR 1878	Mt. Pleasant
009090	JOHNSON, Betsey A.	7y	C	D.C.	15 SEP 1876	Beckett's
020070	JOHNSON, Bettie A.	37y	C	Va.	11 MAY 1879	Baptist
009760	JOHNSON, Betty	16y	C	Va.	20 NOV 1876	Mt. Pleasant
006697	JOHNSON, Beverly	70y	C	Va.	16 MAR 1876	Mt. Zion
011612	JOHNSON, Blanch M.	1y	C	D.C.	16 MAY 1877	Alexandria, Va.
012227	JOHNSON, Bula	7m	C	D.C.	05 JUL 1877	Bell's Farm
016759	JOHNSON, Burnett	1y	C	D.C.	25 JUL 1878	Mt. Olivet
020164	JOHNSON, Calvin R.	59y	W	Ohio	21 MAY 1879	Glenwood
002513	JOHNSON, Carrie	11m	C	D.C.	11 MAR 1875	Young Mens
016129	JOHNSON, Carrie	1y	C	D.C.	12 JUN 1878	Mt. Zion
008137	JOHNSON, Carrie E.	1y	C	D.C.	10 JUL 1876	Young Mens
007299	JOHNSON, Cassil	8y	C	D.C.	14 MAY 1876	Young Mens
003139	JOHNSON, Catharine	108y	C	Va.	26 APR 1875	Benton Station, Va.
005783	JOHNSON, Catharine	73y	W	Va.	18 DEC 1875	Prospect Hill
005055	JOHNSON, Catherine	50y	W	Md.	15 SEP 1875	Oak Hill
016740	JOHNSON, Catherine	52y	C	D.C.	24 JUL 1878	Potters Field
004993	JOHNSON, Catherne	4m	C	D.C.	11 SEP 1875	Potters Field
007057	JOHNSON, Charles	10m	M	D.C.	20 APR 1876	Graceland
006339	JOHNSON, Charles	20y	C	Va.	13 FEB 1876	Young Mens
006134	JOHNSON, Charles	45y	C	Va.	25 JAN 1876	Washington Asylum
016791	JOHNSON, Charles	10y	C	Va.	27 JUL 1878	Potters Field
020109	JOHNSON, Charles	14y	M	D.C.	15 MAY 1879	Harmony
018500	JOHNSON, Charles K.	3y	W	D.C.	29 DEC 1878	Congressional/Oak Hill
018585	JOHNSON, Charlie	1y	C	D.C.	06 JAN 1879	Potters Field
001921	JOHNSON, Charlot	5y	C	Md.	27 JAN 1875	Mt. Olivet
014600	JOHNSON, Charlotte R.	17y	C	Md.	30 JAN 1878	Harmony
005446	JOHNSON, Chas.	5d	C	D.C.	13 NOV 1875	Mt. Olivet
007799	JOHNSON, Chas.	8m	C	D.C.	23 JUN 1876	Ebenezer
002209	JOHNSON, Chas. Henry	10d	C	D.C.	17 FEB 1875	Potters Field
014307	JOHNSON, Chas. T.	5m	C	D.C.	03 JAN 1878	Mt. Olivet
000224	JOHNSON, Clara w/o Philip	60y	C	Md.	17 AUG 1874	Mt. Pleasant
001281	JOHNSON, Clarence	26y	W	D.C.	01 DEC 1874	Soldier's Home
021162	JOHNSON, Clarence	9m	C	D.C.	30 JUL 1879	Young Mens
007630	JOHNSON, Clifford	2m	W	D.C.	13 JUN 1876	Congressional
013589	JOHNSON, Cora	4m	C	D.C.	22 OCT 1877	Beckett's
020484	JOHNSON, Cornelia Kate	4y	C	D.C.	17 JUN 1879	Young Mens
012012	JOHNSON, David	80y	C	Va.	22 JUN 1877	Potters Field
002271	JOHNSON, David C.	5m	C	D.C.	21 FEB 1875	Mt. Zion
016609	JOHNSON, Delbert	2y	C	D.C.	15 JUL 1878	Harmony
003189	JOHNSON, Edgar	2y	C	D.C.	01 MAY 1875	Harmony
013379	JOHNSON, Edie	3y	C	D.C.	02 OCT 1877	Potters Field
012017	JOHNSON, Edith V.	7m	W	D.C.	22 JUN 1877	Mt. Olivet
010910	JOHNSON, Edmond	c.66y	C	Md.	08 MAR 1877	Harmony
012299	JOHNSON, Edmond W.	1y	W	D.C.	10 JUL 1877	Glenwood
012616	JOHNSON, Edw.	5d	C	D.C.	30 JUL 1877	Potters Field
008689	JOHNSON, Edward	72y	C	Md.	15 AUG 1876	Harmony
018895	JOHNSON, Edward	9y	C	D.C.	31 JAN 1879	Potters Field

No.	Name	Age	Race	Birth	Death Date	Burial Place
007610	JOHNSON, Edward Bostick	3m	W	D.C.	12 JUN 1876	Oak Hill
019182	JOHNSON, Edward T.	42y	C	D.C.	24 FEB 1879	Harmony
009205	JOHNSON, Elisabeth	70y	C	Va.	26 SEP 1876	Young Mens
007575	JOHNSON, Eliza	14y	C	Va.	06 AUG 1876	Beckett's
006366	JOHNSON, Eliza	2d	C	D.C.	15 FEB 1876	Ebenezer
008425	JOHNSON, Eliza	3m	C	D.C.	26 JUL 1876	Young Mens
012598	JOHNSON, Eliza	39y	C	Md.	29 JUL 1877	Harmony
020657	JOHNSON, Eliza	37y	C	Md.	28 JUN 1879	Potters Field
003138	JOHNSON, Eliza Ann	3y	C	D.C.	26 APR 1875	Potters Field
007203	JOHNSON, Elizabeth	2y	C	D.C.	04 MAY 1876	Mt. Zion
012895	JOHNSON, Elizabeth	1y	W	D.C.	21 AUG 1877	Prospect Hill
017825	JOHNSON, Elizabeth	1y	C	D.C.	21 OCT 1878	Mt. Zion
020966	JOHNSON, Elizabeth	8m	C	D.C.	16 JUL 1879	Payne's
020978	JOHNSON, Elizabeth A.	68y	W	D.C.	17 JUL 1879	Mt. Olivet
006235	JOHNSON, Ella	1y	C	D.C.	04 FEB 1876	Baptist
012148	JOHNSON, Ella	22d	C	D.C.	01 JUL 1877	Mt. Zion
020861	JOHNSON, Ella	1y	C	D.C.	09 JUL 1879	Moore's
000056	JOHNSON, Ellen	7m	C	D.C.	04 AUG 1874	Young Mens
001560	JOHNSON, Ellen	3m	C	D.C.	01 JAN 1875	Young Mens
016213	JOHNSON, Emer	6m	C	D.C.	18 JUN 1878	Beckett's
000197	JOHNSON, Emma	10m	C	D.C.	15 AUG 1874	Mt. Pleasant
017588	JOHNSON, Emma	30y	C	Va.	01 OCT 1878	Beckett's
020965	JOHNSON, Emma	5m	C	D.C.	16 JUL 1879	Payne's
009735	JOHNSON, Emma B.	1y	W	D.C.	19 NOV 1876	Methodist
001995	JOHNSON, Emma Jane	5m	C	D.C.	02 FEB 1875	Moore's
010356	JOHNSON, Emma V.	5y	C	D.C.	21 JAN 1877	Mt. Zion
003683	JOHNSON, Emmaline	40y	C	Md.	17 JUN 1875	Ebenezer
001925	JOHNSON, Enie	9m	C	D.C.	28 JAN 1875	Harmony
011775	JOHNSON, Eudora Virginia	22y	C	Va.	02 JUN 1877	Harmony
006197	JOHNSON, Eva Irene	2m	W	D.C.	31 JAN 1876	Mt. Olivet
020886	JOHNSON, Ezekiel	6m	C	D.C.	11 JUL 1879	Beckett's
005717	JOHNSON, Fanny	3d	C	D.C.	10 DEC 1875	Mt. Pleasant
014932	JOHNSON, Florence	28y	C	Va.	03 MAR 1878	Potters Field
004479	JOHNSON, Florence E.	2m	W	D.C.	06 AUG 1875	Mt. Olivet
008474	JOHNSON, Florence L.	3m	C	D.C.	29 JUL 1876	Mt. Zion
007579	JOHNSON, Frances	2y	C	D.C.	10 JUN 1876	Graceland
004274	JOHNSON, Frank	9m	C	D.C.	24 JUL 1875	Young Mens
007862	JOHNSON, Frank	5m	M	D.C.	26 JUN 1876	Ebenezer
014727	JOHNSON, Frank	4y	C	D.C	09 FEB 1878	Potters Field
000342f	JOHNSON, Frank Sumner	6m	--	--	26 AUG 1875	Rock Creek
008025	JOHNSON, Frederick	1y	C	Md.	05 JUL 1876	Beckett's
015583	JOHNSON, Frederick	1y	M	D.C.	02 MAY 1878	Beckett's
020086	JOHNSON, Frederick	1y	C	D.C	13 MAY 1879	Moore's
001964	JOHNSON, Geo.	12y	C	D.C.	31 JAN 1875	Young Mens
000100	JOHNSON, George	35y	C	Va.	08 AUG 1874	Washington Asylum
000244	JOHNSON, George	1m	W	D.C.	19 AUG 1874	Mt. Olivet
000495	JOHNSON, George	40y	C	Va.	12 SEP 1874	Washington Asylum
004931	JOHNSON, George	11y	C	Md.	06 SEP 1875	Reform School, D.C.
018265	JOHNSON, George Durham	33y	M	Pa.	07 DEC 1878	Harmony
000341	JOHNSON, George Ella	1y	C	D.C.	28 AUG 1874	Beckett's
010347	JOHNSON, George R.	20y	W	D.C.	20 JAN 1877	Oak Hill
008803	JOHNSON, George Thomas	11y	C	D.C.	24 AUG 1876	Harmony
012545	JOHNSON, George W.	7m	C	D.C.	27 JUL 1877	Mt. Zion
017449	JOHNSON, George Wesley	2m	C	D.C.	18 SEP 1878	Payne's
003240	JOHNSON, Georgeanna	1y	C	D.C.	06 MAY 1875	Mt. Zion
007779	JOHNSON, Georgie Viola	9m	C	D.C.	22 JUN 1876	Moore's

District of Columbia Death Records, August 1, 1874 to July 31, 1879   179

No.	Name	Age	Race	Birth	Death Date	Burial Place
018403	JOHNSON, Gertrude	7m	C	D.C.	20 DEC 1878	Beckett's
017796	JOHNSON, Gertrude	14d	W	D.C.	19 OCT 1878	Oak Hill
017356	JOHNSON, Gertrude	8m	C	D.C.	09 SEP 1878	Mt. Pleasant
018080	JOHNSON, Gindina E.	57y	C	Va.	17 NOV 1878	Glenwood
016233	JOHNSON, Glasel	3m	C	Va.	20 JUN 1878	Payne's
020899	JOHNSON, Grace	4m	C	D.C.	12 JUL 1879	Potters Field
018078	JOHNSON, Hannah	42y	W	Pa.	17 NOV 1878	Glenwood/Philadelphia
004779	JOHNSON, Harriet	1y	W	D.C.	27 AUG 1875	Montgomery Co., Md.
013652	JOHNSON, Harriet	13y	C	D.C.	27 OCT 1877	Payne's
020715	JOHNSON, Harriet	37y	W	Pa.	02 JUL 1879	Mt. Olivet
003548	JOHNSON, Harrison Hemsley	4y	C	D.C.	07 JUN 1875	Harmony
013588	JOHNSON, Harry	2y	C	D.C.	22 OCT 1877	Beckett's
018102	JOHNSON, Harry	1y	M	D.C.	20 NOV 1878	Graceland
013988	JOHNSON, Hattie	2m	C	D.C.	02 DEC 1877	Potters Field
015396	JOHNSON, Hattie	6m	C	D.C.	14 APR 1878	Payne's
018715	JOHNSON, Hattie	5m	C	D.C.	18 JAN 1879	Beckett's
004275	JOHNSON, Hattie F.	7m	W	D.C.	24 JUL 1875	Episcopal Georgetown
005455	JOHNSON, Helen	74y	C	Pa.	14 NOV 1875	Harmony
003881	JOHNSON, Hellen L.M.	3m	C	D.C.	27 JUN 1875	Harmony
002936	JOHNSON, Henrietta	29y	W	Va.	10 APR 1875	Oak Hill
010185	JOHNSON, Henrietta	c.100y	C	D.C.	06 JAN 1877	Mt. Zion
019717	JOHNSON, Henrietta	31y	C	Md.	10 APR 1879	Holy Rood
000519	JOHNSON, Henry	68y	C	Md.	15 SEP 1874	Mt. Zion
000522	JOHNSON, Henry	76y	W	Md.	15 SEP 1874	Holy Rood
015322	JOHNSON, Henry	6y	C	D.C.	08 APR 1878	Potters Field
014835	JOHNSON, Henry	1m	C	D.C.	21 FEB 1878	Beckett's
018139	JOHNSON, Henry	60y	C	Md.	24 NOV 1878	Potters Field
016475	JOHNSON, Henry Blake	5y	W	Pa.	06 JUL 1878	Mt. Olivet
018096	JOHNSON, Hester	50y	C	Md.	19 NOV 1878	Potters Field
005114a	JOHNSON, Horace	2m	C	D.C.	12 OCT 1875	Potters Field
018501	JOHNSON, Hubert M.	9y	W	D.C.	29 DEC 1878	Congressional
003999	JOHNSON, Ida	4m	C	D.C.	04 JUL 1875	Mt. Pleasant
009607	JOHNSON, Ida	6y	C	D.C.	03 NOV 1876	Young Mens
019672	JOHNSON, Ida Clay	28y	W	D.C.	06 APR 1879	Congressional
001472	JOHNSON, Idea May	12m	C	D.C.	24 DEC 1874	Harmony
016191	JOHNSON, Infant of Abe	8d	C	D.C.	16 JUN 1878	Young Mens
013137	JOHNSON, Infant of Abert	8h	C	D.C.	09 SEP 1877	Potters Field
012325	JOHNSON, Infant of Anna	15d	C	D.C.	12 JUL 1877	Potters Field
012587	JOHNSON, Infant of Annie	13d	C	D.C.	28 JUL 1877	Potters Field
011962	JOHNSON, Infant of Burnett	5d	C	D.C.	19 JUN 1877	Mt. Pleasant
006598	JOHNSON, Infant of Charles	1h	C	D.C.	08 MAR 1876	Mt. Zion
010198	JOHNSON, Infant of Charles	20h	C	D.C.	07 JAN 1877	Moore's
014267	JOHNSON, Infant of David	2m	C	D.C.	30 DEC 1877	Mt. Zion
017070	JOHNSON, Infant of Delphine	20h	C	D.C.	16 AUG 1878	Mt. Zion
004781	JOHNSON, Infant of Dennis	1d	C	D.C.	27 AUG 1875	Ebenezer
008053	JOHNSON, Infant of Dennis	1d	C	D.C.	06 JUL 1876	Ebenezer
011309	JOHNSON, Infant of E.	6d	C	D.C.	12 APR 1877	Young Mens
005228	JOHNSON, Infant of Elizabeth	5d	C	D.C.	30 SEP 1875	Harmony
011697	JOHNSON, Infant of Fannie	9h	C	D.C.	25 MAY 1877	Potters Field
003038	JOHNSON, Infant of Geo.	12h	C	D.C.	18 APR 1875	Harmony
004204	JOHNSON, Infant of George	5m	C	D.C.	19 JUL 1875	Potters Field
020658	JOHNSON, Infant of Gwinette	6d	C	D.C.	28 JUN 1879	Payne's
008777	JOHNSON, Infant of Hattie	1m	C	D.C.	22 AUG 1876	Ebenezer
021038	JOHNSON, Infant of J.D.	8m	C	D.C.	21 JUL 1879	Mt. Zion
021051	JOHNSON, Infant of J.D.	2d	C	D.C.	22 JUL 1879	Mt. Zion
003420	JOHNSON, Infant of James	3d	C	D.C.	24 MAY 1875	Potters Field

No.	Name	Age	Race	Birth	Death Date	Burial Place
019069	JOHNSON, Infant of Jas.	1d	C	D.C.	14 FEB 1879	Potters Field
012930	JOHNSON, Infant of John	1d	C	D.C.	24 AUG 1877	Young Mens
010008	JOHNSON, Infant of John	14d	C	D.C.	19 DEC 1876	Young Mens
009803	JOHNSON, Infant of John H.	8d	C	D.C.	26 NOV 1876	Potters Field
006509	JOHNSON, Infant of Joseph	4d	C	D.C.	29 FEB 1876	Baptist
004903	JOHNSON, Infant of Joshua	2h	W	D.C.	04 SEP 1875	Mt. Olivet
006422	JOHNSON, Infant of Julia	15h	C	D.C.	20 FEB 1876	Mt. Zion
019322	JOHNSON, Infant of Maria A.	1m	C	D.C.	08 MAR 1879	Potters Field
010733	JOHNSON, Infant of Marshal	5m	C	D.C.	22 FEB 1877	Young Mens
002577	JOHNSON, Infant of Moses	2d	C	D.C.	15 MAR 1875	Ebenezer
010131	JOHNSON, Infant of Ottawa	6d	C	D.C.	31 DEC 1876	Potters Field
002662	JOHNSON, Infant of Peter	1d	C	D.C.	21 MAR 1875	Ebenezer
019388	JOHNSON, Infant of Peter	6m	C	D.C.	13 MAR 1879	Beckett's
006978	JOHNSON, Infant of Robert	1m	C	D.C.	10 APR 1876	Young Mens
002092	JOHNSON, Infant of Sarah	1m	C	D.C.	09 FEB 1875	Potters Field
016231	JOHNSON, Infant of Smith	2m	C	D.C.	20 JUN 1878	Mt. Pleasant
008324	JOHNSON, Infant of Thomas	9d	C	D.C.	19 JUL 1876	Ebenezer
015936	JOHNSON, Infant of Thomas	9d	C	D.C.	31 MAY 1878	Mt. Olivet
004007	JOHNSON, Infant of Thomas	9h	C	D.C.	05 JUL 1875	Young Mens
018364	JOHNSON, Infant of Wash.	7d	C	D.C.	17 DEC 1878	Potters Field
000739	JOHNSON, Infant of Wm.	4d	C	D.C.	07 OCT 1874	Potters Field
003025	JOHNSON, Infant of Wm.	1m	C	D.C.	17 APR 1875	Ebenezer
005722	JOHNSON, Isaac	c.60y	C	Va.	11 DEC 1875	Washington Asylum
003211	JOHNSON, Isaac	33y	C	Va.	04 MAY 1875	Potters Field
005456	JOHNSON, Isaac	60y	M	Md.	14 NOV 1875	Mt. Olivet
005304	JOHNSON, Isaac	11m	C	D.C.	29 OCT 1875	Ebenezer
007626	JOHNSON, Isaac	102y	C	Va.	13 JUN 1876	Young Mens
020002	JOHNSON, Isaac	80y	C	Va.	05 MAY 1879	Young Mens
014422	JOHNSON, J. Robert	3m	C	D.C.	14 JAN 1878	Young Mens
000469	JOHNSON, James	3y	M	D.C.	10 SEP 1874	Washington Asylum
003113	JOHNSON, James	1y	C	D.C.	25 APR 1875	Beckett's
008746	JOHNSON, James	22y	C	Va.	20 AUG 1876	Young Mens
008010	JOHNSON, James	6d	C	D.C.	04 JUL 1876	Young Mens
006874	JOHNSON, James	51y	C	Va.	31 MAR 1876	Potters Field
013392	JOHNSON, James	1y	C	D.C.	03 OCT 1877	Jones Chapel
018361	JOHNSON, James	50y	C	Md.	17 DEC 1878	Prince George's Co., Md.
020071	JOHNSON, James	10y	C	D.C.	11 MAY 1879	Mt. Pleasant
003936	JOHNSON, James A.	33y	C	Md.	30 JUN 1875	Baltimore, Md.
017722	JOHNSON, James Atwood	1y	C	D.C.	13 OCT 1878	Beckett's
010314	JOHNSON, James Edw.	2y	C	D.C.	17 JAN 1877	Potters Field
003980	JOHNSON, James H.	9d	C	D.C.	03 JUL 1875	Beckett's
017503	JOHNSON, James Henry Buchanan	1y	C	D.C.	23 SEP 1878	Potters Field
012917	JOHNSON, James Hnery	2y	C	D.C.	23 AUG 1877	Young Mens
000201	JOHNSON, James M.	3m	C	D.C.	15 AUG 1874	Ebenezer
008210	JOHNSON, James Marshall	7m	W	D.C.	12 JUL 1876	Mt. Olivet
010510	JOHNSON, Jane Elizabeth	5y	C	D.C.	04 FEB 1877	Young Mens
016633	JOHNSON, Jane M.	39y	W	Md.	17 JUL 1878	Oak Hill
017992	JOHNSON, Jennie	c.23y	C	Va.	09 NOV 1878	Mt. Pleasant
001207	JOHNSON, Jerry	37y	C	Va.	21 NOV 1874	Washington Asylum
011894	JOHNSON, Jerry	7m	C	D.C.	14 JUN 1877	Potters Field
019743	JOHNSON, Jno. W.	55y	C	Va.	12 APR 1879	Harmony
001379	JOHNSON, John	9m	C	D.C.	13 DEC 1874	Young Mens
000868	JOHNSON, John	58y	C	D.C.	19 OCT 1874	Holy Rood
007045	JOHNSON, John	40y	C	Va.	18 APR 1876	Harmony
008272	JOHNSON, John	48y	C	Va.	15 JUL 1876	Mt. Pleasant Plain
012163	JOHNSON, John	7m	C	D.C.	01 JUL 1877	Mt. Zion

District of Columbia Death Records, August 1, 1874 to July 31, 1879   181

No.	Name	Age	Race	Birth	Death Date	Burial Place
017964	JOHNSON, John	51y	W	Nor.	06 NOV 1878	Soldier's Home
018546	JOHNSON, John	85y	C	Md.	02 JAN 1879	Potters Field
009335	JOHNSON, John E.	10m	C	D.C.	07 OCT 1876	Beckett's
001636	JOHNSON, John Francis Jacob	3m	M	D.C.	07 JAN 1875	Mt. Olivet
020863	JOHNSON, John Henry	9m	C	D.C.	09 JUL 1879	Jones Chapel
003650f	JOHNSON, John McFarland	78y	W	Va.	15 JUN 1875	Oak Hill
015543	JOHNSON, John W.A.	11m	C	D.C.	28 APR 1878	Mt. Zion
008972	JOHNSON, Joseph	6d	C	D.C.	05 SEP 1876	Potters Field
014137	JOHNSON, Joseph	2y	C	D.C.	19 DEC 1877	Beckett's
015534	JOHNSON, Joseph	11m	C	D.C.	27 APR 1878	Mt. Olivet
015851	JOHNSON, Joseph	35y	C	Va.	26 MAY 1878	Harmony
017490	JOHNSON, Joseph	45y	C	Va.	22 SEP 1878	Harmony
020735	JOHNSON, Joseph	7m	C	D.C.	03 JUL 1879	Young Mens
020178	JOHNSON, Joseph	56y	C	La.	23 MAY 1879	Beckett's
000860	JOHNSON, Joseph Franklin	3m	C	D.C.	19 OCT 1874	Mt. Pleasant
007023	JOHNSON, Josephine	18y	W	Va.	16 APR 1876	Glenwood
003350	JOHNSON, Judge	75y	C	Va.	17 MAY 1875	Ebenezer
016707	JOHNSON, Julia A.	1m	C	D.C.	21 JUL 1878	Mt. Pleasant
008590	JOHNSON, Julia Ann	9y	C	Va.	07 AUG 1876	Potters Field
012019	JOHNSON, Katie	4y	C	D.C.	23 JUN 1877	Beckett's
004379	JOHNSON, Kittury	84y	W	Md.	30 JUL 1875	New Market, Md.
007204	JOHNSON, Laura	6m	M	D.C.	04 MAY 1876	Mt. Pleasant Plain
003491	JOHNSON, Laura Virginia	3y	C	D.C.	30 MAY 1875	Young Mens
015477	JOHNSON, Lavina	8m	C	D.C.	22 APR 1878	Moore's
004880	JOHNSON, Lavinia	1y	C	D.C.	02 SEP 1875	Ebenezer
018002	JOHNSON, Lemuel	40y	C	Md.	10 NOV 1878	Belt's Farm
004813	JOHNSON, Lewis	80y	C	Va.	29 AUG 1875	Washington Asylum
018003	JOHNSON, Lewis	2m	C	D.C.	10 NOV 1878	Mt. Pleasant
016675	JOHNSON, Lewis Benton	2m	W	D.C.	19 JUL 1878	Congressional
006262	JOHNSON, Lillie	5m	C	D.C.	07 FEB 1876	Ebenezer
016542	JOHNSON, Lillie	1y	C	D.C.	10 JUL 1878	Potters Field
009945	JOHNSON, Lillie Jane	5m	C	D.C.	13 DEC 1876	Ebenezer
010856	JOHNSON, Lizzie	22y	C	Md.	03 MAR 1877	Ebenezer
014401	JOHNSON, Louis F.	24y	M	Va.	12 JAN 1878	Harmony
011000	JOHNSON, Louisa	1y	C	D.C.	16 MAR 1877	Ebenezer
018264	JOHNSON, Louisa	c.40y	C	Va.	07 DEC 1878	Harmony
018362	JOHNSON, Louisa	46y	C	Ky.	17 DEC 1878	Harmony
005366	JOHNSON, Louise	14y	C	Va.	05 NOV 1875	Potters Field
001903	JOHNSON, Lucas	1y	C	D.C.	26 JAN 1875	Mt. Olivet
006004	JOHNSON, Lucian	4d	C	D.C.	12 JAN 1876	Young Mens
002871	JOHNSON, Lucy	5y	C	Va.	04 APR 1875	Harmony
004814	JOHNSON, Lucy	4y	C	D.C.	29 AUG 1875	Mt. Pleasant
002280	JOHNSON, Lucy	45y	C	Va.	22 FEB 1875	Young Mens
018706	JOHNSON, Lucy	7d	C	D.C.	17 JAN 1879	Potters Field
019321	JOHNSON, Lucy Ann	40y	C	Va.	08 MAR 1879	Young Mens
006034	JOHNSON, Luella	1y	C	D.C.	15 JAN 1876	Beckett's
002659	JOHNSON, Luvinia	4y	C	D.C.	20 MAR 1875	Mt. Zion
012108	JOHNSON, M.E.	6m	W	D.C.	28 JUN 1877	Mt. Olivet
016813	JOHNSON, Mabel Garnett	7m	W	D.C.	29 JUL 1878	Congressional
000892	JOHNSON, Maisy	1m	M	D.C.	21 OCT 1874	Potters Field
005620	JOHNSON, Major	30y	C	Va.	01 DEC 1875	Mt. Zion
002226	JOHNSON, Marcia T.	3y	W	D.C.	18 FEB 1875	Oak Hill
000554	JOHNSON, Margaret	2m	C	D.C.	18 SEP 1874	Potters Field
018022	JOHNSON, Margaret	31y	C	Md.	11 NOV 1878	Beckett's
008379	JOHNSON, Maria B.	1y	C	D.C.	22 JUL 1876	Harmony
001354	JOHNSON, Mariah Louisa	6d	C	D.C.	10 DEC 1874	Mt. Olivet

District of Columbia Death Records, August 1, 1874 to July 31, 1879

No.	Name	Age	Race	Birth	Death Date	Burial Place
013514	JOHNSON, Marie	15m	C	D.C.	14 OCT 1877	Young Mens
020077	JOHNSON, Martha	7y	C	D.C.	12 MAY 1879	Mt. Pleasant
002335	JOHNSON, Martha Ann	7y	C	Md.	27 FEB 1875	Mt. Olivet
013435	JOHNSON, Martha Ann	68y	W	Md.	08 OCT 1877	Oak Hill
000604	JOHNSON, Mary	1m	C	D.C.	22 SEP 1874	Harmony
002145	JOHNSON, Mary	2y	C	D.C.	13 FEB 1875	Young Mens
004276	JOHNSON, Mary	2m	C	D.C.	24 JUL 1875	Potters Field
005128a	JOHNSON, Mary	26y	W	Va.	13 OCT 1875	Young Mens
005109	JOHNSON, Mary	5y	C	N.C.	20 SEP 1875	Mt. Pleasant
006283	JOHNSON, Mary	35y	W	Va.	09 FEB 1876	Washington Asylum
006263	JOHNSON, Mary	5m	C	D.C.	07 FEB 1876	Ebenezer
011299	JOHNSON, Mary	37y	C	Va.	11 APR 1877	Mt. Pleasant
010404	JOHNSON, Mary	6m	C	D.C.	25 JAN 1877	Mt. Olivet
012554	JOHNSON, Mary	25y	C	Va.	27 JUL 1877	Potters Field
013972	JOHNSON, Mary	36y	C	Va.	30 NOV 1877	Harmony
017955	JOHNSON, Mary	60y	C	Md.	05 NOV 1878	Beckett's
020833	JOHNSON, Mary	30y	C	D.C.	08 JUL 1879	Beckett's
020426	JOHNSON, Mary	9m	C	D.C.	13 JUN 1879	Mt. Pleasant
019963	JOHNSON, Mary	7d	C	D.C.	02 MAY 1879	Potters Field
002238	JOHNSON, Mary E.	6m	C	D.C.	19 FEB 1875	Ebenezer
011835	JOHNSON, Mary E.	c.36y	M	D.C.	08 JUN 1877	Mt. Pleasant Plain
015969	JOHNSON, Mary E.	11m	C	D.C.	02 JUN 1878	Mt. Zion
002402	JOHNSON, Mary J.	1m	C	D.C.	02 MAR 1875	Ebenezer
013169	JOHNSON, Mary Jane	35y	C	Va.	12 SEP 1877	Potters Field
018190	JOHNSON, Mary Jane	58y	C	Va.	28 NOV 1878	Mt. Zion
010189	JOHNSON, Mary Lucy	9y	C	D.C.	06 JAN 1877	Ebenezer
016741	JOHNSON, Mary S.	2y	C	D.C.	24 JUL 1878	Mt. Zion
003146	JOHNSON, Mary Selina	6y	W	D.C.	27 APR 1875	Congressional
009401	JOHNSON, Matilda C.	75y	W	Md.	13 OCT 1876	Congressional
013776	JOHNSON, Matilda Florence	1y	W	Md.	09 NOV 1877	Oak Hill
014147	JOHNSON, Mattie	4y	C	D.C.	20 DEC 1877	Young Mens
000593	JOHNSON, Melvina	1y	C	D.C.	21 SEP 1874	Potters Field
014469	JOHNSON, Millie	22y	C	Md.	18 JAN 1878	Young Mens
020612	JOHNSON, Molly	31y	W	Eng.	25 JUN 1879	Potters Field
002377	JOHNSON, Morgana	13m	C	D.C.	02 MAR 1875	Mt. Pleasant
001173	JOHNSON, Moses	20y	C	Va.	17 NOV 1874	Potters Field
018896	JOHNSON, Nellie	4y	W	D.C.	31 JAN 1879	Congressional/Oak Hill
014400	JOHNSON, Nettie	7y	W	Va.	12 JAN 1878	Alexandria, Va.
007595	JOHNSON, Noble	3m	C	D.C.	11 JUN 1876	Ebenezer
005471	JOHNSON, Ogleton	76y	C	D.C.	16 NOV 1875	Mt. Olivet
006959	JOHNSON, Peyton	5m	C	D.C.	07 APR 1876	Moore's
018678	JOHNSON, Philip	c.70y	C	Va.	15 JAN 1879	Mt. Pleasant
007564	JOHNSON, Precilla	38y	C	Va.	09 JUN 1876	Beckett's
013198	JOHNSON, Priscilla	20y	C	Md.	14 SEP 1877	Potters Field
000243	JOHNSON, Racheal	4y	C	D.C.	19 AUG 1874	Graceland
011053	JOHNSON, Rachel Ann	13m	M	D.C.	20 MAR 1877	Potters Field
017184	JOHNSON, Rebecca	35y	C	Md.	25 AUG 1878	Jones Chapel
008712	JOHNSON, Richard	35y	C	D.C.	17 AUG 1876	Beckett's
009484	JOHNSON, Richard	75y	C	Md.	21 OCT 1876	Harmony
016942	JOHNSON, Richard	28y	C	Md.	07 AUG 1878	Beckett's
016456	JOHNSON, Richard	1y	C	D.C.	05 JUL 1878	Baptist
010650	JOHNSON, Richard Andrew	1y	C	D.C.	16 FEB 1877	Ebenezer
005029a	JOHNSON, Richard G.	38y	C	D.C.	02 OCT 1875	Mt. Olivet
001713	JOHNSON, Robert	11d	C	D.C.	13 JAN 1875	Potters Field
005142	JOHNSON, Robert	25y	C	Md.	23 SEP 1875	Potters Field
018081	JOHNSON, Robert	35y	C	Va.	17 NOV 1878	Potters Field

District of Columbia Death Records, August 1, 1874 to July 31, 1879   183

No.	Name	Age	Race	Birth	Death Date	Burial Place
020613	JOHNSON, Robert	2y	C	D.C.	25 JUN 1879	Young Mens
020716	JOHNSON, Robert Tucker	1m	W	D.C.	02 JUL 1879	Alexandria, Va.
007331	JOHNSON, Robt. Jas.	12y	C	D.C.	18 MAY 1876	Young Mens
009161	JOHNSON, Rosa	2y	C	D.C.	22 SEP 1876	Harmony
010408	JOHNSON, Rosa	5m	C	D.C.	26 JAN 1877	Young Mens
011976	JOHNSON, Rosa	7y	M	Md.	20 JUN 1877	Mt. Pleasant
008281	JOHNSON, Rosa May	4m	C	D.C.	15 JUL 1876	Beckett's
015469	JOHNSON, Rosa Virginia	7m	W	D.C.	21 APR 1878	Methodist
014189	JOHNSON, Rosena	7y	W	D.C.	24 DEC 1877	Tennallytown
016246	JOHNSON, Sally	47y	C	Va.	21 JUN 1878	Harmony
000447	JOHNSON, Samuel	1y	C	D.C.	07 SEP 1874	Beckett's
017664	JOHNSON, Samuel	19y	C	Va.	07 OCT 1878	Payne's
014956	JOHNSON, Samuel Elias Isaiah	10y	C	D.C.	05 MAR 1878	Potters Field
003880	JOHNSON, Samuel Thdeus	3m	C	D.C.	27 JUN 1875	Young Mens
015971	JOHNSON, Samuel William	1y	C	D.C.	02 JUN 1878	Mt. Pleasant
010018	JOHNSON, Sarah	19y	C	Va.	20 DEC 1876	Young Mens
017255	JOHNSON, Sarah	18y	C	Va.	30 AUG 1878	Harmony
018333	JOHNSON, Sarah	30y	C	Va.	14 DEC 1878	Payne's
020714	JOHNSON, Sarah	7m	C	D.C.	02 JUL 1879	Potters Field
019309	JOHNSON, Sarah	93y	C	Va.	07 MAR 1879	Graceland
004315	JOHNSON, Sarah A.	78y	C	Md.	26 JUL 1875	Potters Field
008553	JOHNSON, Sarah Edna	9m	W	D.C.	04 AUG 1876	Poughkeepsie, N.Y.
007447	JOHNSON, Sarah Maria	11m	C	D.C.	31 MAY 1876	Ebenezer
005229a	JOHNSON, Sarah S.	10m	C	D.C.	21 OCT 1875	Beckett's
013271	JOHNSON, Scipio	40y	C	S.C.	21 SEP 1877	Potters Field
007418	JOHNSON, Sidney	71y	W	D.C.	27 MAY 1876	Glenwood
014564	JOHNSON, Soloman	1y	C	D.C.	26 JAN 1878	Payne's
014709	JOHNSON, Solomon	9m	C	D.C.	08 FEB 1878	Beckett's
003271	JOHNSON, Stella	3m	C	D.C.	09 MAY 1875	Mt. Olivet
010039	JOHNSON, Susan	4d	C	D.C.	21 DEC 1876	Potters Field
020435	JOHNSON, Susan	40y	C	Md.	14 JUN 1879	Payne's
009783	JOHNSON, Susan Rebecca	17y	C	Md.	24 NOV 1876	Young Mens
017129	JOHNSON, Tamer	90y	C	Md.	21 AUG 1878	Harmony
012101	JOHNSON, Theresa	76y	W	Va.	28 JUN 1877	Waterford, Va.
006798	JOHNSON, Thomas	48y	C	Md.	24 MAR 1876	Potters Field
018535	JOHNSON, Thomas	60y	C	Md.	01 JAN 1879	Prince George's Co., Md.
010254	JOHNSON, Thomas Howard	9m	C	D.C.	11 JAN 1877	Mt. Pleasant
010253	JOHNSON, Thomas M.	57y	W	Va.	11 JAN 1877	Presbyterian
013670	JOHNSON, Thos.	43y	W	D.C.	29 OCT 1877	Oak Hill
011997	JOHNSON, Tighlman	32y	C	Md.	21 JAN 1877	Potters Field
010887	JOHNSON, Timandria	46y	W	Md.	06 MAR 1877	Congressional
003300	JOHNSON, Virginia	25y	C	Va.	12 MAY 1875	Harmony
007822	JOHNSON, Virginia	8y	C	D.C.	24 JUN 1876	Harmony
009232	JOHNSON, Virginia	3m	C	D.C.	28 SEP 1876	Mt. Pleasant
020340	JOHNSON, Volney H.	73y	W	N.H.	09 JUN 1879	Congressional
019357	JOHNSON, W.	20d	W	D.C.	10 MAR 1879	Graceland
013434	JOHNSON, W.H.	1m	C	D.C.	08 OCT 1877	Young Mens
012896	JOHNSON, W.J.	22m	C	D.C.	21 AUG 1877	Beckett's
001214	JOHNSON, Walter	7m	M	D.C.	23 NOV 1874	Young Mens
018381	JOHNSON, Walter	2y	C	D.C.	19 DEC 1878	Potters Field
012713	JOHNSON, Walter B.	61y	W	Md.	07 AUG 1877	Congressional
005015	JOHNSON, Warner	16y	C	Va.	12 SEP 1875	Washington Asylum
005746	JOHNSON, William	7d	C	D.C.	14 DEC 1875	Young Mens
003629	JOHNSON, William	1y	C	D.C.	13 JUN 1875	Ebenezer
003429	JOHNSON, William	36y	W	D.C.	25 MAY 1875	Glenwood
006960	JOHNSON, William	72y	W	Del.	07 APR 1876	Wilmington, Del.

District of Columbia Death Records, August 1, 1874 to July 31, 1879

No.	Name	Age	Race	Birth	Death Date	Burial Place
008216	JOHNSON, William	8m	C	D.C.	12 JUL 1876	Young Mens
009711	JOHNSON, William	1y	C	D.C.	17 NOV 1876	Ebenezer
013836	JOHNSON, William	24y	C	Va.	16 NOV 1877	Harmony
014890	JOHNSON, William	1y	C	D.C.	27 FEB 1878	Young Mens
014891	JOHNSON, William	77y	C	Va.	27 FEB 1878	Young Mens
016290	JOHNSON, William	6d	C	D.C.	24 JUN 1878	Mt. Olivet
016147	JOHNSON, William	7m	C	D.C.	13 JUN 1878	Mt. Olivet
019943	JOHNSON, William	20y	C	Va.	30 APR 1879	Beckett's
004727	JOHNSON, William Anderson	11m	M	D.C.	23 AUG 1875	Mt. Zion
009107	JOHNSON, William Henry	1y	C	D.C.	17 SEP 1876	Mt. Zion
011972	JOHNSON, William Henry	2m	C	D.C.	19 JUN 1877	Washington Asylum
000074	JOHNSON, William M., Jr.	6m	C	D.C.	06 AUG 1874	Mt. Pleasant
003856	JOHNSON, Willie	2m	C	D.C.	26 JUN 1875	Harmony
014493	JOHNSON, Wm.	80y	C	Va.	20 JAN 1878	Beckett's
012575	JOHNSON, Wm. H.	1y	C	D.C.	28 JUL 1877	Mt. Olivet
015512	JOHNSON, Wm. H.	6m	C	Va.	25 APR 1878	Mt. Pleasant
010455	JOHNSON, Wm. Henry	11m	C	D.C.	30 JAN 1877	Ebenezer
016192	JOHNSON, Wm. Henry	2y	C	D.C.	16 JUN 1878	Young Mens
019925	JOHNSON, Zachariah	50y	C	Va.	28 APR 1879	Potters Field
014749	JOHNSTON, Alexander	46y	W	Ohio	12 FEB 1878	Glenwood
013513	JOHNSTON, Annie	32y	C	Va.	14 OCT 1877	Mt. Pleasant
009751	JOHNSTON, Armstead	90y	C	Va.	20 NOV 1876	Potters Field
021175	JOHNSTON, Birdie Finette	8y	W	Va.	31 JUL 1879	Graceland
000801	JOHNSTON, Edward	9d	C	D.C.	14 OCT 1874	Young Mens
004199	JOHNSTON, Ella	2y	C	Md.	19 JUL 1875	Ebenezer
009234	JOHNSTON, Emily	80y	C	Va.	29 SEP 1876	Potters Field
012746	JOHNSTON, Henry	45y	C	U.S.	09 AUG 1877	Potters Field
010052	JOHNSTON, James	23y	W	Va.	22 DEC 1876	Potters Field
010771	JOHNSTON, James	65y	W	Ire.	24 FEB 1877	Congressional
013845	JOHNSTON, James Alexander	4y	C	D.C.	17 NOV 1877	Harmony
004098	JOHNSTON, James Lomax	5m	C	D.C.	12 JUL 1875	Congressional
001640	JOHNSTON, Jane A.	44y	W	N.Y.	07 JAN 1875	Chicago, Ill.
008941	JOHNSTON, Jennette	c.68y	W	Scot.	02 SEP 1876	Baltimore, Md.
014239	JOHNSTON, Jermima	85y	C	Va.	28 DEC 1877	Potters Field
006143	JOHNSTON, John W.	11m	C	D.C.	26 JAN 1876	Harmony
007978	JOHNSTON, Louisa	3m	C	D.C.	03 JUL 1876	Chappel's
010228	JOHNSTON, Maggie Elizabeth	18d	W	D.C.	08 JAN 1877	Glenwood
015162	JOHNSTON, Margaret	6y	W	D.C.	23 MAR 1878	Glenwood
002223	JOHNSTON, Matilda	10m	C	D.C.	18 FEB 1875	Mt. Pleasant
015808	JOHNSTON, Pricila	4m	C	D.C.	22 MAY 1878	Brightwood
012772	JOHNSTON, Robt.	3m	C	D.C.	11 AUG 1877	Beckett's
009043	JOHNSTON, Thomas	65y	C	Md.	12 SEP 1876	Potters Field
020860	JOHNSTON, Walter	5m	C	D.C.	09 JUL 1879	Brightwood
012069	JOHNSTON, William Thomas	2m	W	D.C.	26 JUN 1877	Congressional
002371	JOHNSTONE, Grafton	63y	C	Md.	01 MAR 1875	Brightwood
000923	JOICE, Infant of Letta	4d	C	D.C.	24 OCT 1874	Mt. Pleasant
007611	JOICE, Oliver	1y	C	D.C.	12 JUN 1876	Moore's
014847	JOLLY, John	68y	W	D.C.	22 FEB 1878	Congressional
009361	JONES, Aby	2d	C	D.C.	10 OCT 1876	Young Mens
015970	JONES, Albert Marcellus	22y	C	D.C.	02 JUN 1878	Harmony
011061	JONES, Alex A.	1y	C	D.C.	21 MAR 1877	Harmony
011957	JONES, Alfred	61y	C	Va.	18 JUN 1877	Harmony
003501	JONES, Alice	4m	C	D.C.	01 JUN 1875	Young Mens
008123	JONES, Alice	6m	C	D.C.	10 JUL 1876	Falls Church, Va.
018441	JONES, Alice	3w	C	D.C.	23 DEC 1878	Potters Field
008480	JONES, Alonza	1y	W	Md.	29 JUL 1876	Skagg's

District of Columbia Death Records, August 1, 1874 to July 31, 1879   185

No.	Name	Age	Race	Birth	Death Date	Burial Place
002717	JONES, Alvergus	5m	C	D.C.	24 MAR 1875	Potters Field
006631	JONES, Andrew	1y	C	D.C.	10 MAR 1876	Young Mens
019853	JONES, Andrew	52y	C	D.C.	21 APR 1879	Harmony
004778	JONES, Ann Eliza	77y	W	N.Y.	27 AUG 1875	Oak Hill
006896	JONES, Annie	2y	C	D.C.	02 APR 1876	Ebenezer
016802	JONES, Annie	1y	C	D.C.	28 JUL 1878	Harmony
018756	JONES, Annie E.	32y	C	Va.	21 JAN 1879	Alexandria, Va.
003142	JONES, Anthony	27y	C	Mo.	26 APR 1875	Potters Field
020003	JONES, Arthur Leon	6d	W	D.C.	05 MAY 1879	Congressional
019166	JONES, Arthur W.	3y	W	D.C.	23 FEB 1879	Congressional
005322	JONES, Augustine	26y	C	Va.	31 OCT 1875	Ebenezer
018838	JONES, Austen	2y	C	D.C.	27 JAN 1879	Mt. Pleasant
003015	JONES, Barton	6y	C	Va.	17 APR 1875	Young Mens
011291	JONES, Bena M.	18y	C	D.C.	10 APR 1877	Harmony
021039	JONES, Benjamin	2y	C	D.C.	21 JUL 1879	Harmony
013149	JONES, Bertha	11m	C	D.C.	10 SEP 1877	Mt. Zion
010088	JONES, Bertie	1y	C	D.C.	27 DEC 1876	Mt. Zion
017839	JONES, Betsey	10m	C	D.C.	23 OCT 1878	Mt. Pleasant
007924	JONES, Blanch	4m	M	D.C.	29 JUN 1876	Young Mens
018725	JONES, Burtha	6m	C	Md.	19 JAN 1879	Mt. Pleasant
013844	JONES, Carrie Chester	7m	W	D.C.	17 NOV 1877	Oak Hill
001394	JONES, Catherine	60y	W	Va.	15 DEC 1874	Congressional
003631f	JONES, Catherine	23y	C	Va.	13 JUN 1875	Harmony
012730	JONES, Catherine	8y	W	Md.	08 AUG 1877	Piney Grove, Md.
010655	JONES, Catherine Lavinia	3y	C	D.C.	16 FEB 1877	Harmony
001965	JONES, Charles	9m	C	D.C.	31 JAN 1875	Mt. Olivet
020791	JONES, Charles	53y	C	Va.	06 JUL 1879	Potters Field
001348	JONES, Charles C.	9m	C	D.C.	09 DEC 1874	Mt. Zion
005168a	JONES, Charles Thomas Sinclair	10m	C	D.C.	16 OCT 1875	Mt. Pleasant Plain
011359	JONES, Charles Wesley	10d	C	D.C.	17 APR 1877	Potters Field
015895	JONES, Chas.	4m	W	D.C.	29 MAY 1878	Congressional
005253	JONES, Christiana	55y	C	Va.	24 OCT 1875	Mt. Pleasant
012549	JONES, Cornelius	1m	C	D.C.	27 JUL 1877	Washington Asylum
007881	JONES, Daisey	2m	C	D.C.	27 JUN 1876	Ebenezer
016131	JONES, Daniel	54y	C	Va.	12 JUN 1878	Beckett's
018948	JONES, Daniel	48y	C	Va.	04 FEB 1879	Potters Field
019080	JONES, Daniel M.	69y	W	N.Y.	15 FEB 1879	Glenwood
007657	JONES, David Daniel	7m	M	D.C.	15 JUN 1876	Mt. Pleasant
020924	JONES, Dora	13m	C	D.C.	14 JUL 1879	Mt. Zion
020940	JONES, Dorothea	45y	C	Va.	15 JUL 1879	Washington Asylum
008774	JONES, Edward	1y	C	D.C.	22 AUG 1876	Beckett's
017568	JONES, Edward	6y	M	D.C.	29 SEP 1878	Mt. Pleasant
003490	JONES, Edwin F.	9m	W	D.C.	30 MAY 1875	Mt. Olivet
011081	JONES, Eleanor	22y	C	Va.	22 MAR 1877	Harmony
010980	JONES, Eliza	81y	C	Va.	15 MAR 1877	Young Mens
010945	JONES, Eliza	75y	C	Pa.	12 MAR 1877	Potters Field
015335	JONES, Eliza	20y	C	D.C.	09 APR 1878	Young Mens
002622	JONES, Elizabeth	58y	W	Eng.	17 MAR 1875	Congressional
011949	JONES, Elizabeth	30y	C	Md.	17 JUN 1877	Potters Field
011065	JONES, Elizabeth	54y	W	Md.	21 MAR 1877	Presbyterian
007360	JONES, Ellen	55y	C	Md.	21 MAY 1876	Potters Field
015743	JONES, Ellen	60y	C	Va.	16 MAY 1878	Holy Rood
019437	JONES, Ellen	45y	C	Md.	17 MAR 1879	Young Mens
019915	JONES, Ellen, Mrs.	c.60y	C	Md.	27 APR 1879	Harmony
019018	JONES, Emma	22y	C	Va.	10 FEB 1879	Young Mens
013558	JONES, Fannie	29y	C	Va.	18 OCT 1877	Mt. Pleasant

District of Columbia Death Records, August 1, 1874 to July 31, 1879

No.	Name	Age	Race	Birth	Death Date	Burial Place
004258	JONES, Fannie Berkly	5m	C	D.C.	23 JUL 1875	Harmony
001938	JONES, Fanny	10m	C	D.C.	29 JAN 1875	Mt. Zion
003709	JONES, Frankie	11m	C	D.C.	19 JUN 1875	Mt. Olivet
016289	JONES, Frederick William	8m	C	D.C.	24 JUN 1878	Young Mens
011769	JONES, George	53y	C	Va.	01 JUN 1877	Young Mens
008173	JONES, George A.	29y	W	D.C.	11 JUL 1876	Congressional
009774	JONES, George W.	26y	C	Va.	22 NOV 1876	Beckett's
019562	JONES, George W.	4m	W	D.C.	26 MAR 1879	Potters Field
020874	JONES, Gertrude	1y	C	D.C.	10 JUL 1879	Beckett's
002951	JONES, Hanorah	16y	M	Va.	11 APR 1875	Mt. Zion
013515	JONES, Harrie Thaddeus	13y	W	D.C.	14 OCT 1877	Oak Hill
003401	JONES, Harriet	78y	C	Md.	22 MAY 1875	Beckett's
021037	JONES, Harriet	50y	C	Va.	21 JUL 1879	Beckett's
010035	JONES, Harry	1y	W	D.C.	20 DEC 1876	Mt. Olivet
005679	JONES, Henry	15m	W	D.C.	07 DEC 1875	Congressional
012128	JONES, Henry	90y	C	Va.	29 JUN 1877	Potters Field
004520	JONES, Hetty	1y	C	D.C.	09 AUG 1875	Potters Field
008773	JONES, Horace	50y	C	Md.	22 AUG 1876	Harmony
003118	JONES, Ida	3m	C	D.C.	25 APR 1875	Young Mens
008621	JONES, Ida	7m	C	D.C.	09 AUG 1876	Ebenezer
020216	JONES, Ida Veronica	3m	W	U.S.	28 MAY 1879	Mt. Olivet
009170	JONES, Infant	18d	C	D.C.	22 SEP 1876	Potters Field
011488	JONES, Infant of Barbara	6d	C	D.C.	02 MAY 1877	Ebenezer
014728	JONES, Infant of Dennis	28h	C	D.C.	09 FEB 1878	Young Mens
017965	JONES, Infant of Emma	3d	C	D.C.	06 NOV 1878	Potters Field
020832	JONES, Infant of Frank	1m	C	D.C.	08 JUL 1879	Mt. Olivet
017045	JONES, Infant of Georgeanna	2d	C	D.C.	14 AUG 1878	Potters Field
005457	JONES, Infant of Kate	5d	W	D.C.	14 NOV 1875	Potters Field
018502	JONES, Infant of Maria	5min	C	D.C.	29 DEC 1878	Potters Field
009551	JONES, Infant of Robert	8d	C	D.C.	27 OCT 1876	Potters Field
019796	JONES, Infant of Thomas	5m	C	D.C.	16 APR 1879	Mt. Zion
014819	JONES, Infant of William	9d	C	D.C.	19 FEB 1878	Young Mens
018120	JONES, Infant of Wm.	5min	C	D.C.	22 NOV 1878	Beckett's
011533	JONES, James	10y	C	Md.	06 MAY 1877	Harmony
004292	JONES, James S.	56y	W	Del.	25 JUL 1875	Glenwood
005917	JONES, Jane Ann	75y	W	Va.	02 JAN 1876	Presbyterian
008315	JONES, Jerome A.	4m	C	D.C.	18 JUL 1876	Harmony
000814	JONES, Jno. H.	1y	C	D.C.	15 OCT 1874	Mt. Olivet
005303	JONES, John	17y	C	Va.	29 OCT 1875	Mt. Pleasant
011562	JONES, John A.	1y	C	D.C.	11 MAY 1877	Young Mens
007778	JONES, John Alfred	10d	C	D.C.	22 JUN 1876	Moore's
016656	JONES, John H.	3y	C	D.C.	18 JUL 1878	Beckett's
008719	JONES, John Henry	6m	C	D.C.	18 AUG 1876	Potters Field
018023	JONES, John Henry	4m	C	Md.	11 NOV 1878	Potters Field
009391	JONES, John Joseph	10d	C	D.C.	12 OCT 1876	Mt. Olivet
015769	JONES, John W.	26y	W	Va.	19 MAY 1878	Congressional
011759	JONES, John Washington T.	16y	C	D.C.	01 JUN 1877	Harmony
005261	JONES, Johnnie	4y	C	D.C.	25 OCT 1875	Mt. Pleasant
009813	JONES, Joseph	57y	W	Eng.	27 NOV 1876	Congressional
015428	JONES, Joseph	5w	C	D.C.	17 APR 1878	Harmony
004495	JONES, Joseph H.	5w	W	D.C.	07 AUG 1875	Congressional
005124	JONES, Josephine	6y	C	D.C.	21 SEP 1875	Young Mens
020597	JONES, Julius	1m	W	D.C.	24 JUN 1879	Congressional
019895	JONES, Julius Ellis Walters	1y	C	D.C.	25 APR 1879	Potters Field
000242	JONES, Junius	2m	C	D.C.	19 AUG 1874	Young Mens
005141a	JONES, Laura	8m	C	D.C.	21 SEP 1875	Ebenezer

District of Columbia Death Records, August 1, 1874 to July 31, 1879   187

No.	Name	Age	Race	Birth	Death Date	Burial Place
012082	JONES, Laura	1m	C	D.C.	27 JUN 1877	Potters Field
017504	JONES, Laura D.	6y	C	Va.	23 SEP 1878	Va.
005155	JONES, Lilly	1y	C	D.C.	24 SEP 1875	Young Mens
006448	JONES, Lindsey M.	48y	W	Va.	23 FEB 1876	Piney Point, Md.
000726	JONES, Louisa	3m	W	--	05 OCT 1874	Mt. Olivet
012197	JONES, Louisa	2y	C	D.C.	03 JUL 1877	Potters Field
011043	JONES, Louisa	8m	C	D.C.	19 MAR 1877	Harmony
010637	JONES, Louisa P., Mrs.	37y	C	Va.	15 FEB 1877	Young Mens
014869	JONES, Lucian	61y	C	Va.	25 FEB 1878	Holy Rood
004200	JONES, Lucy	40y	M	Md.	19 JUL 1875	Potters Field
002496	JONES, Lucy	18m	M	D.C.	09 MAR 1875	Potters Field
020582	JONES, Lucy	31y	C	Va.	23 JUN 1879	Young Mens
019343	JONES, Lucy A.	56y	W	Va.	09 MAR 1879	Oak Hill
002932	JONES, Lucy A.R.	17m	C	D.C.	09 APR 1875	Harmony
003516	JONES, Lucy Ann	45y	M	Va.	03 JUN 1875	Mt. Zion
018182	JONES, Lula	6m	C	D.C.	27 NOV 1878	Payne's
016520	JONES, Lulius E.	27y	C	D.C.	09 JUL 1878	Young Mens
012996	JONES, Maggie	16m	W	D.C.	28 AUG 1877	Glenwood
013862	JONES, Mahala	73y	C	Va.	19 NOV 1877	Young Mens
012978	JONES, Margaret	13m	C	D.C.	27 AUG 1877	Potters Field
010118	JONES, Margrete	15y	C	Va.	30 DEC 1876	Harmony
016517	JONES, Maria Wells	39y	C	Md.	09 JUL 1878	Harmony
004565	JONES, Martha	1y	C	D.C.	12 AUG 1875	Ebenezer
021050	JONES, Martha Ann	2y	C	D.C.	22 JUL 1879	Mt. Olivet
001200	JONES, Mary	3y	C	D.C.	20 NOV 1874	Mt. Zion
003089	JONES, Mary	1y	C	D.C.	22 APR 1875	Mt. Pleasant
005264	JONES, Mary	1d	C	D.C.	25 OCT 1875	Mt. Olivet
007164	JONES, Mary	20y	C	Va.	30 APR 1876	Young Mens
011438	JONES, Mary	20y	C	D.C.	27 APR 1877	Young Mens
010258	JONES, Mary	2y	C	D.C.	12 JAN 1877	Freedmen's Village, Va.
014988	JONES, Mary	65y	C	Md.	08 MAR 1878	Potters Field
019447	JONES, Mary	3y	C	D.C.	18 MAR 1879	Mt. Pleasant
020179	JONES, Mary	23d	W	D.C.	23 MAY 1879	Mt. Olivet
018609	JONES, Mary A.	55y	W	Md.	08 JAN 1879	Oak Hill
011143	JONES, Mary E.	1y	C	D.C.	28 MAR 1877	Mt. Pleasant
016072	JONES, Mary Eliz.	4y	C	Va.	08 JUN 1878	Young Mens
011707	JONES, Mary Emma	6m	C	D.C.	26 MAY 1877	Moore's
010854	JONES, Mary Hannah	42y	C	Md.	03 MAR 1877	Moore's
014370	JONES, Mary J.	84y	C	Va.	09 JAN 1878	Harmony
016859	JONES, Mary Malinda Sluby	16y	C	D.C.	01 AUG 1878	Harmony
005168	JONES, Mary Virginia	2m	C	D.C.	25 SEP 1875	Harmony
001662	JONES, Matilda	4m	W	D.C.	09 JAN 1875	Mt. Olivet
009117	JONES, Mattie	1y	C	D.C.	17 SEP 1876	Ebenezer
020629	JONES, Milton	9y	C	D.C.	26 JUN 1879	Young Mens
005190	JONES, Miss	--	--		-- --- 1875	--
017946	JONES, Nancy	84y	C	Md.	04 NOV 1878	Smith's
008789	JONES, Nathan	1m	C	Md.	23 AUG 1876	Harmony
017775	JONES, Noah	88y	C	Md.	17 OCT 1878	Jones Chapel
013615	JONES, Octavia	8y	C	D.C.	24 OCT 1877	Mt. Zion
012452	JONES, Phillis	72y	C	Va.	21 JUL 1877	Charlottesville, Va.
006087	JONES, Priscilla	11m	C	D.C.	21 JAN 1876	Young Mens
014482	JONES, Raphael	8d	C	D.C.	19 JAN 1878	Harmony
016148	JONES, Raymond Francis	6m	W	D.C.	13 JUN 1878	Oak Hill
001133	JONES, Robert	26y	C	Va.	13 NOV 1874	Washington Asylum
003574	JONES, Robert	35y	C	Md.	08 JUN 1875	Beckett's
017737	JONES, Robert	24y	C	Va.	14 OCT 1878	Potters Field

No.	Name	Age	Race	Birth	Death Date	Burial Place
021136	JONES, Robert	1y	C	D.C.	28 JUL 1879	Young Mens
009505	JONES, Robert H.	5d	C	D.C.	23 OCT 1876	Mt. Zion
020163	JONES, Robert L.	43y	W	Eng.	21 MAY 1879	Glenwood
012666	JONES, Rosa L.	2y	C	D.C.	04 AUG 1877	Ebenezer
012055	JONES, Rosanna	8m	C	D.C.	25 JUN 1877	Mt. Olivet
014942	JONES, Rose	c.40y	C	Va.	04 MAR 1878	Beckett's
017355	JONES, Rose, Mrs.	24y	W	D.C.	09 SEP 1878	Mt. Olivet
008623	JONES, Sarah	1m	C	D.C.	09 AUG 1876	Young Mens
019684	JONES, Sarah	25y	C	Md.	07 APR 1879	Young Mens
002269	JONES, Sarah Ann	45y	W	Md.	21 FEB 1875	Presbyterian
006589	JONES, Sarah C.	55y	W	Md.	07 MAR 1876	Oak Hill
001548	JONES, Sarah R.	38y	W	Mich.	31 DEC 1874	Glenwood
015257	JONES, Selvin	7m	C	D.C.	01 APR 1878	Young Mens
013002	JONES, Silas	12h	C	D.C.	27 AUG 1877	Potters Field
007281	JONES, Stephen	27y	C	Va.	12 MAY 1876	Harmony
016957	JONES, Susan Willis	48y	C	Md.	08 AUG 1878	Baltimore
013685	JONES, Thomas	48y	W	Ire.	31 OCT 1877	Mt. Olivet
001620f	JONES, Thornton	49y	W	Va.	05 JAN 1875	Congressional
006067	JONES, Toliver	18y	C	Md.	19 JAN 1876	Young Mens
004807f	JONES, Violetta L.	c.37y	W	D.C.	28 AUG 1875	Congressional
001170	JONES, Walter S.	30y	C	D.C.	17 NOV 1874	Harmony
011083	JONES, Webster	5m	W	D.C.	23 MAR 1877	Columbus, Ohio
000851	JONES, William	27y	C	Va.	18 OCT 1874	Harmony
005416	JONES, William	65y	C	Md.	10 NOV 1875	Harmony
008364	JONES, William	3y	C	D.C.	21 JUL 1876	Potters Field
007628	JONES, William	43y	C	Md.	13 JUN 1876	Baltimore, Md.
007499	JONES, William	11m	C	D.C.	04 JUN 1876	Mt. Olivet
007482	JONES, William	80y	C	Va.	03 JUN 1876	Potters Field
009031	JONES, William	12d	C	D.C.	11 SEP 1876	Ebenezer
010471	JONES, William	11y	C	D.C.	01 FEB 1877	Harmony
013748	JONES, William	15m	C	D.C.	06 NOV 1877	Potters Field
016021	JONES, William	9m	C	D.C.	05 JUN 1878	Harmony
012105	JONES, William B.	4m	C	D.C.	28 JUN 1877	Mt. Zion
002963	JONES, William E.	6d	W	D.C.	11 APR 1875	Mt. Olivet
014583	JONES, William Osborn	77y	W	Md.	28 JAN 1878	Glenwood
003832	JONES, William W.	6m	C	D.C.	25 JUN 1875	Harmony
009472	JONES, Willie	1y	C	D.C.	20 OCT 1876	Young Mens
015201	JONES, Wm. Henry	48y	C	Md.	27 MAR 1878	Mt. Olivet
006897	JORDAN, Alice	35y	W	Va.	02 APR 1876	Potters Field
011436	JORDAN, Charles	22y	C	Md.	27 APR 1877	Potters Field
017653	JORDAN, Chas.	3y	C	D.C.	06 OCT 1878	Moore's
016518	JORDAN, Daisy	2m	C	D.C.	09 JUL 1878	Beckett's
007123	JORDAN, Elizabeth	42y	C	Md.	26 APR 1876	Young Mens
017714	JORDAN, Eva	6m	C	D.C.	12 OCT 1878	Moore's
015054	JORDAN, Geo. Washington	54y	C	Md.	13 MAR 1878	Harmony
013854	JORDAN, Hays	9m	C	D.C.	18 NOV 1877	Moore's
000724	JORDAN, Henry	5y	C	Va.	05 OCT 1874	Potters Field
006895	JORDAN, Infant of Alice	10h	W	D.C.	02 APR 1876	Potters Field
009396	JORDAN, Infant of West	7h	C	D.C.	12 OCT 1876	Young Mens
018164	JORDAN, Infant of Wm.	2d	C	D.C.	26 NOV 1878	Beckett's
003937	JORDAN, Jernetta	1m	C	D.C.	30 JUN 1875	Harmony
013671	JORDAN, Lillie	3y	M	D.C.	29 OCT 1877	Harmony
002995	JORDAN, Lilly	7y	C	D.C.	15 APR 1875	Harmony
000234	JORDAN, Louisa	29y	C	Va.	18 AUG 1874	Harmony
019654	JORDAN, Marceline	47y	M	D.C.	04 APR 1879	Harmony
012167	JORDAN, Millie	85y	C	Va.	02 JUL 1877	Potters Field

District of Columbia Death Records, August 1, 1874 to July 31, 1879

No.	Name	Age	Race	Birth	Death Date	Burial Place
008914	JORDAN, Oscar	12y	W	Md.	01 SEP 1876	Rock Creek
016928	JORDAN, Thomas W.	58y	W	Va.	06 AUG 1878	Smithfield, Va.
004378	JORDAN, Willie	13y	C	Va.	30 JUL 1875	Ebenezer
010992	JORDEN, Andrew	9m	C	D.C.	15 MAR 1877	Ebenezer
013404	JORDEN, Celistene	1y	C	D.C.	04 OCT 1877	Alexandria, Va.
021176	JORDON, Andrew	4m	W	D.C.	31 JUL 1879	Mt. Olivet
018245	JOROLOMAN, David	30y	W	N.Y.	05 DEC 1878	Soldier's Home
014445	JOSEPH, Sister Gonsales	35y	W	France	16 JAN 1878	Mt. Olivet
013355	JOSETTI, Martin Luther Bernhard	61y	W	Ger.	30 SEP 1877	Prospect Hill
005321	JOST, Anna Margaret	50y	W	Ger.	31 OCT 1875	Prospect Hill
007710	JOURDAN, Albert	9m	C	D.C.	18 JUN 1876	Young Mens
008257	JOUY, Clara Virginia	9y	W	D.C.	14 JUL 1876	Oak Hill
017974	JOY, Albert Franklin	3y	W	D.C.	07 NOV 1878	Methodist
007945	JOY, Chas. Byron	2d	W	D.C.	01 JUL 1876	Mt. Olivet
017396	JOY, Elizabeth	1h	W	D.C.	13 SEP 1878	Mt. Olivet
014318	JOY, Emma Blanch	14d	W	D.C.	04 JAN 1878	Methodist
017254	JOY, Estelle Elizabeth	1y	W	D.C.	30 AUG 1878	Mt. Olivet
017776	JOY, Fannie	23y	W	D.C.	17 OCT 1878	Mt. Olivet
010392	JOY, Harriet R.	9y	C	D.C.	24 JAN 1877	Mt. Pleasant
004124	JOY, John	1h	W	D.C.	14 JUL 1875	Mt. Olivet
011402	JOY, Joseph	76y	W	Md.	23 APR 1877	Mt. Olivet
017395	JOY, Mary	1h	W	D.C.	13 SEP 1878	Mt. Olivet
019831	JOY, Sarah	5m	C	D.C.	19 APR 1879	Mt. Pleasant
019505	JOY, William Lawrence	1y	W	D.C.	22 MAR 1879	Mt. Olivet
008055	JOYCE, Catheran	19m	C	D.C	07 JUL 1876	Ebenezer
016899	JOYCE, Ellen	29y	W	N.Y.	04 AUG 1878	Unadilla, N.Y.
002302	JOYCE, Infant of Frank	4m	C	D.C.	24 FEB 1875	Ebenezer
012939	JOYCE, Infant of William	36h	C	D.C.	24 AUG 1877	Potters Field
013023	JOYCE, Lillie Victoria	3m	C	D.C.	30 AUG 1877	Beckett's
007677	JOYCE, Margaret	33y	C	D.C.	16 JUN 1876	Harmony
014115	JOYCE, William Ward	10y	W	D.C.	16 DEC 1877	Mt. Olivet
006112	JUDD, Susannah	50y	W	Eng.	23 JAN 1876	Oak Hill
019490	JUDGE, Fannie M.	46y	W	Md.	21 MAR 1879	Glenwood
007679	JUDKINS, Mamie	6m	C	D.C.	16 JUN 1876	Young Mens
003953	JUDSON, Calferni	11m	W	Va.	01 JUL 1875	Graceland
014882	JULIHN, Mena Mathilda	9y	W	D.C.	26 FEB 1878	Oak Hill
007202	JUNEMAN, Wilbur	6y	W	Ger.	04 MAY 1876	Prospect Hill
003187	JURLEY, Aloysious	3y	W	D.C.	01 MAY 1875	Mt. Olivet
016417	JUSTICE, David J.	47y	W	N.C.	03 JUL 1878	Cong./Lexington, Ky.

K

No.	Name	Age	Race	Birth	Death Date	Burial Place
014041	KAHLERT, George C.	3m	W	D.C.	08 DEC 1877	Congressional
016022	KAHLERT, George Goodall	3y	W	D.C.	05 JUN 1878	Congressional
006392	KAIM, Louis	18y	W	D.C.	17 FEB 1876	Glenwood
014249	KAIN, Johan Georg	17y	W	D.C.	29 DEC 1877	Prospect Hill
020120	KAISER, Adam	50y	W	Ger.	16 MAY 1879	Glenwood
013981	KAISER, Catherine	9y	W	D.C.	01 DEC 1877	St. Mary's
005747	KAISER, Geo.	19y	W	D.C.	14 DEC 1875	Prospect Hill
010873	KAISER, George Edward	10m	W	D.C.	05 MAR 1877	Prospect Hill
018152	KAISER, Harriet Ann	17y	W	D.C.	25 NOV 1878	Glenwood
004369	KAISER, John	11d	W	D.C.	29 JUL 1875	Prospect Hill
014570	KAISER, John F.	6m	W	D.C.	27 JAN 1878	Oak Hill
011496	KAISER, Osker	15y	W	Ger.	03 MAY 1877	Presbyterian
013499	KAISER, William	9y	W	D.C.	13 OCT 1877	St. Mary's

No.	Name	Age	Race	Birth	Death Date	Burial Place
020758	KALDENBACH, Andrew E.	5y	W	D.C.	04 JUL 1879	Methodist
004381	KALDENBACK, Charles A.	6m	W	D.C.	30 JUL 1875	Methodist
016979	KALDENBAUCH, Joseph	71y	W	D.C.	09 AUG 1878	Mt. Olivet
012747	KALDENKIRCHEN, Louis Von	45y	W	Hol.	09 AUG 1877	St. Mary's
018839	KALL, Barbra	95y	W	Ger.	27 JAN 1879	Prospect Hill
015233	KAMPF, Ferdinand	36y	W	Ger.	30 MAR 1878	Prospect Hill
001421	KANE, Bridget	5y	W	D.C.	17 DEC 1874	Mt. Olivet
020925	KANE, Catherine	80y	W	Ire.	14 JUL 1879	Mt. Olivet
019448	KANE, Charles	c.60y	C	--	18 MAR 1879	Potters Field
000328	KANE, James	50y	W	Ire.	26 AUG 1874	Mt. Olivet
019081	KANE, John Patrick	2y	W	D.C.	15 FEB 1879	Mt. Olivet
019473	KANE, Julia Ann	75y	W	Va.	20 MAR 1879	Presbyterian
019109	KANE, Julia Elizabeth	1y	W	D.C.	18 FEB 1879	Mt. Olivet
015407	KANE, Martha	58y	W	Ire.	15 APR 1878	Glenwood
015202	KANE, Mary	70y	W	Ire.	27 MAR 1878	Holy Rood
016073	KANE, Mary, Mrs.	78y	W	Ire.	08 JUN 1878	Mt. Olivet
008478	KANE, Minnieta	10m	W	D.C.	29 JUL 1876	Presbyterian
014820	KANE, Peter	33y	W	La.	19 FEB 1878	Mt. Olivet
016671	KANE, William	58y	W	Va.	26 JUL 1878	Alexandria, Va.
011724	KANROKU, Ichiku	21y	W	Jap.	27 MAY 1877	Oak Hill
004073	KAPPLER, William Joseph	10m	W	D.C.	10 JUL 1875	St. Mary's
011164	KARCHER, Anna	45y	W	Ger.	30 MAR 1877	Congressional
020834	KARNER, Ermina S.	44y	W	D.C.	08 JUL 1879	Alexandria, Va.
012257	KAUFFMANN, Phillips	17y	W	Ohio	08 JUL 1877	Oak Hill
004025f	KAUFMAN, Isaac	82y	W	Ger.	06 JUL 1875	Jewish
007247	KAUFMANN, Mina	52y	W	Ger.	08 MAY 1876	Washington Hebrew
002579	KAVANAGH, Richard Vincent	9m	W	Va.	15 MAR 1875	Mt. Olivet
019344	KAVANAUGH, James	37y	W	Ire.	09 MAR 1879	Soldier's Home
005673	KAVANAUGH, Mary	2y	W	Pa.	06 DEC 1875	Mt. Olivet
018041	KAYSER, Charles W.	20y	W	D.C.	13 NOV 1878	Oak Hill
016980	KAYSER, Joseph A., Jr.	8m	W	D.C.	09 AUG 1878	Glenwood
002152	KEACH, Elizabeth	61y	W	Eng.	14 FEB 1875	Oak Hill
019438	KEADY, Julia	48y	W	Ire.	17 MAR 1879	Holy Rood
013932	KEALCY, Mary C.	25y	W	D.C.	26 NOV 1877	Mt. Olivet
002177	KEALEY, Catherine J.	47y	W	Me.	15 FEB 1875	Mt. Olivet
014431	KEALEY, William	48y	W	Can.	15 JAN 1878	Mt. Olivet
003900	KEALING, Jane	c.45y	C	Va.	28 JUN 1875	Mt. Pleasant
015279	KEANE, Catharine	1m	W	D.C.	03 APR 1878	Mt. Olivet
020406	KEANE, Mary Cath:	8m	W	D.C.	12 JUN 1879	Mt. Olivet
002670	KEARNES, John	24y	W	Ire.	21 MAR 1875	Holy Rood
011312	KEARNEY, Annie S.	1y	W	D.C.	12 APR 1877	Mt. Olivet
012541	KEATING, Margaret	60y	W	Ire.	26 JUL 1877	Mt. Olivet
011774	KEATON, Patrick	60y	W	Ire.	02 JUN 1877	Mt. Olivet
010363	KECK, John N.	2y	W	D.C.	21 JAN 1877	Mt. Olivet
012021	KEE, Charly	1y	C	D.C.	23 JUN 1877	Mt. Olivet
009727	KEE, Henrieta	15y	C	Md.	18 NOV 1876	Mt. Olivet
017491	KEECH, Infant of Cora B.	3h	W	D.C.	22 SEP 1878	Oak Hill/Greenmount
018309	KEEFE, George Conrad	4m	W	D.C.	11 DEC 1878	Mt. Olivet
008678	KEEFE, Harry A.	23y	W	D.C.	13 AUG 1876	Mt. Olivet
018651	KEEFE, John	11y	W	D.C.	12 JAN 1879	Mt. Olivet
012210	KEEFE, John Henry	6m	W	D.C.	04 JUL 1877	Mt. Olivet
000741	KEEFE, Mary	73y	W	Ire.	07 OCT 1874	Mt. Olivet
013488	KEEFE, Willie McElroy	20y	W	D.C.	12 OCT 1877	Mt. Olivet
016388	KEEFER, Ireene	6m	W	D.C.	01 JUL 1878	Glenwood
010868	KEEFER, Katie Agnuss	1y	W	D.C.	05 MAR 1877	Congressional
008974	KEEFFE, Edmond	50y	W	Ire.	05 SEP 1876	Mt. Olivet

District of Columbia Death Records, August 1, 1874 to July 31, 1879

No.	Name	Age	Race	Birth	Death Date	Burial Place
004994	KEEGIN, Thomas John	1y	W	D.C.	11 SEP 1875	Mt. Olivet
007483	KEELER, Eben	8y	W	D.C.	03 JUN 1876	Mt. Olivet
010519	KEENAN, Mary	51y	W	Ire.	04 FEB 1877	Holy Rood
021124	KEENE, Mary E.	68y	W	Md.	27 JUL 1879	Glenwood
020717	KEENEY, Adelbert D.	36y	W	Pa.	02 JUL 1879	Hospital
014269	KEESEY, Lydia Ann	18y	W	Va.	30 DEC 1877	Graceland
001702	KEESHAN, William	36y	W	Ire.	12 JAN 1875	Washington Asylum
011796	KEESTER, Richard	46y	W	Md.	04 JUN 1877	Prospect Hill
004882	KEETH, Eliza A.	1y	C	D.C.	02 SEP 1875	Mt. Olivet
014066	KEGAN, Mary E.	2y	W	D.C.	11 DEC 1875	Holy Rood
001701	KEGIN, George	4m	C	D.C.	11 JAN 1875	Young Mens
011103	KEHLER, Catharina	18y	W	D.C.	24 MAR 1877	Prospect Hill
019141	KEHLER, John H., Rev.	82y	W	Md.	21 FEB 1879	Shepherdstown, W.Va.
016944	KEIFE, Katie	2y	W	D.C.	07 AUG 1878	Mt. Olivet
017876	KEIFER, Charles	30y	W	Ger.	27 OCT 1878	Prospect Hill
001012	KEILHOLTZ, Emma F.	24y	W	D.C.	01 NOV 1874	Congressional
005837	KEIM, Henry	61y	W	Ger.	23 DEC 1875	Potters Field
005473	KEITHLEY, Mary J.	2y	W	D.C.	16 NOV 1875	Methodist
019268	KEITHLEY, Milton	3y	W	D.C.	03 MAR 1879	Congressional
001751	KEITHLEY, Richard	46y	W	D.C.	16 JAN 1875	Congressional
018897	KEITHLEY, Susan E.	11y	W	D.C.	31 JAN 1879	Congressional
017738	KELEHER, Johannah	11m	W	D.C.	14 OCT 1878	Holy Rood
010857	KELEHER, Mathew J.	26y	W	Mass.	03 MAR 1877	Mt. Olivet
017068	KELL, Andrew J.	26y	W	Va.	16 AUG 1878	Mt. Olivet
008047	KELLEHER, Johannah	36y	W	Ire.	06 JUL 1876	Mt. Olivet
013199	KELLER, Adolph H.	2y	W	D.C.	14 SEP 1877	Prospect Hill
000875	KELLER, Barbary	38y	W	Ger.	20 OCT 1874	Prospect Hill
007398	KELLER, Catharine B.	71y	W	Ger.	24 MAY 1876	Prospect Hill
020172	KELLER, Charles Lawrence	3y	W	D.C.	22 MAY 1879	Mt. Olivet
003384	KELLER, Charles S.	4m	W	D.C.	21 MAY 1875	Congressional
001056	KELLER, James Alfred	16y	W	D.C.	05 NOV 1874	Rock Creek
003133f	KELLER, James H.H.	45y	W	D.C.	26 APR 1875	Congressional
012251	KELLER, Margaret E.	16m	W	D.C.	07 JUL 1877	Rock Creek
003438	KELLEY, Ann	54y	W	Ire.	25 MAY 1875	Mt. Olivet
003175	KELLEY, Anna	132y	C	Md.	30 APR 1875	Mt. Olivet
012109	KELLEY, Earnest	8m	W	D.C.	28 JUN 1877	Mt. Pleasant
006943	KELLEY, Ellen	62y	W	Ire.	06 APR 1876	Mt. Olivet
010449	KELLEY, Ellen	46y	M	Va.	30 JAN 1877	Harmony
010202	KELLEY, Henry	4y	C	Md.	07 JAN 1877	Mt. Olivet
007802	KELLEY, Infant of John	1d	W	D.C.	23 JUN 1876	Mt. Olivet
000504	KELLEY, J.W.	46y	W	Ver.	13 SEP 1874	Congressional
003342	KELLEY, James	83y	W	Ire.	16 MAY 1875	Mt. Olivet
007099	KELLEY, James	6d	C	D.C.	24 APR 1876	Potters Field
011784	KELLEY, James	66y	W	Ire.	03 JUN 1877	Mt. Olivet
002991	KELLEY, John W.	66y	W	Va.	14 APR 1875	Congressional
011206	KELLEY, Margareth	45y	W	Ire.	03 APR 1877	Mt. Olivet
014201	KELLEY, Mary	8m	C	D.C.	25 DEC 1877	Young Mens
006942	KELLEY, Mary Matilda	2y	M	D.C.	06 APR 1876	Harmony
007659	KELLEY, Nathaniel	11m	M	D.C.	15 JUN 1876	Mt. Pleasant
004126	KELLEY, Rose Ellen	3m	W	D.C.	14 JUL 1875	Mt. Olivet
019100	KELLOGG, Mary A.	1m	W	D.C.	17 FEB 1879	Glenwood/Benson,Ver.
017470	KELLUM, Zarbable	73y	W	Va.	20 SEP 1878	Congressional
004953	KELLY, Andrew J.	4y	W	D.C.	08 SEP 1875	Mt. Olivet
005283	KELLY, Annie	10y	W	D.C.	27 OCT 1875	Mt. Olivet
003632	KELLY, Caroline C.	27y	W	Mass.	13 JUN 1875	Glenwood
016943	KELLY, Catharine	80y	W	Ire.	07 AUG 1878	Mt. Olivet

No.	Name	Age	Race	Birth	Death Date	Burial Place
013629	KELLY, Catharine Ann	c.82y	W	Ire.	25 OCT 1877	Glenwood
012773	KELLY, Charles	39y	C	Md.	11 AUG 1877	Potters Field
001414f	KELLY, Charles A.	54y	W	Md.	02 OCT 1860	Mt. Olivet
003672	KELLY, Charles Frances	5d	W	D.C.	17 JUN 1875	Glenwood
017554	KELLY, Edmund	5d	W	D.C.	28 SEP 1878	Mt. Olivet
008495	KELLY, Ellen	66y	W	Ire.	30 JUL 1876	Mt. Olivet
008725	KELLY, Francis	35y	W	Ire.	18 AUG 1876	Mt. Olivet
011868	KELLY, Infant of John F.	17h	W	D.C.	11 JUN 1877	Mt. Olivet
005030a	KELLY, James	50y	W	Ire.	02 OCT 1875	Mt. Olivet
015448	KELLY, James	2m	C	D.C.	19 APR 1878	Mt. Olivet
016657	KELLY, James	10m	W	D.C.	18 JUL 1878	Mt. Olivet
010587	KELLY, James Daniel	2m	W	D.C.	11 FEB 1877	Mt. Olivet
008056	KELLY, James O.	3m	W	D.C.	07 JUL 1876	Congressional
003741	KELLY, Jane	60y	W	Ire.	21 JUN 1875	Mt. Olivet
004677	KELLY, Jno. Thomas	1y	W	DC.	20 AUG 1875	Mt. Olivet
020241	KELLY, John	19y	W	D.C.	31 MAY 1879	Mt. Olivet
020520	KELLY, Joseph	61y	W	Ire.	19 JUN 1879	Soldier's Home
016249	KELLY, Lillie	23y	C	Va.	21 JUN 1878	Mt. Pleasant
013339	KELLY, Louis	1m	W	D.C.	28 SEP 1877	Mt. Olivet
009129	KELLY, Margaret	37y	W	Md.	19 SEP 1876	Mt. Olivet
020119	KELLY, Mary B.	25y	W	D.C.	16 MAY 1879	Glenwood
009805	KELLY, Mary E.	6y	W	D.C.	26 NOV 1876	Holy Rood
003833	KELLY, Mary Ellen	6y	W	D.C.	25 JUN 1876	Mt. Olivet
008860	KELLY, Mathew	76y	W	Ire.	28 AUG 1876	Mt. Olivet
001519	KELLY, Michl.	66y	W	Ire.	28 DEC 1874	New Cathedral, Md.
006377	KELLY, Thomas Clinton	32y	W	D.C.	16 FEB 1876	Oak Hill
011745	KELP, Catherine	c.66y	W	Ger.	30 MAY 1877	Prospect Hill
019308	KELPHY, Bernard Franklin	9m	W	D.C	07 MAR 1879	Congressional
005560	KELT, John	34y	W	Scot.	25 NOV 1875	Hospital
001074	KELTON, Ellen	18y	C	Va.	07 NOV 1874	Beckett's
015817	KEMON, Grace Lee	13d	W	D.C.	23 MAY 1878	Glenwood
011470	KEMP, Ida	5y	W	D.C.	30 APR 1877	Holy Rood
016420	KEMPER, Mary	44y	W	Va.	03 JUL 1878	Harmony
010982	KENDALL, Louis	65y	C	D.C.	15 MAR 1877	Ebenezer
019019	KENDIG, Samuel B.	67y	W	N.Y.	10 FEB 1879	Seneca, N.Y.
011555	KENDLE, James Thornton	50y	W	Va.	09 MAY 1877	Fredericksburg, Va.
003348	KENDRICK, Ann L.	75y	W	D.C.	17 MAY 1875	Congressional
011624	KENEALLY, Michael	75y	W	Ire.	17 MAY 1877	Mt. Olivet
018536	KENEDY, Margaret A.	73y	W	D.C.	01 JAN 1879	Glenwood
004112	KENGLA, Clara E.	1y	W	D.C.	13 JUL 1875	Holy Rood
004380	KENNARD, Thomas A.	42y	W	Md.	30 JUL 1875	Baltimore, Md.
014268	KENNEALY, Bridget	40y	W	Ire.	30 DEC 1877	Mt. Olivet
001545	KENNEDAY, Thomas D.	9y	W	D.C.	31 DEC 1874	Mt. Olivet
004782	KENNEDY, Agnes M.	1y	W	D.C.	27 AUG 1875	Mt. Olivet
000172	KENNEDY, Albert	45y	C	Va.	13 AUG 1874	Washington Asylum
001888	KENNEDY, Elenora	60y	C	D.C.	25 JAN 1875	Young Mens
000684	KENNEDY, Elizabeth T.	55y	W	D.C.	01 OCT 1874	Mt. Olivet
014673	KENNEDY, James	65y	W	Ire.	05 FEB 1878	Potters Field
019622	KENNEDY, James	6d	W	D.C.	01 APR 1879	Mt. Olivet
009961	KENNEDY, Mary Ann	24y	W	D.C.	14 DEC 1876	Mt. Olivet
005203a	KENNEDY, Molly	22y	W	D.C.	19 OCT 1875	Potters Field
019243	KENNER, Joseph	2y	C	D.C.	01 MAR 1879	Mt. Pleasant
011541	KENNETT, Alexander	47y	W	Ohio	07 MAY 1877	Washington Asylum
003938	KENNEY, James	c.35y	W	Ire.	30 JUN 1875	Mt. Olivet
001733	KENNEY, Patrick	48y	W	Ire.	14 JAN 1875	Mt. Olivet
017993	KENNY, Andrew	6m	C	D.C.	09 NOV 1878	Payne's

District of Columbia Death Records, August 1, 1874 to July 31, 1879   193

No.	Name	Age	Race	Birth	Death Date	Burial Place
007694	KENNY, Frances E.	3m	W	N.Y.	17 JUN 1876	N.Y. City
004074	KENNY, Patrick	1m	W	D.C.	10 JUL 1875	Mt. Olivet
010406	KENNY, Wm.	21y	W	N.Y.	25 JAN 1877	N.Y. City
005301	KENT, Abraham	35y	C	Va.	29 OCT 1875	Young Mens
020811	KENT, Blanche Demont	5m	M	D.C.	07 JUL 1879	Harmony
008922	KENT, Ella	13m	C	D.C.	01 SEP 1876	Mt. Olivet
004834	KENT, George Washington	22y	C	Md.	30 AUG 1875	Young Mens
015300	KENT, Joseph	60y	C	Va.	06 APR 1878	Potters Field
018357	KENT, Joseph F.	3m	C	D.C.	16 DEC 1878	Mt. Olivet
002858	KENT, Mary J.	34y	W	Md.	03 APR 1875	Rock Creek
010108	KENT, Priscilla	26y	C	Va.	29 DEC 1876	Young Mens
005092a	KEOFE, Jeremy	15d	W	D.C.	09 OCT 1875	Mt. Olivet
016676	KEOGH, Alice E.	34y	W	Md.	19 JUL 1878	Mt. Olivet
008045	KEOGH, Simon Walker	8m	W	D.C.	06 JUL 1876	Mt. Olivet
011054	KEON, Patrick	51y	W	Ire.	20 MAR 1877	Soldier's Home
009818	KEOUGH, William Francis	7m	W	D.C.	28 NOV 1876	Mt. Olivet
009745	KEPER, Christian	70y	W	Ger.	19 NOV 1876	Potters Field
019101	KEPNER, Robert B.	53y	W	Pa.	17 FEB 1879	Halifax, Pa.
016349	KEPPEL, David	53y	W	Ire.	28 JUN 1878	Holy Rood
006020	KEPPEL, Jacob	73y	W	Ger.	14 JAN 1876	Congressional
007053	KERN, Agnes Amalie	50y	W	Sax.	19 APR 1876	Prospect Hill
001312	KERN, Jane	48y	W	D.C.	05 DEC 1874	Mt. Olivet
006246	KERNWEIN, Amelia	13y	W	D.C.	05 FEB 1876	Prospect Hill
020339	KEROHR, Clarance Bernard	8m	W	D.C.	08 JUN 1879	Mt. Olivet
011903	KERR, Annie Couper	62y	W	Del.	14 JUN 1877	New Castle, Del.
000701	KERR, Conrad	9m	W	D.C.	03 OCT 1874	Prospect Hill
014571	KERR, John Bozman	68y	W	Md.	27 JAN 1878	Eastern Shore, Md.
003921	KERR, Marianne	76y	W	D.C.	29 JUN 1875	Oak Hill
006590	KERRIGAN, Mary Ann	c.21y	W	Mass.	07 MAR 1876	Mt. Olivet
004714	KERSEY, Dasey	1y	W	D.C.	22 AUG 1875	Congressional
010762	KERSHAW, Mary	64y	W	Eng.	24 FEB 1877	Rock Creek
014989	KESLER, John	48y	W	Ger.	08 MAR 1878	Hospital
009304	KESSLER, John B.	43y	W	Ger.	04 OCT 1876	St. Mary's
017809	KESSLER, Marie Louise	55y	W	Switz.	20 OCT 1878	Prospect Hill
007286	KETCHUM, Jesse J.	40y	C	Ber.	12 MAY 1876	Graceland
020502	KETTLER, Henrietta Rosa	4m	W	D.C.	18 JUN 1879	Prospect Hill
013479	KETTLER, Robert	13y	C	Va.	11 OCT 1877	Young Mens
012532	KETTNER, Ida	3y	W	D.C.	26 JUL 1877	Presbyterian
006322	KEY, Annie	6m	M	D.C.	12 FEB 1876	Potters Field
017203	KEY, Appilonia	25y	C	Md.	26 AUG 1878	Harmony
003857	KEY, Edwin	7m	C	D.C.	26 JUN 1875	Mt. Pleasant
017425	KEY, James B.	27y	C	Md.	16 SEP 1878	Young Mens
018286	KEY, John	4m	M	D.C.	09 DEC 1878	Mt. Olivet
016052	KEY, Mary Ann	50y	C	D.C.	07 JUN 1878	Mt. Pleasant
020165	KEYES, Maggie	29y	W	D.C.	21 MAY 1879	Baltimore, Md.
000072	KEYS, Chas. M.	--	--	--	06 AUG 1874	--
015267	KEYS, Francis Sylvster	1y	C	D.C.	02 APR 1878	Beckett's
000663	KEYS, John	38y	W	Ire.	28 SEP 1874	Mt. Olivet
003373	KEYS, Kittin	12d	C	D.C.	20 MAY 1875	Ebenezer
002574	KEYS, May	5y	W	D.C.	15 MAR 1875	Mt. Olivet
008968	KEYSER, Blanch May	20d	W	D.C.	04 SEP 1876	Martinsburg, W.Va.
017460	KEYSER, John R.L.	10y	W	D.C.	19 SEP 1878	Oak Hill
002485	KIBBEY, William	6d	W	D.C.	09 MAR 1875	Congressional
003691	KICKERRON, Chara	1y	C	D.C.	18 JUN 1875	Ebenezer
013919	KIDD, John Robt.	26y	W	Mo.	25 NOV 1877	Congressional
004566	KIDD, Mattie Virginia	1y	W	D.C.	12 AUG 1875	Congressional

No.	Name	Age	Race	Birth	Death Date	Burial Place
016677	KIDDIE, Isabella Anderson	58y	W	Scot.	19 JUL 1878	Congressional
014920	KIDNEY, William	36y	W	Ire.	02 MAR 1878	Soldier's Home
019732	KIDRICK, David	21y	C	Va.	11 APR 1879	Mt. Zion
014284	KIDRICK, Maggie	13y	C	D.C.	01 JAN 1878	Mt. Zion
014565	KIDWELL, Catharine	22y	W	Md.	26 JAN 1878	Rock Creek
009028	KIDWELL, Elizabeth	48y	W	Va.	11 SEP 1876	Congressional
002752	KIDWELL, George	59y	W	Md.	26 MAR 1875	Oak Hill
009418	KIDWELL, George H.	c.60y	W	Va.	15 OCT 1876	Congressional
018934	KIDWELL, Howard	18y	W	Md.	03 FEB 1879	Mt. Olivet
010445	KIDWELL, Jennie E.	25y	W	Va.	29 JAN 1877	Congressional
009612	KIDWELL, Jeremiah L.	43y	W	D.C.	04 NOV 1876	Congressional
013797	KIDWELL, Mary	35y	W	Md.	11 NOV 1877	Tennallytown
011660	KIDWELL, Mary Catharine	66y	W	Md.	20 MAY 1877	Congressional
014298	KIDWELL, Richard	1y	W	D.C.	02 JAN 1878	Tennallytown
001092	KIDWELL, Sarah Elizabeth	8m	W	D.C.	09 NOV 1874	Congressional
019422	KIDWELL, Thos.	33y	C	Md.	16 MAR 1879	Beckett's
003639	KIEFER, Johanna	31y	W	Ire.	14 JUN 1875	Holy Rood
007658	KIEFER, John Jacob	41y	W	Ger.	15 JUN 1876	Congressional
009463	KIERNAN, Mary	1y	W	D.C.	19 OCT 1876	Mt. Olivet
016912	KILGOUR, Henrietta	23y	W	D.C.	05 AUG 1878	Congressional
017761	KILLAFOYLE, Nancy	60y	W	Ire.	16 OCT 1878	Mt. Olivet
008545	KILLIAN, John George Leo<u>naker</u>	7d	W	D.C.	03 AUG 1876	Glenwood
011978	KILLIGAN, David J.	1y	W	D.C.	20 JUN 1877	Mt. Olivet
016592	KILMARTIN, Catharine Isabel	2m	W	D.C.	14 JUL 1878	Mt. Olivet
010036	KILP, Anthony Joseph	57y	W	Ger.	20 DEC 1876	Prospect Hill
019226	KIMBALL, Infant of Geo. W.	9d	W	D.C.	27 FEB 1879	North Ansen, Me.
004008	KIMBALL, Mary	25y	C	Md.	05 JUL 1875	Mt. Zion
011492	KIMBALL, Sarah Francis	45y	W	N.Y.	02 MAY 1877	Kalamazoo, Mich.
013329	KIMMEL, Daniel Blandy	16y	W	Md.	27 SEP 1877	Congressional
016913	KIMMEL, William	6m	W	D.C.	05 AUG 1878	Congressional
006935	KIMMELL, Laura A.	40y	W	Md.	05 APR 1876	Congressional
012333	KIMMELL, Lilly May	5y	W	D.C.	12 JUL 1877	Glenwood
009150	KINDELL, Thornton	4d	C	D.C.	21 SEP 1876	Mt. Pleasant
013821	KING, aaron	63y	W	N.J.	14 NOV 1877	Soldier's Home
009383	KING, Addie Greenwood	7y	W	R.I.	11 OCT 1876	Newport, R.I.
021023	KING, Alfonso	9m	C	D.C.	20 JUL 1879	Beckett's
018413	KING, Alice	42y	W	Eng.	21 DEC 1878	Glenwood
013500	KING, Ann Maria	38y	W	D.C.	13 OCT 1877	Oak Hill/Arlington
020284	KING, Annie M.	6y	W	D.C.	03 JUN 1879	Rock Creek
020436	KING, Betsey C.	5m	C	D.C.	14 JUN 1879	Potters Field
015098	KING, Capitolia	4m	W	D.C.	17 MAR 1878	Mt. Olivet
006046	KING, Catharine E.	46y	W	Md.	17 JAN 1876	Congressional
006088	KING, Catharine, Mrs.	c.70y	W	Md.	21 JAN 1876	Rock Creek
010096	KING, Charity	65y	C	Tenn.	28 DEC 1876	Baptist
008538	KING, Charles H.	9m	C	D.C.	03 AUG 1876	Potters Field
008539	KING, Charles Henry	8m	C	D.C.	03 AUG 1876	Ebenezer
019474	KING, Charles James	52y	W	Md.	20 MAR 1879	Rock Creek
002637	KING, Chesterfield	24y	C	Va.	18 MAR 1875	Harmony
002421	KING, Corydon T.	42y	W	N.Y.	04 MAR 1875	Middletown, N.Y.
018726	KING, E. Hume	26y	W	D.C.	19 JAN 1879	Mt. Olivet
013113	KING, Eliza	75y	C	Md.	07 SEP 1877	Potters Field
015793	KING, Elizabeth, Mrs.	65y	W	U.S.	21 MAY 1878	Tennallytown
018561	KING, Ellen	37y	W	Va.	04 JAN 1879	Potters Field
000144	KING, Emma A.	13m	W	D.C.	11 AUG 1874	Oak Hill
012302	KING, Eugene	4y	C	D.C.	10 JUL 1877	Harmony
019284	KING, Fanie	28y	C	Va.	05 MAR 1879	Ebenezer

District of Columbia Death Records, August 1, 1874 to July 31, 1879

No.	Name	Age	Race	Birth	Death Date	Burial Place
011536	KING, George	6d	C	D.C.	07 MAY 1877	Ebenezer
019731	KING, George	8m	C	D.C.	11 APR 1879	Jones Chapel
015347	KING, George B. McClenen	16y	W	D.C.	10 APR 1878	Rock Creek
008632	KING, George T.	11y	W	D.C.	09 AUG 1876	Glenwood
016133	KING, Gertrude	4m	C	D.C.	12 JUN 1878	Beckett's
003756	KING, Hattie	90y	C	Md.	21 JUN 1875	Ebenezer
010209	KING, Henry B.	1h	W	D.C.	07 JAN 1877	Mt. Olivet
005672	KING, Honora	4m	W	D.C.	06 DEC 1875	Mt. Olivet
010186	KING, Infant of Clara	3d	C	D.C.	06 JAN 1877	Young Mens
008091	KING, Infant of J.D.	1m	W	D.C.	09 JUL 1876	Westmoreland Co., Va.
012398	KING, Infant of Mary Josephine	5min	W	D.C.	17 JUL 1877	Mt. Olivet
014285	KING, Infant of John	5d	C	D.C.	01 JAN 1878	Harmony
013291	KING, Isadore Estella	1y	W	D.C.	24 SEP 1877	Mt. Olivet
009529	KING, Isadore Serra	29y	W	D.C.	25 OCT 1876	Mt. Olivet
012667	KING, James	c.75y	W	Md.	04 AUG 1877	Tennallytown
013837	KING, James	26y	W	D.C.	16 NOV 1877	Mt. Olivet
007780	KING, James G.	1y	W	D.C.	22 JUN 1876	Oak Hill
014710	KING, John Edward	3m	C	D.C.	08 FEB 1878	Montgomery Co., Md.
007339	KING, John T.	55y	W	Md.	19 MAY 1876	Congressional
004111	KING, John W.	5d	W	D.C.	13 JUL 1875	Prince George's Co., Md.
001203	KING, Joseph	61y	W	Me.	21 NOV 1874	Newport, R.I.
008322	KING, Joseph W.	65y	W	N.Y.	19 JUL 1876	Congressional
011845	KING, Kate	32y	C	Va.	09 JUN 1877	Harmony
001156	KING, Lan[nard]	24y	W	Ire.	16 NOV 1874	Mt. Olivet
004863	KING, Laura	8m	C	D.C.	01 SEP 1876	Ebenezer
007964	KING, Lewis	1y	C	D.C.	02 JUL 1876	Ebenezer
006881	KING, Lola	2y	W	D.C.	01 APR 1876	Oak Hill
005662	KING, Louisa	45y	W	D.C.	05 DEC 1875	Holy Rood
006638	KING, Martha Ellen	7m	M	D.C.	11 MAR 1876	Harmony
001202	KING, Mary	12d	C	D.C.	21 NOV 1874	Harmony
011621	KING, Mary	75y	W	Va.	16 MAY 1877	Oak Hill
016591	KING, Mary	64y	W	D.C.	14 JUL 1878	Rock Creek
002944	KING, Mary E.	27y	W	Md.	11 APR 1875	Montgomery Co., Md.
017202	KING, Mary E.	37y	W	D.C.	26 AUG 1878	Carroll Chapel
000873	KING, Mary Elizabeth	21y	W	D.C.	20 OCT 1874	Congressional
012934	KING, Mary Jane	38y	W	Md.	24 AUG 1877	St. Albans
012404	KING, Mary Josephine	35y	W	Ire.	17 JUL 1877	Mt. Olivet
000151	KING, Mary Julia	4m	C	D.C.	11 AUG 1874	Queen's Chapel, Md.
010601	KING, Mattie	2d	W	D.C.	12 FEB 1877	Oak Hill
015709	KING, Mollie Newton	26y	W	D.C.	13 MAY 1878	Mt. Olivet
005129	KING, Moses	10d	C	D.C.	13 OCT 1875	Ebenezer
020885	KING, Nellie V.	1y	W	D.C.	11 JUL 1879	Oak Hill
015850	KING, Peter	48y	C	Va.	26 MAY 1878	Harmony
017703	KING, Ralph	77y	W	Ga.	11 OCT 1878	Brooklyn, N.Y.
007189	KING, Richard	37y	W	D.C.	02 MAY 1876	Md.
012981	KING, Robert H.	1m	W	D.C.	27 AUG 1877	Graceland
011241	KING, Roland	11d	W	D.C.	06 APR 1877	Oak Hill
008402	KING, Rose Ann	32y	W	Pa.	24 JUL 1876	Mt. Olivet
016832	KING, Sarah	44y	W	Va.	30 JUL 1878	Suffolk, Va.
002024	KING, Sarah S.	83y	W	Pa.	04 FEB 1875	Congressional
006168	KING, Thomas	72y	W	D.C.	28 JAN 1876	Rock Creek
014870	KING, Thomas	1y	C	D.C.	25 FEB 1878	Beckett's
015849	KING, W.B.	76y	W	Va.	26 MAY 1878	Methodist
004755	KING, William	4d	C	D.C.	25 AUG 1875	Ebenezer
003279	KING, William	35y	C	Md.	10 MAY 1875	Ebenezer
010013	KING, William	2y	W	D.C.	19 DEC 1876	Mt. Olivet

No.	Name	Age	Race	Birth	Death Date	Burial Place
013955	KING, William	35y	W	Ire.	28 NOV 1877	Mt. Olivet
014653	KING, William	4y	C	D.C.	03 FEB 1878	Harmony
017683	KING, William	13m	W	D.C.	09 OCT 1878	Mt. Olivet
016929	KING, William N.	58y	W	Md.	06 AUG 1878	Methodist
013272	KINGDOM, Oscar	2y	W	D.C.	21 SEP 1877	Baltimore, Md.
012229	KINGDON, Eugene	3m	W	D.C.	05 JUL 1877	Baltimore, Md.
012043	KINGDON, Herbert	2m	W	D.C.	24 JUN 1877	Baltimore, Md.
006720	KINGMAN, Cordelia Ball	73y	W	Va.	18 MAR 1876	Congressional
019506	KINGSLY, Bertha A.	4m	W	D.C.	22 MAR 1879	Mt. Olivet
005188a	KINKLEY, Frank Dashield	3y	W	D.C.	18 OCT 1875	Loudoun Park, Md.
003307	KINNAHAN, Margreat	45y	W	Ire.	13 MAY 1875	Mt. Olivet
001073	KINNAHAN, Peter	62y	W	Ire.	07 NOV 1874	Mt. Olivet
013676	KINNEY, Frak	3y	C	Pa.	30 OCT 1877	Payne's
003804	KINNEY, Joseph Fredrick	3y	W	D.C.	24 JUN 1875	Prospect Hill
004506	KINNEY, Madeline	6w	W	D.C.	08 AUG 1875	Glenwood
011261	KINNEY, Mary Cagewell	62y	W	Me.	07 APR 1877	Oak Hill
014742	KINSINGER, Larman J.	1y	W	D.C.	11 FEB 1878	Alexandria, Va.
012005	KINSLEY, John A.	24y	W	D.C.	22 JUN 1877	Mt. Olivet
015408	KINSLY, Martha	56y	W	Ire.	15 APR 1878	Mt. Olivet
019400	KINSMAN, Elinor	66y	W	Me.	14 MAR 1879	Portland, Me.
005219a	KINSOLVING, Adeline	5m	W	D.C.	20 OCT 1875	Oak Hill
003227	KINTZ, Martha A.	50y	W	Md.	05 MAY 1875	Congressional
004544	KINZER, Ellen	7d	W	D.C.	11 AUG 1875	Glenwood
017011	KINZIE, Emma	2y	W	D.C.	11 AUG 1878	Mt. Olivet
004545	KIPLINGER, Amelia	22y	W	D.C.	11 AUG 1875	Waltham, Mass.
004228	KIRBY, Katie	1m	W	D.C.	21 JUL 1875	Mt. Olivet
007137	KIRBY, Patrick	74y	W	Ire.	27 APR 1876	Mt. Olivet
001969	KIRBY, Solomon	75y	W	Md.	01 FEB 1875	Congressional
001775	KIRK, Delia Hodges, Mrs.	74y	W	Mass.	18 JAN 1875	Glenwood
019183	KIRK, George Manuel	2y	W	D.C.	24 FEB 1879	Glenwood
017527	KIRK, John	28y	W	--	25 SEP 1878	Mt. Olivet
003000	KIRK, Lulu Agnes	4m	W	D.C.	15 APR 1875	Glenwood
016250	KIRKENDALL, Richard	56y	C	Va.	21 JUN 1878	Hospital
006979	KIRKLAND, Jane	59y	W	Ire.	10 APR 1876	Mt. Olivet
010695	KIRKLEY, Joseph Albaugh	7y	W	D.C.	19 FEB 1877	Loudoun Park, Md.
018716	KIRKWOOD, Ira	12y	W	D.C.	18 JAN 1879	Congressional
015535	KIRWAN, Catherine	47y	W	Ire.	27 APR 1878	Mt. Olivet
010221	KIRZINSKY, Amanda	19y	W	Md.	08 JAN 1877	Prospect Hill
017216	KISSNER, Gertrude	54y	W	Ger.	27 AUG 1878	St. Mary's
010128	KITCHEN, Jesse W.	59y	W	Va.	30 DEC 1876	Presbyterian
014892	KITTINGER, Henry Cress	65y	W	Pa.	27 FEB 1878	Trenton, N.J.
006323	KIVLAHAN, Sister Mary Teresa	40y	W	Ire.	12 FEB 1876	Mt. Olivet
005990	KLEIN, Henry	53y	W	Ger.	10 JAN 1876	Prospect Hill
000231	KLEINSCHMIDT, Carl	9m	W	D.C.	18 AUG 1874	Oak Hill
007522	KLEINSCHMIDT, Hermann	5m	W	D.C.	06 JUN 1876	Oak Hill
013305	KLEINSCHMIDTZ, Rudolph V.	3m	W	D.C.	25 SEP 1877	Oak Hill
010809	KLEISS, Alice	74y	W	Ire.	28 FEB 1877	Mt. Olivet
002929	KLENE, Peter	77y	W	France	09 APR 1875	Mt. Olivet
010440	KLINE, Caroine	45y	W	Ger.	29 JAN 1877	Mt. Olivet
009750	KLINE, Mary A.	72y	W	N.J.	20 NOV 1876	Nokesville, Va.
003737	KLINE, Peter	3m	W	D.C.	21 JUN 1875	Mt. Olivet
017012	KLINE, Salvadore	18m	W	D.C.	11 AUG 1878	Mt. Olivet
010752	KLINE, Susan R.	28y	W	Md.	23 FEB 1877	Mt. Olivet
000765	KLINE, Valentine Henry	3m	W	D.C.	09 OCT 1874	Mt. Olivet
014511	KLINKENS, Elizabeth	4y	C	D.C.	21 JAN 1878	Beckett's
013124	KLINKETT, Caroline Thomas	2y	C	D.C.	08 SEP 1877	Beckett's

District of Columbia Death Records, August 1, 1874 to July 31, 1879   197

No.	Name	Age	Race	Birth	Death Date	Burial Place
014900	KLOFFER, Richard Everett	24y	W	D.C.	28 FEB 1878	Congressional
019120	KLOMAN, Louise	5m	W	Ill.	19 FEB 1879	Prospect Hill
019953	KLOTZ, Arthur H.	3m	W	D.C.	01 MAY 1879	Prospect Hill
019710	KLOTZ, Leela	3y	W	D.C.	09 APR 1879	Glenwood/Mt. Olivet
012756	KLUCKHUHN, Ida	9m	W	D.C.	10 AUG 1877	Prospect Hill
002695	KLUG, Annie Margaretta	75y	W	Ger.	22 MAR 1875	St. Mary's
007695	KNAPP, Auren	53y	W	Conn.	17 JUN 1876	Glenwood
007428	KNETTLE, Rosanna	79y	W	Pa.	28 MAY 1876	Oak Hill
018949	KNIESE, Mary	5y	W	D.C.	04 FEB 1879	Prospect Hill
002889	KNIGHT, Annie, Mrs.	50y	W	Va.	06 APR 1875	Prospect Hill
003123f	KNIGHT, Caleb	52y	W	U.S.	26 APR 1875	Congressional
012489	KNIGHT, Catharine	3m	W	U.S.	23 JUL 1877	Mt. Olivet
006309	KNIGHT, Edward	6m	C	D.C.	11 FEB 1876	Ebenezer
015763	KNIGHT, Edward	40y	C	N.C.	18 MAY 1878	Mt. Pleasant
010694	KNIGHT, Fanny	47y	W	DC.	19 FEB 1877	Holy Rood
015986	KNIGHT, Frank	1y	C	D.C.	03 JUN 1878	Young Mens
007145	KNIGHT, Franklin Lafayette	51y	W	Me.	28 APR 1876	Rock Creek
001255	KNIGHT, John	72y	W	Del.	28 NOV 1874	Congressional
013051	KNIGHT, John J.	10m	W	D.C.	01 SEP 1877	Mt. Olivet
019413	KNIGHT, Lewis E.	4d	W	D.C.	15 MAR 1879	Holy Rood
003805	KNIGHT, Maggie R.	2m	C	D.C.	24 JUN 1875	Ebenezer
010366	KNIGHT, Margaret	3m	C	D.C.	21 JAN 1877	Mt. Olivet
006157	KNIGHT, Mary	18d	W	D.C.	27 JAN 1876	Mt. Olivet
009221	KNIGHT, Mary	3m	W	U.S.	28 SEP 1876	Mt. Olivet
007468	KNIGHT, William Harding	28y	W	D.C.	02 JUN 1876	Congressional
019771	KNODE, Sarah	63y	W	Md.	14 APR 1879	Hagerstown, Md.
020759	KNOL, Joseph August	2m	W	D.C.	04 JUL 1879	St. Mary's
009549	KNORR, Barbara	53y	W	Ger.	27 OCT 1876	Prospect Hill
014286	KNOTT, Armstead	8y	W	D.C.	01 JAN 1878	Presbyterian
017526	KNOTT, Bessie A.	10m	W	D.C.	25 SEP 1878	Oak Hill
016280	KNOTT, Ervin	6d	W	D.C.	23 JUN 1878	Holy Rood
018547	KNOTT, James Wm.	11m	W	D.C.	02 JAN 1879	Mt. Olivet
018287	KNOTT, Luke	29y	W	Md.	09 DEC 1878	Mt. Olivet
016491	KNOTT, Mary	30y	W	Va.	07 JUL 1878	Holy Rood
009386	KNOTT, Mattie	17m	W	D.C.	12 OCT 1876	Congressional
014572	KNOTT, Randolph A.	8m	W	D.C.	27 JAN 1878	Presbyterian
020979	KNOTT, Rosa Adelaide	31y	W	Va.	17 JUL 1879	Richmond, Va.
015163	KNOTT, Walter P.	9y	W	D.C.	23 MAR 1878	Presbyterian
019576	KNOWLES, Lydia	85y	W	Md.	28 MAR 1879	Oak Hill
003519	KNOWLES, Mary Ann	35y	W	Can.	03 JUN 1875	Mt. Olivet
003630f	KNOWLES, Robert	1m	W	D.C.	13 JUN 1875	Mt. Olivet
007845	KNOWLES, Warren Newman	1y	W	D.C.	25 JUN 1876	Oak Hill
011325	KNOX, John J.	42y	W	N.Y.	13 APR 1877	Clarkston, Mich.
004293f	KNOX, John Jay	9m	W	D.C.	25 JUL 1875	Oak Hill
014812	KNOX, Mary J.	26y	W	Va.	18 FEB 1878	Congressional
007801	KNOX, Otto	2m	W	D.C.	23 JUN 1876	Graceland
011991	KOCH, Emma	8m	W	D.C.	21 JUN 1877	Prospect Hill
017760	KOCH, Geo. H.	35y	W	Ger.	16 OCT 1878	Hospital
018266	KOERBER, Anna Maria, Mrs.	56y	W	Ger.	07 DEC 1878	Prospect Hill
015478	KOERTH, Marcella Gabriella	1m	W	D.C.	22 APR 1878	Mt. Olivet
020812	KOHL, Henry	46y	W	Ger.	07 JUL 1879	Mt. Olivet
002848	KOHLER, Amelia	9h	W	D.C.	02 APR 1875	Prospect Hill
020217	KOHLER, Louise M.	31y	W	D.C.	28 MAY 1879	Prospect Hill
016694	KOHLER, William	3m	W	D.C.	20 JUL 1878	Prospect Hill
012280	KOLB, Francis W.	3m	W	D.C.	09 JUL 1877	Glenwood
006787	KOLB, Johana	43y	W	Ger.	23 MAR 1876	Glenwood

District of Columbia Death Records, August 1, 1874 to July 31, 1879

No.	Name	Age	Race	Birth	Death Date	Burial Place
012245	KOLBE, Henry	77y	W	Ger.	06 JUL 1877	Soldier's Home
003982	KOLTMAN, Christian	2y	W	D.C.	03 JUL 1875	Prospect Hill
001351	KONDRUP, Johan Cornelius	45y	W	Den.	10 DEC 1874	Congressional
001824	KONIG, Lenhart	52y	W	Prus.	21 JAN 1875	Prospect Hill
003563	KOON, Mary F.	5y	C	D.C.	07 JUN 1875	Young Mens
000391	KOONES, Josephene S., Mrs.	48y	W	N.J.	31 AUG 1874	Congressional
018151	KOONTZ, Charles Thomas	2y	W	D.C.	25 NOV 1878	Baltimore, Md.
011300	KOONTZ, George S.	1y	W	D.C.	11 APR 1877	Glenwood
019285	KOONTZ, James Henry	38y	W	Md.	05 MAR 1879	Frederick, Md.
002049	KOONTZ, Minnie E.	1y	W	D.C.	06 FEB 1875	Glenwood
002628	KOPPEL, Joseph	24h	W	D.C.	18 MAR 1875	Mt. Olivet
002872	KOPPEL, Mary Agnes	29y	W	S.C.	04 APR 1875	Charleston, S.C.
014763	KORFF, Sarah E.L.	1y	W	D.C.	14 FEB 1878	Oak Hill
008629	KORN, Paul	40y	W	Ger.	09 AUG 1876	Prospect Hill
008613	KOSACK, Edward	5d	W	D.C.	08 AUG 1876	Prospect Hill
013366	KOSACK, Otto	40y	W	Ger.	01 OCT 1877	Prospect Hill
017956	KOSS, William	3y	W	D.C.	05 NOV 1878	Prospect Hill
010703	KOUCHER, Mary	28y	W	Ger.	20 FEB 1877	Prospect Hill
020628	KRACKER, Henry	37y	W	Ger.	26 JUN 1879	Prospect Hill
019577	KRAEMER, Lule	2m	W	D.C.	28 MAR 1879	Prospect Hill
003617	KRAEMER, Mathilde	6m	W	D.C.	12 JUN 1875	Prospect Hill
009468	KRAEUTLER, Adolph	43y	W	Ger.	20 OCT 1876	Prospect Hill
005220	KRAFFT, Mary C.	65y	W	Md.	29 SEP 1875	Glenwood
005485	KRAFT, Barbra	73y	W	Ger.	17 NOV 1875	Prospect Hill
013686	KRAFT, Catherine E.	4y	W	D.C.	31 OCT 1877	Congressional
009820	KRAFT, Christopher	51y	W	Ger.	28 NOV 1876	Mt. Olivet
000881	KRAFT, Conrad	72y	W	Ger.	21 OCT 1874	Prospect Hill
008278	KRAFT, George W.	1m	W	D.C.	15 JUL 1876	Glenwood
017256	KRAFT, Nellie D.P.	1y	W	D.C.	30 AUG 1878	Glenwood
019570	KRAMER, Margaret	2y	C	D.C.	27 MAR 1879	Mt. Zion
016419	KRAMER, Roselinda	44y	W	Ger.	03 JUL 1878	St. Mary's
000577	KRANBRICHT, William C.	10m	W	D.C.	20 SEP 1874	Congressional
017723	KRANSKOPF, Peter	39y	W	Md.	13 OCT 1878	Baltimore, Md.
014270	KRASS, Ann	4m	W	D.C.	30 DEC 1877	Mt. Olivet
013731	KRAUS, Henry	20y	W	D.C.	04 NOV 1877	Oak Hill
016264	KRAUSE, Margaret Francis	45y	W	D.C.	22 JUN 1878	Congressional
003058	KRAUSE, William	5y	W	D.C.	20 APR 1875	Glenwood
018334	KREAGER, Otto	31y	W	Ger.	14 DEC 1878	Washington Asylum
020997	KREANN, Maggie P.	24y	W	D.C.	18 JUL 1879	Holy Rood
014446	KRESS, Catharine	29y	W	Ire.	16 JAN 1878	Mt. Olivet
020087	KRESS, Frederick	50y	W	Ger.	13 MAY 1879	Prospect Hill
014901	KRETSCHMAN, Susan J.	24y	W	D.C.	28 FEB 1878	Congressional
008129	KREUTER, Henry	1y	W	D.C.	10 JUL 1876	Glenwood
012875	KREUTER, Louis Wm.	8d	W	D.C.	19 AUG 1877	Glenwood
018679	KRIGBAUM, William F.	2y	W	D.C.	15 JAN 1879	Sunburg, Pa.
016418	KRITER, Wilhemmiene	66y	W	Ger.	03 JUL 1878	Prospect Hill
004316	KROHR, Charles Robert	3y	W	D.C.	26 JUL 1875	Mt. Olivet
020359	KROHR, Flora	9m	W	D.C.	09 JUN 1879	Mt. Olivet
015504	KROUS, Allen J.F.	3y	W	Md.	24 APR 1878	Prospect Hill
016316	KROUSE, James	6m	W	D.C.	26 JUN 1878	Glenwood
003729	KRUMB, Conrad	13y	W	N.J.	20 JUN 1875	Prospect Hill
007882	KUHN, Henry G.	14m	W	D.C.	27 JUN 1876	Congressional
011340	KUHN, Infant of James	5min	W	D.C.	15 APR 1877	Holy Rood
018207	KUHN, John A.	35y	W	Md.	30 NOV 1878	Mechanicstown, Md.
018861	KUHN, Joseph E.	42y	W	Md.	28 JAN 1879	Mechanictown, Md.
021067	KUHN, Mina Alice	2y	W	D.C.	23 JUL 1879	Glenwood

District of Columbia Death Records, August 1, 1874 to July 31, 1879   199

No.	Name	Age	Race	Birth	Death Date	Burial Place
006273	KUHNER, William Andrew	3m	W	N.Y.	08 FEB 1876	Prospect Hill
004357	KUHNS, Ida N.	6m	W	D.C.	28 JUL 1875	Presbyterian
004764	KUHNS, Julia A.	35y	W	Va.	26 AUG 1875	Presbyterian
018342	KUHNS, W.H.	38y	W	Pa.	15 DEC 1878	Oak Hill
008579	KULP, John	80y	W	Pa.	06 AUG 1876	Congressional
001142	KULUESOUSKI, Mary Josephine	49y	W	Switz.	14 NOV 1874	Mt. Olivet
009506	KUMMER, Jacob	63y	W	Ger.	23 OCT 1876	St. Mary's
002479	KUNKE, Ludwig	30y	W	Ger.	08 MAR 1875	Congressional
018165	KURTZ, Conrad	69y	W	Ger.	26 NOV 1878	Soldier's Home
013532	KURTZ, John D., Col.	56y	W	D.C.	16 OCT 1877	Oak Hill
006463	KURTZ, William C.	59y	W	D.C.	24 FEB 1876	Mt. Olivet
005406	KURTZE, Charles F.	37y	W	Ger.	09 NOV 1875	Hospital
005367	KUSTER, Ferdinand	47y	W	Ger.	05 NOV 1875	Prospect Hill
002294	KUTZ, Infant of Benjamin	2h	W	D.C.	23 FEB 1875	Mt. Olivet
017773	KUTZ, Rosanna	74y	W	Pa.	17 OCT 1878	Wilkesbarre, Pa.
010827	KYLE, Carrie Ella	1y	W	D.C.	01 MAR 1877	Congressional

L

No.	Name	Age	Race	Birth	Death Date	Burial Place
004416	LABALETTE, Charlotte Lucretia	20m	C	D.C.	02 AUG 1875	Harmony
018586	LACEY, Alfred Burton Hart	44y	W	Del.	06 JAN 1879	Congressional
010487	LACEY, Alice	17y	C	Va.	02 FEB 1877	Potters Field
011191	LACEY, Catharine	38y	C	Va.	02 APR 1877	Ebenezer
010522	LACEY, Frankie D.	10m	W	D.C.	04 FEB 1877	Congressional
008637	LACEY, Minnie A.	8m	W	D.C.	10 AUG 1876	Holy Rood
006975	LACEY, Roberta	15y	M	Va.	09 APR 1876	Harmony
014432	LACKEY, Francis Z.	1y	W	D.C.	15 JAN 1878	Mt. Olivet
006206	LACORD, James	65y	W	Ire.	01 FEB 1876	Mt. Olivet
001754	LACY, Annie Elizabeth	25y	W	Va.	16 JAN 1875	Congressional
014821	LACY, Edw.	33y	W	D.C.	19 FEB 1878	Congressional
001350	LACY, Infant of James	12d	C	D.C.	09 DEC 1874	Mt. Pleasant
019423	LACY, John Francis	5y	C	D.C.	16 MAR 1879	Hillsdale
009099	LACY, Joseph	36y	C	Va.	16 SEP 1876	Washington Asylum
012267	LACY, Lillie	4m	C	D.C.	08 JUL 1877	Potters Field
013092	LACY, Mary Jane, Mrs.	51y	W	Va.	05 SEP 1877	Congressional
011771	LACY, Sarah	6m	C	D.C.	01 JUN 1877	Mt. Pleasant
005067	LACY, Walter of George	6y	C	D.C.	16 SEP 1875	Potters Field
015809	LADD, Caroline A.	30y	W	Va.	22 MAY 1878	Congressional
001453f	LADD, Mrs.	75y	W	Va.	17 DEC 1874	Congressional
005155a	LADEN, Michal	13y	W	D.C.	15 OCT 1875	Mt. Olivet
017631	LADSON, Eliza Euphemia	41y	W	D.C.	04 OCT 1878	Congressional
015753	LAHEY, Agnes	3m	W	D.C.	17 MAY 1878	Mt. Olivet
011228	LAINER, Mary R.	5y	W	D.C.	05 APR 1877	Holy Rood
011839	LAING, Richard	10m	W	D.C.	08 JUN 1877	Congressional
006499	LAIR, Virginia Ann	76y	C	Va.	28 FEB 1876	Young Mens
006599	LAKE, Charles	2y	W	D.C.	08 MAR 1876	Glenwood
005919	LAKE, Eli	60y	W	N.Y.	02 JAN 1876	Glenwood
007088	LAKE, Eliza J.	58y	W	Eng.	23 APR 1876	Congressional
014711	LAKE, Fannie E.	30y	W	D.C.	08 FEB 1878	Glenwood
007362	LAKE, James C.	6m	W	D.C.	21 MAY 1876	Glenwood
005207	LAKE, Mary	58y	W	N.Y.	28 SEP 1875	Glenwood
001820	LAKENAN, Mary Ann	56y	W	Va.	21 JAN 1875	Glenwood
020614	LALLEY, Mary Agnes	8m	W	Md.	25 JUN 1879	Mt. Olivet
018783	LALLY, Michael	50y	W	Ire.	23 JAN 1879	Wilmington, Del.
010122	LAMB, Eleanor A.	3y	W	D.C.	30 DEC 1876	Congressional

No.	Name	Age	Race	Birth	Death Date	Burial Place
003362	LAMB, Johanna	27y	W	N.Y.	19 MAY 1875	Mt. Olivet
002866	LAMBERT, Mary	84y	C	Va.	04 APR 1875	Harmony
011732	LAMBERT, Rosetta	41y	W	Md.	28 MAY 1877	Holy Rood
003637	LAMBRECHT, Fredrich	5m	W	D.C.	14 JUN 1875	Prospect Hill
003784	LAMBRECHT, Katie	5m	W	D.C.	23 JUN 1875	Prospect Hill
009811	LAMBRIGHT, Geo. C.	36y	W	D.C.	27 NOV 1876	Oak Hill
014028	LAMPH, James	47y	W	Ire.	07 DEC 1877	Mt. Olivet
012523	LAMPHERE, Mary L.	1m	W	D.C.	25 JUL 1877	Mt. Olivet
010426	LAMSON, Harry Franklin	8y	W	D.C.	28 JAN 1877	Oak Hill
012591	LAMSON, Robert Laurence	6m	W	D.C.	29 JUL 1877	Oak Hill
003367	LANCASTER, Catharine	81y	C	D.C.	19 MAY 1875	Mt. Pleasant
013170	LANCASTER, Chas. H.	1y	C	D.C.	12 SEP 1877	Beckett's
014573	LANCASTER, Emanuel F.	44y	W	Md.	27 JAN 1878	Baltimore, Md.
008607	LANCASTER, Gertrude	7m	C	D.C.	08 AUG 1876	Ebenezer
015631	LANCASTER, Hillary	50y	C	Md.	06 MAY 1878	Mt. Olivet
002891	LANCASTER, James	23y	C	Md.	06 APR 1875	Ebenezer
007178	LANCASTER, James	1y	M	D.C.	01 MAY 1876	Potters Field
012313	LANCASTER, James	5d	C	D.C.	11 JUL 1877	Young Mens
011044	LANCASTER, James	7m	C	D.C.	19 MAR 1877	Mt. Olivet
011024	LANCASTER, Louisa	7y	C	D.C.	18 MAR 1877	Mt. Olivet
018324	LANCASTER, Martha	30y	C	Md.	13 DEC 1878	Beckett's
006961	LANCASTER, Rosene	1y	C	D.C.	07 APR 1876	Mt. Olivet
009641	LANCASTER, Sarah	25y	C	D.C.	08 NOV 1876	Potters Field
016375	LANCASTER, Sarah C.	8m	C	D.C.	30 JUN 1878	Beckett's
019897	LANCASTER, Thomas	60y	C	Md.	25 APR 1879	Mt. Olivet
004835	LANCASTER, William H.	1y	C	D.C.	30 AUG 1875	Beckett's
004201	LANCASTER, Wm. W.	12d	C	D.C.	19 JUL 1875	Mt. Olivet
005368	LANCKTON, Arabella M.	2y	W	D.C.	05 NOV 1875	Oak Hill
004599	LANDGRAAF, Annie Marguerite	30y	W	Ger.	14 AUG 1875	Prospect Hill
003150	LANDON, Clinton H.	44y	W	N.Y.	26 APR 1875	Hospital
002885	LANDON, Wm. Henry	1y	W	D.C.	05 APR 1875	Harmony
013672	LANDRAN, Rosa	1y	C	D.C.	29 OCT 1877	Potters Field
007420	LANDRAN, Walter	11m	C	D.C.	27 MAY 1876	Potters Field
010418	LANDRICK, Alice E.	20y	C	Va.	27 JAN 1877	Brightwood
001934	LANDRS, Carie, Mrs.	20y	C	Va.	28 JAN 1875	Mt. Pleasant
003091	LANDSDALE, Annie	35y	M	D.C.	22 APR 1875	Potters Field
009884	LANDSON, George	7y	C	D.C.	06 DEC 1876	Potters Field
004521	LANE, Annie	1y	C	D.C.	09 AUG 1875	Young Mens
013630	LANE, Annie R.	1y	C	D.C.	25 OCT 1877	Mt. Zion
001911	LANE, Charles H.	63y	W	Md.	27 JAN 1875	Congressional
003298	LANE, Charlotte A., Mrs.	29y	W	D.C.	12 MAY 1875	Mt. Olivet
003578	LANE, Emma	8y	C	D.C.	09 JUN 1875	Young Mens
011010	LANE, Francis W.	52y	W	Va.	16 MAR 1877	Congressional
018537	LANE, Harriet	52y	C	Va.	01 JAN 1879	Mt. Zion
004915	LANE, Infant of Julia	18m	C	D.C.	05 SEP 1875	Freedmen's Village
018727	LANE, James	10y	C	D.C.	19 JAN 1879	Harmony
015226	LANE, Jennie Stevenson	10y	W	Del.	29 MAR 1878	Wilmington, Del.
000812	LANE, Jessie	23y	C	Va.	15 OCT 1874	Washington Asylum
004783	LANE, John	10y	W	D.C.	27 AUG 1875	Mt. Olivet
008249	LANE, Joseph	15d	W	D.C.	13 JUL 1876	Mt. Olivet
005799	LANE, Julia	10m	C	D.C.	19 DEC 1875	Washington Asylum
003327	LANE, Martha E.	48y	W	Md.	14 MAY 1875	Presbyterian
017283	LANE, Mattie L.	20m	W	D.C.	01 SEP 1878	Congressional
005056	LANE, Nellie	1y	C	D.C.	15 SEP 1875	Ebenezer
011280	LANE, Valeria B.	5y	W	Conn.	09 APR 1877	Carlisle, Pa.
000905	LANER, Adam	4y	W	D.C.	23 OCT 1874	Mt. Olivet

District of Columbia Death Records, August 1, 1874 to July 31, 1879   201

No.	Name	Age	Race	Birth	Death Date	Burial Place
006449	LANG, John	50y	W	Ger.	23 FEB 1876	St. Mary's
011158	LANG, Lizzie	1y	W	D.C.	30 MAR 1877	Prospect Hill
002373	LANGHORN, Thos.	2y	W	D.C.	01 MAR 1875	Congressional
003148	LANGLEY, Ann V.	21y	W	D.C.	27 APR 1875	Congressional
013517	LANGLEY, Augustus McKendree	27y	W	D.C.	14 OCT 1877	Oak Hill
010241	LANGLEY, Edna Malvern	1y	W	D.C.	09 JAN 1877	Congressional
001029	LANGLEY, Ella N.	22y	W	Md.	03 NOV 1874	Baltimore, Md.
018201	LANGLEY, John H.	35y	W	D.C.	29 NOV 1878	Congressional
002218	LANGLEY, Lizzie	2m	C	D.C.	18 FEB 1875	Beckett's
013699	LANGLEY, Lula Edith	3y	W	D.C.	01 NOV 1877	Congressional
002032	LANGLEY, Martha C.	75y	W	Md.	05 FEB 1875	Congressional
018885	LANGLEY, Mary E.	69y	W	Md.	30 JAN 1879	Mt. Olivet
006571	LANGLEY, Mary M.	64y	W	Md.	06 MAR 1876	Methodist
000389	LANGLEY, Mary V.	1y	W	D.C.	31 AUG 1874	Congressional
002758	LANGLEY, Robert Croggon	1y	W	D.C.	27 MAR 1875	Glenwood
004546	LANGLEY, Samuel Edwd. Andrews	1y	W	D.C.	11 AUG 1875	Congressional
004160	LANGLEY, Walter	4d	W	D.C.	16 JUL 1875	Congressional
018862	LANGLEY, William H.	9m	C	D.C.	28 JAN 1879	Payne's
020699	LANGLY, Charles W.	3m	W	D.C.	01 JUL 1879	Mt. Olivet
015336	LANGSTON, Matilda	22y	C	Md.	09 APR 1878	Potters Field
013239	LANHAM, Andrew	25y	W	D.C.	18 SEP 1877	Congressional
005347	LANHAM, Dora Lerona	6y	W	D.C.	03 NOV 1875	Alexandria, Va.
001134	LANHAM, Emma E.	1m	W	D.C.	13 NOV 1874	Broad Creek Church
009377	LANHAM, Margaret	64y	W	D.C.	11 OCT 1876	Congressional
017426	LANNAGHAN, Bartley	43y	W	N.Y.	16 SEP 1878	Mt. Olivet
015348	LANSBURGH, Bernard	10m	W	D.C.	10 APR 1878	Washington Hebrew
015752	LANSBURGH, Genevieve	2y	W	D.C.	17 MAY 1878	Washington Hebrew
002039	LANSDALE, Annie May	4y	W	D.C.	05 FEB 1875	Mt. Olivet
009666	LANSDALE, Asbury	55y	C	Md.	10 NOV 1876	Ebenezer
011131	LANSDALE, E. Jane	5y	W	D.C.	27 MAR 1877	Congressional
000510	LANSDALE. U.F.	39y	W	D.C.	14 SEP 1874	Congressional
017780	LANSTON, Infant of Talbot	1h	W	D.C.	18 JAN 1875	Presbyterian
018652	LANTEL, John Henry	12y	W	D.C.	12 JAN 1879	Prospect Hill
015987	LANTNER, George	58y	W	Ger.	03 JUN 1878	Glenwood
014771	LANTNER, Mary E.	31y	W	D.C.	15 FEB 1878	Glenwood
011904	LAPHAM, Charles N., Jr.	1y	W	D.C.	14 JUN 1877	Glenwood
012160	LAPORTE, Ann	70y	W	D.C.	01 JUL 1877	Mt. Olivet
005937	LARCOMBE, Frances	37y	W	Ire.	04 JAN 1876	Glenwood/Congressional
015641	LARCOMBE, Laura C.	27y	W	D.C.	07 MAY 1878	Oak Hill
011066	LARE, Jane	26y	W	Pa.	21 MAR 1877	Mt. Olivet
010978	LARGE, Ebenezer	52y	W	N.J.	15 MAR 1877	Lambertville, N.J.
010979	LARGE, John A.	23y	W	N.J.	15 MAR 1877	Lambertville, N.J.
001367	LARGE, Theodore	38y	W	N.J.	11 DEC 1874	Lambertville, N.J.
012483	LARKIN, Johanna	45y	W	Ire.	23 JUL 1877	Holy Rood
003594	LARKINS, Claude M.	7m	C	D.C.	10 JUN 1875	Beckett's
017344	LARWILL, Susan Christmas	83y	W	Pa.	07 SEP 1878	Wooster, Ohio
010584	LASIER, Harriet Chase	34y	W	Ver.	11 FEB 1877	Rock Creek
008684	LASKEY, Bertie	1d	W	D.C.	14 AUG 1876	Congressional
014459	LASKEY, Mary	19y	W	D.C.	17 JAN 1878	Glenwood
018125	LASKEY, Richard H.	15y	W	D.C.	23 NOV 1878	Congressional
006968	LASSILLE, Hyacinthe	70y	W	Ind.	08 APR 1876	Oak Hill
020639	LATHAM, Ida May	4y	W	D.C	27 JUN 1879	Methodist
004579	LATHAN, Lottie E.	16m	W	D.C.	13 AUG 1875	Methodist
011582	LATHMORE, Elmira	23y	C	Va.	13 MAY 1877	Ebenezer
003432	LATHROP, Esther Maria Green	34y	W	Pa.	25 MAY 1875	Sullivan Co., Pa.
003625	LATHROP, Mary	1m	W	D.C.	13 JUN 1875	Sullivan Co., Pa.

District of Columbia Death Records, August 1, 1874 to July 31, 1879

No.	Name	Age	Race	Birth	Death Date	Burial Place
011362	LATON, Mary	9y	C	D.C.	17 APR 1877	Mt. Zion
013182	LATTIMORE, Finley C., Dr.	43y	W	Ind.	13 SEP 1877	Graceland
012162	LATTIMORE, Fredk.	1m	C	D.C.	01 JUL 1877	Ebenezer
011916	LATTIMORE, Martha W.P.	73y	W	Ky.	15 JUN 1877	North Vernon, Ind.
002276	LATTIMORE, Walter F.	4y	W	D.C.	22 FEB 1875	Glenwood
009848	LAUB, Charles H.	71y	W	D.C.	02 DEC 1876	Oak Hill
002465	LAUCK, Ann H.	46y	W	D.C.	07 MAR 1875	Glenwood
009229	LAUCK, Franklin	6m	W	D.C.	28 SEP 1876	Presbyterian
013705	LAUCK, Robert L.	9d	W	D.C.	02 NOV 1877	Presbyterian
009349	LAUER, Aman	8d	W	D.C.	09 OCT 1876	St. Mary's
000415	LAUER, Bernhardt	32y	W	Ger.	03 SEP 1874	St. Mary's
018622	LAUER, Geo. W.	14y	W	D.C.	09 JAN 1879	Presbyterian
000195	LAUER, Rosena R.	1y	W	D.C.	15 AUG 1874	St. Mary's
015909	LAUPP, Edward	9m	W	D.C.	30 MAY 1878	Prospect Hill
020078	LAUPP, Infant of Charles	6d	W	D.C.	12 MAY 1879	Prospect Hill
007429	LAURANCE, Edward	4y	W	D.C.	28 MAY 1876	Mt. Olivet
014190	LAURITZEN, Kate Ealand	33y	W	D.C.	24 DEC 1877	Glenwood
010023	LAUSON, Infant of Jesse	7d	C	D.C.	20 DEC 1876	Potters Field
013908	LAUTNER, Mary	4y	W	D.C.	24 NOV 1877	Mt. Olivet
012678	LAUXMANN, Christina	77y	W	Ger.	05 AUG 1877	Prospect Hill
005860	LAVENDER, James	66y	W	Eng.	25 DEC 1875	Glenwood
005110	LAVENDER, James	16y	W	D.C.	20 SEP 1875	Prospect Hill
017797	LAVENDER, James	43y	W	Can.	19 OCT 1878	Prospect Hill
006592	LAVENDER, Robert	5d	W	D.C.	07 MAR 1876	Glenwood
020308	LAVERONE, Joseph	17y	W	Italy	05 JUN 1879	St. Mary's
011622	LAW, Isaiah	55y	W	Ire.	17 MAY 1877	Soldier's Home
016717	LAW, Sarah C.	35y	W	N.J.	22 JUL 1878	Mt. Olivet
003377	LAWLER, Mary Irene	1y	W	D.C.	20 MAY 1875	Mt. Olivet
003095	LAWLOR, Ellen, Mrs.	28y	W	Ire.	23 APR 1875	Mt. Olivet
021024	LAWRENCE, Mary A.	79y	W	Eng.	20 JUL 1879	Congressional
009833	LAWRENCE, Minnie	9y	W	D.C.	30 NOV 1876	Oak Hill
010473	LAWRENCE, Robert B.	49y	W	N.Y.	01 FEB 1877	Glenwood
009299	LAWRENCE, William Henry	13y	C	Va.	04 OCT 1876	Potters Field
018747	LAWRIE, John W.	29y	W	D.C.	20 JAN 1879	Glenwood
008897	LAWS, Henry Ezeholtz	8m	C	D.C.	31 AUG 1876	Young Mens
004172	LAWS, Pinkanetta	18m	C	D.C.	17 JUL 1875	Mt. Pleasant Plain
003217	LAWSON, Ann Eliza Rebecca	2m	C	D.C.	04 MAY 1875	Moore's
020521	LAWSON, Cora Bell	1m	C	D.C.	19 JUN 1879	Moore's
019733	LAWSON, Eliza	5y	C	D.C.	11 APR 1879	Beckett's
017397	LAWSON, Emily	1y	C	D.C.	13 SEP 1878	Mt. Zion
000052	LAWSON, Fanny	3y	C	D.C.	04 AUG 1874	Mt. Pleasant
004151	LAWSON, Ida	1y	C	D.C.	16 JUL 1875	Young Mens
014019	LAWSON, Infant of Matthew	21d	C	D.C.	06 DEC 1877	Potters Field
019700	LAWSON, Josephine	3y	C	D.C.	08 APR 1879	Beckett's
010812	LAWSON, Margaret E.	9y	C	D.C.	28 FEB 1877	Mt. Zion
015632	LAWSON, Maria	4y	C	D.C.	06 MAY 1878	Beckett's
006591	LAWSON, Nancy	35y	C	Va.	07 MAR 1876	Potters Field
012935	LAWSON, Robert	6d	C	D.C.	24 AUG 1877	Potters Field
009649	LAWSON, Stanley	40y	C	D.C.	09 NOV 1876	Harmony
009777	LAWSON, Walter Piat	3y	W	D.C.	23 NOV 1876	Glenwood
007248	LAWSON, William	6m	C	D.C.	08 MAY 1876	Young Mens
003657	LAWSON, William S.	65y	W	Ga.	15 JUN 1875	Glenwood
005798	LAWSON, Wm.	59y	W	Va.	19 DEC 1875	Methodist
002469	LAWTON, John	31y	W	Md.	07 MAR 1875	Soldiers' Home
005135a	LAWYER, Eliza L.	3y	W	D.C.	13 OCT 1875	Oak Hill
005373	LAY, Sylvester	47y	W	N.Y.	06 NOV 1875	Albany, N.Y.

No.	Name	Age	Race	Birth	Death Date	Burial Place
001491	LAYTON, Julia W.	34y	W	D.C.	26 DEC 1874	Laurel, Md.
017295	LAYTON, Minnie	18y	C	Va.	02 SEP 1878	Mt. Zion
005337	LAZENBERRY, Janetta	24y	C	Va.	02 NOV 1875	Berry's
013749	LAZENBY, Amos A.	56y	W	Md.	06 NOV 1877	Glenwood
017272	LEA, William G.	43y	W	Va.	31 AUG 1878	Rock Creek
009310	LEACH, Chas. E.	2y	W	D.C.	05 OCT 1876	Congressional
005241	LEACH, Wm.	63y	W	Md.	22 OCT 1875	Congressional
000322	LEAHY, Ewd.	11m	W	D.C.	26 AUG 1874	Mt. Olivet
009242	LEAHY, Mary C.	1m	W	D.C.	29 SEP 1876	Mt. Olivet
019150	LEANNARDA, Mary A.	45y	W	N.J.	22 FEB 1879	Congressional
014319	LEAR, George	65y	C	Va.	04 JAN 1878	Potters Field
014729	LEARCH, William J.	27y	W	Pa.	09 FEB 1878	Rock Creek
002151	LEARSHOTT, George F.	22d	W	D.C.	14 FEB 1875	Glenwood
011307	LEATHERS, Savilla B.	25y	W	Md.	12 APR 1877	Glenwood
005053a	LECKRON, Daniel H.	69y	W	Md.	04 OCT 1875	Oak Hill
018363	LECLAIR, Mathew	54y	W	Ger.	17 DEC 1878	Holy Rood
014836	LeCOMPTE, Anna C.	63y	W	Va.	21 FEB 1878	Mt. Olivet
004837	LeCOMPTE, S.B.	32y	W	N.Y.	30 AUG 1875	Mt. Olivet
009613	LeCONTE, William	30y	W	Ga.	04 NOV 1876	Oak Hill
020471	LEDDY, Hugh	86y	W	Ire.	16 JUN 1879	Mt. Olivet
006918	LEDDY, Owen	85y	W	Ire.	04 APR 1876	Mt. Olivet
020408	LEDERER, Annie	5m	W	D.C.	12 JUN 1879	Congressional
020503	LEDERO, Christian	6m	W	D.C.	18 JUN 1879	Congressional
018935	LEE, Adam	c.50y	C	Md.	03 FEB 1879	Beckett's
005847	LEE, Albert	26h	C	D.C.	24 DEC 1875	Ebenezer
008438	LEE, Alexander	46y	C	Md.	27 JUL 1876	Harmony
016006	LEE, Alfred	2m	C	D.C.	04 JUN 1878	Beckett's
011331	LEE, Alma	2y	C	D.C.	14 APR 1877	Beckett's
002679	LEE, Annie	70y	C	Va.	21 MAR 1875	Ebenezer
020072	LEE, Annie Maria	9y	C	D.C.	11 MAY 1879	Graceland
013223	LEE, Annie, Mrs.	72y	C	Md.	16 SEP 1877	Harmony
016833	LEE, Antony	74y	C	Md.	30 JUL 1878	Mt. Olivet
007249	LEE, Bertha	6m	M	D.C.	08 MAY 1876	Harmony
009458	LEE, Bertha	1y	W	D.C.	18 OCT 1876	Baltimore, Md.
015417	LEE, Catharine	42y	C	Md.	16 APR 1878	Macedonia
020381	LEE, Catharine	71y	C	Va.	10 JUN 1879	Mt. Pleasant
017569	LEE, Catharine, Mrs.	45y	W	Va.	29 SEP 1878	Fairfax, Va.
009163	LEE, Chapman	88y	W	Conn.	22 SEP 1876	Patterson, N.Y.
013893	LEE, Charles	5y	C	D.C.	23 NOV 1877	Mt. Pleasant Plain
005882	LEE, Charles C.	28y	C	Va.	28 DEC 1875	Harmony
002915	LEE, Charles H.	43y	C	Md.	07 APR 1875	Harmony
002536	LEE, Charley	2m	C	D.C.	12 MAR 1875	Holy Rood
010196	LEE, Cora	22y	C	S.C.	06 JAN 1877	Mt. Olivet
010372	LEE, Daniel	c.8y	C	D.C.	22 JAN 1877	Young Mens
001552	LEE, Delia	c.100y	C	Md.	01 JAN 1875	On the Farm
005102	LEE, Edia	4m	W	D.C.	19 SEP 1875	Congressional
006352	LEE, Edward	49y	C	D.C.	14 FEB 1876	Harmony
005417	LEE, Edward Butler	76y	C	D.C.	10 NOV 1875	Mt. Olivet
017693	LEE, Elizabeth	39y	C	D.C.	10 OCT 1878	Mt. Zion
013451	LEE, Ellen	60y	C	Md.	09 OCT 1877	Baptist
007058	LEE, Emma	19y	C	Md.	20 APR 1876	Potters Field
001841	LEE, Florence	9m	C	D.C.	22 JAN 1875	Ebenezer
009015	LEE, Florence E.	13m	C	D.C.	09 SEP 1876	Ebenezer
012716	LEE, Frances	1m	W	D.C.	07 AUG 1877	Mt. Olivet
012130	LEE, Francis	1m	C	D.C.	29 JUN 1877	Ebenezer
021041	LEE, Frank Abram	9m	C	D.C.	21 JUL 1879	Payne's

No.	Name	Age	Race	Birth	Death Date	Burial Place
019142	LEE, George	2m	W	D.C.	21 FEB 1879	Graceland
012822	LEE, George F.	1y	C	D.C.	15 AUG 1877	Mt. Pleasant
007100	LEE, George Robt.	2y	C	Md.	24 APR 1876	Harmony
005323	LEE, George W.	65y	C	Md.	31 OCT 1875	Hospital
018782	LEE, Gilbert Marion	8m	C	D.C.	23 JAN 1879	Beckett's
012715	LEE, Hannah	c.102y	C	Md.	07 AUG 1877	Mt. Olivet
003835	LEE, Harriett	70y	M	Va.	25 JUN 1875	Mt. Zion
000150	LEE, Henreetha	24y	C	D.C.	11 AUG 1874	Harmony
015596	LEE, Infant of Archibald	14d	C	D.C.	03 MAY 1878	Payne's
003621	LEE, Infant of Carrie	7d	C	D.C.	12 JUN 1875	Potters Field
020504	LEE, Infant of Cordelia	--	C	D.C.	18 JUN 1879	Payne's
015553	LEE, Infant of G.W.	6d	C	D.C.	29 APR 1878	Beckett's
016234	LEE, Infant of John	1m	C	D.C.	20 JUN 1878	Harmony
013380	LEE, Infant of Josephine	3m	C	D.C.	02 OCT 1877	Potters Field
007255	LEE, Infant of William	9m	C	D.C.	09 MAY 1876	Young Mens
009356	LEE, John	80y	C	Md.	09 OCT 1876	Harmony
014202	LEE, John	26y	C	Va.	25 DEC 1877	Beckett's
018236	LEE, John	51y	C	Md.	04 DEC 1878	Mt. Olivet
019323	LEE, John F.	77y	C	Md.	08 MAR 1879	Mt. Zion
004335	LEE, John R.	5m	C	D.C.	27 JUL 1875	Ebenezer
012051	LEE, Joseph D.	87y	W	Ky.	25 JUN 1877	Congressional
014308	LEE, Julia	1y	C	D.C.	03 JAN 1878	Beckett's
000209	LEE, Katharine	17m	C	D.C.	16 AUG 1874	Mt. Zion
005738	LEE, Laura	18y	C	Va.	13 DEC 1875	Young Mens
014862	LEE, Lavenia	3y	C	D.C.	24 FEB 1878	Young Mens
017337	LEE, Lavinia	24y	C	D.C.	06 SEP 1878	Young Mens
004932	LEE, Lewis	45y	C	D.C.	06 SEP 1875	Mt. Zion
002278	LEE, Lizzie	6m	C	D.C.	22 FEB 1875	Mt. Pleasant
021052	LEE, Lottie	2y	W	Va.	22 JUL 1879	Methodist
005561	LEE, Lucy	1y	C	D.C.	25 NOV 1875	Young Mens
009013	LEE, Luvenia	42y	C	D.C.	09 SEP 1876	Harmony
013200	LEE, Mamie	7y	C	Md.	14 SEP 1877	Young Mens
002443	LEE, Maria	2y	C	D.C.	05 MAR 1875	Young Mens
010239	LEE, Martha S.	30y	C	Va.	09 JAN 1877	Mt. Zion
001460	LEE, Mary	35y	C	Va.	22 DEC 1874	Potters Field
011338	LEE, Mary	40y	W	Ire.	15 APR 1877	Mt. Olivet
015610	LEE, Mary	78y	W	Ire.	04 MAY 1878	Mt. Olivet
011945	LEE, Mary Ann	1d	C	D.C.	17 JUN 1877	Ebenezer
019832	LEE, Mary Frances	1y	C	D.C.	19 APR 1879	Beckett's
007437	LEE, Mary W.A.	7m	W	D.C.	30 MAY 1876	Congressional
008828	LEE, Mathew	1y	M	D.C.	26 AUG 1876	Potters Field
000287	LEE, Maud E.	1y	C	D.C.	22 AUG 1874	Mt. Pleasant
009881	LEE, Nancy	76y	C	Va.	06 DEC 1876	Mt. Zion
020583	LEE, Nettie	1y	C	D.C.	23 JUN 1879	Payne's
009319	LEE, Phil	33y	C	D.C.	06 OCT 1876	Harmony
006310	LEE, Philip	25y	C	Md.	11 FEB 1876	Potters Field
000545	LEE, Reverdy	1y	C	D.C.	17 SEP 1874	Beckett's
019045	LEE, Reverdy	55y	C	Md.	12 FEB 1879	Beckett's
003550	LEE, Riley	19y	C	Va.	07 JUN 1875	Mt. Zion
002761	LEE, Robert	2y	C	D.C.	27 MAR 1875	Harmony
006709	LEE, Robert	25y	C	Va.	17 MAR 1876	Mt. Pleasant
011350	LEE, Robert	37y	C	Va.	16 APR 1877	Young Mens
002699	LEE, Robt. E.	28y	C	Md.	22 MAR 1875	Potters Field
015479	LEE, Rose	3y	C	D.C.	22 APR 1878	Payne's
001166f	LEE, Samuel H.	220y	W	Va.	17 NOV 1874	Rehobeth, Va.
016890	LEE, Sarah	36y	C	Md.	03 AUG 1878	Mt. Olivet

District of Columbia Death Records, August 1, 1874 to July 31, 1879

No.	Name	Age	Race	Birth	Death Date	Burial Place
018470	LEE, Sarah A.	54y	C	Md.	26 DEC 1878	Mt. Olivet
016227	LEE, Sarah E.	4m	C	D.C.	19 JUN 1878	Beckett's
015755	LEE, Selesten	1y	C	D.C.	17 MAY 1878	Harmony
020792	LEE, Susan	19y	C	D.C.	06 JUL 1879	Harmony
010199	LEE, Thomas	89y	C	Va.	07 JAN 1877	Young Mens
009149	LEE, Walker	31y	C	Va.	21 SEP 1876	Mt. Zion
019209	LEE, Walter	2m	C	D.C.	26 FEB 1879	Potters Field
015365	LEE, William	1y	C	D.C.	11 APR 1878	Mt. Pleasant
002232	LEE, William H.	c.65y	M	D.C.	19 FEB 1875	Harmony
011257	LEE, William Henry	c.12y	C	Md.	07 APR 1877	Ebenezer
002120	LEE, William Thomas	1y	C	D.C.	11 FEB 1875	Ebenezer
000728	LEE, Willie	1m	W	DC.	06 OCT 1874	Young Mens
015337	LEE, Willie	1y	C	D.C.	09 APR 1878	Beckett's
007660	LEE, Wm.	3y	C	D.C.	15 JUN 1876	Potters Field
008356	LEE, Zachariah	6m	C	D.C.	20 JUL 1876	Mt. Olivet
017160	LEECH, Hiram P.	61y	W	N.Y.	23 AUG 1878	Glenwood
003059	LEECH, Robert	c.50y	W	Pa.	20 APR 1875	Glenwood
004904	LEEDE, Albert	28y	W	Ger.	04 SEP 1875	Prospect Hill
001260	LEEHY, Mary	104y	W	Ire.	29 NOV 1874	Mt. Olivet
019991	LEEK, Susana	1y	C	D.C.	04 MAY 1879	Harmony
012757	LEESE, Andrew B.	5m	W	D.C.	10 AUG 1877	Glenwood
019477	LEESMITZER, Earnest Julius	74y	W	Ger.	20 MAR 1879	Congressional
008624	LEETCH, George	6y	W	Ill.	09 AUG 1876	Presbyterian
017106	LeFAIRE, Felicite	69y	W	France	19 AUG 1878	Baltimore, Md.
006198	LEFFINGWELL, Joseph L.	5m	W	D.C.	31 JAN 1876	Baltimore, Md.
001447	LEFTON, Annie	45y	W	Pa.	20 DEC 1874	Rock Creek
020682	LEFTRIDGE, Anna Maria	15m	M	D.C.	30 JUN 1879	Mt. Olivet
004033	LEGG, Aretas M., Jr.	2m	W	D.C.	07 JUL 1875	Skeneateles, N.Y.
015184	LEGG, Daisy	1y	W	N.Y.	25 MAR 1878	Spafford, N.Y.
011519	LEGGINS, Willie	10m	C	D.C.	05 MAY 1877	Macedonia
008953	LEHMAN, Edward	23y	W	Ger.	03 SEP 1876	Potters Field
010974	LEHMANN, John Theo.	23y	W	D.C.	14 MAR 1877	St. Mary's
015818	LEIBKERT, Ernest C.G.	4m	W	D.C.	23 MAY 1878	Prospect Hill
000273	LEIBRANDT, Ella	17y	C	Va.	21 AUG 1874	Beckett's
016981	LEICHT, Margaret V.	9m	W	D.C.	09 AUG 1878	Glenwood
002505	LEINS, Bertram	54y	W	Ger.	10 MAR 1875	Mt. Olivet
015668	LEINTZ, Mary E.	1y	W	D.C.	09 MAY 1878	Oak Hill
016103	LEIPOLD, Carl Shuman	3m	W	D.C.	10 JUN 1878	Rock Creek
009910	LEISHEAR, Edward M.	10m	W	D.C.	09 DEC 1876	Oak Hill
020615	LEISHEAR, Elizabeth	79y	W	Md.	25 JUN 1879	Presbyterian
017059	LEISHEAR, Francis	18y	W	D.C.	15 AUG 1878	Holy Rood
004277	LEISHEAR, Mary E.	17y	W	D.C.	24 JUL 1875	Oak Hill
003202	LEISHEAR, Mildred V.	12y	W	D.C.	03 MAY 1875	Oak Hill
011301	LEITENBERGER, Mary	13d	W	D.C.	11 APR 1877	Graceland
011172	LEJ, John	35y	W	Ger.	31 MAR 1877	Washington Asylum
009214	LEMAR, Josephine	20y	C	Ga.	27 SEP 1876	Potters Field
008754	LEMEA, Elizabeth	6m	W	Va.	20 AUG 1876	Mt. Olivet
009447	LEMMON, Hanah	19y	C	D.C.	17 OCT 1876	Mt. Zion
002129	LEMMON, John C.	28y	W	N.Y.	12 FEB 1875	Buffalo, N.Y.
006068	LEMMON, Lettie, Mrs.	48y	M	S.C.	19 JAN 1876	Mt. Zion
010157	LEMMONS, Isaiah	44y	C	D.C.	03 JAN 1877	Mt. Zion
002056	LEMMONS, Sarah	2m	C	D.C.	06 FEB 1875	Young Mens
007469	LEMON, Infant of Jennie	3m	C	D.C.	02 JUN 1876	Ebenezer
014408	LEMON, Jane	78y	W	Scot.	13 JAN 1878	Mt. Olivet
011266	LEMON, Moses	6m	C	D.C.	08 APR 1877	Mt. Zion
018936	LEMONS, John Henry	6m	C	D.C.	03 FEB 1879	Potters Field

No.	Name	Age	Race	Birth	Death Date	Burial Place
010028	LEMORE, Robert, Sr.	80y	C	Va.	20 DEC 1876	Harmony
017131	LEMOS, Austin	1y	C	D.C.	21 AUG 1878	Harmony
011872	LENDER, Jules C.	51y	W	France	12 JUN 1877	Congressional
005195	LENMAN, Charles	53y	W	D.C.	27 SEP 1875	Graceland
004496	LENMAN, Mary B.	10d	W	D.C.	07 AUG 1875	Prospect Hill
014162	LENNONS, Joseph	25y	C	D.C.	21 DEC 1877	Beckett's
018827	LENNOX, Robert W.	40y	W	Ohio	26 JAN 1879	Columbus, Ohio
002382	LENOIR, Walker T.	4m	W	D.C.	02 MAR 1875	Glenwood
014309	LENOX, Charles Alexander	8d	C	D.C.	03 JAN 1878	Baptist
010337	LENOX, Fred H.	1y	C	D.C.	19 JAN 1877	Potters Field
010203	LENOX, Wm. A.	4y	C	D.C.	07 JAN 1877	Baptist
009780	LENTZ, Mary Christine Koehnlein	20y	W	N.Y.	23 NOV 1876	Prospect Hill
014798	LENZ, Wilhelmina M.	1y	W	D.C.	17 FEB 1878	Prospect Hill
005876	LEONARD, Agnes Violetta	4w	W	D.C.	27 DEC 1875	Mt. Olivet
019007	LEONARD, Catheirne	66y	W	Ire.	09 FEB 1879	Mt. Olivet
013306	LEONARD, Cornelius	c.70y	W	Ire.	25 SEP 1877	Mt. Olivet
010877	LEONARD, Elizabeth	95y	W	Pa.	06 MAR 1877	Holy Rood
015910	LEONARD, Joseph	7m	W	D.C.	30 MAY 1878	Newark, N.J.
009887	LEONARD, Mary	3y	W	D.C.	06 DEC 1876	Newark, N.J.
018487	LEOPARD, Martin	86y	W	Ger.	28 DEC 1878	Potters Field
007884	LEPLEY, Infant of M.G.	6h	W	D.C.	27 JUN 1876	Mt. Olivet
011292	LERCH, Ora N.	6y	W	Va.	10 APR 1877	Congressional
018538	LESCH, Bartholomew	4y	W	D.C.	01 JAN 1879	St. Mary's
007291	LESH, Margaret B.	10y	W	Pa.	13 MAY 1876	Newport, Pa.
018653	LESLER, Hannah	1y	C	D.C.	12 JAN 1879	Beckett's
003332	LESLIE, Nellie	23y	W	N.C.	15 MAY 1875	Congressional
006882	LESSON, E.G.	+47y	W	Pol.	01 APR 1876	Hospital
006788	LESTER, May	4m	C	D.C.	23 MAR 1876	Ebenezer
001463	LESTER, William	4m	C	D.C.	23 DEC 1874	Beckett's
002799	LETCHER, Lilly Ann	14m	C	D.C.	30 MAR 1875	Mt. Zion
008454	LETCHER, Lue Francis I.B.	11m	C	D.C.	28 JUL 1876	Mt. Zion
004480	LEUTNER, Annie	1y	W	D.C.	06 AUG 1875	Congressional
013545	LEVALLEY, Charles	43y	W	U.S.	17 OCT 1877	Hospital
007066	LEVI, Edward	6w	C	D.C.	21 APR 1876	Potters Field
007216	LEVI, Infant of Jacob	10d	W	D.C.	05 MAY 1876	Jewish
009772	LEVI, Mary	66y	C	Md.	22 NOV 1876	Potters Field
013327	LEVIN, Infant of Annie	9d	C	D.C.	27 SEP 1877	Potters Field
007217	LEVY, Martha	c.50y	C	Va.	05 MAY 1876	Mt. Zion
008854	LEWEL, Sophia	75y	C	Md.	28 AUG 1876	Young Mens
014800	LEWIS, Ada	11y	W	Va.	17 FEB 1878	Graceland
011630	LEWIS, Albert	28y	C	Va.	17 MAY 1877	Mt. Olivet
014902	LEWIS, Andrew	40y	C	Va.	28 FEB 1878	Potters Field
003715	LEWIS, Andrew	60y	C	Va.	19 JUN 1875	Beckett's
014801	LEWIS, Anna F., Mrs.	41y	W	Va.	17 FEB 1878	Congressional
004628	LEWIS, Annie	4y	C	D.C.	16 AUG 1875	Young Mens
015480	LEWIS, Annie May	2y	W	D.C.	22 APR 1878	Oak Hill
000753	LEWIS, Annie, Mrs.	43y	W	Va.	08 OCT 1874	Congressional
005651	LEWIS, Anthony	1m	C	D.C.	04 DEC 1875	Ebenezer
019623	LEWIS, Arthur	35y	C	Va.	01 APR 1879	Potters Field
011151	LEWIS, Asa	53y	W	N.Y.	29 MAR 1877	Soldier's Home
013820	LEWIS, Bettie	22y	C	Va.	14 NOV 1877	Beckett's
012288	LEWIS, Birty	9m	C	D.C.	09 JUL 1877	Ebenezer
019401	LEWIS, Caroline	45y	C	Va.	14 MAR 1879	Potters Field
002286	LEWIS, Caroline E.	65y	C	Va.	23 FEB 1875	Harmony
005092	LEWIS, Carry	1y	C	D.C.	18 SEP 1875	Mt. Pleasant
003627	LEWIS, Catharine	84y	W	Ire.	13 JUN 1875	Glenwood

District of Columbia Death Records, August 1, 1874 to July 31, 1879

No.	Name	Age	Race	Birth	Death Date	Burial Place
020681	LEWIS, Charles	25y	C	Va.	30 JUN 1879	Young Mens
014077	LEWIS, Charles	5m	C	D.C.	12 DEC 1877	Potters Field
005032	LEWIS, Charles Sumner	1m	M	D.C.	13 SEP 1875	Young Mens
016557	LEWIS, Chas. Henry	1y	C	D.C.	11 JUL 1878	Mt. Pleasant
014096	LEWIS, Clara Eva	6y	W	Va.	14 DEC 1877	Norfolk, Va.
008221	LEWIS, Clinton	1y	W	D.C.	12 JUL 1876	Alexandria, Va.
020638	LEWIS, Coleman	9d	C	D.C.	27 JUN 1879	Potters Field
001430	LEWIS, Daniel	53y	C	Va.	18 DEC 1874	Young Mens
000108	LEWIS, Daniel	8m	C	D.C.	08 AUG 1874	Young Mens
020455	LEWIS, Eddie	4m	C	D.C.	15 JUN 1879	Young Mens
004101	LEWIS, Edward	8d	C	D.C.	12 JUL 1875	Beckett's
011445	LEWIS, Eliza	84y	C	Md.	28 APR 1877	Baltimore, Md.
004893	LEWIS, Eliza	5y	C	D.C.	03 SEP 1875	Potters Field
010738	LEWIS, Eliza, Mrs.	50y	W	Va.	22 FEB 1877	Congressional
007310	LEWIS, Elizabeth	53y	W	Ky.	15 MAY 1876	Graceland
007332	LEWIS, Elizabeth	2m	C	D.C.	18 MAY 1876	Ebenezer
002975	LEWIS, Elizabeth Della	11m	C	D.C.	13 APR 1875	Baptist
012410	LEWIS, Fanny	27y	C	Md.	18 JUL 1877	Potters Field
005271	LEWIS, Francis	8d	C	D.C.	26 OCT 1875	Ebenezer
003591	LEWIS, Francis B.	18y	C	D.C.	10 JUN 1875	Harmony
017069	LEWIS, Geo. Henry	2y	W	D.C.	16 AUG 1878	Rock Creek
016996	LEWIS, George	1d	C	D.C.	10 AUG 1878	Potters Field
005407	LEWIS, George	1m	C	D.C.	09 NOV 1875	Beckett's
007726	LEWIS, George Thomas	41y	W	D.C.	19 JUN 1876	Oak Hill
013283	LEWIS, Harriet	35y	C	Md.	23 SEP 1877	Beckett's
017599	LEWIS, Henrietta	19y	C	Md.	02 OCT 1878	Macedonia
018995	LEWIS, Henry	50y	C	Va.	08 FEB 1879	Potters Field
004100	LEWIS, Henry	5y	C	D.C.	12 JUL 1875	Ebenezer
018525	LEWIS, Henry	60y	C	Va.	31 DEC 1878	Graceland
000406	LEWIS, Ida	1y	C	D.C.	02 SEP 1874	Young Mens
014799	LEWIS, Infant of C.F.	9h	W	D.C.	17 FEB 1878	Congressional
003331	LEWIS, Infant of E.M. & E.R.	1h	W	D.C.	15 MAY 1875	Congressional
010040	LEWIS, Infant of Henry	2d	C	D.C.	21 DEC 1876	Potters Field
007823	LEWIS, Infant of Margaret	12h	C	D.C.	24 JUN 1876	Potters Field
001161	LEWIS, Infant of Randolph	7d	C	D.C.	16 NOV 1874	Mt. Zion
017398	LEWIS, Infant of Simon	8d	C	D.C.	13 SEP 1878	Mt. Pleasant
009958	LEWIS, Infant of Thomas	2d	C	D.C.	14 DEC 1876	Young Mens
019718	LEWIS, James	23y	C	Va.	10 APR 1879	Graceland
004980	LEWIS, James	27y	C	Va.	10 SEP 1875	Ebenezer
010925	LEWIS, James A.	1y	C	D.C.	09 MAR 1877	Harmony
020927	LEWIS, James Aubern	8m	W	D.C.	14 JUL 1879	Congressional
001406	LEWIS, James Edmond	2m	C	D.C.	16 DEC 1874	Beckett's
003406	LEWIS, James Henry	1y	W	D.C.	23 MAY 1875	Congressional
014957	LEWIS, James Wheeler	2m	M	D.C.	05 MAR 1878	Potters Field
017906	LEWIS, Jerome	5d	C	D.C.	30 OCT 1878	Beckett's
016817	LEWIS, Jno. R.	28y	W	Md.	29 JUL 1878	Oak Hill
011994	LEWIS, John	11m	C	D.C.	21 JUN 1877	Ebenezer
016091	LEWIS, John	3m	C	D.C.	09 JUN 1878	Payne's
020887	LEWIS, John	1y	C	D.C.	11 JUL 1879	Payne's
010714	LEWIS, John F.	1m	W	D.C.	20 FEB 1877	Congressional
004715	LEWIS, John H.	2y	C	D.C.	22 AUG 1875	Mt. Zion
004528	LEWIS, John H.	1y	C	Va.	10 AUG 1875	Ebenezer
015349	LEWIS, John S.	18y	C	Va.	10 APR 1878	Potters Field
007109	LEWIS, Joseph	5m	M	D.C.	25 APR 1876	Mt. Zion
006836	LEWIS, Joseph	27y	C	La.	27 MAR 1876	Ebenezer
005723	LEWIS, Joseph	2m	W	D.C.	11 DEC 1875	Oak Hill

District of Columbia Death Records, August 1, 1874 to July 31, 1879

No.	Name	Age	Race	Birth	Death Date	Burial Place
009537	LEWIS, Joseph	1y	C	D.C.	26 OCT 1876	Beckett's
012390	LEWIS, Joseph	4m	C	D.C.	16 JUL 1877	Potters Field
019883	LEWIS, Joseph	1y	C	D.C.	24 APR 1879	Mt. Pleasant
013563	LEWIS, Joseph C.	71y	W	Ohio	19 OCT 1877	Congressional
006722	LEWIS, Joseph S.	4m	C	D.C.	18 MAR 1876	Young Mens
009871	LEWIS, Josephine	22y	C	Md.	05 DEC 1876	Harmony
019872	LEWIS, Joshua	1y	C	D.C.	23 APR 1879	Good Hope
010518	LEWIS, Julia Douglass	10m	W	D.C.	04 FEB 1877	Rock Creek
005111	LEWIS, Laura Jane	31y	W	D.C.	20 SEP 1875	Presbyterian
006670	LEWIS, Lawrence	56y	W	Va.	14 MAR 1876	Glenwood
015677	LEWIS, Lilly	3y	C	D.C.	10 MAY 1878	Mt. Pleasant
018043	LEWIS, Lucinda	110y	C	Va.	13 NOV 1878	Arlington, Va.
004815	LEWIS, Lucy	1y	C	D.C.	29 AUG 1875	Mt. Zion
015972	LEWIS, Lucy Ann	5m	C	D.C.	02 JUN 1878	Potters Field
013415	LEWIS, Maggie	1m	C	D.C.	06 OCT 1877	Moore's
003364	LEWIS, Mamia	10h	W	D.C.	19 MAY 1875	Alexandria, Va.
000433	LEWIS, Maria	17y	C	D.C.	05 SEP 1874	Nonesuch Farm
018382	LEWIS, Martha	48y	W	D.C.	19 DEC 1878	Glenwood
006835	LEWIS, Mary	23y	C	Va.	27 MAR 1876	Young Mens
015505	LEWIS, Mary	38y	W	Pol.	24 APR 1878	Washington Hebrew
021040	LEWIS, Mary	8m	C	D.C.	21 JUL 1879	Mt. Pleasant
004446	LEWIS, Mary	27y	C	Va.	04 AUG 1875	Harmony
007567	LEWIS, Mary A.	2y	C	D.C.	09 JUN 1876	Graceland
017406	LEWIS, Mary Cecelia	6d	W	D.C.	14 SEP 1878	Mt. Olivet
011975	LEWIS, Mary Elizabeth	2m	C	D.C.	20 JUN 1877	Ebenezer
003712	LEWIS, Mary Eulalia	3y	M	D.C.	19 JUN 1875	Mt. Olivet
016506	LEWIS, Mary M.	75y	W	Va.	08 JUL 1878	Congressional
006708	LEWIS, Melinda	30y	C	D.C.	17 MAR 1876	Family Ground
016849	LEWIS, Minnie	1y	C	D.C.	31 JUL 1878	Young Mens
011787	LEWIS, Nancy	5d	C	D.C.	03 JUN 1877	Potters Field
018884	LEWIS, Nora	4y	W	D.C.	30 JAN 1879	Mt. Olivet
016816	LEWIS, Nora	23y	C	Va.	29 JUL 1878	Potters Field
010237	LEWIS, Rachel E.	38y	C	D.C.	09 JAN 1877	Mt. Zion
019699	LEWIS, Rebertie	8m	C	D.C.	08 APR 1879	Mt. Olivet
008020	LEWIS, Richard	26y	C	Va.	04 JUL 1876	Young Mens
015301	LEWIS, Robert	39y	C	Va.	06 APR 1878	Alexandria, Va.
017350	LEWIS, Robt.	1y	C	D.C.	08 SEP 1878	Potters Field
008890	LEWIS, Robt.	3y	C	D.C.	31 AUG 1876	Beckett's
005871	LEWIS, Rosa	16y	C	Va.	26 DEC 1875	Mt. Pleasant
013138	LEWIS, Rose	61y	C	Va.	09 SEP 1877	Beckett's
011403	LEWIS, Rosetta	6m	C	D.C.	23 APR 1877	Ebenezer
017777	LEWIS, Samuel	28y	C	D.C.	17 OCT 1878	Potters Field
003382	LEWIS, Samuel	11m	C	D.C.	20 MAY 1875	Young Mens
018515	LEWIS, Sarah	c.50y	W	Ohio	30 DEC 1878	Congressional
003328	LEWIS, Sarah	19y	C	Va.	14 MAY 1875	Potters Field
005621	LEWIS, Stacy B.	60y	W	Mass.	01 DEC 1875	Oak Hill
009688	LEWIS, Susan E.	23y	C	Va.	13 NOV 1876	Harmony
011502	LEWIS, Theodore	4m	C	D.C.	04 MAY 1877	Young Mens
001520	LEWIS, Thomas	69y	C	Md.	28 DEC 1874	Potters Field
019624	LEWIS, Thurston	c.24y	C	Va.	01 APR 1879	Payne's
013516	LEWIS, Walter	2m	W	D.C.	14 OCT 1877	Congressional
015724	LEWIS, William	4m	W	D.C.	14 MAY 1878	Oak Hill
016176	LEWIS, William	2m	C	D.C.	15 JUN 1878	Potters Field
017848	LEWIS, Wm.	11m	C	D.C.	24 OCT 1878	Mt. Pleasant
011374	LEWIS, Wm. H.	12m	W	D.C.	19 APR 1877	Congressional
004113	LEWIS, Wm. Henry	2m	C	D.C.	13 JUL 1875	Mt. Pleasant

No.	Name	Age	Race	Birth	Death Date	Burial Place
000524	LEYHEADY, Martin	25y	W	Ire.	15 SEP 1874	Mt. Olivet
011373	LIBBEY, Clara	2d	W	D.C.	19 APR 1877	Oak Hill
000265	LIBBEY, Joseph	5y	W	D.C.	21 AUG 1874	Oak Hill
001405	LIBBY, Charles	14m	W	N.Y.	16 DEC 1874	Mt. Olivet
003056	LIBBY, James Smith	22y	W	N.Y.	20 APR 1875	Mt. Olivet
008528	LIBBY, Mary Rebecca	47y	W	D.C.	02 AUG 1876	Oak Hill
018268	LIBRON, Olmsted	50y	C	Va.	07 DEC 1878	Potters Field
016570	LICTURE, Alice	11m	W	D.C.	12 JUL 1878	Mt. Olivet
017094	LIEGNEL, Emila	15d	W	D.C.	18 AUG 1878	Mt. Olivet
000153	LIGGANS, Martha	85y	C	Va.	11 AUG 1874	Young Mens
010467	LIGGINS, Benjamin	85y	C	Va.	01 FEB 1877	Potters Field
003079	LIGHTER, Annie E.	16y	W	D.C.	21 APR 1875	Methodist
016556	LIGHTFOOT, Beckey	9m	C	D.C.	11 JUL 1878	Mt. Pleasant
016292	LIGHTFOOT, Daniel	68y	W	Va.	24 JUN 1878	Oak Hill
017739	LIGHTFOOT, Daniel M.	40y	W	D.C.	14 OCT 1878	Holy Rood
002186	LIGHTFOOT, John	1m	C	D.C.	15 FEB 1875	Mt. Pleasant
016876	LIGHTFOOT, Wm. J.	32y	W	Va.	02 AUG 1878	Leesburg, Va.
014021	LILES, Henry	64y	C	Md.	06 DEC 1877	Alexandria, Va.
004562	LILFILLIN, Archibald	44y	W	N.Y.	12 AUG 1875	Potters Field
006854	LILLIAN, Emma	1y	W	D.C.	29 MAR 1876	Mt. Olivet
002780	LILLY, Louisa	9m	W	D.C.	29 MAR 1875	Prospect Hill
017310	LIMERICK, William	15m	W	D.C.	03 SEP 1878	Glenwood
017262	LIMIRICK, Annie R.	3y	W	D.C.	30 AUG 1878	Glenwood
016481	LIMMERMACHER, Catharina	68y	W	Ger.	06 JUL 1878	Prospect Hill
013245	LIMTUCCI, Isabella	14y	W	D.C.	18 SEP 1877	Mt. Olivet
017374	LINCOLN, Augustin H.	43y	W	N.Y.	11 SEP 1878	Oak Hill
012090	LINCOLN, Charlott	5m	C	D.C.	27 JUN 1877	Young Mens
001363	LINCOLN, Richard F.	33y	W	Me.	11 DEC 1874	Congressional
018310	LINDENKOHL, Ludwig	2y	W	D.C.	11 DEC 1878	Glenwood
018841	LINDERMAN, Henry Richard	53y	W	Md.	27 JAN 1879	Bethlehem, Pa.
000761	LINDSAY, Anna	20y	M	Va.	09 OCT 1874	Mt. Zion
005230a	LINDSAY, Christianna	55y	C	Md.	21 OCT 1875	Potters Field
013467	LINDSAY, Infant of Warner	1d	C	D.C.	10 OCT 1877	Beckett's
010765	LINDSEY, James	10y	C	Va.	24 FEB 1877	Ebenezer
015148	LINDSEY, Margaret	70y	W	Ire.	22 MAR 1878	Convent
000390	LINDSEY, Nellie	14d	C	D.C.	31 AUG 1874	Beckett's
013888	LINDSEY, Olive	3y	W	N.Y	22 NOV 1877	Brooklyn, N.Y.
015027	LINDSLEY, Charles	6m	C	D.C.	11 MAR 1878	Beckett's
016053	LINGENBAUGH, Lewis	8m	W	D.C.	07 JUN 1878	Mt. Olivet
014574	LINGER, Maria	52y	W	Ger.	27 JAN 1878	Glenwood
014381	LINGFIELD, Thomas C.	12m	W	D.C.	10 JAN 1878	Fairfax Co., Va.
006850	LINGHAM, Alice M.	80y	M	Ga.	28 MAR 1876	Young Mens
010357	LINK, Frederick	28y	W	Ger.	21 JAN 1877	Potters Field
007697	LINKINS, James H.	7w	W	D.C.	17 JUN 1876	Holy Rood
004612	LINKINS, Mary Elizabeth	22y	W	D.C.	15 AUG 1875	Congressional
007321	LINKINS, Mary J.	38y	W	Ire.	16 MAY 1876	Holy Rood
017864	LINKINS, Nelie	7y	W	D.C.	26 OCT 1878	Holy Rood
009994	LINSAY, Flora	23y	C	S.C.	18 DEC 1876	Columbia, S.C.
013777	LINSLEY, Catharine	70y	C	Md.	09 NOV 1877	Potters Field
011187	LINSY, William	2y	C	D.C.	01 APR 1877	Ebenezer
014350	LINTZ, Samuel	40y	W	Ger.	07 JAN 1878	Washington Hebrew
001684	LIPPETT, James F.	9y	W	D.C.	10 JAN 1875	Congressional
013038	LIPPHARD, Alma	22y	W	Eng.	31 AUG 1877	Congressional
005296	LIPPHARD, Matilda	10d	W	D.C.	28 OCT 1875	Congressional
012202	LIPPOLD, Lena M.	3m	W	D.C.	03 JUL 1877	Glenwood
003636	LIPSCOMB, Bertha Elinor	16d	W	D.C.	14 JUN 1875	Oak Hill

District of Columbia Death Records, August 1, 1874 to July 31, 1879

No.	Name	Age	Race	Birth	Death Date	Burial Place
018925	LIPSCOMB, Jesse O.	5y	W	D.C.	02 FEB 1879	Oak Hill
013183	LIPSCOMB, Laura E.	22y	W	D.C.	13 SEP 1877	Congressional
012461	LISH, John L.	3m	W	D.C.	22 JUL 1877	St. Mary's
013436	LISHEAR, Infant of Wm.	2h	W	D.C.	08 OCT 1877	Oak Hill
005892	LISLES, Loyd H.	1y	C	D.C.	29 DEC 1875	Holy Rood
008067	LISTON, Mary	4m	W	D.C.	08 JUL 1876	Mt. Olivet
005875	LITCHFIELD, H.T.	66y	W	N.Y.	27 DEC 1875	Congressional
002564	LITCHFIELD, William E.	34y	W	N.Y.	14 MAR 1875	Congressional
000616	LITHEBETH, Magry H.	2y	C	D.C.	23 SEP 1874	Beckett's
004010	LITLOW, Ophelia Camilla	44y	W	Md.	05 JUL 1875	Middletown, Md.
017117	LITSINGER, Thomas Edgar	3y	W	D.C.	20 AUG 1878	Congressional
016834	LITTLE, Clara May	3y	W	D.C.	30 JUL 1878	Congressional
007015	LITTLE, Edward A.	35y	W	Me.	14 APR 1876	Auburn, Me.
016793	LITTLE, Edward H.	15m	W	D.C.	27 JUL 1878	Congressional
008466	LITTLE, Isaac	77y	W	Eng	29 JUL 1876	Brooklyn, N.Y.
008888	LITTLE, John	71y	W	D.C.	30 AUG 1876	Congressional
003922	LITTLE, John O.	32y	W	D.C.	29 JUN 1875	Congressional
010412	LITTLE, Maggie Belle	3y	W	Me.	26 JAN 1877	Congressional
008079	LITTLE, Martha	21y	C	Md.	08 JUL 1876	Potters Field
017450	LITTLE, Wm.	63y	W	Pa.	18 SEP 1878	Potters Field
012073	LITTLETON, Blanche	6m	W	D.C.	26 JUN 1877	Glenwood
008233	LITTLETON, Fredrick	1y	W	D.C.	13 JUL 1876	Glenwood
005575	LITTLETON, George	26y	W	D.C.	26 NOV 1875	Glenwood/Rock Creek
017185	LITTLETON, Laura V.	37y	W	Va.	25 AUG 1878	Glenwood
006158	LITTLETON, William	2m	W	D.C.	27 JAN 1876	Glenwood
000034	LIVELY, Annie Liza	35y	C	D.C.	02 AUG 1874	Harmony
019536	LIVELY, Charles	35y	C	Va.	24 MAR 1879	Harmony
020998	LIVELY, Sarah	7y	C	D.C.	18 JUL 1879	Harmony
010130	LIVERPOOL, Marie	3y	C	D.C.	31 DEC 1876	Harmony
007725	LIVINGSTON, Worthington	21d	W	D.C.	19 JUN 1876	Baltimore, Md.
015042	LLOYD, Caroline	26y	W	D.C.	12 MAR 1878	Mt. Olivet
005861	LLOYD, Charles Sumner	18m	C	D.C.	25 DEC 1875	Harmony
019131	LLOYD, Henry Clifton	4y	W	D.C.	20 FEB 1879	Mt. Olivet
012997	LLOYD, John H.	3m	W	D.C.	28 AUG 1877	Congressional
005975	LLOYD, Richard	1m	M	D.C.	08 JAN 1876	Harmony
003769	LLOYD, Thomas E.	46y	W	D.C.	22 JUN 1875	Oak Hill
004062	LOBDELL, Daniel G.	c.67y	W	N.Y.	09 JUL 1875	Albany, N.Y.
014460	LOCHREY, Sarah Jane	54y	W	D.C.	17 JAN 1878	Mt. Olivet
008387	LOCHTE, Henry	9m	W	D.C.	22 JUL 1876	Mt. Olivet
020180	LOCKE, Nettie	1y	W	D.C.	23 MAY 1879	Congressional
010226	LOCKE, Richard	3m	W	D.C.	08 JAN 1877	Methodist
000885	LOCKE, William Q.	33y	W	Md.	21 OCT 1874	Mt. Olivet
000184	LOCKEY, Joshua	7m	W	D.C.	14 AUG 1874	Congressional
000555	LOCKEY, Martha B.	28y	W	N.Y.	18 SEP 1874	Congressional
007645	LOCKLEY, Annie	63y	C	Md.	14 JUN 1876	Potters Field
015754	LOCKWOOD, Adelaide Elizabeth	1m	W	D.C.	17 MAY 1878	St. Mary's
011420	LOCKWOOD, Ezekiel	74y	W	N.Y.	25 APR 1877	Congressional
017983	LOCKWOOD, Lilly	6m	C	D.C.	08 NOV 1878	Moore's
006964	LOCLAGER, John	79y	W	Switz.	07 APR 1876	Prospect Hill
007155	LOECRAFT, B.F.	32y	W	N.Y.	29 APR 1876	Mt. Olivet
002339	LOEFFLER, Laura E.	1y	W	D.C.	27 FEB 1875	Prospect Hill
018972	LOEFFLER, Maud	3y	W	D.C.	06 FEB 1879	Prospect Hill
006284	LOEHBILLER, Charles	44y	W	Ger.	09 FEB 1876	St. Mary's
004000	LOEW, Oscar Fredrick	11d	W	D.C.	04 JUL 1875	Prospect Hill
011909	LOFF, John	6m	W	D.C.	15 JUN 1877	Mt. Olivet
020342	LOGAN, Anna Eliza	8m	C	D.C.	08 JUN 1879	Beckett's

District of Columbia Death Records, August 1, 1874 to July 31, 1879   211

No.	Name	Age	Race	Birth	Death Date	Burial Place
012156	LOGAN, Ellen	30y	C	D.C.	01 JUL 1877	Mt. Zion
008077	LOGAN, Janett	60y	C	Md.	08 JUL 1876	Mt. Olivet
002969	LOGAN, John	35y	M	Va.	12 APR 1875	Ebenezer
020928	LOGAN, Mamie	5m	W	D.C.	14 JUL 1879	Glenwood
014674	LOGAN, Margret	21y	C	D.C.	05 FEB 1878	Mt. Olivet
019537	LOGAN, Mary Catherine	43y	W	Md.	24 MAR 1879	Glenwood
015597	LOGAN, Mary M.	49y	C	Md.	03 MAY 1878	Mt. Olivet
010940	LOHL, Esther Otlea	1y	W	D.C.	11 MAR 1877	Presbyterian
020341	LOLLA, Clara	1m	C	D.C.	08 JUN 1879	Payne's
015598	LOLLER, Jenny	7m	C	D.C.	03 MAY 1878	Payne's
010709	LOMAS, Wilhelmina M.	71y	W	Ger.	20 FEB 1877	Congressional
000255	LOMAX, Anna	9m	C	D.C.	20 AUG 1874	Beckett's
019476	LOMAX, Arthur	1y	M	D.C.	20 MAR 1879	Mt. Pleasant
000641f	LOMAX, Charles	25y	C	--	26 SEP 1874	Mt. Pleasant
017492	LOMAX, Infant of Alice	14d	C	D.C.	22 SEP 1878	Potters Field
005312	LOMAX, Infant of Daniel	21d	C	D.C.	30 OCT 1875	Ebenezer
000558	LOMAX, Joshua	60y	C	Va.	18 SEP 1874	Young Mens
001270	LOMAX, Margretta Rose	13m	W	D.C.	29 NOV 1874	Congressional
002408	LOMAX, Mary	7m	C	D.C.	03 MAR 1875	Mt. Pleasant
017204	LOMAX, Mary	2y	M	D.C.	26 AUG 1878	Mt. Pleasant
011145	LOMAX, Milly	c.90y	C	Va.	29 MAR 1877	Harmony
017665	LOMAX, Napoleon Stark	7m	C	D.C.	07 OCT 1878	Mt. Pleasant
010648	LOMAX, Rosa	6m	C	D.C.	15 FEB 1877	Mt. Pleasant Plain
014730	LOMAX, Sally	90y	C	Va.	09 FEB 1878	Harmony
008827	LOMAX, William	14m	C	D.C.	26 AUG 1876	Ebenezer
016900	LOMAX, William	1y	C	D.C.	04 AUG 1878	Beckett's
020698	LOMAX, William	5y	C	D.C.	01 JUL 1879	Beckett's
019916	LOMBARDI, Charles Godfrey	33y	W	D.C.	27 APR 1879	Congressional
006721	LONE, Jeanette	1y	C	D.C.	18 MAR 1876	Ebenezer
014521	LONG, Andrew K.	36y	W	Pa.	22 JAN 1878	Oak Hill
016149	LONG, Catherine	2y	W	D.C.	13 JUN 1878	Prospect Hill
000713	LONG, Daniel	47y	W	Ire.	04 OCT 1874	Mt. Olivet
004009	LONG, Dennis	5d	W	D.C.	05 JUL 1875	Mt. Olivet
008086	LONG, Elizabeth	85y	W	D.C.	08 JUL 1876	Congressional
015574	LONG, Eugene L.	28y	W	Md.	01 MAY 1878	Holy Rood
003954	LONG, Frances Cora	5y	W	D.C.	01 JUL 1875	Glenwood
018153	LONG, Harry	8y	W	D.C.	25 NOV 1878	Congressional
012835	LONG, Johanna	9y	W	D.C.	14 AUG 1877	Mt. Olivet
012823	LONG, Michael	35y	W	Ire.	15 AUG 1877	Mt. Olivet
019210	LONG, Nora	62y	W	Ire.	26 FEB 1879	Holy Rood
014977	LONG, Sarer M.	43y	W	Pa.	07 MAR 1878	Rock Creek
017130	LONGDON, Mary Wheelock	2m	W	D.C.	21 AUG 1878	Rock Creek
018097	LONGHEAD, Jos. P.	55y	W	Pa.	19 NOV 1878	Philadelphia, Pa.
015777	LONGSON, Emily Agnes	53y	W	D.C.	20 MAY 1878	Holy Rood
007696	LONGSTREET, James A.	6m	W	D.C.	17 JUN 1876	Mt. Olivet
018633	LONGWILL, William	50y	W	Scot.	10 JAN 1879	Soldier's Home
009980	LONN, Esther Rebecke	3y	W	D.C.	16 DEC 1876	Congressional
009959	LONYERS, Infant of George	4d	C	D.C.	14 DEC 1876	Jones Chapel
004016	LOONEY, John	4h	W	D.C.	06 JUL 1875	Mt. Olivet
014829	LOONEY, William	15m	W	D.C.	20 FEB 1878	Mt. Olivet
001915	LORAIN, William J.	4y	W	N.Y.	27 JAN 1875	West Point, N.Y.
001066	LORCH, Herman Gotta	64y	W	Ger.	06 NOV 1874	Jewish
017159	LORD, Ida	6y	W	D.C.	23 AUG 1878	Congressional
013201	LORD, Julia Hoover	18y	W	D.C.	14 SEP 1877	Glenwood
002783	LORENZO, Cherubine Felix	6d	W	D.C.	29 MAR 1875	Mt. Olivet
007387	LORICK, Julia	37y	W	Md.	23 MAY 1876	Mt. Olivet

No.	Name	Age	Race	Birth	Death Date	Burial Place
016421	LORNE, John Henry	22h	W	D.C.	03 JUL 1878	Glenwood
003212	LOTON, Christina	2y	C	D.C.	04 MAY 1875	Young Mens
010017	LOTTA, Sister Mary	32y	W	France	19 DEC 1876	Mt. Olivet
016457	LOTTER, Marion	7m	W	Ill.	05 JUL 1878	St. Mary's
019809	LOUDEN, Annette	2y	C	D.C.	17 APR 1879	Mt. Pleasant
002430	LOUDON, Barbara	c.75y	C	Md.	05 MAR 1875	Mt. Olivet
008000	LOUDON, Chrisianna	17y	C	Md.	04 JUL 1876	Harmony
001719	LOUGHBOROUGH, Anna R.	60y	W	Va.	13 JAN 1876	Holy Rood
000960	LOUGHLIN, Willie	2y	W	D.C.	28 OCT 1874	Mt. Olivet
006285	LOUGRES, Mary	16d	C	D.C.	09 FEB 1876	Payne's
005279	LOUIS, Charles Henry	9m	C	D.C.	27 OCT 1875	Young Mens
020040	LOUIS, Infant of Henryetta	2d	C	D.C.	08 MAY 1879	Moore's
016997	LOUIS, Sophia	70y	C	Va.	10 AUG 1878	Harmony
006548	LOUNDES, Charles	86y	C	Md.	04 MAR 1876	Potters Field
016571	LOUNDES, Samuel	22y	C	Md.	12 JUL 1878	Potters Field
010724	LOUXMAN Willie	1y	W	D.C.	21 FEB 1877	Congressional
007375	LOVE, Ann	68y	W	Ire.	22 MAY 1876	Mt. Olivet
000638	LOVE, Emma L.	27y	W	N.J.	25 SEP 1874	Glenwood
008432	LOVE, Ida C.	5y	W	W.Va.	26 JUL 1876	Leesburg, Va.
014665	LOVE, Luther K., Dr.	69y	W	Md.	04 FEB 1878	Glenwood
018237	LOVE, Mary	9y	W	D.C.	04 DEC 1878	Congressional
005427	LOVE, Mildred E.	3m	W	Va.	11 NOV 1875	Woodbridge, Va.
018707	LOVEJOY, John Singleton	48y	W	D.C.	17 JAN 1879	Mt. Olivet
010064	LOVELACE, Harriet	70y	C	Md.	25 DEC 1876	Mt. Olivet
001848	LOVELACE, Mary, Mrs.	85y	W	Conn.	23 JAN 1875	Richmond, Mass.
010110	LOVELESS, James	39y	C	Va.	29 DEC 1876	Potters Field
004678	LOVELL, Joseph	79y	W	N.Y.	20 AUG 1875	Oak Hill
010495	LOVEN, Mary Ann	7m	C	D.C.	03 FEB 1877	Mt. Olivet
014855	LOVING, Infant of Martha	1h	C	D.C.	23 FEB 1878	Harmony
012289	LOVING, Samuel	2½d	C	D.C.	10 JUL 1877	Harmony
003599	LOW, Hannah	30y	W	Ire.	11 JUN 1875	Mt. Olivet
017493	LOWBER, Ellen A.	53y	W	Can.	22 SEP 1878	Glenwood
002473	LOWE, Bertha J.	9m	W	D.C.	08 MAR 1875	Glenwood
007883	LOWE, Catherine	4m	C	D.C.	27 JUN 1876	Mt. Zion
007500	LOWE, Catherine B.	3m	W	D.C.	04 JUN 1876	Holy Rood
012679	LOWE, Edward	67y	W	Md.	05 AUG 1877	Potters Field
006441	LOWE, Francis A.	1y	W	D.C.	22 FEB 1876	Congressional
016030	LOWE, George	85y	C	Va.	06 JUN 1878	Potters Field
008967	LOWE, Jane C.	19m	W	D.C.	04 SEP 1876	Glenwood
020392	LOWE, Joseph F.	37y	W	Md.	11 JUN 1879	Baltimore, Md.
020875	LOWE, Maggie E.	3y	W	D.C.	10 JUL 1879	Baltimore, Md.
015418	LOWE, Mary	9y	W	D.C.	16 APR 1878	Congressional
010503	LOWE, Nathan	73y	W	Md.	03 FEB 1877	Potters Field
015564	LOWE, Phoebe	76y	C	D.C.	30 APR 1878	Harmony
004598	LOWE, Rose Lina	6m	W	D.C.	14 AUG 1875	Holy Rood
018071	LOWENSTEIN, John Frederick	2y	W	D.C.	16 NOV 1878	Mt. Olivet
009919	LOWN, Lotta Celistia	4y	W	D.C.	10 DEC 1876	Congressional
002546	LOWNDES, Gertrude	3y	W	D.C.	13 MAR 1875	Presbyterian
016521	LOWNDES, Wm. H.	1y	C	D.C.	09 JUL 1878	Beckett's
016281	LOWNS, Mary	8m	C	D.C.	23 JUN 1878	Beckett's
010061	LOWREY, William E.	45y	W	D.C.	24 DEC 1876	Oak Hill
001815	LOWRIE, James	41y	W	Scot.	20 JAN 1875	Glenwood
012396	LOWRY, Beverly G.	8m	W	Va.	16 JUL 1877	Stafford Co., Va.
007566	LOWRY, Geo.	5d	W	D.C.	09 JUN 1876	Holy Rood
011303	LOWRY, James H.	81y	W	D.C.	11 APR 1877	Oak Hill
007661	LOWRY, John	11d	W	D.C.	15 JUN 1876	Holy Rood

District of Columbia Death Records, August 1, 1874 to July 31, 1879

No.	Name	Age	Race	Birth	Death Date	Burial Place
004836	LOWRY, Louisa	4w	W	D.C.	30 AUG 1875	Glenwood
017694	LOWRY, Rebecca	77y	W	D.C.	10 OCT 1878	Oak Hill
003333	LUBER, George	14m	W	D.C.	15 MAY 1875	St. Mary's
014078	LUBEY, Timothy	42y	W	Ire.	12 DEC 1877	Mt. Olivet
004358	LUCAS, Alfred	1y	M	D.C.	28 JUL 1875	Young Mens
010446	LUCAS, Alfred	28y	C	Va.	30 JAN 1877	Ebenezer
009217	LUCAS, Andew	4m	C	D.C.	27 SEP 1876	Ebenezer
013778	LUCAS, Arena	1y	C	D.C.	09 NOV 1877	Beckett's
012714	LUCAS, Arthur	10y	C	W.Va.	07 AUG 1877	Potters Field
012731	LUCAS, Charles	50y	C	Va.	08 AUG 1877	Mt. Pleasant
004185	LUCAS, Chas.	3m	M	D.C.	18 JUL 1875	Harmony
008980	LUCAS, E.M.	55y	W	Va.	06 SEP 1876	Graceland
014601	LUCAS, Elijah	50y	C	Va.	30 JAN 1878	Young Mens
007905	LUCAS, Ellen	6m	W	D.C.	28 JUN 1876	Glenwood
017439	LUCAS, Ellen	80y	C	Md.	17 SEP 1878	Harmony
012004	LUCAS, Flavius	35y	C	Va.	22 JUN 1877	Ebenezer
012265	LUCAS, Georgiana	14y	C	Md.	08 JUL 1877	Young Mens
020967	LUCAS, Hattie	18m	C	D.C.	16 JUL 1879	Graceland
002164	LUCAS, Infant of Thos.	1h	C	D.C.	14 FEB 1875	Potters Field
003834	LUCAS, Infant of William	21d	C	D.C.	25 JUN 1875	--
007512	LUCAS, John A.	32y	C	D.C.	05 JUN 1876	Harmony
019020	LUCAS, Lizzie	29y	W	D.C.	10 FEB 1879	Graceland
001412	LUCAS, Margaret	26y	W	Ire.	16 DEC 1874	Glenwood
008535	LUCAS, Margaret	14m	C	D.C.	02 AUG 1876	Potters Field
007981	LUCAS, Maria	70y	C	D.C.	03 JUL 1876	Harmony
012668	LUCAS, Mary	97y	W	Eng.	04 AUG 1877	Congressional
014629	LUCAS, Mary	26y	C	Va.	01 FEB 1878	Harmony
001878	LUCAS, Mary E.	6m	C	D.C.	24 JAN 1875	Harmony
008346	LUCAS, Mary E.	37y	W	Va.	20 JUL 1876	Presbyterian
003448	LUCAS, Mary Frances	1y	C	D.C.	26 MAY 1875	Potters Field
014863	LUCAS, Mary T.	36y	W	Me.	24 FEB 1878	Mt. Olivet
010955	LUCAS, Nancy	31y	W	Ala.	12 MAR 1877	Graceland
004629	LUCAS, Nathaniel	1y	M	D.C.	16 AUG 1875	Mt. Pleasant
008839	LUCAS, Thomas	35y	C	Va.	27 AUG 1876	Harmony
017715	LUCAS, Thomas A.	1y	M	Va.	12 OCT 1878	Westmoreland Co., Va.
006226	LUCAS, Willie	8m	C	D.C.	03 FEB 1876	Ebenezer
014494	LUCAS, Wm.	40y	C	Va.	20 JAN 1878	Potters Field
009676	LUCCHASI, Mary	76y	W	Ire.	11 NOV 1876	Congressional
018728	LUCK, Irene	17m	W	D.C.	19 JAN 1879	Glenwood
017541	LUCK, John	1y	C	D.C.	26 SEP 1878	Beckett's
014419	LUCK, Thomas	40y	C	Va.	14 JAN 1878	Potters Field
013240	LUCKET, Infant of William	7h	C	D.C.	18 SEP 1877	Young Mens
005518	LUCKET, Martha	13m	C	D.C.	20 NOV 1875	Ebenezer
011219	LUCKETT, Alexander	48y	W	Va.	05 APR 1877	Congressional
020736	LUCKETT, Ella R.	1y	W	D.C.	03 JUL 1879	Oak Hill
002081	LUCKETT, George Washington	18m	W	D.C.	08 FEB 1875	Congressional
009021	LUCKETT, L.M.	1m	W	D.C.	10 SEP 1876	Presbyterian
003003	LUCKETT, Susan	35y	C	Md.	15 APR 1875	Thomas'
014615	LUCKY, Sarah A.	1m	W	D.C.	31 JAN 1878	Congressional
010934	LUCUS, Adison	1m	C	D.C.	09 MAR 1877	Potters Field
016332	LUCUS, Charles	4m	M	D.C.	27 JUN 1878	Harmony
018973	LUCUS, Ellen	1m	W	D.C.	06 FEB 1879	Mt. Olivet
016792	LUCUS, Lucinda	75y	C	Va.	27 JUL 1878	Harmony
016374	LUCUS, Nancy	36y	C	D.C.	30 JUN 1878	Graceland
011522	LUCUS, Polley	80y	C	Va.	05 MAY 1877	Mt. Pleasant
018898	LUCUS, Robt. H.	6y	C	D.C.	31 JAN 1879	Mt. Pleasant/Graceland

No.	Name	Age	Race	Birth	Death Date	Burial Place
000870	LUDERS, Lewis	62y	W	Ger.	20 OCT 1874	Prospect Hill
010322	LUDGATE, Edward	2y	W	D.C.	17 JAN 1877	Holy Rood
020088	LUDWIG, Phillip	48y	W	Ger.	13 MAY 1879	St. Mary's
008686	LUGENBEEL, Edith Hamilton	14m	W	D.C.	14 AUG 1876	Tennallytown
008196	LUKEI, Willie	7m	W	D.C.	12 JUL 1876	Presbyterian
003526	LUKES, Olmsead	25y	C	Va.	04 JUN 1875	Potters Field
016193	LUKOWITZ, Ernest Eli	2h	W	D.C.	16 JUN 1878	Graceland
020263	LUNDY, Agnes	2y	C	D.C.	01 JUN 1879	Beckett's
004794	LUNDY, Infant of Henry	1m	C	D.C.	28 AUG 1875	Potters Field
012475	LUNDY, Infant of Henry	18d	C	D.C.	22 JUL 1877	Potters Field
020437	LUNDY, Infant of Henry	3m	C	D.C.	14 JUN 1879	Potters Field
015958	LUNEY, Mary	35y	C	Md.	01 JUN 1878	Young Mens
000552	LUNSFORD, Wm. W.	1y	W	D.C.	18 SEP 1874	Oak Hill
007363	LUNT, William	60y	W	Can.	21 MAY 1876	Glenwood
017847	LUSBEY, Amelia A.	21y	W	D.C.	24 OCT 1878	Congressional
000404	LUSBEY, William	9m	W	D.C.	02 SEP 1874	Glenwood
020208	LUSBY, Infant of Robt.	14d	W	D.C.	27 MAY 1879	Potters Field
016476	LUSBY, James Edward	17y	W	D.C.	06 JUL 1878	Congressional
009647	LUSBY, John	45y	W	Md.	08 NOV 1876	Rock Creek
004464	LUSBY, Lillie M.	14m	W	D.C.	05 AUG 1875	Congressional
004127	LUSBY, Maggie	9m	W	D.C.	14 JUL 1875	Glenwood
000791	LUSBY, Maggie A., Mrs.	28y	W	D.C.	12 OCT 1874	Glenwood
018680	LUSBY, Martha G.	5y	W	D.C.	15 JAN 1879	Congressional
018840	LUSBY, Mary M.	7y	W	D.C.	27 JAN 1879	Congressional
020640	LUSBY, Robert H.	4m	W	D.C.	27 JUL 1879	Congressional
020486	LUSKEY, Clarence	6m	W	D.C.	17 JUN 1879	Congressional
019071	LUTZ, Helen Galt	1y	W	D.C.	14 FEB 1879	Oak Hill
008120	LYCETT, Gracie	10m	W	Md.	10 JUL 1876	Baltimore, Md.
015203	LYCETT, W.C.	52y	W	Eng.	27 MAR 1878	Glenwood
011691	LYDAN, John	42y	W	Ire.	24 MAY 1877	Mt. Olivet
011761	LYDDAN, George Edgar	2y	W	Va.	01 JUN 1877	Mt. Olivet
016982	LYDDANE, Louis K.	3m	W	D.C.	09 AUG 1878	Holy Rood
004793	LYDON, James	11m	W	D.C.	28 AUG 1875	Mt. Olivet
010292	LYLE, George	76y	W	Pa.	14 JAN 1877	Pittsburgh, Pa.
010021	LYLE, Mary	1y	C	D.C.	20 DEC 1876	Mt. Olivet
006477	LYLE, Wm. R.	26y	C	Md.	26 FEB 1876	Harmony
000104f	LYLES, Dennis B.	38y	W	D.C.	08 AUG 1874	Oak Hill
003533	LYLES, Emma	9y	C	D.C.	05 JUN 1875	Macedonia
012339	LYLES, Fred.	11m	C	D.C.	12 JUL 1877	Young Mens
002510	LYLES, Infant of Geo. W.	2h	W	D.C.	11 MAR 1875	Congressional
001211	LYLES, Jeney	21y	C	Va.	22 NOV 1874	Young Mens
008559	LYLES, John, Jr.	1y	C	D.C.	05 AUG 1876	Young Mens
016522	LYLES, John Samuel	6m	C	D.C.	09 JUL 1878	Moore's
000246	LYLES, Lilley	1y	C	D.C.	19 AUG 1874	Mt. Pleasant
011272	LYLES, William Arther Edw.	9m	C	N.Y.	09 APR 1877	Moore's
015836	LYMAN, Ida E.	10m	W	D.C.	25 MAY 1878	Oak Hill
000237	LYMAN, Maria W.	57y	W	Ver.	18 AUG 1874	Glenwood
003748	LYNCH, Agatha Cecelia	58y	W	D.C.	21 JUN 1875	Mt. Olivet
014864	LYNCH, Charles Edward	3m	W	D.C.	24 FEB 1878	Mt. Olivet
004995	LYNCH, Edward	56y	W	Ire.	11 SEP 1875	Brooklyn, N.Y.
003086f	LYNCH, Elizabeth	30y	W	D.C.	22 APR 1875	Congressional
010894	LYNCH, Ellenora	19y	W	D.C.	07 MAR 1877	Congressional
000030	LYNCH, Francis P.	11m	W	D.C.	02 AUG 1874	Mt. Olivet
013653	LYNCH, Hanora	28y	W	Ire.	27 OCT 1877	Mt. Olivet
018253	LYNCH, James	61y	W	Ire.	06 DEC 1878	Congressional
009522	LYNCH, Johana	102y	W	Ire.	25 OCT 1876	Mt. Olivet

District of Columbia Death Records, August 1, 1874 to July 31, 1879

No.	Name	Age	Race	Birth	Death Date	Burial Place
013292	LYNCH, John	6y	W	D.C.	24 SEP 1877	Mt. Olivet
002712	LYNCH, John W.	19y	W	La.	24 MAR 1875	Mt. Olivet
001972	LYNCH, Maria	40y	C	Md.	31 JAN 1875	Mt. Pleasant
003706	LYNCH, Mary Lizzie	2m	W	D.C.	19 JUN 1875	Congressional
011685	LYNCH, Patrick	84y	W	Ire.	23 MAY 1877	Soldier's Home
011121	LYNCH, Richard	1y	W	D.C.	26 MAR 1877	Mt. Olivet
011217	LYNCH, Robert Walter	1m	W	D.C.	05 APR 1877	Bladensburg, Md.
004996	LYNCH, Susan Jane	18y	W	D.C.	11 SEP 1875	Mt. Olivet
011588	LYNCH, Thomas	36y	W	Ire.	13 MAY 1877	Mt. Olivet
008875	LYNCH, Willie	5d	W	D.C.	29 AUG 1876	Mt. Olivet
011984	LYNCH, Wm.	5h	W	D.C.	21 JUN 1877	Mt. Olivet
018267	LYNHAM, Henry	40y	W	Can.	07 DEC 1878	Graceland
005462	LYNN, John	40y	W	Ire.	15 NOV 1875	Mt. Olivet
010715	LYNN, Mary M.	16y	W	Va.	20 FEB 1877	Manassas Station, Va.
010946	LYNN, Seymour	19y	W	Va.	12 MAR 1877	Manassas, Va.
020980	LYON, Jessie	6m	W	D.C.	17 JUL 1879	Congressional
017831	LYON, John	51y	W	Ger.	22 OCT 1878	Congressional
003100	LYONS, Evan	70y	W	W.Va.	23 APR 1875	Oak Hill
013933	LYONS, George Alexander	7m	C	D.C.	26 NOV 1877	Mt. Zion
001857	LYONS, Harriet	15d	C	D.C.	23 JAN 1875	Macedonia
004392	LYONS, J.Q.M.	31y	W	Eng.	31 JUL 1875	Congressional
007565	LYONS, James	11m	W	D.C.	09 JUN 1876	Mt. Olivet
015043	LYONS, John	16y	W	Ire.	12 MAR 1878	Mt. Olivet
013086	LYONS, John J.	64y	W	Ire.	04 SEP 1877	Mt. Olivet
001935	LYONS, Joseph C.	c.45y	W	N.Y.	28 JAN 1875	Glenwood
017740	LYONS, Lilly Cook	9d	W	D.C.	14 OCT 1878	Oak Hill
002655	LYONS, Margaret	87y	W	Ire.	20 MAR 1875	Mt. Olivet
014772	LYONS, Richard	3y	C	D.C.	15 FEB 1878	Mt. Pleasant
001582	LYSLE, Sally Ann	26y	C	Md.	02 JAN 1875	Moore's
012371	LYSLES, Prissilla	3m	C	D.C.	15 JUL 1877	Mt. Olivet

M

No.	Name	Age	Race	Birth	Death Date	Burial Place
018461	MACABEE, Margrate	78y	C	Md.	25 DEC 1878	Mt. Zion
011952	MACALE, Eveline	17y	M	D.C.	18 JUN 1877	Harmony
005418	MACARTNEY, Minerva Wilson	44y	W	Pa.	10 NOV 1875	Congressional
001216	MaCARTY, Daniel J.	6w	W	D.C.	23 NOV 1874	Oak Hill
010931	MACARTY, Mizpah	1y	W	D.C.	09 MAR 1877	Oak Hill
002067	MacCHATY, Denis	14m	W	D.C.	07 FEB 1875	Mt. Olivet
001757	MacDOUGALL, Eva S.	31y	W	N.Y.	16 JAN 1875	Auburn, N.Y.
012173	MACE, John	2½d	W	D.C.	02 JUL 1877	Congressional
005895	MACE, William	52y	W	D.C.	29 DEC 1875	Glenwood
007226	MacFARLAND, Joseph	35y	W	U.S.	06 MAY 1876	Oak Hill
010095	MacGILL, William Augustus	48y	W	Md.	28 DEC 1876	Congressional
004864	MacGROTTY, Edwin	17y	W	N.Y.	01 SEP 1875	Congressional
002168	MacGROTTY, Edwin Albert	4y	W	D.C.	15 FEB 1875	Congressional
008075	MACGUIRE, Elizabeth	32y	W	Md.	08 JUL 1876	Baltimore, Md.
019211	MACK, Anna	1d	C	D.C.	26 FEB 1879	Payne's
019276	MACK, Annie	18y	C	Md.	04 MAR 1879	Harmony
009120	MACK, Annie D.	2y	C	D.C.	18 SEP 1876	Mt. Olivet
020393	MACK, Daniel	7m	C	D.C.	11 JUN 1879	Beckett's
009546	MACK, David B.	38y	W	Ohio	27 OCT 1876	Waneson, Ohio
002006	MACK, David Elcie	10m	C	D.C.	03 FEB 1875	Ebenezer
021150	MACK, Elizabeth M.	10m	W	D.C.	29 JUL 1879	Glenwood
018223	MACK, Ignatius Harrison	7m	C	D.C.	02 DEC 1878	Mt. Olivet

No.	Name	Age	Race	Birth	Death Date	Burial Place
018316	MACK, Jane	55y	C	Va.	12 DEC 1878	Moore's
016151	MACK, John	40y	W	Ire.	13 JUN 1878	Hospital
003861	MACK, Magdalena	4m	C	D.C.	26 JUN 1875	Mt. Olivet
014838	MACK, Mary	1y	W	D.C.	21 FEB 1878	Mt. Olivet
001796	MACK, Philip	65y	C	Md.	19 JAN 1875	Ebenezer
015726	MACK, Walter T.	8y	W	D.C.	14 MAY 1878	Oak Hill
000089	MACK, Wm. Henry	1m	C	D.C.	07 AUG 1874	Potters Field
002179	MACKALL, Helen M.	19y	W	D.C.	15 FEB 1875	Oak Hill
007987	MACKALL, Louis	74y	W	D.C.	03 JUL 1876	Oak Hill
019227	MACKALL, Martha Elizabeth	67y	W	Pa.	27 FEB 1879	Oak Hill
012264	MACKAY, Elsie	50y	C	Va.	08 JUL 1877	Arlington
006847	MACKDANIEL, Nancy	33y	C	Va.	28 MAR 1876	Lynchburg, Va.
003452	MACKENEY, Thomas	36	W	N.Y.	27 MAY 1875	Holy Rood
003923	MACKERTEE, Charles A.	7m	C	D.C.	29 JUN 1875	Mt. Zion
020361	MACKEY, Charlotte Abigail	40y	W	S.C.	09 JUN 1879	Glenwood
006450	MACKEY, Harriet Mary	31y	W	S.C.	23 FEB 1876	Glenwood
021027	MACKLE, Charlie	1m	C	D.C.	20 JUL 1879	Beckett's
010234	MACKLE, James	49y	C	Md.	09 JAN 1877	Potters Field
009498	MACKNAMARRA, Ellen	23y	W	Eng.	22 OCT 1876	Mt. Olivet
012456	MACLE, Harry	7m	C	D.C.	21 JUL 1877	Potters Field
014359	MACOL, James	22y	C	Md.	08 JAN 1878	Young Mens
010534	MACOL, John	c.38y	C	Md.	06 FEB 1877	Young Mens
013822	MACOMB, Richard A.	35y	W	D.C.	14 NOV 1877	Oak Hill
019965	MACON, Albert	15y	C	D.C.	02 MAY 1879	Mt. Zion
004259	MACOO, Polly	80y	C	Va.	23 JUL 1875	Ebenezer
017118	MacPHERSON, Cluny James	5y	W	Eng.	20 AUG 1878	Congressional
017550	MADDEN, Emma	1y	C	Va.	27 SEP 1878	Potters Field
008487	MADDEN, John E.	24y	W	N.Y.	30 JUL 1876	Congressional
016317	MADDEN, Sarah Ann	9m	C	D.C.	26 JUN 1878	Beckett's
016458	MADDOX, Dolly	21y	C	Md.	05 JUL 1878	Prince George's Co., Md.
020912	MADDOX, Emma L.	5y	C	D.C.	13 JUL 1879	Harmony
014848	MADDOX, Maria	33y	C	Va.	22 FEB 1878	Harmony
004278	MADDOX, Milton	46y	W	Md.	24 JUL 1875	Presbyterian
006754	MADDOX, Sarah	65y	W	Del.	20 MAR 1876	Congressional
010641	MADDOX, Susan	76y	W	Md.	15 FEB 1877	Congressional
014616	MADES, Charles	2y	W	D.C.	31 JAN 1878	Prospect Hill
014277	MADES, Christopher	44y	W	Ger.	31 DEC 1877	Prospect Hill
015565	MADIGAN, David	84y	W	Ire.	28 APR 1878	Mt. Olivet
010037	MADIGAN, Michael	78y	W	Ire.	20 DEC 1876	Mt. Olivet
005179a	MADIGAN, Patrick	7d	W	D.C.	17 OCT 1875	Mt. Olivet
018996	MADISON, Elizabeth	47y	C	D.C.	08 FEB 1879	Harmony
018061	MADISON, Florence	4y	C	D.C.	15 NOV 1878	Fairfax Co., Va.
017994	MADISON, George	81y	W	Ger.	09 NOV 1878	Hospital
003862	MADISON, Infant of Eliza	9m	C	D.C.	26 JUN 1875	Potters Field
010297	MADISON, Infant of Sallie	4d	C	D.C.	15 JAN 1877	Ebenezer
015274	MADISON, Jas.	6m	C	D.C.	03 APR 1878	Beckett's
016104	MADISON, John	83y	C	Va.	10 JUN 1878	Mt. Pleasant
000639	MADISON, Paulena	1y	C	D.C.	25 SEP 1874	Young Mens
020110	MADISON, Robert	6m	C	D.C.	15 MAY 1879	Beckett's
018637	MADRID, Rutherford	6m	C	D.C.	10 JAN 1879	Payne's
018005	MAEDER, Atilia	1y	W	D.C.	10 NOV 1878	Prospect Hill
000964	MAGAR, Chloe	59y	W	Md.	28 OCT 1874	Congressional
010633	MAGEE, Susan St. Clair	67y	W	N.Y.	15 FEB 1877	Oak Hill
006113	MAGEE, William C.	71y	W	Md.	24 JAN 1876	Oak Hill
018695	MAGIE, Haines H.	74y	W	N.J.	16 JAN 1879	Chicago, Ill.
020285	MAGILL, John Whitehead	48y	W	Pa.	03 JUN 1879	Oak Hill

District of Columbia Death Records, August 1, 1874 to July 31, 1879   217

No.	Name	Age	Race	Birth	Death Date	Burial Place
012865	MAGILL, Mary Frances	10m	W	D.C.	18 AUG 1877	Congressional
017451	MAGNIER, Eliza	73y	W	Md.	18 SEP 1878	Insane Asylum
005131a	MAGRATH, Mary Ann	1y	W	U.S.	13 OCT 1875	Mt. Olivet
005448	MAGRUDER, Anna Stella	5m	C	D.C.	13 NOV 1875	Ebenezer
013889	MAGRUDER, Annie F.	1y	C	D.C.	22 NOV 1877	Harmony
009282	MAGRUDER, Annie Louiza	10d	C	D.C.	03 OCT 1876	Ebenezer
008655	MAGRUDER, Belford	55y	W	D.C.	11 AUG 1876	Glenwood
017589	MAGRUDER, Catharine	74y	C	D.C.	01 OCT 1878	Harmony
019507	MAGRUDER, Celia	1y	C	D.C.	22 MAR 1879	Beckett's
017060	MAGRUDER, Charles Grafton	2m	C	D.C.	15 AUG 1878	Beckett's
014712	MAGRUDER, Dennis	52y	C	Md.	08 FEB 1878	Mt. Olivet
016492	MAGRUDER, Florence	8m	C	D.C.	07 JUL 1878	Mt. Olivet
018926	MAGRUDER, Fred	16m	C	D.C.	02 FEB 1879	Potters Field
003860	MAGRUDER, George Washington	5m	C	D.C.	26 JUN 1875	Mt. Zion
020013	MAGRUDER, Harry	19m	C	D.C.	06 MAY 1879	Potters Field
019451	MAGRUDER, Jeremiah	6y	C	D.C.	18 MAR 1879	Mt. Olivet
013706	MAGRUDER, Jessie	3y	W	D.C.	02 NOV 1877	Glenwood
015695	MAGRUDER, Laura	2y	C	D.C.	12 MAY 1878	Mt. Olivet
011022	MAGRUDER, Louisa	76y	W	D.C.	17 MAR 1877	Oak Hill
018405	MAGRUDER, Millicent A.	64y	W	D.C.	20 DEC 1878	Oak Hill
007569	MAGRUDER, Rachel A.	9m	C	D.C.	09 JUN 1876	Harmony
012645	MAGRUDER, Richard P.	4m	C	D.C.	02 AUG 1877	Ebenezer
015544	MAGRUDER, Samuel C.	42y	W	D.C.	28 APR 1878	Rock Creek
000401	MAGUDER, Emilie	30y	W	Md.	01 SEP 1874	Oak Hill
007101	MAGUIRE, Bernard	4m	W	D.C.	24 APR 1876	Mt. Olivet
006264	MAGUIRE, Ferd B.	10y	W	D.C.	07 FEB 1876	Congressional
018042	MAGUIRE, Maggie B.	18y	W	D.C.	13 NOV 1878	Mt. Olivet
002533	MAGUIRE, Matilda P.	23y	W	D.C.	12 MAR 1875	Mt. Olivet
002824	MAHANNAH, Alphonzo	49y	W	N.Y.	31 MAR 1875	Hospital
016266	MAHER, Annie	19y	W	D.C.	22 JUN 1878	Mt. Olivet
013767	MAHER, Catharine	c.50y	W	Ire.	08 NOV 1877	Mt. Olivet
020049	MAHER, James	19y	W	D.C.	09 MAY 1879	Mt. Olivet
005184	MAHER, John	80y	W	Ire.	26 SEP 1875	Mt. Olivet
006651	MAHER, Mina	36y	W	Ger.	12 MAR 1876	St. Mary's
009885	MAHER, Saher	57y	W	Ire.	06 DEC 1876	Mt. Olivet
008797	MAHLER, Carl Ferdinand	5w	W	D.C.	23 AUG 1876	Rock Creek
001230	MAHONEY, Alice M.	11m	W	D.C.	25 NOV 1874	Congressional
015014	MAHONEY, Annie	23y	W	Ire.	10 MAR 1878	Mt. Olivet
004739	MAHONEY, Baby	2y	C	D.C.	24 AUG 1875	Ebenezer
020876	MAHONEY, Chas. W.	6m	C	D.C.	10 JUL 1879	Holy Rood
016032	MAHONEY, Ed	1y	W	D.C.	06 JUN 1878	Mt. Olivet
018277	MAHONEY, Flornce	21y	W	Ire.	08 DEC 1878	Mt. Olivet
003318	MAHONEY, George	32y	C	D.C.	14 MAY 1875	Mt. Zion
005031a	MAHONEY, George	1m	C	D.C.	02 OCT 1875	Mt. Zion
013171	MAHONEY, Hannah	4y	W	D.C.	12 SEP 1877	Mt. Olivet
010677	MAHONEY, John Wesley	3y	C	D.C.	18 FEB 1877	Beckett's
012982	MAHONEY, Julia	9m	W	D.C.	27 AUG 1877	Mt. Olivet
007714	MAHONEY, Marion	4d	C	D.C.	18 JUN 1876	Potters Field
008230	MAHONEY, Mary E.	1m	C	D.C.	13 JUL 1876	Young Mens
015121	MAHONEY, Robert	40y	C	Md.	19 MAR 1878	Potters Field
006236	MAHONEY, William B.	26y	W	D.C.	04 FEB 1876	Mt. Olivet
004243	MAHONY, Georgissa	11m	W	D.C.	22 JUL 1875	Presbyterian
019865	MAHONY, Mary	13y	C	D.C.	22 APR 1879	Mt. Olivet
011797	MAHORNEY, Charles Eugene	3m	W	D.C.	04 JUN 1877	Congressional
007568	MAHORNEY, Henrietta	17y	C	D.C.	09 JUN 1876	Holy Rood
014215	MAHORNEY, Ida E.	1y	W	D.C.	26 DEC 1877	Oak Hill

No.	Name	Age	Race	Birth	Death Date	Burial Place
001602	MAHORNEY, John F.	5m	M	Md.	03 JAN 1875	Holy Rood
016094	MAHORNEY, Mary Ellen	3m	W	D.C.	09 JUN 1878	Congressional
019461	MAHORNEY, Mealia	23y	C	Md.	19 MAR 1879	Mt. Zion
012733	MAHORNEY, Warren	60y	C	Va.	08 AUG 1877	Holy Rood
000164	MAHORNY, Mary Alice	2y	W	D.C.	13 AUG 1874	Presbyterian
005439	MAIER, C.G. Lavinia?	9m	W	D.C.	12 NOV 1875	Prospect Hill
007333	MAIN, Eliza Agnes	6m	W	D.C.	18 MAY 1876	Mt. Olivet
015215	MAIN, Mary	68y	W	Can.	28 MAR 1878	Congressional
014675	MAJOR, Olivia Sophia	c.20y	W	D.C.	05 FEB 1878	Rock Creek
004679	MAJOR, Susan A.	53y	W	D.C.	20 AUG 1875	Rock Creek
011458	MAKAL, Mary J.	39y	C	Va.	29 APR 1877	Mt. Zion
019152	MAKEL, Infant of Susie	9d	C	D.C.	22 FEB 1879	Payne's
005310	MALCOM, Frank	7y	W	D.C.	30 OCT 1875	Glenwood
003010	MALEZIEUX, Lucien	50y	W	France	16 APR 1875	Mt. Olivet
008631	MALLE, Edward J.	25y	W	France	09 AUG 1876	Cleveland, Ohio
019854	MALLON, William	7y	W	D.C.	21 APR 1879	Congressional
010867	MALLOY, Gerald	51y	W	Ire.	04 MAR 1877	Mt. Olivet
001427	MALLOY, John Joseph	67y	W	D.C.	18 DEC 1874	Congressional
005275	MALLOY, Mary	28y	W	Ire.	26 OCT 1875	Hospital
001922	MALONE, Ara Marian	1y	W	D.C.	28 JAN 1875	Mt. Olivet
005033	MALONE, Marian Crowe, Mrs.	47y	W	Ire.	13 SEP 1875	Mt. Olivet
017505	MALONE, Mary Jane	31y	W	Ire.	23 SEP 1878	Mt. Olivet
013814	MALONE, Patrick E.	28y	W	Ire.	13 NOV 1877	Mt. Olivet
001373	MALONE, Thomas	31y	W	Ire.	12 DEC 1874	Mt. Olivet
019788	MALONE, William A.	34y	W	Pa.	15 APR 1879	Philadelphia, Pa.
000419	MALONEY, Bridget	11y	W	D.C.	03 SEP 1874	Mt. Olivet
009084	MALONEY, James	13m	W	D.C.	15 SEP 1876	Mt. Olivet
004639	MALONEY, Mary	1h	W	D.C.	17 AUG 1875	Mt. Olivet
009922	MALONEY, Mary	65y	W	Ire.	10 DEC 1876	Mt. Olivet
001894	MALONEY, Nora	86y	W	Ire.	26 JAN 1875	Mt. Olivet
004548	MALONEY, Patrick	45y	W	Ire.	11 AUG 1875	Mt. Olivet
015764	MALONEY, Peter	74y	W	Ire.	18 MAY 1878	Mt. Olivet
012603	MALONY, Annie	1y	W	D.C.	30 JUL 1877	Mt. Olivet
001095	MALORY, John	1y	W	D.C.	09 NOV 1874	Mt. Olivet
012360	MALVERN, Belle	7m	C	D.C.	14 JUL 1877	Young Mens
018815	MALVIN, Blanch M.	1y	C	D.C.	25 JAN 1879	Harmony
011125	MANCO, William Thomas	1y	W	D.C.	27 MAR 1877	Mt. Olivet
018103	MANDERS, Mary	44y	W	Va.	20 NOV 1878	Mt. Olivet
008287	MANDINFORD, Julia A.	28y	W	Pa.	16 JUL 1876	Congressional
001851	MANGAN, Annie May	11m	W	D.C.	23 JAN 1875	Mt. Olivet
019111	MANGAN, Jennie	31y	W	D.C.	18 FEB 1879	Mt. Olivet
014944	MANGAN, John	48y	W	Ire.	04 MAR 1878	Mt. Olivet
020782	MANGAN, Sarah	36y	W	Ire.	05 JUL 1879	Mt. Olivet
004728	MANGEN, Samuel	18y	W	D.C.	23 AUG 1875	Mt. Olivet
000698	MANGEN, Timothy	33y	W	Ire.	03 OCT 1874	Mt. Olivet
001058	MANGON, Johanna	30y	W	Ire.	05 NOV 1874	Mt. Olivet
010729	MANGUM, Elizabeth	29y	W	D.C.	22 FEB 1877	Mt. Olivet
009382	MANGUM, Emeline R.	23y	W	D.C.	11 OCT 1876	Congressional
004279	MANGUM, John	9m	W	D.C.	24 JUL 1875	Mt. Olivet
003739f	MANGUM, Nancy Elen	43y	W	D.C.	21 JUN 1875	Addison's Chapel
004114	MANGUM, William Hamilton	11m	W	D.C.	13 JUL 1875	Congressional
011632	MANHARDT, Daniel	56y	W	Ger.	17 MAY 1877	Soldier's Home
017494	MANHOP, William	14m	C	D.C.	22 SEP 1878	Beckett's
008879	MANKIN, Mary Ann	50y	C	Va.	30 AUG 1876	Beckett's
003012	MANKINS, Theressa	27y	W	D.C.	16 APR 1875	Congressional
005496	MANLEY, Joseph	12d	C	D.C.	18 NOV 1875	Potters Field

District of Columbia Death Records, August 1, 1874 to July 31, 1879   219

No.	Name	Age	Race	Birth	Death Date	Burial Place
004695	MANLY, Josephine	9y	W	Va.	21 AUG 1875	Alexandria, Va.
003463	MANN, Gertrude	4m	C	D.C.	28 MAY 1875	Young Mens
009062	MANN, Martha	2y	C	D.C.	14 SEP 1876	Young Mens
007439	MANN, Mary Ann	5d	W	D.C.	30 MAY 1876	Mt. Olivet
014530	MANN, Mary E.	60y	W	Md.	23 JAN 1878	Millington, Md.
001724	MANNING, Elizabeth	29y	W	Ire.	14 JAN 1875	Mt. Olivet
019046	MANNING, Francis A.	63y	W	Pa.	12 FEB 1879	Mt. Olivet
015338	MANNING, Hiram D.	42y	W	Ohio	09 APR 1878	Hospital, Government
006257	MANNING, Michael Charles	4y	W	D.C.	06 FEB 1876	Mt. Olivet
002634	MANNING, Patrick Ignatius	2m	W	D.C.	18 MAR 1875	Mt. Olivet
010870	MANNIX, John	45y	W	Ire.	05 MAR 1877	Fredericksburg, Va.
017025	MANSFIELD, Charles F.	30y	W	D.C.	12 AUG 1878	Mt. Olivet
003746	MANSFIELD, Edward	15d	W	D.C.	21 JUN 1875	Congressional
002467	MANSFIELD, Job C.	60y	W	Md.	07 MAR 1875	Congressional
018974	MANSFIELD, John Fenton	10m	W	D.C.	06 FEB 1879	Mt. Olivet
013807	MANSFIELD, John Thomas	58y	W	D.C.	12 NOV 1877	Methodist, East
010540	MANSFIELD, Mary	4m	W	D.C.	06 FEB 1877	Congressional
007180	MANSFIELD, Wm. E.	11m	W	D.C.	01 MAY 1876	Methodist
008344	MANSON, Sarah	32y	C	Va.	20 JUL 1876	Beckett's
006863	MANSON, Wm.	107y	C	Va.	30 MAR 1876	Beckett's
019964	MANUEL, Lewis	82y	C	Va.	02 MAY 1879	Mt. Pleasant
004161	MANUEL, Mary	11m	C	D.C.	16 JUL 1875	Potters Field
002087	MAPPEL, Eliza	4d	W	D.C.	08 FEB 1875	Potters Field
001619	MARBURY, Ellen L.	44y	W	D.C.	05 JAN 1875	Oak Hill
002729	MARBURY, Emily	54y	W	D.C.	25 MAR 1875	Oak Hill
007907	MARBURY, John	84y	W	Md.	28 JUN 1876	Oak Hill
003793	MARBURY, Maggie	9y	C	D.C.	23 JUN 1875	Young Mens
006047	MARCERON, Elenora J.	1y	W	D.C.	17 JAN 1876	Mt. Olivet
012157	MARCERON, Marion J.	2m	W	D.C.	01 JUL 1877	Mt. Olivet
012444	MARCERON, Martha E.	40y	W	Md.	20 JUL 1877	Mt. Olivet
009111	MARCHE, Robert M.	13y	W	Va.	17 SEP 1876	Congressional
006969	MARCY, Lucy Ann	63y	W	D.C.	08 APR 1876	Oak Hill
010800	MARDERS, Ida	7y	W	D.C.	27 FEB 1877	Congressional
008192	MARDERS, James William	11m	W	D.C.	11 JUL 1876	Congressional
003704	MARDERS, Maggie May	1½m	W	D.C.	19 JUN 1875	Congressional
019955	MARDERS, Margaret D.	34y	W	Md.	01 MAY 1879	Congressional
016877	MARDERS, Martha	58y	W	Va.	02 AUG 1878	Congressional
018611	MARDERS, William H.	41y	W	Va.	08 JAN 1879	Congressional
016095	MARDIS, Larance R.	5m	W	D.C.	09 JUN 1878	Congressional
020362	MARECK, Wilhelmina	4m	W	D.C.	09 JUN 1879	Prospect Hill
007761	MARICK, Frank	1m	W	D.C.	21 JUN 1876	Prospect Hill
008717	MARINELLA, Joseph	4m	W	D.C.	17 AUG 1876	St. Mary's
010544	MARKHAM, Flora P.	30y	W	D.C.	06 FEB 1877	Rock Creek
008277	MARKHAM, Winifred	104y	W	Ire.	15 JUL 1876	Mt. Olivet
015122	MARKOE, Mary G.	66y	W	Md.	19 MAR 1878	West River, Md.
007597	MARKOLF, Philip Henry	1y	W	D.C.	11 JUN 1876	Prospect Hill
015611	MARKRITER, Barbara	89y	W	Ger.	04 MAY 1878	Mt. Olivet
014017	MARKRITER, Julia Gracie	20d	W	D.C.	06 DEC 1877	Mt. Olivet
003116	MARKS, Annie	8y	C	N.Y.	25 APR 1875	Mt. Pleasant
016251	MARKS, Julia P.	85y	W	Ver.	21 JUN 1878	Oak Hill
004883	MARKS, Maga M.	45y	C	Va.	02 SEP 1875	Young Mens
015398	MARKS, Margaret J.	70y	W	Fla.	14 APR 1878	Congressional
020760	MARKS, Pearl Magdaline	1y	W	D.C.	04 JUL 1879	Congressional
013125	MARKS, Saml. N.	1y	W	D.C.	08 SEP 1877	Methodist
005877	MARKS, Susannah F.	32y	W	D.C.	27 DEC 1875	Congressional
005419	MARLEY, George W.	c.30y	W	Ire.	10 NOV 1875	Mt. Olivet

District of Columbia Death Records, August 1, 1874 to July 31, 1879

No.	Name	Age	Race	Birth	Death Date	Burial Place
019899	MARLL, Elizabeth H.	84y	W	Va.	25 APR 1879	Oak Hill
005220a	MARLOW, George F.	4y	W	Va.	20 OCT 1875	Leesburg, Va.
011770	MARLOW, John W.	72	W	Md.	01 JUN 1877	Glenwood
020166	MARLOW, Joseph	13m	C	D.C.	21 MAY 1879	Mt. Olivet
005894	MARLOW, Julianna B. Howard	52y	W	Md.	29 DEC 1875	Glenwood
009542	MARLOW, Louisa	75y	C	Md.	26 OCT 1876	Ebenezer
019954	MARLOW, Mary Agnes	7y	C	D.C.	01 MAY 1879	Mt. Olivet
004382	MARLOW, Mary Elizabeth	12m	C	D.C.	30 JUL 1875	Mt. Olivet
015409	MARLOW, Peter	c.59y	C	Md.	15 APR 1878	Harmony
004220	MARLOW, Stepny	74y	C	Md.	20 JUL 1875	Marlow's Farm
005595	MARLOW, William H.	30y	W	Md.	28 NOV 1875	Congressional
010188	MARMADUKE, Elizabeth	49y	W	Va.	06 JAN 1877	Congressional
018209	MARMADUKE, Henry Norwood	3y	W	Va.	30 NOV 1878	Graceland
003005	MARONEY, Mich. H.	c.45y	W	Ire.	15 APR 1875	Mt. Olivet
013812	MARROW, Infant of Thomas	6d	C	D.C.	13 NOV 1877	Chappel's
012118	MARRS, Lucy Ann	52y	C	Va.	29 JUN 1877	Ebenezer
020941	MARRS, Maria	7m	C	D.C.	15 JUL 1879	Mt. Pleasant
016803	MARRY, Celia	48y	C	Va.	28 JUL 1878	Harmony
004295	MARS, Fany	6y	C	D.C.	25 JUL 1875	Young Mens
016742	MARS, Mary Ann	11m	C	D.C.	24 JUL 1878	Mt. Zion
005474	MARS, Sarah	34y	C	Pa.	16 NOV 1875	Mt. Zion
020189	MARS, Thomas	55y	C	Va.	24 MAY 1879	Beckett's
017576	MARSDEN, Joseph Francis	13m	W	D.C.	30 SEP 1878	Mt. Olivet
003708	MARSH, Jessie	19d	W	D.C.	19 JUN 1875	Congressional
003592	MARSH, Martha	30y	W	Ger.	10 JUN 1875	Congressional
001408	MARSH, Mary Cordelia	16y	W	N.Y.	16 DEC 1874	Mt. Olivet
013480	MARSHAL, Ada	11m	C	D.C.	11 OCT 1877	Beckett's
000815	MARSHAL, George Henry	4m	C	D.C.	15 OCT 1874	Mt. Pleasant
009903	MARSHAL, George Thos.	21d	C	D.C.	08 DEC 1876	Mt. Olivet
018325	MARSHAL, Infant of Edward	11d	C	D.C.	13 DEC 1878	Mt. Olivet
018254	MARSHAL, Infant of Sandy	3d	C	D.C.	06 DEC 1878	Mt. Olivet
007225	MARSHAL, Leona	62y	W	Md.	06 MAY 1876	Rock Creek
011027	MARSHAL, nfant of John	7d	C	D.C.	18 MAR 1877	Ebenezer
009640	MARSHALL, Betsy	90y	W	Md.	08 NOV 1876	Potters Field
009944	MARSHALL, Caroline	35y	C	Md.	13 DEC 1876	Mt. Olivet
001345	MARSHALL, Cecilia	30y	C	Md.	09 DEC 1874	Thomas'
019491	MARSHALL, Charles	2y	C	D.C.	21 MAR 1879	Beckett's
015988	MARSHALL, Clarisa	3m	C	D.C.	03 JUN 1878	Mt. Olivet
020813	MARSHALL, DeWitt C.	c.50y	W	N.Y.	07 JUL 1879	Poughkeepsie, N.Y.
016092	MARSHALL, Edward	2y	C	D.C.	09 JUN 1878	Mt. Olivet
020438	MARSHALL, Edwd.	1y	C	D.C.	14 JUN 1879	Mt. Olivet
001067	MARSHALL, Elizabeth	3y	C	D.C.	06 NOV 1874	Harmony
005299	MARSHALL, Emily	19y	C	Va.	29 OCT 1875	Baptist
006500	MARSHALL, Francis Ann	1y	C	D.C.	28 FEB 1876	Ebenezer
002052	MARSHALL, Frank	1y	C	D.C.	06 FEB 1875	Beckett's
001395	MARSHALL, Gabriel	55y	C	Va.	15 DEC 1874	Harmony
002745	MARSHALL, Geo. R.	1y	C	D.C.	26 MAR 1875	Harmony
016658	MARSHALL, George	1y	C	D.C.	18 JUL 1878	Rock Creek
018814	MARSHALL, George	8m	C	D.C.	25 JAN 1879	Potters Field
008376	MARSHALL, Georgia	8y	C	D.C.	22 JUL 1876	Moore's
017750	MARSHALL, Hannah	80y	C	Va.	15 OCT 1878	Harmony
017297	MARSHALL, Harriet Ann	1y	C	D.C.	02 SEP 1878	Mt. Olivet
017364	MARSHALL, Henrietta	c.82y	C	Md.	10 SEP 1878	Harmony
008258	MARSHALL, Henry [illegible]	6y	W	D.C.	14 JUL 1876	Glenwood
002124	MARSHALL, Isaac	82y	C	Md.	11 FEB 1875	Potters Field
016958	MARSHALL, James Benjamin	1y	C	D.C.	08 AUG 1878	Moore's

District of Columbia Death Records, August 1, 1874 to July 31, 1879   221

No.	Name	Age	Race	Birth	Death Date	Burial Place
002116	MARSHALL, John Charles Thos.	1y	C	D.C.	11 FEB 1875	Harmony
000278	MARSHALL, John H.	2m	C	D.C.	22 AUG 1874	Mt. Olivet
016932	MARSHALL, Julia	6m	C	D.C.	06 AUG 1878	Beckett's
016678	MARSHALL, Julia	18m	C	D.C.	19 JUL 1878	Mt. Olivet
009450	MARSHALL, Kate, Mrs.	40y	W	Mich.	18 OCT 1876	Glenwood
007580	MARSHALL, Lucy Ann	17y	C	Pa.	10 JUN 1876	Young Mens
020382	MARSHALL, Mariah Antoinette	2y	C	D.C.	10 JUN 1879	Graceland
005519	MARSHALL, Mary	4m	C	D.C.	20 NOV 1875	Mt. Olivet
005044a	MARSHALL, Mary F.	15y	C	Md.	03 OCT 1875	Ebenezer
001525	MARSHALL, Mary V.	33y	C	D.C.	28 DEC 1874	Harmony
000852	MARSHALL, Melvina	1y	C	D.C.	18 OCT 1874	Mt. Olivet
000824	MARSHALL, Robert	78y	C	Va.	16 OCT 1874	Potters Field
000359f	MARSHALL, Sarah A.	30y	W	Md.	29 AUG 1874	Mt. Olivet
016558	MARSHALL, Sarah Elen	6m	W	D.C.	11 JUL 1878	Western Cemetery, Md.
014287	MARSHALL, Sarah Ellen	38y	W	Md.	01 JAN 1878	Loudoun Park, Balt., Md.
009861	MARSHALL, Susan	28y	C	Va.	04 DEC 1876	Mt. Zion
012951	MARSHALL, Walter	14m	C	D.C.	25 AUG 1877	Mt. Olivet
000732	MARSHALL, William H.	11m	C	D.C.	06 OCT 1874	Harmony
010078	MARSLAND, Elizabeth	58y	W	Eng.	26 DEC 1876	Oak Hill
000262	MARSTON, Thomas Hand	57y	W	Pa.	20 AUG 1874	Philadelphia, Pa.
010735	MARTAIN, William	2y	C	D.C.	22 FEB 1877	Ebenezer
020456	MARTIN, Agnes W.	57y	W	Ire.	15 JUN 1879	Congressional
011412	MARTIN, Alfred	10m	C	D.C.	24 APR 1877	Young Mens
020073	MARTIN, Alfred A.	20y	W	D.C.	11 MAY 1879	Mt. Zion
009835	MARTIN, Ann	35y	W	Ire.	30 NOV 1876	Mt. Olivet
014839	MARTIN, B., Mrs.	54y	C	Md.	21 FEB 1878	Mt. Zion
016054	MARTIN, Bessie	9m	C	D.C.	07 JUN 1878	Mt. Pleasant
003043	MARTIN, Bridget	23y	W	Ire.	19 APR 1875	Mt. Olivet
019325	MARTIN, Carrie	3y	C	D.C.	08 MAR 1879	Mt. Zion
018034	MARTIN, Catharina	85y	W	Ger.	12 NOV 1878	Congressional
005730	MARTIN, Charlott S.	78y	W	Md.	12 DEC 1875	Rock Creek
000293	MARTIN, Christian	13y	W	D.C.	23 AUG 1874	Carroll Chapel, Md.
003052	MARTIN, Danl. W.	40y	W	N.Y.	20 APR 1875	Prospect Hill
014687	MARTIN, Edward	1y	W	D.C.	06 FEB 1878	Mt. Olivet
005145a	MARTIN, Ellanor	69y	W	Ire.	14 OCT 1875	Mt. Olivet
011710	MARTIN, Ellen, Miss	25y	W	Ire.	26 MAY 1877	Mt. Olivet
011426	MARTIN, Eva E.	15y	W	Md.	25 APR 1877	Glenwood
019478	MARTIN, Francis	3m	W	D.C.	20 MAR 1879	Mt. Olivet
012520	MARTIN, Fredrick	40y	W	N.Y.	25 JUL 1877	Congressional
018681	MARTIN, George	2y	W	D.C.	15 JAN 1879	Prospect Hill
014584	MARTIN, George E.	23y	W	N.Y.	28 JAN 1878	Rochester, N.Y.
019425	MARTIN, H.F.F., Mrs.	51y	W	D.C.	16 MAR 1879	Glenwood
009211	MARTIN, Henry S.	72y	W	N.Y.	27 SEP 1876	Alexandria, Va.
013616	MARTIN, Infant of Delia	61h	C	D.C.	24 OCT 1877	Harmony
016959	MARTIN, Infant of John	12h	C	D.C.	08 AUG 1878	Potters Field
003312	MARTIN, James	6m	C	D.C.	13 MAY 1875	Mt. Olivet
013408	MARTIN, James	31y	W	Ire.	05 OCT 1877	Hospital, Government
002550f	MARTIN, James H.	61y	W	Md.	13 MAR 1875	Congressional
016544	MARTIN, James, Jr.	23y	W	D.C.	10 JUL 1878	Glenwood
007484	MARTIN, Jas. Thomas	5m	C	D.C.	03 JUN 1876	Mt. Zion
018776	MARTIN, Jessie F.	11m	W	D.C.	22 JAN 1879	Congressional
001415	MARTIN, John	41y	W	Ire.	17 DEC 1874	Washington Asylum
004077	MARTIN, John	46y	W	Ire.	10 JUL 1875	Mt. Olivet
011816	MARTIN, John	57y	W	Ire.	06 JUN 1877	Soldier's Home
013349	MARTIN, Katie C.	40y	W	Va.	29 SEP 1877	Glenwood
005550	MARTIN, Lucy	c.60y	C	Md.	24 NOV 1875	Mt. Zion

District of Columbia Death Records, August 1, 1874 to July 31, 1879

No.	Name	Age	Race	Birth	Death Date	Burial Place
007750	MARTIN, Luther	7m	W	D.C.	20 JUN 1876	Rock Creek
000219	MARTIN, Mary	40y	C	Md.	17 AUG 1874	Mt. Zion
019324	MARTIN, Mary	5y	C	D.C.	08 MAR 1879	Mt. Zion
015878	MARTIN, Mary Eleanora	5m	W	D.C.	28 MAY 1878	Prospect Hill
009968	MARTIN, Mary Elizabeth	18y	C	Va.	15 DEC 1876	Young Mens
012775	MARTIN, Mary Ellen	9m	W	D.C.	11 AUG 1877	Mt. Olivet
018288	MARTIN, Mary Jane	38y	W	Eng.	09 DEC 1878	Mt. Olivet
013760	MARTIN, Mary Josephine	8d	W	D.C.	07 NOV 1877	Mt. Olivet
014129	MARTIN, McKay	55y	W	Md.	18 DEC 1877	Tennallytown
008468	MARTIN, Michael	8y	W	D.C.	29 JUL 1876	Baltimore, Md.
019215	MARTIN, Millard Fillmore	30d	W	D.C.	26 FEB 1879	Methodist
002757	MARTIN, Patrick	36y	W	Ire.	27 MAR 1875	Mt. Olivet
020668	MARTIN, Peter	81y	W	Eng.	29 JUN 1879	Potters Field
003924	MARTIN, Robert	1m	C	D.C.	29 JUN 1875	Young Mens
000854	MARTIN, Rosena	54y	W	Ire.	19 OCT 1874	N.Y.
017600	MARTIN, Rosetta	80y	C	Va.	02 OCT 1878	Beckett's
010410	MARTIN, Ruben	7m	C	D.C.	26 JAN 1877	Young Mens
011956	MARTIN, Rutherford	3m	C	D.C.	18 JUN 1877	Mt. Zion
019326	MARTIN, Samuel, Jr.	8m	C	D.C.	08 MAR 1879	Mt. Zion
002790	MARTIN, Sarah Ida	13y	C	Md.	29 MAR 1875	Mt. Zion
008445	MARTIN, Susan	59y	W	Va.	27 JUL 1876	Alexandria, Va.
000459	MARTIN, William	9d	M	D.C.	09 SEP 1874	Mt. Olivet
019345	MARTIN, William	2y	C	D.C.	08 MAR 1879	Mt. Zion
012297	MARTIN, Wm. H.	50y	C	D.C.	10 JUL 1877	Mt. Olivet
004795	MARTIN, Zachary	84y	W	Ger.	28 AUG 1875	Congressional
003909a	MARTON, Robt.	7w	C	D.C.	28 JUN 1875	Young Mens
016152	MARTYN, Walter H.	7m	W	D.C.	13 JUN 1878	Congressional
006522	MARVINE, Archibald	27y	W	N.Y.	02 MAR 1876	Auburn, N.Y.
021083	MARY, Sister Patrick	26y	W	Ire.	24 JUL 1879	Mt. Olivet
010423	MASINO, Rose	22d	W	D.C.	27 JAN 1877	St. Mary's
008241	MASINO, Teresa	26d	W	D.C.	13 JUL 1876	St. Mary's
012015	MASON, Aaron	70y	C	Md.	22 JUN 1877	Mt. Olivet
014642	MASON, Amanda	21y	W	D.C.	02 FEB 1878	Mt. Olivet
012774	MASON, Amelia	74y	C	Va.	11 AUG 1877	Young Mens
017899	MASON, Catharine	30y	C	D.C.	29 OCT 1878	Mt. Zion
005623	MASON, Charles W.	45y	C	Va.	01 DEC 1875	Brentsville, Va.
001325	MASON, Eliza V.	1m	C	D.C.	06 DEC 1874	Mt. Pleasant
001253	MASON, Ellen	42y	C	W.Va.	28 NOV 1874	Mt. Olivet
019143	MASON, Emeline	11m	C	D.C.	21 FEB 1879	Mt. Zion
012301	MASON, Emma	11y	C	D.C.	10 JUL 1877	Thomas'
002174	MASON, Gabriella	7d	M	D.C.	15 FEB 1875	Mt. Zion
012536	MASON, Hannah	59y	C	D.C.	14 JUL 1877	Harmony
013617	MASON, Harriett	50y	C	D.C.	24 OCT 1877	Mt. Olivet
002027	MASON, Infant Jas. G.	6½h	W	D.C.	04 FEB 1875	Congressional
010596	MASON, Infant of Aaron	6d	C	D.C.	12 FEB 1877	Harmony
008561	MASON, Infant of J.M.	5d	C	D.C.	05 AUG 1876	Young Mens
004867	MASON, James H.A.	3y	M	D.C.	01 SEP 1875	Young Mens
020836	MASON, James Madison	35y	W	Ind.	08 JUL 1879	Oak Hill
010627	MASON, John	27y	C	Md.	14 FEB 1877	Beckett's
011392	MASON, John Francis	2m	C	D.C.	22 APR 1877	Mt. Zion
018731	MASON, John Francis	1y	C	D.C.	19 JAN 1879	Beckett's
007762	MASON, Joseph	4m	C	D.C.	21 JUN 1876	Mt. Olivet
009643	MASON, Joseph	8m	C	D.C.	08 NOV 1876	Harmony
005103	MASON, Joseph Lowry	9m	M	D.C.	19 SEP 1875	Mt. Zion
017696	MASON, Lloyd	9m	C	D.C.	10 OCT 1878	Mt. Zion
015044	MASON, Maggie Ann	4y	W	D.C.	12 MAR 1878	Mt. Olivet

District of Columbia Death Records, August 1, 1874 to July 31, 1879   223

No.	Name	Age	Race	Birth	Death Date	Burial Place
005520	MASON, Martha	35y	W	Va.	20 NOV 1875	Alexandria, Va.
016031	MASON, Martha	2m	M	D.C.	06 AUG 1878	Mt. Olivet
004630	MASON, Mary	7d	M	D.C.	16 AUG 1875	Potters Field
020487	MASON, Mary	35y	C	Va.	17 JUN 1879	Potters Field
003587	MASON, Mary Ann	44y	W	Ire.	10 JUN 1875	Mt. Olivet
021125	MASON, Mary E.F.	8m	C	D.C.	27 JUL 1879	Mt. Olivet
014360	MASON, Mary Francis	5y	C	D.C.	08 JAN 1878	Mt. Zion
014856	MASON, Rachel	95y	C	Md.	23 FEB 1878	Mt. Zion
019213	MASON, Rebecca A.	3y	C	D.C.	26 FEB 1879	Payne's
012548	MASON, Richard Thomas	4y	C	D.C.	27 JUL 1877	Thomas'
010670	MASON, Salie T.	40y	W	Va.	17 FEB 1877	Louisa Co., Va.
009448	MASON, Sandy	56y	C	Md.	18 OCT 1876	Mt. Olivet
002344	MASON, Sarah	c.70y	C	D.C.	27 FEB 1875	Mt. Zion
002153	MASON, Sue Tyler	30y	W	Va.	14 FEB 1875	Jonesborough, Tenn.
012805	MASON, Thomas	53y	W	Ire.	14 AUG 1877	Mt. Olivet
010859	MASON, Thomas Edna	7m	W	Pa.	04 MAR 1877	Mt. Olivet
003475	MASON, Ulyses	4y	C	D.C.	29 MAY 1875	Mt. Zion
005777	MASON, William	7y	C	Va.	17 DEC 1875	Fleetwood, Va.
005230	MASON, William Alexander	12d	C	D.C.	30 SEP 1875	Young Mens
001936	MASSA, Margaret	2y	C	D.C.	28 JAN 1875	Arlington
003535	MASSY, Mary	43y	C	D.C.	05 JUN 1875	Mt. Pleasant
005838	MASTERSON, Hugh	2m	W	D.C.	23 DEC 1875	Holy Rood
009731	MASTIN, Ann V.	36y	W	D.C.	18 NOV 1876	Presbyterian
009315	MATHERS, Wm.	49y	C	Md.	05 OCT 1876	Potters Field
000078	MATHEW, Joseph William	4y	C	D.C.	06 AUG 1874	Harmony
012425	MATHEW, Rose	54y	W	Ire.	19 JUL 1877	Mt. Olivet
000768	MATHEWS, Albert	22y	C	Md.	09 OCT 1874	Thomas'
014040	MATHEWS, Amos Theodore	3y	C	D.C.	08 DEC 1877	Harmony
009566	MATHEWS, Charity	68y	C	Md.	29 OCT 1876	Mt. Olivet
005249	MATHEWS, Christian	64y	W	Switz.	23 OCT 1875	Prospect Hill
001980	MATHEWS, Clara	10m	C	D.C.	01 FEB 1875	Mt. Olivet
018598	MATHEWS, Clara M.	7m	C	D.C.	07 JAN 1879	Potters Field
019021	MATHEWS, Edward	5m	C	D.C.	10 FEB 1879	Beckett's
015258	MATHEWS, Ella Virginia	6m	C	D.C.	01 APR 1878	Holy Rood
018225	MATHEWS, Ellen	35y	C	Md.	02 DEC 1878	Potters Field
008925	MATHEWS, Gloinny	100y	C	Md.	02 SEP 1876	Moore's
001916	MATHEWS, John	55y	C	Md.	27 JAN 1875	Washington Asylum
011181	MATHEWS, John Wilson	2m	C	D.C.	01 APR 1877	Mt. Zion
000635	MATHEWS, Joseph	18y	C	D.C.	25 SEP 1874	Beckett's
010529	MATHEWS, Laura C.	5m	C	D.C.	05 FEB 1877	Brightwood
000332	MATHEWS, Martha	1y	C	D.C.	27 AUG 1874	Beckett's
011466	MATHEWS, Mary	1d	W	D.C.	30 APR 1877	Mt. Olivet
016523	MATHEWS, Mary	3y	C	D.C.	09 JUL 1878	Mt. Pleasant
004981	MATHEWS, Mary Carroline	2y	C	D.C.	10 SEP 1875	Ebenezer
018516	MATHEWS, Mary E.	1m	C	D.C.	30 DEC 1878	Holy Rood
010194	MATHEWS, Mary Ellen	23y	W	Ire.	06 JAN 1877	Mt. Olivet
015275	MATHEWS, Mary Jane	8y	C	D.C.	03 APR 1878	Harmony
009988	MATHEWS, Moran	53y	W	N.Y.	17 DEC 1876	Congressional
013846	MATHEWS, William	1y	C	D.C.	17 NOV 1877	Beckett's
001595	MATHEWS, William Y.	2m	C	D.C.	03 JAN 1875	Beckett's
017375	MATINGLY, Thomas	7y	W	D.C.	11 SEP 1878	Tennallytown,Protestant
001356	MATSON, Lucy	42y	W	Ver.	10 DEC 1874	Graceland
016679	MATTENLY, Joseph	11m	C	D.C.	19 JUL 1878	Potters Field
004497	MATTERN, Julia M.	13m	W	D.C.	07 AUG 1875	Prospect Hill
018208	MATTERN, Maggie	8y	W	D.C.	30 NOV 1878	Prospect Hill
015545	MATTHEWS, Anna Elizabeth	49y	W	D.C.	28 APR 1878	Oak Hill

District of Columbia Death Records, August 1, 1874 to July 31, 1879

No.	Name	Age	Race	Birth	Death Date	Burial Place
015727	MATTHEWS, Annie E.	1y	C	D.C.	14 MAY 1878	Young Mens
012014	MATTHEWS, Bessie	7m	W	Va.	22 JUN 1877	Congressional
009152	MATTHEWS, Charles S.	1y	C	Va.	21 SEP 1876	Ebenezer
012898	MATTHEWS, Charly Ashton	1y	C	Md.	21 AUG 1877	Montgomery Co., Md.
000313	MATTHEWS, Clarence	1m	C	D.C.	25 AUG 1874	Beckett's
007846	MATTHEWS, Earnest	3m	C	D.C.	25 JUN 1876	Ebenezer
004935	MATTHEWS, Gus	1y	C	D.C.	06 SEP 1875	Potters Field
012602	MATTHEWS, Infant of Robert	2h	C	D.C.	29 JUL 1877	Potters Field
015350	MATTHEWS, Isaac	8d	C	D.C.	10 APR 1878	Harmony
007783	MATTHEWS, James	11m	C	D.C.	22 JUN 1876	Harmony
012042	MATTHEWS, John	45y	W	U.S.	24 JUN 1877	Soldier's Home
016680	MATTHEWS, John	1y	W	D.C.	19 JUL 1878	Mt. Olivet
005080a	MATTHEWS, John R.	2y	C	D.C.	07 OCT 1875	Beckett's
010361	MATTHEWS, John T.	46y	C	D.C.	21 JAN 1877	Harmony
004128	MATTHEWS, Joseph	7m	C	D.C.	14 JUL 1875	Freedmen's Village, Va.
009159	MATTHEWS, Lillie	10m	C	D.C.	22 SEP 1876	Young Mens
013367	MATTHEWS, Mary E.	17y	C	Md.	01 OCT 1877	Cox's Station, Md.
013162	MATTHEWS, Sarah	36y	C	D.C.	11 SEP 1877	Washington Asylum
009851	MATTHEWS, Susie	2m	C	D.C.	03 DEC 1876	Young Mens
004448	MATTHEWS, William	1y	C	D.C.	04 AUG 1875	Moore's
006615	MATTHEWS, William	39y	C	Md.	09 MAR 1876	Potters Field
005043a	MATTINGLY, Alice H.	3m	W	D.C.	03 OCT 1875	Oak Hill
009127	MATTINGLY, Ella Rives	35y	W	Va.	18 SEP 1876	Richmond, Va.
007969	MATTINGLY, Ida	1y	W	D.C.	02 JUL 1876	Waterford, Va.
018610	MATTINGLY, Infant of T.O.	1h	W	D.C.	08 JAN 1879	Presbyterian
010100	MATTINGLY, Mary Ann	16h	W	D.C.	28 DEC 1876	Presbyterian
014713	MATTINGLY, Mary Clara Bell	1m	W	D.C.	08 FEB 1878	Presbyterian
013761	MATTINGLY, William	62y	W	D.C.	07 NOV 1877	Presbyterian
001568	MATYSE, Godfrey	40y	W	Switz.	01 JAN 1875	Prospect Hill
018033	MAURER, Chas. Henry	1d	W	D.C.	12 NOV 1878	Tennallytown, Md.
000136	MAURER, Mary	24y	W	Md.	10 AUG 1874	Mt. Olivet
014654	MAUREY, Thomas	75y	W	Ire.	03 FEB 1878	Mt. Olivet
003357	MAURY, Inglis	8m	W	D.C.	18 MAY 1875	Oak Hill
019687	MAUS, Philip	5y	W	Pa.	07 APR 1879	Prospect Hill
006099	MAUSS, Infant of R.G.	18d	W	D.C.	22 JAN 1876	Prospect Hill
010810	MAXWELL, Alice	73y	C	Md.	28 FEB 1877	Potters Field
018587	MAXWELL, Chas. S.	60y	W	Md.	06 JAN 1879	Glenwood
011221	MAXWELL, Delia	40y	W	Ire.	05 APR 1877	St. Peter's, Balt., Md.
011028	MAXWELL, Ellen	11m	W	N.Y.	18 MAR 1877	Mt. Olivet
018599	MAXWELL, Infant of Susan	15min	C	D.C.	07 JAN 1879	Potters Field
008389	MAXWELL, Jane, Mrs.	66y	W	Ire.	23 JUL 1876	Glenwood
015280	MAXWELL, Protus	94y	W	Md.	03 APR 1878	Mt. Olivet
014522	MAY, Ann Elizabeth	78y	W	Md.	22 JAN 1878	Holy Rood
000490	MAY, Catharine Hite	74y	W	Va.	12 SEP 1874	Congressional
012488	MAY, James H.	52y	W	D.C.	23 JUL 1877	Methodist
017798	MAY, John M.	57y	W	Ger.	19 OCT 1878	Holy Rood
015973	MAY, Lulu	2m	W	D.C.	02 JUN 1878	Alexandria
016624	MAY, Margaret	30y	W	Pa.	16 JUL 1878	Mt. Olivet
020781	MAY, Martha M.	6m	W	D.C.	05 JUL 1879	Methodist, E.
006515	MAYBERY, Robert	2y	C	D.C.	01 MAR 1876	Ebenezer
015442	MAYBURN, Rebecca	4y	C	D.C.	18 APR 1878	Young Mens
011440	MAYER, Susan	3d	W	D.C.	27 APR 1877	Congressional
011472	MAYER, Susanna	9d	W	D.C.	01 MAY 1877	Congressional
018154	MAYHEW, George	70y	W	D.C.	25 NOV 1878	Congressional
002080	MAYHEW, Wm. H.	21y	W	D.C.	08 FEB 1875	Mt. Olivet
012983	MAYNARD, Ephraim Wesley	20y	W	N.J.	27 AUG 1877	Mt. Clair, N.J.

District of Columbia Death Records, August 1, 1874 to July 31, 1879   225

No.	Name	Age	Race	Birth	Death Date	Burial Place
015323	MAYO, Martha	9m	C	D.C.	08 APR 1878	Potters Field
000134	MAYS, Salvador	45y	C	D.C.	10 AUG 1874	Holy Rood
006169	McABEE, Mary E.	4m	C	D.C.	28 JAN 1876	Swartz's
000754	McABEE, O.S.	60y	W	Md.	08 OCT 1874	Congressional
004838	McADAMS, Frank	27y	W	Md.	30 AUG 1875	Hospital
006510	McALISTER, John	2y	W	D.C.	29 FEB 1876	Presbyterian
014903	McALLISTER, Cecelia Leton	62y	W	N.Y.	28 FEB 1878	Oak Hill
004933	McALLISTER, Johanna Janet	17d	W	D.C.	06 SEP 1875	Prospect Hill
009182	McANALLY, John T.	48y	W	Ire.	24 SEP 1876	Mt. Olivet
013590	McARDLE, Elizabeth Amelia	13y	W	D.C.	22 OCT 1877	Philadelphia, Pa.
000166	McARTHUR, Howard	10m	W	D.C.	13 AUG 1874	Mt. Olivet
001799	McARTHY, John	60y	W	Ire.	19 JAN 1875	Mt. Olivet
002474	McARVY, Mary	3m	W	D.C.	08 MAR 1875	Mt. Olivet
006199	McAULCIFF, Johanna	7d	W	D.C.	31 JAN 1876	Mt. Olivet
006416	McAULEY, Richard	55y	W	Ire.	19 FEB 1876	Mt. Olivet
010721	McAULIFFE, Cornelius	32y	W	Ire.	21 FEB 1877	Mt. Olivet
000271	McAULIFFE, Johana	8h	W	D.C.	21 AUG 1874	Mt. Olivet
010581	McAULIFFE, Johanna	1y	W	D.C.	10 FEB 1877	Holy Rood
015937	McAULIFFE, Michael	5m	W	D.C.	31 MAY 1878	Mt. Olivet
012717	McAVOY, Wm. Z.	6m	W	D.C.	07 AUG 1877	Mt. Olivet
008979	McBETH, Mary Frances	38y	C	S.C.	06 SEP 1876	Harmony
014495	McBRIDE, Anna Maria	17y	W	D.C.	20 JAN 1878	Glenwood
021081	McBRIDE, Edward D.	6m	W	D.C.	24 JUL 1879	Glenwood
013211	McBRIDE, William	2d	W	D.C.	15 SEP 1877	Glenwood
016610	McBURNEY, Jas.	3y	W	D.C.	15 JUL 1878	Mt. Olivet
017886	McBURNEY, Margaret	7y	W	D.C.	28 OCT 1878	Mt. Olivet
014163	McBURNEY, Margaret C.	21y	W	Ire.	21 DEC 1877	Mt. Olivet
010553	McBURNEY, Mary Ann	3m	W	D.C.	07 FEB 1877	Mt. Olivet
018962	McCABE, James	1m	W	D.C.	05 FEB 1879	Mt. Olivet
010166	McCABE, Patrick	50y	W	Ire.	03 JAN 1877	Carroll Chapel, Md.
009085	McCABE, William B.	1y	W	D.C.	15 SEP 1876	Mt. Olivet
007537	McCAFFERTY, William	69y	W	Md.	07 JUN 1876	Congressional
015460	McCAFFREY, Beatrice, Sister	58y	W	Ire.	20 APR 1878	Convent
021099	McCALLEN, Bridget	10m	W	D.C.	25 JUL 1879	Mt. Olivet
015506	McCANLEY, George	57y	C	D.C.	24 APR 1878	Congressional
014203	McCANN, Annie	20y	W	Va.	25 DEC 1877	Holy Rood
012057	McCANN, David Charles	29y	W	D.C.	25 JUN 1877	Oak Hill
000432	McCANN, Henry C.	32y	W	D.C.	05 SEP 1874	Oak Hill
015865	McCARTHEY, Margaret C.	5m	W	D.C.	27 MAY 1878	Mt. Olivet
003559	McCARTHY, Agnes	7d	W	D.C.	07 JUN 1875	Mt. Olivet
017132	McCARTHY, Bidget Cecelia	20y	W	D.C.	21 AUG 1878	Mt. Olivet
017667	McCARTHY, Elizabeth	3y	W	D.C.	07 OCT 1878	Mt. Olivet
016998	McCARTHY, Ellen	23y	W	Va.	10 AUG 1878	Holy Rood
005204a	McCARTHY, Emily	2y	W	D.C.	19 OCT 1875	Mt. Olivet
013546	McCARTHY, Forence	4y	W	D.C.	17 OCT 1877	Mt. Olivet
005016	McCARTHY, Jeremiah	56y	W	Ire.	12 SEP 1875	Holy Rood
015554	McCARTHY, John	50y	W	Ire.	29 APR 1878	Mt. Olivet
018682	McCARTHY, John	1y	W	D.C.	15 JAN 1879	Mt. Olivet
006919	McCARTHY, John Francis	9m	W	D.C.	04 APR 1876	Holy Rood
008873	McCARTHY, Maggie H.	1y	W	D.C.	29 AUG 1876	Glenwood
006464	McCARTHY, Margaret	65y	W	Ire.	24 FEB 1876	Mt. Olivet
009898	McCARTHY, Mary, Mrs.	50y	W	Ire.	07 DEC 1876	Mt. Olivet
001007	McCARTHY, Michael	40y	W	Ire.	01 NOV 1874	Mt. Olivet
001567	McCARTHY, Michel	2m	W	D.C.	01 JAN 1875	Mt. Olivet
010459	McCARTNEY, Sarah Jane	c.72y	W	Ire.	30 JAN 1877	Wilmington, Del.

No.	Name	Age	Race	Birth	Death Date	Burial Place
011260	McCARTY, Ann, Mrs.	59y	W	Ire.	07 APR 1877	Mt. Olivet
008626	McCARTY, Anna Rebecca	19m	W	D.C.	09 AUG 1876	Holy Rood
001370	McCARTY, Denis	35y	W	Ire.	12 DEC 1874	Mt. Olivet
008756	McCARTY, Dennis	14m	W	D.C.	20 AUG 1876	Mt. Olivet
007781	McCARTY, Frank Thomas	5m	W	Md.	22 JUN 1876	Glenwood
008140	McCARTY, Hanora	38y	W	Ire.	10 JUL 1876	Mt. Olivet
014512	McCARTY, John	41y	W	Ire.	21 JAN 1878	Holy Rood
018775	McCARTY, Susanna W.	70y	W	Mass.	22 JAN 1879	Rock Creek
012669	McCARTY, Walter H.	1m	W	D.C.	04 AUG 1877	Prospect Hill
012606	McCATHRAN, Mary	72y	W	Va.	30 JUL 1877	Methodist
003549	McCATHREN, James R.	77y	W	N.Y.	07 JUN 1875	Methodist E.
014743	McCAULEY, Ann	83y	W	Md.	11 FEB 1878	Laurel, Md.
016253	McCAULEY, Joseph R.	2m	W	D.C.	21 JUN 1878	Holy Rood
008248	McCAULEY, Mary E.	25d	W	D.C.	13 JUL 1876	Holy Rood
017257	McCAULEY, Richard H.	1y	W	Eng.	30 AUG 1878	Oak Hill
003940	McCAULY, Lota	4m	W	D.C.	30 JUN 1875	Holy Rood
006616	McCAULY, William	85y	C	Va.	09 MAR 1876	Potters Field
020616	McCAY, Eliza	50y	C	Va.	25 JUN 1879	Harmony
020209	McCENEY, Ethel	1y	W	D.C.	27 MAY 1879	Rock Creek
009681	McCHESNEY, Emma	22y	W	D.C.	12 NOV 1876	Rock Creek
017161	McCLAIN, Thomas	53y	W	Eng.	23 AUG 1878	Washington Asylum
012191	McCLANE, Mary	7m	W	D.C.	03 JUL 1877	Ebenezer
005169a	McCLELLAN, Maggie Belle	1y	W	D.C.	16 OCT 1875	Glenwood
005324	McCLELLAND, Clara Maud	3y	W	D.C.	31 OCT 1875	Glenwood
007047	McCLELLAND, Emma Amelia	42y	W	Eng.	18 APR 1876	Glenwood
006186	McCLELLAND, John Wm.	51y	W	N.Y.	30 JAN 1876	Glenwood
013393	McCLELLON, Bridget	55y	W	Ire.	03 OCT 1877	Mt. Olivet
002539	McCLERNEN, Mary E.	6m	W	Ky.	12 MAR 1875	Glenwood
009490	McCLORY, Daniel	38y	W	Ire.	22 OCT 1876	Mt. Olivet
020600	McCOLGAN, James	50y	W	Ire.	24 JUN 1879	Mt. Olivet
005057	McCOLGAN, Mary	65y	W	Ire.	15 SEP 1875	Baltimore, Md.
002705	McCONNELL, John	50y	W	Ire.	23 MAR 1875	Mt. Olivet
007992	McCONNELL, Morris	73y	W	Pa.	03 JUL 1876	Glenwood
005475	McCONNELL, Raymond	1y	W	D.C.	16 NOV 1875	Mt. Olivet
003248	McCONVEY, Francis Joseph	10y	W	D.C.	07 MAY 1875	Mt. Olivet
004052	McCONVEY, Isabella C.	2y	W	D.C.	08 JUL 1875	Mt. Olivet
015481	McCONVILLE, John	58y	W	Ire.	22 APR 1878	Soldier's Home
000856	McCOOK, Kate	20y	W	D.C.	19 OCT 1874	Mt. Olivet
016265	McCOOL, Mary Gabriel	72y	W	Ire.	22 JUN 1878	Convent
004865	McCOREY, Francis	75y	W	Ire.	01 SEP 1875	Glenwood
005221	McCORMIC, Ada V.	2m	W	D.C.	29 SEP 1875	Tennallytown
005428	McCORMICK, Benjamin	46y	W	Ohio	11 NOV 1875	Glenwood
008665	McCORMICK, Edward Patrick	2y	W	D.C.	12 AUG 1876	Mt. Olivet
003697	McCORMICK, Elizabeth Blair	58y	W	Md.	18 JUN 1875	Congressional
006898	McCORMICK, Eva	35y	W	D.C.	02 APR 1876	Congressional
008185	McCORMICK, Harry	6y	W	D.C.	11 JUL 1876	Mt. Olivet
005640	McCORMICK, Hugh	61y	W	Ire.	03 DEC 1875	Holy Rood
017716	McCORMICK, James	31y	W	Va.	12 OCT 1878	Mt. Olivet
002156	McCORMICK, Josephine	4m	W	D.C.	14 FEB 1875	Glenwood
013720	McCORMICK, Mamie	4y	W	D.C.	03 NOV 1877	Mt. Olivet
017358	McCORMICK, Margaret	37y	W	Ire.	09 SEP 1878	Mt. Olivet
007631	McCORMICK, Margaret L.	34y	W	D.C.	13 JUN 1876	Congressional
009327	McCORMICK, Maud Nellie	4y	W	D.C.	07 OCT 1876	Glenwood
004115	McCORWIE, Katie	13y	W	Md.	13 JUL 1875	Mt. Olivet
002833	McCOY, Annet	63y	C	Va.	01 APR 1875	Graceland
017601	McCOY, Charles	2y	C	D.C.	02 OCT 1878	Mt. Pleasant

District of Columbia Death Records, August 1, 1874 to July 31, 1879

No.	Name	Age	Race	Birth	Death Date	Burial Place
012568	McCOY, Nancey	103y	C	Va.	27 JUL 1877	Harmony
018646	McCOY, Susan	37y	C	Md.	11 JAN 1879	Young Mens
008062	McCREARY, Forence	1d	W	D.C.	07 JUL 1876	Baltimore, Md.
008114	McCREARY, M.J.	27y	W	Md.	09 JUL 1876	Baltimore, Md.
010245	McCREIGHT, Emma	90y	W	Ire.	10 JAN 1877	Mt. Olivet
003269	McCRISTAL, John	43y	W	Md.	09 MAY 1875	Glenwood
007351	McCUBBIN, Mary Ellen	38y	W	D.C.	20 MAY 1876	Glenwood
009954	McCUBBIN, Nicholas	76y	W	Md.	13 DEC 1876	Congressional
020244	McCUE, Maggie	19y	W	D.C.	31 MAY 1879	Holy Rood
010571	McCULLEN, John	46y	W	Pa.	09 FEB 1877	Congressional
009840	McCULLIS, Lafayette	c.60y	W	U.S.	01 DEC 1876	Springfield, Ill.
003335	McCULLOH, Mary	1y	W	Md.	15 MAY 1875	Baltimore, Md.
009307	McCULLOUGH, James	56y	W	Ire.	05 OCT 1876	Congressional
020309	McCULLOUGH, Philip Martin	41y	W	Md.	05 JUN 1879	Glenwood
014205	McCULLOUGH, Sarah	48y	W	Va.	25 DEC 1877	Congressional
004230f	McCURDY, Charles S.	11m	W	Md.	21 JUL 1875	Oak Hill
018785	McCURDY, Jesse R.	75y	W	Pa.	23 JAN 1879	Oak Hill
005848	McDADE, Robert Lee	8y	W	D.C.	24 DEC 1875	Congressional
011112	McDANIEL, Ann, Mrs.	98y	W	D.C.	25 MAR 1877	Mt. Olivet
002139	McDANIEL, George R.	58y	W	D.C.	12 FEB 1875	Holy Rood
008863	McDANIEL, John Henry	9y	W	D.C.	28 AUG 1876	Holy Rood
015725	McDANIEL, John Robin	70y	W	Va.	14 MAY 1878	Lynchburg, Va.
000142	McDANIEL, Walter	18y	W	D.C.	11 AUG 1874	Holy Rood
014204	McDERMOT, Hugh F.	47y	W	D.C.	25 DEC 1877	Mt. Olivet
000499	McDERMOTT, Annie Celia	11y	W	D.C.	13 SEP 1874	Mt. Olivet
018127	McDERMOTT, Elizabeth R.	27y	W	D.C.	23 NOV 1878	Mt. Olivet
016252	McDERMOTT, George, Lt.	42y	W	Ire.	21 JUN 1878	Mt. Olivet
008170	McDERMOTT, Margaret Ella	10m	W	D.C.	11 JUL 1876	Mt. Olivet
009294	McDERMOTT, Mary F.	1y	W	D.C.	04 OCT 1876	Holy Rood
015952	McDERMOTT, Michael	74y	W	Ire.	01 JUN 1878	Mt. Olivet
008886	McDERMOTT, Patrick	7y	W	Scot.	30 AUG 1876	Mt. Olivet
020121	McDEVITT, Ann	64y	W	Ire.	16 MAY 1879	Mt. Olivet
004567	McDEVITT, James	28y	W	Pa.	12 AUG 1875	Hospital
005769	McDEVITT, John	77y	W	Ire.	16 DEC 1875	Mt. Olivet
014914	McDEVITT, John	47y	W	Pa.	01 MAR 1878	Mt. Olivet
005209	McDEVITT, Maud	1y	W	D.C.	28 SEP 1875	Mt. Olivet
003883	McDONAH, Mary A.	7d	W	D.C.	27 JUN 1875	Holy Rood
015951	McDONALD, Ann Belle	65y	W	Va.	01 JUN 1878	Congressional
000257	McDONALD, Betsey	35y	C	Va.	20 AUG 1874	Mt. Pleasant
009656	McDONALD, Bridget	29y	W	Ire.	09 NOV 1876	Ithaca, N.Y.
013518	McDONALD, Charles Summer	1y	C	D.C.	14 OCT 1877	Beckett's
004934	McDONALD, Christopher	72y	W	Ire.	06 SEP 1875	Mt. Olivet
017577	McDONALD, Edward Logan	11h	W	D.C.	30 SEP 1878	Rock Creek
012260	McDONALD, Eliza	38y	W	Ire.	08 JUL 1877	Mt. Olivet
003317	McDONALD, Hanora	10y	W	D.C.	14 MAY 1875	Mt. Olivet
014252	McDONALD, Harry	1m	W	D.C.	29 DEC 1877	Rock Creek
011396	McDONALD, Infant of Ella	2h	W	D.C.	22 APR 1877	Glenwood
019578	McDONALD, Jenie	9d	W	D.C.	28 MAR 1879	Mt. Olivet
020814	McDONALD, Jessie V.	22m	W	D.C.	07 JUL 1879	Glenwood
017063	McDONALD, Jno. B.	10m	W	D.C.	15 AUG 1878	Mt. Olivet
015099	McDONALD, John Henry	6m	W	D.C.	17 MAR 1878	Queen's Chapel, Md.
011319	McDONALD, Mary	55y	W	Ire.	13 APR 1877	Mt. Olivet
016559	McDONALD, Mary	65y	W	Ire.	11 JUL 1878	Mt. Olivet
006698	McDONALD, Peter	35y	W	Scot.	16 MAR 1876	Potters Field
005135	McDONALD, Richard	8m	W	D.C.	22 SEP 1875	Mt. Olivet
016023	McDONALD, William J.	64y	W	D.C.	05 JUN 1878	Congressional

District of Columbia Death Records, August 1, 1874 to July 31, 1879

No.	Name	Age	Race	Birth	Death Date	Burial Place
000312	McDONNELL, Catharine, Mrs.	52y	W	Ire.	25 AUG 1874	Mt. Olivet
004076	McDONNELL, Daniel	48y	W	Ire.	10 JUL 1875	Mt. Olivet
002801	McDONOUGH, Bridget	40y	W	Ire.	30 MAR 1875	Holy Rood
006944	McDONOUGH, Sarah M.	50y	W	D.C.	06 APR 1876	Congressional
001748	McDOUGALL, Twin of Clinton D.	2h	W	D.C.	15 JAN 1875	Auburn, N.Y.
001747	McDOUGALL, Twin of Clinton D.	2h	W	D.C.	15 JAN 1875	Auburn, N.Y.
004017	McDOWELL, Infant of Matilda	1m	C	D.C.	06 JUL 1875	Ebenezer
011133	McDUELL, Eliza	86y	W	Mass.	28 MAR 1877	Glenwood
000015	McDUELL, Robert Somerville	5y	W	D.C.	02 AUG 1874	Glenwood
007067	McELFRESH, George Spindler	c.64y	W	Md.	21 APR 1876	Congressional
015770	McELHANY, Lorenzo	26y	W	U.S.	19 MAY 1878	Soldier's Home
003806	McELLIGETT, Julia	2m	W	D.C.	24 JUN 1875	Mt. Olivet
013863	McELROY, John A.	2y	W	D.C.	19 NOV 1877	Congressional
007613	McELROY, Mary A.	40y	C	Md.	12 JUN 1876	Potters Field
006451	McELWEE, Jane	80y	W	Ire.	23 FEB 1876	Philadelphia, Pa.
015669	McENEANY, Mary Jane	13y	W	D.C.	09 MAY 1878	Mt. Olivet
011104	McENERY, Johanna	23y	W	Ire.	24 MAR 1877	Mt. Olivet
020901	McENROE, Nicholas	34y	W	Ire.	12 JUL 1879	Hospital/Newark, N.J.
010875	McENTEE, Bridget	45y	W	Ire.	05 MAR 1877	Mt. Olivet
004997	McENTEE, Mary Ann	15y	W	Va.	11 SEP 1875	Mt. Olivet
020942	McENTEE, Thos.	74y	W	Ire.	15 JUL 1879	Mt. Olivet
019773	McEUEN, Carrie Walker	6y	W	D.C.	14 APR 1879	Oak Hill
000632	McEUEN, Jennie C.	29y	W	Va.	24 SEP 1874	Oak Hill
002010	McEWEN, Edgar Hyland	2y	W	D.C.	03 FEB 1875	Glenwood
004075	McEWEN, Hyland L.	11m	W	D.C.	10 JUL 1875	Glenwood
018183	McFARLAND, Andrew	33y	W	D.C.	27 NOV 1878	Delta, Pa.
018663	McFARLAND, Blanche Beatrice	7y	W	D.C.	13 JAN 1879	Oak Hill
017083	McFARLAND, Sarah Elizabeth	20y	W	Va.	17 AUG 1878	Glenwood
016214	McFARLAND, William	84y	W	Md.	18 JUN 1878	Congressional
007927	McFARLAND, William Joseph	5m	W	D.C.	29 JUN 1876	Holy Rood
000981	McGAHN, Frank	44y	W	Ire.	28 OCT 1874	Mt. Olivet
007536	McGARRITY, Catherine	70y	W	Ire.	07 JUN 1876	Holy Rood
010069	McGARVEY, Annie	15y	W	D.C.	25 DEC 1876	Holy Rood
001009	McGARVEY, Martie	48y	W	Ire.	01 NOV 1874	Mt. Olivet
004508	McGAY, James	67y	W	Ire.	08 AUG 1875	Glenwood
008270	McGEE, James H.	1y	C	D.C.	15 JUL 1876	Ebenezer
002466	McGEE, Millie	9y	W	La.	07 MAR 1875	Presbyterian
005348	McGEE, Patrick	38y	W	Ire.	03 NOV 1875	Soldier's Home
014883	McGILL, Gertrude L.	3y	W	D.C.	26 FEB 1878	Oak Hill
015397	McGILL, Isabella	c.50y	W	Pa.	14 APR 1878	Mt. Olivet
020835	McGILL, John	2d	W	D.C.	08 JUL 1879	Holy Rood
000261	McGILL, Lilly V.	20y	W	D.C.	20 AUG 1874	Mt. Olivet
001764f	McGILL, Robt. Tyler	80y	W	Md.	07 JAN 1875	Oak Hill
019538	McGILL, Sallie Wilson	3y	W	D.C.	24 MAR 1879	Glenwood
002590	McGILL, Stephen	1y	W	D.C.	16 MAR 1875	Holy Rood
008065	McGILTON, Thomas	4m	W	D.C.	08 JUL 1876	Mt. Olivet
007936	McGINNELL, Alice	3m	W	D.C.	30 JUN 1876	Holy Rood
007236	McGINNELL, Patrick	86y	W	Ire.	07 MAY 1876	Holy Rood
017854	McGINNES, James	40y	W	Ire.	25 OCT 1878	Mt. Olivet
002792	McGINNESS, Mary Rose	6m	W	D.C.	30 MAR 1875	Mt. Olivet
002367	McGINNIS, Mary	6m	W	D.C.	01 MAR 1875	Holy Rood
004509	McGINNIS, Saml. N.	52y	W	Va.	08 AUG 1875	Westmoreland Co., Va.
017724	McGIVENS, Joseph C.	8y	W	D.C.	13 OCT 1878	Mt. Olivet
015852	McGLATHERY, Virginia Ann	30y	W	Va.	26 MAY 1878	Glenwood
004431	McGLENNON, Jane	75y	W	Ire.	03 AUG 1875	Mt. Olivet
006681	McGLONE, Michael	52y	W	Ire.	15 MAR 1876	Soldier's Home

District of Columbia Death Records, August 1, 1874 to July 31, 1879   229

No.	Name	Age	Race	Birth	Death Date	Burial Place
006800	McGLUE, Gaynor Esther	3y	W	D.C.	24 MAR 1876	Graceland
014550	McGOLRICK, Eliza	38y	W	Ire.	25 JAN 1878	Mt. Olivet
001649	McGOLRICK, Owen	41y	W	Ire.	08 JAN 1875	Mt. Olivet
012361	McGOLRICK, William G.	c.55y	W	Ire.	15 JUL 1877	Mt. Olivet
012486	McGOWAN, Francis Daniel	1y	W	D.C.	23 JUL 1877	Mt. Olivet
008698	McGOWAN, John	9d	W	D.C.	15 AUG 1876	Mt. Olivet
001912	McGOWAN, Mary A.	1d	W	D.C.	27 JAN 1875	Mt. Olivet
006228	McGOWAN, Sarah Virginia	40y	W	Va.	03 FEB 1876	Congressional
011140	McGOWAN, William	45y	W	Ire.	28 MAR 1877	Soldier's Home
007782	McGRATH, Infant of Wm.	23d	W	D.C.	22 JUN 1876	Congressional
011270	McGRATH, John F.	5y	W	Ohio	08 APR 1877	Mt. Olivet
010890	McGRATH, Washington	21y	W	Pa.	07 MAR 1877	Glenwood
011003	McGRAW, Ann	58y	W	Ire.	16 MAR 1877	Mt. Olivet
013838	McGRAW, Eliza Ann	55y	W	Ky.	16 NOV 1877	Mt. Olivet
018784	McGRAW, Hugh	35y	W	N.Y.	23 JAN 1879	Mt. Olivet
005438	McGRAW, James, Sr.	59y	W	Ire.	12 NOV 1875	Mt. Olivet
019744	McGRAW, Margaret	54y	W	Ire.	12 APR 1879	Mt. Olivet
018757	McGRAW, Thos.	21y	W	D.C.	21 JAN 1879	Mt. Olivet
005463	McGRAW, William	62y	W	Ire.	15 NOV 1875	Mt. Olivet
016945	McGRAW, William Henry	7y	W	D.C.	07 AUG 1878	Mt. Olivet
013341	McGREAL, Lucinda	57y	W	D.C.	28 SEP 1877	Mt. Olivet
020181	McGREEVIEF, Nellie	2y	W	D.C.	23 MAY 1879	Congressional
016318	McGRUDER, Harry	1y	C	D.C.	26 JUN 1878	Beckett's
021082	McGRUDER, James	8m	C	D.C.	24 JUL 1879	Potters Field
002942	McGRUE, Alice V.	22y	W	D.C.	10 APR 1875	Congressional
000731	McGUGIEN, Mary	56y	W	Ire.	06 OCT 1874	Mt. Olivet
019686	McGUIGAN, Wm. Alexander	12y	W	D.C.	07 APR 1879	Congressional
013011	McGUIN, Mary Angela	11m	W	D.C.	29 AUG 1877	Mt. Olivet
002096	McGUIRE, Alexander	19y	C	Md.	09 FEB 1875	Mt. Zion
002095	McGUIRE, Catharine	4y	W	D.C.	09 FEB 1875	Mt. Olivet
013012	McGUIRE, Emmet P.	12y	W	D.C.	29 AUG 1877	Mt. Olivet
020427	McGUIRE, James Jacob	58y	C	Va.	13 JUN 1879	Potters Field
001867	McGUIRE, John	63y	W	Ire.	24 JAN 1875	Washington Asylum
016422	McGUIRE, Margaret D.	68y	W	Ire.	03 JUL 1878	Oak Hill
000878	McGUIRE, Mary	50y	C	Va.	20 OCT 1874	Mt. Pleasant
014602	McGUIRE, Mary	70y	W	Ire.	30 JAN 1878	Potters Field
009359	McGUIRE, Patk.	48y	W	Ire.	09 OCT 1876	Mt. Olivet
016031	McGUIRE, Percy	5m	W	D.C.	06 JUN 1878	Mt. Olivet
003686	McGUIRE, Rosana	6m	W	D.C.	18 JUN 1875	Mt. Olivet
017205	McHENRY, Hanora	35y	W	Ire.	26 AUG 1878	Mt. Olivet
000037	McHUGH, Julia	1y	W	D.C.	03 AUG 1874	Mt. Olivet
020505	McHUGH, Margaret Ann	3y	W	D.C.	18 JUN 1879	Mt. Olivet
020719	McHUGH, Mary I.	8m	W	D.C.	02 JUL 1879	Mt. Olivet
021000	McINEREY, John	21d	W	D.C.	18 JUL 1879	Mt. Olivet
010407	McINERNEY, James	1y	W	D.C.	25 JAN 1877	Mt. Olivet
015492	McINTEE, Mark	44y	W	Ire.	23 APR 1878	Mt. Olivet
010602	McINTIRE, Caroline R.	70y	W	D.C.	12 FEB 1877	Glenwood
003185	McINTIRE, Howard Garns	2y	W	D.C.	01 MAY 1875	Congressional
003776	McINTOSH, Agnes	5m	W	D.C.	22 JUN 1875	Congressional
001240	McINTOSH, Ann E.	40y	W	Va.	27 NOV 1874	Mt. Olivet
019635	McINTOSH, David	35y	W	Can.	02 APR 1879	Glenwood
010206	McINTOSH, Edward	60y	W	Ire.	07 JAN 1877	Mt. Olivet
019008	McINTOSH, Elijah	33y	C	Tenn.	09 FEB 1879	Beckett's
012998	McINTOSH, Irvin R.	30y	W	D.C.	28 AUG 1877	Oak Hill
005938	McINTOSH, Norval L.	2y	W	D.C.	04 JAN 1876	Congressional
010682	McKAIG, Joseph	2y	C	D.C.	18 FEB 1877	Baptist

No.	Name	Age	Race	Birth	Death Date	Burial Place
013897	McKALL, Infant of Leml.	10d	C	D.C.	23 NOV 1877	Beckett's
005596	McKANDRESS, Brian	56y	W	Ire.	28 NOV 1875	Mt. Olivet
010564	McKAY, Eugene A.	7m	C	D.C.	08 FEB 1877	Baptist, Georgetown
003030	McKAY, John B.	45y	W	Scot.	18 APR 1875	Glenwood
013139	McKEAN, Mary	4m	W	D.C.	09 SEP 1877	Oak Hill
005130a	McKEAN, Mary Frances	82y	W	Md.	13 OCT 1875	Oak Hill
011783	McKEAN, Rosa May	2y	W	D.C.	03 JUN 1877	Glenwood
018645	McKEE, Andrew Wylie	48y	W	W.Va.	11 JAN 1879	Oak Hill
019571	McKEE, John	58y	W	Ire.	27 MAR 1879	Baltimore, Md.
012897	McKEEVER, Catharine	5m	W	D.C.	21 AUG 1877	Mt. Olivet
012847	McKEEVER, Cora Elizebeth	19y	W	D.C.	16 AUG 1877	Mt. Olivet
012853	McKEEVER, Julia	3y	W	D.C.	17 AUG 1877	Mt. Olivet
007270	McKEEVER, Thomas	53y	W	Ire.	11 MAY 1876	Mt. Olivet
002323	McKELDEN, Frederick E.	1m	W	D.C.	26 FEB 1875	Oak Hill
014085	McKELDEN, Mary Ann	66y	W	Mass.	13 DEC 1877	Glenwood
003901	McKELDEN, S.A. Roszell	22y	W	D.C.	28 JUN 1875	Glenwood
020595	McKELDIN, Harry E.	2d	W	D.C.	24 JUN 1879	Baltimore, Md.
019426	McKELDRIN, Adrian Calvin	17m	W	D.C.	16 MAR 1879	Baltimore, Md.
000340	McKENDRY, Wallace	37y	W	Mass.	27 AUG 1874	Canton, Mass.
013242	McKENNA, Bernard	34y	W	Md.	18 SEP 1877	Baltimore, Md.
013093	McKENNA, Linda F.	11m	W	Co.	05 SEP 1877	Oak Hill
012169	McKENNA, Mary Elizabeth	15y	W	N.Y.	02 JUL 1877	Mt. Olivet
017591	McKENNE, Martha	66y	W	D.C.	01 OCT 1878	Mt. Olivet
006006	McKENNEY, Anna	41y	W	Va.	13 JAN 1876	Oak Hill
012952	McKENNEY, Betsy	78y	W	Va.	25 AUG 1877	Congressional
002388	McKENNEY, Hall	5y	W	D.C.	02 MAR 1875	Glenwood
005178a	McKENNEY, James H.	56y	W	Va.	17 OCT 1875	Congressional
008193	McKENNEY, Mary Ann Lee	70y	W	D.C.	12 JUL 1876	Congressional
010389	McKENNY, John	20y	W	Mass.	24 JAN 1877	Mt. Olivet
015778	McKENY, Thomas F.	27d	W	D.C.	20 MAY 1878	Holy Rood
007125	McKENZIE, Adam	c.35y	C	U.S.	26 APR 1876	Hospital
020050	McKENZIE, Alexander L.	60y	W	Va.	09 MAY 1879	Alexandria, Va.
007292	McKENZIE, Infant of David	1h	W	D.C.	13 MAY 1876	Methodist
000363	McKENZIE, Mary A.	1m	C	D.C.	29 AUG 1874	Beckett's
012748	McKENZIE, Sarah Anna, Mrs.	24y	W	D.C.	09 AUG 1877	Congressional
019462	McKENZIE, Sarah Virginia	8m	C	D.C.	19 MAR 1879	Graceland
019917	McKENZIE, Thos. Jefferson	c.75y	C	D.C.	27 APR 1879	Beckett's
001884f	McKERRICHER, Betsey	45y	W	Scot.	25 JAN 1875	Glenwood
012244	McKIM, John	2m	W	D.C.	06 JUL 1877	Congressional
004336	McKIM, Lucy May	10m	W	D.C.	27 JUL 1875	Congressional
011127	McKIMMIE, Margaret Ann	23m	W	D.C.	27 MAR 1877	Rock Creek
010542	McKINLEY, Mary E.	31y	W	D.C.	06 FEB 1877	Presbyterian
008218	McKINLEY, Sarah E.	5m	W	D.C.	12 JUL 1876	Holy Rood
018573	McKINNY, James	5m	C	D.C.	05 JAN 1879	Payne's
003687	McKINNY, Margaret	68y	W	Ire.?	18 JUN 1875	Congressional
003088	McKINSEY, Henry S.	2y	C	D.C.	22 APR 1875	Harmony
012332	McKIRSON, Ann H.	69y	W	Del.	12 JUL 1877	New Castle, Del.
005015a	McKLIMSLEY, Jennie	18y	C	Va.	01 OCT 1875	Potters Field
009342	McKNEW, Nathan Clarendon	7y	W	D.C.	08 OCT 1876	Oak Hill
009662	McKNIGHT, Birtha May	6m	W	D.C.	10 NOV 1876	Presbyterian
004174	McKNIGHT, Samuel	63y	W	Ire.	15 JUL 1875	Presbyterian
016150	McLAIN, Effie	3m	W	D.C.	13 JUN 1878	Oak Hill
019450	McLAIN, Ellen Elizabeth	12y	W	D.C.	18 MAR 1879	Glenwood
008544	McLAIN, Franklin	50y	W	Pa.	03 AUG 1876	Hospital
017296	McLAIN, Geo. H.	3m	W	D.C.	02 SEP 1878	Graceland
003685	McLAIN, Patrick	65y	W	Ire.	18 JUN 1875	Mt. Olivet

District of Columbia Death Records, August 1, 1874 to July 31, 1879   231

No.	Name	Age	Race	Birth	Death Date	Burial Place
013779	McLAMORE, James	48y	W	Tenn	09 NOV 1877	Soldier's Home
016659	McLANE, Honora	17y	W	D.C.	18 JUL 1878	Mt. Olivet
012680	McLAUGHLIN, Joseph	3m	W	D.C.	05 AUG 1877	Mt. Olivet
018787	McLAUGHLIN, Thomas	45y	W	Ire.	23 JAN 1879	Mt. Olivet
014420	McLEAN, David F.	18y	W	D.C.	14 JAN 1878	Glenwood
015810	McLEAN, George	7m	W	D.C.	22 MAY 1878	Prospect Hill
005254	McLEAN, Julia Ann	11m	C	D.C.	24 OCT 1875	Harmony
018443	McLEAN, Robert	56y	W	Eng.	23 DEC 1878	Baltimore, Md.
010371	McLELLAND, George William	73y	W	Me.	22 JAN 1877	Congressional
001495	McLEOD, Cath.	67y	W	Ire.	26 DEC 1874	Mt. Olivet
011238	McLEOD, Charles	33y	W	Scot.	06 APR 1877	Washington Asylum
010138	McLEOD, Matthew Miles	85y	W	Ire.	31 DEC 1876	Holy Rood
008836	McMAHAN, Thomas, M.D.	c.75y	W	Ire.	26 AUG 1876	Congressional
013585	McMAHON, Alice Cecelia	2y	W	D.C.	21 OCT 1877	Mt. Olivet
002846	McMAHON, Elizabeth	c.70y	W	Ire.	02 APR 1875	Mt. Olivet
002207	McMAHON, James	25y	W	Ire.	17 FEB 1875	Mt. Olivet
009923	McMAHON, John	68y	W	Ire.	10 DEC 1876	Mt. Olivet
008663	McMAHON, Mary	1y	W	D.C.	12 AUG 1876	Mt. Olivet
009045	McMAHON, Mary	2h	W	D.C.	12 SEP 1876	Mt. Olivet
006549	McMAHON, Owen	39y	W	Ire.	04 MAR 1876	Mt. Olivet
013559	McMAHON, Patrick	6y	W	D.C.	18 OCT 1877	Mt. Olivet
020210	McMAHON, Sarah A.	47y	W	Ire.	27 MAY 1879	Mt. Olivet
007885	McMAHON, Thomas Peter	6y	W	N.Y.	27 JUN 1876	Mt. Olivet
011017	McMAKIN, Andrew	26y	W	Pa.	17 MAR 1877	Philadelphia, Pa.
009419	McMASTER, Ella S.	33y	W	Pa.	16 OCT 1876	Pittsburgh, Pa.
019196	McMECHAN, Margaret	72y	W	Ire.	25 FEB 1879	Mt. Olivet
001274	McMENAMIN, Joseph	4y	W	D.C.	30 NOV 1874	Mt. Olivet
011432	McMENAMIN, Maggie G.	1d	W	D.C.	26 APR 1877	Glenwood
006227	McMILLAN, Mary Roseburg	40y	W	Pa.	03 FEB 1876	Pittsburgh, Pa.
012718	McMULLIN, Mursilla	1y	W	N.Y.	07 AUG 1877	Potters Field
004143	McMURRAY, Ellen D.	c.37y	W	Pa.	15 JUL 1875	Mt. Olivet
018869	McNABB, Patrick	33y	W	Ire.	29 JAN 1879	Congressional
002348f	McNAHANY, Marie	3y	W	D.C.	23 JAN 1875	Mt. Olivet
013934	McNAIR, Augusta M.	74y	W	D.C.	26 NOV 1877	Oak Hill
002603	McNAIR, Dunning R.	78y	W	Pa.	16 MAR 1875	Congressional
012899	McNALLEY, Elizabeth A.	1y	W	D.C.	21 AUG 1877	Mt. Olivet
017471	McNALLEY, Gertrude	4y	W	D.C.	20 SEP 1878	Mt. Olivet
011038	McNALLY, James Francis	2y	W	R.I.	19 MAR 1877	Mt. Olivet
012103	McNALLY, John F.	18y	W	N.Y.	28 JUN 1877	Providence, R.I.
013342	McNALLY, Patrick	46y	W	Ire.	28 SEP 1877	Hospital
010089	McNALLY, Sarah	4m	W	D.C.	27 DEC 1876	Graceland
005549	McNAMARA, Annie Maria	19y	W	D.C.	24 NOV 1875	Mt. Olivet
014837	McNAMARA, Ellen	43y	W	Ire.	21 FEB 1878	Mt. Olivet
002808	McNAMARA, Frances	11d	W	D.C.	31 MAR 1875	Mt. Olivet
005034	McNAMARA, James	35y	W	Ire.	13 SEP 1875	Mt. Olivet
014332	McNAMARA, John	16y	W	Ire.	05 JAN 1878	Mt. Olivet
007825	McNAMARA, Joseph	8d	W	D.C.	24 JUN 1876	Mt. Olivet
011659	McNAMARA, Mararet	59y	W	Ire.	20 MAY 1877	Mt. Olivet
003132	McNAMARA, Margret Bernadine	22y	W	D.C.	26 APR 1875	Mt. Olivet
017832	McNAMARA, Michael	19y	W	D.C.	22 OCT 1878	Mt. Olivet
005157a	McNAMARA, Patrick	87y	W	Ire.	15 OCT 1875	Mt. Olivet
014965	McNAMARA, Patrick	18y	W	Ire.	06 MAR 1878	Mt. Olivet
018460	McNAMARA, Peter	52y	W	Ire.	25 DEC 1878	Mt. Olivet
017062	McNAMARA, Timothy	17y	W	D.C.	15 AUG 1878	Mt. Olivet
018004	McNAMARA, Timothy	29y	W	Ire.	10 NOV 1878	Hospital
019239	McNAMARA, William Blake	2y	W	D.C.	28 FEB 1879	Mt. Olivet

No.	Name	Age	Race	Birth	Death Date	Burial Place
001300	McNAMARY, Ann	1min	W	D.C.	04 DEC 1874	Mt. Olivet
005205a	McNAMEE, Alice E.	18y	W	D.C.	19 OCT 1875	Mt. Olivet
017877	McNAMEE, Catherine	68y	W	Ire.	27 OCT 1878	Mt. Olivet
014470	McNAMEE, Mary Agnes	18d	W	D.C.	18 JAN 1878	Mt. Olivet
004730	McNAMEE, Mary Ann	2y	W	D.C.	23 AUG 1875	Mt. Olivet
011556	McNAUGHTON, John D.	34y	W	N.Y.	09 MAY 1877	Caledonia, N.Y.
004549	McNEAL, Almira	3m	C	D.C.	11 AUG 1875	Harmony
019819	McNEAL, Infant of Jas.	1h	C	D.C.	18 APR 1879	Harmony
008017	McNEAL, James E.	27d	C	D.C.	04 JUL 1876	Harmony
015794	McNEANY, Margaret	24y	W	Ire.	21 MAY 1878	Holy Rood
012485	McNEARNEY, Julia	7y	W	D.C.	23 JUL 1877	Mt. Olivet
010030	McNEILL, Eugenia Binnington	28y	W	Md.	20 DEC 1876	Glenwood
015173	McNEIR, Joseph	58y	W	Md.	24 MAR 1878	Glenwood
009910a	McNEIR, M.E., Mrs.	55y	W	Md.	09 DEC 1876	Presbyterian
019874	McNELLY, Martha	34y	W	Md.	23 APR 1879	Congressional
005338	McNERHANY, Mary	1y	W	D.C.	02 NOV 1875	Holy Rood
020245	McNERHANY, Rachel F.	34y	W	Md.	31 MAY 1879	Rock Creek
016708	McNIELL, Amy Burke	79y	W	U.S.	21 JUL 1878	Oak Hill
001760	McNULLY, Agnus	1y	W	D.C.	16 JAN 1875	Graceland
009993	McNULTY, Mary Elizabeth	3y	W	N.Y.	17 DEC 1876	Mt. Olivet
011201	McPHERSON, Ellis	26d	C	D.C.	03 APR 1877	Washington Asylum
011543	McPHERSON, Humphrey	5y	C	D.C.	07 MAY 1877	Graceland
001812f	McPHERSON, John, Capt.	60y	W	D.C.	20 JAN 1875	Congressional
009879	McPHERSON, Mary Ann	70y	W	Va.	05 DEC 1876	Oak Hill
019546	McPHERSON, Mary Elizabeth	51y	W	Md.	25 MAR 1879	Congressional
016402	McPHERSON, May E.	11m	C	D.C.	02 JUL 1878	Mt. Pleasant
008966	McPHERSON, Richard	46y	C	Md.	04 SEP 1876	Beckett's
004481	McPHERSON, Rosella	2w	W	D.C.	06 AUG 1875	Congressional
015247	McPHERSON, Sallie H.	22y	W	D.C.	31 MAR 1878	Oak Hill
007365	McPHERSON, Walter B.	13m	C	D.C.	21 MAY 1876	Potters Field
007033	McQUADE, Owen	33y	W	Ire.	17 APR 1876	Mt. Olivet
018246	McQUAID, Annie	33y	W	Ire.	05 DEC 1878	Mt. Olivet
020599	McQUAY, arthur	7m	C	D.C.	24 JUN 1879	Mt. Pleasant
005705	McQUILLAN, Ann M.	77y	W	D.C.	09 DEC 1875	Mt. Olivet
001428	McQUILLAN, Edward M.	37y	W	D.C.	18 DEC 1874	Mt. Olivet
006144	McQUINN, Josephine	37y	W	Va.	26 JAN 1876	Hospital
018384	McREADY, Caroline	1y	W	Md.	19 DEC 1878	Presbyterian
018442	McREADY, Frederick W.	3y	W	Md.	23 DEC 1878	Presbyterian
017618	McSHANE, Patrick	53y	W	Ire.	03 OCT 1878	Mt. Olivet
007847	McSTAY, Winnie	6m	W	D.C.	25 JUN 1876	Holy Rood
015079	McSWENEY, Josephine Mary	10m	W	D.C.	15 MAR 1878	Mt. Olivet
000583	McTAULTY, Mytie	1y	W	Va.	21 SEP 1874	Graceland
012218	McVARRY, Mary J.	14d	W	D.C.	04 JUL 1877	Mt. Olivet
020659	McVEA, Elizabeth K.	73y	W	Va.	28 JUN 1879	Congressional
010284	McWILLIAMS, Thomas M.	46y	W	Eng.	13 JAN 1877	Oak Hill
010963	McWILLIAMS, William	37y	W	Can.	14 MAR 1877	Soldier's Home
009901	MEAD, Elizabeth	74y	W	N.Y.	07 DEC 1876	Glenwood
020394	MEAD, George T.	4y	W	D.C.	11 JUN 1879	Oak Hill
011749	MEAD, John W.	63y	W	Md.	30 MAY 1877	Congressional
002516	MEAD, Louis A.	27y	W	D.C.	11 MAR 1875	Congressional
016293	MEAD, Simeon	70y	W	N.J.	24 JUN 1878	Glenwood
011863	MEADE, Eliza S.	14m	C	D.C.	11 JUN 1877	Mt. Pleasant
019238	MEADOWS, John Henry	2y	C	D.C.	28 FEB 1879	Graceland
020926	MEADS, Wm. H.	40y	W	Md.	14 JUL 1879	Baltimore, Md.
007698	MEAHLER, Anna	1y	W	D.C.	17 JUN 1876	St. Mary's

District of Columbia Death Records, August 1, 1874 to July 31, 1879

No.	Name	Age	Race	Birth	Death Date	Burial Place
002085	MEANS, Wm.	45y	C	D.C.	08 FEB 1875	Harmony
021011	MEANY, Margret	55y	W	Ire.	19 JUL 1879	Mt. Olivet
013381	MECHAN, Jullia	68y	W	Ire.	02 OCT 1877	Mt. Olivet
006736	MECKLIN, Alex. H.	72y	W	D.C.	19 MAR 1876	Congressional
003518	MECKLIN, Mary	10m	C	D.C.	03 JUN 1875	Potters Field
014371	MEDAIRY, Alpheus W.	1y	W	D.C.	09 JAN 1878	Glenwood
007538	MEDAIRY, William L.	4y	W	D.C.	07 JUN 1876	Glenwood
004370	MEDALION, Ida R.	44y	C	D.C.	29 JUL 1875	Young Mens
008066	MEDLER, Harry Martin	5m	W	D.C.	08 JUL 1876	Glenwood
011647	MEDLEY, Chas. H.A.	1y	C	D.C.	19 MAY 1877	Mt. Olivet
014288	MEDLEY, Mary	45y	C	Va.	01 JAN 1878	Young Mens
008938	MEED, William	51y	C	Md.	02 SEP 1876	Young Mens
002504	MEEDS, Benjamin N.	38y	W	Pa.	10 MAR 1875	Graceland
011216	MEEDS, Catherine	85y	C	Va.	04 APR 1877	Harmony
009932	MEEHN, Catherine	c.30y	W	Ire.	11 DEC 1876	Mt. Olivet
010045	MEEK, Fielding Bradford	59y	W	Ind.	21 DEC 1876	Congressional
002687	MEEM, William A.	30y	W	D.C.	22 MAR 1875	Holy Rood
011789	MEHLER, Mary Annie	10y	W	D.C.	03 JUN 1877	St. Mary's
004085	MEHLING, Andrew	14m	W	D.C.	11 JUL 1875	St. Mary's
017232	MEILENHEIM, Victor	2y	W	D.C.	28 AUG 1878	St. Mary's
004998	MEINCKHEIM, George	55y	W	Ger.	11 SEP 1875	Presbyterian
020900	MEINEY, Mary	59y	W	Ire.	12 JUL 1879	Mt. Olivet
011569	MEINKING, Friedrich Willgain	60y	W	Ger.	12 MAY 1877	Prospect Hill
006799	MELDON, May E.	25y	W	Ohio	24 MAR 1876	Mt. Olivet
012039	MELLINGTON, Walter	5m	W	D.C.	24 JUN 1877	Presbyterian
011657	MELLIS, John	54y	W	Scot.	20 MAY 1877	Glenwood
009655	MELVIN, Infant of William H.	3d	C	D.C.	09 NOV 1876	Harmony
020242	MELVIN, Mary Cordelia	14y	W	Md.	31 MAY 1879	Hampstead, Md.
007646	MEMBRY, Peter	49y	C	Ga.	14 JUN 1876	Ebenezer
014148	MENDEL, Charles	8d	W	D.C.	20 DEC 1877	Prospect Hill
014121	MENDEL, Fred C.	35y	W	Ger.	17 DEC 1877	Prospect Hill
015123	MENDLE, Jennie	2y	W	D.C.	19 MAR 1878	Potters Field
000700	MENGER, Henrietta	78y	W	Ger.	03 OCT 1874	Prospect Hill
002602	MENOCAL, George H.	4m	W	D.C.	16 MAR 1875	Glenwood
007156	MENSING, Mary	76y	W	Ger.	29 APR 1876	Prospect Hill
002882	MENY, Ann	65y	W	Ire.	05 APR 1875	Holy Rood
017096	MERCER, Belle	4m	C	D.C.	18 AUG 1878	Young Mens
018006	MERCER, Charlie	7d	C	D.C.	10 NOV 1878	Payne's
016850	MERCER, Edward	1y	C	D.C.	31 JUL 1878	Payne's
015866	MERCER, Emma	16y	C	Va.	27 MAY 1878	Beckett's
009960	MERCER, Infant of Thomas	10h	W	D.C.	14 DEC 1876	Beckett's
010256	MERCER, Jas.	14d	W	D.C.	11 JAN 1877	Holy Rood
002884	MERCER, Matilda	11y	M	Va.	05 APR 1875	Young Mens
015028	MERCER, Thomas Swann	57y	W	Va.	11 MAR 1878	West River, Md.
003111	MERCERY, Henry	1y	W	D.C.	25 APR 1875	Mt. Olivet
014379	MERCHANT, Katie J.	8m	W	D.C.	10 JAN 1878	Manassas, Va.
013586	MERCHANT, Maud Smith	3y	W	D.C.	21 OCT 1877	Rock Creek
002881	MEREDITH, Eliza	68y	C	Va.	05 APR 1875	Harmony
004219	MEREDITH, George W.	7d	W	D.C.	20 JUL 1875	Ebenezer
011369	MEREDITH, Henry	87y	C	Md.	19 APR 1877	Mt. Olivet
010840	MEREDITH, Henry	10y	C	Md.	02 MAR 1877	Mt. Olivet
017047	MEREDITH, Mary	c.80y	C	Va.	14 AUG 1878	Good Hope
005563	MEREDITH, Mary E.	10m	C	D.C.	25 NOV 1875	Mt. Olivet
018051	MEREDITH, Philip	65y	C	Va.	14 NOV 1878	Harmony
020457	MEREDITH, Sallie H.	76y	W	Va.	15 JUN 1879	Congressional
007399	MEREDITH, Sarah Falitia	19y	M	Va.	24 MAY 1876	Harmony

District of Columbia Death Records, August 1, 1874 to July 31, 1879

No.	Name	Age	Race	Birth	Death Date	Burial Place
005083	MERGENT, Priscilla	6m	C	D.C.	17 SEP 1875	Potters Field
005093	MERGENT, Washington	50y	C	Va.	18 SEP 1875	Potters Field
006837	MERIDETH, Victoria	24y	C	Md.	27 MAR 1876	Ebenezer
020981	MERILLAT, Mary M.	64y	W	D.C.	17 JUL 1879	Glenwood
015536	MERIWEATHER, Arethusa Webb	22y	W	Ky.	27 APR 1878	Oak Hill
012826	MERRILL, John	c.50y	W	Mass.	15 AUG 1877	Concord, N.H.
016836	MERRILL, Maud E.	4y	W	D.C.	30 JUL 1878	Oak Hill
019214	MERRIMAN, Alphonse	7m	W	D.C.	26 FEB 1879	Mt. Olivet
005156a	MERRIMAN, Wm.	6y	W	D.C.	15 OCT 1875	Mt. Olivet
011183	MERRITT, Emma	23y	C	Md.	01 APR 1877	Harmony
012134	MERRITT, Emma	3m	C	D.C.	30 JUN 1877	Potters Field
008337	MERRITT, George	8m	C	D.C.	19 JUL 1876	Potters Field
001772	MERRITT, Howland T.	5m	W	D.C.	18 JAN 1875	Congressional
012222	MERRITT, Marian	3m	M	D.C.	05 JUL 1877	Beckett's
006114	MERRIWEATHER, Joseph B.	7m	C	D.C.	23 JAN 1876	Mt. Olivet
007973	MERRY, Mildred	9m	C	D.C.	02 JUL 1876	Ebenezer
005112	MERTL, Minnie	84y	W	Ire.	20 SEP 1875	Mt. Olivet
017865	MERTS, Elizabeth	33y	W	D.C.	26 OCT 1878	Holy Rood
017427	MERTS, James F.	2m	W	D.C.	16 SEP 1878	Holy Rood
013823	MERTZ, Jas. F.	1y	W	D.C.	14 NOV 1877	Holy Rood
014351	MERWIN, Phineas	50y	W	N.Y.	07 JAN 1878	Glenwood
012281	MESSER, Maggie	1y	W	D.C.	09 JUL 1877	Congressional
006614	MESSERSMITH, George	77y	W	Ger.	09 MAR 1876	Congressional
009270	MESSIAH, Washington	61y	C	Va.	02 OCT 1876	Ebenezer
001122	METZ, Joseph	45y	W	Ger.	24 NOV 1874	N.Y. City
008892	MEWS, George	45y	C	Va.	31 AUG 1876	Potters Field
016333	MEWS, Maria	6m	C	D.C.	27 JUN 1878	Beckett's
007906	MEYER, Annie	54y	W	France	28 JUN 1876	Presbyterian
017359	MEYER, C.E.	85y	W	Ger.	09 SEP 1878	Prospect Hill
018126	MEYER, Charles	40y	W	Ger.	23 NOV 1878	Hospital, Government
004816	MEYER, Ella	1y	W	D.C.	29 AUG 1875	Presbyterian
020094	MEYER, Frederick	43y	W	Ger.	14 MAY 1879	Congressional
002215	MEYER, Fredrick F.	2y	W	D.C.	18 FEB 1875	Congressional
013894	MEYER, Louis	3y	W	D.C.	23 NOV 1877	Washington Hebrew
011882	MEYER, Mary Carrie	1y	W	D.C.	13 JUN 1877	Congressional
010469	MEYER, Rosa B.	4m	W	D.C.	01 FEB 1877	Prospect Hill
019059	MEYERS, Benjamin S.	50y	W	D.C.	13 FEB 1879	Congressional
009705	MEYERS, Emma Josephine	13m	C	D.C.	15 NOV 1876	Mt. Olivet
018730	MEYERS, Garrett	4y	C	D.C.	19 JAN 1879	Payne's
010889	MEYERS, John Edward	12h	M	D.C.	06 MAR 1877	Mt. Olivet
019009	MEYERS, William	2y	C	D.C.	09 FEB 1879	Payne's
008090	MICHAEL, John Bennett	12m	W	D.C.	09 JUL 1876	Mt. Olivet
006884	MICHAEL, Rosina	78y	M	Va.	01 APR 1876	Potters Field
011020	MICHAELSON, Augusta	51y	W	Ger.	17 MAR 1877	Prospect Hill
008350	MICHELBACHER, George	47y	W	Ger.	20 JUL 1876	Prospect Hill
015204	MICHELUS, Ferdinand	59y	W	Ger.	27 MAR 1878	Prospect Hill
011853	MICKELBACKER, E. Caroline	10m	W	D.C.	09 JUN 1877	Prospect Hill
008217	MICKENS, John	7m	C	D.C.	12 JUL 1876	Beckett's
020360	MICKIN, Susan	26y	C	Va.	09 JUN 1879	Beckett's
003108	MIDDLETON, Annie	38y	C	Md.	24 APR 1875	Ebenezer
009204	MIDDLETON, Annie	19y	C	D.C.	25 SEP 1876	Potters Field
004229	MIDDLETON, Clacia	9d	C	D.C.	21 JUL 1875	Mt. Olivet
003626	MIDDLETON, Daniel [Lemuel]	68y	W	D.C.	13 JUN 1875	Oak Hill
017666	MIDDLETON, Eliza	32y	C	Md.	07 OCT 1878	Beckett's
000631	MIDDLETON, Elizabeth	23y	C	Md.	24 SEP 1874	Beckett's
001592	MIDDLETON, Frank	43y	C	Md.	02 JAN 1875	Beckett's

District of Columbia Death Records, August 1, 1874 to July 31, 1879

No.	Name	Age	Race	Birth	Death Date	Burial Place
000344	MIDDLETON, George Heury	1y	C	D.C.	28 AUG 1874	Mt. Olivet
006682	MIDDLETON, Henry	79y	W	N.C.	15 MAR 1876	Charleston, S.C.
009187	MIDDLETON, Infant of Albert	10min	C	D.C.	24 SEP 1876	Potters Field
020059	MIDDLETON, John Albert	19m	C	D.C.	10 MAY 1879	Mt. Olivet
004915	MIDDLETON, John W.	1y	C	D.C.	05 SEP 1875	Harmony
002088	MIDDLETON, Maria	18m	M	D.C.	08 FEB 1875	Mt. Olivet
013382	MIDDLETON, Maria	60y	C	Va.	02 OCT 1877	Potters Field
009461	MIDDLETON, Martha	71y	W	Eng.	19 OCT 1876	Congressional
003178	MIDDLETON, Moses	1m	C	D.C.	30 APR 1875	Ebenezer
005278	MIDDLETON, Otho K.	20d	C	D.C.	27 OCT 1875	Harmony
003569	MIDDLETON, Robert	2y	M	D.C.	08 JUN 1875	Mt. Pleasant
004447	MIDDLETON, Rose	2m	C	D.C.	04 AUG 1875	Young Mens
017329	MIDDLETON, Rose Emma	3y	C	D.C.	05 SEP 1878	Mt. Olivet
000350	MIDDLETON, Sharlott	67y	C	Md.	28 AUG 1874	Mt. Zion
004242	MIDDLETON, Susan	60y	C	U.S.	22 JUL 1875	Potters Field
005144a	MIDDLETON, Wm. A.	6d	C	D.C.	14 OCT 1875	Ebenezer
020218	MIDLETON, Edward A.	2y	C	D.C.	28 MAY 1879	Beckett's
002994	MIDLETON, Samuel	6m	C	D.C.	15 APR 1875	Beckett's
015248	MIGLETON, John	55y	C	Va.	31 MAR 1878	Mt. Pleasant Plain
008208	MILANS, Anna Bella	22y	W	Pa.	12 JUL 1876	Congressional
010813	MILBURN, Infant of Mary	8d	C	D.C.	28 FEB 1877	Potters Field
001254	MILBURN, Margaret	72y	W	Va.	28 NOV 1874	Glenwood
012401	MILBURN, Mary	50y	C	Md.	17 JUL 1877	Mt. Olivet
018226	MILBURN, Samuel	82y	W	Md.	02 DEC 1878	Holy Rood
005274	MILES, Alice	89y	C	Md.	26 OCT 1875	Ebenezer
015642	MILES, Clarence	1y	C	D.C.	07 MAY 1878	Young Mens
015678	MILES, Emily	45y	C	Md.	10 MAY 1878	Beckett's
015989	MILES, Geo. W.	6m	W	D.C.	03 JUN 1878	Glenwood
003794	MILES, Jacob	80y	C	Va.	23 JUN 1875	Potters Field
003939	MILES, John Benjamin	9m	C	D.C.	30 JUN 1875	Beckett's
000417	MILES, John Mason	2y	W	D.C.	03 SEP 1874	Mt. Olivet
011459	MILES, Josephine	40y	W	D.C.	29 APR 1877	Potters Field
018060	MILES, Maria Ann	89y	W	Md.	15 NOV 1878	Mt. Olivet
005458	MILES, Mary Elizabeth	17y	C	D.C.	14 NOV 1875	Mt. Zion
020395	MILES, Mary Margaret Rosale	7m	W	D.C.	11 JUN 1879	Glenwood
006814	MILES, Mary Salestine	20y	M	Md.	25 MAR 1876	Beckett's
015599	MILES, Peter	27y	C	Va.	03 MAY 1878	Mt. Pleasant Plain
005183	MILES, Thomas H.	78y	W	Md.	26 SEP 1875	Mt. Olivet
019151	MILES, William	60y	C	Va.	22 FEB 1879	Potters Field
008383	MILFORD, Sarah	1m	C	D.C.	22 JUL 1876	Beckett's
013643	MILHORN, Clifton	1y	W	D.C.	26 OCT 1877	Glenwood
005114	MILLARD, Annie	10m	C	D.C.	20 SEP 1875	Young Mens
013742	MILLARD, Grace L.	20y	W	Va.	05 NOV 1877	Alexandria, Va.
010972	MILLARD, Ida Blanche	23y	W	Mass.	14 MAR 1877	Glenwood
005170a	MILLARD, Margaret	25y	C	Md.	16 OCT 1875	Mt. Pleasant
004002	MILLARD, Sarhea	13m	C	D.C.	04 JUL 1875	Beckett's
003747	MIILER, William	3m	W	D.C.	21 JUN 1875	Mt. Olivet
006136	MILLER, Agnes	48y	W	Eng.	25 JAN 1876	Congressional
009850	MILLER, Alice	8y	C	Va.	03 DEC 1876	Ebenezer
007046	MILLER, Alice E.	1m	W	D.C.	18 APR 1876	Congressional
010065	MILLER, Amelia	43y	C	Va.	25 DEC 1876	Young Mens
003969	MILLER, Anna F.	37y	W	Pa.	02 JUL 1875	Philadelphia, Pa.
004173	MILLER, Anna Margaret	3w	W	D.C.	17 JUL 1875	Philadelphia, Pa.
004580	MILLER, Baylss	84y	M	Va.	13 AUG 1875	Mt. Pleasant
012140	MILLER, Benjamin F.	6m	W	D.C.	30 JUN 1877	Oak Hill
009302	MILLER, Caspar	76y	W	Ger.	04 OCT 1876	Mt. Olivet

District of Columbia Death Records, August 1, 1874 to July 31, 1879

No.	Name	Age	Race	Birth	Death Date	Burial Place
002459	MILLER, Catherine	31y	W	D.C.	07 MAR 1875	St. Mary's
009765	MILLER, Catherine	3m	W	D.C.	21 NOV 1876	Congressional
005106a	MILLER, Charles	20y	W	Pa.	11 OCT 1875	Prospect Hill
020701	MILLER, Charles G.	37y	W	Ger.	01 JUL 1879	Prospect Hill
014754	MILLER, Charles Lewis	22y	W	N.Y.	13 FEB 1878	Congressional
005107a	MILLER, Chas. H.	9y	W	D.C.	11 OCT 1875	Prospect Hill
005288	MILLER, Chloe Ann	40y	C	Md.	28 OCT 1875	Beckett's
009844	MILLER, Christian	45y	W	Ger.	02 DEC 1876	Mt. Olivet
014803	MILLER, Christian	65y	W	Ger.	17 FEB 1878	Congressional
005294	MILLER, Clifford Morrison	1m	W	D.C.	28 OCT 1875	Congressional
015744	MILLER, Cornelius F.	54y	W	Md.	16 MAY 1878	Piscataway, Md.
015410	MILLER, Dehlia	16y	C	Va.	15 APR 1878	Potters Field
004294	MILLER, Delaware E.	8m	W	D.C.	25 JUL 1875	Presbyterian
013732	MILLER, Fannie Irma	2y	W	D.C.	04 NOV 1877	Glenwood
000624	MILLER, Frederick	34y	W	Switz.	24 SEP 1874	Washington Asylum
000236	MILLER, George	46y	W	Mass.	18 AUG 1874	Glenwood
005800	MILLER, George	70y	W	D.C.	19 DEC 1875	Glenwood
012876	MILLER, George	10d	W	D.C.	19 AUG 1877	Mt. Olivet
015373	MILLER, George	8y	C	D.C.	12 APR 1878	Potters Field
017024	MILLER, George	4y	C	D.C.	12 AUG 1878	Payne's
007311	MILLER, Gertrude	2m	W	D.C.	15 MAY 1876	Mt. Olivet
004949	MILLER, Henry	27d	W	D.C.	07 SEP 1875	Congressional
007614	MILLER, Henry	8m	C	D.C.	12 JUN 1876	Mt. Pleasant
011601	MILLER, Henry	43y	W	D.C.	15 MAY 1877	Glenwood
015399	MILLER, J. Harry S.	39y	W	Pa.	14 APR 1878	Congressional
005818	MILLER, Jacob	47y	W	Ger.	21 DEC 1875	Prospect Hill
008635	MILLER, Jacob	32y	W	Md.	10 AUG 1876	Mt. Olivet
000767	MILLER, James	66y	W	Ire.	09 OCT 1874	Rock Creek
015055	MILLER, James	41y	C	D.C.	13 MAR 1878	Mt. Pleasant
005759	MILLER, James J.	24y	C	Md.	15 DEC 1875	Young Mens
011705	MILLER, Jane	1d	W	D.C.	26 MAY 1877	Congressional
003485	MILLER, John	41y	W	Ger.	30 MAY 1875	Prospect Hill
011709	MILLER, John	21d	W	D.C.	26 MAY 1877	Congressional
005681	MILLER, John Andrew	1y	C	Va.	07 DEC 1875	Harmony
002154	MILLER, John Benjamin	36y	W	Scot.	14 FEB 1875	Glenwood
002731	MILLER, John Forest	4m	W	D.C.	25 MAR 1875	Presbyterian
018986	MILLER, John William	4y	W	D.C.	07 FEB 1879	St. Mary's
005221a	MILLER, Joseph	16y	C	Va.	20 OCT 1875	Mt. Pleasant
019898	MILLER, Joseph	6m	C	D.C.	25 APR 1879	Harmony
010846	MILLER, Louis	29y	W	Ger.	03 MAR 1877	Washington Asylum
001856	MILLER, Lucinda	17y	C	Md.	23 JAN 1875	Ebenezer
018404	MILLER, Luther	30y	C	Ohio	20 DEC 1878	Potters Field
009826	MILLER, Margaret A.	8d	W	D.C.	29 NOV 1876	Presbyterian
009943	MILLER, Mary B., Mrs.	72y	W	Pa.	12 DEC 1876	St. Clairsville, Ohio
019370	MILLER, Mary C.	30y	W	Ger.	12 MAR 1879	Congressional
005510	MILLER, Mary E.	c.38y	W	D.C.	19 NOV 1875	Prospect Hill
016634	MILLER, Nancy	79y	C	Va.	17 JUL 1878	Young Mens
016835	MILLER, Nicholas	57y	W	France	30 JUL 1878	Potters Field
005113	MILLER, Robert F.	7m	W	Md.	20 SEP 1875	Mt. Olivet
005731	MILLER, Robert R.	14d	W	D.C.	12 DEC 1875	Holy Rood
008186	MILLER, Sarah Jane	35y	W	Pa.	11 JUL 1876	Littleston, Pa.
015138	MILLER, Shelton	c.70y	C	Va.	21 MAR 1878	Young Mens
003229	MILLER, Thomas William	9d	C	D.C.	05 MAY 1875	Beckett's
013808	MILLER, V.S.	52y	W	Va.	12 NOV 1877	Lucust Hill, Va.
008504	MILLER, Wesley	35y	C	Md.	31 JUL 1876	Harmony
012352	MILLER, William V.	1y	W	D.C.	13 JUL 1877	St. Mary's

District of Columbia Death Records, August 1, 1874 to July 31, 1879

No.	Name	Age	Race	Birth	Death Date	Burial Place
004465	MILLER, Willie	1y	W	Pa.	05 AUG 1875	Philadelphia, Pa.
014271	MILLER, Wm. Hays	29y	W	Md.	30 DEC 1877	Petersburg, Pa.
020913	MILLES, Louis	46y	C	Md.	13 JUL 1879	Payne's
014840	MILLETT, Wm.	25y	C	Va.	21 FEB 1878	Young Mens
009268	MILLFORD, Jane	17y	C	D.C.	01 OCT 1876	Beckett's
003858	MILLIGAN, Genevieve	1m	W	D.C.	26 JUN 1875	Mt. Olivet
014802	MILLIGAN, Infant	12h	W	D.C.	17 FEB 1878	Glenwood
017507	MILLIGAN, William F.	21y	W	Ky.	23 SEP 1878	Mt. Olivet
009467	MILLIKEN, Eddie M.	6y	W	Me.	19 OCT 1876	Oak Hill
018300	MILLIKEN, Marion Louise	5y	W	D.C.	10 DEC 1878	Glenwood
018326	MILLIKEN, Nannie Lorine	1y	W	D.C.	13 DEC 1878	Glenwood
009788	MILLIONS, Lila	9y	C	D.C.	24 NOV 1876	Ebenezer
018050	MILLS, Albert J.	2y	W	D.C.	14 NOV 1878	Holy Rood
007947	MILLS, Barrett	5m	W	D.C.	01 JUL 1876	Congressional
000654f	MILLS, Catherine	28y	W	Va.	28 SEP 1874	Mt. Olivet
019253	MILLS, Catherine A.	57y	W	Va.	02 MAR 1879	Congressional
017947	MILLS, Chamberlain	48y	W	Va.	04 NOV 1878	Alexandria, Va.
014594	MILLS, Charles C.	8y	W	D.C.	29 JAN 1878	Holy Rood
003510	MILLS, Cora Louisa	1y	W	D.C.	02 JUN 1875	Congressional
019144	MILLS, Elizabeth	59y	C	Md.	21 FEB 1879	Mt. Zion
017590	MILLS, Elizziebeth	2y	W	D.C.	01 OCT 1878	Mt. Olivet
008542	MILLS, Ella	2y	W	D.C.	03 AUG 1876	Mt. Olivet
008563	MILLS, James A.	55y	C	Md.	05 AUG 1876	Mt. Olivet
001448	MILLS, James K.	44y	W	Ill.	20 DEC 1874	Springfield, Mass.
017841	MILLS, Jenny	8m	W	D.C.	23 OCT 1878	Mt. Olivet
000379	MILLS, Joseph Rawlings	11m	W	D.C.	30 AUG 1874	Presbyterian
008033	MILLS, Laura V.	3m	W	D.C.	05 JUL 1876	Alexandria, Va.
005706	MILLS, Mary Agnes	37y	W	D.C.	09 DEC 1875	Presbyterian
005125	MILLS, Mary S.	9m	W	D.C.	21 SEP 1875	Holy Rood
017119	MILLS, Sadie	10m	C	D.C.	20 AUG 1878	Mt. Pleasant
013687	MILNE, Jean May	25d	W	D.C.	31 OCT 1877	Glenwood
018985	MILSTEAD, Caroline	31y	W	D.C.	07 FEB 1879	Congressional
010087	MILSTEAD, Horatio	47y	W	Md.	27 DEC 1876	Potters Field
006883	MILSTEAD, Thomas Alfred	8m	W	D.C.	01 APR 1876	Congressional
006639	MILSTEAD, Wm. B.	42y	W	D.C.	11 MAR 1876	Congressional
010210	MILTON, Annie C.	5m	W	D.C.	07 JAN 1877	Congressional
005740	MILTON, Frances	2½d	C	D.C.	13 DEC 1875	Ebenezer
013997	MILTON, Mary T.	2y	W	D.C.	03 DEC 1877	Mt. Olivet
017948	MINDER, Elizabeth	50y	W	Ger.	04 NOV 1878	Prospect Hill
009816	MINER, Ann	22y	C	Va.	28 NOV 1876	Potters Field
011046	MINER, Infant of Ann	8m	C	D.C.	19 MAR 1877	Potters Field
005231a	MINER, Nancy	60y	M	Va.	21 OCT 1875	Young Mens
016512	MINER, Rebecca	24y	C	D.C.	09 JUL 1878	Harmony
012172	MINES, Dorothy	9m	C	D.C.	02 JUL 1877	Harmony
002686	MINITOR, Honora	c.54y	W	Ire.	22 MAR 1875	Mt. Olivet
002892	MINNETREE, Jane M., Miss	66y	W	Md.	06 APR 1875	Glenwood
001501	MINNIHAN, Michael	35y	W	Ire.	17 DEC 1874	Hospital
018167	MINNIS, Edward Francis	2m	C	D.C.	26 NOV 1878	Moore's
017579	MINNIS, Infant of Richd.	1d	C	D.C.	30 SEP 1878	Moore's
014841	MINNIS, Mary Jane	6y	C	D.C.	21 FEB 1878	Good Hope
012984	MINNITOR, Thomas	15y	W	D.C.	27 AUG 1877	Mt. Olivet
011715	MINNIX, John P.	38y	W	Va.	26 MAY 1877	Congressional
003455	MINNS, Nancy	45y	C	Va.	27 MAY 1875	Young Mens
018914	MINOR, Bettie	24y	C	Va.	01 FEB 1879	Beckett's
017084	MINOR, Clarrington	5y	C	D.C.	17 AUG 1878	Harmony
019082	MINOR, Edward	40y	C	Va.	15 FEB 1879	Beckett's

No.	Name	Age	Race	Birth	Death Date	Burial Place
019252	MINOR, Edward	6m	C	D.C.	02 MAR 1879	Mt. Zion
017643	MINOR, Ella	1y	C	D.C.	05 OCT 1878	Beckett's
019358	MINOR, Emma	4y	M	D.C.	10 MAR 1879	Mt. Zion
020700	MINOR, Fanny	80y	C	Va.	01 JUL 1879	Young Mens
001689	MINOR, Harriet	25y	C	Md.	10 JAN 1875	Young Mens
002960	MINOR, Hattie B.	5m	C	D.C.	11 APR 1875	Mt. Zion
008343	MINOR, James	11m	C	D.C.	20 JUL 1876	Young Mens
016093	MINOR, James T.	3m	C	D.C.	09 JUN 1878	Harmony
008710	MINOR, Jesse Francis	6m	C	D.C.	17 AUG 1876	Mt. Pleasant
000116	MINOR, Julia	1y	C	D.C.	09 AUG 1874	Beckett's
008034	MINOR, Lewis	6m	C	D.C.	05 JUL 1876	Potters Field
005082	MINOR, Louisa V.	43y	C	D.C.	17 SEP 1875	Harmony
019655	MINOR, Marietta S.	45y	W	Va.	04 APR 1879	Rock Creek
000744	MINOR, Mary	29y	C	D.C.	07 OCT 1874	Mt. Pleasant Plain
019873	MINOR, Mary	27y	C	Va.	23 APR 1879	Harmony
020584	MINOR, William	48y	C	Va.	23 JUN 1879	Harmony
002693	MINOR, Wm. Henry	52	C	D.C.	22 MAR 1875	Mt. Pleasant
011162	MINOR, Wm. Minor	12y	C	D.C.	30 MAR 1877	Beckett's
014227	MINTONY, Josephine	24y	W	N.Y.	27 DEC 1877	Brooklyn, N.Y.
016390	MIRIAM, Annette Rose	1y	W	D.C.	01 JUL 1878	Congressional
006727	MISTULI, Joseph	24y	W	Switz.	18 MAR 1876	Prospect Hill
005058	MITCHALL, Infant of John	9d	C	D.C.	15 SEP 1875	Ebenezer
001742	MITCHEL, Charley	1y	C	D.C.	15 JAN 1875	Mt. Pleasant
011846	MITCHEL, George W.	32y	C	Va.	09 JUN 1877	Methodist, Alex., Va.
000081	MITCHEL, John Thomas	10m	C	D.C.	06 AUG 1874	Beckett's
018289	MITCHEL, Martha	8m	C	D.C.	09 DEC 1878	Mt. Pleasant
013416	MITCHEL, Nannett	1m	W	D.C.	06 OCT 1877	Graceland
015443	MITCHELL, Albert B.	26y	W	D.C.	18 APR 1878	Mt. Olivet
016334	MITCHELL, Augustus M.	23y	W	D.C.	27 JUN 1878	Oak Hill
008500	MITCHELL, Bell	9m	C	D.C.	31 JUL 1876	Potters Field
018600	MITCHELL, Cecilia Bernadette	1y	W	D.C.	07 JAN 1879	Mt. Olivet
012999	MITCHELL, Charles	c.100y	C	Md.	28 AUG 1877	Harmony
014731	MITCHELL, Charles S.	1y	C	D.C.	09 FEB 1878	Mt. Zion
007294	MITCHELL, Daniel	35y	W	Ire.	13 MAY 1876	Hospital
003713	MITCHELL, Delia H.	22y	W	D.C.	19 JUN 1875	Congressional
005105a	MITCHELL, Ellen	66y	C	D.C.	11 OCT 1875	Mt. Olivet
012388	MITCHELL, Fanny Pearl	17d	C	D.C.	16 JUL 1877	Mt. Pleasant
004703	MITCHELL, Francis	1y	C	D.C.	21 AUG 1875	Ebenezer
011751	MITCHELL, Gertie	2y	W	D.C.	31 MAY 1877	Presbyterian
020641	MITCHELL, Henry	8m	C	D.C.	27 JUL 1879	Payne's
011718	MITCHELL, James	22y	C	Va.	27 MAY 1877	Potters Field
017095	MITCHELL, Jno. Robert	4d	W	D.C.	18 AUG 1878	Glenwood
018554	MITCHELL, John	72y	W	Eng.	03 JAN 1879	Soldier's Home
019244	MITCHELL, John Robert	25y	C	Va.	01 MAR 1879	Westmoreland Co., Va.
010861	MITCHELL, Joseph E.	28d	C	D.C.	04 MAR 1877	Holy Rood
000917	MITCHELL, Laura	25y	C	S.C.	24 OCT 1874	Beckett's
001621	MITCHELL, Maggie A.	24y	W	D.C.	05 JAN 1875	Mt. Olivet
020837	MITCHELL, Marcy Mayo	7m	W	D.C.	08 JUL 1879	Methodist
011951	MITCHELL, Margaret	79y	W	D.C.	18 JUN 1877	Presbyterian
014566	MITCHELL, Mary E.S. de'Courcy	59y	W	Md.	26 JAN 1878	Baltimore, Md.
005266	MITCHELL, Matilda E., Mrs.	73y	W	Va.	25 OCT 1875	Congressional
001418	MITCHELL, Minnie	8m	C	Va.	17 DEC 1874	Beckett's
014921	MITCHELL, Nancy	55y	C	Md.	02 MAR 1878	Harmony
008609	MITCHELL, Nelly	10m	C	D.C.	08 AUG 1876	Mt. Zion
001942	MITCHELL, Polly	20m	C	D.C.	29 JAN 1875	Potters Field
008734	MITCHELL, Sarah V.	25y	C	Va.	19 AUG 1876	Hamilton, Va.

District of Columbia Death Records, August 1, 1874 to July 31, 1879   239

No.	Name	Age	Race	Birth	Death Date	Burial Place
021025	MITCHELL, Selina Ann	8m	C	D.C.	20 JUL 1879	Graceland
005893	MITCHELL, Thomas	50y	C	Va.	29 DEC 1875	Alexandria, Va.
013224	MITCHELL, Thos. C.	65y	W	Ire.	16 SEP 1877	Mt. Olivet
000485	MITCHELL, Walter	8y	C	D.C.	12 SEP 1874	Beckett's
009002	MITZLER, August	47y	W	Ger.	08 SEP 1876	Prospect Hill
014433	MIX, Charles E.	67y	W	Conn.	15 JAN 1878	Oak Hill
020793	MOCKABEE, Annie Catherine	7m	W	D.C.	06 JUL 1879	Congressional
019479	MOCKABEE, Geo. W.	1m	W	D.C.	20 MAR 1879	Congressional
017840	MOCKEBEE, Margaret Sophia	65y	W	Md.	23 OCT 1878	Congressional
009870	MOCOY, Sarah	65y	W	Md.	05 DEC 1876	Shoemaker
013895	MOFFAT, Mary E.	34y	W	N.Y.	23 NOV 1877	Congressional
007513	MOHORNEY, Henry	80y	C	Md.	05 JUN 1876	Mt. Olivet
020536	MOHUN, Francis	69y	W	Ire.	20 JUN 1879	Congressional
000351	MOLL, Andrew	1y	C	D.C.	28 AUG 1874	Beckett's
003131	MOLLER, Americus	6m	C	D.C.	26 APR 1875	Mt. Pleasant
012273	MOLONEY, John	36y	W	Ire.	09 JUL 1877	Mt. Olivet
013184	MOLROW, Katharina	1y	W	D.C.	13 SEP 1877	Prospect Hill
001470	MOLTON, Adelaide	9y	C	D.C.	24 DEC 1874	Young Mens
008814	MOLTON, Gertrude	10m	C	D.C.	25 AUG 1876	Potters Field
009457	MOLTON, Julia	9y	C	Va.	18 OCT 1876	Young Mens
017506	MOLTON, Matilda	4y	C	D.C.	23 SEP 1878	Young Mens
019286	MONAGHAN, James	45y	W	Ire.	05 MAR 1879	Mt. Olivet
014079	MONGOMERY, George	1y	C	D.C.	12 DEC 1877	Potters Field
003738	MONROE, Arthur S.	4m	W	D.C.	21 JUN 1875	Congressional
013644	MONROE, Charles	3m	C	D.C.	26 OCT 1877	Washington Asylum
003188	MONROE, Elizabeth	77y	W	Va.	01 MAY 1875	Prospect Hill
018937	MONROE, Elizabeth	68y	C	Va.	03 FEB 1879	Payne's
009240	MONROE, James	11y	C	D.C.	29 SEP 1876	Mt. Zion
007364	MONROE, Lucinda	63y	C	Va.	21 MAY 1876	Potters Field
017913	MONROE, Oscar	25y	C	Va.	31 OCT 1878	Potters Field
014871	MONROE, Richard	1y	C	D.C.	25 FEB 1878	Beckett's
017284	MONROE, Sarah	8d	C	D.C.	01 SEP 1878	Beckett's
009895	MONROE, Sterne	c.40y	C	Va.	07 DEC 1876	Potters Field
010569	MONTAGUE, Corraza	16m	C	D.C.	09 FEB 1877	Young Mens
002375	MONTAGUE, H.	26y	C	Mass.	01 MAR 1875	Mt. Pleasant
002560	MONTAGUE, James	55y	C	Va.	13 MAR 1875	Mt. Zion
018526	MONTAGUE, Lewis	31y	C	Va.	31 DEC 1878	Harmony
008853	MONTAGUE, Nanie C.	1y	C	D.C.	28 AUG 1876	Beckett's
011105	MONTAGUE, Thomas Francis	30y	W	Pa.	24 MAR 1877	Soldier's Home
011544	MONTEGRIFFO, Pauline	10m	W	D.C.	08 MAY 1877	St. Mary's
011311	MONTGOMERY, Elias Henry	1y	C	D.C.	12 APR 1877	Ebenezer
018915	MONTGOMERY, Henrietta	63y	W	Md.	01 FEB 1879	White Plain Station
020286	MONTGOMERY, James William	6m	C	D.C.	05 JUN 1879	Harmony
014830	MONTGOMERY, Mary Ellen	33y	W	Md.	20 FEB 1878	Congressional
006753	MONTGOMERY, Matilda Eliza	50y	W	Ala.	20 MAR 1876	Oak Hill/Canada
009570	MONTGOMERY, Rebecca	15m	C	D.C.	29 OCT 1876	Beckett's
018085	MONTGOMERY, Sarah E.	3y	C	D.C.	18 NOV 1878	Holy Rood
003681	MOOD, Sarah	58y	W	Va.	17 JUN 1875	Westmoreland Co., Va.
001064	MOODEY, Jacob	25y	C	Md.	06 NOV 1874	Potters Field
010844	MOODY, Annie L.	9y	W	D.C.	02 MAR 1877	Presbyterian
014773	MOODY, Theodore Lyman	73y	W	Me.	15 FEB 1878	Rock Creek
003482	MOODY, Wm.	2y	C	D.C.	29 MAY 1875	Ebenezer
013798	MOOG, Lewis	6d	C	D.C.	11 NOV 1877	Prospect Hill
011119	MOON, Mary Ann	76y	W	Ire.	26 MAR 1877	Oak Hill
004417	MOONEY, Joseph	11m	W	D.C.	02 AUG 1875	Mt. Olivet
015537	MOONEY, Patrick	45y	W	Ire.	27 APR 1878	Hospital, Government

District of Columbia Death Records, August 1, 1874 to July 31, 1879

No.	Name	Age	Race	Birth	Death Date	Burial Place
012242	MOOR, Charlott	4m	C	D.C.	06 JUL 1877	Harmony
001895	MOOR, Clara	35y	C	Ohio	26 JAN 1875	Washington Asylum
018191	MOORE, Ada C.	36y	W	Va.	28 NOV 1878	Graceland/Woodlawn
000424	MOORE, Adda	2y	C	D.C.	04 SEP 1874	Moore's
014310	MOORE, Aleane	25y	W	Md.	03 JAN 1878	Leonardtown, Md.
012732	MOORE, Alexander	15y	C	Va.	08 AUG 1877	Ebenezer
015710	MOORE, Annie	2m	W	D.C.	13 MAY 1878	Graceland
008598	MOORE, Caroline Cottringer	80y	W	Pa.	07 AUG 1876	Mt. Olivet
020598	MOORE, Catherine	64y	W	Md.	24 JUN 1879	Barnabas Church
012631	MOORE, Charlotte	15y	C	D.C.	01 AUG 1877	Ebenezer
016581	MOORE, Christiana	2y	W	D.C.	13 JUL 1878	Rock Creek
012292	MOORE, Corwin Neville	1m	W	D.C.	10 JUL 1877	Congressional
005536	MOORE, Douglass	57y	W	Md.	22 NOV 1875	Glenwood
003744	MOORE, Elenora	1m	C	D.C.	21 JUN 1875	Harmony
007863	MOORE, Emma Estelle	8m	W	D.C.	26 JUN 1876	Mt. Olivet
011809	MOORE, Flora	77y	C	D.C.	05 JUN 1877	Harmony
004063	MOORE, Frederick Dimmitt	1y	W	D.C.	09 JUL 1875	Cincinnati, Ohio
009436	MOORE, Geo. W.	4y	C	Md.	16 OCT 1876	Potters Field
002175	MOORE, Henry	62y	C	Va.	15 FEB 1875	Washington Asylum
020224	MOORE, Infant of Geo. D.	6h	W	D.C.	29 MAY 1879	St. Mary's
011728	MOORE, Infant of George	½h	C	D.C.	28 MAY 1877	Beckett's
012342	MOORE, Infant of J.H.	5d	C	D.C.	13 JUL 1877	Ebenezer
012936	MOORE, Infant of Jas. W.	4d	W	D.C.	24 AUG 1877	Mt. Olivet
006367	MOORE, Infant of Martin	4d	C	D.C.	15 FEB 1876	Ebenezer
008264	MOORE, James	5m	C	D.C.	14 JUL 1876	Young Mens
019424	MOORE, James Alexander	41y	C	Va.	16 MAR 1879	Young Mens
002060	MOORE, John	60y	W	Pa.	07 FEB 1875	Washington Asylum
002770	MOORE, John	32y	W	Ire.	28 MAR 1875	Mt. Olivet
005597	MOORE, John	87y	W	Md.	28 NOV 1875	Oak Hill
010593	MOORE, John M.	40y	C	Va.	12 FEB 1877	Harmony
003181	MOORE, John Thomas	5m	W	D.C.	30 APR 1875	Congressional
017602	MOORE, Lena Grant	8d	W	D.C.	02 OCT 1878	Congressional
018044	MOORE, Linnie	70y	M	Md.	13 NOV 1878	Beckett's
017995	MOORE, Louise	28y	M	D.C.	09 NOV 1878	Young Mens
019110	MOORE, Lucy	35y	W	Va.	18 FEB 1879	Harmony
003434	MOORE, Marcia R.	4y	W	D.C.	25 MAY 1875	Glenwood
014007	MOORE, Margaretta	57y	C	Md.	04 DEC 1877	Moore's
004018	MOORE, Margrata	4m	C	D.C.	06 JUL 1875	Moore's
001310	MOORE, Martha Ann	32y	C	--	05 DEC 1874	Beckett's
010101	MOORE, Mary C.	83y	W	Va.	28 DEC 1876	Oak Hill
003386	MOORE, Mary Jane	60y	C	Md.	21 MAY 1875	Mt. Olivet
006207	MOORE, Michael	56y	W	Ire.	01 FEB 1876	Mt. Olivet
002441	MOORE, Mollie	19y	W	D.C.	05 MAR 1875	Glenwood
019734	MOORE, Nancy	82y	C	Va.	11 APR 1879	Alexandria, Va.
012558	MOORE, Robert	1y	C	D.C.	27 JUL 1877	Young Mens
013010	MOORE, Sarah	5m	C	D.C.	29 AUG 1877	Potters Field
018224	MOORE, Sarah	81y	C	D.C.	02 DEC 1878	Potters Field
019212	MOORE, Sarah	80y	C	Va.	26 FEB 1879	Graceland
020999	MOORE, Sarah W.	76	W	N.H.	18 JUL 1879	Oak Hill
014699	MOORE, Selena	24y	C	Va.	07 FEB 1878	Young Mens
016672	MOORE, William Appleton	7m	W	D.C.	26 JUL 1878	Congressional
000682	MOORE, William Henry	8m	C	D.C.	01 OCT 1874	Harmony
006550	MOORE, William Henry	20y	M	D.C.	04 MAR 1876	Harmony
005954	MOORE, Willis	54y	M	Va.	06 JAN 1876	Young Mens
015100	MOORES, Ella Lula	4y	W	D.C.	17 MAR 1878	Glenwood
012528	MORAN, Bessie	1y	W	D.C.	25 JUL 1877	Oak Hill

District of Columbia Death Records, August 1, 1874 to July 31, 1879

No.	Name	Age	Race	Birth	Death Date	Burial Place
010388	MORAN, Eddie Lee	1y	W	D.C.	23 JAN 1877	Congressional
009839	MORAN, Eliza	48y	W	Ire.	01 DEC 1876	Oak Hill
004507	MORAN, Ella	1y	W	D.C.	08 AUG 1875	Mt. Olivet
005355	MORAN, John	43y	W	Ire.	04 NOV 1875	Holy Rood
004729	MORAN, Julia	2m	W	D.C.	23 AUG 1875	Holy Rood
005562	MORAN, Lauretia	5m	W	D.C.	25 NOV 1875	Holy Rood
005387	MORAN, Margaret	3y	W	D.C.	07 NOV 1875	Holy Rood
006767	MORAN, Wiliam Richard	31y	W	D.C.	21 MAR 1876	Congressional
000140	MORAN, Wilson	1y	W	D.C.	11 AUG 1874	Holy Rood
004866	MORAN, Wm. Plume	7m	W	D.C.	01 SEP 1875	Oak Hill
004954	MORCOE, Sarah Ann	30y	W	Md.	08 SEP 1875	Glenwood
005976	MOREHEAD, Armstead Henly	59y	W	Va.	08 JAN 1876	Front Royal, Va.
014228	MOREHEAD, Catharine	5m	C	D.C.	27 DEC 1877	Potters Field
009652	MOREHEAD, Edmonia	2y	C	Md.	09 NOV 1876	Potters Field
009249	MOREHEAD, Geo. W.	53y	C	D.C.	30 SEP 1876	Potters Field
009563	MORELAND, Caroline	52y	W	Md.	28 OCT 1876	Rock Creek
015670	MORELAND, John Randolph	1y	W	D.C.	09 MAY 1878	Rock Creek
018654	MORELAND, Mary A.	36y	W	D.C.	12 JAN 1879	Carroll Chapel
014915	MORELAND, Walter Allison	1m	W	D.C.	01 MAR 1878	Rock Creek
013241	MORELL, John	22y	W	Ire.	18 SEP 1877	Congressional
021053	MORGAN, Albert	4m	C	D.C.	22 JUL 1879	Mt. Olivet
002575	MORGAN, Alice E.	5y	W	D.C.	15 MAR 1875	Francistown, N.H.
012607	MORGAN, Arogona Amelia	4m	W	D.C.	30 JUL 1877	Congressional
020838	MORGAN, Benjamin	55y	C	S.C.	08 JUL 1879	Potters Field
001527	MORGAN, Elizebeth	47y	C	Va.	28 DEC 1874	Mt. Zion
014130	MORGAN, Eugene F.	1m	W	D.C.	18 DEC 1877	Holy Rood
002574	MORGAN, Florence	3y	W	D.C.	15 MAR 1875	Francistown, N.H.
016960	MORGAN, Francis	6y	W	D.C.	08 AUG 1878	Oak Hill
007824	MORGAN, George	5m	W	D.C.	24 JUN 1876	Mt. Olivet
015728	MORGAN, George S.R.	73y	W	D.C.	14 MAY 1878	Oak Hill
019926	MORGAN, Hampton	28y	C	Va.	28 APR 1879	Payne's
001822	MORGAN, Infant of Daniel	10h	C	D.C.	21 JAN 1875	Mt. Zion
007501	MORGAN, James	39y	W	Ire.	04 JUN 1876	Mt. Olivet
009094	MORGAN, Joseph C.	6m	W	D.C.	16 SEP 1876	Philadelphia, Pa.
016818	MORGAN, Julia	17m	W	D.C.	29 JUL 1878	Mt. Olivet
017578	MORGAN, Lawrence	32y	W	Md.	30 SEP 1878	Baltimore, Md.
013231	MORGAN, Lucy	60y	C	Va.	17 SEP 1877	Potters Field
020761	MORGAN, Lucy E.	6m	W	D.C.	04 JUL 1879	Oak Hill
012551	MORGAN, Margarett	18d	W	D.C.	27 JUL 1877	Congressional
009480	MORGAN, Mary	76y	W	Ire.	21 OCT 1876	Holy Rood
018335	MORGAN, Mary	65y	W	Va.	14 DEC 1878	Graceland
011308	MORGAN, Mary Elizabeth	c.3y	C	D.C.	22 APR 1877	Young Mens
017186	MORGAN, Nelson	90y	C	Va.	25 AUG 1878	Beckett's
006433	MORGAN, Rachael	39y	C	Va.	21 FEB 1876	Young Mens
001485	MORGAN, Sally	2y	M	D.C.	25 DEC 1874	Potters Field
003674	MORGAN, William	1d	W	D.C.	17 JUN 1875	Graceland
010680	MORGAN, William	20y	W	D.C.	18 FEB 1877	Mt. Olivet
008558	MORGAN, William E.	c.4m	W	D.C.	04 AUG 1876	Glenwood
017311	MORGAN, William S.	77y	W	W.Va.	03 SEP 1878	Congressional
017957	MORGANTHAL, Betty	54y	W	Ger.	05 NOV 1878	Washington Hebrew
011973	MORGENTHOL, Bernhard	39y	W	Ger.	19 JUN 1877	Washington Hebrew
015339	MORIARTY, Mary A.	2y	W	D.C.	09 APR 1878	W. Manchester, Conn.
018729	MORISON, Sarah	65y	C	Va.	19 JAN 1879	Mt. Zion
004894	MORLER, William	1y	C	D.C.	03 SEP 1875	Ebenezer
010113	MORLEY, Mary, Mrs.	55y	W	Ire.	29 DEC 1876	Mt. Olivet
003882	MORONEY, Cathrine	56y	W	Ire.	27 JUN 1875	Mt. Olivet

No.	Name	Age	Race	Birth	Death Date	Burial Place
015507	MORR, Samuel Stuart, Jr.	3y	W	D.C.	24 APR 1878	Mt. Olivet
004765	MORRICE, Marcillas	36y	W	Md.	26 AUG 1875	Mt. Olivet
009301	MORRIS, Catherine	1m	W	D.C.	04 OCT 1876	Mt. Olivet
007004	MORRIS, David	59y	W	N.Y.	12 APR 1876	Hospital
014842	MORRIS, Edith F.	2y	C	D.C.	21 FEB 1878	Mt. Zion
014603	MORRIS, Eliza A.	71y	W	D.C.	30 JAN 1878	Congressional
004619f	MORRIS, George Upham, Capt.	45y	W	Mass.	15 AUG 1875	Oak Hill
020660	MORRIS, Gilbert	8m	W	D.C.	28 JUN 1879	Graceland
007470	MORRIS, Hanah	41y	M	D.C.	02 JUN 1876	Harmony
016743	MORRIS, Harriet	86y	W	R.I.	24 JUL 1878	Oak Hill
001750	MORRIS, Henry	5m	C	D.C.	16 JAN 1875	Young Mens
002322	MORRIS, James	79y	W	Ire.	25 FEB 1875	Hospital
003313	MORRIS, John	23m	C	Va.	13 MAY 1875	Potters Field
002047	MORRIS, John H.	7d	W	D.C.	06 FEB 1875	Mt. Olivet
014822	MORRIS, Julia Elizabeth, Mrs.	32y	C	D.C.	19 FEB 1878	Harmony
009525	MORRIS, Louisa	70y	C	D.C.	25 OCT 1876	Mt. Olivet
019475	MORRIS, Mamie	20m	C	D.C.	20 MAR 1879	Mt. Pleasant
010316	MORRIS, Margaret	18y	M	Md.	17 JAN 1877	Moore's
012438	MORRIS, Martha E.	8y	C	D.C.	20 JUL 1877	Mt. Zion
003254	MORRIS, Mary Elizabeth	22y	W	Pa.	07 MAY 1875	Congressional
011993	MORRIS, Peter	1y	C	D.C.	21 JUN 1877	Ebenezer
010403	MORRIS, Virginia	16y	C	D.C.	25 JAN 1877	Harmony
010739	MORRIS, W.H.	16y	W	Del.	22 FEB 1877	Glenwood
008514	MORRIS, Walter J.	2m	W	D.C.	01 AUG 1876	Mt. Olivet
007596	MORRIS, William	30y	W	Me.	11 JUN 1876	Potters Field
020718	MORRIS, William	59y	C	Va.	02 JUL 1879	Potters Field
009165	MORRIS, Wm.	2m	W	D.C.	22 SEP 1876	Graceland
012670	MORRISEY, Thomas	55y	W	Ire.	04 AUG 1877	Mt. Olivet
013210	MORRISON, Anna	14d	C	D.C.	15 SEP 1877	Potters Field
016593	MORRISON, Emma Virginia	1y	W	Md.	14 JUL 1878	Congressional
013340	MORRISON, Hester A.R.	60y	W	Va.	28 SEP 1877	Congressional
011944	MORRISON, Infant of Solomon	2h	C	D.C.	17 JUN 1877	Young Mens
001259	MORRISON, John T.	50y	W	Ind.	28 NOV 1874	Indianapolis, Ind.
020343	MORRISON, Mary Benigna	50y	W	Ire.	08 JUN 1879	Convent
019295	MORRISON, Minnie	1y	W	D.C.	06 MAR 1879	Potters Field
005849	MORRISON, Obediah Hall	52y	W	N.H.	24 DEC 1875	Glenwood
020794	MORRISON, Ralph E.	7m	W	D.C.	06 JUL 1879	Glenwood
010685	MORRISON, Wallace R.	19m	W	D.C.	18 FEB 1877	Oak Hill
006216	MORRISSEY, Margaret	23y	C	Va.	02 FEB 1876	Potters Field
011514	MORRISY, Elizabeth	47y	W	Va.	04 MAY 1877	Fredericksburg, Va.
013163	MORROW, George	77y	W	Ire.	11 SEP 1877	Soldier's Home
017555	MORROW, James	37y	W	Va.	28 SEP 1878	Congressional
008335	MORROW, Joseph Howard	2y	C	D.C.	19 JUL 1876	Potters Field
012126	MORSE, Blanch	7m	C	D.C.	29 JUN 1877	Harmony
010286	MORSE, Delia C.	41y	W	N.Y.	14 JAN 1877	Congressional
016389	MORSELL, Elizabeth E.	61y	W	Md.	01 JUL 1878	Oak Hill
019251	MORSHEL, Allen	13m	C	D.C.	02 MAR 1879	Young Mens
002810	MORTEN, John	36y	C	Va.	31 MAR 1875	Beckett's
007933	MORTIMER, William	6d	W	D.C.	30 JUN 1876	Alexandria, Va.
012824	MORTIMER, Wm.	98y	W	Va.	15 AUG 1877	Mt. Olivet
001490	MORTIN, Wm. G.M.	5½y	W	D.C.	26 DEC 1874	Graceland
015823	MORTON, Charles	33y	W	Mich.	24 MAY 1878	Soldier's Home
019884	MORTON, Dina	39y	C	Va.	24 APR 1879	Harmony
008029	MORTON, Eva E.	6m	C	D.C.	05 JUL 1876	Mt. Zion
009330	MORTON, George A.	3y	C	Va.	07 OCT 1876	Young Mens
000795	MORTON, Georgiana	12y	C	D.C.	13 OCT 1874	Harmony

District of Columbia Death Records, August 1, 1874 to July 31, 1879   243

No.	Name	Age	Race	Birth	Death Date	Burial Place
018423	MORTON, Gertie	1y	M	D.C.	22 DEC 1878	Potters Field
015837	MORTON, Henry Stewart	6y	C	Va.	25 MAY 1878	Beckett's
006516	MORTON, Infant	5d	C	D.C.	01 MAR 1876	Mt. Pleasant
002798	MORTON, Infant of Edward	1½d	C	D.C.	30 MAR 1875	Mt. Pleasant
005391	MORTON, Infant of Glenmore	14d	C	D.C.	08 NOV 1875	Mt. Zion
005420	MORTON, Infant of Julia	5m	C	D.C.	10 NOV 1875	Potters Field
005048	MORTON, Infant of Robert	23h	C	D.C.	15 SEP 1875	Young Mens
007946	MORTON, Joseph	c.80y	C	Va.	01 JUL 1876	Potters Field
011421	MORTON, Joseph	3m	C	D.C.	25 APR 1877	Young Mens
001694	MORTON, Margaret Ellen	12d	C	D.C.	11 JAN 1875	Beckett's
009203	MORTON, Martha	1y	C	D.C.	25 SEP 1876	Beckett's
003698	MORTON, Mary	50y	C	Va.	18 JUN 1875	Mt. Pleasant
019591	MORTON, Thomas	1y	C	D.C.	29 MAR 1879	Payne's
005680	MORTON, William	37y	C	Va.	07 DEC 1875	Ebenezer
003782	MOSEE, Richard	45y	C	Va.	23 JUN 1875	Beckett's
003983	MOSEL, Benjamin	8y	C	Va.	03 JUL 1875	Alexandria, Va.
015684	MOSELEY, Martha W.	75y	W	Va.	11 MAY 1878	Norfolk, Va.
015259	MOSELEY, Mary Francis	10m	M	D.C.	01 APR 1878	Young Mens
021137	MOSHENVEL, Harry	4m	W	D.C.	28 JUL 1879	Prospect Hill
013350	MOSHER, Eliza Mary	80y	W	D.C.	29 SEP 1877	Holy Rood
016930	MOSHER, George P.	78y	W	R.I.	06 AUG 1878	Soldier's Home
004547	MOSHER, Infant of D.C.	1m	W	Md.	11 AUG 1875	Oak Hill
000282	MOSHER, Nelly Brent	3y	W	DC	22 AUG 1874	Carroll Chapel, Md.
016773	MOSHER, Theodore	53y	W	D.C.	26 JUL 1878	Carroll Chapel
010451	MOSHER, William Longford	1m	W	D.C.	30 JAN 1877	Rock Creek
001970	MOSS, Ellen Jeanette	1y	W	D.C.	01 FEB 1875	Oak Hill
010396	MOSS, Emily Latimer	1y	W	Va.	24 JAN 1877	Fauquier Co., Va.
005817	MOSS, Jane G.	62y	W	D.C.	21 DEC 1875	Mt. Olivet
012953	MOSS, Louise	45y	C	Va.	25 AUG 1877	Harmony
015600	MOSS, Mary	9m	W	D.C.	03 MAY 1878	Gainesville, Pa.
014461	MOTEN, Albert E.	11m	W	D.C.	17 JAN 1878	Mt. Pleasant
017357	MOTEN, Benj.	56y	C	Md.	09 SEP 1878	Harmony
005222	MOTEN, Harry	18y	C	Va.	29 SEP 1875	Harmony
004359	MOTON, Caroline	30y	C	Va.	28 JUL 1875	Ebenezer
003785	MOTON, George E.	6m	M	D.C.	23 JUN 1875	Mt. Zion
019818	MOTON, Infant of Silas	1d	C	D.C.	18 APR 1879	Potters Field
006404	MOTON, John Henry	5y	C	D.C.	18 FEB 1876	Young Mens
008292	MOTON, Wesley	1y	C	Va.	16 JUL 1876	Potters Field
001823	MOTTO, Paul	66y	W	Tenn.	21 JAN 1875	Presbyterian
000901	MOULDEN, Florence	3y	W	D.C.	22 OCT 1874	Glenwood
011197	MOULDEN, George	2y	C	D.C.	02 APR 1877	Harmony
015685	MOULDEN, Hazleton Evans	3d	W	D.C.	11 MAY 1878	Glenwood
010251	MOULDIN, Beorganna	5y	C	D.C.	11 JAN 1877	Ebenezer
000527	MOULDING, Thomas	52y	W	Va.	16 SEP 1874	Mt. Olivet
004614	MOULTHROP, Selina Ash	72y	W	Conn.	15 AUG 1875	New Haven, Conn.
000080	MOULTON, Carrie	15m	C	D.C.	06 AUG 1874	Young Mens
006405	MOULTON, Charles F.	4m	W	D.C.	18 FEB 1876	Oak Hill
001011	MOULTON, Eveline	19y	C	Va.	01 NOV 1874	Harmony
003554	MOULTON, Herbert Beecher	2y	W	D.C.	07 JUN 1875	Glenwood
018694	MOULTON, Infant of Martha	6d	C	D.C.	16 JAN 1879	Payne's
005051	MOULTON, Infant of Robt.	2h	C	D.C.	15 SEP 1875	Young Mens
008452	MOULTON, John	1y	C	Va.	28 JUL 1876	Young Mens
004202	MOULTON, Julia	c.36y	M	Va.	19 JUL 1875	Young Mens
017495	MOULTON, Kate	20y	C	Va.	22 SEP 1878	Potters Field
014131	MOULTON, Martha	20y	C	Va.	18 DEC 1877	Beckett's
020243	MOULTON, Nelson	70y	C	Va.	31 MAY 1879	Harmony

No.	Name	Age	Race	Birth	Death Date	Burial Place
001484	MOULTON, Odoway	3m	C	D.C.	25 DEC 1874	Potters Field
004001	MOULTON, Rebecca	53y	C	Va.	04 JUL 1875	Young Mens
012217	MOULTON, Rose	10m	C	D.C.	04 JUL 1877	Young Mens
009050	MOULTON, Sarah	30y	W	Eng.	13 SEP 1876	Rock Creek
018671	MOULTON, Silas	39y	C	Ga.	14 JAN 1879	Potters Field
010696	MOULTON, Starr F.	1m	W	D.C.	19 FEB 1877	Oak Hill
018786	MOXLEY, Harry Ed	15d	W	D.C.	23 JAN 1879	Congressional
018623	MOXLEY, Infant of Edward	1d	W	D.C.	09 JAN 1879	Congressional
021098	MOXLEY, Joseph	22y	C	Va.	25 JUL 1879	Potters Field
013437	MOYNAHAN, Daniel H.	19y	W	Va.	08 OCT 1877	Mt. Olivet
014352	MOYNEHAN, Joseph	56y	W	Ire.	07 JAN 1878	Mt. Olivet
009354	MUDD, Annie B.	22y	W	D.C.	09 OCT 1876	Presbyterian
012900	MUDD, Charlotte	75y	C	Md.	21 AUG 1877	Potters Field
006370	MUDD, Daniel E.	57y	W	D.C.	13 FEB 1876	Congressional
018269	MUDD, Sarah	53y	W	D.C.	07 DEC 1878	Presbyterian
009878	MUDENIAN, Infant of Mary	36h	W	D.C.	05 DEC 1876	Glenwood
008285	MUDDGETT, Lutteanitt H.	8y	W	D.C.	16 JUL 1876	Congressional
010610	MUDGEN, SArah	18y	C	Va.	13 FEB 1877	Potters Field
008305	MUELLER, Ellis	1y	W	D.C.	17 JUL 1876	Prospect Hill
017285	MUELLER, Peter Joseph	2y	W	D.C.	01 SEP 1878	St. Mary's
011116	MUETT, Henry	55y	W	Ger.	26 MAR 1877	Potters Field
008726	MUGG, John Henry	1y	W	D.C.	18 AUG 1876	Congressional
015324	MUIR, Lewis	48y	W	Ger.	08 APR 1878	Soldier's Home
004849	MULCAHEY, Annie	11m	W	D.C.	31 AUG 1875	Mt. Olivet
007713	MULCAHY, Patrick	46y	W	Ire.	18 JUN 1876	Mt. Olivet
011989	MULCARE, Manuel	46y	W	Ire.	21 JUN 1877	Mt. Olivet
000442	MULCHALEY, Dan'l.	9y	W	D.C.	06 SEP 1874	Mt. Olivet
003884	MULDOON, John Francis	3m	W	D.C.	27 JUN 1875	Mt. Olivet
020865	MULLALY, Charles W.	35y	W	N.Y.	09 JUL 1879	Mt. Olivet
021028	MULLALY, Edward	4m	W	D.C.	20 JUL 1879	Mt. Olivet
015411	MULLEN, Basil	82y	C	Md.	15 APR 1878	Mt. Olivet
017061	MULLEN, Bridgett A.	47y	W	Ire.	15 AUG 1878	Mt. Olivet
001809	MULLEN, Infant of Angelica	4d	C	D.C.	20 JAN 1875	Mt. Olivet
008252	MULLEN, Nancy	65y	M	Va.	13 JUL 1876	Mt. Pleasant
001919	MULLEN, Richmond B.	24y	C	D.C.	27 JAN 1875	Mt. Olivet
006378	MULLEN, William	6d	W	D.C.	16 FEB 1876	Balls Cross Roads, Va.
008330	MULLIGAN, Edward E.	10m	W	D.C.	19 JUL 1876	Mt. Olivet
010919	MULLIKEN, Nathaniel	76y	W	Md.	08 MAR 1877	Glenwood
010425	MULLIKEN, Sarah, Mrs.	74y	W	Md.	28 JAN 1877	Methodist
007681	MULLOY, Kate Esther	16y	W	Mich.	16 JUN 1876	Glenwood
021084	MULLOY, Thos. J.	70y	W	D.C.	24 JUL 1879	Mt. Olivet
012354	MULONY, Michael	1y	W	D.C.	14 JUL 1877	Mt. Olivet
012825	MULVIHILL, Edward	10m	W	D.C.	15 AUG 1877	Mt. Olivet
011173	MUNCASTER, Charles N.	6y	W	D.C.	31 MAR 1877	Congressional
002054	MUNDAY, Charles	24y	C	Va.	06 FEB 1875	Harmony
000461	MUNDELL, Joseph	65y	W	Ire.	09 SEP 1874	Congressional
017241	MUNDHEIM, Simon	c.70y	W	Ger.	29 AUG 1878	Washington Hebrew
012120	MUNGEN, Ellen Cecelia Ragan	29y	W	D.C.	29 JUN 1877	Congressional
016545	MUNN, Cupid	80y	C	Va.	10 JUL 1878	Potters Field
015325	MUNN, E.H.	61y	W	N.Y.	08 APR 1878	Congressional
017695	MUNN, Melinda	70y	C	Va.	10 OCT 1878	Potters Field
019371	MUNN, Sarah	c.37y	W	Ire.	12 MAR 1879	Mt. Olivet
004613	MUNNYOS, Mary Wilson	22y	W	Pa.	15 AUG 1875	Mt. Olivet
018794	MUNOZ, Jacoba Rodriguez de	45y	W	Cuba	24 JAN 1879	Holy Rood
011377	MUNROE, Alfred	6m	C	D.C.	20 APR 1877	Harmony
007680	MUNROE, Betsy	1y	C	N.C.	16 JUN 1876	Beckett's

District of Columbia Death Records, August 1, 1874 to July 31, 1879   245

No.	Name	Age	Race	Birth	Death Date	Burial Place
017034	MUNROE, George	23y	C	Va.	13 AUG 1878	Payne's
007352	MUNROE, John	9y	C	N.C.	20 MAY 1876	Beckett's
007406	MUNROE, Minnie	5y	C	N.C.	25 MAY 1876	Potters Field
004716	MUNSCH, William Cornelius	28d	W	D.C.	22 AUG 1875	Prospect Hill
007293	MUNTS, Archie	50y	C	Va.	13 MAY 1876	Potters Field
002977	MURCHANT, Benjamin	5m	C	D.C.	13 APR 1875	Ebenezer
008203	MURDOCK, Sarah A.	18y	W	Md.	12 JUL 1876	Holy Rood
019449	MURDOCK, William	4m	W	D.C.	18 MAR 1879	Mt. Olivet
007826	MURGRUTER, Denley	14m	C	D.C.	24 JUN 1876	Ebenezer
012487	MURPHEY, Agnes	1y	W	D.C.	23 JUL 1877	Mt. Olivet
002452	MURPHEY, Michael	37y	W	Md.	06 MAR 1875	Holy Rood
005146a	MURPHY, Alice	50y	W	Ire.	14 OCT 1875	Mt. Olivet
007327	MURPHY, Barney	1½d	W	D.C.	17 MAY 1876	Mt. Olivet
018166	MURPHY, Barthamew	26y	W	Ire.	26 NOV 1878	Mt. Olivet
004144	MURPHY, Buelah Louise	19d	W	D.C.	15 JUL 1875	Rock Creek
005054a	MURPHY, Catharine Virga.	32y	W	D.C.	04 OCT 1875	Congressional
016423	MURPHY, Catherine E.	3m	W	D.C.	03 JUL 1878	Mt. Olivet
003968	MURPHY, Catherine Elizabeth	4m	W	D.C.	02 JUL 1875	Mt. Olivet
002667	MURPHY, Charlie	8m	C	D.C.	21 MAR 1875	Mt. Pleasant
013202	MURPHY, Charlie	2y	W	D.C.	14 SEP 1877	Mt. Olivet
012223	MURPHY, Daniel	4y	W	D.C.	05 JUL 1877	Mt. Olivet
015696	MURPHY, Daniel	2y	W	D.C.	12 MAY 1878	Mt. Olivet
011019	MURPHY, Deborah	74y	W	Ire.	17 MAR 1877	Mt. Olivet
016477	MURPHY, Edwin	3m	W	D.C.	06 JUL 1878	Mt. Olivet
010555	MURPHY, Elizabeth	66y	W	Ire.	07 FEB 1877	Mt. Olivet
014483	MURPHY, Elizabeth	10y	C	D.C.	19 JAN 1878	Harmony
007388	MURPHY, Elizabeth V.	12y	W	D.C.	23 MAY 1876	Holy Rood
015908	MURPHY, Ellen	72y	W	Ire.	30 MAY 1878	Mt. Olivet
008371	MURPHY, Fannie Bell	3y	W	D.C.	22 JUL 1876	Glenwood
013368	MURPHY, Francis	74y	W	Ire.	01 OCT 1877	Mt. Olivet
000951	MURPHY, Infant of Jas. M.	8d	C	D.C.	27 OCT 1874	Mt. Olivet
019592	MURPHY, James	40y	W	Ire.	29 MAR 1879	Mt. Olivet
018414	MURPHY, James P.	4m	W	D.C.	21 DEC 1878	Mt. Olivet
008779	MURPHY, Jane T.	22y	W	Pa.	22 AUG 1876	Mt. Olivet
006755	MURPHY, Johanna	75y	W	Ire.	20 MAR 1876	Mt. Olivet
007322	MURPHY, John	18h	W	D.C.	16 MAY 1876	Mt. Olivet
012429	MURPHY, John	1m	W	D.C.	19 JUL 1877	Mt. Olivet
011953	MURPHY, John	68y	W	Ire.	18 JUN 1877	Mt. Olivet
019228	MURPHY, John	48y	W	Ire.	27 FEB 1879	Soldier's Home
014978	MURPHY, Joseph	1y	W	D.C.	07 MAR 1878	Mt. Olivet
018842	MURPHY, Kate	28y	W	D.C.	27 JAN 1879	Mt. Olivet
012344	MURPHY, Lillie	17d	W	D.C	13 JUL 1877	Methodist
003759	MURPHY, Margaret	29y	W	Ire.	22 JUN 1875	Potters Field
018488	MURPHY, Margaret	13y	W	D.C.	28 DEC 1878	Mt. Olivet
012345	MURPHY, Margaret P.	10m	W	D.C.	13 JUL 1877	Mt. Olivet
001547	MURPHY, Margret	15y	W	Ire.	31 DEC 1874	Mt. Olivet
013768	MURPHY, Mary	1m	W	D.C.	08 NOV 1877	Mt. Olivet
008275	MURPHY, Mary Anne Elizabeth	4m	W	D.C.	15 JUL 1876	Mt. Olivet
008576	MURPHY, Mary C.	9m	W	D.C.	06 AUG 1876	Mt. Olivet
017242	MURPHY, Myrtle	32y	W	R.I.	29 AUG 1878	Holy Rood
017810	MURPHY, Nelie	3y	W	D.C.	20 OCT 1878	Congressional
017785	MURPHY, Patrick	64y	W	Ire.	18 OCT 1878	Mt. Olivet
001263	MURPHY, Thomas	45y	W	Ire.	29 NOV 1874	Mt. Olivet
003660	MURPHY, Thomas	25y	W	N.Y.	15 JUN 1875	Soldier's Home
005208	MURPHY, Thomas	31y	W	Ire.	28 SEP 1875	Mt. Olivet
011249	MURPHY, Thomas	45y	W	Ire.	06 APR 1877	Soldier's Home

No.	Name	Age	Race	Birth	Death Date	Burial Place
009087	MURPHY, Thos.	31y	W	Ire.	15 SEP 1876	Baltimore, Md.
018528	MURPHY, Timothy	7y	W	D.C.	31 DEC 1878	Mt. Olivet
014990	MURPHY, William	c.61y	W	Ire.	08 MAR 1878	Rock Creek
020537	MURPHY, William	50y	W	Ire.	20 JUN 1879	Soldier's Home
019563	MURPHY, Wm.	1y	W	D.C.	26 MAR 1879	Mt. Olivet
000202	MURRAY, Alexander	6m	W	D.C.	16 AUG 1874	Holy Rood
017966	MURRAY, Alice E.	6m	M	D.C.	06 NOV 1878	Harmony
014544	MURRAY, Charles	35y	C	Md.	24 JAN 1878	Harmony
010706	MURRAY, Clara M.	8m	W	D.C.	20 FEB 1877	Congressional
019625	MURRAY, Edward	61y	W	U.S.	01 APR 1879	Soldier's Home
021026	MURRAY, Edward	3m	C	D.C.	20 JUL 1879	Mt. Olivet
007227	MURRAY, Emma B.	1y	W	D.C.	06 MAY 1876	Congressional
014462	MURRAY, Florence Cambell	50y	W	Md.	17 JAN 1878	Oak Hill
013769	MURRAY, Ida	4y	C	D.C.	08 NOV 1877	Harmony
010783	MURRAY, Isabella C.	67y	W	Eng.	26 FEB 1877	Holy Rood
016819	MURRAY, James Arthur	17h	W	D.C.	29 JUL 1878	Mt. Olivet
002970	MURRAY, James W.	39y	W	N.Y.	12 APR 1875	Glenwood
013707	MURRAY, Jeannette	2d	C	D.C.	02 NOV 1877	Beckett's
014958	MURRAY, Mary	60y	W	Ire.	05 MAR 1878	Mt. Olivet
005826	MURRAY, Mary Ann	32y	W	D.C.	22 DEC 1875	Holy Rood
007197	MURRAY, Mary E.	5d	W	D.C.	03 MAY 1876	Arlington, Va.
007632	MURRAY, Mary Gertrude	3d	W	D.C.	13 JUN 1876	Baltimore, Md.
002206	MURRAY, Mary Josephine	10m	W	D.C.	17 FEB 1875	Holy Rood
020864	MURRAY, Pauline	14d	W	D.C.	09 JUL 1875	Congressional
000216	MURRAY, Ralph Edward	1y	W	D.C.	17 AUG 1874	Congressional
005156	MURRY, George Henry	9m	C	D.C.	24 SEP 1875	Young Mens
015351	MURRY, Henry	65y	C	Va.	10 APR 1878	Potters Field
001721	MURRY, Jefferson	77y	C	Va.	14 JAN 1875	Washington Asylum
006838	MURRY, John, Sr.	74y	W	Ire.	27 MAR 1876	Mt. Olivet
000314	MURTAGH, James	33y	W	Ire.	25 AUG 1874	Holy Rood
001680	MURTAGH, Lizzie	33y	W	Ire.	10 JAN 1875	Mt. Olivet
011068	MURTAUGH, Ellen	3y	W	D.C.	21 MAR 1877	Holy Rood
019673	MURTH, Margaret	6m	W	D.C.	06 APR 1879	Mt. Olivet
002841	MURTH, Patrick	65y	W	Ire.	02 APR 1875	Mt. Olivet
002431	MUSTIN, Sophia W.	76y	W	Md.	05 MAR 1875	Glenwood
007165	MUTH, Henry Reginal	1y	W	D.C.	30 APR 1876	Glenwood
002012	MUTH, John	7d	W	D.C.	03 FEB 1875	St. Mary's
000003	MYER, Concordia W.	85y	W	Pa.	01 AUG 1874	Congressional
004203f	MYER, Franklin S.	79y	W	Pa.	19 JUL 1875	Glenwood
004260	MYER, George	4m	W	D.C.	23 JUL 1875	Prospect Hill
009264	MYERS, Agnes	2y	C	D.C.	01 OCT 1876	Mt. Zion
009598	MYERS, Benjamin	10m	C	D.C.	02 NOV 1876	Mt. Olivet
004955	MYERS, Clarence H.	1y	W	D.C.	08 SEP 1875	Graceland
001729	MYERS, Edward	11m	W	D.C.	14 JAN 1875	Mt. Olivet
001697f	MYERS, Eliza	--	--	--	19 JAN 1875	--
011682	MYERS, Ella	6m	C	D.C.	23 MAY 1877	Mt. Olivet
003773	MYERS, Elvina	7m	W	D.C.	22 JUN 1875	Glenwood
008683	MYERS, Fanny	29y	C	Va.	14 AUG 1876	Mt. Zion
018449	MYERS, Frankie	14y	W	Md.	24 DEC 1878	Baltimore, Md.
003032	MYERS, Infant of Harriet	1h	C	D.C.	18 APR 1875	Potters Field
010165	MYERS, Infant of Jane	6d	C	D.C.	03 JAN 1877	Potters Field
003085	MYERS, Johanah	24y	W	D.C.	22 APR 1875	Mt. Olivet
018527	MYERS, Katie M.	2y	W	D.C.	31 DEC 1878	Congressional
014018	MYERS, Margaret Eveline	28y	W	N.Y.	06 DEC 1877	Glenwood
014531	MYERS, Margrett	65y	W	Ire.	23 JAN 1878	Mt. Olivet
015555	MYERS, Maud	10m	C	--	29 APR 1878	Potters Field

District of Columbia Death Records, August 1, 1874 to July 31, 1879   247

No.	Name	Age	Race	Birth	Death Date	Burial Place
017935	MYERS, Mrs.	35y	W	Ire.	03 NOV 1878	Mt. Olivet
020197	MYERS, Neal P.	2d	W	D.C.	25 MAY 1879	Glenwood
012316	MYERS, Richd.	63y	C	Va.	11 JUL 1877	Young Mens
010671	MYERS, Samuel	11m	C	D.C.	17 FEB 1877	Mt. Zion
000528	MYERS, Thomas	8m	W	D.C.	16 SEP 1874	Congressional
005196	MYERS, Thomas H.	2y	W	D.C.	27 SEP 1875	Glenwood
014933	MYERS, Virginia M.	44y	W	D.C.	03 MAR 1878	Congressional
005739	MYERS, William J.	4y	W	D.C.	13 DEC 1875	Mt. Olivet
018843	MYGATT, Charles	75y	W	Conn.	27 JAN 1879	Glenwood
000084	MYRES, Charles	54y	W	Ger.	06 AUG 1874	Washington Asylum
003284	MYRES, Cora Lee	2m	W	D.C.	11 MAY 1875	Mt. Olivet
010015	MYRES, Edward	3y	W	D.C.	19 DEC 1876	Prospect Hill
018574	MYRES, John	5y	C	D.C.	05 JAN 1879	Holy Rood

N

No.	Name	Age	Race	Birth	Death Date	Burial Place
009047	NACE, Adia G.	1y	W	D.C.	12 SEP 1876	Prospect Hill
020472	NAILER, Arthur L.	7m	C	D.C.	16 JUN 1879	Harmony
001093	NAILER, Mary Magdelene	5m	M	D.C.	09 NOV 1874	Mt. Zion
018588	NAILOR, Allison, Sr.	70y	W	Va.	06 JAN 1879	Rock Creek
008122	NAILOR, Carrie	8m	W	D.C.	10 JUL 1876	Harmony
013708	NAILOR, Henrietta	38y	W	D.C.	02 NOV 1877	Congressional
009434	NAILOR, Joanna	1y	C	D.C.	16 OCT 1876	Mt. Zion
001369	NAILOR, John H.	29y	W	D.C.	12 DEC 1874	Rock Creek
003701	NAILOR, Louisa	75y	C	Va.	19 JUN 1875	Harmony
001150	NAILOR, Martha Magdalen	5m	C	D.C.	14 NOV 1874	Mt. Zion
016961	NAILOR, Mary Edna	1y	W	D.C.	08 AUG 1878	Mt. Olivet
012531	NAILOR, May	4m	C	D.C.	26 JUL 1877	Ebenezer
020298	NAILOR, Minnie	35y	M	Md.	04 JUN 1879	Mt. Zion
010318	NAILOR, Walter	1y	W	D.C.	17 JAN 1877	Mt. Olivet
016933	NAILOR, Willie Ernest	5y	W	D.C.	06 AUG 1878	Mt. Olivet
017919	NAIRN, Fanny Young	41y	W	Ill.	01 NOV 1878	Oak Hill
003454	NAIRN, Joseph W.	51y	W	D.C.	27 MAY 1875	Rock Creek
004116	NALLE, Charles William	54y	C	Va.	13 JUL 1875	Harmony
013481	NALLEY, Benjamin	1y	W	D.C.	11 OCT 1877	Congressional
001803	NALLEY, Mary Ann	1m	W	D.C.	20 JAN 1875	Mt. Olivet
005521	NALLEY, Sarah Ann	66y	W	Md.	20 NOV 1875	Congressional
004296	NALLEY, Virginia Augusta	45y	W	D.C.	25 JUL 1875	Glenwood
006551	NALLY, Charles F.	27y	W	D.C.	04 MAR 1876	Mt. Olivet
014132	NALLY, Emma R.	19y	W	D.C.	18 DEC 1877	Congressional
008835	NALLY, Minnie Eleanora	11m	W	Md.	26 AUG 1876	Rock Creek
002665	NAPER, Tamer	18y	C	Va.	21 MAR 1875	Mt. Pleasant
020409	NASH, Arena	6m	C	D.C.	12 JUN 1879	Beckett's
016546	NASH, Elvia	84y	C	Va.	10 JUL 1878	Harmony
007908	NASH, James F.	3m	C	D.C.	28 JUN 1876	Mt. Zion
020219	NASH, Martha	37y	C	D.C.	28 MAY 1879	Mt. Zion
000291	NASH, William	9m	C	D.C.	23 AUG 1874	Harmony
019762	NAU, Ludwig	4m	W	D.C.	13 APR 1879	Prospect Hill
016033	NAUCK, John Daniel	67y	W	Prus.	06 JUN 1878	Prospect Hill
014434	NAUDAIN, Mary V.	28y	W	D.C.	15 JAN 1878	Glenwood
001120	NAUMAN, Caspar	37y	W	Ger.	12 NOV 1874	Oak Hill
016744	NAYLER, Wm. Earl	1m	W	D.C.	24 JUL 1878	Oak Hill
009076	NAYLOR, Elizabeth P.S.	39y	W	D.C.	14 SEP 1876	Congressional
019845	NAYLOR, George H.	48y	C	Md.	20 APR 1879	Harmony
009216	NAYLOR, John Wesley	7m	C	D.C.	27 SEP 1876	Harmony

No.	Name	Age	Race	Birth	Death Date	Burial Place
019992	NAYLOR, Laura E.	47y	W	N.Y.	04 MAY 1879	Lancaster, N.Y.
012627	NcNEIR, M.C.	55y	W	Md.	09 DEC 1876	Presbyterian
014496	NEAGLE, Kate	25y	W	Ire.	20 JAN 1878	Mt. Olivet
006258	NEAL, George	38y	C	Md.	06 FEB 1876	Potters Field
021116	NEAL, Harry	1y	W	D.C.	26 JUL 1879	Congressional
015133	NEAL, Henry	8y	C	D.C.	20 MAR 1878	Beckett's
013438	NEAL, Lemuel	2m	C	D.C.	08 OCT 1877	Beckett's
011568	NEAL, Mary E.	8m	C	D.C.	12 MAY 1877	Mt. Olivet
002716	NEAL, Mary Etta	2y	C	D.C.	24 MAR 1875	Mt. Pleasant
017243	NEAL, Rosella	1y	M	D.C.	29 AUG 1878	Young Mens
001930	NEAL, William Henry	18y	M	D.C.	28 JAN 1875	Mt. Olivet
004337	NEAL, Willie	9m	C	D.C.	27 JUL 1875	Young Mens
007102	NEALE, Isabella P.	34y	W	Mass.	24 APR 1876	Natick, Mass.
014551	NEALE, John Edmund	74y	W	Md.	25 JAN 1878	Mt. Olivet
015493	NEALE, Lewis	51y	C	Md.	23 APR 1878	Holy Rood
017725	NEALE, M. Gertrude	2m	W	D.C.	13 OCT 1878	Mt. Olivet
010464	NEALE, Mary A.	1y	C	D.C.	31 JAN 1877	Ebenezer
006756	NEALE, Mary S.	77y	W	Va.	20 MAR 1876	Convent
005108a	NEALE, Sarah H.	58y	W	Eng.	11 OCT 1875	Oak Hill
010928	NEBBITT, Robert	6y	C	Md.	09 MAR 1877	Mt. Olivet
017890	NEBITT, Dora V.	3m	C	D.C.	28 OCT 1878	Beckett's
011025	NEBITT, John Francis	1y	C	D.C.	18 MAR 1877	Mt. Olivet
007803	NEEDFELDT, William E.L.	3m	W	D.C.	23 JUN 1876	Glenwood
000566	NEEL, Margaret	75y	W	Pa.	19 SEP 1874	Chesnut Level, Pa.
018247	NEENAN, John	48y	W	Ire.	05 DEC 1878	Mt. Olivet
019719	NEFF, Benedict	64y	W	Ger.	10 APR 1879	St. Mary's
018299	NEFF, Mary	5y	W	D.C.	10 DEC 1878	St. Mary's
019277	NEIDOMANSKI, Infant of F.G.	2d	W	D.C.	04 MAR 1879	Congressional
019287	NEIDOMANSKI, Infant of F.J.	3d	W	D.C.	05 MAR 1879	Congressional
007048	NEIGLE, William F.	36y	W	Ger.	18 APR 1876	Hospital
017958	NEIL, Annie	60y	C	D.C.	05 NOV 1878	Potters Field
003777	NEIL, Caroline	25y	C	Va.	22 JUN 1875	Young Mens
016403	NEIL, Charles	8m	C	D.C.	02 JUL 1878	Mt. Olivet
019145	NEIL, Cora	13m	C	D.C.	21 FEB 1879	Young Mens
011129	NEIL, Emeline	55y	C	Va.	27 MAR 1877	Harmony
000897	NEIL, Jeremiah	80y	C	Md.	22 OCT 1874	Mt. Olivet
005190a	NEIL, Julia	58y	M	Md.	18 OCT 1875	Holy Rood
007237	NEIL, Mary	17y	C	Md.	07 MAY 1876	Mt. Olivet
010217	NEIL, Mary A.	3y	C	D.C.	08 JAN 1877	Ebenezer
002203	NEIL, Thomas	56y	W	Eng.	17 FEB 1875	Glenwood
020233	NEILL, Edward	3y	C	D.C.	30 MAY 1879	Young Mens
016902	NEITZE, George Frederick	25y	W	D.C.	04 AUG 1878	Prospect Hill
006478	NEITZEY, Elizabeth	39y	W	D.C.	26 FEB 1876	Prospect Hill
016612	NEITZEY, Louisia Elizabeth	14m	W	D.C.	15 JUL 1878	Prospect Hill
012428	NELL, Sophia O.	9m	W	D.C.	19 JUL 1877	Prospect Hill
016319	NELLIGAN, Alexander O.	8y	W	Va.	26 JUN 1878	Congressional
001745	NELSON, Agnes	35y	C	Va.	15 JAN 1875	Harmony
015045	NELSON, Alfred	62y	C	Va.	12 MAR 1878	Harmony
014272	NELSON, Amos	4m	M	D.C.	30 DEC 1877	Young Mens
016361	NELSON, Andrew	7m	C	D.C.	29 JUN 1878	Beckett's
004640	NELSON, Betsie	1y	C	D.C.	17 AUG 1875	Mt. Zion
000825	NELSON, Caroline	55y	M	Va.	16 OCT 1874	Beckett's
018184	NELSON, Catherine	6m	C	D.C.	27 NOV 1878	Harmony
014311	NELSON, Daniel	2y	C	D.C.	03 JAN 1878	Young Mens
020410	NELSON, Daniel	2y	C	D.C.	12 JUN 1879	Potters Field
000977	NELSON, Edward	1y	C	D.C.	29 OCT 1874	Harmony

District of Columbia Death Records, August 1, 1874 to July 31, 1879

No.	Name	Age	Race	Birth	Death Date	Burial Place
020157	NELSON, Elizabeth	7y	C	D.C.	20 MAY 1879	Beckett's
012537	NELSON, Elwyn C.	1y	C	D.C.	26 JUL 1877	Beckett's
018052	NELSON, Frederick	1y	W	D.C.	14 NOV 1878	Presbyterian
003425	NELSON, George	5m	C	D.C.	24 MAY 1875	Beckett's
009277	NELSON, George	77y	W	Md.	02 OCT 1876	Baltimore, Md.
019372	NELSON, Georgeanna	19y	C	Md.	12 MAR 1879	Potters Field
013394	NELSON, Gracy	3y	W	D.C.	03 OCT 1877	Presbyterian
004522	NELSON, Harry Augustus	1y	C	D.C.	09 AUG 1875	Beckett's
000286	NELSON, Infant (illeg.)	7d	C	D.C.	22 AUG 1874	Young Mens
009040	NELSON, Infant of Daniel	1m	C	D.C.	12 SEP 1876	Young Mens
014447	NELSON, Infant of Henry	2d	C	D.C.	16 JAN 1878	Beckett's
001357	NELSON, Infant of James	3d	C	D.C.	10 DEC 1874	Mt. Pleasant Plain
017144	NELSON, Infant of Mary	5d	C	D.C.	22 AUG 1878	Young Mens
015824	NELSON, Infant of Morris	4d	C	D.C.	24 MAY 1878	Potters Field
009979	NELSON, Infant of William	5d	C	D.C.	16 DEC 1876	Ebenezer
005707	NELSON, Jacob	4m	C	D.C.	09 DEC 1875	Young Mens
005632	NELSON, Jacob	8m	C	D.C.	02 DEC 1875	Ebenezer
008070	NELSON, John P.	39y	C	N.Y.	08 JUL 1876	Holy Rood
006801	NELSON, Jos.	3y	C	D.C.	24 MAR 1876	Ebenezer
014230	NELSON, Joseph	78y	C	Va.	27 DEC 1877	Baptist
005392	NELSON, Lars	26y	W	Ger.	08 NOV 1875	Washington Asylum
016561	NELSON, Lemanda	15y	C	Va.	11 JUL 1878	Mt. Pleasant
018950	NELSON, Lizzie	68y	C	Va.	04 FEB 1879	Young Mens
001859	NELSON, Louisa	105y	C	Va.	23 JAN 1875	Potters Field
013052	NELSON, Mary	9y	C	D.C.	01 SEP 1877	Potters Field
012693	NELSON, Mary Gracy	11m	C	D.C.	06 AUG 1877	Young Mens
017258	NELSON, Paul Daniel	13y	C	D.C.	30 AUG 1878	Mt. Pleasant
013000	NELSON, Pery	21y	C	Md.	28 AUG 1877	Mt. Zion
013556	NELSON, Rachel	43y	M	Md.	30 SEP 1877	Mt. Zion
013700	NELSON, Robert	23y	C	Va.	01 NOV 1877	Beckett's
013307	NELSON, Robert Edward	2m	C	D.C.	25 SEP 1877	Young Mens
011480	NELSON, Samuel	76y	W	Va.	01 MAY 1877	Congressional
014229	NELSON, Sarah	5y	M	D.C.	27 DEC 1877	Young Mens
013574	NELSON, Susan Hayden	64y	W	Me.	20 OCT 1877	Oak Hill
013439	NELSON, William	73y	C	Va.	08 OCT 1877	Young Mens
002522	NELSON, William F., Rev.	66y	W	N.Y.	11 MAR 1875	Oak Hill
010882	NELSON, [Mary] Lorinda	41y	W	Va.	06 MAR 1877	Mt. Olivet
010348	NEPUTH, Mary Barker	3y	W	D.C.	20 JAN 1877	Prospect Hill
008351	NERVIS, Mary	9m	C	D.C.	20 JUL 1876	Harmony
000198	NERVIS, Sarah Lavinia	7m	M	D.C.	15 AUG 1874	Harmony
011526	NESBETT, William H.	2y	C	D.C.	06 MAY 1877	Mt. Olivet
008391	NESLINI, Mary Francis	9m	W	D.C.	23 JUL 1876	St. Mary's
014484	NETTER, Charles	c.30y	C	D.C.	19 JAN 1878	Hospital, Government
011196	NETTER, Fred	3y	C	D.C.	02 APR 1877	Potters Field
014139	NETTER, James	8m	C	D.C.	19 DEC 1877	Beckett's
007785	NETTER, Jane	24y	C	Md.	22 JUN 1876	Potters Field
000591	NETTER, Wm. Aaron	1y	C	D.C.	21 SEP 1874	Beckett's
011093	NEU, George	37y	W	Ger.	23 MAR 1877	Prospect Hill
012632	NEUHANS, August	4m	W	D.C.	01 AUG 1877	Prospect Hill
014320	NEUHAUS, Anna	7m	W	D.C.	04 JAN 1878	Prospect Hill
017525	NEUTER, Charles	51y	W	Sax.	25 SEP 1878	Prospect Hill
001205	NEVELTON, Wm. Henry	1y	C	D.C.	21 NOV 1874	Harmony
007078	NEVIT, James	64y	C	D.C.	22 APR 1876	Mt. Zion
018406	NEVITT, Nancy	30y	C	Md.	20 DEC 1878	Harmony
002062	NEVIUS, Norman Austin	3y	W	D.C.	07 FEB 1875	Glenwood
001583	NEWBOLD, Eliza Belle	4y	W	D.C.	02 JAN 1875	Glenwood

District of Columbia Death Records, August 1, 1874 to July 31, 1879

No.	Name	Age	Race	Birth	Death Date	Burial Place
001860	NEWBURN, Naltion?	85y	C	S.C.	23 JAN 1875	Young Mens
008775	NEWBY, James B.	1y	C	D.C	22 AUG 1876	Harmony
020156	NEWCOMER, Selma A.	32y	W	Ill.	20 MAY 1879	Congressional
003781	NEWELL, Louisa	34y	W	Md.	23 JUN 1875	Congressional
007909	NEWMAN, Amy Lucas	1y	W	D.C.	28 JUN 1876	Methodist
011489	NEWMAN, Balisora	11y	C	D.C.	02 MAY 1877	Young Mens
012529	NEWMAN, Caroline	45y	C	Va.	25 JUL 1877	Harmony
015249	NEWMAN, Charles	42y	W	N.Y.	31 MAR 1878	Mt. Olivet
017604	NEWMAN, Charles Francis	4y	W	Md.	02 OCT 1878	Mt. Olivet
015125	NEWMAN, Charles Richard	19d	C	D.C.	19 MAR 1878	Harmony
011447	NEWMAN, Elizabeth R.	32y	W	Md.	28 APR 1877	Baltimore, Md.
015124	NEWMAN, Ella	7m	C	D.C.	19 MAR 1878	Beckett's
016695	NEWMAN, Emily	23y	C	Va.	20 JUL 1878	Beckett's
017603	NEWMAN, Emma	5y	C	D.C.	02 OCT 1878	Beckett's
016074	NEWMAN, Infant of George	8d	C	D.C.	08 JUN 1878	Beckett's
018477	NEWMAN, John	38y	M	Md.	27 DEC 1878	Mt. Olivet
016377	NEWMAN, Louisa	11m	W	D.C.	30 JUN 1878	Prospect Hill
003395	NEWMAN, Lucinda V.	14y	M	Va.	22 MAY 1875	Young Mens
012183	NEWMAN, Mary	5m	M	D.C.	02 JUL 1877	Harmony
016267	NEWMAN, Mary	3y	C	D.C.	22 JUN 1878	Harmony
017786	NEWMAN, Mary	13y	C	D.C.	18 OCT 1878	Beckett's
003009	NEWMAN, Mary Elizabeth	46y	W	Md.	16 APR 1875	Oak Hill
007068	NEWMAN, Mary Ellen	1m	C	D.C.	21 APR 1876	Catholic, Md. X Roads
017778	NEWMAN, Mary, Jr.	3y	W	D.C.	17 OCT 1878	Mt. Olivet
017787	NEWMAN, Mattie S.	8y	C	D.C	18 OCT 1878	Harmony
011405	NEWMAN, Thomas L.	37y	W	D.C.	23 APR 1877	Presbyterian
016635	NEWMAN, Thomas Russell	1m	W	D.C.	17 JUL 1878	Mt. Olivet
017717	NEWMAN, Thos.	3y	C	D.C.	12 OCT 1878	Beckett's
014029	NEWMAN, William T.	22y	W	Va.	07 DEC 1877	Congressional
017259	NEWMAN, Willie	4m	C	D.C.	30 AUG 1878	Beckett's
020585	NEWMANN, Richard Clinton	33y	C	Md.	23 JUN 1879	St. Aloysius, Md.
005186	NEWMON, William	35y	C	Md.	26 SEP 1875	Harmony
017556	NEWNAN, William A.	1y	C	D.C.	28 SEP 1878	Mt. Olivet
010294	NEWRY, Charles	46y	W	Ire.	15 JAN 1877	Soldier's Home
018655	NEWTON, Albert	37y	C	Va.	12 JAN 1879	Harmony
010649	NEWTON, Albert S.	32y	W	N.J.	15 FEB 1877	Oak Hill
002556	NEWTON, Arby	10m	C	D.C.	13 MAR 1875	Mt. Pleasant
005062a	NEWTON, Barbara	80y	C	Md.	05 OCT 1875	Mt. Olivet
011322	NEWTON, Calvin P.	76y	W	Ver.	13 APR 1877	Washington Asylum
006523	NEWTON, Catherine	1y	C	D.C.	02 MAR 1876	Young Mens
003201	NEWTON, Charles	88y	W	Md.	03 MAY 1875	Mt. Olivet
019934	NEWTON, Charles A.	6y	C	D.C.	29 APR 1879	Graceland
002760	NEWTON, Daniel P.	33y	C	D.C.	27 MAR 1875	Harmony
016901	NEWTON, Edward	5m	C	D.C.	04 AUG 1878	Potters Field
010665	NEWTON, Horace	1y	C	D.C	17 FEB 1877	Young Mens
002342	NEWTON, Ignatius A.	79y	W	Md.	27 FEB 1875	Glenwood
001235	NEWTON, Infant of Charles	12d	C	D.C.	26 NOV 1874	Harmony
019463	NEWTON, Infant of Alfred	3d	C	D.C.	19 MAR 1879	Potters Field
003127	NEWTON, Isaac	46y	W	Tenn.	26 APR 1875	Washington Asylum
019966	NEWTON, Jno. C.	74y	W	Md.	02 MAY 1879	Holy Rood
016376	NEWTON, John Henson	2y	C	D.C.	30 JUN 1878	Mt. Olivet
014191	NEWTON, Josephine	15y	C	D.C.	24 DEC 1877	Moore's
009051	NEWTON, Mary	13m	W	D.C.	13 SEP 1876	Potters Field
015174	NEWTON, Mary Rosalia	22y	W	D.C.	24 MAR 1878	Congressional
014463	NEWTON, Reul	34y	W	Mich.	17 JAN 1878	South Bend, Ind.
016424	NEWTON, Thomas	70y	W	Va.	03 JUL 1878	Hospital

District of Columbia Death Records, August 1, 1874 to July 31, 1879   251

No.	Name	Age	Race	Birth	Death Date	Burial Place
012609	NICHLOS, Mary	4m	W	D.C.	30 JUL 1877	Mt. Olivet
006452	NICHOLAS, Jacob	52y	W	Ger.	23 FEB 1876	Prospect Hill
010561	NICHOLAS, Samuel	46y	C	Va.	08 FEB 1877	Young Mens
004402	NICHOLAS, Walter	2y	C	D.C.	01 AUG 1875	Ebenezer
008669	NICHOLS, Edonborough	1y	C	D.C.	13 AUG 1876	Beckett's
006021	NICHOLS, Elizabeth	30y	M	Ga.	14 JAN 1876	Young Mens
006815	NICHOLS, Elizabeth B.	38y	W	Me.	25 MAR 1876	Glenwood
006699	NICHOLS, Icelean L.	4y	C	D.C.	16 MAR 1876	Harmony
013575	NICHOLS, John	33y	W	D.C.	20 OCT 1877	Potters Field
019296	NICHOLS, Joseph	3m	C	D.C.	06 MAR 1879	Beckett's
000298	NICHOLS, Reuben	1y	C	D.C.	24 AUG 1874	Young Mens
016804	NICHOLS, Susan Ann	66y	W	Conn.	28 JUL 1878	Woodlawn, N.Y.
001324	NICHOLS, Thomas L.	71y	W	Va.	06 DEC 1874	Presbyterian
000135	NICHOLS, Tilda	1y	C	D.C.	10 AUG 1874	Beckett's
003642	NICHOLS, Warner Beebe	36y	W	Mass.	14 JUN 1875	Arlington, Va.
015879	NICHOLS, William Dupee	3m	C	D.C.	28 MAY 1878	Harmony
006379	NICHOLSON, Annie D.	5y	W	D.C.	16 FEB 1876	Rock Creek
009634	NICHOLSON, James	48y	W	Ire.	06 NOV 1876	Philadelphia, Pa.
018128	NICHOLSON, John McGowan	8m	W	D.C.	23 NOV 1878	Rock Creek
004186	NICHOLSON, Margaret A.	4y	W	D.C.	18 JUL 1875	Congressional
006864	NICHOLSON, Sally	59y	W	D.C.	30 MAR 1876	Holy Rood
019519	NICHOLSON, Walter	66y	W	D.C.	23 MAR 1879	Congressional
018007	NICHOLSON, Wm.	71y	W	Eng.	10 NOV 1878	Mt. Olivet
018696	NICKELSON, Elizabeth	46y	W	Md.	16 JAN 1879	Presbyterian
005185	NICKINS, Mollie	20y	C	Va.	26 SEP 1875	Hews, Warrenton, Va.
019184	NICKOLS, Washington	12y	C	D.C.	24 FEB 1879	Potters Field
013989	NICKSON, Frank	2m	C	D.C.	02 DEC 1877	Beckett's
013591	NICOLAY, George Bates	2m	W	D.C.	22 OCT 1877	Oak Hill
016611	NICOLS, Marie	2m	W	D.C.	15 JUL 1878	Mt. Olivet
015449	NIEDFELDT, John P.	7y	W	N.J.	19 APR 1878	Glenwood
016493	NILAND, Anne	8m	C	D.C.	07 JUL 1878	Holy Rood
007077	NILAND, Margaret	4m	W	D.C.	22 APR 1876	Holy Rood
000301	NILES, Henry Clay	39y	W	N.Y.	24 AUG 1874	Congressional
006710	NISSLEIN, Mary	4d	W	D.C.	17 MAR 1876	St. Mary's
006962	NISSLEIN, Mary M.	32y	W	Scot.	07 APR 1876	St. Mary's
006135	NOCABE, Hennie	69y	C	Md.	25 JAN 1876	Mt. Pleasant
008467	NOCK, Emily F.	28y	W	Va.	29 JUL 1876	Oak Hill
007784	NOCK, Horace N.	3m	W	D.C.	22 JUN 1876	Oak Hill
008618	NODINE, Abigail E.	68y	W	Conn.	08 AUG 1876	Oak Hill
011364	NOELE, Sarah A.	60y	W	Va.	17 APR 1877	Glenwood
018828	NOERR, Andrew	49y	W	D.C.	26 JAN 1879	Glenwood
009534	NOERR, Catharine	72y	W	Md.	26 OCT 1876	Glenwood
001532	NOES, James	14y	C	Ky.	29 DEC 1874	Potters Field
001099	NOKES, Edward	9m	C	D.C.	09 NOV 1874	Beckett's
003302	NOKES, Henson	56y	C	Va.	13 MAY 1875	Ebenezer
004889f	NOKES, James	63y	W	Va.	02 SEP 1875	Congressional
004917	NOKES, Margaret	36y	W	D.C.	05 SEP 1875	Congressional
018562	NOKES, Melvina	69y	C	Va.	04 JAN 1879	Harmony
009752	NOKES, Norval L.	3y	W	D.C.	20 NOV 1876	Congressional
014552	NOLAN, Cathran	33y	C	D.C.	25 JAN 1878	Mt. Olivet
011611	NOLAN, Celestine	3m	C	D.C.	16 MAY 1877	Mt. Zion
011540	NOLAN, Edward F.	27y	W	N.Y.	07 MAY 1877	Mt. Olivet
004868	NOLAN, George W.	3w	C	D.C.	01 SEP 1875	Mt. Zion
015615	NOLAN, James	52y	W	Ire.	04 MAY 1878	Mt. Olivet
005189a	NOLAN, Mary	9y	W	D.C.	18 OCT 1875	Mt. Olivet
017908	NOLAN, Nannie	35y	W	Ire.	30 OCT 1878	New Cathedral, Md.

No.	Name	Age	Race	Birth	Death Date	Burial Place
011099	NOLAN, Patrick	84y	W	Ire.	24 MAR 1877	Mt. Olivet
008115	NOLAN, Philip	90y	C	Va.	09 JUL 1876	Harmony
016582	NOLAND, Franklin Pierce	21y	W	Va.	13 JUL 1878	Congressional
004641	NOLEN, George Augustus	44y	W	Mass.	17 AUG 1875	Glenwood
004655	NOLEN, Nellie Patton	31y	W	Pa.	18 AUG 1875	Glenwood
002643	NOLLAN, Ann, Mrs.	48y	W	Ire.	19 MAR 1875	Philadelphia, Pa.
002316	NOLTE, John	65y	W	Ger.	25 FEB 1875	St. Mary's
016999	NOONAN, Agnes	18m	W	D.C.	10 AUG 1878	Mt. Olivet
010834	NOONAN, James	53y	W	Ire.	02 MAR 1877	Holy Rood
001220	NOONAN, Kate	14y	W	Fla.	24 NOV 1874	Trinity B.G.
015795	NOONAN, Margaret	2m	C	D.C.	21 MAY 1878	Mt. Olivet
000099	NOONAN, Mary A.	29y	W	Ire.	07 AUG 1874	Holy Rood
007440	NORBECK, John	4m	W	D.C.	30 MAY 1876	Congressional
018517	NORCOM, James	68y	W	N.C.	30 DEC 1878	Glenwood
017145	NORGLE, Lillie	8d	W	D.C.	22 AUG 1878	Prospect Hill
004797	NORIS, Beney	15d	C	D.C.	28 AUG 1875	Ebenezer
002126	NORMAN, Calvin	18y	M	Va.	11 FEB 1875	Young Mens
016731	NORMAN, Charley	18d	C	D.C.	23 JUL 1878	Beckett's
011636	NORMAN, Geo. Augustine	4m	C	D.C.	18 MAY 1877	Holy Rood
016560	NORMAN, Harriett A.	42y	C	D.C.	11 JUL 1878	Mt. Zion
018478	NORMAN, Infant of Christopher	1d	C	D.C.	27 DEC 1878	Mt. Pleasant
010154	NORMAN, John Stewart	60y	W	Va.	02 JAN 1877	Stevensburg, Va.
020877	NORMAN, Mary Magdaline	6m	C	D.C.	10 JUL 1879	Potters Field
005770	NORRIS, Annie	1y	C	D.C.	16 DEC 1875	Ebenezer
002587	NORRIS, Eliza	72y	C	Va.	15 MAR 1875	Potters Field
013053	NORRIS, Elizabeth	45y	C	D.C.	01 SEP 1877	Mt. Zion
005966	NORRIS, Harriet Ann	1y	C	D.C.	07 JAN 1876	Beckett's
011897	NORRIS, Harriet Ann	1m	C	D.C.	14 JUN 1877	Mt. Zion
004244f	NORRIS, Infant of Emiline	6m	W	Md.	22 JUL 1875	Rock Creek
004078	NORRIS, Infant of Francis	7d	C	D.C.	10 JUL 1875	Ebenezer
011045	NORRIS, Infant of Nace	5d	C	D.C.	19 MAR 1877	Mt. Olivet
020488	NORRIS, Isaac	48y	C	Va.	17 JUN 1879	Harmony
016718	NORRIS, John	36y	W	D.C.	22 JUL 1878	Oak Hill
015029	NORRIS, John M.	43y	C	Md.	11 MAR 1878	Beckett's
013935	NORRIS, John T.	52y	W	Md.	26 NOV 1877	Oak Hill
004418	NORRIS, Mark	67y	C	Md.	02 AUG 1875	Harmony
006502	NORRIS, Mary Catharine	6m	C	D.C.	28 FEB 1876	Moore's
010457	NORRIS, Mary E.	5y	W	Md.	30 JAN 1877	Greenmount, Balt., Md.
020914	NORRIS, Robert A.	8m	W	D.C.	13 JUL 1879	Congressional
003344	NORRIS, Sandy	5y	C	Md.	16 MAY 1875	Mt. Zion
008407	NORRIS, Sarah E.	11m	C	D.C.	24 JUL 1876	Beckett's
020149	NORTH, Frank S.	2y	C	D.C.	19 MAY 1879	Holy Rood
018024	NORTON, Amy	9m	W	D.C.	11 NOV 1878	Congressional
001271	NORTON, Anna	9d	W	D.C.	29 NOV 1874	Rock Creek
005529	NORTON, Annie	1y	W	D.C.	21 NOV 1875	Mt. Olivet
011931	NORTON, Augustus	44y	W	Md.	16 JUN 1877	Rock Creek
006501	NORTON, Eli P.	55y	W	Ohio	28 FEB 1876	Congressional
020383	NORTON, Francis	9d	W	D.C.	10 JUN 1879	Prospect Hill
006779	NORTON, Hervey J.	60y	W	Mass.	22 MAR 1876	Pittsfield, Mass.
008523	NORTON, Infant of John	1m	W	D.C.	02 AUG 1876	Rock Creek
001821	NORTON, James Arthur	4y	W	D.C.	21 JAN 1875	Congressional
012918	NORTON, Kate E.	25y	W	D.C.	23 AUG 1877	Mt. Olivet
004796	NORTON, Lewis Almer	3m	W	D.C.	28 AUG 1875	Congressional
010686	NORTON, Lizzie	41y	W	D.C.	18 FEB 1877	Holy Rood
008207	NORTON, Lucretia	46y	W	Mass.	12 JUL 1876	Carroll Chapel, Md.
004053	NORTON, Lucy E.	2m	W	D.C.	08 JUL 1875	Congressional

District of Columbia Death Records, August 1, 1874 to July 31, 1879   253

No.	Name	Age	Race	Birth	Death Date	Burial Place
005055a	NORTON, Margaret	65y	M	Va.	04 OCT 1875	Mt. Olivet
003306	NORTON, Minttie	35y	C	Md.	13 MAY 1875	Ebenezer
011567	NORTON, Robert H.	30y	C	D.C.	11 MAY 1877	Young Mens
003174	NORTON, William	20y	C	Md.	30 APR 1875	Washington Asylum
015116	NORWOOD, Eva	11m	W	Md.	18 MAR 1878	Frederick Co., Md.
010395	NORWOOD, Joseph	15y	C	D.C.	24 JAN 1877	Baptist
015283	NORWOOD, Joseph S.	53y	W	Va.	04 APR 1878	Potters Field
004129	NORWOOD, Magdaline	2m	W	U.S.	14 JUL 1875	Mt. Olivet
007848	NORWOOD, Mary D.	68y	W	Va.	25 JUN 1876	Congressional
001477	NORWOOD, Virginia E.	45y	W	D.C.	25 DEC 1874	Glenwood
019346	NOSKE, Henriette M.	8m	W	D.C.	09 MAR 1879	Prospect Hill
020902	NOTHEY, Charles	1m	W	D.C.	12 JUL 1879	Graceland
003500	NOTT, Jinnie	24y	W	D.C.	31 MAY 1875	Glenwood
006423	NOTT, Robert	34y	W	D.C.	20 FEB 1876	Glenwood
008243	NOURSE, Charles Howard, Rev.	64y	W	D.C.	13 JUL 1876	Montgomery Co., Md.
011380	NOURSE, Elizabeth J., Mrs.	65y	W	Va.	20 APR 1877	Montgomery Co., Md.
001668	NOYES, Charles	14y	C	Va.	09 JAN 1875	Fairfax C.H., Va.
017644	NUGENT, Elizabeth	49y	W	Md.	05 OCT 1878	Potters Field
014164	NUGENT, John	20y	W	Ire.	21 DEC 1877	Mt. Olivet
015216	NUGENT, Ludwell S.	7m	C	D.C.	28 MAR 1878	Harmony
016075	NUGENT, Rebecca	83y	C	D.C.	08 JUN 1878	Mt. Zion
013564	NUGENT, Wm.	3d	C	D.C.	19 OCT 1877	Potters Field
005187	NUISOM, Daisie	10m	C	D.C.	26 SEP 1875	Mt. Zion
021100	NUTHALL, Ann M.	1y	W	D.C.	25 JUL 1879	Mt. Olivet
013770	NYE, Jonas W.	82y	W	Mass.	08 NOV 1877	Glenwood

O

008908	O'BEIRNE, Olivia Henrietta	10m	W	D.C.	01 SEP 1876	N.Y.
014402	O'BRIAN, John	6m	W	D.C.	12 JAN 1878	Mt. Olivet
017949	O'BRIEN, Bridget	83y	W	Ire.	04 NOV 1878	Mt. Olivet
020601	O'BRIEN, Daniel	5m	W	D.C.	24 JUN 1879	Holy Rood
005839	O'BRIEN, Daniel J.	2y	W	D.C.	23 DEC 1875	Holy Rood
006511	O'BRIEN, Ellen	3y	W	Md.	29 FEB 1876	Holy Rood
004696	O'BRIEN, Georgianna Willett	1y	W	D.C.	21 AUG 1875	Glenwood
009430	O'BRIEN, Hannah	65y	W	Ire.	16 OCT 1876	Mt. Olivet
017097	O'BRIEN, John	53y	W	Ire.	18 AUG 1878	Mt. Olivet
017035	O'BRIEN, Mary	1y	W	D.C.	13 AUG 1878	Holy Rood
011418	O'BRIEN, Mary B.	1y	W	D.C.	24 APR 1877	Holy Rood
020720	O'BRIEN, Mary Susannah	1m	W	D.C.	02 JUL 1879	Mt. Olivet
005878	O'BRIEN, Mary T.	32y	W	Ire.	27 DEC 1875	Mt. Olivet
016562	O'BRIEN, Nichols	33y	W	Scot.	11 JUL 1878	Mt. Olivet
005828	O'BRIEN, Octavia	24y	C	D.C.	22 DEC 1875	Mt. Pleasant Plain
002754	O'BRIEN, Owen	33y	W	Md.	27 MAR 1875	Congressional
014744	O'BRIEN, Rose	2m	W	D.C.	11 FEB 1878	Holy Rood
019674	O'BRIEN, Thomas	29y	W	Ire.	06 APR 1879	Mt. Olivet
007389	O'BRIEN, William	75y	W	Md.	23 MAY 1876	Catholic, Geo. College
014216	O'BRIEN, William	22y	W	D.C.	26 DEC 1877	Holy Rood
012402	O'BRIEN, William	5d	W	D.C.	17 JUL 1877	Holy Rood
017878	O'BRINE, Michael	42y	W	Ire.	27 OCT 1878	Holy Rood
002834	O'CALLAGHAN, Mary	3y	W	D.C.	01 APR 1875	Mt. Olivet
009771	O'CONNEL, Infant of Danl.	10min	W	D.C.	22 NOV 1876	Mt. Olivet
015521	O'CONNELL, Bridget	22y	W	Md.	26 APR 1878	Mt. Olivet
007786	O'CONNELL, Ida Lillian	1y	W	D.C.	22 JUN 1876	Mt. Olivet
017428	O'CONNELL, Ida Lillian	1y	W	D.C.	16 SEP 1878	Mt. Olivet

District of Columbia Death Records, August 1, 1874 to July 31, 1879

No.	Name	Age	Race	Birth	Death Date	Burial Place
004297	O'CONNELL, James Edward	10m	W	D.C.	25 JUL 1875	Holy Rood
020396	O'CONNELL, JOhn	39y	W	Ire.	11 JUN 1879	N.Y.
008167	O'CONNELL, Michael	31y	W	Ire.	11 JUL 1876	Mt. Olivet
016035	O'CONNELL, Nellie	8m	W	D.C.	06 JUN 1878	Mt. Olivet
019945	O'CONNELL, Sister Ann Louise	60y	W	Ire.	30 APR 1879	Mt. Olivet
005440	O'CONNELL, Wm.	32y	W	Ire.	12 NOV 1875	Mt. Olivet
020578	O'CONNER, Bessey	10m	W	D.C.	23 JUN 1879	Young Mens
015175	O'CONNER, Jeremiah	45y	W	Ire.	24 MAR 1878	Mt. Olivet
019993	O'CONNER, Patrick Daniel	2m	W	N.J.	04 MAY 1879	Mt. Olivet
005408	O'CONNER, Terrance	65y	W	Ire.	09 NOV 1875	Mt. Olivet
005043	O'CONNOR, Alice	5m	W	D.C.	14 SEP 1875	Mt. Olivet
013452	O'CONNOR, Annie	3y	W	D.C.	09 OCT 1877	Mt. Olivet
006700	O'CONNOR, Bridget	84y	W	Ire.	16 MAR 1876	Mt. Olivet
019373	O'CONNOR, Elizabeth	60y	W	Ire.	12 MAR 1879	Mt. Olivet
005232a	O'CONNOR, John	24y	W	Ire.	21 OCT 1875	Mt. Olivet
009768	O'CONNOR, John	21y	W	Ire.	21 NOV 1876	Mt. Olivet
017098	O'CONNOR, John	13y	W	D.C.	18 AUG 1878	Mt. Olivet
002558	O'CONNOR, Mary	28y	W	Ire.	13 MAR 1875	Mt. Olivet
006920	O'CONNOR, Mary	55y	W	Ire.	04 APR 1876	Mt. Olivet
008820	O'CONNOR, Mary	17y	W	D.C.	25 AUG 1876	Mt. Olivet
017312	O'CONNOR, Mary L.	1y	W	D.C.	03 SEP 1878	Mt. Olivet
002115	O'CONNOR, Michael	21y	W	Ire.	11 FEB 1875	N.Y. City
008039	O'CONNOR, Michael	c.10y	W	D.C.	05 JUL 1876	Mt. Olivet
014105	O'CONNOR, Michael	28y	W	D.C.	15 DEC 1877	Mt. Olivet
018997	O'CONNOR, Sarah	20y	W	Ire.	08 FEB 1879	Mt. Olivet
014403	O'CONNOR, Timothy	31y	W	Ire.	12 JAN 1878	Mt. Olivet
012671	O'CONNOR, William H.	3m	W	D.C.	04 AUG 1877	Mt. Olivet
006855	O'DAIR, Infant of Andrew	13h	W	D.C.	29 MAR 1876	Potters Field
012081	O'DAY, Ann	1m	C	D.C.	27 JUN 1877	Mt. Olivet
000996	O'DAY, Bridget	50y	W	Ire.	31 OCT 1874	Holy Rood
015080	O'DAY, Ellen	79y	W	Ire.	15 MAR 1878	Mt. Olivet
000920	O'DAY, Peter	15y	W	D.C.	24 OCT 1874	Holy Rood
015326	O'DEA, Thomas	50y	W	Ire.	08 APR 1878	Holy Rood
016034	O'DONALD, Ellen	6m	C	D.C.	06 JUN 1878	Mt. Olivet
006406	O'DONALD, James	71y	W	Md.	18 FEB 1876	Mt. Olivet
005748	O'DONALD, Margaret	76y	W	Pa.	14 DEC 1875	Mt. Olivet
007943	O'DONALD, Michel	1y	W	D.C.	30 JUN 1876	Mt. Olivet
006908	O'DONNELL, Anthony Nathan	10m	W	D.C.	03 APR 1876	Mt. Olivet
012272	O'DONNELL, James	9m	W	D.C.	08 JUL 1877	Mt. Olivet
012240	O'DONNOGHUE, Aloysious R.	11m	C	D.C.	06 JUL 1877	Holy Rood
016036	O'DONNOGHUE, Sarah	73y	W	Ire.	06 JUN 1878	Holy Rood
017849	O'DONOGHUE, Louisa	16y	W	D.C.	24 OCT 1878	Mt. Olivet
003103f	O'DONOGHUE, Redmond	43y	W	Ire.	23 APR 1875	Holy Rood
003128	O'DONOHUE, Ellen	65y	W	Ire.	26 APR 1875	Holy Rood
001404	O'DONOHUGH, John	6m	W	D.C.	16 DEC 1874	Holy Rood
008511	O'DONOHUGH, Mary Ann	6w	W	D.C.	01 AUG 1876	Holy Rood
015601	O'DRISCOLL, Elizabeth Agnes	35y	W	D.C.	03 MAY 1878	Mt. Olivet
006768	O'DWYER, Catherine	56y	W	Ire.	21 MAR 1876	Mt. Olivet
001002	O'DWYER, John, Col.	42y	W	Ire.	01 NOV 1874	Mt. Olivet
002031	O'DWYER, Katie	1y	W	D.C.	05 FEB 1875	Mt. Olivet
004444	O'GRADY, John G.	5y	W	D.C.	04 AUG 1875	Mt. Olivet
002489	O'HAGAN, Elizabeth	6m	W	D.C.	09 MAR 1875	Mt. Olivet
019866	O'HAGAN, George Bernard	8m	W	D.C.	22 APR 1879	Mt. Olivet
016490	O'HAGAN, Thos. Leo.	2m	W	D.C.	07 JUL 1878	Mt. Olivet
010833	O'HARA, Martin	1y	W	D.C.	02 MAR 1877	Mt. Olivet
008174	O'HARA, Mary	65y	W	Ire.	11 JUL 1876	Mt. Olivet

District of Columbia Death Records, August 1, 1874 to July 31, 1879

No.	Name	Age	Race	Birth	Death Date	Burial Place
014058	O'HARA, Michael	32y	W	Scot.	10 DEC 1877	Soldier's Home
020473	O'HARE, Catherine	76y	W	Md.	16 JUN 1879	Mt. Olivet
004668	O'HARE, Mary	16y	W	Md.	19 AUG 1875	Texas, Balt. Co., Md.
016660	O'HARRA, Robert	33y	W	Pa.	18 JUL 1878	Hospital
017384	O'HEARN, Jane	44y	W	Ire.	12 SEP 1878	Mt. Olivet
003754	O'KEARNEY, Annie	36y	W	Ire.	21 JUN 1875	Mt. Olivet
015234	O'LEARY, Ann	50y	W	Ire.	30 MAR 1878	Mt. Olivet
009194	O'LEARY, Annie	15y	W	D.C.	24 SEP 1876	Mt. Olivet
008418	O'LEARY, Ellen	83y	W	Ire.	25 JUL 1876	Mt. Olivet
013328	O'LEARY, Ellen	60y	W	Ire.	27 SEP 1877	Mt. Olivet
000067	O'LEARY, John	50y	W	Ire.	05 AUG 1874	Mt. Olivet
018155	O'LEARY, Katie	19y	W	N.Y.	25 NOV 1878	Mt. Olivet
007728	O'LEARY, Thomas	50y	W	Ire.	19 JUN 1876	Mt. Olivet
016709	O'LOUGHLIN, May H.	3y	W	D.C.	21 JUL 1878	Mt. Olivet
010789	O'MARA, Mary	90y	W	Ire.	26 FEB 1877	Mt. Olivet
008405	O'MARRA, Thomas	27y	W	Ire.	24 JUL 1876	N.Y.
013956	O'NEAL, Albert Ignatius	5y	W	D.C.	28 NOV 1877	Holy Rood
012758	O'NEAL, Edward	35y	W	Ire.	10 AUG 1877	Mt. Olivet
004466	O'NEAL, John	8y	W	D.C.	05 AUG 1875	Mt. Olivet
006524	O'NEAL, Maria	55y	C	Va.	02 MAR 1876	Mt. Olivet
018601	O'NEAL, Mary	81y	W	Ire.	07 JAN 1879	Mt. Olivet
017668	O'NEIL, Bernard A.	1y	W	D.C.	07 OCT 1878	Holy Rood
020428	O'NEIL, Edward	10y	W	D.C.	13 JUN 1879	Mt. Olivet
015643	O'NEIL, Elizabeth	78y	W	Ire.	07 MAY 1878	Mt. Olivet
001175	O'NEIL, Hanorah	25y	W	D.C.	18 NOV 1874	Mt. Olivet
008385	O'NEIL, Irene	11m	C	D.C.	22 JUL 1876	Ebenezer
016837	O'NEIL, John	43y	W	Ire.	30 JUL 1878	Mt. Olivet
011898	O'NEIL, Mary Margaret (twin)	3m	C	D.C.	14 JUN 1877	Congressional
005104	O'NEILL, Anne Eliza	1y	W	D.C.	19 SEP 1875	Congressional
000307	O'NEILL, Elizabeth	74y	W	Ire.	24 AUG 1874	N.Y.
014991	O'NEILL, Elizabeth	50y	W	Ire.	08 MAR 1878	Mt. Olivet
001209	O'NEILL, Emmet F.	7y	W	Va.	22 NOV 1874	Congressional
010329	O'NEILL, Francis John	11m	W	D.C.	18 JAN 1877	Mt. Olivet
006075	O'NEILL, Gracie	3y	W	D.C.	20 JAN 1876	Congressional
019197	O'NEILL, John	50y	W	S.C.	25 FEB 1879	Mt. Olivet
012190	O'NEILL, Katie	3m	W	D.C.	03 JUL 1877	Congressional
005879	O'NEILL, Lizzie	8y	W	D.C.	27 DEC 1875	Mt. Olivet
004966	O'NEILL, Mabel	3d	W	D.C.	09 SEP 1875	Congressional
001396	O'NEILL, Michel	3d	W	D.C.	15 DEC 1874	Mt. Olivet
001579	O'NEILL, Mrs. N.	55y	W	Ire.	02 JAN 1875	Mt. Olivet
001897	O'NEILL, Sarah F.	14m	W	D.C.	26 JAN 1875	Congressional
019153	O'NIEL, Daniel	28y	W	D.C.	22 FEB 1879	Mt. Olivet
005850	O'NIEL, Mary	57y	W	Ire.	24 DEC 1875	Mt. Olivet
019848	O'REILLY, Ellinore	33y	W	Pa.	20 APR 1879	Mt. Olivet
003732	O'REYNOLDS, Wm. Henry	7m	W	D.C.	20 JUN 1875	Presbyterian
006145	O'RILEY, William	16y	W	D.C.	26 JAN 1876	Mt. Olivet
010370	O'RILEY, Winfer, Mrs.	70y	W	Ire.	22 JAN 1877	Mt. Olivet
016037	O'ROURKE, John	40y	W	Ire.	06 JUN 1878	Mt. Olivet
011425	O'SHEA, Cornelius	19y	W	N.Y.	25 APR 1877	Mt. Olivet
015633	O'SHEA, Margaret	3y	W	D.C.	06 MAY 1878	Mt. Olivet
017217	O'SULLIVAN, Annie	10d	W	D.C.	27 AUG 1878	Mt. Olivet
009732	O'SULLIVAN, John	51y	W	Ire.	18 NOV 1876	Holy Rood
011765	O'SULLIVAN, Patrick	1d	W	D.C.	01 JUN 1877	Holy Rood
006060	O'TOOLE, John	44y	W	Ire.	18 JAN 1876	Mt. Olivet
000023	O'TOOLE, Mary	45y	W	Ire.	02 AUG 1874	Mt. Olivet
011052	O'TOOLE, Mary, Mrs.	59y	W	Ire.	20 MAR 1877	Holy Rood

No.	Name	Age	Race	Birth	Death Date	Burial Place
015235	O'TOOLE, Wm.	11y	W	D.C.	30 MAR 1878	Mt. Olivet
019121	OAKLEY, Charles M.	28y	W	Va.	19 FEB 1879	Congressional
000590	OAKLEY, James A.	7d	W	D.C.	21 SEP 1874	Methodist
007238	OBER, Francis S.	44y	W	Ala.	07 MAY 1876	Congressional
004982	OBER, Mary M.	8y	W	D.C.	10 SEP 1875	Congressional
019146	OCHMANN, Mary A.	2y	W	D.C.	21 FEB 1879	Congressional
008311	OCKERSHAUSEN, Carl	37y	W	Ger.	18 JUL 1876	Presbyterian
001800	ODDIE, Ann Eliza	80y	W	N.Y.	19 JAN 1875	Yonkers, N.Y.
014097	ODEN, Infant of Lettie	12h	C	D.C.	14 DEC 1877	Potters Field
017345	OEHMAN, Louisa Victoria	3y	W	D.C.	07 SEP 1878	Congressional
000300	OEHMANN, Anna Elizabeth	1y	W	D.C.	24 AUG 1874	Congressional
017762	OERTLY, Bartholomew	51y	W	Switz.	16 OCT 1878	Oak Hill
010176	OFFER, Elizibeth	80y	C	D.C.	05 JAN 1877	Harmony
008986	OFFER, Henry	c.76y	C	Md.	06 SEP 1876	Harmony
017133	OFFERMAN, George H.	27y	W	Ger.	21 AUG 1878	Prospect Hill
019229	OFFLEY, Emily M.	2y	W	D.C.	27 FEB 1879	Oak Hill
006170	OFFRMAN, Bethe	45y	W	D.C.	28 JAN 1876	Tennallytown Methodist
004261f	OFFUTT, Amy	5m	W	D.C.	23 JUL 1875	Holy Rood
001650	OFFUTT, Elizabeth A.	57y	W	D.C.	08 JAN 1875	Oak Hill
017399	OFFUTT, George W.	27y	W	D.C.	13 SEP 1878	Holy Rood
019833	OFFUTT, George W.	52y	W	D.C.	19 APR 1879	Holy Rood
006572	OFFUTT, Infant of F. Ignatius	15min	W	D.C.	06 MAR 1876	Mt. Olivet
016524	OFFUTT, Zachariah M.	75y	W	Md.	09 JUL 1878	College/Holy Rood
013279	OGLE, Alice C.	3y	W	D.C.	22 SEP 1877	Holy Rood
014916	OGLE, Annie V.	45y	W	Va.	01 MAR 1878	Oak Hill
017273	OGLE, Rachel L.	3m	W	D.C.	31 AUG 1878	Holy Rood
018156	OGLETON, Charles H.	1m	C	D.C.	25 NOV 1878	Mt. Zion
000270	OGLETON, Dorho	6d	C	D.C.	21 AUG 1874	Mt. Zion
004467	OGLETON, John H.	9m	C	D.C.	05 AUG 1875	Mt. Zion
004581	OHL, Emma C.	4y	W	Md.	13 AUG 1875	Prospect Hill
009100	OHMER, Susan	48y	W	D.C.	16 SEP 1876	Paton, Ohio
017170	OLDBERG, Rudolph	28y	W	Swed.	24 AUG 1878	Oak Hill
009799	OLDEN, Geo.	1m	C	D.C.	25 NOV 1876	Beckett's
001641	OLDEN, Infant of Fred K.	4h	C	D.C.	07 JAN 1875	Potters Field
009794	OLDEN, Mary	7y	C	D.C.	25 NOV 1876	Swartz's
005930	OLDEN, Mary E.	15d	C	D.C.	03 JAN 1876	Ebenezer
002620	OLIFFE, Annie	2y	W	Md.	17 MAR 1875	Methodist
002380	OLIVE, Annie	48y	W	N.Y.	02 MAR 1875	Glenwood
005945	OLIVE, Henry	56y	W	Va.	05 JAN 1876	Glenwood
017169	OLIVER, Addie Serena	5m	W	D.C.	24 AUG 1878	Congressional
002419	OLIVER, George N.	8y	C	D.C.	04 MAR 1875	Mt. Pleasant
001014	OLIVER, George S.	6m	W	D.C.	02 NOV 1874	Congressional
001710	OLIVER, Harold E.	1m	W	D.C.	13 JAN 1875	Glenwood
018140	OLIVER, Henrietta	92y	C	Md.	24 NOV 1878	College
001381	OLIVER, Infant of Thomas	2h	W	D.C.	14 DEC 1874	Mt. Olivet
007998	OLIVER, Jessie L.	10m	W	D.C.	04 JUL 1876	Congressional
011411	OLIVER, Mary	44y	W	Md.	24 APR 1877	Glenwood
001882	OLIVER, Sarah Ann	51y	W	Md.	25 JAN 1875	Mt. Olivet
007441	OLIVER, Verlinda Wren	73y	W	Va.	30 MAY 1876	Glenwood
017605	OLLIFFE, Wm. R.	9y	W	D.C.	02 OCT 1878	Methodist
009683	OLLIVER, Eveline A.	57y	W	Va.	13 NOV 1876	Oak Hill
012491	OLMSTEAD, Mary	22y	C	Va.	23 JUL 1877	Potters Field
011549	OPPERMAN, Caroline	14d	W	D.C.	09 MAY 1877	Prospect Hill
016636	OPREY, Frederic J.	3y	W	D.C.	17 JUL 1878	Holy Rood
004680	ORANGE, Angelina	11m	W	D.C.	20 AUG 1875	Congressional
014849	ORDWAY, Richmond	5y	W	D.C.	22 FEB 1878	Concord, N.H.

District of Columbia Death Records, August 1, 1874 to July 31, 1879   257

No.	Name	Age	Race	Birth	Death Date	Burial Place
011505	OREM, William E.	2y	W	D.C.	04 MAY 1877	Congressional
003707f	ORENDORF, Lucinda Anne	1y	W	Md.	19 JUN 1875	Baltimore, Md.
000427	ORION, Dominic	10m	W	D.C.	04 SEP 1874	St. Mary's
017120	ORME, Ulysses	1y	C	D.C.	20 AUG 1878	Mt. Pleasant
006711	ORMES, Infant of William	1d	C	D.C.	17 MAR 1876	Potters Field
018998	ORMSBY, William E.	28y	W	U.S.	08 FEB 1879	Soldier's Home
012368	ORRELL, Mary A.	2y	W	D.C.	15 JUL 1877	Oak Hill
006535	ORSBURN, Louisa	5m	C	D.C.	03 MAR 1876	Mt. Pleasant
007049	ORTON, William Henry	1y	W	D.C.	18 APR 1876	Oak Hill
016681	OSBORN, Margarett A.	29y	W	D.C.	19 JUL 1878	Oak Hill
008610	OSBOURNE, Caroline	37y	M	Va.	08 AUG 1876	Harmony
007054	OSGOOD, Cyrus K.	c.58y	W	Me.	19 APR 1876	Savannah, Ga.
011165	OSHANS, Mary J.	7d	W	D.C.	30 MAR 1877	Mt. Olivet
000869	OSSIRE, William Henry	35y	W	Pa.	20 OCT 1874	Oak Hill
001331	OSTERHOLD, Wohlrad	30y	W	Ger.	07 DEC 1874	Prospect Hill
014804	OSWALD, Winfield	9m	W	D.C.	17 FEB 1876	Mt. Olivet
020702	OSWEIL, John Frances	2y	W	D.C.	01 JUL 1879	Mt. Olivet
014688	OSWELL, Mary	23y	W	Md.	06 FEB 1878	Mt. Olivet
006299	OSWILL, Blanche Estella	3m	W	D.C.	10 FEB 1876	Congressional
008627	OSWILL, Elizebeth	27y	W	N.Y.	09 AUG 1876	Mt. Olivet
006340	OTERO, Laura	18m	W	N.M.	13 FEB 1876	Mt. Olivet
005325	OTIS, Frances M.	1y	W	D.C.	31 OCT 1875	Congressional
017592	OTIS, Horace	42y	W	N.Y.	01 OCT 1878	Hospital
019918	OTIS, Ida R.	24y	W	D.C.	27 APR 1879	Glenwood
001947	OTIS, Infant of H.G.	2½d	W	D.C.	29 JAN 1875	Congressional
020250	OTIS, James F.	39y	W	Me.	01 JUN 1879	Portsmouth, N.H.
015308	OTISS, Thomas	32y	W	Va.	07 APR 1878	Methodist
009420	OTT, Mary Ann	67y	W	Md.	16 OCT 1876	Glenwood
001508	OTT, William	30y	W	Md.	27 DEC 1874	Glenwood
009865	OUDEN, Boss	18y	C	Va.	04 DEC 1876	Baptist
013232	OUDEN, Lucy Ann	44y	C	Va.	17 SEP 1877	Baptist
011573	OURAND, Elijah	76y	W	Md.	12 MAY 1877	Rock Creek
019072	OURAND, Franck L., Jr.	2y	W	D.C.	14 FEB 1879	Congressional
003144	OURAND, W.H.E.	35y	W	D.C.	27 APR 1875	Congressional
000930	OURDAN, Joseph J.P.	71y	W	France	25 OCT 1874	Oak Hill
009569	OUTKELT, Mary	50y	W	Ohio	29 OCT 1876	Zanesville, Ohio
013126	OVERTON, Mary Ellen	23y	C	Va.	08 SEP 1877	Mt. Pleasant
005421	OVERTON, Mildred F.	1y	C	D.C.	10 NOV 1875	Mt. Zion
013094	OVERTURF, Thomas	38y	W	Pa.	05 SEP 1877	Hospital, Government
011576	OWDRICK, Benjamin	19y	C	D.C.	12 MAY 1877	Potters Field
014872	OWEN, Edward	84y	W	Wales	25 FEB 1878	Glenwood
000324	OWENS, Archie	10y	C	D.C.	26 AUG 1874	Mt. Zion
007699	OWENS, Caroline H.	c.42y	W	Va.	17 JUN 1876	Mt. Olivet
017975	OWENS, Charles Edward	7y	W	D.C.	07 NOV 1878	Glenwood
001608	OWENS, Chas. E.	70y	W	Md.	04 JAN 1875	Mt. Olivet
020310	OWENS, Edward Jane	32y	W	D.C.	05 JUN 1879	Glenwood
002499	OWENS, Elizabeth	16y	W	D.C.	10 MAR 1875	Addison's Chapel
005476	OWENS, Elizabeth	44y	W	D.C.	16 NOV 1875	Addison's Chapel
017452	OWENS, Elizabeth	55y	C	D.C.	18 SEP 1878	Mt. Pleasant
020029	OWENS, Elizabeth	43y	C	D.C.	07 MAY 1879	Harmony
008282	OWENS, Infant of Marshal	3d	C	D.C.	15 JUL 1876	Mt. Zion
017531	OWENS, Infant of Thomas	1d	C	D.C.	25 SEP 1878	Mt. Zion
015450	OWENS, James Olander	10m	W	D.C.	19 APR 1878	Mt. Olivet
005784	OWENS, James W.	64y	W	Va.	18 DEC 1875	Soldier's Home
006671	OWENS, Margaret	35y	W	Md.	14 MAR 1876	Mt. Olivet
009104	OWENS, Mary	64y	W	Md.	17 SEP 1876	Potters Field

No.	Name	Age	Race	Birth	Death Date	Burial Place
015081	OWENS, Rich. B.	70y	W	Md.	15 MAR 1878	Glenwood
020982	OWENS, Sarah Jane	37y	W	D.C.	17 JUL 1879	Mt. Olivet
014372	OWENS, Stephen	19d	C	D.C.	09 JAN 1878	Harmony
004550	OWNES, Infant of Stephen	5d	C	D.C.	11 AUG 1875	Harmony
011896	OWSLEY, Infant of R.G.	2m	C	D.C.	14 JUN 1877	Ebenezer
004419	OXLEY, Charles	5m	W	D.C.	02 AUG 1875	Oak Hill
006963	OXLEY, Elizabeth	77y	W	Md.	07 APR 1876	Glenwood
000115	OXLEY, Lillie	3y	W	D.C.	09 AUG 1874	Oak Hill
004231	OXLEY, Lulie	5m	W	D.C.	21 JUL 1875	Oak Hill
018372	OYSTER, Mary Eva	26y	W	D.C.	18 DEC 1878	Prospect Hill
020474	OYSTER, Mary Rosa	6m	W	D.C.	16 JUN 1879	Prospect Hill

P

No.	Name	Age	Race	Birth	Death Date	Burial Place
006077	PACE, David	61y	W	Wales	20 JAN 1876	Congressional
008906	PACH, Moses	5m	W	D.C.	31 AUG 1876	Hebrew
011580	PADDON, Charles Raymond	3y	W	D.C.	13 MAY 1877	Glenwood
005663	PADGET, Lilly Aramina	1y	W	D.C.	05 DEC 1875	Congressional
019867	PADGETT, Agnes	1m	W	D.C.	22 APR 1879	Mt. Olivet
018870	PADGETT, Benard	5m	W	D.C.	29 JAN 1879	Congressional
008316	PADGETT, George	7m	W	D.C.	18 JUL 1876	Congressional
021139	PADGETT, H.D.	1y	W	D.C.	28 JUL 1879	Mt. Olivet
008099	PADGETT, Susanna	41y	W	D.C.	09 JUL 1876	Congressional
003796	PADGETT, William H.	73y	W	Md.	23 JUN 1875	Congressional
009555	PADGETT, William H.	53y	W	Md.	27 OCT 1876	Mt. Olivet
016362	PADGODD, Margarith	83y	W	Md.	29 JUN 1878	Mt. Olivet
005642	PAGE, Alice Lucinda	5m	C	D.C.	03 DEC 1875	Mt. Pleasant
008341	PAGE, Charles Henry	75y	W	Va.	20 JUL 1876	Oak Hill
020397	PAGE, Crater	76y	C	Va.	11 JUN 1879	Potters Field
014750	PAGE, Emily B.	34y	C	Va.	12 FEB 1878	Mt. Zion
015046	PAGE, Frank	7m	C	D.C.	12 MAR 1878	Harmony
016525	PAGE, Hattie	18m	C	D.C.	09 JUL 1878	Mt. Pleasant
001642f	PAGE, Henry L.	68y	W	Mass.	07 JAN 1875	Congressional
008572	PAGE, James	9m	C	D.C.	06 AUG 1876	Young Mens
007701	PAGE, John	1y	C	D.C.	17 JUN 1876	Holy Rood
012612	PAGE, Lucinda	23y	C	Va.	30 JUL 1877	Harmony
014676	PAGE, Lucy A.	30y	C	Va.	05 FEB 1878	Mt. Pleasant
011428	PAGE, Maria C., Mrs.	55y	W	N.Y.	25 APR 1877	Congressional
001893	PAGE, Martha	8m	C	D.C.	26 JAN 1875	Young Mens
009590	PAGE, Peter	80y	C	Va.	01 NOV 1876	Young Mens
009164	PAGE, Quincy L.	51y	W	N.H.	22 SEP 1876	Congressional
019402	PAGE, R. Arnold	30y	W	D.C.	14 MAR 1879	Congressional
005369	PAGE, Robert Carter	63y	W	Va.	05 NOV 1875	Glenwood
018788	PAGE, Thomas H.	9m	C	D.C.	23 JAN 1879	Mt. Zion
019977	PAGE, William	19d	C	D.C.	03 MAY 1879	Payne's
004175	PAGE, William H.	29y	W	Va.	17 JUL 1875	Glenwood
004149f	PAGELS, Florence Gaston	7m	W	Md.	15 MAY 1875	Oak Hill
007926	PAIGN, William	½d	C	D.C.	29 JUN 1876	Beckett's
005100a	PAIN, Anna	6d	C	D.C.	10 OCT 1875	Potters Field
020167	PAIN, Elizbeth	10y	C	D.C.	21 MAY 1879	Beckett's
014182	PAINE, Harrison	1y	C	D.C.	23 DEC 1877	Mt. Zion
019032	PAINE, Robert	59y	C	Va.	11 FEB 1879	Potters Field
000640	PAINE, Wm.	14d	C	D.C.	25 SEP 1874	Beckett's
006856	PALM, Sarah	c.40y	C	Va.	29 MAR 1876	Mt. Pleasant Plain
019047	PALMER, Abiah P.	19y	W	Va.	12 FEB 1879	Glenwood

District of Columbia Death Records, August 1, 1874 to July 31, 1879

No.	Name	Age	Race	Birth	Death Date	Burial Place
005093a	PALMER, Benjamin F.	35y	W	D.C.	09 OCT 1875	Congressional
019391	PALMER, David Parsons	67y	W	N.Y.	13 MAR 1879	Glenwood
003120	PALMER, Ernst	8y	M	D.C.	25 APR 1875	Young Mens
012236	PALMER, Henry	70y	C	Md.	06 JUL 1877	Harmony
001343	PALMER, Hester Ann	41y	M	Va.	09 DEC 1874	Mt. Pleasant
000606	PALMER, Infant of Wm. B.	6d	C	D.C.	22 SEP 1874	Potters Field
014755	PALMER, James Hervey	36y	W	Ohio	13 FEB 1878	Oak Hill
004603f	PALMER, John	2y	W	D.C.	14 AUG 1875	St. Mary's
000752	PALMER, Lizzie	30y	M	Va.	08 OCT 1874	Washington Asylum
016594	PALMER, Mary Ann	30y	C	Va.	14 JUL 1878	Mt. Pleasant
006341	PALMER, Mirah	19y	C	Va.	13 FEB 1876	Mt. Pleasant Plain
012305	PALMER, Moses	62y	M	Va.	10 JUL 1877	Harmony
017530	PALMER, Presley	3y	C	D.C.	25 SEP 1878	Payne's
001904	PALMER, Robert	42y	C	Va.	26 JAN 1875	Mt. Pleasant
010463	PALMER, Sarah Ann	1y	C	D.C.	31 JAN 1877	Ebenezer
005066a	PALMER, W.G.	40y	W	Va.	05 OCT 1875	Potters Field
002632	PALMER, William Franklin	5m	W	D.C.	18 MAR 1875	Congressional
017048	PALMER, Wm.	3m	C	D.C.	14 AUG 1878	Beckett's
002672	PALYLUSE, Winfield Jeremiah	16y	W	D.C.	21 MAR 1875	Glenwood
007615	PANCOAST, Charles Albert	6m	W	Wisc.	12 JUN 1876	Newark, N.J.
017171	PANIELL, Michael	42y	W	Ire.	24 AUG 1878	Soldier's Home
008893	PANIER, Monroe	35y	W	Va.	31 AUG 1876	Potters Field
000592	PANNELL, Alice Augusta	14d	C	D.C.	21 SEP 1874	Beckett's
017813	PARISH, Albert Irving	7y	W	D.C.	20 OCT 1878	Oak Hill
012164	PARISH, Mary	1y	W	D.C.	01 JUL 1877	Congressional
004482	PARISH, R.	9m	W	D.C.	06 AUG 1875	Oak Hill
013601	PARK, Ann	71y	W	Eng.	23 OCT 1877	Boston, Mass.
002825	PARK, George A.	30y	W	Mass.	01 APR 1875	Boston, Mass.
020522	PARK, Maria	89y	C	Va.	19 JUN 1879	Beckett's
003903	PARK, William	1y	W	D.C.	28 JUN 1875	Ebenezer
020168	PARKE, Harry	2y	C	D.C.	21 MAY 1879	Young Mens
001437	PARKE, Thomas T.	30y	W	D.C.	20 DEC 1874	Oak Hill
017891	PARKE, Wm.	10h	W	D.C.	28 OCT 1878	Parkersburg, Pa.
005522	PARKER, Adeline L.	55y	W	N.H.	20 NOV 1875	Oak Hill
006161	PARKER, Alfred	70y	C	Va	27 JAN 1876	Potters Field
013896	PARKER, Alfred	4m	C	D.C.	23 NOV 1877	Harmony
015482	PARKER, Ann Sebena	11m	C	D.C.	22 APR 1878	Mt. Zion
010782	PARKER, Ann Sophia	62y	W	D.C.	26 FEB 1877	Congressional
001632	PARKER, Anna	3y	C	D.C.	06 JAN 1875	Harmony
009836	PARKER, Anna B.	3y	W	Minn.	30 NOV 1876	Graceland
016489	PARKER, Anna E. [Hicks]	1m	C	D.C.	07 JUL 1878	Harmony
019288	PARKER, Annie	2y	C	D.C.	05 MAR 1879	Beckett's
010331	PARKER, Arobell	12y	C	Ohio	18 JAN 1877	Harmony
008548	PARKER, Augusta	2y	C	D.C.	04 AUG 1876	Beckett's
019656	PARKER, Chadrick	1y	C	D.C.	04 APR 1879	Mt. Pleasant
014714	PARKER, Charles	6m	C	D.C.	08 FEB 1878	Potters Field
015990	PARKER, Charlott	22y	C	Va.	03 JUN 1878	Harmony
008520	PARKER, Christiana	26y	C	Va.	01 AUG 1876	Harmony
006408	PARKER, Courtney	73y	C	Va.	18 FEB 1876	Harmony
002623	PARKER, David	55y	C	Va.	17 MAR 1875	Beckett's
009564	PARKER, Edward	1y	C	D.C.	28 OCT 1876	Ebenezer
020287	PARKER, Edward	7m	C	D.C.	03 JUN 1879	Harmony
009828	PARKER, Ellen	30y	C	Va.	29 NOV 1876	Harmony
012023	PARKER, Ellen	40y	C	Md.	23 JUN 1877	Harmony
015185	PARKER, Ellen E., Mrs.	46y	W	N.H.	25 MAR 1878	Windsor, Ver.
020569	PARKER, Ernest	10m	C	D.C.	22 JUN 1879	Beckett's

District of Columbia Death Records, August 1, 1874 to July 31, 1879

No.	Name	Age	Race	Birth	Death Date	Burial Place
010073	PARKER, Frances A.	21y	C	Va.	26 DEC 1876	Beckett's
009853	PARKER, Frank	4y	C	D.C.	03 DEC 1876	Harmony
004839	PARKER, Geo. B.	72y	C	Va.	30 AUG 1875	Ebenezer
009925	PARKER, George	76y	W	Md.	10 DEC 1876	Congressional
017866	PARKER, George	7y	W	D.C.	26 OCT 1878	Graceland/Glenwood
005852	PARKER, George Thomas	11m	C	D.C.	24 DEC 1875	Holy Rood
005429	PARKER, Gertrude	4m	C	D.C.	11 NOV 1875	Young Mens
004657	PARKER, Harriet	28y	C	Va.	18 AUG 1875	Mt. Pleasant
016076	PARKER, Harry	13m	C	D.C.	08 JUN 1878	Harmony
018733	PARKER, Harry Dunlap	9y	W	W.Va.	19 JAN 1879	Wheeling, W.Va.
020878	PARKER, Hattie H.	2y	C	D.C.	10 JUL 1879	Mt. Pleasant
011820	PARKER, Henly Ray	6y	M	Ohio	06 JUN 1877	Harmony
004262	PARKER, Hennetta	1y	W	D.C.	23 JUL 1875	Glenwood
004799	PARKER, Henrietta	1y	C	D.C.	28 AUG 1875	Young Mens
009725	PARKER, Ida	7y	C	D.C.	18 NOV 1876	Beckett's
014098	PARKER, Infant of Francis	6d	C	D.C.	14 DEC 1877	Potters Field
003628	PARKER, Infant of Frank	11d	C	D.C.	13 JUN 1875	Harmony
016078	PARKER, Infant of George	1y	C	D.C.	08 JUN 1878	Potters Field
009747	PARKER, Infant of James	10d	C	D.C.	20 NOV 1876	Potters Field
008644	PARKER, Infant of William	24h	C	D.C.	11 AUG 1876	Potters Field
011808	PARKER, Jesse Lee	2y	C	D.C.	05 JUN 1877	Brightwood
014966	PARKER, John	1y	C	D.C.	06 MAR 1878	Mt. Pleasant Plain
010624	PARKER, Kate	2d	C	D.C.	14 FEB 1877	Beckett's
010900	PARKER, Lena	7y	C	--	07 MAR 1877	Potters Field
019521	PARKER, Lettie	1y	C	D.C.	23 MAR 1879	Young Mens
010019	PARKER, Lucinda	110y	C	Va.	20 DEC 1876	Potters Field
005840	PARKER, Mabel A.	7y	W	D.C.	23 DEC 1875	Glenwood
000453	PARKER, Margaret	1m	W	--	08 SEP 1874	Mt. Olivet
000130	PARKER, Mary	2½m	C	D.C.	10 AUG 1874	Beckett's
009917	PARKER, Mary	2m	C	D.C.	10 DEC 1876	Ebenezer
018999	PARKER, Mary Augusta	65y	W	Va.	08 FEB 1879	Oak Hill
004682	PARKER, Mary Eliza	8m	C	D.C.	20 AUG 1875	Potters Field
008864	PARKER, Mary Stanton Waterman	8h	W	D.C.	28 AUG 1876	Prospect Hill
005064a	PARKER, Nathan	17y	C	Va.	05 OCT 1875	Moore's
008866	PARKER, Philip	1y	C	D.C.	29 AUG 1876	Harmony
002734	PARKER, Phillip	43y	C	D.C.	25 MAR 1875	Mt. Zion
008799	PARKER, Richard E.	8m	W	D.C.	23 AUG 1876	Congressional
006945	PARKER, Robert	24y	C	Va.	06 APR 1876	Potters Field
007459	PARKER, Sarah Ann	62y	W	D.C.	01 JUN 1876	Mt. Zion
006407	PARKER, Sarah J.	25y	M	D.C.	18 FEB 1876	Mt. Olivet
013243	PARKER, Sarah W.	24y	W	D.C.	18 SEP 1877	Oak Hill
001665	PARKER, Sophia Elizabeth	6m	W	D.C.	09 JAN 1875	Congressional
009658	PARKER, Thomas	17y	C	D.C.	09 NOV 1876	Mt. Olivet
008022	PARKER, Thos. J.	13m	W	D.C.	05 JUL 1876	Glenwood
012694	PARKER, Virginia	30y	C	Va.	06 AUG 1877	Potters Field
012119	PARKER, William	36y	C	Va.	29 JUN 1877	Ebenezer
020489	PARKER, William	40y	W	Scot.	17 JUN 1879	Soldier's Home
019520	PARKER, William	52y	C	Va.	23 MAR 1879	Harmony
004582	PARKER, William J.	8m	C	D.C.	13 AUG 1875	Ebenezer
009668	PARKER, Wm. H.	29y	C	D.C.	11 NOV 1876	Mt. Zion
005761	PARKER, Wm. Henry Washington	6d	C	D.C.	15 DEC 1875	Harmony
006159	PARKHURST, John Warren	1m	W	D.C.	27 JAN 1876	Glenwood
003182	PARKINSON, Anthony	48y	W	Eng.	30 APR 1875	Congressional
019060	PARKINSON, Edwin	26y	W	D.C.	13 FEB 1879	Mt. Olivet
011664	PARKINSON, William	15d	W	D.C.	21 MAY 1877	Montgomery Co., Md.
002150	PARKS, Annie M.	34y	W	Eng.	14 FEB 1875	Graceland

District of Columbia Death Records, August 1, 1874 to July 31, 1879

No.	Name	Age	Race	Birth	Death Date	Burial Place
015030	PARKS, Geo. Francis	1y	C	D.C.	11 MAR 1878	Young Mens
001542	PARKS, Infant of Frederick J.	1d	W	D.C.	31 DEC 1874	Graceland
016851	PARKS, Josephine	30y	C	Md.	31 JUL 1878	Harmony
010943	PARKS, Julia S., Mrs.	43y	W	Mass.	11 MAR 1877	Palmer, Mass.
001516	PARKS, Margaret, Mrs.	73y	W	Md.	28 DEC 1874	Congressional
011138	PARKS, Maria	33y	C	Md.	28 MAR 1877	Ebenezer
008956	PARKS, Sarah	22y	C	Md.	03 SEP 1876	Arlington
009162	PARKS, Sarah J.	21d	C	D.C.	22 SEP 1876	Arlington, Va.
021138	PARLIN, Stella Baudrey	1y	W	Mo.	28 JUL 1879	Methodist Episcopal
019774	PARRIS, Mary Francis	52y	W	D.C.	14 APR 1879	Congressional
008871	PARRIS, Susan A.	38y	C	Va.	29 AUG 1876	Harmony
012370	PARRON, Jno. Thos.	11m	C	D.C.	15 JUL 1877	Mt. Olivet
012791	PARROTT, Joseph G.	6y	W	D.C.	13 AUG 1877	Presbyterian
018248	PARROTT, Julia A.	54y	C	Va.	05 DEC 1878	Mt. Zion
001275	PARRY, Alfred H.	68y	C	Va.	30 NOV 1874	Beckett's
005939	PARRY, Bertie	7y	C	D.C.	04 JAN 1876	Ebenezer
003538	PARRY, Lucinda	70y	C	Md.	05 JUN 1875	Ebenezer
018899	PARRY, Rebecca	c.70y	C	Md.	31 JAN 1879	Beckett's
016206	PARRY, Richard H.	11m	W	D.C.	17 JUN 1878	Glenwood
010231	PARSON, Portia A.	1y	W	D.C.	09 JAN 1877	Rock Creek
008082	PARSONS, Edward T.	34y	W	Ky.	08 JUL 1876	Louisville, Ky.
012492	PARSONS, Infant of James L.	8d	W	D.C.	23 JUL 1877	Congressional
005293	PARSONS, James L.	3m	W	D.C.	28 OCT 1875	Congressional
012578	PARSONS, Mary Eva	4m	W	D.C.	28 JUL 1877	Congressional
011700	PARTELLO, William Philip	52y	W	N.Y.	25 MAY 1877	Glenwood
001570	PARTRIDGE, L.H.	44y	W	Me.	01 JAN 1875	Congressional
005576	PARUM, Mary	3y	C	D.C.	26 NOV 1875	Young Mens
014782	PASCHAL, Geo. W.	65y	W	Ga.	16 FEB 1878	Oak Hill
001442	PASCO, Cora Elizabeth	3d	W	D.C.	20 DEC 1874	Oak Hill
008336	PASCO, Frances M.	1y	W	D.C.	19 JUL 1876	Oak Hill
010554	PASCO, George	5y	W	D.C.	07 FEB 1877	Oak Hill
000518	PASQUITH, Frances	58y	W	Va.	15 SEP 1874	Northumb. Co., Va.
013440	PASSENO, Mary A.	24y	W	D.C.	08 OCT 1877	Holy Rood
012734	PATCH, Charles S.	1y	W	D.C.	08 AUG 1877	Congressional
001836	PATCH, Edward H.	1y	W	D.C.	22 JAN 1875	Congressional
009669	PATEN, Stephen	45y	C	Va.	11 NOV 1876	Mt. Zion
012085	PATRICK, Ida	7y	C	D.C.	27 JUN 1877	Mt. Zion
007025	PATRICK, Lucy H.	41y	W	N.Y.	16 APR 1876	Ballston, N.Y.
010990	PATRICK, Wm. M.	57y	C	Va.	15 MAR 1877	Mt. Pleasant
020111	PATTEE, Maude Greenleaf	2y	W	D.C.	15 MAY 1879	Graceland
016282	PATTEN, John D.	72y	W	Mass.	23 JUN 1878	Oak Hill
018327	PATTEN, Mary A.	6y	W	D.C.	13 DEC 1878	Mt. Pleasant
002831	PATTERSON, Abigal, Mrs.	51y	W	Md.	01 APR 1875	Presbyterian
008158	PATTERSON, Alexander	35y	C	Va.	10 JUL 1876	Harmony
010483	PATTERSON, Charles Henry	50y	W	D.C.	02 FEB 1877	Young Mens
006989	PATTERSON, Cornelius	11m	C	D.C.	11 APR 1876	Mt. Pleasant
001876	PATTERSON, Cornelius S.	13m	C	N.Y.	24 JAN 1875	Ebenezer
013013	PATTERSON, Elizabeth Ann	7y	W	D.C.	29 AUG 1877	Glenwood
001148	PATTERSON, Elizabeth	3y	C	D.C.	14 NOV 1874	Mt. Pleasant
008251	PATTERSON, George E.	4w	W	D.C.	13 JUL 1876	Oak Hill
006274	PATTERSON, Gertrude R.	3m	C	D.C.	08 FEB 1876	Ebenezer
005422	PATTERSON, Harriet	75y	C	Md.	10 NOV 1875	Mt. Olivet
012435	PATTERSON, James Lewis	1y	W	D.C.	19 JUL 1877	Oak Hill
007341	PATTERSON, John	63y	W	Mass.	19 MAY 1876	Potters Field
018249	PATTERSON, John	23y	C	Va.	05 DEC 1878	Potters Field
002308	PATTERSON, John E.	3y	W	Va.	24 FEB 1874	Graceland

District of Columbia Death Records, August 1, 1874 to July 31, 1879

No.	Name	Age	Race	Birth	Death Date	Burial Place
008490	PATTERSON, Mary	30y	C	Va.	30 JUL 1876	Mt. Pleasant
017570	PATTERSON, Richard	5y	C	D.C.	29 SEP 1878	Mt. Pleasant
009650	PATTERSON, Salina	60y	C	Md.	09 NOV 1876	Potters Field
005946	PATTERSON, Sarah	1m	C	D.C.	05 JAN 1876	Ebenezer
018975	PATTERSON, Susan	35y	C	Va.	06 FEB 1879	Mt. Pleasant
013688	PATTERSON, Thomas M.	5m	W	D.C.	31 OCT 1877	Oak Hill
018844	PATTISON, John R.	45y	W	N.Y.	27 JAN 1879	Brooklyn, N.Y.
017909	PATTON, Ellen	66y	W	Md.	30 OCT 1878	Port Deposit, Md.
002493	PATTON, Richard	11m	C	D.C.	09 MAR 1875	Mt. Pleasant
014448	PATTON, Thomas	18m	C	D.C.	16 JAN 1878	Mt. Pleasant
000543	PATTY, Richard	1y	C	D.C.	17 SEP 1874	Beckett's
000299	PAUL, Alexander H.	69y	W	D.C.	24 AUG 1874	Oak Hill
005409	PAUL, Mary Ann	62y	W	D.C.	09 NOV 1875	Oak Hill
000355	PAUL, Mary Ricard	33y	W	D.C.	29 AUG 1874	Baltimore, Md.
008245	PAUL, Morine	3m	C	N.J.	13 JUL 1876	Young Mens
006380	PAULGLASS, Jessie Vernon	2m	W	D.C.	16 FEB 1876	Glenwood
012061	PAULUS, Infant of John	4d	W	D.C.	26 JUN 1877	Prospect Hill
007951	PAULUS, Joachim M.	9h	W	D.C.	01 JUL 1876	Prospect Hill
002507	PAULUS, John	41y	W	Ger.	10 MAR 1875	Hospital
018647	PAULUS, John H.	7d	W	D.C.	11 JAN 1879	Prospect Hill
002235	PAVARINI, Angeline	1y	W	D.C.	19 FEB 1875	St. Mary's
007864	PAXTON, Hannah	72y	W	Md.	26 JUN 1876	Tennallytown
016228	PAXTON, Richard D.	17d	W	D.C.	19 JUN 1878	Rock Creek
000487	PAXTON, Sarah C.	17y	W	D.C.	12 SEP 1874	Tennallytown
001782	PAYNE, Anna	6m	W	Md.	18 JAN 1875	Presbyterian
007282	PAYNE, Arthur T.	22y	C	Va.	12 MAY 1876	Mt. Pleasant
014945	PAYNE, Bessie Louisa	2y	C	D.C.	04 MAR 1878	Mt. Zion
018407	PAYNE, Charlotte	10m	C	D.C.	20 DEC 1878	Beckett's
017187	PAYNE, Cornelius	1y	C	D.C.	25 AUG 1878	Mt. Zion
006342	PAYNE, Ella J.	10y	W	D.C.	13 FEB 1876	Holy Rood
015451	PAYNE, Ellen	55y	C	Md.	19 APR 1878	Payne's
020538	PAYNE, Ellen H.	31y	C	Miss.	20 JUN 1879	Harmony
016526	PAYNE, Frederick	72y	C	Va.	09 JUL 1878	Potters Field
009926	PAYNE, George G.	19y	W	D.C.	10 DEC 1876	Oak Hill
017496	PAYNE, Harriett	77y	W	Md.	22 SEP 1878	Rock Creek
013369	PAYNE, Henry Franklin	1y	C	D.C.	01 OCT 1877	Potters Field
012284	PAYNE, Infant of Charles	26d	C	D.C.	09 JUL 1877	Fairfax Co., Va.
001829	PAYNE, Infant of Frank	5h	C	D.C.	21 JAN 1875	Potters Field
006696	PAYNE, Infant of Jas.	21d	C	D.C.	16 MAR 1876	Beckett's
005851	PAYNE, Jackson	6m	C	D.C.	24 DEC 1875	Mt. Zion
009212	PAYNE, James	32y	W	D.C.	27 SEP 1876	Tennallytown
014745	PAYNE, James	2y	M	D.C.	15 FEB 1878	Young Mens
013673	PAYNE, James M.	49y	W	N.Y.	29 OCT 1877	Horsehead, N.Y.
016934	PAYNE, Johanna Eliz.	7m	C	D.C.	06 AUG 1878	Payne's
006471	PAYNE, Joseph	20y	C	Va.	25 FEB 1876	Mt. Zion
010212	PAYNE, Joseph	72y	W	Md.	07 JAN 1877	Tennallytown
012320	PAYNE, Joseph	11m	C	D.C.	11 JUL 1877	Potters Field
017000	PAYNE, Louisiana	1m	C	Va.	10 AUG 1878	Beckett's
005723	PAYNE, Martha	2d	C	D.C.	12 DEC 1875	Ebenezer
021085	PAYNE, Mary	15y	C	D.C.	24 JUL 1879	Potters Field
000213	PAYNE, Mary A.	19m	W	D.C.	16 AUG 1874	Tennallytown
015779	PAYNE, Mary Jane	4y	C	Md.	20 MAY 1878	Mt. Pleasant
012095	PAYNE, Mary L.	10m	C	D.C.	27 JUN 1877	Ebenezer
005242	PAYNE, Nelly	77y	C	Va.	22 OCT 1875	Potters Field
001478	PAYNE, Olive	1y	C	D.C.	25 DEC 1874	Mt. Olivet
016774	PAYNE, Reberta	1m	C	D.C.	26 JUL 1878	Beckett's

District of Columbia Death Records, August 1, 1874 to July 31, 1879   263

No.	Name	Age	Race	Birth	Death Date	Burial Place
019666	PAYNE, Thomas	39y	C	Va.	05 APR 1879	Harmony
012179	PAYNE, Walker	4m	C	D.C.	02 JUL 1877	Potters Field
009908	PAYNE, William	1y	C	D.C.	09 DEC 1876	Harmony
007983	PAYNE, William	1y	C	D.C.	03 JUL 1876	Mt. Zion
005997	PAYNE, William H.	27y	W	D.C.	11 JAN 1876	Oak Hill
015991	PAYNE, Wm.	45y	C	Va.	03 JUN 1878	Young Mens
018575	PAYNTER, Jos. H.	2y	M	D.C.	05 JAN 1879	Mt. Pleasant
010393	PAYTON, Alfred M.	7y	C	D.C.	24 JAN 1877	Mt. Zion
012888	PAYTON, Charles	24y	C	Va.	20 AUG 1877	Mt. Olivet
019389	PAYTON, Fannie	10y	C	Wisc.	13 MAR 1879	Mt. Pleasant
007017	PAYTON, Infant of Sarah E.	c.3m	W	D.C.	14 APR 1876	Potters Field
007523	PAYTON, Robert	8y	C	D.C.	06 JUN 1876	Mt. Olivet
013039	PAYTON, Thos.	5m	C	D.C.	31 AUG 1877	Harmony
016178	PAYTON, Wm.	3m	C	D.C.	15 JUN 1878	Potters Field
001864	PEABODY, John L.	3d	W	D.C.	24 JAN 1875	Congressional
004731	PEACH, Georgeanna	19y	C	Md.	23 AUG 1875	Mt. Olivet
012623	PEACH, John Henry	58y	C	Md.	31 JUL 1877	Ebenezer
012525	PEACOCK, Dickerson	11m	W	Md.	25 JUL 1877	Rock Creek
014086	PEAK, Alice Janet	6y	W	D.C.	13 DEC 1877	Methodist
015711	PEAK, Sarah	45y	W	Md.	13 MAY 1878	Congressional
006816	PEAKE, Henry F.	17y	W	D.C.	25 MAR 1876	Congressional
018424	PEAKE, Ida Virginia	4y	W	D.C.	22 DEC 1878	Congressional
014013	PEAKE, James William	1y	W	D.C.	05 DEC 1877	Methodist
018612	PEAKE, Wm.	78y	W	Md.	08 JAN 1879	Mt. Olivet
013689	PEAL, Anna	16y	C	D.C.	31 OCT 1877	Harmony
019102	PEALE, Richard	20y	C	D.C.	17 FEB 1879	Harmony
012052	PEALER, William	7m	W	D.C.	25 JUN 1877	Congressional
000651	PEARCE, Augusta F.	21y	W	Ohio	28 SEP 1874	Pawling, N.Y.
006160	PEARCE, John	c.50y	W	D.C.	27 JAN 1876	Congressional
013547	PEARL, Aann	27y	W	Md.	17 OCT 1877	Congressional
011167	PEARL, Albert L.	7m	W	D.C.	30 MAR 1877	Congressional
018105	PEARL, Marcus	68y	W	Conn.	20 NOV 1878	Oak Hill
003426	PEARL, Norman	18d	W	D.C.	25 MAY 1875	Congressional
010722	PEARSON, Peter Meem	76y	W	D.C.	21 FEB 1877	Oak Hill
013260	PEARSON, Walter H.	38y	W	D.C.	20 SEP 1877	Oak Hill
013024	PECK, Anna Sprigg	1m	W	D.C.	30 AUG 1877	Oak Hill
014321	PECK, Emma	1y	C	D.C.	04 JAN 1878	Beckett's
007598	PECK, Frederick Reginald	18y	W	Mo.	11 JUN 1876	Glenwood
006100	PECK, Ida Blanche	3y	W	D.C.	22 JAN 1876	Glenwood
006116	PECK, Maud E.	1y	W	D.C.	23 JAN 1876	Glenwood
002765	PECK, William H.	27y	C	Md.	27 MAR 1875	Ebenezer
015494	PECK, Willm.	1d	W	D.C.	23 APR 1878	Glenwood
015031	PEEK, Violet	2y	C	D.C.	11 MAR 1878	Beckett's
015566	PEEL, Blancburn	2y	C	D.C.	30 APR 1878	Harmony
017430	PEEL, Marietta	11m	C	D.C.	16 SEP 1878	Harmony
001974	PEEL, Richard	35y	C	Md.	01 FEB 1875	Potters Field
016007	PEELE, Maria	36y	C	U.S.	04 JUN 1878	Harmony
020506	PEER, John	50y	W	N.Y.	18 JUN 1879	Glenwood
018589	PEER, Mattie Bruce	11d	C	D.C.	06 JAN 1879	Harmony
005158a	PEGG, Lizzie	8y	W	D.C.	15 OCT 1875	Congressional
010629	PEIFER, James A.	c.50y	W	Pa.	14 FEB 1877	Bethlehem, Pa.
018202	PEIRCE, Samuel	82y	W	N.Y.	29 NOV 1878	Congressional
009916	PEIRCE, Sarah	6m	C	D.C.	10 DEC 1876	Harmony
000978	PEIRSON, Charles A.	21y	C	D.C.	29 OCT 1874	Mt. Olivet
006562	PEIRSON, Ollive E.	5m	C	D.C.	05 MAR 1876	Mt. Olivet
004656	PELANZE, John A.	42y	W	Pa.	18 AUG 1875	Philadelphia, Pa.

No.	Name	Age	Race	Birth	Death Date	Burial Place
014700	PELHAM, Infant of Burk	1h	C	D.C.	07 FEB 1878	Potters Field
011195	PELHAM, Nathaniel	1y	C	D.C.	02 APR 1877	Young Mens
003236	PELHAM, William	1y	C	D.C.	06 MAY 1875	Mt. Pleasant
015974	PELOUZE, Louis Henry	47y	W	Pa.	02 JUN 1878	Philadelphia, Pa.
005065a	PELTZ, Rosa	6m	W	Md.	05 OCT 1875	Peltz's Farm[1]
012427	PEN, Martha	38y	C	Md.	19 JUL 1877	Ebenezer
015056	PENDERGASS, John	70y	W	Ire.	13 MAR 1878	Mt. Olivet
010828	PENDLE, Malinda	10y	C	Va.	02 MAR 1877	Arlington, Va.
015471	PENDLETON, Alfred	65y	C	Va.	21 APR 1878	Mt. Pleasant
019113	PENDLETON, Esora	1y	C	D.C.	18 FEB 1879	Beckett's
000430	PENDLETON, Florance	6m	C	D.C.	04 SEP 1874	Beckett's
017718	PENDLETON, Gertrude	12m	C	D.C.	12 OCT 1878	Payne's
017842	PENDLETON, Lucy	2m	C	D.C.	23 OCT 1878	Potters Field
017811	PENDLETON, Mamie	1½m	C	D.C.	20 OCT 1878	Potters Field
000515	PENDLETON, Mary	14m	C	D.C.	15 SEP 1874	Mt. Pleasant
015880	PENDLETON, Sallie	1m	C	D.C.	28 MAY 1878	Beckett's
000114	PENEBEKER, Amen	2y	W	Pa.	09 AUG 1874	Lewistown, Pa.
013602	PENN, Ada J.	17y	W	Va.	23 OCT 1877	Congressional
010278	PENN, Mary, Mrs.	27y	W	Va.	13 JAN 1877	Alexandria, Va.
002405	PENNEBAKER, Clinton McClarty	5y	W	D.C.	03 MAR 1875	Louisville, Ky.
008451	PENNELLO, Gaeton	32y	W	Italy	28 JUL 1876	St. Mary's
010600	PENNEY, Geo. W.	50y	W	Ver.	12 FEB 1877	Holy Rood
020987	PENNEY, Rosa	7m	C	D.C.	17 JUL 1879	Washington Asylum
012143	PENNY, Fannie	10m	C	D.C.	30 JUN 1877	Young Mens
009141	PENNY, George M.	4d	W	D.C.	20 SEP 1876	Congressional
010997	PENTZ, Charles A.	28y	W	Md.	16 MAR 1877	Greenmount, Balt., Md.
010482	PEOPLES, Freddy	1y	C	D.C.	02 FEB 1877	Potters Field
006725	PEOPLES, Infant of Henry	1d	C	D.C.	18 MAR 1876	Potters Field
012600	PEPPER, Catharine	83y	W	Ire.	29 JUL 1877	Mt. Olivet
005068	PEPPER, Matthew	42y	W	Ire.	16 SEP 1875	Mt. Olivet
007764	PERCY, Ida	8m	W	D.C.	21 JUN 1876	Mt. Olivet
009494	PERHAM, John	46y	W	Ire.	22 OCT 1876	Soldier's Home
000966	PERKINS, Albert	1m	C	D.C.	28 OCT 1874	Potters Field
005624	PERKINS, Eddie	9m	C	D.C.	01 DEC 1875	Ebenezer
000819	PERKINS, Effie May	2m	W	D.C.	16 OCT 1874	Congressional
005542	PERKINS, Ella	1y	W	D.C.	23 NOV 1875	Methodist
006188	PERKINS, Francis	6m	W	D.C.	30 JAN 1876	Congressional
014935	PERKINS, Jessie	1y	C	D.C.	03 MAR 1878	Beckett's
016661	PERKINS, Luceanna	5m	C	D.C.	18 JUL 1878	Mt. Pleasant
003272	PERKINS, Mary Lillian	2m	W	D.C.	09 MAY 1875	Mt. Olivet
010915	PERKINS, Matilda	1y	W	D.C.	08 MAR 1877	Young Mens
020274	PERKINS, Rose Syebell	10m	W	D.C.	02 JUN 1879	Mt. Olivet
014604	PERKINS, Washington	79y	C	Va.	30 JAN 1878	Mt. Zion
002746	PERKINS, William Franklin	28y	W	D.C.	26 MAR 1875	Congressional
006162	PERKINS, Willie Ernest	4y	W	D.C.	27 JAN 1876	Congressional
007312	PERKINS, Wilmur	8m	W	D.C.	15 MAY 1876	Congressional
019289	PERKS, Josephine A.	7m	W	D.C.	05 MAR 1879	Potters Field
011877	PERLEY, Eliza Frances	67y	W	Ire.	12 JUN 1877	Congressional
000303f	PERRIE, Charles F.	38y	W	Md.	24 AUG 1874	Glenwood
020888	PERRIE, George A.	68y	W	Md.	11 JUL 1879	Glenwood
003352	PERRING, George	6y	W	Va.	17 MAY 1875	Graceland
012376	PERRITT, Ashby	1y	C	D.C.	15 JUL 1877	Young Mens
006115	PERRY, Annie E.	10y	M	D.C.	23 JAN 1876	Harmony

[1] Located in Silver Hill, Prince George's Co., Md.

District of Columbia Death Records, August 1, 1874 to July 31, 1879

No.	Name	Age	Race	Birth	Death Date	Burial Place
007682	PERRY, Augustus Emory	56y	W	Md.	16 JUN 1876	Rock Creek
012618	PERRY, Bertha	1y	C	D.C.	31 JUL 1877	Ebenezer
021001	PERRY, Carrie	1y	C	D.C.	18 JUL 1879	Payne's
018816	PERRY, Elias	90y	C	Md.	25 JAN 1879	Beckett's
000454	PERRY, Emma	20y	W	Va.	08 SEP 1874	Hayfield Farm, Va.
015388	PERRY, Ferdinand Lawson	9d	C	D.C.	13 APR 1878	Mt. Zion
007715	PERRY, Frank W.	31y	W	D.C.	18 JUN 1876	Cleveland, Ohio
001299	PERRY, Infant of Robert	4m	C	Md.	03 DEC 1874	Beckett's
020559	PERRY, Jesse Jeremiah	4m	C	D.C.	21 JUN 1879	Harmony
008911	PERRY, Joseph Elijah	5d	C	D.C.	01 SEP 1876	Potters Field
005297	PERRY, Lettie Cecelia	14y	C	Md.	29 OCT 1875	Beckett's
015992	PERRY, Lucy A.	26y	W	Ohio	03 JUN 1878	Marietta, Ohio
003345	PERRY, Margaret	5m	C	D.C.	16 MAY 1875	Ebenezer
012400	PERRY, Samuel T.	64y	W	Md.	17 JUL 1877	Glenwood
012007	PERRY, Sarah	1y	C	D.C.	22 JUN 1877	Ebenezer
013973	PERRY, Theron S.	8y	W	Va.	30 NOV 1877	Graceland
015955	PERRY, William	60y	C	Md.	01 JUN 1878	Potters Field
012198	PERRY, William Samuel	2y	C	Md.	03 JUL 1877	Ebenezer
002789	PERSON, Lewis	70y	C	Va.	29 MAR 1875	Mt. Zion
012113	PESHALL, Charles	c.70y	W	Ire.	29 JUN 1877	Rock Creek
001654	PETERS, Cornelius	25y	C	D.C.	08 JAN 1875	Mt. Olivet
019112	PETERS, Florence	1y	C	D.C.	18 FEB 1879	Mt. Zion
016478	PETERS, Genette	11m	W	D.C.	06 JUL 1878	Mt. Olivet
007436	PETERS, Infant of Emmit	4h	C	D.C.	29 MAY 1876	Mt. Pleasant
014165	PETERS, John B.	72y	W	Pa.	21 DEC 1877	Glenwood
001039	PETERS, Minnie	2y	W	D.C.	04 NOV 1874	Prospect Hill
019745	PETERS, Richard	33y	C	Va.	12 APR 1879	Mt. Pleasant
008331	PETERSON, Fredrick	42y	W	Swed.	19 JUL 1876	Washington Asylum
009202	PETERSON, Harriet	26d	C	D.C.	25 SEP 1876	Potters Field
006552	PETERSON, Mary	95y	M	Va.	04 MAR 1876	Potters Field
007340	PETERSON, Monroe	17y	C	Va.	19 MAY 1876	Potters Field
010968	PETERSON, Rudolph	2m	W	D.C.	14 MAR 1877	Prospect Hill
015139	PETERSON, Samuel	42y	C	Md.	21 MAR 1878	Potters Field
017606	PETERSON, Wm.	17y	C	Va.	02 OCT 1878	Beckett's
006466	PETIT, Florence	1y	M	D.C.	24 FEB 1876	Young Mens
000045	PETTES, Bertha	7d	C	D.C.	03 AUG 1874	Beckett's
018450	PETTIS, Betty	22y	M	Va.	24 DEC 1878	Young Mens
004956	PETTIS, Florence	8d	C	DC.	08 SEP 1875	Beckett's
012542	PETTIT, John D.	90y	W	Pa.	26 JUL 1877	Washington Asylum
004280	PETTIT, Mary E.	5m	W	D.C.	24 JUL 1875	Congressional
021177	PETTY, Alma Maria	6y	W	D.C.	31 JUL 1879	Mt. Olivet
018462	PEYSER, Theodore	1y	W	Va.	25 DEC 1878	Adas Israel
015205	PEYTON, Bentley	2m	C	D.C.	27 MAR 1878	Potters Field
015117	PEYTON, Carrie	3y	C	D.C.	18 MAR 1878	Young Mens
020331	PEYTON, Henry F.	3m	C	D.C.	07 JUN 1879	Holy Rood
006921	PEYTON, Howe	c.75y	C	U.S.	04 APR 1876	Potters Field
006922	PEYTON, Isaiah	1y	C	D.C.	04 APR 1876	Moore's
008650	PEYTON, Joseph Ireland	6m	W	D.C.	11 AUG 1876	Congressional
017654	PEYTON, Lucie A.	27y	W	D.C.	06 OCT 1878	Congressional
019919	PEYTON, Nellie	2y	W	D.C.	27 APR 1879	Mt. Pleasant
015281	PEYTON, Randolph	30y	C	D.C.	03 APR 1878	Moore's
007941	PEYTON, Virginia	33y	C	Va.	30 JUN 1876	Ebenezer
008861	PFEFFERKORN, Edgar R.	6m	W	D.C.	28 AUG 1876	Congressional
012349	PFELTZ, George C.	18d	W	D.C.	13 JUL 1877	Laurel, Md.
020321	PFIEL, Fritz Wilhelm	1y	W	D.C.	06 JUN 1879	Prospect Hill
011524	PFILE, Caroline E.	6y	W	D.C.	06 MAY 1877	Presbyterian

No.	Name	Age	Race	Birth	Death Date	Burial Place
011589	PFILE, Wilhelmina	11y	W	D.C.	14 MAY 1877	Presbyterian
020669	PFLIEGER, Julius	8m	W	D.C.	29 JUN 1879	Prospect Hill
015896	PFLIEGER, Leonard	9m	W	D.C.	29 MAY 1878	Prospect Hill
017134	PFLUGER, George E.	18d	W	D.C.	21 AUG 1878	Glenwood
018939	PFLUGER, John	19y	W	D.C.	03 FEB 1879	Glenwood
003885	PFLUGER, Mary	4m	W	D.C.	27 JUN 1875	Prospect Hill
002877	PFLUGER, Mary T. Ella	1y	W	D.C.	05 APR 1875	Glenwood
012954	PHALEN, Infant of Lt. Thos.	3½h	W	D.C.	25 AUG 1877	Mt. Olivet
013920	PHALON, Mary Jane	37y	W	Can.	25 NOV 1877	Mt. Olivet
013721	PHASANT, Lizzie Dora	1y	M	D.C.	03 NOV 1877	Mt. Olivet
006780	PHELAN, John	45y	W	Ire.	22 MAR 1876	Holy Rood
007539	PHELPS, Bernard Payne Holloway	4m	W	D.C.	07 JUN 1876	Glenwood
019269	PHELPS, Herbert	1y	W	D.C.	03 MAR 1879	Mt. Olivet
015667	PHELPS, Infant of Wendel	1m	C	D.C.	09 MAY 1878	Potters Field
016839	PHELPS, Mary	1y	W	D.C.	30 JUL 1878	Mt. Olivet
012168	PHELPS, Mary A.	27y	W	Ill.	02 JUL 1877	Lockport, Ill.
016820	PHENIX, Bettie	2y	C	D.C.	29 JUL 1878	Mt. Zion
013102	PHENIX, Rachael Emily	18y	C	Va.	06 SEP 1877	Mt. Zion
008240	PHIERSON, Lizzie	30y	W	D.C.	13 JUL 1876	Mt. Olivet
003176	PHILIP, Charles Worthington	7y	W	D.C.	30 APR 1875	Oak Hill
003115	PHILIP, William Henry, Jr.	4y	W	N.Y.	25 APR 1875	Oak Hill
013104	PHILIPPI, Maria Barbe	59y	W	France	06 SEP 1877	Mt. Olivet
000915	PHILIPS, John	6d	C	D.C.	24 OCT 1874	Young Mens
018987	PHILIPS, Malvina	6y	W	D.C.	07 FEB 1879	Tennallytown
003886	PHILIPS, Roderick	2m	W	D.C.	27 JUN 1875	Mt. Olivet
013743	PHILIPS, Sarah Francis	12y	C	D.C.	05 NOV 1877	Mt. Zion
018062	PHILLIPPS, Henry M.	29y	W	D.C.	15 NOV 1878	Congressional
015186	PHILLIPS, Anna	65y	W	Conn.	25 MAR 1878	Oak Hill
020943	PHILLIPS, Bertie	18m	C	D.C.	15 JUL 1879	Mt. Pleasant
004717	PHILLIPS, Billy Randolph	1y	C	Va.	22 AUG 1875	Young Mens
002282	PHILLIPS, Carrie H.	14d	W	D.C.	22 FEB 1875	Glenwood
007271	PHILLIPS, Cornelius	4y	C	D.C.	11 MAY 1876	Harmony
014805	PHILLIPS, Edward	41y	W	Va.	17 FEB 1878	Mt. Olivet
019763	PHILLIPS, Frank S.	2y	W	Va.	13 APR 1879	Congressional
010811	PHILLIPS, Hazel	1m	C	--	28 FEB 1877	Mt. Olivet
001537	PHILLIPS, James	3y	C	Va.	30 DEC 1874	Young Mens
003506	PHILLIPS, John	3m	W	D.C.	02 JUN 1875	Mt. Olivet
018471	PHILLIPS, John G.	31y	W	Md.	26 DEC 1878	Baltimore, Md.
016662	PHILLIPS, John Wesley	8d	C	D.C.	18 JUL 1878	Mt. Zion
014904	PHILLIPS, Llewellyn	9y	W	D.C.	28 FEB 1878	Oak Hill
003887	PHILLIPS, Margaret	30y	W	D.C.	27 JUN 1875	Rock Creek
002239	PHILLIPS, Martha	15d	C	D.C.	19 FEB 1875	Young Mens
007034	PHILLIPS, Mary A.	2d	W	D.C.	17 APR 1876	Glenwood
013809	PHILLIPS, Minor	8m	C	D.C.	12 NOV 1877	Mt. Zion
006857	PHILLIPS, Sarah	50y	C	Va.	29 MAR 1876	Young Mens
011264	PHILLIPS, William	88y	W	Md.	07 APR 1877	Soldier's Home
019167	PHILLIPS, Wm. T.	20y	W	N.J.	23 FEB 1879	Glenwood
003774	PHILP, Minnie Florence	4m	W	D.C.	22 JUN 1875	Congressional
009674	PHILPITT, Rudolph	42h	W	D.C.	11 NOV 1876	Glenwood
006230	PHILPOTT, Leonard E.	65y	W	Md.	03 FEB 1876	Holy Rood
011084	PHINNEY, Caroline D.	8y	W	R.I.	23 MAR 1877	Newport, R.I.
015939	PHINNY, John	70y	C	Va.	31 MAY 1878	Mt. Pleasant
004631	PHOENIX, John	1y	C	D.C.	16 AUG 1875	Mt. Zion
015612	PHUMPHREY, Frederick R.	7m	W	D.C.	04 MAY 1878	Prospect Hill
015430	PICKARD, Josiah, P.M.	35y	W	Eng.	17 APR 1878	Congressional
000497	PICKENS, Samuel	5m	W	D.C.	13 SEP 1874	Presbyterian

District of Columbia Death Records, August 1, 1874 to July 31, 1879

No.	Name	Age	Race	Birth	Death Date	Burial Place
019967	PICKRELL, Adolphus H.	11m	W	D.C.	02 MAY 1879	Oak Hill
006839	PIDCOCK, Gustavus Hobb	2y	W	D.C.	27 MAR 1876	Prospect Hill
019675	PIDCOCK, Thomas Henry	6y	W	D.C.	06 APR 1879	Prospect Hill
009504	PIEMOUNT, William	58y	C	Va.	23 OCT 1876	Harmony
000736	PIERCE, Daniel	84y	W	Mass.	07 OCT 1874	Congressional
016878	PIERCE, James Franklin	24y	W	D.C.	02 AUG 1878	Congressional
010911	PIERCE, John	8m	C	D.C.	08 MAR 1877	Young Mens
000836	PIERCE, John R.	54y	W	Md.	17 OCT 1874	Congressional
002894	PIERCE, Mary E.	31y	W	D.C.	06 APR 1875	Congressional
011450	PIERCE, Maud Alberta	6y	W	D.C.	28 APR 1877	Congressional
014857	PIERCE, Nannie Louise	9m	C	D.C.	23 FEB 1878	Harmony
001549	PIERCE, Percilla	8d	C	D.C.	31 DEC 1874	Young Mens
009233	PIERCERN, Amelia	65y	C	Va.	28 SEP 1876	Harmony
004157	PIERRE, Charles	1y	C	D.C.	16 JUL 1875	Harmony
004718	PIERRE, Florentina	4y	C	D.C.	22 AUG 1875	Harmony
003633	PIERRE, Johnathan	46y	C	D.C.	13 JUN 1875	Harmony
005326	PIERRE, Wm. E.	1y	C	D.C.	31 OCT 1875	Harmony
001251	PIERSON, Aaron	30y	C	Va.	28 NOV 1874	Washington Asylum
001572	PIERSON, Andrew	8m	C	D.C.	01 JAN 1875	Mt. Olivet
019605	PIERSON, Tiny, Mrs.	98y	C	Md.	30 MAR 1879	West River, Md.
010103	PIGG, John F.	24y	W	D.C.	28 DEC 1876	Congressional
005144	PIGGOT, Wm. Peyton	20m	W	Va.	23 SEP 1875	Congressional
016459	PIKE, Frances Ann	24y	W	Eng.	05 JUL 1878	Oak Hill
020458	PIKE, Mabel	1m	W	D.C.	15 JUN 1879	Glenwood
019480	PILCHER, Sidney C.	13y	W	Va.	20 MAR 1879	Congressional
014106	PILLING, Emma Y.	30y	W	Wisc.	15 DEC 1877	Delevan, Wisc.
007005	PILLING, Hellen	3m	W	D.C.	12 APR 1876	Glenwood
002742	PILLING, Nettie	1y	W	D.C.	26 MAR 1875	Glenwood
018425	PIMPER, George	1y	W	D.C.	22 DEC 1878	Oak Hill
020944	PINCKNEY, Georgeanna C.	3m	C	D.C.	15 JUL 1879	Beckett's
005732	PINDEL, Emley	40y	C	D.C.	12 DEC 1875	Baltimore, Md.
020264	PINDLE, Lucy Sibyl	19m	W	D.C.	01 JUN 1879	Rock Creek
018732	PINE, Eva Maria	7y	W	D.C.	19 JAN 1879	Congressional
020344	PINKET, John H.	14d	C	D.C.	08 JUN 1879	Beckett's
016404	PINKNER, Eleanor	8m	C	D.C.	02 JUL 1878	Beckett's
001016	PINKNEY, Elizebeth	37y	C	Md.	02 NOV 1874	Brandywine, Md.[1]
007662	PINKNEY, Harriet Ann	20y	C	Md.	15 JUN 1876	Harmony
013654	PINKNEY, John	5d	C	D.C.	27 OCT 1877	Beckett's
003902	PINKNEY, Lucinda	10m	C	D.C.	28 JUN 1875	Harmony
021126	PINKNEY, Mary	35y	W	Md.	27 JUL 1879	Congressional
020968	PINKNEY, Mary Ann	3m	C	D.C.	16 JUL 1879	Mt. Pleasant
001861	PINKNEY, William	2y	C	D.C.	23 JAN 1875	Young Mens
006187	PINKWOOD, Edward	1y	C	D.C.	30 JAN 1876	Harmony
010924	PINKWOOD, Thomas	75y	C	Va.	09 MAR 1877	Young Mens
005641	PINN, George	4y	C	Va.	03 DEC 1875	Mt. Pleasant
019789	PINN, William	76y	C	Va.	15 APR 1879	Harmony
001400	PINTER, Hester	87y	W	Va.	15 DEC 1874	Congressional
009880	PINTER, Winnie	94y	C	Md.	06 DEC 1876	Mt. Zion
018938	PINYON, Alexander	1m	C	D.C.	03 FEB 1879	Potters Field
004918	PIPER, Charlotte	55y	C	D.C.	05 SEP 1875	Mt. Olivet
000383	PIPER, Mary G.	15y	W	Pa.	31 AUG 1874	Mt. Olivet
003761	PISTORIO, Lillian M.	7y	W	D.C.	22 JUN 1875	Congressional
001778	PISTORIO, Ettie	1y	W	D.C.	18 JAN 1875	Congressional

[1] Located in Prince George's Co., Md.

No.	Name	Age	Race	Birth	Death Date	Burial Place
020539	PISTORIO, Lillie Blanche	10m	W	D.C.	20 JUN 1879	Congressional
016320	PITCHER, Edward	45y	C	Va.	26 JUN 1878	Mt. Pleasant
005940	PITCHER, Hatty	16m	C	D.C.	04 JAN 1876	Mt. Pleasant
006125	PITNEY, John	1h	W	D.C.	24 JAN 1876	Prospect Hill
003904	PITTS, Alser	3y	C	D.C.	28 JUN 1875	Beckett's
004232	PITTS, Hanson	2y	C	D.C.	21 JUL 1875	Beckett's
003765	PITTS, Ida May	7m	W	D.C.	22 JUN 1875	Mt. Pleasant Plain
005486	PITTS, Martha	35y	C	Va.	17 NOV 1875	Ebenezer
017764	PITTS, Nathan	53y	C	Md.	16 OCT 1878	Harmony
017812	PITTS, Sarah	11m	C	D.C.	20 OCT 1878	Mt. Pleasant
012289	PITTS, Sarah M.	22y	W	S.C.	10 APR 1877	Mt. Olivet
005808	PITZINGER, Annie Catharine	1y	W	Md.	20 DEC 1875	Elkridge, Md.
016719	PITZINGER, Margaret	80y	W	Ger.	22 JUL 1878	Congressional
002447	PIXLEY, Laura E.	3y	W	N.J.	06 MAR 1875	Graceland
011384	PIXON, James A.	4y	M	D.C.	21 APR 1877	Harmony
006189	PLACE, Agnes	8d	W	D.C.	30 JAN 1876	Mt. Olivet
006124	PLACE, Mary	36y	W	Ire.	24 JAN 1876	Mt. Olivet
013519	PLANT, Abbie Marshal	12y	W	D.C.	14 OCT 1877	Mt. Olivet
006061	PLANT, Alice A.M.	66y	W	Va.	18 JAN 1876	Congressional
003287	PLANT, Alice M.	30y	W	D.C.	11 MAY 1875	Congressional
013482	PLANT, Arthur Temple	10y	W	D.C.	11 OCT 1877	Mt. Olivet
015470	PLANT, Eliza Ann	69y	W	D.C.	21 APR 1878	Oak Hill
009767	PLANT, George E.	1m	W	D.C.	21 NOV 1876	Congressional
000180	PLATER, Douglass	20y	C	Va.	13 AUG 1874	Mt. Pleasant
000309	PLATER, Sandy	28y	C	Va.	24 AUG 1874	Mt. Pleasant
007205	PLATO, Thomas	40y	C	D.C.	04 MAY 1876	Mt. Pleasant
017472	PLATT, Mary Olive	2m	W	D.C.	20 SEP 1878	Glenwood
009873	PLEASANT, James	65y	C	Md.	05 DEC 1876	Washington Asylum
013762	PLEASANT, Lulla	4y	M	D.C.	07 NOV 1877	Mt. Olivet
020272	PLEASANTS, Benjamin Franklin	84y	W	Va.	02 JUN 1879	Oak Hill
010385	PLENTY, Robert	70y	C	Va.	23 JAN 1877	Potters Field
019604	PLOWDEN, James	66y	W	Md.	30 MAR 1879	Potters Field/Mt. Olivet
016637	PLOWDEN, Lottie	2m	C	D.C.	17 JUL 1878	Payne's
004383	PLOWMAN, Margaret Ann	38y	W	D.C.	30 JUL 1875	Congressional
004393	PLOWMAN, Mary	47y	W	At Sea	31 JUL 1875	Glenwood
019720	PLOWMAN, Thomas M.	50y	W	Pa.	10 APR 1879	Philadelphia, Pa.
004420	PLOWMAN, William	c.50y	W	D.C.	02 AUG 1875	Glenwood
009432	PLUGGE, Frederick William	47y	W	D.C.	16 OCT 1876	Prospect Hill
019944	PLUMBER, Robert	1y	C	D.C.	30 APR 1879	Young Mens
004318	PLUMERS, Infant of Hennie	11m	C	D.C.	26 JUL 1875	Potters Field
013502	PLUMLEY, Infant of Jno. A.	2d	W	D.C.	13 OCT 1877	Graceland
001105	PLUMLY, George M.	1m	W	D.C.	10 NOV 1874	Graceland
001117	PLUMMER, Charles S.	1m	C	Va.	12 NOV 1874	Arlington, Va.
016254	PLUMMER, Infant of Betsey	9m	C	Ohio	21 JUN 1878	Harmony
004551	PLUMMER, Mary	1y	C	D.C.	11 AUG 1875	Young Mens
020138	PLUMMER, Moses	4y	C	D.C.	18 MAY 1879	Mt. Pleasant
011725	PLUMSELL, Thomas	86y	W	Md.	27 MAY 1877	Congressional
012322	PLUNKET, John	74y	W	Ire.	12 JUL 1877	Methodist
007448	POCK, John F.	18y	W	D.C.	31 MAY 1876	Tennallytown
016745	POEBLES, Mattie	14m	C	D.C.	24 JUL 1878	Beckett's
012646	POHLMAN, George W.	7m	W	D.C.	02 AUG 1877	Graceland
016821	POINDEXTER, Eli	5m	C	D.C.	29 JUL 1878	Payne's
000647	POINDEXTER, Nellie	1m	C	D.C.	27 SEP 1874	Harmony
013990	POINDEXTER, Thomas	1y	C	D.C.	02 DEC 1877	Young Mens
012672	POINTIS, Henry Arthur	8m	W	D.C.	04 AUG 1877	Congressional
006737	POISY, Alexander	32y	C	Md.	19 MAR 1876	Payne's

District of Columbia Death Records, August 1, 1874 to July 31, 1879

No.	Name	Age	Race	Birth	Death Date	Burial Place
004798	POLAND, Alexander	23y	W	Va.	28 AUG 1875	Leesburg, Va.
001308	POLAND, Josephine [Pettit]	23y	W	D.C.	05 DEC 1874	Presbyterian
001618	POLAND, Nanie W.	11y	W	Va.	05 JAN 1875	Leesburg, Va.
003808f	POLAND, William Joseph	7m	W	Va.	24 JUN 1875	Presbyterian
014666	POLETTI, John A.	43y	W	D.C.	19 FEB 1878	Mt. Olivet
012787	POLK, Harriet	36y	C	Tenn.	12 AUG 1877	Harmony
009482	POLKATY, James K.	56y	C	Md.	21 OCT 1876	Mt. Olivet
006508	POLLAND, James	22y	W	Md.	29 FEB 1876	Calvert Co., Md.
012027	POLLARD, Albert Sydney	2y	W	D.C.	23 JUN 1877	Oak Hill
011142	POLLARD, Edward	22y	C	Va.	28 MAR 1877	Potters Field
001004	POLLARD, Infant of James	5½m	C	D.C.	01 NOV 1874	Beckett's
012152	POLLARD, Jackson	c.45y	C	U.S.	01 JUL 1877	Potters Field
017763	POLLARD, Jno. Wesley	18y	C	Md.	16 OCT 1878	Harmony
008645	POLLARD, John	c.35h	C	Va.	11 AUG 1876	Young Mens
005809	POLLARD, Rebecca	18m	C	D.C.	20 DEC 1875	Young Mens
003925	POLLARD, Sarah	30y	C	Va.	29 JUN 1875	Ebenezer
001763	POLLEN, Medorrah A.	1m	C	D.C.	16 JAN 1875	Young Mens
007146	POLLEY, Charles Richard	2y	W	D.C.	28 APR 1876	Congressional
002933	POLLEY, Mary Analoston	2y	W	D.C.	09 APR 1875	Presbyterian
010716	POLOWSKI, Jane	3y	W	I.T.	20 FEB 1877	Mt. Olivet
004869	POMEROY, Nellie	6y	W	D.C.	01 SEP 1875	Rock Creek
008963	POMEROY, William	73y	W	Va.	04 SEP 1876	Mt. Olivet
008152	POND, Amanda	33y	W	Pa.	10 JUL 1876	Mt. Olivet
007300	POND, Fanny	8y	C	Ky.	14 MAY 1876	Harmony
008732	PONEY, William Henry	14d	M	D.C.	19 AUG 1876	Mt. Olivet
001204	POOL, Laura, of Reuben B.	5d	W	D.C.	21 NOV 1874	Glenwood
009535	POOLE, Anna	39y	W	Ire.	26 OCT 1876	Mt. Olivet
017013	POOLE, David	64y	W	Pa.	11 AUG 1878	Congressional
017780	POOLE, Etha E.	40y	W	Mass.	17 OCT 1878	Worcester, Mass.
017571	POOLE, John Albert	3y	W	D.C.	29 SEP 1878	Beckett's
016378	POOLE, Sarah	35y	C	Va.	30 JUN 1878	Mt. Pleasant
008537	POOR, Mark Aloysius	1y	W	D.C.	02 AUG 1876	Holy Rood
017429	POOR, Mary E.	1m	W	D.C.	16 SEP 1878	Holy Rood
001738	POOR, Mattie Lindsay	57y	W	Va.	15 JAN 1875	Oak Hill
003184	POOR, William A.	65y	W	Va.	01 MAY 1875	Congressional
014140	POOR, Wm. F.	17y	W	D.C.	19 DEC 1877	Holy Rood
019847	POORE, Emily	29y	W	Mass.	20 APR 1879	West Newburyport,
004317	POORE, Francis	58y	W	D.C.	26 JUL 1875	Holy Rood
000450	POORE, Joseph M.	1y	W	D.C.	08 SEP 1874	Carroll Chapel, Md.
003424	POORE, Sarah	56y	W	D.C.	24 MAY 1875	Holy Rood
021103	POORE, Wm.	7d	W	D.C.	25 JUL 1879	Holy Rood
002544	POPE, Allice	20y	C	D.C.	13 MAR 1875	Mt. Zion
005778	POPE, Anna	14d	W	D.C.	17 DEC 1875	Methodist
001862	POPE, Delia	4y	C	D.C.	23 JAN 1875	Holy Rood
002040	POPE, Kate	2y	C	D.C.	05 FEB 1875	Holy Rood
003237	POPKINS, Catherine	87y	W	Va.	06 MAY 1875	Congressional
001445	PORKINSON, Mary Isabella	4y	W	D.C.	20 DEC 1874	St. John's, Md.
019363	PORT, Ellen, Mrs.	52y	W	Eng.	11 MAR 1879	Glenwood
010818	PORTER, Gertrude	6m	C	D.C.	01 MAR 1877	Ebenezer
013921	PORTER, Ida	2y	C	D.C.	25 NOV 1877	Mt. Zion
005084	PORTER, Infant of Wm.	5d	C	D.C.	17 SEP 1875	Ebenezer
014361	PORTER, James E.	47y	W	Md.	08 JAN 1878	Baltimore, Md.
007827	PORTER, Lula A.	9m	W	D.C.	24 JUN 1876	Presbyterian
009451	PORTER, Mary, Mrs.	76y	W	Md.	18 OCT 1876	Methodist, East
001365	PORTER, N.	48y	W	Md.	11 DEC 1874	Congressional
007763	PORTER, Susan	8y	C	Va.	21 JUN 1876	Mt. Olivet

District of Columbia Death Records, August 1, 1874 to July 31, 1879

No.	Name	Age	Race	Birth	Death Date	Burial Place
006487	PORTER, Virginia	1y	M	D.C.	27 FEB 1876	Potters Field
006286	PORTER, Walter	6m	C	Va.	09 FEB 1876	Harmony
011011	PORTHOUSE, Thomas	59y	W	Eng.	16 MAR 1877	Soldier's Home
011353	POSE, RICHARD	4d	C	D.C.	16 APR 1877	Ebenezer
014389	POSEY, Alice R.	3y	W	D.C.	11 JAN 1878	Glenwood
007016	POSEY, Ann	73y	W	Md.	14 APR 1876	Congressional
005192	POSEY, Eliza	36y	C	D.C.	18 OCT 1875	Harmony
017914	POSEY, Ella	8w	W	D.C.	31 OCT 1878	Congressional
017529	POSEY, Eugene	3m	C	D.C.	25 SEP 1878	Harmony
017788	POSEY, Ganville Alexander	9m	C	D.C.	18 OCT 1878	Harmony
011255	POSEY, Henson R.	22y	M	Md.	07 APR 1877	Graceland
005063a	POSEY, Infant of George	25d	C	D.C.	05 OCT 1875	Mt. Zion
004683	POSEY, Mary Cecilia	3m	M	D.C.	20 AUG 1875	Harmony
002676	POSEY, Sidney	9m	W	Md.	21 MAR 1875	Charles Co., Md.
008202	POSEY, Wealthy	60y	C	Va.	12 JUL 1876	Potters Field
000218	POSEY, William H.	1m	C	D.C.	17 AUG 1874	Mt. Zion
001695	POSEY, Wm. Henry	40y	C	D.C.	11 JAN 1875	Mt. Olivet
009183	POSS, Howard D.	17d	W	D.C.	24 SEP 1876	Oak Hill
009389	POST, Christina	1y	W	D.C.	12 OCT 1876	St. Mary's
003888	POST, Infant of Albert H.	11d	W	D.C.	27 JUN 1875	Glenwood
010216	POST, Mary	30y	W	Va.	07 JAN 1877	Baltimore, Md.
002189	POTE, Carrie	4m	W	D.C.	16 FEB 1875	Congressional
009267	POTE, Philip	48y	W	Pa.	01 OCT 1876	Congressional
010728	POTTER, Abby	4y	W	N.Y.	22 FEB 1877	Oak Hill
014701	POTTER, Alamena C., Mrs.	55y	W	Mass.	07 FEB 1878	Schenectady, N.Y.
001959	POTTER, Elizabeth	22y	W	D.C.	31 JAN 1875	Glenwood
017996	POTTER, Joseph	13d	W	D.C.	09 NOV 1878	Holy Rood
018505	POTTER, Scott Hayes	1y	W	D.C.	29 DEC 1878	Columbus, Ohio
001908	POTTER, William	1y	C	D.C.	27 JAN 1875	Mt. Olivet
005955	POTTS, Robert Mull	25y	W	N.J.	06 JAN 1876	Oak Hill
014008	POTZLER, Chas.	1y	W	D.C.	04 DEC 1877	Prospect Hill
015956	POTZLER, John	3y	W	D.C.	01 JUN 1878	Prospect Hill
017218	POULLEUX, Joseph	52y	W	France	27 AUG 1878	Mt. Olivet
011132	POULTON, Harry L.	5m	W	Va.	27 MAR 1877	Glenwood
005016a	POULTON, Harry Maltravers	17y	W	D.C.	01 OCT 1875	Glenwood
006229	POWEL, Fannie	21y	C	Va.	03 FEB 1876	Beckett's
011512	POWELL, Alexander	27y	C	Va.	04 MAY 1877	Potters Field
012337	POWELL, Annie S.	4y	W	D.C.	12 JUL 1877	Congressional
014217	POWELL, Archer	1y	C	D.C.	26 DEC 1877	Potters Field
015771	POWELL, Bertha	1y	W	D.C.	19 MAY 1878	Congressional
019834	POWELL, Charles	1y	C	D.C.	19 APR 1879	Payne's
005143	POWELL, Charles Henry	1y	C	D.C.	23 SEP 1875	Young Mens
020570	POWELL, Emma J.	21d	C	D.C.	22 JUN 1879	Beckett's
007865	POWELL, Estella	12m	M	D.C.	26 JUN 1876	Mt. Pleasant Plain
007457	POWELL, Francis H.	9m	W	D.C.	01 JUN 1876	Mt. Olivet
014149	POWELL, Geo.	35y	C	Md.	20 DEC 1877	Payne's
020299	POWELL, Infant of Gabriel	36h	C	D.C.	04 JUN 1879	Potters Field
011451	POWELL, James R.	6y	W	D.C.	28 APR 1877	Congressional
012719	POWELL, John	6m	C	D.C.	07 AUG 1877	Young Mens
001111f	POWELL, John Hepburn	1y	W	Va.	01 MAR 1874	Oak Hill
014206	POWELL, John Thomas	26y	M	Va.	25 DEC 1877	Va.
017385	POWELL, Leana	60y	C	Va.	12 SEP 1878	Mt. Pleasant
014843	POWELL, Lucinda	63y	W	Md.	21 FEB 1878	Glenwood
017669	POWELL, Mary	35y	C	Va.	07 OCT 1878	Beckett's
016307	POWELL, Mary E.	31y	M	Pa.	25 JUN 1878	Young Mens
012517	POWELL, Mary Rose	8y	C	D.C.	25 JUL 1877	Ebenezer

District of Columbia Death Records, August 1, 1874 to July 31, 1879   271

No.	Name	Age	Race	Birth	Death Date	Burial Place
011073	POWELL, Moses	62y	C	Md.	22 MAR 1877	Mt. Pleasant
020198	POWELL, Nelson	2y	C	D.C.	25 MAY 1879	Payne's
001321	POWELL, Prudence E.	61y	W	Va.	07 DEC 1874	Methodist
015780	POWELL, Richard	66y	W	Pa.	20 MAY 1878	Philadelphia, Pa.
016055	POWELL, Susan	30y	C	Va.	07 JUN 1878	Potters Field
018504	POWELL, Virginia A.	54y	W	Va.	29 DEC 1878	Congressional
012701	POWELL, William H.	2y	W	D.C.	06 AUG 1877	Congressional
008984	POWELL, Zadoc A.	2y	W	D.C.	06 SEP 1876	Mt. Olivet
014390	POWER, Effie June	3y	W	D.C.	11 JAN 1878	Presbyterian
017188	POWER, Mary	1y	W	D.C.	25 AUG 1878	Mt. Olivet
019775	POWER, Mic.	78y	W	Ire.	14 APR 1879	Mt. Olivet
016962	POWERS, Andrew	1y	C	D.C.	08 AUG 1878	Beckett's
016903	POWERS, Francis	1y	W	D.C.	04 AUG 1878	Mt. Olivet
013150	POWERS, Infant of Caroline	20d	C	D.C.	10 SEP 1877	Payne's
010749	POWERS, James A.	51y	W	D.C.	23 FEB 1877	Congressional
020475	POWERS, Samuel	9m	C	D.C.	16 JUN 1879	Beckett's
003807	POYNTON, Jennie Frances	6m	W	D.C.	24 JUN 1875	Glenwood
020795	POYNTON, Robert Forsyth	5m	W	D.C.	06 JUL 1879	Glenwood
019657	PRATER, Susan	5y	C	D.C.	04 APR 1879	Potters Field
008133	PRATHER, Aurther	16y	C	Md.	10 JUL 1876	Mt. Olivet
001167	PRATHER, Benjamin A.	41y	W	Md.	17 NOV 1874	Glenwood
020558	PRATHER, Blanche E.	23d	W	D.C.	21 JUN 1879	Congressional
010825	PRATHER, Caroline [or Mary]	5y	M	D.C.	01 MAR 1877	Mt. Olivet
018976	PRATHER, Cornelia	12y	C	D.C.	06 FEB 1879	Potters Field
019846	PRATHER, Florence	1y	C	D.C.	20 APR 1879	Young Mens
009329	PRATHER, Hamilton	40y	C	Md.	07 OCT 1876	Harmony
003109	PRATHER, Infant of R.G.	2d	W	D.C.	25 APR 1875	Congressional
006672	PRATHER, Leonard B.	64y	W	Md.	14 MAR 1876	Glenwood
010862	PRATHER, Mary Ann	78y	W	Md.	04 MAR 1877	Oak Hill
016294	PRATHER, Mary C.	9m	W	D.C.	24 JUN 1878	Congressional
004681	PRATHER, Oliver A.	59d	W	D.C.	20 AUG 1875	Congressional
000412	PRATT, Anson	25y	C	Va.	02 SEP 1874	Beckett's
007570	PRATT, Betsey	22y	C	U.S.	09 JUN 1876	Potters Field
016379	PRATT, Edith May	2y	W	D.C.	30 JUN 1878	Congressional
019185	PRATT, Florent J.	1y	C	D.C.	24 FEB 1879	Payne's
017704	PRATT, George P.	6d	C	D.C.	11 OCT 1878	Harmony
003224	PRATT, Ida	10m	C	D.C.	05 MAY 1875	Mt. Pleasant
015772	PRATT, Infant of William	8h	C	D.C.	19 MAY 1878	Mt. Pleasant
002413	PRATT, Jared	60y	W	Conn.	04 MAR 1875	West Meriden, Conn.
019797	PRATT, Julia	75y	C	Va.	16 APR 1879	Harmony
009425	PRATT, Martha Elizabeth	2y	W	D.C.	16 OCT 1876	Jones Chapel
018489	PRATT, Philip	10m	W	D.C.	28 DEC 1878	Congressional
018383	PRATT, Sally	30y	C	Md.	19 DEC 1878	Baltimore, Md.
005880	PRATT, Sarah J.B.	61y	W	Me.	27 DEC 1875	Oak Hill
000448	PRATT, William Anson	1y	C	D.C.	07 SEP 1874	--
012098	PREBANA, Carolina	60y	W	Ger.	27 JUN 1877	Washington Hebrew
001651	PRELESS, Armina	6y	C	D.C.	08 JAN 1875	Prospect Hill
005191	PRENDABLE, Elizabeth	3y	W	D.C.	18 OCT 1875	Mt. Olivet
013172	PRENDER, John W.	48y	W	Ire.	12 SEP 1877	Congressional
009744	PRENTICE, Sarah	46y	W	Ohio	19 NOV 1876	Cleveland, Ohio
017481	PRENTISS, Wm. Henry	81y	W	D.C.	21 SEP 1878	Glenwood
009324	PRERY, Franklin P.	24y	W	D.C.	06 OCT 1876	Congressional
017031	PRESCOE, Annie	1y	C	D.C.	13 AUG 1878	Harmony
015472	PRESCOE, Clarence	3y	M	D.C.	21 APR 1878	Potters Field
015712	PRESERE, Alphonzo	9y	C	Md.	13 MAY 1878	Harmony
021102	PRESTON, Barbary, Mrs.	27y	W	Ber.	25 JUL 1879	Mt. Olivet

District of Columbia Death Records, August 1, 1874 to July 31, 1879

No.	Name	Age	Race	Birth	Death Date	Burial Place
014380	PRESTON, Beatrix Katherine	4y	W	D.C.	10 JAN 1878	Oak Hill
003427	PRESTON, Charlotte M.	40y	W	N.E.	25 MAY 1875	Augusta, Ga.
010102	PRESTON, Herbert	2y	W	D.C.	28 DEC 1876	Mt. Olivet
006712	PRESTON, Hyacinthe	2d	W	D.C.	17 MAR 1876	Oak Hill
015938	PRESTON, Mary Gertrude	7y	W	D.C.	31 MAY 1878	Baltimore, Md.
006076	PRESTON, Samuel A.	72y	W	Ire.	20 JAN 1876	Walnut Grove, Va.
014906	PREU, Wm.	6y	W	N.Y.	28 FEB 1878	St. Mary's
017465	PREYRE, Rosa M.	32y	W	Peru	20 SEP 1878	Mt. Olivet
012866	PRICE, Alexander	22y	C	Va.	18 AUG 1877	Potters Field
015164	PRICE, Alice	68y	C	Va.	23 MAR 1878	Baltimore, Md.
018683	PRICE, Ariana	35y	C	Va.	15 JAN 1879	Mt. Pleasant
010505	PRICE, Celia	18y	C	Va.	03 FEB 1877	Potters Field
010904	PRICE, Charles Weber	4y	W	D.C.	07 MAR 1877	Mt. Olivet
000196	PRICE, Chas. David	10m	W	D.C.	15 AUG 1874	Glenwood
005045a	PRICE, Duke William	1m	C	D.C.	03 OCT 1875	Ebenezer
001578	PRICE, Edgar	38y	C	Va.	02 JAN 1875	Alexandria, Va.
018717	PRICE, Edward	8m	C	D.C.	18 JAN 1879	Young Mens
009983	PRICE, Elizabeth	5y	C	D.C.	17 DEC 1876	Ebenezer
001576	PRICE, Enoch	73y	W	Wales	02 JAN 1875	Tennallytown
000702f	PRICE, Fannie Wilson	28y	W	Md.	03 OCT 1874	Glenwood
009347	PRICE, Francis R.	3m	C	D.C.	09 OCT 1876	Ebenezer
019644	PRICE, George	11m	C	D.C.	03 APR 1879	Mt. Pleasant
017528	PRICE, Harriet Ann Rebecca	30y	C	Md.	25 SEP 1878	Harmony
006841	PRICE, Infant of William	1d	C	D.C.	27 MAR 1876	Young Mens
009400	PRICE, Infant of W.Z.	12h	W	D.C.	13 OCT 1876	Alexandria, Va.
014775	PRICE, James H.	2y	W	D.C.	15 FEB 1878	Mt. Pleasant
004338	PRICE, Jas. B.	8m	W	D.C.	27 JUL 1875	Alexandria, Va.
006265	PRICE, Jas. Henry	1y	C	D.C.	07 FEB 1876	Potters Field
001840	PRICE, John	3d	C	D.C.	22 JAN 1875	Mt. Pleasant
012624	PRICE, Lousa	8m	C	D.C.	31 JUL 1877	Brightwood
010038	PRICE, Mary Ann	7m	C	D.C.	21 DEC 1876	Macedonia
006163	PRICE, Mary E., Mrs.	43y	W	D.C.	27 JAN 1876	Alexandria, St. Paul's
018290	PRICE, Miller	1m	W	D.C.	09 DEC 1878	Mt. Olivet
002358	PRICE, Rebecca	6m	C	D.C.	28 FEB 1875	Mt. Pleasant Plain
016838	PRICE, Robert	85y	C	Md.	30 JUL 1878	Harmony
005132a	PRICE, Sara	40y	C	Va.	13 OCT 1875	Potters Field
004298	PRICE, Stephen	81y	W	N.B.	25 JUL 1875	Glenwood
013025	PRICE, Thomas S.	4y	C	D.C.	30 AUG 1877	Mt. Olivet
020251	PRICE, William	12d	C	D.C.	02 JUN 1879	Baptist
020384	PRICE, Willie Ann	11m	C	D.C.	10 JUN 1879	Potters Field
011460	PRICE, Wilmer Z.	38y	W	Va.	29 APR 1877	Alexandria, Va.
012149	PRICE, Wm. H.	5m	C	D.C.	01 JUL 1877	Ebenezer
013151	PRICE, Wm. H.	15d	C	D.C.	10 SEP 1877	Beckett's
019048	PRIER, George W.	11m	C	D.C.	12 FEB 1879	Beckett's
020983	PRIMROSE George	67y	C	Md.	17 JUL 1879	Graceland
010795	PRIMUS, Hattie	2y	C	--	27 FEB 1877	Potters Field
008790	PRINCE, Cornelius	6m	C	D.C.	23 AUG 1876	Ebenezer
021012	PRINCE, Wm.	5m	W	D.C.	19 JUL 1879	Congressional
019230	PRINGLE, Elizabeth	c.70y	W	D.C.	27 FEB 1879	Glenwood
001088	PRINKERT, Mary	1y	W	D.C.	08 NOV 1874	Prospect Hill
005551	PRIOR, James	8d	C	D.C.	24 NOV 1875	Beckett's
014241	PRITCHARD, Stephen	2y	W	D.C.	28 DEC 1877	Beckett's
020211	PROCTOR, Alexander H.	17y	W	D.C.	27 MAY 1879	Oak Hill
018278	PROCTOR, Edward August	15m	C	D.C.	08 DEC 1878	Harmony
007421	PROCTOR, Infant of Walker	13d	C	D.C.	27 MAY 1876	Young Mens
008733	PROCTOR, Isabella	24y	M	Md.	19 AUG 1876	Harmony

District of Columbia Death Records, August 1, 1874 to July 31, 1879   273

No.	Name	Age	Race	Birth	Death Date	Burial Place
000911	PROCTOR, James	33y	W	D.C.	23 OCT 1874	Congressional
006393	PROCTOR, James Edward	1y	W	N.Y.	17 FEB 1876	Potters Field
008194	PROCTOR, John C.	43y	W	Md.	12 JUL 1876	Congressional
016946	PROCTOR, John Sherman	2y	C	D.C.	07 AUG 1878	Mt. Pleasant
002702	PROCTOR, Lucretia	39y	C	Md.	23 MAR 1875	Mt. Olivet
005956	PROCTOR, Mary E.	38y	C	Md.	06 JAN 1876	Mt. Olivet
015957	PROCTOR, Samuel C.	33y	W	Va.	01 JUN 1878	Alexandria, Va.
009300	PROCTOR, Stella M.	1y	W	D.C.	04 OCT 1876	Glenwood
002470	PROPHETER, George W.	41y	W	Ohio	28 FEB 1875	Hospital
002390	PROSPERI, Mary Elen	40y	W	D.C.	02 MAR 1875	Congressional
005197	PROUTT, Albert D.	5m	W	D.C.	27 SEP 1875	Alexandria, Va.
002703	PRUETT, Clara L.	8m	W	D.C.	23 MAR 1875	Congressional
017835	PRUSCHER, Rosa Katie	2y	W	D.C.	23 OCT 1878	St. Mary's
012133	PRUSHEIM, Henry	18y	W	D.C.	30 JUN 1877	Prospect Hill
007700	PRYER, Charles	1y	C	D.C.	17 JUN 1876	Mt. Zion
019390	PRYOR, Charles Aaron	5m	M	D.C.	10 MAR 1879	Harmony
012161	PRYOR, Clarissa	7m	M	D.C.	01 JUL 1877	Harmony
009706	PULLEN, James	75y	W	Eng.	15 NOV 1876	Methodist
003699	PULLEN, Thomas	2m	W	D.C.	19 JUN 1875	Mt. Olivet
017984	PULLIN, Louisa	54y	W	Va.	08 NOV 1878	Congressional
009949	PULMAN, Nellie Oliver	3y	W	Va.	13 DEC 1876	Congressional
001249	PUMPHREY, Agnes Geraldine	3y	W	D.C.	28 NOV 1874	Congressional
007050	PUMPHREY, Annie	3m	W	D.C.	18 APR 1876	Congressional
020150	PUMPHREY, Eliza	63y	W	D.C.	19 MAY 1879	Congressional
009786	PUMPHREY, Ida	25y	W	D.C.	24 NOV 1876	Glenwood
000998	PUMPHREY, James Barnett	45y	W	D.C.	31 OCT 1874	Congressional
002396	PUMPHREY, Lewis S.	4m	W	D.C.	02 MAR 1875	Congressional
006434	PUMPHRY, Anna E.	22y	W	Va.	21 FEB 1876	Congressional
003645	PURCELL, Alice V.	2y	W	D.C.	14 JUN 1874	Methodist
008706	PURCELL, Andrew P.	16y	W	D.C.	16 AUG 1876	Congressional
009044	PURCELL, Ida	4y	W	D.C.	12 SEP 1876	Congressional
000749	PURCELL, Jane E.	8d	W	D.C.	08 OCT 1874	Congressional
020051	PURCELL, John	55y	W	Ire.	09 MAY 1879	Mt. Olivet
000948	PURCELL, Kaitley H.	4y	W	D.C.	27 OCT 1874	Mt. Olivet
019347	PURCELL, Mary	c.36y	W	N.C.	09 MAR 1879	Methodist
006465	PURCELL, Mary Frances Eliza	57y	W	Va.	24 FEB 1876	Congressional
011212	PURCELLA, Angiolina	2y	W	D.C.	04 APR 1877	St. Mary's
015613	PURDY, Frederick	3m	W	D.C.	04 MAY 1878	Glenwood
014655	PURDY, Gilbert	2y	W	D.C.	03 FEB 1878	Glenwood
012735	PURDY, Martha A., Mrs.	52y	W	Va.	08 AUG 1877	Glenwood
004510	PURDY, Nathaniel	74y	W	N.Y.	08 AUG 1875	Flint Hill, Fairfax Co.
014715	PURDY, Nathaniel	4y	W	D.C.	08 FEB 1878	Glenwood
020490	PURDY, Ralph	3m	W	D.C.	17 JUN 1879	Glenwood
017697	PURHAM, W.J.	67y	W	Pa.	10 OCT 1878	Congressional
019083	PURSELL, Julia E.	68y	W	D.C.	15 FEB 1879	Congressional
007524	PURVIS, Harriet	8m	W	D.C.	06 JUN 1876	Graceland
001671	PUTMAN, Sallie	33y	W	Md.	10 JAN 1875	Frederick, Md.
015292	PUTNAM, Aaron	85y	C	Md.	05 APR 1878	Potters Field
000678	PUTSCHE, Henrietta Matilda	9m	W	D.C.	30 SEP 1874	Prospect Hill
014471	PYE, Charles H., Dr.	46y	W	Md.	18 JAN 1878	Charles Co., Md.
015165	PYFER, E.L., Mrs.	81y	W	D.C.	23 MAR 1878	Presbyterian
020273	PYFER, Hannah Melville	64y	W	D.C.	02 JUN 1879	Presbyterian/Oak Hill
009358	PYLE, George M.	25y	W	Pa.	09 OCT 1876	Concord Station, Pa.
001000	PYLE, Mary	53y	W	Pa.	01 NOV 1874	New Waterford, Ohio
012078	PYLES, Wm. F.	1y	C	Md.	27 JUN 1877	Bladensburg, Md.
011484	PYNCHEON, Francis M.	35y	W	Ohio	01 MAY 1877	Wellsville, Wis.

District of Columbia Death Records, August 1, 1874 to July 31, 1879

No.	Name	Age	Race	Birth	Death Date	Burial Place
021101	PYNE, James	5d	C	D.C.	25 JUL 1879	Beckett's
000127	PYNN, Alice	1y	C	D.C.	10 AUG 1874	Harmony
000743	PYWELL, Robert E.	10y	W	D.C.	07 OCT 1874	Rock Creek

Q

No.	Name	Age	Race	Birth	Death Date	Burial Place
002661	QUACKENBUSH, Nicholas	70y	W	N.Y.	20 MAR 1875	Albany, N.Y.
020411	QUAILLS, Thomas	20y	M	D.C.	12 JUN 1879	Graceland
015584	QUAILS, Elizabeth	1y	C	D.C.	02 MAY 1878	Mt. Pleasant
013855	QUALLS, Lee A.	2m	C	D.C.	18 NOV 1877	Young Mens
019855	QUALLS, Maggie	1y	C	D.C.	21 APR 1879	Potters Field
014716	QUALLS, Oliver	1y	C	D.C.	08 FEB 1878	Beckett's
003486	QUALLS, William	8d	C	D.C.	30 MAY 1875	Ebenezer
008693	QUANDA, Lizzie	1y	C	D.C.	15 AUG 1876	Mt. Olivet
004957	QUANDER, Ann	70y	C	Va.	08 SEP 1875	Harmony
016438	QUANDER, Henry	4m	C	D.C.	04 JUL 1878	Mt. Olivet
013409	QUANDER, Infant of Nancy	8d	C	D.C.	05 OCT 1877	Potters Field
011240	QUANTRILL, Harry	14d	W	D.C.	06 APR 1877	Glenwood
002433	QUANTRILL, Thomas Ritchie	15d	W	D.C.	05 MAR 1875	Glenwood
016207	QUARELS, William Henry	7m	C	D.C.	17 JUN 1878	Mt. Pleasant Plain
006652	QUARLES, Hattie	4y	C	D.C.	12 MAR 1876	Mt. Pleasant
006573	QUAWS, Jane R.	9m	C	D.C.	06 MAR 1876	Ebenezer
006661	QUEEN, Alice	9m	C	D.C.	13 MAR 1876	Mt. Olivet
020683	QUEEN, Bertha	2m	C	D.C.	30 JUN 1879	Potters Field
021068	QUEEN, Charlott	71y	W	D.C.	23 JUL 1879	Mt. Olivet
000441	QUEEN, Clarence	3m	C	D.C.	06 SEP 1874	Beckett's
009995	QUEEN, Ella	1y	C	D.C.	18 DEC 1876	Mt. Olivet
004529	QUEEN, Emma Jane	2y	C	Md.	10 AUG 1875	Brightwood
019359	QUEEN, Flerman	1y	C	D.C.	10 MAR 1879	Harmony
008735	QUEEN, Florence Perry	5m	C	D.C.	19 AUG 1876	Harmony
007376	QUEEN, H.	70y	C	Md.	22 MAY 1876	X Roads Church, Md.
005530	QUEEN, Jane Elizabeth	60y	W	Md.	21 NOV 1875	Beantown, Md.
016914	QUEEN, Joseph	13m	C	D.C.	05 AUG 1878	Mt. Olivet
020095	QUEEN, Laura	1y	C	D.C.	14 MAY 1879	St. Matthews, Md.
017670	QUEEN, Livinia	1y	C	D.C.	07 OCT 1878	Arlington, Va.
013261	QUEEN, Lucus	2y	C	D.C.	20 SEP 1877	Beckett's
006035	QUEEN, Margaret	56y	W	D.C.	15 JAN 1876	Congressional
017593	QUEEN, Mary	33y	C	Md.	01 OCT 1878	Mt. Olivet
014059	QUEEN, Mary Josephine, Sister	82y	W	Md.	10 DEC 1877	Convent
005339	QUEEN, Minty	c.85y	C	Md.	02 NOV 1875	Harmony
004936	QUEEN, Rebecca	7m	C	D.C.	06 SEP 1875	Ebenezer
003013	QUEEN, Richard R.	60y	C	Md.	16 APR 1875	Mt. Olivet
015352	QUEEN, Sarah S. [Emily]	37y	W	Md.	10 APR 1878	Holy Rood
005169	QUEEN, Teresa	1d	C	D.C.	25 SEP 1875	Potters Field
000760	QUEENE, Mariah J.	23y	C	D.C.	08 OCT 1874	Mt. Zion
019790	QUELLS, Elizabeth	3m	C	D.C.	15 APR 1879	Beckett's
010042	QUESENBERRY, William	39y	C	Va.	21 DEC 1876	Young Mens
003682	QUIET, Georgiana	2m	C	D.C.	17 JUN 1875	Harmony
007866	QUIET, William	12m	C	D.C.	26 JUN 1876	Potters Field
008902	QUIGLEY, Clara E.	62y	W	N.C.	31 AUG 1876	Pensacola, Fla.
016008	QUILL, Bridget	5m	W	D.C.	04 JUN 1878	Mt. Olivet
007828	QUILL, Dennis, Jr.	11d	W	D.C.	24 JUN 1876	Mt. Olivet
012500	QUILL, James P.	1y	W	D.C.	24 JUL 1877	Mt. Olivet
011780	QUILL, Thomas	78y	W	Ire.	02 JUN 1877	Mt. Olivet
007910	QUILLER, Rosa	2y	C	D.C.	28 JUN 1876	Ebenezer

District of Columbia Death Records, August 1, 1874 to July 31, 1879   275

No.	Name	Age	Race	Birth	Death Date	Burial Place
006875	QUILLING, Thomas	47y	W	Ire.	31 MAR 1876	Potters Field
002567	QUILLS, Henry	2y	C	D.C.	14 MAR 1875	Ebenezer
017124	QUINCY, Eliza	83y	C	D.C.	20 AUG 1878	Harmony
014497	QUINCY, Thomas Holland	67y	W	Mass.	20 JAN 1878	Congressional
000367	QUINES, Mamy	8m	C	D.C.	29 AUG 1874	Beckett's
017880	QUINLAIN, Sarah E.	9y	W	D.C.	27 OCT 1878	Mt. Olivet
015853	QUINLAN, Mary	49y	W	Ire.	26 MAY 1878	Mt. Olivet
011616	QUINLAN, Mary S.	c.55y	W	Ire.	16 MAY 1877	Mt. Olivet
019613	QUINLIN, Josephine	9m	W	Va.	31 MAR 1879	Mt. Olivet
002514	QUINN, David	66y	W	Pa.	11 MAR 1875	Middletown, Ohio
017879	QUINN, Edward	45y	W	Ire.	27 OCT 1878	Mt. Olivet
015192	QUINN, Infant of Harry E.	12h	W	D.C.	26 MAR 1878	Rock Creek
004823f	QUINN, John	13y	W	Va.	29 AUG 1875	Mt. Olivet
016840	QUINN, Joseph	1y	W	D.C.	30 JUL 1878	Mt. Olivet
003422	QUINN, Mary Ann	25y	W	Pa.	24 MAY 1875	Mt. Olivet
013140	QUINN, Willie	1y	W	D.C.	09 SEP 1877	Holy Rood
013503	QUINTER, Cordelia	1y	W	D.C.	13 OCT 1877	Rock Creek
013619	QUINTER, Emily	3y	W	D.C.	24 OCT 1877	Rock Creek
013441	QUINTER, Janett	10y	W	D.C.	08 OCT 1877	Rock Creek
013565	QUINTER, Washington	6y	W	D.C.	19 OCT 1877	Rock Creek
021151	QUIRIS, Selistine	1y	C	D.C.	29 JUL 1879	Beckett's
000500	QUIRK, Margaret	36y	W	Can.	13 SEP 1874	Potters Field
019122	QUIRK, Mary	3y	W	D.C.	19 FEB 1879	Mt. Olivet
008361	QUIRUS, Richard	1y	C	D.C.	20 JUL 1876	Ebenezer
019764	QUISENBERRY, Shelton	22y	C	Va.	13 APR 1879	Bealton Station, Va.

R

000691	RABBI, Frank	3y	W	Va.	01 OCT 1874	Prospect Hill
012025	RABBITT, Susan T.	3m	W	D.C.	23 JUN 1877	Mt. Olivet
009020	RABE, Sebastian	39y	W	Ger.	10 SEP 1876	Prospect Hill
004658	RABIT, Mary T.	11m	W	D.C.	18 AUG 1875	Mt. Olivet
018141	RACKS, Louis	6d	C	D.C.	24 NOV 1878	Mt. Pleasant
016527	RACKS, Moses	2m	C	D.C.	09 JUL 1878	Beckett's
010315	RADCLIFF, Mary Ann	35y	W	--	17 JAN 1877	Potters Field
012122	RADCLIFF, Warren	2y	W	D.C.	29 JUN 1877	Congressional
005611	RADCLIFFE, John	65y	W	Va.	30 NOV 1875	Mt. Olivet
006381	RADCLIFFE, Julia A.	67y	W	Va.	16 FEB 1876	Glenwood
000155	RADCLIFFE, Mary	53y	C	Va.	11 AUG 1874	Young Mens
002075	RADOLPH, Infant of Randolph	3d	W	D.C.	08 FEB 1875	Graceland
004600	RADY, Henry	91y	W	Ire.	14 AUG 1875	Mt. Olivet
013533	RADY, Maurice	11y	W	D.C.	16 OCT 1877	Mt. Olivet
014617	RAEBURN, Winona S.	7y	W	Va.	31 JAN 1878	Graceland
006343	RAGAN, Andrew Jackson	20y	W	D.C.	13 FEB 1876	Congressional
002755	RAGAN, Conner	90y	W	Ire.	27 MAR 1875	Mt. Olivet
008943	RAGAN, Elizebeth	37y	W	Pa.	03 SEP 1876	Congressional
010822	RAGAN, Grace	26d	W	D.C.	01 MAR 1877	Congressional
020300	RAGAN, Infant of Columbus	23d	W	D.C.	04 JUN 1879	Mt. Olivet
006101	RAGAN, Joseph F.	5y	W	D.C.	22 JAN 1876	Holy Rood
020572	RAGAN, Margaret	17d	W	D.C.	22 JUN 1879	Mt. Olivet
005133a	RAGAN, Mary Eliza	9y	W	D.C.	13 OCT 1875	Congressional
009429	RAGAN, Susan	2y	W	D.C.	16 OCT 1876	Congressional
006128	RAGEAN, Clarence	2y	W	D.C.	24 JAN 1876	Mt. Olivet
012634	RAGLAND, Alice C.	8y	W	D.C.	01 AUG 1877	Congressional
013066	RAGLAND, James J.	48y	W	Va.	03 SEP 1877	Richmond, Va.

No.	Name	Age	Race	Birth	Death Date	Burial Place
000746	RAGOT, Ilata	20d	W	Pa.	08 OCT 1874	Holy Rood
001657	RAILEY, Mary Elizabeth	4d	C	D.C.	08 JAN 1875	Mt. Olivet
005602	RAINES, Catherine	6m	C	D.C.	29 NOV 1875	Potters Field
006247	RAINES, Cynthia F.	c.52y	W	Ala.	05 FEB 1876	Congressional
004163	RAINEY, Harry	4y	W	D.C.	16 JUL 1875	Mt. Olivet
000571	RAINEY, Jane	1y	W	Md.	20 SEP 1874	Graceland
003253	RAINEY, Losana	3m	W	D.C.	07 MAY 1875	Mt. Olivet
015911	RAINEY, Maggie	6m	C	D.C.	30 MAY 1878	Mt. Pleasant
009829	RAINEY, Samuel	30y	W	Ire.	30 NOV 1876	Mt. Olivet
001188	RAINEY, Samuel A.	41y	W	Ire.	19 NOV 1874	Mt. Olivet
008887	RAINY, Samuel	6m	W	D.C.	30 AUG 1876	Mt. Olivet
015268	RALLS, George	9m	C	D.C.	02 APR 1878	Mt. Olivet
009198	RALSTON, Allen	60y	C	Va.	25 SEP 1876	Potters Field
004158	RAMBO, Martha	6m	W	Md.	16 JUL 1875	Congressional
008237	RAMSAY, David Peter	46y	W	D.C.	13 JUL 1876	Oak Hill
014107	RAMSBURG, Jacob	66y	W	Md.	15 DEC 1877	Oak Hill
016460	RAMSEY, George D.	37y	W	D.C.	05 JUL 1878	Oak Hill/Harrisburg, Pa.
001290	RAMSEY, Grace	72y	W	Eng.	02 DEC 1874	Congressional
009411	RAMSEY, Lydia	40y	C	D.C.	14 OCT 1876	Young Mens
012512	RANDALL, Benjamin	6d	C	D.C.	24 JUL 1877	Potters Field
001320	RANDALL, Eliza G.	40y	W	Ver.	06 DEC 1874	Wells River, Ver.
008040	RANDALL, Ellen	26y	C	Va.	05 JUL 1876	Beckett's
008685	RANDALL, Emily Munroe	71y	W	D.C.	14 AUG 1876	Oak Hill
015940	RANDALL, George Augustin Wash.	79y	W	Va.	31 MAY 1878	Glenwood
018046	RANDALL, Harry	48y	C	Va.	13 NOV 1878	Mt. Pleasant
017234	RANDALL, Henrietta	10d	C	D.C.	28 AUG 1878	Mt. Zion
010560	RANDALL, Henry K.	83y	W	Md.	08 FEB 1877	Oak Hill
006530	RANDALL, Infant of Wm.	4d	C	D.C.	03 MAR 1876	Ebenezer
009651	RANDALL, Infant of William	3h	C	D.C.	09 NOV 1876	Ebenezer
001013	RANDALL, Martha Washington	70y	W	Va.	02 NOV 1874	Glenwood
018086	RANDALL, Richard Griffith	38y	W	Ind.	18 NOV 1878	Rock Creek
010533	RANDALL, Thomas	84y	W	Md.	05 FEB 1877	Annapolis, Md.
008582	RANDELL, J.	23y	C	Va.	07 AUG 1876	Mt. Pleasant
009423	RANDOLPH, Frank	4m	C	D.C.	16 OCT 1876	Potters Field
017003	RANDOLPH, Ida	8m	C	D.C.	10 AUG 1878	Potters Field
016321	RANDOLPH, Joseph	7m	C	D.C.	26 JUN 1878	Mt. Pleasant
013357	RANDOLPH, Mary	23y	C	Va.	30 SEP 1877	Alexandria, Va.
011008	RANDOLPH, Mary E.	34y	C	Md.	16 MAR 1877	Beckett's
006865	RANDOLPH, Nathan E.	6m	C	D.C.	30 MAR 1876	Harmony
012306	RANDOLPH, Rutherford	6m	C	D.C.	10 JUL 1877	Harmony
012967	RANDOLPH, Sarah Lingan	83y	W	Md.	26 AUG 1877	Oak Hill
002950	RANDOLPH, Tabuns	1y	C	D.C.	11 APR 1875	Young Mens
000267	RANDOLPH, William	8m	W	D.C.	21 AUG 1874	Congressional
008191	RANKIN, Arthur	10m	C	D.C.	11 JUL 1876	Young Mens
012563	RANKIN, Bertha	9y	C	N.J.	27 JUL 1877	Young Mens
014884	RANKIN, Edward	74y	C	Va.	26 FEB 1878	Young Mens
009793	RANKIN, Lavinia	28y	C	Va.	25 NOV 1876	Young Mens
008997	RANKIN, Louisa	4y	C	D.C.	07 SEP 1876	Ebenezer
006525	RANKIN, Paul	30y	C	Va.	02 MAR 1876	Hillsdale
011534	RANKIN, Robert	36y	C	Va.	06 MAY 1877	Mt. Pleasant
011566	RANKIN, Walter Newton	19y	W	Ver.	11 MAY 1877	Oak Hill
012594	RANSELL, Joseph	26y	C	D.C.	29 JUL 1877	Potters Field
016583	RANSENN, Josephine	17d	C	D.C.	13 JUL 1878	Mt. Zion
001752	RANSOM, John	3y	C	D.C.	16 JAN 1875	Beckett's
008573	RANSOM, Mary E.	3y	C	D.C.	06 AUG 1876	Ebenezer
010511	RANSOM, Thomas	78y	C	Va.	04 FEB 1877	Ebenezer

District of Columbia Death Records, August 1, 1874 to July 31, 1879

No.	Name	Age	Race	Birth	Death Date	Burial Place
013284	RANSOME, James Henry	12y	M	Md.	23 SEP 1877	Beckett's
004086	RAPER, Infant of Leonard	12d	W	D.C.	11 JUL 1875	Glenwood
013244	RAPHE, Maria	c.75y	C	Va.	18 SEP 1877	Harmony
020929	RAPP, Blanch F.	5m	W	D.C.	14 JUL 1879	Buckhannon, W.Va.
002887	RASNER, Charles	1d	W	D.C.	06 APR 1875	Holy Rood
005145	RATCLIFF, Alexander	31y	W	D.C.	23 SEP 1875	Congressional
003409	RATCLIFFE, Daniel	9y	M	D.C.	23 MAY 1875	Mt. Olivet
014993	RATCLIFFE, Ida	3y	W	D.C.	08 MAR 1878	Oak Hill
014992	RATCLIFFE, Mary A.	1y	W	D.C.	08 MAR 1878	Oak Hill
014048	RATHBONE, Joseph Arthur	6y	W	D.C.	09 DEC 1877	Congressional
012760	RATTO, Anna	c.75y	W	Italy	10 AUG 1877	St. Mary's
000215	RATTO, John	23m	W	D.C.	17 AUG 1874	St. Mary's
015825	RATZ, Sophia	44y	W	Ger.	24 MAY 1878	Prospect Hill
011892	RAU, Ada	4m	W	D.C.	14 JUN 1877	Prospect Hill
011849	RAU, Jessie Mary Jane	4m	W	D.C.	09 JUN 1877	Prospect Hill
000111	RAU, Sarah	30y	W	D.C.	08 AUG 1874	Tennallytown
002370	RAUBB, Spencer	68y	C	Va.	01 MAR 1875	Harmony
015176	RAWLETT, Phillip	38y	W	Va.	24 MAR 1878	Congressional
013105	RAWLINGS, Edwin Albert	1y	W	S.C.	06 SEP 1877	Glenwood/Rock Creek
013829	RAWLINGS, Elizabeth T.	24y	W	D.C.	15 NOV 1877	Congressional
003205	RAWLINGS, Richard M.H.	22y	W	D.C.	03 MAY 1875	Glenwood/Rock Creek
006575	RAWLINGS, Robert	85y	W	Va.	06 MAR 1876	Oak Hill
003711	RAWLINS, Dennis	1m	C	D.C.	19 JUN 1875	Potters Field
015047	RAWLINS, James	2y	M	D.C.	12 MAR 1878	Young Mens
013963	RAX, Elizabeth	8d	C	D.C.	29 NOV 1877	Beckett's
013501	RAX, Griffin	2y	C	D.C.	13 OCT 1877	Beckett's
007599	RAY, Chauncey S.	7m	W	D.C.	11 JUN 1876	Congressional
000288	RAY, Edward	1m	W	D.C.	22 AUG 1874	Glenwood
008562	RAY, Henley	33y	C	Va.	05 AUG 1876	Harmony
010917	RAY, Hobert B.	2y	W	D.C.	08 MAR 1877	Congressional
006409	RAY, James	58y	W	Md.	18 FEB 1876	Holy Rood
005683	RAY, Mary	21d	W	D.C.	07 DEC 1875	Glenwood
013489	RAY, Michel E.	3y	W	D.C.	12 OCT 1877	Holy Rood
007103	RAYBURN, Chas.	7m	C	D.C.	24 APR 1876	Young Mens
002989	RAYGAN, Daniel	2m	W	D.C.	14 APR 1875	Holy Rood
003668	RAYMOND, Emily	1m	M	D.C.	16 JUN 1875	Harmony
016363	RDMOND, Sidney	2m	M	D.C.	29 JUN 1878	Beckett's
004800	REA, Thos. W.	35y	W	Ire.	28 AUG 1875	Rock Creek
010308	READ, Chas.	2y	C	Md.	16 JAN 1877	Baltimore, Md.
020151	READ, Frances Rebecca	49y	W	D.C.	19 MAY 1879	Oak Hill
009172	READ, Harriet Fanning	61y	W	Mass.	22 SEP 1876	Oak Hill
012792	READ, Ovely S.	14m	C	Md.	13 AUG 1877	Mt. Zion
000208	READ, Silvester	15m	W	D.C.	16 AUG 1874	Beckett's
020839	READER, George Lewis	10m	C	D.C.	08 JUL 1879	Mt. Olivet
004958	READER, John H.	4y	C	D.C.	08 SEP 1875	Mt. Olivet
004583	READER, Louis	9m	C	D.C.	13 AUG 1875	Mt. Olivet
011602	READY, William	2m	W	D.C.	15 MAY 1877	Holy Rood
017233	REAGAN, James M.	36y	W	D.C.	28 AUG 1878	Mt. Olivet
000718	REAGAN, Katherine	9y	W	D.C.	05 OCT 1874	Mt. Olivet
020122	REAGAN, Maggie	3y	W	D.C.	16 MAY 1879	Holy Rood
005537	REARDEN, Sarah Cathern	10y	W	D.C.	22 NOV 1875	Glenwood
006980	REARDON, Cornelius	34y	W	Ire.	10 APR 1876	Hospital
002185	REARSON, Peter W.	31y	W	D.C.	15 FEB 1875	Oak Hill
020227	REAU, Richard	25y	C	Md.	30 MAY 1879	Harmony
015236	REAVER, Eliza	74y	W	D.C.	30 MAR 1878	Oak Hill
011324	REDD, Mary Jane B.	49y	W	Ky.	13 APR 1877	Graceland/Woodlawn

District of Columbia Death Records, August 1, 1874 to July 31, 1879

No.	Name	Age	Race	Birth	Death Date	Burial Place
001393	REDDALL, William C.	62y	W	Va.	15 DEC 1874	Oak Hill
016335	REDDEN, Hager	74y	C	Md.	27 JUN 1878	Graceland
008917	REDDEN, Infant of Wm.	5d	W	D.C.	01 SEP 1876	Holy Rood
020004	REDDICK, Nelson	6m	C	D.C.	05 MAY 1879	Moore's
020252	REDDIN, Albert	2y	C	D.C.	01 JUN 1879	Moore's
018887	REDDING, Mary	47y	W	Ire.	30 JAN 1879	Mt. Olivet
011517	REDDY, Margaret	5y	W	D.C.	05 MAY 1877	Holy Rood
003029	REDICK, Anna	1y	C	D.C.	18 APR 1875	Young Mens
019522	REDICK, Dicy	11m	C	D.C.	23 MAR 1879	Mt. Pleasant
013014	REDICK, Harriet Ann	3m	C	D.C.	29 AUG 1877	Belt's
020385	REDIE, James	4y	C	D.C.	10 JUN 1879	Moore's
011305	REDMAN, Ada	5m	C	D.C.	12 APR 1877	Ebenezer
016860	REDMAN, George	50y	C	Va.	01 AUG 1878	Beckett's
004884	REDMAN, Mary	56y	C	Va.	02 SEP 1875	Mt. Pleasant
020946	REDMAN, Noble	68y	C	Va.	15 JUL 1879	Mt. Pleasant
016572	REDMON, Benj.	10m	C	D.C.	12 JUL 1878	Beckett's
016721	REDMON, Julia	75y	C	Va.	22 JUL 1878	Mt. Zion
004449	REDMON, Robert	18y	C	Md.	04 AUG 1875	Potters Field
016194	REDMON, Robert C.	8m	C	D.C.	16 JUN 1878	Beckett's
006617	REDMOND, Clara	1y	C	D.C.	09 MAR 1876	Ebenezer
015838	REDMOND, Infant of Ferdinand	9m	C	D.C.	25 MAY 1878	Beckett's
013839	REDWAY, Norton Faulkner	7y	W	Pa.	16 NOV 1877	Glenwood
015854	REDWAY, Rosa L.	22y	W	N.Y.	26 MAY 1878	Rock Creek
020322	REECE, Hattie	5m	C	D.C.	06 JUN 1879	Young Mens
017684	REED, Andrew, Jr.	5d	C	D.C.	09 OCT 1878	Mt. Zion
007407	REED, Annie	2y	W	D.C.	25 MAY 1876	Prospect Hill
020412	REED, Benjamin	1y	C	D.C.	12 JUN 1879	Beckett's
008420	REED, Bushrod M.	43y	W	Va.	25 JUL 1876	Oak Hill
005393	REED, Bushrod Washington	68y	W	Va.	08 NOV 1875	Rock Creek
019011	REED, Caroline	70y	W	D.C.	09 FEB 1879	Rock Creek
001432	REED, Elizabeth Rebecca	3m	C	D.C.	19 DEC 1874	Beckett's
020866	REED, Evelyn Palmer	1y	W	D.C.	09 JUL 1879	Congressional
017174	REED, Fanny	83y	C	Va.	24 AUG 1878	Harmony
002629	REED, Homer L.	19y	W	Wisc.	18 MAR 1875	Alexandria Co., Va.
003251	REED, Infant of John	5d	C	D.C.	07 MAY 1875	Young Mens
017002	REED, Jno.	10m	W	D.C.	10 AUG 1878	St. Mary's
013982	REED, John W.	2y	C	D.C.	01 DEC 1877	Mt. Zion
010223	REED, Joseph F.	29y	W	Md.	08 JAN 1877	Glenwood
019593	REED, Julia A.	48y	W	Va.	29 MAR 1879	Congressional
006435	REED, Levi	5d	C	D.C.	21 FEB 1876	Payne's
003412	REED, Mary	63y	C	Md.	23 MAY 1875	Harmony
008453	REED, Mary	48y	C	Va.	28 JUL 1876	Beckett's
020288	REED, Maurice	6d	W	D.C.	03 JUN 1879	Presbyterian
000051	REED, Millvinia	65y	C	Va.	04 AUG 1874	Harmony
008896	REED, Noble Harris	5m	C	D.C.	31 AUG 1876	Young Mens
008409	REED, Samuel	6m	C	D.C.	24 JUL 1876	Young Mens
005207a	REED, Sarah	60y	C	Md.	19 OCT 1875	Bennings Bridge
005171	REED, Thomas	1y	C	D.C.	25 SEP 1875	Ebenezer
010050	REED, William B.	67y	W	Va.	22 DEC 1876	Congressional
001078	REED, William N.	20y	W	Va.	07 NOV 1874	Westmoreland Co., Va.
019114	REEDER, Austin	3m	C	D.C.	18 FEB 1879	Mt. Olivet
005116a	REEDER, Charles William	7y	C	D.C.	12 OCT 1875	Mt. Olivet
004483	REEDER, Ellen	22d	C	D.C.	06 AUG 1875	Mt. Olivet
012408	REEDER, Gertrude	9m	C	D.C.	17 JUL 1877	Mt. Zion
007663	REEDER, John	15d	C	D.C.	15 JUN 1876	Mt. Olivet
015032	REEDER, John	3m	C	U.S.	11 MAR 1878	Mt. Olivet

District of Columbia Death Records, August 1, 1874 to July 31, 1879

No.	Name	Age	Race	Birth	Death Date	Burial Place
018951	REEDER, Lula	15m	C	D.C.	04 FEB 1879	Mt. Olivet
019493	REEDER, Mary Ann	1m	C	D.C.	21 MAR 1879	Moore's
014435	REEDER, Michael	1m	C	D.C.	15 JAN 1878	Mt. Olivet
020903	REEDER, Phillip	1m	C	D.C.	12 JUL 1879	Mt. Olivet
004130	REEDER, Samuel D.	2y	W	D.C.	14 JUL 1875	Congressional
014423	REEDER, William	1m	C	D.C.	14 JAN 1878	Mt. Olivet
018871	REESE, Edward William	23y	W	D.C.	29 JAN 1879	Glenwood
011658	REESE, Joseph Pennington	1y	W	D.C.	20 MAY 1877	Congressional
020680	REESE, Moses	7m	W	Ky.	30 JUN 1879	Washington Hebrew
008601	REEVES, Arthur	2y	W	D.C.	07 AUG 1876	Glenwood
019327	REEVES, Emily Danniels	1m	W	D.C.	08 MAR 1879	Glenwood
008812	REEVES, John	45y	C	Va.	25 AUG 1876	Mt. Pleasant
003970	REEVES, Leonard	50y	W	Md.	02 JUL 1875	Mt. Olivet
002000	REEVES, Maud	2y	W	D.C.	02 FEB 1875	Glenwood
013560	REEVES, Nicholas	69y	C	Va.	18 OCT 1877	Potters Field
000806	REEVES, Sarah	50y	C	Va.	14 OCT 1874	Young Mens
009758	REEVES, Sarah	48y	W	Va.	20 NOV 1876	Mt. Olivet
002555	REEVES, Willie	15m	C	D.C.	13 MAR 1875	Mt. Pleasant
018506	REGAN, Annie	24y	W	D.C.	29 DEC 1878	Mt. Olivet
009605	REGAN, Harry	8m	W	D.C.	03 NOV 1876	Mt. Olivet
016336	REGAN, Johanna	50y	W	Ire.	27 JUN 1878	Mt. Olivet
001132	REGAN, John	35y	W	Ire.	01 NOV 1874	Mt. Olivet
017207	REGAN, Richard	1y	W	D.C.	26 AUG 1878	Mt. Olivet
012331	REGAN, Robt. Rutherford	2y	W	Wyo.	12 JUL 1877	Oak Hill
003247	REGLE, Frederick	59y	W	Ger.	06 MAY 1875	Hospital
004421	REH, Julius Wm.	1m	W	D.C.	02 AUG 1875	Prospect Hill
016161	REID, George W.	2y	C	D.C.	14 JUN 1878	Mt. Zion
012854	REID, Mable	21d	W	D.C.	17 AUG 1877	Glenwood
019299	REID, Margaret Cora	26y	W	D.C.	06 MAR 1879	Oak Hill
018427	REID, Margaret, Mrs.	39y	W	Md.	22 DEC 1878	Mt. Olivet, Balto., Md.
012901	REID, Sarah A.	49y	W	Va.	21 AUG 1877	Congressional
007752	REID, W.W.	22y	W	Va.	20 JUN 1876	Westmoreland Co., Va.
001179	REIDER, Calbert	7d	C	D.C.	18 NOV 1874	Mt. Zion
004886	REIDER, James Edward	9y	C	D.C.	02 SEP 1875	Moore's
007206	REIDER, William Agust	8m	C	D.C.	04 MAY 1876	Moore's
016405	REIDY, Catherine	61y	W	Ire.	02 JUL 1878	Mt. Olivet
012225	REIDY, Mary	62y	W	Ire.	05 JUL 1877	Mt. Olivet
019186	REILEY, John	43y	W	Ire.	24 FEB 1879	Mt. Olivet
009579	REILEY, Margaret	15y	W	Ire.	30 OCT 1876	Holy Rood
011941	REILLY, Bernard	46y	W	N.Y.	17 JUN 1877	Congressional
013709	REILLY, Jas. F.	28y	W	Md.	02 NOV 1877	Mt. Olivet
006600	REILLY, Josephine	24y	W	D.C.	08 MAR 1876	Congressional
003341	REILY, William	43y	W	Ire.	16 MAY 1875	Mt. Olivet
020642	REINBURG, John Harris	3m	W	D.C.	27 JUN 1879	Congressional
007647	REINBURG, Louis, Sr.	68y	W	Ger.	14 JUN 1876	Congressional
020969	REINDL, Andrew	58y	W	Bav.	16 JUL 1879	Congressional
013910	REINGRUBER, John W.T.	7y	W	D.C.	24 NOV 1877	Holy Rood
013840	REINGRUBER, Richard T.	2y	W	D.C.	16 NOV 1877	Holy Rood
004573f	REINHARD, Israel	76y	W	Pa.	12 AUG 1875	Oak Hill
000373	REINHART, Casper	47y	W	Ger.	30 AUG 1874	Prospect Hill
001378	REINKARDT, Louis	1y	W	D.C.	13 DEC 1874	Prospect Hill
019010	REINKERD, Wilhelmina Catherine	1y	W	D.C.	09 FEB 1879	Prospect Hill
006126	REINOHL, Cecilia E. Parker	15m	W	D.C.	24 JAN 1876	Oak Hill
011224	REINOHL, Grace Louisa	1y	W	D.C.	05 APR 1877	Oak Hill
010112	REINTAUS, Louise	67y	W	Ger.	29 DEC 1876	Congressional
004616	REINTZEL, Charles H.	2y	W	D.C.	15 AUG 1875	Oak Hill

No.	Name	Age	Race	Birth	Death Date	Burial Place
013810	REIS, Fannie	42y	W	Ger.	12 NOV 1877	Washington Hebrew
008095	REIS, Joseph	4m	W	D.C.	09 JUL 1876	Washington Hebrew
012434	REIS, Leon	3m	W	D.C.	19 JUL 1877	Washington Hebrew
006738	REISE, Catherine A.	19y	W	D.C.	19 MAR 1876	Congressional
006062	REISIGER, Infant of Jacob H.	12d	W	D.C.	18 JAN 1876	Prospect Hill
019364	REISS, Adeline Lowe, Mrs.	54y	W	Md.	11 MAR 1879	Congressional
004617	REITH, Dorothea Ann	11m	W	D.C.	15 AUG 1875	St. Mary's
007035	REITHMULLER, Annie	7y	W	D.C.	17 APR 1876	St. Mary's
005327	REITMULLER, Ignatious	48y	W	Ger.	31 OCT 1875	St. Mary's
009004	REITZEL, Julian A.	8m	W	D.C.	08 SEP 1876	Prospect Hill
007006	REMELSPECK, George	30y	W	Ger.	12 APR 1876	Hospital
006674	REMINGTON, Edmund A.	30y	W	N.Y.	14 MAR 1876	Canandaigua, N.Y.
013103	REMP, Dora	1y	W	D.C.	06 SEP 1877	Prospect Hill
000239	RENEHAN, Agnes B.	6m	W	D.C.	19 AUG 1874	Mt. Olivet
011859	RENNIE, Jane	1y	W	D.C.	10 JUN 1877	Graceland
002553	RENNIS, Alies	9y	W	Eng.	13 MAR 1875	Graceland
009699	RENTCH, Jarvis Nevin	28y	W	W.Va.	15 NOV 1876	Congressional
021013	RENTER, Arthur	9m	W	D.C.	19 JUL 1879	Mt. Olivet
017779	REPPETTI, Richard	7m	W	D.C.	17 OCT 1878	Congressional
016638	RESPOLL, Lucy	8m	C	D.C.	17 JUL 1878	Harmony
005684	REY, Mary Jane	52y	W	Va.	07 DEC 1875	Richmond, Va.
001849	REYBURN, Florence	8m	C	D.C.	23 JAN 1875	Mt. Pleasant
019735	REYNOE, Jane	63y	W	L.I.	11 APR 1879	Congressional
004999	REYNOLD, Thomas	1y	C	D.C.	11 SEP 1875	Young Mens
016179	REYNOLDS, Alice	35y	C	D.C.	15 JUN 1878	Mt. Zion
017172	REYNOLDS, Charles	1y	C	D.C.	24 AUG 1878	Potters Field
010085	REYNOLDS, Charlotte	73y	W	Conn.	26 DEC 1876	Congressional
020459	REYNOLDS, Edna Marie	8m	W	D.C.	15 JUN 1879	Graceland
009889	REYNOLDS, Emmanuel	9m	W	D.C.	06 DEC 1876	Congressional
009660	REYNOLDS, Evelyn Dante	4y	W	D.C.	09 NOV 1876	Congressional
007683	REYNOLDS, Infant of Robert	1m	W	D.C.	16 JUN 1876	Graceland
013095	REYNOLDS, Laura Blanch	14d	W	D.C.	05 SEP 1877	Congressional
005157	REYNOLDS, Luvenia	58y	C	Va.	24 SEP 1875	Potters Field
017274	REYNOLDS, Mary	11m	W	D.C.	31 AUG 1878	Mt. Olivet
013164	REYNOLDS, Mary Genevia	19d	W	D.C.	11 SEP 1877	Congressional
001068	REYNOLDS, Maud L.A.	6m	W	D.C.	06 NOV 1874	Congressional
011750	REYNOLDS, Michael	50y	W	Ire.	31 MAY 1877	Holy Rood
005718	REYNOLDS, Naomi	41y	W	Eng.	10 DEC 1875	Glenwood
019297	REYNOLDS, Wm.	6d	C	D.C.	06 MAR 1879	Payne's
001496	REYNOR, Charles	14m	W	D.C.	26 DEC 1874	Congressional
002697	REZDICK, Mary Ann	4y	C	D.C.	22 MAR 1875	Harmony
007089	RHINE, Mary	3m	W	Md.	23 APR 1876	Glenwood
000662	RHINEHART, Katharine	73y	W	Ger.	28 SEP 1874	Prospect Hill
009493	RHODES, Daniel	65y	W	Md.	22 OCT 1876	Frederick, Md.
006266	RHODES, Edward W.	2m	W	D.C.	07 FEB 1876	Holy Rood
016775	RHODES, Elizabeth A.	15y	C	D.C.	26 JUL 1878	Mt. Zion
015671	RHODES, Eugene B.	7m	W	D.C.	09 MAY 1878	Congressional
015639	RHODES, Infant of Alexander	8d	C	D.C.	07 MAY 1878	Payne's
005199	RHODES, James	29y	M	Va.	27 SEP 1875	Washington Asylum
006259	RHODES, James W.	3y	W	D.C.	06 FEB 1876	Mt. Olivet
014643	RHODES, Sarah E.	32y	W	D.C.	02 FEB 1878	Congressional
007442	RHODES, Virga.	4m	W	D.C.	30 MAY 1876	Mt. Pleasant
019000	RHODES, William	4m	C	D.C.	08 FEB 1879	Potters Field
013999	RHONE, Julis	2y	C	D.C.	03 DEC 1877	Mt. Pleasant
019147	RICARD, Joseph	28y	W	D.C.	21 FEB 1879	Rock Creek
002630	RICE, Arttie	2y	W	D.C.	18 MAR 1875	Jewish

District of Columbia Death Records, August 1, 1874 to July 31, 1879

No.	Name	Age	Race	Birth	Death Date	Burial Place
006041	RICE, Caroline	77y	W	Ger.	16 JAN 1876	Hebrew
012633	RICE, Charles	1y	C	Pa.	01 AUG 1877	Harmony
012059	RICE, Edward V.	2m	W	D.C.	26 JUN 1877	Mt. Olivet
004234	RICE, Infant of Wm. H.	2m	W	D.C.	21 JUL 1875	Oberlin, Ohio
006410	RICE, James	c.35y	C	Va.	18 FEB 1876	Ebenezer
006789	RICE, James K.	46y	W	N.Y.	23 MAR 1876	Congressional
020089	RICE, Jane, Mrs.	72y	W	Mass.	13 MAY 1879	Graceland
000478	RICE, Josaphine A.	31y	W	Mass.	11 SEP 1874	Graceland
019627	RICE, Mary J.	69y	W	Va.	01 APR 1879	Holy Rood
020005	RICE, Mary J.	1y	C	D.C.	05 MAY 1879	Beckett's
010662	RICE, William	2y	W	D.C.	16 FEB 1877	Congressional
006312	RICE, Winnie Ann	3y	C	D.C.	11 FEB 1876	Potters Field
008565	RICH, Eugene	2y	C	D.C.	05 AUG 1876	Harmony
003863	RICH, Henry	6m	W	D.C.	26 JUN 1875	Adas Israel
003618	RICH, Luther James	5m	C	D.C.	12 JUN 1875	Young Mens
010303	RICH, Mary	85y	W	Eng.	15 JAN 1877	Brooklyn, N.Y.
003163	RICH, Nancy	23y	C	Va.	29 APR 1875	Young Mens
004756	RICH, Odalia	2y	C	D.C.	25 AUG 1875	Young Mens
004983	RICH, Thomas	54y	W	D.C.	10 SEP 1875	Congressional
017162	RICH, William	29y	C	Va.	23 AUG 1878	Young Mens
011341	RICHARD, Lilly E.	1y	C	D.C.	15 APR 1877	Harmony
001258	RICHARDS, Alexander	55y	C	Va.	28 NOV 1874	Potters Field
011648	RICHARDS, Channing	7m	W	D.C.	19 MAY 1877	Graceland
013185	RICHARDS, Edward	60y	C	Va.	13 SEP 1877	Young Mens
013453	RICHARDS, Elizabeth	86y	W	Mass.	09 OCT 1877	Oak Hill
000995	RICHARDS, John H.D.	50y	W	N.J.	31 OCT 1874	Mt. Olivet
011368	RICHARDS, Mary E.	2m	W	D.C.	18 APR 1877	Holy Rood
006632	RICHARDS, Sylvester	34y	C	N.C.	10 MAR 1876	Ebenezer
016308	RICHARDS, William E.	53y	W	Md.	25 JUN 1878	Congressional
009371	RICHARDS, Wm. H.	25y	W	Md.	11 OCT 1876	Mt. Olivet
013504	RICHARDSON, Ada	1y	C	D.C.	13 OCT 1877	Beckett's
001182	RICHARDSON, Albert	15y	C	Va.	19 NOV 1874	Graceland
019034	RICHARDSON, Alice	9y	C	D.C.	11 FEB 1879	Mt. Olivet
007716	RICHARDSON, E.S.	9m	C	Md.	18 JUN 1876	Annapolis, Md.
002649	RICHARDSON, Elizabeth	1y	C	D.C.	19 MAR 1875	Mt. Pleasant
009809	RICHARDSON, Ellen	9m	C	D.C.	27 NOV 1876	Potters Field
012455	RICHARDSON, Emma	21y	C	Md.	21 JUL 1877	Harmony
005853	RICHARDSON, George Washington	43y	W	D.C.	24 DEC 1875	Mt. Olivet
015127	RICHARDSON, Harriet Ann	1d	C	D.C.	19 MAR 1878	Payne's
010872	RICHARDSON, Harriet Ellen	76y	W	Md.	05 MAR 1877	Holy Rood
008985	RICHARDSON, Henry	2m	C	D.C.	06 SEP 1876	Potters Field
003644	RICHARDSON, Infant of Henry	7m	C	D.C.	14 JUN 1874	Mt. Olivet
002338	RICHARDSON, Infant of James	2y	C	D.C.	27 FEB 1875	Potters Field
019636	RICHARDSON, Infant of Philip	3m	C	D.C.	02 APR 1879	Beckett's
018255	RICHARDSON, Infant of Wm.	6d	C	D.C.	06 DEC 1878	Beckett's
010183	RICHARDSON, Isaac George	11d	C	D.C.	05 JAN 1877	Glenwood
007228	RICHARDSON, Jane	72y	W	Va.	06 MAY 1876	Warrenton, Va.
017461	RICHARDSON, Jane	80y	C	Va.	19 SEP 1878	Arlington
003060	RICHARDSON, Joseph	3y	C	D.C.	20 APR 1875	Mt. Pleasant
019278	RICHARDSON, Margaret Mary	2y	C	D.C.	04 MAR 1879	Alexandria, Va.
006713	RICHARDSON, Mary	1m	C	D.C.	17 MAR 1876	Mt. Zion
012681	RICHARDSON, Mary E.	50y	W	Md.	05 AUG 1877	Mt. Olivet
012451	RICHARDSON, Mary E.	10m	C	D.C.	21 JUL 1877	Beckett's
003466	RICHARDSON, Mary Jane	16d	C	D.C.	28 MAY 1875	Potters Field
008994	RICHARDSON, Matilda	47y	W	S.C.	07 SEP 1876	Potters Field
018129	RICHARDSON, Samuel S.	22y	W	D.C.	23 NOV 1878	Glenwood

District of Columbia Death Records, August 1, 1874 to July 31, 1879

No.	Name	Age	Race	Birth	Death Date	Burial Place
010916	RICHARDSON, Susan	18m	C	D.C.	08 MAR 1877	Harmony
006069	RICHARDSON, Susan E.	59y	W	Md.	19 JAN 1876	Mt. Olivet
020840	RICHARDSON, Susan E.	6m	C	D.C.	08 JUL 1879	Annapolis, Md.
006344	RICHARDSON, Terecia	35y	C	Md.	13 FEB 1876	Ebenezer
008369	RICHARDSON, Thomas	14m	C	D.C.	21 JUL 1876	Beckett's
015126	RICHARDSON, Thomas B.	3y	W	D.C.	19 MAR 1878	Graceland
009576	RICHARDSON, Willeetta P.	20y	W	Md.	30 OCT 1876	Clarkesville, Md.
008600	RICHEY, Helen	4m	W	D.C.	07 AUG 1876	Glenwood
010490	RICHEY, John	69y	W	Pa.	03 FEB 1877	Glenwood
018518	RICHMOND, Geo. W.	8y	W	Md.	30 DEC 1878	Mt. Olivet
018664	RICHMOND, Hannah	36h	W	D.C.	13 JAN 1879	Mt. Olivet
017799	RICHOLD, Moses	68y	W	Ger.	19 OCT 1878	Washington Hebrew
017814	RICHTER, Anna	6y	W	D.C.	20 OCT 1878	Prospect Hill
017867	RICHTER, Clare	2y	W	D.C.	26 OCT 1878	Prospect Hill
017833	RICHTER, Detie	2y	W	D.C.	22 OCT 1878	Prospect Hill
001157	RICHTER, Elizabeth	64y	W	Ger.	16 NOV 1874	St. Mary's
003055	RICHTER, Frank	1m	W	D.C.	20 APR 1875	Congressional
008824	RICHTER, James	9y	W	D.C.	25 AUG 1876	Congressional
004569	RICHTER, Mary	1y	W	D.C.	12 AUG 1875	Mt. Olivet
017121	RICHTER, Nettie	7m	W	D.C.	20 AUG 1878	Mt. Olivet
000845	RICHTER, Peter	64y	W	Ger.	18 OCT 1874	St. Mary's
011919	RICHTER, Robt. Otto	40y	C	Ger.	15 JUN 1877	Arlington
002645	RICHTER, Veronica	40y	W	D.C.	19 MAR 1875	Congressional
017036	RICKER, Albert	2y	W	D.C.	13 AUG 1878	Graceland
000036	RICKER, Elizabeth May	1y	W	D.C.	03 AUG 1874	Congressional
001765	RICKER, Laurence Hunter	4y	W	D.C.	17 JAN 1875	Congressional
000987	RICKER, Samuel	74y	W	Me.	30 OCT 1874	Cincinnati, Ohio
001810	RICKER, Susan Ellenor	24y	W	Md.	20 JAN 1875	Congressional
004757	RICKERT, Marietta	3d	C	D.C.	25 AUG 1875	Mt. Zion
009672	RICKETS, Maggie M.	10d	C	D.C.	11 NOV 1876	Mt. Zion
001892	RICKETTS, Asa	61y	W	Md.	26 JAN 1875	Glenwood
014299	RICKS, Ellen	77y	W	Va.	02 JAN 1878	Mt. Pleasant
000734	RICKSEY, Johnny	11m	C	D.C.	06 OCT 1874	Mt. Pleasant Plain
012806	RIDDLE, E.	6w	C	D.C.	14 AUG 1877	Mt. Zion
015941	RIDDLE, Mary Ellen	28y	W	D.C.	31 MAY 1878	Glenwood
000018	RIDDLE, Mary Magdelene	82y	W	Md.	02 AUG 1874	Baltimore, Md.
020074	RIDDLE, William	53y	W	Md.	11 MAY 1879	Potters Field/Congressional
004247	RIDDLEMOSER, Johnie	21y	W	Md.	22 JUL 1875	Glenwood
002694	RIDDLES, Lilly	4m	C	D.C.	22 MAR 1875	Mt. Zion
004371	RIDDLES, Margaret	16y	M	Va.	29 JUL 1875	Mt. Zion
002822	RIDDLES, Thos.	43y	C	Va.	31 MAR 1875	Mt. Zion
011207	RIDENOUR, John William	49y	W	Md.	04 APR 1877	Forestville, Md.
002368	RIDEOUT, Augustus G.	1y	C	D.C.	01 MAR 1875	Montgomery Co., Md.
014067	RIDER, John	60y	W	Ire.	11 DEC 1877	Mt. Olivet
008651	RIDERS, Justina	70y	W	Ger.	11 AUG 1876	Prospect Hill
017418	RIDGELEY, John Robert	1y	W	D.C.	15 SEP 1878	Payne's
001637	RIDGELY, Ann Chase	85y	W	Md.	07 JAN 1875	Oak Hill
007664	RIDGELY, Frank Black	10m	W	D.C.	15 JUN 1876	Glenwood
002814	RIDGELY, Matilda L.	84y	W	Md.	31 MAR 1875	Oak Hill
005981	RIDGELY, William G.	49y	W	D.C.	09 JAN 1876	Oak Hill
017049	RIDGEWAY, Emma Louisa	c.8y	M	D.C.	14 AUG 1878	Mt. Pleasant
004991f	RIDGEWAY, Susan of Basil	3y	W	Md.	10 SEP 1875	Congressional
013780	RIDGLEY, Ann	6y	C	D.C.	09 NOV 1877	Payne's
008891	RIDGLEY, John	69y	C	Md.	31 AUG 1876	Potters Field
000888	RIDGLEY, Maria Selman, Mrs.	78y	W	Md.	21 OCT 1874	Oak Hill
015993	RIDGLEY, Robert	23y	C	Md.	03 JUN 1878	Payne's

District of Columbia Death Records, August 1, 1874 to July 31, 1879

No.	Name	Age	Race	Birth	Death Date	Burial Place
020123	RIDGWAY, Charlott J.	49y	W	N.Y.	16 MAY 1879	Glenwood
017376	RIDLEY, Jane	76y	W	Md.	11 SEP 1878	Mt. Olivet
003292	RIDOUT, Eli	3y	C	Md.	12 MAY 1875	Young Mens
004498	RIDOUT, Martha	14y	C	Md.	07 AUG 1875	Mt. Pleasant
008599	RIDWELL, Mary	18y	W	Va.	07 AUG 1876	Congressional
007147	RIEFKOGEL, Minnie	25y	W	Ger.	28 APR 1876	Prospect Hill
004871	RIELLY, Bernard	4y	W	D.C.	01 SEP 1875	Congressional
005269	RIELLY, James	25d	W	D.C.	25 OCT 1875	Mt. Olivet
012340	RIFFLE, Cecelia	2m	W	D.C.	12 JUL 1877	Mt. Olivet
007460	RIGGLES, Ellen Josephine	3m	W	Md.	01 JUN 1876	Glenwood
021178	RIGGLES, Lottie	14m	C	D.C.	31 JUL 1879	Harmony
007600	RIGGLES, Mariah Banfield	26y	W	D.C.	11 JUN 1876	Oak Hill
009311	RIGGLES, William	52y	W	D.C.	05 OCT 1876	Oak Hill
014353	RIGGLES, William Richard	5y	W	Va.	07 JAN 1878	Glenwood
001112	RIGGS, Bowswell	24y	W	France	12 OCT 1874	Oak Hill
006913	RIGGS, Elmer Curtis	6m	W	D.C.	04 APR 1876	Congressional
011758	RIGGS, George	37y	C	Md.	31 MAY 1877	Mt. Zion
007408	RIGGS, Marion Irving	2y	W	D.C.	25 MAY 1876	Glenwood
006990	RIGGS, Mary	22y	C	D.C.	11 APR 1876	Mt. Olivet
008581	RIGHTOUT, Nathan	79y	C	Md.	07 AUG 1876	Young Mens
005017a	RILATT, James	29y	W	Pa.	01 OCT 1875	Mt. Olivet
021002	RILEY, Austin	5m	W	D.C.	18 JUL 1879	Tennallytown
010443	RILEY, Carrie B.	2y	W	D.C.	29 JAN 1877	Oak Hill
017386	RILEY, Clifton	1y	W	D.C.	12 SEP 1878	Tennallytown
005084a	RILEY, Elizabeth	36y	W	D.C.	08 OCT 1875	Methodist
003020	RILEY, Elizebeth	4w	W	D.C.	17 APR 1875	Methodist Tennallytown
004905	RILEY, Emily	41y	C	Va.	04 SEP 1875	Young Mens
019810	RILEY, Fannie Ridgely	5y	W	Md.	17 APR 1879	Waterbury, Md.
016663	RILEY, Francis	64y	W	Ire.	18 JUL 1878	Mt. Olivet
005643	RILEY, Infant of J.B.	8h	W	D.C.	03 DEC 1875	Glenwood
007449	RILEY, Infant of Nicholas	2d	W	D.C.	31 MAY 1876	Mt. Olivet
007443	RILEY, Infant of Nicholas	1d	W	D.C.	30 MAY 1876	Mt. Olivet
018197	RILEY, Infant of Perry	5d	C	D.C.	29 NOV 1878	Harmony
003864	RILEY, James	3m	W	N.Y.	26 JUN 1875	Mt. Olivet
013936	RILEY, James A.	55y	W	D.C.	26 NOV 1877	Holy Rood
016038	RILEY, James W.	10m	W	D.C.	06 JUN 1878	Mt. Olivet
005057a	RILEY, Jane	33y	W	Md.	04 OCT 1875	Oak Hill
018902	RILEY, John	31y	W	Ire.	15 JAN 1879	Congressional
019154	RILEY, John Campbell	50y	W	D.C.	22 FEB 1879	Oak Hill
011766	RILEY, Joseph	c.28y	W	Md.	01 JUN 1877	Baltimore, Md.
011970	RILEY, Joseph S.	3m	W	D.C.	19 JUN 1877	Glenwood
002122	RILEY, Joshua	75y	W	Md.	11 FEB 1875	Oak Hill
008360	RILEY, Larry	43y	W	Ire.	20 JUL 1876	Mt. Olivet
009288	RILEY, Liddie	c.50y	C	Md.	03 OCT 1876	Mt. Zion
014391	RILEY, Lucy	16y	C	Va.	11 JAN 1878	Harmony
013998	RILEY, Margaret	5y	W	D.C.	03 DEC 1877	Holy Rood
019856	RILEY, Margaret	48y	W	D.C.	21 APR 1879	Mt. Olivet
014677	RILEY, Mary	45y	M	Va.	05 FEB 1878	Young Mens
014150	RILEY, Michael	33y	W	Ire.	20 DEC 1877	Soldier's Home
018901	RILEY, osemary	5m	W	D.C.	31 JAN 1879	Mt. Olivet
006574	RILEY, Patrick	39y	W	Ire.	06 MAR 1876	Hospital
008707	RILEY, Richard	24y	W	Ire.	16 AUG 1876	Hospital
001600	RILEY, T.W.	34y	W	D.C.	03 JAN 1875	Congressional
015624	RILEY, William	7m	C	D.C.	05 MAY 1878	Baptist
005921	RIMM, Ethelbert	84y	W	Ger.	02 JAN 1876	Soldier's Home
000040	RIND, James M.	32	W	D.C.	03 AUG 1874	Oak Hill

No.	Name	Age	Race	Birth	Death Date	Burial Place
017741	RINER, Ursula	36y	W	Switz.	14 OCT 1878	Prospect Hill
010345	RING, Solomon	25y	C	N.C.	20 JAN 1877	Harmony
013186	RIORDAN, Francis	3y	W	D.C.	13 SEP 1877	Mt. Olivet
002128	RIORDAN, John	38y	W	Ire.	12 FEB 1875	Glenwood
020684	RIORDEN, Michael	79y	W	Va.	30 JUN 1879	Glenwood
010302	RIORDON, Florence C.	1y	W	D.C.	15 JAN 1877	Baltimore, Md.
007932	RISER, Anna Mary	6y	W	D.C.	29 JUN 1876	St. Mary's
006353	RISER, Cath.	8d	W	D.C.	14 FEB 1876	St. Mary's
019033	RISER, Julia A.	37y	W	Ger.	11 FEB 1879	St. Mary's
018344	RITCHERSON, John	32y	C	Md.	15 DEC 1878	Mt. Olivet
011371	RITCHISON, Peter	22y	W	D.C.	19 APR 1877	Addison's Chapel
003926	RITTER, Albert	4m	C	D.C.	29 JUN 1875	Holy Rood
011333	RITTER, Frederick William	79y	W	N.Y.	14 APR 1877	Congressional
011740	RITTER, Henry Powers	47y	C	Va.	29 MAY 1877	Congressional
006739	RITTER, John Rufus	25y	W	D.C.	19 MAR 1876	Congressional
008296	RITTER, Thersa M.	5m	W	D.C.	17 JUL 1876	Oak Hill
008895	RITTER, William H.	1y	C	D.C.	31 AUG 1876	Beckett's
006007	RITTERSHOEFER, Thekla Selma	27y	W	Ger.	13 JAN 1876	Glenwood
019885	RITTUE, Lida	7y	W	D.C.	24 APR 1879	Presbyterian
010971	RIVERS, Ann Eliza	86y	C	Va.	14 MAR 1877	Congressional
007328	RIVERS, Chas.	15d	C	D.C.	17 MAY 1876	Potters Field
014300	RIVERS, John T.	36y	C	Md.	02 JAN 1878	Young Mens
006936	RIVERS, Richard	1y	C	D.C.	05 APR 1876	Potters Field
001443	RIVES, Jefferson	27y	W	D.C.	20 DEC 1874	Congressional
006311	RIXEY, Mary	3m	C	D.C.	11 FEB 1876	Young Mens
017260	RIXEY, Robert	30y	C	Va.	30 AUG 1878	Harmony
013710	RIXIE, James	19y	C	Va.	02 NOV 1877	Potters Field
005578	RLLINS, Arthur	10m	C	D.C.	26 NOV 1875	Young Mens
000248	ROACH, Alfred Emory	2y	W	D.C.	19 AUG 1874	Glenwood
001817	ROACH, Catharine	63y	W	Ire.	21 JAN 1875	Mt. Olivet
008521	ROACH, Catharine	10y	W	N.Y.	02 AUG 1876	Mt. Olivet
013872	ROACH, Edward	22y	W	D.C.	20 NOV 1877	Mt. Olivet
019187	ROACH, Thomas	74y	W	Md.	24 FEB 1879	Glenwood
004684	ROACH, William	70y	W	Ire.	20 AUG 1875	Mt. Olivet
005709	ROACHE, Margaret	75y	W	Ire.	09 DEC 1875	Mt. Olivet
006923	ROACHE, Michael	70y	W	Ire.	04 APR 1876	Mt. Olivet
004205	ROADES, Abraham	9m	C	D.C.	19 JUL 1875	Young Mens
016720	ROAN, Infant of Jno.	1h	C	D.C.	22 JUL 1878	Mt. Pleasant
005330	ROAN, Lucy	10d	C	D.C.	01 NOV 1875	Young Mens
006778	ROAN, Robert	19y	C	Va.	22 MAR 1876	Young Mens
012878	ROAN, William	10m	C	D.C.	19 AUG 1877	Ebenezer
005374	Roane, John Harry	1y	W	D.C.	06 NOV 1875	Glenwood
014218	ROANE, Ella	19y	C	La.	26 DEC 1877	Harmony
008802	ROANE, Henry Eugene	1y	C	D.C.	24 AUG 1876	Harmony
007851	ROANE, Infant of Martha	6h	C	D.C.	25 JUN 1876	Ebenezer
011521	ROANE, John B.	42y	C	D.C.	05 MAY 1877	Glenwood
007850	ROANE, Martha	36y	C	D.C.	25 JUN 1876	Ebenezer
005206a	ROANE, Mary	11m	C	D.C.	19 OCT 1875	Ebenezer
005056a	ROBB, Mary E.W.	13y	W	D.C.	04 OCT 1875	Methodist
001128	ROBB, Samuel W.	23y	W	D.C.	11 NOV 1874	Methodist
010458	ROBBINS, Infant of N.A.	5d	W	D.C.	30 JAN 1877	Glenwood
009011	ROBBINS, James	80y	W	Ire.	09 SEP 1876	College
013040	ROBBINS, Jane	53y	W	Va.	31 AUG 1877	Mt. Olivet
009520	ROBBINS, Nathan Haile	45y	W	Conn.	25 OCT 1876	Congressional/Arlington
018845	ROBBINS, Theresa	32y	W	D.C.	27 JAN 1879	Holy Rood
019290	ROBBINSON, Elizabeth	8m	C	D.C.	05 MAR 1879	Young Mens

District of Columbia Death Records, August 1, 1874 to July 31, 1879   285

No.	Name	Age	Race	Birth	Death Date	Burial Place
009093	ROBERSON, Catharine	27y	C	Va.	16 SEP 1876	Harmony
019579	ROBERSON, Catherin	2y	C	Md.	28 MAR 1879	Mt. Zion
012611	ROBERT, Joseph	39y	W	France	30 JUL 1877	Mt. Olivet
001941	ROBERTS, Benjamin Stone	64y	W	Ver.	29 JAN 1875	Oak Hill
007514	ROBERTS, Eva Grinnell	1y	W	D.C.	05 JUN 1876	Glenwood
000735	ROBERTS, George	69y	W	Mass.	07 OCT 1874	Mt. Olivet
016268	ROBERTS, Katie A.	6m	W	D.C.	22 JUN 1878	Holy Rood
004870	ROBERTS, Louisa	c.33y	W	D.C.	01 SEP 1875	Glenwood
015773	ROBERTS, Mariah Ann	2y	C	D.C.	19 MAY 1878	Beckett's
010243	ROBERTS, W.H.	32y	W	D.C.	10 JAN 1877	Holy Rood
001494	ROBERTS, William J.	25y	W	Wales	26 DEC 1874	Baltimore, Md.
005117a	ROBERTSON, Charles E.	1y	W	D.C.	12 OCT 1875	Congressional
002751	ROBERTSON, Edward	99y	C	Va.	25 MAR 1875	Potters Field
000764	ROBERTSON, Eliza Ann	72y	W	Md.	09 OCT 1874	Congressional
012695	ROBERTSON, George	70y	C	Va.	06 AUG 1877	Beckett's
009580	ROBERTSON, Gilbert	9d	W	D.C.	30 OCT 1876	College
004885	ROBERTSON, Infant of Amelia	21d	C	D.C.	02 SEP 1875	Potters Field
009996	ROBERTSON, Infant of William	1m	C	D.C.	18 DEC 1876	Ebenezer
000345	ROBERTSON, James	56y	W	Va.	28 AUG 1874	Oak Hill
004817	ROBERTSON, James Edward	1y	C	D.C.	29 AUG 1875	Payne's
011987	ROBERTSON, Martha	4y	C	Va.	21 JUN 1877	Ebenezer
014436	ROBERTSON, Mary	78y	W	Va.	15 JAN 1878	Glenwood
004937	ROBERTSON, Mildred	32y	C	Va.	06 SEP 1875	Young Mens
002774	ROBERTSON, Rosie	8d	W	D.C.	28 MAR 1875	Methodist
011594	ROBERTSON, Samuel Richmond	30y	W	D.C.	14 MAY 1877	Congressional
010380	ROBERTSON, Solomon	50y	C	Va.	23 JAN 1877	Potters Field
017727	ROBERTSON, Somerville	33y	W	Md.	13 OCT 1878	Glenwood
016984	ROBERTSON, William	7y	M	D.C.	09 AUG 1878	Holy Rood
007012	ROBESON, Sarah C.	20h	C	D.C.	13 APR 1876	Harmony
004532	ROBETS, Kate G.	1y	W	D.C.	10 AUG 1875	Congressional
013001	ROBEY, Catharine	76y	W	Md.	28 AUG 1877	Congressional
010328	ROBEY, John A.	33y	W	D.C.	18 JAN 1877	Congressional
007110	ROBEY, John Thomas	22d	W	D.C.	25 APR 1876	Congressional
017580	ROBEY, Loseanna	1y	W	D.C.	30 SEP 1878	Dumfries, Va.
007111	ROBEY, Moses Wesley	22d	W	D.C.	25 APR 1876	Congressional
021152	ROBEY, Richard R.	11m	W	D.C.	29 JUL 1879	Congressional
021014	ROBEY, Winfield Scott	31y	W	D.C.	19 JUL 1879	Congressional
014392	ROBINSON, Albert M., Jr.	18d	W	D.C.	11 JAN 1878	Congressional
016195	ROBINSON, Ambrose	1y	C	D.C.	16 JUN 1878	Beckett's
008291	ROBINSON, Andora	1m	M	D.C.	16 JUL 1876	Potters Field
020815	ROBINSON, Anna	40y	C	Md.	07 JUL 1879	Young Mens
020014	ROBINSON, Anna S.	36y	W	Md.	06 MAY 1879	Oak Hill
006070	ROBINSON, Annie, of Charles Baum	8y	C	D.C.	19 JAN 1876	Potters Field
014068	ROBINSON, Arthur Nicholson	6m	C	D.C.	11 DEC 1877	Graceland
011139	ROBINSON, Ashley	27y	C	Fla.	28 MAR 1877	Harmony
017206	ROBINSON, Augusta M.	56y	W	Va.	26 AUG 1878	Congressional
015015	ROBINSON, Benjamin	18y	C	Va.	10 MAR 1878	Beckett's
004246	ROBINSON, Bettie	74y	C	Va.	22 JUL 1875	Potters Field
009392	ROBINSON, Beverly	80y	C	Va.	12 OCT 1876	Potters Field
014393	ROBINSON, Cara	2y	M	D.C.	11 JAN 1878	Payne's
017173	ROBINSON, Charlotte	22y	C	Va.	24 AUG 1878	Fairfax Co., Va.
005198	ROBINSON, Chas.	4m	C	D.C.	27 SEP 1875	Potters Field
003927	ROBINSON, Christianna V.	44y	W	Va.	29 JUN 1875	Congressional
005430	ROBINSON, Daniel	26y	C	Md.	11 NOV 1875	Payne's
000388	ROBINSON, Edward	7d	C	D.C.	31 AUG 1874	Mt. Pleasant
017508	ROBINSON, Edward	1y	C	D.C.	23 SEP 1878	Young Mens

District of Columbia Death Records, August 1, 1874 to July 31, 1879

No.	Name	Age	Race	Birth	Death Date	Burial Place
019403	ROBINSON, Edward	12m	C	D.C.	14 MAR 1879	Mt. Pleasant
016983	ROBINSON, Elijah	6m	C	D.C.	09 AUG 1878	Payne's
012213	ROBINSON, Eliza	35y	C	Va.	04 JUL 1877	Potters Field
005277	ROBINSON, Eliza M.	6y	W	D.C.	27 OCT 1875	Beckett's
009408	ROBINSON, Elizabeth	40y	W	Md.	14 OCT 1876	Potters Field
012937	ROBINSON, Ethan	1y	C	D.C.	24 AUG 1877	Brightwood
012968	ROBINSON, Etta	1y	W	D.C.	26 AUG 1877	Oak Hill
018529	ROBINSON, Feilding	29y	C	Va.	31 DEC 1878	Young Mens
019492	ROBINSON, Florence Elizabeth	8m	C	D.C.	21 MAR 1879	Young Mens
004469	ROBINSON, George	1y	C	D.C.	05 AUG 1875	Young Mens
015898	ROBINSON, Georgietta	3m	C	D.C.	29 MAY 1878	Beckett's
015522	ROBINSON, Gertrude	9m	C	D.C.	26 APR 1878	Young Mens
017401	ROBINSON, Grandison	52y	C	Va.	13 SEP 1878	Mt. Pleasant
007485	ROBINSON, Harriet	41y	C	Va.	03 JUN 1876	Young Mens
014394	ROBINSON, Harry James	48y	W	Eng.	11 JAN 1878	Rochester, N.Y.
002953	ROBINSON, Henry	1m	W	D.C.	11 APR 1875	Mt. Olivet
008347	ROBINSON, Henry Jerome	11m	W	D.C.	20 JUL 1876	Mt. Olivet
000484	ROBINSON, Ida	2m	C	D.C.	12 SEP 1874	Young Mens
009969	ROBINSON, Ida	56m	C	D.C.	15 DEC 1876	Ebenezer
013468	ROBINSON, Infant of Alfred	4m	C	D.C.	10 OCT 1877	Beckett's
020602	ROBINSON, Infant of Amelia	4m	C	D.C.	24 JUN 1879	Jones Chapel
013750	ROBINSON, Infant of Burnett	3d	C	D.C.	06 NOV 1877	Beckett's
001561	ROBINSON, Infant of J.H.	2m	C	D.C.	01 JAN 1875	Harmony
002554	ROBINSON, Infant of Julia	14d	M	D.C.	13 MAR 1875	Mt. Pleasant
016963	ROBINSON, Infant of Peter	7d	C	D.C.	08 AUG 1878	Beckett's
014138	ROBINSON, Infant of William	8d	C	D.C.	19 DEC 1877	Potters Field
010985	ROBINSON, Isaac F.	9d	C	D.C.	15 MAR 1877	Beckett's
000570	ROBINSON, James	24y	C	Va.	19 SEP 1874	Beckett's
002954	ROBINSON, James	29y	C	S.C.	11 APR 1875	Potters Field
007059	ROBINSON, James	6y	C	Va.	20 APR 1876	Young Mens
006127	ROBINSON, James	70y	C	Va.	24 JAN 1876	Ebenezer
011188	ROBINSON, James	56y	C	Va.	01 APR 1877	Ebenezer
020703	ROBINSON, James Thomas	3m	C	D.C.	01 JUL 1879	Young Mens
001383	ROBINSON, Jane	87y	C	Va.	14 DEC 1874	Mt. Olivet
009559	ROBINSON, Jane	60y	C	Va.	28 OCT 1876	Mt. Pleasant
005899	ROBINSON, John	27y	M	Va.	30 DEC 1875	Mt. Olivet
004087	ROBINSON, John	1m	W	D.C.	11 JUL 1875	Congressional
009387	ROBINSON, John	90y	C	Va.	12 OCT 1876	Beckett's
010583	ROBINSON, John	40y	C	Va.	11 FEB 1877	Ebenezer
001577	ROBINSON, John Gavin, Jr.	39y	W	D.C.	02 JAN 1875	Congressional
006200	ROBINSON, John Gavin	78y	W	Md.	31 JAN 1876	Congressional
006300	ROBINSON, Jordan	35y	C	Va.	10 FEB 1876	Young Mens
016710	ROBINSON, Julius	1y	C	D.C.	21 JUL 1878	Beckett's
005862	ROBINSON, Kate Isabel	17y	W	N.Y.	25 DEC 1875	Brooklyn, N.Y.
004919	ROBINSON, Laura W.	22y	C	D.C.	05 SEP 1875	Mt. Pleasant
008691	ROBINSON, Leuisia	56y	C	Va.	15 AUG 1876	Ebenezer
005708	ROBINSON, Lucinda	9d	C	D.C.	09 DEC 1875	Ebenezer
010895	ROBINSON, Margaret	29y	W	D.C.	07 MAR 1877	Potters Field
005300	ROBINSON, Maria	7d	C	D.C.	29 OCT 1875	Ebenezer
011609	ROBINSON, Maria	5m	W	D.C.	16 MAY 1877	Congressional
021054	ROBINSON, Maria	57y	C	Va.	22 JUL 1879	Graceland
008928	ROBINSON, Mariah	32y	C	Va.	02 SEP 1876	Harmony
001333	ROBINSON, Martha	60y	C	Va.	07 DEC 1874	Potters Field
011211	ROBINSON, Martha	7y	C	D.C.	04 APR 1877	Ebenezer
002041	ROBINSON, Mary	4m	C	D.C.	05 FEB 1875	Young Mens
018817	ROBINSON, Mary	8y	W	D.C.	25 JAN 1879	Congressional

District of Columbia Death Records, August 1, 1874 to July 31, 1879

No.	Name	Age	Race	Birth	Death Date	Burial Place
008188	ROBINSON, Mary A.R.	11m	C	D.C.	11 JUL 1876	Mt. Zion
001773	ROBINSON, Mary Ann Eliz.	6y	W	D.C.	18 JAN 1875	Congressional
017532	ROBINSON, Mary C.	24y	W	D.C.	25 SEP 1878	Congressional
002222	ROBINSON, Mary Isabella	65y	W	Va.	18 FEB 1875	Congressional
004079	ROBINSON, Mary Jane	2y	C	D.C.	10 JUL 1875	Macedonia
020540	ROBINSON, Mary Ruth	19m	C	D.C.	20 JUN 1879	Young Mens
000065	ROBINSON, Maud Celest	13y	C	D.C.	05 AUG 1874	Mt. Pleasant
018479	ROBINSON, Maude	14y	W	D.C.	27 DEC 1878	Oak Hill
014108	ROBINSON, Mollie	11m	C	D.C.	15 DEC 1877	Potters Field
011499	ROBINSON, Moses W.	c.32y	C	Va.	03 MAY 1877	Young Mens
004432	ROBINSON, Nancy	45y	C	Va.	03 AUG 1875	Beckett's
018530	ROBINSON, Natan	7y	C	D.C.	31 DEC 1878	Potters Field
020945	ROBINSON, Nina	3w	C	D.C.	15 JUL 1879	Beckett's
004531	ROBINSON, Peter	19y	M	Va.	10 AUG 1875	Potters Field
012094	ROBINSON, Peter	6m	C	D.C.	27 JUN 1877	Ebenezer
002733	ROBINSON, Peter B.	77y	W	Va.	25 MAR 1875	Congressional
002065	ROBINSON, Pricella	c.45y	C	Va.	07 FEB 1875	Baptist Church Potomac
005035	ROBINSON, Rebecca	2y	C	D.C.	13 SEP 1875	Young Mens
008729	ROBINSON, Robert	2m	C	D.C.	19 AUG 1876	Young Mens
003941	ROBINSON, Roberta	21d	M	D.C.	30 JUN 1875	Mt. Pleasant
005158	ROBINSON, Roberta	2m	C	D.C.	24 SEP 1875	Ebenezer
007911	ROBINSON, Rose	5m	C	D.C.	28 JUN 1876	Ebenezer
003234	ROBINSON, Rose A.	2y	C	D.C.	05 MAY 1875	Harmony
008430	ROBINSON, Rose Lee	3y	C	D.C.	26 JUL 1876	Baptist
000605	ROBINSON, Sarah	45y	C	Va.	22 SEP 1874	Mt. Pleasant
017726	ROBINSON, Sonny	6y	C	Md.	13 OCT 1878	Beckett's
006008	ROBINSON, Sophia	3y	C	D.C.	13 JAN 1876	Potters Field
009124	ROBINSON, Spencer	95y	C	Va.	18 SEP 1876	Mt. Pleasant
007179	ROBINSON, Thomas	75y	C	Va.	01 MAY 1876	Mt. Zion
010674	ROBINSON, Thomas H.	45y	W	Md.	17 FEB 1877	Congressional
018795	ROBINSON, Valentine S.	9m	W	D.C.	24 JAN 1879	Congressional
021069	ROBINSON, W.J.E.	8m	C	D.C.	23 JUL 1879	Beckett's
014151	ROBINSON, Walter	1y	C	D.C.	20 DEC 1877	Young Mens
007633	ROBINSON, William	1y	C	D.C.	13 JUN 1876	Mt. Pleasant
017001	ROBINSON, William	65y	W	Eng.	10 AUG 1878	Mt. Olivet
020253	ROBINSON, William	18y	C	Va.	01 JUN 1879	Brightwood
018359	ROBINSON, William Henry	49y	C	Va.	16 DEC 1878	Harmony
017431	ROBINSON, William Henry	11d	C	D.C.	16 SEP 1878	Mt. Pleasant
005967	ROBINSON, Willis	1y	M	D.C.	07 JAN 1876	Young Mens
003477	ROBINSON, [Sarah]	11m	C	D.C.	29 MAY 1875	Ebenezer
007158	ROBIRON, Tennley Johnson	5y	C	D.C.	29 APR 1876	Harmony
010097	ROBISON, Birty	2y	C	D.C.	28 DEC 1876	Ebenezer
006970	ROBISON, Mary	73y	W	Va.	08 APR 1876	Oak Hill
014994	ROBSON, Henry	30y	C	Ky.	08 MAR 1878	Mt. Olivet
001050	ROBSON, Mary	3y	C	Md.	04 NOV 1874	Potters Field
015118	ROBY, Dorcett	c.67y	W	Md.	18 MAR 1878	Congressional
006022	ROBY, Elizabeth	79y	W	Va.	14 JAN 1876	Rock Creek
010382	ROBY, Elizabeth L.	18y	W	D.C.	23 JAN 1877	Congressional
005685	ROCHE, Catherine Teresa	49y	W	Ire.	07 DEC 1875	Mt. Olivet
016208	ROCHE, David	51y	W	Ire.	17 JUN 1878	Mt. Olivet
011676	ROCHE, Mary A.	54y	W	Mo.	22 MAY 1877	Oak Hill
011578	ROCHE, Mary C.	34y	W	D.C.	13 MAY 1877	Holy Rood
000435f	ROCHE, Mary, Mrs.	69y	--	Ire.	05 SEP 1874	Mt. Olivet
009058	ROCHE, Wm.	62y	W	Ire.	13 SEP 1876	Mt. Olivet
005598	ROCHEM, George	2y	W	D.C.	28 NOV 1875	Mt. Olivet
000670	ROCK, Cath.	3y	W	Ger.	29 SEP 1874	Prospect Hill

No.	Name	Age	Race	Birth	Death Date	Burial Place
008339	ROCK, Ernest Osborne	5m	W	D.C.	19 JUL 1876	Oak Hill
006137	ROCKEY, Mary	31y	W	Ger.	25 JAN 1876	Presbyterian
017676	ROCKEY, Sadie	1y	W	D.C.	08 OCT 1878	Presbyterian
017997	ROCKS, Amelia	45y	C	Va.	09 NOV 1878	Young Mens
004281f	ROCOFORD, John	6m	W	D.C.	24 JUL 1875	Holy Rood
008052	RODDERICK, Nellie	9m	W	D.C.	06 JUL 1876	Mt. Olivet
004468	RODENBURG, Henry	51y	W	Ger.	05 AUG 1875	Graceland
011999	RODERICK, Ugona H.	5m	W	D.C.	21 JUN 1877	Harper's Ferry, Va.
019946	RODGERS, Alfred, Lt. U.S.A.	31y	W	La.	30 APR 1879	Cincinnati, Ohio
006899	RODGERS, Amelia	53y	W	N.J.	02 APR 1876	Congressional
009106	RODGERS, Ellen	58y	W	Va.	17 SEP 1876	Aquia Creek, Va.
016879	RODGERS, Harriet	8d	C	D.C.	02 AUG 1878	Baptist, First
017432	RODGERS, James A.	11m	C	D.C.	16 SEP 1878	Harmony
019791	RODGERS, Julia A.	59y	C	Va.	15 APR 1879	Harmony
016915	RODGERS, Mary	3y	C	D.C.	05 AUG 1878	Mt. Olivet
008930	RODGERS, Rose	6d	C	D.C.	02 SEP 1876	Beckett's
017014	RODGERS, Samuel	28y	C	N.Y.	11 AUG 1878	Beckett's
013026	RODIER, Mary Francis	43y	W	D.C.	30 AUG 1877	Holy Rood
018927	RODNEY, William	73y	W	Del.	02 FEB 1879	Congressional
020796	RODRICK, Eva Julia	2m	W	D.C.	06 JUL 1879	Harpers Ferry, W.Va.
002198	ROE, Beverly Webb	5d	W	D.C.	17 FEB 1875	Jenkins' Farm
019688	ROE, Catharine E.	31y	W	Can.	07 APR 1879	Congressional
019254	ROELKER, Alfred P.	2y	W	D.C.	02 MAR 1879	Oak Hill
005171a	ROERS, Daisy	8m	C	D.C.	16 OCT 1875	Ebenezer
001334	ROESE, Annie	30y	W	Md.	07 DEC 1874	Prospect Hill
020060	ROGERS, Annie	60y	C	D.C.	10 MAY 1879	Mt. Pleasant
004552	ROGERS, Augustus	5m	W	D.C.	11 AUG 1875	Congressional
002320	ROGERS, Celia	4m	C	D.C.	25 FEB 1875	Ebenezer
012049	ROGERS, Frank	11m	W	D.C.	25 JUN 1877	Congressional
010367	ROGERS, James E.	28y	W	Va.	21 JAN 1877	Leesburg, Va.
015538	ROGERS, John	32y	W	Eng.	27 APR 1878	Mt. Olivet
007925	ROGERS, John J.	6m	W	D.C.	29 JUN 1876	Congressional
007751	ROGERS, Julia Ann	43y	W	Scot.	20 JUN 1876	Mt. Olivet
012462	ROGERS, Maggie E.R.	1y	W	D.C.	22 JUL 1877	Congressional
007729	ROGERS, Thomas S.	5m	W	D.C.	19 JUN 1876	Glenwood
003001	ROGERS, Timothy	58y	C	S.C.	15 APR 1875	Harmony
008469	ROGINSKI, Elijah P.	8d	W	D.C.	29 JUL 1876	Jewish
013734	ROHR, Frederick G.	45y	W	Ger.	04 NOV 1877	Prospect Hill
005073a	ROHRER, John E.	33y	W	Md.	06 OCT 1875	Oak Hill
005118a	ROHRER, Mary	20y	W	Ger.	12 OCT 1875	Prospect Hill
004669	ROLA, William Edward	10m	C	D.C.	19 AUG 1875	Ebenezer
001444	ROLAN, Martha Ellen	4y	W	D.C.	20 DEC 1874	Congressional
012249	ROLAND, George W.	1y	W	D.C.	07 JUL 1877	Congressional
020816	ROLAND, James A.	1m	W	D.C.	07 JUL 1879	Broad Creek Church
018358	ROLAND, James Herbert	6y	W	D.C.	16 DEC 1878	Congressional
017219	ROLLENS, John	60y	W	D.C.	27 AUG 1878	Rock Creek
013735	ROLLER, Emily Rosina	4y	W	D.C.	04 NOV 1877	Glenwood
010129	ROLLER, William	60y	W	Va.	31 DEC 1876	Potters Field
007765	ROLLINGS, Fannie Louise	c.21m	W	D.C.	21 JUN 1876	Oak Hill
020061	ROLLINGS, Washington	48y	W	D.C.	10 MAY 1879	Glenwood
013330	ROLLINS, Albert Eugene	2m	C	D.C.	27 SEP 1877	Potters Field
005543	ROLLINS, Charles J.	1y	W	D.C.	23 NOV 1875	Congressional
000563	ROLLINS, Infant of James	20h	C	D.C.	19 SEP 1874	Mt. Pleasant Plain
009703	ROLLINS, Lewis	23y	C	Va.	15 NOV 1876	Potters Field
018602	ROLLINS, Margaret	47y	C	Va.	07 JAN 1879	Harmony
010653	ROLLINS, Martha Ann	52y	W	D.C.	16 FEB 1877	Glenwood

District of Columbia Death Records, August 1, 1874 to July 31, 1879					289

No.	Name	Age	Race	Birth	Death Date	Burial Place
018886	ROLLINS, Mary Francis	1y	W	D.C.	30 JAN 1879	Methodist
012877	ROLLINS, Peter	1y	C	D.C.	19 AUG 1877	Beckett's
006208	ROLLINS, Philip	c.40y	C	Va.	01 FEB 1876	Young Mens
002157	ROLLINS, Richard	1y	C	D.C.	14 FEB 1875	Ebenezer
013454	ROLLINS, Sarah	34y	C	Md.	09 OCT 1877	Potters Field
000310	ROLLINS, Stephen	59y	W	Va.	25 AUG 1874	Washington Asylum
006488	ROLLINS, William G.	1m	C	D.C.	27 FEB 1876	Young Mens
014689	ROLLS, John William	4y	C	D.C.	06 FEB 1878	Payne's
000623	RONEY, George W.	21y	W	D.C.	24 SEP 1874	Presbyterian
010369	ROOM, Wm. Edward	4m	W	D.C.	22 JAN 1877	Jersey City
014575	ROOME, Samuel Seabury	36y	W	N.Y.	27 JAN 1878	Brooklyn, N.Y.
016180	ROONEY, Eugene	21y	W	Md.	15 JUN 1878	Mt. Olivet
006769	ROONEY, Mitchell	29y	W	Pa.	21 MAR 1876	Congressional
006089	ROOSA, Charles	7y	W	D.C.	21 JAN 1876	Mt. Olivet
004436f	ROOSE, Frank	2m	W	D.C.	10 AUG 1875	Glenwood
018426	ROOTS, Hayes	1y	C	D.C.	22 DEC 1878	Potters Field
000880	ROPE, William	1m	W	D.C.	21 OCT 1874	Prospect Hill
005134a	RORDOUT, Ann	34y	C	Va.	13 OCT 1875	Young Mens
008898	ROSA, Catherine	66y	C	Va.	31 AUG 1876	Potters Field
016010	ROSE, August	9y	W	D.C.	04 JUN 1878	Prospect Hill
009118	ROSE, Cassey A.	3y	C	D.C.	18 SEP 1876	Ebenezer
011506	ROSE, Frank Obed	9m	W	D.C.	04 MAY 1877	Mt. Olivet/Congressional
010330	ROSE, George	2m	W	D.C.	18 JAN 1877	Prospect Hill
005653	ROSE, Mary	14y	C	Md.	04 DEC 1875	Potters Field
006618	ROSE, William	2y	W	D.C.	09 MAR 1876	Prospect Hill
000105	ROSE, Willie R.	11m	W	D.C.	08 AUG 1874	Congressional
020762	ROSENKRANTZ, Anna M.	1y	C	D.C.	04 JUL 1879	Mt. Olivet
020661	ROSENTHOL, Jacob W.	9m	W	D.C.	28 JUN 1879	Washington Hebrew
003928	ROSHORE, George Bailey	3m	W	D.C.	29 JUN 1875	Mt. Olivet
015309	ROSIER, Nathan	78y	C	Md.	07 APR 1878	Graceland
005801	ROSS, Alberta	8m	C	D.C.	19 DEC 1875	Potters Field
005094	ROSS, Ann	48y	C	Va.	18 SEP 1875	Mt. Pleasant Plain
012221	ROSS, Belle M.	7m	W	D.C.	04 JUL 1877	Prospect Hill
006217	ROSS, Betsey	85y	C	Va.	02 FEB 1876	Beckett's
018748	ROSS, Charles	20y	C	Md.	20 JAN 1879	Potters Field
007886	ROSS, Dacy	1y	W	D.C.	27 JUN 1876	Prospect Hill
000280	ROSS, David	26y	C	Md.	22 AUG 1874	Potters Field
020131	ROSS, Elisabeth Ann	45y	W	Va.	17 MAY 1879	Congressional
018900	ROSS, Emma Teney	33y	W	N.H.	31 JAN 1879	Oak Hill/Manchester, N.H.
012798	ROSS, Eva Mullinaux	1y	W	D.C.	14 AUG 1877	Congressional
002829	ROSS, Frank	1y	M	Va.	01 APR 1875	Mt. Pleasant
000579	ROSS, George	60y	C	Md.	20 SEP 1874	Mt. Olivet
002103	ROSS, George	80y	C	Md.	09 FEB 1875	Ebenezer
004615	ROSS, Harriet	40y	C	Md.	15 AUG 1875	Harmony
008085	ROSS, Harry	1y	C	D.C.	08 JUL 1876	Young Mens
020603	ROSS, Hellenna	11m	C	D.C.	24 JUN 1879	Payne's
015975	ROSS, Infant of H.E.	7d	C	D.C.	02 JUN 1878	Harmony
001950	ROSS, Infant of Henry	13d	W	D.C.	30 JAN 1875	Prospect Hill
015412	ROSS, Infant of John	1m	C	D.C.	15 APR 1878	Potters Field
018490	ROSS, Infant of Thomas	36h	C	D.C.	28 DEC 1878	Beckett's
010929	ROSS, Infant of William	9d	C	D.C.	09 MAR 1877	Potters Field
016364	ROSS, James	37y	C	D.C.	29 JUN 1878	Hospital
014030	ROSS, Jane	2y	C	D.C.	07 DEC 1877	Harmony
008670	ROSS, Jesse	20y	C	U.S.	13 AUG 1876	Potters Field
010525	ROSS, John B.	8y	C	D.C.	05 FEB 1877	Harmony
010524	ROSS, Laura	6m	C	D.C.	05 FEB 1877	Beckett's

No.	Name	Age	Race	Birth	Death Date	Burial Place
003035	ROSS, Lucy	75y	C	Va.	18 APR 1875	Washington Asylum
007090	ROSS, Malinda V.	13m	C	D.C.	23 APR 1876	Harmony
014173	ROSS, Maria	16y	M	D.C.	22 DEC 1877	Harmony
017542	ROSS, Mary A.	33y	W	Md.	26 SEP 1878	Rock Creek
004568	ROSS, Mary C.	11y	C	D.C.	12 AUG 1875	Harmony
015686	ROSS, Nettie	9m	C	D.C.	11 MAY 1878	Potters Field
008671	ROSS, Sarah	2y	C	D.C.	13 AUG 1876	Mt. Olivet
017557	ROSS, Susan	45y	C	Va.	28 SEP 1878	Beckett's
000798	ROSS, Thadeus A. Alexander	1y	C	D.C.	13 OCT 1874	Young Mens
015227	ROSS, Theo.	44y	C	D.C.	29 MAR 1878	Harmony
007256	ROSS, Thomas	4y	C	D.C.	09 MAY 1876	Young Mens
014498	ROSS, Thomas	2m	C	D.C.	20 JAN 1878	Beckett's
005523	ROSS, Thomas Fenwell	1y	C	D.C.	20 NOV 1875	Ebenezer
015260	ROSS, William	70y	C	Va.	01 APR 1878	Potters Field
002685	ROSS, William S.	62y	W	N.J.	22 MAR 1875	Oak Hill
008996	ROSSI, Albert	1y	M	D.C.	07 SEP 1876	Potters Field
016009	ROTH, Florence H.	19y	W	Pa.	04 JUN 1878	Marietta, Pa.
019956	ROTH, Frances	8y	W	D.C.	01 MAY 1879	St. Mary's
009859	ROTH, Infant of Conrad	4h	W	D.C.	03 DEC 1876	Prospect Hill
020737	ROTH, Leonard	11m	W	D.C.	03 JUL 1879	Prospect Hill
001273	ROTHBURG, Infant of Abraham	10d	C	D.C.	30 NOV 1874	Potters Field
010541	ROTHMUND, Sarah	44y	W	Md.	06 FEB 1877	Prospect Hill
015269	ROTHSTEIN, Anna Elizabeth	8m	W	D.C.	02 APR 1878	Prospect Hill
010991	ROTHWELL, Annie	4m	W	D.C.	15 MAR 1877	Congressional
006395	ROUDEBUSH, Infant of C.M.	6d	W	D.C.	17 FEB 1876	Covington, Ky.
006301	ROUDEBUSH, Infant of M.	4h	W	D.C.	10 FEB 1876	Glenwood
007849	ROUNDS, Frank	40y	C	D.C.	25 JUN 1876	Potters Field
015431	ROUNDS, James	74y	C	D.C.	17 APR 1878	Potters Field
002893	ROUSE, William	45y	C	Va.	06 APR 1875	Washington Asylum
016479	ROUSSEAU, Edward B.	2y	W	D.C.	06 JUL 1878	Mt. Olivet
013343	ROUTENBERG, William F.	37y	W	Ger.	28 SEP 1877	Oak Hill
012092	ROUZER, Lilly May	7m	W	D.C.	27 JUN 1877	Cong./Rock Creek
013603	ROVER, John W., Rev., S.J.	32y	W	D.C.	23 OCT 1877	College, Georgetown
020731	ROWANS, Julia	6m	W	D.C.	03 JUL 1879	Mt. Olivet
005652	ROWE, A. Ellen	3	W	D.C.	04 DEC 1875	Glenwood
020571	ROWE, Blanche D.	11m	W	D.C.	22 JUN 1879	Congressional
012955	ROWE, Francis	13y	W	D.C.	25 AUG 1877	Mt. Olivet
014242	ROWE, John L.	16y	W	D.C.	28 DEC 1877	Mt. Olivet
000471	ROWE, L. Wood, Mrs.	54y	C	Md.	10 SEP 1874	Beckett's
017616	ROWE, William	8y	W	Va.	03 OCT 1878	Potters Field
002895	ROWELLE, Robert	19d	W	D.C.	06 APR 1875	Congressional
018916	ROWEN, James F.	7d	C	D.C.	01 FEB 1879	Westmoreland Co., Va.
013856	ROWLES, Gracie	7m	W	D.C.	18 NOV 1877	Presbyterian
015881	ROWLEY, Georgiana Augusta	44y	W	Ohio	28 MAY 1878	Oak Hill
006394	ROWLS, William H.	1y	W	D.C.	17 FEB 1876	Rock Creek
005682	ROWSEE, Willie	1m	W	D.C.	07 DEC 1875	Mt. Zion
020507	ROWSER, Gertrude	1m	C	D.C.	18 JUN 1879	Mt. Pleasant
002240	ROWSIE, Mary E.	3m	C	D.C.	19 FEB 1875	Mt. Zion
019248	ROWZEE, Martin Luther	10m	W	D.C.	02 MAR 1879	Glenwood/Graceland
002437	ROWZER, Daniel	56y	C	Va.	05 MAR 1875	Washington Asylum
000509	ROY, Agnes	62y	W	Md.	14 SEP 1874	Baltimore, Md.
016350	ROY, Alexander	78y	W	Md.	28 JUN 1878	Oak Hill
005072a	ROY, Charles Clifton Brown	2m	C	D.C.	06 OCT 1875	Mt. Pleasant
003393f	ROY, James	33y	C	Va.	19 MAY 1875	Potters Field
019050	ROY, John	1y	C	D.C.	12 FEB 1879	Beckett's
015444	ROY, John H.	6m	C	D.C.	18 APR 1878	Beckett's

District of Columbia Death Records, August 1, 1874 to July 31, 1879   291

No.	Name	Age	Race	Birth	Death Date	Burial Place
013203	ROY, Mary M.	1y	C	D.C.	14 SEP 1877	Beckett's
018408	ROY, Thornton	19y	C	Md.	20 DEC 1878	Mt. Pleasant
005920	ROYCE, Albert Willis	1y	W	D.C.	02 JAN 1876	Glenwood
008444	ROYCE, Helen	2m	W	D.C.	27 JUL 1876	Congressional
002581	ROYSTER, Lucian P.	17y	W	Va.	15 MAR 1875	Richmond, Va.
015781	ROZIER, Hannibal	22y	C	D.C.	20 MAY 1878	Mt. Olivet
002654	ROZZELL, Edmund James	14y	W	D.C.	20 MAR 1875	Glenwood
007435	RUBINCAM, Mary A.	c.45y	W	Pa.	29 MAY 1876	Philadelphia, Pa.
017379	RUCKDASCHEL, Mary	18d	W	D.C.	12 SEP 1878	Prospect Hill
007390	RUCKEL, Joseph S.	56y	W	N.Y.	23 MAY 1876	N.Y.
003416	RUCKER, Manda	6y	C	Va.	23 MAY 1875	Young Mens
003158	RUCKER, Mary	3y	C	D.C.	28 APR 1875	Young Mens
017085	RUDD, B.F.	3y	W	Va.	17 AUG 1878	Alexandria, Va.
000645	RUDD, Edward B.	1y	C	D.C.	26 SEP 1874	Harmony
019626	RUDD, Fannie Mary	1y	W	D.C.	01 APR 1879	Alexandria, Va.
006673	RUDD, Infant of Theodore M.	2d	W	D.C.	14 MAR 1876	Alexandria, Va.
014499	RUDD, Katie	3y	C	D.C.	20 JAN 1878	Young Mens
000146	RUDY, Infant	6d	W	D.C.	11 AUG 1874	Mt. Olivet
000695	RUE, Edward	10m	W	D.C.	02 OCT 1874	Congressional
005349	RUE, Infant of M.F.	2h	W	D.C.	03 NOV 1875	Congressional
000723	RUESS, Anita	4m	W	D.C.	05 OCT 1874	Prospect Hill
020617	RUFF, Hrary	1y	W	D.C.	25 JUN 1879	Mt. Olivet
007887	RUFFIN, Benjamin	1m	C	D.C.	27 JUN 1876	Holy Rood
009071	RUFFIN, Infant of Henry	6d	C	D.C.	14 SEP 1876	Young Mens
015353	RUFFIN, Willie	14y	W	D.C.	10 APR 1878	Beckett's
013781	RULLMAN, Frederick W.	1m	W	D.C.	09 NOV 1877	Baltimore, Md.
019408	RUMBY, Cora Lee	2y	C	Va.	15 MAR 1879	Potters Field
000872	RUMMER, Francisca	60y	W	Ger.	20 OCT 1874	St. Mary's
000959	RUMSEY, James G.	67y	W	Ver.	28 OCT 1874	N.Y. City
004034	RUMSEY, Mary	c.45y	W	Va.	07 JUL 1875	Glenwood
013549	RUNDELL, James	60y	W	Va.	17 OCT 1877	Potters Field
016696	RUOTT, George	23y	W	Ohio	20 JUL 1878	Soldier's Home
004233	RUPP, Albert	40y	W	Ger.	21 JUL 1875	Prospect Hill
017617	RUPP, H. Frederick	67y	W	Ger.	03 OCT 1878	Prospect Hill
003575	RUPP, Mary	10m	W	D.C.	08 JUN 1875	Prospect Hill
005170	RUPPEL, John Adam	1m	W	D.C.	25 SEP 1875	St. Mary's
016351	RUPPEL, William	4m	W	D.C.	28 JUN 1878	St. Mary's
019216	RUPPERT, Elizebeth	4y	W	D.C.	26 FEB 1879	Mt. Olivet
019188	RUPPERT, Frederick William	1y	W	D.C.	24 FEB 1879	St. Mary's
018888	RUPPERT, Mary Elizabeth	40y	W	Ger.	30 JAN 1879	St. Mary's
018130	RUSH, Annie	27y	W	D.C.	23 NOV 1878	Methodist
011683	RUSH, Ellen Rebecca	2y	C	D.C.	23 MAY 1877	Beckett's
017026	RUSH, George W.	4y	W	D.C.	12 AUG 1878	Glenwood
017543	RUSH, Noble	12y	W	D.C.	26 SEP 1878	Methodist
010708	RUSH, Oscar	18m	W	D.C.	20 FEB 1877	Glenwood
017400	RUSH, T.E.	9m	W	D.C.	13 SEP 1878	Glenwood
007976	RUSS, Benton	2m	W	D.C.	03 JUL 1876	Congressional
003228	RUSS, John Thomas	3y	C	Va.	05 MAY 1875	Mt. Olivet
004245	RUSSEL, Infant of Ms.	c.4m	W	D.C.	22 JUL 1875	Graceland
015068	RUSSEL, William	67y	C	Va.	14 MAR 1878	Beckett's
005286	RUSSELL, Eliza J.	c.67y	W	Va.	27 OCT 1875	Warrenton, Va.
000107	RUSSELL, Emeline	95y	C	Md.	08 AUG 1874	Harmony
004530	RUSSELL, Hallie	2y	C	D.C.	10 AUG 1875	Potters Field
010886	RUSSELL, Hattie	9d	C	D.C.	06 MAR 1877	Potters Field
005085	RUSSELL, Infant of Joseph	24h	W	D.C.	17 SEP 1875	Potters Field
007157	RUSSELL, J. Chas.	1h	W	D.C.	29 APR 1876	Mt. Olivet

No.	Name	Age	Race	Birth	Death Date	Burial Place
006275	RUSSELL, Janet, Mrs.	71y	W	Md.	08 FEB 1876	Congressional
010055	RUSSELL, Malinda	86y	C	Md.	24 DEC 1876	Young Mens
007471	RUSSELL, Mary	50-60y	C	Md.	02 JUN 1876	Hospital
001461	RUSSELL, Mary Elizabeth	7m	C	D.C.	22 DEC 1874	Young Mens
006840	RUSSELL, Randolph	9m	W	Md.	27 MAR 1876	Mt. Olivet
000138	RUSSELL, Robert J.	34y	W	Can.	11 AUG 1874	Glenwood
019900	RUSSELL, Thomas F.	13y	W	Iowa	25 APR 1879	Mt. Olivet
012911	RUSSELL, Thornton	49y	C	Va.	21 AUG 1877	Harmony
017321	RUSSELL, William	55y	W	Md.	04 SEP 1878	Congressional
004670	RUSSELL, Wm. C.	9m	W	D.C.	19 AUG 1875	Glenwood
015149	RUSSELL, Wm. Montgomery	10y	W	D.C.	22 MAR 1878	Congressional
016056	RUSTIC, Wm. Alex.	8y	C	D.C.	07 JUN 1878	St. Mary's Co., Md.
011357	RUSTIN, Anna Lee	2y	M	D.C.	16 APR 1877	Beckett's
002920	RUSTIN, John	9h	C	D.C.	08 APR 1875	Mt. Olivet
013054	RUSTIN, Lewis	9y	C	D.C.	01 SEP 1877	Mt. Olivet
013631	RUSTIN, Maria	44y	C	D.C.	25 OCT 1877	Beckett's
015653	RUSTON, Basil	90y	C	D.C.	08 MAY 1878	Mt. Olivet
015679	RUSTON, Cassandria	40y	C	Md.	10 MAY 1878	All Saints, Md.
001005	RUSTON, Matilda	50y	C	Md.	01 NOV 1874	Mt. Olivet
011827	RUSTON, William Thomas	49y	C	Md.	07 JUN 1877	Mt. Olivet
010494	RUSTON, Winny	60y	C	Md.	03 FEB 1877	Beckett's
003049	RUTDGE, Alice Ekin	53y	W	Eng.	19 APR 1875	Congressional
013114	RUTH, Apollonia	38y	W	Ger.	07 SEP 1877	St. Mary's
001077	RUTH, George Paul	4y	W	D.C.	07 NOV 1874	St. Mary's
000826	RUTH, Mary	2m	W	D.C.	16 OCT 1874	St. Mary's
013316	RUTH, Matilda Amelia	19d	W	D.C.	26 SEP 1877	St. Mary's
015270	RUTHERDALE, Jennie	23y	W	D.C.	02 APR 1878	Congressional
015994	RUTHERFORD, Edward	3m	W	D.C.	03 JUN 1878	Congressional
006653	RUTHERFORD, James A.	19y	W	Wisc.	12 MAR 1876	Jefferson, Wisc.
012433	RUTHERFORD, Julia C.	5m	W	D.C.	19 JUL 1877	Graceland
000609	RUTHERFORD, William	37y	W	Ire.	23 SEP 1874	N.Y.
009600	RUTHERFORD, William	23y	W	D.C.	02 NOV 1876	Congressional
005222a	RUTIGAN, Mary Ellen	5m	W	D.C.	20 OCT 1875	Holy Rood
013548	RUYNS, Charles A.	34y	W	France	17 OCT 1877	Mt. Olivet
005577	RYAN, Agnes Ann	5y	W	Va.	26 NOV 1875	Congressional
000827	RYAN, Anna Gertrude	27y	W	D.C.	16 OCT 1874	Congressional
017910	RYAN, Bertha R.	2y	W	D.C.	30 OCT 1878	Mt. Olivet
014354	RYAN, Catharine	2m	W	D.C.	07 JAN 1878	Mt. Olivet
001802	RYAN, Catherine	54y	W	Ire.	19 JAN 1875	Mt. Olivet
013152	RYAN, Cathrine	75y	W	Ire.	10 SEP 1877	Mt. Olivet
016861	RYAN, Charles	2y	W	D.C.	01 AUG 1878	Mt. Olivet
020541	RYAN, Cornelius S.	9m	W	D.C.	20 JUN 1879	Mt. Olivet
005881	RYAN, Edwin	5d	W	D.C.	27 DEC 1875	Mt. Olivet
009759	RYAN, Ellen	42y	W	Ire.	20 NOV 1876	Mt. Olivet
001301	RYAN, Hanora	65y	W	Ire.	04 DEC 1874	Mt. Olivet
011152	RYAN, Henry	5m	W	D.C.	29 MAR 1877	Mt. Olivet
019404	RYAN, James D.	25y	W	D.C.	14 MAR 1879	Mt. Olivet
010988	RYAN, Jeremiah F.	3y	W	Pa.	15 MAR 1877	Mt. Olivet
003745	RYAN, John	40y	W	Ire.	21 JUN 1875	Mt. Olivet
010787	RYAN, John	2m	W	D.C.	26 FEB 1877	Mt. Olivet
019658	RYAN, John	1d	W	D.C.	04 APR 1879	Mt. Olivet
015644	RYAN, Joseph	2m	W	D.C.	07 MAY 1878	Mt. Olivet
004235	RYAN, Joseph J.	1y	W	D.C.	21 JUL 1875	Mt. Olivet
018336	RYAN, Julia	8y	W	D.C.	14 DEC 1878	Holy Rood
013722	RYAN, Kate	24y	W	Ire.	03 NOV 1877	Mt. Olivet
013490	RYAN, Kate	20y	W	D.C.	12 OCT 1877	Mt. Olivet

District of Columbia Death Records, August 1, 1874 to July 31, 1879   293

No.	Name	Age	Race	Birth	Death Date	Burial Place
016365	RYAN, Katie	9m	W	D.C.	29 JUN 1878	Mt. Olivet
019689	RYAN, Katie	1y	W	D.C.	07 APR 1879	Holy Rood
005210	RYAN, Louisa	1y	W	Va.	28 SEP 1875	Mt. Olivet
007935	RYAN, Margaret	4d	W	D.C.	30 JUN 1876	Holy Rood
003383	RYAN, Marguerite	70y	W	Ire.	21 MAY 1875	Mt. Olivet
013186a	RYAN, Mary	52y	W	Ire.	13 SEP 1877	Mt. Olivet
018343	RYAN, Mary Joseph	5y	W	D.C.	15 DEC 1878	Mt. Olivet
005270	RYAN, Michael	20y	W	D.C.	25 OCT 1875	Mt. Olivet
008302	RYAN, Sarah E.	40y	W	Md.	17 JUL 1876	Mt. Olivet
000400	RYDER, Jane	59y	C	Md.	01 SEP 1874	Harmony
001190	RYON, Ellen	47y	W	Md.	19 NOV 1874	Congressional
019994	RYON, Margarett Lillian	6m	W	D.C.	04 MAY 1879	Congressional
015897	RYON, Raymond P.	1m	W	D.C.	29 MAY 1878	Mt. Olivet
001652	RYON, Thomas Courtney	1y	W	D.C.	08 JAN 1875	Congressional
020721	RYRILY, Lucy	8m	C	D.C.	02 JUL 1879	Mt. Olivet
001814	RYTHER, Edwin A.	52y	W	Mass.	20 JAN 1875	Congressional

S

No.	Name	Age	Race	Birth	Death Date	Burial Place
015826	SACHO, Rebecca	8y	W	D.C.	24 MAY 1878	Prospect Hill
016380	SACHS, Elizabeth	22y	W	D.C.	30 JUN 1878	Prospect Hill
015354	SACKER, Caroline	c.60y	C	Md.	10 APR 1878	Beckett's
000167	SADGRUAE, Raphael A.	1y	C	N.C.	13 AUG 1874	Harmony
005957	SADLER, John M.	32y	W	Md.	06 JAN 1876	Congressional
014009	SADLER, Mary Ann	75y	W	Md.	04 DEC 1877	Mt. Olivet
004671	SAFFELL, Mary	9d	W	D.C.	19 AUG 1875	Mt. Olivet
016367	SAGE, Gustavus A.	70y	W	Pa.	29 JUN 1878	Congressional
013873	SAGE, Mary	4y	W	D.C.	20 NOV 1877	Payne's
005188	SAHN, Justus Rudolph	37y	W	Ger.	26 SEP 1875	Prospect Hill
017190	SAILER, Charles	10h	W	D.C.	25 AUG 1878	Congressional
010126	SALAMON, Levi	5y	W	D.C.	30 DEC 1876	Washington Hebrew
020722	SALE, Eliza	3m	C	D.C.	02 JUL 1879	Beckett's
016862	SALES, Earnest	6m	C	D.C.	01 AUG 1878	Beckett's
013922	SALES, Nellie	9y	C	D.C.	25 NOV 1877	Payne's
016529	SALES, Richard	2y	C	D.C.	09 JUL 1878	Potters Field
005233a	SALES, William	31y	C	Va.	21 OCT 1875	Gardner's Farm[1]
011678	SALTCORN, Frederick	37y	W	Ger.	22 MAY 1877	Washington Asylum
019978	SALTER, Francis	48y	W	Eng.	03 MAY 1879	Flint Hill, Va.
000677	SAMPPLE, Caroline	41y	M	Va.	30 DEC 1874	Mt. Zion
017731	SAMPSON, Infant of John P.	2w	C	D.C.	14 OCT 1878	Beckett's
015483	SAMPSON, Phebe E., Mrs.	72y	W	Mass.	22 APR 1878	Plympton, Mass.
004938	SAMPSON, Rubina	3m	C	D.C.	06 SEP 1875	Mt. Zion
012970	SAMSON, Emily Jane	61y	W	Md.	26 AUG 1877	Methodist
001353	SAMUELS, Irena A.	4y	W	D.C.	10 DEC 1874	Congressional
012020	SANDAS, Thomas	81y	C	Va.	23 JUN 1877	Harmony
018665	SANDERS, August	9m	W	D.C.	13 JAN 1879	Mt. Pleasant
012868	SANDERS, Charles H.	5y	C	D.C.	18 AUG 1877	Young Mens
006924	SANDERS, Clara	16y	C	D.C.	04 APR 1876	Harmony
018965	SANDERS, Delenia	2m	C	D.C.	05 FEB 1879	Mt. Zion
015150	SANDERS, Ella	9m	C	D.C.	22 MAR 1878	Harmony
002137	SANDERS, Evelina	10m	C	D.C.	12 FEB 1875	Moore's
009810	SANDERS, George	c.40y	C	U.S.	27 NOV 1876	Potters Field
009063	SANDERS, Ida	4y	C	D.C.	14 SEP 1876	Mt. Pleasant

[1] Located near Uniontown, D.C.

No.	Name	Age	Race	Birth	Death Date	Burial Place
014145	SANDERS, Infant of Clem	5h	C	D.C.	20 DEC 1877	Potters Field
017351	SANDERS, Margaret Ann	6m	C	D.C.	08 SEP 1878	Beckett's
003666	SANDERS, Mary Jane	23y	C	Va.	16 JUN 1875	Potters Field
016296	SANDERS, Maud E.	6m	C	D.C.	24 JUN 1878	Mt. Olivet
010956	SANDERS, Nancy	99y	C	D.C.	12 MAR 1877	Young Mens
020254	SANDERS, Nancy	75y	M	W.Va.	01 JUN 1879	Harmony
011701	SANDERS, Richard	c.47y	W	Va.	25 MAY 1877	Mt. Olivet
005210a	SANDERS, Roy	57y	C	Va.	19 OCT 1875	Ebenezer
010024	SANDERS, Walter	2y	M	D.C.	20 DEC 1876	Beckett's
009260	SANDERS, Willie	14d	C	D.C.	01 OCT 1876	Ebenezer
008527	SANDERSON, Georgianna McGowan	1y	W	D.C.	02 AUG 1876	Mt. Olivet
019051	SANDERSON, Lemuel Walton	6y	W	Pa.	12 FEB 1879	Congressional
012063	SANDERSON, Samuel H.	65y	W	D.C.	26 JUN 1877	Congressional
018964	SANDICK, William	67y	C	Md.	05 FEB 1879	Potters Field
013293	SANDIFORD, Mary	91y	W	Va.	24 SEP 1877	Oak Hill
018718	SANDS, Anna E.	44y	W	D.C.	18 JAN 1879	Congressional
009680	SANDS, Bridget	30y	W	Ire.	12 NOV 1876	Mt. Olivet
011510	SANDS, Charles Morrison	21y	W	Md.	04 MAY 1877	Oak Hill
017800	SANDS, Edward L.	65y	W	Md.	19 OCT 1878	Oak Hill
020904	SANDS, John	65y	W	Ire.	12 JUL 1879	Mt. Olivet
003363	SANDS, Margaret	80y	W	Md.	19 MAY 1875	Mt. Olivet
016117	SANDS, Morris C.	3y	W	Md.	11 JUN 1878	Glenwood
016508	SANDY, Charlotte Delilah	81y	W	Va.	08 JUL 1878	Methodist, E.
007283	SANFORD, Julia Ellis	2½m	W	D.C.	12 MAY 1876	Congressional
005931	SANFORD, Lizzie	5d	C	D.C.	03 JAN 1876	Young Mens
012720	SANFORD, Sallie	76y	W	N.Y.	07 AUG 1877	Congressional
000252	SANFORD, Willie	16d	C	D.C.	20 AUG 1874	Young Mens
005604	SANGER, Bertha	30y	W	Ger.	29 NOV 1875	Orthodox Hebrew
014116	SANGER, Jacob	1y	W	D.C.	16 DEC 1877	Jewish
010860	SANGER, Martha W.	63y	W	Va.	04 MAR 1877	Oak Hill
020879	SANGER, Ralph	1y	W	D.C.	10 JUL 1879	Oak Hill
018666	SANGER, Tette	29y	W	Ger.	13 JAN 1879	Adas Israel
017135	SANNER, Elizabeth V.	46y	W	Md.	21 AUG 1878	Glenwood
014014	SANTEE, John W.	6y	W	D.C.	05 DEC 1877	Mt. Olivet
020970	SAPPINGTON, John	40y	W	Md.	16 JUL 1879	Annapolis Junction
003889	SARCHER, James W.	80y	C	Md.	27 JUN 1875	Ebenezer
006654	SARGENT, James Whitcomb	58y	W	N.H.	12 MAR 1876	Falls Church, Va.
001993	SARGENT, Nathan	80y	W	Ver.	02 FEB 1875	Rock Creek
014783	SARGENT, Rosina	79y	W	Mass.	16 FEB 1878	Rock Creek
005075a	SARTAIN, Jane Ann	16y	W	Va.	06 OCT 1875	Rock Creek
002940	SARTEN, Benj.	1y	W	D.C.	10 APR 1875	Rock Creek
004985	SAUER, George	17y	W	Pa.	10 SEP 1875	Mt. Olivet
020311	SAUL, Katie	7m	W	D.C.	05 JUN 1879	Prospect Hill
013470	SAUNDERS, Albert Neville	6y	W	D.C.	10 OCT 1877	Leesburg, Va./Rock Creek
020323	SAUNDERS, Anne	6m	C	D.C.	06 JUN 1879	Beckett's
004188	SAUNDERS, Annie	53y	C	N.C.	18 JUL 1875	Potters Field
019886	SAUNDERS, Anthony	44y	C	Md.	24 APR 1879	Potters Field
003614	SAUNDERS, Caroline	4m	C	D.C.	12 JUN 1875	Mt. Pleasant
012379	SAUNDERS, Charles	76y	C	Va.	16 JUL 1877	Potters Field
002131	SAUNDERS, Edward W.	23y	M	Pa.	12 FEB 1875	Young Mens
013212	SAUNDERS, Frances	72y	C	Va.	15 SEP 1877	Harmony
015366	SAUNDERS, George	40y	C	Va.	11 APR 1878	Harmony
013469	SAUNDERS, Henrietta Frances	5y	W	D.C.	10 OCT 1877	Leesburg, Va.
001307	SAUNDERS, Henry	39y	C	Md.	05 DEC 1874	Harmony
014813	SAUNDERS, Ida Cordelia	21y	W	D.C.	18 FEB 1878	Glenwood
002753	SAUNDERS, Infant of Henry	1h	C	D.C.	26 MAR 1875	Ebenezer

District of Columbia Death Records, August 1, 1874 to July 31, 1879   295

No.	Name	Age	Race	Birth	Death Date	Burial Place
003378	SAUNDERS, Irene	47y	C	D.C.	20 MAY 1875	Mt. Olivet
013317	SAUNDERS, J.E.	1y	C	D.C.	26 SEP 1877	Harmony
019035	SAUNDERS, James Stevenson	48y	W	Md.	11 FEB 1879	Laurel, Md.
019036	SAUNDERS, John	25y	C	Va.	11 FEB 1879	Potters Field
000320	SAUNDERS, John A.	3y	W	Md.	26 AUG 1874	Laurel, Md.
013534	SAUNDERS, Mary	16y	C	D.C.	16 OCT 1877	Mt. Olivet
003905	SAUNDERS, Mary Mordina	1y	C	D.C.	28 JUN 1875	Harmony
020544	SAUNDERS, Maud Unity	8m	W	Va.	20 JUN 1879	Glenwood
014585	SAUNDERS, Rachel	28y	C	D.C.	28 JAN 1878	Harmony
007730	SAUNDERS, Richard L.	65y	C	Md.	19 JUN 1876	Mt. Pleasant
006910	SAUNDERS, Siddy	2y	C	D.C.	03 APR 1876	Mt. Pleasant
020364	SAUNDERS, Winn V.	4m	W	D.C.	09 JUN 1879	Rock Creek
005579	SAUNDERS, Wm. T.	5y	C	D.C.	26 NOV 1875	Harmony
000800	SAUR, George C.G.	59y	W	Ger.	14 OCT 1874	Prospect Hill
007665	SAUTER, Frank	1y	W	D.C.	15 JUN 1876	Mt. Olivet
013864	SAUTER, Margaret Elizabeth	11y	W	D.C.	19 NOV 1877	Mt. Olivet
013874	SAUTER, Mary Magdalen	8y	W	D.C.	20 NOV 1877	Mt. Olivet
004698	SAUTER, Wm.	2y	W	D.C.	21 AUG 1875	Mt. Olivet
020460	SAVAGE, Hester Ann	24y	C	D.C.	15 JUN 1879	Mt. Zion
021127	SAVAGE, James Edward	2m	W	D.C.	27 JUL 1879	Alexandria, Va.
001575	SAVAGE, Mary	2m	W	D.C.	01 JAN 1875	Alexandria, Va.
007979	SAVAGE, Robt. E.	13d	W	D.C.	03 JUL 1876	Alexandria, Va.
011713	SAVAGE, Rosetta	54y	C	Md.	26 MAY 1877	Mt. Zion
017892	SAVAN, John	60y	C	D.C.	28 OCT 1878	Mt. Pleasant
014513	SAVOY, Duriell	3m	C	D.C.	21 JAN 1878	Harmony
004089	SAVOY, Infant of Alexander	6m	C	D.C.	11 JUL 1875	Moore's
018758	SAVOY, Maria V.	23y	M	Va.	21 JAN 1879	Harmony
017977	SAVOY, William L.	24y	C	Md.	07 NOV 1878	Mt. Olivet
001318	SAWYER, Aholia Joseph	58y	W	N.H.	06 DEC 1874	Mt. Olivet
018988	SAWYER, Emma	52y	C	Va.	07 FEB 1879	Young Mens
004685	SAWYER, Frederick P.	58y	W	Ver.	20 AUG 1875	Oak Hill
009365	SAWYER, William	67y	C	Md.	10 OCT 1876	Mt. Pleasant
015310	SAXTON, Charles E.	18y	W	D.C.	07 APR 1878	Congressional
021107	SAXTON, Jacob T.	69y	W	N.Y.	25 JUL 1879	Glenwood
013857	SAXTON, Robert	72y	W	Md.	18 NOV 1877	Congressional
019927	SAXTON, Robert Franklin	6h	W	D.C.	28 APR 1879	Congressional
018540	SAXTY, Aylmer	14m	W	D.C.	01 JAN 1879	Glenwood
014087	SAXTY, Geo. H.	53y	W	Eng.	13 DEC 1877	Prospect Hill
005047a	SAYLES, Joseph Peyton	1y	C	D.C.	03 OCT 1875	Danford's Farm
007685	SAYLES, Margaret Ann	11m	C	D.C.	16 JUN 1876	Ebenezer
009488	SAYRE, Charles L.R.	27y	W	N.Y.	22 OCT 1876	Congressional
000042	SAYRE, LeRoy	12d	W	D.C.	03 AUG 1874	Washington Asylum
018590	SAYRE, William	66y	W	N.Y.	06 JAN 1879	Congressional
006453	SCAGGS, Alvia	1h	W	D.C.	23 FEB 1876	Glenwood
009886	SCALA, Blanche	4y	W	D.C.	06 DEC 1876	Congressional
002079	SCALES, Carrie	14y	C	N.C.	08 FEB 1875	Harmony
011778	SCALES, Nelson	50y	C	Va.	02 JUN 1877	Potters Field
000247	SCANLON, Catherine	18y	W	D.C.	19 AUG 1874	Mt. Olivet
000098	SCANLON, Johana	6d	W	D.C.	07 AUG 1874	Mt. Olivet
001292	SCANLON, Mary	90y	W	Ire.	02 DEC 1874	Mt. Olivet
015177	SCANLON, Mary	1y	W	D.C.	24 MAR 1878	Mt. Olivet
006397	SCANLON, Mary Ellen	8m	W	D.C.	17 FEB 1876	Mt. Olivet
019270	SCANLON, Mary Ellen	5y	W	D.C.	03 MAR 1879	Mt. Olivet
001181	SCANLON, Patrick	89y	W	Ire.	19 NOV 1874	Mt. Olivet
003349	SCANLON, Patrick	60y	W	Ire.	17 MAY 1875	Mt. Olivet
007461	SCANLON, Susan	36y	W	Pa.	01 JUN 1876	Mt. Olivet

No.	Name	Age	Race	Birth	Death Date	Burial Place
005376	SCHACHAN, August	53y	W	Ger.	06 NOV 1875	Washington Asylum
012829	SCHADE, John W.M.	53y	W	Ger.	15 AUG 1877	Prospect Hill
015915	SCHAEFER, J. George	12y	W	D.C.	30 MAY 1878	Prospect Hill
009431	SCHAEFER, John Thomas	24y	W	D.C.	16 OCT 1876	St. Mary's
010071	SCHAEFER, Joseph William	17y	W	D.C.	25 DEC 1876	St. Mary's
007541	SCHAEFFER, Chas. N.	21m	W	D.C.	07 JUN 1876	Congressional
019645	SCHAEFFER, Frederick	80y	W	Ger.	03 APR 1879	Prospect Hill
017433	SCHAEFFER, Infant of Geo.	½h	W	D.C.	16 SEP 1878	St. Mary's
017434	SCHAEFFER, Infant of Geo.	½h	W	D.C.	16 SEP 1878	St. Mary's
014979	SCHAEFFER, Martha	78y	W	Md.	07 MAR 1878	Congressional
009963	SCHAFER, Frederick	41y	W	Ger.	14 DEC 1876	Prospect Hill
018035	SCHAFER, George	50y	W	Ger.	12 NOV 1878	Prospect Hill
010114	SCHAFER, Lizzie	23y	W	Md.	29 DEC 1876	Prospect Hill
014133	SCHAFFER, George	3y	W	D.C.	18 DEC 1877	Prospect Hill
013791	SCHAFFERT, Mina	21y	W	Ger.	10 NOV 1877	Prospect Hill
015680	SCHAFHIRT, Arthur	2y	W	D.C.	10 MAY 1878	Rock Creek
018337	SCHAIBLE, Gottfried	27y	W	Ger.	14 DEC 1878	Prospect Hill
014678	SCHARF, Eugene Arnold Young	8y	W	Md.	05 FEB 1878	Oak Hill
007486	SCHAUB, Katie	15min	W	D.C.	03 JUN 1876	St. Mary's
004394	SCHAUB, Lorenz	11d	W	D.C.	31 JUL 1875	St. Mary's
014069	SCHAYER, Eugene F.	2y	W	D.C.	11 DEC 1877	Glenwood
017881	SCHECKERS, Albert	12y	W	Md.	27 OCT 1878	Rock Creek
017882	SCHEIDE, George W.	52y	W	Pa.	27 OCT 1878	Hospital, Government
010080	SCHEIDEGGER, Emma M.	28y	W	Pa.	26 DEC 1876	St. Mary's
019452	SCHEIFLEY, Jacob	56y	W	Pa.	18 MAR 1879	Rogers Ford, Pa.
006537	SCHELL, Maggie C.	3y	W	Pa.	03 MAR 1876	Graceland
007766	SCHEMMERHORN, George	36y	W	N.Y.	21 JUN 1876	Mt. Olivet
017015	SCHENIG, Charles	36y	W	Ger.	11 AUG 1878	Potters Field
015943	SCHEPPECK, Charles	3m	W	D.C.	31 MAY 1878	Prospect Hill
012635	SCHERER, Henry	4y	W	Md.	01 AUG 1877	Presbyterian
009442	SCHERMONT, Peter	60y	W	Ger.	17 OCT 1876	Potters Field
018345	SCHERRER, Mary	40y	W	Ger.	15 DEC 1878	Holy Rood
018967	SCHICK, Elise	32y	W	Ger.	05 FEB 1879	Prospect Hill
017844	SCHLAICH, Frederick	53y	W	Ger.	23 OCT 1878	Prospect Hill
015237	SCHLEICHEIRS, Infant of Gustav	8d	W	D.C.	30 MAR 1878	Congressional
018635	SCHLEICHER, Gustave	56y	W	Ger.	10 JAN 1879	San Antonio, Tex.
014656	SCHLEUTER, Mary	3y	W	D.C.	03 FEB 1878	Prospect Hill
015293	SCHLOFSER, William	40y	W	D.C.	05 APR 1878	Glenwood
015082	SCHLONEBERG, Infant of Abner	12d	W	D.C.	15 MAR 1878	Washington Hebrew
001515	SCHLOSEN, Eva S.	3y	W	D.C.	28 DEC 1874	Glenwood
020169	SCHLOSHER, Jane	39y	W	Pa.	21 MAY 1879	Mt. Olivet
017440	SCHLOSSER, Amelia	4y	W	D.C.	17 SEP 1878	Glenwood
005069	SCHLOSSER, Elizabeth	60y	W	Ger.	16 SEP 1875	Mt. Olivet
000200	SCHLOSSER, Eva	61y	W	Ger.	15 AUG 1874	Glenwood
001929	SCHLOSSER, Peter	11h	W	D.C.	28 JAN 1875	Prospect Hill
018492	SCHLOTTERBECK, Annie Margaretha	10y	W	D.C.	28 DEC 1878	Prospect Hill
014152	SCHLOTTERBECK, Christina Salome	1y	W	D.C.	20 DEC 1877	Prospect Hill
005267	SCHMIDT, Benjamin C.	5m	W	D.C.	25 OCT 1875	Prospect Hill
000070	SCHMIDT, Christian Fred.	56y	W	Ger.	05 AUG 1874	Prospect Hill
009134	SCHMIDT, Ernest Ludwig	52y	W	Ger.	19 SEP 1876	Prospect Hill
004986	SCHMIDT, Frank M.	55y	W	Ger.	10 SEP 1875	Hospital
005725	SCHMIDT, Johanna J. Fredericka	66y	W	Ger.	11 DEC 1875	Prospect Hill
008781	SCHMIDT, Junella	1y	W	D.C.	22 AUG 1876	Congressional
006724	SCHMIDT, Margaretha	73y	W	Ger.	18 MAR 1876	Prospect Hill
011560	SCHMIDT, Odelia	73y	W	Ger.	10 MAY 1877	St. Mary's
005048a	SCHMIDT, Thomas	49y	W	Eng.	03 OCT 1875	Mt. Olivet

District of Columbia Death Records, August 1, 1874 to July 31, 1879

No.	Name	Age	Race	Birth	Death Date	Burial Place
002985	SCHMIDTMAER, Infant of Hammond	1h	W	D.C.	14 APR 1875	Prospect Hill
020476	SCHMITH, Jos. B.	8m	W	D.C.	16 JUN 1879	Mt. Olivet
000865	SCHMITTIS, Annie B.	12y	C	Va.	19 OCT 1874	Beckett's
018104	SCHNEBEL, Fred H.	26y	W	Ger.	20 NOV 1878	Prospect Hill
015585	SCHNEIDER, Catherine	46y	W	Italy	02 MAY 1878	Mt. Olivet
000783	SCHNEIDER, John Francis	3y	W	D.C.	12 OCT 1874	Prospect Hill
011283	SCHNEIDER, Joseph L.	82y	W	Ger.	09 APR 1877	Soldier's Home
016310	SCHNEIDER, William	4m	W	D.C.	25 JUN 1878	Prospect Hill
010691	SCHOEPFLEN, Louis	44y	W	Ger.	19 FEB 1877	Prospect Hill
000811	SCHOEPP, John	50y	W	Ger.	15 OCT 1874	Prospect Hill
016283	SCHOFIELD, Mary Elizabeth	59y	W	Md.	23 JUN 1878	Mt. Olivet
001777	SCHONBORN, Anton Henry	7y	W	D.C.	18 JAN 1875	Congressional
018577	SCHOOFIELD, Elizabeth	82y	W	D.C.	05 JAN 1879	Congressional
015016	SCHOOLCRAFT, Mary H.R.	60y	W	S.C.	10 MAR 1878	Congressional
015228	SCHORN, J. Reynold	37y	W	Prus.	29 MAR 1878	Congressional
004321	SCHOTT, Arthur Charles Victor	61y	W	Ger.	26 JUL 1875	Oak Hill
019074	SCHOUBORN, Albert	10y	W	D.C.	14 FEB 1879	Prospect Hill
014437	SCHRAM, Isaac C.	54y	W	N.Y.	15 JAN 1878	Hospital, Government
009897	SCHREIBER, Eliza	54y	W	Ger.	07 DEC 1876	Oak Hill
007167	SCHREINER, Anna Mary	82y	W	Md.	30 APR 1876	Oak Hill
009012	SCHREINER, Edward Stanley	34y	W	Pa.	09 SEP 1876	Glenwood
017816	SCHREPPLER, John	68y	W	Ger.	20 OCT 1878	Mt. Olivet
008074	SCHRIVER, Luther	1y	W	D.C.	08 JUL 1876	Methodist
011251	SCHRIVER, Mary	40y	W	Md.	07 APR 1877	Congressional
009526	SCHROAKOPF, Emil F.	46y	W	Ger.	25 OCT 1876	St. Mary's
002393	SCHUERGER, John And.	3m	W	D.C.	02 MAR 1875	Prospect Hill
001644	SCHUH, Sarah E.	26y	W	D.C.	07 JAN 1875	Prospect Hill
003971	SCHULTE, Rosanna	5m	W	D.C.	02 JUL 1875	Mt. Olivet
012636	SCHULTZ, Margaretha	73y	W	Ger.	01 AUG 1877	Prospect Hill
000354	SCHULTZ, Mary	30y	W	Ire.	29 AUG 1874	Mt. Olivet
003956	SCHULTZE, August H.	4m	W	D.C.	01 JUL 1875	Prospect Hill
002262	SCHULTZE, Gertrud	20y	W	Ger.	21 FEB 1875	Prospect Hill
001571	SCHULZE, Daniel	35y	W	Ger.	01 JAN 1875	Congressional
018292	SCHUSTER, Anna	8y	W	D.C.	09 DEC 1878	Prospect Hill
018613	SCHUSTER, Ernestine	40y	W	Ger.	08 JAN 1879	Prospect Hill
011394	SCHWAB, Elizabeth	39y	W	Ger.	22 APR 1877	Mt. Olivet
016683	SCHWABE, Conrad	2y	W	D.C.	19 JUL 1878	Prospect Hill
001060	SCHWAKOPF, Magdalena Pauline	1y	W	D.C.	05 NOV 1874	St. Mary's
009046	SCHWAKOPF, Mary L.	1y	W	D.C.	12 SEP 1876	St. Mary's
000876	SCHWARTZ, Augustus Chas.	58y	W	Bav.	20 OCT 1874	Mt. Olivet/Rock Creek
002011	SCHWARTZ, Catharina	8d	W	D.C.	03 FEB 1875	Prospect Hill
003093	SCHWARTZ, Charles	39y	W	Switz.	23 APR 1875	Prospect Hill
013782	SCIPICO, Virginia	22y	C	Va.	09 NOV 1877	Richmond, Va.
016368	SCOBB, Joseph	3m	W	D.C.	29 JUN 1878	Mt. Olivet
003811	SCOTT, Adell	4m	C	D.C.	24 JUN 1875	Young Mens
006553	SCOTT, Albert	19y	C	Va.	04 MAR 1876	Mt. Zion
012024	SCOTT, Allen	23y	C	Va.	23 JUN 1877	Mt. Zion
009562	SCOTT, Amelia	38y	C	Pa.	28 OCT 1876	Philadelphia, Pa.
002365	SCOTT, Anderson	26y	C	Md.	28 FEB 1875	Potters Field
019607	SCOTT, Ann	95y	W	Md.	30 MAR 1879	Oak Hill
002797	SCOTT, Annie	13d	C	D.C.	30 MAR 1875	Potters Field
010741	SCOTT, Benjamin	14d	C	D.C.	22 FEB 1877	Young Mens
013154	SCOTT, Benjamin F.	1y	W	D.C.	10 SEP 1877	Oak Hill
016136	SCOTT, Bessie Nicholson	8y	W	Ky.	12 JUN 1878	Oak Hill
009156	SCOTT, Carrie	1y	C	D.C.	21 SEP 1876	Young Mens
012956	SCOTT, Catherine	70y	C	D.C.	25 AUG 1877	Beckett's

No.	Name	Age	Race	Birth	Death Date	Burial Place
012269	SCOTT, Catherine	4m	C	D.C.	08 JUL 1877	Harmony
000125	SCOTT, Charles	26y	C	Va.	10 AUG 1874	Mt. Olivet
014362	SCOTT, Charles	27y	C	Va.	08 JAN 1878	Beckett's
019091	SCOTT, Charles A.	7m	C	D.C.	16 FEB 1879	Beckett's
001779	SCOTT, Charles E.	2m	W	DC.	18 JAN 1875	Congressional
016682	SCOTT, Chas. R.	7m	C	D.C.	19 JUL 1878	Beckett's
001807	SCOTT, Clara V.	5y	W	D.C.	20 JAN 1875	Congressional
016625	SCOTT, Clarence	4m	W	D.C.	16 JUL 1878	Presbyterian
003541	SCOTT, Daniel	35y	C	Ky.	06 JUN 1875	Potters Field
002557	SCOTT, David	40y	C	D.C.	13 MAR 1875	Potters Field
006971	SCOTT, Edward	4y	M	D.C.	08 APR 1876	Ebenezer
015556	SCOTT, Edward	42y	C	Md.	29 APR 1878	Potters Field
015432	SCOTT, Eliza	57y	C	Va.	17 APR 1878	Beckett's
000063	SCOTT, Ella	17y	C	U.S.	05 AUG 1874	Harmony
018819	SCOTT, Ellen	78y	W	Md.	25 JAN 1879	Congressional
017352	SCOTT, Elvina	10y	C	D.C.	08 SEP 1878	Beckett's
019628	SCOTT, Emerline	18m	C	D.C.	01 APR 1879	Beckett's
009308	SCOTT, Emma	c.39y	M	Va.	05 OCT 1876	Mt. Zion
012254	SCOTT, Francis Elizabeth	1y	C	D.C.	07 JUL 1877	Ebenezer
012471	SCOTT, Francis Jasper	8m	W	D.C.	22 JUL 1877	Congressional
008084	SCOTT, Garland	56y	C	Va.	08 JUL 1876	Potters Field
009313	SCOTT, Genevieve	2m	C	D.C.	05 OCT 1876	Mt. Zion
002819	SCOTT, Geo. Holman	1y	C	D.C.	31 MAR 1875	Mt. Pleasant
008935	SCOTT, George	2y	W	D.C.	02 SEP 1876	Congressional
015033	SCOTT, George	29y	C	Va.	11 MAR 1878	Beckett's
001061f	SCOTT, George R.	8m	M	Va.	05 NOV 1874	Beckett's
006771	SCOTT, George W.	42y	W	Pa.	21 MAR 1876	Oak Hill
021086	SCOTT, Guy	7m	W	D.C.	24 JUL 1879	Oak Hill
008737	SCOTT, Harriet	35y	C	Va.	19 AUG 1876	Manassas Junction, Va.
009000	SCOTT, Harriet	2y	M	D.C.	08 SEP 1876	Potters Field
011092	SCOTT, Harriet	10m	C	D.C.	23 MAR 1877	Young Mens
011179	SCOTT, Harriet A., Mrs.	31y	W	Mich.	31 MAR 1877	Oak Hill
012921	SCOTT, Harry	10m	W	D.C.	23 AUG 1877	Congressional
017071	SCOTT, Hattie	1y	C	D.C.	16 AUG 1878	Beckett's
012648	SCOTT, Henry	6y	C	D.C.	02 AUG 1877	Mt. Zion
014322	SCOTT, Henry	37y	C	Va.	04 JAN 1878	Mt. Olivet
016480	SCOTT, Henry	4m	W	D.C.	06 JUL 1878	Congressional
018759	SCOTT, Herman	7m	C	D.C.	21 JAN 1879	Harmony
019464	SCOTT, Hestilla	2y	C	D.C.	19 MAR 1879	Beckett's
015634	SCOTT, Ida	40y	C	Va.	06 MAY 1878	Harmony
018941	SCOTT, Infant of Bertie	24h	C	D.C.	03 FEB 1879	Potters Field
015914	SCOTT, Infant of Charles	6d	C	D.C.	30 MAY 1878	Mt. Olivet
001247	SCOTT, Infant of Isham	3d	C	D.C.	27 NOV 1874	Mt. Zion
004119	SCOTT, Infant of Lee	11d	C	D.C.	13 JUL 1875	Moore's
013751	SCOTT, Infant of Sallie	6d	C	D.C.	06 NOV 1877	Beckett's
008713	SCOTT, Infant of Sarah	6d	C	D.C.	17 AUG 1876	Potters Field
016916	SCOTT, James	7m	C	D.C.	05 AUG 1878	Mt. Zion
013620	SCOTT, James A.	46y	W	D.C.	24 OCT 1877	Congressional
019849	SCOTT, James Dudley	65y	C	Va.	20 APR 1879	Young Mens
015484	SCOTT, James H.	9y	C	Ohio	22 APR 1878	Young Mens
012392	SCOTT, James Hays	4m	C	D.C.	16 JUL 1877	Potters Field
006643	SCOTT, Jennie	2y	C	D.C.	11 MAR 1876	Harmony
000993	SCOTT, Jessie	7m	W	D.C.	31 OCT 1874	Congressional
002486	SCOTT, Jimmie	5m	C	D.C.	09 MAR 1875	Potters Field
009512	SCOTT, John	4y	C	D.C.	23 OCT 1876	Mt. Olivet
017246	SCOTT, John Edward	10m	W	D.C.	29 AUG 1878	Oak Hill

District of Columbia Death Records, August 1, 1874 to July 31, 1879

No.	Name	Age	Race	Birth	Death Date	Burial Place
012116	SCOTT, John Frederick	10m	C	D.C.	29 JUN 1877	Beckett's
017275	SCOTT, John Wesley	1y	C	D.C.	31 AUG 1878	Moore's
004301	SCOTT, Joseph	40y	C	Md.	25 JUL 1875	Potters Field
008620	SCOTT, Joseph	6m	C	D.C.	09 AUG 1876	Mt. Olivet
002192	SCOTT, Joshua	14d	C	D.C.	16 FEB 1875	Ebenezer
005375	SCOTT, Julia	57y	W	Va.	06 NOV 1875	Mt. Olivet
006248	SCOTT, Julia	10y	C	D.C.	05 FEB 1876	Ebenezer
007239	SCOTT, Julia	65y	W	D.C.	07 MAY 1876	Hospital
018293	SCOTT, Lavinia	70y	C	Va.	09 DEC 1878	Washington Asylum
003838	SCOTT, Lillie	2m	W	D.C.	25 JUN 1875	Congressional
015057	SCOTT, Louis	9d	C	D.C.	13 MAR 1878	Payne's
006424	SCOTT, Lucius	38y	C	Va.	20 FEB 1876	Harmony
008297	SCOTT, Martha	5m	C	D.C.	17 JUL 1876	Young Mens
008328	SCOTT, Mary	11d	C	D.C.	19 JUL 1876	Beckett's
005223	SCOTT, Mary Clara Prissilla	3y	W	D.C.	29 SEP 1875	Glenwood
008477	SCOTT, Mary Elizabeth	5m	C	D.C.	29 JUL 1876	Beckett's
013153	SCOTT, Mary M.	7d	C	D.C.	10 SEP 1877	Potters Field
006071	SCOTT, Matilda	50y	C	D.C.	19 JAN 1876	Holy Rood
012212	SCOTT, Milton H.	9m	W	D.C.	04 JUL 1877	Congressional
016864	SCOTT, Noah Davis	5y	C	D.C.	01 AUG 1878	Young Mens
009213	SCOTT, Patsy	60y	C	Va.	27 SEP 1876	Young Mens
019271	SCOTT, Polly	115y	C	Va.	03 MAR 1879	Harmony
001635	SCOTT, Richard Gerry	30y	W	Conn.	07 JAN 1875	Glenwood
019836	SCOTT, Robert H.	17y	W	D.C.	19 APR 1879	Congressional
018493	SCOTT, Rosa	c.70y	C	Va.	28 DEC 1878	Young Mens
015508	SCOTT, Russell	3y	C	D.C.	24 APR 1878	Beckett's
016297	SCOTT, Rutherford	1y	C	D.C.	24 JUN 1878	Young Mens
007649	SCOTT, Samuel B.	24y	W	D.C.	14 JUN 1876	Congressional
004470	SCOTT, Samuel G.	46y	C	Va.	05 AUG 1875	Mt. Pleasant
008646	SCOTT, Sophia	25y	C	Va.	11 AUG 1876	Harmony
008206	SCOTT, Susan	1y	C	D.C.	12 JUL 1876	Potters Field
011988	SCOTT, Thornton	28y	C	Va.	21 JUN 1877	Mt. Zion
003942	SCOTT, Walter Lee	6m	W	D.C.	30 JUN 1875	Mt. Olivet
007274	SCOTT, William	63y	C	Va.	11 MAY 1876	Harmony
018874	SCOTT, William H.	1d	W	D.C.	29 JAN 1879	Congressional
006436	SCOTT, William Henry	1y	C	D.C.	21 FEB 1876	Ebenezer
012617	SCOTT, William Joseph	5m	C	D.C.	31 JUL 1877	Ebenezer
004511	SCOTT, Willie	5m	C	D.C.	08 AUG 1875	Mt. Olivet
017671	SCRAGGS, Mary Jane	36y	C	Tenn.	07 OCT 1878	Harmony
011063	SCRAGGS, Willie	2y	C	D.C.	21 MAR 1877	Ebenezer
019722	SCRANAGE, Gurtrude	13m	C	D.C.	10 APR 1879	Mt. Pleasant
015645	SCRANAGE, Isaac	18m	C	D.C.	07 MAY 1878	Mt. Pleasant
019547	SCRANAGE, Virginia	5y	C	D.C.	25 MAR 1879	Mt. Pleasant
002766	SCRANAGE, Wm.	2y	C	D.C.	27 MAR 1875	Mt. Pleasant
008622	SCRANGE, Albert	10m	C	D.C.	09 AUG 1876	Mt. Pleasant
010405	SCRIBNER, Elizabeth	51y	W	Md.	25 JAN 1877	Rock Creek
017111	SCRIBNER, Ella Piatt	8m	W	D.C.	19 AUG 1878	Rock Creek
004700	SCRIVENER, Kate Eugenia	1y	W	D.C.	21 AUG 1875	Glenwood
015434	SCRIVENER, Lewis Clayton	2m	W	D.C.	16 APR 1878	Presbyterian
013677	SCRIVENER, Wm. H.	22y	W	D.C.	30 OCT 1877	Congressional
014784	SCRIVER, Geo. W.	44y	W	D.C.	16 FEB 1878	Glenwood
017189	SCRIVNER, Gertie	4y	W	D.C.	25 AUG 1878	Presbyterian
019062	SCRIVNER, Lewis H.	63y	W	Md.	13 FEB 1879	Congressional
012086	SCROGGIN, Phillip	39y	C	Va.	27 JUN 1877	Harmony
013535	SCROGGINS, Eddie	2y	C	D.C.	16 OCT 1877	Congressional
015284	SCROGGINS, Edward	3m	C	D.C.	04 APR 1878	Beckett's

No.	Name	Age	Race	Birth	Death Date	Burial Place
019748	SCROGGINS, Martha	3w	W	D.C.	12 APR 1879	Congressional
008910	SCROGGINS, Philip	18m	C	D.C.	01 SEP 1876	Harmony
009798	SCROGGINS, Sarah	c.35y	C	Va.	25 NOV 1876	Harmony
019747	SCROPPS, Robert	7m	C	D.C.	12 APR 1879	Beckett's
010346	SCRUBBS, Martha	8y	C	Va.	20 JAN 1877	Mt. Olivet
019606	SCRUGS, William	30y	C	Va.	30 MAR 1879	Beckett's
001924	SCUNLOW, Johanna	10m	W	D.C.	28 JAN 1875	Mt. Olivet
016640	SEAL, Annie	2m	W	D.C.	17 JUL 1878	Congressional
000185	SEAL, Ellen	1y	W	D.C.	14 AUG 1874	Mt. Olivet
010338	SEAL, Mary	1y	W	D.C.	19 JAN 1877	Congressional
006383	SEALS, Charles	20y	C	Va.	16 FEB 1876	Alexandria, Va.
019169	SEALS, Mary	50y	C	Va.	23 FEB 1879	Harmony
011113	SEALS, Spencer	9m	C	Wyo.	25 MAR 1877	Mt. Zion
008654	SEAMAN, John George	76y	W	N.Y.	11 AUG 1876	Ridgewood, N.Y.
008785	SEARLES, Jessie R.	16m	W	D.C.	22 AUG 1876	Congressional
008253	SEARS, Infant of Samuel	1d	C	D.C.	14 JUL 1876	Ebenezer
020182	SEARS, Mary E.	45y	W	Va.	23 MAY 1879	Oak Hill
016323	SEARS, Rebeca	77y	W	D.C.	26 JUN 1878	Oak Hill
017551	SEATON, Jane Elizabeth Sprigg	49y	W	D.C.	27 SEP 1878	Congressional
016805	SEBASTIAN, Ann Maria	61y	W	Va.	28 JUL 1878	Alexandria, Va.
001839f	SEBASTIAN, Catherine E.	64y	W	Md.	22 JAN 1875	Holy Rood
019375	SEBASTIAN, Charles W.	7m	W	D.C.	12 MAR 1879	Presbyterian
008862	SEBASTIAN, Richard W.	64y	W	Va.	28 AUG 1876	Alexandria, Va.
014967	SEBASTIAN, Wm. T.	1y	W	D.C.	06 MAR 1878	Holy Rood
012807	SEBASTIN, William	3m	W	D.C.	14 AUG 1877	Graceland
012387	SEBRING, Charles P.	11m	W	D.C.	16 JUL 1877	Graceland
012048	SEBRING, Narcissa LaRue	28y	W	Ia.	25 JUN 1877	Graceland
003714	SEDGEWICK, Mrs. Thos. Stewart	40y	W	D.C.	19 JUN 1875	Oak Hill
008722	SEDGWICK, Elizebeth	1y	C	D.C.	18 AUG 1876	Mt. Zion
003638	SEDGWICK, Juan Stewart	20d	W	D.C.	14 JUN 1875	Oak Hill
006937	SEDRICKS, John Clifton	5m	C	D.C.	05 APR 1876	Mt. Pleasant
020783	SEDWICK, Richard T.	5m	C	D.C.	05 JUL 1879	Mt. Zion
003136	SEEFERS, John	4y	C	D.C.	26 APR 1875	Beckett's
008236	SEEHY, Mary Griswold	40y	W	Conn.	13 JUL 1876	Congressional
010794	SEELEY, Annie	36y	W	Pa.	26 FEB 1877	Philadelphia, Pa.
013592	SEGERSON, Ellen	85y	W	Ire.	22 OCT 1877	Holy Rood
000918	SEIBERS, Charles	14y	W	D.C.	24 OCT 1874	Mt. Olivet
008530	SEIBERT, Frances	22y	W	Md.	02 AUG 1876	St. Mary's
008011	SEILER, Francis S.	79y	W	Ger.	04 JUL 1876	Prospect Hill
012347	SEILER, John	66y	W	Eng.	13 JUL 1877	Soldier's Home
021164	SEILER, John A.	3y	W	D.C.	30 JUL 1879	Prospect Hill
006826	SEIVERS, Infant of Henry	26d	W	D.C.	26 MAR 1876	Prospect Hill
010377	SELBY, George E.	10m	W	D.C.	22 JAN 1877	Methodist
008032	SELBY, Jesse S.	5m	W	D.C.	05 JUL 1876	Congressional
017742	SELBY, John	65y	W	Md.	14 OCT 1878	Methodist
004959	SELBY, John Layton	17y	W	Md.	08 SEP 1875	Congressional
000217	SELBY, Mable	1y	W	D.C.	17 AUG 1874	Glenwood
003987	SELBY, Sarah F.	26y	W	D.C.	03 JUL 1875	Congressional
006517	SELDEN, Emily	60y	W	Va.	01 MAR 1876	Congressional
009955	SELDEN, Sophia	75y	M	Va.	14 DEC 1876	Harmony
005101a	SELKE, Mary Caroline	3y	W	Mass.	10 OCT 1875	Mt. Olivet
003290	SELKIRK, Robt.	43y	W	N.Y.	12 MAY 1875	Graceland
018317	SELMON, Moses	1y	C	D.C.	12 DEC 1878	Payne's
015048	SELVY, Caroline	2y	C	D.C.	12 MAR 1878	Harmony
006324	SELVY, James	49y	C	Md.	12 FEB 1876	Harmony
008118	SEMBLER, Annie Kathrina	22y	W	Ger.	10 JUL 1876	Prospect Hill

District of Columbia Death Records, August 1, 1874 to July 31, 1879 301

No.	Name	Age	Race	Birth	Death Date	Burial Place
010775	SEMBLY, Infant of Joseph	½h	C	D.C.	25 FEB 1877	Young Mens
006619	SEMLEY, Anna	1y	C	D.C.	09 MAR 1876	Young Mens
011194	SEMMES, Hattie	1y	C	D.C.	02 APR 1877	Ebenezer
018903	SEMMS, Rosa	1y	C	D.C.	31 JAN 1879	Payne's
009951	SENER, Henry Sharp	2y	W	D.C.	13 DEC 1876	Graceland/Glenwood
003065f	SENGSTACK, C.P.	40y	W	D.C.	12 APR 1875	Oak Hill
019001	SENGTELLER, Henry	17y	W	D.C.	08 FEB 1879	Glenwood
003608	SENSENEY, George E.	22y	W	D.C.	11 JUN 1875	Holy Rood
006025	SERGEANT, Adaline	68y	W	D.C.	14 JAN 1876	Congressional
017046	SERONI, Frank	11m	W	D.C.	14 AUG 1878	Mt. Olivet
010001	SERRER, Annie Belle	8y	W	Va.	18 DEC 1876	Graceland/Glenwood
018539	SERRIN, Etta Isabell	8y	W	D.C.	01 JAN 1879	Presbyterian
018798	SERRIN, John Edward	1y	W	D.C.	24 JAN 1879	Presbyterian
017453	SERRIN, Sarah L.	3y	W	D.C.	18 SEP 1878	Oak Hill
001144	SERRIN, Thomas	50y	W	D.C.	14 NOV 1874	Oak Hill
010572	SERRIN, Walter	3m	W	D.C.	09 FEB 1877	Presbyterian
007113	SERVOSS, Silas M.B.	40y	W	N.Y.	25 APR 1876	Oak Hill
008580	SESSFORD, Arthur	12m	W	D.C.	06 AUG 1876	Congressional
017330	SESSFORD, Joseph	61y	W	D.C.	05 SEP 1878	Congressional
015419	SESSFORD, Josephine A.	51y	W	Md.	16 APR 1878	Glenwood
017377	SESSFORD, Sarah E.	50y	W	Pa.	11 SEP 1878	Mt. Olivet
002718	SETTLE, Alexander Lawson	65y	W	Va.	24 MAR 1875	Holy Rood
013087	SETTLE, Curtis	4y	C	D.C.	04 SEP 1877	Beckett's
010386	SETTLE, George	42y	C	Va.	23 JAN 1877	Potters Field
011005	SETTLERS, Jane	70y	C	Va.	16 MAR 1877	Harmony
020905	SETTLERS, Walter	14d	C	D.C.	12 JUL 1879	Potters Field
013141	SEUROT, Albert	29y	W	France	09 SEP 1877	Hospital, Government
000133	SEWEL, Elizabeth	50y	M	D.C.	10 AUG 1874	Holy Rood
010427	SEWELL, Aggie Blair	14y	C	Md.	28 JAN 1877	Harmony
010907	SEWELL, Anna	85y	C	D.C.	08 MAR 1877	Potters Field
012920	SEWELL, Eliza	51y	C	Va.	23 AUG 1877	Baptist
007168	SEWELL, Julius	22y	M	D.C.	30 APR 1876	Ebenezer
019711	SEWELL, Margaret	65y	C	Md.	09 APR 1879	Mt. Zion
014373	SEWELL, Maria	5y	C	D.C.	09 JAN 1878	Beckett's
014449	SEWELL, Susie	24y	C	D.C.	16 JAN 1878	Harmony
001538	SEWLL, Nancy	34y	C	Va.	30 DEC 1874	Harmony
011422	SEXTON, Catherine	4m	W	D.C.	25 APR 1877	Mt. Olivet
008312	SEYBERT, Llwellen	26y	W	Mo.	18 JUL 1876	Congressional
006171	SEYBERT, Oscar T.	6m	W	D.C.	28 JAN 1876	Potters Field
010559	SEYBOLT, John W.	27y	W	D.C.	08 FEB 1877	Congressional
012777	SEYMOUR, Richard	82y	C	Va.	11 AUG 1877	Harmony
015625	SHAAFF, Mary Athenia	71y	W	Ga.	05 MAY 1878	Congressional
008162	SHACKELFORD, Mary Ann	76y	W	Va.	11 JUL 1876	Congressional
014117	SHACKELFORD, Sarah A.	35y	W	Va.	16 DEC 1877	Stafford Co., Va.
002987	SHACKLEFORD, James	73y	W	Va.	14 APR 1875	Congressional
000693	SHADE, George	29y	W	D.C.	02 OCT 1874	Congressional
002993	SHADERICH, Annie	1y	C	D.C.	14 APR 1875	Mt. Zion
019170	SHAEFER, Mary Angelia	1m	W	D.C.	23 FEB 1879	Mt. Olivet
006417	SHAFER, Mary M.	52y	W	D.C.	19 FEB 1876	Congressional
012856	SHAFER, Rosie E.	12y	W	D.C.	17 AUG 1877	Congressional
004340	SHAMAL, H[illegible]	19y	C	Md.	27 JUL 1875	Beckett's
007264	SHANAHAN, James	53y	W	Ire.	10 MAY 1876	Baltimore, Md.
019093	SHANAHAN, Michael	33y	W	Ire.	16 FEB 1879	Mt. Olivet
004620	SHANDLER, Joseph Allen	7m	C	D.C.	16 AUG 1875	Young Mens
008224	SHANDS, Infant of Alice	7h	C	D.C.	13 JUL 1876	Ebenezer
011768	SHANDS, Willie	12d	C	D.C.	01 JUN 1877	Ebenezer

No.	Name	Age	Race	Birth	Death Date	Burial Place
020930	SHANE, Elizabeth	71y	W	Ger.	14 JUL 1879	Mt. Olivet
014166	SHANE, Uriah	c.70y	W	Ire.	21 DEC 1877	Soldier's Home
005291	SHANHOUSE, Robert	16y	C	N.C.	28 OCT 1875	Mt. Pleasant
011794	SHANKIN, Henrietta	2y	C	D.C	04 JUN 1877	Ebenezer
014657	SHANKLAND, Infant of John	6d	C	D.C.	03 FEB 1878	Potters Field
011354	SHANKLAND, James	6d	C	D.C.	16 APR 1877	Potters Field
008776	SHANKLAND, Philip	2y	C	D.C.	22 AUG 1876	Ebenezer
015389	SHANKLIN, Allen	1y	C	D.C.	13 APR 1878	Beckett's
005698	SHANKLIN, George	61y	C	Va.	08 DEC 1875	Harmony
005831	SHANKLIN, Infant of Nancy	7d	C	D.C.	22 DEC 1875	Potters Field
006757	SHANKLIN, Infant of Meredith	36h	C	D.C.	20 MAR 1876	Ebenezer
010740	SHANKLIN, John S.	39y	W	Ind	22 FEB 1877	Crawfordsville, Ind.
019374	SHANKLIN, Meredith	47y	C	Va.	12 MAR 1879	Potters Field
001759	SHANKLIN, Peggy	85y	M	Va.	16 JAN 1875	Beckett's
008279	SHANKLIN, Thos.	19y	C	Va.	15 JUL 1876	Ebenezer
000574f	SHANKLIN, Winnie	90y	C	Va.	20 SEP 1874	Harmony
005315	SHANKLIN, Wm.	75y	C	Va.	30 OCT 1875	Ebenezer
021106	SHANKLING, Alphonzy	9m	C	D.C.	25 JUL 1879	Beckett's
020508	SHANKS, Bessie May	6m	W	D.C.	18 JUN 1879	Glenwood
018830	SHANKS, Catharine N.	83y	W	D.C.	26 JAN 1879	Congressional
014219	SHANKS, Harvey	2y	W	D.C.	26 DEC 1877	Holy Rood
005136	SHANKS, Mary E.	62y	W	Md.	22 SEP 1875	Holy Rood
019310	SHARP, Albert	1y	C	D.C.	07 MAR 1879	Swartz's
005224a	SHARP, James Carroll	4m	C	D.C.	20 OCT 1875	Swartz's
016918	SHARP, Mary	20y	C	--	05 AUG 1878	Beckett's
018963	SHARPS, Wm. H.	1y	C	D.C.	05 FEB 1879	Payne's
019541	SHAW, Albert	2m	W	D.C.	24 MAR 1879	Potters Field
020739	SHAW, Candice	78y	C	Va.	03 JUL 1879	Harmony
005350	SHAW, Charles Edwin	9d	W	D.C.	03 NOV 1875	Congressional
013690	SHAW, Clara Anna	1y	W	Ia.	31 OCT 1877	Presbyterian
008283	SHAW, David	16d	W	D.C.	15 JUL 1876	Mt. Olivet
013525	SHAW, Eliza Ann	c.45y	C	Md.	15 OCT 1877	Harmony
012065	SHAW, Ellen M.	35y	W	Pa.	26 JUN 1877	Congressional
011406	SHAW, Emmus V.	34y	W	Md.	23 APR 1877	Annapolis, Md.
012001	SHAW, Infant of Alfred	½h	W	D.C.	22 JUN 1877	Congressional
007516	SHAW, Infant of Delia	10h	C	D.C.	05 JUN 1876	Beckett's
012957	SHAW, Infant of Oliver	20h	W	D.C.	25 AUG 1877	Cumberland, Md.
019887	SHAW, James W.	42y	W	Ohio	24 APR 1879	Glenwood
015420	SHAW, John M.	44y	W	Me.	16 APR 1878	Prospect Hill
000092	SHAW, Joseph A.	8m	C	D.C.	07 AUG 1874	Mt. Olivet
006758	SHAW, Lucy	73y	C	Md.	20 MAR 1876	Rock Creek
009254	SHAW, Margret	112y	C	Md.	30 SEP 1876	Mt. Pleasant
001928	SHAW, Nicholas Snethen	59y	W	Md.	28 JAN 1875	Resin Shaw's B.G.
015206	SHAW, Susannah Elizabeth (Custis)	41y	W	D.C.	27 MAR 1878	Glenwood
004585	SHEA, Anna	1y	W	D.C.	13 AUG 1875	Mt. Olivet
012253	SHEA, Bartholomew	58y	W	Ire.	07 JUL 1877	Mt. Olivet
003446	SHEA, Cornelius	35y	W	Ire.	26 MAY 1875	Mt. Olivet
005085a	SHEA, David	55y	W	Ire.	08 OCT 1875	Mt. Olivet
017100	SHEA, Infant of Daniel	½h	W	D.C.	18 AUG 1878	Holy Rood
017099	SHEA, Infant of Daniel	½h	W	D.C.	18 AUG 1878	Holy Rood
018624	SHEA, John	60y	W	Ire.	09 JAN 1879	Mt. Olivet
020586a	SHEA, John	10d	W	D.C.	23 JUN 1879	Mt. Olivet
006396	SHEA, Joseph	15d	W	D.C.	17 FEB 1876	Mt. Olivet
014450	SHEA, Mary	56y	W	Ire.	16 JAN 1878	Mt. Olivet
000221	SHEA, Mary, Mrs.	35y	W	Ire.	17 AUG 1874	Mt. Olivet
013058	SHEA, Patrick	55y	W	Ire.	02 SEP 1877	Mt. Olivet

District of Columbia Death Records, August 1, 1874 to July 31, 1879

No.	Name	Age	Race	Birth	Death Date	Burial Place
013712	SHEA, Stephen	12h	W	D.C.	02 NOV 1877	Holy Rood
013674	SHEA, Thomas	4m	W	D.C.	29 OCT 1877	Mt. Olivet
013604	SHEA, Thomas P.	1y	W	D.C.	23 OCT 1877	Mt. Olivet
020289	SHEA, William Charles	9m	W	D.C.	03 JUN 1879	Mt. Olivet
003208	SHEAHAN, Annie	15m	W	D.C.	03 MAY 1875	Mt. Olivet
002972	SHEAHAN, Daniel	45y	W	Ire.	12 APR 1875	Mt. Olivet
019646	SHEAHAN, Michael Dominic	8m	W	D.C.	03 APR 1879	Mt. Olivet
004697	SHEAN, Charles	4y	W	D.C.	21 AUG 1875	Alexandria Co., Va.
008160	SHEAR, Mary, Mrs.	80y	W	Ver.	11 JUL 1876	Albany, N.Y.
011026	SHEARN, Mary	2y	W	D.C.	18 MAR 1877	Mt. Olivet
014020	SHECKELS, Elizabeth	c.35y	W	D.C.	06 DEC 1877	Congressional
011013	SHEDD, Harry	2y	W	D.C.	16 MAR 1877	Graceland
019777	SHEDERIC, Elisabeth	10m	C	D.C.	14 APR 1879	Mt. Zion
011234	SHEDRICK, Infant of Andrew	5d	C	D.C.	06 APR 1877	Potters Field
006578	SHEED, Deborah A.	86y	W	Pa.	06 MAR 1876	Rock Creek
008104	SHEEDY, Martin	79y	W	Ire.	09 JUL 1876	Mt. Olivet
017163	SHEEHAN, Mary	17y	W	D.C.	23 AUG 1878	Mt. Olivet
006576	SHEEHAN, Michael	87y	W	Ire.	06 MAR 1876	Mt. Olivet
017719	SHEEHAN, Patrick	21y	W	Ire.	12 OCT 1878	Mt. Olivet
009220	SHEHAN, Ellen	1y	W	D.C.	28 SEP 1876	Mt. Olivet
011148	SHEHAN, Patrick	25y	W	Ire.	29 MAR 1877	Mt. Olivet
002923	SHEIR, John Frederick	3y	W	D.C.	08 APR 1875	Mt. Olivet
019245	SHEKELL, Benjamin Owen	73y	W	N.Y.	01 MAR 1879	Mt. Olivet
005017	SHEKELL, Sarah Ann	68y	W	D.C.	12 SEP 1875	Mt. Olivet
007829	SHELDON, Lucinda	22y	C	Va.	24 JUN 1876	Ebenezer
000483	SHELTAN, Anne	40y	C	Va.	12 SEP 1874	Harmony
007830	SHELTON, Charles T.	10m	W	D.C.	24 JUN 1876	Congressional
000352	SHELTON, Infant of George	8h	C	D.C.	28 AUG 1874	Beckett's
015495	SHELTON, Martha	5m	C	D.C.	23 APR 1878	Mt. Zion
013455	SHELTON, Mary S.	25y	W	D.C.	09 OCT 1877	Congressional
005449	SHELTON, Mary Susan	1y	C	D.C.	13 NOV 1875	Ebenezer
020324	SHELTON, Robert Lee	21y	C	Va.	06 JUN 1879	Beckett's
013752	SHELTON, Thomas C.	39y	C	D.C.	06 NOV 1877	Mt. Zion
016042	SHELTON, Thomas F.	7m	W	D.C.	06 JUN 1878	Congressional
018291	SHELTON, William	45y	C	Va.	09 DEC 1878	Herndon, Va.
001080	SHEPARD, Sylvia Ann	99y	C	Va.	08 NOV 1874	Harmony
001535	SHEPERD, Winney	30y	C	Va.	29 DEC 1874	Beckett's
009344	SHEPHARD, David A.	76y	W	N.Y.	08 OCT 1876	Congressional
015285	SHEPHARD, William Dunn	67y	W	Pa.	04 APR 1878	Congressional
020007	SHEPHERD, Albertha	1y	C	D.C.	05 MAY 1879	Young Mens
020075	SHEPHERD, Fannie N.	25y	C	Va.	11 MAY 1879	Graceland
002890	SHEPHERD, Joseph	85y	W	Md.	06 APR 1875	Methodist
002383	SHEPHERD, Mary E.	3y	C	Va.	02 MAR 1875	Young Mens
006147	SHEPHERD, Mary E.	4y	W	D.C.	26 JAN 1876	Congressional
007938	SHEPHERD, Minnie V.	2y	W	D.C.	30 JUN 1876	Methodist
020140	SHEPHERD, Robert	7d	C	D.C.	18 MAY 1879	Graceland
007273	SHEPHERD, Sadie	3m	C	D.C.	11 MAY 1876	Young Mens
005356	SHEPHERD, Sanford	2y	C	D.C.	04 NOV 1875	Young Mens
001489	SHEPHERD, Susan Davidson	65y	W	Md.	26 DEC 1874	Rock Creek
004819	SHEPHERD, Theresa	11m	C	D.C.	29 AUG 1875	Mt. Olivet
003191	SHEPHERD, William	64y	W	N.Y.	01 MAY 1875	Hospital
020440	SHEPLEY, Jas. H.	43y	W	Me.	14 JUN 1879	Holy Rood/Arlington
019935	SHEPPARD, Hannah M.	54y	W	N.J.	29 APR 1879	Congressional
013318	SHEPPARD, Louisa	4y	C	D.C.	26 SEP 1877	Mt. Pleasant
011726	SHEPPARD, Sophie D.	17y	W	N.J.	27 MAY 1877	Congressional
010135	SHEPPERD, Emma L.	33y	W	D.C.	31 DEC 1876	Oak Hill

No.	Name	Age	Race	Birth	Death Date	Burial Place
001858f	SHEPPERSON, G.W.	27y	W	Va.	23 JAN 1875	Congressional
008990	SHERBERTH, Elizabeth	57y	W	Md.	07 SEP 1876	Mt. Olivet
012808	SHERER, John B.	1y	W	D.C.	14 AUG 1877	Mt. Olivet
014917	SHERIDAN, John A.	9y	W	D.C.	01 MAR 1878	Mt. Olivet
013262	SHERIDAN, Sister Sybillina	39y	W	N.Y.	20 SEP 1877	Mt. Olivet
007314	SHERIER, Catharine	30y	W	Va.	15 MAY 1876	Walker Chapel, Va.
001097	SHERIER, Ida	12y	W	Va.	09 NOV 1874	Va.
007702	SHERIER, Norah	1y	W	D.C.	17 JUN 1876	Walker Chapel, Va.
015913	SHERIFF, Eleanor	78y	W	Md.	30 MAY 1878	Congressional
004967	SHERMAN, Ada Elizabeth	20y	W	Conn.	09 SEP 1875	Oak Hill
015713	SHERMAN, Elgar H.	40y	W	Ala.	13 MAY 1878	Congressional
019311	SHERMAN, Hannah	55y	W	Va.	07 MAR 1879	Glenwood
019540	SHERMAN, Henry	71y	W	N.Y.	24 MAR 1879	Oak Hill
020984	SHERMAN, John T.	40y	W	Ohio	17 JUL 1879	Hospital
018709	SHERMONG, Wm.	44y	W	Ger.	17 JAN 1879	Hospital
008767	SHERR, Infant of Julius	4d	W	D.C.	21 AUG 1876	Prospect Hill
019509	SHERROD, Dempsey Barnes	50y	W	N.C.	22 MAR 1879	Congressional
013691	SHERWIN, Walter R.	7m	W	D.C.	31 OCT 1877	Accotink, Va.
020931	SHERWOOD, Ella Jane	14y	W	Va.	14 JUL 1879	Alexandria, Va.
007218	SHERWOOD, Emma Frances	11m	W	D.C.	05 MAY 1876	Presbyterian
007104	SHERWOOD, Frederick Donald	6y	W	D.C.	24 APR 1876	Congressional
016041	SHERWOOD, Ida Jane	5m	W	D.C.	06 JUN 1878	Glenwood
010831	SHERWOOD, James	1y	W	Pa.	02 MAR 1877	Graceland
010880	SHERWOOD, Lena	25y	W	Ger.	06 MAR 1877	St. Mary's
019615	SHERWOOD, Lena E.	2y	W	D.C.	31 MAR 1879	St. Mary's
003723	SHERWOOD, Odallie	1y	W	D.C.	20 JUN 1875	Congressional
006384	SHERWOOD, Wilhelmina	24d	W	D.C.	16 FEB 1876	Glenwood
002614	SHEURER, Infant of Andrew	1d	W	D.C.	17 MAR 1875	Presbyterian
013736	SHIBE, George	39y	W	Pa.	04 NOV 1877	Prospect Hill
006911	SHIELDS, Allen T.	2y	C	D.C.	03 APR 1876	Young Mens
017834	SHIELDS, Andrew B.	1m	C	D.C.	22 OCT 1878	Harmony
010588	SHIELDS, Charles Edward	4m	C	D.C.	11 FEB 1877	Harmony
011200	SHIELDS, Emma	10m	C	D.C.	03 APR 1877	Harmony
020275	SHIELDS, Eugene	3y	C	D.C.	02 JUN 1879	Harmony
005592	SHIELDS, Isaac Edward	12h	C	D.C.	28 NOV 1875	Harmony
003405	SHIELDS, James	3y	W	Md.	23 MAY 1875	Col'd Fields, Md.
017581	SHIELDS, Kate	24y	W	D.C.	30 SEP 1878	Mt. Olivet
020644	SHIELDS, Lewis	1y	C	D.C.	27 JUN 1879	Harmony
010864	SHIELDS, Noah	40y	C	Va.	04 MAR 1877	Harmony
012941	SHIELDS, Roberta B.	11m	M	D.C.	24 AUG 1877	Beckett's
005511	SHIELDS, Samuel	1y	C	D.C.	19 NOV 1875	Harmony
016584	SHIELDS, Thomas Henry	9d	C	D.C.	13 JUL 1878	Potters Field
003731	SHIELDS, Walter	4m	C	D.C.	20 JUN 1875	Ebenezer
015058	SHILLING, Omar George	5y	W	N.Y.	13 MAR 1878	Congressional
009175	SHIMS, Willis	55y	C	Va.	23 SEP 1876	Harmony
005273	SHINER, John Freeman Lincoln	1m	C	D.C.	26 OCT 1875	Beckett's
001121	SHINER, Sarah E.J.	20d	C	D.C.	12 NOV 1874	Beckett's
001616	SHINN, Martha	35y	W	Va.	05 JAN 1875	Alexandria, Va.
020724	SHINNTER, William	4m	C	D.C.	02 JUL 1879	Harmony
007334	SHIPLEY, Infant of Fernando	1h	C	D.C.	18 MAY 1876	Potters Field
010106	SHIPLEY, John William	5m	W	D.C.	28 DEC 1876	Glenwood
018194	SHIPLEY, Moses	60y	C	Va.	28 NOV 1878	Mt. Olivet
020191	SHIPLEY, Sarah Francis	11m	W	D.C.	24 MAY 1879	Mt. Olivet
021003	SHIPMAN, Laura	23d	C	D.C.	18 JUL 1879	Graceland
009659	SHIPPEN, Bessie	14y	C	Va.	09 NOV 1876	Harmony
002988	SHIVAS, Alexander Eaken	62y	W	Pa.	14 APR 1875	Mt. Holly, N.J.

District of Columbia Death Records, August 1, 1874 to July 31, 1879   305

No.	Name	Age	Race	Birth	Death Date	Burial Place
009701	SHLASSER, Henrietta	3y	W	D.C.	15 NOV 1876	Mt. Olivet
019877	SHOEMAKER, Abner C.	13y	W	D.C.	23 APR 1879	Holy Rood
003955	SHOEMAKER, Annie F.	6m	W	D.C.	01 JUL 1875	Presbyterian
002446	SHOEMAKER, Bertha	2y	W	D.C.	06 MAR 1875	Presbyterian
018749	SHOEMAKER, Celia	20y	C	Va.	20 JAN 1879	Mt. Zion
008069	SHOEMAKER, Eddward, Jr.	17y	W	D.C.	08 JUL 1876	Oak Hill
017389	SHOEMAKER, Ella	3m	W	D.C.	12 SEP 1878	Presbyterian
016229	SHOEMAKER, George	41y	W	D.C.	19 JUN 1878	Oak Hill
000228	SHOEMAKER, Grace	9m	W	D.C.	18 AUG 1874	Congressional
002594f	SHOEMAKER, H. Dixon	4y	--	Va.	-- DEC 1871	Rock Creek
004872	SHOEMAKER, Jasper William	2m	W	D.C.	01 SEP 1875	Oak Hill
020032	SHOEMAKER, Mary Augusta	34y	W	N.Y.	07 MAY 1879	New Drop, N.Y.
011671	SHOEMAKER, Mary Ellen	14y	W	D.C.	22 MAY 1877	Oak Hill
010127	SHOEMAKER, Oliver G.	7y	W	D.C.	30 DEC 1876	Oak Hill
000608	SHOEMAKER, Susan W.	1y	W	D.C.	23 SEP 1874	Oak Hill
002593f	SHOEMAKER, Thos. F., Jr.	3y	--	D.C.	-- FEB 1875	Rock Creek
002592f	SHOEMAKER, Wm. H.	1½y	--	D.C.	-- FEB 1875	Rock Creek
010137	SHOMO, J. Schuyler	9y	W	D.C.	31 DEC 1876	Congressional
016947	SHONE, Josephine	50y	W	D.C.	07 AUG 1878	Glenwood
009795	SHOOLER, Rosa L.	3y	W	Va.	25 NOV 1876	Spring Hill, Va.
011287	SHORES, Alinda	29y	C	Va.	10 APR 1877	Mt. Zion
014995	SHORT, Eliz. Henrietta Hortense	1y	W	D.C.	08 MAR 1878	Mt. Olivet
019712	SHORT, Margaret Ellen	5y	W	N.Y.	09 APR 1879	Mt. Olivet
016722	SHORT, Sarah	1y	C	D.C.	22 JUL 1878	Beckett's
003810	SHORTER, Abraham	112y	C	Md.	24 JUN 1875	Potters Field
002412	SHORTER, Ada	3y	C	D.C.	03 MAR 1875	Ebenezer
008633	SHORTER, Alfred	44y	C	Va.	10 AUG 1876	Young Mens
019092	SHORTER, Arie	4m	C	D.C.	16 FEB 1879	Potters Field
020542	SHORTER, Ellen	49y	C	D.C.	20 JUN 1879	Harmony
013566	SHORTER, Florence E.	1y	C	D.C.	19 OCT 1877	Harmony
013841	SHORTER, Frank	7y	C	D.C.	16 NOV 1877	Mt. Pleasant
005674	SHORTER, Henry	4m	C	D.C.	06 DEC 1875	Potters Field
007912	SHORTER, Infant of John	2d	C	D.C.	28 JUN 1876	Ebenezer
015959	SHORTER, Infant of Henry	7d	C	D.C.	01 JUN 1878	Potters Field
007767	SHORTER, James	42y	C	Md.	21 JUN 1876	Potters Field
003070	SHORTER, Jane	15y	C	Md.	21 APR 1875	Mt. Olivet
010785	SHORTER, John	2y	C	D.C.	26 FEB 1877	Ebenezer
013771	SHORTER, John	c.60y	C	Md.	08 NOV 1877	Young Mens
016270	SHORTER, John	1y	C	D.C.	22 JUN 1878	Holy Rood
017313	SHORTER, Maria	40y	C	D.C.	03 SEP 1878	Potters Field
007079	SHORTER, Mary	69y	C	Md.	22 APR 1876	Holy Rood
019103	SHORTER, Mary A.	1y	C	D.C.	17 FEB 1879	Harmony
019171	SHORTER, Nelson	70y	C	D.C.	23 FEB 1879	Mt. Olivet
021105	SHORTER, Richard Francis	18y	c	Md.	25 JUL 1879	Good Hope
005019a	SHORTER, Robert	29y	C	Pa.	01 OCT 1875	Harmony
012468	SHORTER, William E.	1y	C	D.C.	22 JUL 1877	Harmony
014644	SHORTS, Carrie	1y	C	D.C.	02 FEB 1878	Harmony
003601	SHRAVE, William	6m	W	D.C.	11 JUN 1875	Glenwood
018193	SHRECK, Mary J., Mrs.	45y	W	Md.	28 NOV 1878	Baltimore, Md.
016528	SHREEVES, Angeline R.	1y	C	D.C.	09 JUL 1878	Mt. Pleasant
020723	SHREVE, George Eliott	15d	W	D.C.	02 JUL 1879	Glenwood
016595	SHREVE, Mary Ann	23y	W	Del.	14 JUL 1878	Glenwood
020523	SHREVE, Mollie Isabella	22y	W	D.C.	19 JUN 1879	Glenwood
003985	SHRIVE, Robert	7d	W	D.C.	03 JUL 1875	Glenwood
005208a	SHRUGRUE, Johanna	90y	W	Ire.	19 OCT 1875	Holy Rood
002420	SHRYER, Susan	74y	W	Md.	04 MAR 1875	Congressional

No.	Name	Age	Race	Birth	Death Date	Burial Place
007400	SHUGHRUE, Kate	6y	W	D.C.	24 MAY 1876	Mt. Olivet
017967	SHUGRUE, Jas.	62y	W	Ire.	06 NOV 1878	Mt. Olivet
008834	SHULTZ, Annie	3w	W	D.C.	26 AUG 1876	Prospect Hill
019936	SHULTZ, Ferdinand	60y	W	Ger.	29 APR 1879	Hospital
009231	SHULTZ, George	3m	W	D.C.	28 SEP 1876	St. Mary's
013249	SHUMAN, Armin	10y	W	Va.	19 SEP 1877	Prospect Hill
020511	SMURM, Minnie	1m	W	D.C.	18 JUN 1879	Congressional
007867	SHUSTER, Samuel Paul	80y	W	N.J.	26 JUN 1876	Oak Hill
005147a	SIBLEY, Greenbery	40y	W	Md.	14 OCT 1875	Glenwood
010638	SIBLEY, Solomon	71y	W	Md.	15 FEB 1877	Glenwood
007515	SIDNEY, Cassy B.	1y	C	D.C.	05 JUN 1876	Harmony
000357	SIDNEY, Flornce	4y	C	D.C.	29 AUG 1874	Harmony
013142	SIDNEY, Judy	27y	C	Va.	09 SEP 1877	Harmony
007140	SIDNEY, Richard	74y	C	Va.	27 APR 1876	Harmony
000594	SIDNOR, Edward Augustus	1y	C	D.C.	22 SEP 1874	Beckett's
011457	SIDNOR, Infant of Jacob	9d	C	D.C.	29 APR 1877	Beckett's
007913	SIEBERT, Nellie	5m	W	D.C.	28 JUN 1876	Glenwood
005664	SIEVER, Nelly	7d	W	D.C.	05 DEC 1875	Prospect Hill
008479	SIEVERS, Louise	8m	W	D.C.	29 JUL 1876	Prospect Hill
013425	SIGGERS, Mary Ellen	44y	W	N.Y.	07 OCT 1877	Congressional
017619	SIGMUND, Christian	62y	W	Md.	03 OCT 1878	Oak Hill
021021	SIGNEY, Margret Louisa	1y	W	D.C.	20 JUL 1879	Mt. Olivet
009244	SIGNOR, Emma E.	2y	W	D.C.	30 SEP 1876	Congressional
006072	SIGNOR, Katie Virginia	1m	W	D.C.	19 JAN 1876	Congressional
000295	SIGOURNEY, Daniel	15d	W	D.C.	23 AUG 1874	Congressional
004672	SIGOURNEY, Jane A.	5m	W	D.C.	19 AUG 1875	Congressional
011088	SIKEN, Phillip	8m	W	D.C.	23 MAR 1877	Mt. Olivet
003728	SILBY, Margaret	2m	C	D.C.	20 JUN 1875	Mt. Olivet
016641	SILENCE, George Henry	9d	W	D.C.	17 JUL 1878	Va.
016077	SILL, Margaret W.	58y	W	Mass.	08 JUN 1878	Newark, N.J.
005830	SILLERS, Violet	1y	W	D.C.	22 DEC 1875	Mt. Olivet
003157	SILLS, Emily	78y	C	Va.	28 APR 1875	Cephas Farm
011247	SILLS, Mary	7y	C	Mass.	06 APR 1877	Harmony
011163	SILLSBEE, John O.	42y	W	N.Y.	30 MAR 1877	Washington Asylum
011666	SILSBY, Isaac	68y	W	Mass.	21 MAY 1877	Oak Hill
011332	SILVA, Branger	65y	C	D.C.	14 APR 1877	Slager, Md.
004818	SILVESTER, Mattie Elizebeth	9d	C	D.C.	29 AUG 1875	Ebenezer
013783	SILVY, Eliza M.	25y	C	Va.	09 NOV 1877	Harmony
014253	SIMES, Emma	3y	C	D.C.	29 DEC 1877	Young Mens
012036	SIMES, Laura	25y	C	Md.	24 JUN 1877	Jones Chapel
016863	SIMES, Stephen	46y	C	Md.	01 AUG 1878	Young Mens
000405	SIMMAKER, Leonard	64y	W	Ger.	02 SEP 1874	Prospect Hill
003387	SIMMES, Daniel	c.75y	C	Md.	21 MAY 1875	Beckett's
017817	SIMMES, Henry	60y	C	Va.	20 OCT 1878	Potters Field
007666	SIMMES, Martha	30y	M	Md.	15 JUN 1876	Young Mens
009779	SIMMES, Sarah	23y	C	D.C.	23 NOV 1876	Potters Field
018008	SIMMONS, Ann	80y	W	Va.	10 NOV 1878	Graceland
001507	SIMMONS, Augustus	74y	W	Md.	27 DEC 1874	Glenwood
002633	SIMMONS, Charles A.	3y	W	D.C.	18 MAR 1875	Glenwood
002710	SIMMONS, Charles H.	3y	W	D.C.	23 MAR 1875	Oak Hill
006146	SIMMONS, Cresie	71y	C	Va.	26 JAN 1876	Harmony
012277	SIMMONS, Henry G.	4y	W	D.C.	09 JUL 1877	Presbyterian
000976	SIMMONS, Henry P.	14y	W	D.C.	29 OCT 1874	Congressional
006723	SIMMONS, Martha E.	4y	W	D.C.	18 MAR 1876	Presbyterian
019746	SIMMONS, Maud W.	5m	C	Fla.	12 APR 1879	Harmony
020313	SIMMONS, Primus M.	1y	C	D.C.	05 JUN 1879	Graceland

District of Columbia Death Records, August 1, 1874 to July 31, 1879

No.	Name	Age	Race	Birth	Death Date	Burial Place
020276	SIMMONS, Samuel	2y	W	D.C.	02 JUN 1879	Oak Hill
012307	SIMMONS, Thomas	7m	C	D.C.	10 JUL 1877	Young Mens
020133	SIMMONS, William H.	68y	W	Va.	17 MAY 1879	Oak Hill
001769	SIMMS, Abert Eugene	4m	C	D.C.	17 JAN 1875	Mt. Pleasant
007166	SIMMS, Adaline	30y	C	Va.	30 APR 1876	Young Mens
013879	SIMMS, Adam	43y	C	Md.	21 NOV 1877	Young Mens
007540	SIMMS, Adia Rebeca	11m	C	D.C.	07 JUN 1876	Ebenezer
005018a	SIMMS, Amanda	23y	C	Md.	01 OCT 1875	Thomas'
017176	SIMMS, Antony	82y	C	Md.	24 AUG 1878	Mt. Olivet
002404	SIMMS, Charles	45y	W	Md.	03 MAR 1875	Mt. Olivet
015828	SIMMS, Charles Neville	61y	W	Va.	24 MAY 1878	Oak Hill
000823	SIMMS, Charlotte	76y	M	Md.	16 OCT 1874	Potters Field
018708	SIMMS, David	70y	C	Md.	17 JAN 1879	Potters Field
015839	SIMMS, Edward Alexander	13d	C	D.C.	25 MAY 1878	Young Mens
004422	SIMMS, Eliza Catherine	20y	C	Va.	02 AUG 1875	Ebenezer
016295	SIMMS, Emma	1y	C	D.C.	24 JUN 1878	Beckett's
007928	SIMMS, Fanny	64y	C	Va.	29 JUN 1876	Potters Field
019616	SIMMS, Genevieve	2y	W	D.C.	31 MAR 1879	Mt. Olivet
002735	SIMMS, Harriett A.	4m	C	D.C.	25 MAR 1875	Beckett's
020053	SIMMS, Henry	c.35y	W	--	09 MAY 1879	Potters Field
005477	SIMMS, Ida	4y	C	D.C.	16 NOV 1875	Oxen Hill, Md.
003866	SIMMS, Infant of Daniel	15min	C	D.C.	26 JUN 1875	Nonesuch
018415	SIMMS, Infant of Henry	5min	C	D.C.	21 DEC 1878	Potters Field
000947	SIMMS, Infant of Isabella	30d	C	D.C.	27 OCT 1874	Washington Asylum
000384	SIMMS, Infant of Mary Allen	--	M	D.C.	31 AUG 1874	Potters Field
006180	SIMMS, Infant of Siras	5d	C	D.C.	29 JAN 1876	Ebenezer
015765	SIMMS, Jane	29y	C	Va.	18 MAY 1878	Young Mens
013784	SIMMS, John F.	1y	C	D.C.	09 NOV 1877	Payne's
019837	SIMMS, Joseph	1m	W	U.S.	19 APR 1879	Mt. Olivet
020206	SIMMS, Julia	c.28y	C	Va.	26 MAY 1879	Harmony
017646	SIMMS, Lewis	8y	C	D.C.	05 OCT 1878	Mt. Pleasant
008001	SIMMS, Lizzie	2m	C	D.C.	04 JUL 1876	Harmony
005854	SIMMS, Martha	33y	C	Md.	24 DEC 1875	Moore's
014355	SIMMS, Mary	13y	C	D.C.	07 JAN 1878	Sol. G. Brown's
020031	SIMMS, Mary Ann	24y	C	Md.	07 MAY 1879	Potters Field
004785	SIMMS, Nelson	18y	C	D.C.	27 AUG 1875	Potters Field
005829	SIMMS, Phillip	70y	C	Md.	22 DEC 1875	Jones Chapel
014595	SIMMS, Reuben	75y	C	Va.	29 JAN 1878	Potters Field
011867	SIMMS, Richard Henry	9m	C	D.C.	11 JUN 1877	Mt. Olivet
015827	SIMMS, Rosetta	20y	C	Md.	24 MAY 1878	Harmony
003836	SIMMS, Samuel	10m	C	D.C.	25 JUN 1875	Harmony
006641	SIMMS, Solomon	3y	C	D.C.	11 MAR 1876	Mt. Pleasant
019231	SIMMS, Sophia	c.50y	C	Md.	27 FEB 1879	Beckett's
006740	SIMMS, Sylvester E.	6m	C	D.C.	19 MAR 1876	Holy Rood
020063	SIMMS, Thomas	3m	C	D.C.	10 MAY 1879	Beckett's
007733	SIMMS, Thomas H.	18m	C	D.C.	19 JUN 1876	Beckett's
018366	SIMMS, William	53y	M	Md.	17 DEC 1878	Hospital, Government
016891	SIMMS, Willis	53y	C	Md.	03 AUG 1878	Hillsdale
003726	SIMON, Lewis	16y	W	Md.	20 JUN 1875	St. Mary's
021087	SIMONDS, Sarah A.	66y	W	D.C.	24 JUL 1879	Mt. Olivet
006442	SIMONDS, Stephen	68y	W	D.C.	22 FEB 1876	Methodist, East
008460	SIMONS, Charles Augustus	11m	C	D.C.	28 JUL 1876	Potters Field
001158	SIMONS, Elizabeth	63y	W	D.C.	16 NOV 1874	Presbyterian
005726	SIMONS, Florance A.	3m	W	D.C.	11 DEC 1875	Congressional
020386	SIMONS, John	31y	W	D.C.	10 JUN 1879	Methodist
004720	SIMONS, Thos. J.	47y	W	Va.	22 AUG 1875	Alexandria, Va.

No.	Name	Age	Race	Birth	Death Date	Burial Place
017037	SIMONTON, Florida	48y	W	D.C.	13 AUG 1878	Congressional
011057	SIMONTON, Mary	66y	W	Va.	21 MAR 1877	Washington Asylum
005780	SIMPSON, Alice	1y	C	D.C.	17 DEC 1875	Washington Asylum
021140	SIMPSON, Ann	70y	C	Va.	28 JUL 1879	Potters Field
006354	SIMPSON, Arthur O.	3y	W	D.C.	14 FEB 1876	Addison's Chapel
003623	SIMPSON, Estelle	30y	W	Can.	13 JUN 1875	Congressional
006790	SIMPSON, Fannia	3y	C	D.C.	23 MAR 1876	Ebenezer
017298	SIMPSON, Francis	69y	W	Va.	02 SEP 1878	Tennallytown
000517	SIMPSON, Franck	2y	W	N.Y.	15 SEP 1874	Baltimore, Md.
006209	SIMPSON, George Bayne	1y	W	D.C.	01 FEB 1876	Addison's Chapel
020430	SIMPSON, Grace	2½m	W	D.C.	13 JUN 1879	Graceland
010930	SIMPSON, Hannah	14d	C	D.C.	09 MAR 1877	Moore's
004984	SIMPSON, Infant of Benjamin	1m	C	D.C.	10 SEP 1875	Potters Field
001991	SIMPSON, Infant of Carrie	8d	C	D.C.	02 FEB 1875	Potters Field
009648	SIMPSON, Joseph	14d	C	D.C.	09 NOV 1876	Young Mens
007731	SIMPSON, Lilly May	10m	W	D.C.	19 JUN 1876	Bell Church, Md.
002090f	SIMPSON, Mary	62y	W	Eng.	12 OCT 1864	Congressional
000889	SIMPSON, Mary Ellen	4y	W	D.C.	21 OCT 1874	Barnabas Church
002722	SIMPSON, Nancy	75y	C	Md.	24 MAR 1875	Mt. Zion
009328	SIMPSON, Rebecca, Mrs.	35y	W	D.C.	07 OCT 1876	Oak Hill
012385	SIMPSON, Sophia B.	23y	C	D.C.	16 JUL 1877	Harmony
015375	SIMPSON, Walter	5y	W	D.C.	12 APR 1878	Congressional
003598f	SIMPSON, William T.	80y	W	Va.	10 JUN 1875	Congressional
019875	SIMS, Annie	4m	W	D.C.	23 APR 1879	Congressional
019366	SIMS, Annie R.	21y	W	Md.	11 MAR 1879	Congressional
005109a	SIMS, Charlotte Anne	4y	C	D.C.	11 OCT 1875	Ebenezer
001180	SIMS, Edward	35y	C	D.C.	19 NOV 1874	Mt. Olivet
011226	SIMS, Elias	3y	C	D.C.	05 APR 1877	Ebenezer
008068	SIMS, Ellen	1m	C	D.C.	08 JUL 1876	Moore's
014207	SIMS, Florence	5y	W	D.C.	25 DEC 1877	Glenwood
004019	SIMS, George Francis	5m	C	D.C.	06 JUL 1875	Ebenezer
015083	SIMS, Hattie	2m	C	D.C.	15 MAR 1878	Beckett's
004020	SIMS, Henrietta	7m	C	D.C.	06 JUL 1875	Mt. Olivet
004961f	SIMS, Henry	50y	C	Md.	08 SEP 1875	Thomas'
000494	SIMS, Infant (illeg.)	6m	C	D.C.	12 SEP 1874	Potters Field
007138	SIMS, Infant of Robert	2m	C	D.C.	27 APR 1876	Potters Field
019061	SIMS, James	20y	C	Md.	13 FEB 1879	Beckett's
004534	SIMS, John	62y	C	Md.	10 AUG 1875	Stanton Ave./Good Hope
015882	SIMS, Laura Alberta	11m	C	D.C.	28 MAY 1878	Payne's
001730	SIMS, Maggie	1y	C	D.C.	14 JAN 1875	Mt. Olivet
016057	SIMS, Mary Francis	38y	C	D.C.	07 JUN 1878	Mt. Pleasant
002114	SIMS, Rachel	50y	C	Md.	11 FEB 1875	Young Mens
013173	SIMS, Theo.	1y	C	D.C.	12 SEP 1877	Young Mens
010953	SIMS, William	7y	C	D.C.	12 MAR 1877	Ebenezer
010669	SIMS, Wm. Henry	1y	C	D.C.	17 FEB 1877	Ebenezer
016024	SINCELL, Mary Ann	3y	W	D.C.	06 JUN 1878	Glenwood
004850	SINCLAIR, Elen	72y	C	Md.	31 AUG 1875	Mt. Zion
003084	SINCLAIR, Harriet W.	63y	W	Va.	22 APR 1875	Oak Hill
003264	SINCLAIR, James	35y	W	N.Y.	08 MAY 1875	Hospital
003315	SINCLAIR, James Alexander	3y	W	Mass.	14 MAY 1875	Baltimore, Md.
017498	SINCLAIRE, Cecelia	75y	W	S.C.	22 SEP 1878	Graceland
005394	SINGLETON, Mary	39y	C	Va.	08 NOV 1875	Mt. Zion
000374	SINGLETON, Matilda	2y	C	D.C.	30 AUG 1874	Macedonia
006490	SINGLETON, Rebecca V.	17y	C	Va.	27 FEB 1876	Mt. Zion
006577	SINGLETON, Sallie S.	c.36y	W	Md.	06 MAR 1876	Oak Hill
008026	SINGLETON, Waltimore Sylvester	1y	C	D.C.	05 JUL 1876	Holy Rood

District of Columbia Death Records, August 1, 1874 to July 31, 1879

No.	Name	Age	Race	Birth	Death Date	Burial Place
006276	SINKFIELD, Minney	1y	C	Va.	08 FEB 1876	Fairfax Co., Va.
000277	SINON, John Thomas	42y	W	D.C.	21 AUG 1874	Glenwood
007191	SIOUSSA, John	63y	W	D.C.	02 MAY 1876	Glenwood
001425	SIOUSSA, Mary	c.50y	W	D.C.	18 DEC 1874	Glenwood
005622	SIPE, Louisa A.	63y	W	Md.	01 DEC 1875	Congressional
010332	SIPHAS, Paul	c.50y	W	Hung.	19 JAN 1877	Hospital, Government
000071	SIPPLES, C. Nace	40y	M	Va.	05 AUG 1874	Washington Asylum
002391	SIS, Sarah Catherine	31y	W	Md.	02 MAR 1875	Holy Rood
004404	SISSON, Augusta V.	25y	W	Va.	01 AUG 1875	Congressional
016163	SISSON, Francis Hoag	45y	W	N.Y.	14 JUN 1878	Glenwood
008567	SISSON, Infant of J. Henry	30min	W	D.C.	05 AUG 1876	Mt. Olivet
015557	SISSON, John C	12y	W	Va.	29 APR 1878	Congressional
009778	SISSON, Martha A.	65y	C	Md.	23 NOV 1876	Addison's Farm
002904	Sister Virginia	34y	W	France	07 APR 1875	Mt. Olivet
005724	SIVAS, [Illegible]	c.70y	C	--	11 DEC 1875	Potters Field
004740	SKEHEN, John	82y	W	Ire.	24 AUG 1875	Mt. Olivet
006425	SKELTON, Francis P.	36y	W	W.Va.	20 FEB 1876	Congressional
012673	SKIDMORE, Eliza J.	22y	W	Md.	04 AUG 1877	Oak Grove, Md.
009757	SKIDMORE, Emma	4y	W	D.C.	20 NOV 1876	Congressional
012855	SKIDMORE, Henry	9m	W	D.C.	17 AUG 1877	Brick Church, Md.
006991	SKIDMORE, Laura V.	18y	W	D.C.	11 APR 1876	Congressional
009376	SKIDMORE, Louis F.	51y	W	Va.	11 OCT 1876	Congressional
015302	SKINNER, Adele	11y	W	D.C.	06 APR 1878	Tennallytown
004319	SKINNER, Benjamin H.	71y	W	Conn.	26 JUL 1875	Glenwood
009437	SKINNER, Betsey	85y	C	Va.	16 OCT 1876	Beckett's
015059	SKINNER, George	45y	W	U.S.	13 MAR 1878	Glenwood
013319	SKINNER, Infant of Elizabeth	1m	C	D.C.	26 SEP 1877	Moore's
012166	SKINNER, James	1y	W	D.C.	01 JUL 1877	Mt. Olivet
005686	SKINNER, Jane	90y	C	Va.	07 DEC 1875	Potters Field
011754	SKINNER, John	11m	C	D.C.	31 MAY 1877	Ebenezer
009545	SKINNER, Mary Ellen	11m	C	D.C.	26 OCT 1876	Mt. Zion
000096	SKINNER, Matilda	3w	W	D.C.	07 AUG 1874	Prospect Hill
000060	SKINNER, Willie	11m	C	D.C.	04 AUG 1874	Washington Asylum
015060	SKIPPON, Sarah E.	c.45y	W	Va.	13 MAR 1878	Glenwood
018417	SKOURK, Abraham David	28y	W	Rus.	21 DEC 1878	Adas Israel
018719	SLACK, Carl Stanly	6m	W	D.C.	18 JAN 1879	Congressional
012033	SLACK, G.A.	1m	W	D.C.	24 JUN 1877	Holy Rood
005172	SLADE, Charles H.	1y	C	D.C.	25 SEP 1875	Mt. Pleasant
012986	SLADE, Henrietta Brown	14d	M	D.C.	27 AUG 1877	Harmony
003865	SLADE, Henry M.	46y	W	Ver.	26 JUN 1875	Middleburg, Ver.
010140	SLAGLE, John W.	52y	W	Va.	01 JAN 1877	Graceland
005982	SLAGLE, John Wall	18y	W	Va.	09 JAN 1876	Glenwood
008057	SLATER, Ann	45y	W	Eng.	07 JUL 1876	Mt. Olivet
000316	SLATER, Annie, Mrs.	41y	C	Md.	25 AUG 1874	Harmony
003233	SLATER, Caroline	52y	C	Md.	05 MAY 1875	Harmony
007753	SLATER, Caroline	1m	C	D.C.	20 JUN 1876	Ebenezer
015602	SLATER, Charles	40y	C	Md.	03 MAY 1878	Upton Run, Md.
010343	SLATER, Emma	6m	D.C.		20 JAN 1877	Harmony
012596	SLATER, Estelle F.	2m	W	D.C.	29 JUL 1877	Presbyterian
020842	SLATER, Geo. E.	10m	C	D.C.	08 JUL 1879	Mt. Pleasant
016613	SLATER, Hannah	110y	C	Md.	15 JUL 1878	Mt. Zion
008368	SLATER, Henrietta	75y	C	D.C.	21 JUL 1876	Mt. Zion
003028	SLATER, Infant of Alice	2h	C	D.C.	17 APR 1875	Potters Field
012828	SLATER, James Francis	42y	M	Va.	15 AUG 1877	Harmony
004236	SLATER, John Souder	38y	W	Va.	21 JUL 1875	Congressional
008377	SLATER, Louis	24y	C	Va.	22 JUL 1876	Mt. Zion

District of Columbia Death Records, August 1, 1874 to July 31, 1879

No.	Name	Age	Race	Birth	Death Date	Burial Place
011762	SLATER, Margaret E.	7y	W	D.C.	01 JUN 1877	Congressional
001784	SLATER, Martha	20y	C	Md.	18 JAN 1875	Jones Chapel
002673	SLATER, Rachal	16m	C	D.C.	21 MAR 1875	Harmony
012759	SLATER, Susan	6m	W	D.C.	10 AUG 1877	Graceland
013875	SLATER, William Risler	22y	W	N.J.	20 NOV 1877	Frenchtown, N.J.
008142	SLATTERY, Michael Francis	1y	W	D.C.	10 JUL 1876	Mt. Olivet
016426	SLATTERY, Sarah	40y	W	Ire.	03 JUL 1878	Mt. Olivet
011491	SLATUR, Louisa	60y	C	Md.	02 MAY 1877	Jones Chapel
009445	SLAUGHTER, Alice Bulah	3y	W	Va.	17 OCT 1876	Potters Field
012383	SLAUGHTER, Clara	7m	C	D.C.	16 JUL 1877	Mt. Olivet
002914	SLAUGHTER, Elijah	1y	C	D.C.	07 APR 1875	Mt. Zion
009415	SLAUGHTER, Ernest Summer	7m	C	D.C.	15 OCT 1876	Harmony
019073	SLAUGHTER, Furry B.	11m	C	D.C.	14 FEB 1879	Mt. Zion
001594	SLAUGHTER, George A.	2y	M	Va.	02 JAN 1875	Potters Field
005804	SLAUGHTER, Harriet B.	1y	C	D.C.	20 DEC 1875	Mt. Olivet
020139	SLAUGHTER, Infant of Susan	1h	C	D.C.	18 MAY 1879	Potters Field
002624	SLAUGHTER, James D.	32y	W	N.Y.	16 MAR 1875	Hospital
012604	SLAUGHTER, Lenny	4m	C	D.C.	30 JUL 1877	Young Mens
017408	SLAUGHTER, Maria	30y	C	Va.	14 SEP 1878	Beckett's
016494	SLAUGHTER, Martha Ellen	1y	C	D.C.	07 JUL 1878	Beckett's
006412	SLAUGHTER, Mary Jane	3y	C	D.C.	18 FEB 1876	Beckett's
002015	SLAUGHTER, Reuben	22y	M	Va.	03 FEB 1875	Potters Field
005180a	SLAVEN, Samuel S.	9m	W	D.C.	17 OCT 1875	Graceland
013471	SLENTZ, Georgeana Washington	34y	W	Pa.	10 OCT 1877	Gettysburg, Pa.
018797	SLICK, Otilda A.	20y	W	Va.	24 JAN 1879	Glenwood
021108	SLICK, Saml. E.	6m	W	D.C.	25 JUL 1879	Glenwood
007971	SLIDE, Louise Brown	14d	C	D.C.	02 JUL 1876	Harmony
019659	SLIGHT, Jane F.	44y	W	D.C.	04 APR 1879	Congressional
016215	SLINEY, Rose Standish	4y	W	D.C.	18 JUN 1878	Rock Creek
001910	SLINTER, Josephine	45y	C	D.C.	27 JAN 1875	Harmony
004088	SLOAN, John	14m	W	D.C.	11 JUL 1875	Mt. Olivet
017365	SLOANE, Maggie A.	34y	W	N.Y.	10 SEP 1878	Rock Creek
016822	SLOSSER, Margaret E.	7m	W	D.C.	29 JUL 1878	Glenwood
005340	SLOUGH, R.E.	5y	W	D.C.	02 NOV 1875	Congressional
001036	SLOUTEN, Lewis	6d	C	D.C.	03 NOV 1874	Beckett's
007169	SLYE, Nannie	1y	W	D.C.	30 APR 1876	Congressional
019256	SLYER, Luther Samuel	29y	W	W.Va.	02 MAR 1879	Martinsburg, W.Va.
015496	SLYER, Sarah	69y	W	W.Va.	23 APR 1878	Martinsburg, W.Va.
001285	SMACKRUM, Hannah	75y	C	Md.	02 DEC 1874	Addison's, Reason
006102	SMACKUM, Amelia	24y	C	Md.	22 JAN 1876	Mt. Zion
005200	SMACKUM, George E.	1m	C	D.C.	27 SEP 1875	Young Mens
017244	SMACKUM, Mary L.	6d	C	D.C.	29 AUG 1878	Holy Rood
006218	SMACKUM, Mary M.	45y	C	Md.	02 FEB 1876	Holy Rood
006411	SMALL, Catherine Elizabeth	1y	C	D.C.	18 FEB 1876	Holy Rood
011056	SMALL, David	35y	W	Scot.	21 MAR 1877	Glenwood
020152	SMALL, Fannie J.	42y	W	Md.	19 MAY 1879	Baltimore, Md.
014679	SMALL, Infant of James	1d	W	D.C.	05 FEB 1878	Congressional
010847	SMALLWOOD, Alexander	50y	C	Md.	03 MAR 1877	Oxen Hill, Md.
009502	SMALLWOOD, Benjamin	3y	C	D.C.	22 OCT 1876	Beckett's
011674	SMALLWOOD, Bessie Ann	2y	C	D.C.	22 MAY 1877	Mt. Olivet
018491	SMALLWOOD, Charity	c.80y	C	Md.	28 DEC 1878	Harmony
019481	SMALLWOOD, Charles	6m	C	D.C.	20 MAR 1879	Harmony
010478	SMALLWOOD, Eldora	11m	M	D.C.	02 FEB 1877	Potters Field
020076	SMALLWOOD, Eliza Catherine	37y	C	Md.	11 MAY 1879	Mt. Pleasant
004887	SMALLWOOD, Emeline	20y	C	D.C.	02 SEP 1875	Ebenezer
005654	SMALLWOOD, Fannie	16m	C	D.C.	04 DEC 1875	Harmony

District of Columbia Death Records, August 1, 1874 to July 31, 1879   311

No.	Name	Age	Race	Birth	Death Date	Burial Place
009812	SMALLWOOD, Gertrude	3y	W	D.C.	27 NOV 1876	Congressional
004701	SMALLWOOD, Henrietta	78y	C	Md.	21 AUG 1875	Mt. Pleasant
006992	SMALLWOOD, Infant of Charles	1d	C	D.C.	11 APR 1876	Potters Field
020630	SMALLWOOD, James	80y	C	Md.	26 JUN 1879	Van Buren
003580	SMALLWOOD, James F.	7m	C	D.C.	09 JUN 1875	Mt. Olivet
017322	SMALLWOOD, James M.	29y	C	D.C.	04 SEP 1878	Mt. Pleasant
008442	SMALLWOOD, John	66y	C	D.C.	27 JUL 1876	Harmony
009524	SMALLWOOD, Joseph	60y	C	D.C.	25 OCT 1876	Mt. Zion
018863	SMALLWOOD, Laura	25y	C	Md.	28 JAN 1879	Mt. Olivet
017387	SMALLWOOD, Lottie	5y	C	D.C.	12 SEP 1878	Mt. Zion
005699	SMALLWOOD, Margret B.J.	2m	C	D.C.	08 DEC 1875	Mt. Olivet
009252	SMALLWOOD, Mary A.	3y	C	D.C.	30 SEP 1876	Mt. Olivet
020738	SMALLWOOD, Mary Jane	11m	C	D.C.	03 JUL 1879	Mt. Pleasant
016391	SMALLWOOD, Minnett	8d	C	D.C.	01 JUL 1878	Mt. Olivet
016162	SMALLWOOD, Moses	67y	C	Md.	14 JUN 1878	Young Mens
020985	SMALLWOOD, Ned	65y	C	Va.	17 JUL 1879	Potters Field
008182	SMALLWOOD, Patsey	70y	C	D.C.	11 JUL 1876	Harmony
012827	SMALLWOOD, Rachel	76y	C	Md.	15 AUG 1877	Potters Field
003542	SMALLWOOD, William H.	33y	C	D.C.	06 JUN 1875	Mt. Olivet
010690	SMALLWOOD, William H.	57y	C	D.C.	19 FEB 1877	Mt. Olivet
013248	SMALLWOOD, William H.	57y	C	D.C.	19 FEB 1877	Mt. Olivet
004450	SMILER, Eaver	4m	C	D.C.	04 AUG 1875	Harmony
011339	SMILER, Sarha	4y	C	D.C.	15 APR 1877	Harmony
001109	SMITH, Abraham	35y	C	Va.	10 NOV 1874	Arlington, Va.
012969	SMITH, Abraham	27y	C	W.Va.	26 AUG 1877	Potters Field
014690	SMITH, Abram Gurney	52y	W	N.Y.	06 FEB 1878	Glenwood
002658	SMITH, Ada Ford	1m	W	D.C.	20 MAR 1875	Graceland
017998	SMITH, Adeline	54y	W	Ohio	09 NOV 1878	Congressional
000113	SMITH, Albert	24d	W	D.C.	09 AUG 1874	Mt. Olivet
013772	SMITH, Albert L.	6d	C	D.C.	08 NOV 1877	Mt. Zion
015996	SMITH, Alex	11y	C	D.C.	03 JUN 1878	Mt. Pleasant
002048	SMITH, Alexander	c.60y	M	U.S.	06 FEB 1875	Ebenezer
010271	SMITH, Alfred	50y	C	Md.	12 JAN 1877	Thomas'
000103	SMITH, Alice	2m	C	D.C.	08 AUG 1874	Beckett's
017976	SMITH, Amanda M.	48y	W	N.Y.	07 NOV 1878	Oak Hill
007126	SMITH, Amelia	76y	C	Va.	26 APR 1876	Harmony
012879	SMITH, Andrew	15y	C	Md.	19 AUG 1877	Mt. Zion
012749	SMITH, Andrew King	76y	W	Va.	09 AUG 1877	Congressional
000883	SMITH, Ann	73y	W	Md.	21 OCT 1874	Congressional
005223a	SMITH, Ann	76y	W	Va.	20 OCT 1875	Glenwood
019776	SMITH, Ann M.	38y	C	Va.	14 APR 1879	Mt. Olivet
008464	SMITH, Ann Rebecca	33y	C	D.C.	29 JUL 1876	Ebenezer
000329	SMITH, Anna	14y	C	D.C.	26 AUG 1874	Young Mens
000397	SMITH, Annie	6m	W	D.C.	01 SEP 1874	Holy Rood
019217	SMITH, Annie Baldwin	11m	W	D.C.	26 FEB 1879	Mt. Olivet
012067	SMITH, Annie E.	5m	C	D.C.	26 JUN 1877	Mt. Olivet
013593	SMITH, Annie E.	36y	W	Va.	22 OCT 1877	Clark's Gap, Va.
005287	SMITH, Annie Genevieve	2y	W	D.C.	28 OCT 1875	Holy Rood
016439	SMITH, Annie V.	11m	W	D.C.	04 JUL 1878	Mt. Olivet
006993	SMITH, Athansius	8m	C	D.C.	11 APR 1876	Ebenezer
010034	SMITH, Atken	54y	W	Mass.	20 DEC 1876	Provincetown, Mass.
008289	SMITH, Augustus	12d	C	D.C.	16 JUL 1876	Mt. Olivet
014049	SMITH, Augustus	1d	W	D.C.	09 DEC 1877	Prospect Hill
008187	SMITH, Avangerline	9m	C	D.C.	11 JUL 1876	Harmony
004732	SMITH, Azchar	4m	C	D.C.	23 AUG 1875	Beckett's
010807	SMITH, Belle	2y	M	D.C.	28 FEB 1877	Jones Chapel

No.	Name	Age	Race	Birth	Death Date	Burial Place
011465	SMITH, Bertha C.R.	11y	W	Md.	30 APR 1877	Holy Rood
009293	SMITH, Bertie Ann	2y	C	D.C.	04 OCT 1876	Harmony
019539	SMITH, Betsey	55y	C	Va.	24 MAR 1879	Potters Field
018684	SMITH, Blanche	11m	C	D.C.	15 JAN 1879	Potters Field
002410	SMITH, Carlotta	5m	C	D.C.	03 MAR 1875	Mt. Olivet
004920	SMITH, Catharine	57y	W	Ger.	05 SEP 1875	Mt. Olivet
018904	SMITH, Catharine R.	83y	W	Md.	31 JAN 1879	Congressional
004644	SMITH, Catherine	1y	C	Pa.	17 AUG 1875	Ebenezer
019550	SMITH, Catherine E.	76y	W	Pa.	25 MAR 1879	Glenwood
003026	SMITH, Cecelia	25y	C	Va.	17 APR 1875	Mt. Pleasant
005388	SMITH, Charity Ann	3y	C	D.C.	07 NOV 1875	Beckett's
002106	SMITH, Charles	8y	W	D.C.	10 FEB 1875	Glenwood
019524	SMITH, Charles H.	60y	W	Va.	23 MAR 1879	Richmond, Va.
015166	SMITH, Charles M., Jr.	22y	W	Ohio	23 MAR 1878	Congressional
010622	SMITH, Chas.	29y	C	Md.	14 FEB 1877	Potters Field
010117	SMITH, Clara	75y	C	Va.	30 DEC 1876	Mt. Zion
020618	SMITH, Clara R.	2½m	C	D.C.	25 JUN 1879	Young Mens
019614	SMITH, Corinne	1m	C	D.C.	31 MAR 1879	Harmony
010246	SMITH, Cornelia	26y	C	D.C.	10 JAN 1877	Mt. Olivet
015523	SMITH, Cornelius	8m	C	DC.	26 APR 1878	Harmony
009918	SMITH, Covington, Mrs.	81y	W	D.C.	10 DEC 1876	Oak Hill
020190	SMITH, David	1y	C	D.C.	24 MAY 1879	Beckett's
007018	SMITH, David Rodolph	43y	W	N.Y.	14 APR 1876	Congressional
017856	SMITH, Dora	c.30y	C	Va.	25 OCT 1878	Beckett's
004570	SMITH, Dorie	10m	W	DC.	12 AUG 1875	Prospect Hill
007170	SMITH, Draper Carpenter	43y	W	R.I.	30 APR 1876	Providence, R.I.
007684	SMITH, Earnest H.	10d	C	D.C.	16 JUN 1876	Young Mens
001051	SMITH, Eddie	2m	W	D.C.	05 NOV 1874	Glenwood
002270	SMITH, Eddie	1y	C	D.C.	21 FEB 1875	Ebenezer
010269	SMITH, Eddie	24h	W	D.C.	12 JAN 1877	Congressional
016269	SMITH, Edith A.	1m	W	D.C.	22 JUN 1878	Oak Hill
013187	SMITH, Edward, Jr.	16y	W	D.C.	13 SEP 1877	Mt. Olivet
002739	SMITH, Edward Starr	58y	W	N.Y.	25 MAR 1875	Oak Hill
000697	SMITH, Elicia	65y	W	Md.	02 OCT 1874	Congressional
013233	SMITH, Eliza	65y	C	Md.	17 SEP 1877	Mt. Zion
021104	SMITH, Eliza	40y	C	Md.	25 JUL 1879	Beckett's
020225	SMITH, Eliza	32y	C	Md.	29 MAY 1879	Halls Station, Md.
012593	SMITH, Elizabeth	8m	W	D.C.	29 JUL 1877	Mt. Olivet
013655	SMITH, Elizabeth	97y	W	Va.	27 OCT 1877	Presbyterian
005586	SMITH, Elizabeth Mattingly	33y	W	Ky.	27 NOV 1875	Holy Rood
004222	SMITH, Ella	15m	C	D.C.	20 JUL 1875	Harmony
020052	SMITH, Ellie	18y	C	D.C.	09 MAY 1879	Harmony
008778	SMITH, Elsie	40y	C	Va.	22 AUG 1876	Arlington, Va.
020212	SMITH, Emelia	49y	W	Ger.	27 MAY 1879	Potters Field
012498	SMITH, Emily	1m	C	D.C.	23 JUL 1877	Young Mens
008927	SMITH, Emma	7m	C	D.C.	02 SEP 1876	Moore's
021179	SMITH, Emma	21y	C	Va.	31 JUL 1879	Harmony
005231	SMITH, Erma	6y	C	D.C.	30 SEP 1875	Harmony
012494	SMITH, Eugene	2m	W	U.S.	23 JUL 1877	Mt. Olivet
003809	SMITH, Florence	6m	C	D.C.	24 JUN 1875	Mt. Olivet
004766	SMITH, Florence H.	1y	W	D.C.	26 AUG 1875	Glenwood
005710	SMITH, Francis Edward	11m	C	D.C.	09 DEC 1875	Mt. Olivet
018451	SMITH, Frank	75y	C	Md.	24 DEC 1878	Beckett's
005018	SMITH, Frederick	1y	C	D.C.	12 SEP 1875	Mt. Olivet
012940	SMITH, Frederick	3m	C	D.C.	24 AUG 1877	Young Mens
013536	SMITH, Frederick	52y	C	Md.	16 OCT 1877	Mt. Olivet

District of Columbia Death Records, August 1, 1874 to July 31, 1879

No.	Name	Age	Race	Birth	Death Date	Burial Place
010033	SMITH, Geo. B.	67y	W	Va.	20 DEC 1876	Glenwood
005532	SMITH, George	25y	C	Va.	21 NOV 1875	Ebenezer
016904	SMITH, George	2y	C	D.C.	04 AUG 1878	Potters Field
016135	SMITH, George	39y	C	Va.	12 JUN 1878	Potters Field
015654	SMITH, George	4m	C	D.C.	08 MAY 1878	Harmony
001835f	SMITH, George A.	27y	W	D.C.	21 JAN 1875	Glenwood
019721	SMITH, George Albert	17y	C	D.C.	10 APR 1879	Young Mens
007502	SMITH, George C.	29y	W	Md.	04 JUN 1876	Prospect Hill
020290	SMITH, George Francis	6m	W	D.C.	03 JUN 1879	Congressional
017191	SMITH, George M.	2y	W	D.C.	25 AUG 1878	Methodist
003984	SMITH, George Morris	3m	W	D.C.	03 JUL 1875	Congressional
007139	SMITH, George W.	32y	C	Ohio	27 APR 1876	Harmony
013606a	SMITH, George Walker	7m	C	D.C.	23 OCT 1877	Beckett's
013491	SMITH, George Walter	7m	C	D.C.	23 OCT 1877	Beckett's
018131	SMITH, Gerard V.	13y	W	D.C.	23 NOV 1878	Rock Creek
010236	SMITH, Gertrude	3y	C	D.C.	09 JAN 1877	Mt. Pleasant
002064	SMITH, Hamilton	70y	W	N.H.	07 FEB 1875	Oak Hill
000733f	SMITH, Harriet, Mrs.	c.70y	W	D.C.	06 OCT 1874	Rock Creek
015311	SMITH, Harry Steel	2y	W	D.C.	07 APR 1878	Congressional
011656	SMITH, Hattia Ann	6y	C	D.C.	20 MAY 1877	Moore's
020030	SMITH, Hattie	16m	C	D.C.	07 MAY 1879	Mt. Pleasant
015473	SMITH, Helen	53y	C	D.C.	21 APR 1878	Mt. Olivet
006909	SMITH, Henry	52y	M	D.C.	03 APR 1876	Harmony
009905	SMITH, Henry	27y	W	U.S.	08 DEC 1876	Washington Asylum
009197	SMITH, Henry	35y	C	Md.	25 SEP 1876	Mt. Pleasant
012502	SMITH, Henry	9m	C	D.C.	24 JUL 1877	Potters Field
012346	SMITH, Henry	32y	C	Md.	13 JUL 1877	Beckett's
013632	SMITH, Henry	1m	W	D.C.	25 OCT 1877	Potters Field
009426	SMITH, Henry Wm.	18y	W	Ohio	16 OCT 1876	Mt. Olivet
008540	SMITH, Hester Ann	45y	C	D.C.	03 AUG 1876	Harmony
007787	SMITH, Howard	10m	W	D.C.	22 JUN 1876	Baltimore, Md.
007250	SMITH, Ida	7y	W	D.C.	08 MAY 1876	Congressional
004320	SMITH, Infant of Alexander	5d	C	D.C.	26 JUL 1875	Young Mens
001030	SMITH, Infant of Andrew	8d	C	D.C.	03 NOV 1874	Young Mens
005159	SMITH, Infant of Anie	2m	C	D.C.	24 SEP 1875	Potters Field
016080	SMITH, Infant of Ben	4m	C	D.C.	09 JUN 1878	Beckett's
015782	SMITH, Infant of E.W.	12h	W	D.C.	20 MAY 1878	Graceland
002350	SMITH, Infant of Emanuel	15min	C	D.C.	28 FEB 1875	Ebenezer
016823	SMITH, Infant of Frank	1d	C	D.C.	29 JUL 1878	Mt. Zion
004968	SMITH, Infant of George	21d	C	D.C.	09 SEP 1875	Brightwood
007450	SMITH, Infant of George	21d	C	D.C.	31 MAY 1876	Mt. Pleasant
017175	SMITH, Infant of Gilbert	5h	C	D.C.	24 AUG 1878	Beckett's
016134	SMITH, Infant of Hamilton	3d	C	D.C.	12 JUN 1878	Harmony
001670	SMITH, Infant of Harriet	3d	C	D.C.	09 JAN 1875	Potters Field
001669	SMITH, Infant of Harriet	2½d	C	D.C.	09 JAN 1875	Potters Field
001574	SMITH, Infant of Henry	2d	C	D.C.	01 JAN 1875	Potters Field
005117	SMITH, Infant of J.B.	16h	W	D.C.	20 SEP 1875	Oak Hill
002030	SMITH, Infant of James	5min	W	D.C.	05 FEB 1875	Glenwood
014424	SMITH, Infant of John	38y	C	D.C.	14 JAN 1878	Harmony
001349	SMITH, Infant of John	14d	C	D.C.	09 DEC 1874	Mt. Pleasant
006526	SMITH, Infant of Joseph	11d	C	D.C.	02 MAR 1876	Young Mens
009536	SMITH, Infant of Lee	5d	C	D.C.	26 OCT 1876	Ebenezer
014785	SMITH, Infant of Lousa	1m	C	D.C.	16 FEB 1878	Potters Field
010659	SMITH, Infant of Reuben	1d	C	D.C.	16 FEB 1877	Potters Field
010878	SMITH, Infant of Rose	4h	C	D.C.	06 MAR 1877	Potters Field
007991	SMITH, Infant of S.E.	1d	W	D.C.	03 JUL 1876	Oak Hill

No.	Name	Age	Race	Birth	Death Date	Burial Place
003243	SMITH, Infant of Sarah	1d	C	D.C.	06 MAY 1875	Ebenezer
001611	SMITH, Infant of Thomas	4h	C	D.C.	04 JAN 1875	Young Mens
012736	SMITH, Infant of Thomas	2d	C	D.C.	08 AUG 1877	Montgomery Co., Md.
008018	SMITH, Infant of Thomas	15min	W	D.C.	04 JUL 1876	Glenwood
006817	SMITH, Infant of Thos.	2d	C	Md.	25 MAR 1876	Montgomery Co., Md.
000370	SMITH, Infant of Wilson	2m	C	D.C.	30 AUG 1874	Mt. Pleasant Plain
002135	SMITH, Infant of Wm.	4d	C	D.C.	12 FEB 1875	Potters Field
014556	SMITH, Infant of Wm.	9m	C	D.C.	25 JAN 1878	Potters Field
001996	SMITH, Isaiah	8m	C	D.C.	02 FEB 1875	Beckett's
019508	SMITH, Ithaniel	44y	C	Va.	22 MAR 1879	Harmony
000866	SMITH, J.C.	75y	C	Va.	19 OCT 1874	Penny Hill
005095	SMITH, James	18m	C	D.C.	18 SEP 1875	Brightwood Methodist
007229	SMITH, James	66y	W	Scot.	06 MAY 1876	Glenwood
014208	SMITH, James	27y	C	Va.	25 DEC 1877	Potters Field
012293	SMITH, James	7y	C	D.C.	10 JUL 1877	Ebenezer
011590	SMITH, James	8m	C	D.C.	14 MAY 1877	Ebenezer
001978	SMITH, James A.	18m	W	D.C.	01 FEB 1875	Glenwood
011150	SMITH, James A.	1y	C	D.C.	29 MAR 1877	Holy Rood
005116	SMITH, James Edward	1y	W	D.C.	20 SEP 1875	Congressional
005810	SMITH, James Henry	2y	C	D.C.	20 DEC 1875	Washington Asylum
003797	SMITH, Jane	21y	C	Md.	23 JUN 1875	Mt. Zion
003492	SMITH, Jane	50y	C	Va.	30 MAY 1875	Potters Field
012335	SMITH, Jane	1y	C	D.C.	12 JUL 1877	Harmony
017950	SMITH, Jane	34y	C	Va.	04 NOV 1878	Young Mens
017767	SMITH, Jane D.	3y	W	D.C.	16 OCT 1878	Graceland/Glenwood
000833	SMITH, Jas. P.	1y	W	D.C.	17 OCT 1874	Mt. Olivet
011779	SMITH, Jasper A.	4d	W	D.C.	02 JUN 1877	Mt. Olivet
012504	SMITH, Jenine	8m	C	D.C.	24 JUL 1877	Young Mens
002976	SMITH, Jennie	16y	C	Va.	13 APR 1875	Harmony
006642	SMITH, Jennie	1y	C	D.C.	11 MAR 1876	Ebenezer
001035	SMITH, Jeramiah M.	59y	W	Va.	03 NOV 1874	Fairfax Co., Va.
018169	SMITH, Jeremiah	1y	C	D.C.	26 NOV 1878	Mt. Olivet
011077	SMITH, Jesse	5m	M	D.C.	22 MAR 1877	Harmony
003511	SMITH, Jno.	3m	C	D.C.	02 JUN 1875	Ebenezer
004080	SMITH, John	3m	W	D.C.	10 JUL 1875	Congressional
008571	SMITH, John	20y	W	Swe.	05 AUG 1876	Washington Asylum
009582	SMITH, John	13h	W	D.C.	31 OCT 1876	Mt. Olivet
012889	SMITH, John	12y	C	D.C.	20 AUG 1877	Harmony
010342	SMITH, John	40y	W	Ga.	20 JAN 1877	Potters Field
015539	SMITH, John	39y	C	S.C.	27 APR 1878	Potters Field
019132	SMITH, John	1y	C	D.C.	20 FEB 1879	Mt. Pleasant
020643	SMITH, John B.H.	5m	C	D.C.	27 JUN 1879	Mt. Olivet
014532	SMITH, John Cross	c.75y	W	Md.	23 JAN 1878	Congressional
000939	SMITH, John F.	29y	W	Md.	26 OCT 1874	Mt. Olivet
018873	SMITH, John H.	14y	C	Va.	29 JAN 1879	Arlington
000174	SMITH, John J.	11m	C	D.C.	13 AUG 1874	Young Mens
001006	SMITH, John T.	40y	W	D.C.	01 NOV 1874	Congressional
018953	SMITH, John T.	87y	C	U.S.	04 FEB 1879	Harmony
013424	SMITH, John Wesley	1m	C	D.C.	07 OCT 1877	Beckett's
011943	SMITH, Jonathan Moody	73y	W	Mass.	17 JUN 1877	Congressional
009709	SMITH, Joseph	14d	C	D.C.	16 NOV 1876	Mt. Olivet
010319	SMITH, Joseph	87y	W	Mass.	17 JAN 1877	Oak Hill
014312	SMITH, Joseph H.	43y	C	D.C.	03 JAN 1878	Mt. Zion
020948	SMITH, Judith Bussey	57y	W	Me.	15 JUL 1879	Boston, Mass.
017136	SMITH, Julia	63y	W	Va.	21 AUG 1878	Mt. Olivet
008566	SMITH, Katie	76y	C	Va.	05 AUG 1876	Harmony

District of Columbia Death Records, August 1, 1874 to July 31, 1879   315

No.	Name	Age	Race	Birth	Death Date	Burial Place
008977	SMITH, Katie	7y	C	D.C.	05 SEP 1876	Mt. Zion
003430	SMITH, Laura	21y	C	Md.	25 MAY 1875	Mt. Olivet
017005	SMITH, Laura	26y	C	Va.	10 AUG 1878	Mt. Olivet
004081	SMITH, Levi	28y	C	Va.	10 JUL 1875	Ebenezer
005201	SMITH, Levina	9m	C	D.C.	27 SEP 1875	Potters Field
017050	SMITH, Lewellyn	9m	C	D.C.	14 AUG 1878	Beckett's
001455	SMITH, Lewis M., Dr.	33y	W	Pa.	21 DEC 1874	York, Pa.
008536	SMITH, Lile Virginia	10m	W	D.C.	02 AUG 1876	Presbyterian
014050	SMITH, Liley	c.40y	C	Va.	09 DEC 1877	Beckett's
017765	SMITH, Lillie	2y	C	D.C.	16 OCT 1878	Harmony
021055	SMITH, Lillie	1m	C	D.C.	22 JUL 1879	Washington Asylum
000704	SMITH, Liza	3y	C	D.C.	03 OCT 1874	Young Mens
017462	SMITH, Louis Franklin	2y	C	D.C.	19 SEP 1878	Harmony
001873f	SMITH, Louis Martin	55y	W	D.C.	24 JAN 1875	Oak Hill
004248	SMITH, Louisa	2y	C	D.C.	22 JUL 1875	Young Mens
009476	SMITH, Lucretia	8m	C	D.C.	21 OCT 1876	Ebenezer
009280	SMITH, Lucy	23y	C	Va.	03 OCT 1876	Potters Field
016905	SMITH, Lucy	1y	C	D.C.	04 AUG 1878	Mt. Zion
018928	SMITH, Luther	41y	W	Me.	02 FEB 1879	Hospital, Government
004719	SMITH, Mabel Morrell	2y	W	D.C.	22 AUG 1875	Congressional
004064	SMITH, Magdaline	6m	W	D.C.	09 JUL 1875	Mt. Olivet
005086a	SMITH, Magdaline	5m	C	D.C.	08 OCT 1875	Mt. Olivet
016865	SMITH, Maggie	18y	C	D.C.	01 AUG 1878	Mt. Olivet
000992	SMITH, Margaret	26c	C	D.C.	31 OCT 1874	Potters Field
010152	SMITH, Margaret	59y	W	Spain	02 JAN 1877	Mt. Olivet
017209	SMITH, Margaret	3y	C	D.C.	26 AUG 1878	Beckett's
021056	SMITH, Margaret	30y	W	Md.	22 JUL 1879	Frederick, Md.
000589f	SMITH, Margaret Wooten	62y	W	Md.	21 SEP 1874	Rock Creek
013964	SMITH, Maria Ann	30y	C	Va.	29 NOV 1877	Potters Field
007788	SMITH, Marion	39y	C	Md.	22 JUN 1876	Mt. Pleasant
011265	SMITH, Martha	9m	C	D.C.	08 APR 1877	Ebenezer
011355	SMITH, Martha	1y	C	D.C.	16 APR 1877	Young Mens
011829	SMITH, Martha	7m	C	D.C.	07 JUN 1877	Harmony
015005	SMITH, Martha	8m	C	D.C.	09 MAR 1878	Potters Field
018672	SMITH, Martha	5y	C	D.C.	14 JAN 1879	Mt. Pleasant
014936	SMITH, Martha A.	51y	W	Md.	03 MAR 1878	Prospect Hill
020645	SMITH, Martinia H.	53y	W	Md.	27 JUN 1879	Mt. Olivet
003906	SMITH, Mary	2m	W	N.Y.	28 JUN 1875	Holy Rood
009009	SMITH, Mary	c.66y	W	Ohio	09 SEP 1876	Congressional
012207	SMITH, Mary	35y	C	D.C.	04 JUL 1877	Potters Field
012209	SMITH, Mary	50y	C	Md.	04 JUL 1877	Harmony
010989	SMITH, Mary	66y	C	D.C.	15 MAR 1877	Mt. Zion
020124	SMITH, Mary	10m	C	D.C.	16 MAY 1879	Payne's
005159a	SMITH, Mary A.	69y	W	D.C.	15 OCT 1875	Oak Hill
005115	SMITH, Mary A.	34y	C	Va.	20 SEP 1875	Young Mens
009158	SMITH, Mary Ann Elizabeth	1y	C	D.C.	22 SEP 1876	Young Mens
015017	SMITH, Mary Ann	22y	W	Md.	10 MAR 1878	Mt. Olivet
017620	SMITH, Mary Ann	2m	C	D.C.	03 OCT 1878	Mt. Olivet
003353	SMITH, Mary Covington	39y	W	D.C.	17 MAY 1875	Congressional
002050	SMITH, Mary E.	5y	C	D.C.	06 FEB 1875	Harmony
006655	SMITH, Mary Emma	6m	C	D.C.	12 MAR 1876	Mt. Zion
004801	SMITH, Mary Hasiffa	1y	W	D.C.	28 AUG 1875	Mt. Olivet
009088	SMITH, Mary Jane	19d	C	D.C.	15 SEP 1876	Ebenezer
003195	SMITH, Mary Louisa	1y	C	D.C.	02 MAY 1875	Mt. Olivet
021153	SMITH, Mary M.B.	27y	W	D.C.	29 JUL 1879	Congressional
014485	SMITH, Mary, Mrs.	85y	W	Va.	19 JAN 1878	Harmony

No.	Name	Age	Race	Birth	Death Date	Burial Place
007112	SMITH, Mary S.	4m	C	D.C.	25 APR 1876	Harmony
002674	SMITH, Mathew	5y	C	D.C.	21 MAR 1875	Mt. Olivet
002902	SMITH, Matilda	c.80y	C	D.C.	07 APR 1875	Smith's
001966	SMITH, Matilda	65y	C	Md.	31 JAN 1875	Jones Chapel
009644	SMITH, Matilda Ann	7m	C	D.C.	08 NOV 1876	Young Mens
002086f	SMITH, Matilda R., Mrs.	72y	--	Va.	08 FEB 1875	--
013621	SMITH, Millie	28y	C	Va.	24 OCT 1877	Young Mens
019090	SMITH, Milly	1y	C	D.C.	16 FEB 1879	Mt. Pleasant
016040	SMITH, Milton	1½h	C	D.C.	06 JUN 1878	Mt. Zion
005046a	SMITH, Mollie	2y	C	D.C.	03 OCT 1875	Ebenezer
012565	SMITH, Moranda B.	63y	W	D.C.	27 JUL 1877	Alexandria, Va.
001531f	SMITH, Morgan L.	--	--	--	18 DEC 1874	--
016011	SMITH, Moses	45y	C	Va.	04 JUN 1878	Beckett's
001486f	SMITH, Nancy	72y	C	Va.	25 DEC 1874	Harmony
009914	SMITH, Nancy	80y	C	Md.	10 DEC 1876	Mt. Pleasant
009673	SMITH, Nancy	18y	C	Md.	11 NOV 1876	Arlington
012466	SMITH, Nancy	1y	C	D.C.	22 JUL 1877	Ebenezer
006325	SMITH, Nathaniel	100y	C	Md.	12 FEB 1876	Ebenezer
013824	SMITH, Nellie	100y	C	Va.	14 NOV 1877	Young Mens
013923	SMITH, Nellie	5y	C	Va.	25 NOV 1877	Mt. Zion
005922	SMITH, Patrick	36y	W	Ire.	02 JAN 1876	Holy Rood
013792	SMITH, Patrick	7d	W	D.C.	10 NOV 1877	Holy Rood
002112	SMITH, Peter M.	43y	C	Md.	10 FEB 1875	Mt. Olivet
014905	SMITH, Philip	11m	C	D.C.	28 FEB 1878	Beckett's
001096	SMITH, Phoebe	50y	C	Va.	09 NOV 1874	Beckett's
002400	SMITH, Priscilla	24y	C	Md.	02 MAR 1875	Ebenezer
016965	SMITH, Rachael	38y	C	Va.	08 AUG 1878	Harmony
011213	SMITH, Rachel	53y	C	Va.	04 APR 1877	Moore's
000046	SMITH, Richard	1y	C	D.C.	04 AUG 1874	Young Mens
010181	SMITH, Richard S.	44y	C	Mass.	05 JAN 1877	Harmony
007852	SMITH, Robert	1m	C	Va.	25 JUN 1876	Ebenezer
006078	SMITH, Rosa	29y	C	Va.	20 JAN 1876	Harmony
012657	SMITH, Rose	c.82y	C	Va.	03 AUG 1877	Harmony
008433	SMITH, Rose Emma	3y	C	D.C.	26 JUL 1876	Ebenezer
015178	SMITH, Rosetta	50y	M	Va.	24 MAR 1878	Graceland
003126	SMITH, Rosina	1y	C	D.C.	26 APR 1875	Mt. Pleasant
018818	SMITH, Sallie E.	16y	W	Md.	25 JAN 1879	Oak Hill
005193a	SMITH, Samuel	6d	C	D.C.	18 OCT 1875	Beckett's
021163	SMITH, Sarah	20y	C	D.C.	30 JUL 1879	Harmony
003795	SMITH, Sarah Ann	13d	C	D.C.	23 JUN 1875	Potters Field
010312	SMITH, Sarah E.	54y	W	Eng.	16 JAN 1877	Glenwood
005889	SMITH, Selina	2y	C	D.C.	28 DEC 1875	Ebenezer
001043	SMITH, Seriah E.	25y	C	Md.	04 NOV 1874	Mt. Olivet
011545	SMITH, Solomon	10m	C	D.C.	08 MAY 1877	Ebenezer
020062	SMITH, Sonny	2y	C	D.C.	10 MAY 1879	Potters Field
001116	SMITH, Sophia	16y	C	Md.	12 NOV 1874	Harmony
002398	SMITH, Susan	28y	C	Va.	02 MAR 1875	Ebenezer
010604	SMITH, Susan	16y	M	D.C.	13 FEB 1877	Potters Field
011532	SMITH, Susan	20y	C	Md.	06 MAY 1877	Ebenezer
000787	SMITH, Tamer	32y	C	Va.	12 OCT 1874	Harmony
010502	SMITH, Thomas	68y	W	Ire.	03 FEB 1877	Soldier's Home
020509	SMITH, Thomas	16m	C	D.C.	18 JUN 1879	Beckett's
019947	SMITH, Thomas H.	29y	C	D.C.	30 APR 1879	Mt. Olivet
002108	SMITH, Thomas Joyes	16y	C	Va.	10 FEB 1875	Macedonia
010786	SMITH, Thornton	4y	C	Va.	26 FEB 1877	Ebenezer
007127	SMITH, Thos. Wilson	2y	W	D.C.	26 APR 1876	Glenwood

District of Columbia Death Records, August 1, 1874 to July 31, 1879   317

No.	Name	Age	Race	Birth	Death Date	Burial Place
008456	SMITH, William	3m	C	D.C.	28 JUL 1876	Mt. Zion
008443	SMITH, William	59y	W	Ger.	27 JUL 1876	Soldier's Home
017146	SMITH, William	5m	C	D.C.	22 AUG 1878	Holy Rood
019736	SMITH, William	9d	W	D.C.	11 APR 1879	Mt. Olivet
020199	SMITH, William	27y	C	Md.	25 MAY 1879	Payne's
006683	SMITH, William Arthur	5m	M	D.C.	15 MAR 1876	Young Mens
004494	SMITH, William Baker	63y	W	Va.	07 AUG 1875	Congressional
009642	SMITH, William E.	2y	W	D.C.	08 NOV 1876	Glenwood
011690	SMITH, William Henry	1m	C	D.C.	24 MAY 1877	Mt. Olivet
016366	SMITH, William Henry	1y	C	Va.	29 JUN 1878	Beckett's
010902	SMITH, William Isac	8y	C	D.C.	07 MAR 1877	Young Mens
006382	SMITH, Willie	11m	C	D.C.	16 FEB 1876	Young Mens
009227	SMITH, Willie	1y	C	D.C.	28 SEP 1876	Mt. Pleasant
016964	SMITH, Willie	11m	C	D.C.	08 AUG 1878	Mt. Pleasant
014873	SMITH, Willie	8m	C	D.C.	25 FEB 1878	Potters Field
018952	SMITH, Willie	18m	C	D.C.	04 FEB 1879	Potters Field
005105	SMITH, Wm.	1m	W	D.C.	19 SEP 1875	Navy Yard Methodist
012652	SMITH, Wm.	6y	C	D.C.	03 AUG 1877	Macedonia
015069	SMITH, Wm.	14y	M	Va.	14 MAR 1878	Payne's
003986	SMITH, Wm. H.	40y	W	D.C.	03 JUL 1875	Congressional
012703	SMITH, Wm. Henry	11y	W	D.C.	06 AUG 1877	Congressional
021042	SMITHERS, Elizabeth	21d	C	D.C.	21 JUL 1879	Harmony
008259	SMITHERS, Jane	23y	C	D.C.	14 JUL 1876	Harmony
005118	SMITHING, Wm. H.	41y	W	D.C.	20 SEP 1875	Glenwood
016153	SMITHSON, Cora C.A.	5m	W	D.C.	13 JUN 1878	Congressional
008008	SMITHSON, George W.	11m	W	D.C.	04 JUL 1876	Congressional
013662	SMOOT, Edw. Arthur	4m	W	D.C.	28 OCT 1877	Mt. Olivet
000182	SMOOT, Henry	9m	C	D.C.	14 AUG 1874	Harmony
016337	SMOOT, Infant of John	1h	C	D.C.	27 JUN 1878	Mt. Pleasant
019937	SMOOT, Rebecca	30y	W	Md.	29 APR 1879	Mt. Olivet
013234	SMOOTT, John	8d	C	D.C.	17 SEP 1877	Young Mens
005146	SMOTHERS, Andrew	6	C	D.C.	23 SEP 1875	Ebenezer
017210	SMOTHERS, Anna Mary	12y	M	D.C.	26 AUG 1878	Payne's
002104	SMOTHERS, Annie	18m	C	D.C.	10 FEB 1875	Mt. Olivet
020947	SMOTHERS, Bettie	25y	C	Md.	15 JUL 1879	Harmony
021070	SMOTHERS, Birdie	21d	C	D.C.	23 JUL 1879	Harmony
011464	SMOTHERS, Infant of Geo.	9d	C	D.C.	30 APR 1877	Mt. Olivet
012150	SMYTH, Minnie	11m	W	D.C.	01 JUL 1877	Congressional
018734	SMYTH, Stuart James	72y	W	Ire.	19 JAN 1879	Mt. Olivet
020492	SMYTHE, Margaret	1y	W	D.C.	17 JUN 1879	Congressional
007648	SNEAD, Chas. B.	7m	W	Md.	14 JUN 1876	Baltimore, Md.
009629	SNEE, Thomas	49y	W	Ire.	06 NOV 1876	Mt. Olivet
015452	SNEED, Rebecca	1y	C	Va.	19 APR 1878	Potters Field
016425	SNEIDER, Joseph	5m	C	D.C.	03 JUL 1878	Mt. Olivet
015167	SNODEN, Tuker	11m	C	D.C.	23 MAR 1878	Harmony
015840	SNOOK, Laura Virginia	27y	W	Va.	25 MAY 1878	Congressional
013456	SNOW, Thomas P.	55y	W	U.S.	09 OCT 1877	Congressional
020312	SNOWDEN, Carrie	10m	C	D.C.	05 JUN 1879	Skagg's
017101	SNOWDEN, Charles	10m	C	D.C.	18 AUG 1878	Mt. Pleasant
015179	SNOWDEN, Charles	3y	C	D.C.	24 MAR 1878	Potters Field
015995	SNOWDEN, Francis	25y	C	Va.	03 JUN 1878	Potters Field
014333	SNOWDEN, Henry	40y	C	D.C.	05 JAN 1878	Potters Field
003064	SNOWDEN, Infant of Jas.	2d	C	D.C.	20 APR 1875	Mt. Zion
016639	SNOWDEN, Infant of Florence	3m	C	D.C.	17 JUL 1878	Potters Field
005779	SNOWDEN, James	5d	C	D.C.	17 DEC 1875	Harmony
020006	SNOWDEN, Martha Ann	7y	C	D.C.	05 MAY 1879	Payne's

No.	Name	Age	Race	Birth	Death Date	Burial Place
005232	SNOWDEN, Martha Ellen	3m	C	D.C.	30 SEP 1875	Mt. Zion
008998	SNOWDEN, Mary Ida Elizabeth	2y	C	D.C.	07 SEP 1876	Mt. Pleasant
013785	SNOWDEN, Philip Thomas	71y	W	Md.	09 NOV 1877	Columbus, Ohio
017261	SNOWDEN, Rosa	38y	C	Md.	30 AUG 1878	Harmony
009978	SNOWDEN, Samuel	3m	C	D.C.	16 DEC 1876	Potters Field
006023	SNOWDEN, Susan	99y	C	Md.	14 JAN 1876	Young Mens
016495	SNYDAM, James C.	32y	W	Pa.	07 JUL 1878	Congressional
017177	SNYDER, Asa P.	41y	W	Del.	24 AUG 1878	Congressional
013055	SNYDER, Eliza	41y	W	D.C.	01 SEP 1877	Presbyterian
017545	SNYDER, Infant of Wm. F.	2d	W	D.C.	26 SEP 1878	Congressional
016664	SNYDER, Jacob A.	6m	W	D.C.	18 JUL 1878	Presbyterian
003558	SNYDER, Jno. W.H.F.	6m	C	D.C.	07 JUN 1875	Mt. Olivet
008656	SNYDER, John Wesley	2m	C	D.C.	12 AUG 1876	Mt. Olivet
003493f	SNYDER, Mary Ellen	8m	W	D.C.	12 JAN 1863	Oak Hill
003493f	SNYDER, Mollie	6m	W	Md.	09 JAN 1865	Oak Hill
012141	SNYDER, Wm. M.	3w	W	D.C.	30 JUN 1877	Presbyterian
009195	SODA, Susan	60y	W	Va.	25 SEP 1876	Alexandria, Va.
018603	SOHL, John	3y	W	D.C.	07 JAN 1879	Prospect Hill
014922	SOHON, Eva	2y	W	D.C.	02 MAR 1878	Mt. Olivet
019077	SOLARI, Giozeppe	44y	W	Italy	15 FEB 1879	Mt. Olivet
017509	SOLES, Esther	25h	W	D.C.	23 SEP 1878	Mt. Olivet
017122	SOLLERS, Catharine	22m	W	D.C.	20 AUG 1878	Mt. Olivet
017932	SOLOMAN, Greenbury	78y	C	Va.	03 NOV 1878	Mt. Olivet
003002	SOLOMAN, Madorow	5y	C	D.C.	15 APR 1875	Mt. Pleasant
010250	SOLOMON, Carrie	2y	W	D.C.	10 JAN 1877	Washington Hebrew
005000	SOLOMON, Ellis	8m	W	D.C.	11 SEP 1875	Hebrew
001613	SOLOMON, Infant of Elias	8d	W	D.C.	04 JAN 1875	Adas Israel
010983	SOLOMON, Infant of Thomas	2d	C	D.C.	15 MAR 1877	Moore's
011681	SOLOMON, Mary Lizzie	3m	W	D.C.	23 MAY 1877	Potters Field
004784	SOLOMONS, Ada An	1y	C	D.C.	27 AUG 1875	Moore's
007354	SOMERS, Robert J.	1y	W	D.C.	20 MAY 1876	Mt. Olivet
019676	SOMERS, Rosa	5y	W	D.C.	06 APR 1879	Hebrew
000475	SOMERVILL, John H.	10d	C	D.C.	11 SEP 1874	Beckett's
017388	SOMERVILL, Prescilla B.	56y	W	Md.	12 SEP 1878	Oak Hill
007754	SOMERVILLE, Arthur	2m	C	D.C.	20 JUN 1876	Mt. Olivet
012778	SOMERVILLE, Elizabeth	20y	C	Va.	11 AUG 1877	Ebenezer
013561	SOMERVILLE, Jessie Todd	10m	W	D.C.	18 OCT 1877	Congressional
019439	SOMERVILLE, Mary	1y	W	D.C.	17 MAR 1879	Mt. Olivet
020632	SOMERVILLE, Susan	55y	C	Va.	26 JUN 1879	Beckett's
010926	SOMMERS, John	c.80y	W	Prus.	09 MAR 1877	Glenwood
015006	SOMMERS, Warrington	41y	W	Pa.	09 MAR 1878	Graceland
004632	SOMMERSCALES, Lydia Ann	7m	W	D.C.	16 AUG 1875	Glenwood
011741	SOMMERVILLE, Robert A.	60y	W	Va.	29 MAY 1877	Presbyterian
007732	SONDER, Julia Ann	50y	W	Md.	19 JUN 1876	Baltimore, Md.
002874	SONDHEIMER, Elizabeth	3m	W	D.C.	04 APR 1875	Jewish
012448	SONNENIAN, Lizzie	1y	W	D.C.	20 JUL 1877	Prospect Hill
020332	SOPER, Helen M.	70y	W	Md.	07 JUN 1879	Soper's
001658	SOPER, Josephine Pauline	3y	W	D.C.	08 JAN 1875	Mt. Olivet
019104	SOPER, Julia M.	5y	W	D.C.	17 FEB 1879	Congressional
002078	SOPER, Thomas Jerome	5m	W	Md.	08 FEB 1875	Mt. Olivet
015282	SORRELL, Arthur Raymond	7y	W	D.C.	03 APR 1878	Congressional
015945	SORRELL, Elizabeth H.	21d	W	D.C.	31 MAY 1878	Congressional
004035	SORRELL, Georgietta	3m	C	D.C.	07 JUL 1875	Presbyterian
006656	SORRELL, James H.	30y	W	D.C.	12 MAR 1876	Congressional
003388	SOULE, Samuel Mitchell	76y	W	Me.	21 MAY 1875	Congressional
008798	SOUTHALL, Robert P.	39y	W	Va.	23 AUG 1876	Oak Hill

District of Columbia Death Records, August 1, 1874 to July 31, 1879

No.	Name	Age	Race	Birth	Death Date	Burial Place
010977	SOUTHALL, Vernon	7m	C	D.C.	14 MAR 1877	Mt. Pleasant
010391	SOUTHARD, Mary	3m	C	D.C.	24 JAN 1877	Moore's
018185	SOUTHERN, Letty	4y	C	D.C.	27 NOV 1878	Potters Field
002381	SOUTHEY, Margreat	3m	W	D.C.	02 MAR 1875	Holy Rood
016116	SOUTHRON, Lucy	45y	C	Va.	11 JUN 1878	Young Mens
014334	SOUTHWICK, Emily	56y	W	Eng.	05 JAN 1878	Rock Creek
003305	SPAIGHT, Hannah	3y	W	D.C.	13 MAY 1875	Mt. Olivet
005160a	SPALDING, Cecilia	34y	W	Pa.	15 OCT 1875	Congressional
005531	SPALDING, Henry	43y	W	R.I.	21 NOV 1875	Mont Clair, N.J.
011376	SPALDING, Ignatius	55y	C	Md.	19 APR 1877	Mt. Olivet
015614	SPALDING, Joseph	3y	W	D.C.	04 MAY 1878	Holy Rood
005243	SPALDING, Mary Ann	66y	W	Va.	22 OCT 1875	Mt. Olivet
005512	SPARKS, Anthony	72y	W	Eng.	19 NOV 1875	Glenwood
006981	SPARKS, Catherine	29y	W	Ire.	10 APR 1876	Baltimore, Md.
017900	SPARKS, Claudie Ann	49y	W	Md.	29 OCT 1878	Methodist
015034	SPARKS, Elizabeth	68y	W	Eng.	11 MAR 1878	Glenwood
020363	SPARKS, Elizebeth	17y	W	D.C.	09 JUN 1879	Methodist
002254	SPARKS, Frances	1y	C	D.C.	20 FEB 1875	Ebenezer
019482	SPARKS, Francis	22y	W	D.C.	20 MAR 1879	Methodist
015061	SPARKS, Frank	6m	W	D.C.	13 MAR 1878	Graceland
013847	SPARKS, Harry	22d	W	D.C.	17 NOV 1877	Glenwood
013472	SPARKS, Thomas	64y	C	Va.	10 OCT 1877	Macedonia
014409	SPARKS, Virginia	40y	C	Va.	13 JAN 1878	Beckett's
018346	SPARKS, William	20y	W	D.C.	15 DEC 1878	Methodist
009682	SPARRIER, Joseph	1d	W	D.C.	12 NOV 1876	Mt. Olivet
012076	SPARROW, Benjamin	2m	C	D.C.	26 JUN 1877	Ebenezer
011558	SPARROW, Daniel	26d	C	D.C.	10 MAY 1877	Ebenezer
011413	SPARROW, Georgianna	26y	C	Md.	24 APR 1877	Ebenezer
004840	SPARROW, Ida (twin)	11d	C	D.C.	30 AUG 1875	Ebenezer
013308	SPARROW, Joseph	1w	C	D.C.	25 SEP 1877	Payne's
017004	SPARROW, Manuel	2y	C	D.C.	10 AUG 1878	Mt. Zion
010169	SPARROW, R.B.	22d	C	D.C.	04 JAN 1877	Harmony
009593	SPARROW, William T.	38y	W	Md.	01 NOV 1876	Middletown, Md.
010437	SPATES, Charles F.	31y	W	Va.	29 JAN 1877	Congressional
012682	SPATES, Margaret A.	66y	W	Gr.	05 AUG 1877	Prospect Hill
007962	SPEAKE, Clifton Bowman	7m	W	D.C.	02 JUL 1876	Baltimore, Md.
006048	SPEAKS, Caroline	28y	M	Md.	17 JAN 1876	Young Mens
006426	SPEAKS, George	23y	W	Md.	20 FEB 1876	Congressional
004339	SPEAKS, Hattie	4m	C	D.C.	27 JUL 1875	Young Mens
008097	SPEAKS, Henry	72y	C	Md.	09 JUL 1876	Mt. Olivet
002468	SPEAKS, Infant of Mary	21d	C	D.C.	07 MAR 1875	Payne's
000942	SPEAKS, John, Jr.	7m	C	D.C.	26 OCT 1874	Mt. Olivet
004300	SPEAKS, Josephine	22y	C	D.C.	25 JUL 1875	Mt. Zion
000057	SPEAKS, Mary	4y	C	Md.	04 AUG 1874	Potters Field
003750	SPEAKS, Richard	2d	C	D.C.	21 JUN 1875	Ebenezer
008616	SPEAR, Bertha	3d	W	D.C.	08 AUG 1876	Hebrew
016309	SPEAR, Oliver	4m	W	D.C.	25 JUN 1878	Flint Hill, Va.
021117	SPEARE, Lula May	1y	W	D.C.	26 JUL 1879	Congressional
009657	SPEDDEN, Ellen F.	43y	W	Md.	09 NOV 1876	Baltimore, Md.
011965	SPEDDEN, Jesse Lare	4y	W	D.C.	19 JUN 1877	Oak Hill
015312	SPEDDEN, Mary Shaw	34y	W	D.C.	07 APR 1878	Oak Hill
000249	SPEEKS, Al bert	1y	C	D.C.	19 AUG 1874	Potters Field
007525	SPEER, Wm. D.	15m	W	D.C.	06 JUN 1876	Flint Hill, Va.[1]

---

[1] Place of burial given as Flint Hill burial ground near Fairfax C.H., Va.

District of Columbia Death Records, August 1, 1874 to July 31, 1879

No.	Name	Age	Race	Birth	Death Date	Burial Place
006267	SPEIDEN, Addie Elizabeth	9y	W	D.C.	07 FEB 1876	Congressional
015101	SPELSHAUSE, Lizzabeth	6d	W	D.C.	17 MAR 1878	Rock Creek
010712	SPELSHOUSE, Edward	1m	W	D.C.	20 FEB 1877	Prospect Hill
020246	SPENCE, Ellen Reid	46y	W	Scot.	31 MAY 1879	Lowell, Mass.
018365	SPENCE, Ernest R.W.	21y	W	D.C.	17 DEC 1878	Glenwood
013793	SPENCE, T.A.	67y	W	Md.	10 NOV 1877	Snow Hill, Md.
001449	SPENCER, Catharine	63y	W	Ire.	20 DEC 1874	Congressional
020413	SPENCER, Charles W.	29y	W	N.Y.	12 JUN 1879	Graceland
012647	SPENCER, Daniel	6m	C	D.C.	02 AUG 1877	Mt. Olivet
008587	SPENCER, Delia	1y	C	D.C.	07 AUG 1876	Potters Field
002900	SPENCER, Eva May	9y	W	D.C.	06 APR 1875	Oak Hill
011041	SPENCER, Jane	60y	C	Md.	19 MAR 1877	Potters Field
000283	SPENCER, John	4m	C	D.C.	22 AUG 1874	Mt. Olivet
018036	SPENCER, Julia	1m	C	D.C.	12 NOV 1878	Beckett's
002033	SPENCER, Kate	20y	W	D.C.	05 FEB 1875	Glenwood
017192	SPENCER, Lucinda	40y	C	Va.	25 AUG 1878	Beckett's
011254	SPENCER, Martha	26y	C	Md.	07 APR 1877	Mt. Olivet
002267	SPENCER, Mary	1y	C	D.C.	21 FEB 1875	Mt. Pleasant
018228	SPENCER, Mary	10m	C	D.C.	02 DEC 1878	Young Mens
017645	SPENCER, Matilda	1y	C	D.C.	05 OCT 1878	Union Baptist
004207	SPENCER, Ruby L.	3w	W	D.C.	19 JUL 1875	Oak Hill
017858	SPENCER, Susan	2m	C	D.C.	25 OCT 1878	Potters Field
002769	SPIESS, Dorothea Louise	2m	W	D.C.	28 MAR 1875	Prospect Hill
002102	SPIGGS, George	6y	C	D.C.	09 FEB 1875	Young Mens
001076	SPILLER, Ann	38y	C	Pa.	07 NOV 1874	Beckett's
014645	SPILLMAN, Ann Ogden	85y	W	Va.	02 FEB 1878	Presbyterian
004618	SPILLMAN, James A.	11y	W	D.C.	15 AUG 1875	Holy Rood
015976	SPILLMAN, James F.	6m	W	D.C.	02 JUN 1878	Congressional
002201	SPILLMAN, Lettie A.	22m	W	D.C.	17 FEB 1875	Congressional
002481	SPILLMAN, Stokey E.	3y	W	D.C.	09 MAR 1875	Congressional
008410	SPILMAN, Annie L.	1y	W	D.C.	24 JUL 1876	Holy Rood
013692	SPILMAN, Grace	18m	W	D.C.	31 OCT 1877	Graceland
018494	SPILWELL, Sally	75y	C	Va.	28 DEC 1878	Potters Field
009145	SPLANE, Bridget	80y	W	Ire.	20 SEP 1876	Long Island, N.Y.
012192	SPOTTSWOOD, Silvey	45y	C	Va.	03 JUL 1877	Potters Field
011501	SPRADLEY, James	70y	C	Va.	03 MAY 1877	Potters Field
020543	SPRAGUE, Rachel	10m	C	D.C.	20 JUN 1879	Mt. Pleasant
013027	SPRANDEL, Julius	39y	W	Ger.	30 AUG 1877	Glenwood
004601	SPRASSER, John	3y	W	D.C.	14 AUG 1875	Prospect Hill
002134	SPRIEG, Austin	6m	C	D.C.	12 FEB 1875	Moore's
010628	SPRIGG, Edward	2y	C	D.C.	14 FEB 1877	Ebenezer
007939	SPRIGG, Mary Ellen	2y	C	D.C.	30 JUN 1876	Mt. Olivet
020132	SPRIGGS, Florence	3y	C	D.C.	17 MAY 1879	Mt. Pleasant
020670	SPRIGGS, Frank	24y	C	Md.	29 JUN 1879	Potters Field
011591	SPRIGGS, Mamie	6m	C	D.C.	14 MAY 1877	Young Mens
008048	SPRIGGS, Mary	22y	C	Md.	06 JUL 1876	Potters Field
011443	SPRIGGS, Mary	72y	C	Va.	27 APR 1877	Mt. Olivet
011899	SPRIGGS, Philip	58y	C	Md.	14 JUN 1877	Harmony
011929	SPRIGS, Virgil	3m	C	D.C.	16 JUN 1877	Potters Field
002449	SPRINGER, Henry C.	7m	C	Md.	06 MAR 1875	Baltimore, Md.
018227	SPRINGMAN, Emma F.	19y	W	D.C.	02 DEC 1878	Beltsville, Md.
020255	SPROESSER, Caroline	3m	W	D.C.	01 JUN 1879	Prospect Hill
018311	SPROESSER, Louis	10m	W	D.C.	11 DEC 1878	Prospect Hill
004299	SPROSSER, Fred	11m	W	D.C.	25 JUL 1875	Prospect Hill
015440	SQUIER, Robert, Rev.	80y	C	Md.	18 APR 1878	Baltimore, Md.
007353	ST. CLAIR, Allen Jefferson	1y	C	Ala.	20 MAY 1876	Harmony

District of Columbia Death Records, August 1, 1874 to July 31, 1879　　　　321

No.	Name	Age	Race	Birth	Death Date	Burial Place
018203	ST. CLAIR, Clara E.	5m	C	D.C.	29 NOV 1878	Harmony
000203	ST. CLAIR, Katie F.	34y	W	Va.	16 AUG 1874	Alexandria, Va.
019821	ST. CLAIR, Nellie	2m	W	U.S.	18 APR 1879	Mt. Olivet
001828	ST. CLAIR, Rosanna, Mrs.	55y	W	Va.	21 JAN 1875	Congressional
017110	ST. LANCE, Faith De	38y	W	Brazil	19 AUG 1878	Mt. Olivet
007051	STACEY, Edward Porter	4m	W	D.C.	18 APR 1876	Woodland, Philadelphia
012890	STACK, Thomas W.	27y	W	Ver.	20 AUG 1877	Mt. Olivet
019246	STAFFORD, Mrs.	28y	W	D.C.	01 MAR 1879	Mt. Olivet
001042	STAHL, Fred	6d	W	D.C.	04 NOV 1874	Prospect Hill
016440	STAHL, John	25y	W	D.C.	04 JUL 1878	Mt. Olivet
013924	STAHL, Magdalene	57y	W	Ger.	25 NOV 1877	Prospect Hill
007114	STAHL, Michael	24h	W	D.C.	25 APR 1876	Prospect Hill
011961	STAHL, William H.	13y	W	Va.	19 JUN 1877	Graceland
011902	STAILEY, John H.	63y	W	Pa.	14 JUN 1877	Congressional
009608	STAILEY, Valentine Tarleton	3y	W	D.C.	03 NOV 1876	Glenwood
020234	STALK, John	68y	W	Md.	30 MAY 1879	Congressional
006649	STALL, Hannah	35y	C	Md.	12 MAR 1876	Potters Field
002046	STALLCUP, John	23y	W	Va.	06 FEB 1875	Congressional
007036	STALLINGS, James O.	32y	W	D.C.	17 APR 1876	Oak Hill
011557	STALLINS, Joseph	2d	C	D.C.	10 MAY 1877	Beckett's
018444	STAMPS, Joseph	42d	C	D.C.	23 DEC 1878	Potters Field
019037	STANARD, Josephe	24y	C	Va.	11 FEB 1879	Mt. Zion
009097	STANDARD, Howard	20d	M	D.C.	16 SEP 1876	Harmony
008742	STANDEN, Ellen	3m	W	D.C.	19 AUG 1876	Mt. Olivet
007734	STANFORD, Infant of W.M.	16h	W	D.C.	19 JUN 1876	Congressional
002795	STANLEY, Ella Bell	1m	W	D.C.	30 MAR 1875	Glenwood
003649	STANLEY, John Thomas	51y	W	D.C.	15 JUN 1875	Congressional
002519f	STANLEY, Thomas	94y	W	Eng.	11 MAR 1875	Congressional
001523	STANSBURY, George	65y	C	Md.	28 DEC 1874	Potters Field
019189	STANSBURY, Howard M.	26y	W	D.C.	24 FEB 1879	Congressional
014996	STANSBURY, Margaret, Mrs.	52y	W	Ire.	08 MAR 1878	Mt. Olivet
015567	STANT, Emily	21y	W	Pa.	30 APR 1878	Congressional
009067	STANT, Harris	14d	W	D.C.	14 SEP 1876	Methodist
004950	STANTON, Edward	4y	C	D.C.	07 SEP 1875	Ebenezer
013015	STANTON, Edwin L.	35y	W	Ohio	29 AUG 1877	Oak Hill
014764	STANTON, Infant of Andrew	12h	C	D.C.	14 FEB 1878	Mt. Olivet
011606	STANTON, John	40y	W	U.S.	15 MAY 1877	Soldier's Home
019405	STANTON, Margaret A.	44y	C	N.Y.	14 MAR 1879	Graceland
016760	STANTON, Martha	c.40y	C	Va.	25 JUL 1878	Beckett's
020266	STANTON, Rosannah	69y	W	Ire.	01 JUN 1879	Holy Rood
011175	STAPLER, Infant of Caroline	2d	W	D.C.	31 MAR 1877	Prospect Hill
018132	STARK, Jane	62y	M	Va.	23 NOV 1878	Harmony
013763	STARKE, Mary A.	78y	C	D.C.	07 NOV 1877	Beckett's
013331	STARKES, Ann	1y	C	D.C.	27 SEP 1877	Harmony
013526	STARKES, Jane E.	13y	M	D.C.	15 OCT 1877	Harmony
010417	STARKEY, George L.	34y	W	Me.	27 JAN 1877	Glenwood
012056	STARKS, Eugene Max	1m	C	D.C.	25 JUN 1877	Beckett's
015509	STARKS, Susan	c.60y	C	Va.	24 APR 1878	Young Mens
006172	STARKWEATHER, H.H.	49y	W	Conn.	28 JAN 1876	Norwich, Conn.
017016	STARNER, Infant of Chs.	12h	W	D.C.	11 AUG 1878	Rock Creek
011390	STARR, Gertrude	9m	W	D.C.	22 APR 1877	Tennallytown
014631	STARR, Infant of Jesse C.	4d	W	D.C.	01 FEB 1878	Tennallytown
018940	STATELY, Elizabeth	42y	C	D.C.	03 FEB 1879	Graceland
009160	STATELY, Mariah	56y	C	Va.	22 SEP 1876	Young Mens
016058	STATON, Georgia A.	22y	W	D.C.	07 JUN 1878	Presbyterian
011232	STATZ, John	45y	W	Ger.	05 APR 1877	St. Mary's

No.	Name	Age	Race	Birth	Death Date	Burial Place
007323	STATZ, Mary Elizabeth	2y	W	D.C.	16 MAY 1876	St. Mary's
002725	STEADY, James	30y	C	Va.	24 MAR 1875	Beckett's
007889	STEARN, Henry R.	3m	W	D.C.	27 JUN 1876	Congressional
011176	STEARNS, Ralph E.	2y	W	D.C.	31 MAR 1877	Graceland
019594	STEAURT, Southall	33y	C	Va.	29 MAR 1879	Graceland
003812	STEAVENSON, Richard	5m	C	D.C.	24 JUN 1875	Mt. Zion
016530	STECK, Katherine	18m	W	Md.	09 JUL 1878	Prospect Hill
020740	STEEL, Edward	1m	C	D.C.	03 JUL 1879	Mt. Olivet
015856	STEEL, Rebecca	88y	W	Va.	26 MAY 1878	Oak Hill
020784	STEELE, Mary Mills	7m	W	D.C.	05 JUL 1879	Glenwood
013235	STEELE, Peter C.	34y	W	Va.	17 SEP 1877	Fairfax, Va.
010298	STEELYARDS, James H.	1y	C	D.C.	15 JAN 1877	Beckett's
004360	STEELYARDS, Laura E.	11d	C	D.C.	28 JUL 1875	Ebenezer
020818	STEEP, George W.	2y	W	D.C.	07 JUL 1879	Glenwood
020439	STEEVER, Edgar Zell	67y	W	Pa.	14 JUN 1879	Oak Hill
009180	STEGMAIER, Michael	51y	W	Ger.	23 SEP 1876	St. Mary's
012524	STEGMAIER, Theresa	51y	W	Ger.	25 JUL 1877	St. Mary's
011278	STEIN, Celia	13y	W	D.C.	09 APR 1877	Jewish
002460	STEIN, Clara	9m	W	D.C.	07 MAR 1875	Washington Hebrew
009776	STEIN, John J.	44y	W	Bav.	22 NOV 1876	Congressional
004974f	STEIN, John M.	18y	W	Md.	09 SEP 1875	Baltimore, Md.
008265	STEINBERGEN, Hattie	1y	W	D.C.	14 JUL 1876	Washington Hebrew
005431	STEINLE, Edw.	10m	W	D.C.	11 NOV 1875	Congressional
008147	STELLE, Isaac	84y	W	N.J.	10 JUL 1876	New Brunswick, N.J.
007554	STELLO, Henry	50y	W	Ger.	08 JUN 1876	Prospect Hill
000158	STENBAER, George	4y	W	W.D.	12 AUG 1874	Glenwood
017698	STEPHENS, Alberta Victoria	3y	C	D.C.	10 OCT 1878	Harmony
006090	STEPHENS, Anna	78y	W	N.J.	21 JAN 1876	Glenwood
020763	STEPHENS, Lida Elizabeth	4m	C	D.C.	04 JUL 1879	Harmony
017473	STEPHENSON, Charles W.	3y	C	D.C.	20 SEP 1878	Young Mens
007888	STEPHENSON, Edmonia Virginia	32y	C	Va.	27 JUN 1876	Harmony
017544	STEPHENSON, Eugene	41y	C	D.C.	26 SEP 1878	Harmony
010062	STEPHENSON, George Benjamin	70y	W	Va.	24 DEC 1876	Oak Hill
000431	STEPHENSON, John Henry	6m	C	D.C.	04 SEP 1874	Potters Field
002925	STEPHENSON, Lavinia	25y	C	Md.	08 APR 1875	Mt. Zion
002856	STEPHENSON, Lola Virginia	30y	W	D.C.	03 APR 1875	Glenwood
005044	STEPHENSON, Malinda C.	47y	W	Va.	14 SEP 1875	Congressional
008950	STEPHENSON, Theodore	1y	C	Va.	03 SEP 1876	Mt. Zion
005700	STEPHENSON, William	9m	W	D.C.	08 DEC 1875	Glenwood
014031	STEPHENSON, Wm. Fletcher	2m	C	D.C.	07 DEC 1877	Young Mens
008584	STEPNY, Charlotte	23y	M	D.C.	07 AUG 1876	Harmony
014118	STEPTOE, Dorinda	55y	C	Va.	16 DEC 1877	Harmony
017766	STERICK, Laura Jane	2y	W	Pa.	16 OCT 1878	Presbyterian
002965	STERLING, Jonathan	34y	C	Va.	11 APR 1875	Young Mens
019292	STERNE, William Van Aken	1y	W	D.C.	05 MAR 1879	Glenwood
015453	STERRIT, John	50y	C	Mass.	19 APR 1878	Thomas'
020631	STETSON, Walter	4y	W	D.C.	26 JUN 1879	Glenwood
008429	STETTINIUS, Samuel	73y	W	D.C.	26 JUL 1876	Congressional
007422	STEUART, Thomas J.	5y	W	D.C.	27 MAY 1876	Congressional
004118	STEVENS, Elisha	c.75y	W	Conn.	13 JUL 1875	Congressional
015796	STEVENS, Frederick A.	3y	W	D.C.	21 MAY 1878	Glenwood
015586	STEVENS, George	1y	C	D.C.	02 MAY 1878	Mt. Olivet
010837	STEVENS, Harry	1m	C	D.C.	02 MAR 1877	Young Mens
005633	STEVENS, Marietta	52y	W	Ohio	02 DEC 1875	Congressional
006368	STEVENS, Mary Ann	55y	W	Conn.	15 FEB 1876	Norwalk, Conn.
002378	STEVENS, Matilda	74y	W	Md.	02 MAR 1875	Fairfax Co., Va.

District of Columbia Death Records, August 1, 1874 to July 31, 1879   323

No.	Name	Age	Race	Birth	Death Date	Burial Place
009471	STEVENS, Percy C.	4y	W	D.C.	20 OCT 1876	Glenwood
011511	STEVENS, Rebecca	80y	W	Ver.	04 MAY 1877	Glenwood
018829	STEVENSON, Emma	1y	C	D.C.	26 JAN 1879	Beckett's
002292	STEVENSON, John	45y	C	Va.	23 FEB 1875	Potters Field
004206	STEVENSON, Lucy	1y	C	D.C.	19 JUL 1875	Moore's
012037	STEVENSON, Sarah P.	63y	C	D.C.	24 JUN 1877	Harmony
005331	STEVENSON, William Ellsworth	11m	C	D.C.	01 NOV 1875	Harmony
002138	STEVERSON, Rachel A.	6y	C	D.C.	12 FEB 1875	Young Mens
002093	STEVERSON, Willie Alfred	1y	C	D.C.	09 FEB 1875	Mt. Pleasant
018796	STEVESON, Fredrick	2m	C	D.C.	24 JAN 1879	Mt. Pleasant
011089	STEVESON, Jennie	4m	C	D.C.	23 MAR 1877	Ebenezer
009938	STEWARD, Adeline	6m	C	D.C.	12 DEC 1876	Mt. Pleasant
012985	STEWARD, Emanuel	2y	C	D.C.	27 AUG 1877	Potters Field
017178	STEWARD, Infant of Issabel	21d	C	D.C.	24 AUG 1878	Jones Chapel
004584	STEWARD, Martha Jane	26y	C	Va.	13 AUG 1875	Harmony
017407	STEWARD, Oregon Nevada	2m	C	D.C.	14 SEP 1878	Harmony
016573	STEWART, Alfred R.	1y	C	D.C.	12 JUL 1878	Payne's
011080	STEWART, Alice	26y	C	Md.	22 MAR 1877	Potters Field
002583	STEWART, Andrew	35y	C	Va.	15 MAR 1875	Beckett's
019548	STEWART, Anna M.	3m	C	D.C.	25 MAR 1879	Mt. Olivet
001872	STEWART, Betsey	101y	C	Md.	24 JAN 1875	Potters Field
019365	STEWART, Blanche [Maud]	1y	C	D.C.	11 MAR 1879	Potters Field
007986	STEWART, Charles	4y	C	D.C.	03 JUL 1876	Union Baptist
006858	STEWART, Charles Francis	6m	C	D.C.	29 MAR 1876	Mt. Pleasant
004987	STEWART, Charles M.	3y	W	D.C.	10 SEP 1875	Congressional
000365	STEWART, Chas.	90y	C	Va.	29 AUG 1874	Washington Asylum
001020	STEWART, Chas.	17y	C	Va.	02 NOV 1874	Beckett's
018386	STEWART, Clara Stuart	4y	C	D.C.	19 DEC 1878	Beckett's
012867	STEWART, Cora	8y	C	Va.	18 AUG 1877	Harmony
011281	STEWART, Corra A. Lutia	2y	W	D.C.	09 APR 1877	Holy Rood
016585	STEWART, Custar	1y	W	Md.	13 JUL 1878	Taymens, Md.
004249	STEWART, Dora	11y	C	Va.	22 JUL 1875	Mt. Zion
018473	STEWART, Dulphy	3m	C	D.C.	26 DEC 1878	Young Mens
003147	STEWART, Eddie	7d	C	D.C.	27 APR 1875	Potters Field
007414	STEWART, Edward	70y	C	Va.	26 MAY 1876	Beckett's
002917	STEWART, Edward Carrington Palmer	2y	W	D.C.	08 APR 1875	Congressional
006210	STEWART, Elenander	37y	C	Md.	01 FEB 1876	Moore's
014632	STEWART, Elizabeth	65y	C	Md.	01 FEB 1878	Beckett's
012902	STEWART, Euphemia	2y	C	D.C.	21 AUG 1877	Young Mens
004906	STEWART, Florence C.	8m	C	D.C.	04 SEP 1875	Harmony
006079	STEWART, Frances M.	3y	W	D.C.	20 JAN 1876	Glenwood
014756	STEWART, Francis	6m	W	D.C.	13 FEB 1878	Mt. Olivet
011865	STEWART, Frank	6m	C	D.C.	11 JUN 1877	Potters Field
015497	STEWART, Frank	8m	C	D.C.	23 APR 1878	Mt. Olivet
013656	STEWART, Freddie	1y	C	D.C.	27 OCT 1877	Beckett's
015855	STEWART, George	1y	C	D.C.	26 MAY 1878	Mt. Zion
019075	STEWART, George	40y	C	Va.	14 FEB 1879	Petersburg, Va.
015119	STEWART, Georgiana	23y	C	Va.	18 MAR 1878	Young Mens
005553	STEWART, Harry	8d	C	D.C.	24 NOV 1875	Harmony
000047	STEWART, Hattie	1y	C	D.C.	04 AUG 1874	Beckett's
006190	STEWART, Hattie	3m	C	D.C.	30 JAN 1876	Potters Field
011893	STEWART, Hellen	6m	W	D.C.	14 JUN 1877	Holy Rood
005634	STEWART, Henry	23y	C	Md.	02 DEC 1875	Harmony
002530	STEWART, Henry	2y	C	D.C.	12 MAR 1875	Young Mens
015912	STEWART, Henry	5m	C	D.C.	30 MAY 1878	Mt. Olivet
004131	STEWART, Infant of Martha	2m	C	D.C.	14 JUL 1875	Potters Field

District of Columbia Death Records, August 1, 1874 to July 31, 1879

No.	Name	Age	Race	Birth	Death Date	Burial Place
019525	STEWART, Infant of Tom. K.	5min	W	D.C.	23 MAR 1879	Glenwood
007735	STEWART, Infant of Wm.	4m	C	D.C.	19 JUN 1876	Mt. Olivet
015374	STEWART, Izea	2y	C	D.C.	12 APR 1878	Mt. Pleasant
005441	STEWART, Jacob B.	60y	W	N.Y.	12 NOV 1875	Hospital
014100	STEWART, James Wilson	54y	W	Ire.	14 DEC 1877	Mt. Olivet
004939	STEWART, Jane	55y	C	Va.	06 SEP 1875	Potters Field
002340	STEWART, John	11m	C	D.C.	27 FEB 1875	Mt. Olivet
014605	STEWART, John	65y	C	Md.	30 JAN 1878	Young Mens
015729	STEWART, John	2m	W	D.C.	14 MAY 1878	Holy Rood
017632	STEWART, John	55y	C	Md.	04 OCT 1878	Harmony
010998	STEWART, John Adams	51y	W	Md.	16 MAR 1877	Oak Hill
020686	STEWART, John W.	5m	W	D.C.	30 JUN 1879	Mt. Olivet
018472	STEWART, Joseph Augustus	2y	C	D.C.	26 DEC 1878	Payne's
012942	STEWART, Laura	1y	C	D.C.	24 AUG 1877	Potters Field
011040	STEWART, Laura	3y	C	D.C.	19 MAR 1877	Ebenezer
015140	STEWART, Leo	7d	C	D.C.	21 MAR 1878	Mt. Zion
008856	STEWART, Leonard Calendar	1y	C	D.C.	28 AUG 1876	Harmony
000297	STEWART, Lloyd	4m	C	D.C.	23 AUG 1874	Mt. Pleasant
013815	STEWART, Lloyd	32y	C	Md.	13 NOV 1877	Harmony
018355	STEWART, Lloyd	42y	W	D.C.	19 DEC 1878	Mt. Olivet
015513	STEWART, Lona F.	3m	W	D.C.	25 APR 1878	Congressional
012938	STEWART, Louise	9d	C	D.C.	24 AUG 1877	Mt. Olivet
006179	STEWART, Lucinda	1y	C	D.C.	29 JAN 1876	Mt. Pleasant
013473	STEWART, Mack	31y	C	Va.	10 OCT 1877	Potters Field
017672	STEWART, Mamie	10y	W	D.C.	07 OCT 1878	Graceland
013723	STEWART, Margaret	52y	W	Md.	03 NOV 1877	Mt. Olivet
001901	STEWART, Martha	25y	C	Md.	26 JAN 1875	Mt. Olivet
006201	STEWART, Martha	15y	C	Va.	31 JAN 1876	Mt. Pleasant
017409	STEWART, Martha	40y	C	Va.	14 SEP 1878	Young Mens
019198	STEWART, Martha	4m	C	D.C.	25 FEB 1879	Mt. Zion
003837	STEWART, Mary	9y	C	D.C.	25 JUN 1875	Ebenezer
009409	STEWART, Mary	1y	W	D.C.	14 OCT 1876	Graceland
018480	STEWART, Mary A.	1y	C	D.C.	27 DEC 1878	Mt. Zion
009756	STEWART, Mary J.	7y	W	D.C.	20 NOV 1876	Congressional
019876	STEWART, Mattie	1y	C	D.C.	23 APR 1879	Graceland
019580	STEWART, Phebe	70y	C	Md.	28 MAR 1879	Beckett's
005094a	STEWART, Robert	26y	C	Va.	09 OCT 1875	Potters Field
017815	STEWART, Robert Lincoln	14y	W	Md.	20 OCT 1878	Baltimore, Md.
004699	STEWART, Rosalind	11m	W	D.C.	21 AUG 1875	Mt. Olivet
015942	STEWART, Samuel	29y	C	N.Y.	31 MAY 1878	Potters Field
004250	STEWART, Sarah	10m	C	D.C.	22 JUL 1875	Beckett's
006866	STEWART, Sarah	9m	W	D.C.	30 MAR 1876	Mt. Olivet
009332	STEWART, Sarah A.	5m	C	D.C.	07 OCT 1876	Piney Grove
009416	STEWART, Susan	64y	C	Va.	15 OCT 1876	Beckett's
020841	STEWART, Thadeus Stevens	1y	C	D.C.	08 JUL 1879	Mt. Pleasant
007444	STEWART, Thomas	33y	C	U.S.	30 MAY 1876	Harmony
011250	STEWART, Thomas	8m	C	Md.	07 APR 1877	Harmony
017608	STEWART, Tiny	3y	C	D.C.	02 OCT 1878	Young Mens
013848	STIARWALT, Mattie Lovell	11y	W	Ohio	17 NOV 1877	Bellefontaine, Ohio
000001	STICKELL, Harrison T.	2w	W	Md.	01 AUG 1874	Baltimore, Md.
004065	STICKNEY, John	26d	W	D.C.	09 JUL 1875	Glenwood
015376	STIDHAM, Blanche	4y	W	D.C.	12 APR 1878	Rock Creek
005968	STILES, Charles C.	29y	W	Mass.	07 JAN 1876	Glenwood
003890	STILLARD, Infant of Daniel	7m	C	D.C.	27 JUN 1875	Ebenezer
002224	STILSON, Nancy	40y	W	N.Y.	18 FEB 1875	Glenwood
001732	STIMSON, Edward H.	6m	W	D.C.	14 JAN 1875	Congressional

District of Columbia Death Records, August 1, 1874 to July 31, 1879

No.	Name	Age	Race	Birth	Death Date	Burial Place
009500	STINCHCOMB, John H.	16m	W	D.C.	22 OCT 1876	Mt. Olivet
008200	STINER, Amanda	20y	C	Md.	12 JUL 1876	Mt. Pleasant
015355	STINOCKLE, Andrias	20y	W	D.C.	10 APR 1878	St. Mary's
002867	STINZING, Maggie	21d	W	D.C.	04 APR 1875	Glenwood
017855	STIRS, Mary	70y	C	Va.	25 OCT 1878	Harmony
014010	STOBESAND, Aleiza	6y	W	D.C.	04 DEC 1877	Oak Hill
012431	STOCK, Blanche	9m	W	D.C.	19 JUL 1877	Glenwood
003275	STOCKED, Lloyd	70y	C	D.C.	09 MAY 1875	Potters Field
003943f	STOCKING, Wilbur Fisk	33y	W	Conn.	30 JUN 1875	Oak Hill
012637	STOCKMAN, Coar H.	7y	W	D.C.	01 AUG 1877	Oak Hill
011523	STOCKMAN, Lillian G.	2y	W	D.C.	06 MAY 1877	Holy Rood
018279	STOCKS, Martha	76y	C	Md.	08 DEC 1878	Mt. Zion
019551	STOCKTON, Phillip	46y	W	Pa.	25 MAR 1879	Baltimore, Md.
020986	STOCKTON, William	11m	W	D.C.	17 JUL 1879	Potters Field
017918	STODDARD, Mary E.	37y	C	Md.	01 NOV 1878	Harmony
000381	STODDART, Infant of M.C.	11d	W	D.C.	31 AUG 1874	Glenwood
000349	STOERMER, Annie	2m	W	D.C.	28 AUG 1874	Prospect Hill
007295	STOERTZER, Julius	34y	W	Ger.	13 MAY 1876	Prospect Hill
017901	STOKES, Rosa	2d	W	D.C.	29 OCT 1878	Glenwood
017497	STOLL, George	24y	W	Switz.	22 SEP 1878	Soldier's Home
018445	STOLPE, Edward	42d	W	D.C.	23 DEC 1878	Prospect Hill
017655	STONE, Albertie	29y	C	Va.	06 OCT 1878	Mt. Pleasant
006946	STONE, August	47y	W	Pa.	06 APR 1876	Mt. Olivet
002682f	STONE, Brinton	5m	--	Md.	05 AUG 1871	Oak Hill
001826	STONE, Brinton	33y	W	Pa.	21 JAN 1875	Congressional
002683f	STONE, Brinton[1]	8m	--	Md.	-- JUL 1870	Oak Hill
020685	STONE, Cecelia	1m	W	D.C.	30 JUN 1879	Mt. Olivet
002935f	STONE, Charles S.	24y	W	Va.	10 APR 1875	Glenwood
004512	STONE, Harret C.	1y	W	D.C.	08 AUG 1875	Presbyterian
014923	STONE, John	65y	W	Me.	02 MAR 1878	Hospital, Government
003543f	STONE, John G., Mrs.	60y	W	Va.	06 DEC 1872	Oak Hill
001614	STONE, Rachel	72y	W	D.C.	04 JAN 1875	Congressional
013965	STONE, Sarah F.	33y	W	Va.	29 NOV 1877	Presbyterian/RockCreek
002681f	STONE, Thysa[2]	5m	--	Md.	-- MAR 1869	Oak Hill
017331	STONER, Emma, Mrs.	46y	W	Ohio	05 SEP 1878	Canton, Ohio
008321	STONER, Henry	1y	W	D.C.	18 JUL 1876	Congressional
019190	STONER, Martha	c.75y	W	Pa.	24 FEB 1879	McVeytown, Pa.
018966	STORAM, Edwin K.	6m	C	D.C.	05 FEB 1879	Harmony
008016	STORKS, Gus Her.	2m	C	D.C.	04 JUL 1876	Young Mens
008235	STORM, John	36y	W	Ire.	13 JUL 1876	Hospital
009184	STORM, Leo	12y	W	Va.	24 SEP 1876	Presbyterian
011855	STORRS, Cordial, Sr.	91y	W	Conn.	09 JUN 1877	Glenwood
007526	STORUM, James Garrett	4m	C	D.C.	06 JUN 1876	Harmony
012336	STORY, L.L.	3m	W	D.C.	12 JUL 1877	Glenwood
011477	STORY, William	62y	W	Ire.	01 MAY 1877	Congressional
015250	STOTSENBURY, Nellie Denham	4y	W	Del.	31 MAR 1878	Wilmington, Del.
015400	STOTT, Mary Irene	7y	W	D.C.	14 APR 1878	Rock Creek
011199	STOTTS, Augemma	94y	C	Va.	02 APR 1877	Harmony
005905	STOTTS, Jane Eliza	17y	C	Va.	31 DEC 1875	Moore's
011862	STOUDER, Mary	21y	W	Ire.	11 JUN 1877	Mt. Olivet
005552	STOUGHTON, Agustus Burbanks	65y	W	Pa.	24 NOV 1875	Mt. Olivet
007868	STOUT, Burd Helen	7m	W	Va.	26 JUN 1876	Congressional

[1] Removed to Oak Hill from Coatesville, Pa.
[2] Removed to Oak Hill from Coatesville, Pa.

District of Columbia Death Records, August 1, 1874 to July 31, 1879

No.	Name	Age	Race	Birth	Death Date	Burial Place
012919	STOW, Hester	80y	W	N.Y.	23 AUG 1877	Congressional
015120	STRACHAN, Bettie	44y	C	Va.	18 MAR 1878	Harmony
017208	STRACHAN, Charles S.	7y	C	D.C.	26 AUG 1878	Harmony
005771	STRADER, Sarah B.	69y	W	Pa.	16 DEC 1875	Louisville, Ky.
020950	STRAIGHT, Beatrice Louise	3m	W	D.C.	15 JUL 1879	Graceland
015960	STRAIGHT, Mary Edith	8m	W	D.C.	01 JUN 1878	Graceland
019440	STRAIT, Cora	11m	C	D.C.	17 MAR 1879	Potters Field
003654	STRAITNER, Jeremiah	2y	C	D.C.	15 JUN 1875	Mt. Pleasant
019199	STRAITS, Cecelia	1y	C	D.C.	25 FEB 1879	Mt. Pleasant
003143	STRANGE, Catherine	50y	C	Va.	27 APR 1875	Winchester, Va.
001416	STRATTON, Ella G.	3y	W	D.C.	17 DEC 1874	Congressional
005772	STRAUB, Frank	45y	W	Ger.	16 DEC 1875	Prospect Hill
020797	STRAUGHTER, Mary	1y	C	D.C.	06 JUL 1879	Young Mens
008531	STRAUM, Elisabeth Adelaide	1y	W	N.C.	02 AUG 1876	Oak Hill
005819	STRAUS, Grace	3y	W	D.C.	21 DEC 1875	Washington Hebrew
016746	STRAUSS, Arthur	9y	W	D.C.	24 JUL 1878	Jewish
004642	STRAUSS, Leon	1y	W	D.C.	17 AUG 1875	Hebrew, P.G. Co., Md.
016507	STRAUTHER, Nicholas	78y	C	Va.	08 JUL 1878	Potters Field
009814	STRAWTHER, Annie	32y	C	Va.	28 NOV 1876	Alexandria, Va.
012080	STRAWTHER, Matthew	4m	C	D.C.	27 JUN 1877	Beckett's
009530	STREAKS, Martha	42y	W	Md.	25 OCT 1876	Congressional
004221	STREEKS, Hacker	3m	W	D.C.	20 JUL 1875	Congressional
009548	STREEKS, Mary Ann	19y	W	D.C.	27 OCT 1876	Congressional
008359	STREET, Catherine E.	1y	W	D.C.	20 JUL 1876	Mt. Olivet
008226	STREET, Charles Ezra	21d	W	D.C.	13 JUL 1876	Congressional
000729	STREET, Priscilla	75y	M	Va.	06 OCT 1874	Washington Asylum
006536	STREET, William H.	1y	W	D.C.	03 MAR 1876	Congressional
002826	STREITBERGER, Infant of Henry	2m	W	D.C.	01 APR 1875	Prospect Hill
002946	STREITENBERGER, Edward	2y	W	D.C.	11 APR 1875	Prospect Hill
011096	STRICKHART, Clara W.	3m	W	D.C.	23 MAR 1877	Congressional
006103	STRICKHART, Laura Leola	3m	W	D.C.	22 JAN 1876	Congressional
017323	STRIDER, Maggie	4y	W	D.C.	04 SEP 1878	Congressional
011932	STRIEBY, Emma	3m	W	D.C.	16 JUN 1877	Glenwood
006925	STRIFFLER, Leopold	3y	W	D.C.	04 APR 1876	Prospect Hill
004643	STRIFFLER, Sophia	1y	W	D.C.	17 AUG 1875	Prospect Hill
008150	STRIFFLER, William	14d	W	D.C.	10 JUL 1876	Prospect Hill
017179	STRIVERS, Lucy	2m	C	D.C.	24 JUL 1878	Beckett's
003560	STROBEL, John G.	60y	W	Ger.	07 JUN 1875	Prospect Hill
020399	STROBLE, Henry Julius	3m	W	D.C.	11 JUN 1879	Prospect Hill
005524	STRONG, Edmund	37y	W	N.Y.	20 NOV 1875	Hospital
015587	STRONG, Mary	80y	C	Va.	02 MAY 1878	Mt. Pleasant Plain
013225	STROTHER, Hetty Ann	1m	C	D.C.	16 SEP 1877	Beckett's
000139	STROTHER, James	10y	C	Va.	11 AUG 1874	Beckett's
018416	STROTHER, James	70y	C	Va.	21 DEC 1878	Young Mens
005601	STROTHER, Mary	25y	C	Va.	29 NOV 1875	Mt. Zion
014786	STROTHER, Rebecca	4y	C	D.C.	16 FEB 1878	Potters Field
005351	STROTHER, Thos. Wesley	15d	C	D.C.	03 NOV 1875	Beckett's
006037	STROTHERS, Mary	7m	M	Va.	15 JAN 1876	Middleburg, Va.
009733	STROUT, Lewis F.	35y	W	Me.	19 NOV 1876	Congressional
014410	STUART, Catherine	65y	W	N.Y.	13 JAN 1878	Congressional
007955	STUART, Catherine M.	2y	C	D.C.	01 JUL 1876	Mt. Olivet
016137	STUART, Charles N.	18y	W	D.C.	12 JUN 1878	Congressional
020096	STUART, Chas. A.	36y	W	D.C.	14 MAY 1879	Congressional
000521	STUART, Delansteen	2y	C	D.C.	15 SEP 1874	Harmony
005036	STUART, Effie	2y	W	D.C.	13 SEP 1875	Congressional
014553	STUART, Frederic Donald	63y	C	N.Y.	25 JAN 1878	Congressional

District of Columbia Death Records, August 1, 1874 to July 31, 1879   327

No.	Name	Age	Race	Birth	Death Date	Burial Place
016935	STUART, John	22y	W	D.C.	06 AUG 1878	Congressional
018889	STUART, Laura V.	18m	C	D.C.	30 JAN 1879	Young Mens
006489	STUART, Malvina	44y	M	Va.	27 FEB 1876	Young Mens
005067a	STUART, Mary D.	38y	W	D.C.	05 OCT 1875	Congressional
020880	STUART, Mary E.	6m	W	D.C.	10 JUL 1879	Glenwood
012145	STUART, William	2m	C	D.C.	30 JUN 1877	Young Mens
015672	STUART, William M.	64y	W	Mass.	09 MAY 1878	Newark, N.J.
007687	STUBBS, Mary J.	10m	W	Md.	17 JUN 1876	St. John's Church, Md.
006036	STULL, Mariah	84y	W	D.C.	15 JAN 1876	Presbyterian
018142	STUMBLER, John	46y	W	Ger.	24 NOV 1878	Hospital, Government
008064	STUMP, Henry	8m	W	D.C.	08 JUL 1876	Prospect Hill
007060	STURGIS, Charles B.	7y	W	D.C.	20 APR 1876	Holy Rood
017921	STURM, Louise	5y	W	Md.	01 NOV 1878	Baltimore, Md.
007391	STUTELEY, Bertie	2m	C	D.C.	23 MAY 1876	Beckett's
003094	STUTLEY, William	24h	C	D.C.	23 APR 1875	Beckett's
016209	STUTLY, Morris	14d	C	D.C.	17 JUN 1878	Beckett's
002069	STUTZ, Catharine	16y	W	D.C.	07 FEB 1875	Prospect Hill
013527	SUBBLE, Margaret	38y	C	Md.	15 OCT 1877	Beckett's
002636	SUDLER, Henrietta M.T.	73y	W	Md.	18 MAR 1875	Oak Hill
000178	SUIDAM, Catharin	1y	W	D.C.	13 AUG 1874	Washington
011290	SUIT, Bertie	30y	W	Md.	10 APR 1877	Congressional
010754	SUIT, Jane E.	68y	W	Md.	23 FEB 1877	Marlboro, Md.
010450	SUIT, John Smith	26y	W	Md.	30 JAN 1877	Congressional
019348	SUIT, Lizzie	13m	W	D.C.	09 MAR 1879	Mt. Olivet
013410	SUIT, William	17y	W	D.C.	05 OCT 1877	Mt. Olivet
005209a	SULIVAN, Charles H.	1y	C	D.C.	19 OCT 1875	Jones Chapel
020141	SULIVAN, Maggie A.	5y	W	D.C.	18 MAY 1879	Mt. Olivet
020112	SULIVAN, Michael	3y	W	D.C.	15 MAY 1879	Mt. Olivet
000962	SULIVAN, William	5d	W	D.C.	28 OCT 1874	Mt. Olivet
012087	SULLIVAN, Annie	24y	W	Mass.	27 JUN 1877	Mt. Olivet
020265	SULLIVAN, Catharine Sophia	13y	W	D.C.	01 JUN 1879	Mt. Olivet
004322	SULLIVAN, Catherine	1y	W	D.C.	26 JUL 1875	Holy Rood
009102	SULLIVAN, Catherine S.	50y	W	Ire.	16 SEP 1876	Holy Rood
005644	SULLIVAN, Christina	83y	W	Ire.	03 DEC 1875	Convent
017482	SULLIVAN, Cornelius	56y	W	Ire.	21 SEP 1878	Mt. Olivet
020671	SULLIVAN, Daisy	8m	W	D.C.	29 JUN 1879	Glenwood
009581	SULLIVAN, Daniel	45y	W	Ire.	31 OCT 1876	Mt. Olivet
013358	SULLIVAN, Danis	30y	W	Ire.	30 SEP 1877	Mt. Olivet
014702	SULLIVAN, Dennis J.	19y	W	Ire.	07 FEB 1878	Mt. Olivet
000175	SULLIVAN, Edw.	80y	W	Ire.	13 AUG 1874	Mt. Olivet
010973	SULLIVAN, Elizabeth	45y	W	Ire.	14 MAR 1877	Mt. Olivet
011220	SULLIVAN, Ellen	31y	W	Ire.	05 APR 1877	Potters Field
016917	SULLIVAN, Eugene Aloysius	10m	W	D.C.	05 AUG 1878	Mt. Olivet
016181	SULLIVAN, Florence A.	27y	W	Va.	15 JUN 1878	Mt. Olivet
008749	SULLIVAN, Geo. E.	8m	C	D.C.	20 AUG 1876	Graceland
014757	SULLIVAN, Hanora A.	23y	W	Va.	13 FEB 1878	Holy Rood
014751	SULLIVAN, Henry William	2y	W	D.C.	12 FEB 1878	Glenwood
000809	SULLIVAN, Hugh Eugene	1y	W	D.C.	15 OCT 1874	Mt. Olivet
008358	SULLIVAN, Ida	3m	W	D.C.	20 JUL 1876	Presbyterian
017685	SULLIVAN, Jane	65y	W	Ire.	09 OCT 1878	Mt. Olivet
018507	SULLIVAN, Jeremiah	15y	W	D.C.	29 DEC 1878	Mt. Olivet
005250	SULLIVAN, Jerry	1y	W	D.C.	23 OCT 1875	Mt. Olivet
004451	SULLIVAN, Johanna	6m	W	D.C.	04 AUG 1875	Mt. Olivet
010051	SULLIVAN, John	37y	W	Ire.	22 DEC 1876	Hospital
010362	SULLIVAN, John	30y	W	Ire	21 JAN 1877	Hospital, Government
017533	SULLIVAN, John	64y	W	Ire.	25 SEP 1878	Holy Rood

District of Columbia Death Records, August 1, 1874 to July 31, 1879

No.	Name	Age	Race	Birth	Death Date	Burial Place
021181	SULLIVAN, John	60y	W	Ire.	31 JUL 1879	Mt. Olivet
008367	SULLIVAN, John D.	28y	W	U.S.	21 JUL 1876	Congressional
012309	SULLIVAN, Joseph	1m	W	D.C.	10 JUL 1877	Mt. Olivet
019549	SULLIVAN, Joseph	2d	W	D.C.	25 MAR 1879	Mt. Olivet
000685	SULLIVAN, Katey	15y	W	Can.	01 OCT 1874	Congressional
000077	SULLIVAN, Mary	53y	W	Ire.	06 AUG 1874	Mt. Olivet
006024	SULLIVAN, Mary	62y	W	Ire.	14 JAN 1876	Mt. Olivet
008462	SULLIVAN, Mary	7m	W	D.C.	28 JUL 1876	Mt. Olivet
015474	SULLIVAN, Mary	11m	C	D.C.	21 APR 1878	Potters Field
019820	SULLIVAN, Mary	69y	W	Ire.	18 APR 1879	Mt. Olivet
018872	SULLIVAN, Mary	2y	C	D.C.	29 JAN 1879	Mt. Pleasant
019279	SULLIVAN, Mary	67y	W	Ire.	04 MAR 1879	Mt. Olivet
000625	SULLIVAN, Mary A.	1y	W	D.C.	24 SEP 1874	Mt. Olivet
000187	SULLIVAN, Mary Ann	21y	W	D.C.	14 AUG 1874	Mt. Olivet
016665	SULLIVAN, Mary Ann	80y	W	Ire.	19 JUL 1878	Holy Rood
014339	SULLIVAN, Mary E.	45y	W	Md.	06 JAN 1878	Oak Hill
005423	SULLIVAN, Mary Ellen	5y	W	D.C.	10 NOV 1875	Mt. Olivet
020134	SULLIVAN, Patk.	1m	W	D.C.	17 MAY 1879	Mt. Olivet
000805	SULLIVAN, Patrick	58y	C	Ire.	14 OCT 1874	Mt. Olivet
002644	SULLIVAN, Patrick	65y	W	Ire.	19 MAR 1875	Mt. Olivet
009691	SULLIVAN, Patrick	49y	W	Ire.	13 NOV 1876	Mt. Olivet
018192	SULLIVAN, Timity	9m	W	D.C.	28 NOV 1878	Mt. Olivet
008962	SULLIVAN, William J.	8m	W	D.C.	04 SEP 1876	Mt. Olivet
017607	SUMLY, Eliza	32y	C	D.C.	02 OCT 1878	Beckett's
006885	SUMMER, Arand M.	3m	W	D.C.	01 APR 1876	Jewish
009872	SUMMER, Ellen	4d	C	D.C.	05 DEC 1876	Mt. Olivet
016106	SUMMER, George N.	1y	W	D.C.	10 JUN 1878	Conduit Rd.
006355	SUMMER, Joseph	30y	C	N.C.	14 FEB 1876	Potters Field
005309	SUMMERS, Aquilla T.	76y	W	Va.	30 OCT 1875	Congressional
003907	SUMMERS, Charles	1m	C	D.C.	28 JUN 1875	Potters Field
005289	SUMMERS, Daniel E.	21d	C	D.C.	28 OCT 1875	Fentonsville, Va.[1]
007342	SUMMERS, David	37y	C	Pa.	19 MAY 1876	Potters Field
006345	SUMMERS, John	50y	W	Md.	13 FEB 1876	Congressional
006983	SUMMERS, John A.	58y	W	Md.	10 APR 1876	Mt. Olivet
011049	SUMMERS, Louisa	80y	W	Md.	20 MAR 1877	Forestville, Md.
009675	SUMMERS, Mary B.	45y	W	Md.	11 NOV 1876	Congressional
005081a	SUMMERS, Rebecca	66y	W	Md.	07 OCT 1875	Congressional
001994	SUMMERS, Thomas	78y	W	Md.	02 FEB 1875	Forestville, Md.
011375	SUMMERS, Wm.	55y	C	Va.	19 APR 1877	Mt. Pleasant
014567	SUMMY, Herbert Irwin	5y	W	D.C.	26 JAN 1878	Rock Creek
012702	SUMNER, Chas.	1y	C	D.C.	06 AUG 1877	Beckett's
014099	SUMNER, Hester A.	58y	W	N.Y.	14 DEC 1877	Glenwood
010416	SUMNER, Infant of Richard	23y	C	D.C.	27 JAN 1877	Ebenezer
017245	SUPPES, John Burke	9m	W	D.C.	29 AUG 1878	Prospect Hill
001139	SUPPLEE, Percy	8m	W	D.C.	14 NOV 1874	Congressional
012391	SURRICKS, Wm. C.T.	6m	C	D.C.	16 JUL 1877	Young Mens
019850	SURTIN, Mariah, Mrs.	73y	W	Va.	20 APR 1879	Congressional
008109	SUSTRATT, Frederick	c.38y	W	Ger.	09 JUL 1876	Congressional
004263	SUTHARD, Albert	5m	C	D.C.	23 JUL 1875	Moore's
021180	SUTHERLAND, Peter	17y	W	Va.	31 JUL 1879	Fairfax Co., Va.
014425	SUTPHIN, William A.	42y	W	N.J.	14 JAN 1878	Sumerville, N.J.
006202	SUTPIN, Ann Cecelia	50y	W	Md.	31 JAN 1876	Baltimore, Md.
015018	SUTTON, Agnes Louisa	1y	C	D.C.	10 MAR 1878	Mt. Olivet

[1] Located in Fairfax Co., Va.

District of Columbia Death Records, August 1, 1874 to July 31, 1879   329

No.	Name	Age	Race	Birth	Death Date	Burial Place
015313	SUTTON, Elizabeth Lavinia	8y	W	D.C.	07 APR 1878	Congressional
017038	SUTTON, Infant of John	15min	C	D.C.	13 AUG 1878	Mt. Olivet
017072	SUTTON, Mary	3d	C	D.C.	16 AUG 1878	Mt. Olivet
014787	SUTTON, Mary	51y	W	Ger.	16 FEB 1878	Glenwood
014691	SUTTON, Peter Joseph	1m	W	D.C.	06 FEB 1878	Congressional
016596	SUTTON, Richard	70y	W	Eng.	14 JUL 1878	Congressional
002540	SUTTON, Stanley Ross	18y	C	Va.	12 MAR 1875	Potters Field
019765	SUYDAM, James Cameron	18m	W	D.C.	13 APR 1879	Congressional
019723	SWAGART, Joseph	79y	W	Md.	10 APR 1879	Congressional
001362	SWAGGART, Joseph Franklin	6d	W	D.C.	11 DEC 1874	Congressional
001655	SWAILES, Samuel A.	3y	C	D.C.	08 JAN 1875	Mt. Zion
001761	SWAIN, Moses P.	68y	W	N.J.	16 JAN 1875	Graceland
019835	SWAINGAN, Earnest D.	6m	C	D.C.	19 APR 1879	Holy Rood
019255	SWAINGAN, Harry J.	2y	C	D.C.	02 MAR 1879	Holy Rood
000210	SWAN, Alice M.	10m	W	D.C.	16 AUG 1874	Mt. Olivet
006640	SWAN, Bessie C.	10m	W	D.C.	11 MAR 1876	Prince William Co., Va.
020183	SWAN, Emely	60y	C	Md.	23 MAY 1879	Moore's
009575	SWAN, Melissa Jane, Mrs.	35y	W	Ky.	30 OCT 1876	Carrollton, Ky.
013213	SWAN, Rosana, Mrs.	36y	C	D.C.	15 SEP 1877	Harmony
013937	SWANEY, John	40y	W	Va.	26 NOV 1877	Fairfax Co., Va.
014363	SWANN, Florence E.	13y	W	Md.	08 JAN 1878	Preston, Va.[1]
013605	SWANN, Margaret Jane	44y	W	Ire.	23 OCT 1877	Rock Creek
017843	SWANN, William Henry	18m	C	D.C.	23 OCT 1878	Beckett's
014533	SWART, Nicholas A.	38y	W	N.Y.	23 JAN 1878	Schenectady, N.Y.
020949	SWARTONT, Mable E.	9m	W	D.C.	15 JUL 1879	Congressional
018082	SWAYGART, Freddi K.	6y	W	D.C.	17 NOV 1878	Prospect Hill
020033	SWAYZE, George Green	33y	W	N.J.	07 MAY 1879	Oak Hill
020817	SWEENEY, Catharin	4m	W	D.C.	07 JUL 1879	Mt. Olivet
008795	SWEENEY, Catharine	9d	W	D.C.	23 AUG 1876	Mt. Olivet
007789	SWEENEY, Infant of George	3m	C	D.C.	22 JUN 1876	Mt. Zion
009737	SWEENEY, Pat.	1y	W	D.C.	19 NOV 1876	Mt. Olivet
004423	SWEENY, Bridget	71y	W	Ire.	02 AUG 1875	Mt. Olivet
008630	SWEENY, Chas. Jos.	14m	W	D.C.	09 AUG 1876	Mt. Olivet
018576	SWEENY, Edward	30y	W	Pa.	05 JAN 1879	Binghampton, N.Y.
011310	SWEENY, Mary Frances	1y	C	D.C.	12 APR 1877	Moore's
006770	SWEENY, Morris Morton	4m	W	D.C.	21 MAR 1876	Mt. Olivet
020491	SWEET, Georgeana	8m	C	D.C.	17 JUN 1879	Congressional
003154	SWEET, Wm. E.	2h	W	D.C.	28 APR 1875	Glenwood
015655	SWEETMAN, Margret	69y	C	Md.	08 MAY 1878	Mt. Olivet
000792	SWEETNEY, Mamie Elizabeth	1y	C	D.C.	12 OCT 1874	Beckett's
020586	SWEETNING, Louis	7m	C	D.C.	23 JUN 1879	Mt. Olivet
020015	SWEETNING, Martha	30y	C	Md.	06 MAY 1879	Mt. Olivet
013711	SWEETWINE, Infant of William	1m	C	D.C.	02 NOV 1877	Beckett's
005947	SWEETWINE, Wliliam	18d	C	D.C.	05 JAN 1876	Ebenezer
003586	SWETLAND, Mary A.	39y	W	N.Y.	10 JUN 1875	Saratoga Co., N.Y.
014534	SWIFT, Willie	2y	W	D.C.	23 JAN 1878	Congressional
004264	SWINDELLS, Frederick E.	4m	W	D.C.	23 JUL 1875	Oak Hill
006219	SWINDELLS, Rachel M.	5y	W	D.C.	02 FEB 1876	Oak Hill
002237	SWINDELLS, Samuel	73y	W	Eng.	19 FEB 1875	Lancaster, Pa.
006005	SYBERT, Lloyd	2y	C	D.C.	12 JAN 1876	Potters Field
001010	SYBERT, William Henry	2y	C	D.C.	01 NOV 1874	Mt. Zion
018634	SYDNOR, Hattie	8m	M	D.C.	10 JAN 1879	Beckett's
010296	SYDNOR, William H	35y	C	Va.	15 JAN 1877	Harmony

---

[1] "Preston" plantation was located in Alexandria Co., Va., the home of the Charles Alexander family and descendants.

No.	Name	Age	Race	Birth	Death Date	Burial Place
013088	SYKES, Jesse	69y	C	Va.	04 SEP 1877	Union Baptist
010750	SYLVESTER, David M.	44y	W	Md.	23 FEB 1877	Mt. Olivet
019749	SYLVESTER, George, Dr.	65y	W	Md.	12 APR 1879	Congressional
016322	SYMMES, George	78y	C	Md.	26 JUN 1878	Beckett's
017510	SYPHAX, Daniel	42y	C	Va.	23 SEP 1878	Harmony
009710	SYPHAX, Eliza	68y	C	Va.	16 NOV 1876	Mt. Zion
009622	SYPHAX, Francis	19y	C	Va.	05 NOV 1876	Harmony
009131	SYPHAX, Joseph	2m	M	D.C.	19 SEP 1876	Harmony
020510	SYPHAX, Louisa	28y	C	Va.	18 JUN 1879	Harmony
004533	SYPHAX, Richard L.	1y	C	D.C.	10 AUG 1875	Mt. Pleasant
000774	SYPLER, Edward P.	c.30y	W	N.J.	10 OCT 1874	Morrisville, N.J.

T

No.	Name	Age	Race	Birth	Death Date	Burial Place
003410	TABB, Franklin	2y	C	D.C.	23 MAY 1875	Harmony
003280f	TABBS, Annie Cornelia	13y	M	Md.	10 MAY 1875	Mt. Olivet
002296	TABBS, Joseph Ignatius	5d	C	D.C.	23 FEB 1875	Mt. Olivet
005251	TABLER, William J.	57y	W	D.C.	23 OCT 1875	Glenwood
010309	TABOR, Mary Eunice	17d	W	D.C.	16 JAN 1877	Congressional
001361	TABOTT, Louisa	16m	C	D.C.	11 DEC 1874	Young Mens
000665	TABS, Mary B.	1y	C	Md.	29 SEP 1874	Mt. Olivet
006702	TAFF, George D.	4m	W	D.C.	16 MAR 1876	Congressional
019690	TAFFE, James	61y	W	Ire.	07 APR 1879	Hospital/Mt. Olivet
005711	TAFT, Reuben	75y	W	Ver.	09 DEC 1875	Congressional
017368	TAGGERT, Mary Ann	10d	W	D.C.	10 SEP 1878	Mt. Olivet
007284	TAIT, Alexander Glenholm	30y	W	D.C.	12 MAY 1876	Mt. Olivet
013344	TAIT, Elizabeth	17y	C	Va.	28 SEP 1877	Beckett's
000607	TAIT, Jane	87y	W	Scot.	23 SEP 1874	Congressional
013633	TAIT, William	21y	C	Va.	25 OCT 1877	Beckett's
017699	TALBERT, Charles O.	1y	C	D.C.	10 OCT 1878	Mt. Pleasant
009697	TALBERT, Delia	8m	C	D.C.	14 NOV 1876	Ebenezer
008982	TALBERT, George W.	2h	W	D.C.	06 SEP 1876	Congressional
011485	TALBERT, George W.	50y	W	Md.	01 MAY 1877	Rock Creek
020687	TALBERT, George W.	7m	W	D.C.	30 JUN 1879	Congressional
014042	TALBERT, John Walter	6d	C	D.C.	08 DEC 1877	Harmony
004132	TALBERT, Laura	1y	C	D.C.	14 JUL 1875	Mt. Pleasant
008392	TALBERT, Louis Henry	1y	C	D.C.	23 JUL 1876	Harmony
002816f	TALBERT, Margarett	90y	W	Md.	31 MAR 1875	Rock Creek
009462	TALBERT, Mary Ann	24y	C	Va.	19 OCT 1876	Harmony
012721	TALBERT, Washington	11h	W	D.C.	07 AUG 1877	Congressional
013825	TALBOT, Adella	9y	C	D.C.	14 NOV 1877	Mt. Pleasant Plain
010119	TALBOT, Annie	1y	C	D.C.	30 DEC 1876	Young Mens
012638	TALBOT, Carrie E.	1y	C	Md.	01 AUG 1877	Ebenezer
001062	TALBOT, Infant of Hester	7d	C	D.C.	05 NOV 1874	Potters Field
014183	TALBOT, John	45y	W	Prus.	23 DEC 1877	Soldier's Home
017868	TALBOT, Margaretta	11w	C	D.C.	26 OCT 1878	Young Mens
001960	TALBOT, Mary E.	1y	C	D.C.	31 JAN 1875	Harmony
005194a	TALBOT, Mime L.	11d	M	D.C.	18 OCT 1875	Harmony
015485	TALBOTT, Amelia	53y	C	D.C.	22 APR 1878	Mt. Olivet
003725	TALBOTT, Francis	8m	C	D.C.	20 JUN 1875	Mt. Pleasant
007703	TALBOTT, Joseph	c.3m	C	D.C.	17 JUN 1876	Mt. Pleasant
015656	TALBOTT, Linda	9m	C	D.C.	08 MAY 1878	Mt. Pleasant
018968	TALBURTT, Jennie Laselle	34y	W	D.C.	05 FEB 1879	Mt. Olivet
000585	TALCOTT, Josephine	1d	W	D.C.	21 SEP 1874	Glenwood
000935	TALCOTT, Maria Louisa	40y	W	Va.	26 OCT 1874	Glenwood

District of Columbia Death Records, August 1, 1874 to July 31, 1879

No.	Name	Age	Race	Birth	Death Date	Burial Place
005554	TALIFARO, Maria	21y	C	Va.	24 NOV 1875	Ebenezer
004303	TALLEY, Helen L.	52y	C	D.C.	25 JUL 1875	Harmony
008286	TANCO, Clara	1y	C	D.C.	16 JUL 1876	Mt. Pleasant
003521	TANNER, Alfred	4m	W	D.C.	04 JUN 1875	Prospect Hill
003408	TANNER, Henry	16y	W	Switz.	23 MAY 1875	Congressional
017884	TANNER, John Thomas	4m	W	D.C.	27 OCT 1878	Mt. Olivet
001239	TANSIL, Allen Sherman	3y	C	D.C.	26 NOV 1874	Harmony
019948	TAPER, Francis	1y	C	D.C.	30 APR 1879	Graceland
004036	TAPER, Nancy	1y	C	D.C.	07 JUL 1875	Harmony
021088	TAPLETT, William	50y	C	Va.	24 JUL 1879	Potters Field
002916	TAPPAN, Charles	94y	W	Mass.	08 APR 1875	Boston, Mass.
009712	TAPPAN, George Raymond	2y	W	D.C.	17 NOV 1876	Glenwood
000171	TAPSICO, Mary Washington	4m	M	D.C.	13 AUG 1874	Young Mens
010333	TARGEE, Daniel	65y	W	Ger.	19 JAN 1877	Soldier's Home
018244	TARMON, Jane E., Mrs.	56y	W	Va.	05 DEC 1878	Congressional
017903	TARRELL, Ellen	8d	W	D.C.	29 OCT 1878	Mt. Olivet
009940	TARRISS, Marie L.	2y	W	Pa.	12 DEC 1876	Presbyterian
004524	TASCO, Mary Ann	1m	C	D.C.	09 AUG 1875	Potters Field
003957	TASCOR, Henry	50y	C	Md.	01 JUL 1875	Potters Field
004721	TASKALL, Annie	35y	M	U.S.	22 AUG 1875	Potters Field
001716	TASKER, Charlotte	20y	C	Md.	13 JAN 1875	Mt. Pleasant
002204	TASKER, Edith A.	4m	W	D.C.	17 FEB 1875	Glenwood
008083	TASKER, Rachael	40y	C	Va.	08 JUL 1876	Mt. Pleasant
013214	TASKER, Spencer	30y	C	Va.	15 SEP 1877	Arlington
005119	TASKER, Willie	10m	C	D.C.	20 SEP 1875	Mt. Pleasant
007961	TASSMAN, Martha Magdalena	11m	W	D.C.	01 JUL 1876	Congressional
001804	TASTER, Horner	c.100y	C	Va.	20 JAN 1875	Washington Asylum
011873	TATE, Etta	2y	W	D.C.	12 JUN 1877	Congressional
001624	TATE, Sarah	34y	C	Va.	05 JAN 1875	Beckett's
009864	TATE, William A.	6y	C	D.C.	04 DEC 1876	Ebenezer
009208	TATTZAY [Apache Indian Chief]	22y	--	Ariz.	26 SEP 1876	Congressional
007007	TAUBERSMITH, Ernst August	16m	W	D.C.	13 APR 1876	Prospect Hill
015041	TAUNTON, Infant of Ruben	5d	C	D.C.	12 MAR 1878	Potters Field
000642	TAVENNER, Sallie J., Mrs.	41y	W	Va.	26 SEP 1874	Congressional
006684	TAYLER, George	27y	W	Ohio	15 MAR 1876	Youngstown, Ohio
019617	TAYLER, Louisa	17y	C	Va.	31 MAR 1879	Freedmen's Village, Va.
008246	TAYLER, Mariah	6m	C	D.C.	13 JUL 1876	Beckett's
000064	TAYLER, Richard	11m	C	D.C.	05 AUG 1874	Young Mens
002345	TAYLOE, Geo. W.	9d	C	D.C.	27 FEB 1875	Potters Field
014523	TAYLOR, Abraham	45y	C	Va.	22 JAN 1878	Payne's
014524	TAYLOR, Adaline	c.70y	C	Va.	22 JAN 1878	Beckett's
009952	TAYLOR, Alfred	45y	W	Eng.	13 DEC 1876	Congressional
009973	TAYLOR, Alice, Mrs.	30y	W	Md.	15 DEC 1876	Congressional
013865	TAYLOR, Andrew D.	45y	W	Va.	19 NOV 1877	Glenwood
006418	TAYLOR, Ann	30y	C	Pa.	19 FEB 1876	Potters Field
001277	TAYLOR, Ann Maria	71y	W	Md.	30 NOV 1874	Mt. Olivet
012793	TAYLOR, Annie Crawford	24y	W	Ohio	13 AUG 1877	Oak Hill
020604	TAYLOR, Armstead	9m	C	D.C.	24 JUN 1879	Payne's
015558	TAYLOR, Atha J.	28y	W	Md.	29 APR 1878	Glenwood
011156	TAYLOR, Benjamin	2y	C	D.C.	29 MAR 1877	Harmony
009614	TAYLOR, Bertha	2d	C	D.C.	04 NOV 1876	Beckett's
015378	TAYLOR, Bertie	8m	W	D.C.	12 APR 1878	Glenwood
006386	TAYLOR, Betsey	25y	C	Va.	16 FEB 1876	Young Mens
006867	TAYLOR, Bettie	3y	C	D.C.	30 MAR 1876	Beckett's
007230	TAYLOR, Caroline	23y	C	Md.	06 MAY 1876	Mt. Olivet
020867	TAYLOR, Caroline	1y	C	D.C.	09 JUL 1879	Mt. Pleasant

No.	Name	Age	Race	Birth	Death Date	Burial Place
008929	TAYLOR, Carrie	1m	C	D.C.	02 SEP 1876	Beckett's
014122	TAYLOR, Charles	22y	C	Va.	17 DEC 1877	Beckett's
019979	TAYLOR, Charles D.	1y	W	D.C.	03 MAY 1879	Presbyterian
019660	TAYLOR, Charlotte	7y	C	D.C.	04 APR 1879	Mt. Pleasant
009692	TAYLOR, Clara	2m	C	D.C.	14 NOV 1876	Potters Field
003471	TAYLOR, Clarrie J.	6m	W	D.C.	29 MAY 1875	Congressional
014874	TAYLOR, Custis Lee	5y	C	D.C.	25 FEB 1878	Holy Rood
013505	TAYLOR, Daniel A.	20y	C	D.C.	13 OCT 1877	Payne's
010643	TAYLOR, Delora	65y	C	Va.	15 FEB 1877	Mt. Zion
019906	TAYLOR, Duana	52y	C	Va.	26 APR 1879	Beckett's
006859	TAYLOR, Edom	29y	C	Va.	29 MAR 1876	Ebenezer
015049	TAYLOR, Edward	2y	M	D.C.	12 MAR 1878	Young Mens
003390	TAYLOR, Eliza B., Mrs.	56y	C	Va.	21 MAY 1875	Harmony
010326	TAYLOR, Elizabeth	40y	C	Va.	18 JAN 1877	Alexandria, Va.
004251	TAYLOR, Eller	1y	C	D.C.	22 JUL 1875	Harmony
020277	TAYLOR, Emma Miller	3y	W	D.C.	02 JUN 1879	Glenwood
006314	TAYLOR, Fannie Ann	1y	C	D.C.	11 FEB 1876	Ecton's B.G.
008121	TAYLOR, Fannie B.	1m	W	D.C.	10 JUL 1876	Congressional
020016	TAYLOR, Fedrick	2y	C	D.C.	06 MAY 1879	Young Mens
005357	TAYLOR, Francis	39y	M	Va.	04 NOV 1875	Harmony
008830	TAYLOR, Francis	3m	C	D.C.	26 AUG 1876	Potters Field
002037	TAYLOR, Francis Ellen	8m	C	D.C.	05 FEB 1875	Mt. Olivet
016407	TAYLOR, Franklin	3m	W	D.C.	02 JUL 1878	Graceland
020764	TAYLOR, Franklin	8m	C	D.C.	04 JUL 1879	Harmony
006685	TAYLOR, Frederick	7m	C	D.C.	15 MAR 1876	Chappel's
003343	TAYLOR, George	54y	C	Va.	16 MAY 1875	Potters Field
009912	TAYLOR, George	57y	W	Ger.	09 DEC 1876	Ebenezer
006620	TAYLOR, George F.	14m	C	D.C.	09 MAR 1876	Young Mens
007804	TAYLOR, Gertrude	7m	C	D.C.	23 JUN 1876	Young Mens
007915	TAYLOR, Gertrude	18d	C	D.C.	28 JUN 1876	Potters Field
012809	TAYLOR, Gertrude	3m	C	D.C.	14 AUG 1877	Ebenezer
017220	TAYLOR, Gertrude P.	1y	W	N.C.	27 AUG 1878	Congressional
017801	TAYLOR, Griffin	8y	C	D.C.	19 OCT 1878	Beckett's
002559	TAYLOR, Harrett Elizabeth	7y	C	D.C.	13 MAR 1875	Harmony
001065	TAYLOR, Harriet	65y	C	Md.	06 NOV 1874	Beckett's
016761	TAYLOR, Harriet	1y	C	D.C.	25 JUL 1878	Mt. Pleasant
011912	TAYLOR, Harrison	50y	C	Va.	15 JUN 1877	Potters Field
005086	TAYLOR, Henry	5y	M	D.C.	17 SEP 1875	Potters Field
007504	TAYLOR, Henry C.	63y	W	Eng.	04 JUN 1876	Pokepsie, N.Y.
005352	TAYLOR, Hunter	28y	W	D.C.	03 NOV 1875	Glenwood
019552	TAYLOR, Ida	2y	C	D.C.	25 MAR 1879	Potters Field
007635	TAYLOR, Infant of Ann	½h	C	D.C.	13 JUN 1876	Mt. Zion
014184	TAYLOR, Infant of Annie	8d	C	D.C.	23 DEC 1877	Potters Field
013978	TAYLOR, Infant of Charles	2m	C	D.C.	01 DEC 1877	Potters Field
011023	TAYLOR, Infant of Francis M.	2d	W	D.C.	18 MAR 1877	Howard
010999	TAYLOR, Infant of Francis M.	10h	W	D.C.	16 MAR 1877	Howard's
003568	TAYLOR, Infant of George	5h	W	D.C.	08 JUN 1875	Congressional
010488	TAYLOR, Infant of Jane	1m	C	D.C.	03 FEB 1877	Ebenezer
016937	TAYLOR, Infant of Jordan	26h	C	D.C.	06 AUG 1878	Potters Field
010433	TAYLOR, Infant of Lucy	¼d	C	D.C.	29 JAN 1877	Potters Field
015377	TAYLOR, Infant of Nero	34h	C	D.C.	12 APR 1878	Potters Field
006104	TAYLOR, Infant of Thomas	11h	W	D.C.	22 JAN 1876	Oxen Hill, Md.
003600	TAYLOR, Infant of W.S.	½h	C	D.C.	11 JUN 1875	Ebenezer
013059	TAYLOR, Infant of Wm. H. (twin)	3m	C	D.C.	02 SEP 1877	Richmond, Va.
012625	TAYLOR, James	2y	C	D.C.	31 JUL 1877	Ebenezer
015102	TAYLOR, James	70y	C	Va.	17 MAR 1878	Moore's

District of Columbia Death Records, August 1, 1874 to July 31, 1879   333

No.	Name	Age	Race	Birth	Death Date	Burial Place
014554	TAYLOR, James Arthur	7m	C	D.C.	25 JAN 1878	Potters Field
006657	TAYLOR, James Bell	16y	W	D.C.	12 MAR 1876	Oak Hill
000245	TAYLOR, James Ernest	11m	C	D.C.	19 AUG 1874	Harmony
002464	TAYLOR, James H.	5m	C	D.C.	07 MAR 1875	Ebenezer
010579	TAYLOR, James L.	9y	C	D.C.	10 FEB 1877	Mt. Zion
001492	TAYLOR, Jane	1y	C	D.C.	26 DEC 1874	Potters Field
011442	TAYLOR, Jane	58y	W	Md.	27 APR 1877	Congressional
017006	TAYLOR, Jane R.	85y	W	Ire.	10 AUG 1878	Oak Hill
001606	TAYLOR, Jennie	7d	C	D.C.	04 JAN 1875	Beckett's
014997	TAYLOR, Jerry	1y	C	D.C.	08 MAR 1878	Young Mens
007960	TAYLOR, Jesse	7m	M	Va.	01 JUL 1876	Young Mens
013991	TAYLOR, Jno.	50y	C	Md.	02 DEC 1877	Moore's
005161a	TAYLOR, John	25y	C	Va.	15 OCT 1875	Harmony
012003	TAYLOR, John	60y	C	Va.	22 JUN 1877	Beckett's
011706	TAYLOR, John	6d	C	D.C.	26 MAY 1877	Ebenezer
016107	TAYLOR, John	11m	C	D.C.	10 JUN 1878	Chapman Family
015867	TAYLOR, John	80y	C	Md.	27 MAY 1878	Harmony
020819	TAYLOR, John	22y	C	Va.	07 JUL 1879	Young Mens
002020	TAYLOR, John F.	6m	C	D.C.	04 FEB 1875	Mt. Zion
014340	TAYLOR, John James	50y	C	Va.	06 JAN 1878	Harmony
018212	TAYLOR, Joseph	1y	C	D.C.	01 DEC 1878	Moore's
017883	TAYLOR, Josephine	3y	C	D.C.	27 OCT 1878	Young Mens
017051	TAYLOR, Kate L.	32y	W	D.C.	14 AUG 1878	Glenwood
008711	TAYLOR, L. Lyttleton	3m	C	D.C.	17 AUG 1876	Beckett's
013975	TAYLOR, Lena	7y	C	D.C.	30 NOV 1877	Beckett's
020906	TAYLOR, Leonard	47y	C	D.C.	12 JUL 1879	Young Mens
015514	TAYLOR, Lewis	111y	C	Va.	25 APR 1878	Mt. Zion
010255	TAYLOR, Lina	71y	C	Va.	11 JAN 1877	Jones Chapel
009862	TAYLOR, Lucy	104y	C	Va.	04 DEC 1876	Potters Field
013678	TAYLOR, Lucy	25y	C	Va.	30 OCT 1877	Potters Field
005332	TAYLOR, Mahala Ann	1y	C	D.C.	01 NOV 1875	Young Mens
000132	TAYLOR, Malinda, Mrs.	45y	C	Va.	10 AUG 1874	Young Mens
005060	TAYLOR, Mari	3y	C	D.C.	15 SEP 1875	Beckett's
008574	TAYLOR, Martha Matilda	20y	C	Va.	06 AUG 1876	Ebenezer
000083	TAYLOR, Mary	25y	C	Va.	06 AUG 1874	Beckett's
008606	TAYLOR, Mary Ann Elizabeth	11m	C	D.C.	08 AUG 1876	Ebenezer
009191	TAYLOR, Mary Augusta	8d	W	D.C.	24 SEP 1876	Harper's Ferry, Va.
010994	TAYLOR, Mary E.	8y	C	D.C.	15 MAR 1877	Tennallytown
004971	TAYLOR, Mary Elizabeth	10d	C	D.C.	09 SEP 1875	Ebenezer
018250	TAYLOR, Mary Lillian	2y	W	Md.	05 DEC 1878	Mt. Olivet/Arlington
008589	TAYLOR, Matilda	28y	C	Md.	07 AUG 1876	Ebenezer
013679	TAYLOR, Matthew	17y	C	Va.	30 OCT 1877	Young Mens
005127	TAYLOR, Minnie	11m	M	D.C.	21 SEP 1875	Young Mens
004500	TAYLOR, Minor	21y	C	Va.	07 AUG 1875	Ebenezer
015524	TAYLOR, Minor	50y	C	Va.	26 APR 1878	Prince George's Co., Md.
005162a	TAYLOR, Nathan	50y	C	Va.	15 OCT 1875	Beckett's
010808	TAYLOR, Peter	54y	C	Va.	28 FEB 1877	Ebenezer
016369	TAYLOR, Rachael	35y	C	Va.	29 JUN 1878	Beckett's
006803	TAYLOR, Richard	8d	C	D.C.	24 MAR 1876	Beckett's
006703	TAYLOR, Richard	10y	M	Va.	16 MAR 1876	Potters Field
020843	TAYLOR, Richard Edward	7m	C	D.C.	08 JUL 1879	Harmony
002001	TAYLOR, Robert	17d	C	D.C.	01 FEB 1875	Union Town, D.C.
014875	TAYLOR, Robert Walker	65y	W	Pa.	25 FEB 1878	Youngstown, Ohio
017052	TAYLOR, Rose	22y	C	Va.	14 AUG 1878	Mt. Pleasant
006467	TAYLOR, Rosetta	7m	C	D.C.	24 FEB 1876	Ebenezer
016824	TAYLOR, Samuel	6m	C	D.C.	29 JUL 1878	Mt. Pleasant

No.	Name	Age	Race	Birth	Death Date	Burial Place
002476	TAYLOR, Samuel Henderson	4y	W	Va.	08 MAR 1875	Congressional
008805	TAYLOR, Sarah Ann	1m	C	D.C.	24 AUG 1876	Eckton's Place
001792	TAYLOR, Seymour	c.35y	C	La.	19 JAN 1875	Mt. Pleasant
003562	TAYLOR, Silas	25y	C	Va.	07 JUN 1875	Ebenezer
013576	TAYLOR, Solomon	9y	C	D.C.	20 OCT 1877	Beckett's
017441	TAYLOR, Susan, Mrs.	27y	W	Va.	17 SEP 1878	Potters Field
001342	TAYLOR, Thomas	24y	C	Md.	09 DEC 1874	Beckett's
000321	TAYLOR, Thomas Simpson	6d	C	D.C.	26 AUG 1874	Harmony
006580	TAYLOR, Travers	70y	C	Va.	06 MAR 1876	Harmony
003226	TAYLOR, William	1y	C	D.C.	05 MAY 1875	Young Mens
004921	TAYLOR, William	65y	C	Va.	05 SEP 1875	Potters Field
008811	TAYLOR, William	4m	C	D.C.	25 AUG 1876	Potters Field
006026	TAYLOR, William	2m	W	Va.	14 JAN 1876	Mt. Olivet
008157	TAYLOR, William	30y	C	Va.	10 JUL 1876	Young Mens
007916	TAYLOR, William	14d	C	D.C.	28 JUN 1876	Young Mens
008946	TAYLOR, William	42y	C	Md.	03 SEP 1876	Beckett's
010841	TAYLOR, William Albert	18y	M	D.C.	02 MAR 1877	Mt. Pleasant
005128	TAYLOR, William H.	2y	C	D.C.	21 SEP 1875	Ebenezer
009089	TAYLOR, Winnie	8d	C	D.C.	15 SEP 1876	Ebenezer
011792	TAYLOR, Wm.	2y	C	D.C.	03 JUN 1877	Potters Field
016985	TAYLOR, Wm.	13m	C	D.C.	09 AUG 1878	Beckett's
006579	TAYLOR, Zachariah	2y	C	D.C.	06 MAR 1876	Chappel's
006760	TEABOWER, Margaret	1y	W	D.C.	19 MAR 1876	Prospect Hill
001059	TEACHAM, Burr	4y	W	D.C.	05 NOV 1874	Congressional
014153	TEACKLE, Harriet	80y	W	Md.	20 DEC 1877	Oak Hill
017017	TEEPLE, Edna Burford	10m	W	D.C.	11 AUG 1878	Congressional
006009	TEEPLE, Edna H.	11m	W	D.C.	13 JAN 1876	Congressional
015841	TEEPLE, Mary R.	28y	W	D.C.	25 MAY 1878	Congressional
003695	TELLS, Joseph	2d	C	D.C.	18 JUN 1875	Ebenezer
018025	TEMPLE, Bettie	4y	C	D.C.	11 NOV 1878	Young Mens
004021	TEMPLE, Franklin Whitlock	5m	W	Md.	06 JUL 1875	Baltimore, Md.
003149	TEMPLE, George	4y	C	Tenn.	27 APR 1875	Mt. Olivet
004969	TEMPLE, Lillie	3y	C	Md.	09 SEP 1875	Mt. Olivet
005002	TEMPLE, Louisa	7y	C	Md.	11 SEP 1875	Mt. Olivet
018373	TEMPLETON, Archibald	1y	W	D.C.	18 DEC 1878	Congressional
020034	TENALLY, Ellen Maria	28y	W	D.C.	07 MAY 1879	Mt. Olivet
016967	TENALLY, Wm. Henry	47y	W	D.C.	08 AUG 1878	Rock Creek
010020	TENEL, Beatrice	27y	M	D.C.	20 DEC 1876	Mt. Olivet
000931	TENLEY, Margaret W.	66y	W	Pa.	25 OCT 1874	Glenwood
004741	TENLY, John	3m	W	D.C.	24 AUG 1875	Mt. Olivet
000840	TENNANT, John Alexander	9m	W	D.C.	17 OCT 1874	Holy Rood
000955	TENNEY, Furnando	10m	C	D.C.	27 OCT 1874	Mt. Pleasant
009698	TENNEY, John	74y	W	D.C.	14 NOV 1876	Oak Hill
005395	TENNISON, David	90y	C	Va.	08 NOV 1875	Brightwood
000855	TENNY, Caroline	67y	W	Mass.	19 OCT 1874	Oak Hill
001256	TENNYSON, Earnist	4m	C	D.C.	28 NOV 1874	Holy Rood
006791	TENNYSON, Flora	23y	C	D.C.	23 MAR 1876	Mt. Olivet
008044	TENPIN, Starling	64y	C	Va.	05 JUL 1876	Potters Field
009323	TENTLOFF, Randolph	22y	W	Ger.	06 OCT 1876	Prospect Hill
018339	TERFLINGER, Addie D.	29y	W	N.B.	14 DEC 1878	Congressional
018531	TERNELL, Francis P.	2y	W	D.C.	31 DEC 1878	Mt. Olivet
003664	TERRELL, Charles	3m	C	D.C.	16 JUN 1875	Ebenezer
014680	TERRELL, Eliza	68y	C	Va.	05 FEB 1878	Mt. Olivet
019595	TERRELL, Eugene	5m	C	D.C.	29 MAR 1879	Payne's
005020a	TERRELL, James	45y	C	D.C.	01 OCT 1875	Potters Field
005564	TERRELL, Robert	62y	C	Va.	25 NOV 1875	Harmony

District of Columbia Death Records, August 1, 1874 to July 31, 1879

No.	Name	Age	Race	Birth	Death Date	Burial Place
004722	TERRY, Arthur W.	9m	C	D.C.	22 AUG 1875	Harmony
013018	TERRY, Clara	5d	W	D.C.	30 AUG 1877	Glenwood
020827	TERRY, Elizabeth L.	5m	W	D.C.	08 JUL 1879	Mt. Olivet
000990	TERRY, Florinda	2m	C	D.C.	31 OCT 1874	Beckett's
019052	TERRY, Infant of James	12d	C	D.C.	12 FEB 1879	Beckett's
001212	TERRY, James Henry Otho	11m	W	D.C.	22 NOV 1874	Glenwood
016119	TERRY, James Youngs	22d	W	D.C.	11 JUN 1878	Glenwood
009997	TERRY, Scipio	10m	C	D.C.	18 DEC 1876	Ebenezer
017594	TERRY, Wm.	41y	M	Va.	01 OCT 1878	Harmony
010639	TESTE, Peter	87y	W	France	15 FEB 1877	Soldier's Home
009171	TETEDOUX, Apolline Guilford	52y	W	Ohio	22 SEP 1876	Cincinnati, Ohio
009921	TEW, Frederick William	5y	W	D.C.	10 DEC 1876	Glenwood
006503	THALMON, Joseph	65y	W	Switz.	28 FEB 1876	Mt. Olivet
011577	THARP, Mary A.	1y	W	D.C.	13 MAY 1877	Mt. Olivet
002022	THAYER, James H.	45y	W	N.Y.	04 FEB 1875	Graceland
008638	THEACKER, Pauline	2m	W	D.C.	10 AUG 1876	Glenwood
020688	THEALL, Benjamin F.	15d	W	D.C.	30 JUN 1879	Graceland
006091	THECKER, Henry	67y	W	D.C.	21 JAN 1876	Oak Hill
016597	THILL, Catharine L.	1y	W	D.C.	14 JUL 1878	St. Mary's
019510	THISSELL, Addie M.	4m	W	D.C.	23 MAR 1879	Congressional
008822	THISSELL, Infant	9h	W	D.C.	25 AUG 1876	Congressional
018977	THMAS, Lydia Elizabeth Elen	2y	W	D.C.	06 FEB 1879	Graceland
001956	THOMA, William	59y	W	Ger.	30 JAN 1875	Oak Hill
003044	THOMAS, Adline	50y	C	Md.	19 APR 1875	Ebenezer
016748	THOMAS, Albert	34y	M	Md.	24 JUL 1878	Harmony
002724	THOMAS, Alice	3y	W	D.C.	24 MAR 1875	Rock Creek
015646	THOMAS, Alice Roberta	6m	C	D.C.	07 MAY 1878	Potters Field
012107	THOMAS, Alice Virginia (twin)	4m	W	D.C.	28 JUN 1877	Mt. Olivet
007451	THOMAS, Andrew	9m	C	D.C.	31 MAY 1876	Mt. Pleasant
010413	THOMAS, Ann	2m	W	U.S.	26 JAN 1877	Mt. Olivet
006926	THOMAS, Annie	23y	C	Md.	04 APR 1876	Young Mens
015783	THOMAS, Annie	7m	C	D.C.	20 MAY 1878	Mt. Olivet
013826	THOMAS, Annie C.	2y	C	D.C.	14 NOV 1877	Mt. Zion
015486	THOMAS, Archie	8m	C	D.C.	22 APR 1878	Young Mens
009239	THOMAS, Augusta Lee Washington	1y	C	D.C.	29 SEP 1876	Young Mens
003509	THOMAS, B.F.	6h	M	D.C.	02 JUN 1875	Young Mens
001341	THOMAS, Benjamin	70y	C	Va.	08 DEC 1874	Potters Field
017442	THOMAS, Bettie	9y	C	Va.	17 SEP 1878	Potters Field
020090	THOMAS, Blanch	7m	C	D.C.	13 MAY 1879	Beckett's
007472	THOMAS, Bruce P.	c.36y	W	Ala.	02 JUN 1876	Congressional
011593	THOMAS, Caroline	44y	M	N.C.	14 MAY 1877	Beckett's
008509	THOMAS, Carrie	5d	C	D.C.	31 JUL 1876	Mt. Zion
019191	THOMAS, Carrie Caroline	6y	C	D.C.	24 FEB 1879	Young Mens
001267	THOMAS, Catharine	11y	C	Md.	29 NOV 1874	Beckett's
012460	THOMAS, Charles	88y	M	Md.	21 JUL 1877	Potters Field
014633	THOMAS, Charles	81y	W	Pa.	01 FEB 1878	Congressional
011620	THOMAS, Charles C.	3y	M	Md.	16 MAY 1877	Glenwood
019200	THOMAS, Charles Nicholas	1y	C	D.C.	25 FEB 1879	Mt. Pleasant
000810	THOMAS, Charlotte R.	24d	W	D.C.	15 OCT 1874	Congressional
002230	THOMAS, Clarinda	12m	C	D.C.	19 FEB 1875	Mt. Pleasant
001032	THOMAS, Clementia	1y	1y	D.C.	03 NOV 1874	Congressional
015340	THOMAS, Cora	1y	M	D.C.	09 APR 1878	Beckett's
002997	THOMAS, Cyrus A.	34y	W	N.Y.	15 APR 1875	Buffalo, N.Y.
009422	THOMAS, Edward	5m	C	D.C.	16 OCT 1876	Smith's
013106	THOMAS, Elisha	24y	W	D.C.	06 SEP 1877	Congressional
001387	THOMAS, Eliza	16m	C	D.C.	14 DEC 1874	Mt. Olivet

District of Columbia Death Records, August 1, 1874 to July 31, 1879

No.	Name	Age	Race	Birth	Death Date	Burial Place
009837	THOMAS, Eliza	78y	C	Md.	01 DEC 1876	Mt. Olivet
012127	THOMAS, Eliza R.	21d	M	D.C.	29 JUN 1877	Beckett's
015657	THOMAS, Elizabeth	2y	C	D.C.	08 MAY 1878	Mt. Olivet
013395	THOMAS, Elizabeth Ida	1y	C	D.C.	03 OCT 1877	Mt. Olivet
008658	THOMAS, Ellen	45y	C	Md.	12 AUG 1876	Ebenezer
009708	THOMAS, Emily Ann	64y	W	Md.	16 NOV 1876	Mt. Olivet
016338	THOMAS, Emma Luvenia	10m	W	D.C.	27 JUN 1878	Rock Creek
016196	THOMAS, Emma Virginia	14y	W	D.C.	16 JUN 1878	Oak Hill
013332	THOMAS, Fannie	38y	C	Md.	27 SEP 1877	Beckett's
019247	THOMAS, Ferdinand C.	4y	C	D.C.	01 MAR 1879	Young Mens
007207	THOMAS, Frances J.	32y	C	U.S.	04 MAY 1876	Harmony
018134	THOMAS, Francis	4m	C	D.C.	23 NOV 1878	Holy Rood
003219	THOMAS, Frank	82y	C	Md.	05 MAY 1875	Mt. Olivet
002551	THOMAS, George	68y	W	Va.	13 MAR 1875	Congressional
008838	THOMAS, George	3m	C	D.C.	27 AUG 1876	Ebenezer
011296	THOMAS, George	57y	C	Md.	10 APR 1877	Potters Field
001557	THOMAS, George Columbus	37y	C	D.C.	01 JAN 1875	Young Mens
005594	THOMAS, Grace	6y	W	D.C.	28 NOV 1875	Hancock, Md.
009957	THOMAS, Hamilton	22y	C	D.C.	14 DEC 1876	Potters Field
003278	THOMAS, Harry	17d	W	D.C.	10 MAY 1875	Presbyterian
020512	THOMAS, Hattie Anna	12y	C	Md.	18 JUN 1879	Mt. Olivet
004011	THOMAS, Hellen	14d	C	D.C.	05 JUL 1875	Potters Field
000600	THOMAS, Henry	60y	M	Md.	22 SEP 1874	Mt. Zion
005734	THOMAS, Henry	1y	C	D.C.	12 DEC 1875	Mt. Zion
017235	THOMAS, Henry	40y	M	Ohio	28 AUG 1878	Insane Asylum
021118	THOMAS, Henry	2y	C	D.C.	26 JUL 1879	Young Mens
007555	THOMAS, Henry J.	3m	W	D.C.	08 JUN 1876	Congressional
010849	THOMAS, Ida V.	2m	C	D.C.	03 MAR 1877	Harmony
018204	THOMAS, Infant	2d	C	D.C.	29 NOV 1878	Mt. Olivet
019392	THOMAS, Infant of Annie	8d	C	D.C.	13 MAR 1879	Potters Field
017276	THOMAS, Infant of Catharine	3m	C	D.C.	31 AUG 1878	Mt. Olivet
009453	THOMAS, Infant of Eugene	4d	M	D.C.	18 OCT 1876	Young Mens
020368	THOMAS, Infant of Jno.	2h	C	D.C.	09 JUN 1879	Harmony
012559	THOMAS, Infant of Laura	9d	C	D.C.	27 JUL 1877	Potters Field
003622	THOMAS, Infant of Maria	5d	C	D.C.	12 JUN 1875	Young Mens
008423	THOMAS, Infant of Mary Ellen	15min	C	D.C.	26 JUL 1876	Potters Field
011034	THOMAS, Infant of Robert	23d	C	D.C.	19 MAR 1877	Mt. Zion
013811	THOMAS, Infant of Susan	3h	C	D.C.	12 NOV 1877	Potters Field
010760	THOMAS, Infant of William	7d	C	D.C.	24 FEB 1877	Young Mens
007704	THOMAS, Irene	4m	C	D.C.	17 JUN 1876	Mt. Olivet
015159	THOMAS, Isabel	1y	C	D.C.	23 MAR 1878	Moore's
005120	THOMAS, Isabella	1y	C	D.C.	20 SEP 1875	Harmony
006139	THOMAS, James	8m	C	D.C.	25 JAN 1876	Ebenezer
017857	THOMAS, James	24y	C	Va.	25 OCT 1878	Mt. Zion
003814	THOMAS, James L.	24d	C	D.C.	24 JUN 1875	Ebenezer
012830	THOMAS, James L.	1y	C	D.C.	15 AUG 1877	Potters Field
004283	THOMAS, Jane	42y	C	Md.	24 JUL 1875	Potters Field
008813	THOMAS, Jane	2y	C	D.C.	25 AUG 1876	Ebenezer
005082a	THOMAS, Jas. K.	5d	W	D.C.	07 OCT 1875	Presbyterian
000264	THOMAS, Jerome	1y	C	D.C.	20 AUG 1874	Prince George's Co., Md.
000434	THOMAS, Jesse G.	2m	C	D.C.	05 SEP 1874	Harmony
004003	THOMAS, John	10m	C	D.C.	04 JUL 1875	Young Mens
013294	THOMAS, John	1y	C	D.C.	24 SEP 1877	Young Mens
014555	THOMAS, John	c.30y	M	Va.	25 JAN 1878	Potters Field
010027	THOMAS, John A.	1y	C	D.C.	20 DEC 1876	Young Mens
016408	THOMAS, John Dill	45y	W	Del.	02 JUL 1878	Rock Creek

District of Columbia Death Records, August 1, 1874 to July 31, 1879   337

No.	Name	Age	Race	Birth	Death Date	Burial Place
001197	THOMAS, John the Baptist	20d	C	D.C.	20 NOV 1874	Holy Rood
007977	THOMAS, John W.	10m	W	D.C.	03 JUL 1876	Oak Hill
009875	THOMAS, Joseph	14d	W	D.C.	05 DEC 1876	Mt. Olivet
018481	THOMAS, Julia	84y	C	Md.	27 DEC 1878	Harmony
014500	THOMAS, Katie	17y	C	Va.	20 JAN 1878	Mt. Zion
004702	THOMAS, Katie E.	2y	W	D.C.	21 AUG 1875	Presbyterian
008148	THOMAS, Laura	7y	C	D.C.	10 JUL 1876	Moore's
012079	THOMAS, Levi S.	55y	W	N.Y.	27 JUN 1877	Corning, N.Y.
015251	THOMAS, Lilie	2y	C	D.C.	31 MAR 1878	Harmony
004484	THOMAS, Lillie S.	1y	C	D.C.	06 AUG 1875	Harmony
002397	THOMAS, Lorenzo	70y	W	Del.	02 MAR 1875	Oak Hill
004452	THOMAS, Louis Wm.	12m	C	D.C.	04 AUG 1875	Mt. Zion
019257	THOMAS, Louisa G.	20y	C	N.C.	02 MAR 1879	Payne's
015356	THOMAS, Louisa Virginia	10m	C	D.C.	10 APR 1878	Mt. Zion
003433	THOMAS, Lucinda	60y	C	Md.	25 MAY 1875	Mt. Olivet
007343	THOMAS, Margaret	34y	C	D.C.	19 MAY 1876	Young Mens
020798	THOMAS, Margaret	54y	M	Va.	06 JUL 1879	Graceland
003124	THOMAS, Margarett Ann	21y	W	D.C.	26 APR 1875	Oak Hill
019218	THOMAS, Maria	6m	C	D.C.	26 FEB 1879	Mt. Zion
012177	THOMAS, Martha Ellen	5y	C	D.C.	02 JUL 1877	Ebenezer
020443	THOMAS, Martin Fielding	20d	W	D.C.	14 JUN 1879	Mt. Olivet
001647	THOMAS, Mary	22y	C	Md.	07 JAN 1875	Harmony
007301	THOMAS, Mary	55y	C	Md.	14 MAY 1876	Mt. Olivet
009599	THOMAS, Mary	27y	C	Ga.	02 NOV 1876	Potters Field
015977	THOMAS, Mary	2y	C	D.C.	02 JUN 1878	Moore's
017951	THOMAS, Mary	1y	C	D.C.	04 NOV 1878	Mt. Olivet
018157	THOMAS, Mary	8y	C	D.C.	25 NOV 1878	Mt. Zion
018347	THOMAS, Mary Cecelia	23y	C	Md.	15 DEC 1878	Mt. Olivet
020017	THOMAS, Mary Eliza	19m	C	D.C.	06 MAY 1879	Mt. Olivet
003755	THOMAS, Mary Elizabeth	4m	M	D.C.	21 JUN 1875	Ebenezer
005037	THOMAS, Mary Jane	1y	C	D.C.	13 SEP 1875	Beckett's
012880	THOMAS, Mary L.	2y	C	Va.	19 AUG 1877	Potters Field
009257	THOMAS, Mary Levy	10d	C	D.C.	01 OCT 1876	Ebenezer
018171	THOMAS, Mary Louisa	1y	C	D.C.	26 NOV 1878	Beckett's
005377	THOMAS, Mary M.	23y	W	Va.	06 NOV 1875	Congressional
012959	THOMAS, Mary M.	10m	M	Va.	25 AUG 1877	Harmony
000671	THOMAS, Mason N.	14y	C	Va.	29 SEP 1874	Tennallytown
009689	THOMAS, Matilda	c.26y	M	Md.	13 NOV 1876	Harmony
020366	THOMAS, Maud G.	8m	C	D.C.	09 JUN 1879	Mt. Pleasant
018474	THOMAS, Michael	87y	C	Va.	26 DEC 1878	Potters Field
011286	THOMAS, Nathaniel	5m	C	D.C.	10 APR 1877	Young Mens
005032a	THOMAS, Netty	4m	C	D.C.	02 OCT 1875	Ebenezer
005666	THOMAS, Noah	10m	C	D.C.	05 DEC 1875	Mt. Olivet
017985	THOMAS, Noble John	57y	W	Va.	08 NOV 1878	Congressional
020041	THOMAS, Philip	1y	C	D.C.	08 MAY 1879	Potters Field
019838	THOMAS, Philip Kearney	39y	W	Mich.	19 APR 1879	Oak Hill
003867	THOMAS, Phillip E.	6m	C	D.C.	26 JUN 1875	Mt. Olivet
006519	THOMAS, Rebecca	48y	C	D.C.	01 MAR 1876	Beckett's
014451	THOMAS, Richard Daniel	2m	C	D.C.	16 JAN 1878	Young Mens
005525	THOMAS, Samuel	25y	C	Md.	20 NOV 1875	Mt. Olivet
015568	THOMAS, Sarah Brooke Lee	68y	W	D.C.	30 APR 1878	Mt. Olivet
002921	THOMAS, Sarah Eliza	5d	C	D.C.	08 APR 1875	--
005059	THOMAS, Sarah Jane	1y	W	D.C.	15 SEP 1875	Congressional
007634	THOMAS, Sherman	5m	C	D.C.	13 JUN 1876	Young Mens
006886	THOMAS, Sinthia A.	41y	W	Va.	01 APR 1876	Harmony
004523	THOMAS, Sophia	24y	C	Md.	09 AUG 1875	Mt. Olivet

No.	Name	Age	Race	Birth	Death Date	Burial Place
009091	THOMAS, Sophia L.	5m	C	D.C.	15 SEP 1876	Mt. Olivet
011875	THOMAS, Susan	c.80y	C	Md.	12 JUN 1877	Mt. Pleasant
012365	THOMAS, Theodore M.	3m	W	D.C.	15 JUL 1877	Presbyterian
001452	THOMAS, Thomas H.	34y	C	Va.	20 DEC 1874	Harmony
002923a	THOMAS, Washington	4d	C	D.C.	08 APR 1875	Ebenezer
004177	THOMAS, William	19y	W	Md.	17 JUL 1875	Mt. Olivet
002771	THOMAS, William	82y	W	N.Y.	28 MAR 1875	Oak Hill
008125	THOMAS, William	6m	C	D.C.	10 JUL 1876	Mt. Zion
009804	THOMAS, William	22y	C	Md.	26 NOV 1876	Ebenezer
012869	THOMAS, William	24y	C	Va.	18 AUG 1877	Mt. Pleasant
012262	THOMAS, William	3m	C	D.C.	08 JUL 1877	Beckett's
019581	THOMAS, William	1y	C	D.C.	28 MAR 1879	Potters Field
011563	THOMAS, William Chr. Col.	2y	C	D.C.	11 MAY 1877	Young Mens
017123	THOMAS, William H.	1y	C	D.C.	20 AUG 1878	Mt. Olivet
006313	THOMAS, William Henry	57y	C	Md.	11 FEB 1876	Harmony
006073	THOMAS, William Henry	8m	M	D.C.	19 JAN 1876	Young Mens
009748	THOMAS, William Henry	7m	C	D.C.	20 NOV 1876	Young Mens
016182	THOMAS, William Henry	11m	C	D.C.	15 JUN 1878	Potters Field
004802	THOMAS, William S.	22y	C	Md.	28 AUG 1875	Harmony
000477	THOMAS, Wm.	6d	W	D.C.	11 SEP 1874	Rock Creek
017435	THOMAS, Wm. Henry	2y	C	D.C.	16 SEP 1878	Young Mens
005265	THOMPKINS, Robert	1y	C	D.C.	25 OCT 1875	Ebenezer
008648	THOMPSON, Addi C.	1y	C	Va.	11 AUG 1876	Holmead's
015128	THOMPSON, Amanda	67y	W	Md.	19 MAR 1878	Congressional
017346	THOMPSON, Anne Eliza	61y	W	Md.	07 SEP 1878	St. Mary's Co., Md.
004265	THOMPSON, Benedict	32y	W	Md.	23 JUL 1875	Mt. Olivet
017802	THOMPSON, Benj.	69y	W	Va.	19 OCT 1878	Congressional
019105	THOMPSON, Benjamin F.	27y	W	D.C.	17 FEB 1879	Oak Hill
001159	THOMPSON, Bessie Lee	2m	W	D.C.	16 NOV 1874	Glenwood
019360	THOMPSON, Beverly Hendee	5y	W	Calif.	10 MAR 1879	Philadelphia, Pa.
015461	THOMPSON, Boswell	70y	C	Va.	20 APR 1878	Potters Field
000957f	THOMPSON, Charles E.	2y	W	Md.	27 OCT 1874	Oak Hill
001622	THOMPSON, Daniel	35y	C	Va.	05 JAN 1875	Mt. Pleasant
018388	THOMPSON, Dolly	1y	C	D.C.	19 DEC 1878	Mt. Olivet
014278	THOMPSON, Eliza	70y	C	Va.	31 DEC 1877	Alexandria, Va.
002625f	THOMPSON, Eliza[1]	35y	--	Eng.	-- --- 1850	Oak Hill
019724	THOMPSON, Ella	3y	W	D.C.	10 APR 1879	Mt. Pleasant
009583	THOMPSON, Ellen	5y	C	D.C.	31 OCT 1876	Beckett's
019298	THOMPSON, Ellen	5y	C	D.C.	06 MAR 1879	Payne's
020988	THOMPSON, Etta	2m	C	D.C.	17 JUL 1879	Harmony
016906	THOMPSON, Eugen	1y	C	D.C.	04 AUG 1878	Beckett's
012831	THOMPSON, Fanny	11m	W	D.C.	15 AUG 1877	Holy Rood
018238	THOMPSON, Franklin	1y	C	D.C.	04 DEC 1878	Beckett's
013577	THOMPSON, G. Richard	42y	W	D.C.	20 OCT 1877	Congressional
007240	THOMPSON, Gilbert Thornton	1d	W	D.C.	07 MAY 1876	Oak Hill
000498	THOMPSON, Harry	11m	W	D.C.	13 SEP 1874	Locust Farm, Va.[2]
010713	THOMPSON, Harry Baker	3m	W	D.C.	20 FEB 1877	Glenwood
000204	THOMPSON, Harry L.	4y	W	D.C.	16 AUG 1874	Congressional
004282	THOMPSON, Hattie	4y	C	D.C.	24 JUL 1875	Harmony
010950	THOMPSON, Helen	64y	W	D.C.	12 MAR 1877	Graceland
001479	THOMPSON, Henry	26y	W	Eng.	25 DEC 1874	Washington Asylum
013188	THOMPSON, Infant of A.	5h	W	D.C.	13 SEP 1877	Methodist

[1] Removed to Oak Hill from Holmead's.
[2] Located in Westmoreland Co., Va.

District of Columbia Death Records, August 1, 1874 to July 31, 1879   339

No.	Name	Age	Race	Birth	Death Date	Burial Place
003330	THOMPSON, Infant of Ebenezer	7h	C	D.C.	15 MAY 1875	Ebenezer
004988	THOMPSON, Infant of Elenora	1d	M	D.C.	10 SEP 1875	Ebenezer
005295	THOMPSON, Infant of Jno. C.	12d	W	D.C.	28 OCT 1875	Westmoreland, Va.
018604	THOMPSON, Infant of Wm.	1d	W	D.C.	07 JAN 1879	Potters Field
005762	THOMPSON, James	63y	W	D.C.	15 DEC 1875	Mt. Olivet
010921	THOMPSON, James A.	2y	C	D.C.	09 MAR 1877	Holy Rood
000794	THOMPSON, James O.	23y	W	D.C.	13 OCT 1874	Graceland
015525	THOMPSON, Jas. Ernest	1m	W	D.C.	26 APR 1878	Glenwood
008840	THOMPSON, John	4y	C	D.C.	27 AUG 1876	Potters Field
007128	THOMPSON, John A.	31y	W	Ohio	26 APR 1876	Glenwood
013060	THOMPSON, John F.	22y	C	Md.	02 SEP 1877	Harmony
019095	THOMPSON, John H.	3y	C	D.C.	16 FEB 1879	Mt. Pleasant
001355	THOMPSON, Joseph	10m	C	D.C.	10 DEC 1874	Young Mens
013744	THOMPSON, Joseph	40y	C	Va.	05 NOV 1877	Young Mens
008169	THOMPSON, Josephine	14d	C	D.C.	11 JUL 1876	Young Mens
020079	THOMPSON, Josephine	2y	C	D.C.	12 MAY 1879	Beckett's
006518	THOMPSON, Judy	c.45y	C	Va.	01 MAR 1876	Ebenezer
000315	THOMPSON, Julia	9m	C	D.C.	25 AUG 1874	Harmony
016920	THOMPSON, Julia	35y	C	Md.	05 AUG 1878	Harmony
018213	THOMPSON, Julia A.	7w	W	D.C.	01 DEC 1878	Holy Rood
016852	THOMPSON, Kate	30y	C	Va.	31 JUL 1878	Harmony
008763	THOMPSON, Lillie	9m	C	D.C.	21 AUG 1876	Young Mens
014545	THOMPSON, Louana	1y	M	D.C.	24 JAN 1878	Harmony
019094	THOMPSON, Lucy Ann	8m	C	D.C.	16 FEB 1879	Mt. Pleasant
011431	THOMPSON, Margarite	40y	W	D.C.	26 APR 1877	Potters Field
016867	THOMPSON, Martha	2y	C	D.C.	01 AUG 1878	Payne's
010485	THOMPSON, Martha Ann	76y	W	D.C.	02 FEB 1877	Holy Rood
015944	THOMPSON, Mary	21d	W	D.C.	31 MAY 1878	Holy Rood
002257	THOMPSON, Mary E.	10m	C	D.C.	20 FEB 1875	Mt. Pleasant
014136	THOMPSON, Mary S.	25y	W	D.C.	19 DEC 1877	Glenwood
011686	THOMPSON, Mic.	70y	W	Ire.	24 MAY 1877	Mt. Olivet
008913	THOMPSON, Richard	85y	W	Md.	01 SEP 1876	Glenwood
004304	THOMPSON, Robert	44y	C	Va.	25 JUL 1875	Harmony
010726	THOMPSON, Roberta	2y	C	D.C.	21 FEB 1877	Young Mens
014876	THOMPSON, Rosena	5y	C	Va.	25 FEB 1878	Langley, Va.
003792	THOMPSON, Sarah	10m	C	D.C.	23 JUN 1875	Potters Field
014501	THOMPSON, Susan	2y	C	D.C.	20 JAN 1878	Mt. Olivet
003024	THOMPSON, Susette	7m	W	D.C.	17 APR 1875	Congressional
018760	THOMPSON, Theadore	18y	M	Va.	21 JAN 1879	Young Mens
004022	THOMPSON, Thomas	38y	W	W.I.	06 JUL 1875	Washington Asylum
014998	THOMPSON, Thomas	28y	C	Va.	08 MAR 1878	Harmony
012106	THOMPSON, Virginia	8m	W	D.C.	28 JUN 1877	Westmoreland Co., Va.
002478	THOMPSON, William	3y	W	D.C.	08 MAR 1875	Presbyterian
016966	THOMPSON, William	89y	W	Eng.	08 AUG 1878	Congressional
008727	THOMPSON, William Fairfax	19y	W	Md.	18 AUG 1876	Rock Creek
002626f	THOMPSON, William[1]	40y	--	Eng.	-- --- 1851	Oak Hill
017180	THOMPSON, Willie	7m	C	D.C.	24 AUG 1878	Potters Field
020461	THOMPSON, Wm.	41y	C	D.C.	15 JUN 1879	Mt. Olivet
019453	THOMSON, Edward Francis, Jr.	2y	W	D.C.	18 MAR 1879	Mt. Olivet
011858	THONE, Amy	1y	C	D.C.	10 JUN 1877	Harmony
000969	THONE, John F.	17d	C	D.C.	29 OCT 1874	Beckett's
017559	THORN, John F.	25y	W	Md.	28 SEP 1878	Oak Hill
002651	THORN, Thomas	37y	W	D.C.	20 MAR 1875	Glenwood

[1] Removed to Oak Hill from Holmead's.

District of Columbia Death Records, August 1, 1874 to July 31, 1879

No.	Name	Age	Race	Birth	Death Date	Burial Place
003588	THORNETT, Elizabeth	85y	W	Eng.	10 JUN 1875	Congressional
003081	THORNLEY, Victora	10m	C	D.C.	21 APR 1875	Baptist, Georgetown
006356	THORNTON, Ann Thomas	1m	C	D.C.	14 FEB 1876	Mt. Pleasant
016441	THORNTON, Annie	1y	C	D.C.	04 JUL 1878	Beckett's
018508	THORNTON, Anrena	5m	C	D.C.	29 DEC 1878	Mt. Pleasant
008116	THORNTON, Betty	10y	C	Va.	09 JUL 1876	Ebenezer
019811	THORNTON, Edmond	62y	C	Va.	17 APR 1879	Harmony
002971	THORNTON, Elizabeth	2y	C	D.C.	12 APR 1875	Young Mens
016747	THORNTON, Ella	4y	C	D.C.	24 JUL 1878	Harmony
003077	THORNTON, Evelina	5m	C	D.C.	21 APR 1875	Young Mens
010461	THORNTON, Ida	11d	C	D.C.	31 JAN 1877	Ebenezer
018720	THORNTON, Infant of Aaron	5d	C	D.C.	18 JAN 1879	Young Mens
014254	THORNTON, Infant of John	17h	C	D.C.	29 DEC 1877	Beckett's
003694	THORNTON, James	32y	C	Va.	18 JUN 1875	Beckett's
005003	THORNTON, James	2y	C	D.C.	11 SEP 1875	Ebenezer
019134	THORNTON, John	73y	W	Ire.	20 FEB 1879	Holy Rood
002811	THORNTON, John M.	61y	W	Pa.	31 MAR 1875	Congressional
020441	THORNTON, Julia	1d	C	D.C.	14 JUN 1879	Mt. Pleasant Plain
016164	THORNTON, Mahala	70y	C	Va.	14 JUN 1878	Potters Field
000102	THORNTON, Malvina	100y	C	Va.	08 AUG 1874	Mt. Pleasant
011553	THORNTON, Manemia	70y	C	Va.	09 MAY 1877	Young Mens
020365	THORNTON, Martha	18y	C	Va.	09 JUN 1879	Harmony
010373	THORNTON, Mary	18y	C	Va.	22 JAN 1877	Young Mens
018789	THORNTON, Mildred	47y	C	Va.	23 JAN 1879	Graceland
002009	THORNTON, Nancy	70y	C	Va.	03 FEB 1875	Young Mens
006743	THORNTON, Nellie A.	7y	C	D.C.	19 MAR 1876	Ebenezer
000655	THORNTON, Philip	70y	C	Va.	28 SEP 1874	Baptist
005665	THORNTON, Sarah	50y	C	Va.	05 DEC 1875	Ebenezer
011831	THORNTON, Sarah	c.72y	C	Va.	07 JUN 1877	Beckett's
018088	THORNTON, Sarah Ann	c.30y	C	Md.	18 NOV 1878	Harmony
004145	THORNTON, William	1y	C	D.C.	15 JUL 1875	Macedonia
002668	THORNTON, William	85y	C	Va.	21 MAR 1875	Ebenezer
012516	THORNTON, William	1y	C	D.C.	25 JUL 1877	Harmony
009702	THORPE, Sarah E.	51y	W	Eng.	15 NOV 1876	Congressional
011947	THRIFT, Robert G.	40y	W	Md.	17 JUN 1877	Germantown, Md.
016235	THROCKMORTON, Richd. B.	48y	C	W.Va.	20 JUN 1878	Harmony
017558	THROOP, John	10y	W	D.C.	28 SEP 1878	Congressional
006512	THROOP, Sella May	7m	W	D.C.	29 FEB 1876	Congressional
010162	THURMAN, Amalia	1m	W	D.C.	03 JAN 1877	Congressional
000900	THURMAN, John	71y	W	N.Y	22 OCT 1874	N.Y.
004686	THURMAN, John	33y	W	Md.	20 AUG 1875	Mt. Olivet
004940	THURSTON, Frank A.	9d	W	D.C.	06 SEP 1875	Glenwood
015774	THYSON, Mary Margarette	14m	W	D.C.	19 MAY 1878	Mt. Olivet
003944	THYSON, William Lawrence	7m	M	D.C.	30 JUN 1875	Mt. Olivet
002573	TIBBETS, Ivanna Fog	21y	W	N.Y.	15 MAR 1875	Great Falls, N.H.
006568	TIBBS, Infant of Nimrod	6d	C	D.C.	06 MAR 1876	Potters Field
012761	TIBBS, Lucius	5m	C	D.C.	10 AUG 1877	Potters Field
001593	TIBBS, Lydia Ann	18y	M	--	02 JAN 1875	Potters Field
000457	TIBBS, Mary Ida	1y	C	D.C.	08 SEP 1874	Mt. Olivet
007069	TIBBS, Thomas	26y	C	Md.	21 APR 1876	Potters Field
001755	TICHENOR, Geo. W., Sr.	55y	W	N.J.	16 JAN 1875	Congressional
009671	TIDBALL, John	52y	C	Va.	11 NOV 1876	Mt. Pleasant
011856	TIDINGS, Joseph Clinton	7m	C	D.C.	10 JUN 1877	Ebenezer
012597	TIERNEY, Jas. B.	29y	W	N.H.	29 JUL 1877	Mt. Olivet
015714	TIERNEY, Margaret	49y	W	Ire.	13 MAY 1878	Mt. Olivet
007219	TIERNEY, Thomas	57y	W	Ire.	05 MAY 1876	Mt. Olivet

District of Columbia Death Records, August 1, 1874 to July 31, 1879

No.	Name	Age	Race	Birth	Death Date	Burial Place
012762	TIGHLMAN, Joseph	21y	C	Md.	10 AUG 1877	Potters Field
012382	TIGHLMAN, Mabel A.	2m	C	D.C.	16 JUL 1877	Mt. Zion
016409	TIGNOR, John Lewis	11m	C	D.C.	02 JUL 1878	Harmony
011528	TILGHMAN, Carrie	1y	C	D.C.	06 MAY 1877	Moore's
006427	TILGHMAN, Elizabeth	1y	C	D.C.	20 FEB 1876	Ebenezer
018387	TILGHMAN, Elizabeth	64y	C	Va.	19 DEC 1878	Young Mens
020414	TILGHMAN, Elizabeth	10m	C	D.C.	12 JUN 1879	Young Mens
004037	TILGHMAN, George	20y	C	Md.	07 JUL 1875	Harmony
004187	TILGHMAN, Infant of John H.	2d	C	D.C.	18 JUL 1875	Young Mens
013773	TILGHMAN, Infant of J.H.	7d	C	D.C.	08 NOV 1877	Young Mens
017147	TILGHMAN, Priscilla	9d	C	D.C.	22 AUG 1878	Young Mens
007527	TILGHMAN, Richard Allen	5m	C	D.C.	06 JUN 1876	Mt. Zion
002253	TILL, Benjamin	20y	C	S.C.	20 FEB 1875	Washington Asylum
010976	TILLEY, George Arrable	23y	W	R.I.	14 MAR 1877	Congressional
020462	TILLIEUX, Mary	6m	W	D.C.	15 JUN 1879	Congressional
005590	TILLMAN, Amelia	3m	C	D.C.	28 NOV 1875	Ebenezer
007503	TILLMAN, Juda	c.75y	C	Va.	04 JUN 1876	Beckett's
001462	TILLMAN, Nathaniel	42y	C	Md.	23 DEC 1874	Harmony
015062	TILLOTSON, John	40y	W	Md.	13 MAR 1878	Potters Field
010376	TILLS, John Wesley	4m	C	D.C.	22 JAN 1877	Harmony
014192	TILLS, Mary E.	c.20y	C	Md.	24 DEC 1877	Harmony
010208	TILTON, Charles	45y	C	Va.	07 JAN 1877	Potters Field
018133	TILTON, James	59y	W	Del.	23 NOV 1878	Oak Hill
019123	TILTON, Wrennetta E.	29y	W	Ark.	19 FEB 1879	Congressional
000961	TIMMINS, Charles	46y	W	Ire.	28 OCT 1874	Mt. Olivet
019172	TIMS, Codelia	25y	C	Va.	23 FEB 1879	Baptist
003066f	TINKER, Stanton	1y	W	Ver.	08 JAN 1875	Oak Hill
012683	TINNEY, Charles	9m	C	D.C.	05 AUG 1877	Ebenezer
016005	TINNEY, Dennis	1y	C	D.C.	04 JUN 1878	Mt. Pleasant
006741	TINNEY, Harriet Labertha	3m	M	D.C.	19 MAR 1876	Mt. Pleasant
019822	TINNEY, Joseph H.	22y	C	D.C.	18 APR 1879	Harmony
016806	TINNEY, Simeal	26y	C	D.C.	28 JUL 1878	Payne's
012290	TINNEY, Susan A.	56y	C	D.C.	10 JUL 1877	Mt. Pleasant
005001	TINSEL, Geo. W.	32y	W	Md.	11 SEP 1875	Glenwood
009271	TIPPETT, Mary E.	24y	W	D.C.	02 OCT 1876	Glenwood
011351	TIPPETT, Susan Rebecca	40y	W	D.C.	16 APR 1877	Congressional
012750	TIPPETTS, Mary Ann	70y	W	Md.	09 AUG 1877	Potters Field
013174	TISSLNER, Rose Ann	65y	W	Md.	12 SEP 1877	Prospect Hill
012330	TITLOW, Alice M.	20d	W	D.C.	12 JUL 1877	Congressional
009086	TITTLER, Henry H.	38y	W	Ohio	15 SEP 1876	Hospital, Government
020560	TOBIAS, Mr.	c.60y	C	U.S.	21 JUN 1879	Potters Field
004099	TOBIN, Cathrine	45y	W	Ire.	12 JUL 1875	Mt. Olivet
010304	TOBIN, Emma Jane	3y	W	D.C.	15 JAN 1877	Mt. Olivet
011230	TOBIN, George	55y	W	Ire.	05 APR 1877	Mt. Olivet
013370	TOBIN, James	46y	W	Ire.	01 OCT 1877	Holy Rood
006621	TOBIN, John	81y	W	Ire.	09 MAR 1876	Mt. Olivet
012540	TOBIN, Margaret A.	2m	W	D.C.	26 JUL 1877	Holy Rood
002671	TOBIN, Sallie, Mrs.	63y	W	Ire.	21 MAR 1875	Mt. Olivet
009654	TOBIN, Thomas Walter	6y	W	D.C.	09 NOV 1876	Mt. Olivet
004922	TOBIN, William	69y	W	Ire.	05 SEP 1875	Mt. Olivet
005625	TOBY, Frederick A.	55y	W	Ger.	01 DEC 1875	Baltimore
008112	TODD, Bernard	42y	W	Aus.	09 JUL 1876	Congressional
006947	TODD, Helen Bruce	44y	W	Scot.	06 APR 1876	Congressional
018121	TODD, Mary	87y	W	Mass.	22 NOV 1878	Oak Hill
009095	TODD, William Bruce	46y	W	Scot.	16 SEP 1876	Congressional
015050	TOLAND, Female	10y	W	D.C.	12 MAR 1878	Mt. Olivet

No.	Name	Age	Race	Birth	Death Date	Burial Place
015063	TOLAND, Margaret	1y	W	D.C.	13 MAR 1878	Mt. Olivet
019133	TOLAVER, Mamie Elizh.	1y	C	D.C.	20 FEB 1879	Payne's
005071	TOLBERT, Celia	100y	M	Md.	16 SEP 1875	Mt. Olivet
015261	TOLBERT, Sarah	27y	C	D.C.	01 APR 1878	Potters Field
020524	TOLIVER, Edward	4m	C	D.C.	19 JUN 1879	Young Mens
007285	TOLIVER, Eliza	10m	C	D.C.	12 MAY 1876	Holy Rood
006211	TOLIVER, Ella	2y	C	D.C.	01 FEB 1876	Potters Field
011977	TOLIVER, Frank	1y	C	D.C.	20 JUN 1877	Ebenezer
011102	TOLIVER, Geo. S.	17y	C	Va.	24 MAR 1877	Graceland
020125	TOLIVER, Infant of Sarah	15h	C	D.C.	16 MAY 1879	Potters Field
017390	TOLIVER, Infant of William	5d	C	D.C.	12 SEP 1878	Harmony
000994	TOLIVER, Infant of William	6d	C	D.C.	31 OCT 1874	Harmony
002140	TOLIVER, James H.	6m	C	D.C.	12 FEB 1875	Young Mens
016723	TOLIVER, May	18m	C	D.C.	22 JUL 1878	Young Mens
013143	TOLIVER, Patsy	c.50y	C	Va.	09 SEP 1877	Harmony
018210	TOLIVER, Sallie	4y	C	D.C.	30 NOV 1878	Young Mens
008021	TOLIVER, Susan	55y	C	Va.	04 JUL 1876	Young Mens
020398	TOLLIS, Edward	100y	C	D.C.	11 JUN 1879	Mt. Zion
019155	TOLLIVAR, Ruben	35y	C	Va.	22 FEB 1879	Graceland
016138	TOLLIVER, Edward	8m	C	D.C.	12 JUN 1878	Young Mens
009478	TOLLIVER, Edwin	1m	C	D.C.	21 OCT 1876	Harmony
000689	TOLLIVER, Emily	39y	C	Va.	01 OCT 1874	Young Mens
012810	TOLLIVER, Major	45y	C	Md.	14 AUG 1877	Potters Field
007026	TOLLIVER, Mariah	11y	C	Va.	16 APR 1876	Young Mens
007392	TOLLIVER, Milly	18y	C	Va.	23 MAY 1876	Young Mens
009362	TOLLIVER, Robert	1y	C	D.C.	10 OCT 1876	Potters Field
009405	TOLLIVER, Sallie	39y	C	Va.	14 OCT 1876	Young Mens
010764	TOLLIVER, Zachariah	75y	C	Va.	24 FEB 1877	Potters Field
007401	TOLOVER, Mary Lizzie	9m	C	D.C.	24 MAY 1876	Ebenezer
002860	TOLSON, Cathrine	16y	C	D.C.	03 APR 1875	Young Mens
011006	TOLSON, Eugene	22y	W	D.C.	16 MAR 1877	Congressional
005019	TOLSON, Francis Albert	1m	C	D.C.	12 SEP 1875	Ebenezer
013371	TOLSON, Infant of Millie	12h	C	D.C.	01 OCT 1877	Potters Field
012030	TOLSON, Jesse	55y	C	Md.	23 JUN 1877	Potters Field
002190	TOLSON, John F.	21d	W	D.C.	16 FEB 1875	Congressional
006965	TOLSON, Josie	3y	C	D.C.	07 APR 1876	Mt. Olivet
016794	TOLSON, Mary Edith	9m	W	D.C.	27 JUL 1878	Congressional
006437	TOLSON, Melinda	85y	C	Va.	21 FEB 1876	Ebenezer
002617	TOLSON, Rachel M.A.	43y	W	D.C.	17 MAR 1875	Congressional
003016	TOLSON, Randall	45y	C	Va.	17 APR 1875	Washington Asylum
016406	TOLSON, Rebecca	17d	C	D.C.	02 JUL 1878	Harmony
011937	TOLSON, Thomas	38y	C	Md.	17 JUN 1877	Ebenezer
018520	TOMLINSON, Richard	38y	W	N.Y.	30 DEC 1878	Graceland
004323	TOMPKINS, Mary	19y	W	Md.	26 JUL 1875	Port Tobacco, Md.
002709	TOMPKINS, Richard P.	14m	W	D.C.	23 MAR 1875	Glenwood
020442	TOMPKINS, Robert B.	44y	W	N.Y.	14 JUN 1879	Congressional
005498	TOMPKINS, Walton	10m	C	D.C.	18 NOV 1875	Young Mens
009743	TONER, Isaac	3m	C	D.C.	19 NOV 1876	Ebenezer
012341	TONER, Virginia	24y	M	Va.	13 JUL 1877	Harmony
005923	TONNET, Alexander P.	36y	W	N.Y.	02 JAN 1876	Mt. Olivet
012158	TONNEY, Mary M.	5m	C	D.C.	01 JUL 1877	Mt. Olivet
006701	TONSEL, Edward	2½m	C	D.C.	16 MAR 1876	Potters Field
016574	TOOLAN, Ellen	28y	W	Ire.	12 JUL 1878	Mt. Olivet
014717	TOOLAN, Ellen, Mrs.	55y	W	Ire.	08 FEB 1878	Mt. Olivet
003027	TOOLEY, Peter	63y	W	Ire.	17 APR 1875	Hospital
010224	TOOMBS, Wm. Edward	10m	W	D.C.	08 JAN 1877	Congressional

District of Columbia Death Records, August 1, 1874 to July 31, 1879   343

No.	Name	Age	Race	Birth	Death Date	Burial Place
007377	TOOMEY, Bridget	45y	W	Ire.	22 MAY 1876	Mt. Olivet
016442	TOOMEY, Francis Raymond	9m	W	D.C.	04 JUL 1878	Mt. Olivet
019312	TOOMEY, Maria Bernedet	15m	W	D.C.	07 MAR 1879	Mt. Olivet
003813	TOOMEY, Mary Pauline	5m	W	D.C.	24 JUN 1875	Mt. Olivet
002563	TOOMEY, Wm.	9m	W	Va.	14 MAR 1875	Mt. Olivet
016165	TOPHAM, Richard	15d	W	D.C.	14 JUN 1878	Graceland
018799	TOPPIN, John	30y	C	D.C.	24 JAN 1879	Harmony
011810	TOPPIN, Mary Elizabeth	25y	C	D.C.	05 JUN 1877	Harmony
006742	TOPPING, Samuel Ecelston	21y	W	D.C.	19 MAR 1876	Mt. Olivet
002061	TORBERT, James M.	3y	W	D.C.	07 FEB 1875	Congressional
019667	TORBERT, Peyton	4y	W	D.C.	05 APR 1879	Congressional
018711	TORREY, Erasmus	70y	W	N.H.	17 JAN 1879	Congressional
002561f	TOTTEN, Julia R.	--	--	U.S.	10 MAR 1875	Congressional
016853	TOUMEY, James E.	11y	C	Va.	31 JUL 1878	Payne's
019201	TOUNLY, Harrison	55y	C	Va.	25 FEB 1879	Mt. Pleasant
000451	TOWEL, Sally	7m	C	D.C.	08 SEP 1874	Mt. Pleasant
011786	TOWERS, Cornelia Francis	56y	W	Va.	03 JUN 1877	Congressional
002307	TOWERS, Mary E vlyn	2y	W	D.C.	24 FE B 1875	Glenwood
014174	TOWERS, Mary Mitchell Moore	65y	W	Md.	22 DEC 1877	Glenwood
012426	TOWLES, Caroline	63y	C	Va.	19 JUL 1877	Arlington
000233	TOWLES, Charles	1y	C	D.C.	18 AUG 1874	Beckett's
000742	TOWLES, James Brook, Jr.	33y	W	D.C.	07 OCT 1874	Glenwood
007853	TOWLES, Lucius Leland	6m	W	D.C.	25 JUN 1876	Glenwood
012246	TOWLES, Margaret Ann	7m	C	D.C.	06 JUL 1877	Young Mens
011646	TOWNLEY, Charlotte	24y	W	D.C.	19 MAY 1877	Congressional
003018	TOWNLEY, Eliza Jane	1y	W	D.C.	17 APR 1875	Holy Rood
018563	TOWNLEY, Eugene A.	53y	W	D.C.	04 JAN 1879	Congressional
012403	TOY, Louisa	10y	M	D.C.	17 JUL 1877	Harmony
001771	TOYER, Elizabeth	75	M	Md.	17 JAN 1875	Washington Asylum
014209	TOYER, James	6m	C	D.C.	25 DEC 1877	Potters Field
011960	TOYER, Willie	3y	C	D.C.	18 JUN 1877	Potters Field
021004	TRACEY, Arunah	34y	W	Me.	18 JUL 1879	Glenwood
008242	TRACY, Ann, Mrs.	64y	W	Va.	13 JUL 1876	Oak Hill
010257	TRACY, John Brederick	30y	W	N.J.	11 JAN 1877	Newark, N.J.
013041	TRAMBLE, Frank	27y	W	Va.	31 AUG 1877	Congressional
002820	TRAMBLE, Hester Ella	1y	C	D.C.	31 MAR 1875	Mt. Pleasant
015730	TRAMMELL, Eliza	4y	C	D.C.	14 MAY 1878	Mt. Zion
010777	TRAPP, Caspar	35y	W	Ger.	25 FEB 1877	St. Mary's
014472	TRASK, William E.	65y	W	Ver.	18 JAN 1878	Windsor, Ver.
008081	TRAUB, Sophia	18y	W	Ger.	08 JUL 1876	Prospect Hill
019572	TRAVER, Kate	30y	W	D.C.	27 MAR 1879	Oak Hill
007148	TRAVERS, Doctor	40y	C	Va.	28 APR 1876	Mt. Pleasant
014752	TRAVERS, Ernest R.	1m	W	D.C.	12 FEB 1878	Graceland
007037	TRAVERS, Malvina	66y	C	Va.	17 APR 1876	Alexandria, Va.
005126	TRAVERS, Mary Ann	1y	C	D.C.	21 SEP 1875	Young Mens
019012	TRAVES, May	7y	W	D.C.	09 FEB 1879	Glenwood
000193	TREADWAY, Anjanett	57y	W	Mass.	15 AUG 1874	Glenwood
011168	TRECO, Myra	31y	W	Va.	30 MAR 1877	Wirts?, Va.
008800	TREMBLY, Trasy Leroy	2y	W	D.C.	23 AUG 1876	Congressional
005061	TRENT, Fredric	1y	M	D.C.	15 SEP 1875	Graceland
014606	TRENT, Richard Felix	2y	W	Mich.	30 JAN 1878	Oak Hill
010084	TRETLER, John	68y	W	DC.	26 DEC 1876	Glenwood
004267f	TREVOR, Annie	20y	W	D.C.	23 JUL 1875	Glenwood
009801	TREW, George W.	39y	W	Va.	25 NOV 1876	Westmoreland Co., Va.
008365	TREXELL, Marian B.	4y	W	D.C.	21 JUL 1876	Presbyterian
001279	TRIBBY, Charles	46y	W	Va.	01 DEC 1874	Congressional

No.	Name	Age	Race	Birth	Death Date	Burial Place
004266	TRICE, Catherine Teresa	2y	M	D.C.	23 JUL 1875	Holy Rood
020367	TRICE, Henrietta Gertrude	2y	C	D.C.	09 JUN 1879	Young Mens
005136a	TRICE, Laurence	4d	C	D.C.	13 OCT 1875	Ebenezer
016614	TRICE, Tibatha	9m	M	D.C.	15 JUL 1878	Holy Rood
016881	TRICKSON, William Belfield	3y	C	D.C.	02 AUG 1878	Harmony
002807f	TRIMBLE, Moffatt Ogilby	3y	W	Ky.	08 OCT 1861	Oak Hill
008041	TRIMBLY, Norman R.	1m	W	D.C.	05 JUL 1876	Congressional
012958	TRIMMON, Jno. Joseph	13m	C	D.C.	25 AUG 1877	Mt. Olivet
000455	TRINE, Mary	11m	W	D.C.	08 SEP 1874	Mt. Olivet
003380	TRIPLET, Frances	54y	C	Va.	20 MAY 1875	Graceland
000818	TRIPLET, Obadiah	35y	C	Va.	16 OCT 1874	Beckett's
014667	TRIPLET, Rebecca	22m	C	D.C.	04 FEB 1878	Beckett's
009397	TRIPLETT, Infant of John	13h	C	D.C.	12 OCT 1876	Beckett's
003325	TRIPLETT, Kate	3y	C	D.C.	14 MAY 1875	Mt. Olivet
010768	TRIPLETT, Mary Oscieola	22y	W	Va.	24 FEB 1877	Triplett's nr. Alexandria[1]
000480	TRIPLETT, Stephen	1m	C	D.C.	11 SEP 1874	Mt. Olivet
014732	TRIPLETT, Thomas Jefferson	78y	W	Md.	09 FEB 1878	Glenwood
009630	TRISTAN, James	56y	W	Ire.	06 NOV 1876	Mt. Olivet
017019	TRODDEN, John	c.32y	W	N.Y.	11 AUG 1878	Mt. Olivet
020951	TROOK, Susan C., Mrs.	80y	W	Va.	15 JUL 1879	Congressional
010259	TROTTMAN, Samuel	33y	C	N.C.	12 JAN 1877	Ebenezer
007831	TROUFELD, Mary	2m	W	D.C.	24 JUN 1876	Ebenezer
009617	TROXELL, Wyvil	27y	W	Md.	04 NOV 1876	Oak Hill
019124	TRUE, Milton W.	6m	W	D.C.	19 FEB 1879	Wirt's Wharf, Va.
019427	TRUEWORTHY, Viola	3m	W	D.C.	16 MAR 1879	Oak Hill
018614	TRUNDLE, Martha C.	32y	W	Md.	08 JAN 1879	Holy Rood
019949	TRUNNEL, Lucey V.	9y	W	D.C.	30 APR 1879	Glenwood
000408	TRUNNEL, Mary Elanor	72y	W	Ire.	02 SEP 1874	Glenwood
002604	TRUNNEL, William H.	40y	W	Md.	16 MAR 1875	Presbyterian
014788	TRUNNELL, Charles A.	23y	W	D.C.	16 FEB 1878	Holy Rood
004767	TRUSTY, Annie	1y	C	D.C.	26 AUG 1875	Mt. Zion
012903	TRUWORTHY, Irene Iola	2y	W	D.C.	21 AUG 1877	Congressional
002669	TRZECIAK, John	48y	W	Prus.	21 MAR 1875	Prospect Hill
005038	TUBMAN, Charles H.	30y	C	Md.	13 SEP 1875	Potters Field
017959	TUBMAN, Girtrude	8m	C	D.C.	05 NOV 1878	Mt. Pleasant
018111	TUBMAN, Mary	6y	C	Md.	21 NOV 1878	Potters Field
002202	TUBMAN, Meverill Hewitt	5m	W	D.C.	17 FEB 1875	Glenwood
005655	TUCKER, Catharine	21y	C	Va.	04 DEC 1875	Harmony
010866	TUCKER, Celinda Ann	51y	W	Mass.	04 MAR 1877	Congressional
006792	TUCKER, Charles C.	46y	W	N.Y.	23 MAR 1876	Oak Hill
009981	TUCKER, Edith	2y	W	D.C.	16 DEC 1876	Glenwood
003297	TUCKER, Emma	53y	W	D.C.	12 MAY 1875	Congressional
013550	TUCKER, Fenton S.	39y	W	Va.	17 OCT 1877	Congressional
009592	TUCKER, George W.	32y	W	D.C.	01 NOV 1876	Congressional
018710	TUCKER, Infant of William	14h	C	D.C.	17 JAN 1879	Mt. Pleasant
018170	TUCKER, Jennet	c.80y	W	D.C.	26 NOV 1878	Congressional
009285	TUCKER, Josephine	7d	W	D.C.	03 OCT 1876	Glenwood
001741	TUCKER, L.	6m	C	D.C.	15 JAN 1875	Harmony
005129a	TUCKER, Lillie E.	1y	W	D.C.	21 SEP 1875	Congressional
000788	TUCKER, Mary	24y	C	Md.	12 OCT 1874	Potters Field
011921	TUCKER, Permelia	10m	C	D.C.	15 JUN 1877	Ebenezer
016118	TUCKER, Richard Powell	9y	W	D.C.	11 JUN 1878	Mt. Olivet
008667	TUCKER, Thomas	63y	C	Va.	13 AUG 1876	Mt. Zion

[1] Place of burial in given as Mrs. Jane Triplett, 5 miles from Alexandria.

District of Columbia Death Records, August 1, 1874 to July 31, 1879

No.	Name	Age	Race	Birth	Death Date	Burial Place
004302	TUCKER, William	5m	W	D.C.	25 JUL 1875	Glenwood
018009	TUCKER, William	65y	W	Md.	10 NOV 1878	Congressional
001052	TUCKER, William D.	22y	W	D.C.	05 NOV 1874	Congressional
004803	TUCKSON, Joseph Luciene	2y	C	D.C.	28 AUG 1875	Harmony
000850	TUCKSON, Martha	35y	C	Va.	18 OCT 1874	Harmony
012437	TUCKSON, Nelly R.	7m	C	D.C.	20 JUL 1877	Harmony
003130	TUCKSON, Stewart	75y	C	Va.	26 APR 1875	Harmony
013983	TUEL, John E.	50y	W	D.C.	01 DEC 1877	N.Y.
000780	TULL, Eliza A.	72y	W	Md.	11 OCT 1874	Mt. Olivet
019383	TULLE, Christian	39y	W	Ger.	13 MAR 1879	Hospital, Government
007571	TULLEY, James	4m	W	D.C.	09 JUN 1876	Holy Rood
014943	TULLY, Mary	37y	W	Ire.	04 MAR 1878	Mt. Olivet
012071	TULLY, Mary E.	9m	W	D.C.	26 JUN 1877	Holy Rood
004176	TUNE, Lula Maude	11m	W	D.C.	17 JUL 1875	Congressional
019823	TUNE, S.T.	55y	W	Va.	18 APR 1879	Congressional
018864	TUNSTALL, James Henry	5d	C	D.C.	28 JAN 1879	Potters Field
012696	TUNSTEN, Henrietta	3y	C	D.C.	06 AUG 1877	Young Mens
012409	TUNSTOL, Nannie	4m	M	D.C.	17 JUL 1877	Potters Field
004970	TUPPER, Francis M.	10m	W	D.C.	09 SEP 1875	Congressional
017552	TUPPER, Harriet	39y	W	Md.	27 SEP 1878	Congressional
013713	TUPPER, Mady liola	1m	W	D.C.	02 NOV 1877	Congressional
013442	TURBEY, Nancy Ann	50y	W	Va.	08 OCT 1877	Presbyterian
016880	TURKENTON, Catharine	1m	W	D.C.	02 AUG 1878	Holy Rood
010815	TURKENTON, Edelbert J.	2d	W	D.C.	01 MAR 1877	Holy Rood
010479	TURNBULL, Mary Nisbet	45y	W	D.C.	02 FEB 1877	Oak Hill
004742	TURNBURKE, Caroline	9m	W	D.C.	24 AUG 1875	Mt. Olivet
014789	TURNBURKE, George	56y	W	Port.	16 FEB 1878	Glenwood
018761	TURNER, Aaron	c.70y	C	Va.	21 JAN 1879	Young Mens
011848	TURNER, Alberta Jennings	6m	C	D.C.	09 JUN 1877	Harmony
010048	TURNER, Alice	11m	W	D.C.	22 DEC 1876	Congressional
020915	TURNER, Alta	6m	W	D.C.	13 JUL 1879	Congressional
004395	TURNER, Ann	65y	C	Md.	31 JUL 1875	Harmony
010591	TURNER, Anne	22y	W	Md.	11 FEB 1877	Carroll Chapel, Md.
016866	TURNER, Beatrice	5m	C	D.C.	01 AUG 1878	Methodist, E.
017609	TURNER, Bertha	1y	C	D.C.	02 OCT 1878	Payne's
019511	TURNER, Bettie	c.26y	C	--	22 MAR 1879	Potters Field
006662	TURNER, Celia	65y	M		13 MAR 1876	Mt. Olivet
005226a	TURNER, Charlotte	3y	C	D.C.	20 OCT 1875	Potters Field
019957	TURNER, Daniel	8y	C	D.C.	01 MAY 1879	Beckett's
009665	TURNER, Eliza	5d	C	D.C.	10 NOV 1876	Ebenezer
010158	TURNER, Eliza	c.18y	C	Md.	03 JAN 1877	Scagg's
017920	TURNER, Elizabeth B.	19y	W	Va.	01 NOV 1878	Garrisonville, Va.
020400	TURNER, Esther	85y	C	Md.	11 JUN 1879	Potters Field
016210	TURNER, Eugene	7m	C	D.C.	17 JUN 1878	Mt. Pleasant
005225a	TURNER, Geo. Henry	32y	C	Md.	20 OCT 1875	Mt. Pleasant Plain
002229	TURNER, George H.	14d	W	D.C.	19 FEB 1875	Congressional
008475	TURNER, Gertrude	11m	C	D.C.	29 JUL 1876	Young Mens
018446	TURNER, Harry	2y	C	D.C.	23 DEC 1878	Beckett's
004758	TURNER, Henry	8m	C	D.C.	25 AUG 1875	Mt. Olivet
018636	TURNER, Infant of Charles	½d	C	D.C.	10 JAN 1879	Potters Field
013966	TURNER, Infant of Rebecca	3d	C	D.C.	29 NOV 1877	Potters Field
009724	TURNER, Infant of Thomas	½h	C	D.C.	18 NOV 1876	Potters Field
008434	TURNER, Isaiah	1y	C	D.C.	26 JUL 1876	Mt. Zion
019258	TURNER, Jacob	6m	C	D.C.	02 MAR 1879	Beckett's
006563	TURNER, James Henry	8m	C	D.C.	05 MAR 1876	Young Mens
005045	TURNER, James L.	3y	W	D.C.	14 SEP 1875	Congressional

No.	Name	Age	Race	Birth	Death Date	Burial Place
021043	TURNER, Jenette	1m	W	D.C.	21 JUL 1879	Mt. Olivet
017366	TURNER, Jennetta	11m	C	D.C.	10 SEP 1878	Mt. Pleasant
009787a	TURNER, Jerry	35y	C	Md.	24 NOV 1876	Potters Field
011673	TURNER, John	9m	C	D.C.	22 MAY 1877	Harmony
006818	TURNER, Julia	80y	C	Va.	25 MAR 1876	Beckett's
019240	TURNER, Junius Thomas	11m	W	D.C.	28 FEB 1879	Congressional
020587	TURNER, Leona	9m	W	D.C.	23 JUN 1879	Graceland
016461	TURNER, Lily	4m	C	D.C.	05 JUL 1878	Young Mens
002778	TURNER, Louisa	30y	C	Md.	28 MAR 1875	Harmony
020142	TURNER, Lucinda	53y	M	Md.	18 MAY 1879	Young Mens
007335	TURNER, Lucy Ann	6m	C	D.C.	18 MAY 1876	Potters Field
012910	TURNER, Maggie	6m	C	D.C.	22 AUG 1877	Mt. Zion
013753	TURNER, Martha	40y	C	Md.	06 NOV 1877	Moore's
009596	TURNER, Mary	72y	C	Va.	02 NOV 1876	Beckett's
013165	TURNER, Mary Bernadine	3m	C	D.C.	11 SEP 1877	Mt. Olivet
012496	TURNER, Mary Emma	2y	W	D.C.	23 JUL 1877	Rock Creek
014831	TURNER, Mary Ida	1y	C	D.C.	20 FEB 1878	Beckett's
000941	TURNER, Mary M.	5m	M	D.C.	26 OCT 1874	Harmony
012595	TURNER, Mary V.	32y	C	Md.	29 JUL 1877	Lanham Station, Md.
009255	TURNER, Milly	22y	C	Va.	30 SEP 1876	Beckett's
000339	TURNER, Nelson	13y	C	D.C.	27 AUG 1874	Beckett's
018917	TURNER, Perry	c.65y	C	Va.	01 FEB 1879	Young Mens
007755	TURNER, Rebecca Jane	2m	C	D.C.	20 JUN 1876	Moore's
017582	TURNER, Reuben	80y	C	Md.	30 SEP 1878	Potters Field
003011	TURNER, Robert	1y	C	D.C.	16 APR 1875	Ebenezer
005070	TURNER, Robert	43y	C	Md.	16 SEP 1875	Potters Field
015797	TURNER, Robert	13m	C	D.C.	21 MAY 1878	Beckett's
015421	TURNER, Sallie	21y	C	Va.	16 APR 1875	Payne's
017211	TURNER, Sarah Ann	66y	C	Md.	26 AUG 1878	Beckett's
009584	TURNER, Thomas	2y	C	D.C.	31 OCT 1876	Young Mens
017018	TURNER, Thomas	62y	C	Va.	11 AUG 1878	Beckett's
008560	TURNER, William	45y	C	Md.	05 AUG 1876	Harmony
011015	TURNER, William	2m	W	D.C.	17 MAR 1877	Rock Creek
006346	TURNER, William E.	2y	C	D.C.	13 FEB 1876	Young Mens
004688f	TURNER, William W.	26y	C	Md.	20 AUG 1875	Lanham's Station, Md.
000035	TURTCHELL, Mary A.	38y	W	Me.	03 AUG 1874	Graceland
020561	TURTON, Ferdinand	27y	W	D.C.	21 JUN 1879	Oak Hill
001639	TURTON, William	19y	W	Md.	07 JAN 1875	Congressional
005049a	TURVEY, Francis	14m	W	D.C.	03 OCT 1875	Holy Rood
006138	TURVEY, Wm. L.	29y	W	D.C.	25 JAN 1876	Holy Rood
009316	TUTLE, Emma	23y	C	Md.	05 OCT 1876	Anne Arundel Co., Md.
000912	TUTTEL, Alexander	8d	C	D.C.	23 OCT 1874	Potters Field
004485	TUTTLE, Ann	9y	C	Md.	06 AUG 1875	Potters Field
005211	TUTTLE, Mary Agnes	3y	C	Md.	28 SEP 1875	Potters Field
005499	TWEEDY, Arian E.	43y	W	D.C.	18 NOV 1875	Oak Hill
003531	TWIMAN, Robert	4y	C	D.C.	05 JUN 1875	Young Mens
017518	TWINE, Sandy	4m	C	D.C.	24 SEP 1878	Mt. Pleasant
015916	TWINE, Thomas Andrew	27y	M	D.C.	30 MAY 1878	Harmony
012794	TWINE, William Arthur	3m	C	D.C.	13 AUG 1877	Mt. Pleasant
009167	TYALOR, A.J.	45y	C	Va.	22 SEP 1876	Young Mens
001528	TYCER, Henry	49y	W	D.C.	28 DEC 1874	Glenwood
015004	TYFORD, Emily P.	4m	W	D.C.	09 MAR 1878	Cold Spring, N.Y.
017902	TYLER, Ada	5m	C	D.C.	29 OCT 1878	Young Mens
007366	TYLER, Annie	3m	C	D.C.	21 MAY 1876	Ebenezer
017367	TYLER, Carrie	6w	M	D.C.	10 SEP 1878	Mt. Olivet
015379	TYLER, Charles	75y	C	Va.	12 APR 1878	Potters Field

District of Columbia Death Records, August 1, 1874 to July 31, 1879   347

No.	Name	Age	Race	Birth	Death Date	Burial Place
017768	TYLER, Charles Thornton	30y	W	Va.	16 OCT 1878	Congressional
005969	TYLER, Clara	c.85y	C	Md.	07 JAN 1876	Mt. Zion
003775	TYLER, Daniel	69y	W	Me.	22 JUN 1875	Glenwood
017247	TYLER, Eliza	c.35y	C	Md.	29 AUG 1878	Beckett's
001057	TYLER, Ella	6y	C	D.C.	05 NOV 1874	Young Mens
012124	TYLER, Ellenora Ann	10m	C	D.C.	29 JUN 1877	Beckett's
001250	TYLER, Fannie	110y	C	Md.	28 NOV 1874	Mt. Olivet
019637	TYLER, Harry	1y	C	D.C.	02 APR 1879	Young Mens
018591	TYLER, Henry	1y	C	D.C.	06 JAN 1879	Beckett's
016059	TYLER, Ida Bell	5y	C	D.C.	07 JUN 1878	Harmony
007805	TYLER, Infant of Luke	3d	C	D.C.	23 JUN 1876	Mt. Pleasant
002967	TYLER, James	27y	C	Md.	12 APR 1875	Washington Asylum
003929	TYLER, James	1y	C	D.C.	29 JUN 1875	Ebenezer
000610	TYLER, Joseph	28y	C	Va.	23 SEP 1874	Washington Asylum
012375	TYLER, Joseph	1y	M	D.C.	15 JUL 1877	Young Mens
009413	TYLER, Lizzie	4m	W	D.C.	15 OCT 1876	Graceland
016919	TYLER, Mary	55y	C	Va.	05 AUG 1878	Mt. Zion
017347	TYLER, Mary	10m	C	D.C.	07 SEP 1878	Beckett's
018548	TYLER, Mary	4m	C	D.C.	02 JAN 1879	Harmony
016509	TYLER, Mary L.	25y	M	D.C.	08 JUL 1878	Harmony
008197	TYLER, Mary M.	57y	W	Md.	12 JUL 1876	Oak Hill
015857	TYLER, Maud	10m	W	D.C.	26 MAY 1878	Congressional
010504	TYLER, Milly	21d	M	D.C.	03 FEB 1877	Ebenezer
020226	TYLER, Reuben	6d	C	D.C.	29 MAY 1879	Beckett's
009055	TYLER, Sam'l	14y	C	Va.	13 SEP 1876	Young Mens
008517	TYLER, Sarah	60y	C	Md.	01 AUG 1876	Mt. Zion
009092	TYLER, Sarah	c.50y	C	Va.	16 SEP 1876	Potters Field
015262	TYLER, Thomas	35y	C	Md.	01 APR 1878	Harmony
007914	TYLER, Thomas F.	57y	W	Md.	28 JUN 1876	Mt. Zion
009146	TYLER, Viana	31y	W	U.S.	20 SEP 1876	Soldier's Home
002503	TYLOR, Delia	1m	C	D.C.	10 MAR 1875	Beckett's
016352	TYNAN, Catherine	54y	W	Ire.	28 JUN 1878	Mt. Olivet
007736	TYRENE, Elizabeth	1y	C	D.C.	19 JUN 1876	Ebenezer
009936	TYRING, Cecilia	c.45y	C	Va.	12 DEC 1876	Beckett's
014109	TYSER, Samuel	68y	W	Md.	15 DEC 1877	Oak Hill
006385	TYSON, Emma	1y	C	D.C.	16 FEB 1876	Mt. Zion
011938	TYSON, Rachel L.	72y	W	Pa.	17 JUN 1877	Oak Hill

U

No.	Name	Age	Race	Birth	Death Date	Burial Place
005978	UBER, Mary	2y	W	D.C.	08 JAN 1876	Prospect Hill
012348	UBHOFF, Christian	50y	W	Ger.	13 JUL 1877	Oak Hill
009920	ULLMAN, Ella	1y	W	D.C.	10 DEC 1876	Mt. Olivet
005487	ULTZ, Harry Vanderbilt	5y	W	Ia.	17 NOV 1875	Fairfield, Ia.
017391	UMBELS, Betsy	97y	C	Va.	12 SEP 1878	Harmony
005977	UNDERDUE, Sampson	14d	C	D.C.	08 JAN 1876	Mt. Zion
010098	UNDERDUE, William	7d	C	D.C.	28 DEC 1876	Mt. Zion
009464	UNDERWOOD, Laura	1y	W	D.C.	19 OCT 1876	Middleburg, Va.
003791	Unknown	38y	C	U.S.	23 JUN 1875	Mt. Zion
005087a	Unknown	65y	W	U.S.	08 OCT 1875	Potters Field
010814	Unknown	c.60y	C	--	01 MAR 1877	Potters Field
015193	Unknown	50-60y	W	U.S.	26 MAR 1878	Potters Field
017512	Unknown Child	4y	W	D.C.	24 SEP 1878	Young Mens
004659	Unknown Infant	28d	W	D.C.	18 AUG 1875	Methodist
002639	Unknown Infant	1h	C	D.C.	-- MAR 1875	Potters Field

District of Columbia Death Records, August 1, 1874 to July 31, 1879

No.	Name	Age	Race	Birth	Death Date	Burial Place
001899f	Unknown Infant	1y	W	Pa.	01 DEC 1871	Oak Hill
000004	Unknown Infant	--	W	D.C.	01 AUG 1874	Oak Hill
000652	Unknown Infant	c.3m	W	D.C.	28 SEP 1874	Potters Field
000538	Unknown Infant	1d	M	D.C.	17 SEP 1874	Potters Field
000622	Unknown Infant	1d	C	D.C.	24 SEP 1874	Potters Field
002912	Unknown Infant	--	C	D.C.	07 APR 1875	Potters Field
003121	Unknown Infant	1m	C	D.C.	25 APR 1875	Potters Field
004723	Unknown Infant	1h	C	D.C.	22 AUG 1875	Potters Field
004571	Unknown Infant	½h	W	D.C.	12 AUG 1875	Potters Field
005645	Unknown Infant	½h	W	D.C.	03 DEC 1875	Potters Field
005856	Unknown Infant	2d	C	D.C.	24 DEC 1875	Mt. Zion
005855	Unknown Infant	4m	C	D.C.	24 DEC 1875	Mt. Pleasant
005820	Unknown Infant	c.3m	W	D.C.	21 DEC 1875	Potters Field
002005	Unknown Infant	10min	C	D.C.	03 FEB 1875	Potters Field
002351	Unknown Infant	½h	C	D.C.	28 FEB 1875	Potters Field
002299	Unknown Infant	3h	C	D.C.	24 FEB 1875	Potters Field
003988	Unknown Infant	2d	C	D.C.	03 JUL 1875	Potters Field
003552	Unknown Infant	5m	C	U.S.	07 JUN 1875	Ebenezer
003676	Unknown Infant	½h	C	D.C.	17 JUN 1875	Potters Field
002608	Unknown Infant	1h	C	D.C.	16 MAR 1875	Potters Field
002480	Unknown Infant	1h	W	D.C.	08 MAR 1875	Potters Field
002463	Unknown Infant	½h	W	D.C.	07 MAR 1875	Potters Field
003119	Unknown Infant	1m	W	D.C.	31 MAR 1875	Potters Field
003329	Unknown Infant	1m	C	D.C.	15 MAY 1875	Potters Field
005464	Unknown Infant	--	C	--	15 NOV 1875	Potters Field
005255	Unknown Infant	½d	W	D.C.	24 OCT 1875	Potters Field
005106	Unknown Infant	1d	C	D.C.	19 SEP 1875	Potters Field
007173	Unknown Infant	1m	C	D.C.	30 APR 1876	Washington Asylum
007149	Unknown Infant	1h	C	D.C.	28 APR 1876	Potters Field
007172	Unknown Infant	1h	C	D.C.	30 APR 1876	Potters Field
008748	Unknown Infant	1m	C	D.C.	20 AUG 1876	Potters Field
010022	Unknown Infant	2w	C	D.C.	20 DEC 1876	Potters Field
009843	Unknown Infant	5m	C	D.C.	02 DEC 1876	Potters Field
006302	Unknown Infant	c.1m	C	D.C.	10 FEB 1876	Potters Field
006010	Unknown Infant	16d	W	D.C.	13 JAN 1876	Potters Field
008043	Unknown Infant	½h	W	D.C.	05 JUL 1876	Potters Field
008087	Unknown Infant	1d	C	D.C.	08 JUL 1876	Potters Field
008153	Unknown Infant	1m	M	D.C.	10 JUL 1876	Potters Field
008327	Unknown Infant	14d	C	D.C.	19 JUL 1876	Potters Field
007737	Unknown Infant	2d	C	D.C.	10 JUN 1876	Potters Field
006728	Unknown Infant	1h	C	D.C.	19 MAR 1876	Potters Field
006842	Unknown Infant	c.3m	C	D.C.	27 MAR 1876	Potters Field
007208	Unknown Infant	1d	C	D.C.	04 MAY 1876	Potters Field
007181	Unknown Infant	1d	W	D.C.	01 MAY 1876	Potters Field
007257	Unknown Infant	c.3m	C	D.C.	09 MAY 1876	Potters Field
009623	Unknown Infant	½h	W	D.C.	05 NOV 1876	Potters Field
009646	Unknown Infant	1h	W	D.C.	08 NOV 1876	Potters Field
009827	Unknown Infant	1d	C	D.C.	29 NOV 1876	Potters Field
009037	Unknown Infant	--	C	D.C.	12 SEP 1876	Potters Field
009017	Unknown Infant	--	C	D.C.	10 SEP 1876	Potters Field
011342	Unknown Infant	1y	C	D.C.	15 APR 1877	Potters Field
011417	Unknown Infant	½h	C	D.C.	24 APR 1877	Potters Field
013017	Unknown Infant	1min	C	D.C.	29 AUG 1877	Potters Field
012858	Unknown Infant	1h	C	D.C.	16 AUG 1877	Potters Field
012870	Unknown Infant	1min	W	D.C.	18 AUG 1877	Potters Field
012790	Unknown Infant	4m	C	U.S.	13 AUG 1877	Potters Field

District of Columbia Death Records, August 1, 1874 to July 31, 1879   349

No.	Name	Age	Race	Birth	Death Date	Burial Place
010472	Unknown Infant	7m	C	--	01 FEB 1877	Potters Field
010774	Unknown Infant	½h	W	--	25 FEB 1877	Potters Field
010274	Unknown Infant	½h	W	D.C.	13 JAN 1877	Potters Field
010182	Unknown Infant	10min	C	D.C.	05 JAN 1877	Potters Field
010218	Unknown Infant	6w	C	D.C.	08 JAN 1877	Potters Field
010447	Unknown Infant	5d	C	D.C.	30 JAN 1877	Potters Field
012189	Unknown Infant	--	W	D.C.	03 JUL 1877	Potters Field
012569	Unknown Infant	1d	C	D.C.	27 JUL 1877	Potters Field
012459	Unknown Infant	15min	W	D.C.	21 JUL 1877	Potters Field
012045	Unknown Infant	½h	C	D.C.	25 JUN 1877	Potters Field
013869	Unknown Infant	1m	C	D.C.	20 NOV 1877	Potters Field
013301	Unknown Infant	21d	C	D.C.	25 SEP 1877	Potters Field
015287	Unknown Infant	½h	C	D.C.	04 APR 1878	Potters Field
015286	Unknown Infant	1min	C	D.C.	04 APR 1878	Potters Field
015390	Unknown Infant	1h	C	D.C.	13 APR 1878	Potters Field
015559	Unknown Infant	1d	C	D.C.	29 APR 1878	Potters Field
016868	Unknown Infant	--	W	D.C.	01 AUG 1878	Potters Field
016907	Unknown Infant	--	W	D.C.	01 AUG 1878	Potters Field
017053	Unknown Infant	--	C	D.C.	14 AUG 1878	Potters Field
018312	Unknown Infant	1h	W	D.C.	11 DEC 1878	Potters Field
014733	Unknown Infant	½h	W	D.C.	09 FEB 1878	Potters Field
014502	Unknown Infant	4h	W	D.C.	20 JAN 1878	Potters Field
014464	Unknown Infant	24h	C	D.C.	17 JAN 1878	Potters Field
016427	Unknown Infant	5m	C	D.C.	03 JUL 1878	Potters Field
015682	Unknown Infant	6m	C	--	11 MAY 1878	Payne's
015889	Unknown Infant	3m	W	D.C.	29 MAY 1878	Potters Field
015842	Unknown Infant	3m	W	D.C.	26 MAY 1878	Jones Chapel
017625	Unknown Infant	c.1d	C	D.C.	03 OCT 1878	Potters Field
017743	Unknown Infant	--	C	D.C.	14 OCT 1878	Potters Field
019691	Unknown Infant	few min	W	D.C.	07 APR 1879	Potters Field
019629	Unknown Infant	--	C	D.C.	01 APR 1879	Potters Field
018751	Unknown Infant	3d	W	D.C.	20 JAN 1879	Washington Asylum
018750	Unknown Infant	1d	C	D.C.	20 JAN 1879	Potters Field
018712	Unknown Infant	5m	C	D.C.	17 JAN 1879	Potters Field
021089	Unknown Infant	few min	W	D.C.	24 JUL 1879	Potters Field
020291	Unknown Infant	few min	C	D.C.	03 JUN 1879	Potters Field
020369	Unknown Infant	few min	C	D.C.	09 JUN 1879	Potters Field
020634	Unknown Infant	--	C	D.C.	26 JUN 1879	Potters Field
019259	Unknown Infant	½h	C	D.C.	02 MAR 1879	Potters Field
019494	Unknown Infant	3min	C	D.C.	21 MAR 1879	Potters Field
020097	Unknown Infant	few min	M	D.C.	14 MAY 1879	Potters Field
019995	Unknown Infant	--	W	D.C.	04 MAY 1879	Potters Field
020153	Unknown Infant	4m	W	D.C.	19 MAY 1879	Potters Field
019968	Unknown Infant	few min	W	D.C.	02 MAY 1879	Potters Field
008250	UPPERMAN, Charles Henry	11m	W	D.C.	13 JUL 1876	Graceland
010497	UPPERMAN, Edwin W.	1y	W	D.C.	03 FEB 1877	Glenwood
005147	UPPERMAN, Marion E.	52y	W	D.C.	23 SEP 1875	Presbyterian
006479	UPSHER, James	5y	C	D.C.	26 FEB 1876	Mt. Olivet
003839	UPSHUR, Charlot	48y	C	Va.	25 JUN 1875	Young Mens
017443	UPSHUR, Walte D.	19y	C	Va.	17 SEP 1878	Richmond, Va.
007769	UPTURE, Ella	4y	C	D.C.	21 JUN 1876	Ebenezer
007768	UPTURE, Matilda	2y	C	D.C.	21 JUN 1876	Ebenezer
006520	USHER, Ada	1y	W	D.C.	01 MAR 1876	Congressional

V

No.	Name	Age	Race	Birth	Death Date	Burial Place
013909	VAGIL, Infant of Oscar	8d	C	D.C.	24 NOV 1877	Potters Field
007378	VALENTINE, Aletta J.	65y	W	N.Y.	22 MAY 1876	N.Y. City
001556	VALENTINE, John	78y	W	Va.	01 JAN 1875	Glenwood
007806	VALIENT, Mary Perlie	15d	W	D.C.	23 JUN 1876	Baltimore, Md.
013745	VAN ARNUM, Hattie Ann	9y	W	D.C.	05 NOV 1877	Glenwood
007402	VAN BARBER, Benj.	c.25y	C	Va.	24 MAY 1876	Young Mens
021165	VAN BERGEN, Ada	1y	W	D.C.	30 JUL 1879	St. Mary's
020347	VAN BRAKLE, Mary Ann	66y	M	N.M.	08 JUN 1879	Mt. Olivet
013799	VAN BUREN, Carrie	1m	C	D.C.	11 NOV 1877	Hillsdale
002696	VAN BUREN, George H.	43y	W	N.Y.	22 MAR 1875	Glenwood
002646	VAN BUREN, James H.	8y	C	D.C.	19 MAR 1875	Moore's
020525	VAN BUREN, John	7m	C	D.C.	19 JUN 1879	Hillsdale
008989	VAN BUREN, Wm. Henry	2w	C	D.C.	06 SEP 1876	Moore's
014576	VAN BUSKIRK, John M.	44y	W	N.Y.	27 JAN 1878	Oak Hill
019219	VAN DEUSEN, Walter E.	28y	W	U.S.	26 FEB 1879	Soldier's Home
020741	VAN DEVENTER, Willie P.	8y	W	D.C.	03 JUL 1879	Glenwood
019260	VAN DOREN, John	30d	W	D.C.	02 MAR 1879	Mt. Olivet
014525	VAN DOREN, Lancing	38y	W	N.Y.	22 JAN 1878	Ottawa, Ill.
018942	VAN FLEET, Mary S.	27y	W	Va.	03 FEB 1879	Congressional
003958	VAN HORN, Infant of Edgar	15d	W	D.C.	01 JUL 1875	Mt. Olivet
020765	VAN REUTH, Floris	35y	W	Eng.	04 JUL 1879	Graceland/Rock Creek
000489	VAN RISWICK, John Thompson	65y	W	Md.	12 SEP 1874	Mt. Olivet
013226	VAN RISWICK, Leo	25y	W	D.C.	16 SEP 1877	Mt. Olivet
017728	VAN SCHRIVER, Irene	80y	W	Ky.	13 OCT 1878	Oak Hill
018752	VAN SLYKE, Martin	66y	W	N.Y.	20 JAN 1879	Mt. Olivet
014758	VAN TASSEL, Emma L.	20y	W	N.Y.	13 FEB 1878	Congressional
002044	VANANKEN, David	c.70y	W	U.S.	06 FEB 1875	Potters Field
007930	VANATTA, Daisy May	1y	W	Pa.	29 JUN 1876	Graceland
013816	VANDERBILT, William	1m	W	D.C.	13 NOV 1877	Mt. Olivet
013042	VANDERPOEL, Levingston	33y	C	N.Y.	31 AUG 1877	Harmony
015997	VANDERWERKEN, James B.	48y	W	N.Y.	03 JUN 1878	Oak Hill
015575	VANDEVEER, Helen Gutherie	31y	W	N.J.	01 MAY 1878	Jersey City, N.J.
000464	VANDT?, John H.	25h	W	D.C.	09 SEP 1874	Rock Creek
009830	VANE, George	10d	C	D.C.	30 NOV 1876	Potters Field
005424	VANSCIVER, Alice	2y	W	D.C.	10 NOV 1875	Presbyterian
018350	VANSCIVER, Jacob	35y	W	N.J.	15 DEC 1878	Soldier's Home
004384	VANSCIVER, James	6m	W	D.C.	30 JUL 1876	Presbyterian
003790	VANSCIVER, John	49y	W	D.C.	23 JUN 1875	Oak Hill
009243	VANSCIVER, Lotta	8m	W	D.C.	30 SEP 1876	--
001909	VANSCIVER, Rose Emma	22y	W	D.C.	27 JAN 1875	Tennallytown
007832	VANSCIVER, Samuel	47y	W	D.C.	24 JUN 1876	Presbyterian
004586	VANSCRIVER, Lillie May	2y	W	D.C.	13 AUG 1875	Presbyterian
008619	VANT, Richard	51y	W	Eng.	08 AUG 1876	Congressional
010937	VARNELL, Edward	10y	W	D.C.	11 MAR 1877	Holy Rood
020952	VARNELL, George E.	3m	W	D.C.	15 JUL 1879	Holy Rood
008031	VARNER, Rachael	2m	C	D.C.	05 JUL 1876	Young Mens
008333	VATTEEN, Elizabeth	43y	W	Ire.	19 JUL 1876	N.Y. City
014193	VAUGHAN, John	48y	W	Eng.	24 DEC 1877	Congressional
011385	VAUGHAN, Margaret	20d	W	D.C.	21 APR 1877	Mt. Olivet
011274	VAUGHAN, William E.	50y	W	N.C.	09 APR 1877	Congressional
009541	VAUGHN, Ary Ann	60y	C	Va.	26 OCT 1876	Freedmen's Village
019701	VAUGHN, Ida May	22y	W	D.C.	08 APR 1879	Congressional
003495	VAUGHN, Martha	16y	C	Va.	31 MAY 1875	Freedmen's Village
005021a	VAUX, Harry Lyman	1y	W	D.C.	01 OCT 1875	Oak Hill

District of Columbia Death Records, August 1, 1874 to July 31, 1879

No.	Name	Age	Race	Birth	Death Date	Burial Place
007869	VEIHMEYER, Anna	16y	W	D.C.	26 JUN 1876	Glenwood
017686	VEIHMEYER, Cora E.	4y	W	D.C.	09 OCT 1878	Glenwood
017444	VEIHMEYER, David	1y	W	D.C.	17 SEP 1878	Glenwood
005612	VEIHMEYER, Eve	78y	W	Pa.	30 NOV 1875	Glenwood
005565	VEIHMEYER, Lillie Agnes	3m	W	D.C.	25 NOV 1875	Glenwood
019125	VEIHMEYER, Martin	39y	W	Md.	19 FEB 1879	Glenwood
016025	VEIRCORN, Fredrick	6m	W	D.C.	05 JUN 1878	Prospect Hill
001257f	VENABLE, Sarah E.	39y	W	D.C.	28 NOV 1874	Methodist
018625	VENABLE, Wm. F.	1y	W	D.C.	09 JAN 1879	Mt. Olivet
019582	VENNATAR, George	10h	W	D.C.	28 MAR 1879	Congressional
007423	VERMILIAN, Oliver Eugene	5m	W	D.C.	27 MAY 1876	Congressional
017673	VERMILLION, Clarence	13d	W	D.C.	07 OCT 1878	Congressional
013426	VERMILLION, Harry	4y	W	D.C.	07 OCT 1877	Congressional
013417	VERMILLION, Mattie	6y	W	D.C.	06 OCT 1877	Congressional
007160	VERMILLION, Nicholas	71y	W	Md.	29 APR 1876	Congressional
001875	VERMILLION, Otha T.	76y	W	D.C.	24 JAN 1875	Congressional
008329	VERMILLION, Rebecca	5y	W	D.C.	19 JUL 1876	Catholic
007542	VERMILLION, Sarah	75y	W	Md.	07 JUN 1876	Frederick, Md.
015635	VERNON, James	7m	M	D.C.	06 MAY 1878	Young Mens
006357	VERRILL, Miranda	74y	W	Me.	14 FEB 1876	Congressional
002244f	VESSEL, Charles Henry	18m	--	D.C.	19 FEB 1875	Harmony
011708	VESSEY, Leonard	48y	W	Eng.	26 MAY 1877	Oak Hill
017324	VIERCORN, Mamie	8y	W	D.C.	04 SEP 1878	Prospect Hill
012041	VIGEL, Eliza, Miss	c.42y	C	D.C.	24 JUN 1877	Harmony
014959	VIGER, Charles	13y	C	D.C.	05 MAR 1878	Young Mens
010941	VIGGS, Lemuel	17y	C	Md.	11 MAR 1877	Ebenezer
017483	VIGLE, Austen	21y	C	D.C.	21 SEP 1878	Harmony
012334	VIGLE, Lucy	68y	C	Md.	12 JUL 1877	Mt. Zion
016712	VIGOL, Martha Ellen	25y	C	Va.	21 JUL 1878	Harmony
015883	VILES, Eliza Pierce	66y	W	Mass.	28 MAY 1878	Glenwood
000572	VINCENT, Infant of Lee	7d	C	D.C.	20 SEP 1874	Harmony
001402	VINEL, Thomas	8y	M	Md.	15 DEC 1874	Potters Field
003117	VINY, Mary	21y	M	Va.	25 APR 1875	Potters Field
005675	VITT, John	55y	W	Ger.	06 DEC 1875	Baltimore, Md.
015884	VODRAY, Wellington	17m	M	D.C.	28 MAY 1878	Harmony
004888	VOEGLER, William	3y	W	D.C.	02 SEP 1875	Prospect Hill
018112	VOGELWEYD, John F.	4y	W	D.C.	21 NOV 1878	Prospect Hill
018123	VOGELWEYD, William	7y	W	D.C.	22 NOV 1878	Prospect Hill
016776	VOGLE, Kateran	5y	W	D.C.	26 JUL 1878	Glenwood
004147f	VOGT, John	14d	W	D.C.	15 JUL 1875	Prospect Hill
011901	VOIGT, Fred. W.	49y	W	Prus.	14 JUN 1877	Prospect Hill
005353	VOIGT, John Jacob	6y	W	D.C.	03 NOV 1875	St. Mary's
014011	VOIGT, Sophie	5y	W	D.C.	04 DEC 1877	Prospect Hill
004133	VOLK, George Sherwood	2m	W	D.C.	14 JUL 1875	Congressional
017263	VOLKER, Rosanna	10m	W	D.C.	30 AUG 1878	Congressional
007636	VOLLAND, Annie	5m	W	D.C.	13 JUN 1876	Prospect Hill
019901	VOLLBRIGHT, August	65y	W	Ger.	25 APR 1879	Prospect Hill
002221	VOLLBRIGHT, Wilimina	65y	W	Ger.	18 FEB 1875	Prospect Hill
021044	VON GROBE, Alexander	32y	W	Prus.	21 JUL 1879	Soldier's Home
008916	VONTY, Paul Hamilton	11m	W	D.C.	01 SEP 1876	Alexandria, Va.
000143	VORNHOF, Rosina	66y	W	Ger.	11 AUG 1874	Prospect Hill
018338	VOW, Jane	64y	C	Va.	14 DEC 1878	Mt. Zion
013028	VOWEL, Robert Lewis	23y	C	D.C.	30 AUG 1877	Harmony

No.	Name	Age	Race	Birth	Death Date	Burial Place
W						
018565	WADDEN, Eddie	2y	C	D.C.	04 JAN 1879	Beckett's
017818	WADDEY, Charles	6y	C	D.C.	20 OCT 1878	Macedonia
005111a	WADDIS, Octavia	26y	C	Md.	11 OCT 1875	Young Mens
014814	WADDY, Infant of W. & C.	6m	C	D.C.	18 FEB 1878	Macedonia
021090	WADE, Bessy	17m	C	D.C.	24 JUL 1879	Mt. Olivet
006480	WADE, Glenwood	30y	C	Va.	26 FEB 1876	Potters Field
003216	WADE, Llzzle	11y	C	D.C.	04 MAY 1875	Potters Field
017338	WADE, Louisa	6y	C	Va.	06 SEP 1878	Young Mens
010261	WADE, Nellie	8m	C	D.C.	12 JAN 1877	Potters Field
017287	WADKIN, Infant of Sally	10min	C	D.C.	01 SEP 1878	Potters Field
000118	WAGGEMANN, Clara	25y	W	Md.	09 AUG 1874	St. Mary's
018832	WAGGENER, Hanson	66y	W	W.Va.	26 JAN 1879	Rock Creek
016511	WAGNER, Annie E.	8y	W	D.C.	08 JUL 1878	Prospect Hill
004675	WAGNER, Annie Regina	1y	W	D.C.	19 AUG 1875	Prospect Hill
014089	WAGNER, Bertha J.	5y	W	D.C.	13 DEC 1877	Prospect Hill
012832	WAGNER, Carl L.	44y	W	Ger.	15 AUG 1877	St. Mary's
014937	WAGNER, Catharine M.	4m	W	D.C.	03 MAR 1878	Glenwood
001643	WAGNER, Christian	56y	W	Ger.	07 JAN 1875	Prospect Hill
002008	WAGNER, Elisabeth	75y	W	Ger.	03 FEB 1875	Prospect Hill
010420	WAGNER, Frederick	19d	W	D.C.	27 JAN 1877	Prospect Hill
001113	WAGNER, George S.	32y	W	Pa.	12 NOV 1874	York, Pa.
014043	WAGNER, Jacob	41y	W	D.C.	08 DEC 1877	Glenwood
008168	WAGNER, John	67y	W	Ger.	11 JUL 1876	Prospect Hill
006439	WAGNER, John William	16m	W	D.C.	21 FEB 1876	Prospect Hill
017064	WAGNER, Magia V.E.	1y	W	D.C.	15 AUG 1878	Oak Hill
009272	WAGNER, Mary Lenora	10m	W	D.C.	02 OCT 1876	Methodist
004223	WAGNER, Mary Whilmine	55y	W	Ger.	20 JUL 1875	Congressional
003532	WAGNER, Sarah	45y	W	N.Y.	05 JUN 1875	Potters Field
006326	WAHL, George	65y	W	Md.	12 FEB 1876	Glenwood
000653	WAHL, Sophia	73y	W	Ger.	28 SEP 1874	Prospect Hill
020663	WAHLY, Mary	8y	W	Mich.	28 JUN 1879	Rock Creek
003684	WAIL, Fred	58y	W	Ger.	17 JUN 1875	Prospect Hill
002549	WAILES, Ellen Cole	1y	W	D.C.	13 MAR 1875	Glenwood
018849	WAILES, Martha	76y	W	Ire.	27 JAN 1879	Glenwood
000473	WAILES, Stephen Newton	16y	W	D.C.	11 SEP 1874	Glenwood
002144	WAINWRIGHT, Samuel	85y	W	Eng.	13 FEB 1875	Rock Creek
011548	WAINWRIGHT, Sophia Dallas	17d	W	D.C.	09 MAY 1877	Congressional
005088a	WAIT, Infant of Saml. C.	1½d	W	D.C.	08 OCT 1875	Graceland
009824	WAITE, Annie	33y	W	N.Y.	29 NOV 1876	Mt. Olivet
001098	WAITE, Julia Ann	60y	W	Md.	09 NOV 1874	Glenwood
004134	WAITE, Matthew	83y	W	Eng.	14 JUL 1875	Glenwood
006929	WAITER, Walker	33y	M	Va.	04 APR 1876	Harmony
005046	WALCH, Annie	10m	W	D.C.	14 SEP 1875	Mt. Olivet
014618	WALDEA, Charles	40y	W	Ger.	31 JAN 1878	Hospital, Government
018831	WALDREN, Infant of Precilla	5d	C	D.C.	26 JAN 1879	Potters Field
019878	WALDRON, Albert	32y	W	N.Y.	23 APR 1879	Hospital, Government
014220	WALES, Helen	36y	C	N.Y.	26 DEC 1877	Young Mens
014681	WALES, Rachel	70+y Md.		Md.	05 FEB 1878	Potters Field
020019	WALKENIGHT, Mary Jane	73y	W	Pa.	06 MAY 1879	Oak Hill
012129	WALKER, Andrew	28y	C	Va.	29 JUN 1877	Potters Field
012123	WALKER, Ann	c.63y	C	Md.	29 JUN 1877	Harmony
018656	WALKER, Anna	2y	C	D.C.	12 JAN 1879	Beckett's
000999	WALKER, Benjamin	4y	W	Va.	31 OCT 1874	Fairfax Co., Va.
012137	WALKER, Catharine	1y	C	D.C.	30 JUN 1877	Ebenezer

District of Columbia Death Records, August 1, 1874 to July 31, 1879   353

No.	Name	Age	Race	Birth	Death Date	Burial Place
014395	WALKER, Chas. Edward	36y	W	D.C.	11 JAN 1878	Glenwood
014396	WALKER, Chas. Howard	10m	W	D.C.	11 JAN 1878	Graceland
007061	WALKER, Claracy Martha Sharp	1y	C	Md.	20 APR 1876	Harmony
000863f	WALKER, Edward	7y	W	D.C.	19 OCT 1874	Congressional
014051	WALKER, Eliza E.	33y	C	Va.	09 DEC 1877	Harmony
018374	WALKER, Elizabeth	76y	W	D.C.	18 DEC 1878	Congressional
021005	WALKER, Ella	2m	C	D.C.	18 JUL 1879	Brightwood
006704	WALKER, Emily	54y	C	Va.	16 MAR 1876	Harmony
018135	WALKER, Fannie Martha	42y	W	Miss.	23 NOV 1878	Oak Hill
005741	WALKER, Fanny	25y	W	Va.	13 DEC 1875	Mt. Olivet
012649	WALKER, George	16y	C	Va.	02 AUG 1877	Ebenezer
000559	WALKER, George Ellsworth	3m	C	D.C.	19 SEP 1874	Mt. Pleasant
021045	WALKER, George S.	7m	W	D.C.	21 JUL 1879	Mt. Olivet
007070	WALKER, George Tucker	2d	W	D.C.	21 APR 1876	Mt. Olivet
008858	WALKER, Gideon L.	63y	W	N.Y.	28 AUG 1876	Congressional
016044	WALKER, Hannah	10y	W	Eng.	06 JUN 1878	Oak Hill
009907	WALKER, Infant of Hellen	1d	C	D.C.	09 DEC 1876	Young Mens
010355	WALKER, Infant of Robert	15h	C	D.C.	21 JAN 1877	Potters Field
000668	WALKER, Infant of Robert	2d	C	D.C.	29 SEP 1874	Mt. Pleasant
014301	WALKER, Infant of Robt.	5d	C	D.C.	02 JAN 1878	Potters Field
002330	WALKER, James	24y	C	Va.	26 FEB 1875	Mt. Pleasant
005162	WALKER, James	4y	C	D.C.	24 SEP 1875	Ebenezer
017635	WALKER, James	12y	C	D.C.	04 OCT 1878	Young Mens
005211a	WALKER, James H.	57y	W	Md.	19 OCT 1875	Oak Hill
004841	WALKER, Jno. H.	60y	C	Va.	30 AUG 1875	Potters Field
004805	WALKER, John	45y	W	Scot.	29 AUG 1875	Mt. Olivet
007452	WALKER, John C.	39y	W	D.C.	31 MAY 1876	Congressional
012583	WALKER, John Jacob Conroy	5m	C	D.C.	28 JUL 1877	Holy Rood
003484	WALKER, John M.L.	10y	W	D.C.	30 MAY 1875	Congressional
000862f	WALKER, John W.	45y	W	D.C.	19 OCT 1874	Congressional
004486	WALKER, Joseph	4y	C	Va.	06 AUG 1875	Young Mens
006388	WALKER, Julia	84y	C	Va.	16 FEB 1876	Harmony
019542	WALKER, Lucy	1m	C	D.C.	24 MAR 1879	Mt. Olivet
018721	WALKER, Margerate	30y	C	Md.	18 JAN 1879	Hagerstown, Md.
014745	WALKER, Maria E.	68y	W	Eng.	11 FEB 1878	Congressional
014374	WALKER, Mariah	75y	C	Va.	09 JAN 1878	Mt. Olivet
003291	WALKER, Martha A.L.	15y	C	Va.	12 MAY 1875	Ebenezer
001605	WALKER, Mary	7y	C	Va.	03 JAN 1875	Young Mens
013345	WALKER, Mary Ann	69y	W	Va.	28 SEP 1877	Oak Hill
012526	WALKER, Mary E.	7d	C	D.C.	25 JUL 1877	Ebenezer
017102	WALKER, Mary J.	1y	M	Md.	18 AUG 1878	Graceland
011469	WALKER, Matilda	7y	C	D.C.	30 APR 1877	Harmony
002123	WALKER, Matilda Sinclair	2y	C	D.C.	11 FEB 1875	Potters Field
004851	WALKER, Mattie	2y	C	D.C.	31 AUG 1875	Young Mens
004090	WALKER, Minnie	2m	C	D.C.	11 JUL 1875	Ebenezer
004786	WALKER, Nettie	1y	W	D.C.	27 AUG 1875	Congressional
010354	WALKER, Patsy	40y	C	Va.	21 JAN 1877	Young Mens
006890	WALKER, Rachel	75y	C	Va.	01 APR 1876	Alexandria, Va.
007193	WALKER, Richard	35y	C	Va.	02 MAY 1876	Young Mens
003090	WALKER, Rosa	25y	M	Va.	22 APR 1875	Potters Field
019868	WALKER, Rosanna E.	72y	W	Va.	22 APR 1879	Glenwood
005227a	WALKER, Saml.	7d	C	D.C.	20 OCT 1875	Harmony
009492	WALKER, Simpson A.	64y	W	Pa.	22 OCT 1876	Oak Hill
005285	WALKER, Susie	4y	C	D.C.	27 OCT 1875	Mt. Olivet
007071	WALKER, Thomas Edward	2d	W	D.C.	21 APR 1876	Mt. Olivet
007931	WALKER, Walter Warren	24y	M	Va.	29 JUN 1876	Young Mens

No.	Name	Age	Race	Birth	Death Date	Burial Place
004907	WALKER, William	2y	C	D.C.	04 SEP 1875	Young Mens
001816	WALKER, Willie	2y	C	D.C.	20 JAN 1875	Beckett's
014885	WALKER, Willie	1m	C	D.C.	26 FEB 1878	Young Mens
012369	WALKER, Wm.	14d	C	D.C.	15 JUL 1877	Potters Field
019840	WALKER, Wm.	1y	C	D.C.	19 APR 1879	Mt. Pleasant
004372	WALKINS, Samuel	7d	C	D.C.	29 JUL 1875	Ebenezer
003050	WALL, Ellen	54y	W	Ire.	19 APR 1875	Mt. Olivet
017221	WALL, John H.	2m	W	D.C.	27 AUG 1878	Presbyterian
012310	WALL, Joseph P.	3y	W	Mo.	11 JUL 1877	Winchester, Va.
009320	WALL, Julia	2y	C	D.C.	06 OCT 1876	Ebenezer
012282	WALL, M.A., Mrs.	67y	W	Md.	09 JUL 1877	Presbyterian
005370	WALL, Treadwell S.	53y	W	Va.	05 NOV 1875	Winchester, Va.
008721	WALL, William Dennison	1y	C	D.C.	18 AUG 1876	Graceland
005656	WALL, William L.	49y	W	D.C.	04 DEC 1875	Mt. Olivet
005290	WALLA, Mary	2m	C	D.C.	28 OCT 1875	Ebenezer
005097a	WALLACE, Archibald Walker	22y	W	Scot.	09 OCT 1875	Oak Hill
000690	WALLACE, Benj. S.	42y	C	D.C.	01 OCT 1874	Harmony
010252	WALLACE, Bessie	5m	C	D.C.	11 JAN 1877	Young Mens
018294	WALLACE, Bud	1y	C	D.C.	09 DEC 1878	Potters Field
008447	WALLACE, Clinton Ross	1y	W	D.C.	27 JUL 1876	Oak Hill
016353	WALLACE, Henry	35y	C	D.C.	28 JUN 1878	Harmony
012586	WALLACE, Infant of Christiana	2h	C	D.C.	28 JUL 1877	Beckett's
008564	WALLACE, Infant of Linton	5d	C	D.C.	05 AUG 1876	Ebenezer
015527	WALLACE, Infant of Louise	1h	C	D.C.	26 APR 1878	Potters Field
019512	WALLACE, Infant of Mildred	34h	C	D.C.	22 MAR 1879	Beckett's
014790	WALLACE, Isham	16y	C	Va.	16 FEB 1878	Payne's
017687	WALLACE James Nagley	3m	W	D.C.	09 OCT 1878	Mt. Olivet
005189	WALLACE, Jennie	40y	C	Md.	26 SEP 1875	Potters Field
009345	WALLACE, John	3y	C	D.C.	08 OCT 1876	Potters Field
014619	WALLACE, John Dandridge	42y	M	D.C.	31 JAN 1878	Harmony
003607	WALLACE, Lizzie	2m	C	D.C.	11 JUN 1875	Ebenezer
003196f	WALLACE, Martha	38y	W	Md.	02 MAY 1875	Glenwood
010197	WALLACE, Mary Ann	38y	W	Ire.	06 JAN 1877	Mt. Olivet
009157	WALLACE, Mary C.	4y	M	D.C.	21 SEP 1876	Mt. Olivet
007557	WALLACE, Mary Spriggs	8m	C	D.C.	08 JUN 1876	Mt. Olivet
016795	WALLACE, Moses, Jr.	18m	C	D.C.	27 JUL 1878	Mt. Pleasant
009571	WALLACE, Richard	13d	C	D.C.	29 OCT 1876	Mt. Olivet
013029	WALLACE, Richard	65y	C	Md.	30 AUG 1877	Potters Field
010576	WALLACE, Sally	c.80y	C	Va.	10 FEB 1877	Harmony
018409	WALLACE, Samuel Albert	3y	W	D.C.	20 DEC 1878	Graceland
006481	WALLACE, William	2m	C	D.C.	26 FEB 1876	Young Mens
009128	WALLACH, Ethel Howard	1y	W	D.C.	19 SEP 1876	Oak Hill
015515	WALLACH, Samuel	73y	W	Ger.	25 APR 1878	Washington Hebrew
000715	WALLACK, Robert	74y	W	Mass.	05 OCT 1874	Congressional
002097	WALLER, Annie	19y	C	Va.	09 FEB 1875	Ebenezer
005719	WALLER, Charles	24y	C	Va.	10 DEC 1875	Mt. Olivet
016684	WALLER, Cora	1y	C	D.C.	19 JUL 1878	Beckett's
009251	WALLER, Cordelia	1y	C	D.C.	30 SEP 1876	Young Mens
005119a	WALLER, James	1m	C	D.C.	12 OCT 1875	Ebenezer
010645	WALLER, Mary Ellen	2y	W	D.C.	15 FEB 1877	Mt. Olivet
004873	WALLER, Phebe Ellen	2y	C	D.C.	01 SEP 1875	Young Mens
010462	WALLING, David	74y	W	Md.	31 JAN 1877	Presbyterian
017700	WALLINGSFORD, Joseph Owen	46y	W	Md.	10 OCT 1878	Congressional
020035	WALLIS, Mary Ann	94y	W	Md.	07 MAY 1879	Oak Hill
019702	WALLIS, Sarah C.	83y	W	Va.	08 APR 1879	Congressional
018301	WALLIS, William	91y	W	Md.	10 DEC 1878	Congressional

District of Columbia Death Records, August 1, 1874 to July 31, 1879

No.	Name	Age	Race	Birth	Death Date	Burial Place
007141	WALLS, Annie E.	35y	C	Md.	27 APR 1876	Mt. Pleasant Plain
007265	WALLS, Victoria A.	1m	C	D.C.	10 MAY 1876	Young Mens
009899	WALMSLEY, Anna L.	17y	W	D.C.	07 DEC 1876	Glenwood
010350	WALMSLEY, Theodore	45y	W	Md.	20 JAN 1877	Glenwood
012165	WALSH, Agnes Annina	8m	W	D.C.	01 JUL 1877	Mt. Olivet
002074	WALSH, Agnes O.	1m	W	D.C.	08 FEB 1875	Mt. Olivet
004268	WALSH, Amelia	1y	C	D.C.	23 JUL 1875	Ebenezer
016968	WALSH, Earnest Jeffers	8m	W	D.C.	08 AUG 1878	Congressional
018047	WALSH, Edmond	54y	W	Ire.	13 NOV 1878	Soldier's Home
000612	WALSH, Eugene	5y	W	D.C.	23 SEP 1874	Mt. Olivet
018944	WALSH, Fannie Parmelee	11y	W	N.Y.	03 FEB 1879	Lansingburgh, N.Y.
001476	WALSH, Francis Stuart	63y	W	Ire.	24 DEC 1874	Mt. Olivet
013250	WALSH, Frederic	5y	W	D.C.	19 SEP 1877	Holy Rood
013320	WALSH, George F.	1y	W	D.C.	26 SEP 1877	Holy Rood
015064	WALSH, Helen Ivey	33y	W	D.C.	13 MAR 1878	Mt. Olivet
002919	WALSH, Henry Stuart	11m	W	D.C.	08 APR 1875	Oak Hill
005702	WALSH, James	72y	W	Ire.	08 DEC 1875	Soldier's Home
003266	WALSH, James	55y	W	Ire.	09 MAY 1875	Mt. Olivet
008983	WALSH, John	24y	W	Ire.	06 SEP 1876	Mt. Olivet
014980	WALSH, John	1h	W	D.C.	07 MAR 1878	Mt. Olivet
005501	WALSH, John L.	58y	W	Ire.	18 NOV 1875	Mt. Olivet
004503f	WALSH, Joseph	1y	W	D.C.	07 AUG 1875	Holy Rood
009707	WALSH, Julia	38y	W	Ire.	16 NOV 1876	Mt. Olivet
013227	WALSH, Kate	32y	W	Ire.	16 SEP 1877	Mt. Olivet
000822	WALSH, Margaret	45y	W	Ire.	16 OCT 1874	Mt. Olivet
012562	WALSH, Mary	58y	W	D.C.	27 JUL 1877	Congressional
019839	WALSH, Mary	16y	W	N.J.	19 APR 1879	Holy Rood
003989	WALSH, Mary C.	23y	W	Ire.	03 JUL 1875	Mt. Olivet
014255	WALSH, Mathew K.	55y	W	Ire.	29 DEC 1877	Mt. Olivet
012922	WALSH, Michael	6y	W	D.C.	23 AUG 1877	Holy Rood
014586	WALSH, Stuart	1m	W	D.C.	28 JAN 1878	Mt. Olivet
019280	WALSH, Willie	1y	W	D.C.	04 MAR 1879	Mt. Olivet
018850	WALSH, William F.	9y	W	D.C.	27 JAN 1879	Congressional
001709	WALSKY, C.	4m	W	D.C.	13 JAN 1875	Jewish
019023	WALSON, Minnie	1y	C	D.C.	10 FEB 1879	Holy Rood
005781	WALSTON, Ann Maria	13y	C	D.C.	17 DEC 1875	Holy Rood
016921	WALSTON, Geo. L.	4m	C	D.C.	05 AUG 1878	Holy Rood
013427	WALSTON, George	46y	C	Md.	07 OCT 1877	Holy Rood
021129	WALSTON, Henry	14y	C	D.C.	15 FEB 1879	Potters Field
000398	WALTER, Frank	6m	W	D.C.	01 SEP 1874	St. Mary's
001648	WALTER, Fredie Emelia	4m	W	Va.	08 JAN 1875	Congressional
019825	WALTER, John	69y	W	Ger.	18 APR 1879	St. Mary's
013858	WALTERS, Catherine Pauline	26y	W	D.C.	18 NOV 1877	Mt. Olivet
005890	WALTERS, Frederick	7m	C	D.C.	28 DEC 1875	Mt. Pleasant
002258	WALTERS, Robert	60y	C	Va.	20 FEB 1875	Young Mens
005396	WALTERS, Sarah E.	26y	W	Md.	08 NOV 1875	Christiana, Del.
016186	WALTHEN, Johanna	19d	W	D.C.	15 JUN 1878	Tennallytown
012006	WALTMEYER, Bertie	8y	W	D.C.	22 JUN 1877	Mt. Olivet
007488	WALTON, Infant of Lucy	36h	C	D.C.	03 JUN 1876	Potters Field
000008	WALTON, Susan	2y	W	D.C.	01 AUG 1874	Congressional
011934	WALTZ, Henry	8m	W	D.C.	16 JUN 1877	St. Mary's
007380	WANE, Mary Jane	6d	M	D.C.	22 MAY 1876	Ebenezer
017074	WANES, Martha Ellen	2y	C	D.C.	16 AUG 1878	Potters Field
005121a	WANES, Rebecca	38y	C	Md.	12 OCT 1875	Mt. Zion
020547	WANN, Isaac	54y	C	N.C.	20 JUN 1879	Harmony
014221	WANNALL, Jennette	49y	W	Mass.	26 DEC 1877	Glenwood

District of Columbia Death Records, August 1, 1874 to July 31, 1879

No.	Name	Age	Race	Birth	Death Date	Burial Place
004501	WANSER, William	1y	C	D.C.	07 AUG 1875	Ebenezer
015647	WANSER, William	1y	C	D.C.	07 MAY 1878	Mt. Pleasant
008499	WANSTALL, Emily E.	1y	W	D.C.	31 JUL 1876	Oak Hill
005959	WANTON, Benjamin	53y	C	Md.	06 JAN 1876	Harmony
010091	WANTON, Mary Elizabeth	64y	W	Va.	27 DEC 1876	Congressional
018989	WANZER, Frank	50y	C	Va.	07 FEB 1879	Harmony
020158	WANZER, John H.	3m	C	D.C.	20 MAY 1879	Young Mens
001518	WANZER, Levi	1m	C	D.C.	28 DEC 1874	Washington Asylum
000582	WARD, Alice R.	56y	W	Md.	21 SEP 1874	Baltimore, Md.
003340	WARD, Ann O.	39y	W	Ire.	16 MAY 1875	Mt. Olivet
008945	WARD, Blanch E.	1y	W	D.C.	03 SEP 1876	Congressional
002610	WARD, Chas.	13m	W	D.C.	16 MAR 1875	Glenwood
014620	WARD, Edmond Wilson	14d	W	D.C.	31 JAN 1878	Tennallytown
013418	WARD, Effie E.	1m	W	D.C.	06 OCT 1877	Congressional
005933	WARD, Eliza	38y	W	Ire.	03 JAN 1876	Rock Creek
002317	WARD, Elizabeth	34y	C	Va.	25 FEB 1875	Young Mens
004023	WARD, Elizabeth	4m	C	D.C.	06 JUL 1875	Young Mens
007080	WARD, Ellen	54y	W	D.C.	22 APR 1876	Congressional
000548	WARD, Emily Ann	24y	W	Eng.	17 SEP 1874	Rock Creek
004487	WARD, Emma	1y	M	D.C.	06 AUG 1875	Harmony
014503	WARD, Georgiana	c.62y	W	D.C.	20 JAN 1878	Glenwood
015498	WARD, Henry	9m	C	D.C.	23 APR 1878	Mt. Pleasant Plain
000183	WARD, Isabella	14m	W	D.C.	14 AUG 1874	Mt. Olivet
000975	WARD, John	64y	W	Ire.	29 OCT 1874	Mt. Olivet
014514	WARD, John H.T.	56y	W	Md.	21 JAN 1878	Glenwood
000709f	WARD, John Joseph	8m	W	Va.	04 OCT 1874	Holy Rood
010191	WARD, Julia Howe	2y	W	D.C.	06 JAN 1877	Congressional
015391	WARD, Louisa	84y	C	Va.	13 APR 1878	Mt. Pleasant
019750	WARD, Mabel	2y	W	D.C.	12 APR 1879	Congressional
000396	WARD, Margaret	46y	W	Ire.	01 SEP 1874	Mt. Olivet
010892	WARD, Margaret	78y	W	Ire.	07 MAR 1877	Mt. Olivet
019038	WARD, Mary	24y	W	Md.	11 FEB 1879	Washington Asylum
000882	WARD, Mary Lawrence	59y	W	N.Y.	21 OCT 1874	Oak Hill
007585	WARD, Mary R.	2d	W	D.C.	10 JUN 1876	Graceland
009847	WARD, May	3y	W	D.C.	02 DEC 1876	Rock Creek
003374	WARD, Minnie Parker	2y	C	Md.	20 MAY 1875	Macedonia
014776	WARD, Ralph	56y	C	Md.	15 FEB 1878	Beckett's
005857	WARD, Robert	23y	C	Md.	24 DEC 1875	Thomas'
001982f	WARD, Susan V.	78y	--	D.C.	01 FEB 1875	Glenwood
008441	WARD, William	30y	C	D.C.	27 JUL 1876	Mt. Olivet
010177	WARD, William	40y	W	Ire.	05 JAN 1877	Holy Rood
003223	WARD, William Edward	28y	W	Va.	05 MAY 1875	Glenwood
004554	WARD, William Hamlin	11m	W	D.C.	11 AUG 1875	Mt. Olivet
001717	WARDELL, C.A.	76y	W	Eng.	13 JAN 1875	Oak Hill
004842	WARDELL, James	74y	W	Conn.	30 AUG 1875	Brandford, Conn.
015238	WARDEN, Wm.	69y	W	Ire.	30 MAR 1878	Congressional
005342	WARDER, William	55y	W	Va.	02 NOV 1875	Glenwood
000347	WARE, Amanda	17m	C	Va.	28 AUG 1874	Beckett's
009279	WARE, Andrew	2y	C	D.C.	02 OCT 1876	Ebenezer
007008	WARE, Ann	65y	C	Md.	12 APR 1876	Ebenezer
016778	WARE, Ann Elizabeth	6m	C	D.C.	26 JUL 1878	Mt. Pleasant
019824	WARE, Celia	75y	C	Va.	18 APR 1879	Graceland
006663	WARE, Charles	c.20y	C	Md.	13 MAR 1876	Mt. Olivet
003891	WARE, Francis	13m	C	Va.	27 JUN 1875	Macedonia
005863	WARE, Herbert	11m	C	D.C.	25 DEC 1875	Beckett's
009496	WARE, Infant of Robert	7d	C	D.C.	22 OCT 1876	Beckett's

District of Columbia Death Records, August 1, 1874 to July 31, 1879

No.	Name	Age	Race	Birth	Death Date	Burial Place
000128	WARE, James	22y	C	Md.	10 AUG 1874	Potters Field
001391	WARE, James	22y	C	Md.	14 DEC 1874	Beckett's
016026	WARE, James W.	5m	C	D.C.	05 JUN 1878	Beckett's
003320	WARE, Julia Ann	64y	W	Md.	14 MAY 1875	Cox's Station, Md.
005172a	WARE, Laura	2y	C	D.C.	16 OCT 1875	Ebenezer
008492	WARE, Richard S.	7m	C	D.C.	30 JUL 1876	Ebenezer
011178	WARE, Robert F.	8m	C	D.C.	31 MAR 1877	Ebenezer
001906	WARE, Susan	25y	C	Va.	26 JAN 1875	Ebenezer
005160	WARE, Thomas	46y	W	N.Y.	24 SEP 1875	Washington Asylum
000982	WARE, Townly	80y	C	Md.	30 OCT 1874	Beckett's
009283	WARE, William	4m	C	D.C.	03 OCT 1876	Moore's
007209	WARE, Wm. H.	5m	C	D.C.	04 MAY 1876	Potters Field
019414	WARFEL, Rosa	10y	W	Ohio	15 MAR 1879	Worcester, Ohio
020917	WARFIELD, Elwood R.	6m	W	D.C.	13 JUL 1879	Presbyterian
000952	WARFIELD, Ernie	1y	C	D.C.	27 OCT 1874	Beckett's
012178	WARFIELD, Susan Maud	2m	W	D.C.	02 JUL 1877	Presbyterian
013156	WARFIELD, William H.	3y	C	Md.	10 SEP 1877	Potters Field
015546	WARNER, Adolphus	5m	C	D.C.	28 APR 1878	Young Mens
003840	WARNER, Amy	60y	C	Va.	25 JUN 1875	Potters Field
012303	WARNER, David	4y	C	D.C.	10 JUL 1877	Mt. Zion
015422	WARNER, George David	3m	W	D.C.	16 APR 1878	Bristol, R.I.
018136	WARNER, Gertrude	2y	C	D.C.	23 NOV 1878	Harmony
015441	WARNER, Infant of Jo.	7d	C	D.C.	18 APR 1878	Potters Field
003678	WARNER, Jacob Dedicate Wilson	6m	W	D.C.	17 JUN 1875	Methodist
003702	WARNER, Joseph Pence Wilson	6m	W	D.C.	19 JUN 1875	Methodist
005020	WARNER, Julia	1y	W	D.C.	12 SEP 1875	Oak Hill
017369	WARNER, Leonard F.	9m	W	D.C.	10 SEP 1878	Holy Rood
020767	WARNER, Mary Ann	1y	W	D.C.	04 JUL 1879	Methodist, E.
002843	WARNER, Mary Peters	65y	W	D.C.	02 APR 1875	Congressional
002089f	WARNER, Mary Virginia	48y	W	Va.	08 FEB 1875	Oak Hill
000943	WARNER, Wm. P.	34y	W	Pa.	26 OCT 1874	Congressional
003670	WARREN, Alice Ann	24y	M	Md.	17 JUN 1875	Mt. Olivet
001517	WARREN, Caroline	2y	C	D.C.	28 DEC 1874	Mt. Olivet
004341	WARREN, Charity	63y	C	Md.	27 JUL 1875	Mt. Olivet
000944	WARREN, Clara	2y	C	D.C.	26 OCT 1874	Potters Field
011905	WARREN, Ella	1y	C	D.C.	15 JUN 1877	Ebenezer
009636	WARREN, Emma	20y	C	Va.	07 NOV 1876	Young Mens
005667	WARREN, Ernest	2y	W	D.C.	05 DEC 1875	Mt. Olivet
015961	WARREN, Estella	7w	C	D.C.	01 JUN 1878	Moore's
012357	WARREN, Harriet	32y	C	Md.	14 JUL 1877	Mt. Olivet
016908	WARREN, Henry	31y	C	Md.	04 AUG 1878	Va.
005263	WARREN, Infant of Wm.	15h	C	D.C.	25 OCT 1875	Potters Field
014535	WARREN, Joseph Thomas	8d	C	D.C.	23 JAN 1878	Beckett's
006603	WARREN, Julia E.	6m	W	D.C.	08 MAR 1876	Methodist
017137	WARREN, Lewis	11m	C	D.C.	21 AUG 1878	Beckett's
009138	WARREN, Louiza	24y	C	Md.	20 SEP 1876	Ebenezer
017633	WARREN, Mary L.	21d	C	D.C.	04 OCT 1878	Mt. Olivet
011154	WARREN, Minnie	c.29y	W	U.S.	29 MAR 1877	Mt. Olivet
019053	WARREN, Rosa Palini	2m	C	D.C.	12 FEB 1879	Potters Field
014946	WARREN, Willis	6m	C	D.C.	04 MAR 1879	Mt. Olivet
018214	WARRING, Wm., Jr.	20y	C	D.C.	01 DEC 1878	Graceland
015868	WASHINGTON, Ada	2y	M	Va.	27 MAY 1878	Jones Chapel
016312	WASHINGTON, Albert	1m	C	D.C.	25 JUN 1878	Mt. Olivet
003289	WASHINGTON, Alice	3y	C	D.C.	11 MAY 1875	Harmony
018800	WASHINGTON, Alice V.	1y	C	D.C.	24 JAN 1879	Mt. Zion
009177	WASHINGTON, Aloysius	2m	C	D.C.	23 SEP 1876	Beckett's

No.	Name	Age	Race	Birth	Death Date	Burial Place
011513	WASHINGTON, Andrew	7y	C	R.I.	04 MAY 1877	Young Mens
012367	WASHINGTON, Annie	18y	C	Va.	15 JUL 1877	Mt. Zion
019261	WASHINGTON, Annie	26y	C	Md.	02 MAR 1879	Chalmond Point, Md.
002835	WASHINGTON, Armistead	5m	M	D.C.	01 APR 1875	Mt. Pleasant
017402	WASHINGTON, Augustus	63y	C	Va.	13 SEP 1878	Harmony
018978	WASHINGTON, Aurena	4m	C	D.C.	06 FEB 1879	Potters Field
016841	WASHINGTON, Baptist	1y	C	D.C.	30 JUL 1878	Young Mens
006387	WASHINGTON, Basket	2m	C	D.C.	16 FEB 1876	Potters Field
004237	WASHINGTON, Benjamin Calvin	14y	C	Va.	21 JUL 1875	Young Mens
005137	WASHINGTON, Betty	1y	C	D.C.	22 SEP 1875	Beckett's
007891	WASHINGTON, Burford	45y	C	Va.	27 JUN 1876	Harmony
008307	WASHINGTON, Calvin	12y	C	Va.	17 JUL 1876	Mt. Pleasant
012610	WASHINGTON, Charles	10m	C	D.C.	30 JUL 1877	Young Mens
011035	WASHINGTON, Charles	38y	C	D.C.	19 MAR 1877	Harmony
020662	WASHINGTON, Charles	6y	C	D.C.	28 JUN 1879	Young Mens
004433	WASHINGTON, Charles Henry	17m	C	D.C.	03 AUG 1875	Mt. Olivet
000318	WASHINGTON, Charlotte	8y	C	D.C.	25 AUG 1874	Mt. Pleasant Plain
020785	WASHINGTON, Clem	38y	C	Md.	05 JUL 1879	Mt. Olivet
020018	WASHINGTON, Dora	2y	C	D.C.	06 MAY 1879	Young Mens
003910	WASHINGTON, Edie	18y	C	Va.	28 JUN 1875	Beckett's
016110	WASHINGTON, Edmund	12h	C	D.C.	10 JUN 1878	Beckett's
015887	WASHINGTON, Edward	5m	M	D.C.	28 MAY 1878	Jones Chapel
020546	WASHINGTON, Edward	34y	C	Va.	20 JUN 1879	Harmony
007425	WASHINGTON, Eli	30y	C	Va.	27 MAY 1876	Potters Field
002357	WASHINGTON, Eliza	53y	C	D.C.	28 FEB 1875	Young Mens
003602	WASHINGTON, Elizabeth	4d	C	D.C.	11 JUN 1875	Moore's
020619	WASHINGTON, Elizabeth	35y	C	Va.	25 JUN 1879	Harmony
001783	WASHINGTON, Ella	3y	C	D.C.	18 JAN 1875	Ebenezer
005587	WASHINGTON, Ellen	4y	C	Md.	27 NOV 1875	Brightwood
011497	WASHINGTON, Ellen	60y	C	Va.	03 MAY 1877	Hospital
013484	WASHINGTON, Eugene	7y	C	D.C.	11 OCT 1877	Beckett's
016869	WASHINGTON, Eugene	6m	C	D.C.	01 AUG 1878	Mt. Pleasant
017279	WASHINGTON, Florence	6m	C	D.C.	31 AUG 1878	Young Mens
018555	WASHINGTON, Florence	17y	C	D.C.	03 JAN 1879	Harmony
010460	WASHINGTON, Frank	48y	C	Va.	31 JAN 1877	Young Mens
013383	WASHINGTON, Frank	6y	C	D.C.	02 OCT 1877	Beckett's
017610	WASHINGTON, Frank	7y	C	D.C.	02 OCT 1878	Mt. Olivet
009854	WASHINGTON, Frank J.	5y	C	D.C.	03 DEC 1876	Mt. Olivet
013947	WASHINGTON, Geo.	40y	C	D.C.	27 NOV 1877	Potters Field
000131	WASHINGTON, George	1m	C	D.C.	10 AUG 1874	Beckett's
000109	WASHINGTON, George	55y	C	N.C.	08 AUG 1874	Potters Field
006994	WASHINGTON, George	80y	C	Ala.	11 APR 1876	Potters Field
008355	WASHINGTON, George	8m	C	D.C.	20 JUL 1876	Young Mens
009736	WASHINGTON, George	40y	C	D.C.	19 NOV 1876	Young Mens
018429	WASHINGTON, George	3m	C	D.C.	22 DEC 1878	Mt. Pleasant
016762	WASHINGTON, George	1y	C	D.C.	25 JUL 1878	Young Mens
016120	WASHINGTON, George	14y	M	Va.	11 JUN 1878	Potters Field
015151	WASHINGTON, George	1y	C	D.C.	22 MAR 1878	Mt. Pleasant
018763	WASHINGTON, George	35y	C	Md.	21 JAN 1879	Harmony
020588	WASHINGTON, George	25y	C	D.C.	23 JUN 1879	Potters Field
019465	WASHINGTON, George	1y	C	D.C.	19 MAR 1879	Mt. Olivet
020769	WASHINGTON, George Henry	6m	C	D.C.	04 JUL 1879	Beckett's
000368	WASHINGTON, George M.	36y	C	Va.	29 AUG 1874	Mt. Zion
010550	WASHINGTON, Georgianna	23y	C	Va.	07 FEB 1877	Harmony
016443	WASHINGTON, Gertrude	2m	C	D.C.	04 JUL 1878	Beckett's
020742	WASHINGTON, Gertrude	13m	C	D.C.	03 JUL 1879	Mt. Olivet

District of Columbia Death Records, August 1, 1874 to July 31, 1879

No.	Name	Age	Race	Birth	Death Date	Burial Place
000235	WASHINGTON, Harriet	2y	C	D.C.	18 AUG 1874	Young Mens
010582	WASHINGTON, Harriet	52y	C	Va.	11 FEB 1877	Falls Church, Va.
018556	WASHINGTON, Infant of Charles	½d	W	D.C.	03 JAN 1879	Graceland
003959	WASHINGTON, Infant of Edmund	4d	C	D.C.	01 JUL 1875	Ebenezer
012933	WASHINGTON, Infant of Ferdinand	1d	C	D.C.	24 AUG 1877	Mt. Zion
012527	WASHINGTON, Infant of George	8d	C	D.C.	25 JUL 1877	Potters Field
019786	WASHINGTON, Infant of James	7d	C	D.C.	15 APR 1879	Graceland
019173	WASHINGTON, Infant of John	8d	C	D.C.	23 FEB 1879	Mt. Pleasant
004724	WASHINGTON, Infant of John	6d	C	D.C.	22 AUG 1875	Beckett's
007890	WASHINGTON, Infant of Julia	2d	C	D.C.	27 JUN 1876	Potters Field
014364	WASHINGTON, Infant of Richard	9d	C	D.C.	08 JAN 1878	Beckett's
010679	WASHINGTON, Infant of Samuel	7d	C	D.C.	18 FEB 1877	Young Mens
013849	WASHINGTON, Infant of Thomas	5d	C	D.C.	17 NOV 1877	Young Mens
011807	WASHINGTON, Infant of Thomas	9h	C	D.C.	05 JUN 1877	Potters Field
018923	WASHINGTON, Infant of William	8d	C	D.C.	02 FEB 1879	Potters Field
009070	WASHINGTON, James	9m	C	D.C.	14 SEP 1876	Potters Field
004208	WASHINGTON, James H.	1m	C	D.C.	19 JUL 1875	Ebenezer
004951	WASHINGTON, Jane	53y	C	Va.	07 SEP 1875	Mt. Zion
005163	WASHINGTON, Jane	3d	C	D.C.	24 SEP 1875	Young Mens
002149	WASHINGTON, John	25y	C	Va.	14 FEB 1875	Washington Asylum
007424	WASHINGTON, John	6d	C	D.C.	27 MAY 1876	Ebenezer
011940	WASHINGTON, John	65y	C	Md.	17 JUN 1877	Mt. Olivet
017278	WASHINGTON, John	c.19y	C	--	31 AUG 1878	Beckett's
021119	WASHINGTON, John	19y	C	Va.	26 JUL 1879	Washington Asylum
000757	WASHINGTON, John A.	65y	C	D.C.	08 OCT 1874	Potters Field
016575	WASHINGTON, John Francis	8m	C	D.C.	12 JUL 1878	Beckett's
004587	WASHINGTON, John H.	30y	C	Va.	13 AUG 1875	Harmony
021142	WASHINGTON, John W.	1y	C	D.C.	28 JUL 1879	Beckett's
018280	WASHINGTON, Joshua	64y	C	Va.	08 DEC 1878	Harmony
012698	WASHINGTON, Julia	9m	C	D.C.	06 AUG 1877	Mt. Pleasant
002457	WASHINGTON, Lemuel	9m	C	D.C.	06 MAR 1875	Young Mens
020704	WASHINGTON, Lewis	55y	C	Va.	01 JUL 1879	Beckett's
017236	WASHINGTON, Lizzie	10d	C	D.C.	28 AUG 1878	Beckett's
018673	WASHINGTON, Lizzie	25y	C	Md.	14 JAN 1879	Payne's
019778	WASHINGTON, Lou Emma	1y	C	D.C.	14 APR 1879	Mt. Olivet
008926	WASHINGTON, Louisa A.	1y	M	D.C.	02 SEP 1876	Harmony
015454	WASHINGTON, Lucinda	c.23y	C	D.C.	19 APR 1878	Young Mens
016750	WASHINGTON, Lucinda	1y	C	D.C.	24 JUL 1878	Beckett's
012495	WASHINGTON, Lucy	6m	C	D.C.	23 JUL 1877	Mt. Zion
010850	WASHINGTON, Lucy	19m	C	D.C.	03 MAR 1877	Young Mens
012796	WASHINGTON, Lucy Ellen	4y	M	D.C.	13 AUG 1877	Ebenezer
021015	WASHINGTON, Mabell E.	7m	C	D.C.	19 JUL 1879	Young Mens
018564	WASHINGTON, Mahala	10m	C	D.C.	04 JAN 1879	Payne's
010692	WASHINGTON, Maria	7m	C	D.C.	19 FEB 1877	Ebenezer
014515	WASHINGTON, Maria	65y	C	Md.	21 JAN 1878	Beckett's
017286	WASHINGTON, Maria	47y	C	Va.	01 SEP 1878	Mt. Pleasant
001303	WASHINGTON, Mary	28y	C	Va.	04 DEC 1874	Beckett's
003868	WASHINGTON, Mary	3d	C	D.C.	26 JUN 1875	Beckett's
005701	WASHINGTON, Mary E.	1y	C	D.C.	08 DEC 1875	Brightwood
016777	WASHINGTON, Mary E.	1y	C	D.C.	26 JUL 1878	Harmony
016410	WASHINGTON, Mary Eliza	3y	C	D.C.	02 JUL 1878	Smith's
005998	WASHINGTON, Mary Elizabeth	8m	C	D.C.	11 JAN 1876	Potters Field
009035	WASHINGTON, Mildred	6m	C	D.C.	11 SEP 1876	Young Mens
008738	WASHINGTON, Montague	9m	M	D.C.	19 AUG 1876	Young Mens
001037	WASHINGTON, Nancy	1y	C	D.C.	03 NOV 1874	Mt. Zion
002387	WASHINGTON, Nannie	17y	C	Va.	02 MAR 1875	Mt. Zion

No.	Name	Age	Race	Birth	Death Date	Burial Place
011731	WASHINGTON, Rinaldo Walter	9m	C	D.C.	28 MAY 1877	Ebenezer
017621	WASHINGTON, Rosa	12m	C	D.C.	03 OCT 1878	Beckett's
015899	WASHINGTON, Rosetta	3m	C	D.C.	29 MAY 1878	Mt. Olivet
015401	WASHINGTON, Saml.	31y	C	Va.	14 APR 1878	Young Mens
000082	WASHINGTON, Samuel	1y	C	D.C.	06 AUG 1874	Beckett's
006049	WASHINGTON, Samuel	81y	C	Va.	17 JAN 1876	Harmony
018762	WASHINGTON, Samuel	11m	C	D.C.	21 JAN 1879	Potters Field
011613	WASHINGTON, Sarah	4m	C	D.C.	16 MAY 1877	Ebenezer
015141	WASHINGTON, Sarah	23y	C	Va.	21 MAR 1878	Potters Field
018990	WASHINGTON, Simon	3m	C	D.C.	07 FEB 1879	Potters Field
006773	WASHINGTON, Sophia	28y	C	Md.	21 MAR 1876	Harmony
015603	WASHINGTON, Sophia	25y	C	D.C.	03 MAY 1878	Beckett's
020477	WASHINGTON, Sophia	25y	C	Va.	16 JUN 1879	Beckett's
009454	WASHINGTON, Taylor	c.40y	C	Va.	18 OCT 1876	Harmony
002306	WASHINGTON, Thos.	1y	C	D.C.	24 FEB 1875	Harmony
002578	WASHINGTON, Thos. Jefferson	29y	C	Va.	15 MAR 1875	Harmony
016576	WASHINGTON, W.H.	18y	C	Va.	12 JUL 1878	Harmony
007275	WASHINGTON, William T.	3m	C	D.C.	11 MAY 1876	Mt. Olivet
016341	WASHINGTON, Wm. B.	4m	C	D.C.	27 JUN 1878	Beckett's
008422	WASHINGTON, Wm. F.	2y	C	D.C.	25 JUL 1876	Ebenezer
005924	WASHINGTON, Wm. Henry	1y	M	D.C.	02 JAN 1876	Young Mens
008036	WASHINGTON, Wm. Henry	8d	C	D.C.	05 JUL 1876	Ebenezer
018801	WASSER, Joseph	85y	W	Switz.	24 JAN 1879	Mt. Olivet
003489	WATERKINS, Addison	7y	C	Va.	30 MAY 1875	Young Mens
003507	WATERS, Anna G.	17y	C	Mass.	02 JUN 1875	Harmony
004361	WATERS, Benjamin	1y	C	D.C.	28 JUL 1875	Young Mens
006231	WATERS, Bertha	4y	W	D.C.	03 FEB 1876	Mt. Olivet
005676	WATERS, Elizabeth	3h	C	D.C.	06 DEC 1875	Ebenezer
019793	WATERS, Ethel Brooks	1y	W	D.C.	15 APR 1879	Glenwood
009014	WATERS, Harriet	35y	C	Va.	09 SEP 1876	Young Mens
006793	WATERS, Henry	38y	C	Md.	23 MAR 1876	Mt. Olivet
007572	WATERS, Isaiah	2y	M	D.C.	09 JUN 1876	Potters Field
007302	WATERS, John	4y	C	D.C.	14 MAY 1876	Mt. Pleasant
015869	WATERS, John Golden	49y	W	N.J.	27 MAY 1878	Hopewell, N.J.
014777	WATERS, John J.	34y	W	D.C.	15 FEB 1878	Congressional
010805	WATERS, Joseph B.	5m	C	D.C.	28 FEB 1877	Mt. Olivet
008636	WATERS, Julia	2½d	W	D.C.	10 AUG 1876	Mt. Olivet
002711	WATERS, Lizzie	c.100y	C	Va.	23 MAR 1875	Harmony
011966	WATERS, Loraine	6y	W	D.C.	19 JUN 1877	Glenwood
016697	WATERS, Lydia Ann	19y	C	Md.	20 JUL 1878	Beckett's
009984	WATERS, Maggie	2m	C	D.C.	17 DEC 1876	Ebenezer
013764	WATERS, Maria	1m	W	D.C.	07 NOV 1877	Mt. Olivet
012857	WATERS, Sallie	1y	W	D.C.	17 AUG 1877	Presbyterian
008354	WATERS, William	4m	W	D.C.	20 JUL 1876	Congressional
007966	WATKINS, Elizabeth	4m	C	D.C.	02 JUL 1876	Ebenezer
007355	WATKINS, George Simpson	73y	W	Pa.	20 MAY 1876	Glenwood
002949	WATKINS, Harry Tolbert	7m	W	D.C.	11 APR 1875	Presbyterian
014858	WATKINS, John	1y	M	D.C.	23 FEB 1878	Potters Field
019888	WATKINS, Mary	7m	C	D.C.	24 APR 1879	Mt. Pleasant
002275f	WATKINS, Robert M.	65y	C	Md.	22 FEB 1875	Harmony
017314	WATKINS, Sallie	20y	C	Va.	03 SEP 1878	Young Mens
004305	WATKINS, Sarah	1y	C	D.C.	25 JUL 1875	Young Mens
013567	WATKINS, Simon	27y	W	Va.	19 OCT 1877	Potters Field
005864	WATKINS, Susana	49y	C	D.C.	25 DEC 1875	Harmony
005785	WATKINS, Thomas Coke	75y	W	Md.	18 DEC 1875	Baltimore, Md.
011001	WATSON, Alfred	3y	C	D.C.	16 MAR 1877	Young Mens

No.	Name	Age	Race	Birth	Death Date	Burial Place
018475	WATSON, Alphonso	3y	W	D.C.	26 DEC 1878	Congressional
004895	WATSON, Ann	60y	C	Va.	03 SEP 1875	Washington Asylum
010855	WATSON, Arminta	21y	C	Va.	03 MAR 1877	Mt. Pleasant
021058	WATSON, David	2y	C	D.C.	22 JUL 1879	Young Mens
016271	WATSON, Edgar J.	1m	W	D.C.	22 JUN 1878	Glenwood
002851	WATSON, Ella	15y	C	Va.	02 APR 1875	Harmony
011857	WATSON, Ella	23y	C	Va.	10 JUN 1877	Baptist
015616	WATSON, Emily Will.	3y	W	D.C.	04 MAY 1878	Glenwood
003496	WATSON, George A.	4m	C	D.C.	31 MAY 1875	Mt. Olivet
004435	WATSON, Infant of Alx.	7d	W	D.C.	03 AUG 1875	Congressional
004453	WATSON, Jenny	84y	M	Md.	04 AUG 1875	Potters Field
010613	WATSON, Louisa	c.55y	C	Va.	13 FEB 1877	Baptist
019980	WATSON, Maria A.	65y	W	Md.	03 MAY 1879	Mt. Olivet
011313	WATSON, Mary A.	70y	W	Pa.	12 APR 1877	Franklinville, Pa.
008901	WATSON, Mary B.	36y	W	D.C.	31 AUG 1876	Convent
011153	WATSON, Minte	9m	C	D.C.	29 MAR 1877	Young Mens
004820	WATSON, Richard	35y	M	Va.	29 AUG 1875	Potters Field
003561	WATSON, Rosa	49y	W	Ire.	07 JUN 1875	Mt. Olivet
012833	WATSON, Rosa	18y	C	Va.	15 AUG 1877	Staunton, Va.
003257	WATSON, Sarah E.	1m	C	D.C.	07 MAY 1875	Mt. Pleasant
004660	WATSON, Thomas H.	37d	W	D.C.	18 AUG 1875	Glenwood
020314	WATSON, Viola E.	7m	W	D.C.	05 JUN 1879	Norfolk, Va.
008595	WATTER, Mary	1d	W	D.C.	07 AUG 1876	Congressional
006912	WATTS, Belinda	4y	C	D.C.	03 APR 1876	Small Pox Grounds
016167	WATTS, Charles	8m	C	Md.	14 JUN 1878	Mt. Pleasant
010563	WATTS, Charles Henry	11m	C	D.C.	08 FEB 1877	Ebenezer
012066	WATTS, George	3m	C	D.C.	26 JUN 1877	Mt. Zion
017869	WATTS, George William	23y	C	D.C.	26 OCT 1878	Harmony
016324	WATTS, James Henry	23y	C	Ala.	26 JUN 1878	Beckett's
015103	WATTS, John R.	5y	W	D.C.	17 MAR 1878	Oak Hill
005489	WATTS, Peter	57y	C	Va.	17 NOV 1875	Potters Field
000971	WATTS, Sandy A.	4m	C	D.C.	29 OCT 1874	Beckett's
014859	WATTS, Solomon	4d	C	D.C.	23 FEB 1878	Beckett's
002360	WATTS, Willie	4y	C	D.C.	28 FEB 1875	Potters Field
013359	WAUGH, George	70y	C	Va.	30 SEP 1877	Young Mens
019115	WAUGH, Lucy	18y	C	D.C.	18 FEB 1879	Harmony
018578	WAUGH, Mary E.	3y	C	Va.	05 JAN 1879	Young Mens
011642	WAUGH, William B.	c.60y	W	Md.	18 MAY 1877	Congressional
003499	WAYLEN, George Ellsworth	2m	C	D.C.	31 MAY 1875	Mt. Pleasant
000906	WAYMAN, Geo. Thomas	1y	C	D.C.	23 OCT 1874	Mt. Zion
010656	WAYNE, Mary Elizabeth	7y	C	D.C.	16 FEB 1877	Young Mens
012884	WAYNE, Sarah	12d	C	D.C.	19 AUG 1877	Beckett's
013984	WAYNES, Lewis	41y	C	Va.	01 DEC 1877	Mt. Zion
001513	WEAL, Infant of Elias	8h	W	D.C.	28 DEC 1874	Tennallytown
018187	WEATHERS, James	25y	C	Va.	27 NOV 1878	Potters Field
011564	WEATHERS, Mary D.	2y	C	D.C.	11 MAY 1877	Beckett's
013634	WEAVER, Cecelia	35y	C	Md.	25 OCT 1877	Mt. Pleasant
010105	WEAVER, Charles Edwin	7y	W	N.Y.	28 DEC 1876	Prospect Hill
009939	WEAVER, Douglas	7d	C	D.C.	12 DEC 1876	Mt. Zion
020844	WEAVER, Elizabeth	90y	W	Md.	08 JUL 1879	Oak Hill
003770	WEAVER, Elmina S.	2m	C	D.C.	22 JUN 1875	Graceland
020042	WEAVER, Ida C.	25y	W	Pa.	08 MAY 1879	Oak Hill
002907	WEAVER, James Henry	9m	W	D.C.	07 APR 1875	Oak Hill
016482	WEAVER, John	7y	C	D.C.	06 JUL 1878	Young Mens
012268	WEAVER, Joseph	4y	C	D.C.	08 JUL 1877	Mt. Zion
010961	WEAVER, Leonna	3y	M	D.C.	14 MAR 1877	Mt. Pleasant

District of Columbia Death Records, August 1, 1874 to July 31, 1879

No.	Name	Age	Race	Birth	Death Date	Burial Place
016370	WEAVER, Margaret	3m	W	D.C.	29 JUN 1878	St. Mary's
005410	WEAVER, Zenus	25y	M	Md.	09 NOV 1875	Baltimore, Md.
014634	WEBB, Charles H.	36y	W	Me.	01 FEB 1878	Hospital
014473	WEBB, Edwin Bathurst	5y	W	Tenn.	18 JAN 1878	Oak Hill
005182a	WEBB, Elen	45y	C	Va.	17 OCT 1875	Beckett's
020744	WEBB, Eliza W.	63y	W	S.C.	03 JUL 1879	Oak Hill
004674	WEBB, Francis	8d	C	D.C.	19 AUG 1875	Beckett's
008472	WEBB, George	72y	C	Va.	29 JUL 1876	Potters Field
015499	WEBB, George Spencer	1m	C	D.C.	23 APR 1878	Beckett's
007463	WEBB, Infant of A.W.	8d	W	D.C.	01 JUN 1876	Glenwood
000369	WEBB, Infant of George	0	C	D.C.	30 AUG 1874	Beckett's
004952	WEBB, Infant of George P.	1h	C	D.C.	07 SEP 1875	Ebenezer
005513	WEBB, Jas. Henry	7m	C	D.C.	19 NOV 1875	Potters Field
011136	WEBB, Jas. T.	7m	C	D.C.	28 MAR 1877	Ebenezer
020932	WEBB, John	10m	C	D.C.	14 JUL 1879	Young Mens
001705	WEBB, John Freeman	76y	W	Conn.	12 JAN 1875	Oak Hill
018846	WEBB, Louisa	20y	C	S.C.	27 JAN 1879	Potters Field
009852	WEBB, Peter	20y	C	Va.	03 DEC 1876	Mt. Olivet
009018	WEBB, Rebecca	1y	C	D.C.	10 SEP 1876	Ebenezer
014243	WEBB, Waverley	65y	C	Va.	28 DEC 1877	Potters Field
006889	WEBB, William	6d	C	D.C.	01 APR 1876	Ebenezer
020043	WEBEL, John	9m	W	D.C.	08 MAY 1879	Prospect Hill
011389	WEBER, Charles	41y	W	D.C.	22 APR 1877	Glenwood
005690	WEBER, Conrad	47y	W	Ger.	07 DEC 1875	Hospital
009421	WEBER, Elisabeth	32y	W	Md.	16 OCT 1876	Glenwood
013474	WEBER, Rose L.	2y	W	D.C.	10 OCT 1877	Mt. Olivet
008411	WEBER, Washington W.	5m	W	D.C.	24 JUL 1876	Prospect Hill
020444	WEBSTER, Addison	81y	C	Va.	14 JUN 1879	Harmony
011803	WEBSTER, Alexander	30y	C	D.C.	05 JUN 1877	Potters Field
014736	WEBSTER, Arrabella	74y	C	Va.	10 FEB 1878	Harmony
006564	WEBSTER, Caroline	71y	C	Md.	05 MAR 1876	Harmony
003004	WEBSTER, Eliza A.	9y	C	D.C.	15 APR 1875	Ebenezer
015698	WEBSTER, Elizabeth	67y	W	N.Y.	12 MAY 1878	Graceland
013635	WEBSTER, Ella	6y	C	D.C.	25 OCT 1877	Harmony
001833	WEBSTER, Harriet	13y	C	D.C.	21 JAN 1875	Beckett's
005749	WEBSTER, Henry	32y	W	Scot.	14 DEC 1875	Hamilton, Can.
009679	WEBSTER, Hester	14m	C	D.C.	12 NOV 1876	Harmony
005884	WEBSTER, Infant of Fletcher	4d	C	D.C.	28 DEC 1875	Mt. Pleasant
000428	WEBSTER, James	2y	C	D.C.	04 SEP 1874	Beckett's
017622	WEBSTER, Jane	38y	C	D.C.	03 OCT 1878	Mt. Zion
004386	WEBSTER, John	11m	C	D.C.	30 JUL 1875	Ebenezer
016342	WEBSTER, Joseph F.	1y	C	D.C.	27 JUN 1878	Mt. Olivet
013866	WEBSTER, Josephine	5d	C	D.C.	19 NOV 1877	Beckett's
019415	WEBSTER, Josephine	9m	C	D.C.	15 MAR 1879	Graceland
019203	WEBSTER, Lucretia Ann	65y	C	Md.	25 FEB 1879	Harmony
005252	WEBSTER, Margaret S.	52y	W	Ger.	23 OCT 1875	Prospect Hill
016027	WEBSTER, Martha	39y	C	Md.	05 JUN 1878	Mt. Pleasant
015885	WEBSTER, Mary	4y	C	D.C.	28 MAY 1878	Mt. Pleasant
004989	WEBSTER, Mary E.	4y	W	D.C.	10 SEP 1875	Methodist
014383	WEBSTER, Mary Ellen	2y	C	D.C.	10 JAN 1878	Beckett's
007833	WEBSTER, Phebe A.	67y	W	Pa.	24 JUN 1876	Glenwood
008881	WEBSTER, Rebecca Jane	28y	C	D.C.	30 AUG 1876	Harmony
001171	WEBSTER, Sarah	36y	C	D.C.	17 NOV 1874	Harmony
018615	WEBSTER, Sharlott	78y	C	D.C.	08 JAN 1879	Mt. Zion
001411	WEBSTER, Victoria	15m	W	D.C.	16 DEC 1874	Navy Yard Methodist
020664	WEBSTER, William	11m	C	D.C.	28 JUN 1879	Harmony

District of Columbia Death Records, August 1, 1874 to July 31, 1879

No.	Name	Age	Race	Birth	Death Date	Burial Place
009228	WEBSTER, William E.	49y	W	N.H.	28 SEP 1876	Concord, N.H.
016197	WEDDING, Norman Clarridge	2y	W	Va.	16 JUN 1878	Alexandria, Va.
006454	WEDGE, Barbara	35y	C	Va.	23 FEB 1876	Ebenezer
010276	WEDGE, Edward	35y	C	Md.	13 JAN 1877	Mt. Zion
016986	WEDGE, George	21y	C	D.C.	09 AUG 1878	Harmony
004645	WEEDEN, Lillie	11m	W	D.C.	17 AUG 1875	Congressional
004189	WEEDEN, May	10m	W	D.C.	18 JUL 1875	Congressional
002924	WEEDEN, William	80y	C	Va.	08 APR 1875	Mt. Pleasant
019272	WEEDON, Mary Bernadine	1y	C	D.C.	03 MAR 1879	Mt. Olivet
002840	WEEKS, Albert M.	33y	W	Va.	02 APR 1875	Prince William Co., Va.
008920	WEEKS, Ann Maria	1y	C	D.C.	01 SEP 1876	Young Mens
007192	WEEKS, Arthur	2y	C	D.C.	02 MAY 1876	Young Mens
012474	WEEKS, Jane R.	1y	C	D.C.	22 JUL 1877	Ebenezer
007315	WEEKS, Margaret	24y	W	N.Y.	15 MAY 1876	Long Island, N.Y.
007517	WEEKS, Thomas	5y	W	Va.	05 JUN 1876	Prince William Co., Va.
019950	WEEMS, Hurbet H.	2y	C	D.C.	30 APR 1879	Mt. Pleasant
015917	WEEMS, John W.	78y	C	Md.	30 MAY 1878	Mt. Olivet
000017	WEGE, Anna	9m	W	D.C.	02 AUG 1874	Prospect Hill
010444	WEGE, Emma F.	5m	W	D.C.	29 JAN 1877	Prospect Hill
016236	WEGE, John L.	31y	W	Ger.	20 JUN 1878	Prospect Hill
010419	WEGE, Louis	26y	W	Ger.	27 JAN 1877	Prospect Hill
014289	WEIDE, George	43y	W	Ger.	01 JAN 1878	Prospect Hill
020562	WEIDEMAN, Arther S.	4m	W	D.C.	21 JUN 1879	Prospect Hill
008320	WEIDEMAN, Estella S.M.	1m	W	D.C.	18 JUL 1876	Prospect Hill
020278	WEIGAND, Michael	72y	W	Ger.	02 JUN 1879	St. Mary's
002178	WEIGEL, George L.	5m	W	D.C.	15 FEB 1875	Prospect Hill
003596f	WEIGHTMAN, Mary	48y	W	D.C.	10 JUN 1875	Congressional
006220	WEIGHTMAN, Roger C.	89y	W	Va.	02 FEB 1876	Congressional
019951	WEIGLE, Harriet M.	58y	W	Pa.	30 APR 1879	New Oxford, Pa.
017212	WEIL, Rieke	c.52y	W	Ger.	26 AUG 1878	Washington Hebrew
000325f	WEILER, Willie [Wm. P.]	[6m]	--	--	26 AUG 1874	Oak Hill
009042	WEIRDMAN, John Henry	6m	W	D.C.	12 SEP 1876	Prospect Hill
002488	WEIRICH, C.G.	30y	W	W.Va.	09 MAR 1875	Council Bluff, Ia.
001502	WEIRMAN, John M.	37y	W	Pa.	19 DEC 1874	Hospital
009008	WEIRMAN, Mary	78y	W	Pa.	09 SEP 1876	Lancaster, Pa.
008205	WEIRTS, Lustave	45y	W	Ger.	12 JUL 1876	Potters Field
006900	WEISBACKER, Albert	63y	W	Ger.	02 APR 1876	Mt. Olivet
002582	WEISBATH, Dorothea	65y	W	Ger.	15 MAR 1875	Glenwood
001160	WEISENTHAL, Herman	26y	W	Ger.	16 NOV 1874	Prospect Hill
013419	WEISMAN, Minnie	20y	W	Md.	06 OCT 1877	Prospect Hill
006239	WEISS, Chs. N.	28y	W	Ger.	04 FEB 1876	Prospect Hill
002543	WEISS, Henry Lewis	3y	W	D.C.	13 MAR 1875	Prospect Hill
005941	WEITZEL, Conrad	58y	W	Ger.	04 JAN 1876	Prospect Hill
019792	WEITZELL, Elizabeth	5y	W	D.C.	15 APR 1879	Prospect Hill
002313	WEITZELL, Mary C.	30y	W	D.C.	25 FEB 1875	Holy Rood
000773	WELCH, Anna Maria	4y	C	D.C.	10 OCT 1874	Potters Field
015380	WELCH, Anne G.	12d	W	D.C.	12 APR 1878	Oak Hill
018143	WELCH, Daniel	63y	W	Pa.	24 NOV 1878	Bellefonte, Pa.
012577	WELCH, Edw.	1y	W	D.C.	28 JUL 1877	Ebenezer
002117	WELCH, Eugen	9m	C	D.C.	11 FEB 1875	Beckett's
005500	WELCH, Gardiner	65y	W	Mass.	14 NOV 1875	Hospital
011064	WELCH, Henry	40y	C	N.C.	21 MAR 1877	Young Mens
002931	WELCH, Hubbard Prince	32y	W	Va.	09 APR 1875	Oak Hill
017624	WELCH, James	75y	W	Pa.	03 OCT 1878	Prince George's Co., Md.
018010	WELCH, Mary Lucinda	37y	C	Md.	10 NOV 1878	Mt. Pleasant
001135	WELCH, Michael	55y	W	Ire.	13 NOV 1874	Holy Rood

No.	Name	Age	Race	Birth	Death Date	Burial Place
003624	WELCH, Michael	1y	W	D.C.	13 JUN 1875	Mt. Olivet
016381	WELCH, Sue	1y	W	Md.	30 JUN 1878	Baltimore, Md.
003483f	WELCH, William	36y	W	Ire.	29 MAY 1875	Hospital
010903	WELCH, Willie	14d	W	D.C.	07 MAR 1877	Graceland
002773	WELCKER, John	38y	W	Ger.	28 MAR 1875	N.Y. City
012070	WELCKER, Peter Anderson	3m	W	D.C.	26 JUN 1877	Prospect Hill
017454	WELDEN, Louisa	33y	C	D.C.	18 SEP 1878	Young Mens
003684	WELDEN, William	8m	C	D.C.	10 JUN 1875	Mt. Pleasant
018890	WELDON, Mary	96y	C	Md.	30 JAN 1879	Mt. Olivet
006557	WELLFORD, Rebecca	83y	W	Md.	04 MAR 1876	Oak Hill
019857	WELLNER, William	49y	W	Ger.	21 APR 1879	Prospect Hill
010213	WELLS, Danl.	71y	W	Eng.	07 JAN 1877	Oak Hill
003301	WELLS, Edward	17y	C	Md.	12 MAY 1875	Mt. Olivet
015604	WELLS, Edward H.	34y	W	Del.	03 MAY 1878	Oak Hill
002767	WELLS, Edward Lloyd	72y	W	Del.	28 MAR 1875	Oak Hill
013754	WELLS, Elizabeth Estell	7d	W	D.C.	06 NOV 1877	Mt. Olivet
008543	WELLS, Fanny	32y	W	U.S.	03 AUG 1876	Potters Field
004942	WELLS, Frank	10m	C	Pa.	06 SEP 1875	Mt. Olivet
005224	WELLS, Herbert	8m	W	D.C.	29 SEP 1875	Congressional
008874	WELLS, Infant of Fanny	3m	W	U.S.	29 AUG 1876	Potters Field
015918	WELLS, J.T.	21y	W	Pa.	30 MAY 1878	Oak Hill
012883	WELLS, Louisa	23y	C	Va.	19 AUG 1877	Potters Field
016272	WELLS, Lucy	13y	C	D.C.	22 JUN 1878	Young Mens
003869	WELLS, Lula	3y	C	D.C.	26 JUN 1875	Beckett's
017474	WELLS, Maria	38y	C	Md.	20 SEP 1878	Mt. Olivet
016892	WELLS, Martha	24y	C	Va.	03 AUG 1878	Mt. Pleasant
017730	WELLS, Martha A.	48y	W	Va.	13 OCT 1878	Rock Creek
020370	WELLS, Mary B.	6y	W	Va.	09 JUN 1879	Fairfax Station, Va.
020126	WELLS, Mary Ellen	1m	C	D.C.	16 MAY 1879	Beckett's
020953	WELLS, Morris	4y	C	D.C.	15 JUL 1879	Baptist
006851	WELLS, Victoria	c.24y	C	Md.	28 MAR 1876	Harmony
000660	WELLS, William Allen	66y	W	Conn.	28 SEP 1874	Glenwood
019647	WELSCH, Mary Anna	1y	W	D.C.	03 APR 1879	Mt. Olivet
013155	WELSH, Alford C.	21y	W	Md.	10 SEP 1877	Glenwood
006238	WELSH, Bartly	45y	W	Ire.	04 FEB 1876	Holy Rood
002197	WELSH, Catharine	64y	W	Ire.	17 FEB 1875	Mt. Olivet
002216	WELSH, Catharine	2y	W	D.C.	18 FEB 1875	Mt. Olivet
013016	WELSH, Ellen	56y	W	Ire.	29 AUG 1877	Mt. Olivet
020971	WELSH, Harry	15y	M	Pa.	16 JUL 1879	Graceland
004054	WELSH, Margaret	10y	W	Ire.	08 JUL 1875	Mt. Olivet
019393	WELSH, Martha	3y	C	D.C.	13 MAR 1879	Mt. Pleasant
015784	WELSH, Mary Dominica, Sister	70y	W	Pa.	20 MAY 1878	Convent
004209	WELSH, Michael	21y	W	D.C.	19 JUL 1875	Mt. Olivet
020635	WELSH, Morgan J.	4y	W	D.C.	26 JUN 1879	Holy Rood
012751	WELSH, Patrick	10m	W	D.C.	09 AUG 1877	Holy Rood
012944	WELSH, Thomas	40y	W	Ire.	24 AUG 1877	Washington Asylum
006117	WENDEHUTH, Rebecca	44y	W	Ger.	23 JAN 1876	Prospect Hill
008366	WENGER, John	53y	W	Ger.	21 JUL 1876	Prospect Hill
008810	WERNER, Hermann	28y	W	Ger.	24 AUG 1876	Congressional
008932	WESER, John Francis	3y	W	D.C.	02 SEP 1876	Mt. Olivet
003960	WESLEY, John William	12d	W	D.C.	01 JUL 1875	St. Mary's
000168	WESSEL, Antone David	5d	W	D.C.	13 AUG 1874	Prospect Hill
011294	WEST, Adora	2y	C	D.C.	10 APR 1877	Harmony
009888	WEST, Ann E.	59y	W	Va.	06 DEC 1876	Glenwood
020689	WEST, Charles Fletcher	7y	W	D.C.	30 JUN 1879	Oak Hill
013483	WEST, Charles Sumner	8y	C	D.C.	11 OCT 1877	Mt. Olivet

District of Columbia Death Records, August 1, 1874 to July 31, 1879   365

No.	Name	Age	Race	Birth	Death Date	Burial Place
003137	WEST, Clarisa	62y	M	Md.	26 APR 1875	Young Mens
016724	WEST, David	10m	C	D.C.	22 JUL 1878	Beckett's
021120	WEST, Ellen	45y	C	Md.	26 JUL 1879	Hillsdale
005735	WEST, Emily Jane	3y	C	D.C.	12 DEC 1875	Young Mens
020143	WEST, Emma N.	8y	C	D.C.	18 MAY 1879	Potters Field
003696	WEST, Eugene	6m	C	D.C.	18 JUN 1875	Beckett's
012834	WEST, Eveline	76y	C	Va.	15 AUG 1877	Mt. Olivet
001999	WEST, Francis	9m	M	D.C.	02 FEB 1875	Potters Field
018954	WEST, George	32y	C	Va.	04 FEB 1879	Young Mens
005691	WEST, Harry Stewart	1y	W	D.C.	07 DEC 1875	Nokesville, Va.
000646	WEST, Henreter, Mrs.	45y	C	Md.	26 SEP 1874	Beckett's
008588	WEST, Ida	4m	C	D.C.	07 AUG 1876	Potters Field
000927	WEST, Infant of Julia	8½h	C	D.C.	23 OCT 1874	Potters Field
003635	WEST, James E.	8m	C	D.C.	13 JUN 1875	Young Mens
008882	WEST, Jenny	28y	C	Va.	30 AUG 1876	Young Mens
005689	WEST, John	7y	C	Md.	07 DEC 1875	Young Mens
018122	WEST, John	58y	W	Pa.	22 NOV 1878	Prince George's Co., Md.
002865	WEST, John H.	63y	C	Va.	03 APR 1875	Young Mens
002647	WEST, Lewis	79y	C	Md.	19 MAR 1875	Young Mens
006347	WEST, Lilly	10m	C	D.C.	13 FEB 1876	Potters Field
019202	WEST, Louisa	4y	C	D.C.	25 FEB 1879	Prince George's Co., Md.
006995	WEST, Lydia	3y	C	D.C.	11 APR 1876	Mt. Zion
007637	WEST, Magdalene	4m	W	D.C.	13 JUN 1876	Ebenezer
018430	WEST, Mary	66y	C	Md.	22 DEC 1878	Harmony
001198	WEST, Mary Ann	57y	W	Va.	20 NOV 1874	Falls Church, Va.
020020	WEST, Mary Ann	73y	W	Md.	06 MAY 1879	Baltimore, Md.
018626	WEST, Samuel	4m	C	D.C.	09 JAN 1879	Harmony
001565	WEST, Stillman	66y	W	Ver.	01 JAN 1875	Farm near Bennings
015858	WEST, Thomas	60y	C	Md.	26 MAY 1878	Potters Field
004759	WEST, Victoria	10m	C	D.C.	25 AUG 1875	Young Mens
017028	WEST, Washington	17y	C	Md.	12 AUG 1878	Moore's
019907	WEST, William	80y	C	Va.	26 APR 1879	Mt. Pleasant
020606	WEST, William Callender	54y	W	N.Y.	24 JUN 1879	Congressional/N.Y.
017969	WEST, Wm.	6m	C	D.C.	06 NOV 1878	Potters Field
014313	WESTERMAN, Willie J.	2y	W	D.C.	03 JAN 1878	Presbyterian
016483	WESTERN, Charles	22d	W	D.C.	06 JUL 1878	Prospect Hill
016185	WESTERN, Charlotte	19y	W	Pa.	15 JUN 1878	Prospect Hill
015569	WESTFALL, Philip Winslow	8y	W	D.C.	30 APR 1878	Amenia, N.Y.
020766	WESTON, John	39y	C	Va.	04 JUL 1879	Potters Field
020346	WESTPHALL, August H.	48y	W	Prus.	08 JUN 1879	Prospect Hill
009667	WESTWOOD, John Hardy	78y	W	Md.	10 NOV 1876	Greenmount, Balt., Md.
007929	WESTWOOD, Susan	8m	W	D.C.	29 JUN 1876	Baltimore, Md.
012943	WESTWOOD, Wm. Penn	2m	W	D.C.	24 AUG 1877	Baltimore, Md.
000575	WEYGANT, Charles Wine	5m	W	D.C.	20 SEP 1874	Congressional
007807	WEYMAN, Elizabeth Jane	53y	W	S.W.	23 JUN 1876	Glenwood
001604	WHALAN, Hester	3y	W	D.C.	03 JAN 1875	Mt. Olivet
019232	WHALAND, William	9m	W	D.C.	27 FEB 1879	Mt. Olivet
020345	WHALEN, Edgar	20y	W	D.C.	08 JUN 1879	Congressional
004733	WHALEN, Joseph	9y	C	D.C.	23 AUG 1875	Young Mens
014718	WHALEN, Mary	11y	W	D.C.	08 FEB 1878	Mt. Olivet
007586	WHALEN, Susan	40y	W	Md.	10 JUN 1876	Mt. Olivet
005181a	WHALEY, John L.	71y	W	Va.	17 OCT 1875	Congressional
005316	WHARTON, Mary E.	2m	C	D.C.	30 OCT 1875	Holy Rood
010718	WHARTON, Penelope G.	c.59y	W	Eng.	21 FEB 1877	Congressional
018657	WHEAT, Alvenda	23y	W	W.Va.	12 JAN 1879	Glenwood
021016	WHEAT, Jesse Cummins	32y	W	W.Va.	19 JUL 1879	Glenwood

District of Columbia Death Records, August 1, 1874 to July 31, 1879

No.	Name	Age	Race	Birth	Death Date	Burial Place
020548	WHEAT, Marian	8m	W	Va.	20 JUN 1879	Richmond, Va.
011483	WHEATLEY, Caroline	65y	W	Md.	01 MAY 1877	Oak Hill
010400	WHEATLEY, James H.	72y	W	Md.	25 JAN 1877	Holy Rood
004821	WHEATLEY, William Ignatius	61y	W	Md.	29 AUG 1875	Mt. Olivet
012555	WHEEDON, Annie May	5m	C	D.C.	27 JUL 1877	Potters Field
004024	WHEELER, Benjamin	5y	C	D.C.	06 JUL 1875	Young Mens
004743	WHEELER, Daniel E.	11m	W	D.C.	24 AUG 1875	Congressional
000126	WHEELER, Edward	36y	W	N.Y.	10 AUG 1874	Congressional
004284	WHEELER, Ela B. DeFreitas	7m	W	D.C.	24 JUL 1875	Oak Hill
002389	WHEELER, Fanny Osborne	29y	W	N.J	02 MAR 1875	Oak Hill
002483	WHEELER, George	1m	C	D.C.	09 MAR 1875	Holy Rood
015775	WHEELER, George	2m	C	D.C.	19 MAY 1878	Mt. Zion
006491	WHEELER, Georgeanna	14m	C	D.C.	27 FEB 1876	Mt. Olivet
000006	WHEELER, Gordon S.	1y	C	D.C.	01 AUG 1874	Young Mens
003908	WHEELER, Harry Thomas	14d	W	D.C.	28 JUN 1875	Graceland
011819	WHEELER, Ida	11d	W	D.C.	06 JUN 1877	Congressional
007462	WHEELER, Infant of William	8h	W	D.C.	01 JUN 1876	Graceland
015829	WHEELER, Laura	16y	C	D.C.	24 MAY 1878	Young Mens
016339	WHEELER, Margaret	9m	C	D.C.	27 JUN 1878	Mt. Olivet
000088	WHEELER, Mary	35y	M	D.C.	07 AUG 1874	Mt. Olivet
014341	WHEELER, Mary Agnes	2y	C	D.C.	06 JAN 1878	Mt. Olivet
003634	WHEELER, Mary Ellen	11d	C	D.C.	13 JUN 1875	Mt. Olivet
006538	WHEELER, Mary K.	48y	W	N.Y.	03 MAR 1876	Malone, N.Y.
020746	WHEELER, Samuel D.	3m	C	D.C.	03 JUL 1879	Mt. Pleasant
012684	WHEELER, Thomas	6d	C	D.C.	05 AUG 1877	Mt. Olivet
002952	WHEELER, Thos. W.	20y	C	D.C.	11 APR 1875	Mt. Zion
009275	WHEELER, William Henry	4m	C	D.C.	02 OCT 1876	Potters Field
006559	WHEELOCK, Arthur S.	3y	W	D.C.	04 MAR 1876	Congressional
000533f	WHEELOCK, Madison	18m	W	Md.	17 SEP 1874	Congressional
004780	WHEET, Infant of Robert	28h	C	D.C.	27 AUG 1875	Beckett's
009825	WHELAN, Fanny	26y	W	D.C.	29 NOV 1876	Presbyterian
013663	WHELAN, Ruth Ann	26y	W	D.C.	28 OCT 1877	Presbyterian
017677	WHELAN, Thomas	55y	W	Ire.	08 OCT 1878	Mt. Olivet
015294	WHIPPLE, Jenesha	78y	W	Conn.	05 APR 1878	Cazenovia, N.Y.
000776	WHITAKER, Catharine	55y	C	Va.	10 OCT 1874	"On the Farm," Md.
009278	WHITAKER, Samuel	55y	W	Ire.	02 OCT 1876	Mt. Olivet
020247	WHITALL, Mary N.	68y	W	N.J.	31 MAY 1879	Oak Hill
013568	WHITCOMB, Frederick Adolphus	9y	W	D.C.	19 OCT 1877	Glenwood
013948	WHITCOMB, Gustavus Wm.	3y	W	D.C.	27 NOV 1877	Glenwood
018452	WHITE, Aaron	54y	C	U.S.	24 DEC 1878	Beckett's
007344	WHITE, Ada	7m	M	Va.	19 MAY 1876	Young Mens
002736	WHITE, Aley	53y	C	Va.	25 MAR 1875	Beckett's
006398	WHITE, Amanda R.	35y	W	N.J.	17 FEB 1876	Congressional
011399	WHITE, Amy Bradley	51y	W	D.C.	22 APR 1877	Glenwood
011171	WHITE, Ann	1m	W	D.C.	30 MAR 1877	Mt. Olivet
007988	WHITE, Ann Bernedethe	5m	W	D.C.	03 JUL 1876	Mt. Olivet
019135	WHITE, Anthony	50y	C	Va.	20 FEB 1879	Potters Field
020021	WHITE, Becky	4y	C	D.C.	06 MAY 1879	Potters Field
005138	WHITE, Bessie	5m	C	D.C.	22 SEP 1875	Ebenezer
012515	WHITE, C.J.	37y	W	D.C.	24 JUL 1877	Congressional
013115	WHITE, Catharine E.	2y	W	D.C.	07 SEP 1877	Holy Rood
009083	WHITE, Charles	35y	C	D.C.	15 SEP 1876	Ebenezer
013056	WHITE, Charles	1y	C	D.C.	01 SEP 1877	Oak Hill
016109	WHITE, Charles	29y	C	Va.	10 JUN 1879	Young Mens
015263	WHITE, Charles Ignatius, Rev.	71y	W	Md.	01 APR 1878	Mt. Olivet
017299	WHITE, Chas. Henry	18y	W	Pa.	02 SEP 1878	Glenwood

District of Columbia Death Records, August 1, 1874 to July 31, 1879

No.	Name	Age	Race	Birth	Death Date	Burial Place
013552	WHITE, Clara B.	1½d	W	D.C.	17 OCT 1877	Glenwood
003991	WHITE, Dolly	58y	C	Va.	03 JUL 1875	Harmony
003392	WHITE, Elizabeth	60y	C	D.C.	21 MAY 1875	Harmony
021071	WHITE, Elizabeth	25d	W	D.C.	23 JUL 1879	Mt. Olivet
011244	WHITE, Ellen	2d	W	D.C.	06 APR 1877	Mt. Olivet
017978	WHITE, Emma A.	28y	C	Va.	07 NOV 1878	Baptist
000542	WHITE, Emma M.	2y	W	N.Y.	17 SEP 1874	Oak Hill
011720	WHITE, Emma T.	33y	W	D.C.	27 MAY 1877	Holy Rood
007993	WHITE, Enoch	77y	W	Va.	03 JUL 1876	Oak Hill
004454	WHITE, Frances Victoria	18m	C	D.C.	04 AUG 1875	Moore's
005832	WHITE, Francis	4m	C	D.C.	22 DEC 1875	Young Mens
020325	WHITE, Francis	3m	W	D.C.	06 JUN 1879	Mt. Olivet
004238	WHITE, Francis A.	3y	W	D.C.	21 JUL 1875	Holy Rood
017781	WHITE, Frank Young	3y	W	D.C.	17 OCT 1878	Congressional
015801	WHITE, Frederick H.	16m	C	D.C.	21 MAY 1878	Mt. Pleasant
002021	WHITE, George	65y	C	Va.	04 FEB 1875	Harmony
016139	WHITE, George	37y	C	Va.	12 JUN 1878	Mt. Pleasant Plain
012844	WHITE, Harriet	35y	C	Va.	16 AUG 1877	Ebenezer
015134	WHITE, Harry H.	8y	W	D.C.	20 MAR 1878	Glenwood
004572	WHITE, Hattie	1y	C	D.C.	12 AUG 1875	Beckett's
001226	WHITE, Henrietta Pearl	1m	C	D.C.	25 NOV 1874	Young Mens
011866	WHITE, Henry	80y	C	Va.	11 JUN 1877	Potters Field
011785	WHITE, Henry	49y	C	Va.	03 JUN 1877	Young Mens
009653	WHITE, Horace T.	65y	W	Ver.	09 NOV 1876	Bennington, Ver.
001169	WHITE, Infant of Charles	28d	C	D.C.	17 NOV 1874	Potters Field
003663	WHITE, Infant of James	11d	C	D.C.	16 JUN 1875	New Haven
016043	WHITE, Infant of James	18d	C	D.C.	06 JUN 1878	Potters Field
005173	WHITE, Isaac	23d	C	D.C.	25 SEP 1875	Young Mens
014791	WHITE, Ivey	2y	C	D.C.	16 FEB 1878	Harmony
005802	WHITE, James	6m	C	D.C.	19 DEC 1875	Ebenezer
003990	WHITE, James	10d	C	D.C.	03 JUL 1875	Ebenezer
006938	WHITE, James	5y	C	Va.	05 APR 1876	Young Mens
014141	WHITE, James	c.40y	C	N.Y.	19 DEC 1877	Young Mens
002349	WHITE, James H.	1y	C	D.C.	28 FEB 1875	Ebenezer
012843	WHITE, Jane	85y	C	Va.	16 AUG 1877	Young Mens
003162	WHITE, John	75y	W	Eng.	29 APR 1875	Glenwood
005068a	WHITE, John	53y	W	Ire.	05 OCT 1875	Mt. Olivet
006287	WHITE, John	75y	C	Md.	09 FEB 1876	Ebenezer
016779	WHITE, John H.	40y	C	S.C.	26 JUL 1878	Young Mens
011885	WHITE, John Henry	11m	W	N.Y.	14 JUN 1877	Mt. Olivet
013680	WHITE, John Henry	3m	M	D.C.	30 OCT 1877	Beckett's
013859	WHITE, John Thomas	55y	W	Md.	18 NOV 1877	Congressional
000353	WHITE, John Wesly	1m	C	D.C.	28 AUG 1874	Beckett's
000161	WHITE, Jonah Henry	11m	W	Va.	12 AUG 1874	Congressional
002184	WHITE, Joseph A.	8m	C	D.C.	15 FEB 1875	Near Aqueduct Bridge
015104	WHITE, Josephine	4m	W	U.S.	17 MAR 1878	Mt. Olivet
005313	WHITE, L.E.	1y	C	D.C.	30 OCT 1875	Ebenezer
019039	WHITE, Lena	1y	C	D.C.	11 FEB 1879	Beckett's
007092	WHITE, Lewis	2y	C	D.C.	23 APR 1876	Harmony
007618	WHITE, Lily	4m	C	D.C.	12 JUN 1876	Potters Field
021057	WHITE, Lullie	5m	C	D.C.	22 JUL 1879	Young Mens
012552	WHITE, Lullu	6m	W	D.C.	27 JUL 1877	Potters Field
016218	WHITE, Lydia	1m	C	D.C.	18 JUN 1878	Mt. Olivet
004148	WHITE, Mary	20d	W	D.C.	15 JUL 1875	Mt. Olivet
002414	WHITE, Mary	4m	C	D.C.	04 MAR 1875	Mt. Olivet
005459	WHITE, Mary	6m	C	D.C.	14 NOV 1875	Mt. Zion

No.	Name	Age	Race	Birth	Death Date	Burial Place
007705	WHITE, Mary	10d	W	D.C.	17 JUN 1876	Mt. Olivet
005544	WHITE, Mary A.	3y	C	D.C.	23 NOV 1875	Beckett's
000285	WHITE, Mary Ellen	2m	C	D.C.	22 AUG 1874	Beckett's
015626	WHITE, Michael	33y	W	Ire.	05 MAY 1878	Mt. Olivet
010153	WHITE, Milton	30y	W	D.C.	02 JAN 1877	Washington Asylum
017634	WHITE, Peter	50y	C	Va.	04 OCT 1878	Mt. Pleasant
016428	WHITE, Philip	1y	C	D.C.	03 JUL 1878	Mt. Pleasant
005378	WHITE, Rosa	18y	C	Md.	06 NOV 1875	Potters Field
009616	WHITE, Ruth	48y	W	Va.	04 NOV 1876	Oak Hill
020768	WHITE, Ruth E.	6m	W	D.C.	04 JUL 1879	Presbyterian
006820	WHITE, Sarah	3y	C	D.C.	25 MAR 1876	Ebenezer
017705	WHITE, Sarah R.	9m	C	D.C.	11 OCT 1878	Beckett's
002678	WHITE, Solomon	20y	C	Va.	21 MAR 1875	Young Mens
009116	WHITE, Susan	16y	C	Md.	17 SEP 1876	Mt. Olivet
015886	WHITE, Susan	5m	W	D.C.	28 MAY 1878	Mt. Olivet
003718	WHITE, Theodore	3m	C	D.C.	19 JUN 1875	Harmony
020159	WHITE, Thomas P.	c.48y	W	Md.	20 MAY 1879	Mt. Olivet
012362	WHITE, William	60y	W	Ire.	15 JUL 1877	Mt. Olivet
012102	WHITE, William H.	24y	C	S.C.	28 JUN 1877	Young Mens
006148	WHITE, William P., Jr.	1y	W	D.C.	26 JAN 1876	Congressional
015207	WHITE, Willis	1y	C	D.C.	27 MAR 1878	Beckett's
019040	WHITE, Wm.	49y	C	Va.	11 FEB 1879	Harmony
010647	WHITE, Wm. Henry	3m	W	D.C.	15 FEB 1877	Mt. Olivet
019454	WHITE, Wylie	25y	C	Va.	18 MAR 1879	Potters Field
001446	WHITEHEAD, Catherine	33y	W	Ire.	20 DEC 1874	Mt. Olivet
003173	WHITEHEAD, Harry	4m	W	D.C.	30 APR 1875	Mt. Olivet
000793	WHITEHEAD, Lawrence B.	3y	C	Va.	13 OCT 1874	Mt. Pleasant
000938	WHITEING, Thomas	10y	C	Va.	26 OCT 1874	Beckett's
005812	WHITELEY, Jefferson	40y	C	Va.	20 DEC 1875	Young Mens
020705	WHITEMORE, Clara B.	28y	W	W.Va.	01 JUL 1879	Congressional
008596	WHITEMORE, Nellie Fenton	1y	W	D.C.	07 AUG 1876	Alexandria, Va.
001543	WHITESICK, James	5y	W	Ky.	31 DEC 1874	Franklin, Ky.
021091	WHITESIDE, John W.	11y	W	D.C.	24 JUL 1879	Brookeville, Md.
013166	WHITFIELD, Mary Elizabeth	2y	C	D.C.	11 SEP 1877	Macedonia
007949	WHITING, Catharine	68y	C	Va.	01 JUL 1876	Harmony
004787	WHITING, Elizabeth Sullivan	51y	W	Pa.	27 AUG 1875	Oak Hill
016013	WHITING, Georgia	9m	C	D.C.	04 JUN 1878	Mt. Zion
014806	WHITING, Henry	70y	C	U.S.	17 FEB 1878	Potters Field
019523	WHITING, Lydia	6y	C	Md.	23 MAR 1879	Mt. Olivet
008375	WHITING, Mary	5y	C	D.C.	22 JUL 1876	Young Mens
001087	WHITING, Rachel Ann	30y	C	Md.	08 NOV 1874	Beckett's
006887	WHITING, Richard H.	21y	W	D.C.	01 APR 1876	Oak Hill
018509	WHITING, Robert	50y	C	Va.	29 DEC 1878	Alexandria, Va.
001656	WHITLEY, Wilson	20y	C	Va.	08 JAN 1875	Harmony
001374	WHITLING, Cornelia	6m	C	D.C.	13 DEC 1874	Harmony
020080	WHITLOCK, Martha A.	58y	W	Va.	12 MAY 1879	Petersburg, Va.
003892	WHITLOE, F.J.	2m	M	D.C.	27 JUN 1875	Holy Rood
014577	WHITLOW, Carrie	8m	C	D.C.	27 JAN 1878	Mt. Pleasant
011663	WHITLOW, Harriet	1y	C	D.C.	21 MAY 1877	Mt. Pleasant
003239	WHITLOW, Julia M.	21y	M	D.C.	06 MAY 1875	Holy Rood
009948	WHITLOW, Thomas Grant	14m	C	D.C.	13 DEC 1876	Harmony
007997	WHITLOW, Wilson Young	8m	C	D.C.	04 JUL 1876	Harmony
015271	WHITLY, Ernest	8m	C	D.C.	02 APR 1878	Harmony
020526	WHITMAN, Elma May	3m	W	D.C.	19 JUN 1879	Congressional
007996	WHITMORE, Alvah D.H.	10m	W	D.C.	04 JUL 1876	Graceland
007558	WHITMORE, Louis Eugene	8m	W	D.C.	08 JUN 1876	Graceland

District of Columbia Death Records, August 1, 1874 to July 31, 1879

No.	Name	Age	Race	Birth	Death Date	Burial Place
015673	WHITNEY, Ann	54y	W	Md.	09 MAY 1878	Baltimore, Md.
015487	WHITNEY, Catharine Moore	68y	W	N.C.	22 APR 1878	Rock Creek
019920	WHITNEY, George H.	44y	W	N.Y.	27 APR 1879	Baltimore, Md.
006928	WHITNEY, Infant of A.C.	4d	W	D.C.	04 APR 1876	Congressional
003249	WHITNEY, Infant of Jessie	1d	C	D.C.	07 MAY 1875	Ebenezer
003909	WHITNEY, John Francis	4m	C	D.C.	28 JUN 1875	Young Mens
019022	WHITON, Anna	6m	C	D.C.	10 FEB 1879	Mt. Zion
019668	WHITON, Lewis C.	c.50y	W	Mass.	05 APR 1879	Boston, Mass.
015402	WHITTELSEY, Louise M., Mrs.	56y	W	N.Y.	14 APR 1878	Oak Hill
005354	WHITTHAFT, William George	22y	W	D.C.	03 NOV 1875	Glenwood
007584	WHITTIER, Cyrus M.	39y	W	Me.	10 JUN 1876	Congressional
016825	WHITTING, Caroline	50y	C	Va.	29 JUL 1878	Young Mens
018943	WHITTINGTON, Dora	22y	C	Md.	03 FEB 1879	Payne's
019969	WHITTINGTON, Gracie G.	4m	C	D.C.	02 MAY 1879	Payne's
009894	WHITTINGTON, Joseph F.	6m	C	D.C.	07 DEC 1876	Ebenezer
003930	WHITTINGTON, Lettie	91y	C	Md.	29 JUN 1875	Mt. Pleasant
010270	WHITTLESEY, Annie Stratton	25y	W	D.C.	12 JAN 1877	Congressional
019367	WHITTLESEY, Jane N.	28y	W	D.C.	11 MAR 1879	Congressional
002300	WHITTON, James	31y	C	Va.	24 FEB 1875	Harmony
020918	WHITTY, Jasper M.	44y	W	Ire.	13 JUL 1879	Mt. Olivet
015800	WHITTY, Timothy	10d	W	D.C.	21 MAY 1878	Mt. Olivet
001151	WHOLLY, James W.	28y	W	Mass.	15 NOV 1874	Malden, Mass.
016392	WHORLY, Elizebeth	10m	W	D.C.	01 JUL 1878	St. Mary's
003671	WHORTON, Infant of John	7d	W	D.C.	17 JUN 1875	Glenwood
009519	WHUSTON, William P.	65y	W	Ga.	24 OCT 1876	Oak Hill
020799	WICK, Infant of Wm.	14d	W	D.C.	06 JUL 1879	Prospect Hill
018195	WICKES, Maria M.	37y	W	N.Y.	28 NOV 1878	Mt. Olivet
020415	WICKS, Maria Louisa	32y	C	Va.	12 JUN 1879	Mt. Pleasant Plain
018790	WICKS, Martha Ann	10m	C	D.C.	23 JAN 1879	Mt. Olivet
008936	WIDDICOMBE, Robert	77y	W	Eng.	02 SEP 1876	Congressional
010145	WIDMAYER, Charles	1m	W	D.C.	01 JAN 1877	Prospect Hill
005442	WIDMEYER, Christian Jacob	6d	W	D.C.	12 NOV 1875	Prospect Hill
013190	WIDMEYER, Francis C.	1y	W	D.C.	13 SEP 1877	Mt. Olivet
014981	WIDMEYER, Geo.	1m	W	D.C.	07 MAR 1878	Prospect Hill
005984	WIEDERMAN, Debora Jane	4w	W	D.C.	09 JAN 1876	Mt. Olivet
009700	WIESSNER, Anton	22y	W	Md.	15 NOV 1876	P.G. Co., Md., farm
009470	WIETBERGER, Verlinda Mary	75y	W	D.C.	20 OCT 1876	Rock Creek
000256	WIGGINS, Amos	1y	C	D.C.	20 AUG 1874	Beckett's
003946f	WIGGINS, John	35y	C	Va.	30 JUN 1875	Ebenezer
005926	WIGGINS, John	10d	C	D.C.	02 JAN 1876	Ebenezer
016155	WIGGINTON, Wm. E.	7y	C	D.C.	13 JUN 1878	Mt. Pleasant
007870	WILCKINS, Manda	3m	W	D.C.	26 JUN 1876	Congressional
007055	WILCOX, Edwin G.	53y	W	Conn.	19 APR 1876	Oak Hill
005555	WILCOXEN, Esther	72y	W	W.Va.	24 NOV 1875	Congressional
008640	WILD, Francis	74y	W	Ger.	10 AUG 1876	Baltimore
005173a	WILDER, Sarah Hill	74y	W	Mass.	16 OCT 1875	West Roxbury, Mass.
019495	WILER, Joseph	7y	W	D.C.	21 MAR 1879	Mt. Olivet
020036	WILES, Charles H.	8y	W	Md.	07 MAY 1879	Graceland
000531	WILEY, Agnes	29d	C	D.C.	16 SEP 1874	Mt. Zion
001843	WILEY, Clarence	7m	C	D.C.	22 JAN 1875	Young Mens
015367	WILEY, Edward	10d	W	D.C.	11 APR 1878	Congressional
019692	WILEY, Infant of Edward F.	4h	W	D.C.	07 APR 1879	Congressional
005087	WILEY, Infant of W.L.	8h	W	D.C.	09 SEP 1875	Near Sandy Spring, Md.
000908	WILEY, Nelson	75y	C	Va.	23 OCT 1874	Potters Field
007999	WILIAMS, James	2m	C	D.C.	04 JUL 1876	Ebenezer
020889	WILIAMS, Nettie	1y	C	D.C.	11 JUL 1879	Mt. Pleasant

District of Columbia Death Records, August 1, 1874 to July 31, 1879

No.	Name	Age	Race	Birth	Death Date	Burial Place
011074	WILIAMS, Percey	2m	C	D.C.	22 MAR 1877	Young Mens
004012	WILINGTON, Allen B.	3y	W	D.C.	05 JUL 1875	Mt. Olivet
008525	WILKE, Lena Elma Alice	7m	W	D.C.	02 AUG 1876	Mt. Olivet
007603	WILKERSON, Henry James	10m	C	D.C.	11 JUN 1876	Ebenezer
020646	WILKERSON, Maurice Sistan	1m	W	D.C.	27 JUN 1879	Graceland
003655	WILKERSON, Sarah Ann	6m	M	D.C.	15 JUN 1875	Young Mens
018349	WILKERSON, Susan	92y	C	Md.	15 DEC 1878	Holy Rood
010565	WILKES, Charles	78y	W	N.Y.	08 FEB 1877	Oak Hill
017870	WILKES, Edward T.	5y	C	D.C.	26 OCT 1878	Graceland
013925	WILKEY, Benjamin J.	37y	W	Pa.	25 NOV 1877	Mt. Olivet
016184	WILKINS, Anna Maria	1y	W	D.C.	15 JUN 1878	Oak Hill
010535	WILKINS, Betsy	19y	C	Va.	06 FEB 1877	Mt. Pleasant Plain
016807	WILKINS, Daisy	14d	W	D.C.	28 JUL 1878	Congressional
002425	WILKINS, Geo. E.	2y	C	D.C.	04 MAR 1875	Young Mens
003815	WILKINS, Kate E.	25y	W	Ire.	24 JUN 1875	Glenwood
012256	WILKINS, Lillie M.	1m	W	D.C.	07 JUL 1878	Congressional
001329	WILKINS, William E.	4m	W	D.C.	07 DEC 1874	Glenwood
002013	WILKINSON, Howard Lemuel	11d	C	D.C.	03 FEB 1875	Harmony
015859	WILKINSON, John F.	4m	C	D.C.	26 MAY 1878	Harmony
021154	WILKINSON, Mary A.	65y	C	Pa.	29 JUL 1879	Harmony
012882	WILKINSON, Robert Henry	18m	M	D.C.	19 AUG 1877	Harmony
013067	WILLARD, Annie	8m	W	D.C.	03 SEP 1877	Mt. Olivet
017237	WILLARD, Forrest H.	4y	W	Va.	28 AUG 1878	Glenwood
018980	WILLARD, Mary V.	37y	W	D.C.	06 FEB 1879	Holy Rood
006237	WILLARD, Saml.	54y	W	N.Y.	04 FEB 1876	Graceland
010687	WILLENBUCHER, Eugenie Elis.	6d	W	D.C.	18 FEB 1877	Prospect Hill
005821	WILLETT, John A.	57y	W	Md.	21 DEC 1875	Congressional
000556	WILLETT, Rachel M.	55y	W	Md.	18 SEP 1874	Glenwood
003534	WILLETT, Sarah	73y	C	D.C.	05 JUL 1875	Oak Hill
005022a	WILLEY, Penney	96y	C	N.C.	01 OCT 1875	Young Mens
003733	WILLIAM, George	1y	W	D.C.	21 JUN 1875	Union Town, Md.
020743	WILLIAM, Norman	12y	C	D.C.	03 JUL 1879	Mt. Olivet
009296	WILLIAM, Penny	75y	C	Va.	04 OCT 1876	Va.
002165	WILLIAM, Sarah Jane	19y	C	D.C.	14 FEB 1875	Harmony
000199	WIILIAMS, Infant	3d	C	D.C.	15 AUG 1874	Potters Field
014587	WILLIAMS, Abel	1y	W	D.C.	28 JAN 1878	Congressional
010358	WILLIAMS, Abraham	90y	C	D.C.	21 JAN 1877	Mt. Zion
018072	WILLIAMS, Abraham	1m	C	D.C.	16 NOV 1878	Potters Field
005688	WILLIAMS, Adam	34y	C	Md.	07 DEC 1875	Young Mens
001017	WILLIAMS, Adelle	29y	M	Va.	02 NOV 1874	Potters Field
009547	WILLIAMS, Albert	7d	C	D.C.	27 OCT 1876	Ebenezer
010066	WILLIAMS, Alice	13y	C	Va.	25 DEC 1876	Potters Field
018418	WILLIAMS, Alphons S.	68y	W	Conn.	21 DEC 1878	Detroit, Mich.
019096	WILLIAMS, Amelia	1m	C	D.C.	16 FEB 1879	Mt. Pleasant Plain
015217	WILLIAMS, Amelia Ann	5y	C	D.C.	28 MAR 1878	Young Mens
005161	WILLIAMS, Andrew J.	24y	C	Va.	24 SEP 1875	Harmony
013551	WILLIAMS, Anna	32y	C	Md.	17 OCT 1877	Young Mens
016256	WILLIAMS, Anna M.	18y	C	Md.	21 JUN 1878	Beckett's
000169	WILLIAMS, Annie	17y	C	Md.	13 AUG 1874	Harmony
006472	WILLIAMS, Annie	4m	C	D.C.	25 FEB 1876	Mt. Zion
009790	WILLIAMS, Archie	35y	C	Md.	24 NOV 1876	Harmony
005760	WILLIAMS, Arthur	4m	C	D.C.	15 DEC 1875	Potters Field
002502	WILLIAMS, Arthur	5m	C	D.C.	10 MAR 1875	Mt. Zion
004633	WILLIAMS, Arthur A.	25y	M	D.C.	16 AUG 1875	Mt. Zion
017054	WILLIAMS, Arthur Eugene	9m	C	D.C.	14 AUG 1878	Harmony
002817	WILLIAMS, Arthur T.	5m	C	D.C.	31 MAR 1875	Ebenezer

District of Columbia Death Records, August 1, 1874 to July 31, 1879   371

No.	Name	Age	Race	Birth	Death Date	Burial Place
010288	WILLIAMS, Augustus	5m	C	D.C.	14 JAN 1877	Mt. Olivet
004190	WILLIAMS, Barbara	62y	W	Ger.	18 JUL 1875	St. Mary's
007917	WILLIAMS, Betsy	60y	C	Md.	28 JUN 1876	Harmony
001315	WILLIAMS, Betsy Thomas	4m	C	D.C.	05 DEC 1874	Harmony
010454	WILLIAMS, Blanch Elizabeth	2y	C	D.C.	30 JAN 1877	Mt. Olivet
004102	WILLIAMS, Brooke Beale	23y	W	D.C.	12 JUL 1875	Oak Hill
005196a	WILLIAMS, Catharine	32y	C	Va.	18 OCT 1875	Young Mens
011572	WILLIAMS, Catharine	c.25y	C	Va.	12 MAY 1877	Ebenezer
017859	WILLIAMS, Cato	13d	C	D.C.	25 OCT 1878	Beckett's
011508	WILLIAMS, Celia	80y	C	Md.	04 MAY 1877	Mt. Zion
002171	WILLIAMS, Charity	80y	C	Md.	15 FEB 1875	Ebenezer
011256	WILLIAMS, Charles	21y	C	Md.	07 APR 1877	Ebenezer
016219	WILLIAMS, Charles	5m	C	D.C.	18 JUN 1878	Mt. Pleasant
020745	WILLIAMS, Charles	11m	C	D.C.	03 JUL 1879	Beckett's
019377	WILLIAMS, Charles E.	33y	W	D.C.	12 MAR 1879	Graceland
000240	WILLIAMS, Charles Jaq.	6m	W	D.C.	19 AUG 1874	Mt. Olivet
005163a	WILLIAMS, Clara M.	2y	C	D.C.	15 OCT 1875	Smith's
011597	WILLIAMS, Colin, Rev.	84y	C	Va.	14 MAY 1877	Baptist
013817	WILLIAMS, Cornelia	14y	M	D.C.	13 NOV 1877	Arlington, Va.
020514	WILLIAMS, Cornelius	11y	C	D.C.	18 JUN 1879	Potters Field
019779	WILLIAMS, Cythia	55y	C	Va.	14 APR 1879	Young Mens
013569	WILLIAMS, Daniel Howard	11m	C	D.C.	19 OCT 1877	Beckett's
005076a	WILLIAMS, David	36y	C	Va.	06 OCT 1875	Mt. Olivet
011644	WILLIAMS, Denis	21y	C	Md.	18 MAY 1877	Mt. Olivet
005096a	WILLIAMS, Dolly Julia	28y	W	Ger.	09 OCT 1875	St. Mary's German
015357	WILLIAMS, Earnest N.	3y	M	D.C.	10 APR 1878	Young Mens
014938	WILLIAMS, Eddie	3y	C	D.C.	03 MAR 1878	Young Mens
019513	WILLIAMS, Eddie	7y	C	D.C.	22 MAR 1879	Harmony
000769	WILLIAMS, Edward	18y	M	D.C.	09 OCT 1874	Mt. Pleasant
003063	WILLIAMS, Edward	35y	W	Pa.	20 APR 1875	Congressional
013251	WILLIAMS, Elijah	1y	C	D.C.	19 SEP 1877	Beckett's
018847	WILLIAMS, Elijah	1y	C	D.C.	27 JAN 1879	Mt. Zion
006772	WILLIAMS, Eliza	22y	C	Va.	21 MAR 1876	Mt. Zion
008976	WILLIAMS, Eliza	75y	C	Va.	05 SEP 1876	Beckett's
021182	WILLIAMS, Eliza	16d	C	D.C.	31 JUL 1879	Beckett's
014320a	WILLIAMS, Eliza Ann	42y	C	Va.	04 JAN 1878	Beckett's
020513	WILLIAMS, Eliza Reeves	73y	W	Mass.	18 JUN 1879	Oak Hill
001998	WILLIAMS, Elizabeth	1y	C	D.C.	02 FEB 1875	Ebenezer
008533	WILLIAMS, Elizabeth	72y	W	Md.	02 AUG 1876	Rock Creek
012737	WILLIAMS, Elizabeth	19d	M	D.C.	08 AUG 1877	Mt. Olivet
016531	WILLIAMS, Elizabeth	5m	C	D.C.	09 JUL 1878	Beckett's
021059	WILLIAMS, Elizabeth	2m	W	D.C.	22 JUL 1879	Graceland
001931f	WILLIAMS, Elizabeth, Miss	80y	W	Md.	28 JAN 1875	Oak Hill
005432	WILLIAMS, Ella	2m	C	D.C.	11 NOV 1875	Young Mens
017027	WILLIAMS, Ella	9y	W	D.C.	12 AUG 1878	Congressional
017193	WILLIAMS, Ella	30y	W	N.Y.	25 AUG 1878	Mt. Pleasant
015570	WILLIAMS, Ella Victoria	3y	M	D.C.	30 APR 1878	Harmony
001591	WILLIAMS, Ellen	c.52y	C	Va.	02 JAN 1875	Jones Chapel
002026	WILLIAMS, Ellen Irderea	1y	C	D.C.	04 FEB 1875	Harmony
003165	WILLIAMS, Ellsworth	14y	W	D.C.	29 APR 1875	Congressional
009515	WILLIAMS, Emma Jane	16y	C	Md.	24 OCT 1876	Young Mens
011825	WILLIAMS, Emmeline	40y	C	Va.	07 JUN 1877	Baptist
000358	WILLIAMS, Emory	3m	W	D.C.	29 AUG 1874	Congressional
003523	WILLIAMS, Erasmus	22y	C	Md.	04 JUN 1875	Harmony
002214	WILLIAMS, Florene B.	1y	W	D.C.	18 FEB 1875	Glenwood
020747	WILLIAMS, Frances Lee	4m	W	D.C.	03 JUL 1879	Presbyterian

No.	Name	Age	Race	Birth	Death Date	Burial Place
016586	WILLIAMS, Francis	7m	C	D.C.	13 JUL 1878	Mt. Olivet
015035	WILLIAMS, Francis J.	10y	C	D.C.	11 MAR 1878	Harmony
000672	WILLIAMS, Frank	3m	M	D.C.	29 SEP 1874	Beckett's
004553	WILLIAMS, Frank	3m	C	D.C.	11 AUG 1875	Potters Field
006358	WILLIAMS, Frank	3y	W	Va.	14 FEB 1876	Methodist Ebenezer
012481	WILLIAMS, Frank J.	11m	C	D.C.	23 JUL 1877	Young Mens
006744	WILLIAMS, Geo. W.	21y	W	N.Y.	19 MAR 1876	Potters Field
006528	WILLIAMS, George	7y	C	D.C.	02 MAR 1876	Young Mens
009406	WILLIAMS, George	4y	C	N.Y.	14 OCT 1876	Mt. Zion
010229	WILLIAMS, George	76y	W	Va.	08 JAN 1877	Alexandria, Va.
010452	WILLIAMS, George	35y	W	Ga.	30 JAN 1877	Congressional
015381	WILLIAMS, George	34y	W	Ire.	12 APR 1878	Mt. Olivet
015822	WILLIAMS, George	1y	C	D.C.	24 MAY 1878	Payne's
017484	WILLIAMS, George A.	1y	C	D.C.	21 SEP 1878	Potters Field
005958	WILLIAMS, George C.	2m	W	D.C.	06 JAN 1876	Graceland
018592	WILLIAMS, George W.	36y	W	D.C.	06 JAN 1879	Glenwood
006492	WILLIAMS, Grace Turner	3y	W	D.C.	27 FEB 1876	Glenwood
009314	WILLIAMS, Gustavius	1y	C	D.C.	05 OCT 1876	Harmony
015229	WILLIAMS, Hannah	14h	W	D.C.	29 MAR 1878	Congressional
015998	WILLIAMS, Hattia	2y	C	D.C.	03 JUN 1878	Beckett's
019630	WILLIAMS, Hattie	4m	C	D.C.	01 APR 1879	Potters Field
010313	WILLIAMS, Hattie Jane	11m	C	D.C.	17 JAN 1877	Mt. Zion
005488	WILLIAMS, Henrietta	37y	C	Va.	17 NOV 1875	Ebenezer
017885	WILLIAMS, Henrietta F.	22y	C	N.C.	27 OCT 1878	Potters Field
005841	WILLIAMS, Henry	21y	M	Va.	23 DEC 1875	Young Mens
005687	WILLIAMS, Henry	44y	C	Md.	07 DEC 1875	Thomas'
008092	WILLIAMS, Henry	4m	C	D.C.	09 JUL 1876	Potters Field
017248	WILLIAMS, Henry	50y	C	Va.	29 AUG 1878	Mt. Pleasant
021155	WILLIAMS, Henry	11m	C	D.C.	29 JUL 1879	Mt. Olivet
005137a	WILLIAMS, Ida Mary	2y	C	D.C.	13 OCT 1875	Ebenezer
015526	WILLIAMS, Infant of Alexander	7d	C	D.C.	26 APR 1878	Potters Field
007573	WILLIAMS, Infant of Barnett	1m	C	D.C.	09 JUN 1876	Young Mens
006746	WILLIAMS, Infant of Eli	1h	C	D.C.	19 MAR 1876	Potters Field
005979	WILLIAMS, Infant of Emma	10h	C	D.C.	08 JAN 1876	Alexandria, Va.
001967	WILLIAMS, Infant of Fred	1m	C	D.C.	31 JAN 1875	Potters Field
007409	WILLIAMS, Infant of George	10d	C	D.C.	25 MAY 1876	Mt. Olivet
009717	WILLIAMS, Infant of Henry	14d	C	D.C.	17 NOV 1876	Potters Field
012891	WILLIAMS, Infant of John	½h	C	D.C.	20 AUG 1877	Baptist
019441	WILLIAMS, Infant of John	7d	C	D.C.	17 MAR 1879	Mt. Zion
013594	WILLIAMS, Infant of John	10d	C	D.C.	22 OCT 1877	Beckett's
017222	WILLIAMS, Infant of Julia	1d	C	D.C.	27 AUG 1878	Mt. Pleasant
019573	WILLIAMS, Infant of Mary V.	14d	C	D.C.	27 MAR 1879	Potters Field
002146	WILLIAMS, Infant of Moses	11m	C	D.C.	13 FEB 1875	Jones Chapel
005983	WILLIAMS, Infant of Oliver	15min	C	D.C.	09 JAN 1876	Ebenezer
002805	WILLIAMS, Infant of Oliver	1h	C	D.C.	30 MAR 1875	Young Mens
007686	WILLIAMS, Infant of Peter	1m	C	D.C.	16 JUN 1876	Mt. Zion
004155	WILLIAMS, Infant of Richard	21d	C	D.C.	16 JUL 1875	Mt. Zion
004120	WILLIAMS, Infant of Robert	2m	C	D.C.	13 JUL 1875	Potters Field
004091	WILLIAMS, Infant of Thomas	1m	C	D.C.	11 JUL 1875	Berry's Farm[1]
009929	WILLIAMS, Infant of Victoria	3d	C	D.C.	11 DEC 1876	Potters Field
015065	WILLIAMS, Infant of William	7d	C	D.C.	13 MAR 1878	Mt. Zion
000512	WILLIAMS, Isaac	11m	C	D.C.	14 SEP 1874	Beckett's
004162	WILLIAMS, Isaac	63y	C	Md.	16 JUL 1875	Potters Field

[1] Located near Tennallytown.

District of Columbia Death Records, August 1, 1874 to July 31, 1879

No.	Name	Age	Race	Birth	Death Date	Burial Place
019677	WILLIAMS, Isaac	39y	W	Md.	06 APR 1879	Tennallytown[1]
014032	WILLIAMS, Isaac Grant	69y	W	Conn.	07 DEC 1877	Congressional
004515	WILLIAMS, Isabella	1y	C	D.C.	08 AUG 1875	Beckett's
017029	WILLIAMS, Israel	1y	C	D.C.	12 AUG 1878	Smith's
004908	WILLIAMS, Jackson	3y	C	D.C.	04 SEP 1875	Harmony
013215	WILLIAMS, James	50y	C	D.C.	15 SEP 1877	Potters Field
019564	WILLIAMS, James	10d	C	D.C.	26 MAR 1879	Beckett's
020081	WILLIAMS, James	2h	C	D.C.	12 MAY 1879	Payne's
014866	WILLIAMS, James Henry	1y	C	D.C.	24 FEB 1878	Payne's
007324	WILLIAMS, Jane	70y	C	Va.	16 MAY 1876	Union
013396	WILLIAMS, Jane	95y	C	Va.	03 OCT 1877	Mt. Zion
015798	WILLIAMS, Jane	29y	C	Va.	21 MAY 1878	Beckett's
016711	WILLIAMS, Jane E.	44y	W	Md.	21 JUL 1878	Addison's
009479	WILLIAMS, Jarrard	52y	C	Md.	21 OCT 1876	Harmony
006527	WILLIAMS, Jemima	26y	C	Md.	02 MAR 1876	Potters Field
010607	WILLIAMS, Jno. H.	5m	C	D.C.	13 FEB 1877	Beckett's
004324	WILLIAMS, John	30y	C	Md.	26 JUL 1875	Potters Field
002541	WILLIAMS, John	9y	C	D.C.	12 MAR 1875	Ebenezer
006303	WILLIAMS, John	33y	W	Md.	10 FEB 1876	Glenwood
006191	WILLIAMS, John	10m	C	D.C.	30 JAN 1876	Harmony
006581	WILLIAMS, John	10m	C	D.C.	06 MAR 1876	Mt. Pleasant Plain
009693	WILLIAMS, John	2y	C	D.C.	14 NOV 1876	Chappel's
012697	WILLIAMS, John	17y	C	D.C.	06 AUG 1877	Mt. Zion
012034	WILLIAMS, John	23y	C	Va.	24 JUN 1877	Ebenezer
020401	WILLIAMS, John	26y	C	Md.	11 JUN 1879	Harmony
017520	WILLIAMS, John Franklin	3y	C	D.C.	24 SEP 1878	Harmony
015799	WILLIAMS, John Henry	2m	C	D.C.	21 MAY 1878	Mt. Pleasant
010853	WILLIAMS, Jos.	4y	C	D.C.	03 MAR 1877	Mt. Zion
005478	WILLIAMS, Joseph	6	C	Va.	16 NOV 1875	Young Mens
008435	WILLIAMS, Joseph	2y	M	D.C.	26 JUL 1876	Potters Field
014033	WILLIAMS, Joseph	22y	C	Ky.	07 DEC 1877	Young Mens
015830	WILLIAMS, Joseph	3d	C	D.C.	24 MAY 1878	Mt. Zion
017729	WILLIAMS, Joseph	1m	C	D.C.	13 OCT 1878	Payne's
016749	WILLIAMS, Josephine	6m	C	D.C.	24 JUL 1878	Beckett's
020845	WILLIAMS, Julia	1m	W	I.T.	08 JUL 1879	Glenwood
020054	WILLIAMS, Julia	38y	C	Va.	09 MAY 1879	Mt. Zion
016273	WILLIAMS, Julia B.	26y	W	D.C.	22 JUN 1878	Congressional
006277	WILLIAMS, Laura	11y	W	D.C.	08 FEB 1876	Mt. Olivet
002291	WILLIAMS, Laurence	19y	M	D.C.	23 FEB 1875	Potters Field
015296	WILLIAMS, Letta	7y	C	D.C.	05 APR 1878	Mt. Pleasant
014465	WILLIAMS, Lillie	1y	C	D.C.	17 JAN 1878	Young Mens
016882	WILLIAMS, Liza	4d	C	D.C.	02 AUG 1878	Potters Field
014256	WILLIAMS, Lizzie	4m	C	D.C.	29 DEC 1877	Beckett's
012099	WILLIAMS, Lorena M.	1m	W	D.C.	28 JUN 1877	Graceland
018048	WILLIAMS, Lucinda B.	76y	W	N.Y.	13 NOV 1878	Canandaigua, N.Y.
008923	WILLIAMS, Lucy	5y	C	D.C.	02 SEP 1876	Chappel's
012193	WILLIAMS, Lucy	50y	C	Va.	03 JUL 1877	Young Mens
012114	WILLIAMS, Lucy	90y	C	Md.	29 JUN 1877	Mt. Olivet
017647	WILLIAMS, Lucy	40y	C	Va.	05 OCT 1878	Mt. Pleasant
015088	WILLIAMS, Lucy Ann	11y	C	D.C.	16 MAR 1878	Harmony
005970	WILLIAMS, Madelen	3m	C	D.C.	07 JAN 1876	Mt. Zion
018348	WILLIAMS, Margaret	29y	W	Ire.	15 DEC 1878	Mt. Olivet
001609	WILLIAMS, Maria Howard	75y	W	Md.	04 JAN 1875	Poolesville, Md.

[1] Grave for Isaac Williams, b. 7 AUG 1839, is found at Eldbrooke Methodist Cemetery.

No.	Name	Age	Race	Birth	Death Date	Burial Place
011186	WILLIAMS, Marietta	7y	C	D.C.	01 APR 1877	Young Mens
006080	WILLIAMS, Marshall	26y	C	N.C.	20 JAN 1876	Harmony
000958	WILLIAMS, Martha	55y	W	Ohio	27 OCT 1874	Glenwood
000779	WILLIAMS, Martha L.	1y	C	D.C.	11 OCT 1874	Harmony
002386	WILLIAMS, Martha R.	11m	C	D.C.	02 MAR 1875	Mt. Pleasant
007617	WILLIAMS, Mary	2m	C	D.C.	12 JUN 1876	Beckett's
007276	WILLIAMS, Mary	75y	W	Md.	11 MAY 1876	Oak Hill
009333	WILLIAMS, Mary	10d	C	D.C.	07 OCT 1876	Mt. Zion
010668	WILLIAMS, Mary	34y	C	Va.	17 FEB 1877	Mt. Pleasant
012132	WILLIAMS, Mary	44y	W	D.C.	30 JUN 1877	Congressional
002440	WILLIAMS, Mary A.	4y	C	D.C.	05 MAR 1875	Mt. Pleasant
006827	WILLIAMS, Mary A.	4y	C	D.C.	26 MAR 1876	Mt. Zion
001696	WILLIAMS, Mary C.	58y	W	Va.	11 JAN 1875	Glenwood
005948	WILLIAMS, Mary C.	48y	W	Md.	05 JAN 1876	Holy Rood
012812	WILLIAMS, Mary DeC.	60y	W	Pa.	14 AUG 1877	Mt. Olivet
002454	WILLIAMS, Mary E.	7d	C	D.C.	06 MAR 1875	Mt. Pleasant
006984	WILLIAMS, Mary E.	3y	C	D.C.	10 APR 1876	Small Pox Grounds
016217	WILLIAMS, Mary E.	1y	C	D.C.	18 JUN 1878	Mt. Zion
015716	WILLIAMS, Mary Ellen	9m	C	D.C.	13 MAY 1878	Payne's
012054	WILLIAMS, Mary Grace	2m	W	D.C.	25 JUN 1877	Congressional
012881	WILLIAMS, Mary Rebecca	6y	C	D.C.	19 AUG 1877	Ebenezer
005033a	WILLIAMS, Mary Rebecka	2y	M	D.C.	02 OCT 1875	Harmony
019302	WILLIAMS, Mattie	6y	C	D.C.	06 MAR 1879	Brightwood
009967	WILLIAMS, Minnie	16y	C	Va.	15 DEC 1876	Jones Chapel
015717	WILLIAMS, Minnie	14m	C	D.C.	13 MAY 1878	Mt. Olivet
013830	WILLIAMS, Mollie	2y	C	Va.	15 NOV 1877	Potters Field
015681	WILLIAMS, Mollie	9m	C	D.C.	10 MAY 1878	Young Mens
020055	WILLIAMS, Moses	62y	C	Va.	09 MAY 1879	Potters Field
001720	WILLIAMS, Nace	60y	C	Md.	14 JAN 1875	Washington Asylum
019106	WILLIAMS, Nellie	90y	C	Md.	17 FEB 1879	Harmony
004405	WILLIAMS, Nelly	86y	M	Ky.	01 AUG 1875	Potters Field
000890	WILLIAMS, Peter	1m	C	D.C.	21 OCT 1874	Beckett's
006901	WILLIAMS, Peyton	14d	C	D.C.	02 APR 1876	Beckett's
015999	WILLIAMS, Rachael	20y	M	Md.	03 JUN 1878	Harmony
000422	WILLIAMS, Rebecca	1y	C	D.C.	03 SEP 1874	Harmony
012605	WILLIAMS, Rebecca Smith	7m	C	D.C.	30 JUL 1877	Potters Field
014486	WILLIAMS, Richard	30y	C	Va.	19 JAN 1878	Mt. Zion
013832	WILLIAMS, Robert	3y	C	D.C.	15 NOV 1877	Young Mens
014693	WILLIAMS, Robert	9y	C	D.C.	06 FEB 1878	Payne's
004514	WILLIAMS, Robert Benj.	5m	C	D.C.	08 AUG 1875	Young Mens
001889	WILLIAMS, Rosa	5d	C	D.C.	26 JAN 1875	Mt. Zion
000534	WILLIAMS, Rosa Matilda	2y	W	D.C.	17 SEP 1874	Mt. Olivet
012329	WILLIAMS, Rose	1y	C	D.C.	12 JUL 1877	Young Mens
013384	WILLIAMS, Rufus	7m	C	D.C.	02 OCT 1877	Beckett's
011100	WILLIAMS, Samuel	48y	C	Md.	24 MAR 1877	Mt. Olivet
000578	WILLIAMS, Sarah	2y	C	D.C.	20 SEP 1874	Mt. Pleasant
012374	WILLIAMS, Sarah	1m	C	D.C.	15 JUL 1877	Mt. Zion
013397	WILLIAMS, Sarah	9m	C	D.C.	03 OCT 1877	Mt. Zion
016626	WILLIAMS, Sarah Ann	28y	M	Del.	16 JUL 1878	Young Mens
020098	WILLIAMS, Sarah Ann	33y	C	Md.	14 MAY 1879	Payne's
009446	WILLIAMS, Sarha, Mrs.	49y	W	Md.	17 OCT 1876	Mt. Olivet
004602	WILLIAMS, Silas	1y	C	D.C.	14 AUG 1875	Potters Field
006821	WILLIAMS, Susan	40y	C	Va.	25 MAR 1876	Potters Field
013475	WILLIAMS, Susan	27y	C	U.S.	10 OCT 1877	Hospital
003947	WILLIAMS, Susannah	1y	C	D.C.	30 JUN 1875	Harmony
015811	WILLIAMS, Thomas	6m	C	D.C.	22 MAY 1878	Young Mens

District of Columbia Death Records, August 1, 1874 to July 31, 1879   375

No.	Name	Age	Race	Birth	Death Date	Burial Place
017519	WILLIAMS, Thomas	22y	C	D.C.	24 SEP 1878	Payne's
002242	WILLIAMS, Walter Henry	2m	C	D.C.	19 FEB 1875	Harmony
012359	WILLIAMS, Washington	3y	C	D.C.	14 JUL 1877	Harmony
002305	WILLIAMS, William	80y	W	Va.	24 FEB 1875	Presbyterian
001667	WILLIAMS, William	75y	C	Md.	09 JAN 1875	Harmony
018256	WILLIAMS, William	21y	C	Va.	06 DEC 1878	Beckett's
003398	WILLIAMS, William A.	1m	C	D.C.	22 MAY 1875	Ebenezer
006714	WILLIAMS, William D.	61y	W	Md.	17 MAR 1876	Mt. Olivet
019013	WILLIAMS, William H.	60y	M	Va.	09 FEB 1879	Graceland
016796	WILLIAMS, William W.	44y	W	D.C.	27 JUL 1878	Congressional
003651	WILLIAMS, Willie	9y	W	D.C.	15 JUN 1875	Congressional
007242	WILLIAMS, Willie	2m	C	D.C.	07 MAY 1876	Mt. Pleasant
019002	WILLIAMS, Winna	60y	C	Va.	08 FEB 1879	Baptist
002354	WILLIAMS, Wm. H.	6m	C	D.C.	28 FEB 1875	Mt. Zion
010107	WILLIAMSON, Adlade	50y	M	Va.	29 DEC 1876	Young Mens
017636	WILLIAMSON, Ann S.	55y	W	Ire.	04 OCT 1878	Mt. Olivet
009322	WILLIAMSON, Elizabeth	2y	C	D.C.	06 OCT 1876	Congressional
008470	WILLIAMSON, Gertrude	1y	C	D.C.	29 JUL 1876	Ebenezer
000511	WILLIAMSON, Infant of Jas.	14d	W	D.C.	14 SEP 1874	Congressional
011471	WILLIAMSON, Margaret M.	55y	W	Pa.	30 APR 1877	Congressional
010222	WILLIAMSON, Marion R.P.	53y	W	Va.	08 JAN 1877	Glenwood
007770	WILLIAMSON, Mary	5y	W	D.C.	21 JUN 1876	Glenwood
007583	WILLIAMSON, Robert Harper	77y	W	Va.	10 JUN 1876	Oak Hill
015718	WILLIAMSON, Thomas	81y	W	Eng.	13 MAY 1878	Glenwood
006593	WILLIAMSON, William E.	19y	W	D.C.	07 MAR 1876	Congressional
000613	WILLIMS, Malinda	7m	C	D.C.	23 SEP 1874	Mt. Olivet
005256	WILLING, Rosa	43y	W	Ger.	24 OCT 1875	Prospect Hill
013842	WILLIS, Clara (Heck)	38y	W	Ger.	16 NOV 1877	Prospect Hill
017086	WILLIS, Corenia	2m	C	D.C.	17 AUG 1878	Beckett's
005358	WILLIS, Elijah	6y	C	D.C.	04 NOV 1875	Young Mens
005195a	WILLIS, Eliza	53y	C	Va.	18 OCT 1875	Washington Asylum
003893	WILLIS, Emma	5m	C	D.C.	27 JUN 1875	Mt. Zion
014893	WILLIS, Frank A.	50y	W	Md.	27 FEB 1878	Oak Hill
010858	WILLIS, George	8m	C	D.C.	04 MAR 1877	Young Mens
009125	WILLIS, George E.	20y	C	Va.	18 SEP 1876	Harmony
011453	WILLIS, Henry	c.70y	C	Md.	28 APR 1877	Ebenezer
009501	WILLIS, Infant of George	6h	C	D.C.	22 OCT 1876	Potters Field
005120a	WILLIS, John W.A.	1y	C	D.C.	12 OCT 1875	Harmony
014658	WILLIS, Josephine	16y	C	Va.	03 FEB 1878	Mt. Zion
016587	WILLIS, Lucy Ann	4m	M	D.C.	13 JUL 1878	Beckett's
018302	WILLIS, Martha Rebecca	8m	W	D.C.	10 DEC 1878	Beckett's
016987	WILLIS, Mary	3m	M	D.C.	09 AUG 1878	Beckett's
014703	WILLIS, Mary Ellen	11m	C	D.C.	07 FEB 1878	Young Mens
012419	WILLIS, Maude L.	3m	W	D.C.	18 JUL 1877	Congressional
006745	WILLIS, Sarah	45y	C	Va.	19 MAR 1876	Beckett's
012811	WILLIS, Sophrinea	15y	M	Va.	14 AUG 1877	Beckett's
007379	WILLIS, Susan	40y	C	Va.	22 MAY 1876	Ebenezer
011135	WILLIS, Thomas	27y	C	Va.	28 MAR 1877	Ebenezer
000857	WILLIS, Wm. H.	9m	C	D.C.	19 OCT 1874	Beckett's
007241	WILLISS, William B.R.	61y	W	Md.	07 MAY 1876	Baltimore, Md.
009110	WILLOUGHBY, Arthur	4m	W	D.C.	17 SEP 1876	Glenwood
000348	WILLS, Annie	3y	C	Md.	28 AUG 1874	Potters Field
016510	WILLS, Annie	18m	C	D.C.	08 JUL 1878	Beckett's
017073	WILLS, Clara	4y	C	D.C.	16 AUG 1878	Harmony
005911	WILLS, Francis	1y	C	D.C.	01 JAN 1876	Ebenezer
000163	WILLS, Grayson	1y	C	Md.	12 AUG 1874	Potters Field

No.	Name	Age	Race	Birth	Death Date	Burial Place
018848	WILLS, Infant of Jas.	8d	C	D.C.	27 JAN 1879	Harmony
014526	WILLS, Margaret	2m	C	U.S.	22 JAN 1878	Mt. Olivet
011495	WILLS, Samuel	6y	M	D.C.	03 MAY 1877	Harmony
015208	WILLSON, Charles E.	37y	W	D.C.	27 MAR 1878	Congressional
011014	WILLSON, Francis McDowell	7y	W	D.C.	16 MAR 1877	Glenwood
017007	WILLSON, Harriet	70y	W	D.C.	10 AUG 1878	Glenwood
003268	WILLSON, Irvin Russell	11m	W	D.C.	09 MAY 1875	Glenwood
003760	WILLSON, Rose	2y	C	D.C.	22 JUN 1875	Ebenezer
011393	WILMIRE, Hannah	35y	W	Ire.	22 APR 1877	Mt. Olivet
001588	WILMOT, Wm.	30y	C	--	02 JAN 1875	Potters Field
010517	WILMUTH, Sarah	28y	W	Ire.	04 FEB 1877	Mt. Olivet
015766	WILSON, Ada	5m	C	D.C.	18 MAY 1878	Beckett's
012153	WILSON, Adaline	50y	C	Va.	01 JUL 1877	Mt. Pleasant
015089	WILSON, Adela	10d	C	D.C.	16 MAR 1878	Mt. Zion
010932	WILSON, Adeline	6y	M	D.C.	09 MAR 1877	Graceland
006556	WILSON, Albert Thomas	21m	W	D.C.	04 MAR 1876	Presbyterian
002868	WILSON, Anna Elizabeth	3y	W	D.C.	04 APR 1875	Holy Rood
005095a	WILSON, Benjamin B.	69y	W	Md.	09 OCT 1875	Congressional
016949	WILSON, Betsey	95y	C	Md.	07 AUG 1878	Mt. Olivet
006602	WILSON, Caroline Virginia	30y	W	Va.	08 MAR 1876	Glenwood
014273	WILSON, Catharine	75y	W	D.C.	30 DEC 1877	Congressional
003170f	WILSON, Catherine	72y	W	Va.	29 APR 1875	Mt. Olivet
001927	WILSON, Catherine	18y	W	D.C.	28 JAN 1875	Glenwood
005712	WILSON, Charles	77y	W	Md.	09 DEC 1875	Frederick, Md.
017595	WILSON, Charles Benton	4y	W	D.C.	01 OCT 1878	Congressional
013274	WILSON, Charles C.	35y	W	N.H.	21 SEP 1877	Topsfield, Mass.
012258	WILSON, Chas.	37y	W	Md.	08 JUL 1877	Oak Hill
015636	WILSON, Clarence	47d	M	D.C.	06 MAY 1878	Beckett's
005677	WILSON, Edward	81y	C	Va.	06 DEC 1875	Mt. Pleasant
006804	WILSON, Elizabeth	40y	W	D.C.	24 MAR 1876	Oak Hill
013831	WILSON, Elizabeth	67y	C	D.C.	15 NOV 1877	Harmony
013295	WILSON, Fanny	30y	W	Md.	24 SEP 1877	Mt. Olivet
003375	WILSON, Frank	c.22y	C	--	20 MAY 1875	Potters Field
007717	WILSON, George Keck	27y	W	Pa.	18 JUN 1876	Allentown, Pa.
002290	WILSON, George S.	9m	W	D.C.	23 FEB 1875	Congressional
013351	WILSON, Harriet C.	2y	C	D.C.	29 SEP 1877	Mt. Olivet
008949	WILSON, Harry	7m	C	D.C.	03 SEP 1876	Ebenezer
020916	WILSON, Harry	11m	C	D.C.	13 JUL 1879	Mt. Olivet
021141	WILSON, Hattie	1w	C	D.C.	28 JUL 1879	Young Mens
011753	WILSON, Henry	25d	C	D.C.	31 MAY 1877	Beckett's
013636	WILSON, Henry	49y	C	Ga.	25 OCT 1877	Beckett's
006759	WILSON, Henry A.	37y	W	Conn.	20 MAR 1876	Mt. Olivet
018428	WILSON, Henry C.	1y	C	D.C.	22 DEC 1878	Harmony
002195f	WILSON, Henry P.C.	74y	W	Md.	16 FEB 1875	Oak Hill
005538	WILSON, Henry, Vice-President	63y	W	N.H.	22 NOV 1875	Natick, Mass.
003771	WILSON, Infant of Alexander	12d	C	D.C.	22 JUN 1875	Young Mens
013189	WILSON, Infant of Eliza	24h	C	D.C.	13 SEP 1877	Potters Field
013976	WILSON, Infant of Mary Eliza	3d	C	D.C.	30 NOV 1877	Potters Field
011391	WILSON, Infant of Perry	4m	M	D.C.	22 APR 1877	Beckett's
011696	WILSON, Infant of Thos.	26d	C	D.C.	25 MAY 1877	Beckett's
012044	WILSON, James	3m	W	D.C.	25 JUN 1877	Mt. Olivet
009986	WILSON, James Gregory	7d	M	D.C.	17 DEC 1876	Philadelphia, Pa.
003662	WILSON, Jessie May	5m	W	D.C.	16 JUN 1875	Glenwood
004673	WILSON, John	26y	C	Md.	19 AUG 1875	Moore's
005991	WILSON, John	67y	C	D.C.	10 JAN 1876	Rock Creek
020725	WILSON, John	2m	W	Pa.	02 JUL 1879	Mt. Olivet

District of Columbia Death Records, August 1, 1874 to July 31, 1879

No.	Name	Age	Race	Birth	Death Date	Burial Place
020478	WILSON, John Colby	66y	W	N.H.	16 JUN 1879	Concord, N.H.
000549f	WILSON, John D.	67y	W	Md.	17 SEP 1874	Congressional
020463	WILSON, John J.	4m	C	D.C.	15 JUN 1879	Mt. Olivet
004941	WILSON, John W.	44y	W	D.C.	06 SEP 1875	Congressional
012795	WILSON, Joseph	24y	W	Eng.	13 AUG 1877	Potters Field
016936	WILSON, Joseph H.	44y	W	D.C.	06 AUG 1878	Oak Hill
008155	WILSON, Leah L.	80y	W	Md.	10 JUL 1876	Congressional
003615	WILSON, Louisa B.	54y	C	D.C.	12 JUN 1875	Holy Rood
002998	WILSON, Lucy, Mrs.	31y	W	Eng.	15 APR 1875	Methodist
005102a	WILSON, Lulie	8m	C	D.C.	10 OCT 1875	Young Mens
019527	WILSON, Marcellus C.	57y	W	Md.	23 MAR 1879	Bladensburg, Md.
004191	WILSON, Margaret A.	4m	W	D.C.	18 JUL 1875	Congressional
013068	WILSON, Maria	69y	C	Va.	03 SEP 1877	Potters Field
011851	WILSON, Martha	5m	C	D.C.	09 JUN 1877	Mt. Pleasant
016642	WILSON, Martha	5d	C	D.C.	17 JUL 1878	Beckett's
006240	WILSON, Mary	3y	C	D.C.	04 FEB 1876	Young Mens
020989	WILSON, Mary	1y	C	D.C.	17 JUL 1879	Potters Field
017277	WILSON, Mary A.	1y	W	D.C.	31 AUG 1878	Glenwood
001952	WILSON, Mary Ann, Mrs.	58y	W	Ire.	30 JAN 1875	Mt. Olivet
000382	WILSON, Mary E.	25y	C	Md.	31 AUG 1874	Mt. Pleasant
020493	WILSON, Mary Ellen	2m	W	D.C.	17 JUN 1879	Potters Field
001762	WILSON, Mary Hamilton	75y	W	D.C.	16 JAN 1875	Oak Hill
012261	WILSON, Mary V.	7m	C	D.C.	08 JUL 1877	Young Mens
015605	WILSON, Nancy	70y	C	Va.	03 MAY 1878	Mt. Olivet
009615	WILSON, Rachal	45y	W	Md.	04 NOV 1876	Congressional
002939	WILSON, Rebecca	1y	C	D.C.	10 APR 1875	Beckett's
003945	WILSON, Rebecca	106y	C	Md.	30 JUN 1875	Holy Rood
006604	WILSON, Robert	71y	W	Eng.	08 MAR 1876	Malvern, Ohio
015180	WILSON, Robert	43y	W	Eng.	24 MAR 1878	Soldier's Home
015756	WILSON, Robert	5m	C	D.C.	17 MAY 1878	Beckett's
010960	WILSON, Robert M.	5y	C	D.C.	13 MAR 1877	Holy Rood
002785	WILSON, Robert S.	1y	C	D.C.	29 MAR 1875	Mt. Pleasant
006927	WILSON, Rosabella	25y	W	D.C.	04 APR 1876	Mt. Olivet
000206	WILSON, Rosea	10m	C	D.C.	16 AUG 1874	Beckett's
000717	WILSON, Samuel	61y	W	Md.	05 OCT 1874	Washington Asylum
008505	WILSON, Samuel	21y	C	Va.	31 JUL 1876	Potters Field
014070	WILSON, Sarah	32y	W	D.C.	11 DEC 1877	Graceland
010938	WILSON, Sarah T.	86y	W	N.H.	11 MAR 1877	Concord, N.H.
006438	WILSON, Susan Calidonia	51y	W	Tenn.	21 FEB 1876	Congressional
010434	WILSON, Thomas Chamberlain	57y	W	Md.	29 JAN 1877	Mt. Olivet
006877	WILSON, Virginia	11y	C	D.C.	31 MAR 1876	Ebenezer
003235f	WILSON, Virginia Frances	36y	W	D.C.	02 NOV 1873	Mt. Olivet
013043	WILSON, Walker	26y	C	Va.	31 AUG 1877	Mt. Pleasant
003789	WILSON, Walter	1y	M	N.Y.	23 JUN 1875	Young Mens
014746	WILSON, Warren Wesley	1y	C	Va.	11 FEB 1878	Potters Field
005110a	WILSON, William	7m	C	D.C.	11 OCT 1875	Ebenezer
008130	WILSON, William Jesse	23y	W	D.C.	10 JUL 1876	Glenwood
014314	WILSON, William Solomon	61y	C	Va.	03 JAN 1878	Young Mens
014323	WILSON, Wm.	70y	W	Md.	04 JAN 1878	Congressional
018168	WILSON, Wm.	59y	C	N.J.	26 NOV 1878	Graceland
009010	WILSON, Wm. J.	4d	C	D.C.	09 SEP 1876	Congressional
006105	WILTS, Georgeanna	c.25y	C	Va.	22 JAN 1876	Ebenezer
007345	WIMMS, Isaac	56y	C	Md.	19 MAY 1876	Mt. Zion
002937	WIND, Robert A.	14y	W	Pa.	10 APR 1875	Oak Hill
009677	WINDFIELD, Martha	9d	C	D.C.	12 NOV 1876	Potters Field
006118	WINDHAM, Virginia	39y	W	D.C.	23 JAN 1876	Oak Hill

District of Columbia Death Records, August 1, 1874 to July 31, 1879

No.	Name	Age	Race	Birth	Death Date	Burial Place
002598	WINDRICH, Mary L.	36y	W	Md.	16 MAR 1875	Prospect Hill
011967	WINFIELD, Annie E.	24y	W	Va.	19 JUN 1877	Glenwood
000557	WINFIELD, Douglas	24y	M	Va.	18 SEP 1874	Harmony
000393	WINFIELD, Infant of Walter	11d	C	D.C.	01 SEP 1874	Mt. Pleasant
002609	WINFIELD, Joseph	2y	C	D.C.	16 MAR 1875	Potters Field
013144	WINFIELD, Lewis Thomas	1y	C	D.C.	09 SEP 1877	Macedonia
007970	WINFIELD, William	5m	C	D.C.	02 JUL 1876	Young Mens
018791	WINGATE, Henry	49y	W	Md.	23 JAN 1879	Oak Hill
017648	WINGFIELD, Fanny	1y	C	D.C.	05 OCT 1878	Beckett's
002898	WINGFIELD, Robt.	20y	C	Va.	06 APR 1875	Ebenezer
004252	WINKFIELD, Mary E.	9m	C	D.C.	22 JUL 1875	Ebenezer
015812	WINN, Elizabeth A.	72y	W	Md.	22 MAY 1878	Baltimore, Md.
000360	WINNER, May Jennett	6m	W	D.C.	29 AUG 1874	Glenwood
010214	WINSLOW, Benjamin F.	67y	W	Ver.	07 JAN 1877	Pittsford, Ver.
006249	WINSLOW, Clara	63y	M	Va.	05 FEB 1876	Harmony
013492	WINSLOW, Ida	22y	C	Va.	12 OCT 1877	Potters Field
000696	WINSLOW, James A.	1m	C	D.C.	02 OCT 1874	Mt. Pleasant
017348	WINSLOW, Lindsey	10d	C	D.C.	07 SEP 1878	Beckett's
017332	WINSLOW, Mary	6d	C	D.C.	05 SEP 1878	Beckett's
012008	WINSLOW, Mary E.	5m	C	D.C.	22 JUN 1877	Ebenezer
017706	WINSLOW, Millie	14y	C	Va.	11 OCT 1878	Beckett's
005657	WINSLOW, Solomon	73y	C	Va.	04 DEC 1875	Harmony
014918	WINSTON, John Henry	10m	C	D.C.	01 MAR 1878	Potters Field
018410	WINSTON, Martha	22y	C	Va.	20 DEC 1878	Gordonsville, Va.
016598	WINSTON, Mary	45y	C	Va.	14 JUL 1878	Young Mens
015813	WINTER, Lee	2y	C	D.C.	22 MAY 1878	Harmony
020990	WINTER, Lucy A.	38y	W	D.C.	17 JUL 1879	Oak Hill
006687	WINTER, Maud A.	4y	W	Md.	15 MAR 1876	Knoxville, Md.
000048	WINTER, Ujeane	7m	C	D.C.	04 AUG 1874	Mt. Olivet
009477	WINTERS, Charles	5m	C	D.C.	21 OCT 1876	Ebenezer
010435	WINTERS, Charles	2y	C	D.C.	29 JAN 1877	Harmony
012040	WINTERS, Daniel	5m	M	D.C.	24 JUN 1877	Harmony
002118	WINTERS, Emma	2y	C	D.C.	11 FEB 1875	Harmony
009060	WINTERS, Fannie	1y	C	D.C.	13 SEP 1876	Harmony
001610	WINTERS, Henry	1y	W	D.C.	04 JAN 1875	Prospect Hill
012639	WINTERS, James Blanchard	5y	C	D.C.	01 AUG 1877	Harmony
005833	WINTERS, Nancy	85y	C	Md.	22 DEC 1875	Holy Rood
005842	WINTERSTEIN, Ida M.	20y	W	Va.	23 DEC 1875	Congressional
017623	WIRT, Wm. B.	65y	C	Va.	03 OCT 1878	Potters Field
008073	WIRTH, Barbary	58y	W	Ger.	08 JUL 1876	Prospect Hill
019908	WIRTH, Joseph	54y	W	Ger.	26 APR 1879	Prospect Hill
016216	WISE, Ann Rebecca	6m	C	D.C.	18 JUN 1878	Mt. Olivet
019799	WISE, Anna Elizabeth	39y	W	Ohio	16 APR 1879	Martinsville, Ohio
009516	WISE, Annie E.	6d	C	D.C.	24 OCT 1876	Mt. Zion
009729	WISE, Cornelia	2y	C	D.C.	18 NOV 1876	Ebenezer
006658	WISE, Francis Mabel	3y	C	D.C.	04 MAR 1876	Mt. Olivet
013191	WISE, Francis Mabel	1y	C	D.C.	13 SEP 1877	Mt. Olivet
004822	WISE, James Harvey	11m	W	D.C.	29 AUG 1875	Mt. Olivet
011733	WISE, John	38y	C	Va.	29 MAY 1877	Potters Field
017410	WISE, John	59y	W	D.C.	14 SEP 1878	Mt. Olivet
018186	WISE, Mamy	8y	C	D.C.	27 NOV 1878	Mt. Pleasant
008497	WISE, Margaret	12h	C	D.C.	30 JUL 1876	Ebenezer
001805	WISE, Marie	59y	C	Va.	20 JAN 1875	Washington Asylum
002243	WISE, Martha	c.26y	C	Md.	19 FEB 1875	Harmony
001456	WISE, Mary	3m	W	D.C.	21 DEC 1874	Mt. Olivet
009001	WISE, Mary	30y	C	Va.	08 SEP 1876	Potters Field

District of Columbia Death Records, August 1, 1874 to July 31, 1879   379

No.	Name	Age	Race	Birth	Death Date	Burial Place
006888	WISE, Patrick	2h	W	D.C.	01 APR 1876	Holy Rood
019526	WISE, Sidney	1y	C	D.C.	23 MAR 1879	Mt. Pleasant
004471	WISE, William G.	11m	W	D.C.	05 AUG 1875	Oak Hill
006129	WISE, William Horace	21y	W	D.C.	24 JAN 1876	Mt. Olivet
010283	WISEKEY, Elizabeth	24d	W	D.C.	13 JAN 1877	St. Mary's
019800	WISEKY, Frank	36y	W	Sax.	16 APR 1879	St. Mary's
017378	WISKEY, Dora	1y	W	Md.	11 SEP 1878	St. Mary's
015252	WISNER, Henry B.	39y	W	Ger.	31 MAR 1878	Holy Rood
017826	WISSINGER, Susan	85y	W	Md.	21 OCT 1878	Oak Hill
007871	WISWALL, Elizabeth A.	40y	W	N.H.	26 JUN 1876	Neusbury, N.Y.
012971	WISWALL, Florence E.	8y	W	D.C.	26 AUG 1877	Oak Hill
012188	WISWALL, Owen L.	6m	W	D.C.	02 JUL 1877	Congressional
007616	WITHERALL, Augusta	33y	W	D.C.	12 JUN 1876	Oak Hill
011777	WITHEROW, Chalesworth	25y	W	Pa.	02 JUN 1877	Oak Hill
006554	WITHEROW, James W.	46y	W	Pa.	04 MAR 1876	Glenwood
001913	WITHEROW, Uriah	4m	W	D.C.	27 JAN 1875	Glenwood
014924	WITHERS, Harry Kerr	2y	W	D.C.	02 MAR 1878	Glenwood
017065	WITHERS, John W.	32y	W	Va.	15 AUG 1878	Glenwood
006985	WITHERS, Margaret H.	66y	W	Va.	10 APR 1876	Glenwood
019313	WITHERSPOON, Annie	3m	C	D.C.	07 MAR 1879	Mt. Olivet
018087	WITMER, Margaret E.B.	49y	W	Md.	18 NOV 1878	Glenwood
001107	WODE, Jane	81y	W	Va.	10 NOV 1874	Congressional
013794	WOLF, Charles Thomas	11m	W	D.C.	10 NOV 1877	Oak Hill
007091	WOLF, Conrad	66y	W	Ger.	23 APR 1876	St. Mary's
000026	WOLF, Ida	9m	W	D.C.	02 AUG 1874	Mt. Olivet
010836	WOLFE, Charles L.	21y	W	Md.	02 MAR 1877	Williamsport, Md.
001553	WOLFE, Lena	23y	W	N.Y.	01 JAN 1875	Pennyann, N.Y.
014123	WOLFE, Michael	73y	W	Ire.	17 DEC 1877	Mt. Olivet
007972	WOLFES, Cath.	1m	W	D.C.	02 JUL 1876	Prospect Hill
008676	WOLFORD, Elsie	4m	W	D.C.	13 AUG 1876	Tennallytown
008696	WOLFORD, Mabel	1y	W	D.C.	15 AUG 1876	Tennallytown
020821	WOLFORD, Susie E.	20y	W	Md.	07 JUL 1879	Graceland
018389	WOLFRAM, Anna Clara	4y	W	D.C.	19 DEC 1878	Prospect Hill
002585	WOLFRAM, Aug.	27y	W	Ger.	15 MAR 1875	Prospect Hill
001886	WOLSTON, Frances Allouise	9m	C	D.C.	25 JAN 1875	Holy Rood
000154	WOLTZ, Abert F.	2m	W	D.C.	11 AUG 1874	Glenwood
004535	WOLTZ, George William	10w	W	D.C.	10 AUG 1875	Glenwood
019301	WOLTZ, Tobias M.	62y	W	D.C.	06 MAR 1879	Rock Creek
006876	WOLZ, Conrad	50y	W	Ger.	31 MAR 1876	Oak Hill
014659	WOLZ, Mary	77y	W	Ger.	03 FEB 1878	Oak Hill
020770	WOMERSLEY, Edward Everett	11m	W	D.C.	04 JUL 1879	Graceland
007367	WOOD, Agnus	2y	C	D.C.	21 MAY 1876	Mt. Olivet
012473	WOOD, Alice Milburn	28y	W	Md.	22 JUL 1877	Congressional
006011	WOOD, Ann	82y	W	Md.	13 JAN 1876	Congressional
005932	WOOD, Ann	75y	W	Va.	03 JAN 1876	Congressional
005925	WOOD, Betsy	104y	C	Md.	02 JAN 1876	Potters Field
010272	WOOD, Betty Ann	19y	C	Va.	13 JAN 1877	Potters Field
006050	WOOD, Blanchard	1y	C	D.C.	17 JAN 1876	Beckett's
012449	WOOD, Cassie	82y	C	Md.	20 JUL 1877	Harmony
002728a	WOOD, Charles	1m	W	D.C.	25 MAR 1875	Mt. Olivet
011942	WOOD, Charles	85y	M	Md.	17 JUN 1877	Mt. Olivet
016060	WOOD, Charles	9m	C	D.C.	07 JUN 1878	Potters Field
004513	WOOD, Charles Fraser	80y	W	Mass.	08 AUG 1875	Glenwood
002045	WOOD, Charles Raymond	1y	W	D.C.	05 FEB 1875	Congressional
010381	WOOD, Charles Wm.	48y	C	Md.	23 JAN 1877	Mt. Olivet
007581	WOOD, Edith	3d	W	D.C.	10 JUN 1876	Congressional

District of Columbia Death Records, August 1, 1874 to July 31, 1879

No.	Name	Age	Race	Birth	Death Date	Burial Place
009054	WOOD, Edward	16m	C	D.C.	13 SEP 1876	Potters Field
002111	WOOD, Elias	1y	C	D.C.	10 FEB 1875	Young Mens
000884	WOOD, Elizabeth Ann	2y	W	D.C.	21 OCT 1874	Methodist
008051	WOOD, Ellen	14y	C	Md.	06 JUL 1876	Potters Field
016780	WOOD, Ellen	17y	W	D.C.	26 JUL 1878	Congressional
013273	WOOD, Emmeline	62y	W	N.Y.	21 SEP 1877	Buffalo, N.Y.
015888	WOOD, Frank	8m	C	D.C.	28 MAY 1878	Mt. Zion
018054	WOOD, George	22y	C	Md.	15 NOV 1878	Young Mens
019428	WOOD, George Buchly	2y	W	D.C.	16 MAR 1879	Congressional
014052	WOOD, Henry Little	6d	C	D.C.	09 DEC 1877	Potters Field
006601	WOOD, Infant of Chas.	2m	C	D.C.	08 MAR 1876	Mt. Olivet
003458	WOOD, Infant of Edward	3m	C	D.C.	28 MAY 1875	Ebenezer
012650	WOOD, Infant of John	14d	C	D.C.	02 AUG 1877	Potters Field
010439	WOOD, Infant of Sidney	3d	C	D.C.	29 JAN 1877	Ebenezer
007129	WOOD, Infant of Sidney	5d	C	D.C.	26 APR 1876	Ebenezer
013420	WOOD, James	33y	W	N.Y.	06 OCT 1877	Soldier's Home
009855	WOOD, James Augustus	1y	C	D.C.	03 DEC 1876	Mt. Olivet
014607	WOOD, James I.	1y	C	D.C.	30 JAN 1878	Mt. Pleasant
010125	WOOD, James Randolph	12d	W	D.C.	30 DEC 1876	Glenwood
002990	WOOD, Jane	46y	C	Md.	14 APR 1875	Ebenezer
012252	WOOD, Jas. Thomas	4m	M	D.C.	07 JUL 1877	Mt. Olivet
005811	WOOD, John	63y	W	Va.	20 DEC 1875	Congressional
009456	WOOD, Laura Gertrude	28y	W	D.C.	18 OCT 1876	Rock Creek
009290	WOOD, Luella	1y	C	D.C.	03 OCT 1876	Ebenezer
007602	WOOD, Maris A., Mrs.	37y	W	D.C.	11 JUN 1876	Congressional
018172	WOOD, Martha Ellen	6y	C	D.C.	26 NOV 1878	Mt. Pleasant
008037	WOOD, Moses	32y	C	D.C.	05 JUL 1876	Potters Field
001026	WOOD, Peter	64y	W	Md.	03 NOV 1874	Woodville, Md.
010205	WOOD, Poindexter	20y	C	Va.	07 JAN 1877	Charlottesville, Va.
006819	WOOD, Rachel	80y	C	Md.	25 MAR 1876	Mt. Olivet
013069	WOOD, Samuel	7y	W	D.C.	03 SEP 1877	Glenwood
014080	WOOD, Sarah	35y	C	Md.	12 DEC 1877	Beckett's
012395	WOOD, Susan J.	5m	W	D.C.	16 JUL 1877	Glenwood
002957	WOOD, Thomas	5m	M	D.C.	11 APR 1875	Harmony
004455	WOOD, Walmuth W.	26y	W	Kan.	04 AUG 1875	Oak Hill
006473	WOOD, William	72y	C	Md.	25 FEB 1876	Mt. Olivet
014865	WOOD, William	14d	W	D.C.	24 FEB 1878	Carroll [Chapel], Md.
018011	WOOD, William Walter	8m	C	D.C.	10 NOV 1878	Mt. Olivet
017264	WOOD, Willie	30h	M	D.C.	30 AUG 1878	Potters Field
015314	WOODARD, Elizabeth J.	c.17y	C	D.C.	07 APR 1878	Harmony
008549	WOODARD, Ella	2y	M	D.C.	04 AUG 1876	Graceland
002588	WOODARD, Lundon	33y	C	Va.	15 MAR 1875	Potters Field
012845	WOODEN, Hardy	30y	C	Va.	16 AUG 1877	Potters Field
004972	WOODEY, Jno. W.	47y	W	Ohio	09 SEP 1875	Mt. Olivet
020200	WOODFORD, Infant of Ella	3d	C	D.C.	25 MAY 1879	Potters Field
018648	WOODFORK, John	4y	C	D.C.	11 JAN 1879	Young Mens
014759	WOODLAND, Edward	77y	C	D.C.	13 FEB 1878	Harmony
013070	WOODLAND, George Edward	9m	C	D.C.	03 SEP 1877	Harmony
010057	WOODLAND, James Henry	4m	C	D.C.	24 DEC 1876	Potters Field
002193	WOODLAND, Joseph	c.90y	C	Md.	16 FEB 1875	Mt. Zion
014504	WOODLAW, Claudia Berdella	1y	C	D.C.	20 JAN 1878	Prince George's Co., Md.
010865	WOODLEY, Caroline, Mrs.	51y	W	Eng.	04 MAR 1877	Rock Creek
001902	WOODROW, Eliza	c.34y	C	Md.	26 JAN 1875	Mt. Olivet
016547	WOODROW, Ernest	1y	C	D.C.	10 JUL 1878	Payne's
002832	WOODROWE, Thomas	95y	C	Md.	01 APR 1875	Potters Field
013606	WOODRUFF, J.B.	66y	W	Conn.	23 OCT 1877	Glenwood

District of Columbia Death Records, August 1, 1874 to July 31, 1879

No.	Name	Age	Race	Birth	Death Date	Burial Place
005341	WOODRUFF, Nancy Amanda	45y	W	N.Y.	02 NOV 1875	Augusta, Ga.
015687	WOODS, Catherine	62y	W	Ire.	11 MAY 1878	Mt. Olivet
004434	WOODS, Edward	37y	W	Ire.	03 AUG 1875	Mt. Olivet
003231	WOODS, James S.	52y	W	Scot.	05 MAY 1875	Congressional
016732	WOODS, James Shepherd	2y	W	D.C.	23 JUL 1878	Congressional
007582	WOODS, Letty	4m	C	Pa.	10 JUN 1876	Young Mens
020545	WOODS, Margaret	3m	C	D.C.	20 JUN 1879	Mt. Olivet
007316	WOODSIDE, Hannah	90y	W	N.Y.	15 MAY 1876	Glenwood
012407	WOODSON, Harriet Elizabeth	5m	C	D.C.	17 JUL 1877	Young Mens
018482	WOODSON, Julia Etta	2y	C	D.C.	27 DEC 1878	Graceland
020972	WOODSON, Robert	5m	C	Va.	16 JUL 1879	Beckett's
020786	WOODWARD, Charles Herbert	17d	W	D.C.	05 JUL 1879	Glenwood
016255	WOODWARD, Charlotte	87y	C	Md.	21 JUN 1878	Mt. Pleasant
011985	WOODWARD, Earnest	7d	C	D.C.	21 JUN 1877	Mt. Zion
016643	WOODWARD, Eliza	88y	W	Mass.	17 JUL 1878	Oak Hill
005626	WOODWARD, Ernest Cameron	2y	W	D.C.	01 DEC 1875	Congressional
006726	WOODWARD, Joseph H.	2m	W	D.C.	18 MAR 1876	Congressional
007556	WOODWARD, Lennon	1y	C	D.C.	08 JUN 1876	Ebenezer
001364	WOODWARD, Luther Rittenhouse	2y	W	D.C.	11 DEC 1874	Congressional
000085	WOODWARD, Maria E.	80y	W	Mass.	07 AUG 1874	Oak Hill
015571	WOODWARD, Rachel	55y	W	D.C.	30 APR 1878	Congressional
004488	WOODWARD, Sabra	88y	W	Conn.	06 AUG 1875	Oak Hill
008154	WOODWARD, Wm. P.	76y	W	Va.	10 JUL 1876	Middlesex Co., Va.
017871	WOODWORTH, Charlie	4m	M	D.C.	26 OCT 1878	Graceland
019406	WOODWORTH, John Maynard	41y	W	N.Y.	14 MAR 1879	Rock Creek
020056	WOODWORTH, Lewis	2d	W	D.C.	09 MAY 1879	Glenwood
015152	WOOLFORD, Thomas E.	52y	W	Md.	22 MAR 1878	Baltimore, Md.
014324	WOOSTER, Cornelia Maria	41y	W	Conn.	04 JAN 1878	Congressional
004385	WOOTTEN, John Richard	4y	W	Ill.	30 JUL 1875	Glenwood
016284	WORMELEY, James	5m	W	D.C.	23 JUN 1878	Young Mens
013205	WORMLEY, Anie	20y	C	Va.	14 SEP 1877	Lancaster Co., Va.
020431	WORMLEY, Benjamin	2m	M	D.C.	13 JUN 1879	Young Mens
016411	WORMLEY, Gertrude	5m	C	D.C.	02 JUL 1878	Young Mens
012584	WORMLEY, Infant of John	6d	C	D.C.	28 JUL 1877	Beckett's
003288f	WORMLEY, Jerry	26y	C	Va.	11 MAY 1875	Beckett's
002910	WORMLEY, Lloyd	15y	C	Va.	07 APR 1875	Mt. Olivet
018979	WORMLEY, Moses	56y	C	Va.	06 FEB 1879	Beckett's
004960	WORMLEY, Rachel Edith	1m	C	D.C.	08 SEP 1875	Harmony
000024	WORMLEY, Rebeca	2y	C	D.C.	02 AUG 1874	Beckett's
010077	WORMLEY, Robert	4y	C	D.C.	26 DEC 1876	Graceland
012621	WORMLY, Lucy B.	6m	C	D.C.	31 JUL 1877	Young Mens
004804	WORMSLY, Fanny Calvert	10m	W	D.C.	28 AUG 1875	Graceland
016854	WORTHINGTON, Ann Hood	87y	W	Md.	31 JUL 1878	Oak Hill
006369	WORTHINGTON, Cora	6y	C	D.C.	15 FEB 1876	Young Mens
011887	WORTHINGTON, Eliza	30y	C	Md.	14 JUN 1877	Young Mens
011427	WORTHINGTON, Irwin Starr	2y	W	D.C.	25 APR 1877	Oak Hill
005072	WORTHINGTON, John Griffith	77y	W	D.C.	16 SEP 1875	Oak Hill
010225	WORTHINGTON, Joseph Walter	9m	W	D.C.	08 JAN 1877	Methodist
002332	WORTHINGTON, Lucy A.	69y	W	D.C.	26 FEB 1875	Oak Hill
016948	WOSSOM, Mary Ella	3m	W	D.C.	07 AUG 1878	Mt. Olivet
006825	WRED, Mary	40y	C	Va.	26 MAR 1876	Harmony
020082	WRIGHT, Agnes	12m	W	U.S.	12 MAY 1879	Mt. Olivet
007650	WRIGHT, Alice Adeline	27y	W	D.C.	14 JUN 1876	Congressional
016340	WRIGHT, Amelia	7m	C	D.C.	27 JUN 1878	Mt. Zion
015699	WRIGHT, Amelia	3m	C	D.C.	12 MAY 1878	Potters Field
013321	WRIGHT, Ann	45y	C	Va.	26 SEP 1877	Harmony

No.	Name	Age	Race	Birth	Death Date	Burial Place
015105	WRIGHT, Austin	7m	W	U.S.	17 MAR 1878	Mt. Olivet
019958	WRIGHT, Caroline	26y	W	Ohio	01 MAY 1879	Cincinnati, Ohio
019300	WRIGHT, Eliza	25y	C	Va.	06 MAR 1879	Young Mens
016061	WRIGHT, Elizabeth	35y	W	Mass.	07 JUN 1878	Potters Field
005465	WRIGHT, Hannah M.	46y	W	Mass.	15 NOV 1875	Glenwood
014325	WRIGHT, Harry	5m	M	D.C.	04 JAN 1878	Young Mens
002566	WRIGHT, Hellen E.	8m	W	D.C.	14 MAR 1875	Fairfax Co., Va.
001022	WRIGHT, Infant of Elvira	2d	C	D.C.	02 NOV 1874	Mt. Pleasant
007473	WRIGHT, Infant of William M.	3h	W	D.C.	02 JUN 1876	Congressional
018579	WRIGHT, James	64y	C	Va.	05 JAN 1879	Mt. Pleasant
002295	WRIGHT, James W.	39y	C	Va.	23 FEB 1875	Mt. Pleasant
018875	WRIGHT, John F.	31y	C	D.C.	29 JAN 1879	Mt. Pleasant
011669	WRIGHT, Juanita Bell	1y	W	D.C.	22 MAY 1877	Congressional
001514	WRIGHT, Julia C.	5y	C.	D.C.	28 DEC 1874	Mt. Zion
010523	WRIGHT, Katie F.	4m	W	D.C.	04 FEB 1877	Congressional
019376	WRIGHT, Katie Irene	2y	W	D.C.	12 MAR 1879	Glenwood
008552	WRIGHT, Levina	22y	C	Va.	04 AUG 1876	Beckett's
015327	WRIGHT, Lewis	71y	W	Va.	08 APR 1878	Congressional
018521	WRIGHT, Lorena Irene	1y	W	D.C.	30 DEC 1878	Congressional
007505	WRIGHT, Mamie	10	W	Md.	04 JUN 1876	Jewish
017934	WRIGHT, Mary	67y	C	Va.	03 NOV 1878	Harmony
016797	WRIGHT, Mary E.	6m	W	D.C.	27 JUL 1878	Congressional
011871	WRIGHT, Mary G.	11m	W	Ohio	12 JUN 1877	Congressional
017968	WRIGHT, Minnie	26y	W	Pa.	06 NOV 1878	Glenwood
010654	WRIGHT, Rebecca M.	27y	W	Ohio	16 FEB 1877	Congressional
010906	WRIGHT, Richard	82y	W	Eng.	08 MAR 1877	Graceland
002813	WRIGHT, Robert	2m	W	Va.	31 MAR 1875	Mt. Olivet
005138a	WRIGHT, Thomas	33y	W	Miss.	13 OCT 1875	Hospital
021128	WRITH, Ferina, Mrs.	73y	W	Ger.	27 JUL 1879	Prospect Hill
002456	WROE, Jane	57y	W	D.C.	06 MAR 1875	Rock Creek
006686	WROE, Richard	c.99y	W	Va.	15 MAR 1876	Rock Creek
018685	WURDEMAN, Henry	5y	W	D.C.	15 JAN 1879	Glenwood
015617	WURDEMAN, Herman H.	49y	W	Ger.	04 MAY 1878	Glenwood
009866	WURDEMAN, Mary	43y	W	Md.	04 MAR 1876	Glenwood
008309	WYATT, Kitty	24y	C	Va.	18 JUL 1876	Caroline Co., Va.
013664	WYATT, Thornton	75y	C	Va.	28 OCT 1877	Beckett's
012904	WYE, Benjamin	1m	C	D.C.	21 AUG 1877	Young Mens
012945	WYE, Georgeanna	c.18y	C	Md.	24 AUG 1877	Young Mens
005225	WYE, Richard	1y	C	D.C.	29 SEP 1875	Harmony
004768	WYE, Samuel Claton	1y	C	D.C.	26 AUG 1875	Young Mens
008534	WYE, Washington	64y	C	Md.	02 AUG 1876	Young Mens
018419	WYETH, Elizabeth	30y	C	Va.	21 DEC 1878	Potters Field
003303f	WYGANTT, Henry H.	--	--	--	12 MAY 1875	--
019713	WYLIE, Abbie	10y	W	Md.	09 APR 1879	Montgomery Co., Md.
006315	WYMAN, Harriet Catharine	37y	W	Mo.	11 FEB 1876	Oak Hill
001316	WYNDAM, Annie	3m	W	D.C.	04 DEC 1874	Congressional
014326	WYNN, Andrew J.	9y	W	D.C.	04 JAN 1878	Congressional
009384	WYNN, Joseph T.	43y	W	N.C.	11 OCT 1876	Congressional
005164a	WYNNE, Mary Craig	1y	W	Va.	15 OCT 1875	Bethel Ch., Fairfax Co.
008303	WYNNE, Thomas	46y	W	Ire.	17 JUL 1876	Soldier's Home
001776	WYVILL, Florence R.	9y	W	D.C.	18 JAN 1875	Glenwood

X

| 005233 | XANDER, Pauline | 3y | W | Ill. | 30 SEP 1875 | Prospect Hill |

District of Columbia Death Records, August 1, 1874 to July 31, 1879

No.	Name	Age	Race	Birth	Death Date	Burial Place
Y						
019693	YANCY, Harris	28y	C	Va.	07 APR 1879	Potters Field
005668	YANSON, Christie	40y	W	Den.	05 DEC 1875	Rock Creek
019233	YARNALL, Mordecai	63y	W	Ohio	27 FEB 1879	Oak Hill
005545	YARNELL, Harry	7m	W	D.C.	23 NOV 1875	Glenwood
009558	YATEMAN, Arther	2d	W	D.C.	28 OCT 1876	Oak Hill
009245	YATES, Annie E.	8y	W	D.C.	30 SEP 1876	Oak Hill
012571	YATES, David	17m	C	D.C.	28 JUL 1877	Ebenezer
015187	YATES, Franklin Pierce	18y	W	Md.	25 MAR 1878	Congressional
005546	YATES, Gideon Demaine	35y	W	Md.	23 NOV 1875	Oak Hill
006164	YATES Harriet B.	5m	W	D.C.	27 JAN 1876	Oak Hill
007393	YATES, Jane Margaret	22y	W	Md.	23 MAY 1876	Congressional
006327	YATES, John Lewis	71y	W	Md.	12 FEB 1876	Mt. Olivet
002595	YATES, John S.	28y	W	Va.	16 MAR 1875	Congressional
004325	YATES, Kate E.	26y	W	Md.	26 JUL 1875	Congressional
007243	YATES, Lewis	4y	W	D.C.	07 MAY 1876	Congressional
005234	YATES, William	49y	W	Mass.	05 SEP 1874	Hospital
006119	YEAGER, Charles	c.30y	W	U.S.	23 JAN 1876	Washington Asylum
016563	YEATMAN, Alfred H.	23y	W	D.C.	11 JUL 1878	Oak Hill
016615	YEATMAN, Catherine	24y	W	Va.	15 JUL 1878	Nomini Ferry, Va.
005164	YEATMAN, Frank R.	18y	W	D.C.	24 SEP 1875	Oak Hill
004342	YEATMAN, Infant of James	14d	C	D.C.	27 JUL 1875	Beckett's
004990	YEATMAN, Marion	2y	C	Va.	10 SEP 1875	Beckett's
016644	YEATMAN, Nellie Louise	8m	W	D.C.	17 JUL 1878	Oak Hill
004502	YEATMAN, Susan Amelia	43y	W	Va.	07 AUG 1875	Glenwood
001544	YEODER, Elizabeth	35y	W	Va.	31 DEC 1874	Glenwood
014302	YERBY, Robet	24y	C	Va.	02 JAN 1878	Potters Field
014635	YERKES, Elizabeth	82y	W	Md.	01 FEB 1878	Glenwood
002978	YERKES, J. Arthur	2y	W	D.C.	13 APR 1875	Oak Hill
020173	YEWELL, John P.	54y	W	Md.	22 MAY 1879	Baltimore
009618	YINGLING, Alfred Hull	1y	W	Pa.	05 NOV 1876	Lewistown, Pa.
016532	YINGLING, E.P.	19m	W	D.C.	08 JUL 1878	Lewistown, Pa.
012206	YOAKIM, Elizabeth	20y	W	Pa.	04 JUL 1877	Prospect Hill
009719	YODER, Annie E.	27y	W	D.C.	17 NOV 1876	Glenwood
017688	YORK, Caroline	4m	C	D.C.	09 OCT 1878	Harmony
008012	YORK, George W.	1y	C	D.C.	04 JUL 1876	Holy Rood
008370	YORK, John	60y	W	Gre.	22 JUL 1876	Boston, Mass.
007381	YORK, Lettie	10y	C	D.C.	22 MAY 1876	Harmony
020954	YORK, Mary Anne	8y	C	N.C.	15 JUL 1879	Harmony
014536	YORK, Oliver	16m	C	D.C.	23 JAN 1878	Harmony
013372	YORK, Thomas	2m	C	Va.	01 OCT 1877	Harmony
002968f	YORPP, S.C. [Charlott], Miss	48y	C	Va.	12 APR 1875	Harmony
003262	YOSHIDA, Waka	2m	J	D.C.	08 MAY 1875	Oak Hill
003102	YOST, Edward	9m	W	D.C.	23 APR 1875	Prospect Hill
011870	YOST, Martha D.	1y	W	D.C.	12 JUN 1877	Prospect Hill
005139	YOUNG, Alber Ewing	16m	W	D.C.	22 SEP 1875	Holy Rood
019349	YOUNG, Albert S.	2y	W	D.C.	09 MAR 1879	Washington Hebrew
001192	YOUNG, Alfred	22y	C	Va.	19 NOV 1874	Young Mens
016751	YOUNG, Annie	76y	C	Md.	24 JUL 1878	Harmony
014692	YOUNG, Annie L.	1y	C	D.C.	06 FEB 1878	Moore's
001914	YOUNG, Benjamin Franklin	26y	W	Va.	27 JAN 1875	Berryville, Va.
012640	YOUNG, Catharina	66y	W	Ger.	01 AUG 1877	Oak Hill
005077a	YOUNG, Charles	7m	C	D.C.	06 OCT 1875	Young Mens
014000	YOUNG, Charles	2y	C	D.C.	03 DEC 1877	Beckett's
018865	YOUNG, Charles	6m	C	D.C.	28 JAN 1879	Young Mens

No.	Name	Age	Race	Birth	Death Date	Burial Place
005058a	YOUNG, Charles Edward	1m	C	D.C.	04 OCT 1875	Young Mens
011665	YOUNG, Charlotte A.	33y	C	D.C.	21 MAY 1877	Piney Grove
005692	YOUNG, Child of Sophia	10y	C	D.C.	07 DEC 1875	Potters Field
002183	YOUNG, Clara	3m	C	D.C.	15 FEB 1875	Ebenezer
004806	YOUNG, Daniel Benjamin	4y	C	D.C.	28 AUG 1875	Thomas'
006781	YOUNG, Doctor	65y	C	Va.	22 MAR 1876	Mt. Pleasant
013263	YOUNG, Eddward	3y	C	D.C.	20 SEP 1877	Young Mens
013701	YOUNG, Eddy	c.3y	W	D.C.	01 NOV 1877	Prospect Hill
013867	YOUNG, Edward	2y	C	D.C.	19 NOV 1877	Moore's
016444	YOUNG, Edward	8m	C	D.C.	04 JUL 1878	Harmony
005234a	YOUNG, Edward Owen	29y	C	D.C.	21 OCT 1875	Mt. Pleasant
005397	YOUNG, Elenorah	1y	C	D.C.	08 NOV 1875	Mt. Olivet
013309	YOUNG, Elisabeth	85y	C	D.C.	25 SEP 1877	Holy Rood
019703	YOUNG, Eliza Winter	67y	W	Eng.	08 APR 1879	Congressional
006529	YOUNG, Ellen L.	16y	W	D.C.	02 MAR 1876	Mt. Olivet
014537	YOUNG, Eloise	6y	W	D.C.	23 JAN 1878	Mt. Olivet
017039	YOUNG, Emma	24y	M	N.C.	13 AUG 1878	Congressional
013938	YOUNG, Emma Jane	12y	C	D.C.	26 NOV 1877	Beckett's
019303	YOUNG, Eva	2y	C	D.C.	06 MAR 1879	Mt. Zion
018876	YOUNG, Ezekiel	55y	W	D.C.	29 JAN 1879	Congressional
020772	YOUNG, Fennamore	10y	C	D.C.	04 JUL 1879	Young Mens
001450	YOUNG, Frank	1m	W	D.C.	20 DEC 1874	Prospect Hill
007771	YOUNG, Frank	9h	W	D.C.	21 JUN 1876	Congressional
006051	YOUNG, Frank E.	11m	C	D.C.	17 JAN 1876	Potters Field
007738	YOUNG, George Washington	1y	C	D.C.	19 JUN 1876	Thomas'
011115	YOUNG, Grace	7m	W	Va.	26 MAR 1877	Mt. Olivet
000387	YOUNG, Harriet Ann	1y	C	D.C.	31 AUG 1874	Thomas'
016000	YOUNG, Henrietta	85y	W	Md.	03 JUN 1878	Mt. Olivet
013800	YOUNG, Henry	70y	C	Md.	11 NOV 1877	Harmony
020037	YOUNG, Henry N.	53y	C	D.C.	07 MAY 1879	Piscataway, Md.
006948	YOUNG, Infant of Henry	30min	C	D.C.	06 APR 1876	Mt. Zion
005693	YOUNG, Infant of Jno.	10y	C	D.C.	07 DEC 1875	Washington Asylum
006052	YOUNG, Infant of John	11m	C	D.C.	17 JAN 1876	Mt. Olivet
010948	YOUNG, Infant of Joseph	4d	C	D.C.	12 MAR 1877	Potters Field
010920	YOUNG, Infant of Lucy	3d	C	D.C.	09 MAR 1877	Potters Field
014335	YOUNG, Infant of Rosetta	10min	C	D.C.	05 JAN 1878	Potters Field
014487	YOUNG, Infant of Rosetta	2w	C	D.C.	19 JAN 1878	Potters Field
015433	YOUNG, Irene	2y	C	D.C.	17 APR 1878	Harmony
014110	YOUNG, Isaac	79y	W	Ger.	15 DEC 1877	Jewish
007419	YOUNG, J.	4y	C	D.C.	27 MAY 1876	Young Mens
008846	YOUNG, Jacob W.	46y	W	N.J.	27 AUG 1876	Phillipsburg, N.J.
002793	YOUNG, James	40y	C	Va.	30 MAR 1875	Harmony
009248	YOUNG, James	2y	C	D.C.	30 SEP 1876	Ebenezer
012779	YOUNG, James	18y	C	Md.	11 AUG 1877	Potters Field
006504	YOUNG, James Edward	1y	C	D.C.	28 FEB 1876	Mt. Zion
010626	YOUNG, Jane	25y	C	Md.	14 FEB 1877	Mt. Olivet
014257	YOUNG, Jennie	8y	C	D.C.	29 DEC 1877	Young Mens
018638	YOUNG, john F.	39y	W	Pa.	10 JAN 1879	Congressional
007718	YOUNG, John	8m	W	D.C.	18 JUN 1876	Congressional
020846	YOUNG, John A.	8m	W	D.C.	08 JUL 1879	Mt. Olivet
009269	YOUNG, John Alex.	5m	C	D.C.	02 OCT 1876	Ebenezer
013275	YOUNG, Josephine Catherine	54y	W	Md.	21 SEP 1877	Congressional
012503	YOUNG, Julia Ann	9m	C	D.C.	24 JUL 1877	Beckett's
004269	YOUNG, Katie	7m	W	D.C.	23 JUL 1875	Mt. Olivet
009728	YOUNG, Lillie Walace	3m	C	Md.	18 NOV 1876	Prince George's Co., Md.
015658	YOUNG, Lucinda	24y	C	Md.	08 MAY 1878	Potters Field

District of Columbia Death Records, August 1, 1874 to July 31, 1879   385

No.	Name	Age	Race	Birth	Death Date	Burial Place
006399	YOUNG, Lydia Ann	8d	M	D.C.	17 FEB 1876	Ebenezer
010981	YOUNG, Malinda	78y	W	Va.	15 MAR 1877	Caroline Co., Va.
011002	YOUNG, Mary	50y	W	Ire.	16 MAR 1877	Mt. Olivet
007266	YOUNG, Mary Catherine	5d	C	D.C.	10 MAY 1876	Ebenezer
020771	YOUNG, Mary E.	11m	C	D.C.	04 JUL 1879	Mt. Zion
016168	YOUNG, Maud F.	5m	W	D.C.	14 JUN 1878	Congressional
001123	YOUNG, Nelson	24y	C	Va.	24 NOV 1874	Young Mens
018196	YOUNG, Nicholas Dominic	86y	W	Md.	28 NOV 1878	Somerset, Ohio
008400	YOUNG, Nicholas Raymond	58y	W	D.C.	24 JUL 1876	Mt. Olivet
015516	YOUNG, Pauline Kandis	3y	C	S.C.	25 APR 1878	Graceland
019003	YOUNG, Richard	50y	W	Eng.	08 FEB 1879	Mt. Olivet
004744	YOUNG, Robert	1y	C	D.C.	24 AUG 1875	Mt. Zion
013296	YOUNG, Robert	1y	C	D.C.	24 SEP 1877	Beckett's
019631	YOUNG, Robert	29y	C	Va.	01 APR 1879	Harmony
020515	YOUNG, Rose	4m	C	D.C.	18 JUN 1879	Payne's
018820	YOUNG, Samuel R.	c.43y	W	Pa.	25 JAN 1879	Oak Hill
019204	YOUNG, Thomas	69y	W	D.C.	25 FEB 1879	Congressional
019596	YOUNG, Thomas	28y	C	Va.	29 MAR 1879	Mt. Pleasant
016577	YOUNG, Warren	73y	W	Mass.	12 JUL 1878	Graceland
005763	YOUNG, William	27y	C	Md.	15 DEC 1875	Small Pox Grounds
010484	YOUNG, William	12y	C	Md.	02 FEB 1877	Ebenezer
018905	YOUNG, William	70y	C	Md.	31 JAN 1879	Mt. Olivet
019996	YOUNG, William Beverly Drinkard	7m	W	D.C.	04 MAY 1879	Congressional/Oak Hill
012846	YOUNG, William F.	3m	C	D.C.	16 AUG 1877	Potters Field
012050	YOUNG, William Henry	5m	C	D.C.	25 JUN 1877	Payne's
005379	YOUNG, Wm. H.	26d	W	D.C.	06 NOV 1875	N.Y.
007543	YOUNGER, Bessie Madora	2y	C	D.C.	07 JUN 1876	Harmony
009207	YOUNGER, Fred S.	4m	C	D.C.	26 SEP 1876	Harmony
020690	YOUNGER, Mary C.	46y	C	Va.	30 JUN 1879	Harmony
002453	YOUNGER, Mary I.S.	33y	C	D.C.	06 MAR 1875	Mt. Olivet
000269	YOUNGHANS, Elizabeth	1y	W	D.C.	21 AUG 1874	St. Mary's
002999	YOUNT, David Percy	1y	W	D.C.	15 APR 1875	Gettysburg, Pa.

Z

016063	ZABARIN, Sally Markoe	73y	W	W.I.	08 JUN 1878	Oak Hill
010620	ZAKLY, Sarah Elizabeth	21y	W	Pa.	14 FEB 1877	Potters Field
013297	ZAMITZER, John	36y	W	Ger.	24 SEP 1877	Soldier's Home
015860	ZANTZINGER, William C.	58y	W	D.C.	26 MAY 1878	Congressional
004178	ZASCO, Richard	6d	M	D.C.	17 JUL 1875	Young Mens
009452	ZEGOWITZ, Barbara F.	5d	W	D.C.	18 OCT 1876	St. Mary's
003766	ZEIRMAN, Charles Henry	28d	W	D.C.	22 JUN 1875	Mt. Olivet
018735	ZEIRMAN, Mary Elizabeth	2y	W	D.C.	19 JAN 1879	Mt. Olivet
000751	ZELLER, Adam	5y	W	D.C.	08 OCT 1874	Prospect Hill
019514	ZELLER, Fred'k. P.	7d	W	D.C.	22 MAR 1879	Prospect Hill
008612	ZELLERE, Joseph L.	13m	W	D.C.	08 AUG 1876	St. Mary's
006521	ZEVELY, Edmund Alexander	32y	W	D.C.	01 MAR 1876	Rock Creek
018012	ZIGLER, George	10y	W	D.C.	10 NOV 1878	Graceland
011284	ZIMMER, Frederick	44y	W	Ger.	09 APR 1877	Prospect Hill
000661	ZIMMERMAN, Charlie Andrew	28y	W	Va.	28 SEP 1874	Glenwood
001269	ZIMMERMAN, Elizabeth	76y	W	Bav.	29 NOV 1874	Prospect Hill
006192	ZIMMERMAN, George W.	7y	W	D.C.	30 JAN 1876	Prospect Hill
015700	ZIMMERMAN, Henry Fairhurst	59y	W	Va.	12 MAY 1878	Glenwood
012580	ZIMMERMAN, Mary E.	28y	W	D.C.	28 JUL 1877	Glenwood
011834	ZOLL, Fredreika	1y	W	D.C.	07 JUN 1877	Prospect Hill

No.	Name	Age	Race	Birth	Death Date	Burial Place
009588	ZUCHNETT, Maggie	3y	W	D.C.	01 NOV 1876	Prospect Hill
012186	ZULICH, Gregorus	10m	W	D.C.	02 JUL 1877	St. Mary's
021046	ZUSCHNITT, Frederic S.	8m	W	D.C.	21 JUL 1879	Prospect Hill

Incomplete Records

000117	[blank], Ann	1m	C	D.C.	09 AUG 1874	Mt. Olivet
010617	[blank], Fannie	5d	W	D.C.	13 FEB 1877	Mt. Olivet
001038	[blank], Francis	1m	W	D.C.	04 NOV 1874	Mt. Olivet
009108	[blank], Francisco	65y	W	Spain	17 SEP 1876	Mt. Olivet
002701	[blank], Joseph	1m	C	D.C.	23 MAR 1875	Mt. Olivet
000326	[blank], Margaret	1m	C	D.C.	26 AUG 1874	Mt. Olivet
002852	[blank], Margaret	1m	C	D.C.	03 APR 1875	Mt. Olivet
003758	[blank], Margaret	3m	C	D.C.	22 JUN 1875	Mt. Olivet
009784	[blank], Mary (a foundling)	2m	C	D.C.	24 NOV 1876	Harmony
007130	[blank], Mary Ann	1m	C	D.C.	27 APR 1876	Mt. Olivet
015903	[blank], Mary Catharine	7m	W	--	30 MAY 1878	Mt. Olivet
012592	[blank], Mary Margaret	1m	C	D.C.	29 JUL 1877	Mt. Olivet
008869	[blank], Metihel	1y	C	D.C.	29 AUG 1876	Young Mens
002471	[blank], Michael	2m	C	D.C.	08 MAR 1875	Mt. Olivet
016105	[blank], Oliver	6w	W	D.C.	10 JUN 1878	Young Mens
017702	[blank], Sister Harriett	31y	W	Bel.	11 OCT 1878	Mt. Olivet
013204	[see No. #11,332 for Branger Silva]					
013116	[see No. #13,186a for Mary Ryan]					

Record Not Used or Missing

002256f	Not Used
004909f	Not Used
004853f	Not Used
005131f	Not Used
005148f	Not Used
005130f	Not Used
005174f	Not Used
005175f	Not Used
005176f	Not Used

001493	No Record
002014	No Record
002506	No Record
004447	No Record
005004	No Record
012745	No Record
017827	No Record
020862	No Record

Appendix

AN ACT to provide for the Registry of Deaths and for other purposes.

Be it enacted by the Board of Aldermen and Board of Common Council of the City of Washington, That whenever any person shall die within the limits of the City of Washington, it shall be the duty of the physician who attended during his or her last sickness, or of the Coroner of Washington County, when the case comes under his notice, to furnish and deliver to the family of the deceased, or to the undertaker or other person having charge of or superintending the burial of the said deceased, a certificate setting forth, as far as the same can be ascertained, the name, sex, color, nativity, occupation, probable age, place of decease, time of, and supposed cause of death, of the person deceased. And it shall be the duty of the physician or coroner, as above stated, to deliver or cause to be delivered the above-named certificate to the party or parties above named, within forth-eight hours after the death of said deceased shall come to their knowledge, and they deliver said certificate sooner if possible, if requested so to do.

Sec. 2. *And be it further enacted,* That no person having the charge, as sexton or otherwise, of any vault, burial-ground, or cemetery within the City of Washington, (including the Intendant of the Washington Asylum,) shall inter or allow to be interred, place or allow to be placed in any vault, burial-ground, or cemetery under their control, the dead body of any person, unless there shall have been delivered to them by the person or persons ordering the said interment, or the placing of a dead body in a vault, a certificate as hereinbefore, or as may be hereafter provided for.

Sec. 3. *And be it further enacted,* That any undertaker or other person removing the dead body of a person who has died in said city, (and which dead body shall not have been previously buried, or been placed in a vault or other receptacle for the temporary deposit of the dead,) to any place beyond the limits of said city, shall deliver or cause to be delivered, the hereinbefore or as may be hereinafter required certificate to the Secretary of the Board of Health, to be left at his residence or place of business on or before the tenth of the succeeding month, to which certificate the date and place of interment shall be attached.

Sec. 4. *And be if further enacted,* In case any person shall die without the attendance of a physician, or if the physician who did attend at the time of the death of said person refuses or neglects to deliver the certificate as hereinbefore required, then the said certificate may be furnished by the Secretary of the Board of Health, any member of the Board of Health, or by any respectable citizen cognizant of the circumstances and causes of death, and should there be no physician, and an inquest be held, and the Coroner refuses or neglects to furnish the certificate as hereinbefore required, then the said certificate may be furnished by either of the parties above enumerated in this section.

Sec. 5. *And be it further enacted,* That every sexton or other person having charge of any vault, burial-ground, or cemetery within the limits of the City of Washington, shall return each and every certificate of death coming into his or their hands, in accordance with the foregoing provisions of this act, and shall deliver or cause such certificate or certificates to be delivered at the residence or office of the Secretary of the Board of Health on or before the tenth of the month following that in which said death shall have occurred.

Sec. 6. *And be it further enacted,* That it shall be the duty of the Secretary of the Board of Health to furnish each and every undertaker within the limits of the City of Washington, with a list, containing the name and residence of each and every member of the Board of Health, and he shall promptly communicate to the aforesaid undertakers any change that may be made therein; he shall also keep on hand, and promptly furnish to undertakers, physicians, and such other persons as may require them, blank forms for such certificates as are hereinbefore required; he shall also furnish each and every physician and undertaker, and also every sexton or other person in charge of any vault, burial-ground, or cemetery within the limits of the City of Washington, with a printed copy of this act, and he shall publish a statistical report of all certificates coming into his hands, on or before the fifteenth of each month, giving numbers of deaths, various causes, ages, &c., and shall also perform such other duties as may be necessary to facilitate a compliance with the provisions of this act.

Sec. 7. *And be it further enacted,* That in case any physician or coroner shall refuse or neglect to deliver such certificates, and at the time and in the manner hereinbefore required, he or they shall forfeit and pay the sum of ten dollars for each and every such neglect, or refusal; said fines to be recovered as other fines for the use and benefit of the Corporation of Washington City; and it is hereby made the duty of the Secretary of the Board of Health to see that the provisions of this section are rigidly enforced.

Sec. 8. *And be it further enacted,* That every undertaker, sexton, or other person removing the dead body of any person beyond the city limits, who shall have died within the City of Washington, except as provided for in section three of this act, or having charge of any vault, burial-ground, or cementer, within the limits of said city, who refuses or neglects to perform any of the duties required of them by the provisions of this act, shall, for each and every such refusal or neglect, forfeit and pay the sum of two dollars; and the Secretary of the Board of Health, for each and every refusal or neglect to perform the duties as hereinbefore required of him shall forfeit and pay the sum of five dollars; said fines as enumerated in this section to be recovered as are other fines for the use and benefit of the Corporation of Washington City.

SEC. 9. *And be it further enacted,* That all acts or parts or acts inconsistent with the provisions of this act be, and the same are hereby, repealed.

Approved January 8, 1868.

Rules, Regulations, and Instructions for the Prevention of the Spread of Epidemic, Infectious and Contagious Diseases in the District of Columbia

5. That all undertakers, or persons acting as undertakers, in the city of Georgetown are hereby required to report to the Board of Health, on or before the tenth day of each month, until otherwise ordered, all interments made by them, together with a certificate from the physician or other responsible person cognizant of the circumstances attending the death of any individual, setting forth the name, sex, color, age, time of and cause of death, and also the place of interment, together with such other facts as may serve to identify the individual and be of service to the Board in preventing the spread of epidemic, infectious or contagious disease.

These regulations the Board of Health will, to conserve the public health, rigidly enforce according to the law conferring the authority and making it the duty of the Board of Health to issue orders, regulations, and instructions as aforesaid.

Chris. C. Cox, M.D.,
President Board of Health, District of Columbia

Attest: D.W. Bliss, M.D., Secretary
Approved: H.D. Cooke, Governor

Other Heritage Books by Wesley E. Pippenger:

Alexandria (Arlington) County, Virginia Death Records, 1853-1896

Alexandria City and Arlington County, Virginia Records Index: Vol. 1

Alexandria City and Arlington County, Virginia Records Index: Vol. 2

Alexandria County, Virginia Marriage Records, 1853-1895

Alexandria Virginia Marriage Index, January 10, 1893 to August 31, 1905

Alexandria, Virginia Marriages, 1870-1892

*Alexandria, Virginia Town Lots, 1749-1801
Together with the Proceedings of the Board of Trustees, 1749-1780*

Alexandria, Virginia Wills, Administrations and Guardianships, 1786-1800

Alexandria, Virginia 1808 Census (Wards 1, 2, 3, and 4)

Alexandria, Virginia Death Records, 1863-1896

Alexandria, Virginia Hustings Court Orders, Volume 1, 1780-1787

Connections and Separations: Divorce, Name Change and Other Genealogical Tidbits from the Acts of the Virginia General Assembly

Daily National Intelligencer *Index to Deaths, 1855-1870*

Daily National Intelligencer, *Washington, District of Columbia Marriages and Deaths Notices (January 1, 1851 to December 30, 1854)*

Dead People on the Move: Reconstruction of the Georgetown Presbyterian Burying Ground, Holmead's (Western) Burying Ground, and Other Removals in the District of Columbia

Death Notices from Richmond, Virginia Newspapers, 1841-1853

District of Columbia Ancestors, A Guide to Records of the District of Columbia

District of Columbia Death Records: August 1, 1874-July 31, 1879

District of Columbia Foreign Deaths, 1888-1923

District of Columbia Guardianship Index, 1802-1928

*District of Columbia Interments (Index to Deaths)
January 1, 1855 to July 31, 1874*

District of Columbia Marriage Licenses, Register 1: 1811-1858

District of Columbia Marriage Licenses, Register 2: 1858-1870

*District of Columbia Marriage Records Index
June 28, 1877 to October 19, 1885: Marriage Record Books 11 to 20*
Wesley E. Pippenger and Dorothy S. Provine

*District of Columbia Marriage Records Index
October 20, 1885 to January 20, 1892: Marriage Record Books 21 to 30*

District of Columbia Probate Records, 1801-1852

District of Columbia: Original Land Owners, 1791-1800

Early Church Records of Alexandria City and Fairfax County, Virginia

Georgetown, District of Columbia 1850 Federal Population Census (Schedule I) and 1853 Directory of Residents of Georgetown

Georgetown, District of Columbia Marriage and Death Notices, 1801-1838

Husbands and Wives Associated with Early Alexandria, Virginia (and the Surrounding Area), 3rd Edition, Revised

Index to District of Columbia Estates, 1801-1929

*Index to Virginia Estates, 1800-1865
Volumes 4, 5 and 6*

John Alexander, a Northern Neck Proprietor, His Family, Friends and Kin

Legislative Petitions of Alexandria, 1778-1861

Pippenger and Pittenger Families

Proceedings of the Orphan's Court, Washington County, District of Columbia, 1801-1808

The Georgetown Courier *Marriage and Death Notices: Georgetown, District of Columbia, November 18, 1865 to May 6, 1876*

The Georgetown Directory for the Year 1830: to which is appended, a Short Description of the Churches, Public Institutions, and the Original Charter of Georgetown, and Extracts of the Laws Pertaining to the Chesapeake and Ohio Canal Company

The Virginia Gazette and Alexandria Advertiser:
Volume 1, September 3, 1789 to November 11, 1790

The Virginia Journal and Alexandria Advertiser:
Volume I (February 5, 1784 to January 27, 1785)

Volume II (February 3, 1785 to January 26, 1786)

Volume III (March 2, 1786 to January 25, 1787)

Volume IV (February 8, 1787 to May 21, 1789)

The Washington and Georgetown Directory of 1853

Tombstone Inscriptions of Alexandria, Volumes 1-4